The Oxford Handbook of Developmental Psychology and the Law

OXFORD LIBRARY OF PSYCHOLOGY

AREA EDITORS:

Clinical Psychology
David H. Barlow

Cognitive Neuroscience
Kevin N. Ochsner and Stephen M. Kosslyn

Cognitive Psychology
Daniel Reisberg

Counseling Psychology
Elizabeth M. Altmaier and Jo-Ida C. Hansen

Developmental Psychology
Philip David Zelazo

Health Psychology
Howard S. Friedman

History of Psychology
David B. Baker

Methods and Measurement
Todd D. Little

Neuropsychology
Kenneth M. Adams

Organizational Psychology
Steve W. J. Kozlowski

Personality and Social Psychology
Kay Deaux and Mark Snyder

Psychology and Law
David DeMatteo and Kyle Scherr

OXFORD LIBRARY OF PSYCHOLOGY

The Oxford Handbook of Developmental Psychology and the Law

Edited by
Allison D. Redlich and Jodi A. Quas

OXFORD
UNIVERSITY PRESS

Oxford University Press is a department of the University of Oxford. It furthers
the University's objective of excellence in research, scholarship, and education
by publishing worldwide. Oxford is a registered trade mark of Oxford University
Press in the UK and certain other countries.

Published in the United States of America by Oxford University Press
198 Madison Avenue, New York, NY 10016, United States of America.

© Oxford University Press 2024

All rights reserved. No part of this publication may be reproduced, stored in
a retrieval system, or transmitted, in any form or by any means, without the
prior permission in writing of Oxford University Press, or as expressly permitted
by law, by license, or under terms agreed with the appropriate reproduction
rights organization. Inquiries concerning reproduction outside the scope of the
above should be sent to the Rights Department, Oxford University Press, at the
address above.

You must not circulate this work in any other form
and you must impose this same condition on any acquirer.

Library of Congress Cataloging-in-Publication Data
Names: Redlich, Allison D., editor. | Quas, Jodi A., author.
Title: The Oxford handbook of developmental psychology and the law /
[edited by] Allison D. Redlich, Jodi A. Quas.
Other titles: Handbook of developmental psychology and the law
Description: 1 Edition. | New York, NY : Oxford University Press, [2024] |
Series: Oxford library of psychology series | Includes index. |
Identifiers: LCCN 2023017835 (print) | LCCN 2023017836 (ebook) |
ISBN 9780197549513 (hardback) | ISBN 9780197549537 (epub) | ISBN 9780197549544
Subjects: LCSH: Developmental psychology. | Law—Psychological aspects. |
Criminal justice, Administration of—Psychological aspects.
Classification: LCC BF713.O92944 2023 (print) | LCC BF713 (ebook) |
DDC 155—dc23/eng/20230630
LC record available at https://lccn.loc.gov/2023017835
LC ebook record available at https://lccn.loc.gov/2023017836

DOI: 10.1093/oxfordhb/9780197549513.001.0001

Printed by Sheridan Books, Inc., United States of America

CONTENTS

List of Contributors ix

Section I • Infant, Child, and Adolescent Development and the Law

1. Infant, Child, and Adolescent Development and the Law: Intersections, Interactions, and Influences 1
   Jodi A. Quas and *Allison D. Redlich*

Subsection 1.1 • Infancy and Childhood

2. The Relational Context of Early Development: Consequences of Maltreatment in Infancy and Effective Early Intervention 7
   Ann M. Stacks, Danielle Rice, Kathleen Allen, and *Eleanor Rabior*
3. Developmental Pathways to Antisocial Behavior: Implications for Juvenile Justice Policy and Practice 37
   Paul J. Frick, Emily C. Kemp, and *Julianne S. Speck*
4. Memory, Suggestibility, and Disclosure Processes: Implications for Children in Legal Settings 57
   Emily M. Slonecker, Alma P. Olaguez, Rachel L. Taffe, and *J. Zoe Klemfuss*
5. The Developmental Science of Children in Criminal and Dependency Court 85
   Rayna Enriquez, Lily F. Brown, Gail S. Goodman, Stacy Metcalf, and *Jodi A. Quas*
6. Attachment and Parenting Time for Children Under 3 Years of Age 109
   William V. Fabricius
7. Child Development and the Family Regulation System 129
   Clare Huntington
8. A Developmental Perspective on Unaccompanied Migrant Youth in the U.S. Immigration Legal System 149
   Kalina M. Brabeck, Deborah Gonzalez, Sarah Rendón García, and *Adrian Pendergast*

9. Adoption   169
   Jesús Palacios, David M. Brodzinsky, and *Harold D. Grotevant*
10. The Promise and Problems of Policy-Minded Developmental Research: Recognizing Our Implicit Value Judgments and the Limits of Our Research   195
    Thomas D. Lyon and *Michael E. Lamb*

Subsection 1.2 • Adolescence
11. Risky and Antisocial Behavior in Adolescence   209
    Michelle E. Manasse and *Cesar J. Rebellon*
12. Adolescent Victims and Witnesses: Disclosures, Memory, and Suggestibility   233
    Joshua Wyman, Rachel Dianiska, Hayden Henderson, and *Lindsay C. Malloy*
13. Police Interviewing and Interrogation of Adolescent Suspects   257
    Hayley M. D. Cleary and *Megan G. Crane*
14. Youth in Juvenile and Criminal Court   279
    Tina M. Zottoli, Tarika Daftary-Kapur, and *Emily Haney-Caron*
15. Alternatives to Traditional Court Processing: Diversion and Specialty Courts   303
    Erika Fountain, Christina Ducat, and *Allison Lloyd*
16. Adolescent Incarceration: Rates, Impact, and Reform   321
    Jodi L. Viljoen, Shanna M. Y. Li, Julia M. Schillaci-Ventura, and *Dana M. Cochrane*
17. Rethinking the Age of Majority   347
    Vivian Hamilton
18. Schools and Juvenile Justice   363
    Adam D. Fine, Kayleigh A. Stanek, and *Andrea N. Montes*
19. Adolescents and Youth Justice: Framing the Developmental Research   385
    Thomas Grisso

Section 2 • Adult Development and the Law
20. Adult Development and the Law: Intersections, Interactions, and Influences   399
    Allison D. Redlich and *Jodi A. Quas*
21. Understanding Deviancy in Adulthood   403
    Chelsey S. Narvey and *Alex R. Piquero*
22. Transitioning to Adulthood in the Legal System: The Creation of Young Adult Courts   423
    Marie L. Gillespie, Nicholas S. Riano, and *Elizabeth Cauffman*

23. Adults With Developmental Disabilities in the Criminal Justice System   449
    Karen L. Salekin and *Mary E. Wood*
24. Pregnancy and Parenting in Prison   477
    Rebecca J. Shlafer, Joanna Woolman, and *Mariann A. Howland*
25. The Impact of Reproductive Rights on Women's Development   493
    Allison M. Whelan and *Michele Bratcher Goodwin*
26. Racial Disparities in Policing: Psychological Consequences Over the Lifespan   517
    Kelly C. Burke, Cynthia J. Najdowski, and *Margaret C. Stevenson*
27. Prisoner Reentry and the Life Course   561
    Thomas P. LeBel and *Matt Richie*
28. Ethical Considerations and Ramifications of Advance Care Planning and End-of-Life Decision Making for Older Adults   587
    Pamela B. Teaster and *E. Carlisle Shealy*
29. Older Adults as Victims and Witnesses   611
    Eve Brank
30. Aging in the Criminal Justice System: A Call for Age-Focused Research, Policy, and Practice   625
    Lindsey E. Wylie and *Sarah Hubner*
31. A Commentary on Adulthood/Aging, Developmental Psychology, and the Law   649
    Nancy Rodriguez and *Katherine Waggoner*

Index   663

CONTRIBUTORS

Kalina M. Brabeck, PhD is Professor in the Department of Counseling, Educational Leadership, and School Psychology at Rhode Island College and a Staff Psychologist in the Latinx Mental Health Program at Lifepsan. Her research, funded by the Foundation for Child Development and Robert Wood Johnson Foundation, explores the intersections among sociostructural challenges (e.g., poverty, racism, immigration status), family processes, and individual mental health. Dr. Brabeck has presented to the Inter-American Human Rights Commission and her work has been cited in the Supreme Court in the case *SCOTUS Texas vs. U.S.* Dr. Brabeck has 20 years of experience providing forensic psychological evaluations and expert testimony in immigration court.

Eve Brank, JD, PhD is Professor of Psychology and courtesy Professor of Law at the University of Nebraska–Lincoln (UNL). She also serves as Director of the Center on Children, Families, and the Law at UNL. Her research and writing have focused mostly on the way the law intervenes in, and sometimes interferes with, family and individual decision making. In particular, she studies the legal requirements of elder caregiving, parental responsibility within the context of the juvenile justice system, and decision making in the context of government searches. Brank is the author of *The Psychology of Family Law* (2019).

David M. Brodzinsky, PhD is Professor Emeritus of Clinical and Developmental Psychology at Rutgers University, New Brunswick, New Jersey. His research and scholarly writings have focused primarily on developmental issues and family relationships impacting adopted children, with a particular interest in how children come to understand and cope with adoption-related loss. This work has resulted in over 120 journal articles, book chapters, and policy briefs, as well as six authored or edited books on adoption. He maintains a clinical practice focusing on the mental health needs of adoption kinship members. In addition, he has been a consultant to numerous public and private adoption agencies and has conducted numerous training workshops on adoption throughout North America and Europe. He is a Fellow of the American Psychological Association and has received national awards for his research and advocacy in adoption.

Lily F. Brown received her undergraduate degree in Psychology from the University of California (UC), Davis, in 2019. She spent 4 years as a researcher in the UC Davis

Developmental Research Center, contributing to research on the relation between trauma and memory, as well as on children's abilities and experiences as victims/witnesses of violence and maltreatment. She was involved in designing and implementing research projects regarding children and the law while publishing empirical studies and chapters on children's memory development and historic child maltreatment cases. She is currently pursuing a doctoral degree in Clinical Psychology at the University of Maine.

Kelly C. Burke, PhD is Assistant Professor at the University of Texas at El Paso. Her research focuses on the role of prejudice, discrimination, and race in juror and police officer decision making. She also examines the influence of body-worn camera footage on jurors' decisions and public perceptions of police. She co-edited the book, *The Legacy of Racism for Children: Psychology, Law, and Public Policy*, and her work has been published in peer-reviewed journals and books and funded by the National Science Foundation, American Psychology–Law Society, and Society for the Psychological Study of Social Issues.

Elizabeth Cauffman, PhD is Professor in the Department of Psychological Science at the University of California, Irvine, and holds courtesy appointments in the School of Education and the School of Law. She has published over 150 articles on the study of contemporary adolescence, including adolescent brain development, risk taking, and juvenile justice. Her research was incorporated into the American Psychological Association's amicus briefs to the U.S. Supreme Court in *Roper v. Simmons*, which abolished the juvenile death penalty, and in *Miller v. Alabama*, which placed limits on life without parole sentences for juveniles. Dr. Cauffman currently directs the Center for Psychology and Law (http://psychlaw.soceco.uci.edu/) as well as the Master of Legal and Forensic Psychology (https://mlfp.soceco.uci.edu/).

Hayley M. D. Cleary, MPP, PhD is Associate Professor of Criminal Justice and Public Policy at Virginia Commonwealth University in Richmond, Virginia. Her research examines adolescent behavior and decision making in legal system contexts, including youth's contact with law enforcement, courts, and corrections. The cornerstone of her research program involves police interrogation of juvenile suspects, and her work appears in psychology, criminal justice, and policy-focused journals. Cleary's research has been funded by the National Science Foundation and the Annie E. Casey Foundation and featured in national news outlets such as the *New York Times*.

Dana M. Cochrane is a PhD student in Clinical Child Psychology at Simon Fraser University. Her research focuses on the intersection between mental health and adolescent offending.

Megan G. Crane is an attorney and Co-Director of the Roderick and Solange MacArthur Justice Center's (MJC) Missouri office, where she runs the MJC Wrongful Conviction Project. Before MJC, Crane was the Codirector of the Center on Wrongful Convictions of Youth (CWCY) at Northwestern Pritzker School of Law, where she represented wrongfully convicted youth, with a focus on youth who falsely confessed. Crane frequently presents about police interrogations and juvenile confessions and regularly assists in litigation as amicus counsel and/or a consultant in litigation involving extreme sentencing of youth and coercive interrogations of youth, including in the U.S. Supreme Court.

Tarika Daftary-Kapur, PhD is Associate Professor of Justice Studies at Montclair State University. She holds a PhD in Psychology and Law from the Graduate Center, City University of New York. Her scholarship and teaching focus on youth in the legal system with an emphasis on improving outcomes for justice-involved youth. Her secondary research focus is guilty plea decision making. She has worked and consulted with jurisdictions around the country on their juvenile and criminal justice policies.

Rachel Dianiska, PhD is a Postdoctoral Fellow at the University of California, Irvine, where she is researching best practices for interviewing adolescent victims and witnesses. She received her PhD in Cognitive Psychology from Iowa State University in 2020. Her program of research broadly investigates the influence of various cognitive processes on issues such as interviewing and credibility assessment, the development of false memories, and the influence of lying on memory for the truth.

Christina Ducat is a second-year PhD student in the Human Services Psychology program (Community track) at the University of Maryland, Baltimore. Her research focuses on the impact of state violence in the legal system on girls and gender nonconforming youth and how youth resist oppression. She received her bachelor's degrees in Applied Psychology, Global Public Health, and Politics from New York University in 2018. After graduating, she spent several years doing advocacy work and organizing with girls involved with the legal system. She also conducted research on the state of girls' incarceration nationally and collaborated with community organizations to promote youth agency and well-being.

Rayna Enriquez is a PhD student in Developmental Psychology at the University of California, Davis. She received a bachelor's degree in Psychology from the University of Southern California, where she began her research on improving maltreated children's interactions with the legal system and their eyewitness testimony in maltreatment cases. Enriquez's current research interests include children's memory capabilities after experiencing a traumatic event and how adults perceive children's memory accounts. Her research also examines memory in neurotypical children compared with children who have been diagnosed with a developmental disorder, such as autism spectrum disorder.

William V. Fabricius, PhD is Associate Professor of Psychology and Affiliated Faculty in Law and Behavioral Science at Arizona State University. His research has been supported by the National Institutes of Health and focuses on social cognitive development in childhood and adolescence, the role of fathers in adolescent and young adult mental and physical health, and social policy regarding child custody after parental divorce. He was instrumental in the passage of reforms to Arizona's child custody statutes in 2013 favoring equal parenting time.

Adam D. Fine, PhD is Assistant Professor in the School of Criminology and Criminal Justice at Arizona State University. He received his doctorate, specializing in developmental psychology and quantitative methods, from the University of California, Irvine. A developmental psychologist conducting research at the intersection of psychology, law, public policy, and criminology, Fine's research broadly focuses on juvenile delinquency and juvenile justice. His current work centers on two areas: how youth develop their perceptions of law enforcement, the law, and the justice system, and how juvenile probation processes affect youth offending, employment, education, and attitudes.

Erika Fountain, PhD is Assistant Professor in the Department of Psychology at the University of Maryland, Baltimore County, earned her PhD in Psychology with a concentration in Human Development and Public Policy from Georgetown University. She incorporates developmental and community psychology, law, and public policy to answer questions about legal decision making, court processes, and attorney–client–family relationships. Additionally, she explores how science can contribute to developmentally informed justice policy. She has testified to state legislators considering juvenile justice policies addressing jurisdiction, confidentiality, and legal protections in interrogation. She has authored op-eds advocating for developmentally informed reforms to youth justice.

Paul J. Frick, PhD ABPP is the Roy Crumpler Memorial Chair and Professor in the Department of Psychology at Louisiana State University. His research interests focus on understanding the different pathways through which youth develop serious antisocial behavior and aggression and the implications of this research for assessment, treatment, and public policy. He received his degree in Clinical Psychology from the University of Georgia.

Marie L. Gillespie, PhD is a Postdoctoral Scholar in the Department of Psychological Science at the University of California, Irvine. She earned her PhD in Clinical Psychology from the University of Southern California in 2019 and specializes in trauma-informed and family-based interventions for youth and families impacted by the criminal justice system. Her research focuses on program evaluation using randomized controlled trial methodology; neuropsychological and forensic assessment; forming interdisciplinary collaborations within community, school, and correctional agencies; and developing psychosocial interventions for youth of color at high risk of system contact.

Deborah Gonzalez, JD is the Director of the Immigration Clinic at Roger Williams' University School of Law, where law students practice law under Gonzalez's supervision in the Immigration Court in Boston, Massachusetts, and before the U.S. Citizenship and Immigration Service in Johnston, Rhode Island. Prior to becoming the Director of the Immigration Clinic, Gonzalez was a partner at Gonzalez Law Offices, Inc. She is a member of the Federal and Rhode Island Bars, Women's Bar Association, Rhode Island Criminal Defense Lawyers Association, Rhode Island Hispanic Bar Association, Hispanic National Bar Association, American Immigration Lawyers Association, and American Bar Association.

Gail S. Goodman, PhD is Distinguished Professor of Psychology at the University of California, Davis. Her research concerns children's and adults' memory for trauma, child sexual abuse, trauma-related developmental psychopathology, forensic interviewing, and effects of legal involvement. She served as President of several divisions of the American Psychological Association (e.g., Developmental Psychology, American Psychology–Law Society) and is a consultant to the Children's Advocacy Center, Sacramento's Child Protective Services. She is internationally known for her research on victims and witnesses, which has been cited multiple times by the U.S. Supreme Court. Dr. Goodman has published widely and received national and international awards and numerous federal grants for her research. She received her PhD from the University of California, Los Angeles.

Michele Bratcher Goodwin is the Linda D. & Timothy J. O'Neill Professor of Constitutional Law and Global Health Policy at Georgetown Law School, where she serves as Co-Faculty Director of the O'Neill Institute. She is the author of numerous books, articles, chapters, and commentaries, and is currently *President* of the Law and Society Association. Her most recent book is *Policing the Womb: Invisible Women and the Criminalization of Motherhood*.

Thomas Grisso, PhD a clinical and forensic psychologist, is Emeritus Professor at the University of Massachusetts Medical School. His research and writing throughout his career have focused on the decision-making capacities of children, adolescents, and adults in legally relevant contexts, including criminal and juvenile courts as well as capacities to make medical decisions. He has also contributed substantially to evidence-based forensic psychological practice, publishing forensic assessment tools and shaping forensic psychology practice standards.

Harold D. Grotevant, PhD holds the Rudd Family Foundation Chair in Psychology at the University of Massachusetts Amherst, where he is the Founding Director of the Rudd Adoption Research Program. His research focuses on relationships in adoptive families (especially open adoption) and on identity development in adolescents and young adults. His work has resulted in over 175 articles and chapters as well as several books. He is a Fellow of the American Psychological Association, the Association for Psychological Science, and the National Council on Family Relations, and recipient of awards for research, teaching, mentoring, outreach, and educational leadership.

Vivian Hamilton is a Professor of Law, Founding Director of the William and Mary Center for Racial and Social Justice, and an affiliate faculty member of the

William and Mary Gender, Sexuality, and Women's Studies Program. Her research focuses on K–12 education and the rights of adolescents and emerging adults, and her work has been published in the *Boston University Law Review, North Carolina Law Review, University of Georgia Law Review,* and others. Professor Hamilton has been elected to the American Bar Foundation and American Law Institute and has served as Chair of the Section on Family and Juvenile Law of the Association of American Law Schools. She earned her BA in History from Yale College and JD from Harvard Law School.

Emily Haney-Caron is an Assistant Professor of Psychology and Director of the Youth Law and Psychology Lab at John Jay College of Criminal Justice. She holds a JD and a PhD in Clinical Psychology from Drexel University, and she completed a predoctoral clinical internship at Brown University Warren Alpert Medical School. Her research, scholarship, policy work, and teaching are all focused on the juvenile legal system, with a primary goal of contributing to system reform to increase racial justice and improve the system's developmental appropriateness. Dr. Haney-Caron is a licensed attorney in Pennsylvania and a licensed psychologist in New York.

Hayden Henderson, PhD is currently pursuing her JD at Stanford Law School and will graduate in spring of 2024. She received her PhD in Psychology from the University of Cambridge in 2019. At Cambridge, she worked with Professor Michael Lamb, examining the treatment of child victims in court. Afterward, she spent 3 years at the University of Southern California working as a postdoctoral research associate with Professor Thomas Lyon, where they explored ways to increase productivity and decrease reluctance in forensic interviews with child and adolescent victims.

Mariann A. Howland, MA is a National Science Foundation Graduate Fellow pursuing a PhD in Developmental and Clinical Psychology in the Institute of Child Development at the University of Minnesota. Her research is broadly centered on risk and resilience during the perinatal period, a sensitive window of development for both women and their children.

Sarah Hubner is a PhD candidate in the Department of Gerontology at the University of Nebraska Omaha. She is a research assistant and part-time instructor in the department and is a member of the CAPACITY lab. Hubner holds an MA in Social Gerontology from the University of Nebraska Omaha in addition to a BS (Human Physiology) and BA (Spanish) from the University of Iowa. Her research interests include cognition, modifiable health behaviors, and cumulative (dis)advantage. Her recent projects focus on technology, cognitive impairment, exercise/nutrition, and the relationships between behavior, health disparities, and morbidity in later life.

Clare Huntington is a Professor of Law at Columbia University. An expert in the fields of family law and poverty law, she serves as an Associate Reporter for the American Law Institute's *Restatement of the Law, Children and the Law*. She was an Attorney Advisor in the Justice Department's Office of Legal Counsel and clerked for

Justice Harry Blackmun and Justice Stephen Breyer of the U.S. Supreme Court, Judge Merrick Garland of the DC Circuit, and Judge Denise Cote of the Southern District of New York. Professor Huntington earned her JD from Columbia Law School and her BA from Oberlin College.

Emily C. Kemp, MA is a PhD student at Louisiana State University (LSU) in the American Psychological Association–accredited doctoral program in Clinical Psychology working in the lab of Dr. Paul Frick. Her research interests include the underlying mechanisms with which elevated callous–unemotional (CU) traits develop, neural and cognitive correlates to conduct disorder and chronic antisocial behavior, and assessment and intervention techniques for youth with elevated CU traits and persistent behavioral problems. She obtained a Bachelor of Science degree with highest honors in Psychology from the University of Texas at Austin in 2014 and a Master of Arts in Psychology from LSU in 2020.

J. Zoe Klemfuss, PhD is Associate Professor of Psychological Science at the University of California, Irvine. Her research focuses on factors that influence how children remember and report about their past experiences, and how these reports are perceived by others. This work is firmly rooted in cognitive and social developmental theory and has direct societal application, for example, in legal settings where a child's testimony may be deciding evidence in a case. Her work is published broadly in top academic journals, books, and online resources and is funded by sources such as the National Institute of Child Health and Human Development.

Michael E. Lamb, PhD is Professor Emeritus of Psychology at the University of Cambridge. He obtained his PhD in Psychology from Yale University. Lamb researches early family relationships, child care, developmental science and related public policy. This work has focused on children's testimony, divorce, child custody, child maltreatment, and the effects of child care on children's psychosocial development. His work on family relationships has focused on the role of parents and the importance of their relationships with children. He has also researched how custody arrangements affect parents' relationships with children and the benefit of shared parenting after divorce. Lamb has extensively researched forensic interviews with allegedly abused children and has developed best practices in regards to interviewing children about abuse. Lamb headed the Section on Social and Emotional Development of the National Institute of Child Health and Human Development for 17 years, has published approximately 700 professional articles and chapters, edited or authored 50 books, and is the Editor of *Psychology, Public Policy, and Law*. In addition, he is the former President of the American Psychological Association's Division on Developmental Psychology and the recipient of lifetime achievement awards from the Association of Psychological Science, the American Psychological Association, the Society for Child Development, and the American Psychology-Law Society as well as four honorary degrees from Universities in North America and Europe.

Thomas P. LeBel, PhD is an Associate Professor and Chair of the Department of Criminal Justice and Criminology in the University of Wisconsin–Milwaukee's Helen Bader School of Social Welfare. His research focuses on prisoner reintegration, desistance from crime, the stigma of incarceration, drug treatment courts, and interventions for criminal justice–involved women with substance use problems.

Shanna M. Y. Li is a master's student in Law and Forensic Psychology at Simon Fraser University. Her research interests include violence risk assessment and racial/ethnic minority youth in the justice system.

Allison Lloyd is a second-year PhD student in the Human Services Psychology program (Community track) at the University of Maryland, Baltimore. She earned her MA in Clinical Psychology at Towson University in 2019. Her current research focuses on trans and gender-expansive youths' perceptions of the police and experiences with school resource officers, and how these perceptions and experiences relate to their well-being. Using an intersectional framework, her research also examines how the nuances of race, gender, and socioeconomic status influence how trans and gender-expansive youth interact with law enforcement, inside and outside of school.

Thomas D. Lyon, JD, PhD is the Judge Edward J. and Ruey L. Guirado Chair in Law and Psychology at the University of Southern California Gould School of Law. A *magna cum laude* graduate of Dartmouth College and Harvard Law School, Lyon received his PhD. in Developmental Psychology from Stanford University. His research goal is to identify the most productive means of questioning children about abuse and violence He is past-president of the American Psychological Association's (APA) Section on Child Maltreatment (Division 37) and a former member of the Board of Directors of the American Professional Society on the Abuse of Children (APSAC). He has published more than 100 papers in peer-reviewed journals, and 30 book chapters and law review articles. He received the APA Award for Outstanding Dissertation in Developmental Psychology and the APSAC Outstanding Research Career Achievement Award. His work has been supported by the National Institutes of Health, the National Science Foundation, the United States Department of Justice, the National Center on Child Abuse and Neglect, the California Endowment, the Haynes Foundation, and the California Office of Emergency Services.

Lindsay C. Malloy, PhD is an Associate Professor at Ontario Tech University specializing in developmental and forensic psychology. She received her PhD in Psychology and Social Behavior from the University of California, Irvine, in 2008. Her research addresses questions concerning children's and adolescents' disclosure of negative or traumatic experiences, investigative interviewing and interrogation techniques, and implications of research findings for the legal system. Dr. Malloy's research has been funded by several U.S. and Canadian federal agencies, and she has received multiple awards for her commitment to conducting scientific research with practical implications for children and families.

Michelle E. Manasse is a Professor in the Department of Sociology, Anthropology, and Criminal Justice at Towson University, where her work primarily focuses on criminological theory testing and elaboration, with a particular emphasis on Agnew's general strain theory and gender. Some of her most recent publications have appeared in *Feminist Criminology* and the *Journal of Research in Crime and Delinquency*.

Stacy Metcalf, PhD is a Research Associate at Evalcorp, Inc. She completed her doctorate in Psychological Science at the University of California, Irvine. She received her bachelor's degree in Psychology from the University of San Francisco and worked in nonprofit, advocacy, and research prior to pursuing graduate school. Metcalf's research examines the experiences and consequences of adversity exposure (e.g., maltreatment) on youth development. To do so, she focuses on two related topics: how maltreatment affects socioemotional functioning and how contextual factors (e.g., policy changes, program implementation, societal events) impact youth's experiences and trajectories.

Andrea N. Montes, PhD is Assistant Professor at Arizona State University's School of Criminology and Criminal Justice. Her work has appeared in *Justice Quarterly*, *Crime and Delinquency*, *Criminology and Public Policy*, and *Criminal Justice and Behavior*. Her research focuses on theories of crime and punishment, crime prevention and school safety, and privatization.

Cynthia J. Najdowski, PhD is Associate Professor of Psychology and Director of the Social–Personality Psychology Doctoral Program at the University at Albany, State University of New York. Her research examines the psychological causes of miscarriages of justice, which occur when innocent individuals are mistakenly entangled in criminal legal systems or when guilty individuals wrongly evade punishment. She is specifically interested in understanding errors that affect marginalized and vulnerable populations. Professor Najdowski has received several nationally competitive grants and scholarly awards, including, most recently, the American Psychological Association Early Career Award for Distinguished Contributions to Psychology in the Public Interest.

Chelsey S. Narvey, PhD is Assistant Professor of Criminology and Criminal Justice at Sam Houston State University. Her research interests include corrections, developmental psychopathology, and criminological theory and policy. She has published on feelings of legitimacy and legal cynicism in correctional settings, as well as on the role of empathy in offending. Some of her work can be found in *Neuroscience and Biobehavioral Reviews*, *Aggression & Violent Behavior*, and *Neuroscience: Theory, Research, and Treatment*.

Alma P. Olaguez earned her PhD in Psychological Science from the University of California, Irvine. She is currently Assistant Professor at California State University Los Angeles. Her primary research interests bridge theoretical research on emotions and decision making and applies it to the legal setting. Specifically, her research examines how jurors' emotional reactions to child witnesses testifying in emotionally evocative cases can influence jurors' decision making and subsequently examines how trial procedures may mitigate the biasing effect of emotions. Her teaching interests include research methods and forensic psychology, in which students can learn about how empirical research in psychology can impact legal proceedings.

Jesús Palacios, PhD is Professor of Developmental and Educational Psychology at the University of Seville, Spain. His interest in human development and the family as a developmental context led him to the field of child abuse and child protection. With a special interest in foster care and adoption, his work has resulted in numerous articles and books. In addition, he has developed working materials for child protection professionals and collaborates with different governments in the promotion of the best child protection regulations and practices. He has actively promoted international adoption research networks and has been involved in the organization of international conferences.

Adrian Pendergast, MS graduated from Rhode Island College with a Master of Science in Clinical Mental Health Counseling in May 2021. Her current clinical work involves youth with problem sexual behaviors and their caregivers. Her research interests include health disparities, the transmission of intergenerational trauma, immigration, and gender and sexuality.

Alex R. Piquero is a Professor in the Department of Sociology and Criminology and Arts and Sciences Distinguished Scholar at the University of Miami (on public service leave while he is the Director of the Burea of Justice Statistics). His research interests include criminal careers, criminological theory, public policy, and quantitative methods. He is Fellow of both the American Society of Criminology and the Academy of Criminal Justice Sciences. In 2019, he received the Academy of Criminal Justice Sciences Bruce Smith Sr. Award for outstanding contributions to criminal justice and in 2020 he received the American Society of Criminology Division of Developmental and Life-Course Criminology Distinguished Achievement Award.

Jodi A. Quas, PhD is a Chancellor's Professor of Psychological Science at the University of California, Irvine, where she pursues research, conducts trainings, and advises on legislation concerning children's eyewitness capabilities, abuse disclosure, and the consequences of legal involvement on youth victims, witnesses, and defendants. She has received numerous awards for her work and student training, including the Nicholas Hobbs Award for Career Contributions from the Society for Child and Family Policy and Practice. As a Fulbright Specialist, she worked in Asunción, Paraguay, training broad government, private, and public audiences on the consequences of maltreatment on children, families, and communities, and on improving identification and protection of victimized youth.

Eleanor Rabior, JD is the Co-Executive Director of the Michigan Children's Law Center, a nonprofit that provides legal services to youth in Wayne County, Michigan.

Rabior is a Lawyer Guardian Ad Litem who represents youth who have been neglected or abused or who have been charged with delinquent behavior both in the courtroom and on appeal. She also represents children on the Wayne County Baby Court docket and has extensive training in trauma and development and is active in training clinicians and attorneys.

Cesar J. Rebellon is Professor in the Department of Criminology, Law, and Society at George Mason University. His research has been funded by the National Science Foundation and focuses on the ways in which family and peer environments contribute to juvenile crime and delinquency, as well as on the ways in which legal socialization affects rule-violating behavior. Some of his most recent publications have appeared in *Deviant Behavior*, *Journal of Child and Family Studies*, *Journal of Social Issues*, and *Victims and Offenders*.

Allison D. Redlich, PhD is Distinguished University Professor at George Mason University in the Department of Criminology, Law, and Society. She received her PhD in Developmental Psychology at the University of California, Davis. Her research focuses on confessions and interrogations, guilty pleas, and wrongful convictions. She is a Fellow of the American Psychological Association, the American Psychology–Law Society (AP-LS), Developmental Psychology (APA Division 7), and the Academy of Experimental Criminology. Professor Redlich is the recipient of two awards for excellence in mentoring and past president of the AP-LS.

Sarah Rendón García, EdM is a doctoral candidate in Human Development, Learning, and Teaching at the Harvard Graduate School of Education. She employs a social–emotional learning framework and dual-generation approach to examine the psychological well-being of families originating from Latin America and impacted by immigration status. Her dissertation focuses on the relationships between child development, the caregiver–child relationship, and children's understanding of immigration status. In addition to drawing on developmental–contextual and attachment theories, her own experiences growing up Latina with undocumented status in the northeast United States informs her work. Her research is generously supported by the Ford and Spencer Foundations.

Nicholas S. Riano, MAS is a PhD student of Psychological Science at the University of California, Irvine. His research focuses on the quality and availability of mental and physical health care for those impacted by the legal system, specifically surrounding metabolic and infectious diseases. He holds a joint appointment in the Department of Psychiatry at the University of California, San Francisco (UCSF), where he works closely with the UCSF PReMIUM Collaborative and the UCSF Center for AIDS Prevention Studies. He received his BA in Psychology from University of California, Berkeley, and his Master's in Criminology, Law, and Society from University of California, Irvine.

Danielle Rice, LMSW, IMH-E® is a workforce development specialist at the Michigan Association for Infant Mental Health and a doctoral student at Wayne State University pursuing a Dual-Title Degree in Social Work and Infant Mental Health. Rice began her career as a foster care worker and then worked as an infant mental health clinician serving families on the Wayne County Baby Court docket. Her research interests include experiences of reflective supervision for clinicians of color and implications for practice with families.

Matt Richie, PhD is an Assistant Professor in the Department of Criminal Justice at the University of Wisconsin–Oshkosh. His research focuses on jail recidivism and operations, desistance from crime, and pretrial/postconviction treatment diversion programming.

Nancy Rodriguez is Professor in the Department of Criminology, Law, and Society at the University of California, Irvine. Her research interests include inequality (race/ethnicity, class, crime and justice) and the collateral consequences of mass incarceration. Throughout her career, Dr. Rodriguez has engaged in use-inspired research and has been part of many successful collaborations with law enforcement, courts, and correctional agencies. In October 2014, Dr. Rodriguez was appointed by President Barack Obama to serve as the Director of the National Institute of Justice (NIJ). As Director of NIJ, she led the development of the agency's first strategic research plans in the areas of corrections, safety, health and wellness, and policing. She worked with federal partners to raise awareness of crime and justice research gaps and collaborated with federal partners to make investments in research and evaluation. Since leaving the NIJ, Dr. Rodriguez has dedicated her time to advancing research in the areas of racial and ethnic disparities and prison violence (with the generous support from the John D. and Catherine T. MacArthur Foundation and Arnold Ventures).

Karen L. Salekin, PhD is Associate Professor at the University of Alabama in the Department of Psychology. Dr. Salekin is a licensed clinical forensic psychologist who has conducted hundreds of forensic assessments; for the past 19 years she has specialized in the assessment of intellectual disability in criminal cases. She has consulted and testified in several capital cases involving intellectual disability determination. Dr. Salekin has assisted the American Psychological Association in the writing of amicus briefs related to the standards of assessment of intellectual disability in capital cases; these briefs were submitted to the Supreme Court of the United States. Dr. Salekin conducts research dedicated to evaluating the interface between the legal system and individuals with intellectual disability. She has published chapters and manuscripts focused within this context and has conducted workshops and trainings for lawyers, psychologists, and graduate students related to the assessment of intellectual disability in adult forensic assessments.

Julia M. Schillaci-Ventura earned her BA in Psychology (Honors First Class with Distinction) from Simon Fraser University. Her primary research interest includes assessing and reducing risk of violence among adolescents.

E. Carlisle Shealy is the Assistant Director at the Center for Gerontology at Virginia Tech. She completed her graduate education at Virginia Tech, earning her Master of Public Health in 2017 and a PhD in Environmental Design and Planning in 2021. While completing her PhD she also earned the Graduate Certificate in Gerontology. Her doctoral research explored the relationship between neighborhood design and walkability to understand the preferences of older adults in senior living communities. Dr. Shealy has a deep interest in end-of-life decision making and surrogate decision making, specifically in rural areas. She has recently contributed to projects on elder abuse, advance care planning, and the exploration of diversity and inclusion among older women of faith.

Rebecca J. Shlafer, PhD, MPH is Assistant Professor in the Department of Pediatrics at the University of Minnesota. She is a developmental child psychologist, with additional training in maternal and child public health. Her community-engaged research uses a health equity framework to examine the intersections of the criminal legal system, child development, and family well-being.

Emily M. Slonecker is Assistant Professor at Cabrini University. She received her PhD in Psychological Science from the University of California, Irvine, with a specialization in developmental psychology and quantitative methodology. She uses an interdisciplinary, cross-cultural framework to explore how cognitive development and autobiographical memory are related to health and well-being across diverse populations and contexts. Previously, Emily earned a BA in Psychology from the University of Maryland and an MA in Social Ecology from UC Irvine. She was also awarded a Post-Baccalaureate Intramural Research Training Award from the National Institute of Child Health and Human Development. Her research is broadly focused on the intersection between culture, cognition, and health.

Julianne S. Speck, BA is a doctoral student at Louisiana State University (LSU) in the American Psychological Association–accredited Clinical Psychology program working in the lab of Dr. Paul Frick. Her research and clinical interests include assessment and intervention for children and adolescents with conduct problems, particularly among youth with elevated callous–unemotional traits and with justice-involved youth. She also has interests in studying the effects of juvenile justice system involvement on youth's adjustment and using this knowledge to improve juvenile justice policy. Speck earned her Bachelor of Arts degree with distinction in Psychology from the University of Delaware in 2016.

Ann M. Stacks, PhD, LMFT, IMH-E® is the Director of the Infant Mental Health Program at Wayne State University's Merrill Palmer Skillman Institute. She holds a research/faculty endorsement from the Michigan Association for Infant Mental Health and has served as the university partner for the Wayne County Baby Court since 2008. Dr. Stacks's research focuses on caregiving that supports social–emotional development in early childhood. She is particularly interested in the protective role that caregiver reflective functioning and sensitivity play in supporting early childhood mental health and interventions that enhance reflective functioning and social–emotional competencies.

Kayleigh A. Stanek is a third-year doctoral student at Arizona State University's School of Criminology and Criminal Justice. Her research focuses on criminal justice responses to victims and victimization, specifically sexual assault and domestic violence. She is also interested in victimization among special populations such as college students, American Indian women, and other minority groups, and offenders and inmates. Among these groups, she is particularly interested in exploring victims' needs in terms of programming and criminal justice responses.

Margaret C. Stevenson, PhD is Associate Professor of Psychology at Kenyon College. She has been awarded various national and institutional grants and awards for scholarship, psychological service, and teaching, and has published over 30 peer-reviewed articles and chapters related to jury decision making and the intersection of children, psychology, race, and the law. She recently published two Oxford University Press edited volumes: *Criminal Juries in the 21st Century* and *The Legacy of Racism for Children*. She currently serves as President of the American Psychological Association Division 37, Child and Family Policy and Practice, Section on Child Maltreatment.

Rachel L. Taffe is a fourth-year undergraduate student double-majoring in Psychological Science and Criminology, Law, and Society at the University of California (UC), Irvine. Broadly, her research interests lie in applied developmental psychology and the reciprocal influences between children and the criminal justice system. After graduating from UC Irvine, Taffe plans to pursue a PhD in Developmental Psychology and a future career in academia.

Pamela B. Teaster is Professor and the Director of the Center for Gerontology at Virginia Tech. She is the North American Representative of the International Network for the Prevention of Elder Abuse, is Immediate Past President of the Board of Trustees for the Center for Guardianship Certification, and serves on the editorial boards of the *Journal of Elder Abuse and Neglect* and the *Journal of Trauma, Violence, and Abuse Review*. Dr. Teaster is a Fellow of the Gerontological Society of America and the Association for Gerontology in Higher Education and is a recipient of the Isabella Horton Grant Award for Guardianship (National College of Probate Judges), the Rosalie Wolf Award for Research on Elder Abuse (NAPSA), the Outstanding Affiliate Member Award (Kentucky Guardianship Association), and the Distinguished Educator Award (Kentucky Association for Gerontology). Former President of the National Committee for the Prevention of Elder Abuse, she has received continuous funding for over 20 years from public and private sources. Her areas of scholarship include the abuse of elders and vulnerable adults, guardianship, end-of-life decision making, ethical treatment of older adults, and public policy and public affairs. She has published over 200 scholarly articles, reports, and book chapters and is the editor/author of six books.

Jodi L. Viljoen was a nationally and internationally recognized expert in adolescent risk assessment and management. She was Professor of Clinical Forensic Psychology at Simon Fraser University and Associate Director of the Institute for the Reduction of Youth Violence. Her research, which focused on adolescent offending, particularly risk assessment, intervention planning, and efforts to manage and reduce reoffense risk, had—and will continue to have—significant impact on youth, their families, communities, and the justice system broadly.

Kathleen Walton Allen, JD is a Referee in the Michigan Third Judicial Circuit, Court, Juvenile Division. She has been licensed as a Michigan attorney for 35 years and a Juvenile Division Referee for 21 years. Referee Allen is the Wayne County Baby Court jurist. She serves on numerous committees, including the State Court Administrative Offices Neglect and Delinquency Court Rules and Court Forms Committee and the Court Improvement Taskforce, which is charged with improving case practice in child protective proceedings, providing training, and addressing barriers to safety, permanency, and well-being. She is also a member of the Child Welfare Quality Service Review team.

Katherine Waggoner is a PhD student in the Department of Criminology, Law, and Society at the University of California, Irvine. She earned a Master of Science in Criminal Justice and Public Safety at the O'Neill School of Public and Environmental Affairs at Indiana University. Her doctoral research primarily focuses on the impact of criminal justice system involvement on identity formation, the navigation of stigmatized identities, and the consequences of criminal justice policy.

Allison M. Whelan is a Sharswood Fellow at the University of Pennsylvania Carey Law School. Previously, Whelan was an associate at Covington & Burling LLP. She clerked for the Honorable Guido Calabresi of the U.S. Court of Appeals for the Second Circuit and the Honorable William J. Kayatta Jr. of the U.S. Court of Appeals for the First Circuit. She is the author of numerous law review articles and book chapters. Whelan holds a JD and an MA in Bioethics from the University of Minnesota.

Mary E. Wood, PhD, ABPP is Assistant Professor of Psychiatry and Behavioral Sciences at Vanderbilt University Medical Center. The majority of her training and interests (clinical and research) fall at the interface of psychology and the law, with a particular emphasis on the appropriate identification, assessment, and treatment of individuals with intellectual disability in forensic settings. Dr. Wood is board certified in forensic psychology by the American Board of Professional Psychology, and she has conducted nearly 1,000 forensic mental health evaluations for juvenile, criminal, and federal courts in several jurisdictions.

Joanna Woolman is Professor of Law and teaches at Mitchell Hamline School of Law in St. Paul, Minnesota. She teaches courses in Feminist Legal Theory, Child Welfare Policy, Criminal Law, and Constitutional Law. She is the Director of the Institute to Transform Child Protection at Mitchell Hamline. Part of the work of the institute is to provide direct legal representation to parents whose children have been removed into the child welfare system.

Lindsey E. Wylie, JD, PhD is a Court Research Associate at the National Center for State Courts and an adjunct instructor in the School of Criminology and Criminal Justice and the Department of Gerontology at the University of Nebraska Omaha. Dr. Wylie holds an MA in Forensic Psychology at John Jay College of Criminal Justice, a JD from the Nebraska College of Law, and a PhD in Social Psychology at the University of Nebraska–Lincoln. Dr. Wylie's work has focused on aging in the legal system, juvenile justice, public health policy, program evaluation, attribution theories and bias, and quantitative methods.

Joshua Wyman, PhD is Assistant Professor at King's University College, Western University. He received his PhD in School and Applied Child Psychology from McGill University in 2019. His research focuses on improving the best practice methods for interviewing children, youth, and older adults in criminal investigations. He has also published work in the areas of deception detection, lie-telling development, and social skills training programs for youth with developmental disabilities. Dr. Wyman is a licensed school and clinical psychologist in Ontario, Canada, and he works with children and youth in school and clinical settings.

Tina M. Zottoli is Associate Professor of Psychology and Director of the Legal Decision Making Lab at Montclair State University. She holds a PhD in Psychology from the City University of New York, John Jay College of Criminal Justice, and is a licensed clinical psychologist in the state of New York. Dr. Zottoli's scholarship focuses on decision making and legal competencies, with emphases on the decisions of adolescent defendants and reducing adverse outcomes for system-involved youth (e.g., wrongful conviction). Her clinical practice focuses on issues pertaining to legal competencies, violence risk, and sentencing mitigation, and she is regularly hired as a consultant in cases involving youth and young adults.

CHAPTER
1

Infant, Child, and Adolescent Development and the Law: Intersections, Interactions, and Influences

Jodi A. Quas and Allison D. Redlich

Abstract

The *Oxford Handbook of Developmental Psychology and the Law* includes two sections. The first section covers the developmental periods of *Infancy and Childhood* and *Adolescence*. The chapters included address a wide range of ways that children and youth come into contact with different facets of the justice system. At times, this contact is direct, with minors being questioned by forensic interviewers (as victims/witnesses or suspects) or participating in immigration, custody, or juvenile or criminal court hearings. At other times, the contact is indirect, with legal decisions being made on behalf of children that have profound implications for their futures. As described in this introductory chapter, the chapters reveal the complexity in children's and adolescents' experiences and the diverse ways that developmental science, law, policy, and practice can be considered in relation to one another.

Key Words: child victims/witnesses, adolescent suspects, adolescent defendants, school-to-prison pipeline, youth diversion programs, youth immigration, youth custody, adoption, child protection

When one considers the interface between developmental science and the law, a few key topics stand out, ones that have received considerable scientific, legislative, and even public attention during the past several decades. These include, most notably, children's memory, suggestibility, and eyewitness capabilities (e.g., Quas et al., 2000; Saywitz et al., 2017), and adolescents' experiences as suspects and defendants, including in interrogations and when involved in the juvenile or criminal systems (Cleary, 2017; Scott & Grisso, 1997). Yet, as the chapters in this volume demonstrate, this interface—even when restricted to just childhood or adolescence—covers a much larger range of topics. This includes, for instance, the consequence of maltreatment and legal interventions on infant and child development, the implications of early-onset antisocial behavior in children for the justice system, and the need for placement decisions to account for a myriad of familial, experiential, and developmental characteristics that can affect the outcomes of those decisions on children. Other examples include unaccompanied minors' understanding of and participation in immigration proceedings, child welfare responses and adoption policies, and the best interest of a child in contested custody cases. The chapters in the first section of the Handbook, while not comprehensive of all ways that children and adolescents might come into contact with different facets of the justice system, showcase both the range and complexity of youth's legal experiences, including how those experiences affect, and are affected by, the law.

Infancy and Childhood

A key theme across many of the chapters in this subsection concerns the links between child maltreatment and legal interventions. This theme is understandable given the sheer numbers of children exposed to maltreatment. Each year in the United States alone, approximately 4 million referrals involving upward of 7–8 million children are made to the authorities concerning suspected maltreatment (Child Maltreatment, 2020), nearly half of which result in social service or legal action. Several chapters focus on the children and families who experience this action.

Two chapters, for instance, direct attention toward the child welfare system, given that this system represents, for many children and families, the first one that responds when suspicions, risks, or evidence of maltreatment emerge. In Chapter 2, Stacks, Rice, Allen, and Rabior review interventions to improve outcomes for infants and toddlers who are exposed to maltreatment and subsequently immersed in the child welfare system. Stacks et al. lay the foundation for why early interventions are especially important. Not only is this age group overrepresented in the child welfare system, but also the rapid developmental changes during this period increase infants' and toddlers' sensitivity to environmental perturbations, leading to especially profound negative effects of maltreatment. That same sensitivity, though, also opens up opportunities for interventions to be maximally beneficial. Stacks et al. close with a discussion of several promising intervention programs supported by child welfare services, which is then followed by a compelling argument for continued legislative support to maintain and expand the programs for larger numbers of infants, toddlers, and families.

In Chapter 7, Huntington takes a different perspective of the child welfare system by focusing on its history, evolution, and current state. Her review highlights significant problems with the "crisis orientation" model followed by many social welfare agencies rather than models that prioritize prevention, and with the long-standing racial and economic inequality that has pervaded child welfare decisions and outcomes. Minoritized children and youth continue to be overrepresented in the child welfare system. They are more likely to be removed, have their relationship to their parents terminated, and exhibit poor short- and long-term outcomes. Huntington closes with a detailed description of why addressing these issues is crucial to foster healthy child development and improve outcomes for entire families.

Two other chapters are also relevant to child maltreatment and legal interventions. Slonecker, Olaguez, Taffe, and Klemfuss (Chapter 4) review the highly influential body of literature on children's eyewitness memory and suggestibility. The chapter begins with a broad overview of areas of consensus that have emerged from this literature, thereby providing some foundational knowledge for readers who may not be especially familiar with the research. The chapter then moves well beyond areas of consensus by first describing ongoing controversies and debates in the field about the accuracy of children's reports about their prior experiences, especially sexual abuse and other forms of maltreatment; and second discussing new research that systematically addresses these debates in ways that has direct implications for legal decision making, both in forensic interviews and trials when children's statements are at issue.

Of note, once children have disclosed maltreatment or other forms of victimization, some become immersed in the criminal justice system. For many, though, the maltreatment occurred in the home and children's legal involvement is in the dependency branch of the juvenile justice system. In aanother chapter focused on maltreatment and the legal system, Enriquez, Brown, Goodman, Metcalf, and Quas (Chapter 5) describe the consequences of this immersion, which, for most children, extends well beyond initial efforts to identify child victims that is, the investigative phase (e.g., a forensic interview). It involves repeated interviews, multiple interactions with social service and legal professionals, attending hearings and testifying, changing placements, receiving services, and reunion or termination of their parents' rights, all of which can last months or years. Enriquez et al. describe these experiences and then describe socioemotional and attitudinal consequences of those experiences, followed by the policy implications.

The remaining four chapters in the *Infancy and Childhood* subsection diverge somewhat from the prior chapters' emphasis on legal responses to suspected child maltreatment and turn to other types of contact children have with the legal system. Fabricius (Chapter 6) and Brabeck, Gonzalez, Rendón García, and Pendergast (Chapter 8) tackle two incredibly important and regularly overlooked populations of legally involved children, namely those involved in family court cases regarding custody and visitation, and those navigating the U.S. immigration system as unaccompanied immigrant youth. The challenges facing these two populations are significant and unique. Fabricius focuses on a decades-old debate concerning fathers, visitation, and custody, specifically on the extent to which young children need to be with their mothers or whether and how much contact with fathers is in the children's, father's, and family's best interest. Fabricius describes the history and significance of the debate along with relevant theory (e.g., attachment theory) and research. He closes with recommendations for legal professionals regarding how to integrate information about placement, fathers, and children's best interests into custody decisions. Brabeck et al. direct attention to youth, many of whom are older children and adolescents, who arrive at U.S. borders as unaccompanied minors, triggering a complicated series of actions by the U.S. government as officials evaluate the youth's experiences, risks, and needs. Decisions must be made about where to house the youth, whether there are available caregivers to take the youth, or whether the youth should be returned to their home country, and if so how. The youth's developmental capacities profoundly shape their understanding and engagement in the immigration system, and that engagement, beyond the youth's experiences, affects the system's responses. As Brabeck et al. explain, the immigration system continues to fail to take youth development into account in its responses and decisions, leading to significant and ongoing trauma, confusion, and adverse outcomes for many of the unaccompanied youth seeking protection from the United States at the borders.

In Chapter 3, Frick, Kemp, and Speck consider antisocial behavior in children as a precursor to and predictor of juvenile justice involvement later in development. The importance of applying a developmental lens to understand antisocial behavior cannot be overstated. That is, a majority of the work on antisocial behavior and justice involvement has focused on adolescents, who certainly are at risk and may well become immersed in the juvenile system because of delinquent acts. Yet, as Frick et al. explain, multiple developmental trajectories, beginning in childhood, can lead to problematic behavior. Juvenile justice actors need to consider these trajectories when making decisions about how best to respond to children, and later to adolescents, who engage in such behavior.

Finally, Palacios, Brodzinsky, and Grotevant (Chapter 9) highlight yet another important way that the legal system affects children, namely via adoption. Certainly, children may be adopted following termination of parental rights due to exposure to maltreatment and parents' failure to meet requirements specified in dependency case plans. Yet, adoption is significantly more complex and diverse, as it can occur at multiple time points in a child's life and with a range of different constellations of adoptive parents. In the chapter, Palacios et al. describe this complexity. The authors first consider how the study of adopted children has led to considerable advances in the field of developmental science, for instance, by helping to address classic questions about nature versus nurture, the influence of early experiences on later functioning, and identity development. Second, the authors discuss adoption practices, including how those practices have evolved into their present form. And third, Palacios et al. turn to how developmental science has informed, and can continue to inform, adoption law and practice. It is through the sharing of information specifically as it relates to adoption that the best decisions for children and their entire families can be made.

The section closes with an especially thoughtful integrative piece by Lyon and Lamb (Chapter 10), leading scholars in law, psychology, and development. Their piece touts the potential value of the research presented in the aforementioned chapters but also discusses the significant need to consider the limitations in the applicability of research as well. Scientists, scholars, and practitioners need to share ideas but also listen and consider their own biases when pursuing legally relevant research and when evaluating and discussing it in legal settings. Doing so will allow for the broadest and best impact possible.

Adolescence

The subsection on adolescent involvement in the legal system also reveals both complexity and diversity in adolescents' experiences as they move into and out of the system. In Chapter 11, Manasse and Rebellon address in detail how risk taking and tendencies toward antisocial behavior can typify some aspects of adolescent development, building on and extending some of the important ideas laid out by Frick et al. in the earlier chapter on antisocial behavior in childhood (Chapter 3). Manasse and Rebellon address the normative aspects of these traits as well as individual difference factors that can enhance or inhibit risky and/or antisocial behavior. The authors delve into the biological, familial, peer, and community influences, providing a comprehensive overview of how youth generally, and some specific subsets of youth, can find themselves in the face of legal involvement. In another chapter also focused on potentially problematic youth behavior, but also on responses that can exacerbate that behavior, Fine, Stanek, and Montes discuss the role of schools in youths' entry into the justice system (Chapter 18). Acknowledging that youth spend a majority of their waking hours in school, Fine and colleagues examine relations between schools and delinquency, programs designed to deter problematic behavior (e.g., zero tolerance) and the presence of policelike officials (e.g., school resource and probation officers) in schools and the likelihood of deterring or furthering justice system involvement. In short, schools, largely meant to protect children and increase safety, can provide a pathway into prison, particularly for minority youth. Fine et al. close with nine recommendations for preventing the school-to-prison pipeline, recommendations that have significant implications for policy and practice.

Other chapters in the *Adolescence* subsection direct attention to youths' experiences and capabilities once they are engaged in the justice system but also to ways of exiting the system. Wyman, Dianiska, Henderson, and Malloy (Chapter 12) and Cleary and Crane (Chapter 13) review what happens when youth are questioned by the police as either victims/witnesses or suspects of crimes,. Wyman et al. highlight the value of considering how adolescents' cognitive and socioemotional development shape their abilities while being questioned and while answering questions. The authors address both the willingness of youth to disclose relevant experiences and their ability to do so accurately and comprehensively. Next, Cleary and Crane discuss many of the same defining characteristics of adolescents reviewed by Wyman et al. (and others in this subsection), here linking those characteristics to juveniles' capabilities and limitations in interrogations. The authors describe current laws pertinent to juvenile suspect interrogations, and how these laws and their underlying assumptions do and do not map onto adolescent development, traits, and abilities (e.g., suggestibility, perceptions of authority). A crucial point made by Cleary and Crane, which is similar to that made in multiple other chapters (e.g., see Huntington, Chapter 7; Fine et al. Chapter 18; and Burke et al., Chapter 26), concerns how youth of color are uniquely affected and are at heightened risk of coerced and false confessions. In essence, both Wyman et al. (Chapter 12) and Cleary and Crane (Chapter 13) demonstrate the inherent risk of errors and reduced accuracy when youth are questioned without adequate safeguards in place.

After being questioned by police as suspects, youths may find themselves in diversion programs or in court as defendants. In Chapter 14, Zottoli, Daftary-Kapur, and Haney-Caron describe how youth defendants navigate their way through the juvenile and criminal justice systems. After charting the history of juvenile involvement in, and treatment by, the courts, Zottoli and colleagues describe the modern "era of developmental science" and its influence on case law from the nation's highest court and on understanding youths as defendants and appropriate sentencing outcomes. In Chapter 15, Fountain, Ducat, and Lloyd discuss less formal, alternative paths out of the court system, via diversion programs specific to youth. Diversionary routes can occur at the prearrest (police) stage, postarrest (court-sponsored programs), or via specialty youth courts, which include juvenile drug courts, juvenile mental health courts, and teen courts. Though designed with good intentions, Fountain and her colleagues describe the possible risks and pitfalls associated with these diversion programs and the general dearth of research demonstrating their effectiveness and fairness. Both Zottoli et al. and Fountain et al. also discuss how youth of color fare as defendants and how they often face disproportionate challenges throughout the court process.

In Chapter 16, Viljoen, Li, Schillaci-Ventura, and Cochrane provide a valuable overview of key aspects of youths' experiences after they are convicted in court, either at trial or via guilty plea—that is, their experiences while incarcerated in youth correctional facilities. Building on some of the contextual framing provided by Zottoli et al. (Chapter 14) regarding youth's experiences in the criminal and juvenile system, Viljoen and colleagues provide a description of the history of custodial options for youth, which move from almshouses and houses of refuges in the 18th and 19th centuries, to increased use of detention in the mid-20th century, to newer declining usage of incarceration in the 21st century. Although on the decline, still about 25% of convicted youth are incarcerated (rates that tend to be higher for youth of color). Viljoen et al. demonstrate the adverse effects of incarceration on recidivism rates, family and peer relations, school success, future employment, physical and mental health, victimization, and overall psychosocial development. They conclude their chapter with strategies to continue the decrease of the incarceration of youth.

Hamilton (Chapter 17) takes a step back and provides a macro-level view of adolescence and the construct of the legal age of majority. She prompts readers to "rethink the age of majority," arguing to abandon the conception of adulthood (currently at age 18 years) as a its own distinct legal status. In brief, she cogently lays out how laws that demarcate youth and adults (e.g., freedom from parental authority, contract rights, and the right to medical and procreative choice) no longer conform to the modern, gradual transitions into adulthood, but rather stem from outdated conceptualizations of discrete events (such as marriage or entry into the workforce). Although Hamilton's focus is not on criminal justice events, such as interrogation-related abilities, courtroom participation, or youth in carceral settings, her chapter provides an important backdrop for understanding and framing the content of the other chapters in the *Adolescence* subsection.

This backdrop is further eloquently described in Grisso's summary of the adolescent section (Chapter 19). He, like Lyon and Lamb (Chapter 10), describes both the enormous potential benefit of the research for improving vulnerable adolescents' encounters and experiences in the justice system and the need for caution and clear explanation of the precise ways in which research can and should be applied. His summary chapter lays out different types of research approaches, each with benefits and limitations. It is up to scientists and practitioners to work together to communicate and understand the different approaches and how best to apply findings to achieve maximum benefit for vulnerable youth.

Summary

In summary, when reviewed as a whole, the chapters included in the *Infancy and Childhood* and *Adolescence* subsections address a wide range of ways that children and youth come into contact with different facets of the justice system. At times, this contact is direct, with minors being questioned by forensic interviewers (as victims/witnesses or suspects) or participating in immigration hearings, custody hearings, or juvenile or criminal court hearings as witnesses or defendants. At other times, though, the contact is indirect, with legal decisions being made on behalf of children that have profound implications for their futures. The authors of the chapters approached the topics from varied disciplines and emphasized different themes (e.g., historical trends versus new promising approaches). We are thrilled that the authors did just this, as it reveals not only the complexity in children's and adolescent's experiences but also the diverse ways that developmental science, law, policy, and practice can be considered in relation to one another. With greater recognition of the different perspectives, findings, and implications, communication between developmental science and the law can be enhanced in ways that ultimately improve youth contact with the legal system and the consequences of that contact.

References

Child Maltreatment. (2020). *Child maltreatment report*. U.S. Department of Health & Human Services, Administration on Children, Youth and Families Children's Bureau.

Cleary, H. (2017). Applying the lessons of developmental psychology to the study of juvenile interrogations: New directions for research, policy, and practice. *Psychology, Public Policy, and Law, 23*(1), 118.

Quas, J. A., Goodman, G. S., Ghetti, S., & Redlich, A. D. (2000). Questioning the child witness: What can we conclude from the research thus far? *Trauma, Violence, & Abuse, 1*(3), 223–249.

Saywitz, K. J., Lyon, T. D., & Goodman, G. S. (2017). When interviewing children: A review and update. In J. Conte & B. Klika (Eds.), *APSAC handbook on child maltreatment* (4th ed., pp. 310–329). Sage.

Scott, E. S., & Grisso, T. (1997). The evolution of adolescence: A developmental perspective on juvenile justice reform. *Journal of Criminal Law and Criminology, 88*, 137–189.

CHAPTER 2

The Relational Context of Early Development: Consequences of Maltreatment in Infancy and Effective Early Intervention

Ann M. Stacks, Danielle Rice, Kathleen Allen, and Eleanor Rabior

Abstract

During pregnancy and the first three years of life, the environment impacts gene expression and neurobiology, which has a cascading effect on health and development across the lifespan. Understanding these effects is critical to assessing and responding to the impact of maltreatment during this developmental window. The current chapter provides this background knowledge. First, the science of child development is presented together with child welfare laws that support the well-being of maltreated children. Next, the impact of maltreatment during the embryonic, fetal, and infant periods of human development is reviewed. Finally, promising relationship-based interventions for maltreating families are described.

Key Words: infant, early childhood, pregnancy, maltreatment, intimate partner violence, substance abuse, abuse or neglect, infant mental health, relationship-based interventions, infant-toddler court teams

> The future of any society depends on its ability to foster the health and well-being of the next generation. Stated simply, today's children will become tomorrow's citizens, workers, and parents. When we fail to provide children with what they need to build a strong foundation for healthy and productive lives, we put our future prosperity and security at risk.
> —National Scientific Council on the Developing Child (2007)

Annual costs associated with substantiated child maltreatment are estimated to be $428 billion (Peterson et al., 2018). There are more than half a million confirmed child abuse cases each year, and over one third of those children are infants and toddlers (U.S. Department of Health and Human Services, 2020, 2021). More than one quarter (28.1%) of all children in foster care are between birth and 2 years old, and the highest victimization rate is for infants under the age of 1 year (U.S. Department of Health and Human Services, 2021).

The fetal period and the first 3 years after birth are considered critical periods of human development. The environment impacts gene expression and the developing brain, starting a cascading effect on physical health and development across the lifespan. Stressors, including abuse, neglect, caregiving instability, and inadequate nutrition early in life, can have a devastating impact on child well-being (National Academies of Science, Engineering, and Medicine, 2019a, 2019b). The means by which the experience of maltreatment impacts well-being requires an understanding of the science of development, including how biological and environmental factors transact to shape human development. This understanding is also essential when considering parenting interventions, especially those designed for the child welfare system (CWS).

Child welfare laws were developed to support the well-being of maltreated children and reduce costs associated with maltreatment. Some of the more comprehensive laws, designed to improve states' abilities to identify and treat victims of maltreatment, first went into effect in 1975. These initially favored removal as a way to intervene. Since then, there has been a shift in the laws, which now focus on preserving the family, identifying early delays, and reducing the time that children spend in out-of-home care as a way to improve children's safety and well-being (Meyers, 2008; see Huntington, Chapter 7, this volume). Because early maltreatment is associated with poorer health and development across the lifespan and poorer parenting in the next generation, it is essential to offer effective services to infants and their families.

The broad goal of the present chapter is to provide a context for interpreting potential child welfare services designed to address the needs of infants, toddlers, and families within the CWS. This chapter begins with a review of the developmental science related to human development from the fetal period through age 3 and legal policies relevant to maltreatment in the early years. These topics provide a context for understanding the long-term negative impact that early maltreatment can have on neurobiological development, physical health, and the development of social–emotional, cognitive, and language skills. The chapter then describes interventions that are effective at improving outcomes for maltreated infants and toddlers, including infant–toddler court teams.

Developmental Issues and Legal Policies Relevant to Maltreatment in Infancy

The environment profoundly influences human development. The transactional model of child development suggests that the quality of parent–child interaction influences and is influenced by children's characteristics. This begins in the prenatal period, where the fetal environment shapes physiological development to prepare the infant to survive in the world. Environmental risks during embryonic and fetal development periods can predispose individuals to poor physical and emotional health into adulthood, via their effect on genes (for reviews, see Lindsay et al., 2019; Robinson et al., 2019; Stevenson et al., 2020). The environment becomes even more important during the first 3 years of life, during which the quality of care that an infant receives is a strong predictor of development and well-being and during which maltreatment experiences exert a profound negative effect. U.S. child welfare laws and policies, including the Child Abuse Prevention and Treatment Act, the Adoption and Safe Families Act, and the Families First Prevention Services Act, are especially relevant to intervening to promote improved outcomes early in life following exposure to maltreatment.

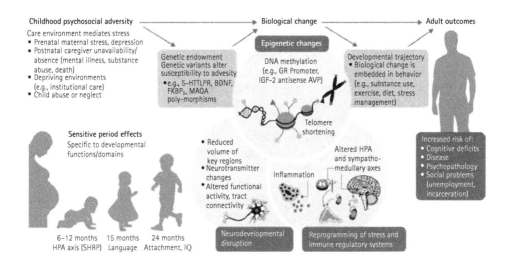

Figure 2.1 Biological Pathways from Early Psychosocial Adversity to Adult Outcomes.

The Science of Early Development

Before discussing child welfare laws and interventions for young maltreated children, it is helpful to understand early development, including how maltreatment and related adversities affect development. The trajectory of a child's development is influenced by the interaction of biological and environmental influences that start before birth and continue throughout the lifespan (Bronfenbrenner & Morris, 2006; National Academies of Science, Engineering, and Medicine, 2019a). The prenatal to early childhood period of development is marked by rapid growth and development of the brain and body and is a critical time for children to get on track to meet their full potential (National Academies of Science, Engineering, and Medicine, 2019b; Nelson et al., 2020).

Both genetics and the environment play a role in early human development (see Figure 2.1). Increasingly, research is concerned with the combined contribution of multiple genes that influence development. For example, more than 900 genes influence temperament (Zwir et al., 2021). Temperament is one's innate biological disposition that impacts behavior, emotional reactions, and affiliations (Cloninger et al., 2019) and how one perceives and responds to the environment, including shyness, activity level, novelty seeking, reactivity, adaptability, persistence, and distractibility. Early temperamental dispositions are stable in infancy (Bornstein et al., 2015), across early childhood (Bornstein et al., 2019; Rothbart, 2007), and into middle childhood (Neppl et al., 2010). Further, certain constellations of infant temperament predict the development of anxiety, depression (Clauss & Blackford, 2012), attention difficulties (Willoughby et al., 2017), and psychopathology (Kostyrka-Allchorne et al., 2020).

Genetics can play a role in physical health, learning, and emotional and behavioral development. The growing field of epigenetics demonstrates that the environment can impact how genes work—whether they are turned "on" or "off" and whether they enable the body to adapt to its environment (Marsit, 2015). Through epigenetic changes, the environment modulates gene expression and shapes brain development, which affects learning and behavior. The pattern of gene expression can increase vulnerability, or it can increase resilience (Kumsta, 2019). For example, stress during pregnancy can impact the methylation of several genes responsible for the regulation of the hypothalamic–pituitary–adrenal (HPA) axis, which is the body's stress response system (for reviews, see Cao-Lei et al., 2020; Glover et al., 2018). Maternal caregiving can also affect how genes are expressed. Krol and colleagues (2019) demonstrated that the oxytocin system, which plays a role in the emergence of complex social behavior, is shaped by the quality of maternal care in the first 6 months of infancy. In the study, the researchers found that higher maternal engagement in play predicted changes in the expression of the oxytocin receptor gene, which in turn was associated with a less difficult infant temperament. Therefore, the caregiving environment can be a powerful force in shaping development because of its impact on developmental outcomes, which are themselves mediated by epigenetic changes.

Development is also shaped by the caregiver–child relationship. Studies demonstrate that parenting can "get under the skin" (McEwen, 2012, pg. 1) and that the quality of early attachment regulates the stress response system, both of which play a role in social–emotional development (Craig et al., 2021). Decades of research show that sensitive parenting is associated with developing a secure attachment relationship, whereas harsh, intrusive, and rejecting parenting is associated with an insecure attachment (Fearon & Belsky, 2018; Lucassen et al., 2011; Madigan et al., 2006). The quality of parenting interactions and attachment both predict brain development (Bernier et al., 2019; Moutsiana et al., 2014, 2015; Taylor-Colls & Fearon, 2015), language development (Madigan, Prime, et al., 2019; Pungello et al., 2009), social–emotional development, and psychopathology (Fearon et al., 2010; Groh et al., 2017). Moreover, positive caregiving is a protective factor against poor developmental outcomes among children placed at-risk. For example, parental reflective functioning and sensitive parenting protect infants who have a difficult temperament from developing behavior problems (Kochanska, 1997; Thomas et al., 2017; Wong et al., 2017). Among children exposed to alcohol prenatally, only those whose parents are insensitive and provide lower levels of cognitive stimulation have IQ deficits (S. W. Jacobson et al., 2004). Maltreated infants and toddlers who had high levels of temperamental and neurodevelopmental risk at the time of their report to Child Protective Services (CPS) showed improvements in their cognitive and behavioral development if they were placed with caregivers who were sensitive and provided high levels of cognitive stimulation (Jaffee, 2007). High-quality childcare characterized by sensitive caregiver–child interactions also supports emotion regulation for at-risk infants and toddlers who have high temperamental and parenting risks (Mortensen & Barnett, 2019).

In early childhood, caregiving quality and attachment predict developmental outcomes and psychopathology and are also associated with parenting and attachment in the next generation. For example, there is a concordance between a mother's attachment to her parents and her infant's attachment (Berthelot et al., 2015; Verhage et al., 2016). The intergenerational transmission of attachment is mediated by several factors, including parental reflective functioning (Slade et al., 2005), mind-mindedness (Arnott & Meins, 2007), and parenting sensitivity (Behrens et al., 2016; Verhage et al., 2016). These malleable factors are targeted in attachment-based interventions, which improve parenting and infant development (see section Interventions for Maltreated Infants). Likewise, research shows that parents who were maltreated as children are at higher risk for dysfunctional parenting (Savage et al., 2019) and maltreating their children (Assink et al., 2018; Bartlett et al., 2017; Madigan, Cyr, et al., 2019). Therefore, the experience of safe, stable, and nurturing relationships has the potential to break the cycle of maltreatment (Schofield et al., 2013).

Unique Needs for Intervention Following Maltreatment in Early Development
Legal and policy interventions need to focus on early development following maltreatment. Supporting optimal child development and interrupting the intergenerational cycle of maltreatment need to begin in pregnancy, when exposure to substances and maternal stress can

impact how genes are expressed and how the brain develops, both of which influence later development. This support needs to continue throughout infancy when interactions with caregivers have the most profound effect on development.

In the late 1990s and early 2000s, there was a notable lack of data about the well-being of children in foster care. Data that were available, though, painted a grim picture for infants. For example, infants had much longer stays in foster care and were less likely to be reunified with their biological parents than older children (Wulczyn et al., 2001, 2002). Babies also experienced the highest rates of repeated abuse (Palusci et al., 2005), and babies who entered care in the first year of life had the highest rates of reentry into care (Courtney, 1995). Data also suggested that infants were suffering from high rates of developmental delay, with only the most severely affected being referred for an assessment (Leslie et al., 2002), despite policy statements from the American Academy of Pediatrics (1994). Finally, even when maltreated infants were identified as delayed, they were not enrolled in treatment (Simms, 1989).

In 1997, Congress approved funding for the Administration for Children and Families to conduct a nationally representative study of children reported to CPS. The National Survey of Child and Adolescent Well-being (NSCAW) sought to determine whether the CWS met the needs of children and families to inform policy decisions. The first cohort, NSCAW I, began in 1999 and included more than 6,200 children followed for up to 6 years. The second cohort, NSCAW II, started in 2008 and followed 5,800 children for 3 years. NSCAW III began in 2017 and is ongoing.

Findings from NSCAW I showed that 35.2% of infants and toddlers reported for maltreatment exhibited developmental delays, and only 12.7% were referred to services to address their delays (Casanueva, Cross, & Ringeisen, 2008). Similarly, Stahmer and colleagues (2005) found a very high need for developmental and behavioral services among maltreated toddlers (41.8%) and preschoolers (68.1%) and that less than one quarter of children under the age of 3 years were receiving these services. In addition to high rates of developmental delays, children who entered foster care in the first year of life showed significant decreases in their language development while they were in care (Stacks et al., 2011). Infants placed in foster care in their first year of life spent nearly 3 years in care (Stacks & Partridge, 2011) and experienced high levels of caregiver instability across early childhood (Casanueva et al., 2014). The NSCAW studies have been valuable in identifying the unique developmental risk of maltreatment in early childhood, helping to determine whether policy changes are leading to improved outcomes, and informing amendments made to child welfare legislation.

Laws and Legal Policies

Maltreatment can profoundly impact development and well-being across the lifespan, and thus it is important to identify which children have been maltreated. The Federal Child Abuse and Prevention Act (CAPTA) requires each state to have provisions or procedures to mandate certain individuals to report abuse or neglect of a child (42 U.S.C. § 5106a(b)(2)(B)(i)). States then specify professionals and other persons who are required to do so. Most states mandate that social workers, teachers, other school personnel, medical professionals, childcare providers, law enforcement officers, and mental health professionals report suspected or known child abuse or neglect. Typically, mandated reporters will have frequent contact with children (Child Welfare Information Gateway, 2019). Unfortunately, there are racial and socioeconomic disparities in the CWS, where Black and American Indian/Alaska Native families are disproportionately represented. Black families are more likely to be reported for maltreatment, more likely to have substantiated cases of maltreatment, and more likely to have children who are placed in out-of-home care. Once in care, the children are less likely to receive services and have longer times to permanency (Child Welfare Information Gateway, 2021; Ingoldsby et al., 2021).

Two sections of CAPTA are specific to infants and toddlers. Section 106(b)(2)(B)(xxi) requires that states have procedures for referring infants whose maltreatment is substantiated to early intervention services funded by Part C of the Individual with Disabilities Act (IDEA) so that their delays are identified and they receive appropriate services (Administration for Children and Families, 2021). Section 5106a(b)(2)(B)(ii)–(iii) mandates states to have a requirement that health care providers make a report to CPS when an infant is born prenatally exposed to drugs and alcohol, including those with fetal alcohol spectrum disorders (FASD). The Comprehensive Addiction and Recovery Act of 2016 (P.L. 114-198) further requires states to develop a "plan of safe care" (POSC) for infants who have been born exposed to or affected by prenatal drug or alcohol use. The plan should address the immediate needs of the infant's safety, health, and development; it must also include the affected parent or caregiver's health and substance abuse treatment needs. In most states, the child welfare agency formulates the POSC, but in some states, the health care provider may initiate the plan as part of the discharge process (Child Welfare Information Gateway, 2020).

In response to the growing number of children languishing in foster care in the 1990s, Congress passed the Adoption and Safe Families Act of 1997 (ASFA; P.L. 105-89) to shorten the length of time that children spend in foster care and facilitate timely placement of foster children into safe, stable, and permanent homes. ASFA set forth timelines for permanency planning hearings to be held within 12 months of the child being placed into foster care to ensure a permanent plan for the child to be returned to the parent, placed for adoption, or placed with a relative or legal guardian. The child welfare agency must also make reasonable efforts to maintain children in their home or alleviate the risks that brought the child into care, except in the case of egregious abuse (e.g., sexual abuse, prior involuntary termination of a sibling, severe and repeated abuse). ASFA set timelines for termination of parental rights, including when (a) the child has been in care for 15 of the past 22 months, (b) the child has been abandoned, or (c) the parent has been convicted of a crime related to family violence (e.g., sexual abuse, murder of a sibling, solicitation of a child). The timelines for termination of parental rights do not apply if the child is in the care of a relative, services have not been provided to the family, or termination is not in the child's best interest.

While the provision of services was an important part of ASFA, before 2018, child welfare agencies could not use federal funding to provide services to children reported for maltreatment or maltreated children residing at home with their parents. For infants and toddlers, this is especially problematic because children with unsubstantiated cases of maltreatment experience equally high rates of developmental delays (Casanueva, Cross, & Ringeisen, 2008). The Families First Prevention Services Act (FFPSA; P.L. 115-123) enacted in 2018 allowed states to use Title IV-E of the Social Security Act funding for time-limited prevention services for children at risk of out-of-home placement, their parents and caregivers, and pregnant and parenting youth. To use these funds, the child must be at imminent risk of entering foster care but, with services, can remain safely in the home or with a kinship placement. These funds can be used for up to 12 months, beginning when the child is identified as a candidate for foster care. Families can also receive preventative services more than once when a child is later identified as a candidate for foster care. Additionally, unlike other Title IV-E requirements for reimbursement, families are eligible for prevention services and programs whether or not they meet the Aid to Families with Dependent Children income eligibility requirements.

The types of services provided to families under the FFPSA include mental health and substance abuse prevention and treatment offered to parents by a qualified clinician, in-home parenting programs, and individual or family counseling. The FFPSA requires services and programs to be trauma informed, they must also meet evidence-based requirements that follow promising or well-supported practices as defined in the FFPSA. The prevention plan must be written to specify what services are needed for the family and must identify the strategy for the child to remain safely at home. The services provided to children, including services that support more sensitive and responsive caregiving during and after involvement in the CWS, can help place children on a healthy developmental trajectory by supporting parenting quality and infant attachment. For infants and toddlers, these policies, which are designed to reduce time in care and placement changes, may support the development of an organized or secure attachment and have long-term implications for well-being.

Forms of Maltreatment

As already explained, the environment strongly affects development in the embryonic and fetal periods and throughout the first 3 years of life. Next, we discuss forms of maltreatment most likely to occur during these developmental windows. Because extant research typically focuses on maltreatment after a child is born, we spend more time describing maltreatment-related influences on prenatal development.

Prenatal Maltreatment

Pregnancy, infancy, and early childhood offer the unique opportunity to prevent adverse maternal and child outcomes (Olds, 2008). When considering the prenatal environment, two experiences in utero, prenatal exposure to substances (PSE) and prenatal exposure to intimate partner violence, *may* be considered maltreatment because of the potential for long-term neurodevelopmental impairments. Pregnancy is a time when women are most likely to successfully stop using substances (see Massey et al., 2015, 2018), yet the fear of encountering the CWS may prevent some women from seeking treatment. It is important to recognize that policies that list these experiences as forms of maltreatment may further the racial and socioeconomic disparities that exist in the CWS and decrease the probability that families will receive timely and appropriate services (see Ingoldsby et al., 2021).

PRENATAL EXPOSURE TO SUBSTANCES

Between 2000 and 2019, there was a 20.4% increase in children being placed into foster care due to parental alcohol or drug abuse (National Center on Substance Abuse and Child Welfare, 2019). More than three quarters of maltreatment victims under the age of 1 year have confirmed exposure to alcohol or drugs (U.S. Department of Health and Human Services, 2021), which can cross the placenta and impact fetal brain and organ development (Behnke et al., 2013; Koponen et al., 2020), resulting in preterm birth and low birth weight (Austin et al., 2022; Corsi et al., 2019). The outcomes of prenatal substance exposure are dependent on the duration and extent and the type of substance(s) used (Anthony et al., 2010).

Prenatal Exposure to Alcohol. Prenatal alcohol exposure (PAE) is the known leading cause of intellectual disabilities (Hoyme et al., 2016; Popova et al., 2016. It is prevalent in child welfare, yet up to 80% of cases are missed, highlighting the importance of routine screening, especially for children who enter the CWS after infancy (Chasnoff et al., 2015; Ingoldsby et al., 2021; Lange et al., 2013). There is a lack of knowledge by child welfare staff about the prevalence and long-term impact of PAE and how to assess for it (Ingoldsby et al., 2021). The damaging effects of PAE appear in many developmental domains, including learning and memory, executive function, attention, and language development, with these extending throughout childhood and into adulthood (J. L. Jacobson et al., 2021; Riley et al., 2011). PAE also impacts sleep movements and sleep quality in utero that extend into infancy (Inkelis & Thomas, 2018; Troese et al., 2008). The structural and functional effects on the brain, organs, and body systems; growth impedance; and neurobehavioral disabilities caused by PAE are known as FASD. Children diagnosed with FASD also have an increased likelihood of experiencing mental health issues, including anxiety, mood disorders, depression, attention-deficit/ hyperactivity disorder (ADHD), substance use, and suicide (Coles et al., 2009; Mattson et al., 2011).

Prenatal Exposure to Cigarettes. Like PAE, prenatal exposure to maternal smoking has been widely studied in human and animal models. While smoking during pregnancy has decreased, nearly 7% of pregnant women report smoking (Azagba et al., 2020). Across studies, maternal smoking during pregnancy is associated with several negative effects, including infant mortality, neurobehavioral and cognitive deficits, congenital heart defects, externalizing behaviors, difficulty with self-regulation, and preterm birth (Bublitz & Stroud, 2011; Cui et al., 2016; Estabrook et al., 2015; L. J. Lee & Lupo, 2013).

Prenatal Exposure to Drugs. It can be challenging to determine the impact of prenatal drug exposure on developmental outcomes because many women who use drugs in pregnancy use more than one drug, plus alcohol and/or cigarettes. Data on prenatal drug exposure (PDE) has not indicated the same severity of neurocognitive, physical, and developmental problems as those reported with FASD. Yet, PDE is still associated with increased and lasting developmental issues. Research on prenatal exposure to opioids, cocaine, and marijuana is reviewed here.

The opioid use disorder (OUD) rate at delivery increased 131% between 2010 and 2017 (Hirai et al., 2021). Women who use opioids during pregnancy are less likely to seek prenatal care, they are at increased risk for postpartum depression and death, and their infants have longer stays in the hospital (Haight et al., 2018). Neonatal abstinence syndrome (NAS) and neonatal opioid withdrawal syndrome (NOWS) are the most common outcomes of prenatal opioid exposure. Approximately 50%–80% of exposed infants will develop NAS, a withdrawal syndrome characterized by tremors, hyperthermia, sweating, irritability, excessive crying, low birth weight, respiratory problems, and seizures (Jansson & Patrick, 2019 Jones et al., 2010). Prenatal opioid exposure has also been associated with congenital heart defects, decreased brain volume, and low birth weight (Patrick et al., 2015; Walhovd et al., 2008). Increasingly research is showing that exposure to opioids in utero is associated with poorer neurocognitive, motor, and behavioral outcomes that persist into childhood; however, there is a wide range of effects among exposed infants based on gene–environment interactions, the caregiving environment after birth, exposure to other substances, and the specific opioid exposure in pregnancy (see Larson et al., 2019, and Yeoh et al., 2019, for systematic reviews).

Common treatment intervention for opioid misuse during pregnancy is medication-assisted treatment (MAT) with methadone or buprenorphine. Both mental health treatment and prenatal care are recommended along with MAT to treat opioid abuse during pregnancy rather than detoxification because of the risk of relapse and stress (Atkins & Durrance, 2020; Terplan et al., 2018). Exposure to MAT during pregnancy can result in NAS; however, the outcomes for mothers and infants are significantly better than those with exposure to heroin and opioid pain relievers (Atkins & Durrance, 2020).

The impact of prenatal exposure to cocaine has been highly studied and is associated with preterm delivery, placental displacement, low birth weight, and smaller head circumference (dos Santos et al., 2018). Bauer and colleagues (2005 found that infants exposed to cocaine in utero had a higher frequency of tremors, irritability, hyperalertness, and autonomic instability. Prenatal cocaine exposure during the first trimester is associated with decreased sociability, increased withdrawal, and increased anxious/depressed symptomatology in children (Richardson et al., 2015). Early behavior, language, and reading problems extend into late adolescence (Landi et al., 2017; Min et al., 2018).

A growing number of states are legalizing the recreational and medicinal use of cannabis, and prenatal cannabis use increased by 170% from 2009 to 2016 (Nashed et al., 2021). Depending on the sample of women studied, cannabis use during pregnancy ranges from 4.2% to 35%, and many women believe that it is relatively safe to use during pregnancy (Ko et al., 2020; Mark et al., 2017; Young-Wolff et al., 2017). Yet, large studies reveal that infants exposed to cannabis in utero are more likely to be born preterm, have low birth weight, and have higher mortality in the first year of life (Shi & Di Liang, 2021). Willford and colleagues (2010) found that children who were prenatally exposed to cannabis had lower scores on tests of visual problem solving, visual–motor coordination, and visual analysis than children who had no prenatal cannabis exposure. Some studies also find that the psychoactive ingredient in cannabis, Δ-9 THC, increases the risk of cognitive impairment and mental health disorders (Nashed et al., 2021). Outcomes vary across studies based on the frequency of use, the concentration of THC and cannabidiol, and whether individuals use other substances concurrently, making it difficult to know the true unique effects of cannabis use in pregnancy.

Polydrug Use. Polydrug use is common among prenatal substance users (Bada et al., 2012). The use of both alcohol and drugs makes it challenging to separate the effects of PAE and PDE (Koponen et al., 2020). Across studies, exposure to multiple drugs is associated with preterm delivery, poor neuroanatomical and cognitive functioning, and behavior problems (Nygaard et al., 2018; Walhovd et al., 2012).

Summary. In sum, infants exposed to both legal and illegal substances have an increased likelihood of involvement with the CWS, yet underdiagnosis and misdiagnosis of FASD remain problematic, especially for children who come to the attention of CPS after infancy. Some states have policies that support substantiating child maltreatment and removing children from the home if they have been exposed to drugs prenatally, which furthers the racial and socioeconomic disparities in child welfare. A disproportionate number of Black and low-income women are reported to CPS because of substance use during pregnancy, particularly if exposed to crack cocaine, which is far less damaging than alcohol, especially in the context of sensitive caregiving. Exposure to maternal smoking is not considered a form of maltreatment, despite effects that are similar to exposure to other drugs. Hospital screens at birth rarely test for alcohol (see Ingoldsby et al., 2021). Policies like the FFPSA, together with the Children's Bureau's priority to address disproportionality, present opportunities for states to reconsider the circumstances under which children who are exposed to substances in utero are removed from their parents' care. Prenatal exposure to substances may be considered a form of maltreatment because of the impact on infant health and well-being and may make prenatally exposed children difficult to parent. However, in the context of sensitive and nurturing parenting, removing a prenatally exposed infant from their parent may result in more harm to the infant.

SUBSTANCE USE ON PARENTING BEHAVIORS

One reason for enduring adverse effects of PAE and PDE may be related to alcohol and drugs' impact on parenting behaviors (see Hans, 2002). Maternal substance use in pregnancy is associated with lower quality parenting (Flykt et al., 2021; Landi et al., 2011; Mayes & Sean, 2002), including intrusive and hostile features in mother–infant interactions (Belt et al., 2012) and maltreatment (Kepple, 2017). One reason for the association between addiction and lower quality parenting is that substance use takes over the brain's reward system and contributes to the continued use of substances, making parents less physically and emotionally available (Everitt & Robbins, 2005; Landi et al., 2011; Rutherford et al., 2011). Some studies suggest a cascading developmental pathway whereby maternal substance use in pregnancy predicts poorer quality parenting, which then predicts poorer social–emotional development (Eiden et al., 2014; Flykt et al., 2021). Flykt and colleagues (2021) also found that those who experienced higher quality parenting in infancy had better social–cognitive outcomes among children with PAE and PDE. This highlights the importance of effective parenting interventions for substance-using women whose children have come to the attention of the CWS. PAE and PDE have direct and indirect impacts on infant well-being and are a risk factor for maltreatment. When prenatal exposure is *defined* as maltreatment, it may be more difficult for families to receive the necessary services and support to address the underlying issue of parental substance abuse and to support child development. Other exposures in utero, like exposure to intimate partner violence, are not considered maltreatment, yet they also significantly impact infants' physical and psychological well-being.

PRENATAL INTIMATE PARTNER VIOLENCE

Approximately 36% of women experience intimate partner violence before and during pregnancy (Bonomi et al., 2006). Meta-analytic findings suggest that exposure to intimate partner violence is associated with poor birth outcomes (Donovan et al., 2016) and low birth weight (Yost et al., 2005); extreme low birth weight is a predictor of a variety of health outcomes in adulthood, including mental health problems (Mathewson et al., 2017), hypertension (Mu et al., 2012), type 2 diabetes (Mi et al., 2017), and cardiovascular structure and function (Harris et al., 2020). Another mechanism by which intimate partner violence may impact child development outcomes is its effect on maternal stress and the fetus's exposure to stress hormones (Martinez-Torteya et al., 2017). Maternal stress during pregnancy due to interpersonal violence can impact the developing fetal brain and stress response system (Davis et al., 2011; Mueller & Tronick, 2020; Ramborger et al., 2018). These changes in prenatal neurohormonal chemistry can be associated with later mental illness, neurodevelopmental disorders, and decreased intellectual functioning (Tuovinen et al., 2021).

Another mechanism by which prenatal exposure to intimate partner violence impacts developmental outcomes is its effect on the caregiving relationship. Levendosky and colleagues (2011) found that infants and young children are indirectly affected by prenatal exposure to intimate partner violence because of the mental health challenges experienced by their mothers. Mothers who have experienced intimate partner violence may have an increased likelihood of difficulty bonding with their infants due to the stress brought on by victimization (Anderson & Van Ee, 2018) and are at increased risk of insecure attachment representations in pregnancy (Huth-Bocks et al., 2004), which in turn impact parental warmth, caregiving, and the development of healthy attachments (Levendosky et al., 2011; Zeanah et al., 1999).

Maltreatment in Infancy

Infants are overrepresented in maltreatment reports and foster care relative to other children and adolescents. Among the 656,243 U.S. children with substantiated maltreatment cases in 2019, 34% were under the age of 4 years (U.S. Department of Health and Human Services, 2021). Just over one-quarter million children entered foster care in 2019; among those, 38% were under the age of 4 years. More than three quarters of the children who enter care in their first year of life have been exposed to drugs or alcohol prenatally (U.S. Department of Health and Human Services, 2020). Next, we discuss the effects of these experiences in detail, focusing on the neurobiological and cognitive effects, as well as the longer term effects, highlighting how maltreatment early in life affects health across the lifespan.

MALTREATMENT AND NEUROBIOLOGICAL DEVELOPMENT

Much of what we know about how perturbations in early caregiving impact neurobiological development are from the animal literature, studies of abandoned infants in institutionalized care, or studies of a combination of early life stressors, including self-reported maltreatment or trauma, across childhood and adolescence. These studies document the negative effect that early stressors, including maltreatment, can have on the structure and function of the brain (see reviews by Agorastos et al., 2019; Herzberg & Gunnar, 2020 Holochwost et al., 2021; Nelson et al., 2019), telomere length (Ridout et al., 2018), inflammation, and cardiovascular risk (Danese et al., 2007, 2009) in adulthood. While studies of documented maltreatment among human infants are limited, the findings largely confirm what is known from the animal and human research on sequelae of early life stress. Maltreated infants are deprived of social and/or physical care that is needed for healthy development, which can result in increased fear and anxiety (Herzberg & Gunnar, 2020), making it a form of toxic stress that has a downstream effect on development (Nelson et al., 2020).

Hypothalamic–Pituitary–Adrenal Axis. Studies of the impact of documented abuse, neglect, and exposure to intimate partner violence in the first 3 years of life show a negative effect on the functioning of the HPA axis, commonly referred to as the stress response system because it regulates the body's response to and recovery from stress. A well-regulated HPA axis shows a peak in cortisol in the morning that declines over the day to almost zero at the onset of sleep. Cortisol levels also rise in response to stressful events throughout the day (Cone et al., 2003). Studies of stress exposure among young children with a history of maltreatment have assessed waking levels of cortisol, patterns of cortisol throughout the day, and cortisol reactivity in response to acute stressors. Studying cortisol in infants is particularly important because atypical patterns of cortisol responses or cortisol levels can be neurotoxic (see Conrad et al., 2017). Across studies, maltreated children tend to show dysregulation of the HPA axis, either high or low morning cortisol, a flat or blunted cortisol response across the day, or cortisol reactivity that is hyper- or hyporesponsive to a stressor. This variability in response may be related to the severity and chronicity of maltreatment, with chronic stress being associated with a more blunted cortisol response, including across the day (Gunnar & Quevedo, 2007; Herzberg & Gunnar, 2020).

Covert maltreatment, like maternal emotional unavailability and frequent corporal punishment in the first year of life, is associated with toddlers' elevated levels of morning cortisol and cortisol hyperreactivity in response to a stressor (Bugental et al., 2003). Other studies suggest that only young children who experienced a combination of physical and sexual abuse or emotional maltreatment have high waking cortisol (Bruce et al., 2009; Cicchetti & Rogosch, 2001; Halldorsdottir et al., 2019). Infants exposed to intimate partner violence show greater stress-induced hyperreactivity if they also experience insensitive maternal care or have greater genetic risk (Halldorsdottir et al., 2019; Hibel et al., 2011).

Among infants in foster care, Dozier and colleagues (2006) found lower values of waking cortisol and blunted cortisol patterns across the day. Meta-analytic findings suggested a small but significant association between maltreatment and blunted wake-up cortisol levels (Bernard, Frost, et al., 2017). Doom and colleagues (2014) studied morning and afternoon cortisol over 20 weeks to better understand discrepant findings. Children who experienced less severe, early-onset, but not recurrent maltreatment showed the most variability in cortisol production. The researchers suggest that this higher variability in cortisol reflects the difficulty that maltreated children may have regulating the HPA axis across the day and in response to stress.

Overall, dysregulation of the HPA axis is thought to be a mechanism by which maltreatment impacts child well-being. Dysregulation of the HPA axis is associated with psychopathology, including internalizing and externalizing behavior problems (Bernard, Zwerling, & Dozier, 2015; Saridjan et al., 2014), impaired self-regulation (Wesarg et al., 2020), difficulties with emotion regulation (Frost et al., 2017), and increased risk for physical and mental health problems into adulthood (Herzberg & Gunnar, 2020; Shonkoff et al., 2012).

Telomere Shortening. Another neurobiological mechanism by which maltreatment impacts health is its impact on telomere length. Telomeres are the caps at the end of chromosomes that protect DNA from damage. Shorter telomere length indicates cellular aging and disease risk (Epel & Prather, 2018; McEachern et al., 2000). Exposure to early life adversities, including family violence, is associated with accelerated telomere shortening (Drury et al., 2014; Shalev et al., 2013). Only one study has assessed the impact of infant maltreatment on telomere length: Asok and colleagues (2013) found that preschool children who were reported to CPS as infants and experienced low levels of parental responsiveness had shorter telomeres than children who had not been referred to CPS. For the children who had been referred to CPS, having a more responsive parent protected against shortened telomere length, showing the importance of parenting interventions for families who have been reported to CPS. Telomere length, like dysregulation of the HPA axis, is a biological mechanism that explains how maltreatment increases the risk for poor physical and mental health across the lifespan (O'Donovan et al., 2012).

MALTREATMENT AND SOCIAL–EMOTIONAL/BEHAVIORAL DEVELOPMENT

Social–emotional development includes the ability to experience, understand, express, and manage strong emotions. It also includes regulating behavior, developing empathy for others, and maintaining relationships. These early social–emotional competencies develop in the context of relationships and are linked to lifelong abilities related to mental health, school success, and successful relationships (see National Scientific Council on the Developing Child, 2004). When infants experience abuse or neglect or witness intimate partner violence, it can profoundly negatively impact their social–emotional competencies, including developing a secure attachment, emotion regulation, and behavior.

Attachment. A well-studied and important social–emotional milestone is the development of a secure attachment. Children are biologically predisposed to develop an attachment with a small number of caregivers to support proximity seeking in times of stress or danger and exploration in times of safety. Children's strategies to maintain proximity underlie the different secure and insecure attachment patterns, and parental sensitivity is the most robust predictor of attachment security. Children develop a secure attachment when parents respond contingently and sensitively to their needs; they develop insecure attachments when their parents are less sensitive to their needs. Disorganized attachment is a type of insecurity where the child's proximity-seeking strategies break down, leaving the child feeling overwhelmed and helpless (see Dozier & Bernard, 2015; George, 2014).

There are high rates of disorganized attachment in maltreated infants and toddlers (Baer & Martinez, 2006; Bernard et al., 2012; Cicchetti & Barnett, 1991; van iJzendoorn et al., 1999). Witnessing intimate partner violence in infancy is also associated with reduced attachment security (McIntosh et al., 2021) and disorganized attachment (Zeanah et al., 1999). Infants with an insecure–disorganized attachment are at the highest risk for internalizing and externalizing psychopathology (Groh et al., 2012, 2017; Madigan et al., 2013, 2016; van iJzendoorn et al., 1999). As such, attachment disorganization may contribute to behavior problems in maltreated children, making attachment-based interventions particularly important. Removing children from their parent's care when they can safely remain in the home with services may also be damaging to children's attachment. Very frequent parent–child visitation or services that allow the young children to remain with their parents should always be prioritized.

Behavior Problems. In addition to experiencing high rates of insecure attachment, maltreated infants are likely to exhibit ongoing behavior problems and difficulties with peers across childhood (Egeland et al., 2002; Raby et al., 2017) and psychopathology and physical health problems in adulthood (Johnson et al., 2017; VanMeter et al., 2021). These early behavior problems can be persistent and predict later psychiatric illness (Briggs-Gowan et al., 2006; Bufferd et al., 2012; Ringeisen et al., 2009) and are particularly concerning for maltreated children because they predict ongoing harsh parenting, lower rates of reunification, and placement disruptions (Aarons et al., 2010; Landsverk et al., 1996; Mortensen & Barnett, 2018). Among infants investigated for maltreatment between 12 and 18 months of age, 47% enter care with elevated social–emotional problems or very low levels of social competence, both of which indicate clinical risk. Still, fewer than 1% were referred to services (Horowitz et al., 2012). Eighteen months following the CPS investigation, the infants' (now toddlers') behavior was reassessed; those with elevated social–emotional problems in infancy were significantly more likely to exhibit clinically significant behavior problems, especially if they were living with a caregiver who was depressed (Horowitz et al., 2014). Similar trends emerged among infants investigated for maltreatment between 19 and 36 months; 10% exhibited clinical symptoms, and only 2.2% received any mental health service (Horowitz et al., 2012). In another study, maltreated infants showed differences relative to nonmaltreated infants in the area of their brain associated with the ability to process affective facial expressions in toddlerhood, with particular sensitivity for seeing angry faces; maltreated children were more familiar with seeing angry faces than nonmaltreated children (Cicchetti & Curtis, 2005). When followed into preschool, the maltreated children continued to show hyperresponsivity to angry expressions (Curtis & Cicchetti, 2011).

Witnessing intimate partner violence in infancy also impacts behavior. Infants who witnessed intimate partner violence in their first year of life exhibit poor emotion regulation (Geyer & Ogbonnaya, 2021). Studies consistently show that the impact of witnessing intimate partner violence on child behavior is via the effect that violence has on parenting. For example, witnessing violence in infancy is associated with higher rates of social–emotional problems, lower positive affect, and more withdrawn behavior when infants are 12 months old, especially if their mothers have high rates of posttraumatic stress disorder hyperarousal symptoms (Ahlfs-Dunn & Huth-Bocks, 2014). Levendosky and colleagues (2006) also found that intimate partner violence is associated with less parenting sensitivity, which in turn predicts persistent externalizing behaviors (Holmes, 2013). Intimate partner violence may be related to toddler behavior problems only when the mothers also report using corporal punishment (Easterbrooks et al., 2018).

MALTREATMENT AND LANGUAGE AND COGNITIVE DEVELOPMENT

Several studies suggest that maltreatment in infancy has an impact on both language and cognitive development that may extend into higher rates of special education services and poor academic performance across childhood and adolescence (Fantuzzo et al., 2011; Raby et al., 2018; Ringeisen et al., 2009). Serious developmental delays are rare in the general population, approximately 2.3%, but substantially higher (e.g., 18.7%) among infants in the CWS (Casanueva et al., 2012; Stacks et al., 2020).

Neglect, in particular, is associated with language and cognitive delays (Fantuzzo et al., 2011; Helton et al., 2018), and language development progresses more slowly for infants whom CPS investigated in their first year of life (Stacks et al., 2011), perhaps due to very low rates of services received by infants in the CWS (Casanueva, Cross, et al., 2008). As with behavioral development, several factors are associated with such delays, including neglect, poverty, family risks, remaining with birth parents, and extended stays in foster care (Fantuzzo et al., 2011; Jaffe & Maikovich-Fong, 2011; Lloyd & Barth, 2011; Scarborough et al., 2009; Scarborough & McCrae, 2010; Zajac et al., 2018). In contrast, higher quality interactions with caregivers appear to buffer these effects (Bernard, Lee, & Dozier, 2017; Jaffee, 2007; Jones-Harden & Whitaker, 2011; Merritt & Klein, 2014; Stahmer, Hurlbert, et al., 2009).

SUMMARY
Research is clear that maltreatment is a stressor that has a negative impact on children's well-being. It is also important to recognize that separation from a parent in early childhood is a stressor that can impact neurobiology, attachment, and behavior problems. As such, it is important to consider whether a child can remain at home with effective services in place.

Interventions for Maltreated Infants
The caregiving environment in the first 3 years of life has a profound and long-lasting impact on development. During this same window, the infant's brain is most malleable, making the first 3 years a sensitive period for intervention. Maltreated infants and their parents must be offered evidence-based services, meaning that research has shown that they are effective (Berliner et al., 2014). Several studies have now documented that the parenting services offered by CWS programs are not individualized or intensive enough to improve parenting or reduce the recurrence of maltreatment (Barth et al., 2005; Casanueva, Martin, et al., 2008; Fuller & Nieto, 2014; Hurlburt et al., 2007). In contrast, relationally based interventions are particularly useful in improving parenting, reducing recidivism, and improving outcomes for children (Lee & Stacks, 2005). One promising example of these programs is infant–toddler court teams. They provide a nonadversarial courtroom with all members trained in the science of development, as well as relationship-based, trauma-informed interventions to parent–infant dyads, and recognize the expertise of an infant mental health clinician on the court team.

Relationship-Based Interventions
Relationship-based interventions are grounded in attachment theory and aim to improve parenting quality and children's social–emotional outcomes, including attachment. Clinicians enhance the parent's ability to reflect on the child's needs and provide sensitive and responsive care (Osofsky & Lieberman, 2011). These interventions often use psychoanalytic approaches to help parents heal the relational trauma from their childhoods that interfere with reflection and sensitive parenting, what Selma Fraiberg called ghosts in the nursery (Fraiberg et al., 1975). Next, we describe several relationship-based interventions shown to improve parent–infant interactions and child development in maltreating families and families with other risks (e.g., maternal depression, adolescent parents, families at high demographic risk).

Attachment and Biobehavioral Catchup (ABC) is a 10-session intervention for parents at high risk for abusing or neglecting their children between the ages of 6 and 36 months. The home-based intervention is delivered weekly with the parent and child together to support a secure infant attachment and child self-regulation. It includes these components: (a) following the child's lead, (b) providing nurturance to the child's distress, and (c) reducing harsh and frightening parenting behavior. ABC is listed as an evidence-based intervention by the National Child Traumatic Stress Network and the California Clearinghouse for Child Welfare and has been offered to foster parent–infant dyads, parents participating in home-based Early Head Start, and CWS-involved infants living with their birth parents (Dozier & Bernard, 2019). The studies show a range of improvements. ABC increased parent sensitivity (Bernard, Simons, & Dozier, 2015; Bick & Dozier, 2013; Yarger et al., 2016), including into middle childhood (Garnett et al., 2020). Parents also showed changes in brain activity related to responses to children's emotions (Bernard, Simons, & Dozier, 2015). Among children, ABC is effective at promoting a secure attachment and reducing disorganized attachment (Bernard et al., 2012; Yarger et al., 2020), again with benefits being sustained into middle childhood (Zajac et al., 2020). ABC also produces positive changes in social–emotional development (Lind et al., 2014, 2020), language development (Bernard, Lee, & Dozier, 2017; Zajac et al., 2018), and executive functioning (Lewis-Morrarty et al., 2012; Lind et al., 2017). Moreover, the intervention supports better regulation of the infants' stress response system (Bernard, Dozier, et al., 2015; Bernard, Hostinar, & Dozier, 2015; Bernard, Simons, & Dozier, 2015). These changes are also sustained into middle childhood (Garnett et al., 2020). Finally, preliminary evidence suggests the ABC intervention is associated with epigenetic changes related to metabolism and neuronal development in children (Hoye et al., 2020), indicating potential long-term benefits.

Child–Parent Psychotherapy (CPP) is a 10–12-month weekly intervention for parents and their children ages birth to 5 years. It aims to promote protective caregiving and secure attachment and interrupts circumstances that impair the parenting behavior and the parent–child relationship. CPP is listed on the Substance Abuse and Mental Health Services Administration National Registry of Evidence-Based and Promising Practices. The efficacy of CPP has been documented in five randomized controlled trials (for a review, see Lieberman et al., 2019), several of which included maltreating parents and their infants as participants. Evidence suggests improved parent–child relationships (Toth et al., 2002), improved child attachment security (Cicchetti et al., 2006; Cicchetti, Rogosch, & Toth, 2011; Toth et al., 2002), and a better regulated child stress response system (Cicchetti, Rogosch, et al., 2011). Further, CPP reduces placement in foster care and the number of placement changes while in foster care (see Lieberman et al., 2019). For young children exposed to intimate partner violence, CPP was effective at reducing children's behavior problems and traumatic stress symptoms (Lieberman et al., 2005).

Infant Mental Health-Home Visiting (IMH-HV) emphasizes both the parent–infant and parent–clinician relationship to address the needs of infants and families at high risk for a variety of concerns, including child maltreatment, infant behavioral or developmental issues, and parent mental health difficulties (Tableman & Ludtke, 2020). Services are home based, 1–2 hours per week from pregnancy to the child's third birthday. Clinicians offer case management services to help parents with material needs, emotional support, developmental guidance, and infant–parent psychotherapy (for a review, see Weatherston et al., 2020). IMH-HV delivered to maltreating parents and their children improved parenting responsivity and reflective functioning (Stacks et al., 2019) and children's language, positive affect, and enthusiasm (Stacks et al., 2020). In a community sample of parents, some of whom were referred by the court, IMH-HV was effective at increasing parent reflective functioning (Stacks et al., 2022) and sensitivity (Rosenblum et al., 2020), reducing child abuse potential (Julian et al., 2021), and promoting infant social–emotional development (Ribaudo et al., 2022).

Promoting First Relationships (PFR) is a 10-week intervention delivered to caregivers and their children, ages birth to 5 years, in the home. Providers use video feedback with parents to help them consider their child's perspective, increase their sensitive responses, and promote their child's emotional and behavioral well-being. Providers also help caregivers reflect on their own needs and feelings and consider their impact on parenting (Kelly et al., 2008). PFR has been evaluated in experimental and quasi-experimental trials with children and their caregivers (foster or biological) reported to the CWS. Findings suggest that PFR improves parenting sensitivity and understanding of children's emotional needs (Oxford, Spieker, et al., 2016; Spieker et al., 2012). Parents who had a history of physical child abuse showed the greatest improvements in sensitivity, which in turn predicted attachment behaviors associated with security (Pasalich et al., 2019). In addition, children placed with foster parents who participated in PFR had more stable placements and were more likely to be adopted (Spieker et al., 2014). Children who participated with their biological parents were less likely to be placed in foster care 1 year following the intervention (Oxford, Spieker, et al., 2016) and demonstrated better stress regulation (Hastings et al., 2019). In addition, children placed into foster care and reunified with their parents showed less separation distress, which in turn predicted fewer sleep (Oxford et al., 2013) and behavior (Oxford, Marcenko, et al., 2016) problems. Children whose families did not participate in PFR demonstrated greater placement instability, less attachment security, and more behavior problems (Pasalich et al., 2016).

In summary, the interventions reviewed are all manualized, have been tested in real-world community settings, and are effective for maltreating parents. All are offered by mental health clinicians who pay special attention to parents' histories of trauma, support parents' understanding of their children's emotional needs, and increase parenting sensitivity as a way to foster infant attachment security and well-being. These interventions are recommended for use by infant–toddler court teams, which began in Miami-Dade County in the 1990s to address the need to support maltreated infants and their parents and reduce the potential for long-term harm (Lecklitner et al., 1999; Lederman & Osofsky, 2004; Malik et al., 2002). According to Zero to Three (2023), there are now infant–toddler court teams across 30 states. Because of these teams' potential, they are reviewed separately next.

Infant–toddler court teams integrate relationship-based interventions into the dependency court to promote emotional well-being. Court teams are led by a science-informed jurist who requires nonadversarial and collaborative interactions among the attorneys, child welfare professionals, and infant mental health clinicians who make up the court team. All court team members are trained in the developmental needs of young children, including the impact of trauma and the importance of attachment relationships. Parent–infant dyads are referred to relationship-based services that are backed by evidence (Casanueva et al., 2013; Miami Child Well-Being Court Initiative, 2013). Evaluations of infant–toddler court teams show promise for improving child welfare outcomes, including safety, permanency, and well-being.

Earlier in this chapter, we reviewed research from the 1990s and 2000s that showed poor outcomes for infants and toddlers who encountered the CWS and noted that services offered to parents and infants were ineffective at improving parenting or child development outcomes. Evaluations from infant–toddler court teams suggest that this is a promising model for improving outcomes, including the following: parenting sensitivity and responsivity (Casanueva et al., 2013; Chinitz et al., 2017; Stacks et al., 2019), child development (Stacks et al., 2020), reunification with biological parents (Casanueva et al., 2013; Chinitz et al., 2017; McCombs-Thornton & Foster, 2012; Stacks et al., 2020), children spend less time in foster care (Faria et al., 2020; Stacks et al., 2020), and children are less likely to experience a recurrence of abuse or neglect (Casanueva et al., 2018; Faria et al., 2020).

Conclusion

Relationship-based and systems integration interventions are promising to support parenting and child well-being among maltreated parent–infant dyads. These interventions present an opportunity to ameliorate the adverse effects of maltreatment on many child outcomes, including neurobiology; emotional, behavioral, and cognitive development; and long-term health outcomes. Interventions that focus on factors that impact the quality of parenting may be most effective in early childhood, which is a critical period for development.

References

Aarons, G. A., James, S., Monn, A. R., Raghavan, R., Wells, R., & Leslie, L. (2010). Disentangling the relationship between behavior problems and placement change in child welfare: A multi-level cross-lag modeling approach. *Journal of the American Academy of Child and Adolescent Psychiatry, 49*(1), 70–80.

Administration for Children and Families. (2021). 2.1I CAPTA, assurances and requirements, referrals to IDEA, Part C. In *Child Welfare Policy Manual*. https://www.acf.hhs.gov/cwpm/public_html/programs/cb/laws_policies/laws/cwpm/policy_dsp.jsp?citID=354

Agorastos, A., Pervanidou, P., Chrousos, G. P., & Baker, D. G. (2019). Developmental trajectories of early life stress and trauma: A narrative review on neurobiological aspects beyond stress system dysregulation. *Frontiers in Psychiatry, 10*(118), 1–25.

Ahlfs-Dunn, S. M., & Huth-Bocks, A. C. (2014). Intimate partner violence and infant socioemotional development: The moderating effects of maternal trauma symptoms. *Infant Mental Health Journal, 35*(4), 322–335. https://doi.org/10.1002/imhj.21453

American Academy of Pediatrics, Committee on Early Childhood, Adoption, and Dependent Care. (1994). Health care of children in foster care. *Pediatrics, 93*(2), 335–338.

Anderson, K., & Van Ee, E. (2018). Mothers and children exposed to intimate partner violence: A review of treatment interventions. *International Journal of Environmental Research and Public Health, 15*(9), 1955.

Anthony, E. K., Austin, M. J., & Cormier, D. R. (2010). Early detection of prenatal substance exposure and the role of child welfare. *Children and Youth Services Review, 32*(1), 6–12.

Arnott, B., & Meins, E. (2007). Links among antenatal attachment representations, postnatal mind-mindedness, and infant attachment security: A preliminary study of mothers and fathers. *Bulletin of the Menninger Clinic, 71*(2), 132–156.

Asok, A., Bernard, K., Roth, T. L., Rosen, J. B., & Dozier, M. (2013). Parental responsiveness moderates the association between early-life stress and reduced telomere length. *Development and Psychopathology, 25*(3), 577–585.

Assink, M., Spruit, A., Schuts, M., Lindauer, R., van der Put, C. E., & Stams, G-J. J. M. (2018). The intergenerational transmission of child maltreatment: A three-level meta-analysis. *Child Abuse & Neglect, 84*, 131–145.

Atkins, D. N., & Durrance, C. P. (2020). State policies that treat prenatal substance use as child abuse or neglect fail to achieve their intended goals. *Health Affairs, 39*(5), 756–763.

Austin, A. E., Gest, C., Atkeson, A., Berkoff, M. C., Puls, H. T., & Shanahan, M. E. (2022). Prenatal substance exposure and child maltreatment: A systematic review. *Child Maltreatment, 27*(2), 290-315.

Azagba, S., Manzione, L., Shan, L., & King, J. (2020). Trends in smoking during pregnancy by socioeconomic characteristics in the United States, 2010–2017. *BMC Pregnancy and Childbirth, 20*, 52.

Bada, H. S., Bann, C. M., Whitaker, T. M., Bauer, C. R., Shankaran, S., LaGasse, L., Lester, B. M., Hammond, J., & Higgins, R. (2012). Protective factors can mitigate behavior problems after prenatal cocaine and other drug exposures. *Pediatrics, 130*(6) e1479-e1488.

Baer, J. C., & Martinez, C. D. (2006). Child maltreatment and insecure attachment: A meta-analysis. *Journal of Reproductive & Infant Psychology, 24*(3), 187–197.

Barth, R. P., Landsverk, J. A., Chamberlain, P., Reid, J., Rolls, J., Hurlburt, M. S., Farmer, E. M. Z., James, S., McCabe, K. M., & Kohl, P. L. (2005). Parent-training programs in child welfare services: Planning for a more evidence-based approach to serving biological parents. *Research on Social Work Practice, 15*(5), 353–371.

Bartlett, J. D., Kotake, C., Fauth, R., & Easterbrooks, M. A. (2017). Intergenerational transmission of child abuse and neglect: Do maltreatment type, perpetrator and substantiation status matter? *Child Abuse & Neglect, 63*, 84–94.

Bauer, C. R., Langer, J. C., Shankaran, S., Bada, H. S., Lester, B., Wright, L. L., Krause-Steinrauf, H., Smeriglio, V. L., Finnegan, L. P., Maza, P. L., & Verter, J. (2005). Acute neonatal effects of cocaine exposure during pregnancy. *Archives of Pediatrics and Adolescent Medicine, 159*(9), 824.

Behnke, M., Smith, V. C., Committee on Substance Abuse, & Committee on Fetus and Newborn. (2013). Prenatal substance abuse: Short- and long-term effects on the exposed fetus. *Pediatrics, 131*(3) e1009-e1024.

Behrens, K. Y., Haltigan, J. D., & Gribneau Bahm, N. I. (2016). Infant attachment, adult attachment and maternal sensitivity: Revisiting the intergenerational transmission gap. *Attachment and Human Development, 18*(4), 337–353.

Belt, R., Flykt, M., Punamäki, R.-L., Pajulo, M., Posa, T., Biringen, Z., & Tamminen, T. (2012). Psychotherapy groups to enhance mental health and early dyadic interaction among drug abusing mothers. *Infant Mental Health Journal, 33*, 520–534.

Berliner, L., Fitzgerald, M. M., Dorsey, S., Chaffin, M., Ondersma, S. J., & Wilson, C. (2014). Report of the APSAC taskforce on evidence-based service planning guidelines for child welfare. *Child Maltreatment, 20*(1), 6–16.

Bernard, K., Dozier, M., Bick, J., & Gordon, K. M. (2015). Normalizing blunted diurnal cortisol rhythms among children at risk for neglect: The effects of an early intervention. *Development and Psychopathology, 27*(3), 829–841.

Bernard, K., Dozier, M., Bick, J., Lewis-Morrarty, E., Lindhiem, O., & Carlson, E. (2012). Enhancing attachment organization among maltreated children: Results of a randomized controlled trial. *Child Development, 83*(2), 623–636.

Bernard, K., Frost, A., Bennett, C. B., & Lindhiem, O. (2017). Maltreatment and diurnal cortisol regulation: A meta-analysis. *Psychoneuroendocrinology, 78*, 57–67.

Bernard, K., Hostinar, C., & Dozier, M. (2015). Intervention effects on diurnal cortisol rhythms of CPS referred infants persist into early childhood: Preschool follow-up results of a randomized clinical trial. *JAMA Pediatrics, 169*(2), 112–119.

Bernard, K., Lee, A. H., & Dozier, M. (2017). Effects of the ABC Intervention on foster children's receptive vocabulary: Follow-up results from a randomized clinical trial. *Child Maltreatment, 22*(2), 174–179.

Bernard, K., Simons, R., & Dozier, M. (2015). Effects of an attachment-based intervention on child protective services-referred mothers' event-related potentials to children's emotions. *Child Development, 86*(6), 1673–1684.

Bernard, K., Zwerling, J., & Dozier, M. (2015). Effects of early adversity on young children's diurnal cortisol rhythms and externalizing behavior. *Developmental Psychobiology, 57*(8), 935–947.

Bernier, A., Dégeilh, F., Leblanc, É., Daneault, V., Bailey, H. N., & Beauchamp, M. H. (2019). Mother-infant interaction and child brain morphology: A multidimensional approach to maternal sensitivity. *Infancy, 24*(2), 120–138.

Berthelot, N., Ensink, K., Bernazzani, O., Normandin, L., Luyten, P., & Fonagy, P. (2015). Intergenerational transmission of attachment in abused and neglected mothers: The role of trauma-specific reflective functioning. *Infant Mental Health Journal, 36*(2), 200–212.

Bick, J., & Dozier, M. (2013). The effectiveness of an attachment-based intervention in promoting foster mothers' sensitivity toward foster infants. *Infant Mental Health Journal, 34*(2), 95–103.

Bonomi, A. E., Thompson, R. S., Anderson, M., Rivara, F. P., Holt, V. L., Carrell, D., & Martin, D. P. (2006). Ascertainment of intimate partner violence using two abuse measurement frameworks. *Injury Prevention: Journal of the International Society for Child and Adolescent Injury Prevention, 12*(2), 121–124.

Bornstein, M. H., Hahn, C-S., Putnick, D. L., & Pearson, R. (2019). Stability of child temperament: Multiple moderation by child and mother characteristics. *British Journal of Developmental Psychology, 37*, 51–67.

Bornstein, M. H., Putnick, D. L., Garstein, M. A., Hahn, C-S., Auestad, N., & Connor, D. L. (2015). Infant temperament: Stability by age, gender, birth order, term status and socioeconomic status. *Child Development, 86*(3), 844–863.

Briggs-Gowan, J. J., Carter, A. S., Skuban, E. M., & Horwitz, S. M. C. (2006). Are infant-toddler social-emotional and behavioral problems transient? *Journal of the American Academy of Child and Adolescent Psychiatry, 47*(7), 849–858.

Bronfenbrenner, U., & Morris, P. (2006). The bioecological model of human development. In R. M. Lerner & W. Damon (Eds.), *Handbook of child psychology: Theoretical models of human development* (pp. 793–828). John Wiley and Sons.

Bruce, J., Fisher, P. A., Pears, K. C., & Levine, S. (2009). Morning cortisol levels in preschool-aged foster children: Differential effects of maltreatment type. *Developmental Psychobiology, 51*, 14–23.

Bublitz, M. H., & Stroud, L. R. (2011). Maternal smoking during pregnancy and offspring brain structure and function: Review and agenda for future research. *Nicotine & Tobacco Research, 14*(4), 388–397.

Bufferd, S. J., Dougherty, L. R., Carlson, G. A., Rose, S., & Klein, D. N. (2012). Psychiatric disorders in preschoolers: Continuity from ages 3–6. *American Journal of Psychiatry, 169*(11), 1157–1164.

Bugental, D. B., Martorell, G. A., & Barraza, V. (2003). The hormonal costs of subtle forms on infant maltreatment. *Hormones and Behavior, 43*(1), 237–244.

Cao-Lei, L., de Rooij, S. R., King, S., Matthews, S. G., Metz, G. A. S., Roseboom, T. J., & Szyf, M. (2020). Prenatal stress and epigenetics. *Neuroscience & Biobehavioral Reviews, 117*, 198–210.

Casanueva, C., Cross, T. P., & Ringeisen, H. (2008). Developmental needs and Individualized Family Service Plans among infants and toddlers in the CWS. *Child Maltreatment, 13*(3), 245–258.

Casanueva, C., Dozier, M., Tueller, S., Dolan, M., Smith, K., Bruce Webb, M., Westbrook, T., & Jones Harden, B. (2014). Caregiver instability and early life changes among infants reported to the CWS. *Child Abuse & Neglect, 38*(3), 498–509.

Casanueva, C., Goldman Fraser, J., Gilbert, A., Maze, C., Katz, L., Ullery, M. A., Stacks, A. M., & Lederman, C. (2013). Evaluation of the Miami Child Well-Being Court Model: Safety, permanency and well-being. *Child Welfare, 92*(3), 73–96.

Casanueva, C., Harris, S., Carr, C., Burfeind, C., & Smith, K. (2018). Helping young maltreated children and their families: Outcomes among families at Safe Babies Court Team sites. *Zero to Three, 38*(6), 29–37.

Casanueva, C., Martin, S. L., Runyan, D. K., Barth, R. P., & Bradley, R. H. (2008). Parenting services for mothers involved with child protective services: Do they change maternal parenting and spanking behaviors with young children? *Children and Youth Services Review, 30*(8), 861–878.

Casanueva, C., Smith, K., Dolan, M., Tueller, S., & Lloyd, S. (2012). *NSCAW II Wave 2 report: Safety* (OPRE Report #2013-07). Office of Planning, Research and Evaluation, Administration for Children and Families, U.S. Department of Health and Human Services.

Chasnoff, I. J., Wells, A. M., & King, L. (2015). Misdiagnosis and missed diagnoses in foster and adopted children with prenatal alcohol exposure. *Pediatrics, 135*(2), 264–270.

Child Abuse Prevention and Treatment Act, 42 U.S.C. §5101 et seq. (2017).

Child Welfare Information Gateway. (2019). *Mandatory reporters of child abuse and neglect*. U.S. Department of Health and Human Services, Children's Bureau.

Child Welfare Information Gateway. (2020). *Plans of safe care for infants with prenatal substance exposure and their families*. U.S. Department of Health and Human Services, Administration for Children and Families, Children's Bureau.

Child Welfare Information Gateway. (2021). *Child welfare practice to address racial disproportionality and disparity*. U.S. Department of Health and Human Services, Administration for Children and Families, Children's Bureau.

Chinitz, S., Guzman, H., Amstutz, J., & Alkon, M. (2017). Improving outcomes for babies and toddlers in child welfare: A model for infant mental health intervention and collaboration. *Child Abuse & Neglect, 7*, 190–198.

Cicchetti, D., & Barnett, D. (1991). Attachment organization in maltreated preschoolers. *Development and Psychopathology, 3*(4), 397–411.

Cicchetti, D., & Curtis, W. J. (2005). An event-related potential study of the processing of affective facial expressions in young children who experienced maltreatment during the first year of life. *Development and Psychopathology, 17*(3), 641–677.

Cicchetti, D., & Rogosch, F. (2001). Diverse patterns of neuroendocrine activity in maltreated children. *Development and Psychopathology, 13*, 677–693.

Cicchetti, D., Rogosch, F. A., & Toth, S. L. (2006). Fostering secure attachment in infants in maltreating families through preventative interventions. *Development and Psychopathology, 18*(3), 623–649.

Cicchetti, D., Rogosch, F. A., & Toth, S. L. (2011). The effects of child maltreatment and polymorphisms of the serotonin transporter and dopamine D4 receptor genes on infant attachment and intervention efficacy. *Development and Psychopathology, 23*(2), 357–372.

Cicchetti, D., Rogosch, F. A., Toth, S. L., & Sturge-Apple, M. L. (2011). Normalizing the development of cortisol regulation in maltreated infants through preventative interventions. *Development and Psychopathology, 23*(3), 789–800.

Clauss, J. A., & Blackford, J. U. (2012). Behavioral inhibition and risk for developing social anxiety disorder: A meta-analytic study. *Journal of the American Academy of Child and Adolescent Psychiatry, 51*(10), 1066–1075.e1.

Cloninger, C. R., Cloninger, K. M., Zwir, I., & Keltikangas-Järvinen, L. (2019). The complex genetics and biology of human temperament: A review of traditional concepts in relation to new molecular findings. *Translational Psychiatry, 9*(1), 1–21.

Coles, C. D., Kable, J. A., & Taddeo, E. (2009). Math performance and behavior problems in children affected by prenatal alcohol exposure: Intervention and follow-up. *Journal of Developmental and Behavioral Pediatrics, 30*(1), 7–15.

Comprehensive Addiction and Recovery Act of 2016, 42 U.S.C. §501 et seq. (2016).

Cone, R. D., Low, M. J., Elmquist, J. K., & Cameron, J. L. (2003). Neuroendocrinology. In P. R. Larsen, H. M Kronenberg, S. Melmed, K. S. & Polonsky, J. D. (Eds.) *Williams textbook of endocrinology* (pp. 81–176). Philadelphia, PA: Saunders.

Conrad, C. D., Oritz, J. B., & Judd, J. M. (2017). Chronic stress and hippocampal dendritic complexity: Methodological and functional considerations. *Physiology & Behavior, 178*, 66–81.

Corsi, D. J., Walsh, L., Weiss, D., Hsu, H., El-Chaar, D., Hawken, S., Fell, D. B., & Walker, M. (2019). Association between self-reported prenatal cannabis use and maternal, perinatal, and neonatal outcomes. *JAMA, 322*(2), 145.

Courtney, M. E. (1995). Reentry to foster care of children returned to their families. *Social Services Review, 69*(4), 226–241.

Craig, F., Tenuta, F., Rizzato, V., Costabile, A., Trabacca, A., & Montrosso, R. (2021). Attachment-related dimensions in the epigenetic era: A systematic review of the human research. *Neuroscience & Behavioral Reviews, 125*, 654–666.

Cui, H., Gong, T.-T., Liu, C-X., & Wu, Q-J. (2016). Associations between passive maternal smoking during pregnancy and preterm birth: Evidence from a meta-analysis of observational studies. *PLos One, 11*(1), e0147848.

Curtis, W. J., & Cicchetti, D. (2011). Affective facial expression processing in young children who have experienced maltreatment during the first year of life: An event-related potential study. *Development and Psychopathology, 23*, 373–395.

Danese, A., Moffitt, T. E., Harrington, H., Milne, B. J., Polanczyk, G., Pariante, C. M., Poulton, R., & Caspi, A. (2009). Adverse childhood experiences and adult risk factors for age-related disease: Depression, inflammation, and clustering of metabolic risk markers. *Archives of Pediatric and Adolescent Medicine, 163*(12), 1135–1143.

Danese, A., Pariante, C. M., Caspi, A., Taylor, A., & Poulton, R. (2007). Childhood maltreatment predicts adult inflammation in a life-course study. *Proceedings of the National Academy of Sciences of the United States of America, 104*(4), 1319–1324.

Davis, E. P., Glynn, L. M., Waffarn, F., & Sandman, C. A. (2011). Prenatal maternal stress programs infant stress regulation. *Journal of Child Psychology and Psychiatry, 52*(2), 119–129.

Donovan, B., Spracklen, C., Schweizer, M., Ryckman, K., & Saftlas, A. (2016). Intimate partner violence during pregnancy and the risk for adverse infant outcomes: A systematic review and meta-analysis. *International Journal of Obstetrics and Gynecology, 123*, 1289–1299.

Doom, J. R., Cicchetti, D., & Rogosch, F. A. (2014). Longitudinal patterns of cortisol regulation differ in maltreated and non-maltreated children. *Journal of the American Academy of Child and Adolescent Psychiatry, 53*(11), 1206–1215.

dos Santos, J. F., de Melo Bastos Cavalcante, C., Barbosa, F. T., Góes Gitaí, D. L., Duzzioni, M., Tilelli, C. Q., Shetty, A. K., & de Castro, O. W. (2018). Maternal, fetal and neonatal consequences associated with the use of crack cocaine during the gestational period: A systematic review and meta-analysis. *Archives of Gynecology and Obstetrics, 298*, 487–503.

Dozier, M., Manni, M., Gordon, M. K., Peloso, E. Gunnar, M. R., Stovall-McClough, K. C., Eldreth, D., & Levine, S. (2006). Foster children's diurnal production of cortisol: An exploratory study. *Child Maltreatment, 11*(2), 189-197.

Dozier, M., & Bernard, K. (2015). Attachment: Normal development, individual differences, and associations with experience. In A. Thaper, D. S. Pine, J. E. Leckman, S. Scott, M. J. Snowling, & E. Taylor (Eds.), *Rutters child and adolescent psychiatry* (6th ed., pp. 65–78). John Wiley & Sons.

Dozier, M., & Bernard, K. (2019). Attachment and biobehavioral catch-up. In C. H. Zeanah (Ed.), *Handbook of infant mental health* (4th ed., pp. 514–526). Guilford Press.

Drury, S. S., Mabile, E., Brett, Z. H., Esteves, K., Jones, E., Shirtcliff, E. A., & Theall, K. P. (2014). The association of telomere length with family violence and disruption. *Pediatrics, 134*(1), e128–e137.

Easterbrooks, M. A., Katz, R. C., & Kotake, C. (2018). Intimate partner violence in the first 2 years of life: Implications for toddlers behavior regulation. *Journal of Interpersonal Violence, 33*(7), 1192–1214.

Egeland, B., Yates, T., Appleyard, K., & van Dulmen, M. (2002). The long-term consequences of maltreatment in the early years. A developmental pathway model to antisocial behavior. *Children's Services: Social Policy, Research, and Practice, 5*(4), 249–260.

Eiden, R. D., Godleski, S., Colder, C. R., & Schuetze, P. (2014). Prenatal cocaine exposure: The role of cumulative environmental risk and maternal harshness in the development of child internalizing behavior problems in kindergarten. *Neurotoxicology and Teratology, 44*, 1–10.

Epel, E. S., & Prather, A. A. (2018). Stress, telomeres, and psychopathology: Toward a deeper understanding of a triad of early aging. *Annual Review of Clinical Psychology, 14*, 371–397.

Estabrook, R., Massey, S. H., Clark, C. A. C., Burns, J. L., Mustanksi, B. S., Cook, E. H., O'Brien, C. O., Makowski, B., Espy, K. A., & Wakschlag, L. S. (2015). Separating family-level and direct exposure effects of smoking during pregnancy on offspring externalizing symptoms: Bridging the behavior genetic and behavior teratologic divide. *Behavioral Genetics, 46*, 389–402.

Everitt, B. J., & Robbins, T. W. (2005). Neural systems of reinforcement for drug addiction: From actions to habits to compulsion. *Nature Neuroscience, 8*(11), 1481–1489.

Families First Prevention Services Act of 2018, 42 U.S.C. §50701 et seq. (2018).

Fantuzzo, J. W., Perlman, S. M., & Dobbins, E. K. (2011). Types and timing of child maltreatment and early school success: A population-based investigation. *Children and Youth Services Review, 33*(8), 1404–1411.

Faria, A.-M., Bowdon, J., Conway-Turner, J., Pan, J., Ryznar, T., Michaelson, L., Derrington, T., & Watson, J. (2020). *The Safe Babies Court Team evaluation: Changing the trajectories of children in foster care*. American Institutes for Research.

Fearon, R. M. P., Bakermans-Kranenburg, M., van IJzendoorn, M., Lapsley, A-M., & Roisman, G. I. (2010). The significance of insecure attachment and disorganization in the development of children's externalizing behavior: A meta-analytic study. *Child Development, 81*(2), 435–456.

Fearon, R. M. P., & Belsky, J. (2018). Precursors of attachment security. In J. Cassidy & P. R. Shaver (Eds.), *Handbook of attachment: Theory, research and clinical applications* (pp. 291–313). Guilford Press.

Flykt, M. S., Lindblom, J., Belt, R., & Punamäki, R-L. (2021). The role of mother's prenatal substance use disorder and early parenting on child social cognition at school age. *Infant and Child Development, 30*(3), e221.

Fraiberg, S., Adelson, E., & Shapiro, V. (1975). Ghosts in the nursery: A psychoanalytic approach to the problems of impaired infant-mother relationships. *Journal of American Academy of Child Psychiatry, 14*(3), 387–421.

Frost, A., Jelinek, C., Bernard, K., Lind, T., & Dozier, M. (2017). Longitudinal associations between low morning cortisol in infancy and anger dysregulation in early childhood in a CPS-referred sample. *Developmental Science, 21*(3), e12573.

Fuller, T., & Nieto, M. (2014). Child welfare services and risk of child maltreatment rereports: Do services ameliorate initial risk? *Children and Youth Services Review, 47*(1), 46–54.

Garnett, M., Bernard, K., Hoye, J., Zajac, L., & Dozier, M. (2020). Parental sensitivity mediates the sustained effect of Attachment and Biobehavioral Catch-up on cortisol in middle childhood: A randomized clinical trial. *Psychoneuroendocrinology, 121*, 104809.

George, C. (2014). Attachment theory: Implications for young children and their parents. In K. Brandt, B. Perry, & E. Tronick (Eds.), *Infant and early childhood mental health* (pp. 97–110). American Psychiatric Publishing.

Geyer, C., & Ogbonnaya, I. N. (2021). The relationship between maternal domestic violence and infant and toddlers' emotional regulation: Highlighting the need for preventative services. *Journal of Interpersonal Violence, 36*(3–4), 1029–1048.

Glover, V., O'Donnell, K. J., O'Connor, T., & Fisher, J. (2018). Prenatal maternal stress, fetal programming, and mechanisms underlying later psychopathology: A global perspective. *Development and Psychopathology, 30*(3), 843–854.

Groh, A. M., Fearon, R. M. P., vanIJzendoorn, M. H., Bakermans-Kranenburg, M. J., & Roisman, G. I. (2017). Attachment in the early life course: Meta-analytic evidence for its role in socioemotional development. *Child Development Perspectives, 11*(1), 70–76.

Groh, A. M., Roisman, G. I., van IJzendoorn, M. H., Bakermans-Kranenburg, M. J., & Fearon, R. P. (2012). The significance of insecure and disorganized attachment for children's internalizing symptoms: A meta-analytic study. *Child Development, 83*(2), 591–610.

Gunnar, M. R., & Quevedo, K. (2007). The neurobiology of stress and development. *Annual Review of Psychology, 27*, 208–211.

Haight, S. C., Ko, J. Y., Tong, V. T., Bohm, M. K., & Callaghan, W. M. (2018). Opioid use disorder documented at delivery hospitalization—United States, 1999–2014. *Morbidity and Mortality Weekly Report, 67*(31), 845.

Halldorsdottir, T., Kurtoic, D., Müller-Myhsok, B., Family Life Project Key Investigators, Binder, E. B., & Blair, C. (2019). Neurobiology of self-regulation: Longitudinal influences of FKBP5and intimate partner violence on emotional and cognitive development in childhood. *American Journal of Psychiatry, 176*(8), 626–634.

Hans, S. L. (2002). Studies of prenatal exposure to drugs: Focusing on parental care of children. *Neurotoxicology and Teratology, 24*(3), 329–337.

Harris, S. L., Bray, H., Troughton, R., Elliott, J., Frampton, C., Horwood, J., & Darlow, B. A. (2020). Cardiovascular outcomes in young adulthood in a population-based very low birthweight cohort. *Journal of Pediatrics, 225*, 74–79.

Hastings, P. D., Kahle, S., Fleming, C., Lohr, M. J., Katz, L. F., & Oxford, M. L. (2019). An intervention that increases parental sensitivity in families referred to child protective services also changes toddlers' parasympathetic regulation. *Developmental Science, 22*(1), e12725.

Helton, J. J., Cross, T. P., Vaughn, M. G., & Gochez-Kerr, T. (2018). Food neglect and infant development. *Infant Mental Health Journal, 39*(2), 231–241.

Herzberg, M. P., & Gunnar, M. R. (2020). Early life stress and brain function: Activity and connectivity associated with processing emotion and reward. *NeuroImage, 209*, 116943.

Hibel, L. C., Granger, D. A., Blair, C., & Cox, M. J. (2011). Maternal sensitivity buffers the adrenocortical implications of intimate partner violence during childhood *Development and Psychopathology, 23*, 689–701.

Hirai, A. H., Ko, J. Y., Owens, P. L., Stocks, C., & Patrick, S. W. (2021). Neonatal abstinence syndrome and maternal opioid-related diagnoses in the US, 2010–2017. *JAMA, 325*(2), 146–155.

Holmes, M. R. (2013). The sleeper effect of intimate partner violence exposure: Long-term consequences on young children's aggressive behavior. *Journal of Child Psychology and Psychiatry, 54*(9), 986–995.

Holochwost, S. J., Wang, G., Kolacz, J., Mills-Koonce, R., Klika, J. B., & Jaffe, S. R. (2021). The neurophysiological embedding of child maltreatment. *Development and Psychopathology, 33*(3), 1107–1137.

Horowitz, S. M., Hurlburt, M. S., Heneghan, A., Zhang, J., Rolls-Reutz, J., Fisher, E., Landsverk, J., & Stein, R. E. K. (2012). Mental health problems in young children investigated by U.S. child welfare agencies. *Journal of the American Academy of Child & Adolescent Psychiatry, 51*(6), 572–581.

Horowitz, S. M., Hurlburt, M. S., Heneghan, A., Zhang, J., Rolls-Reutz, J., Landsverk, J., & Stein, R. E. K. (2014). Persistence of mental health problems in very young children investigated by US child welfare agencies. *Academic Pediatrics, 13*(6), 1–10.

Hoye, J. R., Cheishvili, D., Yarger, H. A., Roth, T. L., Szyf, M., & Dozier, M. (2020). Preliminary indications that the Attachment and Biobehavioral Catch-up Intervention alters DNA methylation in maltreated children. *Development and Psychopathology, 32*(4), 1486–1494.

Hoyme, H. E., Kalberg, W. O., Elliott, A. J., Blankenship, J., Buckley, D., Marais, A.-S., Manning, M. A., Robinson, L. K., Adam, M. P., Abdul-Rahman, O., Jewett, T., Coles, C. D., Chambers, C., Jones, K. L., Adnams, C. M., Shah, P. E., Riley, E. P., Charness, M. E., Warren, K. R., & May, P. A. (2016). Updated clinical guidelines for diagnosing fetal alcohol spectrum disorders. *Pediatrics, 138*(2) e20154256.

Hurlburt, M., Barth, R. P., Leslie, L. K., Landsverk, J. A., & McCrae, J. S. (2007). Building on strengths: Current status and opportunities for improvement of parent training for families in child welfare services. In R. Haskins, F. Wulczyn, & M. B. Webb (Eds.), *Child protection: Using research to improve policy and practice* (pp. 81–106). Brookings Institution.

Huth-Bocks, A. C., Levendosky, A. A., Theran, S. A., & Bogat, G. A. (2004). The impact of domestic violence on mothers' prenatal representations of their infants. *Infant Mental Health Journal, 25*(2), 79-88.

Ingoldsby, E., Richards, T., Usher, K., Wang, K., Morehouse, E., Masters, L., & Kopiec, K. (2021). *Prenatal alcohol and other drug exposures in child welfare study: Final report.* Children's Bureau, Administration for Children and Families, U.S. Department of Health and Human Services.

Inkelis, S. M., & Thomas, J. D. (2018). Sleep in infants and children with prenatal alcohol exposure. *Alcoholism: Clinical and Experimental Research, 42*(8), 1390–1405.

Jacobson, J. L., Akkaya-Hocagil, T., Ryan, L. M., Dodge, N. C., Richardon, G. A., Olson, H. C., Coles, C. D., Day, N. L., Cook, R. J., & Jacobson, S. W. (2021). Effects of prenatal alcohol exposure on cognitive and behavioral development: Findings from a hierarchical meta-analysis of data from six prospective longitudinal U.S. cohorts. *Alcoholism Clinical & Experimental Research, 45*(10), 2040–2058.

Jacobson, S. W., Jacobson, J. L., Sokol, R. J., Chiodo, L. M., & Corbana, R. (2004). Maternal age, alcohol abuse history, and quality of parenting as moderators of the effects of prenatal alcohol exposure on 7.5 year intellectual functioning. *Alcoholism: Clinical and Experimental Research, 28*, 1732–1745.

Jaffee, S. R. (2007). Sensitive, stimulating caregiving predicts cognitive and behavioral resilience in neurodevelopmentally at-risk infants. *Development and Psychopathology, 19*, 631–647.

Jaffee, S. R., & Maikovich-Fong, A. K. (2011). Effects of chronic maltreatment and maltreatment timing on children's behavior and cognitive abilities. *Journal of Child Psychology and Psychiatry, 52*(2), 184–194.

Jansson, L. M. & Patrick, S. W. (2019). Neonatal abstinence syndrome. *Pediatric Clinics, 66*(2), 353-367.

Johnson, W. F., Huelsnitz, C. O., Carlson, E. A., Roisman, G. I., Englund, M. M., Miller, G. E. & Simpson, J. E. (2017). Childhood abuse and neglect and physical health at midlife: Prospective, longitudinal evidence. *Development and Psychopathology, 29*(5), 1935–1946.

Jones, H. E., Harrow, C., O'Grady, K. E., Crocetti, M., Jansson, L. M., & Kaltenback, K. (2010). Neonatal abstinence scores in opioid-exposed and non-exposed neonates: A blinded comparison. *Journal of Opioid Management, 6*(6), 409–413.

Jones-Harden, B., & Whittaker, J. V. (2011). The early home environment and developmental outcomes for young children in the CWS. *Children and Youth Services Review, 33*(8), 1392–1403.

Julian, M. M., Muzik, M., Jester, J. M., Handelazalts, J., Erikson, N., Stringer, M., Brophy-Herb, H., Ribaudo, J., Huth-Bocks, A., Lawler, J., Stacks, A., Rosenblum, K. L., & The Michigan Collaborative for Infant Mental Health Research. (2021). Relationships heal: Reducing harsh parenting and child abuse potential with relationship-based home visiting. *Children and Youth Services Review, 128*, 106135.

Kelly, J. F., Zuckerman, T., & Rosenblatt, S. (2008). Promoting First Relationships: A relationship-focused early intervention approach. *Infants and Young Children, 21*, 285–295.

Kepple, N. J. (2017). The complex nature of parental substance use: Examining past year and prior use behaviors as correlates of child maltreatment frequency. *Substance Use and Misuse, 52*, 811–821.

Ko, J. Y., Coy, K. C., Height, S. C., Haegerich, T. M., Williams, L., Cox, S., Njai, R., & Grant, A. M. (2020). Characteristics of marijuana use during pregnancy – Eight states, pregnancy risk assessment monitoring system 2017. *Morbidity and Mortality Weekly Report, 69*(32), 1058–1063.

Kochanska, G. (1997). Multiple pathways to conscience for children with difficult temperaments: From toddlerhood to age 5. *Developmental Psychology, 35*, 228–240.

Koponen, A. M., Nissinen, N.-M., Gissler, M., Autti-Rämö, I., Sarkola, T., & Kahila, H. (2020). Prenatal substance exposure, adverse childhood experiences and diagnosed mental and behavioral disorders – A longitudinal register-based MATCHED cohort study in Finland. *SSM - Population Health, 11*, 100625.

Kostyrka-Allchorne, K., Wass, S. V., & Sonuga-Barke, E. J. S. (2020). Research review: Do parent ratings of infant negative emotionality and self-regulation predict psychopathology in childhood and adolescence? A systematic review and meta-analysis of prospective longitudinal studies. *Journal of Child Psychology and Psychiatry, 61*(4), 401-416.

Krol, K. M., Moulder, R. G., Lillard, T. S., Grossman, T., & Connely, J. J. (2019). Epigenetic dynamics in infancy and the impact of maternal engagement. *Science Advances, 5*(10), eaay0680.

Kumsta, R. (2019). The role of epigenetics for understanding mental health difficulties and its implications for psychotherapy research. *Psychology and Psychotherapy: Theory, Research and Practice, 92*, 190–207.

Landi, N., Avery, T., Crowley, M. J., Wu, J., & Mayes, L. (2017). Prenatal cocaine exposure impacts language and reading into late adolescence: Behavioral and ERP evidence. *Developmental Neuropsychology, 42*(6), 369–386.

Landi, N., Montoya, J., Kober, H., Rutherford, H. J., Mencl, W. E., Worhunsky, P. D., Potenza, M. N., & Mayes, L. C. (2011). Maternal neural responses to infant cries and faces: Relationships with substance use. *Frontiers in Psychiatry, 2*, 32.

Landsverk, J., Davis, I., Ganger, W., Newton, R., & Johnson, I. (1996). Impact of child psychosocial functioning on reunification from out-of-home placement. *Children and Youth Services Review, 18*(4–5), 447–463.

Lange, S., Shield, K., Rehm, J., & Popova, S. (2013). Prevalence of fetal alcohol spectrum disorders in child care settings: A meta-analysis. *Pediatrics, 132*(4), e980–985.

Larson, J. L., Graham, D. L., Singer, L. T., Beckwith, A. M., Terplan, M., Davis, J. M., Martinez, J., & Bada, H. S. (2019). Cognitive and behavioral impact on children exposed to opioids during pregnancy. *Pediatrics, 144*(2), e20190514.

Lecklitner, G. L., Malik, N. M., Aaron, S. M., & Lederman, C. S. (1999). Promoting safety for abused children and battered mothers: Miami-Dade county's model dependency court intervention program. *Child Maltreatment, 4*(2), 175–182.

Lederman, C. S., & Osofsky, J. D. (2004). Infant mental health interventions in juvenile court: Ameliorating the effects of maltreatment and deprivation. *Psychology, Public Policy, and Law, 10*(1–2), 162–177.

Lee, L. J., & Lupo, P. J. (2013). Maternal smoking during pregnancy and the risk of congenital heart defects in offspring: A systematic review and metaanalysis. *Pediatric Cardiology, 34*, 398–407.

Lee, R. E., & Stacks, A. M. (2005). In whose arms?: Using relational therapy in supervised family visitation with very young children in foster care. *Journal of Family Psychotherapy, 15*, 1–14.

Leslie, L., Gordon, J., Ganger, W., & Gist, K. (2002). Developmental delay in young children in the CWS by initial placement type. *Infant Mental Health Journal, 23*(5), 496–516.

Levendosky, A. A., Bogat, G. A., Huth-Bocks, A. C., Rosenblum, K., & von Eye, A. (2011). The effects of domestic violence on the stability of attachment from infancy to preschool. *Journal of Clinical Child & Adolescent Psychology, 40*(3), 398–410.

Levendosky, A. A., Leahy, K. L., Bogat, G. A., Davidson, W. S., & von Eye, A. (2006). Domestic violence, maternal parenting, maternal mental health, and infant externalizing behavior. *Journal of Family Psychology, 20*, 544–552.

Lewis-Morrarty, E., Dozier, M., Barnard, K., Terraccino, S. M., & Moore, S. V. (2012). Cognitive flexibility and theory of mind outcomes among foster children: Preschool follow-up results of a randomized clinical trial. *Journal of Adolescent Health, 51*(2), S17–S22.

Lieberman, A. F., Dimmler, M. H., & Gosh Ippen, C. M. (2019). Child-Parent Psychotherapy: A trauma-informed treatment for young children and their caregivers. In C. H. Zeanah (Ed.), *Handbook of infant mental health* (4th ed., pp. 485–499). Guilford Press.

Lieberman, A. F., Van Horn, P., & Gosh Ippen, C. (2005). Toward evidence-based treatment: Child-Parent Psychotherapy with preschoolers exposed to martial violence. *Journal of the American Academy of Child & Adolescent Psychiatry, 44*(12), 1241–1248.

Lind, T., Bernard, K., Ross, E., & Dozier, M. (2014). Intervention effects on negative affect of CPS-referred children: Results of a randomized clinical trial. *Child Abuse & Neglect, 38*(9), 1459–1467.

Lind, T., Raby, L., & Dozier, M. (2017). Attachment and biobehavioral catch-up effects on foster toddler executive functioning: Results of a randomized clinical trial. *Development and Psychopathology, 29*, 575-586.

Lind, T., Bernard, K., Yarger, H. A., & Dozier, M. (2020). Promoting compliance in children referred to child protective services: A randomized clinical trial. *Child Development, 91*(2), 563–576.

Lindsay, K. L., Buss, C., Wadhwa, P. D., & Entringer, S. (2019). The interplay between nutrition and stress in pregnancy: Implications for fetal programming of brain development. *Biological Psychiatry, 85*(2), 135–149.

Lloyd, E. C., & Barth, R. P. (2011). Developmental outcomes after five years for foster children returned home, remaining in care, or adopted. *Children and Youth Services Review, 33*, 1383–1391.

Lucassen, N., Tharner, A., van IJzendoorn, M. H., Gakermans-Kranenburg, M. J., Volling, B. L., Verhulst, F. C., Lambregtse-Van den Berg, M. P., & Tiemeier, H. (2011). The association between paternal sensitivity and infant-father attachment security: A meta-analysis of three decades of research. *Journal of Family Psychology, 25*(6), 986–992.

Madigan, S., Atkinson, L., Laurin, K., & Benoit, D. (2013). Attachment and internalizing behavior in early childhood: A meta-analysis. *Developmental Psychology, 49*(4), 672–689.

Madigan, S., Bakermans-Kranenburg, M. J., Van Ijzendoorn, M. H. Moran, G., Pederson, D. R., & Benoit, D. (2006). Unresolved states of mind, anomalous parental behavior, and disorganized attachment: A review and meta-analysis of a transmission gap. *Attachment & Human Development, 8*(2), 89-111.

Madigan, S., Brumariu, L. E., Villani, V., Atkinson, L., & Lyons-Ruth, K. (2016). Representational and questionnaire measures of attachment: A meta-analysis of relations to child internalizing and externalizing problems. *Psychological Bulletin, 142*(4), 367–399.

Madigan, S., Cyr, C., Eirich, R., Fearon, R. M. P., Ly, A., Rash, C., Poole, J. C., & Alink, L. R. A. (2019). Testing the cycle of maltreatment hypothesis: Meta-analytic evidence of the intergenerational transmission of child maltreatment. *Development and Psychopathology 31*(1), 23–51.

Madigan, S., Prime, H., Graham, S. A., Rodrigues, M., Anderson, N., Khoury, J., & Jenkins, J. M. (2019). Parenting behavior and child language: A meta-analysis. *Pediatrics, 144*(4), e20183556.

Malik, N. M., Lederman, C. S., Crowson, M. M., & Osofsky, J. D. (2002). Evaluating maltreated infants, toddlers, and preschoolers in dependency court. *Infant Mental Health Journal, 23*(5), 576–592.

Mark, K., Gryczynski, J., Axenfeld, E., Schwartz, R. P., & Terplan, M. (2017). Pregnant women's current and intended cannabis use in relation to their views toward legalization and knowledge of potential harm. *Journal of Addiction Medicine, 11*(3), 211–216.

Marsit, C. J. (2015). Influence of environmental exposure on human epigenetic regulation. *Journal of Experimental Biology, 218*(1), 71–79.

Martinez-Torteya, C., Bogat, G. A., Lonstein, J. S., Granger, D. A., & Levendosky, A. A. (2017). Exposure to intimate partner violence in utero and infant internalizing behaviors: Moderation by salivary cortisol-alpha amylase asymmetry. *Early Human Development, 113*, 40–48.

Massey, S. H., Newmark, R. L., & Wakschlag, L. S. (2018). Explicating the role of empathic processes in substance use disorders: A conceptual framework and research agenda. *Drug and Alcohol Review, 37*(3), 316–332.

Mathewson, K. J., Chow, C. H., Dobson, K. G., Pope, E. I., Schmidt, L. A., & Van Lieshout, R. J. (2017). Mental health of extremely low birth weight survivors: A systematic review and meta-analysis. *Psychological Bulletin, 143*(4), 347.

Mattson, S. N., Crocker, N., & Nguyen, T. T. (2011). Fetal alcohol spectrum disorders: Neuropsychological and behavioral features. *Neuropsychology Review, 21*(2), 81–101.

Mayes, L. C., & Sean, T. D. (2002). Substance abuse and parenting. In M. H. Bornstein (Ed.), *Handbook of parenting, Vol. 4: Social conditions and applied parenting* (2nd ed., pp. 329–359). Lawrence Erlbaum Associates Publishers.

McCombs-Thornton, K. L., & Foster, E. M. (2012). The effect of the ZERO TO THREE Court Teams initiative on types of exits from the foster care system: A competing risks analysis. *Children and Youth Services Review, 34*(1), 169–178.

McEachern, M. J., Krauskopf, A., & Blackburn, E. H. (2000). Telomeres and their control. *Annual Review of Genetics, 34*, 331–358.

McEwen, B. S. (2012). Brain on stress how the social environment gets under the skin. *Proceedings of the National Academy of Science, 109*(Supplement 2), 17180–17185.

McIntosh, J. E., Tan, E. S., Levendosky, A. A., & Holtzworth-Munroe, A. (2021). Mothers' experience of intimate partner violence and subsequent offspring attachment security ages 1-5 years: A meta-analysis. *Trauma, Violence & Abuse, 22*(4)), 885-899.

Merritt, D.,H., & Klein, S. (2015). Do early care and education services improve language development for maltreated children? Evidence from a national child welfare sample. *Child Abuse & Neglect, 39*, 185–196.

Meyers, J. E. B. (2008). A short history of child protection in America. *Family Law Quarterly, 42*(3), 449–463.

Mi, D., Fang, H., Zhao, Y., & Zhong, L. (2017). Birth weight and type 2 diabetes: A meta-analysis. *Experimental and Therapeutic Medicine, 14*(6), 5313-5320.

Miami Child Well-Being Court Initiative. (2013). *The Miami child well-being court model: Essential elements and implementation guidance* (Prepared by J. Goldman Fraser and C. Casanueva). http://www.floridaschildrenfirst.org/the-miami-child-well-being-court-modeltm-essential-elements-and-implementation-guidance/

Min, M. O., Minnes, S., Park, H., Ridenour, T., Kim, J. Y., Yoon, M., & Singer, L. T. (2018). Developmental trajectories of externalizing behavior from ages 4 to 12: Prenatal cocaine exposure and adolescent correlates. *Drug and Alcohol Dependence, 192*, 223–232.

Mortensen, J. A., & Barnett, M. A. (2018). Emotion regulation, harsh parenting, and teacher sensitivity among socioeconomically disadvantaged toddlers in child care. *Early Education and Development, 29*(2), 143–160.

Mortensen, J. A., & Barnett, M. A. (2019). Intrusive parenting, teacher sensitivity, and negative emotionality on the development of emotion regulation in Early Head Start toddlers. *Infant Behavior and Development, 55*, 10–21.

Moutsiana, C., Fearon, P., Murray, L., Cooper, P., Goodyer, I., Johnstone, T., & Halligan, S. (2014). Making an effort to feel positive: Insecure attachment in infancy predicts the neural underpinnings of emotion regulation in adulthood. *Journal of Child and Psychology and Psychiatry, 55*(9), 999–1008.

Moutsiana, C., Johnstone, T., Murray, L., Fearon, R. M. P., Cooper, P. J., Pliatsikas, C., Goodyer, I., & Halligan, S. L. (2015). Insecure attachment during infancy predicts greater amygdala volumes in early adulthood. *Journal of Child Psychology and Psychiatry, 56*(6), 540–548.

Mu, M., Wang, S-F., Sheng, J., Zhao, Y., Li, H-Z., Hu, C-L., & Tao, F-B. (2012). Birth weight and subsequent blood pressure: A meta-analysis. *Archives of Cardiovascular Diseases, 105*(2), 99–113.

Mueller, I., & Tronick, E. (2020). The long shadow of violence: The impact of exposure to intimate partner violence in infancy and early childhood. *International Journal of Applied Psychoanalytic Studies, 17*(3), 232–245.

Nashed, M. G., Hardy, D. B., & Laviolette, S. R. (2021). Prenatal cannabinoid exposure: Emerging evidence of psychological and neuropsychiatric abnormalities. *Frontiers in Psychiatry*, 11, 624275.

National Academies of Sciences, Engineering, and Medicine. (2019a). *Fostering healthy mental, emotional, and behavioral development in children and youth: A national agenda*. National Academies Press.

National Academies of Sciences, Engineering, and Medicine. (2019b). *Vibrant and healthy kids: Aligning science, practice and policy to advance health equity*. National Academies Press.

National Center on Substance Abuse and Child Welfare. (2019). *Child welfare and alcohol and drug use statistics*. https://ncsacw.samhsa.gov/research/child-welfare-and-treatment-statistics.aspx

National Scientific Council on the Developing Child. (2004). *Children's emotional development is built into the architecture of their brains* (Working Paper No. 2). http://www.developingchild.net

National Scientific Council on the Developing Child. (2007). *The science of early childhood development: Closing the gap between what we know and what we don't*. http://www.developingchild.net

Nelson, C. A., Bhutta, Z. A., Burke Harris, N., Danese, A., & Samara, M. (2020). Adversity in childhood is linked to mental and physical health throughout life. *BMJ, 371*, m3048, 1–9.

Nelson, C. A., Zeanah, C. H., & Fox, N. A. (2019). How early experiences shape human development: The case of psychosocial deprivation. *Neural Plasticity, 2019*, 1676285.

Neppl, T. K., Bonnellan, M. B., Scaramella, L. V., Widaman, K. F., Spilman, S. K., Ontai, L. L., & Conger, R. D. (2010). Differential stability of temperament and personality from toddlerhood to middle childhood. *Journal of Research in Personality, 44*(3), 386–396.

Nygaard, E., Slinning, K., Moe, V., Due-Tønnessen, P., Fjell, A., & Walhovd, K. B. (2018). Neuroanatomical characteristics of youths with prenatal opioid and poly-drug exposure. *Neurotoxicology and Teratology, 68*, 13–26.

O'Donovan, A., Tomiyama, A. J., Lin, J., Puterman, E., Adler, N. E., Kemeny, M., Wolkowitz, O. M., Blackburn, E. H., & Epel, E. S. (2012). Stress appraisals and cellular aging: A key role for anticipatory threat in the relationship between psychological stress and telomere length. *Brain, Behavior, and Immunity, 26*(4), 573–579.

Olds, D. L. (2008). Preventing child maltreatment and crime with prenatal and infancy support of parents: The nurse-family partnership. *Journal of Scandinavian Studies in Criminology and Crime Prevention, 9*(Suppl 1), 2–24.

Osofsky, J. D., & Lieberman, A. F. (2011). A call for integrating a mental health perspective into systems of care for abused and neglected infants and young children. *American Psychologist, 66*(2), 120-128.

Oxford, M. L., Fleming, C. B., Nelson, E. M., Kelly, J. K., & Spieker, S. J. (2013). Randomized trial of Promoting First Relationships: Effects on maltreated toddlers' separation distress and sleep regulation after reunification. *Children and Youth Services Review, 35*(12), 1988–1992.

Oxford, M. L., Marcenko, M., Fleming, C. B., Lohr, M. J., & Spieker, S. J. (2016). Promoting birthparents' relationships with their toddler upon reunification: Results from Promoting First Relationships home visiting program. *Children and Youth Services Review, 61*, 109–116.

Oxford, M. L., Spieker, S. J., Lohr, M. J., & Fleming, C. B. (2016). Promoting First Relationships: Randomized trial of a 10-week home visiting program with families referred to child protective services. *Child Maltreatment, 21*(4), 267–277.

Palusci, V. J., Smith, E. G., & Paneth, N. (2005). Predicting and responding to physical abuse in young children using NCANDS. *Children and Youth Services Review, 27*(6), 667–682.

Pasalich, D. S., Fleming, C. B., Oxford, M. L., Zheng, Y., & Spieker, S. J. (2016). Can parenting intervention prevent cascading effects from placement instability to insecure attachment to externalizing problems in maltreated toddlers? *Child Maltreatment, 21*(3), 175–185.

Pasalich, D. S., Fleming, C. B., Speiker, S. J., Lohr, M. J., & Oxford, M. L. (2019). Does parents' own history of child abuse moderate the effectiveness of the promoting first relationships intervention in child welfare? *Child Maltreatment, 24*(1), 56–65.

Patrick, S. W., Dudley, J., Martin, P. R., Martin, F. E., Warren, M. D., Hartmen, K. E., Wesley, E., Grijalva, C. G., & Cooper, W. O. (2015). Prescription opioid epidemic and infant outcomes. *Pediatrics, 135*(5), 842–850.

Peterson, C., Florence, C., & Klevens, J. (2018). The economic burden of child maltreatment in the United States in 2015. *Child Abuse & Neglect, 86*, 178–183.

Popova, S., Lange, S., Shield, K., Mihic, A., Chudley, A. E., Mukherjee, R. A., Bekmuradov, D., & Rehm, J. (2016). Comorbidity of fetal alcohol spectrum disorder: A systematic review and meta-analysis. *The Lancet, 387*(10022), 978–987.

Pungello, E. P., Iruka, I. U., Dotterer, A. M., Mills-Koonce, R., & Reznick, J. S. (2009). The effects of socioeconomic status, race, and parenting on language development in early childhood. *Developmental Psychology, 45*, 544–557.

Raby, K. L., Labella, M. H., Martin, J., Carlson, E. A., & Roisman, G. I. (2017). Childhood abuse and neglect and insecure attachment states of mind in adulthood: Prospective, longitudinal evidence from a high-risk sample. *Development and Psychopathology, 29*(2), 347–363.

Raby, K. L., Roisman, G. I., Labella, M. H., Martin, J., Fraley, R. C., & Simpson, J. A. (2018). The legacy of early abuse and neglect for social and academic competence from childhood to adulthood. *Child Development, 90*(5), 1684–1701.

Ramborger, M. E., Zubilete, M. A. Z., & Acosta, G. B. (2018). Prenatal stress and its effects of human cognition, behavior, and psychopathology: A review of the literature. *Pediatric Dimensions, 3*(1), 1–6.

Ribaudo, J., Lawler, J. M., Jester, J. M., Riggs, J., Erickson, N. L., Stacks, A. M., Brophy-Herb, H., Muzik, M., & Rosenblum, K. L. (2022). Maternal history of adverse experiences and PTSD symptoms impact toddlers' early socioemotional wellbeing: The benefits of Infant Mental Health Home Visiting. *Frontiers in Psychology, 12*, 792989.

Richardson, G. A., Goldschmidt, L., Larkby, C., & Day, N. L. (2015). Effects of prenatal cocaine exposure on adolescent development. *Neurotoxicology and Teratology, 49*, 41–48.

Ridout, K. K., Levandowski, M., Ridout, S. J., Gantz, L., Goonan, K., Palermo, D., Price, L. H., & Tyrka, A. R. (2018). Early life adversity and telomere length: A meta-analysis. *Molecular Psychiatry, 23*, 858–871.

Riley, E. P., Infante, M. A., & Warren, K. R. (2011). Fetal alcohol spectrum disorders: An overview. *Neuropsychology Review, 21*(2), 73–80.

Ringeisen, H., Casanueva, C., Cross, T. P., & Urato, M. (2009). Mental health and special education services at school entry for children who were involved with the child welfare system as infants. *Journal of Emotional and Behavioral Disorders, 17*(3), 177–192.

Robinson, R., Lahti-Pulkkinen, M., Heinonen, K., Reynolds, R. M., & Räikkönen, K. (2019). Fetal programming of neuropsychiatric disorders by maternal pregnancy depression: A systematic mini review. *Pediatric Research, 85*, 134–145.

Rosenblum, K. L., Muzik, M., Jester, J. M., Huth-Bocks, A., Erickson, N., Ludtke, M., Weatherston, D., Brophy-Herb, H., Tableman, B., Alfafara, E., Waddell, R., & The Michigan Collaborative for Infant Mental Health Research. (2020). Community-delivered infant-parent psychotherapy improves maternal sensitive caregiving: Evaluation of the Michigan model of infant mental health home visiting. *Infant Mental Health Journal, 41*(2), 178–190.

Rothbart, M. K. (2007). Temperament, development, and personality. *Current Directions in Psychological Science, 16*, 207–212.

Rutherford, H. J., Williams, S. K., Moy, S., Mayes, L. C., & Johns, J. M. (2011). Disruption of maternal parenting circuitry by addictive process: Rewiring of reward and stress systems. *Frontiers in Psychiatry, 2*, 37.

Saridjan, N. S., Velders, F. P., Jaddoe, V. W. V., Hofman, A., Verhulst, F. C., & Tiemeier, H. (2014). The longitudinal association of the diurnal cortisol rhythm with internalizing and externalizing problems in preschoolers: The Generation R Study. *Psychoneuroendocrinology, 71*, 147–154.

Savage, L-É., Tarabulsy, G. M., Pearson, J., Collin-Vézina, D., & Gagné, L. M. (2019). Maternal antecedents of childhood maltreatment and later parenting outcome: A meta-analysis. *Development and Psychopathology, 31*(1), 9–21.

Scarborough, A. A., Lloyd, E. C., & Barth, R. P. (2009). Maltreated infants and toddlers: Predictors of developmental delay. *Journal of Developmental and Behavioral Pediatrics, 30*(6), 489–498.

Scarborough, A. A., & McCrae, J. S. (2010). School-age special education outcomes of infants and toddlers investigated for maltreatment. *Children and Youth Services Review, 32*(1), 80–88.

Schofield, T. J., Lee, R. D., & Merrick, M. T. (2013). Safe, stable, nurturing relationships as a moderator of intergenerational continuity of child maltreatment: A meta-analysis. *Journal of Adolescent Health, 53*, S32–S38.

Shalev, I., Moffitt, T. E., Sugden, K., Williams, B., Houts, R. M., Danese, A., Mill, J., Arsenaeault, L., & Caspi, A. (2013). Exposure to violence during childhood is associated with telomere erosion from 5 to 10 years of age: A longitudinal study. *Molecular Psychiatry, 18*(5), 576–581.

Shi, Y., Zhu, B., & Liang, D. (2021). The associations between prenatal cannabis use disorder and neonatal outcomes. *Addiction, 116*(11), 3069-3079.

Shonkhoff, J. P., Garner, A. S., Siegel, B. S., et al., & the Committee on Psychosocial Aspects of Child and Family Health Committee on Early Childhood, Adoption, and Dependent Care Section on Developmental and Behavioral Pediatrics. (2012). The lifelong effects of early childhood adversity and toxic stress. *Pediatrics, 129*, e232–246.

Simms, M. D., (1989). The foster care clinic: A community program to identify treatment needs of children in foster care. *Journal of Developmental and Behavioral Pediatrics, 10*, 121–128.

Slade, A., Grienenberger, J., Bernbach, E., Levy, D., & Locker, A. (2005). Maternal reflective functioning, attachment, and the transmission gap: A preliminary study. *Attachment and Human Development, 7*(3), 289–298.

Spieker, S. J., Oxford, M. L., & Fleming, C. B. (2014). Permanency outcomes for toddlers in child welfare two years after a randomized trial of a parenting intervention. *Child and Youth Services Review, 44*, 201–206.

Spieker, S. J., Oxford, M. L., Kelly, J. B., Nelson, E. M., & Fleming, C. B. (2012). Promoting First Relationships: Randomized trial of a relationship-based intervention for toddlers in child welfare. *Child Maltreatment, 17*(4), 271–286.

Stacks, A. M., Barron, C. C., & Wong, K. (2019). Infant mental health home visiting in the contest of an infant-toddler court team: Changes in parental responsiveness and reflective functioning. *Infant Mental Health Journal, 40*(4), 523–540.

Stacks, A. M., Beeghly, M., Partridge, T., & Dexter, C. (2011). Effects of placement type on the language developmental trajectories of maltreated children from infancy to early childhood. *Child Maltreatment, 16*(4), 287–299.

Stacks, A. M., Jester, J. J., Wong, K., Huth-Bocks, A., Brophy-Herb, H., Lawler, J., Riggs, J., Ribaudo, J., Muzik, M., Rosenblum, K. L., & The Michigan Collaborative for Infant Mental Health Research. (2022). Infant mental health home visiting: Intervention dosage and therapist experience interact to support improvements in maternal reflective functioning. *Attachment & Human Development, 24*(1), 53-75.

Stacks, A. M., & Partridge, T. (2011). Infants placed in foster care prior to their first birthday: Differences in kin and nonkin placements. *Infant Mental Health Journal, 32*(5), 489–508.

Stacks, A. M., Wong, K., Barron, C. C., & Ryznar, T. (2020). Permanency and well-being outcomes for maltreated infants: Pilot results from and infant-toddler court team. *Child Abuse & Neglect, 101*, 104332.

Stahmer, A. C., Hurlburt, M., Horowitz, S. M., Landsverk, J., Zhang, J., & Leslie, L. (2009). Associations between intensity of child welfare involvement and child development among young children in child welfare. *Child Abuse and Neglect, 33*(9), 598–611.

Stahmer, A. C., Leslie, L. K., Hurlburt, M., Barth, R. P., Bruce Webb, M., Landsverk, J., & Zhang, J. (2005). Developmental and behavioral needs and service use for young children in child welfare. *Pediatrics, 116*(4), 891–900.

Stevenson, K., Lillycrop, K. A., & Silver, M. J. (2020). Fetal programming and epigenetics. *Current Opinions in Metabolic Research, 13*, 1–6.

Tableman, B., & Ludtke, M. (2020). Introduction to the special section: The development of infant mental health home visiting in Michigan state government. *Infant Mental Health Journal, 41*(2), 163–165.

Taylor-Colls, S., & Fearon, R. M. P. (2015). The effects of parental behavior on infants' neural processing of emotion expression. *Child Development, 86*(3), 877–888.

Terplan, M., Laird, H. J., Hand, D. J., Wright, T. E., Premkumar, A., Martin, C. E., Meyer, M. C., Jones, H. E., & Krans, E. E. (2018). Opioid detoxification during pregnancy. *Obstetrics and Gynecology, 131*(5), 803–814.

Thomas, J. C., Letourneau, N., Campbell, T. S., Tomfohr-Madsen, L., Giesbrecht, G. F., & APrONStudy Team. (2017). Developmental origins of infant emotion regulation: Mediation by temperamental negativity and moderation by maternal sensitivity. *Developmental Psychology, 53*(4), 611–628.

Toth, S. L., Maughan, A., Manly, J. T., Spagnola, M., & Cicchetti, D. (2002). The relative efficacy of two interventions in altering maltreated preschool children's representational models: Implications for attachment theory. *Development and Psychopathology, 14*(4), 877–908.

Troese, M., Fukumizu, M., Sallinen, B. J., Gilles, A. A., Wellman, J. D., Paul, J. A., Brown, E. R., & Hayes, M. J. (2008). Sleep fragmentation and evidence for sleep debt in alcohol-exposed infants. *Early Human Development, 84*(9), 577–585.

Tuovinen, S., Lahti-Pulkkinen, M., Girchenko, P., Heinonen, K., Lahti, J., Reynolds, R. M., Hämäläinen, E., Villa, P. M., Kajantie, E., Laivuori, H., & Raikkonen, K. (2021). Maternal antenatal stress and mental and behavioral disorders in their children. *Journal of Affective Disorders, 278*, 57–65.

U.S. Department of Health and Human Services, Administration for Children and Families, Administration on Children, Youth and Families, Children's Bureau. (2020). *The AFCARS report*. https://www.acf.hhs.gov/sites/defa ult/files/documents/cb/afcarsreport27.pdf

U.S. Department of Health and Human Services, Administration for Children and Families, Administration on Children, Youth and Families, Children's Bureau. (2021). *Child maltreatment 2019*. https://www.acf.hhs.gov/cb/ research-data-technology/statistics-research/child-maltreatment

van IJzendoorn, M. H., Schuengel, C., & Bakermans-Krannenburg, M. J. (1999). Disorganized attachment in early childhood: Meta-analysis of precursors, concomitants, and sequalae. *Development and Psychopathology, 11*(2), 225–250.

VanMeter, F., Nivison, M. D., Englund, M. M., Carlson, E. A., & Roisman, G. (2021). Childhood abuse and neglect and self-reported symptoms of psychopathology through midlife. *Developmental Psychology, 57*(5), 824–836.

Verhage, M. L., Schuengel, C., Madigan, S., Fearon, R. M. P., Oosterman, M., Cassibba, R., Bakermans-Kranenburg, M. J., & vanIJzendoorn, M. H. (2016). Narrowing the transmission gap: A synthesis of three decades of research on intergenerational transmission of attachment. *Psychological Bulletin, 142*(4), 337–366.

Walhovd, K. B., Moe, V., Slinning, K., Due-Tønnessen, P., Bjørnerud, A., Dale, A. M., van derKouwe, A., Quinn, B. T., Kosofsky, B., Greve, D., & Fischl, B. (2008). Volumetric cerebral characteristics of children exposed to opiates and other substances in utero. *NeuroImage, 36*(4), 1331–1344.

Walhovd, K. B., Watts, R., Amlien, I., & Woodward, L. J. (2012). Neural tract development of infants born to methadone-maintained mothers. *Pediatric Neurology, 47*(1), 1–6.

Weatherston, D. J., Ribaudo, J., & The Michigan Collaborative for Infant Mental Health Research. (2020). The Michigan Infant Mental Health Home Visiting Model. *Infant Mental Health Journal, 41*(2), 166–177.

Wesarg, C., Van Den Akker, A. L., Oei, N. Y. L., Hoeve, M., & Wiers, R. W. (2020). Identifying pathways from early adversity to psychopathology: A review on dysregulated HPA axis functioning and impaired self-regulation in early childhood. *European Journal of Developmental Psychology, 17*(6), 808–827.

Willford, J. A., Chandler, L. S., Goldschmidt, L., & Day, N. L. (2010). Effects of prenatal tobacco, alcohol, and marijuana exposure on processing speed, visual–motor coordination, and interhemispheric transfer. *Neurotoxicology and Teratology, 32*(6), 580–588.

Willoughby, M. T., Gottfredson, N. C., Stifter, C. A., & The Family Life Project Investigators. (2017). Observed temperament from ages 6 to 36 months predicts parent- and teacher-reported attention-deficit/hyperactivity disorder symptoms in first grade. *Development and Psychopathology, 29*(1), 107–120.

Wong, K., Stacks, A. M., Rosenblum, K. L., & Muzik, M. (2017). Reflective functioning moderates the relationship between difficult temperament in infancy and behavior problems in toddlerhood. *Merrill Palmer Quarterly, 63*(1), 54–76.

Wulczyn, F., Hislop, K. B., & Goerge, R. M. (2001). *Foster care dynamics 1983–1998*. Chapin Hall Center for Children.

Wulczyn, F., Hislop, K. B., & Jones Harden, B. (2002). The placement of infants in foster care. *Infant Mental Health Journal, 23*(5), 454–475.

Yarger, H. A., Bronfman, E., Carlson, E., & Dozier, M. (2020). Intervening with Attachment and Biobehavioral Catch-Up to decrease disrupted parenting behavior and attachment disorganization: The role of parental withdrawal. *Development and Psychopathology, 32*(3), 1139–1148.

Yarger, H. A., Hoye, J. R., & Dozier, M. (2016). Trajectories of change in Attachment and Biobehavioral Catch-Up among high-risk mothers: A randomized clinical trial. *Infant Mental Health Journal, 37*(5), 525–536.

Yeoh, S. L., Eastwood, J., Wright, I. M., Morton, R., Melhuish, E., Ward, M., & Oei, J. L. (2019). Cognitive and motor outcomes of children with prenatal opioid exposure: A systematic review and meta-analysis. *Jama Network, 2*(7), e197025.

Yost, N. P., Bloom, S. L., McIntire, D. D., & Leveno, K. J. (2005). A prospective observational study of domestic violence during pregnancy. *Obstetrics & Gynecology, 106*(1), 61–65.

Young-Wolff, K. C., Tucker, L. Y., Alexeeff, S., Armstrong, M. A., Conway, A., & Weisner, C. (2017). Trends in self-reported and biochemically tested marijuana use among pregnant females in California from 2009–2016. *JAMA, 318*, 2490–2491.

Zajac, L., Raby, K. L., & Dozier, M. (2018). Receptive vocabulary development of children placed in foster care and children who remained with birth parents after involvement with child protective services. *Child Maltreatment, 24*(1), 107–112.

Zajac, L., Raby, K. L., & Dozier, M. (2020). Sustained effects on attachment security in middle childhood: results from a randomized clinical trial of the Attachment and Biobehavioral Catch-up (ABC) intervention. *Journal of Child Psychology and Psychiatry, 61*(4), 417–427.

Zeanah, C. H., Danis, B., Hirshberg, L., Benoit, D., Miller, D., & Heller, S. S. (1999). Disorganized attachment associated with partner violence: A research note. *Infant Mental Health Journal, 20*(1), 77–86.

Zero to Three. (2023). *Safe Babies States and Sites* https:/ https://www.zerotothree.org/safe-babies-states-and-sites

Zwir, I., Del-Val, C., Arnedo, J., et al. (2021). Three genetic-environmental networks for human personality. *Molecular Psychiatry, 26*(8), 3858-3875.

Developmental Pathways to Antisocial Behavior: Implications for Juvenile Justice Policy and Practice

Paul J. Frick, Emily C. Kemp, and Julianne S. Speck

Abstract

This chapter illustrates a developmental psychopathology approach to understanding antisocial behavior in children and adolescents. Specifically, the chapter summarizes research suggesting that there are three common ways that various risk factors can influence critical developmental mechanisms that make a child more likely to act in ways that violate the rights of others or that violate major societal norms, both of which can lead to justice system involvement. One such pathway involves youth who do not show serious conduct problems until they approach adolescence and who then seem to experience an exaggeration of typical adolescent rebellion associated with identity formation. Two other pathways involve conduct problems that emerge earlier in development and that are related to either deficits in the typical development of conscience or deficits in the typical ability to appropriately regulate emotions and behaviors. In summarizing the research supporting these different developmental pathways, the chapter illustrates the implications of this approach for research, assessment, and treatment of youth who show serious antisocial behavior, as well as the implications for juvenile justice policy.

Key Words: conduct problems, developmental pathways, age of onset, callous-unemotional traits, treatment, juvenile justice policy

Introduction: The Importance of Integrating Developmental and Clinical Research

Research on antisocial and criminal behavior has long been the focus of psychological as well as sociological and criminological research. This research has uncovered many risk factors that increase a child's likelihood of acting in ways that violate others' rights and/or break major societal norms, including breaking the law. The risk factors cover a wide range of characteristics in the child (e.g., low resting heart rate, low intelligence, poor impulse control, sensation seeking), as well as in the child's prenatal (e.g., exposure to toxins during pregnancy), family (e.g., parental mental health problems, harsh and inconsistent parenting), neighborhood (e.g., exposure to community violence, impoverished living conditions), and broader societal (e.g., media exposure to violence) contexts (see Dodge & Pettit, 2003; Frick, 2006; and Raine, 2002, for reviews). This large body of work importantly shows that theories that seek to explain the causes of antisocial and criminal behavior cannot simply focus on any single risk factor. Similarly, interventions that target only one risk factor (e.g., inconsistent parenting, anger control) are likely to have limited effectiveness for preventing or treating antisocial behavior. Unfortunately, while research has been very successful in documenting the myriad factors that can place a child at risk for problem behavior, it has generally not been as successful at integrating these risk factors into causal models that are useful for both theory and intervention.

Recently, however, there have been attempts to integrate developmental theory with research on risk factors to antisocial behavior to develop more comprehensive causal models. These models are posited to explain how the risk factors for conduct problems may influence key developmental processes that can make the child more likely to act in an antisocial or aggressive manner (Frick & Viding, 2009). Such causal models that take a developmental psychopathological perspective have influenced psychiatric diagnosis in important ways and may have a number of important implications for advancing both understanding and treatment of antisocial behavior. These developmental approaches integrate several important assumptions. First, these approaches recognize that not only do causal theories have to account for the myriad risk factors that can lead to antisocial behavior but also that these factors may vary across individuals. This concept of *equifinality* means that the same outcome (i.e., conduct problems or criminal behavior) can come about through very different causal processes across individuals (Cicchetti & Rogosch, 1996). Equifinality is important for treatment as well because it suggests that treatment needs to be comprehensive to be able to address multiple risk factors but also individualized and tailored to the child's specific needs.

Second, these developmental approaches recognize that there may be some common pathways through which the risk factors negatively influence the developing child. As a result, we may not need to target all risk factors to prevent and treat antisocial behavior. Instead, we can develop treatments that address the specific developmental mechanisms leading to the problem behavior. This possibility is important because we may not be able to eliminate all risk factors. For example, knowing that exposure to toxins prenatally may lead to serious conduct problems in the child has led to some very effective public health interventions to reduce later delinquency by improving prenatal care in pregnant women (Lorber et al., 2019). However, a psychologist working with a child who was exposed to alcohol during pregnancy cannot go back and change this risk factor. Nonetheless, interventions can be implemented to target the developmental mechanisms that were altered by the risk factor. Third, if research can clarify the effects of various risk factors on the developing child, such developmental mechanisms can be targeted both as treatment and as prevention prior to the child developing serious antisocial behavior. Such interventions can prevent the significant impairments that result from such behavior throughout the lifespan.

Based on this promise of the developmental psychopathological perspective, the current chapter reviews research on the causes of antisocial behavior through this perspective. Specifically, rather than providing another review of the large number of risk factors that have been linked to antisocial and aggressive behavior in past research, we instead focus on three ways in which these risk factors can negatively influence the developing child. These common developmental pathways have received strong support from research and, as a result, have recently been integrated into diagnostic classification systems for disorders of conduct. These pathways also have important implications for prevention and treatment of antisocial and criminal behavior in clinical, educational, and forensic settings, which we also highlight in this chapter.

Key Developmental Processes and Causal Theories of Antisocial Behavior

Adolescent Rebellion

There is a long history of research on juvenile antisocial behavior that emphasizes the distinction made based on when the child's behavior problems first emerge during development. This distinction has been variously labeled as the "early-starter" versus "later-starter" pathways (Farrington et al., 1988) or the "childhood-onset" versus "adolescent-onset" pathways (Moffitt, 2018). It recognizes that some children begin to show behavior problems very early in development, as early as preschool. These behavior problems begin as oppositional, angry, and defiant behaviors that worsen in severity over childhood and into adolescence, when it becomes more serious antisocial and aggressive behavior (Rowe et al., 2002). In contrast, other children don't begin showing behavior problems until the onset of adolescence. Importantly, adolescents in juvenile institutions for criminal behavior tend to be about evenly split in terms of their pattern of onset (Moffitt, 2018).

In addition to the different timing of onset, youth in these two subgroups have been shown to have very different outcomes. For example, Farrington et al. (1988) reported that boys who were arrested prior to age 12 showed almost twice as many convictions at two later points in time (between the ages of 16 and 18 and the ages of 22 and 24) than those with later age of first arrest. Similarly, Robins (1966) reported that boys referred to a mental health clinic for antisocial behavior prior to age 11 were twice as likely to receive a diagnosis of an antisocial personality disorder as an adult as compared to boys who began showing antisocial behavior after age 11. In a New Zealand birth cohort of 539 males followed though age 26, 55% of those whose problem behavior started prior to adolescence had a criminal conviction, with an average rate of 6.9 convictions (SD = 11.5), compared to a conviction rate of 34% and an average rate of 3.5 convictions (SD = 10.8) for those whose problem behaviors started during adolescence (Moffitt et al., 2002). The difference between the two groups was even more dramatic for violent convictions through age 32, whereby 32.7% of the males who began showing serious conduct problems prior to adolescence had been convicted of a violent offense, compared to only 10.2% for males who began showing serious conduct problems in adolescence and only 0.4% for males who did not show serious conduct problems in either childhood or adolescence (Odgers et al., 2008). This latter finding on violent offenses is consistent with multiple studies finding that youth who begin showing serious conduct problems in adolescence are less likely to be aggressive through adolescence and into adulthood (Moffitt, 2018).

Thus, the childhood and adolescent subtypes of conduct disorder (CD) show very different trajectories of antisocial behavior, in terms of both their patterns of onset and life-course trajectory. In addition, a rather extensive body of research suggests that the two groups also differ on several dispositional and contextual risk factors that, in combination, seem to implicate different developmental processes leading to the two groups' disruptive behaviors. To summarize these findings, compared to adolescent-onset CD, childhood-onset CD seems to be more strongly related to neuropsychological (e.g., deficits in executive functioning) and cognitive (e.g., low intelligence) risk factors (see Frick & Viding, 2009, and Moffitt, 2018, for reviews). Children in the childhood-onset group also seem to show more temperamental and personality risk factors, such as impulsivity, attention deficits, callous–unemotional (CU) traits, and problems in emotional regulation. Finally, the same group of children show higher rates of family instability and conflict and have parents who use less effective parenting strategies. When children in the adolescent-onset group differ from control children without conduct problems, it is often due to the former showing higher levels of rebelliousness and rejection of conventional values and status hierarchies (Dandreaux & Frick, 2009; Moffitt, 2018).

The different outcomes and risk factors for the two subtypes of antisocial individuals led Moffitt (2018) to propose that children in the adolescent-onset group show an exaggeration of the normative process of adolescent rebellion. That is, most adolescents show some level of rebelliousness to parents and other authority figures (Brezina & Piquero, 2007). This rebelliousness is part of a process by which adolescents begin to develop their autonomous sense of self and unique identity by rejecting traditional status hierarchies. However, despite some level of rebelliousness being developmentally normative, only a small percentage of adolescents show antisocial behavior that is severe enough to lead to a diagnosis of a CD or serious enough to lead to arrest. According to Moffitt (2018), the youth in the adolescent-onset group engages in antisocial and delinquent behaviors as a misguided attempt to obtain a subjective sense of maturity and adult status in a way that is maladaptive (e.g., breaking societal norms). This maladaptive rebellion can be encouraged by an antisocial peer group, can be a result of parents who do not adequately supervise or monitor the adolescent's behavior, can be due to an adolescent's failure to be connected to prosocial institutions (e.g., school, church), or simply can be due to the adolescent having a more rebellious personality (Dandreaux & Frick, 2009).

This conceptualization of the adolescent-onset pattern of antisocial behavior illustrates the developmental psychopathological approach. Multiple risk factors (e.g., delinquent peer affiliation, poor parental monitoring and supervision) are linked to antisocial behavior through their influence on a developmental process (i.e., identity development) that can make this normal developmental process go awry (i.e., maladaptive rebellion) and lead to problematic behavior. Importantly, the contention that the behavior of youth in this group is viewed as an exaggeration of a process specific to adolescence, and not due to an enduring vulnerability, can explain why the antisocial behavior displayed by this group is unlikely to persist beyond adolescence. However, it is important to note that persons in the adolescent-onset group are still more likely to have mental health, occupational, and educational problems in adulthood compared to persons who did not show conduct problems in either childhood or adolescence (Odgers et al., 2008). These problems in adjustment could be due to lingering consequences that persist into adulthood as a result of adolescent antisocial behavior (e.g., a criminal record, dropping out of school, substance abuse), which are considered "snares" that affect adjustment, even once the primary causes of the antisocial behavior are gone (Moffitt, 2018).

Given the importance in distinguishing early and late starting antisocial behavior, age of onset has been used for a number of years to designate distinct groups of children with CD and to designate distinct patterns of criminal behavior in juveniles, although the exact age to make this distinction has varied somewhat from 11 years (Robins, 1966) to 14 years of age (Patterson & Yoerger, 1997; Tibbetts & Piquero, 1999). It was first added to the *Diagnostic and Statistical Manual of Mental Disorders* (DSM) as part of the criteria for CD in its 4th edition (American Psychiatric Association, 1994), and it was retained in its next revision (American Psychiatric Association, 2013). In the DSM, an even earlier age of 10 years was applied as the cut-off for defining the childhood-onset group. This decision was made to have a more conservative cut-off for defining the more severe childhood onset and to limit the number of children potentially misclassified into this group, given the difficulty in accurately determining the age of onset due to problems in retrospective recall of past behaviors (Moffitt et al., 2008). This difficulty in establishing the age of onset has led some to advocate taking a more dimensional approach to using age of onset, rather than using a categorical cut-off for defining early versus later onset (Lahey et al., 1999), which would be consistent with findings that, even within both childhood- and adolescent-onset groups, the earlier the onset of problem behavior, the more severe the behavior problems seem to be (Fairchild et al., 2013).

One additional caution in using the age-of-onset criterion to distinguish important subgroups of youths with antisocial behavior relates to concerns about its applicability to girls (Silverthorn & Frick, 1999). That is, much of the research comparing outcomes between the two groups has focused on boys. What is clear from research is that childhood onset is much rarer in girls, with most antisocial girls displaying an adolescent onset to their antisocial and aggressive behavior (Konrad et al., 2021; Silberg et al., 2015). Despite this later onset, girls who show serious antisocial behavior in adolescence often have a number of dispositional (e.g., poor impulse control, CU traits) and contextual vulnerabilities (e.g., high rates of family dysfunction) that were evident earlier in development, despite not showing early behavior problems (Konrad et al., 2021; Silverthorn et al., 2001). Further, despite this later onset, girls who show serious antisocial behavior in adolescence often show significant adjustment problems in adulthood (Pajer, 1998). Thus, it has been suggested that girls typically follow a "delayed-onset" trajectory of conduct problems, more like childhood-onset boys, that is related to several enduring vulnerabilities that are not manifested as antisocial behavior until adolescence. The absence of childhood displays of conduct problems could be due to stronger cultural sanctions against antisocial and aggressive behavior in girls. Once such behavior emerges, however, it could still lead to chronic problems across the lifespan (Silverthorn & Frick, 1999).

To summarize, despite some cautions in using age of onset to designate a distinct subgroup of adolescents with severe behavior problems, research supports that one common pathway, at least in boys, consists of adolescents who show serious antisocial behavior, which may be an exaggeration of normal adolescent rebellion. Despite being an exaggeration of a normal developmental process, it is still a severe and impairing pattern of behavior that can lead to a host of impairments in adolescence (e.g., legal consequences, school discipline problems, substance use) that can negatively influence the person's transition into adulthood. Finally, by separating out this substantial group of youth who show serious conduct problems, research can focus on a group of youth who begin showing behavior problems prior to adolescence, who are more aggressive and violent, and who are at higher risk for problems throughout the lifespan.

Empathy, Guilt, and the Affective Components of Conscience

From this research on the differences between the childhood- and adolescent-onset subtypes of antisocial behavior, it is evident that the childhood-onset group shows difficulties that are not typically confined to a single developmental stage. Specifically, they tend to start their conduct problems earlier, their adult outcomes tend to be worse, and they show a number of dispositional vulnerabilities that can negatively affect their adjustment across the lifespan (Frick & Viding, 2009). However, even within the childhood-onset group, there is significant variability in the dispositional vulnerabilities and the life course of their behavior problems, which has led to attempts to define additional subgroups within this category. One group that has received substantial support is those who exhibit elevated CU traits (Frick et al., 2014). Specifically, about 20%–30% of preadolescents with serious conduct problems show limited prosocial emotions, defined by a callous lack of empathy, limited guilt and remorse, failure to put forth effort in important activities, and restricted or shallow affect (Frick & Ray, 2015). These traits were included in the DSM-5 and *International Classification of Diseases*, 11th revision (ICD-11), as a specifier for conduct disorders labeled "with limited prosocial emotions" (American Psychiatric Association, 2013; World Health Organization, 2018).

CU traits were included in the DSM-5 based on substantial evidence supporting their clinical and etiological significance for designating a subgroup of children with serious conduct problems. In terms of clinical significance, youth with elevated CU traits show more severe (Ray et al., 2016) and stable (McMahon et al., 2010) conduct problems. Similarly, these youth are more aggressive (including bullying), display more severe aggression that results in more harm to their victims, and show more instrumental (i.e., used for personal gain or dominance) and premeditated aggression (see Frick et al., 2014, for a review). For example, in 150 adolescents arrested for a sexual offense, those who were high on CU traits, as compared to those with low or normative levels, showed more severe aggression in their sexual offending and described more detailed planning in their sexual offenses (Lawing et al., 2010).

In short, CU traits clearly seem to designate a group of youth with conduct problems who are in need of treatment. However, research on youth with elevated CU traits in treatment also suggests that they present quite a treatment challenge. Specifically, research has found that children and adolescents with elevated CU traits are more likely to be aggressive and violent during treatment (White et al., 2013) and are more likely to show poorer treatment outcomes (Frick et al., 2014) than other antisocial youth. Importantly, it is not that children with CU traits do not respond to many evidence-based treatments for conduct problems. Instead, research suggests that they start treatment with more severe behavior problems and, despite improving with treatment, still end treatment with more severe behavior problems (Hawes et al., 2014; Wilkinson et al., 2016).

Children and adolescents with conduct problems and nonelevated CU traits also show a host of other differences. Specifically, the conduct problems of those with elevated CU traits show stronger genetic influences that appear to be independent of conduct problem severity (Viding et al., 2005) and co-occurring problems of impulsivity (Viding et al., 2007). Youth with elevated CU traits also show abnormalities in how they process punishment cues, such as showing an insensitivity to punishment, especially around peers. They are more likely to view aggression as an acceptable method to use for instrumental gain or dominance, and they are more likely than other youth to focus on the positive outcomes of their antisocial behavior. Finally, not only do children and adolescents with elevated CU traits show less sensitivity to punishment than other children with conduct problems, but also they are less fearful (see Frick et al., 2014, for a review of this research).

However, perhaps one of the most consistent findings of how youth with elevated CU traits differ from other antisocial youth is in their reduced reactivity to signs of fear, pain, and distress in others. This difference has been found across multiple methods of measuring emotional reactivity. Specifically, children with elevated CU traits show lower levels of amygdala activation to fearful facial expressions (Viding et al., 2012) and when asked to judge the acceptability of statements that might cause fear in others (e.g., "You better watch your back"; Cardinale et al., 2018). Compared to children with conduct problems and normative levels of CU traits, children with elevated CU traits show reduced attentional orienting to pictures depicting distress (Kimonis et al., 2006), reduced startle potentiation when presented with aversive stimuli or imagining a fearful event (Kimonis et al., 2016), reduced attentional capture (i.e., distraction) to emotional faces (Hodsoll et al., 2014), and reduced attentional engagement to images of people in distress (Kimonis et al., 2016). These emotional deficits can be detected very early in life. For instance, Willoughby and colleagues (2011) reported that 5-year-old children with conduct problems and elevated CU traits were found to be less soothable and to display lower levels of negative reactivity to the still-face paradigm (i.e., parental faces showing no emotion versus positive interaction with infant) as infants (6 months) compared to children with conduct problems but normative levels of CU traits.

A final key difference between youth with and without elevated CU traits is their response to parenting. Specifically, the conduct problems in children with elevated CU traits seem to be less related to hostile and coercive parenting and more strongly related to a lack of warm and responsive parenting (Goulter et al., 2020; Pasalich et al., 2011). A critical issue in this research is that the measures of warm and supportive parent–child relations have varied greatly across studies, including such things as use of positive reinforcement, display of positive affect to the child, degree of parental involvement in the child's activities, degree and quality of parent–child cooperation, and positive communication between parent and child. Clark and Frick (2018) reported results from an ethnically diverse sample of kindergarten students to suggest that distinguishing among these various dimensions of positive parenting may be important. Specifically, they reported that parental use of positive reinforcement was more strongly related (negatively) to teacher-rated conduct problems in children with elevated CU traits, whereas measures of parental warmth were more strongly related (again negatively) to CU traits themselves.

In short, a wealth of research supports the use of CU traits to distinguish clinically relevant groups of children with serious conduct problems. In keeping with the developmental psychopathology approach, the risk factors for conduct problems (e.g., reduced emotional reactivity, fearlessness, parenting characterized by low warmth) appear to be different for this group of youth compared to other children with childhood-onset conduct problems and adolescent-onset conduct problems. Further, these unique risk factors provide clues for what developmental mechanisms may be leading to the behavior problems of this group. Specifically, deficits in guilt and empathy that define CU traits have long been considered the affective components of conscience (Kochanska & Thompson, 1997). Further, there is substantial research on how these components of conscience develop, which provides clues for how they may go awry in children with elevated CU traits.

Empathy. Empathy, defined broadly as the process by which one reacts to, recognizes, and understands the emotional states of others, is a complex ability considered vital to socioemotional development (de Waal & Preston, 2017). Specifically, empathy has been found to play a role in social learning and communication, to motivate a child to display prosocial behavior, and to aid in the establishment of close interpersonal relationships (Decety, 2011; Spinrad & Eisenberg, 2017). As such, empathy is considered a fundamental human trait necessary for both social survival and success (de Waal & Preston, 2017; Decety et al., 2016).

There is also fairly good consensus that empathy is composed of two distinct but interrelated components: affective and cognitive empathy. Affective empathy refers to one's own emotional response elicited by the emotions of others. This emotional responsiveness is conceptualized as both emotional reactivity (e.g., one's negative arousal in response to seeing another person in distress) and emotional contagion (e.g., one's subjective experience of sadness felt when witnessing others' apparent sadness; de Wied et al., 2010). With this, affective empathy is thought to be an automatic and reflexive process that develops early in childhood and is displayed even mere hours after birth (e.g., in the form of reflexive or contagious crying; Blair, 2005; Martin & Clark, 1982, Sagi & Hoffman, 1976). Cognitive empathy refers to the ability to accurately recognize and identify others' emotions (i.e., emotion recognition) and to understand another's perspective (i.e., perspective taking; Decety & Jackson, 2004). Affective and cognitive empathy are considered interrelated, in that when a typically developing young child experiences empathic distress (i.e., affective empathy) in response to seeing a peer cry, this experience is theorized to motivate the child to learn to recognize others' emotions and to adopt their perspective, so that the child may avoid experiencing such aversive feelings in the future (Frick & Kemp, 2021).

The development of empathy is influenced both by dispositional characteristics of the child and by socializing influences of parents and others in the child's psychosocial context. Regarding disposition, children characterized as having a behaviorally uninhibited (Kagan et al., 1988) or fearless (Rothbart, 1981) temperament are more likely to seek out novel and dangerous activities and to show less physiological arousal to unfamiliar people and circumstances, punishment cues, and negative emotional stimuli, such as fear or distress cues. Further, prospective research shows that young children (i.e., preschoolers) who are less behaviorally inhibited and fearful are also less empathetic, according to parent and teacher report, later in childhood (Kimonis et al., 2006; Waller et al., 2016). With regard to socialization, Kochanska and colleagues (see Kochanska & Thompson, 1997; Kochanska & Murray, 2000) have proposed that the parent–child relationship, especially the degree of warmth and responsiveness between parent and child, may be especially important for empathy development in fearless young children. With this, children who are less emotionally aroused by distress in others may still learn to take others' perspectives in the context of a relationship that models empathic concern toward others (see Kochanska, 1995; Kohanska & Thompson, 1997). In support of this possibility, Kochanska and colleagues (2005) reported that in infants as young as 9 months of age with a fearless temperament, warm and responsive parenting predicted greater levels of empathy and other moral emotions (i.e., guilt) at 45 months.

From this description of the temperamental and parental influences on empathy development, it is clear that this research is consistent with many of the characteristics of children with elevated CU traits. That is, the lack of responsiveness to various types of emotional stimuli and to cues to punishment and threat, as well as the importance of warm and responsive parenting, is consistent with the risk factors that have been associated with this group of youth with conduct problems. Importantly, however, a callous lack of empathy is only one defining feature of CU traits, and it is only one aspect of the broader construct of "conscience" that has proven important for the moral regulation of behavior in children.

Conscience. Conscience is a construct defined by emotional, cognitive, and relational processes by which children acquire internal standards for conduct and the ability to regulate their behavior in response to the social demands of a situation (Kochanska & Thompson, 1997). More specifically, the affective components of conscience refer to the moral or prosocial emotions experienced in response to the real or imagined consequences of one's behavior on others. That is, the desire to modify or regulate one's behavior due to its effects on others, and not due only to its effects on oneself, is dependent on the experience of empathic concern toward others. Similarly, the desire to change behavior to avoid displeasing socializing agents (e.g., parents, teachers) is dependent on the recognition of and concern about others' emotions. However, conscience also includes feelings of remorse and guilt over misdeeds, which is necessary for a child to learn to follow social norms and abide by cultural codes of conduct (Kochanska & Thompson, 1997).

Thus, there is a large body of research supporting the importance of a child's development of adequate levels of empathy and guilt for successful socioemotional functioning, and CU traits are defined partly as a deficit in these two components of conscience. In support of this link between CU traits and conscience, Waller and colleagues (2020) conducted a meta-analysis of 59 studies and reported that measures of CU traits showed moderate to large associations with measures of empathy ($\rho = -.57$), as well as with measures of guilt ($\rho = -.40$). Further, while developmental research on empathy and guilt has largely focused on their importance for motivating prosocial behavior and socioaffiliative success, empathy and guilt have also been considered important for inhibiting aggressive behavior. Specifically, both the ability to recognize pain and distress in others (i.e., cognitive empathy) and the experience of being disturbed by such (i.e., affective empathy and guilt) are thought to be critical for a child learning to inhibit behaviors that would cause such negative feelings in others (Frick & Kemp, 2021. Thus, various risk factors (e.g., low emotional responsiveness, lack of parental warmth) can lead to an increased risk for the child developing CU traits. Further, these deficits in the development of the affective components of conscience may be critical for explaining why youth with conduct problems and elevated CU traits are more likely to show a severe pattern of aggressive and violent behavior (Frick et al., 2014).

Emotional and Behavioral Regulation

Research suggests that it is only a minority of children and adolescents with childhood-onset conduct problems who show elevated CU traits and the associated deficits in prosocial emotions (Kahn et al., 2012). Thus, the behavior problems of the majority of youth who start showing conduct problems prior to adolescence are not explained well by the problems in conscience development associated with CU traits. However, by separating out children who show elevated CU traits, research has begun to more clearly define the unique risk factors associated with children in the childhood-onset pathway without elevated CU traits, leading to theories specifying separate developmental mechanisms to explain their antisocial behavior.

Specifically, children with conduct problems who do not show elevated CU traits are less aggressive overall and show less severe aggression. In addition, when they do act aggressively, it tends to be confined to reactive aggression in the context of high emotional arousal and in response to perceived provocation (Frick et al., 2003; Kruh et al., 2005). Children with conduct problems and normative levels of CU traits show other characteristics that have been associated with reactive aggression, such as a hostile attribution bias (Frick et al., 2003), lower levels of verbal intelligence (Loney et al., 1998), and an enhanced emotional response to provocation (Munoz et al., 2008).

As noted earlier, perhaps the clearest difference between antisocial youth with and without elevated CU traits is in their different patterns of emotional reactivity. That is, while children with conduct problems and elevated CU traits show hyporesponsivity to various emotional stimuli, children with conduct problems and normative levels of CU traits seem to show enhanced emotional reactivity across various methods used in research, such as amygdala activation to fearful faces (Viding et al., 2012), startle reflex during fear imagery (Fanti et al., 2016) attentional orienting to pictures depicting distress (Kimonis et al., 2006), and self-report ratings of fear, sensitivity to punishment, and anxiety (Fanti et al., 2016 Frick et al., 1999). To illustrate this, Viding and colleagues (2012) studied functional magnetic resonance imaging responses to fearful and calm faces in a sample of boys (ages 10–16) and reported that amygdala responses to fearful faces (relative to calm faces) were stronger in boys with conduct problems without elevated CU traits than controls but were weaker in boys with conduct problems with elevated CU traits when compared to controls. Similarly, in a sample of children (M age = 11.21; SD = 1.06), Fanti and colleagues (2016) reported that on both physiological (i.e., startle reflex during fear imagery) and behavioral (i.e., ratings of fear and sensitivity to punishment) measures of fearfulness, children with chronic conduct problems with and without elevated CU traits showed opposing responses, with those high on CU traits showing weaker startle reflex and lower ratings of fear and punishment sensitivity and those normative on CU traits showing enhanced physiological responses and higher behavioral ratings. These opposing patterns of emotional reactivity may provide one of the clearest examples of why the developmental psychopathological approach is important for research. That is, if children with serious conduct problems are studied as a single group, these opposing patterns of emotional responding would obscure these very different patterns of reactivity across groups and lead to very inconsistent results in research, not only for studies of emotional responding, but also for studies investigating the molecular, genetic, neurochemical, or neurocognitive underpinnings of these different patterns of reactivity (Fairchild et al., 2019).

Another important difference between children with serious conduct problems with and without elevated CU traits is that the conduct problems in the latter group are more influenced by environmental factors (Viding et al., 2005, 2007). While parental warmth and responsiveness seem to be particularly important for those high on CU traits, harsh and inconsistent parenting are more strongly associated with conduct problems of children without elevated CU traits (Goulter et al., 2020; Pasalich et al., 2011; Waller et al., 2018; Wootton et al., 1997). For example, in a study of 76 adolescents who had been detained for their antisocial behavior, harsh and inconsistent parenting was only related to antisocial behavior in those low on CU traits (Edens et al., 2008).

Thus, there is a wealth of research documenting different risk factors to conduct problems in children with and without elevated CU traits. These different characteristics found in those without elevated CU traits are not suggestive of the same problems in conscience development that were proposed as the developmental mechanisms underlying the behavior of children with elevated CU traits. Specifically, children with serious conduct problems who are not elevated on CU traits do not appear to be emotionally detached from the suffering of others, but they do appear to be highly emotionally reactive and tend to act impulsively and without planning or forethought. These characteristics are suggestive of problems in the development of self-regulation of emotions and behavior (Frick & Morris, 2004; Frick & Viding, 2009).

There are a number of developmental theories for how children develop the capacity to regulate their emotions, defined as the internal and external processes involved in initiating, maintaining, and modulating the occurrence, intensity, and expression of emotions (Grolnick et al., 1996). Important to these theories is that adaptive emotional regulation involves a process of learning how to suppress emotional responses coupled with the child's ability to respond in an adaptive and flexible manner to stressful demands and emotional experiences (Eisengberg & Morris, 2002). Thus, emotional regulation involves not only the intensity, duration, and valence (e.g., sadness, anger, joy) of the emotional reaction but also the child's skills in learning how to regulate these emotions in a socially adaptive manner. Stated differently, emotional regulation involves both emotional reactivity and strategies that the child uses to regulate this reactivity. These strategies may include automatic processes that can be present very early in development, such as shifting attention away from emotionally charged stimuli to more effortful processes such as learning to reframe emotional events in ways that lessen their negative connotations or learning to avoid situations that illicit negative emotions (Graziano et al., 2011). Further, these theories for how a child develops emotional regulation make it clear that strategies involve both processes within the child, such as attentional shifting, and external influences, such as parents and other socializing agents who can model appropriate emotional regulation strategies for their child or who can directly coach a child to respond adaptively to emotional situations.

The types of internal and external processes important for the development of emotional regulation in children make clear how they can go awry in some children and lead to conduct problems. The first internal process relates to the child's temperament. Children can vary greatly in how intensely they react to things, with some children having a tendency that is present early in life to react to many things with intense negative emotions (Rothbart, 1981). Infants who have such reactive temperaments (i.e., those who become angry, upset, or overstimulated from relatively little provocation) have more difficulty developing adaptive regulatory skills to modulate this reactivity (Stifter & Braungart, 1995). These findings would be consistent with research showing that children with conduct problems and nonelevated CU traits show high levels of emotional arousal to various types of emotional stimuli, including perceived provocation from others. The second internal process that has been linked to successful emotional regulation is intelligence and, in particular, verbal intelligence. Specifically, expressive language helps young children to better organize and label their thoughts, emotions, and behaviors; allows the child to "self-soothe" through internal dialogue; and helps the child to evaluate adaptive responses to emotionally charged events (Gözüm & Aktulun, 2021; ten Braak et al., 2019). These findings are consistent with research showing that children with conduct problems and nonelevated CU traits often show impaired verbal intelligence. Finally, most theories of the development of emotional regulation also focus on the role of parents and other socializing agents. Specifically, parents who are overly harsh and show high rates of anger do not provide good models for how to adaptively manage intense negative emotions for their children and they tend to apply punishment for emotions and feelings, rather than coaching their children in effective ways to manage emotions (Spinrad et al., 2020). Also, developmental theories recognize how children's characteristics can interact with parenting in the development of emotional regulation, such that children who respond with intense emotional reactions often evoke harsh responses from their parents (Bohlmann et al., 2015), and highly reactive children become more quickly emotionally overaroused by harsh parenting (Kochanska, 1995). These findings linking harsh parenting to problems in emotional regulation are consistent with research showing that conduct problems in children without elevated CU traits are related to harsh and inconsistent parenting.

Thus, children with conduct problems who do not show elevated CU traits often show a number of internal (e.g., high emotional reactivity, low levels of intelligence) and external (e.g., harsh and inconsistent parenting) risk factors that can increase their likelihood of problems in regulating emotions, leading to conduct problems in the context of high emotional arousal. However, developmental theory also considers other types of self-regulation of behavior that are not directly tied to emotional regulation. Specifically, executive control of behavior refers to the child's ability to regulate their behavior in response to contextual demands or in order to achieve some desired goal (Diamond, 2013). While difficulties in a child's ability to plan, monitor, and alter their behavior can be due to intense emotional arousal, it can also take place in nonemotional situations (Gagne et al., 2021). As was the case with emotional regulation, the development of executive control of behavior involves processes both internal and external to the child. Specifically, a key to most theories of executive control is the ability of the child to inhibit prepotent responses in order to evaluate potential consequences of their actions (i.e., inhibition; Nigg, 2001). Executive control has also been linked to general intelligence, potentially through shared genetic influences (Engelhardt et al., 2016). Finally, harsh and inconsistent parenting has also been associated with problems in executive control (Valcan et al., 2018). This has been suggested to be the result of hostile parenting harming the child's ability to internalize strategies to regulate behavior, resulting in behavioral control through forced compliance to parental demands rather than control based on learning rules and strategies for behavioral regulation (Fay-Stammbach et al., 2014). Again, all of these risk factors (i.e., problems of inhibition, low intelligence, harsh and inconsistent parenting) have also been associated with conduct problems in children without elevated CU traits. As result, the problems in the development of self-regulation for children in this group may not be solely due to problems in the development of emotional regulation but could also involve problems in the executive control of behavior, leading to unplanned impulsive behavior, for which the child may feel remorseful afterward but may have difficulty inhibiting in the future (Frick & Viding, 2009).

Implications and Future Directions

Implications for Research

In this chapter, we have summarized the research supporting a model of antisocial behavior that proposes three common pathways through which various risk factors can influence key developmental mechanisms (i.e., identity development, conscience development, development of self-regulation) that can put the child at risk for displaying behavior that violates the rights of others or major societal norms, including criminal behavior. What is clear from this work is that using antisocial behavior as a unitary outcome in research (i.e., grouping all antisocial individuals together) can lead to very inconsistent findings on the outcomes of persons with serious conduct problems, as well as the risk factors and causal processes leading to their antisocial behavior. That is, an extensive body of research supports the different outcomes of children with childhood-onset versus adolescent-onset antisocial behavior. More recent research has supported potential differences in the outcomes of those with and without elevated CU traits. Further, research clearly shows that children with and without elevated CU traits not only have different risk factors but also can have opposing levels of the same risk factors, such as emotional reactivity. Thus, combining both groups together in research would lead to inconsistent results and possibly erroneous conclusions on what risk factors may be related to antisocial behavior and the strength of their association.

Not only does recognizing the different developmental pathways help to guide research on differences between important subgroups of antisocial individuals, but also it helps to clarify the deficits within each of these subgroups. By separating out the adolescent-onset group from other youth with more dispositional deficits, research can better focus on what factors lead to the exaggerated rebellion displayed by the later onset group (Dandreaux & Frick, 2009). Similarly, by separating out children who show problems in conscience development from those who show problems with emotional and behavioral regulation, research can better define the emotional, cognitive, and neurological process leading to the problems in self-regulation of the latter group (Nigg, 2001). And finally, by focusing on the group with problems in conscience development, research can better define the types of emotional deficits that are most common in this group and how they may change across development. For example, in Waller et al.'s (2020) meta-analysis, associations between CU traits and affective empathy were not moderated by child age, whereas associations with cognitive empathy were stronger in younger children (see also Dadds et al., 2009). Frick and Kemp (2021) suggest that these findings reflect developmental changes in how empathy is related to CU traits. That is, in very young children, deficient affective empathy may reduce intrinsic motivation to develop cognitive empathy skills. However, as youth with elevated CU traits age, they may experience extrinsic motivation to acquire cognitive empathy skills, as these enable them to use social cues to their advantage. Thus, the association between CU traits and affective empathy may be consistent across development, but the association between cognitive empathy and CU traits may change as the child ages.

Implications for Practice

This research on common developmental pathways has some important implications for treatment as well. That is, treatments that focus on enhancing contact with prosocial mentors or prosocial peers have proven to be only moderately successful in reducing antisocial behavior, but their effectiveness for some youth may have been underestimated in past research that has not tried to tailor treatment to the different pathways to antisocial behavior (Frick, 2012; McMahon & Frick, 2019). These interventions could help to reduce risk factors that lead to maladaptive patterns of rebellion, which is characteristic of youth within the adolescent-onset pathway, but do not address problems of emotional regulation and conscience development present in youth with a childhood onset to their antisocial behavior. Similarly, there have been many evidence-based treatments for conduct problems that teach children how to regulate their anger or that focus on reducing harsh and inconsistent parenting (McMahon & Frick, 2019). It is likely that the success of such programs may have been underestimated because treatment trials have typically not distinguished between those without elevated CU traits, whose behavior problems are highly related to problems with emotional regulation and harsh parenting, and those with elevated CU traits, whose behavior problems are associated with other risk factors.

The importance of tailoring treatment to the varying needs of youth with behavior problems is supported by the fact that the most effective treatments for adolescents with severe behavior problems are interventions that are comprehensive (i.e., targeting multiple risk factors) and also individualized to the needs of the youth displaying antisocial behavior (McMahon & Frick, 2019), such as multisystemic therapy (MST, Henggeler et al., 2009) and functional family therapy (FFT; Alexander et al., 2013). The need to tailor some programs specifically for the group of youths with elevated CU traits is illustrated by White and colleagues (2013), who conducted an open trial of FFT provided to 134 adolescents who had been arrested and referred to a community mental health center for treatment. The results showed that levels of CU traits were associated with more severe behavior problems at the start of treatment and more violent acts during treatment. CU traits were also associated with the greatest reductions in antisocial behavior over treatment. Despite this improvement, however, CU traits were still related to more severe antisocial behavior following treatment.

As a result, existing treatments need to be enhanced to address the specific needs of children and adolescents with elevated CU traits. In an example of this approach (see also Elizur et al., 2017, for another example), Kimonis and colleagues (2019) enhanced a standard parent management training program, which is an evidence-based approach to treating conduct problems in young children, in three crucial ways based on research on children with elevated CU traits. First, the team added systematic and explicit teaching of parents on how to increase parental warmth and emotional responsiveness in their interactions with their children. Second, the team shifted emphasis from punishment to reward-oriented discipline by systematically training parents to use both appropriate punishment-based disciplinary strategies (i.e., timeout) and tangible reward-based techniques (i.e., dynamic and individualized token economy). Third, the team delivered an adjunctive module to coach children on how to attend to and recognize emotions in others. In an open trial of 23 families of children ages 3–6 who were referred to a mental health clinic for serious conduct problems with elevated CU traits, Kimonis et al. (2019) reported that the intervention produced decreases posttreatment in children's conduct problems and CU traits and increases in empathy, with "medium" to "huge" effect sizes ($ES = 0.7–2.0$) that were maintained at a 3-month follow-up. By 3 months posttreatment, 75% of treatment completers no longer showed clinically significant conduct problems compared to 25% of dropouts. Importantly, these results need to be replicated in a randomized controlled trial. Further, similar modifications of interventions, like FFT, need to be tested in adolescents. However, the work of Kimonis et al. illustrates how research on developmental pathways to antisocial behavior can be used to enhance treatment.

For treatments to be tailored to different developmental pathways, it is important to have reliable and well-validated methods for assessing CU traits. Much of the research on CU traits has relied on rating scales, completed by either the child or key informants (i.e., parent and teacher; Frick et al., 2014). Early measures of CU traits used subscales from broader measures of psychopathy, which meant they often had only a very few items assessing CU traits, and this resulted in some significant psychometric limitations (Frick & Ray, 2015). However, as it became clear that the dimensions of psychopathy had different associations with conduct problems and, as a result, should not be combined into a total score but measured separately (De Brito et al., 2021), more extended rating scales to specifically assess CU traits were developed. For example, the Inventory of Callous–Unemotional traits (ICU; Kimonis et al., 2008) is a 24-item multi-informant (i.e., self-, parent-, and teacher-report) questionnaire that utilizes a 4-point Likert-type scale (i.e., 0 = "Not at all true" to 3 = "Definitely true") to indicate how accurately each statement describes an individual. Each of the four symptoms of the DSM-5 criteria for "limited prosocial emotions" is assessed by three positively (i.e., in the callous direction) and three negatively (i.e., in the prosocial direction) worded items. The ICU can be used from ages 6 to 21 years, with a preschool version available as well. The ICU has been translated into over 30 languages and used in over 300 published studies. Items have consistently been shown to load on an overarching factor that is reasonably well assessed by a simple summing of items (Ray & Frick, 2020). These total scores have been shown to be reliable across a wide age range (Deng et al., 2019), and they are consistently positively associated with antisocial behavior and negatively associated with empathy and prosocial behavior (Cardinale & Marsh, 2020). Finally, empirically derived cut-scores have been developed to guide use of the ICU (Kemp et al., 2021).

While ratings scales can be useful for many purposes, some clinical and forensic assessments require a more in-depth clinical assessment that allow the clinician more flexibility in obtaining information and for evaluating the veracity of the information being given. Clinician ratings of psychopathy, such as the Psychopathy Checklist: Youth Version (PCL: YV; Forth, 2005), assess the affective dimensions of psychopathy, which largely correspond to CU traits. In addition, the Clinical Assessment of Prosocial Emotions (CAPE-1.1; Frick, 2016) was developed to provide a clinician rating specifically for the four CU symptoms included in the DSM-5 specifier of "with limited prosocial emotions." The CAPE-1.1 requires information from multiple sources. It provides a clinical interview to guide the collection of such information and provides guidance on how to use this information to make judgments on the severity and pervasiveness of the four symptoms of the specifier. While more research is needed to evaluate the reliability and validity of the CAPE, initial tests of its psychometric properties have been promising (see Hawes et al., 2020; Molinuevo et al., 2020).

Implications for Policy

The developmental psychopathology approach to antisocial behavior also has some important implications for juvenile justice policy. Because characteristics of youth in the different pathways seem to make them more or less susceptible to environmental influences, policy research on the effects of justice system involvement needs to consider these differences. For example, persons in the adolescent-onset pathways may be more susceptible to the influence of deviant peers (Moffitt, 2018), whereas some children with elevated CU traits may be less influenced by their peers. Specifically, adolescents with elevated CU traits are more likely to be the leader during crimes committed in groups (Thornton et al., 2015) and appear to be highly influential in the behavior of their peers, while simultaneously being less influenced themselves by those peers' behavior (Kerr et al., 2012). Consistent with these findings, Robertson and colleagues (2020) reported that an adolescent's gun carrying was less influenced by peers' gun carrying if the adolescent was elevated rather than low on CU traits.

These differences in susceptibility to peer influence could lead to differences in the adolescent's responses to contact with the juvenile justice system. To test this directly, Robertson and colleagues (2021) showed that, in a sample of over 1,216 adolescents arrested for the first time for an offense of mild to moderate severity, those adolescents who were formally processed by the juvenile justice system were at increased risk for self-reported delinquency and rearrest when compared to those who were diverted from the justice system after this first arrest, even when controlling for a number of preexisting risk factors for offending. However, this harmful effect of formal processing was only found for those adolescents who were low or normative on CU traits. The authors noted that these findings suggest that past work showing the beneficial effects of diversion may have underestimated these effects for the majority of adolescents who are not elevated on CU traits.

Even more important for juvenile justice policy is the research suggesting that youth in the different pathways to antisocial behavior respond differently to treatment, requiring an individualized approach to intervening with youth in the justice system. This demands individualized needs assessments in order to determine the most appropriate treatment. To accomplish such an assessment, many tools designed to estimate risk in the adolescent for future violence or offending assess many characteristics that help to define the different developmental pathways to antisocial behavior as well. For example, the Structured Assessment of Violence Risk in Youth (SAVRY; Borum, 2006) includes items assessing early initiation of violence (i.e., age of onset) and low empathy/remorse (i.e., CU traits), as well as other key risk factors that can help differentiate among adolescents in these pathways (e.g., anger management problems, poor parental management, strong attachment and bonds, positive attitudes toward authority). However, the developmental psychopathology approach requires a different application of risk assessments, like the SAVRY than has been typically used in many juvenile justice settings. That is, rather than simply rating items and summing them into a total score to determine the adolescent's overall risk level, items need to be reviewed to determine specific areas of need. Then, a system for tailoring treatment to these needs is required. This can be done by referring youth to interventions like FFT or MST, which were developed to be individualized. Alternatively, the justice system can adopt a risk–needs–responsivity model that develops guidelines for identifying certain profiles of needs and having mechanisms for matching youth to appropriate treatments based on this (Nelson & Vincent, 2018). The basic principle to guide this approach, which really highlights the importance of the developmental psychopathology perspective, is that, given that youth develop antisocial behavior through a number of different processes, intervention must be able to be individualized to address the specific developmental mechanisms that lead to the youth's antisocial behavior to be successful.

References

Alexander, J. F., Waldron, H. B., Robbins, M. S., & Neeb, A. A. (2013). *Functional family therapy for adolescent behavior problems*. American Psychological Association.

American Psychiatric Association. (1994). *Diagnostic and statistical manual of mental disorders* (4th ed.). American Psychiatric Publishing.

American Psychiatric Association. (2013). *Diagnostic and statistical manual of mental disorders* (5th ed.). American Psychiatric Publishing.

Blair, R. J. R. (2005). Responding to the emotions of others: Dissociating forms of empathy through the study of typical and psychiatric populations. *Consciousness and Cognition*, *14*(4), 698–718.

Bohlmann, N. L., Maier, M. F., & Palacios, N. (2015). Bidirectionality in self-regulation and expressive vocabulary: Comparisons between monolingual and dual language learners in preschool. *Child development*, *86*(4), 1094-1111.

Borum, R. (2006). Assessing risk for violence among juvenile offenders. In Sparta, S. N., & Koocher, G. P. (Eds.) *The forensic assessment of children and adolescents: Issues and applications*, 190-202. Oxford University Press.

Brezina, T., & Piquero, A. R. (2007). Moral beliefs, isolation from peers, and abstention from delinquency. *Deviant Behavior*, *28*(5), 433–465.

Cardinale, E. M., Breeden, A. L., Robertson, E. L., Lozier, L. M., Vanmeter, J. W., & Marsh, A. A. (2018). Externalizing behavior severity in youths with callous–unemotional traits corresponds to patterns of amygdala activity and connectivity during judgments of causing fear. *Development and Psychopathology*, *30*(1), 191–201.

Cardinale, E. M., & Marsh, A. A. (2020). The reliability and validity of the Inventory of Callous Unemotional Traits: A meta-analytic review. *Assessment, 27*(1), 57–71.

Cicchetti, D., & Rogosch, F. A. (1996). Equifinality and multifinality in developmental psychopathology. *Development and Psychopathology, 8*(4), 597–600.

Clark, J. E., & Frick, P. J. (2018). Positive parenting and callous-unemotional traits: Their association with school behavior problems in young children. *Journal of Clinical Child & Adolescent Psychology, 47*(Suppl 1), S242–S254.

Dadds, M. R., Hawes, D. J., Frost, A. D., Vassallo, S., Bunn, P., Hunter, K., & Merz, S. (2009). Learning to 'talk the talk': The relationship of psychopathic traits to deficits in empathy across childhood. *Journal of child psychology and psychiatry, 50*(5), 599-606.

Dandreaux, D. M., & Frick, P. J. (2009). Developmental pathways to conduct problems: A further test of the childhood and adolescent-onset distinction. *Journal of Abnormal Child Psychology, 37*, 375–385.

De Brito, S. A., Forth, A. E., Baskin-Sommers, A. R., Brazil, I. A., Kimonis, E. R., Pardini, D., Frick, P. J., Blair, R. J. R., & Viding, E. (2021). Psychopathy. *Nature Reviews Disease Primer, 7*, 49.

De Waal, F. B., & Preston, S. D. (2017). Mammalian empathy: Behavioural manifestations and neural basis. *Nature Reviews Neuroscience, 18*(8), 498–509.

de Wied, M., Gispen-de Wied, C., & van Boxtel, A. (2010). Empathy dysfunction in children and adolescents with disruptive behavior disorders. *European Journal of Pharmacology, 626*(1), 97–103.

Decety, J. (2011). The neuroevolution of empathy. *Annals of the New York Academy of Sciences, 1231*(1), 35–45.

Decety, J., Bartal, I. B. A., Uzefovsky, F., & Knafo-Noam, A. (2016). Empathy as a driver of prosocial behaviour: Highly conserved neurobehavioural mechanisms across species. *Philosophical Transactions of the Royal Society B: Biological Sciences, 371*(1686), 20150077.

Decety, J., & Jackson, P. L. (2004). The functional architecture of human empathy. *Behavioral and Cognitive Neuroscience Reviews, 3*(2), 71–100.

Deng, J., Wang, M. C., Zhang, X., Shou, Y., Gao, Y., & Luo, J. (2019). The Inventory of Callous Unemotional Traits: A reliability generalization meta-analysis. *Psychological Assessment, 31*(6), 765.

Diamond, A. (2013). Executive functions. *Annual review of psychology, 64*, 135-168.

Dodge, K. A., & Pettit, G. S. (2003). A biopsychosocial model of the development of chronic conduct problems in adolescence. *Developmental Psychology, 39*(2), 349–371.

Edens, J. F., Poythress, N. G., Lilienfeld, S. O., Patrick, C. J., & Test, A. (2008). Further evidence of the divergent correlates of the Psychopathic Personality Inventory factors: prediction of institutional misconduct among male prisoners. *Psychological assessment, 20*(1), 86.

Eisenberg, N., & Morris, A. S. (2002). Children's emotion-related regulation. In R. V. Kail (Ed.), *Advances in child development and behavior,* Vol. 30, pp. 189–229). Academic Press.

Elizur, Y., Somech, L. Y., & Vinokur, A. D. (2017). Effects of parent training on callous-unemotional traits, effortful control, and conduct problems: Mediation by parenting. *Journal of Abnormal Child Psychology, 45*(1), 15–26.

Engelhardt, L. E., Mann, F. D., Briley, D. A., Church, J. A., Harden, K. P., & Tucker-Drob, E. M. (2016). Strong genetic overlap between executive functions and intelligence. *Journal of Experimental Psychology: General, 145*(9), 1141–1159.

Fairchild, G., Hawes, D. J., Frick, P. J., Copeland, W. E., Odgers, C. L., Franke, B., Freitag, C. M., De Brito, S. A. (2019). Conduct disorder. *Nature Reviews Disease Primers, 5*(1), 1–25.

Fairchild, G., van Goozen, S. H., Calder, A. J., & Goodyer, I. M. (2013). Research review: Evaluating and reformulating the developmental taxonomic theory of antisocial behaviour. *Journal of Child Psychology and Psychiatry, 54*(9), 924–940.

Fanti, K. A., Panayiotou, G., Kyranides, M. N., & Avraamides, M. N. (2016). Startle modulation during violent films: Association with callous–unemotional traits and aggressive behavior. *Motivation and Emotion, 40*, 321-333.

Farrington, D. P., Gallagher, B., Morley, L., Ledger, R. J. S., & West, D. J. (1988). Are there any successful men from criminogenic backgrounds? *Psychiatry, 51*(2), 116–130.

Fay-Stammbach, T., Hawes, D. J., & Meredith, P. (2014). Parenting influences on executive functioning in early childhood: A review. *Child Development Perspectives, 8*(4), 258–264.

Forth, A. E. (2005). Hare psychopathy checklist: Youth version. *Mental Health Screening and Assessment in Juvenile Justice, 9*, 324–338.

Frick, P. J. (2006). Developmental pathways to conduct disorder. *Child and Adolescent Psychiatric Clinics, 15*(2), 311–331.

Frick, P. J. (2012). Developmental pathways to conduct disorder: Implications for future directions in research, assessment, and treatment. *Journal of Clinical Child & Adolescent Psychology, 41*(3), 378–389.

Frick, P. J. (2016). *Clinical assessment of prosocial emotions (CAPE1.1)* [Unpublished test manual].

Frick, P.J., Cornell, A. H., Bodin, S. D., Dane, H. A., Barry, C. T., & Loney, B. R. (2003). Callous-unemotional traits and developmental pathways to severe aggressive and antisocial behavior. *Developmental Psychology, 39*(2), 246-260.

Frick, P. J., & Kemp, E. C. (2021). Conduct disorders and empathy development. *Annual Review of Clinical Psychology, 17*, 391–416.

Frick, P.J., Lilienfeld, S.O., Ellis, M.L, Loney, B.R., & Silverthorn, P. (1999). The association between anxiety and psychopathy dimensions in children. *Journal of Abnormal Child Psychology, 27*, 381-390.

Frick, P. J., & Morris, A. S. (2004). Temperament and developmental pathways to severe conduct problems. *Journal of Clinical Child and Adolescent Psychology, 33*(1), 54-68.

Frick, P. J., & Ray, J. V. (2015). Evaluating callous-unemotional traits as a personality construct. *Journal of Personality, 83*(6), 710–722.

Frick, P. J., Ray, J. V., Thornton, L. C., & Kahn, R. E. (2014). Can callous-unemotional traits enhance the understanding, diagnosis, and treatment of serious conduct problems in children and adolescents? A comprehensive review. *Psychological Bulletin, 140*(1), 1–57.

Frick, P. J., & Viding, E. M. (2009). Antisocial behavior from a developmental psychopathology perspective. *Development and Psychopathology, 21*(4), 1111–1131.

Gagne, J. R., Liew, J., & Nweadinobi, O. K. (2021). How does the broader construct of self-regulation relate to emotional regulation in young children? *Developmental Review, 60*,100965.

Goulter, N., McMahon, R. J., Pasalich, D. S., & Dodge, K. A. (2020). Indirect effects of early parenting on adult antisocial outcomes via adolescent conduct disorder symptoms and callous-unemotional traits. *Journal of Clinical Child & Adolescent Psychology, 49*(6), 930–942.

Gözüm, A. İ. C., & Aktulun, Ö. U. (2021). Relationship between Pre-Schoolers' self-regulation, language, and early academic skills: The mediating role of self-regulation and moderating role of gender. *Current Psychology, 40*(10), 4718-4740.

Graziano, P. A., Calkins, S. D., & Keane, S. P. (2011). Sustained attention development during the toddlerhood to preschool period: Associations with toddlers' emotion regulation strategies and maternal behaviour. *Infant and child development, 20*(6), 389-408.

Grolnick, W. S., Bridges, L. J., & Connell, J. P. (1996). Emotion regulation in two-year-olds: Strategies and emotional expression in four contexts. *Child development, 67*(3), 928-941.

Hawes, D. J., Kimonis, E. R., Mendoza Diaz, A., Frick, P. J., & Dadds, M. R. (2020). The Clinical Assessment of Prosocial Emotions (CAPE 1.1): A multi-informant validation study. *Psychological Assessment, 32*(4), 348.

Hawes, D. J., Price, M. J., & Dadds, M. R. (2014). Callous-unemotional traits and the treatment of conduct problems in childhood and adolescence: A comprehensive review. *Clinical Child and Family Psychology Review, 17*(3), 248–267.

Henggeler, S. W., Schoenwald, S. K., Borduin, C. M., Rowland, M. D., & Cunningham, P. B. (2009). *Multisystemic Therapy for antisocial behavior in children and adolescents* (2nd ed.). Guilford Press.

Hodsoll, S., Lavie, N., & Viding, E. (2014). Emotional attentional capture in children with conduct problems: The role of callous-unemotional traits. *Frontiers in Human Neuroscience, 8*, 570.

Kagan, J., Reznick, J. S., Snidman, N., Gibbons, J., & Johnson M. O. (1988). Childhood derivatives of inhibition and lack of inhibition to the unfamiliar. *Child Devevelopment, 59*(6), 1580-1589.

Kahn, R. E., Frick, P. J., Youngstrom, E., Findling, R. L., & Youngstrom, J. K. (2012). The effects of including a callous-unemotional specifier for the diagnosis of conduct disorder. *Journal of Child Psychology and Psychiatry, 53*(3), 271-282.

Kemp, E. C., Frick, P. J., Matlasz, T. M., Clark, J. E., Robertson, E. L., Ray, J. V., Thornton, L. C., Wall Myers, T. D., Steinberg, L., & Cauffman, E. (2021). Developing cutoff scores for the Inventory of Callous-Unemotional Traits (ICU) in justice-involved and community samples. *Journal of Clinical Child and Adolescent Psychology, 52*(4), 519-532.

Kerr, M., Van Zalk, M., & Stattin, H. (2012). Psychopathic traits moderate peer influence on adolescent delinquency. *Journal of Child Psychology and Psychiatry, 53*(8), 826–835.

Kimonis, E. R., Fanti, K. A., Anastassiou-Hadjicharalambous, X., Mertan, B., Goulter, N., & Katsimicha, E. (2016). Can callous-unemotional traits be reliably measured in preschoolers? *Journal of Abnormal Child Psychology, 44*(4), 625–638.

Kimonis, E. R., Fleming, G., Briggs, N., Brouwer-French, L., Frick, P. J., Hawes, D. J., Bagner, D. M., Thomas, R., & Dadds, M. (2019). Parent-Child Interaction Therapy adapted for preschoolers with callous-unemotional traits: An open trial pilot study. *Journal of Clinical Child & Adolescent Psychology, 48*(Suppl 1), S347–S361.

Kimonis, E. R., Frick, P. J., Fazekas, H., & Loney, B. R. (2006). Psychopathy, aggression, and the processing of emotional stimuli in non-referred girls and boys. *Behavioral Sciences & the Law, 24*(1), 21–37.

Kimonis, E. R., Frick, P. J., Skeem, J. L., Marsee, M. A., Cruise, K., Munoz, L. C., Aucoin, K. J., & Morris, A. S. (2008). Assessing callous–unemotional traits in adolescent offenders: Validation of the Inventory of Callous–Unemotional Traits. *International Journal of Law and Psychiatry, 31*(3), 241–252.

Kochanska, G. (1995). Children's temperament, mothers' discipline, and security of attachment: multiple pathways to emerging internalization. *Child Development, 66*(3), 597-615.

Kochanska, G., Aksan, N., & Carlson, J. J. (2005). Temperament, relationships, and young children's receptive cooperation with their parents. *Developmental Psychology, 41*(4), 648.

Kochanska, G., & Murray, K. T. (2000). Mother–child mutually responsive orientation and conscience development: From toddler to early school age. *Child development, 71*(2), 417-431.

Kochanska, G., & Thompson, R. A. (1997). The emergence and development of conscience in toddlerhood and early childhood. In Grusec, J. E. & Kuczynski, L. (Eds.) *Parenting and children's internalization of values: A handbook of contemporary theory* (pp. 53–77). John Wiley & Sons Inc.

Konrad, K., Kohls, G., Baumann, S., Bernhard, A., Martinelli, A., Ackermann, K., . . . Freitag, C. M. (2021). Sex differences in psychiatric comorbidity and clinical presentation in youths with conduct disorder. *Journal of Child Psychology and Psychiatry, 63*(2), 218-228.

Kruh, I. P., Frick, P. J., & Clements, C. B. (2005). Historical and personality correlates to the violence patterns of juveniles tried as adults. *Criminal Justice and Behavior, 32*(1), 69-96.

Lahey, B. B., Waldman, I. D., & McBurnett, K. (1999). Annotation: The development of antisocial behavior: An integrative causal model. *Journal of Child Psychology and Psychiatry and Allied Disciplines, 40*(5), 669–682.

Lawing, K., Frick, P. J., & Cruise, K. R. (2010). Differences in offending patterns between adolescent sex offenders high or low in callous–unemotional traits. *Psychological Assessment, 22*(2), 298.

Loney, B. R., Frick, P. J., Ellis, M. L., & McCoy, M. G. (1998). Intelligence, psychopathy, and antisocial behavior. *Journal of Psychopathology and Behavioral Assessment, 20,* 231-247.

Lorber, M. F., Olds, D. L., & Donelan-McCall, N. (2019). The impact of a preventive intervention on persistent, cross-situational early onset externalizing problems. *Prevention Science, 20*(5), 684–694.

Martin, G. B., & Clark, R. D. (1982). Distress crying in neonates: Species and peer specificity. *Developmental Psychology, 18*(1), 3.

McMahon, R. J., & Frick, P. J. (2019). Conduct and oppositional disorders. In M. J. Prinstein, E. A. Youngstrom, E. J. Mash, & R. A. Barkley (Eds.), *Treatment of disorders in childhood and adolescence* (pp. 102–172). Guilford Press.

McMahon, R. J., Witkiewitz, K., & Kotler, J. S. (2010). Predictive validity of callous–unemotional traits measured in early adolescence with respect to multiple antisocial outcomes. *Journal of Abnormal Psychology, 119*(4), 752.

Moffitt, T. E. (2018). Male antisocial behaviour in adolescence and beyond. *Nature Human Behaviour, 2*(3), 177-186.

Moffitt, T. E., Arseneault, L., Jaffee, S. R., Kim-Cohen, J., Koenen, K. C., Odgers, C. L., Slutske, W. S., & Viding, E. (2008). Research review: DSM-V conduct disorder: Research needs for an evidence base. *Journal of Child Psychology and Psychiatry, 49*(1), 3–33.

Moffitt, T. E., Caspi, A., Harrington, H., & Milne, B. J. (2002). Males on the life-course-persistent and adolescence-limited antisocial pathways: Follow-up at age 26 years. *Development and Psychopathology, 14*(1), 179–207.

Molinuevo, B., Martínez-Membrives, E., Pera-Guardiola, V., Requena, A., Torrent, N., Bonillo, A., Batalla, I., Torrubia, R., & Frick, P. J. (2020). Psychometric properties of the clinical assessment of prosocial emotions: Version 1.1 (CAPE 1.1) in young males who were incarcerated. *Criminal Justice and Behavior, 47*(5), 547–563.

Munoz, L. C., Frick, P. J., Kimonis, E. R., & Aucoin, K. J. (2008). Types of aggression, responsiveness to provocation, and callous-unemotional traits in detained adolescents. *Journal of Abnormal Child Psychology, 36,* 15-28.

Nelson, R. J., & Vincent, G. M. (2018). Matching services to criminogenic needs following comprehensive risk assessment implementation in juvenile probation. *Criminal Justice and Behavior, 45*(8), 1136-1153.

Nigg, J. T. (2001). Is ADHD a disinhibitory disorder?. *Psychological bulletin, 127*(5), 571.

Odgers, C. L., Moffitt, T. E., Broadbent, J. M., Dickson, N., Hancox, R. J., Harrington, H., Poulton, R., Sears, M. R., Thomson, W. M., & Caspi, A. (2008). Female and male antisocial trajectories: From childhood origins to adult outcomes. *Developmental Psychopathology, 20*(2), 673–716.

Pajer, K. A. (1998). What happens to "bad" girls? A review of the adult outcomes of antisocial adolescent girls. *American Journal of Psychiatry, 155*(7), 862–870.

Pasalich, D. S., Dadds, M. R., Hawes, D. J., & Brennan, J. (2011). Do callous-unemotional traits moderate the relative importance of parental coercion versus warmth in child conduct problems? An observational study. *Journal of Child Psychology and Psychiatry, 52*(12), 1308–1315.

Patterson, G. R., & Yoerger, K. (1997). A developmental model for late-onset delinquency. In D. W. Osgood (Ed.), *Motivation and delinquency* (pp. 119–177). University of Nebraska Press.

Raine, A. (2002). Biosocial studies of antisocial and violent behavior in children and adults: A review. *Journal of Abnormal Child Psychology*, *30*(4), 311–326.

Ray, J. V., & Frick, P. J. (2020). Assessing callous-unemotional traits using the total score from the Inventory of Callous-Unemotional Traits: A meta-analysis. *Journal of Clinical Child and Adolescent Psychology*, *49*(2), 190-199.

Ray, J. V., Thornton, L. C., Frick, P. J., Steinberg, L., & Cauffman, E. (2016). Impulse control and callous-unemotional traits distinguish patterns of delinquency and substance use in justice involved adolescents: Examining the moderating role of neighborhood context. *Journal of Abnormal Child Psychology*, *44*(3), 599–611.

Robertson, E. L., Frick, P. J., Ray, J. V., Thornton, L. C., Wall Myers, T. D., Steinberg, L., & Cauffman, E. (2021). Do callous–unemotional traits moderate the effects of the juvenile justice system on later offending behavior? *Journal of Child Psychology and Psychiatry*, *62*(2), 212–222.

Robertson, E. L., Frick, P. J., Walker, T. M., Kemp, E. C., Ray, J. V., Thornton, L. C., Wall Myers, T. D., Steinberg, L., & Cauffman, E. (2020). Callous-unemotional traits and risk of gun carrying and use during crime. *American Journal of Psychiatry*, *177*(9), 827–833.

Robins, L. N. (1966). *Deviant children grown up: A sociological and psychiatric study of sociopathic personality*. ERIC Institute of Education Series.

Rothbart, M. K. (1981). Measurement of temperament in infancy. *Child Devevelopment*, *52*(2), 569-578.

Rowe, R., Maughan, B., Pickles, A., Costello, E. J., & Angold, A. (2002). The relationship between DSM-IV oppositional defiant disorder and conduct disorder: Findings from the Great Smoky Mountains Study. *Journal of Child Psychology and Psychiatry*, *43*(3), 365–373.

Sagi, A., & Hoffman, M. L. (1976). Empathic distress in the newborn. *Developmental Psychology*, *12*(2), 175.

Silberg, J., Moore, A. A., & Rutter, M. (2015). Age of onset and the subclassification of conduct/dissocial disorder. *Journal of Child Psychology and Psychiatry*, *56*(7), 826–833.

Silverthorn, P., & Frick, P. J. (1999). Developmental pathways to antisocial behavior: The delayed-onset pathway in girls. *Development and Psychopathology*, *11*(1), 101–126.

Silverthorn, P., Frick, P. J., & Reynolds, R. (2001). Timing of onset and correlates of severe conduct problems in adjudicated girls and boys. *Journal of Psychopathology and Behavioral Assessment*, *23*(3), 171–181.

Spinrad, T. L., & Eisenberg, N. (2017). Compassion in children. In Seppälä, E. M., Simon-Thomas, E., Brown, S. L., Worline, M. C., Cameron, C. D., & Doty, J. R. (Eds.) *The Oxford handbook of compassion science* (pp. 53–63). Oxford University Press.

Spinrad, T. L., Morris, A. S., & Luthar, S. S. (2020). Introduction to the special issue: Socialization of emotion and self-regulation: Understanding processes and application. *Developmental Psychology*, *56*(3), 385.

Stifter, C. A., & Braungart, J. M. (1995). The regulation of negative reactivity in infancy: function and development. *Developmental psychology*, *31*(3), 448.

ten Braak, D., Størksen, I., Idsoe, T., & McClelland, M. (2019). Bidirectionality in self-regulation and academic skills in play-based early childhood education. *Journal of Applied Developmental Psychology*, *65*, 101064.

Thornton, L. C., Frick, P. J., Shulman, E. P., Ray, J. V., Steinberg, L., & Cauffman, E. (2015). Callous-unemotional traits and adolescents' role in group crime. *Law and Human Behavior*, *39*(4), 368.

Tibbetts, S. G., & Piquero, A. R. (1999). The influence of gender, low birth weight, and disadvantaged environment in predicting early onset of offending: A test of Moffitt's interactional hypothesis. *Criminology*, *37*(4), 843–878.

Valcan, D. S., Davis, H., & Pino-Pasternak, D. (2018). Parental behaviours predicting early childhood executive functions: A meta-analysis. *Educational Psychology Review*, *30*, 607-649.

Viding, E., Blair, R. J. R., Moffitt, T. E., & Plomin, R. (2005). Evidence for substantial genetic risk for psychopathy in 7-year-olds. *Journal of Child Psychology and Psychiatry*, *46*(6), 592–597.

Viding, E., Frick, P. J., & Plomin, R. (2007). Aetiology of the relationship between callous-unemotional traits and conduct problems in childhood. *British Journal of Psychiatry*, *190*(Suppl 49), s33–s38.

Viding, E., Sebastian, C. L., Dadds, M. R., Lockwood, P. L., Cecil, C. A., De Brito, S. A., & McCrory, E. J. (2012). Amygdala response to preattentive masked fear in children with conduct problems: The role of callous-unemotional traits. *American Journal of Psychiatry*, *169*(10), 1109–1116.

Waller, R., Hyde, L. W., Klump, K. L., & Burt, S. A. (2018). Parenting is an environmental predictor of callous-unemotional traits and aggression: A monozygotic twin differences study. *Journal of the American Academy of Child & Adolescent Psychiatry*, *57*(12), 955-963.

Waller, R., Shaw, D.S., & Hyde, L.W. (2017). Observed fearlessness and positive parenting interact predict childhood callous-unemotional behaviors among low income boys. *Journal of Child Psychology and Psychiatry*, *58*(3), 282-291.

Waller, R,. Wagner, N. J., Barstead, M. G., Subar, A., Petersen, J. L., Hyde, J. S., & Hyde, L. W. (2020.) A meta-analysis of the associations between callous-unemotional traits and empathy, prosociality, and guilt. *Clinical Psychology Review*, *75*, 101809.

White, S. F., Frick, P. J., Lawing, K., & Bauer, D. (2013). Callous-unemotional traits and response to Functional Family Therapy to adolescent offenders. *Behavioral Sciences & the Law, 31*(2), 271–285.

Wilkinson, S., Waller, R., & Viding, E. (2016). Practitioner review: Involving young people with callous unemotional traits in treatment—does it work? A systematic review. *Journal of Child Psychology and Psychiatry, 57*(5), 552–565.

Willoughby, M. T., Waschbusch, D. A., Moore, G. A., & Propper, C. B. (2011). Using the ASEBA to screen for callous unemotional traits in early childhood: Factor structure, temporal stability, and utility. *Journal of Psychopathology and Behavioral Assessment, 33*(1), 19–30.

Wootton, J. M., Frick, P. J., Shelton, K. K., & Silverthorn, P. (1997). Ineffective parenting and childhood conduct problems: The moderating role of callous-unemotional traits. *Journal of Consulting and Clinical Psychology, 65*(2), 301-308.

World Health Organization. (2018). *International classification of diseases* (11th revision).

CHAPTER
4

Memory, Suggestibility, and Disclosure Processes: Implications for Children in Legal Settings

Emily M. Slonecker, Alma P. Olaguez, Rachel L. Taffe, and J. Zoe Klemfuss

Abstract
Children's eyewitness capabilities, suggestibility, and disclosure processes have direct consequences for legal procedures and may shape the progress and outcomes of legal cases. This chapter describes relevant empirical research on child development and explains how research has informed legal practices and policies. In the first of two sections, the chapter provides an overview of children's memory development during childhood and identifies internal and external factors that are related to children's memory errors. The chapter then briefly discusses the field's current knowledge of children's disclosure and recantation processes. In the second section, the topics from the first section are applied to the legal system and their consequences for forensic interviews and courtroom testimony examined. The chapter concludes with implications for the legal field and identifies directions for future research.

Key Words: child eyewitness, memory development, suggestibility, disclosure processes, forensic interviews, courtroom testimony

Children's ability to accurately report information about their experiences not only is important to understand from a developmental perspective but also has direct consequences within the legal system. Countless children are interviewed in legal proceedings across the world each year, with over 4 million children in the United States, Europe, and Canada interviewed annually for maltreatment investigations alone (Public Health Agency of Canada, 2010; U.S. Department of Health & Human Services, 2020; World Health Organization, 2018). These children may be interviewed as witnesses, during custody proceedings, or in immigration courts. However, children's testimony is most often heard in court when they are testifying as victims to alleged crime, meaning their testimony is crucial for the case. Thus, understanding the various factors that create ideal circumstances for children's reporting is necessary for ensuring that fact finders reach a fair and just decision. This chapter will review how research on children's memory development informs our understanding of best practices with child witnesses in forensic interviews and in court.

The chapter is organized into two sections. The first provides an overview of memory development during childhood, factors associated with children's memory errors, and disclosure and recantation processes. The second section then applies these topics to the legal system, including within the forensic interviewing context and within the context of courtroom testimony. The chapter concludes with a discussion of implications for legal policy and practice and with observations and suggestions for future directions in the field.

Memory, Suggestibility, and Disclosure Processes in Childhood

Children experience significant changes in memory capacity and performance across the first decade of life. These changes impact children's ability to report legally relevant experiences and provide accurate event information in the face of potentially suggestive questioning in legal contexts. However, capacity alone is not sufficient for understanding how and when children will accurately and completely report their experiences; children must also be willing to provide relevant information. Multiple factors dictate when and to whom children disclose information about legally relevant events, particularly within the context of abuse or neglect. Some of these factors have also been linked to children's recantations of earlier disclosures, although debates remain in the field regarding how often recantation occurs and how best to distinguish between true and false recantations. In this section we provide an overview of research on normative memory development, factors affecting memory and suggestibility, and factors affecting disclosure and recantation processes during childhood.

Memory Development

Children undergo rapid mnemonic development as they age and demonstrate growth in the ability to report retrieved memories. Here we focus on development in a particularly legally relevant domain—autobiographical memory. Children begin to construct mental, and eventually verbal, representations of past experiences, namely autobiographical memories, within the first years of life (Bloom, 1991; Howe & Courage, 2004; Reese, 2002). Autobiographical memories are recollections of personally experienced events that are associated with a particular time, place, and sense of self (Fivush, 2011; Fivush & Zaman, 2014). On average, when children are asked to describe their earliest autobiographical memories, they mention events that occurred around or after the age of 2 (Howe et al., 2003; Peterson, 2011; Peterson & Warren, 2009; Peterson et al., 2005). Around 2–3 years of age, children also develop the ability to verbally describe their past experiences and recall autobiographical information over short delays (Baker-Ward et al., 1993; Hamond & Fivush, 1991; Reese, 2002).

As children age into middle and late childhood, their recall ability improves, likely aided by the parallel development of interrelated cognitive abilities, such as advances in their knowledge base, reasoning and representational abilities, and information processing speeds (Bjorklund et al., 2009; Ceci et al., 2010; Goswick et al., 2013; Howe et al., 2009; Lyons & Ghetti, 2010). Compared to younger children, older children tend to recall more information about past events (e.g., Goodman et al., 1994; Hamond & Fivush, 1991; Howe et al., 1994; Ornstein, 1995; Ornstein et al., 1998; Peterson, 1999; Peterson & Bell, 1996; Peterson & Whalen, 2001; Pressley & Schneider, 1997; Salmon et al., 2002; Saywitz et al., 1991), provide more accurate information (Bjorklund et al., 1998; Goodman et al., 1994), are better able to identify the source of remembered information (Foley & Johnson, 1985; Lindsay et al., 1991), and are less likely to conflate details across different events (Farrar & Goodman, 1992; Powell et al., 1999).

In addition to developmental improvements in the ability to retain and report accurate information, children experience marked growth in the ability to reject false suggestions about past experiences. Suggestibility broadly refers to "the degree to which the encoding, storage, retrieval, and reporting of events can be influenced by a range of internal and external factors" (Ceci & Bruck, 1995, p. 44) and can be classified as occurring immediately or after a delay. Immediate suggestibility refers to the acceptance of misinformation during a conversation and is often attributed to the use of leading questions (Gudjonsson, 2003; Gudjonsson & Clark, 1986). An example of immediate suggestibility is acquiescing (often falsely) to a question that indicates the expected or desired response (e.g., "George shut the door, didn't he?"). Delayed suggestibility involves incorporating prior suggested information into later reports. This could occur when, for example, the false suggestion that George shut the door is later recalled as having occurred; thus, the inaccuracy is reproduced across subsequent retellings of the event (Loftus, 1979; Ridley & Gudjonsson, 2013; Vagni et al., 2015).

Early childhood is considered to be the developmental period of highest risk for susceptibility to false suggestions. As children enter middle childhood, they generally become less susceptible to suggestion (e.g., Ceci & Bruck, 1993, 1995). However, under some conditions, children become *more* susceptible to suggestibility with age. Specifically, increasing sophistication in children's knowledge can lead to somewhat predictable errors in older, as opposed to younger, children's memory. For example, older children are more likely than younger children to report false memories for items that are semantically related to information they are tasked to recall (e.g., falsely remembering the word "sleep" after hearing words like "pillow," "dreams," "nighttime"; Brainerd & Reyna, 2005). Many theorists identify changes in children's broader knowledge base as the primary mechanism responsible for this increased vulnerability (Bjorklund, 1987; Brainerd & Reyna, 2005; Howe, 2005; Howe & Wilkinson, 2011), although some suggest that increases in children's overall cognitive processing speeds also play a role (Howe, 2005, 2006).

Factors Affecting Memory and Suggestibility

Researchers generally accept that memory improves dramatically across childhood and suggestibility typically peaks in early childhood. However, some aspects of children's memory and suggestibility are still debated, such as how internal and external factors impact children's capabilities (Ceci & Friedman, 2000; Lyon, 1999). To follow we review some key factors that may impact children's memory and suggestibility performance and highlight areas of consensus and debate.

DEMOGRAPHICS

In addition to age, gender and cultural background have been studied as demographic variables associated with children's memory performance and suggestibility. Gender has long been considered an important factor in children's autobiographical memory development. Multiple studies suggest that girls tend to engage in more detailed (Buckner & Fivush, 1998; Peterson, 2011) and complete memory recall than boys (Fivush & Schwarzmueller, 1998; Fivush et al., 2003; Peterson & McCabe, 1983), although these results are somewhat inconsistent across studies (see Grysman & Hudson, 2013, for a review). Researchers posit that these differences reflect socialized gender norms and variation in caregivers' strategies for discussing the past with girls relative to boys (Nelson & Fivush, 2004). In contrast, research on children's suggestibility rarely identifies gender differences (Eisen et al., 2007; Ghetti et al., 2006; Gudjonsson et al., 2016; Kim et al., 2017; Uhl et al., 2016; Volpini et al., 2016; K. L. Warren & Peterson, 2014), an exception being one study that found girls were less likely to acquiesce to misleading questions than boys (Gilstrap & Ceci, 2005).

Children's autobiographical memories can also vary cross-culturally, likely due to cultural variations in self-perception and social structures. Researchers have discovered consistent differences in the structure, content, emotional valence, functional usage, and accessibility of autobiographical memory when comparing group-oriented collectivist populations, like Asians or Asian Americans, to self-oriented individualistic populations, like European

Americans (see Wang, 2021, for a recent discussion). In general, European American children frequently center themselves as the main focal point when asked to describe the past; they tend to recall unique, one-time experiences more so than routine events; their descriptions of the past frequently include references to feelings, thoughts, and desires; and they often report more specific details about events relative to Asian children. In contrast, Asian children often recall more routine events that are centered on social interactions or other people. They usually avoid discussing their subjective feelings about past events and tend to recall more general information rather than specific details (Wang, 2004, 2006). Although European American children often provide more unique memory information when describing the past, children from Asian cultures tend to provide less inaccurate memory information during prompted recall (Klemfuss & Wang, 2017), possibly due to a greater appreciation for the importance of memory accuracy within Asian societies (Wang et al., 2000).

Far less is known about cultural differences in children's false memories, although existing research suggests this is an area ripe for investigation. For example, a study comparing Norwegian and American preschoolers found that Norwegian children were less suggestible than American children (Melinder et al., 2005). Relatedly, Brazilian children were less suggestible than American children when completing a moral judgment task (Saltzstein et al., 2004). However, given the dearth of research on this topic, the exact mechanism(s) responsible for these differences, as well as the existence of similar variations among other populations, is unknown.

EVENT CHARACTERISTICS

Characteristics of the event being recalled, such as the extent of the child's involvement in the event and whether the event occurred once or multiple times, can also influence children's memory. Research comparing children's memory for events they experienced firsthand versus those they passively witnessed is both theoretically important for understanding children's memory processes and practically important from a legal perspective. Though children are frequently called upon to testify as victims/witnesses, they may also be called upon to testify as passive witnesses to alleged transgressions. Research suggests that children generally provide more accurate memory descriptions of personally experienced events as opposed to passively witnessed events (Murachver et al., 1996; Roediger et al., 2004; Rudy & Goodman, 1991; Tobey & Goodman, 1992) and are less susceptible to false memories about experienced events relative to witnessed events (Bruck et al., 2002; Rudy & Goodman, 1991). Thus, greater involvement in an event is associated with better memory and reduced suggestibility in children.

The frequency with which children are exposed to an event can also impact memory. Regrettably, many cases of child sexual abuse involve repeated assaults, and child victims will often experience multiple incidents that are similar in content and context. Over time, children may develop a "script," or a general mental representation of the events that is based on the shared elements of the incidents (Farrar & Goodman, 1992; Hudson et al., 1992; Nelson & Gruendel, 1981). Children who develop generalized memory scripts tend to describe similar incidents with more detail (Bauer & Fivush, 1992; Fivush et al., 1992; Hudson, 1990; Hudson & Nelson, 1986; Powell & Thomson, 2003) and show higher rates of accuracy (McNichol et al., 1999) than children without scripts. In addition, repeated exposure may make children more resistant to suggestive questioning (Connolly & Lindsay, 2001; Gobbo et al., 2002; Powell et al., 1999).

However, repeated experiences can also prove detrimental to children's memory. When children are asked to describe a specific instance of a repeated event, they tend to focus on the characteristics that were similar across incidents and may leave out highly relevant details that were unique to the specific incident in question (Connolly & Lindsay, 2001; McNichol et al., 1999). Repeated exposure can also make it more difficult for children to specify the exact instance in which a unique detail occurred (Johnson et al., 1993; Leichtman et al., 2000; Lindsay & Johnson, 1989; Quas et al., 2000; Roberts & Powell, 2001; Zaragoza & Lane, 1994).

STRESS AND TRAUMA

Many events recalled within the context of the legal system are negative or stressful in nature and potentially traumatic. Researchers have been working to elucidate how stress and trauma, both independently and in conjunction, are related to children's memory performance. Some researchers have found that stress at the time of an event can improve children's memory performance (Goodman et al., 1991; A. R. Warren & Smartwood, 1992), while others have found that stress either inhibits (Bugental et al., 1992; Merritt et al., 1994; Peters, 1991) or is unrelated to children's memory performance (Baker-Ward et al., 1993; Howe et al., 1994). These inconsistencies are likely due to variations in study methodology, such as the type of stressful event explored or differences in the operationalization of stress. For example, many studies ask children to recall naturally occurring stressful events, like medical procedures or accidents (e.g., Burgwyn-Bailes et al., 2001; Peterson & Whalen, 2001), meaning that the intensity, duration, and personal relevance of the stressful events likely vary across and within studies. Moreover, it may be a child's physiological response to a stressful situation, rather than simply the presence of a potentially stressful event, that most strongly influences memory performance.

Using a controlled laboratory stressor rather than naturally occurring experience, Rush and colleagues (2014) randomly assigned children to participate in a high-stress or low-stress task and later assessed their memory for the task. Researchers found no difference in memory performance between stress conditions, and instead found that children with higher levels of arousal during the task exhibited better recall for the event relative to children with lower levels of arousal. That said, children may experience high levels of arousal when recalling a stressful experience (Brenner, 2000; Levine et al., 2008), which is known to be associated with *decreased* memory accuracy in children (Almerigogna et al., 2007; Nathanson & Saywitz, 2003; Quas & Lench, 2007). Therefore, it is also important to consider children's physiological state at retrieval, in addition to encoding.

The association between stress and children's suggestibility is also unclear and seems to be influenced by moderators like stress levels during retrieval, symptoms of psychopathology, and age. For example, children appear to be more suggestible when they experience high state anxiety at retrieval, although the style of the interview (i.e., supportive versus nonsupportive) can reduce children's state anxiety, and therefore reduce suggestibility (Almerigogna et al., 2007; Bettenay et al., 2015). In addition, Eisen and colleagues (2007) found that the association between arousal during a to-be-remembered stressful event and children's suggestibility varied depending on children's dissociation symptoms; increased stress reactivity was associated with an increase in suggestibility for children with high dissociation symptoms but a decrease in suggestibility for children with low dissociation symptoms. The authors offered multiple explanations for these findings, including variations in children's response biases, difficulties in identifying the source of their memory, and differing levels of arousal during retrieval. These potential mechanisms represent important avenues for future work to explore.

Other researchers found developmental differences, such that 7–8-year-olds who had higher arousal during the event had better memory, regardless of whether the event was stressful or not, whereas this pattern was not found for 12–14-year-olds (Quas et al., 2014). Although the exact reason for this discrepancy remains unclear, the authors suggested it was related to age-specific variations in participants' perception of the stressful lab event. The older participants appeared less willing than the younger participants to answer questions about the lab event, meaning they also exhibited a lower level of acquiescence to misleading questions. The authors speculated adolescents may have been more hesitant to talk about the event because they perceived it as a more stressful experience relative to children.

Further complicating the association between stress and memory is the role of trauma. Traumatic events are inherently stressful, but not all stressful events result in trauma. Children are generally better at recalling traumatic experiences over the long term relative to positive or neutral events (Burgwyn-Bailes et al., 2001; Peterson & Bell, 1996; Peterson & Whalen, 2001), but children may also be more likely to provide overly general descriptions of traumatic memories (Williams et al., 2007). Moreover, traumatic events can lead to the development of posttraumatic stress disorder (PTSD), a condition that can further modify the relationship between children's memory and suggestibility.

In a recent study by Vagni and colleagues (2021), suspected victims of child abuse completed a suggestibility task that measured immediate and delayed recall and suggestibility for memory information from a short story (i.e., information unrelated to their abuse). They found that PTSD did not predict deficits in immediate recall but was positively associated with immediate and delayed suggestibility, as well as inaccuracies during delayed recall. These findings suggest that PTSD may not actually inhibit memory on a cognitive level but may make children more susceptible to incorporating misinformation when faced with negative feedback. However, it should be noted that when children with PTSD are asked about trauma-related information, PTSD has been found to enhance, rather than inhibit, recall (Howe et al., 1994).

COGNITIVE FUNCTIONING

The memory system is one piece of a much larger cognitive system that develops rapidly across childhood. Therefore, children's ability to recall information is intrinsically tied to other aspects of their cognition, such as theory of mind (ToM), executive functioning, and intelligence. Children develop ToM, the awareness that other people have unique thoughts and mental states, around the age of 5 (Astington, 1993). ToM contributes to children's memory performance in multiple ways. For example, ToM allows children to develop a basic understanding of how knowledge is acquired, which is necessary for the encoding and retrieval of personal events (Perner & Ruffman, 1995; Welch-Ross, 1995). Once children develop ToM, they also develop the ability to differentiate between new experiences and "reliving" old experiences; they recognize that their description of a former event in the present is just a recollection of a previous experience, rather than a new experience (Flavell, 1988; Perner, 1988). However, parsing out the unique contributions of ToM to memory performance is difficult because there are equally strong associations between ToM and other correlates linked to memory performance, including early language development (e.g., Astington & Jenkins, 1999; Farrar & Maag, 2002) and metacognition—the ability to think about thinking (e.g., Perner & Ruffman, 1995). Thus, findings regarding children's ToM and suggestibility are mixed. Some have found that ToM predicts resistance to suggestive questioning (Bright-Paul et al., 2008), although these associations may be partially explained by age (Karpinski & Scullin, 2009) and/or other cognitive processes (Melinder et al., 2006), while others have failed to find any significant associations (Klemfuss et al., 2016).

Executive functions (EFs), a collection of interrelated cognitive processes required for planning, inhibiting, monitoring, and shifting behavior (Diamond, 2013), also begin to emerge during early childhood, with most children reaching adultlike levels of EF around the age of 12 (Anderson, 2002; Cragg & Nation, 2008; Crone et al., 2006). Research suggests that multiple aspects of EFs, such as the ability to actively hold small chunks of information in the mind, to concentrate on certain information, to plan, and to control our impulses, play a crucial role in the ability to identify and select relevant memory information for retrieval (Conway & Pleydell-Pearce, 2000; Unsworth, 2007; Unsworth & Engle, 2007; Unsworth et al., 2012; Williams et al., 2007). However, most of the empirical evidence for a link between EF and memory recall is based on research in populations suffering from conditions that inhibit normal autobiographical memory performance, such as neurodevelopmental disorders (Fabio & Capri, 2015; Goddard et al., 2014) or psychiatric disorders (Kaczmarczyk et al., 2018; Valentino et al., 2012). Work confirming this association in typically developing children is sparse and conflicting; while some researchers have found associations between autobiographical memory specificity and EF (Nieto et al., 2018; Nixon et al., 2013; Raes et al., 2010), others have found no association (Nuttall et al., 2014).

The relationship between EF and suggestibility in children is also complex. Karpinski and Scullin (2009) found an association between a composite measure of EF and children's resistance to suggestive questioning about a live event, while Melinder et al. (2006) found that children's inhibitory control predicted resistance to suggestive questions about an event seen on video. However, others failed to find an association between children's resistance to questioning about a live event and multiple EF measures, including inhibitory control (Klemfuss et al., 2016; McCrory et al., 2007).

The mixed findings regarding EF may be due to the fact that EF is rarely conceptualized or measured in the same way across studies. Further complicating matters is the murky distinction between EF and intelligence. Intelligence is one of the more robust predictors of event recall in children, such that increases in intelligence are normally associated with improved memory recall (Geddie et al., 2000; Roebers & Schneider, 2001). However, the relationship between intelligence and children's suggestibility is more mixed. Some researchers have found that higher intelligence is associated with reduced suggestibility (Bettenay et al., 2015; Gignac & Powell, 2006; Roma et al., 2011), while others have found no association (Caprin et al., 2016; Gilstrap & Papierno, 2004; Gudjonsson et al., 2016; Melinder et al., 2010). To date, the reason for these inconsistencies is unclear; while this variation may be explained by differences in methodology (i.e., using verbal versus nonverbal measures of intelligence), a recent review on children's suggestibility by Klemfuss and Olaguez (2020) does not reveal a conclusive pattern.

Studies that compare the memory performance of typically developing children to those with intellectual disabilities offer a clearer picture. Children with intellectual disabilities show higher rates of suggestibility compared to age-matched typically developing children (Bowles & Sharman, 2014; Brown et al., 2012; Henry & Gudjonsson, 2007; Milne et al., 2013), suggesting that intelligence does seem related to suggestibility. However, these differences disappear when the samples are matched based on mental age rather than chronological age (Brown et al., 2012; London et al., 2013). Thus, children with intellectual disabilities can likely resist suggestive questioning as well as children without intellectual disabilities if questioning techniques are tailored to their mental, rather than chronological, age (Klemfuss & Olaguez, 2020).

LANGUAGE DEVELOPMENT

Across the span of childhood, language development facilitates increasingly lengthy and detailed recounting of past experiences, and thus, language plays a crucial role in children's ability to describe the past. However, the picture becomes more complex when considering different aspects of language development (e.g., the ability to understand language, narrative skills, language production) and when considering different types of memory reporting (e.g., free recall, direct questioning, suggestive questioning).

Theory regarding the development of autobiographical memory suggests that language development plays a crucial role in improving children's free recall of the past and resistance to suggestive misinformation (e.g., Fivush, 2011). However, empirical results confirming this association are inconsistent. Like general intelligence, language development can be operationalized in a variety of ways, resulting in conflicting findings regarding the relation between language and memory performance. In order to engage in a forensic interview or courtroom testimony, children must use their receptive language skills to understand the person talking to them and their productive language skills to provide a coherent response. Given that these two systems rely on different mechanisms and skills to function (e.g., Smith, 1997), the association between language and memory can vary depending on which linguistic system is being assessed (Klemfuss, 2015). Children's receptive skills may be more important when they are being asked direct questions (e.g., during cross-examination) or when resisting suggestive misinformation, while children's productive skills may be more important when they need to produce a coherent description of the past (e.g., when first disclosing an incident during a forensic interview).

Another aspect of language development that can affect memory and suggestibility is the style in which children learn to discuss the past. Parent–child reminiscing conversations play a crucial role in shaping children's memory performance. Not only do these conversations give children a chance to rehearse and consolidate their memories, but also they frequently expose children to new information about the event in question, teach children which information is most important to discuss, and help children learn new labels and terms for different actions and objects (Fivush & Nelson, 2004; Fivush et al., 1996; Reese, 2002). Research suggests these benefits are particularly pronounced when children's conversational partner uses a highly elaborative conversation style marked by requests for more information, the inclusion of new information, and the frequent use of open-ended "wh-" questions (Farrant & Reese, 2000; Fivush et al., 2006; Kulkofsky et al., 2008; Nelson & Fivush, 2004; Wang et al., 2015). Caregivers who engage in elaborative conversations about the past tend to have children who are more elaborative in independent event conversations and provide lengthier, more detailed accounts of their past experiences relative to children of less elaborative caregivers. That said, children who are particularly proficient narrators may perceive past talk as a more social or collaborative process, causing them to incorporate more false suggestions from conversational partners when discussing the past (Kulkofsky & Klemfuss, 2008).

In recent years, researchers have shifted their focus toward better understanding the association between children's language development and suggestibility, introducing new and exciting areas of inquiry. Whereas having a conversation partner with an elaborative conversation style might assist preschool-aged children's general memory performance, two studies conducted by Principe and colleagues (2013, 2017) suggest this added structure may be detrimental for children's suggestibility. However, other work suggests the association between caregivers' conversation styles and children's memory performance may depend on the context of the conversation (Klemfuss et al., 2016; Slonecker & Klemfuss, 2020, 2021).

PSYCHOSOCIAL FACTORS

Children's memory reports are also influenced by aspects of their social and emotional environment, heuristically labeled as psychosocial factors. Here, we briefly discuss known associations between children's memory performance and attachment styles, as well as child temperament. Given that many children become involved in the legal system due to their experiences with abuse, we also discuss how a history of maltreatment may be related to children's memory performance and suggestibility.

There is some evidence to suggest that children's attachment styles, as well as their caregivers' attachment styles, are related to memory performance through numerous mechanisms. Children's attachment experiences are organized within the memory system to create broad expectations about the formation of social relationships, namely internal working models (Bowlby, 1982; Main, 1995). It is theorized that these schemas influence the way people perceive and describe their experiences and memories, particularly for emotional events (Alexander et al., 2002; Chae et al., 2011). As a result, caregivers' and children's attachment styles may be related to the way caregivers discuss the past with children, how easily children can regulate their emotions during memory encoding and recall, and how willing children are to trust adults and accept misinformation (Alexander et al., 2002; Chae et al., 2011; Goodman et al., 1994, 1997). Research examining emotional events suggests that children with higher positive representations of their parent (e.g., protective, affectionate) are better able to resist false suggestions about emotional events and freely recall more accurate event information (Chae et al., 2014, 2018). Furthermore, a recent study by Lawson and colleagues (2021) suggests caregivers' reminiscing styles may mediate the association between attachment and children's memory performance. Specifically, the researchers found that children's attachment security within the parent–child relationship was associated with higher levels of caregiver-sensitive guidance during reminiscing, which was then associated with children's recall.

Researchers have also found that caregivers' attachment styles play a role in shaping children's memory performance. For example, Chae and colleagues (2014) found that children were more suggestible if their caregiver was high avoidant rather than low avoidant. While Melinder and colleagues (2010) found no association between children's overall suggestibility and caregiver attachment, they did find that interviewers were more likely to ask children misleading questions when discussing a nonstressful event if the child's caregiver was anxiously attached. In other work, children of anxious parents were found to be more prone to memory errors when questioned about stressful events (Alexander et al., 2002; Goodman et al., 1997). Given such variability in findings, the role of attachment in predicting children's memory performance is an important area to investigate further. If these relations are parsed out, forensic interviewers may be able to take additional precautions depending on children's attachment styles.

The associations between child abuse and memory performance are somewhat more clearcut. Abused children tend to overemphasize negative emotional stimuli and misinterpret positive stimuli when encoding an event (McWilliams et al., 2014). As a result, children who have been abused or mistreated often recall less overall information, demonstrate difficulty recalling specific events, and include more inaccurate information in descriptions of the past than children who have not been abused (Alexander et al., 2005; Goodman et al., 2001; Kaczmarczyk et al., 2018; McWilliams et al., 2014; Valentino et al., 2009; Young & Widom, 2014). A history of trauma and abuse is also associated with increased suggestibility in children when questioned about events that are unrelated to the abuse or traumatic event. Like adults (e.g., Drake, 2014; Drake et al., 2008), children who have been sexually abused, maltreated, or neglected show higher levels of both immediate and delayed suggestibility compared to children with no abuse history (Curci et al., 2017; Gudjonsson, 1984; McWilliams et al., 2014; Vagni et al., 2015), suggesting that a history of abuse may influence children's broader mnemonic abilities. However, it is important to note that other researchers have found no association between abuse and suggestibility (Eisen et al., 2007; Goodman et al., 2001), and one study found that suspected victims of maltreatment were less suggestible than children who were not maltreated (Otgaar et al., 2017). Some researchers suggest these conflicting results are related to the mediating role of PTSD, which is itself associated with suggestibility and may or may not develop in children following abuse or neglect (Chae et al., 2011).

Disclosure and Recantation

Most research on children's disclosure and recantation focuses on cases of abuse and neglect. However, the findings from this line of work are still applicable to broader contexts in which children might have a reason to conceal or recant legally relevant information. For example, children are regularly questioned during custody proceedings and asked to disclose information that might significantly impact their living situation (California Family Code § 3042, 1992; Emery et al., 2005). Thus, there are several scenarios in which children may have varying motivations to disclose or recant sensitive information crucial to the investigative process. In the following section, we first briefly discuss why rates of children's disclosure and recantation vary substantially across studies and then review how demographic and case factors can influence children's disclosure and recantation.

Researchers generally agree that children can and do refrain from disclosing information during interviews (London et al., 2005; Malloy et al., 2007). However, estimates of disclosure rates vary significantly, with researchers reporting disclosure rates ranging from 24% to 96% (London et al., 2020; Lyon et al., 2020). This variability can impact how interviewers interpret children's disclosure or lack of disclosure in an interview. For example, if an interviewer believes that 96% of children who have been abused disclose abuse, they may stop pursuing a case if the child involved does not disclose abuse during the initial interview. In contrast, if the interviewer believes that the rate of disclosure during initial interviews is much smaller, the interviewer may recommend additional interviews with the child to encourage disclosure, potentially risking additional opportunities to introduce suggestive information. Thus, understanding why rates of disclosure vary across studies is a pivotal query to explore.

Variation in disclosure rates across studies is likely due to several factors including how disclosure is defined (Lyon et al., 2014), the research methodologies used (London et al., 2008), and the sample composition across studies (e.g., by abuse substantiation, age, gender, ethnicity, perpetrator identity; see London et al., 2008, for a review). Moreover, researchers' estimates are often constrained by an inability to conclusively determine the veracity of children's abuse allegations and the limited availability of information on nonreported instances of abuse (Lyon et al., 2020). Critically, rate estimations are extrapolated from *reported* cases of abuse and do not account for abuse that goes unreported or undetected.

Though disclosure is a complex process, researchers have begun to identify demographic factors that predict disclosure, such as children's age and gender. Prior to reaching adolescence, children are more likely to disclose sexual abuse (Azzopardi et al., 2019; Grandgenett et al., 2019; Malloy et al., 2014) and less likely to disclose physical abuse (Lahtinen et al., 2020). In addition, Leach and colleagues (2017) found that disclosure rates increased up to age 11 and then decreased until age 16 (see Wyman et al., this volume, for an in-depth discussion on adolescent disclosure rates). Regarding gender, some research suggests girls are more likely to disclose than boys (Lahtinen et al., 2020; London et al., 2005).

The likelihood of disclosure can also be influenced by case factors, such as the abuser's relationship to the child and the state of the relationship between the child and parental figures. Generally, the closer the abuser is to the child, the longer it takes for the child to disclose (Hershkowitz et al., 2007; Skinner et al., 2019). For example, intrafamilial abuse has been associated with delayed disclosure (London et al., 2008; Lyon, 2007; Malloy et al., 2011) even when the perpetrator is not a parental figure (Tashjian et al., 2016). In addition, children who fear that their parents will not believe the abuse allegations may instead disclose to nonparental adults or delay disclosure altogether. Unfortunately, this hesitation may only exacerbate parents' skepticism and cause them to question their child's motivations for not disclosing sooner (Hershkowitz et al., 2007). In contrast, children are more likely to disclose abuse in a forensic interview if their caregiver believes the abuse allegations (Grandgenett et al., 2019; Malloy & Mugno, 2016).

Factors that appear to delay disclosure for children have also been linked to reasons that children may recant their allegations. Although recantation appears to be somewhat rare (McGuire & London, 2020), rate estimates range from 4% to 27% (London et al., 2008; Malloy et al., 2007). Malloy and colleagues (2007) suggest that recantation is due in large part to family pressures and children's vulnerability to the influence of adults who do not believe their allegations. In line with delayed disclosure patterns, children are more likely to recant if their family members do not believe their allegations (Malloy et al., 2016) or if they are closely related to the perpetrator (Hays et al., 2017; Malloy et al., 2007). Boys and younger children are also more likely to recant (Hays et al., 2017; Malloy et al., 2007), whereas children removed from the home and/or separated from siblings are less likely to recant (Malloy et al., 2016). Petherick (2020) argues that recantation may reflect a change in the child's belief about the abuse, which may be brought on by external pressure from adults or the inability to find corroborating evidence that supports the child's allegation. Recantations can happen for true allegations of abuse (Malloy et al., 2007), although false allegations do occur at a nonnegligible rate (O'Donohue et al., 2018). Thus, rates of recantations continue to be of interest for researchers and can help legal professionals understand why children may recant abuse allegations at any point in the investigation.

For cases of abuse that reach the courtroom, the ongoing debate regarding disclosure and recantation is often discussed in relation to child sexual abuse accommodation syndrome (CSAAS), a well-known model of victim disclosure behavior (Summit, 1983). The model suggests that children are likely to delay disclosure because the perpetrator is often an adult in a position of trust and power. As a result, children are frequently manipulated to keep the abuse secret and may recant the abuse when faced with the negative consequences of disclosure, such as alienation from a nonoffending parent. Given that the model was only partly based on empirical research, many components of the CSAAS model have been refuted. For example, the original author has since critiqued his inclusion of the word "syndrome" in the model title (*R. v. A. K.* 1999). Nevertheless, prosecutors often call on experts to testify on CSAAS in legal cases and explain to juries why children might delay disclosure or recant their allegations.

However, a recent ruling may soon change this practice. In *New Jersey v. J.L.G.* (2018), the New Jersey Supreme Court rendered testimony based on CSAAS inadmissible in court due to the lack of empirical evidence supporting reasons for recantations (London et al., 2020). Whether recantations can help distinguish between true and false allegations of abuse is still up for contentious debate (see Lyon et al., 2020, and the corresponding response from London et al., 2020). That said, both sides of the aisle agree that more research is urgently needed on the matter, and London et al. (2020) put forth several suggestions for future lines of inquiry on this topic.

Application in the Legal System

In this section we provide an overview of the most prominent interviewing protocols that children are likely to face during forensic interviews and courtroom testimony. We then explain how the research discussed in the first section applies within these legal contexts. Given children's memory skills, individual differences, and vulnerability to suggestibility, certain interviewing practices in both settings may hinder children's ability to answer questions in an accurate, complete, and coherent manner. Children's responses during forensic interviews and during courtroom testimony have a significant impact on whether other adults will deem their narrative as credible and warranting of criminal charges or a conviction. We review how applied research at the intersection of developmental psychology and the law has provided a foundational understanding of what can improve and what can hinder children's reporting in the forensic interviewing context and in courtroom contexts.

Forensic Interviewing

Most of the research on child interviewing practices has been conducted to inform forensic interviews with suspected child victims and witnesses. Here, we briefly describe the most commonly used interviewing protocols and the research that highlights critical components of the protocols, such as question types and interviewer behavior during questioning. We then discuss problematic interviewing practices that are still commonly used within the legal system and potential areas of research that can help distinguish between true and false event reports.

There are several forensic interviewing protocols available, some of which are evidence based. The protocol used during a forensic interview, or whether a protocol is used at all, depends on a range of factors including jurisdiction, type of facility/practitioner (e.g., by a caseworker in the welfare system, by police, or by specialists in child advocacy centers), and the breadth and currency of the practitioner's training. Some of the primary protocols used throughout the world include the Achieving Best Evidence in Criminal Proceedings, the Step-Wise Interview, and the National Institute of Child Health and Development (NICHD) Investigative Protocol.

Across recommended protocols, all include a period of building rapport, using mostly open-ended free recall questions, followed by closed-ended direct questions (Lavoie et al., 2021). In addition, it is common for protocols to include a practice interview phase to familiarize children with the process of formal questioning. For example, in the Narrative Elaboration procedure (Saywitz & Snyder, 1996; Saywitz et al., 1996), children are taught to organize event information into multiple categories (e.g., participants, setting) and given the opportunity to practice this mnemonic strategy at the beginning of the interview process. Practice sessions teach children how to naturally elaborate on their descriptions of the past, and research suggests that children provide more accurate information when interviewing procedures include a practice component (Saywitz et al., 1996; Saywitz & Snyder, 1996).

Like the Narrative Elaboration procedure, the NICHD Protocol also includes a practice component. The NICHD Protocol is widely considered to be the gold standard in child interviewing procedures in the United States and Israel (Lamb et al., 2007). A meta-analysis from Benia et al. (2015) reveals that, compared to other interviewing protocols, the NICHD Protocol elicits more details from children in response to open-ended questions and fewer details in response to suggestive questions. Recently, interviewers have begun implementing the *Revised* NICHD Protocol, which includes a more extensive rapport-building phase at the beginning of the interview and promotes increased emotional support for the child throughout the interview (Ahern et al., 2014; Hershkowitz et al., 2015).

Studies comparing the efficacy of the Revised NICHD Protocol to that of the standard NICHD Protocol reveal numerous benefits of including additional interviewer support. Children interviewed with the Revised NICHD Protocol provide more event details that are relevant for criminal charges (e.g., frequency of contact, touching over or under clothing), are less reluctant to provide information, and eventually disclose abuse with fewer prompts than those interviewed under the standard NICHD Protocol (Ahern et al., 2019; Blasbalg et al., 2019; Hershkowitz et al., 2015). Furthermore, the closeness with which interviewers adhere to the Revised NICHD Protocol's guidelines predicts the likelihood that children will make abuse allegations (Blasbalg et al., 2021).

Interviews following the Revised NICHD Protocol begin with a "ground rules" phase, wherein the interviewer outlines expectations and instructs the child to express when they do not understand a question or do not know the answer. Next, the interviewers engage in rapport building before progressing to questions about the event in question. This next phase includes mostly open-ended questions ("Tell me what happened.") at the beginning of the interview to encourage the child to provide a story and only uses direct questions as necessary ("What did he say next?"). The direct follow-up questions should be used to clarify or elaborate on anything the child disclosed themselves, and questions should only include details the child already provided. Finally, throughout the interview, the interviewer should conduct themselves in a manner that is supportive and welcoming to the child, without giving children contingent feedback that suggests that the interviewer prefers some types of responses over others (Lamb et al., 2007).

Research on the efficacy of the Revised NICHD Protocol suggests that interviewer support may be a key component in establishing rapport and improving interview quality. Interviewer support is expected to facilitate disclosure by increasing children's comfort with the interviewer and willingness to share sensitive information and/or contradict the interviewer if the interviewer is mistaken (Olaguez et al., 2018). While interviewer support has been linked to interviewee well-being and is widely considered to be a beneficial technique in forensic contexts (see Saywitz et al., 2019, for a review), the role that interviewer support has on rapport is still being refined. Operational definitions of interviewer support vary across studies but most often reference interviewer eye contact, vocal intonation, posture, smiling, and rapport building (Carter et al., 1996; Davis & Bottoms, 2002; Eisen et al., 2019; Imhoff & Baker-Ward, 1999; Quas et al., 2005; Sauerland et al., 2018). However, the concept of rapport building is often conflated with interviewer support and some researchers have used the terms interchangeably (Sauerland et al., 2018; Saywitz et al., 2015), while others consider rapport building as just one element of interviewer support (Davis & Bottoms, 2002; Eisen et al., 2019; Quas et al., 2005).

Generally, interviewer support has positive effects on children's memory reports. Supportive interviewers do not negatively impair children's memory reports and help children avoid falling prey to suggestive questions (for a review see Olaguez et al., 2018, and for a meta-analysis see Saywitz et al., 2015). However, additional research with consistent operational definitions of rapport is needed to help clarify how rapport is beneficial in some cases and whether it has the potential to harm children's accuracy in other contexts.

In terms of forensic interviewing practices that are harmful to children's reporting, most involve introducing bias via suggestive questions, option posing questions ("Did he do X or Y?"), and providing reinforcement that is contingent upon children's responses. Research has revealed that when the interviewer provides positive feedback to certain types of responses provided by the child, the child may resort to providing or assenting to incorrect information in order to receive additional positive reinforcement (Olaguez et al., 2018). In some jurisdictions, problematic interviewing practices are even part of the recommended interviewing procedures. In England and Wales, the "20 Principles" protocol includes several principles that are weakly supported by empirical evidence and a few that directly contradict extant research evidence (see Cooper et al., 2018, for a review). One such principle advises against rapport building, which, as previously described, is a highly valuable tool to increase reporting. Another recommended principle is having children recount information following a chronological order; however, the efficacy of this technique has not been adequately tested (Cooper et al., 2018). Similarly, forensic interviewers may inadvertently shape children's reports to fit an existing prosecutorial narrative due to confirmation bias (O'Donohue & Cirlugea, 2021). To mitigate these effects, O'Donohue and Cirlugea (2021) suggest building instructions and practices aimed at reducing confirmation bias directly into interviewing protocols.

The harmful effects of poor interviewing practices are frequently compounded by children's reluctancy to signal confusion during interviews. Often, when children do not understand a question, they will try to provide an answer rather than ask for clarification from the interviewer. This phenomenon is especially prevalent among younger children (Brubacher et al., 2015; Fritzley & Lee, 2003; Fritzley et al., 2013; Henderson & Lyon, 2020) and in novel situations such as forensic and legal questioning (Brubacher et al., 2015). Accordingly, it is essential that interviewers continually monitor children's comprehension and recognize potential signals of misunderstanding (Henderson & Lyon, 2020).

Given that children do not typically signal confusion well, it can be challenging for interviewers to determine whether a child is relaying true or false event information. Researchers have examined the content of children's reports to reveal potential indicators that can help differentiate between true and false reports. In experimental settings, children describing false events provide more details and display greater narrative cohesion than children describing true events (Bruck et al., 2002; Kulkofsky et al., 2008). As suggested by Kulkofsky and colleagues (2008), these findings may reflect children's attempts to model the narrative form in which they were first exposed to the event, which often includes embellishment.

The consistency of children's reports across multiple interviews may also vary depending on whether they are relaying true or false event information. Overall, children interpret repeated questioning as a signal that their original response was "incorrect." Therefore, children tend to provide inconsistent information when asked repeatedly about an event (Cassel et al., 1996; Poole & White, 1991). That said, some research suggests that children describe true events more consistently than false events across multiple interviews (Bruck et al., 2002). Thus, even though young children have the capacity to provide accurate reports of experiences (Leichtman & Ceci, 1995), it can be challenging to determine whether children's responses are based on true events or false events.

Courtroom Testimony
Forensic interviews that result in disclosure and credible allegations of abuse may result in a child being required to present their testimony in court. Though requirements vary by jurisdiction (Henderson et al., 2019; Zajac et al., 2018), children around the world are frequently called upon to provide evidence on the stand. In-court testimony is particularly challenging for young witnesses, starting from the initial process of being deemed competent to provide evidence. Many children undergo competency examinations prior to testifying in court, although evidence suggests that these competency examinations do not appropriately assess children's actual ability to testify. Children who are deemed competent (who can potentially be as young as 2 or 3 years old) then face the challenge of answering questions that are often

developmentally inappropriate in a high-stress environment, which may directly and indirectly impact memory recall.

In terms of competency exams, many children are tested on their understanding of what it means to tell the truth or a lie and their perceived moral obligation to tell the truth on the stand (Lyon, 2011). Yet, children's performance on typical competency questions does not predict how they will perform on the stand. As such, these assessments may bar competent witnesses from testifying and label less able witnesses as competent (Klemfuss & Ceci, 2012). Specifically, experimental research reveals that truth–lie competency (i.e., understanding what "truth" and "lie" means and distinguishing between the two, understanding that one is obligated to tell the truth on the stand) does not reliably predict children's honesty (Lyon, 2011). However, a simplified oath that asks children to promise to tell the truth is relatively effective at increasing children's honesty (Lyon, 2011; Talwar et al., 2002). Considering these findings, competency tests are rarely used in Australia and the United Kingdom's criminal courts, and they have been outright banned in other countries (Lyon, 2011). However, they continue to be a mainstay in U.S. courts.

Whether children can competently testify in court and whether jurors *believe* the child is competent enough to testify are separate constructs. For children to appear credible in court, they are expected to provide coherent accounts of the event, meaning that minimally sufficient responses, or contradictory or inconsistent responses, can decrease children's credibility. The type of questions asked of child witnesses in the courtroom can affect children's responses via the amount of accurate information (Evans & Lyon, 2012) and the amount of detail provided (Stolzenberg et al., 2020), as well as the introduction of miscommunication (Evans et al., 2017; Wylie et al., 2019). Despite legal reform efforts in previous decades, most courtroom questioning is not age appropriate for children (Zajac et al., 2018), with both prosecutors and defense attorneys posing a high percentage of developmentally inappropriate questions to children (Denne et al., 2020; Evans & Lyon, 2012; Skinner et al., 2019). Thus, researchers have identified potential areas of difficulties children may face in the courtroom, including certain question structures, question scope, and the use of certain linguistic terms.

A recent analysis of case transcripts by Stolzenberg and colleagues (2020) demonstrates the impact that question structure can have on children's responses. The researchers found that certain types of closed-ended questions frequently produced responses from children that were detrimental to their credibility. Specifically, statement questions (e.g., "And he hit you?") and indirect yes/no questions (e.g., "Do you remember if X happened?") elicited one-word responses or responses that suggested lack of knowledge (e.g., "I don't know."). Questions that introduce additional ambiguity, such as those beginning with "do you know" or "do you remember," present a particular challenge for children; children may choose to respond to the explicit part of the question (i.e., "I know/remember") rather than the implicit (i.e., "it happened") part of the question (Evans et al., 2017; Wylie et al., 2019). Regarding question scope, both overly broad and overly specific questions are likely to be misinterpreted by children, especially when switching back and forth between the two (Sullivan et al., 2021).

Questions that include certain linguistic terms may elicit confused responses from children as well. For instance, children are more likely to understand the word "tell" as a synonym of "say" rather than as a command, meaning they may misunderstand questions such as "Did your mother tell you what happened?" (Stolzenberg et al., 2020). A child may answer "yes" to this question, thinking they are affirming that their mother "said" what happened. However, jurors may perceive the child's "yes" as an admission that the mother coached or "told" the child what to say about the event. Children also tend to misinterpret attorney questions about sexual abuse mechanics (Sullivan et al., 2021) and exact clothing placement (Stolzenberg et al.,

2017b; Wylie et al., 2021). For example, during questioning about abuse incidents, questions asked about "how" abuse occurred produce responses from children that indicate confusion (Sullivan et al., 2021). On the other hand, "where" questions tend to elicit accurate descriptions of clothing placement from children in actual sexual abuse cases (Stolzenberg et al., 2017b) and experimental research (Wylie et al., 2021). Children's abilities to answer questions in a clear and coherent manner are critical for their perceived credibility, and questioning methods that are considerate of children's response tendencies are most likely to improve their performance.

Implications

There have been several recent advancements in response to the research conducted on children's memory and disclosure processes. Within the broader scope of children's development and well-being, research on the importance of socioemotional support during interviews has inspired revisions to interviewing protocols and sparked interest in developing new methods to increase children's comfort during stressful forensic contexts. For example, concerns about the emotional consequences of testifying have resulted in court accommodations to reduce the potential for distress, such as displaying the child's testimony via Closed-Circuit TV to the courtroom (Protection Of Identity Of Child Witnesses And Victims, 2020). The implementation of Child Advocacy Centers (CACs) across the United States also illustrates acknowledgment of the complexity and specialized training required to properly interview child witnesses.

Researchers are also making strides toward identifying a balance between the acknowledgment of individual differences and standardized practices. Although research suggests demographic variables such as gender and culture are related to children's suggestibility, best practice entails universal interviewing practices. In fact, one of the leading researchers in the area of forensic interviews opined that an increased focus on individual differences shifts attention away from following best practice guidelines that should be beneficial across all children (Lamb et al., 2015). According to Lamb and colleagues (2015), best practice guidelines should supersede considerations of individual difference variables to ensure that the interview is first implemented in a consistent fashion across jurisdictions.

Future Directions

Although our understanding of children's eyewitness testimony has grown in recent decades, there are many areas of research that would benefit from additional inquiry. Researchers have yet to find common ground regarding children's disclosure and recantation rates, suggesting this is an area in dire need of additional exploration. While such topics have proven difficult to empirically study, they have direct consequences regarding the interpretation of victims' postabuse behavior by forensic interviewers, jurors, and other actors within the legal system (see London et al., 2020, for discussion).

Additional research is also needed to verify the impact of controversial forensic interviewing techniques like putative confessions, a technique in which interviewers try to facilitate disclosure by telling the child the alleged perpetrator "told me everything that happened" and wants the child to "tell the truth" (Quas et al., 2018; Stolzenberg et al., 2017a). Although this novel approach appears to improve children's disclosure rates, it may be perceived as a form of deception if the suspect has not actually confessed and increase children's mistrust in adults. Another somewhat less controversial technique is the use of note taking during forensic interviews. Previous work suggests that the often-incomplete nature of interviewers' notes can increase the use of suggestive questioning during forensic interviews (Ceci & Bruck, 2000). However, a recent study found that notes may help interviewers develop prudent follow-up questions that actually improve children's accuracy (Baker et al., 2021). Additional work is needed to discern if there are specific contexts in which novel interviewer techniques may be beneficial.

When considering practices within the courtroom, future work should explore techniques for incentivizing the adoption of empirically based practices among legal actors. For example, courts in the United States still permit children to testify using anatomical dolls ((Protection Of Identity Of Child Witnesses And Victims, 2020).), despite work demonstrating this technique can increase errors in children's memory reports (see Poole & Bruck, 2012, for a review). Recent reviews also suggest that many forensic interviewers do not consistently use empirically based best practices (Johnson et al., 2015; Lamb, 2016) and attorneys often use developmentally inappropriate language when questioning children (Denne et al., 2020; Zajac et al., 2018). Similarly, as researchers develop a better understanding of how involvement in the legal system impacts children's well-being, we must develop actionable interventions in tandem. For example, promising lines of inquiry include the benefits of emotional support dogs in the courtroom (e.g., Spruin et al., 2020). Finally, the recent increase in unaccompanied immigrant children seeking asylum within the United States will likely result in the involvement of many asylum-seeking or refugee children within the legal system. Researchers must help practitioners develop a more nuanced understanding of the challenges of working with this unique population, including language barriers, conflicting cultural identities, trauma exposure, and attachment difficulties (see Quas & Lyon, 2019, for a recent discussion).

Conclusions

Decades after a string of sensational child abuse investigations (e.g., *McMartin v. County of Los Angeles*, 1988; *State of New Jersey v. Margaret Kelly Michaels*, 1993) instigated a new wave of research on child eyewitness testimony, researchers have amassed a far clearer understanding of children's memory, suggestibility, and disclosure processes. As this chapter demonstrates, there is now a growing body of applied work at the intersection of developmental psychology and law that has begun to shape the legal system and allowed researchers to develop evidence-based recommendations for legal practitioners. It is clear that children are capable of providing accurate and useful eyewitness accounts when questioned using developmentally appropriate questioning techniques, both in and out of the courtroom. Justice is best served when children are given the support and guidance needed to accurately voice their experiences, and through the use of evidence-based protocols and resources like CACs, legal practitioners can collect useful forensic information from children while making children's journey through the legal system potentially less challenging. Although many unanswered questions regarding children's eyewitness capabilities remain, developmental researchers have established a strong empirical foundation that can be built up and used to assess current legal practices and, if necessary, establish more efficacious alternatives.

References

Ahern, E. C., Hershkowitz, I., Lamb, M. E., Blasbalg, U., & Karni-Visel, Y. (2019). Examining reluctance and emotional support in forensic interviews with child victims of substantiated physical abuse. *Applied Developmental Science, 23*(3), 227–238.

Ahern, E. C., Hershkowitz, I., Lamb, M. E., Blasbalg, U., & Winstanley, A. (2014). Support and reluctance in the pre-substantive phase of alleged child abuse victim investigative interviews: Revised versus standard NICHD protocols. *Behavioral Sciences and the Law, 32*(6), 762–774.

Alexander, K. W., Quas, J. A., & Goodman, G. S. (2002). Theoretical advances in understanding children's memory for distressing events: The role of attachment. *Developmental Review, 22*, 490–519.

Alexander, K. W., Quas, J. A., Goodman, G. S., Ghetti, S., Edelstein, R. S., Redlich, A. D., Cordon, I. M., & Jones, D. P. H. (2005). Traumatic impact predicts long-term memory for documented child sexual abuse. *Psychological Science, 16*(1), 33–40.

Almerigogna, J., Ost, J., Bull, R., & Akehurst, L. (2007). A state of high anxiety: How non-supportive interviewers can increase the suggestibility of child witnesses. *Applied Cognitive Psychology, 21*(7), 963–974.

Anderson, P. (2002). Assessment and development of executive function (EF) during childhood. *Child Neuropsychology, 8*(2), 71–82.

Astington, J. W. (1993). *The child's discovery of the mind*. Harvard University Press.

Astington, J. W., & Jenkins, J. M. (1999). A longitudinal study of the relation between language and theory-of-mind development. *Developmental Psychology, 35*(5), 1311–1320.

Azzopardi, C., Eirich, R., Rash, C. L., MacDonald, S., & Madigan, S. (2019). A meta-analysis of the prevalence of child sexual abuse disclosure in forensic settings. *Child Abuse & Neglect, 93*, 291–304.

Baker, M., Fessinger, M., McWilliams, K., & Williams, S. (2021). The use of note-taking during forensic interviews: Perceptions and practical recommendations for interviewers. *Developmental Child Welfare, 3*(1), 20–35).

Baker-Ward, L., Gordon, B. N., Ornstein, P. A., Larus, D. M., & Clubb, P. A. (1993). Young children's long-term retention of a pediatric examination. *Child Development, 64*(5), 1519–1533.

Bauer, P. J., & Fivush, R. (1992). Constructing event representations: Building on a foundation of variation and enabling relations. *Cognitive Development, 7*(3), 381–401.

Benia, L. R., Hauck-Filho, N., Dillenburg, M., & Stein, L. M. (2015). The NICHD investigative interview protocol: A meta-analytic review. *Journal of Child Sexual Abuse, 24*(3), 259–279.

Bettenay, C., Ridley, A. M., Henry, L. A., & Crane, L. (2015). Changed responses under cross-examination: The role of anxiety and individual differences in child witnesses. *Applied Cognitive Psychology, 29*(3), 485–491.

Bjorklund, D. F. (1987). How age changes in knowledge base contribute to the development of children's memory: An interpretive review. *Developmental Review, 7*(2), 93–130.

Bjorklund, D. F., Bjorklund, B. R., Brown, R. D., & Cassel, W. S. (1998). Children's susceptibility to repeated questions: How misinformation changes children's answers and their minds. *Applied Developmental Science, 2*(2), 99–111.

Bjorklund, D. F., Dukes, C., & Brown, R. D. (2009). The development of memory strategies. In M. L. Courage & N. Cowan (Eds.), *The development of memory in infancy and childhood* (2nd ed., pp. 145–175). Psychology Press.

Blasbalg, U., Hershkowitz, I., Lamb, M. E., & Karni-Visel, Y. (2021). Adherence to the Revised NICHD Protocol recommendations for conducting repeated supportive interviews is associated with the likelihood that children will allege abuse. *Psychology, Public Policy, and Law, 27*(2) 209–220.

Blasbalg, U., Hershkowitz, I., Lamb, M. E., Karni-Visel, Y., & Ahern, E. C. (2019). Is interviewer support associated with the reduced reluctance and enhanced informativeness of alleged child abuse victims? *Law and Human Behavior, 43*(2), 156–165.

Bloom, L. (1991). *Language development from two to three*. Cambridge University Press.

Bowlby, J. (1982). Attachment and loss: Retrospect and prospect. *American Journal of Orthopsychiatry, 52*(4), 664–678.

Bowles, P. V., & Sharman, S. J. (2014). A review of the impact of different types of leading interview questions on child and adult witnesses with intellectual disabilities. *Psychiatry, Psychology and Law, 21*(2), 205–217.

Brainerd, C. J., & Reyna, V. F. (2005). *The science of false memory*. Oxford University Press.

Brenner, E. (2000). Mood induction in children: Methodological issues and clinical implications. *Review of General Psychology, 4*(3), 264–283.

Bright-Paul, A., Jarrold, C., & Wright, D. B. (2008). Theory-of-mind development influences suggestibility and source monitoring. *Developmental Psychology, 44*(4), 1055–1068.

Brown, D. A., Lewis, C. N., Lamb, M. E., & Stephens, E. (2012). The influences of delay and severity of intellectual disability on event memory in children. *Journal of Consulting and Clinical Psychology, 80*(5), 829–841.

Brubacher, S. P., Poole, D. A., & Dickinson, J. J. (2015). The use of ground rules in investigative interviews with children: A synthesis and call for research. *Developmental Review, 36*, 15–33).

Bruck, M., Ceci, S. J., & Hembrooke, H. (2002). The nature of children's true and false narratives. *Developmental Review, 22*(3), 520–554.

Buckner, J. P., & Fivush, R. (1998). Gender and self in children's autobiographical narratives. *Applied Cognitive Psychology, 12*(4), 407–429.

Bugental, D. B., Blue, J., Cortez, V., Fleck, K., & Rodriguez, A. (1992). Influences of witnessed affect on information processing in children. *Child Development, 63*(4), 774–786.

Burgwyn-Bailes, E., Baker-Ward, L., Gordon, B. N., & Ornstein, P. A. (2001). Children's memory for emergency medical treatment after one year: The impact of individual difference variables on recall and suggestibility. *Applied Cognitive Psychology, 15*(7). S25–S48.

California Family Code § 3042—(2021).Custody of children: Right to custody of a minor child. Available at, https://casetext.com/statute/california-codes/california-family-code/division-8-custody-of-children/part-2-right-to-custody-of-minor-child/chapter-2-matters-to-be-considered-in-granting-custody/section-3042-wishes-of-child-considered#:~:text=Section%203042%20%2D%20Wishes%20of%20child%20considered%20(a)%20If%20a,or%20modifying%20custody%20or%20visitation.

Caprin, C., Benedan, L., Ciaccia, D., Mazza, E., Messineo, S., & Piuri, E. (2016). True and false memories in middle childhood: The relationship with cognitive functioning. *Psychology, Crime & Law, 22*(5), 473–494.

Carter, C. A., Bottoms, B. L., & Levine, M. (1996). Linguistic and socioemotional influences on the accuracy of children's reports. *Law and Human Behavior, 20*(3), 335–357.

Cassel, W. S., Roebers, C. E., & Bjorklund, D. F. (1996). Developmental patterns of eyewitness responses to repeated and increasingly suggestive questions. *Journal of Experimental Child Psychology, 61*(2), 116–133.

Ceci, S. J., & Bruck, M. (1993). Suggestibility of the child witness: A historical review and synthesis. *Psychological Bulletin, 113*(3), 403–439.

Ceci, S. J., & Bruck, M. (1995). *Jeopardy in the courtroom: A scientific analysis of children's testimony*. American Psychology Association.

Ceci, S. J., & Bruck, M. (2000). Why judges must insist on electronically preserved recordings of child interviews. *Court Review, 37*(2), 10–12.

Ceci, S. J., Fitneva, S. A., & Williams, W. M. (2010). Representational constraints on the development of memory and metamemory: A developmental–representational theory. *Psychological Review, 117*(2), 464–495.

Ceci, S., & Friedman, R. D. (2000). The suggestibility of children: Scientific research and legal implications. *Cornell Law Review, 86*(33), 34–108.

Chae, Y., Goodman, G. S., Eisen, M. L., & Qin, J. (2011). Event memory and suggestibility in abused and neglected children: Trauma-related psychopathology and cognitive functioning. *Journal of Experimental Child Psychology, 110*(4), 520–538.

Chae, Y., Goodman, M., Goodman, G. S., Troxel, N., McWilliams, K., Thompson, R. A., Shaver, P. R., & Widaman, K. F. (2018). How children remember the Strange Situation: The role of attachment. *Journal of Experimental Child Psychology, 166*, 360–379.

Chae, Y., Goodman, G. S., Larson, R. P., Augusti, E.-M., Alley, D., VanMeenen, K. M., Culver, M., & Coulter, K. P. (2014). Children's memory and suggestibility about a distressing event: The role of children's and parents' attachment. *Journal of Experimental Child Psychology, 123*, 90–111.

Connolly, D. A., & Lindsay, D. S. (2001). The influence of suggestions on children's reports of a unique experience versus an instance of a repeated experience. *Applied Cognitive Psychology, 15*(2), 205–223.

Conway, M. A., & Pleydell-Pearce, C. W. (2000). The construction of autobiographical memories in the self-memory system. *Psychological Review, 107*(2), 261–288.

Cooper, P., Dando, C., Ormerod, T., Mattison, M., Marchant, R., Milne, R., & Bull, R. (2018). One step forward and two steps back? The "20 Principles" for questioning vulnerable witnesses and the lack of an evidence-based approach. *International Journal of Evidence and Proof, 22*(4), 392–410.

Cragg, L., & Nation, K. (2008). Go or no-go? Developmental improvements in the efficiency of response inhibition in mid-childhood. *Developmental Science, 11*(6), 819–827.

Crone, E. A., Somsen, R. J. M., Zanolie, K., & van der Molen, M. W. (2006). A heart rate analysis of developmental change in feedback processing and rule shifting from childhood to early adulthood. *Journal of Experimental Child Psychology, 95*(2), 99–116.

Curci, A., Bianco, A., & Gudjonsson, G. H. (2017). Verbal ability, depression, and anxiety as correlates of interrogative suggestibility in children exposed to life adversities. *Psychology, Crime & Law, 23*(5), 445–458.

Davis, S. L., & Bottoms, B. L. (2002). Effects of social support on children's eyewitness reports: A test of the underlying mechanism. *Law and Human Behavior, 26*(2), 185 – 215.

Denne, E., Sullivan, C., Ernest, K., & Stolzenberg, S. N. (2020). Assessing children's credibility in courtroom investigations of alleged child sexual abuse: Suggestibility, plausibility, and consistency. *Child Maltreatment, 25*(2), 224–232.

Diamond, A. (2013). Executive functions. *Annual Review of Psychology, 64*(1), 135–168.

Drake, K. E. (2014). The role of trait anxiety in the association between the reporting of negative life events and interrogative suggestibility. *Personality and Individual Differences, 60*, 54–59.

Drake, K. E., Bull, R., & Boon, J. C. W. (2008). Interrogative suggestibility, self-esteem, and the influence of negative life-events. *Legal and Criminological Psychology, 13*(2), 299–307.

Eisen, M. L., Goodman, G. S., Diep, J., Lacsamana, M. T., Olomi, J., Goldfarb, D., & Quas, J. A. (2019). Effects of interviewer support on maltreated and at-risk children's memory and suggestibility. *International Journal on Child Maltreatment: Research, Policy and Practice, 2*, 55–78.

Eisen, M. L., Goodman, G. S., Qin, J., Davis, S., & Crayton, J. (2007). Maltreated children's memory: Accuracy, suggestibility, and psychopathology. *Developmental Psychology, 43*(6), 1275–1294.

Emery, R. E., Otto, R. K., & O'Donohue, W. T. (2005). A critical assessment of child custody evaluations: Limited Science and a flawed system *Psychological Science in the Public Interest, 6*(1), 1–29.

Evans, A. D., & Lyon, T. D. (2012). Assessing children's competency to take the oath in court: The influence of question type on children's accuracy. *Law and Human Behavior, 36*(3), 195–205.

Evans, A. D., Stolzenberg, S. N., & Lyon, T. D. (2017). Pragmatic failure and referential ambiguity when attorneys ask child witnesses "Do You Know/Remember" questions. *Psychol Public Policy Law, 23*, 191–199.

Fabio, R. A., & Capri, T. (2015). Autobiographical memory in ADHD subtypes. *Journal of Intellectual and Developmental Disability, 40*(1), 26–36.

Farrant, K., & Reese, E. (2000). Maternal style and children's participation in reminiscing: Stepping stones in children's autobiographical memory development. *Journal of Cognition and Development, 1*(2), 193–225.

Farrar, M. J., & Goodman, G. S. (1992). Developmental changes in event memory. *Child Development, 63*(1), 173–187.

Farrar, M. J., & Maag, L. (2002). Early language development and the emergence of a theory of mind. *First Language, 22*(2), 197–213.

Fivush, R. (2011). The development of autobiographical memory. *Annual Review of Psychology, 62*(1), 559–582.

Fivush, R., Berlin, L., McDermott Sales, J., Mennuti-Washburn, J., & Cassidy, J. (2003). Functions of parent-child reminiscing about emotionally negative events. *Memory, 11*(2), 179–192.

Fivush, R., Haden, C., & Reese, E. (1996). Remembering, recounting, and reminiscing: The development of autobiographical memory in social context. In D. C. Rubin (Ed.), Remembering our past; Studies in autobiographical memory (pp. 341–359). Cambridge University Press.

Fivush, R., Haden, C. A., & Reese, E. (2006). Elaborating on elaborations: Role of maternal reminiscing style in cognitive and socioemotional development. *Child Development, 77*(6), 1568–1588.

Fivush, R., Kuebli, J., & Clubb, P. A. (1992). The structure of events and event representations: A developmental analysis. *Child Development, 63*(1), 188–201.

Fivush, R., & Nelson, K. (2004). Culture and language in the emergence of autobiographical memory. *Psychological Science, 15*(9), 573–577.

Fivush, R., & Schwarzmueller, A. (1998). Children remember childhood: Implications for childhood amnesia. *Applied Cognitive Psychology, 12*(5), 455–473.

Fivush, R., & Zaman, W. (2014). Gender, subjective perspective, and autobiographical consciousness. In P. J. Bauer & R. Fivush (Eds.), *The Wiley handbook on the development of children's memory* (1st ed., Vol. 2, pp. 586–604). John Wiley & Sons, Ltd.

Flavell, J. H. (1988). The development of children's knowledge about the mind: From cognitive connections to mental representations. In J. W. Astington, P. L. Harris, & D. R. Olson (Eds.), *Developing theories of mind* (pp. 244–267). Cambridge University Press.

Foley, M. A., & Johnson, M. K. (1985). Confusions between memories for performed and imagined actions: A developmental comparison. *Child Development, 56*(5), 1145–1155.

Fritzley, V. H., & Lee, K. (2003). Do young children always say yes to yes-no questions? A metadevelopmental study of the affirmation bias. *Child Development, 74*(5), 1297–1313.

Fritzley, V. H., Lindsay, R. C. L., & Lee, K. (2013). Young children's response tendencies toward yes-no questions concerning actions. *Child Development, 84*(2), 711–725.

Geddie, L., Fradin, S., & Beer, J. (2000). Child characteristics which impact accuracy of recall and suggestibility in preschoolers: Is age the best predictor? *Child Abuse & Neglect, 24*(2), 223–235.

Ghetti, S., Edelstein, R. S., Goodman, G. S., Cordòn, I. M., Quas, J. A., Alexander, K. W., Redlich, A. D., & Jones, D. P. H. (2006). What can subjective forgetting tell us about memory for childhood trauma? *Memory & Cognition, 34*(5), 1011–1025.

Gignac, G. E., & Powell, M. B. (2006). A direct examination of the nonlinear (quadratic) association between intelligence and suggestibility in children. *Applied Cognitive Psychology, 20*(5), 617–623.

Gilstrap, L. L., & Ceci, S. J. (2005). Reconceptualizing children's suggestibility: Bidirectional and temporal properties. *Child Development, 76*(1), 40–53.

Gilstrap, L. L., & Papierno, P. B. (2004). Is the cart pushing the horse? The effects of child characteristics on children's and adults' interview behaviours. *Applied Cognitive Psychology, 18*(8), 1059–1078.

Gobbo, C., Mega, C., & Pipe, M. E. (2002). Does the nature of the experience influence suggestibility? A study of children's event memory. *Journal of Experimental Child Psychology, 81*(4), 502–530.

Goddard, L., Dritschel, B., & Howlin, P. (2014). A preliminary study of gender differences in autobiographical memory in children with an autism spectrum disorder. *Journal of Autism and Developmental Disorders, 44*(9), 2087–2095.

Goodman, G., Hirschman, J., Hepps, D., & Rudy, L. (1991). Children's memory for stressful events. *Merrill-Palmer Quarterly*, *37*(1), 109–157.

Goodman, G. S., Bottoms, B. L., Rudy, L., Davis, S. L., & Schwartz-Kenney, B. M. (2001). Effects of past abuse experiences on children's eyewitness memory. *Law and Human Behavior*, *25*(3), 269–298.

Goodman, G. S., Quas, J. A., Batterman-Faunce, J. M., Riddlesberger, M. M., & Kuhn, J. (1994). Predictors of accurate and inaccurate memories of traumatic events experienced in childhood. *Consciousness and Cognition*, *3*(3–4), 269–294.

Goodman, G. S., Quas, J. A., Batterman-Faunce, J. M., Riddlesberger, M. M., & Kuhn, J. (1997). Children's reactions to and memory for a stressful event: Influences of age, anatomical dolls, knowledge, and parental attachment. *Applied Developmental Science*, *1*(2), 54–75.

Goswick, A. E., Mullet, H. G., & Marsh, E. J. (2013). Suggestibility from stories: Can production difficulties and source monitoring explain a developmental reversal? *Journal of Cognition and Development*, *14*(4), 607–616.

Grandgenett, H. M., Pittenger, S. L., Dworkin, E. R., & Hansen, D. J. (2019). Telling a trusted adult: Factors associated with the likelihood of disclosing child sexual abuse prior to and during a forensic interview. *Child Abuse and Neglect*, *116*(1),104193.

Grysman, A., & Hudson, J. A. (2013). Gender differences in autobiographical memory: Developmental and methodological considerations. *Developmental Review*, *33*(3), 239–272.

Gudjonsson, G. H. (1984). A new scale of interrogative suggestibility. *Personality and Individual Differences*, *5*(3), 303–314.

Gudjonsson, G. H. (2003). *The psychology of interrogations and confessions*. Wiley.

Gudjonsson, G. H., & Clark, N. K. (1986). Suggestibility in police interrogation: A social psychological model. *Social Behaviour*, *1*(2), 83–104.

Gudjonsson, G., Vagni, M., Maiorano, T., & Pajardi, D. (2016). Age and memory related changes in children's immediate and delayed suggestibility using the Gudjonsson Suggestibility Scale. *Personality and Individual Differences*, *102*, 25–29.

Hamond, N. R., & Fivush, R. (1991). Memories of Mickey Mouse: Young children recount their trip to Disneyworld. *Cognitive Development*, *6*, 433–448.

Hays, A., Moniz, S., & Medina, M. P. (2017). *Factors related to recantation in child sexual abuse interviews* (Publication No. 10276893) [Thesis, Brenau University]. ProQuest Dissertations & Theses Global.

Henderson, H. M., Andrews, S. J., & Lamb, M. E. (2019). Examining children in English High Courts with and without implementation of reforms authorized in Section 28 of the Youth Justice and Criminal Evidence Act. *Applied Cognitive Psychology*, *33*(2), 252–264.

Henderson, H. M., & Lyon, T. D. (2020). Children's signaling of incomprehension: The diagnosticity of practice questions during interview instructions. *Child Maltreatment*, *26*(1), 95–104.

Henry, L. A., & Gudjonsson, G. H. (2007). Individual and developmental differences in eyewitness recall and suggestibility in children with intellectual disabilities. *Applied Cognitive Psychology*, *21*(3), 361–381.

Hershkowitz, I., Lamb, M. E., Katz, C., & Malloy, L. C. (2015). Does enhanced rapport-building alter the dynamics of investigative interviews with suspected victims of intra-familial abuse? *Journal of Police and Criminal Psychology*, *30*, 6–14.

Hershkowitz, I., Lanes, O., & Lamb, M. E. (2007). Exploring the disclosure of child sexual abuse with alleged victims and their parents. *Child Abuse and Neglect*, *31*(2), 111–123.

Howe, M. L. (2005). Children (but not adults) can inhibit false memories. *Psychological Science*, *16*(12), 927–931.

Howe, M. L. (2006). Developmentally invariant dissociations in children's true and false memories: Not all relatedness is created equal. *Child Development*, *77*(4), 1112–1123.

Howe, M. L., & Courage, M. L. (2004). Demystifying the beginnings of memory. *Developmental Review*, *24*(1), 1–5.

Howe, M., Courage, M. L., & Edison, S. (2003). When autobiographical memory begins. *Developmental Review*, *23*(4), 471–494.

Howe, M. L., Courage, M. L., & Peterson, C. (1994). How can I remember when "I" wasn't there: Long-term retention of traumatic experiences and emergence of the cognitive self. *Consciousness and Cognition*, *3*(3–4), 327–355.

Howe, M. L., & Wilkinson, S. (2011). Using story contexts to bias children's true and false memories. *Journal of Experimental Child Psychology*, *108*(1), 77–95.

Howe, M. L., Wimmer, M. C., Gagnon, N., & Plumpton, S. (2009). An associative-activation theory of children's and adults' memory illusions. *Journal of Memory and Language*, *60*(2), 229–251.

Hudson, J. A. (1990). Constructive processing in children's event memory. *Developmental Psychology*, *26*(2), 180–187.

Hudson, J. A., Fivush, R., & Kuebli, J. (1992). Scripts and episodes: The development of event memory. *Applied Cognitive Psychology*, *6*(6), 483–505.

Hudson, J., & Nelson, K. (1986). Repeated encounters of a similar kind: Effects of familiarity on children's autobiographic memory. *Cognitive Development*, *1*(3), 253–271.

Imhoff, M. C., & Baker-Ward, L. (1999). Preschoolers' suggestibility: Effects of developmentally appropriate language and interviewer supportiveness. *Journal of Applied Developmental Psychology, 20*(3), 407–429.

Johnson, M. K., Hashtroudi, S., & Lindsay, D. S. (1993). Source monitoring. *Psychological Bulletin, 114*(1), 3–28.

Johnson, M., Magnussen, S., Thoresen, C., Lønnum, K., Burrell, L. V., & Melinder, A. (2015). Best practice recommendations still fail to result in action: A national 10-year follow-up study of investigative interviews in CSA cases. *Applied Cognitive Psychology, 29*(5), 661–668.

Kaczmarczyk, M., Wingenfeld, K., Kuehl, L. K., Otte, C., & Hinkelmann, K. (2018). Childhood trauma and diagnosis of major depression: Association with memory and executive function. *Psychiatry Research, 270*, 880–886.

Karpinski, A. C., & Scullin, M. H. (2009). Suggestibility under pressure: Theory of mind, executive function, and suggestibility in preschoolers. *Journal of Applied Developmental Psychology, 30*(6), 749–763.

Kim, I. K., Kwon, E. S., & Ceci, S. J. (2017). Developmental reversals in report conformity: Psycho-legal implications. *Applied Cognitive Psychology, 31*(2), 128–138.

Klemfuss, J. Z. (2015). Differential contributions of language skills to children's episodic recall. *Journal of Cognition and Development, 16*(4), 608–620.

Klemfuss, J. Z., & Ceci, S. J. (2012). Legal and psychological perspectives on children's competence to testify in court. *Developmental Review, 32*(3), 268–286.

Klemfuss, J. Z., & Olaguez, A. P. (2020). Individual differences in children's suggestibility: An updated review. *Journal of Child Sexual Abuse, 29*(2), 158–182.

Klemfuss, J. Z., Rush, E. B., & Quas, J. A. (2016). Parental reminiscing style and children's suggestibility about an alleged transgression. *Cognitive Development, 40*, 33–45.

Klemfuss, J. Z., & Wang, Q. (2017). Narrative skills, gender, culture, and children's long-term memory accuracy of a staged event. *Journal of Cognition and Development, 18*(5), 577–594.

Kulkofsky, S., & Klemfuss, J. Z. (2008). What the stories children tell can tell about their memory: Narrative skill and young children's suggestibility. *Developmental Psychology, 44*(5), 1442–1456.

Kulkofsky, S., Wang, Q., & Ceci, S. J. (2008). Do better stories make better memories? Narrative quality and memory accuracy in preschool children. *Applied Cognitive Psychology, 22*(1), 21–38.

Lahtinen, H.-M., Laitila, A., Korkman, J., Ellonen, N., & Honkalampi, K. (2020). Children's disclosures of physical abuse in a population-based sample. *Journal of Interpersonal Violence, 37*(5–6), 2011–2036.

Lamb, M. E. (2016). Difficulties translating research on forensic interview practices to practitioners: Finding water, leading horses, but can we get them to drink? *American Psychologist, 71*(8), 710.

Lamb, M. E., Malloy, L. C., Hershkowitz, I., & La Rooy, D. (2015). Children and the law. In M. E. Lamb & R. M. Lerner (Eds.), *Handbook of child psychology and developmental science: Socioemotional processes* (pp. 464–512). John Wiley & Sons.

Lamb, M. E., Orbach, Y., Hershkowitz, I., Esplin, P. W., & Horowitz, D. (2007). Structured forensic interview protocols improve the quality and informativeness of investigative interviews with children: A review of research using the NICHD Investigative Interview Protocol. *Child Abuse & Neglect, 31*, 1201–1231.

Lavoie, J., Wyman, J., Crossman, A. M., & Talwar, V. (2021). Meta-analysis of the effects of two interviewing practices on children's disclosures of sensitive information: Rapport practices and question type. *Child Abuse & Neglect, 113*, 104930.

Lawson, M., Chae, Y., Noriega, I., & Valentino, K. (2021). Parent–child attachment security is associated with preschoolers' memory accuracy for emotional life events through sensitive parental reminiscing. *Journal of Experimental Child Psychology, 209*, 105168.

Leach, C., Powell, M. B., Sharman, S. J., & Anglim, J. (2017). The relationship between children's age and disclosures of sexual abuse during forensic interviews. *Child Maltreatment, 22*(1), 79–88.

Leichtman, M. D., & Ceci, S. J. (1995). The effects of stereotypes and suggestions on preschoolers' reports. *Developmental Psychology, 31*(4), 568–578.

Leichtman, M. D., Pillemer, D. B., Wang, Q., Koreishi, A., & Han, J. J. (2000). When Baby Maisy came to school. *Cognitive Development, 15*(1), 99–114.

Levine, L. J., Burgess, S. L., & Laney, C. (2008). Effects of discrete emotions on young children's suggestibility. *Developmental Psychology, 44*(3), 681–694.

Lindsay, D. S., & Johnson, M. K. (1989). The eyewitness suggestibility effect and memory for source. *Memory & Cognition, 17*(3), 349–358.

Lindsay, D. S., Johnson, M. K., & Kwon, P. (1991). Developmental changes in memory source monitoring. *Journal of Experimental Child Psychology, 52*(3), 297–318.

Loftus, E. F. (1979). *Eyewitness testimony*. Harvard University Press.

London, K., Bruck, M., Ceci, S. J., & Shuman, D. W. (2005). Disclosure of child sexual abuse: What does the research tell us about the ways that children tell? *Psychology, Public Policy, and Law, 11*(1), 194–226.

London, K., Bruck, M., Miller, Q. C., & Ceci, S. J. (2020). Analyzing the scientific foundation of child sexual abuse accommodation syndrome: A reply to Lyon et al. *Behavioral Sciences and the Law*, *38*(6), 648–653.

London, K., Bruck, M., Wright, D. B., & Ceci, S. J. (2008). Review of the contemporary literature on how children report sexual abuse to others: Findings, methodological issues, and implications for forensic interviewers. *Memory*, *16*(1), 29–47.

London, K., Henry, L. A., Conradt, T., & Corser, R. (2013). Suggestibility and individual differences in typically developing and intellectually disabled children. In A. M. Ridley, D. J. La Rooy, & F. Gabbert (Eds.), *Suggestibility in legal contexts: Psychological research and forensic implications* (pp. 129–148). Wiley.

Lyon, T. D. (1999). The new wave of suggestibility research: A critique. *Cornell Law Review*, *84*, 1004–1087.

Lyon, T. D. (2007). False denials: Overcoming methodological biases in abuse disclosure research. In M. E. Pipe, M. E. Lamb, Y. Orbach, & A. C. Cederborg (Eds.), *Child sexual abuse: Disclosure, delay and denial* (pp. 41–63). Psychology Press.

Lyon, T. D. (2011). Assessing the competency of child witnesses: Best practice informed by psychology and law. In M. E. Lamb, D. J. La Rooy, L. C. Malloy, & C. Katz (Eds.), *Children's testimony: A handbook of psychological research and forensic practice* (pp. 69–85). John Wiley & Sons, Ltd.

Lyon, T. D., Wandrey, L., Ahern, E., Licht, R., Sim, M. P. Y., & Quas, J. A. (2014). Eliciting maltreated and nonmaltreated children's transgression disclosures: Narrative practice rapport building and a putative confession. *Child Development*, *85*(4), 1756–1769.

Lyon, T. D., Williams, S., & Stolzenberg, S. N. (2020). Understanding expert testimony on child sexual abuse denial after New Jersey v. J.L.G.: Ground truth, disclosure suspicion bias, and disclosure substantiation bias. *Behavioral Sciences and the Law*, *38*(6), 630–647.

Lyons, K. E., & Ghetti, S. (2010). Metacognitive development in early childhood: New questions about old assumptions. In A. Efklides & P. Misailidi (Eds.), *Trends and prospects in metacognition research* (pp. 259–278). Springer US.

Main, M. (1995). Recent studies in attachment: Overview, with selected implications for clinical work. In S. Goldberg, R. Muir, & J. Kerr (Eds.), *Attachment theory: Social, developmental, and clinical perspectives* (pp. 407–474). Analytic Press.

Malloy, L. C., Brubacher, S. P., & Lamb, M. E. (2011). Expected consequences of disclosure revealed in investigative interviews with suspected victims of child sexual abuse. *Applied Developmental Science*, *15*(1), 8–19.

Malloy, L. C., Lyon, T. D., & Quas, J. A. (2007). Filial dependency and recantation of child sexual abuse allegations. *Journal of the American Academy of Child and Adolescent Psychiatry*, *46*(2), 162–170.

Malloy, L. C., & Mugno, A. P. (2016). Children's recantation of adult wrongdoing: An experimental investigation. *Journal of Experimental Child Psychology*, *145*, 11–21.

Malloy, L. C., Mugno, A. P., Rivard, J. R., Lyon, T. D., & Quas, J. A. (2016). Familial influences on recantation in substantiated child sexual abuse cases. *Child Maltreatment*, *21*(3), 256–261.

Malloy, L. C., Quas, J. A., Lyon, T. D., & Ahern, E. C. (2014). Disclosing adult wrongdoing: Maltreated and nonmaltreated children's expectations and preferences. *Journal of Experimental Child Psychology*, *124*(1), 78–96.

McCrory, E., Henry, L. A., & Happé, F. (2007). Eye-witness memory and suggestibility in children with Asperger syndrome. *Journal of Child Psychology and Psychiatry*, *48*(5), 482–489.

McGuire, K., & London, K. (2020). A retrospective approach to examining child abuse disclosure. *Child Abuse & Neglect*, *99*, 104263.

McMartin v. County of Los Angeles, 202 Cal. App. 3d. (1988).

McNichol, S., Shute, R., & Tucker, A. (1999). Children's eyewitness memory for a repeated event. *Child Abuse & Neglect*, *23*(11), 1127–1139.

McWilliams, K., Goodman, G. S., Lyons, K. E., Newton, J., & Avila Mora, E. (2014). Memory for child sexual abuse information: Simulated memory error and individual differences. *Memory & Cognition*, *42*(1), 151–163.

Melinder, A., Alexander, K., Cho, Y. I. Goodman, G. S., Thoresen, C., Lonnum, K., & Magnussen, S. (2010). Children's eyewitness memory: A comparison of two interviewing strategies as realized by forensic professionals. *Journal of Experimental Child Psychology*, *105*(3), 156–177.

Melinder, A., Endestad, T., & Magnussen, S. (2006). Relations between episodic memory, suggestibility, theory of mind, and cognitive inhibition in the preschool child. *Scandinavian Journal of Psychology*, *47*(6), 485–495.

Melinder, A., Scullin, M. H., Gunnerød, V., & Nyborg, E. (2005). Generalizability of a two-factor measure of young children's suggestibility in Norway and the USA. *Psychology, Crime & Law*, *11*(2), 123–145.

Merritt, K. A., Ornstein, P. A., & Spicker, B. (1994). Children's memory for a salient medical procedure: Implications for testimony. *Pediatrics*, *94*, 17–23.

Milne, R., Sharman, S. J., Powell, M. B., & Mead, S. (2013). Assessing the effectiveness of the cognitive interview for children with severe intellectual disabilities. *International Journal of Disability, Development and Education*, *60*(1), 18–29.

Murachver, T., Pipe, M.-E., Gordon, R., Owens, J. L., & Fivush, R. (1996). Do, show, and tell: Children's event memories acquired through direct experience, observation, and stories. *Child Development, 67*(6), 3029–3044.

Nathanson, R., & Saywitz, K. J. (2003). The effects of the courtroom context on children's memory and anxiety. *Journal of Psychiatry & Law, 31*(1), 67–98.

Nelson, K., & Fivush, R. (2004). The emergence of autobiographical memory: A social cultural developmental theory. *Psychological Review, 111*(2), 486–511.

Nelson, K., & Gruendel, J. M. (1981). Generalized event representations: Basic building blocks of cognitive development. In A. L. Brown & M. E. Lamb (Eds.), *Advances in developmental psychology* (1st ed., Vol. 1, pp. 131–158). Psychology Press.

New Jersey v. J.L.G., 190 A.3d 442 (N.J.) (2018).

Nieto, M., Ros, L., Ricarte, J. J., & Latorre, J. M. (2018). The role of executive functions in accessing specific autobiographical memories in 3- to 6- year-olds. *Early Childhood Research Quarterly, 43*, 23–32.

Nixon, R. D. V., Ball, S. A., Sterk, J., Best, T., & Beatty, L. (2013). Autobiographical memory in children and adolescents with acute stress and chronic posttraumatic stress disorder distrust. *Behaviour Change, 30*(3), 180–198.

Nuttall, A. K., Valentino, K., Comas, M., McNeill, A. T., & Stey, P. C. (2014). Autobiographical memory specificity among preschool-aged children. *Developmental Psychology, 50*(7), 1963–1972.

O'Donohue, W., & Cirlugea, O. (2021). Controlling for confirmation bias in child sexual abuse interviews. *Journal of the American Academy of Psychiatry and the Law, 49*(3), 1–10.

O'Donohue, W., Cummings, C., & Willis, B. (2018). The frequency of false allegations of child sexual abuse: A critical review. *Journal of Child Sexual Abuse, 27*(5), 459–475.

Olaguez, A. P., Castro, A., Cleveland, K. C., Klemfuss, J. Z., & Quas, J. A. (2018). Using implicit encouragement to increase narrative productivity in children: Preliminary evidence and legal implications. *Journal of Child Custody, 15*(4), 286–301.

Ornstein, P. A. (1995). Children's long-term retention of salient personal experiences. *Journal of Traumatic Stress, 8*(4), 581–605.

Ornstein, P. A., Ceci, S. J., & Loftus, E. F. (1998). Adult recollections of childhood abuse: Cognitive and developmental perspectives. *Psychology, Public Policy, and Law, 4*(4), 1025–1051.

Otgaar, H., Howe, M. L., & Muris, P. (2017). Maltreatment increases spontaneous false memories but decreases suggestion-induced false memories in children. *British Journal of Developmental Psychology, 35*(3), 376–391.

Perner, J. (1988). Developing semantics for theories of mind: From propositional attitudes to mental representation. In J. W. Astington, P. L. Harris, & D. R. Olson (Eds.), *Developing theories of mind* (pp. 141–172). Cambridge University Press.

Perner, J., & Ruffman, T. (1995). Episodic memory and autonoetic consciousness: Developmental evidence and a theory of childhood amnesia. *Journal of Experimental Child Psychology, 59*(3), 516–548.

Peters, D. P. (1991). The influence of stress and arousal on the child witness. In J. Doris (Ed.), *The suggestibility of children's recollections* (pp. 60–76). American Psychological Association.

Peterson, C. (1999). Children's memory for medical emergencies: 2 years later. *Developmental Psychology, 35*(6), 1493–1506.

Peterson, C. (2011). Children's memory reports over time: Getting both better and worse. *Journal of Experimental Child Psychology, 109*(3), 275–293.

Peterson, C., & Bell, M. (1996). Children's memory for traumatic injury. *Child Development, 67*(6), 3045–3070.

Peterson, C., Grant, V., & Boland, L. (2005). Childhood amnesia in children and adolescents: Their earliest memories. *Memory, 13*(6), 622–637.

Peterson, C., & McCabe, A. (1983). *Developmental psycholinguistics: Three ways of looking at a child's narrative*. Springer US.

Peterson, C., & Warren, K. L. (2009). Injuries, emergency rooms, and children's memories. In J. A. Quas & R. Fivush (Eds.), *Emotions in memory development: Biological, cognitive, and social considerations* (pp. 60–85). Oxford University Press.

Peterson, C., & Whalen, N. (2001). Five years later: Children's memory for medical emergencies. *Applied Cognitive Psychology, 15*(7), 7–24.

Petherick, W. (2020). Recantations and retractions in child sexual abuse. In I. Bryce & W. Petherick (Eds.), *Child sexual abuse: Forensic issues in evidence, impact, and management* (pp. 435–443). Elsevier.

Poole, D. A., & Bruck, M. (2012). Divining testimony? The impact of interviewing props on children's reports of touching. *Developmental Review, 32*(3), 165–180.

Poole, D. A., & White, L. T. (1991). Effects of question repetition on the eyewitness testimony of children and adults. *Developmental Psychology, 27*(6), 975.

Powell, M. B., Roberts, K. P., Ceci, S. J., & Hembrooke, H. (1999). The effects of repeated experience on children's suggestibility. *Developmental Psychology, 35*(6), 1462–1477.

Powell, M. B., & Thomson, D. M. (2003). Improving children's recall of an occurrence of a repeated event: Is it a matter of helping them to generate options? *Law and Human Behavior, 27*(4), 365–384.

Pressley, M., & Schneider, W. (1997). *Introduction to memory development during childhood and adolescence*. Taylor & Francis.

Principe, G. F., DiPuppo, J., & Gammel, J. (2013). Effects of mothers' conversation style and receipt of misinformation on children's event reports. *Cognitive Development, 28*(3), 260–271.

Principe, G. F., Trumbull, J., Gardner, G., van Horn, E., & Dean, A. M. (2017). The role of maternal elaborative structure and control in children's memory and suggestibility for a past event. *Journal of Experimental Child Psychology, 163*, 15–31.

Protection of Identity of Child Witnesses and Victims, 18 U.S.C. § 3509 (2020)

Public Health Agency of Canada. (2010). *Canadian incidence study of reported child abuse and neglect – 2008: Major findings*.

Quas, J. A., & Lench, H. C. (2007). Arousal at encoding, arousal at retrieval, interviewer support, and children's memory for a mild stressor. *Applied Cognitive Psychology, 21*(3), 289–305.

Quas, J. A., & Lyon, T. D. (2019). *Questioning unaccompanied immigrant children: Lessons from developmental science on forensic interviewing*. SRCD Child Evidence Brief.

Quas, J. A., Rush, E. B., Yim, I. S., & Nikolayev, M. (2014). Effects of stress on memory in children and adolescents: Testing causal connections. *Memory, 22*(6), 616–632.

Quas, J. A., Schaaf, J. M., Alexander, K. W., & Goodman, G. S. (2000). Do you really remember it happening or do you only remember being asked about it happening? Children's source monitoring in forensic contexts. In K. P. Roberts & M. Blades (Eds.), *Children's source monitoring* (1st ed., pp. 197–226). Psychology Press.

Quas, J. A., Stolzenberg, S. N., & Lyon, T. D. (2018). The effects of promising to tell the truth, the putative confession, and recall and recognition questions on maltreated and non-maltreated children's disclosure of a minor transgression. *Journal of Experimental Child Psychology, 166*, 266–279.

Quas, J. A., Wallin, A. R., Papini, S., Lench, H., & Scullin, M. H. (2005). Suggestibility, social support, and memory for a novel experience in young children. *Journal of Experimental Child Psychology, 91*(4), 315–341.

R. v. A. K. (1999), 125, Ontario Court of Appeals 1, Canada

Raes, F., Verstraeten, K., Bijttebier, P., Vasey, M. W., & Dalgleish, T. (2010). Inhibitory control mediates the relationship between depressed mood and overgeneral memory recall in children. *Journal of Clinical Child & Adolescent Psychology, 39*(2), 276–281.

Reese, E. (2002). A model of the origins of autobiographical memory. In J. W. Fagen & H. Hayne (Eds.), *Progress in infancy research* (1st ed., Vol. 2, pp. 1–46). Psychology Press.

Ridley, A. M., & Gudjonsson, G. H. (2013). Suggestibility and individual differences: Psychosocial and memory measures. In A. M. Ridley, F. Gabbert, & D. J. La Rooy (Eds.), *Suggestibility in legal contexts: Psychological research and forensic implications* (pp. 85–106). Wiley Blackwell.

Roberts, K. P., & Powell, M. B. (2001). Describing individual incidents of sexual abuse: A review of research on the effects of multiple sources of information on children's reports. *Child Abuse & Neglect, 25*(12), 1643–1659.

Roebers, C. M., & Schneider, W. (2001). Individual differences in children's eyewitness recall: The influence of intelligence and shyness. *Applied Developmental Science, 5*(1), 9–20.

Roediger, H. L., McDermott, K. B., Pisoni, D. B., & Gallo, D. A. (2004). Illusory recollection of voices. *Memory, 12*(5), 586–602.

Roma, P., Sabatello, U., Verrastro, G., & Ferracuti, S. (2011). Comparison between Gudjonsson Suggestibility Scale 2 (GSS2) and Bonn Test of Statement Suggestibility (BTSS) in measuring children's interrogative suggestibility. *Personality and Individual Differences, 51*(4), 488–491.

Rudy, L., & Goodman, G. S. (1991). Effects of participation on children's reports: Implications for children's testimony. *Developmental Psychology, 27*(4), 527–538.

Rush, E. B., Quas, J. A., Yim, I. S., Nikolayev, M., Clark, S. E., & Larson, R. P. (2014). Stress, interviewer support, and children's eyewitness identification accuracy. *Child Development, 85*(3), 1292–1305.

Salmon, K., Price, M., & Pereira, J. K. (2002). Factors associated with young children's long-term recall of an invasive medical procedure: A preliminary investigation. *Journal of Developmental & Behavioral Pediatrics, 23*(5), 347–352.

Saltzstein, H., Dias, M. da G., & Millery, M. (2004). Moral suggestibility: The complex interaction of developmental, cultural and contextual factors. *Applied Cognitive Psychology, 18*(8), 1079–1096.

Sauerland, M., Brackmann, N., & Otgaar, H. (2018). Rapport: Little effect on children's, adolescents', and adults' statement quantity, accuracy, and suggestibility. *Journal of Child Custody, 15*(4), 268–285.

Saywitz, K. J., Goodman, G. S., Nicholas, E., & Moan, S. F. (1991). Children's memories of a physical examination involving genital touch: Implications for reports of child sexual abuse. *Journal of Consulting and Clinical Psychology, 59*(5), 682–691.

Saywitz, K. J., Larson, R. P., Hobbs, S. D., & Wells, C. R. (2015). Developing rapport with children in forensic interviews: Systematic review of experimental research. *Behavioral Sciences & the Law, 33*, 372–389.

Saywitz, K. J., & Snyder, L. (1996). Narrative elaboration: Test of a new procedure for interviewing children. *Journal of Consulting and Clinical Psychology, 64*(6), 1347–1357.

Saywitz, K. J., Snyder, L., & Lamphear, V. (1996). Helping children tell what happened: A follow-up study of the narrative elaboration procedure. *Child Maltreatment, 1*(3), 200–212.

Saywitz, K. J., Wells, C. R., Larson, R. P., & Hobbs, S. D. (2019). Effects of interviewer support on children's memory and suggestibility: Systematic review and meta-analyses of experimental research. *Trauma, Violence, & Abuse, 20*(1), 22–39.

Skinner, G. C. M., Andrews, S. J., & Lamb, M. E. (2019). The disclosure of alleged child sexual abuse: An investigation of criminal court transcripts from Scotland. *Psychology, Crime and Law, 25*(5), 458–481.

Slonecker, E. M., & Klemfuss, J. Z. (2020). Caregiver-child reminiscing and recounting across contexts. *Cognitive Development, 56*, 100947.

Slonecker, E. M., & Klemfuss, J. Z. (2021, April). *Caregiver-child conversations and autonomy support across contexts* [Poster presentation]. Society for Research in Child Development biennial meeting.

Smith, A. (1997). Development and course of receptive and expressive vocabulary from infancy to old age: Administrations of the Peabody Picture Vocabulary Test, Third edition, and the expressive vocabulary test to the same standardization population of 2725 subjects. *International Journal of Neuroscience, 92*(1–2), 73–78.

Spruin, E., Dempster, T., & Mozova, K. (2020). Facility dogs as a tool for building rapport and credibility with child witnesses. *International Journal of Law, Crime and Justice, 62*, 100407.

State of New Jersey v. Margaret Kelly Michaels, 264 N.J. Super. 579 (1993).

Stolzenberg, S. N., McWilliams, K., & Lyon, T. D. (2017a). Ask versus tell: Potential confusion when child witnesses are questioned about conversations. *Journal of Experimental Psychology: Applied, 23*(4), 447–459.

Stolzenberg, S. N., McWilliams, K., & Lyon, T. D. (2017b). Spatial language, question type, and young children's ability to describe clothing: Legal and developmental implications. *Law and Human Behavior, 41*(4), 398–409.

Stolzenberg, S. N., Morse, S. J., Haverkate, D. L., & Garcia-Johnson, A. M. (2020). The prevalence of declarative and indirect yes/no questions when children testify in criminal cases of child sexual abuse in the United States. *Applied Cognitive Psychology, 34*(1), 194–204.

Sullivan, C., George, S. S., Stolzenberg, S. N., Williams, S., & Lyon, T. D. (2021). Imprecision about body mechanics when child witnesses are questioned about sexual abuse. *Journal of Interpersonal Violence, 37*(13–14), NP12375–NP12397.

Summit, R. C. (1983). The child sexual abuse accommodation syndrome. *Child Abuse & Neglect, 7*(2), 177–193.

Talwar, V., Lee, K., Bala, N., & Lindsay, R. C. L. (2002). Children's conceptual knowledge of lying and its relation to their actual behaviors: Implications for court competence examinations. *Law and Human Behavior, 26*(4), 395–415.

Tashjian, S. M., Goldfarb, D., Goodman, G. S., Quas, J. A., & Edelstein, R. (2016). Delay in disclosure of nonparental child sexual abuse in the context of emotional and physical maltreatment: A pilot study. *Child Abuse & Neglect, 58*, 149–159.

Tobey, A. E., & Goodman, G. S. (1992). Children's eyewitness memory: Effects of participation and forensic context. *Child Abuse & Neglect, 16*(6), 779–796.

Uhl, E. R., Camilletti, C. R., Scullin, M. H., & Wood, J. M. (2016). Under pressure: Individual differences in children's suggestibility in response to intense social influence. *Social Development, 25*(2), 422–434.

Unsworth, N. (2007). Individual differences in working memory capacity and episodic retrieval: Examining the dynamics of delayed and continuous distractor free recall. *Journal of Experimental Psychology: Learning, Memory, and Cognition, 33*(6), 1020–1034.

Unsworth, N., & Engle, R. W. (2007). Individual differences in working memory capacity and retrieval: A cue-dependent search approach. In J. S. Nairne (Ed.), *The foundations of remembering: Essays in honor of Henry L. Roediger, III* (pp. 241–258). Psychology Press.

Unsworth, N., Spillers, G. J., & Brewer, G. A. (2012). The role of working memory capacity in autobiographical retrieval: Individual differences in strategic search. *Memory, 20*(2), 167–176.

U.S. Department of Health & Human Services, Administration for Children and Families, Administration on Children, Youth and Families, Children's Bureau. (2020). *Child maltreatment 2018.*

Vagni, M., Maiorano, T., & Pajardi, D. (2021). Effects of post-traumatic stress disorder on interrogative suggestibility in minor witnesses of sexual abuse. *Current Psychology, 41*, 7681–7694.

Vagni, M., Maiorano, T., Pajardi, D., & Gudjonsson, G. (2015). Immediate and delayed suggestibility among suspected child victims of sexual abuse. *Personality and Individual Differences, 79*, 129–133.

Valentino, K., Bridgett, D. J., Hayden, L. C., & Nuttall, A. K. (2012). Abuse, depressive symptoms, executive functioning, and overgeneral memory among a psychiatric sample of children and adolescents. *Journal of Clinical Child & Adolescent Psychology, 41*(4), 491–498.

Valentino, K., Toth, S. L., & Cicchetti, D. (2009). Autobiographical memory functioning among abused, neglected, and nonmaltreated children: The overgeneral memory effect. *Journal of Child Psychology and Psychiatry, 50*(8), 1029–1038.

Volpini, L., Melis, M., Petralia, S., & Rosenberg, M. D. (2016). Measuring children's suggestibility in forensic interviews. *Journal of Forensic Sciences, 61*(1), 104–108.

Wang, Q. (2004). The emergence of cultural self-constructs: Autobiographical memory and self-description in European American and Chinese children. *Developmental Psychology, 40*(1), 3–15.

Wang, Q. (2006). Relations of maternal style and child self-concept to autobiographical memories in Chinese, Chinese immigrant, and European American 3-year-olds. *Child Development, 77*(6), 1794–1809.

Wang, Q. (2021). The cultural foundation of human memory. *Annual Review of Psychology, 72*, 151–179.

Wang, Q., Koh, J. B. K., Song, Q., & Hou, Y. (2015). Knowledge of memory functions in European and Asian American adults and children: The relation to autobiographical memory. *Memory, 23*(1), 25–38.

Wang, Q., Leichtman, M. D., & Davies, K. I. (2000). Sharing memories and telling stories: American and Chinese mothers and their 3-year-olds. *Memory, 8*, 159–177.

Warren, A. R., & Swartwood, J. N. (1992). Developmental issues in flashbulb memory research: Children recall the Challenger event. In E. Winograd & U. Neisser (Eds.), *Affect and accuracy in recall: Studies of "flashbulb" memories* (pp. 95–120). Cambridge University Press.

Warren, K. L., & Peterson, C. (2014). Exploring parent-child discussions of crime and their influence on children's memory. *Behavioral Sciences & the Law, 32*(6), 686–701.

Welch-Ross, M. K. (1995). Developmental changes in preschoolers' ability to distinguish memories of performed, pretended, and imagined actions. *Cognitive Development, 10*(3), 421–441.

Williams, J. M. G., Barnhofer, T., Crane, C., Hermans, D., Raes, F., Watkins, E., & Dalgleish, T. (2007). Autobiographical memory specificity and emotional disorder. *Psychological Bulletin, 133*(1), 122–148.

World Health Organization. (2018). *European status report on preventing child maltreatment*.

Wylie, B. E., Lyon, T. D., O'Connor, A. M., Aidy, C. L., & Evans, A. D. (2019). Adults' perceptions of children's referentially ambiguous responses. *Psychology, Crime and Law, 25*(7), 729–738.

Wylie, B., Stolzenberg, S. N., McWilliams, K., Evans, A. D., & Lyon, T. D. (2021). Young children's ability to describe intermediate clothing placement. *Child Maltreatment, 26*(1), 87–94.

Young, J. C., & Widom, C. S. (2014). Long-term effects of child abuse and neglect on emotion processing in adulthood. *Child Abuse & Neglect, 38*(8), 1369–1381.

Zajac, R., Westera, N., & Kaladelfos, A. (2018). The "good old days" of courtroom questioning: Changes in the format of child cross-examination questions over 60 years. *Child Maltreatment, 23*(2), 186–195.

Zaragoza, M. S., & Lane, S. M. (1994). Source misattributions and the suggestibility of eyewitness memory. *Journal of Experimental Psychology: Learning, Memory, and Cognition, 20*(4), 934–945.

The Developmental Science of Children in Criminal and Dependency Court

Rayna Enriquez, Lily F. Brown, Gail S. Goodman, Stacy Metcalf, and Jodi A. Quas

> **Abstract**
>
> Children at times play key roles in legal cases as victims of or witnesses to crimes. This is most notable in criminal cases involving alleged sexual abuse. It also occurs with cases involving other types of crimes, both in criminal and juvenile dependency courts, the latter when children are suspected of having been exposed to intrafamilial maltreatment. Involving children is complicated, due to their prior experiences of trauma and their incomplete cognitive or socioemotional development and dependence on family members and legal authorities for assistance. How both the criminal and dependency systems involve children and the consequences of that involvement for children and the pursuit of justice have been heavily debated. This chapter reviews extant research concerning children's participation in criminal and dependency proceedings as victims or witnesses. It includes a discussion of methodological issues that arise when pursuing this research, as well as findings concerning both the socioemotional and attitudinal consequences of children's participation. The chapter closes with suggestions for future research and legal recommendations.
>
> **Key Words:** child victims, legal attitudes, dependency court, criminal court, child maltreatment

In 2005, the Washington State Supreme Court confirmed the conviction of James Woods of two counts of first-degree child molestation after he was accused of sexually abusing his two daughters 4 and 6 years of age. The family had previously encountered the legal system in 2001 when the girls' mother reported to Child Protective Services (CPS) that she found physical signs of abuse (e.g., bruises) on her daughters. CPS investigated, interviewed the girls, determined that the allegations were sufficiently serious, and filed a dependency case. The dependency case ultimately led to the girls' removal from the custody of both biological parents and placement into a foster home. After staying there for a short period of time, the girls began to exhibit sexualized behavior, such as rubbing in between dolls' legs while saying "hold still," "be a good girl," and "stop daddy." The foster parent brought this to the attention of the authorities, and prosecutors eventually decided to criminally charge Woods with two counts of child molestation. After a 3-day pretrial hearing, both girls were deemed competent to testify in the criminal trial, which led to Woods's conviction. Woods appealed on the grounds that the girls' testimony should not have been admitted. The court of appeals and State Supreme

Court disagreed, ruling that the girls were able to provide clear and informative accounts of the abuse. The conviction stood.

The *State of Washington v. Woods* (2005) case illustrates the complex ways in which children who have been subjected to maltreatment may become involved in the legal system in the United States, and how that involvement can last for many years. The girls took part in CPS investigations that led to their involvement in the dependency[1] court system, and in law enforcement investigations that led to their criminal system involvement. The physical abuse was discovered and later corroborated based on physical evidence, whereas the sexual abuse was identified and its veracity based largely on the children's own words.

How being enmeshed in these "systems" affects children has been the focus of considerable legal and scholarly debate (Block et al., 2010; Goodman et al., 1992; Hershkowitz, 2009; Melton & Berliner, 1992; Quas, Cooper, & Wandrey, 2009), and a small but important body of research has been conducted that provides relevant empirical data. In this chapter, we discuss the research and its conclusions. We consider effects that may emerge when children come into contact with the criminal courts (i.e., those concerned with guilt or innocence of adults accused of breaking the law) and also with the dependency courts (i.e., those concerned with child protection, largely in intrafamilial cases of abuse or neglect). We focus on children's legal experiences and the possible emotional and attitudinal consequences of them. We define "children" as those spanning across childhood until 18 years of age. We also focus primarily on legal involvement in the United States and use the legal terms common to U.S. states. We recognize that legal procedures and children's experiences vary across countries, and when relevant research is available from other countries regarding the effects of legal involvement on children, we describe that here as well. Nonetheless, caution should be taken when attempting to interpret findings or apply conclusions broadly.

Methodological Considerations When Studying Children's Legal Involvement

Before describing research on children's legal experiences and their possible effects, it is important to understand methodological issues that arise when attempting to document such experiences and draw conclusions about how they affect children. Such issues begin in the execution of the research itself, given the highly vulnerable population—victimized children immersed in the legal system—on whom the research is taken. Special precautions are needed to ensure that the children are protected when they take part in the research. Access to the children is often limited and, when data are collected, samples may or may not be representative of the population as a whole (e.g., if only children who are functioning well, for instance, are referred for a study). Thus, careful attention needs to be paid to recruitment, data collection, and ultimately the generalizability of any conclusions generated, while also ensuring careful and ethical consideration of the unique needs and vulnerabilities in the children themselves.

---

[1] Writing of this chapter was supported in part by grants to Gail S. Goodman from the National Science Foundation (1424420 and 2037583) and the National Institute of Justice (2013-IJ-CX-0104), and by grants to Jodi A. Quas from the National Science Foundation (SES 1921187) and from UCI (NIH UL1 TR001414). Any opinions, findings, conclusions, or recommendations do not necessarily reflect the views of any of the funders. Correspondence concerning this manuscript should be addressed to Gail S. Goodman, Department of Psychology, University of California, 1 Shields Avenue, Davis, CA 95616 USA (ggoodman@ucdavis.edu) or Jodi A. Quas, Department of Psychological Science, University of California, Irvine, CA (jquas@uci.edu). The name of this court varies depending on the state within the United States. In different states, it is referred to as family court, juvenile court, or dependency court. Our research into these types of courts is most common in California and Florida, and both use the latter term. Thus, we refer to these types of courts as "dependency courts."

Even with this attention and ethical protections, the recruitment process itself can be challenging. Social workers, prosecuting attorneys, and others are vigilant in protecting maltreated children, including from research studies. Attorneys and judges do not readily give researchers access to case files or the courtroom. Dependency cases are particularly likely to have case files sealed. In general, legal professionals want to be convinced that the research will *directly* benefit their clients. If one can obtain these professionals' approvals, informed consent must still be secured. The presiding court judge can at times provide legal permission or consent for research participation if the judge can be convinced of the value of the research. Or, if the child has not been removed from the home, parents can be approached. Their willingness to support the research, or even acknowledge the crime, can be affected by their relationship to the alleged offender (Malloy et al., 2007). For example, in one investigation of child victims' experiences in criminal court, families in intrafamilial (i.e., incest) were less likely than families in extrafamilial cases to agree to participate (Goodman et al., 1992).

Several strategies may be useful in overcoming recruitment challenges. One is to carry out research in places with less restrictive protections and to rely heavily on observational research. For instance, in Florida, most dependency cases are generally open to the public (Fla. Stat. § 39.507(2)), meaning that, for example, researchers can attend and listen to hearings with few legal restrictions precluding them from doing so. It is still beneficial to inform court professionals about ongoing activities and secure their support, but that is much easier when laws are more permissive. Another approach is to partner with legal professionals, such as attorneys or social service workers, and provide assistance in exchange for access (e.g., to deidentified data). Such partnerships take time to develop but can be mutually beneficial given the common goal of intervening and protecting vulnerable children.

Insofar as data are collected, another key issue that arises is that of random assignment. Ethically, one cannot (and would not want to) randomly assign children to maltreatment or legal involvement groups to ascertain how such experiences "affect" children. Therefore, the cause of any group differences or evident outcomes is less clear and may or may not be due to the variables of interest. For instance, findings indicating that children fare poorly following participation in criminal proceedings do not mean that the proceedings themselves "caused" children's poor functioning. Instead, traumas that occurred prior to the case may be playing a key role in leading to specific outcomes. Further, within a sample of legally involved children, differences observed between groups with different experiences (e.g., testifiers versus not, those in cases that end in guilt or acquittals) cannot necessarily be attributed to those experiences, given that other factors (e.g., age, type of evidence, defendant confession) could be confounding and contributing to the observed differences. Because of these confounds, causal inferences about "effects" of specific experiences cannot be reliably determined.

A few research teams have found creative ways to address questions of causality. For example, in a large investigation of the consequences of criminal court involvement on children, Goodman et al. (1992) matched groups of testifiers and non-testifiers on important variables such as age, gender, and initial mental health and then compared functioning between the groups, creating a quasi-experimental design. Other researchers have relied on statistical techniques to adjust for potentially confounding variables (Quas et al., 2005; Runyan et al., 1988; Whitcomb et al., 1991). Propensity score matching has been employed in studies of legally involved samples (e.g., comparisons of outcomes between juvenile offenders who are and are not formally processed following their first contact with the authorities; e.g., Hobbs et al., 2021; Loughran et al., 2010). Propensity score matching is a statistical approach that matches groups a priori. Although this type of matching may help to minimize selection bias in making comparisons about outcomes linked to those groups (Rosenbaum, 2010), it does not fully solve the problem of lack of random assignment (Shadish, 2013).

With time and trust, teams can take advantage of opportunities that arise and allow for some types of random assignment to be implemented (e.g., Goldfarb et al., 2023; Lamb et al., 2007). Finally, experimental analogs of courtroom procedures have permitted tests of courtroom modifications. Random assignment can then be achieved (e.g., Goodman et al., 1998; Nathanson & Saywitz, 2003) and causal inferences drawn.

With these approaches, researchers have been able to generate valuable information about the likely effects of specific aspects of legal involvement and make stronger recommendations about potential interventions. Moreover, when findings using the various methodologies converge on the same patterns, stronger confidence in the conclusions can be drawn, and the courts can be given even more concrete guidance and recommendations regarding how to proceed in a way that facilitates justice and protects children.

Children in Criminal Court

To date, the most salient concerns and debates about children's involvement in the legal system have focused on the criminal courts, that is, when children have been victims of or witnesses to crime and, as a result, become immersed in cases against the alleged perpetrators. Children may be bystander witnesses or victims, and either way, can provide evidence in the case. Regardless of which, though, children themselves arguably are not the central participant. From a legal perspective, in criminal court actions, the defendant is primary, given that their liberty is at stake. Defendants have U.S. constitutional rights at trial (e.g., the Sixth Amendment gives defendants the right to "confront," meaning cross-examine, witnesses at trial); child witnesses and child victims do not have similar U.S. constitutional rights, although some state constitutions include victim rights.

Debates nonetheless focus on whether legal participation by children constitutes a form of secondary victimization, adding to the trauma of the crime itself (Murtha, 2021; Schudson, 1987), or whether the short-term distress experienced by children is inevitable for all witnesses in criminal cases (e.g., Shore, 1985). The dilemma is exemplified in regard to face-to-face confrontation, a right protected not only by the U.S. Constitution's Sixth Amendment but also by several international doctrines (e.g., Section 1, Article 6[3] (2007) in the European Convention on Human Rights). It is a facet of criminal proceedings often considered necessary for justice: According to the U.S. adversarial legal system, it is believed that facing the accuser compels witnesses to speak the truth and permits fact finders to assess witness credibility.

Yet, facing a defendant, especially one who threatened or harmed a victim, or one to whom loyalty is felt, can be quite distressing when the victim is a child (Hobbs & Goodman, 2018; Hobbs et al., 2014). Developmental differences in coping (e.g., Compas et al., 2017) and reasoning about the legal system (e.g., Goldfarb et al., 2017; Grisso et al., 2003) may limit children's understanding of why they must testify. This lack of understanding could lead to challenges for a child if and when the child ends up in court as well as to negative consequences that in some cases may last for years (Quas et al., 2005).

It is worth noting that debates surrounding a child's understanding of the need to testify and subsequent adjustment is largely a U.S.-centered controversy. Although the U.S. Constitution formally enshrines the Sixth Amendment right to face-to-face confrontation, other countries, such as the United Kingdom, Finland, Norway, and Sweden, do not place this same emphasis on the adversarial approach or the explicit need for face-to-face confrontation. Instead, these countries incorporate a variety of approaches to decrease the possible distress a child may experience when providing testimony and possibly seeing the defendant

(Hobbs et al., 2014). Virtually all legal systems have the right to counsel and, in varying degrees, confrontation (van Koppen & Penrod, 2003). But countries unhampered by the Sixth Amendment are more apt to bend to individual children's need for personal security, utilizing alternative options for child witnesses to provide accurate statements to authorities and effective testimony outside the presence of accused perpetrators (Hobbs & Goodman, 2018; Melinder et al., 2021).

The Criminal Court Process

In considering the developmental effects of criminal court involvement on child victims, it is important to understand the basic format of criminal court. Here, we review that format, with an emphasis on how the adversarial court system in the United States emphasizes not just face-to-face confrontation but also cross-examination during that confrontation as key facets (Hobbs & Goodman, 2018). We also primarily emphasize criminal cases involving alleged child sexual abuse, as these are the types of criminal case in which children testify most often (Cross & Whitcomb, 2017; Goodman et al., 1999; Plotnikoff & Woolfson, 2004). However, children also appear as victims or witnesses in other types of criminal cases, such as domestic violence, robberies, thefts, murder, trafficking, and even border crossings.

As Quas and Goodman (2012) point out, how a criminal case progresses depends on a host of factors, some of which include the specifics of the crime itself, the evidence available (e.g., medical evidence, which is infrequent in child sexual abuse cases), and relevant state or federal laws. In general, however, when authorities suspect a crime has occurred, an investigation takes place. Law enforcement or social services may take an initial statement from a child and gather basic details about the crime and perpetrator's identity. This may provide some indight as to whether a child is in current danger of intrafamilial harm, which could trigger a dependency case that would then unfold possibly concurrent with the criminal investigation, as we discuss later.

Children are now regularly interviewed, at times following their initial statements, in more depth at Children's Advocacy Centers (CACs). When the evidence is sufficient and the child appears credible, the alleged perpetrator will be charged and an arraignment hearing is held (without the child's presence) in which the defendant enters an initial plea. Assuming the plea is "not guilty," a preliminary hearing (e.g., in California) or a grand jury hearing (e.g., in New York) is scheduled shortly afterward to demonstrate that a crime was committed and there is sufficient evidence that the defendant may have been involved to proceed to trial. In some of these, a child may be required to testify. Alternatively, or at times in addition, a videotape of an interview with a child can be viewed or the child's "disclosure recipient" (e.g., a nonoffending parent, a teacher, the forensic interviewer) might be required to repeat the child's words, providing "hearsay." Although a defendant's Sixth Amendment constitutional right largely guarantees face-to-face confrontation, defendant constitutional rights typically refer to the trial itself, not to the preliminary hearing.

Next is a discovery phase, during which the prosecutor and defense attorney gather evidence to support their claims. Either at the time of the preliminary hearing or during discovery, if requested by either party, a child may be subjected to evaluations by the judge (e.g., competency hearings) or may be deposed to provide statements. The child may also be interviewed by various professionals (e.g., detectives, attorneys, psychologists) about the crime.

Following discovery, is the next formal hearing, the trial itself, although the date, which is set at the preliminary hearing, is often postponed via continuances, sometimes taking place on the day the trial is supposed to commence. Once the trial begins, continuances can and often do still occur. Continuances mean that a child may have appeared at the courthouse, ready to testify in the case, with all the anxieties and nightmares involved, only to be sent home and required to return on a different day, likely months later, sometimes repeatedly. During the trial, the child may testify under both direct and cross-examination with the defendant a short distance away, a legal experience about which children express great distress (Goodman et al., 1992). Typically, a jury of adult strangers will also be present to evaluate the child's credibility and deliberate on the verdict. In recent years, some child witnesses have the benefit of a support dog hidden from the jury at the child's feet behind the witness stand (Burd & McQuiston, 2019).

Jurors must evaluate the child victims' credibility, often with little knowledge of child maltreatment dynamics. Jurors may hold biases and stereotypes (Goodman-Delahunty et al., 2010; Stolzenberg & Lyon, 2014) or struggle to understand children's reluctance to disclose. St. George et al. (2020), for example, analyzed the types of questions jurors submitted to the court during child sexual abuse criminal trials involving alleged victims ages 5–17 years of age. The jurors asked about such topics as the abuse dynamics, the context surrounding the alleged abuse, and children's disclosure processes, with the questions often reflecting common misconceptions about child sexual abuse, such as whether it is credible to delay disclosure or maintain contact with an alleged perpetrator.

If the defendant is found guilty at the trial, a sentencing hearing will be scheduled, during which the judge will decide on the appropriate punishment. As part of this determination, the child may be asked to testify (again), that is, to provide a victim statement concerning the emotional and other consequences of the sexual assault. Psychologists may also testify about the consequences of the crime on the child or to justify particular punishment of or leniency for the defendant (e.g., to mitigate a sentence because the defendant had been a child victim of abuse). Although the average time between the acceptance for prosecution and the eventual resolution of a criminal case involving a child victim ranges from a year (mainly for cases that are "plea bargained out," which occur in the vast majority of prosecutions) to 2 years (e.g., for cases that go to trial), some cases take longer (Stroud et al., 2000). Furthermore, if a guilty verdict is reached, defendants can (and most do) file an appeal, arguing that some facet of the process violated their constitutional rights to justice. Although the child will not participate directly in the appeal process, in the rare case that the verdict is overturned on appeal, the prosecutor can decide to retry the case and the process starts over again.

During this legal involvement, there are age differences in the experience: Older compared to younger children endure more repeated interviews, are more likely to testify, are more likely to testify for longer durations, and experience harsher questioning when they do appear in criminal court (Goodman et al., 1992; Whitcomb et al., 1991). In contrast, younger children are exposed to a greater number of court continuances, receive less maternal support, are more likely for their legal cases to lack corroborative evidence, and are more likely for their cases to be dismissed or end in an acquittal (Quas & Goodman, 2012). These age differences may result in part from younger children being (or perceived of as being) less complete, less consistent, and more suggestible in their disclosures and forensic interviews (Quas et al., 2007; see Slonecker et al., this volume), making defendants less likely to plea bargain and jurors less likely to reach a guilty verdict.

Socioemotional Outcomes for Children in Criminal Court

Studies on children in criminal court actions concentrate on child victims of sexual abuse, not because other types of cases are unimportant, but because of the relative frequency of proceedings involving charges of child sexual abuse (Cross & Whitcomb, 2017; Goodman et al., 1999). In such cases, children are the critical witnesses. In the United States, studies further focus on whether testifying face to face with the defendant leads to adverse outcomes for children, the defendant, or society, given this rather unique constitutional requirement. This focus stems from legal controversy regarding possible procedural alterations to reduce the need for children to testify while facing the defendant, which is particularly distressing for child victims (Goodman et al., 1992; Hobbs et al., 2014).

In one longitudinal study (Goodman et al., 1992; Quas et al., 2005), child victims' experiences during criminal prosecutions were studied in relation to child, family, abuse, and legal factors. Specifically, Goodman et al. (1992) followed 218 child victims of sexual assault during their participation in criminal prosecutions that took place in the 1980s. When the case was referred for prosecution, detailed information was collected regarding the children, their families, and the offenses that led to the legal case. Of importance methodologically, the Child Behavior Checklist (CBCL; Achenbach, 1991), a gold standard measure of behavioral adjustment, was completed by a nonoffending parent once the case was referred. This permitted the researchers to assess the children's emotional well-being after the sexual assault but before the court cases began. A subsample of the children (4–17 years old) testified in preliminary hearings, trials, and/or sentencing hearings. Among the remaining children who were also involved in child sexual abuse prosecutions but did not testify, a subset was selected that matched the testifiers on key demographic and abuse characteristics and mental health (their CBCL scores) at the start of the case. The testifiers were interviewed immediately before and right after their court appearances, and they were observed while testifying. All children's emotional well-being was again assessed with the CBCL at various points later, including after the case ended, allowing for important comparisons in functioning between the testifiers and matched nontestifiers.

Among the key findings were first, at the start of the prosecution, children in general evidenced considerable emotional disturbance, as reported by their parents, likely due to the combined effects of the sexual abuse, disclosing it to authorities, and beginning the prosecution, along with preexisting problems (which may have been exacerbated by the prosecution). Second, Child Advocacy Centers did not exist at the time of the original study, so most children were interviewed by law enforcement, who were unlikely to have been trained in child-friendly questioning approaches. Moreover, many of these children were interviewed multiple times, an experience considered quite distressing to children (Tedesco & Schnell, 1987). Third, children who testified showed greater emotional distress than those who did not, especially if they testified multiple times, if they lacked maternal support, or if their cases lacked corroborative evidence. Similar findings, that is, child sexual abuse victims evidencing adverse effects of testifying, particularly when they do so more than once, have been uncovered in other studies (Elmi et al., 2018; Runyan, as cited in Whitcomb et al., 1991), as have studies reporting considerable difficulty in children's functioning when they lack caregiver support (e.g., Liang et al., 2006; Malloy & Lyon, 2006; Sas, 1993).

Analyses of the interviews with children before they testified revealed that children's greatest fears involved testifying in front of the defendant (see also Randell et al., 2018). Children expressed concerns about reprisals (e.g., threats against themselves or their loved ones); and that the person might get off scot-free, possibly moving back in next door or within easy reach of the child, the child's loved ones, or other children. Some defendants had violent histories, increasing the children's concerns. Children also reported fears about being cross-examined, being called a liar, or having to describe sexual details in front of strangers. Multiple parents reported that their children had suffered nightmares, had been vomiting, and were terrified. Of importance, children who were the most frightened had the most trouble answering the prosecutors' questions, suggesting that their distress not only affected their well-being but also their ability to communicate, the latter of which has direct implications for the truth-seeking function of a trial, which requires clear communication and reporting from children. Based in part on this finding, the U.S. Supreme Court now permits an exception to the face-to-face confrontation clause of the Sixth Amendment for children who, in child sexual abuse cases, are so traumatized by facing the defendant that they cannot reasonably communicate at trial. The judge is given the power to decide the testimonial needs for closed-circuit television (CCTV) in such cases (Murtha, 2021).

Quas et al. (2005), in a follow-up of the original Goodman et al. (1992) sample, reinterviewed 174 of the former victims a decade later. Children who were involved in severe abuse cases (e.g., closer child–perpetrator relationship, more invasive sexual contact, longer duration of abuse) and who testified more than once reported, as young adults, more defensive avoidance symptoms, which are trauma symptoms that reflect not wanting to think about the past. Note that behavioral adjustment when the case was initially referred for the prosecution was statistically adjusted for in the Quas et al. follow-up study. Thus, significant associations between testifying in childhood and outcomes in adulthood emerged even when behavioral adjustment at the start of the prosecution was taken into consideration.

However, studies exist that have *not* found significant associations between testifying and mental health (e.g., Berliner & Conte, 1995; Henry, 1997; Sas, 1993). For example, Berliner and Conte (1995) reported that the anticipation of testifying was associated with increased distress, even though the act of testifying itself was not traumatic. Indeed, in the Goodman et al. (1992) study, some children emerged from the courtroom saying it was not as bad as they had anticipated (although one young child expressed relief that the defendant was not going to kill her, but rather only kill her mother!). Further, Quas et al. (2005) found evidence that, under certain conditions, not testifying predicted poor outcomes. That is, although testifying repeatedly predicted defensive avoidance among individuals who experienced severe abuse, not testifying predicted defensive avoidance when the abuse was less severe. In the latter cases, children may need to have some clear acknowledgment that not only did the abuse occur but also that the abuse was a sufficient wrong as to warrant public intervention. Testifying may provide such acknowledgment, at least in part. Quas and Goodman (2012) note:

> Should this finding replicate in the future, it implies that uniform bans on children testifying are not only unrealistic, but overly simplistic in attempting to address potential mental health consequences of testifying: At times, even though in the short-term children may be distressed by testifying, it may be better in the long-run for them to have had their day in court. (p. 401)

Legal Questioning of Children in Criminal Court

When children take the stand in criminal court, they will be questioned about salient and potentially distressing experiences, at times committed by loved ones, and possibly about conversations about those experiences afterward (Brown-Schmidt & Benjamin, 2018; Wu et al., 2021). Children are rarely developmentally equipped for the challenges associated with such questioning (Goldfarb & Goodman, 2014). They have limited linguistic abilities to understand the complex and nuanced legal phrasing of questions and limited understanding of legal procedures, and they are highly dependent on adults to help guide their reporting (e.g., Bowlby, 1980; Goodman et al., 1992; Saywitz et al., 1999). Thus, it is important for attorneys to appreciate children's ability to understand pragmatic speech and question types used in courtroom questioning (Evans et al., 2017).

Prosecutors' and defense attorneys' questions. Of note, in court, and in contrast to forensic interviewing contexts, which emphasize the value of open-ended and follow-up prompts questions to elicit detailed narratives from children (Andrews et al., 2015; Evans et al., 2017), prosecutors and defense attorneys ask primarily closed-ended questions (Andrews et al., 2015). Prosecutors may be encouraged to use open-ended questions to prompt child victims to recount their experiences, but prosecutors may also have very clear legal needs regarding what should be described (indeed, preparation and practice with witnesses of all ages before they testify is common practice). Prosecutors may be concerned about children going "off script" and providing irrelevant or potentially conflicting information. Closed-ended questions may, therefore, help guide children's testimony. Prosecutors can request permission from the court to ask leading questions when children are unable to answer open-ended questions (Myers, 2011).

Most concerns about legal questioning, though, have focused on defense attorneys' questioning during cross-examination and its potential effects on children's well-being, but also accuracy and credibility. A primary goal of cross-examination, in general, is to raise doubts about and discredit a witness's testimony, and there is no exception when the witness is a child. Defense attorneys often ask, "That's not what you told the police, is it?" or "Are you sure about that?" (Andrews et al., 2015). Evidence suggests that such strategies are effective: Righarts et al. (2015), for example, found that children's reports decreased significantly during cross-examination relative to direct examination, and children were more likely to recant true experiences during cross-examination. Children also changed their earlier testimony even when their memory remained intact (a pattern also seen in adults during cross-examination; Zajac & Cannon, 2009). It should be noted though that cross-examination has been shown in a mock trial study to increase disclosures of transgressions in children coached to lie and deny them (Fogliati & Bussey, 2015). Whether such would also occur in an actual trial when children were being questioned about a criminal experience is not known.

As a final note, in rare instances in the United States, defendants elect to use their constitutional right to represent themselves in court rather than be represented by a defense attorney, which could mean that the defendant would be able to question witnesses, including potentially a child victim, directly, even if the defendant is violent and accused of murder, child sexual abuse, or other crimes (Hobbs & Goodman 2018; Murtha, 2021). Seeing the defendant in the courtroom and cross-examination are two of the most distressing components of the legal process for children (Eastwood & Patton, 2002; Hobbs et al., 2014; Randell et al., 2018). The combination of these factors—being cross-examined by that very defendant—would almost certainly combine to exacerbate that distress (Hobbs & Goodman, 2018) and may well undermine children's ability to withstand the inquiry. Such a possibility has yet to be tested scientifically and is likely to be quite rare. However, one child experienced such a situation in the Goodman et al. (1992) study. She described it as one of the worst experiences of her life.

Alternate forms of testimony. In light of the distress that recounting traumas like sexual abuse in open court surrounded by strangers in formal attire can cause, provisions and laws across countries now permit children to testify via a number of alternative formats. For instance, the United Kingdom allows child witnesses to be cross examined via CCTV. With this format, the child is available to answer questions, and the judge, attorneys, and jury can see the child, but the child cannot see them. CCTV is also permissible in limited circumstances in the United States, for instance, if the child is so distressed as to be unable to reasonably communicate. However, its actual use may be rare and generally only occurs in child sexual abuse cases (*Maryland v. Craig*, 1990; but see Murtha, 2021). Some Scandinavian countries allow prerecorded forensic interviews to be trial evidence. During the interviews, the judge, prosecutor, and defense can pose questions, but the questioning of the child is via a trained police interviewer who has built rapport with the child. The interview is recorded and entered into evidence at trial (McWilliams et al., 2014). Other special measures proposed and/or used in other countries include screens to shield children while testifying from viewing the defendant.

Despite widespread usage of CCTV in various countries, researchers are concerned that out-of-court testimony lacks the immediacy and emotional impact of live courtroom testimony (Landström et al., 2007; McAuliff & Kovera, 2012). For example, Goodman et al. (1998) and Orcutt et al. (2001) found that children testifying through CCTV were seen by mock jurors as less accurate, less believable, less consistent, less confident, less attractive, and less intelligent than children testifying live in court. At the same time, the mock jurors were no better at determining truthfulness (children who lied versus told the truth) when children testified live in court or through CCTV (Orcutt et al., 2001). Whether the other alternate forms of testimony from children affect fact finders' decisions has not been as extensively studied, although, given their frequency, such investigations would be particularly valuable. Also important will be assessments of children's decisions and desires about testifying. That is, for children, more important than the mode of giving evidence may be for children to have a say in the process by being involved in the decision regarding how to provide their evidence in court. In an early investigation of Australian children involved in criminal proceedings because of sexual abuse, Cashmore (1991) reported that children's observed emotional state and performance as witnesses were influenced more by whether they were able to use CCTV when they wanted to than by whether they did or did not use CCTV. By having a choice, child witnesses are given the power to shape their court experience in the way that best suits their own needs and comfort level.

Attitudinal Outcomes for Children in Criminal Court

What children know and how they feel about the legal system can affect their beliefs about justice. Those beliefs are related to their willingness to engage with law enforcement and the courts (Tyler, 1980; Tyler & Lind, 2001) in a manner similar to that observed in adults (Tyler, 2006), separating feelings about the process (e.g., whether they were treated fairly) and the outcome (whether they like the ultimate decision). Most studies with child victims of sexual abuse reveal that case outcome is most important. Children feel more negative about their courtroom experiences and the legal system generally when the case outcome is lenient (e.g., Goodman et al., 1992; Randell et al., 2018; Sas, 1991). These associations hold both shortly after a case ended and many years later, demonstrating remarkably consistent feelings about the legal experience. Quas et al. (2005) asked young adults who had been involved as children in sexual abuse prosecutions about their perceptions of the fairness of the criminal court, police practices, juvenile courts, and the legal system as a whole. Even when other crucial variables were statistically adjusted for (e.g., age, initial mental health, abuse characteristics), less severe sentences for the defendant predicted more negative feelings.

Yet, children's attitudes can be shaped by additional features of their experiences. For instance, greater abuse severity predicts more negative legal attitudes (Goodman et al., 1992), as does experiencing numerous interviews (Goodman et al., 1992; Tedesco & Schnell, 1987; but see Quas et al., 2005). Testifying at times predicts negative attitudes, but so does not testifying. For instance, Tedesco and Schnell (1987) reported that testifying was associated with more negative perceptions of the legal system several years later (e.g., testifiers were more likely to indicate that the legal system was not helpful, that they felt ambivalent or conflicted about the legal case). Yet, other studies have found that children who did not testify felt worse about not having done so when the case outcome was not guilty (either through a plea bargain or court decision) than when the outcome was guilty (Goodman et al., 1992). Negative feelings about not having testified were also more likely in children with a prior abuse history than in children without such a history. Former victims who had not testified as children have also been shown to continue to feel negatively years later: They reported that the legal system was less fair than the victims who had testified (Quas et al., 2005). These findings are consistent with the procedural justice literature, which suggests that not being part of the process of legal decision making is associated with more negative perceptions of fairness (Tyler, 2006).

Finally, children's age has implications for their legal attitudes. Older children are at increased risk for negative legal attitudes. Older children may recognize the significance of their legal case for themselves, their family, other potential victims, and the defendant (Cashmore & Bussey, 1989; Melton & Berliner, 1992). This recognition may lead to older children's more negative attitudes about the case and their involvement in it. Also, older children are treated more harshly when they testify in court and are more likely to have their credibility challenged (Bottoms & Goodman, 1994; Whitcomb et al., 1991), both of which may increase their negative feelings. Finally, older children have more negative feelings about the legal system's fairness and legitimacy in general (Fagan & Tyler, 2005). These feelings certainly could extend to attitudes toward specific interactions with the legal system. Indeed, in Goodman et al.'s (1992) longitudinal research, adolescents felt the most negative in the short term and years later as adults: Among individuals who did not testify, being older at the time of the case was associated many years later with feeling more negative about not having testified (Quas et al., 2005).

Summary
In summary, children involved in criminal cases are at increased risk of negative emotional and attitudinal outcomes. Testifying, especially multiple times, particularly when children do not have a voice in decisions about how that testimony is provided, is linked to increased distress and behavior problems shortly afterward, with these negative consequences persisting for many years. Children often report feelings of fear and distress before and after testifying in front of their perpetrator, with cross-examination being particularly challenging. Yet, at times, not testifying is associated with negative outcomes, including on children's well-being and attitudes, specifically when the case ends in an acquittal or lenient sentence. Thus, in some situations, children may experience positive feelings after being given the opportunity to tell the judge and jury about their victimization. Finally, the case outcome exerts a powerful and sustained influence on children's legal attitudes. It is important for legal officials to balance protecting children from secondary victimization while still giving them the opportunity to have their voices heard within a defendant's constitutional rights and need for a fair trial. Such a balance may mean involving children in legal actions, but doing so with adequate support and protection, along with explanations and control over what is happening and why.

Children in Dependency Courts

Dependency courts make decisions about the best interests of children following exposure to harm within the family or following parents' failure to protect the children from harm. A crucial part of these decisions concerns whether children should be removed from the home, but also what services the children and parents should receive, and the requirements parents must fulfill to be reunited with their children or for the case itself to be closed. The dependency process bears some similarities to the criminal court process, although there are enough differences that it is worth providing a more detailed explanation before turning to scientific literature on children's involvement in the dependency system. In the United States, dependency-related laws that govern legal responses in cases involving alleged maltreatment primarily occur at the state level. Thus, some inevitable variations exist in our general description across states. When these exist, we rely most heavily on how dependency courts operate in two states with particularly large dependent populations and in which we have collected data in the past: California and Florida.

The Dependency Court Process

Typically, a case is brought to the attention of the dependency court when an allegation of child abuse or neglect is made against a parent or guardian involving a child aged 17 years old or younger. Despite this age cut-off, in some cases (e.g., in extended foster care), individuals older than 17 years of age may also participate. Allegations may include acts of commission (e.g., physical or sexual abuse) or omission (e.g., neglect). The latter often comprises failure to provide or protect, such as failure to keep a child out of danger; failure to protect the child from harm (e.g., by a romantic partner or sibling, which can include exposure to domestic violence between parents); or not providing adequate medical attention or access to schooling. Reports are often made by school staff, counselors, or other professional adults who work with children, or by family members who have concerns and notify law enforcement or child protection.

Such notifications trigger a social service investigation to assess the veracity of the claims and also the ongoing risk to the child. If the risks are deemed sufficiently serious or the child is in imminent danger of harm, social services will file a dependency court petition. The dependency court, a subdivision of juvenile court, then provides a formal assessment of the allegations and determines how best to intervene. In the United States, because parents are direct participants in these cases, they are entitled to several constitutionally afforded due process rights (by the 14th Amendment), state rights, and rights related to their legal relationships with their children (*Meyer v. Nebraska*, 1923; *Troxel v. Granville*, 2000; *Stanley v. Illinois*, 1972). Among the most noteworthy of these are the rights to be present at hearings, to be informed of the state's allegations, and to provide evidence to the court (Child Welfare Information Gateway, 2006; Donnelly & Haralambie, 2005; Fla. Stat. § 39.013, 39.402, 2017). Although not federally mandated, most states also give parents the right to counsel, but the stage at which counsel is appointed varies by state (e.g., some require appointment before children's removal and others not until termination of parental rights proceedings; Sankaran, 2017; see also Shlafer et al., this volume). Parents may hire their own attorney(s). Children also have representation in their cases (e.g., their own attorney or a guardian ad litem), separate from state attorneys (often called "county counsel"), who represent social services (Goodman et al., 2008).

When a social service investigation deems that a child is at significant risk of immediate or serious harm, the child can be temporarily removed from parental custody. When this occurs, the dependency courts will act quickly by holding a hearing within 24–48 hours (similar to a preliminary hearing); this hearing determines whether there is probable cause supporting the premise that the child is at imminent risk of danger and that it is in the "best interest of the child" to remain living away from the home until an adjudication hearing (similar to a trial) is held (Fla. Stat. § 39.507, 2018). In the adjudication hearing, parents have the opportunity to respond to the allegations (i.e., present their side or a defense). If the parents successfully prove their case, the allegations may be dismissed and the case closed. However, if the state (social services) proves their case, the child will be deemed a dependent of the court and may remain in out-of-home care, although some children are returned home under supervision. During a disposition hearing, the courts then give parents a case plan that lists the requirements they must complete for reunification. This hearing may occur during or separate from the adjudication hearing. In some states and in many circumstances, parents participate in both adjudication and disposition hearings, whereas in other states and under some circumstances, the state moves directly to disposition (Shlafer et al., this volume).

Due to the complexity of the hearings and the individual case needs, case durations may vary significantly, from a few months to multiple years. In the United States, most courts, especially in major cities where the population is dense, report excessive case lengths (Quas, Cooper, & Wandrey, 2009; Sedlak et al., 2005). Children in foster care stay in the system for an average of 15.5 months (Child Welfare Information Gateway, 2019). Parents, and sometimes children, are expected to actively participate in their case throughout this time, which involves attending hearings every 6 months, completing requirements (e.g., anger management classes, "clean" drug tests), and at times more. Review hearings monitor case progress (e.g., whether parents are complying with mandated services, whether the child's needs are being met; Office of Children & Families in the Courts, 2009). Case plans often change across the different review hearings, and other requirements may be added, depending on the child's needs or the court's perceptions of the parents' behaviors. Finally, a permanency hearing is held, ideally within a year of the initial hearing—although this ideal is not always met—to determine permanent placement for the child and case resolution (i.e., reunification, guardianship, or adoption; 42 U.S.C. § 675(5)(C)(2020); Wood & Russell, 2011).

Some states permit children to attend their hearings and participate in decision making, to increase their involvement (Quas, Cooper, & Wandrey, 2009; Quas, Wallin et al., 2009). During the hearings, children will listen to attorneys, social workers, judges, and parents discuss the details of their dependency case, the children's needs, and the requirements for parents. Children may be questioned by the judge about experiences of maltreatment with their parents, their experiences in their current placement, or at some ages their placement preferences and what they want as the outcome of the case (Dickerson et al., 2021). This also gives children an opportunity to see their parents if they were removed from the home, which can be a positive, personally meaningful experience for the children (Hobbs et al., 2014). Despite some children being permitted to attend, many are not encouraged to appear, depending upon the state, county, and presiding judge's judgment. Moreover, in Florida, dependency court is open to the public and press, but in most other states, such hearings are private. Thus, whether children attend and who else is or is not present can vary widely across jurisdiction but also over time.

This description is an oversimplification of what, for many children and parents, is a much more complex and lengthy process. Multiple interim hearings may be held to evaluate evidence, claims, or needs. Continuances and modifications of plans are common. Legal professionals and social workers change, and the evidentiary standards for different decisions and outcomes vary (Yoon, 2019). Children and parents need to successfully navigate all of these complexities, and parents need to complete all mandates, to be reunited with their child (Cleveland & Quas, 2022). Meanwhile, the child might endure multiple out-of-home placements, which can have significant adverse effects on children's attachments and mental health (Bederian-Gardner et al., 2018).

Socioemotional Outcomes for Children in Dependency Court
Children's experiences in dependency courts can be dissimilar from those seen in children in criminal courts. Children in dependency courts typically have been removed from the home and experienced considerable trauma as a result. Even maltreated children are attached to their parents (Bowlby, 1980), and many report wanting to go home (Block et al., 2010). At the same time, many also seem to recognize that they may need to live elsewhere for a while, demonstrated by their desire to remain in their out-of-home placement in the short term but return home in the long term (Dickerson et al., 2021). During a dependency case, children have contact with social workers, police officers, investigators, child advocates, judges,

and their own attorneys. These interactions with unfamiliar professionals, at times in formal contexts, are compounded by having to cope with the trauma of maltreatment and removal, underdeveloped cognitive skills, and pressure to provide a reliable and accurate account of their needs and desires and of the events that took place.

Before a dependency case is even opened, the trauma of personally experiencing or witnessing abuse or neglect puts children at a heightened risk for mental and physical health problems (Crooks et al., 2007; Ellis & Wolfe, 2009; Friedrich, 1993). In addition, children report feeling severe distress when making the difficult decision to disclose their allegations (Berliner & Conte, 1995). This decision can be particularly challenging for children who lack maternal support (Bronfenbrenner, 1977; Malloy et al., 2007). That is, maltreatment allegations filed in the dependency court system are often against one or both parents, making familial support complicated (Quas & Sumaroka, 2011). Research has found that children who lacked maternal support for disclosure reported feeling depressed initially and years following the termination of the case (Sas, 1993). In contrast, maternal support during a legal case is associated with positive improvement of children's functioning (Whitcomb et al., 1991). In a dependency case, though, such support is often missing, leading to a potentially greater need for support from social service and legal professionals, who are also charged with ensuring the children's safety and well-being.

Social service and legal professionals rarely need to devote attention to providing support specifically in relation to children taking the stand, given that children rarely actually testify in dependency cases. Moreover, when children do take the stand, courtrooms are closed, with few others present, including few, if any, researchers. Perhaps in part because of the different contexts, the effects of testifying in dependency court do not appear to be similar to those observed in children testifying in criminal court, although scientific research on emotional outcomes after testifying in dependency court is largely nonexistent. In one of the only studies conducted, Runyan et al. (1988) assessed functioning in 75 child sexual abuse victims aged 6–7 years according to a structured psychiatric interview administered when their case was referred for court action and 5 months later. Between the two time points, 12 children testified in the dependency court, 22 children were waiting for criminal proceedings, and 33 children were not involved in criminal proceedings and did not testify in dependency cases. Although nearly all children were distressed at the initial assessment, at the 5-month juncture a higher proportion of children who testified in dependency proceedings showed improved mental health (anxiety) compared to children waiting for criminal proceedings. Runyan et al. concluded that testimony in juvenile court may be beneficial, a trend consistent with Hobbs et al.'s (2014) study, as they found that children in dependency court report less negativity about seeing defendants in court than did children in criminal court. The different structure of the dependency hearings (e.g., less formality) or perhaps the nature of the acts or decisions being rendered, which children may or may not fully understand (Block et al., 2010; Quas, Wallin et al., 2009), may reduce their anxiety.

Social service and legal professionals may provide support to children when taking their statements and by speaking for them in court. Children's statements initially concern their descriptions of the events that led to the case itself. The statements may be presented by the professionals or in written format in lieu of children appearing. Yet, not being present may also be problematic. Scientific research, especially retrospective and qualitative reports, suggests negative consequences when children feel as though they have no voice in their dependency cases. Much more so than some criminal actions, dependency decisions directly and potentially permanently alter children's lives in profound ways (e.g., by affecting with whom children live, the conditions under which they have contact with parents, where they go to school, and even whether and how often they can see their siblings). Children express a strong desire to be involved and have input in decisions, or at least have knowledge of why decisions are made. And, in contrast to concerns about such involvement being harmful or about children being incapable of providing reasonable input, several lines of work suggest the alternative: Not giving children a voice may be worse, and children are valuable sources of information about their needs and desires. Children's input is often sought when evaluating their needs in medical and custodial settings (Barnes, 2007; Coyne et al., 2014; Spinetta et al., 2003; Zimmerman, 1982). In dependency cases, children can provide information that may be unknown, overlooked, or underemphasized by adults (Kelly, 1994), thereby improving decisions. Giving children a voice about, for instance, with whom they would like to live may enhance their feelings of control or empowerment (Merritt, 2008; Pitchal, 2008) over what is a challenging and confusing process (Melinder et al., 2013). Indeed, children as young as 6 can provide reasonable responses when asked about their placement desires, at least when those questions are phrased in an open-ended manner. They often choose placements that are consistent with the types of placements suggested by research as being optimal for children's well-being (i.e., with kin or siblings; Dickerson et al., 2021; Mukhopadhyay et al., 2022).

As already mentioned, in a few jurisdictions, in part to increase children's involvement, children above a particular age, such as 4 or 12 years, semiregularly attend their dependency hearings (Quas, Wallin et al., 2009; Weisz et al., 2011). This involvement may in part facilitate children's ability to connect with their legal representative and ease scheduling demands of visitations or court evaluations. In contrast to concerns about the consequences of such attendance on children (e.g., that it may be traumatic for children to be present in hearings in which their parents' maltreating behaviors are being discussed), evidence indicates that children are not uniformly distressed when they are in attendance (Quas, Wallin et al., 2009). Instead, anxiety is often low beforehand, and even lower afterward (Weisz et al., 2011). Attendance may influence children's feelings in ways that facilitate their acceptance of the decisions, at least when compared to children not attending (Khoury, 2006), and possibly reduce harmful consequences associated with feeling that they had no voice.

It is important to consider potential age effects in children's reactions. Quas, Wallin, and colleagues (2009) assessed 4–15-year-olds' reactions to attending their dependency court cases. When asked immediately afterward about how they felt, younger children whose cases had only recently begun reported more negative feelings than younger children who had been involved for longer and older children, regardless of length of involvement. Whether those feelings in the youngest children are linked to longer term outcomes has not been examined. However, given the other children's reactions and findings from Weisz et al.'s (2011) study, it is likely that, over time, children may feel empowered as a result of attending, and negative feelings would likely be lower than those of younger children not given the opportunity to take part in their hearings, who may be distressed upon learning about decisions well after they took place with no control or input possible.

Attitudinal Outcomes for Children in Dependency Court

Findings are conflicted regarding the extent to which children are involved in their cases and how that involvement affects their attitudes about their experiences in the dependency system. There is, for example, a general assumption that maltreated children are involved, with this involvement reflected in the children disclosing their experiences of abuse or providing information to the courts via social workers or their attorney about their needs (Goldfarb et al., 2019; Pitchal, 2008). Yet, this general legal assumption is inconsistent with children's own feelings and objective reports, as has already been noted. Surveys of former foster children, for example, reveal that many felt they had no voice. In one such investigation, nearly a quarter reported that they had never attended their court hearings, and about half said that they had never or rarely been involved in placement or permanency decisions (Voice for Adoption, 2016). The same survey further suggests that not only were foster children feeling disconnected but also nearly 20% reported that no one had helped explain permanency decisions or helped them change their minds about decisions, over 54% reported never having had the term "permanency" explained to them, and nearly 46% said they were unaware of what their permanency goals were while they were in care. Finally, all voiced strong regret about not being involved in decisions about their futures.

One strategy of increasing children's involvement is to have them attend hearings, a strategy rarely used in most counties across the United States and less common with children under age 12 than with older children (Quas, Cooper, & Wandrey, 2009). Some studies have, however, examined the consequences of attendance in jurisdictions that do allow (or at times mandate) children's attendance. How these children fare in terms of both their distress while in attendance and their attitudes about and understanding of what happened are suggestive of benefits (e.g., Block et al., 2010; Quas, Wallin, et al., 2009). That is, even when children report being nervous or afraid of courtroom procedures (Hobbs et al., 2014), their distress is not uniformly high and experiences are not uniformly negative. In one such investigation, Weisz et al. (2011) compared children's attitudes about their case and hearing between 43 children who had attended the hearing and 50 who had not (ages 8–18 years). Compared to the latter group, children who had attended felt the decisions were more fair and reported greater trust in the judge.

Another means to increase foster youth's "voice" in decisions is through positive interactions with their attorneys. Goldfarb et al. (2019) found that, compared to other foster youth or youth not in foster care, those foster youth with the highest perceived quality of experiences (e.g., frequency of child–attorney contact, an attorney who represented the youth's voice) indicated more positive views of foster care. It will be important in subsequent research to assess whether differences in attitudes are sustained over time or influence long-term feelings in children that they indeed had some voice in their cases, lives, and futures.

Development again, though, is also important to consider. Consistent with research findings in criminal courts (Goodman et al., 1992), in their investigation of children's experiences after attending dependency hearings, Quas, Wallin, et al. (2009) found that older children reported more negative attitudes about their case than younger children. The authors attributed these differences to older children's greater cognitive and socioemotional development that allowed them to understand the implications of the maltreatment that took place, the stress of involving family members, and changes in living arrangements. Similar results have been reported by others (e.g., Block et al., 2010; Goodman et al., 1992). Weisz et al. (2011), for example, found that, among children who attended hearings, older children reported less trust than did younger children. The opposite pattern emerged among children who did not attend hearings—older children reported more trust than younger children. Simply attending, therefore, may not be sufficient for older children to feel more trusting of the judge's decisions. Older children instead may need to be informed and engaged directly.

Summary

Although only a small body of empirical literature has examined maltreated children's reactions to and feelings about dependency court, findings suggest that foster youth's feelings are mixed. Overall children want and benefit from a way to provide input and have a voice in their case, especially regarding their opinions, needs, desires, and futures. Likewise, whereas foster youth being able to attend hearings appears to be preferable to not attending, simply attending hearings is not sufficient, the latter most notably for older children. Across age, children who attend their hearings rarely fully understand what is happening (e.g., Block et al., 2010; Quas, Wallin, et al., 2009) and at times may be more confused about decisions than children who do not attend (Weisz et al., 2011). Thus, attendance would be best accompanied by engagement and explanation. Informing children of their roles in the dependency proceedings and helping them understand individual outcomes and long-term plans are likely imperative to their adjustment and overall success.

Future Directions

For justice—and child protection—to be served, it is an inevitable requirement that children will be involved, to varying extents, in the legal system as victims. Mixed findings about children's involvement indicate that some children feel that their voices were heard after appearing in court (Goodman et al., 1992; Quas et al., 2005; Weisz et al., 2011), whereas other children feel their involvement was harmful to their well-being (Goodman et al., 1992; Henry, 1997). It is important for the courts and legal officials, across systems, to take the time to accommodate each child's individual needs for participation in the legal system and protect the child from revictimization by the courts (Cashmore, 1991). Given that existing research has demonstrated that such involvement can be predictive of important emotional and attitudinal outcomes, the question of how to effectively balance the rights of children as vulnerable witnesses with the truth-seeking function of the legal system, and the goal of procedural justice, warrants further exploration. More specific directions for this exploration are noted here.

First, as the Washington case at the start of this chapter indicates, some children are engaged in both criminal and dependency court. Research is needed with such children. Hobbs et al. (2014) had the rare opportunity to compare children's attitudes toward criminal versus dependency court. Child victims of sexual abuse who testified in criminal court reported greater negativity about seeing defendants in the courtroom than did child victims of maltreatment testifying in dependency court. In addition, regardless of case type, girls were more negative about testifying than boys. Finally, more severe maltreatment and being older were positively associated with negativity about testifying. Runyan et al. (1988) reported that children in dependency court actions who were waiting to testify in criminal court were at particular risk. Whether findings would be additive, though, for children testifying or participating in both is not clear, but it is important to consider given known evidence of cumulative risk on development (Appleyard et al., 2005).

Second, our chapter did not describe in detail interventions designed to reduce negative consequences of legal involvement. One modification is the use of Child Advocacy Centers (CACs), which are multidisciplinary interview centers where children can provide evidence via videotaped forensic interviews that can be reviewed and shown to legal professionals. CACs can decrease the number of people with whom the child must discuss sensitive details related to the crime (Jones et al., 2007; Newman & Dannenfelser, 2005). CACs can also reduce delays between children's reports of maltreatment and indictment hearings, increase access to medical resources, and lessen trauma experienced by the child and family from participation in the legal system (Jones et al., 2007; Saint-Amand et al., 2023; Walsh et al., 2008). Whether and how their use specifically affects children's attitudes about criminal versus dependency cases, especially over time, has yet to be examined empirically but will be important in evaluating their supportive role in legal proceedings.

Third, support persons or support animals may be used to reduce a child witness's distress (McAuliff, 2009; Spruin et al., 2020). Victim witness assistants are active in courts in the United States, in which informational and emotional support is provided to the child throughout legal proceedings (McAuliff et al., 2013). However, research indicates that the presence of a victim support person can diminish jurors' perceptions of credibility of the child witness (Nefas et al., 2008). Whether such a support person would be useful in dependency court (such as a known and trusted guardian ad litem or court-appointed special advocate) who could sit near and help a child provide statements is not clear. It would also be of interest to study the effects of that person's presence on judges' opinions in dependency cases. Perhaps the use of support animals (e.g., support dogs) would be as helpful to children in dependency court as they seem to be for children in criminal court cases (Burd & McQuiston, 2019). All of these issues are worth exploring, in terms of both immediate emotional effects and long-term attitudinal effects.

Educational programs (e.g., Kids Court School) can help reduce children's stress and anxiety about participation in the judicial process (Nathanson & Saywitz, 2015). Several such programs emerged based on research conducted in Canada in which Sas and colleagues (1996) found that deep muscle relaxation, cognitive restructuring, and empowerment training reduced anxiety in children before participating in criminal proceedings, as compared to the high anxiety among children who received standard court preparation. Current Canadian courtroom preparation programs, moreover, have gone even further and adapted their programs to account for developmental variations in children's understanding and needs, with separate programs for younger children and adolescents (e.g., https://ccaa.org/ccaa_curriculum.html). Comprehensive evaluations of these programs over time would be useful in ascertaining whether additional modifications could improve their effects. Moreover, developing and testing modifications for children in dependency court would also be a fruitful direction for legally focused research on vulnerable children.

The implementation of procedures to help child victims in the legal system is not without controversy. The United States may be wise to look internationally and continue to build off the practices of other countries, such as Australia, New Zealand, Norway, Sweden, and the United Kingdom. In such countries, access to special measures or alternative modes of testifying are more easily incorporated as standard procedure (Bull & Davies, 1996; Hobbs et al., 2013; McWilliams et al., 2014; Powell et al., 2016). As evidence accumulates regarding the efficacy of interventions in reducing adverse psychological outcomes for child victims over time, those that show consistent promise with no reductions in judicial fairness should have an increasing presence within the U.S. legal system.

Conclusion

Given the reality of child maltreatment, an important goal when courts intervene should be to minimize the amount of exposure to secondary victimization and further traumatic experiences during court appearances and testimony (Goodman et al., 1992). Children are particularly susceptible to stress in the legal system due to their lack of emotional development, their lack of legal knowledge, and their dependence on adults' assistance with the process (Bowlby, 1980; Goodman et al., 1992; Saywitz et al., 1999). Yet, children may also want to be involved in cases that have the potential to affect their lives and futures, sometimes in profound ways. Participating in the legal process with a limited understanding of its procedures or why participation might be important may not be the optimal solution. Instead, care must be taken to increase children's comfort and knowledge during their participation, to ensure that they have adequate support, and to provide them with opportunities to contribute during courts' decision-making processes. Courts may need to adjust to children's individual needs so that they can participate in legal proceedings in a proactive and safe way (Goldfarb et al., 2015) while maintaining attention toward defendants' rights and judicial responsibility. Doing so will allow children to feel empowered and heard, help them understand outcomes (even those with which they might disagree), and reduce at least some of the distress associated with the legal proceedings over time, all while preserving justice for all.

References

Achenbach, T. M. (1991). *Manual for the Child Behavior Checklist 14-18 and 1991 Profile*. University of Vermont Department of Psychiatry.

Adjudicatory Hearings, Fla. Stat. § 39.507(2) (2018).

Andrews, S. J., Lamb, M. E., & Lyon, T. D. (2015). Question types, responsiveness and self-contradictions when prosecutors and defense attorneys question alleged victims of child sexual abuse. *Applied Cognitive Psychology, 29*, 253–261.

Appleyard, K., Egeland, B., van Dulmen, M., & Sroufe, L. A. (2005). When more is not better: The role of cumulative risk in child behavior outcomes. *Journal of Child Psychology and Psychiatry, 46*, 235–245.

Barnes, V. (2007). Young people's views of children's rights and advocacy services: A case for "caring" advocacy? *Child Abuse Review, 16*, 140–152.

Bederian-Gardner, D., Hobbs, S. D., Ogle, C. M., Goodman, G. S., Cordón, I. M., Bakanosky, S., Narr, R., Chae, Y., Chong, J. Y., & NYTD/CYTD Research Group. (2018). Instability in the lives of foster and nonfoster youth: Mental health impediments and attachment insecurities. *Children and Youth Services Review, 84*, 159–167.

Berliner, L., & Conte, J. R. (1995). The effects of disclosure and intervention on sexually abused children. *Child Abuse & Neglect, 19*, 371–384.

Block, S. D., Oran, H. S., Oran, D., Baumrind, N., & Goodman, G. S. (2010). Abused and neglected children in court: Knowledge and attitudes. *Child Abuse & Neglect, 34*, 659–670.

Bottoms, B. L., & Goodman, G. S. (1994). Perceptions of children's credibility in sexual assault cases. *Journal of Applied Social Psychology, 24*, 702–732.

Bowlby, J. (1980). *Attachment and loss. Vol. 3: Loss, sadness and depression*. Basic Books.

Bronfenbrenner, U. (1977). Toward an experimental ecology of human development. *American Psychologist, 32*, 513–531.

Brown-Schmidt, S., & Benjamin, A. S. (2018). How we remember conversation: Implications in legal settings. *Policy Insights from the Behavioral and Brain Sciences, 5*, 187–194.

Bull, R., & Davies, G. M. (1996). The effects of child witness research on legislation in Great Britain. In B. L. Bottoms & G. S. Goodman (Eds.), *International perspectives on child abuse and children's testimony* (pp. 96–113). Sage.

Burd, K. A., & McQuiston, D. E. (2019). Facility dogs in the courtroom: Comfort without prejudice? *Criminal Justice Review, 44*, 515–536.

Cashmore, J. (1991). *The use of closed-circuit television for child witnesses in the ACT*. Australian Law Reform Commission.

Cashmore, J., & Bussey, K. (1996). Judicial perceptions of child witness competence. *Law & Human Behavior, 3*, 313–334.

Child Welfare Information Gateway. (2006). *Child neglect: A guide for prevention, assessment, and intervention*. Child Welfare Information Gateway, Children's Bureau. https://www.childwelfare.gov/pubPDFs/neglect.pdf

Child Welfare Information Gateway. (2019). *Foster care statistics 2019*. Child Welfare Information Gateway, Children's Bureau. https://www.childwelfare.gov/pubpdfs/foster.pdf

Cleveland, K. C., & Quas, J. A. (2022). What's fair in child welfare? Parent knowledge, attitudes, and experiences. *Child Maltreatment, 27*, 53–65.

Compas, B. E., Jaser, S. S., Bettis, A. H., Watson, K. H., Gruhn, M. A., & Dunbar, P. B. (2017). Coping, emotion regulation, and psychopathology in childhood and adolescence: A meta-analysis and narrative review. *Psychological Bulletin, 143*, 939–991.

Council of Europe. (2007). *Convention on the Protection of Children against Sexual Exploitation and Sexual Abuse*. https://rm.coe.int/1680084822

Coyne, I., Amory, A., Kiernan, G., & Gibson, F. (2014). Children's participation in shared decision-making: Children, adolescents, parents and healthcare professionals' perspectives and experiences. *European Journal of Oncology Nursing, 18*, 273–280.

Crooks, C. V., Scott, K. L., Wolfe, D. A., Chiodo, D., & Killip, S. (2007). Understanding the link between childhood maltreatment and violent delinquency: What do schools have to add? *Child Maltreatment, 12*, 269–280.

Cross, T. P., & Whitcomb, D. (2017). The practice of prosecuting child maltreatment: Results of an online survey of prosecutors. *Child Abuse & Neglect, 69*, 20–28.

Dickerson, K. L., Lyon, T. D., & Quas, J. A. (2021). The role of kinship and siblings in young children's placement preferences. *Journal of Interpersonal Violence, 36*.

Donnelly, A. G., & Haralambie, A. M. (2005). Child welfare constitutional case law. In M. Ventrell & D. N. Duquette (Eds.), *Child welfare law and practice: Representing children, parents, and state agencies in abuse, neglect, and dependency cases* (pp. 185–211). Bradford Publishing.

Eastwood, C., & Patton, W. (2002). *The experiences of child complainants of sexual abuse in the criminal justice system.* https://www.aic.gov.au/sites/default/files/2020-05/eastwood.pdf.

Elmi, A. N., Daignault, I. V., & Hebert, M. (2018). Child sexual abuse victims as witnesses: The influence of testifying on their recovery. *Child Abuse & Neglect, 86*, 22–32.

Ellis, W. E., & Wolfe, D. A. (2009). Understanding the association between maltreatment history and adolescent risk behavior by examining popularity motivations and peer group control. *Journal of Youth and Adolescence, 38*, 1253–1263.

Evans, A. D., Stolzenberg, S. N., & Lyon, T. D. (2017). Pragmatic failure and referential ambiguity when attorneys ask child witnesses "do you know/remember" questions. *Psychology, Public Policy, and Law, 23*, 191–199.

Fagan, J., & Tyler, T. R. (2005). Legal socialization of children and adolescents. *Social Justice Research, 18*, 217–242.

Fogliati, R., & Bussey, K. (2015). The effects of cross-examination on children's coached reports. *Psychology, Public Policy, and Law, 21*, 10–23.

Friedrich, W. N. (1993). Sexual victimization and sexual behavior in children: A review of recent literature. *Child Abuse & Neglect, 17*, 59–66.

Goldfarb, D. A., & Goodman, G. S. (2014). Cross-examination's big effect on the criminal system's smallest witnesses: How the judiciary can alleviate the negative effects of cross-examination. *Chronicle*. London, UK: International Association of Youth and Family Judges and Magistrates.

Goldfarb, D., Goodman, G. S., & Lawler, M. J. (2015). Children's evidence and the convention on the rights of the child: Improving the legal system for children. In S. Mahmoudi, P. Leviner, A. Kaldal, & K. Lainpelto (Eds.), *Child-friendly justice* (pp. 85–109). Koninklijke Brill.

Goldfarb, D., Goodman, G. S., Wang, Y., Fisher, R. P., Vidales, D., Gonzalves, L. C., Wu, Y., Hartman, D. T., Qin, J., & Eisen, M. L. (2023). Adults' memory for a maltreatment-related childhood experience: Interview protocols. *Clinical Psychological Science, 11*(1), 164–182.

Goldfarb, D. A., Lagattuta, K. H., Kramer, H. J., Kennedy, K., & Tashjian, S. M. (2017). When your kind cannot live here: How generic language and criminal sanctions shape social categorization. *Psychological Science, 28*, 1597–1609.

Goldfarb, D. A., Tashjian, S. M., Goodman, G. S., Bederian-Gardner, D., Hobbs, S. D., Cordon, I. M., Ogle, C. M., Bakanosky, S., Narr, R. K., Chae, Y., & the NYTD/CYTD Research Group. (2019). After child maltreatment: The importance of voice for youth in foster care. *Journal of Interpersonal Violence, 36*, NP7388–NP7414.

Goodman-Delahunty, J., Cossins, A., & O'Brien, K. (2010). Enhancing the credibility of complaints in child sexual assault trials: The effect of expert evidence and judicial directions. *Behavioral Sciences & the Law, 28*, 769–783.

Goodman, G. S., Edelstein, R. S., Mitchell, E. B., & Myers, J. E. (2008). A comparison of types of attorney representation for children in California juvenile court dependency cases. *Child Abuse & Neglect, 32*, 497–501.

Goodman, G. S., Quas, J. A., Bulkley, J., & Shapiro, C. (1999). Innovations for child witnesses: A national survey. *Psychology, Public Policy, and Law, 5*, 255–281.

Goodman, G. S., Taub, E. P., Jones, D. P. H., England, P., Port, L. K., Rudy, L., & Prado, L. (1992). Testifying in criminal court: Emotional effects on child sexual assault victims. *Monographs of the Society for Research in Child Development, 57*, i, 1–159.

Goodman, G. S., Tobey, A. E., Batterman-Faunce, J. M., Orcutt, H., Thomas, S., Shapiro, C., & Sachsenmaier, T. (1998). Face-to-face confrontation: Effects of closed-circuit technology on children's eyewitness testimony and jurors' decisions. *Law and Human Behavior, 22*, 165.

Grisso, T., Steinberg, L., Woolard, J., Cauffman, E., Scott, E., Graham, S., Lexcen, F., Reppucci, N. D., & Schwartz, R. (2003). Juveniles' competence to stand trial: A comparison of adolescents' and adults' capacities as trial defendants. *Law and Human Behavior, 27*, 333–363.

Henry, J. (1997). System intervention trauma to child sexual abuse victims following disclosure. *Journal of Interpersonal Violence, 12*, 499–512.

Hershkowitz, I. (2009). Socioemotional factors in child sexual abuse investigations. *Child Maltreatment, 14*, 172–181.

Hobbs, S. D., Bederian-Gardner, D., Ogle, C. M., Bakanosky, S., Narr, R. K., & Goodman, G. S. (2021). Foster youth and at-risk non-foster youth: A propensity score and structural equation modeling analysis. *Children and Youth Services Review, 126*, 106034.

Hobbs, S. D., & Goodman, G. S. (2018). Self-representation: Pro se cross-examination and revisiting trauma upon child witnesses. *International Journal on Child Maltreatment, 1*, 77–95.

Hobbs, S. D., Goodman, G. S., Block, S. D., Oran, D., Quas, J. A., Park, A., Widaman, K. F., & Baumrind, N. (2014). Child maltreatment victims' attitudes about appearing in dependency and criminal courts. *Children and Youth Services Review, 44*, 407–416.

Hobbs, S. D., Johnson, J. L., Goodman, G. S., Bederian-Gardner, D., Lawler, M. J., Vargas, I. D., & Mendoza, M. (2013). Evaluating eyewitness testimony in children. In I. B. Weiner & R. K. Otto (Eds.), *Handbook of forensic psychology* (pp. 561–612). Wiley.

U.S. Code. (2020). Title 42, Section 675(5)(C).

Jones, L. M., Cross, T. P., Walsh, W. A., & Simone, M. (2007). Do children's advocacy centers improve families' experiences of child sexual abuse investigations? *Child Abuse & Neglect, 31*, 1069–1085.

Kelly, J. B. (1994). The determination of child custody. *Future of Children, 4*, 121–142.

Khoury, A. (2006). Seen and heard: Involving children in dependency court. *ABA Child Law Practice, 25*, 145–155.

Lamb, M. E., Orbach, Y., Hershkowitz, I., Esplin, P. W., & Horowitz, D. (2007). A structured forensic interview protocol improves the quality and informativeness of investigative interviews with children: A review of research using the NICHD Investigative Interview Protocol. *Child Abuse & Neglect, 31*, 1201–1231.

Landström, S., Granhag, P. A., & Hartwig, M. (2007). Children's live and videotaped testimonies: How presentation mode affects observers' perception, assessment and memory. *Legal and Criminological Psychology, 12*, 333–347.

Liang, B., Williams, L., & Siegel, J. (2006). Relational outcomes of childhood sexual trauma in female survivors: A longitudinal study. *Journal of Interpersonal Violence, 21*, 1–16.

Loughran, T. A., Mulvey, E. P., Schubert, C. A., Chassin, L. A., Steinberg, L., Piquero, A. R., Fagan, J., Cota-Robles, S., Cauffman, E., & Losoya, D. (2010) Differential effects of adult court transfer on juvenile offender recidivism. *Law and Human Behavior, 34*, 476–488.

Malloy, L. C., & Lyon, T. D. (2006). Caregiver support and child sexual abuse: Why does it matter? *Journal of Child Sexual Abuse, 15*, 97–103.

Malloy, L. C., Lyon, T. D., & Quas, J. A. (2007). Filial dependency and recantation of child sexual abuse allegations. *Journal of the American Academy of Child & Adolescent Psychiatry, 46*, 162–170.

Maryland v. Craig, 487 U.S. 836 (1990). https://www.oyez.org/cases/1989/89-478

McAuliff, B. D. (2009). Judging the validity of psychological science from the bench: A case in point. *Journal of Forensic Psychology Practice, 9*, 310–320.

McAuliff, B., & Kovera, M. B. (2012). Do jurors get what they expect? Traditional versus alternative forms of children's testimony. *Psychology, Crime & Law, 18*, 27–47.

McAuliff, B. D., Nicholson, E., Amarilio, D., & Ravanshenas, D. (2013). Supporting children in U.S. legal proceedings: Descriptive and attitudinal data from a national survey of victim/witness assistants. *Psychology, Public Policy, and Law, 19*, 98–113.

McWilliams, K., Augusti, E. M., Dion, J., Block, S., Melinder, A. M., Cashmore, J., & Goodman, G. S. (2014). Children as witnesses. In G. Melton, A. BenArieh, J. Cashmore, G. S. Goodman, & N. K. Worley (Eds.), *The Sage handbook of child research* (pp. 285–300). Sage.

Melinder, A. M., Baugerud, G. A., Ovenstad, K. S., & Goodman, G. S. (2013). Children's memories of removal: A test of attachment theory. *Journal of Traumatic Stress, 26*, 125–133.

Melinder, A. M., van der Hagen, M. D., & Sandberg, K. (2021). In the best interest of the child: The Norwegian approach to child protection. *International Journal of Child Maltreatment, 4*, 209–230

Melton, G. B., & Berliner, L. (1992). *Preparing sexually abused children for testimony: Children's perceptions of the legal process*. National Center on Child Abuse and Neglect.

Merritt, D. H. (2008). Placement preferences among children living in foster or kinship care: A cluster analysis. *Children and Youth Services Review, 30*, 1336–1344.

Meyer v. State of Nebraska, 262 U.S. 390 (1923). https://www.oyez.org/cases/1900-1940/262us390

Mukhopadhyay, S., Dickerson, K. D., Lyon, T. D., & Quas, J. A. (2022). Foster youth's placement preferences: The roles of kin, siblings, and age. *Child Abuse & Neglect, 131*, 105761.

Murtha, C. (2021). Standing by to protect child abuse victims: Utilizing standby counsel in lieu of personal cross-examination. *Dickinson Law Review, 126*, 249–272.

Myers, J. E. B. (2011). *Myers on evidence of interpersonal violence: Child maltreatment, intimate partner violence, rape, stalking, and elder abuse cases*. Wolters Kluwer Law and Business.

Nathanson, R., & Saywitz, K. J. (2003). The effects of the courtroom context on children's memory and anxiety. *Journal of Psychiatry & Law, 31*, 67–98.

Nathanson, R., & Saywitz, K. J. (2015). Preparing children for court: Effects of a model court education program on children's anticipatory anxiety. *Behavioral Sciences & the Law, 33*, 459–475.

Nefas, C., Neal., E., Maurice, K., & McAuliff, B. D. (2008). Support person use and child victim testimony: Believe it or not. *Behavioral Sciences & the Law, 33*, 508–527.

Newman, B. S., & Dannenfelser, P. L. (2005). Children's protective services and law enforcement: Fostering partnerships in investigations of child abuse. *Journal of Child Sexual Abuse, 14*, 97–111.

Office of Children & Families in the Courts. (2009). *Court processes.* http://www.ocfcpacourts.us/parents-and-families/child-dependency-system/court-processes

Orcutt, H. K., Goodman, G. S., Tobey, A. E., Batterman-Faunce, J. M., & Thomas, S. F. (2001). Detecting deception in children's testimony: Factfinders' abilities to reach the truth in open court and closed-circuit trials. *Law and Human Behavior, 25*, 339–372.

Pitchal, E. S. (2008). Where are all the children? Increasing youth participation in dependency proceedings. *Journal of Juvenile Law and Policy, 12*, 233–264.

Placement in a shelter, Fla. Stat. § 39.013, 39.402 (2017).

Plotnikoff, J., & Woolfson, R. (2004). *In their own words: The experiences of 50 young witnesses in criminal proceedings.* National Society for the Prevention of Cruelty to Children.

Powell, M., Westera, N., Goodman-Delahunty, J., & Pichler, A. (2016). *An evaluation of how evidence is elicited from complainants of child sexual abuse.* Royal Commission Into Institutional Responses to Child Sexual Abuse.

Quas, J. A., Cooper, A., & Wandrey, L. (2009). Child victims in dependency court. In B. L. Bottoms, G. S. Goodman, & C. Nadjowski (Eds.), *Child victims, child offenders: Psychology and law* (pp. 128–149). Guilford Press.

Quas, J. A., & Goodman, G. S. (2012). Consequences of criminal court involvement for child victims. *Psychology, Public Policy, and Law, 18*, 392–414.

Quas, J. A., Goodman, G. S., Ghetti, S., Alexander, K. W., Edelstein, R. S., Redlich, A. D., & Cordón, I. M. (2005). Childhood sexual assault victims: Long-term outcomes after testifying in criminal court. *Monographs of the Society for Research in Child Development, 70*, vii, 1–117.

Quas, J. A., Malloy, L. C., Melinder, A., Goodman, G. S., D'Mello, M., & Schaaf, J. (2007). Developmental differences in the effects of repeated interviews and interviewer bias on young children's event memory and false reports. *Developmental Psychology, 43*, 823–837.

Quas, J. A., & Sumaroka, M. (2011). Consequences of legal involvement on child victims of maltreatment. In M. E. Lamb, D. J. La Rooy, L. C. Malloy, & C. Katz (Eds.), *Children's testimony: A handbook of psychological research and forensic practice* (pp. 323–350). Wiley-Blackwell.

Quas, J. A., Wallin, A. R., Horwitz, B. N., Davis, E., & Lyon, T. D. (2009). Maltreated children's understanding of and emotional reactions to dependency court involvement. *Behavioral Science & the Law, 27*, 97–117.

Randell, I., Seymour, F., Henderson, E., & Blackwell, S. (2018). The experiences of young complainant witnesses in criminal court trials for sexual offences. *Psychiatry, Psychology, and Law, 25*, 357–373.

Righarts, S., Jack, F., Zajac, R., & Hayne, H. (2015). Young children's responses to cross-examination style questioning: The effects of delay and subsequent questioning. *Psychology, Crime & Law, 21*, 274–296.

Rosenbaum, P. R. (2010). *Design of observational studies.* Springer.

Runyan, D. K., Everson, M. D., Edelsohn, G. A., Hunter, W. M., & Coulter, M. L. (1988). Impact of legal intervention on sexually abused children. *Journal of Pediatrics, 113*, 647–653.

Saint-Amand, A., Rimer, P., Nadeau, D., Hebert, J., & Walsh, W. (2023) (Eds.), *Contemporary and innovative practices in child and youth advocacy centre models.* Presses de l'Université du Québec.

Sankaran, V. S. (2017). Child welfare's scarlet letter: How prior termination of parental rights can permanently brand parent as unfit. *New York University Review of Law & Social Change, 41*, 685–706.

Sas, L. D. (1991). *Reducing the system-induced trauma for child sexual abuse victims through court preparation, assessment and follow-up* (Final Report, Project No. 4555-1-125, National Welfare Grants Division, Health and Welfare Canada). London Family Court Clinic.

Sas, L. (1993). *Three years after the verdict: A longitudinal study of the social and psychological adjustment of child witnesses referred to the Child Witness Project.* London Family Court Clinic.

Sas, L. D., Wolfe, D. A., & Gowdey, K. (1996). Children in the courts in Canada. *Criminal Justice and Behavior, 23*, 338–357.

Saywitz, K. J., Snyder, L., & Nathanson, R. (1999). Facilitating the communicative competence of the child witness. *Applied Developmental Science, 3*, 58–68.

Schudson, C. B. (1987). Making courts safe for children. *Journal of Interpersonal Violence, 2*, 120–122.

Sedlak, A. J., Doueck, H. J., Lyons, P., Wells, S. J., Schultz, D., & Gragg, F. (2005). Child maltreatment and the justice system: Predictors of court involvement. *Research on Social Work Practice, 15*, 389–403.

Shadish, W. R. (2013). Propensity score analysis: Promise, reality, and irrational exuberance. *Journal of Experimental Criminology, 9*, 129–144.

Shore, M. F. (1985). The clinician as advocate: Interventions in court settings: Opportunities, responsibilities, and hazards. *Journal of Clinical Child Psychology, 14*, 236–238.

Spinetta, J. J., Masera, G., Jankovic, M., Oppenheim, D., Martins, A. G., Ben Arush, M. W., van Dongen-Melman, J., Epelman, C., Medin, G., Pekkanen, K., Eden, T., & SIOP Working Committee on Psychosocial Issues in Pediatric Oncology. (2003). Valid informed consent and participative decision-making in children with cancer and their parents: A report of the SIOP Working Committee on psychosocial issues in pediatric oncology. *Medical and Pediatric Oncology, 40,* 244–246.

Spruin, E., Mozova, K., Dempster, T., & Freeman, R. (2020). The use of facility dogs to bridge the justice gap for survivors of sexual offending. *Social Sciences, 9*(6), 96.

St. George, S., Garcia-Johnson, A., Denne, E., & Stolzenberg, S. N. (2020). "Did you ever fight back?" Jurors' questions to children testifying in criminal trials about alleged sexual abuse. *Criminal Justice and Behavior, 47,* 1032–1054.

Stanley v. Illinois, 405 U.S. 645 (Ill. 1972). https://www.oyez.org/cases/1971/70-5014

State of Washington v. Woods, 154 Wn.2d 613 (Wash. 2005). https://case-law.vlex.com/vid/114-p-3d-1174-631046883

Stolzenberg, S. N., & Lyon, T. D. (2014). Evidence summarized in attorney's closing arguments predicts acquittals in criminal trials of child sexual abuse. *Child Maltreatment, 19,* 119–129.

Stroud, D. D., Martens, S. L., & Barker, J. (2000). Criminal investigation of child sexual abuse: A comparison of cases referred to the prosecutor to those not referred. *Child Abuse & Neglect, 24,* 689–700.

Tedesco, J. F., & Schnell, S. V. (1987). Children's reactions to sex abuse investigation and litigation. *Child Abuse & Neglect, 11,* 267–272.

Troxel v. Granville, 520 U.S. 57 (2000). https://www.oyez.org/cases/1999/99-138

Tyler, T. R. (1980). Impact of directly and indirectly experienced events: The origin of crime-related judgments and behaviors. *Journal of Personality and Social Psychology, 39,* 13–28.

Tyler, T. R. (2006). Restorative justice and procedural justice: Dealing with rule breaking. *Journal of Social Issues, 62,* 307–326.

Tyler, T. R., & Lind, E. A. (2001). Procedural justice. In J. Sanders & V. L. Hamilton (Eds.), *Handbook of justice research in law* (pp. 65–92). Kluwer.

U.S. Code. (2020). Title 42, Section 675(5)(C).

van Koppen, P. J., & Penrod, S. D. (Eds.). (2003). *Adversarial versus inquisitorial justice: Psychological perspectives on criminal justice systems.* Kluwer Academic/Plenum Publishers.

Voice for Adoption. (2016). *Youth voices for permanency: A courtroom guide on how courts and judges can make a difference.* www.voice-for-adoption.org

Walsh, W. A., Lippert, T., Cross, T. P., Maurice, D. M., & Davison, K. S. (2008). How long to prosecute child sexual abuse for a community using a children's advocacy center and two comparison communities? *Child Maltreatment, 13,* 3–13.

Weisz, V., Wingrove, T., Beal, S. J., & Faith-Slaker, A. (2011). Children's participation in foster care hearings. *Child Abuse & Neglect, 35,* 267–272.

Whitcomb, D., Runyan, D. K., DeVos, E., Hunter, W. M., Cross, T. P., Everson, M. D., Peeler, N. A., Porter, C. Q., Toth, P. A., & Cropper, C. (1991). *Child victims as witnesses: Research and development program.* Office of Juvenile Justice and Delinquency Prevention.

Wood, S., & Russell, J. (2011). Effects of parental and attorney involvement on reunification in juvenile dependency cases. *Children and Youth Services Review, 33,* 1730–1741.

Wu, Y., Goodman, G. S., Goldfarb, D., Wang, Y., Vidales, D., Brown, L., Eisen, M. L., & Qin, J. (2021). Memory accuracy after 20 years for interviews about child maltreatment. *Child Maltreatment, 28,* 85–96.

Yoon, Y. (2019). Building broken children in the name of protecting them: Examining the effects of lower evidentiary standard in temporary child removal cases. *University of Illinois Law Review, 2019,* 743–772.

Zajac, R., & Cannan, P. (2009). Cross-examination of sexual assault complainants: A developmental comparison. *Psychiatry, Psychology and Law, 16*(Suppl 1), S36–S54.

Zimmerman, R. B. (1982). *Foster care in retrospect* (Vol. 14). School of Social Work, Tulane University.

CHAPTER 6

Attachment and Parenting Time for Children Under 3 Years of Age

William V. Fabricius

Abstract

Attachment theory is the current standard model for how infants and toddlers develop emotional connections to their caregivers. This chapter is focused on implications that can be drawn from attachment theory and research for legal policies regarding overnight parenting time for children under 3 years of age whose parents either never cohabitated after the birth of the child or cohabitated for a period of time before separating. First, the basic principles of modern attachment theory are presented, followed by a brief review of research on the importance of the emotional security that children can derive from parent-child relationships for their healthy social, emotional, and stress-related physical health development. Second, the recent heated debate about overnight parenting time for infants and toddlers is reviewed, and the relevant studies and findings are discussed. Third, the implications that can be drawn from the current state of theory and findings are considered, and are found to support policies to encourage equal parenting time for children under 3 years of age. Finally, it is argued that equal parenting time not only serves children's best interest in terms of their long-term health but also serves gender equality. Thus, gender equality could provide the needed principled legal framework on which to found consistent new custody policies presuming equal parenting time.

Key Words: infant attachment, equal parenting time, parent-child relationships, child custody policy, gender equality

In his 2011 book *Family Law and the Indissolubility of Parenthood*, Patrick Parkinson, professor of law at the University of Sydney, developed his thesis that the divorce revolution of the 1960s and 1970s, which sought to establish divorce as a clean dissolution leaving ex-spouses free to pursue separate lives, ran head-on into another great cultural change. The second great change was the realization of the importance of fathers for children's healthy development, which in turn requires acceptance of the "indissolubility of parenthood" after divorce. In many countries now, cultural norms have settled into a view of divorce involving children as not a simple dissolution of an adult relationship, but rather as a restructuring of a continuing adult relationship in order to maintain children's relationships with both parents. Parkinson's thesis is that legal regimes have been unable to keep up with the cultural change. Parkinson argues that no principled legal framework, or "philosophical shift in the meaning of divorce" (p. 42), has emerged on which to found consistent new custody policy, resulting in "either insufficient consensus to achieve reform or unsatisfactory compromises that lead to laws filled with contradictions" (p. 9). Parkinson should know, having played a major role in Australia's 2006 custody statute reforms.

Parkinson's thesis of insufficient legal consensus and unsatisfactory compromises is amply illustrated in the topic of this chapter: attachment and parenting time for children under 3 years of age. The recent historical context of this topic stems from a special issue of *Family Court Review* on "Attachment Theory, Separation, and Divorce" (McIntosh, 2011) that featured interviews with selected attachment researchers (for the longer history, see Warshak, 2018). Kelly (2014), Lamb (2012), and Ludolph (2012) subsequently criticized editor McIntosh for choosing commentators who did not reflect the range of opinions among attachment researchers. The special issue was immediately followed by the 2012 annual Association of Family and Conciliation Courts (AFCC) meeting devoted to the topic "Attachment, Brain Science, and Children of Divorce." Both the special issue and the conference sounded an alarm about overnight parenting time away from the custodial parent (usually the mother) for very young children.

AFCC leadership convened a follow-up think tank meeting in 2013, composed of 19 social scientists and mental health practitioners, 12 legal professionals, and one activist-educator, to evaluate the limited research upon which the alarm was based, and to consider implications for practice and policy. However, the think tank did not reach consensus but instead concluded that research had not settled the issue and eschewed any prescriptions about the ideal amount of overnight parenting time for young children, as reported in a second special issue of *Family Court Review* (Pruett & DiFonzo, 2014).

Nevertheless, three think tank members pursued consensus among themselves (McIntosh et al., 2014; Pruett et al., 2014) and proposed detailed guidelines for individual practice and general policy for children aged birth to 3 that recommended infrequent overnights. At the same time, Warshak (2014) brought the issue to the attention of a wider academic and legal community, resulting in an alternative consensus statement signed by 110 psychologists and family law scholars endorsing frequent overnights during the child's first 3 years as beneficial to the father–child relationship and not harmful to the mother–child relationship. Additionally, Nielsen (2014) argued that advocates opposed to overnight parenting time for infants and toddlers had misrepresented the four empirical studies that had been done on the topic.

Finally, 70 prominent attachment experts issued a consensus statement 10 years after the initial 2011 special issue of *Family Court Review* (Forslund et al., 2021). The attachment experts not only echoed Nielsen's (2014) critique of the misuse of attachment theory in the debates about overnight parenting time but also, importantly, presented the mainstream scientific knowledge about attachment and warned of the dangers of expecting undertrained custody evaluators in individual divorce cases, as well as in child protection cases, to attempt to use the scientific instruments that attachment researchers have developed over the years for research purposes. Those research purposes involve measuring child attachment security and insecurity on the one hand and parent attachment–related behaviors on the other hand, in order to understand the basic mechanisms of attachment development. Forslund et al. (2021) forcefully, and rightfully, pushed back against growing tendencies in child protection agencies worldwide to use ill-defined and subjectively assessed "attachment insecurity" to remove children from their homes or stable foster care placements. The Forslund et al. (2021) critique is a direct descendent of the original critique (Rodham, 1973) of subjectivity and cultural bias in child custody decisions and is the latest in an unbroken series of such critiques since 1973 (e.g., Emery et al., 2005). For our purposes, however, what Forslund et al. (2021) did *not* do was reach consensus on cashing out the substantial wealth of attachment theory and research that has accumulated during the same time period into policy recommendations for overnight parenting time for very young children.

Against this historical backdrop, I begin this chapter with a brief overview of attachment theory. Next, I discuss the research that exists on overnight parenting time for children under 3 years of age. I conclude with a discussion of the implications of attachment theory and research for policies and practices for overnight parenting time for children under 3 years of age.

Attachment Theory

The modern theory of how infants develop attachment relationships with parents was the work of British psychiatrist John Bowlby (1969/1993, 1973, 1980). According to attachment theory, human infants are biologically programmed to begin actively engaging with any and all adults and to slowly develop preferences for, and later attachments to, those adults who care for them. Establishing attachment relationships allows infants to signal when distressed and anticipate and obtain a soothing response from their attachment figures. Cycles of signal and response not only help ensure infants' survival but also build up a feeling of security, termed a secure base, that allows toddlers to begin independently exploring the physical and social worlds with confidence and trust that attachment figures will have their backs, so to speak. Consistent with attachment theory, secure parent–child relationships are among the most reliable predictors of healthy development in many areas, including social skills, mental health, self-esteem, educational attainment, relationship success, and lifetime earnings (Lamb & Lewis, 2010).

Contemporary research has added physical health to the list of positive outcomes of strong parent–child relationships (Ranson & Urichuk, 2008; Troxel & Matthews, 2004). Research on the connection between attachment and physical health suggests that the cycles of infant signal and caregiver response during the development of attachment also serve to establish the set points of the infant's developing biological stress response regulatory system. A well-regulated stress response allows the individual to respond to threats and danger and then quickly recover to healthy, baseline equilibrium when the danger has passed.

The first indications of connections between attachment and physical health were noticed in rat pups who had been repeatedly but briefly, separated from mothers in early infancy as part of other experimental procedures (Caldi et al., 1998). Upon reunion, the separated pups received more maternal soothing behaviors (licking and grooming) than they would have without the repeated separations and reunions. These artificially enhanced cycles of separation and reunion altered the infant pups' brain chemistry, resulting in better regulated responses to future stressors, faster recovery to baseline, milder age-related declines, and longer lives.

The first exploration of the public health literature for links between attachment and chronic, stress-related physical health was reported by Repetti et al. in 2002. They found that large public health studies going back to the 1960s contained evidence that lack of support and deficient nurturing in childhood led, decades later, to higher rates of serious chronic illnesses, including hypertension, heart disease, diabetes, obesity, and some cancers. Other studies reviewed by Repetti et al. (2002) indicated that one link between deficient nurturing and chronic disease lay in dysregulation of children's developing stress response systems. One important component of stress response regulation is the hormone cortisol. The instantaneous secretion of stress hormones such as cortisol helps mobilize an individual for "fight or flight," and the timely reabsorption of stress hormones returns the individual to healthy equilibrium. Dysregulated set points for response and recovery prolong a child's exposure to chronic, low levels of stress hormones, which can disrupt cardiovascular, metabolic, and immune functions. Dysregulation can be established early and then persist. Within the first few months of life, the less sensitivity that mothers display to their infants' signals, the slower the infants' cortisol recovery following a stressful event (Albers et al., 2008). In young adulthood, college students who reported having had poor family relationships in childhood had higher blood pressure and higher cortisol levels in response to stress (Luecken, 1998).

Three important aspects of attachment that are often misunderstood are the universal developmental timing of attachment during the first 2 years, secure versus insecure attachments, and attachments to multiple caregivers.

Developmental timing. During the early months, up to about 6 months of age, infants generally respond indiscriminately to adults, expressing pleasure in interacting and not expressing stress in separating from one caregiver and joining another. The reason for infants' inclusiveness is that during the first 6 months, infants have not yet developed the cognitive capacity to expect different things from caregivers than from strangers. Everything is new and interesting, especially people. From about 7 to 9 months, however, it becomes increasingly apparent that infants are slowly acquiring expectations of specific caregivers, are beginning to be wary of strangers, and are establishing emotional attachments to their caregivers. Between 9 and 24 months, infants are fully engaged in maintaining and benefiting from their attachment relationships. When upset or distressed, they turn to those adults for comfort, and when not upset or distressed, they turn to those adults for playful interactions.

Thus, the period from about 7 months through 24 months is the most important time to avoid unexpected and prolonged separations from regular caregivers. The disappearance of an adult with whom the infant has begun to become attached is experienced by the infant as a prolonged, chronic threat. Acute threats, such as a stranger appearing or a parent leaving the room, can be dealt with by signaling distress and receiving a soothing response. But signals to an *absent* attachment figure go unheeded. The infant's cognitive, emotional, and physiological systems had been learning to anticipate a response from that particular parent, and the prolonged absence of a response throws those systems into disarray. The longer the separation goes on, the more disoriented and abandoned the infant feels, the longer the infant's developing systems are exposed to chronic release of stress hormones, and the more likely the infant is to learn an unconscious and lifelong lesson about the dangers of trusting someone. Bowlby's early research showed that when toddlers were separated from *both* parents for even a few days' hospital stay, intense child distress and disturbances in parent–child relationships persisted for as long as 6 months after the child came home. Those findings led to reforms in pediatric hospital policy that allowed parents to stay with their infants during hospitalizations, a practice that was initially met with resistance from the medical community but is now a social norm. Similar findings regarding separation from *both* parents come from studies of children in Israeli kibbutzim who had slept every night in communal centers away from their parents, a practice that was abandoned by the 1990s. Researchers later found long-lasting disturbances in those children's attachments to their parents (Aviezer et al., 1994, 2002).

Bowlby's early research on orphanages after World War II led to reforms in foster care and adoption policies that emphasize early placement with permanent parents before about 6 months of age, and in the event that is not possible, maintaining the temporary foster parents until about 24 months of age, with permanent placement after that time (for a consensus statement and a current review of effects of early institutionalization see, respectively, Dozier et al., 2014; van IJzendoorn et al., 2020). Confirmation of the importance of establishing and maintaining attachment relationships during the period from about 7 months through 24 months is found in studies of Romanian orphans adopted by British families in the early 1990s. Despite unusually severe deprivation of personalized caregiving in the Romanian orphanages, if infants were adopted before 6 months of age, their daytime cortisol levels and their attachments to adoptive parents did not differ from a control group of adoptive families. Despite the radical change to placement in middle-class British families, if infants were adopted after 6 months of age, daytime cortisol levels and the prevalence of an attachment disorder unique to institutional care were significantly higher than in controls, and cortisol levels and attachment disorder both increased as child age at adoption increased (Gunnar et al., 2001; Rutter et al., 2004). The attachment disorder unique to institutional care seemed to reflect varying degrees of failure to develop attachments to their adoptive parents and was characterized by coy, silly, overexuberant, or overexcited behavior in the presence of strangers.

Secure versus insecure attachments. Although infants are biologically programmed to develop attachments to their caregivers, we have seen that prolonged separations can disrupt attachments in progress, and lack of personalized caregiving can prevent attachment from having a chance to start. But even in normal caregiving environments, not all parent–child attachments are the same. It is a mistake to assume that infants' and toddlers' attachment needs for security will be met simply by having regular, consistent caregiving. Attachments can be secure or insecure, and the regularity and amount of caregiving time by itself is not sufficient for secure attachment to develop. Rates of insecurity vary with cultural differences in childrearing but are always found to be substantial (for cross-cultural review, see Mesman et al., 2016). In middle-class American families, for example, only about two thirds of parent–child attachments are classified as secure. That means that about one third are classified as insecure. A 33% rate of failure to establish secure parent–child attachments shows that attachment development differs from language development. Both are biologically programmed, but it is unheard of that in any population, one third of children would fail to become fluent speakers of the language of their community. Whereas linguistic interaction with caregivers is sufficient for language fluency, social interaction with caregivers is not sufficient for attachment security.

The security or insecurity of any parent–child attachment relationship reflects both individuals' contributions to the relationship. Parents differ in how responsive they are to infant signals, and infants differ in irritability and in how quickly they can be soothed. Insecure attachments are likely to develop when the behaviors of both the parent and the infant result in parents responding less effectively to infant signals. Disrupted cycles of signal and response result. Laboratory procedures administered by trained researchers reveal that some insecurely attached toddlers (labeled insecure-avoidant) neither signal to the parent when distressed nor expect the parent to initiate a soothing response. They act as if they have given up expecting to receive comfort from that parent and instead seem to withhold their painful feelings of distress from that parent. Other insecurely attached toddlers (labeled insecure-resistant) do signal their distress but are not easily comforted when the parent responds. Instead, they show aggressive behaviors toward that parent while the parent attempts to provide a soothing response. In neither case does the child's stress response system easily return to a healthy equilibrium; instead, it is held in disequilibrium by anger. Anger is expressed covertly and overtly, respectively, in both types of insecure attachment styles. The role of anger in the attachment system is not well understood, but it could function as a warning message to the caregiver. Insecure attachments can become more secure during the child's early years, perhaps as some parents get the message and are able to establish more effective cycles of signal and response. By the same token, initially secure attachments can become more insecure, not only as a result of prolonged separations but also as a result of deteriorated parenting. Avoidant and resistant attachment styles are easily observable in adults. Adults with insecure attachment histories are likely prone to attribute negative intentions to their partners and to respond with anger in the form of withdrawal or attack.

Insecure attachments stem from many of the same types of risky family environments that Repetti et al. (2002) found predicted stress-related physical and mental health problems later in life. For example, Flinn and England (1997) reported that abnormal cortisol response profiles, diminished immunity, and frequent illnesses from infancy through adolescence could be traced back to the types of parent–child interaction patterns that interfere with healthy cycles of signal and response and thus foster insecurity (i.e., unavailable or erratic attention from parents; few positive, affectionate interactions; and high levels of negative interactions). On the one hand, family circumstances can make it harder for any parent and infant to establish and maintain a secure attachment. Flinn and England (1997) reported that it was less likely for children to receive positive parenting when mothers had little or no mate or kin support that they could draw on. Both divorce and high parent conflict can also diminish parenting quality (Sturge-Apple et al., 2012), adversely affect children's cortisol reactivity (Davies et al., 2007), and threaten children's emotional security. On the other hand, improvements in family circumstances that lead to decreased conflict can enhance parenting and cause parent–child relationships to become more secure (Cummings & Davies, 2002).

Attachments to multiple caregivers. Infants in two-parent families begin to form attachments to both mothers and fathers at the same time, even though fathers typically spend less time with their infants (see Lamb, 2002, for a review). In an early study, Parke and Sawin (1980) found that, regardless of educational background, new fathers were as effective as mothers in feeding newborns. Since then, researchers have consistently found that fathers and mothers display similar sensitivity to their infants' signals (e.g., Cabrera et al., 2010). Thus, it should be unsurprising that infants are as likely to be securely attached to mothers as they are to be securely attached to fathers. For example, Kochanska and Kim (2013) found that among the 100 children they assessed at 15 months of age, 40 were secure with both mother and father, 18 were insecure with both, and 42 were mixed—16 secure with mother but insecure with father, and 26 secure with father but insecure with mother. Child sex was unrelated to whether the infants were securely attached to mothers or fathers.

Biological and neurological factors underpin equal attachments to mothers and fathers. Biological changes appear to shift men away from mating effort and toward preparation for fatherhood (Bakermans-Kranenburg et al., 2019; Feldman et al., 2019). For example, testosterone levels decline during romantic relationships, continue to decline during the pregnancy, and decline further as men transition to fatherhood (Corpuza & Bugental, 2020; see also Meijer et al., 2019). Similar decrease in testosterone occurs in other paternal mammals (Reburn & Wynne-Edwards, 1999) and in paternal birds (Wingfield & Farner, 1993). Both men and women have higher concentrations of prolactin (linked to paternal responsiveness to baby cries and paternal caregiving in many species) and cortisol (linked to maternal affiliative behaviors toward infants, and likely also to paternal affiliative behaviors) just before the births of their children and lower concentrations of sex steroids (testosterone or estradiol) after birth (Storey et al., 2000). One indicator of a history of early positive father–child social interactions has been found in enhanced rhythmic synchrony of brain activity between fathers and their 5- to 6-year-old children during cooperative problem solving (Nguyen et al., 2021). These findings parallel similar previous findings with mothers. Brain synchrony is thought to be important in facilitating the continuous monitoring of a partner's behavior and one's own intentions and behavior during cooperative social interactions (Perner et al., 2006).

Other studies of the effects of fathers' parenting on child development also attest to the importance of attachments to both parents. In regard to mental health, studies have consistently shown that mother–child and father–child attachment relationships play similar roles in children's development of problem behaviors, depression, and anxiety (Deneault et al., 2021) and further suggest that the mental health benefits of two secure relationships likely outweigh the benefits from only one secure parent–child relationship (Dagan et al., 2021).

Early father involvement is also associated with children's educational attainments, independent of mothers' involvement, child sex, and one- or two-parent family structure (Flouri & Buchanan, 2004).

In addition, recent studies on child stress- and health-related variables reveal effects of fathers' parenting during infancy. For example, high father involvement in infancy is associated with low levels of cortisol in 2-year-olds (Mills-Koonce et al., 2011). Fathers' high involvement and personal commitment to sharing infant care at 12 months of age can blunt the effects of chronic stress, protecting those children who are biologically oversensitive to stress and who otherwise would be at risk for mental health problems at age 9 (Boyce et al., 2006; Roby et al., 2021). At 10 months of age, fathers' sensitive parenting was actually found to be more closely related than mothers' sensitive parenting to infants' ability to successfully manage their emotional reactions to frustrations in a challenging problem-solving task (Martins et al., 2016). At 27 months of age, both mothers' and fathers' parenting behaviors predicted children's ability to self-regulate and manage stress at 4½ and 6 years of age, after controlling for child sex, child temperament, and hereditary effects (Bridgett et al., 2018).

Father–child shared time often emerges as one important aspect of positive father involvement and as such is relevant to the general issue of parenting time after divorce or separation. For example, shared activities, supportive behavior, and feelings of affection on the part of mothers and both biological and stepfathers predict fewer child behavior problems that are linked with dysregulation of the stress response system (Amato & Gilbreth, 1999; Amato & Rivera, 1999). Frequent father engagement in shared activities in adolescence predicts lower cortisol reactivity to stress in young adulthood (Ibrahim et al., 2017). In postdivorce families, higher father support behaviors (i.e., helping, participating in fun activities, and giving positive feedback, advice, and emotional support) bolster adolescents' self-esteem and confidence in their ability to handle problems, which in turn predict better stress-related physical health in young adulthood (Ibrahim et al., 2021).

Summary. During the first 2 years, infants and toddlers begin to develop their first relationships. Given two caregivers, children will develop independent relationships with each, gaining emotional security from both, neither, or only one (for a current review see Dagan & Sagi-Schwartz, 2021). The initial security or insecurity of a parent–child attachment relationship is not set in stone but can change, and security must be maintained by continued responsiveness and availability of the parent. Secure parent–child relationships provide an important component of future mental health and, given the intimate connection between mind and body, future stress-related physical health as well. Courts cannot predict the future of any parent–child relationship, but they can do no harm during the child's early years by prioritizing the continued availability of both parents.

Research on Overnight Parenting Time for Infants and Toddlers

Previous research. Parkinson's thesis about insufficient consensus and unsatisfactory compromises is most clearly illustrated in the flurry of activity in 2014 that was noted above—that is, the guidelines for overnight parenting time for infants and toddlers (McIntosh et al., 2014; Pruett et al., 2014), the alternative consensus statement (Warshak, 2014), and the many critiques of the small empirical base of four studies of overnight parenting time for infants and toddlers (e.g., Nielsen, 2014; see Emery et al., 2016, for a full list of citations).

The insufficient consensus was expressed by Emery et al. (2016), who advised that in the debates about overnight parenting to date, there was "an inadequate body of research upon which to speculate about policy implications" (p. 144). In fact, none of the four studies had found evidence of harm to the mother–child relationship associated with overnight parenting time. The only study that used the gold-standard Strange Situation procedure for assessing attachment in young children (Solomon & George, 1999) found that attachment classifications were *not* significantly different between families with at least one overnight with father per month and those with at least one daytime visit but no overnights; furthermore, within the overnight group, there were no associations between attachment to each parent and any of eight measures of the length, frequency, and age of initiation of overnights. Two of the four studies did not assess attachment with valid measures (McIntosh et al., 2013; Tornello et al., 2013), and the fourth did not assess parent–child relationships at all (Pruett et al., 2004). Other findings among these four studies of associations between overnights and child outcome measures that might be expected to reflect attachment insecurity were limited and contradictory; that is, associations between overnights and difficulty with persistence and more problem behaviors (McIntosh et al., 2013) were contradicted by associations with fewer social problems (Pruett et al., 2004) and more positive behaviors (Tornello et al., 2013), and associations with more wheezing and irritability at age 1 were contradicted by associations with less wheezing and better health at age 2 (McIntosh et al., 2013). At least 39 other statistical tests in these four studies found no associations with overnights, even at the trend level (i.e., p = .10).

Unsatisfactory compromises were evident among the authors of the various guidelines (for a detailed analysis, see Warshak, 2018). Specifically, for birth to 18 months of age, proposals ranged from no overnights, unless it would benefit the mother (McIntosh, 2011), to a limit of one overnight per week for all parents (McIntosh et al., 2014), to a limit of one overnight per week for parents who disagree on the parenting plan and take their cases to court ("Charting Overnight Decisions for Infants and Toddlers (CODIT)" guidelines; see McIntosh et al., 2014). For 2- and 3-year-olds, proposals ranged from one overnight per week for all parents (McIntosh et al., 2015), to a limit of one overnight per week for parents who disagree (Pruett et al., 2014, 2016), to no limit on overnights simply because parents disagree (Kelly, 2014).

Current research. The most recent consensus statement by the attachment research community (Forslund et al., 2021) does not resolve the question of whether equal parenting time during the first years is associated with higher rates of secure attachment:

> What differs among attachment researchers—the current authors included—is whether the relationship with a "most familiar" caregiver may have particular importance as a safe haven in the earliest years of child life, and whether this caregiver—in the context of custody decisions—should consequently be allocated more time with the child until the child's cognitive development makes separations from the most familiar caregiver more tolerable. (p. 12)

For the past 20 years, beginning with Solomon and Biringen (2001), attachment researchers have called for research to answer the question of whether equal parenting time during the first years of life is associated with higher rates of secure attachment; yet, Forslund et al. (2021) noted that "the attachment research community has not done enough research on topics and with samples relevant to court practice (e.g. time-allocation, overnights, and inter-parental conflict in relation to child attachment)" (p. 21). To our knowledge, Fabricius and Suh (2017) is the only new, quantitative study of overnight parenting time for very young children to appear since the original four studies. Attesting to the intense interest and need for research in this area, Fabricius and Suh (2017) was the most downloaded paper from the *Psychology, Public Policy, and Law* journal webpage in 2017 (Michael Lamb, personal communication, March 31, 2018) and reached over 10,000 "reads" on Research Gate by the end of 2021.

Forslund et al. (2021) called for studies that meet at least three requirements: collaboration between attachment experts and practitioners; tests of whether the association between overnights and attachment is influenced by different levels of parental conflict, parental cooperation, and children's developmental age; and careful consideration of the implications for court decisions. Fabricius and Suh (2017) largely met these requirements. We initiated the study in 2012 when the alarm was raised about overnight parenting time for very young children. In line with the call for collaborative research, we consulted in the early stages with Alan Sroufe, who has long been a leading attachment theorist and researcher, as well as a principal contributor to the 2011 special issue of *Family Court Review* (Sroufe & McIntosh, 2011). He suggested to us that any effects of overnight parenting time would have the strongest impact if overnights were initiated during the child's first year. In response, we took the additional time to assemble a sample large enough to allow us to compare families that had initiated overnights during the child's first, second, or third year. We also examined the relation between equal overnight parenting time and attachment at different levels of parent conflict and parent cooperation. Finally, we also consulted with Sroufe on deriving the implications of the findings.

The four previous studies had examined only short-term associations with overnights, in which case it is difficult to distinguish temporary adjustment problems from more enduring effects on parent–child relationships. Attachment theory has always been directed toward explaining how experiences in infancy can propagate effects extending throughout childhood and into adulthood, with the goal of understanding how better to intervene with therapy and policy. Thus, we assessed long-term associations, and we did so by recruiting college students ($N = 116$) whose parents had separated before they were 3 years old. This strategy provided some insight into long-term associations without having to wait 20 years to collect longitudinal data, but it also meant that we did not assess attachment with the standard measures during toddlerhood; consequently, the study fell outside of the focus adopted by Forslund et al. (2021) and received only brief mention there.

The students reported on their *current* relationships with each of their parents. Thus, the data on the dependent variables (i.e., security of parent–child relationships in young adulthood) were not retrospective. Most importantly, we also recruited the parents, and they reported on the predictor variables (i.e., parenting time at the father's home during each of the child's first 3 years) as well as on the various control variables. This met the rigorous requirement of obtaining data on predictor and dependent variables from different reporters, which is not met when mothers report both overnights and child behaviors, as was the case in McIntosh et al. (2013) and Tornello et al. (2013).

The data from the parents were retrospective and thus potentially subject to recall biases. The rigorous requirement for establishing objectivity of retrospective data is that different reporters agree with each other. On all our retrospective variables, mothers' and fathers' independent reports were highly consistent with each other (and also with students' reports where applicable), replicating Fabricius and Luecken's (2007) findings of similar consistency among multiple reporters with a sample such as this one, and providing some assurance of objectivity.

Regarding representativeness, college samples of young adults with divorced parents are sometimes characterized as the "success stories" of children of divorce, but that is not necessarily the case, at least not in terms of mental health. Face-to-face interviews conducted in the 2001–2002 National Epidemiologic Survey on Alcohol and Related Conditions ($N = 43,093$) revealed that almost half of college-aged individuals had a psychiatric disorder in the past year, and the overall rate did not differ between those attending college and those not attending college (Blanco et al., 2008). Laumann-Billings and Emery (2000) also reported that their sample of relatively affluent University of Virginia students did not differ on standard measures of mental health, as well as on a new measure of lingering painful feelings about parents' divorces, from low-income community adolescents and young adults, many of whom had chaotic family backgrounds including abuse and extreme poverty. Whereas Laumann-Billings and Emery's college sample was middle to upper-middle class (mean household income = $105,715), our college samples have been drawn from Arizona State University, whose mission goals include "accessibility to match Arizona's socioeconomic diversity" (https://newamericanuniversity.asu.edu/about/asu-charter-mission-and-goals). That goal is a reality, as reflected in a large sample (N = 1,030) that we obtained in 2006, in which students were asked, for each parent, "What is the financial status of your [mother's/father's] household (including new spouse, if any) right now?" The 10-point scale ranged from "complete poverty" to "very wealthy." The median for mothers' households was at the midpoint of the scale (i.e., "enough money for almost all small extras [i.e., under $50], and very few big extras [over $500]"). The median for fathers' households was one step above ("enough money for all small extras and a few big extras"). The students' reports correlated highly with the Free Application for Federal Student Aid (FAFSA) data on their families' financial situations supplied to us by the university Office of Financial Aid, thus providing some assurance of objectivity.

Returning to the Fabricius and Suh study, students rated five different aspects of their current relationships with each of their parents: attributions of parental blame for family problems (Laumann-Billings & Emery, 2000), representations of parental warmth and responsiveness (Parker, 1989), enjoyment in spending time together, overall closeness of the relationship, and feelings of mattering to parents (Velez et al., 2020). All five measures tapped into two distinct factors, one reflecting mother–child relationships and one reflecting father–child relationships. Students' scores on each factor provided continuous measures that we took to be reasonable indications of how secure they currently felt with each parent.

Parents reported the frequency of parent conflict before and up to 5 years after the separation, their level of education, and whether they had agreed about overnight parenting time (75% of the families) or disagreed (25%). Those who disagreed reported either that they never came to an agreement and one parent got what he or she wanted mostly because the other one gave in, or that the final decision came from mediation, custody evaluation, attorney-led bargaining, or court hearing. Parents further reported that when they disagreed, it was because the father wanted the child to spend more overnights at his home but the mother wanted the child to spend fewer overnights at his home. Parents who disagreed ended up with similar numbers of overnights as parents who agreed, and in both groups, 14% of children had equal overnights with each parent at age 2. Parents also reported the amount of parenting time with the father when the child was 5 to 10 years old and 10 to 15 years old, because controlling for effects of later parenting time is necessary in order to isolate the effects of parenting time during the child's first 3 years.

For father–child relationships, there was a linear, "dose-response" relation between more overnights with fathers, *up to and including equal overnights* at both parents' homes, and correspondingly higher scores on the relationship security factor. For mother–child relationships, there was no decrease in scores on the relationship security factor with increasing overnights; on the contrary, higher scores on the relationship security factor were associated with having *at least two to four overnights per month* with fathers, as well as *more daytime-only parenting time* with fathers. The positive associations between overnight parenting time and long-term quality of both parent–child relationships are to be expected if infants were developing attachment relationships with both parents. As a result, those young adults who, as infants and toddlers, had more equally distributed overnights with both parents felt closer to both of their parents, were more likely to remember each of their parents as having been warm and responsive during their childhood and as having enjoyed spending time together, blamed their parents less for family problems, and were more certain that they mattered to each of their parents.

These findings for both parents held after controlling for children's sex, daytime parenting time with fathers, yearly percentage of parenting time with fathers during childhood and adolescence, parent education, parent conflict up to 5 years after separation, child age at separation, and disagreement about overnights. Controlling for parenting time in childhood and adolescence means that "lost" overnight parenting time in the first 3 years was not made up by parenting time later. There were no benefits to the father–child relationship associated with daytime-only visits, which means that more daytime visits did not make up for fewer overnights.

The same positive associations between overnights and both parent–child relationships were clearly present regardless of whether parents (a) were more versus less educated, (b) had high conflict versus low conflict, (c) had separated when children were under 1 year old versus when children were either 1 or 2 years old, or (d) had agreed about overnight parenting time and thus presumably volunteered for it versus disagreed and had an arrangement imposed unwillingly upon one of them. This means that it is *not* true that overnights only "worked" for parents who were more educated, who had less conflict, whose children were over 1 year of age, or who had agreed about overnights.

Furthermore, when there was high conflict or disagreement about overnights, more overnights were required for father–child relationships to attain the same level of security as when there was low conflict or agreement. Similarly, when parents had less education or had separated during the child's first year, more overnights were required to attain the same level of father–child relationship security as when parents had more education or had separated during the child's second or third year.

There are developmentally plausible processes by which overnights could lead to long-term benefits in security of parent–child relationships. Overnights allow the father to learn about the child by assuming the role of caregiver. In support of this, a review of 14 papers describing the effectiveness of 12 interventions for fathers of infants and toddlers (Magill-Evans et al., 2006) revealed that active participation with or observation of his child enhanced the father's interactions with and positive perceptions of the child. George and Solomon (2008) suggest that the attachment system in children is complemented by a caregiving system in adults. If so, then in the words of the attachment researchers' (Forslund et al., 2021) current consensus statement:

> Seriously depriving a caregiver of time with his/her child and caregiving responsibilities may consequently not only influence the child's ability to develop and maintain an attachment relationship to the caregiver. It may also have untoward effects on the caregiver's caregiving system, which may become thwarted. (p. 14)

Regarding benefits to the mother–child relationship, overnights provide respite from caring for an infant alone, which could help the mother maintain a higher level of responsive parenting. This harkens back to Flinn and England's (1997) findings, reported earlier, that mothers' positive parenting was facilitated by having mate or kin support. Such support, according to these findings, can come in the form of providing practical assistance with childcare.

Translating Attachment Theory and Research Into Policies for Overnight Parenting Time in Infancy and Toddlerhood

Implications from attachment theory. The developmental course of attachment implies that if parents separate during the first 6 months, when infants do not express stress in separating from one caregiver and joining another, no concerns are raised from the perspective of attachment theory about initiating equal overnight parenting time. During the first 6 months, new caregivers can also be introduced. This applies to cases of never-married parents in which the father and mother have not been living together and paternity is established in the early months. Paternity cases typically have been overlooked in policy discussions (Maldonado, 2014), and have fallen outside the focus of discussions of applying attachment theory to policy as well (Kelly & Lamb, 2000). When parents who have never lived together are both able to provide care, then no concerns are raised from the perspective of attachment theory about initiating equal overnight parenting time during the first 6 months.

The developmental course of attachment also implies that the period from about 7 months through 24 months is the most important time to avoid unexpected and prolonged separations from regular caregivers. Most of the proposed guidelines from 2014 assumed that overnights with all fathers should be gradually introduced in some kind of "step-up" plan during this time period. In paternity cases where paternity is established 6 months or more after the child's birth, gradually introducing overnight parenting time with the father would be consistent with attachment theory. However, when fathers have been living with mothers before the separation, "gradual introduction" of overnights means that the child experiences "immediate separation" from the father precisely during the time when abrupt and prolonged separations are to be avoided.

Among some professionals who use attachment theory to advise courts, there has been a persistent bias to put primary emphasis on risk of harm to mother–child attachment security and secondary emphasis on possibility of benefit to father–child attachment security. Kelly and Lamb (2000) explained where this bias originated:

> Thus, the infant or toddler who was accustomed to seeing both parents each day abruptly began seeing one parent, usually the father, only once a week (or once every 2 weeks) for a few hours. This arrangement was often represented by professionals as being in the best interests of the child due to the mistaken understanding, based on Bowlby's earliest speculations, that infants had only one significant or primary attachment. As a result, early child development research followed untested psychoanalytic theory in focusing exclusively on mothers and infants, presuming fathers to be quite peripheral and unnecessary to children's development and psychological adjustment. The resulting custody arrangements sacrificed continuity in infant-father relationships, with long-term socioemotional and economic consequences for children. (p. 304)

Implications from empirical research. In intact families, high-quality attachment research has consistently revealed that infants and toddlers are as likely to be secure with fathers as with mothers. Evidence that traditional visitation schedules have interfered with the development of secure father–child relationships comes from the fact that damaged father–child relationships are the most frequent outcome of divorce (Amato, 2003). Visitation schedules that unwittingly promote insecurity with fathers leave children to depend solely on the mother–child relationship for attachment security. Equal parenting time with both parents gives children a better chance of having at least one or two secure relationships, which is reflected in findings that with equal parenting time, parent–child relationships in young adulthood are similar in divorced and intact families (Fabricius, 2003; Luecken & Fabricius, 2003).

The Fabricius and Suh (2017) study did not find any associations between equal overnights and any long-term harm to either parent–child relationship but instead revealed benefits to both relationships. Thus, the findings constitute a strong rejection of the hypothesis that attachment harm would be associated with overnight parenting time, and they contradict the policy implication that "prior to age 18 months, overnights away from the primary carer [*sic*] should be quite rare" (Sroufe & McIntosh, 2011, p. 472). In discussing the policy implications with us, Sroufe decided, "Your results would of course lead me to temper my conclusions" (personal communication, September 21, 2016).

The Fabricius and Suh (2017) findings do not support policies that would urge parents and courts to generally be cautious about frequent overnights, or to begin with few overnights and gradually "step up" over several years to frequent overnights, when there are no extenuating circumstances such as parent mental illness, previous absence from the child's life, and so forth. The best parent–child relationships in young adulthood were those in which the children were spending equal overnights at both parents' homes before they turned 3. The long-term connection was independent of parenting time in childhood and adolescence and thus constitutes an impressive validation of attachment theory.

The findings also indicate that parent conflict, disagreements about overnights, and children under 1 year of age are not circumstances that should require caution; on the contrary, more overnight parenting time was needed in those cases to achieve the same benefits to the father–child relationship. Importantly, the finding that benefits accrued to both mother–child and father–child relationships even when courts ordered overnight parenting over the mother's objections resembled a similar finding from the classic Stanford Child Custody Study (Maccoby & Mnookin, 1992). Fabricius et al. (2012) reported that in the publicly available data from the Stanford study, the great majority of parents with shared parenting had to accept it after mediation, custody evaluation, trial, or judicial imposition. Nevertheless, those with shared parenting time had the most well-adjusted children years later. These findings provide evidential support for policies to encourage frequent overnight parenting time for infants and toddlers, even when one parent disagrees.

Finally, the opposite policy of postponing overnights would conflict with historically developing social norms. In the 1980s, one third of children under 2 spent overnights with their separated and divorced fathers (Maccoby et al., 1988; Seltzer, 1991). The Fabricius and Suh data reveal that in the mid-1990s, over half of parents of future college students provided overnights when the child was 1 year old, almost two thirds did so when the child was 2, and parents increased rather than decreased overnights during the child's first 3 years, which suggests that parents found overnight parenting time workable.

Conclusions

Empirical basis for custody policy reform: Attachment and health. Attachment theory is one of the great scientific advances, and early on it assumed its place among the great applications of basic science to public health. Infants in pediatric wards had long suffered high rates of failure to thrive and death from unknown causes. Bowlby and his colleagues recognized the power of sudden and protracted interference with infants' biological drive to form attachments. The medical community was unaware of the emotional life of infants, focused instead on protection from germ transmission, and was understandably reluctant to consider that traditional policies of excluding parents from pediatric wards might have unwittingly been causing harm. Films made of the rapid emotional withdrawal of infants in the first few days of complete separation from parents were instrumental in changing policy, and once started, the opening up of pediatric wards to parents quickly spread.

Modern research reveals connections between the more mundane forms of attachment insecurity that arise in typical childrearing contexts, dysregulation of children's stress response systems, and long-term, stress-related, chronic physical and mental health problems (Ranson & Urichuk, 2008; Repetti et al., 2002; Troxel & Matthews, 2004). Chronic diseases are a great cost to individuals and to society. Thus, attachment theory has the potential to make further contributions to public health.

Forslund et al. (2021) missed an opportunity to connect attachment insecurity and physical health. They focused instead on advising courts about the psychology of attachment and the misuse of laboratory measures of attachment, all of which is important and needed, especially in regard to regulating child protection services. But without drawing a connection to physical health, the attachment researchers' consensus statement does little to help family courts weigh the importance of protecting the young child's developing attachment to each parent against myriad other factors that courts are required to consider.

The consistent pattern of previous findings reveals a chain of connections from equal parenting time in childhood, to secure parent–child relationships in young adulthood, to long-term health (for reviews see Fabricius, 2020; Fabricius et al., 2012). The current findings indicate the unique role of equal parenting time in infancy and toddlerhood in laying the foundation for future relationships. The long-term health risk of damaged parent–child relationships should translate into policies that encourage equal parenting time in order to protect the young child's developing attachment to each parent and the child's future health.

In the drive to develop and test attachment theory, researchers had focused almost exclusively on mother–child attachment. The unfortunate effect was that when custody standards switched in the 1970s from the "tender years doctrine" that young children should be placed with mothers to the child's best interests standard, which was meant to be gender neutral, the traditional gender bias in family law was not challenged by the attachment research of the day. Every-other-weekend visits between divorced fathers and their children remained the norm. The public health benefits once afforded by the application of attachment theory to the medical community now need to be extended by similar application to the family law community.

Principled legal basis for custody policy reform: Gender equality. The cultural shift beginning in the 1970s toward recognition of the importance of father involvement in childrearing is directly reflected in public attitudes today favoring equal parenting time after divorce (Braver et al., 2011; Fabricius et al., 2012; Votruba et al., 2014). It is also reflected in the push for legal presumptions favoring equal parenting time currently underway in many countries around the world and recently instituted in Belgium and in six states in the United States (Arizona in 2013 and Kentucky in 2018, followed recently by West Virginia, Arkansas, Missouri, and Florida; for an evaluation of Arizona's law see Fabricius et al., 2018). As Parkinson (2011) notes, however, the legal debates often seem to be framed in terms of a trade-off between freedom to pursue new lives after divorce and continuing ties to ex-spouses in terms of childrearing, or between "mothers' rights" and "fathers' rights."

As often happens in the historical development of new ideas, when two sides have strong but irreconcilable arguments, it signals that both are overlooking something. In this case, both sides are overlooking the very thing that has fueled both, which is the underlying cultural change toward gender equality. Gender equality motivated the changes in legal standards that instituted no-fault divorce and related policies including child support enforcement with the intention of leveling the playing field for both parents to pursue new lives. Gender equality in terms of parenting motivates the current custody reforms favoring equal parenting time.

Gender equality provides the needed principled legal framework on which to found consistent new custody policies presuming equal parenting time. There are strong arguments that equal parenting time supports greater gender equality (David, 2019). Legislation for rebuttable presumptions of equal parenting time would be an unmistakable espousal of gender equality in family law, and would have broader societal effects. It would legitimize and codify expectations and social norms of equal parental responsibility for childcare (Maldonado, 2005); it would counteract the public perception of maternal bias in custody decisions and restore faith in the family courts (Braver et al., 2011); and it would have cascading effects onto other gender equity policies in the workplace.

In the current political climate, it is remarkable that legislation for rebuttable presumptions of equal parenting time has received strong bipartisan support in the six states so far that have passed it. In each case, the groundwork laid by researchers, parents, and advocates in educating legislators and judges about the empirical research on equal parenting time allowed policymakers to realize that the policies of the past were based on a lingering maternal bias in custody decisions.

Equal parenting time serves children's best interests in terms of their long-term health, and it serves gender equality as well. New custody policies presuming equal parenting time will allow ex-spouses to pursue their separate lives on a more equal playing field, while maintaining both parents in their children's lives, from birth onward.

Acknowledgments
Helpful comments and suggestions on an earlier draft were received from Abraham Sagi-Schwartz and Marinus van IJzendoorn.

References
Albers, E. M., Marianne Riksen-Walraven, J., Sweep, F. C., & Weerth, C. D. (2008). Maternal behavior predicts infant cortisol recovery from a mild everyday stressor. *Journal of Child Psychology and Psychiatry, 49*, 97–103.

Amato, P. R. (2003). Reconciling divergent perspectives: Judith Wallerstein, quantitative family research, and children of divorce. *Family Relations, 52*, 332–339.

Amato, P. R., & Gilbreth, J. G. (1999). Nonresident fathers and children's well-being: A meta-analysis. *Journal of Marriage and Family, 61*, 557–573.

Amato, P. R., & Rivera, F. (1999). Paternal involvement and children's behavior problems. *Journal of Marriage and the Family, 61*, 375–384.

Aviezer, O., Sagi, A., & van IJzendoorn, M. H. (2002). Balancing the family and the collective in raising Kibbutz children: Why the communal sleeping experiment was predestined to fail. *Family Process, 41*, 435–454.

Aviezer, O., van IJzendoorn, M. H., Sagi, A., & Schuengel, C. (1994). "Children of the dream" revisited: 70 years of collective early child care in Israeli kibbutzim. *Psychological Bulletin, 116*, 99–116.

Bakermans-Kranenburg, M. J., Lotz, A., Alyousefi-van Dijk, K., & van IJzendoorn, M. H. (2019). Birth of a father: Fathering in the first 1,000 days. *Child Development Perspectives, 13*, 247–253.

Blanco, C., Okuda, M., Wright, C., Hasin, D. S., Grant, B. F., Liu, S. M., & Olfson, M. (2008). Mental health of college students and their non-college-attending peers: Results from the National Epidemiologic Study on Alcohol and Related Conditions. *Archives of General Psychiatry, 65*, 1429–1437.

Bowlby, J. (1999). *Attachment. Attachment and loss* (Vol. 1, 2nd ed.). Basic Books. (Original work published 1969)

Bowlby, J. (1973). *Separation: Anxiety & anger. Attachment and loss* (Vol. 2; International Psycho-analytical Library No. 95). Hogarth Press.

Bowlby, J. (1980). *Loss: Sadness & depression. Attachment and loss* (Vol. 3; International Psycho-analytical Library No. 109). Hogarth Press.

Boyce, W. T., Essex, M. J., Alkon, A., Goldsmith, H. H., Kraemer, H. C., & Kupfer, D. J. (2006). Early father involvement moderates biobehavioral susceptibility to mental health problems in middle childhood. *Journal of the American Academy of Child and Adolescent Psychiatry, 45*, 1510–1520.

Braver, S. L., Ellman, I., Vortuba, A., & Fabricius, W. V. (2011). Lay judgments about child custody after divorce. *Psychology, Public Policy and Law, 17*, 212–240.

Bridgett, D. J., Ganiban, J. M., Neiderhiser, J. M., Natsuaki, M. N., Shaw, D. S., Reiss, D., & Leve, L. D. (2018). Contributions of mothers' and fathers' parenting to children's self-regulation: Evidence from an adoption study. *Developmental Science, 21*, e12692.

Cabrera, N. J., Shannon, J. D., & Tamis-LeMonda, C. (2010). Fathers' influence on their children's cognitive and emotional development: From toddlers to pre-K. *Applied Developmental Science, 11*, 208–213.

Caldi, C., Tannenbaum, B., Sharma, S., Francis, D., Plotsky, P. M., & Meaney, M. J. (1998). Maternal care during infancy regulates the development of neural systems mediating the expression of fearfulness in the rat. *Proceedings of the National Academy of Science of the United States of America, 95*, 5335–5340.

Corpuza, R., & Bugental, D. (2020). Life history and individual differences in male testosterone: Mixed evidence for early environmental calibration of testosterone response to first-time fatherhood. *Hormones and Behavior, 120,* 104684.

Cummings, E. M., & Davies, P. T. (2002). Effects of marital conflict on children: Recent advances and emerging themes in process-oriented research. *Journal of Child Psychology and Psychiatry, 43,* 31–63.

Dagan, O., & Sagi-Schwartz, A. (2021). Early attachment network to multiple caregivers: History, assessment models, and future research recommendations. *New Directions in Child and Adolescent Development, 180,* 9–19.

Dagan, O., Schuengel, C., Verhage, M., van IJzendoorn, M. H., Sagi-Schwartz, A., Madigan, S., Duschinsky, R., Roisman, G. I., Bernard, K., Bakermans-Kranenburg, M., Bureau, J-F., Volling, B. L., Wong, M. S., Colonnesi, C., Brown, G. L., Eiden, R. D., Pasco Fearon, R. M., Oosterman, M., Aviezer, O., & Cummings, E. M. (2021). Configurations of mother-child and father-child attachment as predictors of internalizing and externalizing symptoms: An individual participant data (IPD) meta-analysis. *New Directions for Child and Adolescent Development, 180,* 67–94.

David, H. (2019). Shared parenting in the modern family from a feminist view. *Journal of Interdisciplinary Sciences, 3,* 36–54.

Davies, P. T., Sturge-Apple, M. L., Cicchetti, D., & Cummings, E. M. (2007). The role of child adrenocortical functioning in pathways between interparental conflict and child maladjustment. *Developmental Psychology, 43,* 918–930.

Deneault, A. A., Bakermans-Kranenburg, M. J., Groh, A. M., Pasco Fearon, R. M., & Madigan, S. (2021). Child-father attachment in early childhood and behavior problems: A meta-analysis. *Child and Adolescent Development, 2021,* 43–66.

Dozier, M., Kaufman, J., Kobak, R. R., O'Connor, T. G., Sagi-Schwartz, A., Scott, S., Shauffer, C., Smetana, J., van IJzendoorn, M. H., & Zeanah, C. H. (2014). Consensus statement on group care for children and adolescents. *American Journal of Orthopsychiatry, 84,* 219–225.

Emery, R. E., Holtzworth-Munroe, A., Johnston, J. R., Pedro-Carroll, J. L., Pruett, M. K., Saini, M., & Sandler, I. (2016). "Bending" the evidence for a cause: Scholar-advocacy bias in family law. *Family Court Review, 54,* 134–149.

Emery, R. E., Otto, R. K., & O'Donohue, W. T. (2005). A critical assessment of child custody evaluations: Limited science and a flawed system. *Psychological Science in the Public Interest, 6,* 1–29.

Fabricius, W. V. (2003). Listening to children of divorce: New findings on living arrangements, college support and relocation that rebut Wallerstein, Lewis and Blakeslee. *Family Relations, 52,* 385–396.

Fabricius, W. V. (2020). Equal parenting time: The case for a legal presumption. In J. G. Dwyer (Ed.), *Oxford handbook of children and the law* (pp. 453–475). Oxford University Press.

Fabricius, W. V., Aaron, M., Akins, F. R., Assini, J. J., & McElroy, T. (2018). What happens when there is presumptive 50/50 parenting time? An evaluation of Arizona's new child custody statute. *Journal of Divorce and Remarriage, 59,* 414–428.

Fabricius, W. V., & Luecken, L. J. (2007). Postdivorce living arrangements, parent conflict, and long-term physical health correlates for children of divorce. *Journal of Family Psychology, 21,* 195–205.

Fabricius, W. V., Sokol, K. R., Diaz, P., & Braver, S. L. (2012). Parenting time, parent conflict, parent-child relationships, and children's physical health. In K. Kuehnle & L. Drozd (Eds.), *Parenting plan evaluations: Applied research for the family court* (pp. 188–213). Oxford University Press.

Fabricius, W. V., & Suh, G. W. (2017). Should infants and toddlers not have overnight parenting time with fathers? The policy debate and new data. *Psychology, Public Policy, and Law, 23,* 68–84.

Feldman, R., Braun, K., & Champagne, F. A. (2019). The neural mechanisms and consequences of paternal caregiving. *Nature Reviews Neuroscience, 20,* 205–224.

Flinn, M. V., & England, B. G. (1997). Social economics of childhood glucocorticoid stress responses and health. *American Journal of Physical Anthropology, 102,* 33–53.

Flouri, E., & Buchanan, A. (2004). Early father's and mother's involvement and child's later educational outcomes. *British Journal of Educational Psychology, 74,* 141–153.

Forslund, T., Granqvist, P., van IJzendoorn, M. H., Sagi-Schwartz, A., Glaser, D., Steele, M., Hammarlund, M., Schuengel, C., Bakermans-Kranenburg, M. J., Steele, H., Shaver, P. R., Lux, U., Simmonds, J., Jacobvitz, D., Groh, A. M., Bernard, K., Cyr, C., Hazen, N. L., Foster, S., . . . Duschinsky, R. (2022). Attachment goes to court: Child protection and custody issues. *Attachment & Human Development, 24*(1), 1–52.

George, C., & Solomon, J. (2008). The caregiving system: A behavioral systems approach to parenting. In J. Cassidy & P. R. Shaver (Eds.), *Handbook of attachment: Theory, research, and clinical applications* (pp. 833–856). Guilford Press.

Gunnar, M. R., Morison, S. J., Chisholm, K., & Schuder, M. f2001). Salivary cortisol levels in children adopted from Romanian orphanages. *Developmental Psychopathology, 13*, 611–628.

Ibrahim, M. H., Luecken, L. J., Jewell, S. L., Somers, J. A., Wolchik, S. A., & Sandler, I. N. (2021). Father supportive behaviors and offspring physical health perceptions 15-years after parental divorce. *Family Court Review, 59*, 294–308.

Ibrahim, M. H., Somers, J. A., Luecken, L. J., Fabricius, W. V., & Cookston, J. T. (2017). Father-adolescent engagement in shared activities: Effects on cortisol stress response in young adulthood. *Family Psychology, 31*, 485–494.

Kelly, J. B. (2014). Paternal involvement and child and adolescent adjustment after separation and divorce: Current research and implications for policy and practice. *International Family Law, Policy, & Practice, 2*, 5–23.

Kelly, J. B., & Lamb, M. E. (2000). Using child development research to make appropriate custody and access decisions for young children. *Family Court Review, 38*, 297–311.

Kochanska, G., & Kim, S. (2013). Early attachment organization with both parents and future behavior problems: From infancy to middle childhood. *Child Development, 84*, 283–296.

Lamb, M. E. (2002). Infant-father attachments and their impact on child development. In C. S. Tamis-LeMonda & N. Cabrera (Eds.), *Handbook of father involvement: Multidisciplinary perspectives* (pp. 93–117). Erlbaum.

Lamb, M. (2012). A wasted opportunity to engage with the literature on the implications of attachment research for family court professionals. *Family Court Review, 50*, 481–485.

Lamb, M. E., & Lewis, C. (2010). The development and significance of father–child relationships in two-parent families. In M. E. Lamb (Ed.), *The role of the father in child development* (pp. 94–153). Wiley.

Laumann-Billings, L., & Emery, R. E. (2000). Distress among young adults from divorced families. *Journal of Family Psychology, 14*, 671–687.

Ludolph, P. S. (2012). The special issue on attachment: Overreaching theory and data. *Family Court Review, 50*, 486–495.

Luecken, L. J. (1998). Childhood attachment and loss experiences affect adult cardiovascular and cortisol function. *Psychosomatic Medicine, 60*, 765–772.

Luecken, L. J., & Fabricius, W. V. (2003). Physical health vulnerability in adult children from divorced and intact families. *Journal of Psychosomatic Research, 55*(3), 221–228.

Maccoby, E. E., Charlene, E., Depner, C. E., & Mnookin, R. H. (1988). Custody of children following divorce. In E. M. Hetherington & J. Arasteh (Eds.), *The impact of divorce, single parenting, and stepparenting on children* (pp. 91–114). Erlbaum.

Maccoby, E. E., & Mnookin, R. H. (1992). *Dividing the child: Social and legal dilemmas of custody*. Harvard University Press.

Magill-Evans, J., Harrison, M. J., Rempel, G., & Slater, L. (2006). Interventions with fathers of young children: Systematic literature review. *Journal of Advanced Nursing, 55*, 248–264.

Maldonado, S. (2005). Beyond economic fatherhood: Encouraging divorced fathers to parent. *University of Pennsylvania Law Review, 153*, 921–1009.

Maldonado, S. (2014). Shared parenting and never-married families. *Family Court Review, 52*, 632–638.

Martins, E. C., Soares, I., Martins, C., & Osorio, A. (2016). Infants' style of emotion regulation with their mothers and fathers: Concordance between parents and the contribution of father–infant interaction quality. *Social Development, 25*, 812–827.

McIntosh, J. E. (2011). Guest editor's introduction to special issue on attachment theory, separation, and divorce: Forging coherent understandings for family laws. *Family Court Review, 49*, 418–425.

McIntosh, J. E., Pruett, M. K., & Kelly, J. B. (2014). Parental separation and overnight care of young children: Part II. Putting theory into practice. *Family Court Review, 52*, 256–262.

McIntosh, J., Smyth, B., & Kelaher, M. (2013). Overnight care patterns following parental separation: Associations with emotion regulation in infants and young children. *Journal of Family Studies, 19*, 224–239.

McIntosh, J. E., Smyth, B. M., & Kelaher, M. A. (2015). Responding to concerns about a study of infant overnight care postseparation, with comments on consensus: Reply to Warshak (2014). *Psychology, Public Policy, and Law, 21*, 111–119.

Meijer, W. M., Van IJzendoorn, M. H., & Bakermans-Kranenburg, M. J. (2019). Challenging the challenge hypothesis on testosterone in fathers: A meta-analysis. *Psychoneuroendocrinology, 110*, 104435.

Mesman, J., van IJzendoorn, M. H., & Sagi-Schwartz, A. (2016). Cross-cultural patterns of attachment: Universal and contextual dimensions. In J. Cassidy & P. Shaver (Eds.), *Handbook of attachment: Theory, research, and clinical applications* (3rd ed., pp. 852–877). Guilford.

Mills-Koonce, W. R., Garrett-Peters, P., Barnett, M., Granger, D. A., Blair, C., Cox, M. J., & Family Life Project. (2011). Father contributions to cortisol responses in infancy and toddlerhood. *Developmental Psychology, 47*, 388–395.

Nguyen, T., Schleihauf, H., Kungl, M., Kayhan, E., Hoehl, S., & Vrticka, P. (2021). Interpersonal neural synchrony during father–child problem solving: An fNIRS hyperscanning study. *Child Development, 92*(4), e565–e580.

Nielsen, L. (2014). Woozles: Their role in custody law reform, parenting plans, and family court. *Psychology, Public Policy, and Law, 20*, 164–180.

Parke, R. D., & Sawin, D. B. (1980). The family in early infancy: Social interactional and attitudinal analyses. In F. A. Pedersen (Ed.), *The father–infant relationship: Observational studies in a family setting* (pp. 44–70). Praeger.

Parker, G. (1989). The Parental Bonding Instrument: Psychometric properties reviewed. *Psychiatric Developments, 7*, 317–335.

Parkinson, P. (2011). *Family law and the indissolubility of parenthood*. Cambridge University Press.

Perner, J., Aichhorn, M., Kronbichler, M., Staffen, W., & Ladurner, G. (2006). Thinking of mental and other representations: The roles of left and right temporo-parietal junction. *Social Neuroscience, 1*, 245–258.

Pruett, M. K., Deutsch, R. M., & Drozd, L. (2016). Considerations for step-up planning: When and how to determine the "right" time. In L. Drozd, M. Saini, & N. Olesen (Eds.), *Parenting plan evaluations: Applied research for the family court* (2nd ed., pp. 535–554). Oxford University Press.

Pruett, M. K., & DiFonzo, J. H. (2014). AFCC think tank final report. Closing the gap: Research, policy, practice, and shared parenting. *Family Court Review, 52*, 152–174.

Pruett, M. K., Ebling, R., & Insabella, G. (2004). Critical aspects of parenting plans for young children: Interjecting data into the debate about overnights. *Family Court Review, 42*, 39–59.

Pruett, M. K., McIntosh, J. E., & Kelly, J. B. (2014). Parental separation and overnight care of young children: Part I. Consensus through theoretical and empirical integration. *Family Court Review, 52*, 240–255.

Ranson, K. E., & Urichuk, L. J. (2008). The effect of parent–child attachment relationships on child biopsychosocial outcomes: A review. *Early Child Development and Care, 178*, 129–152.

Reburn, C. J., & Wynne-Edwards, K. E. (1999). Hormonal changes in males of a naturally biparental and a uniparental mammal. *Hormones and Behavior, 35*, 163–176.

Repetti, R. L., Taylor, S. E., & Seeman, T. E. (2002). Risky families: Family social environments and the mental and physical health of offspring. *Psychological Bulletin, 128*, 330–366.

Roby, E., Piccolo, L. R., Gutierrez, J., Kesoglides, N. M., Raak, C. D., Mendelsohn, A. L., & Canfield, C. F. (2021). Father involvement in infancy predicts behavior and response to chronic stress in middle childhood in a low-income Latinx sample. *Developmental Psychobiology, 63*, 1449–1465.

Rodham, H. (1973). Children under the law. *Harvard Educational Review, 43*, 487–514.

Rutter, M., O'Conner, T. G., & the English and Romanian Adoptees (ERA) Study Team (2004). Are there biological programming effects for psychological development? Findings from a study of Romanian adoptees. *Developmental Psychology, 40*(1), 81–94.

Seltzer, J. A. (1991). Relationships between fathers and children who live apart: The father's role after separation. *Journal of Marriage and the Family, 53*, 79–101.

Solomon, J., & Biringen, Z. (2001). Another look at the developmental research: Commentary on Kelly and Lamb's "Using child development research to make appropriate custody and access decisions for young children." *Family Court Review, 39*, 355–364.

Solomon, J., & George, C. (1999). The development of attachment in separated and divorced families. *Attachment & Human Development, 1*, 2–33.

Sroufe, A., & McIntosh, J. (2011). Divorce and attachment relationships: The longitudinal journey. *Family Court Review, 49*, 464–473.

Storey, A. E., Walsh, C. J., Quinton, R. L., & Wynne-Edwards, K. E. (2000). Hormonal correlates of paternal responsiveness in new and expectant fathers. *Evolution and Human Behavior, 21*(2), 79–95.

Sturge-Apple, M. L., Davies, P. T., Cicchetti, D., & Manning, L. G. (2012). Interparental violence, maternal emotional unavailability and children's cortisol functioning in family contexts. *Developmental Psychology, 48*, 237–249.

Tornello, S. L., Emery, R., Rowen, J., Potter, D., Ocker, B., & Xu, Y. (2013). Overnight custody arrangements, attachment, and adjustment among very young children. *Journal of Marriage and Family, 75*, 871–885.

Troxel, W. M., & Matthews, K. A. (2004). What are the costs of marital conflict and dissolution to children's physical health? *Clinical Child and Family Psychology Review, 7*, 29–57.

van IJzendoorn, M. H., Bakermans-Kranenburg, M. J., Duschinsky, R., Goldman, P. S., Fox, N. A., Gunnar, M. R., Johnson, D. E., Nelson, C. A., Reijman, S., Skinner, G. C. M., Zeanah, C. H., & Sonuga-Barke, E. J. S. (2020). Institutionalisation and deinstitutionalisation of children I: A systematic and integrative review of evidence regarding effects on development. *Lancet Psychiatry, 7*, 703–720.

Velez, C. S., Braver, S. L., Cookston, J. T., Fabricius, W. V., & Parke, R. D. (2020). Does mattering to parents "matter" to adolescent mental health? *Family Relations, 69*(1), 180–194.

Votruba, A. M., Ellman, I. M., Braver, S. L., & Fabricius, W. V. (2014). Moral intuitions about fault, parenting, and child custody after divorce. *Psychology, Public Policy, and Law, 20*, 251–262.

Warshak, R. A. (2014). Social science and parenting plans for young children: A consensus report. *Psychology, Public Policy, and Law, 20*, 46–67.

Warshak, R. A. (2018). Night shifts: Revisiting blanket restrictions on children's overnights with separated parents. *Journal of Divorce & Remarriage, 59*(4), 282–323.

Wingfield, J. C., & Farner, D. S. (1993). Endocrinology of reproduction in wild species. In D. S. Farner, J. R. King, & K. C. Parkes (Eds.), *Avian biology* (pp. 164–328). Academic Press.

CHAPTER 7

Child Development and the Family Regulation System

Clare Huntington*

Abstract

Child abuse and neglect clearly harm children, but the risks that accompany involvement with the family regulation system (also known as the child welfare system), especially placement in foster care, also present considerable risks to child development. This chapter describes these competing risks to child development, the legal framework governing the family regulation system, and scholarly debates in the field. It then analyzes the system in the broader context of the legal regulation of children, showing that the family regulation system is out of step with other areas and in need of significant reform. A core problem with the system is its crisis orientation, paying too little attention to family support and the prevention of child maltreatment. Equally problematic, the family regulation system reflects and reinforces racial and economic inequality. Black and Native American children are significantly overrepresented in the system and have worse outcomes than other children. Addressing these issues would help foster healthy child development.

Key Words: child development, foster care, child abuse, child neglect, racial/economic inequality

Child abuse and neglect can have a profound impact on child development, but state intervention through the family regulation system (also known as the child welfare system) also poses substantial risks to children and child development. When state officials determine that a child is experiencing—or is at risk for—abuse and neglect, the local child welfare agency will intervene in the family. Sometimes this intervention consists of supportive services to keep the family together, but intervention can also lead to the removal of the child from the family and placement in foster care. Approximately half the children who are removed from their homes return to the care of a parent, but for many families, removal ends in the termination of parental rights (Children's Bureau, 2020). As noted throughout this chapter, these risks are not distributed evenly across the population. Instead, Black and Native American children are at much greater risk for involvement in the family regulation system and tend to have worse outcomes in the system than other children (Children's Bureau, 2016). Given these high stakes,

---

* This chapter is based on prior work, including the following: Conceptualizing Legal Childhood in the Twenty-First Century, 118 MICH. L. REV. 1371 (2020) (with Elizabeth Scott); Early Childhood Development and the Law, 90 S. CAL. L. REV. 755 (2017); The Child Welfare System and the Limits of Determinacy, 76 LAW & CONTEMP. PROBS. 221 (2014); Mutual Dependency in Child Welfare, 82 NOTRE DAME L. REV. 1485 (2007); and Rights Myopia in Child Welfare, 53 UCLA L. REV. 637 (2006).

and the need to protect all children equally, the challenge for the legal system is to prevent child abuse and neglect by strengthening families and to limit the removal of children to only those cases where it is absolutely necessary.

This chapter begins by describing the competing child development interests and the shifts in legal regulation that reflect these competing interests, often prioritizing one interest and then another. The chapter then identifies the many shortcomings of state intervention, with a focus on child development and racial and economic inequality. After describing scholarly debates about the family regulation system, the chapter concludes with a discussion of the implications for reform, drawing on the work of the American Law Institute's new *Restatement of the Law, Children and the Law.*

Competing Risks to Child Development

As other chapters in this book have made clear, early childhood is a critical period of child development, and yet it is also the period when child abuse and neglect are most common (see Stacks et al., this volume). Young children, particularly those under the age of 2 years, are at the highest risk for maltreatment, making up 28% of victims nationally (Children's Bureau, 2021a). Additionally, nearly half the children who enter foster care are aged 5 or younger (Children's Bureau, 2020). This prevalence of abuse, neglect, and foster care placement during early childhood poses significant risks to healthy child development. This section describes the competing risks to child development: from abuse and neglect, on the one hand, and from foster care placement, on the other. Older children and adolescents are not immune to child abuse and neglect or state intervention, but the risks, needs, and consequences may vary developmentally, requiring separate consideration. This chapter focuses on young children, given the increased risk of maltreatment and prevalence of removal in this age group.

Child Maltreatment and Child Development

A strong, stable, positive relationship between a child and a parent or other primary caregiver is foundational to healthy child development. Unfortunately, the reverse is also true: An abusive or neglectful relationship between a parent and child can have a long-lasting and detrimental impact on child development. To understand why, it is helpful to review some of the basics of early childhood development. Beginning with attachment, research demonstrates that infants and young children seek proximity to a caregiver (often but not always a parent), protest when separated from the parent, and seek out the parent when in danger or need (Ainsworth & Bowlby, 1965; Ainsworth, 1967; Ainsworth et al., 1978; Bowlby, 1969, 1973, 1980). If the parent consistently responds to the child's needs for comfort and reassurance, the child will develop a secure attachment to the parent. By contrast, if the parent is unpredictable and inconsistent, the child may develop an anxious attachment, with the child constantly worried about the parent's presence, attention, and protection. If the parent is reluctant and rejecting, the child may develop an avoidant attachment, rejecting the parent. And if the child does not use any of the other three strategies for relating to attachment figures, the child may develop what is called disorganized attachment. This is most common when the parent is frightened or frightening precisely when the child looks to the parent for reassurance (Shaver et al., 2009).

The attachment between child and parent has ramifications for the child's development. A secure attachment with a caregiver both alleviates stress and, when there is no immediate stress, facilitates engagement with the larger world. When children have this secure base, they confidently explore their surroundings, knowing that they can come back to the caregiver for comfort and familiarity at any time (Ainsworth, 1967; Ainsworth et al., 1978). Securely attached children also learn to regulate their own emotions and solve problems because they feel effective, and they learn that negative emotions can be tolerated and managed. They can test reality because they are able to evaluate their own behaviors and other people's reactions. As a result, they tend to develop good problem-solving skills, emotional balance, and positive expectations for relationships, meaning they can find and absorb positive emotional support, a protective factor against depression and other behavior and mental health problems (Coan, 2018).

By contrast, however, when a parent is abusive or neglectful, children develop an insecure attachment, including disorganized attachment (Carlson, 1998). Abused children may fear a caregiver who is expected to provide them with comfort and safety, creating a conflicting dynamic for the child who may freeze or dissociate in response to the caregiver (Baer & Martinez, 2006). Alternatively, absence by a neglectful caregiver may prevent the child from attaching at the outset (Sroufe, 2005). A disorganized attachment strongly predicts poorer mental health in adolescence (Carlson, 1998), and the other forms of insecure attachment are often linked to a range of social, relationship, and emotion challenges (Cicchetti, 2004).

Attachment patterns also lay the groundwork for an adult's future patterns of relating, because a child's experience of relating to a parent becomes the internal working model for relationships into adulthood (Fraley & Roisman, 2019). Adults who have internalized a secure model of attachment are comfortable with emotional intimacy and can turn to their partners for support. By contrast, adults who have internalized an anxious model of attachment repeatedly seek intimacy and reassurance and worry about being abandoned. Adults who have internalized an avoidant model of attachment have difficulty forming close relationships and do not like to trust or be dependent on others. And the disorganized attachment style in a child is predictive of later difficulties, such as anxiety disorders and serious antisocial behavior problems (Carlson, 1998).

Early childhood is also crucial for brain development, and again child abuse and neglect can have a devastating impact. Genetics and the pre- and postnatal environment both affect brain development (National Scientific Council on the Developing Child, 2010), but a child's relationships are the other key factor. A critical mechanism for making and strengthening neural connections is repeated interactions between an attentive, responsive caregiver and a child. The child initiates interaction through babbling, movements, and facial expressions, and the adult responds with sounds and gestures. This exchange establishes and reinforces neural connections between different areas of the brain and becomes the basis for future communication and social skills (National Scientific Council on the Developing Child, 2010).

To appreciate the role of parents in brain development, it is important to understand that much critical brain development occurs before a child enters formal schooling at age 5. Different capacities develop during "sensitive periods," with the basic neural circuitry for vision and hearing developing shortly before and soon after birth and the circuits used for language and speech production peaking before age 1 (National Scientific Council on the Developing Child, 2010). The higher level circuits used for cognitive functions develop throughout the first several years of life. For example, executive functioning—the brain's ability to hold information in the short term, ignore distractions, and switch gears between contexts and priorities—are developed from birth through late adolescence but with a particularly important period occurring from ages 3 to 5 (National Scientific Council on the Developing Child, 2011).

Early childhood is also a time of vulnerability for neural circuits involved in emotion regulation and response. Learning how to cope with stress is an important part of child development. For example, the temporary disappearance of a caregiver or a minor injury may trigger a child's stress response system, with an increased heart rate and heightened levels of stress hormones. When a caregiver promptly comforts the child, the response system is quickly deactivated, and the child develops an ability to regulate their responses to stressful events (National Scientific Council on the Developing Child, 2005).

By contrast, prolonged, severe, or frequent stress stemming from abuse, neglect, extreme poverty, and maternal clinical depression creates what some researchers call toxic stress (Shonkoff & Bales, 2011), which has a serious adverse impact on brain development. When there is no caring adult able to relieve this stress or when the caregiver is the source of the stress, as in the case of abuse and neglect, the child's stress response remains activated, which over time can overload the developing brain and impede the construction of neural pathways. In extreme cases, toxic stress can lead to the development of a smaller brain. In cases of moderate toxic stress, the brain can change such that it develops a hair trigger for stress, activating the stress response system in reaction to events that others might not perceive as difficult or threatening (National Scientific Council on the Developing Child, 2005). These changes can influence how individuals respond to adversity throughout life (National Scientific Council on the Developing Child, 2005).

This lasting effect is because the neural circuits involved in the transmission of stress signals are particularly flexible during early childhood, meaning that the effect of toxic stress leaves a lasting impression on the creation of these circuits, affecting how easily the stress response is turned on and off (National Scientific Council on the Developing Child, 2005). This, in turn, creates a greater vulnerability later to physical illnesses, such as diabetes, stroke, and cardiovascular disease, and mental illnesses, such as depression and anxiety disorders (National Scientific Council on the Developing Child, 2005). Further, chronically heightened levels of cortisol, the hormone triggered by stress, has consequences for the development of the areas of the brain dedicated to memory and learning, weakening the neural connections to these parts of the brain (National Scientific Council on the Developing Child, 2005). A child's relationship with a caregiver may alter how children regulate production of cortisol, with a responsive caregiver helping to prevent its overproduction, even in children temperamentally predisposed to be anxious who are known to exhibit particularly high levels of cortisol reactions to potential threats. By contrast, when a caregiver is depressed, abusive, or neglectful, a child's cortisol reactions are exaggerated, both during stress and even after the stressful period ends (National Scientific Council on the Developing Child, 2005, 2008). Compromised circuits that may result are harder, although not impossible, to repair later in life (National Scientific Council on the Developing Child, 2005).

The effect of toxic stress is particularly strong early in life when neural circuits are undergoing rapid development (National Scientific Council on the Developing Child, 2005). During these periods, the genetic plan and brain architecture can be significantly modified. By contrast, once a circuit has matured, environment and experiences affect the genetic plan and architecture to a much lesser degree (National Scientific Council on the Developing Child, 2005).

The Adverse Childhood Experiences (ACE) Study documents the long-term impact of child abuse and neglect as well as other childhood experiences (Felitti et al., 1998). The participants in the study reported their childhood exposure to seven different categories of abuse and trauma: psychological abuse, physical abuse, sexual abuse, domestic violence, substance abuse, living with someone mentally ill or suicidal, and living with an ex-prisoner. A person's ACE score correlates with the number of adverse experiences. Researchers found a significant correlation between high ACE scores and future adult health problems such as heart disease, lung disease, cancer, obesity, depression, alcoholism, and drug abuse (Felitti et al., 1998). Part of the explanation is that ACEs can lead to behaviors such as smoking, drug or alcohol abuse, and overeating, because individuals engage in these behaviors as a short-term coping mechanism for intense stress and abuse, and the behaviors then become chronic (Felitti et al., 1998).

But negative health behaviors are not the whole picture. After controlling for age, sex, race, and education as well as traditional risk factors such as smoking, physical inactivity, body mass index, diabetes, and hypertension, participants with a very high ACE score had a 310% increase in their risk of ischemic heart disease, the most common cause of death in the United States, over those who had no history of an ACE (Dong et al., 2004). There is not a complete explanation for this nonbehavioral link, but evidence suggests that ACEs can lead to long-lasting negative chemical changes in the body that affect adult health (Dong et al., 2004; Tough, 2011).

In short, the relationship between a child and a parent or primary caregiver strongly influences child development—for better, and worse—in childhood and ultimately across the entire lifespan.

Risks of State Intervention
As the previous section demonstrated, an abusive or neglectful relationship between a parent and child can have a lasting and highly detrimental impact on child development. But state intervention through the family regulation system poses its own risks to child development. Disruptions to the parent–child relationship—especially during early childhood and even when the parent is not providing what a child needs—can have a long-lasting impact on development (Nickerson et al., 2013). Children who are removed from their homes, and especially if they experience multiple foster placements, often have trouble forming new attachments to caregivers (Gauthier et al., 2004; Penzerro & Lein, 1995); they can develop attachment disorders and distrust of adult caregivers; and they experience behavioral or developmental challenges (Gauthier et al., 2004). More generally, factors such as gender, age, and number of placements influence mental health outcomes for children in foster care (Villegas & Pecora, 2012).

There is evidence that as compared with similarly situated children who were abused or neglected but not placed in foster care, removal of a child does not necessarily improve the outcomes for children (Doyle, 2013). Research exploring the causal effects of foster placement on child outcomes used the naturally randomized assignment of child protection investigators to simulate a controlled lab study (Doyle, 2013). Some investigators are more likely to recommend placement, and thus the study was able to isolate the causal effects of placement, comparing children placed in foster care with those who were similarly situated but not removed from their homes (Doyle, 2013). Results showed a causal relationship between foster placement and the child's involvement with the criminal legal system, as well as an increased need for short-term emergency health care for the child (Doyle, 2013).

The Interrelationship of Child Development and the Family Regulation System

Given the competing risks to child development, one of the central debates in child welfare is how to protect children from abuse and neglect while also minimizing the harms stemming from state intervention, including the placement of children in foster care. As this section describes, lawmakers have toggled back and forth between emphasizing the removal of children from their homes and placement of children in foster care, and emphasizing family preservation, which seeks to keep children at home with supportive services.

This debate affects thousands of families. In 2019, 656,000 children experienced substantiated abuse or neglect, for a maltreatment rate of 8.9 per 1,000 children (Children's Bureau,

2021a). For the children who are in foster care, 32% live with a relative (what is known as kinship foster care), 46% live with an unrelated family, and the remaining live in other settings, including 4% in a group home and 6% in an institution (Children's Bureau, 2020). These risks, of child welfare involvement and foster care placement, do not fall evenly across different groups: Most families involved in the family regulation system are low income and are disproportionately Black and Native American (Children's Bureau, 2016).

This section begins by describing this income and racial inequality and then traces the roots of the family regulation system, showing that it has long focused on low-income, marginalized families. This section then describes the changes in law and policy, which reflect the competing stakes for child development.

Racial Disproportionality and Racial Disparities

Racial and economic inequality is one of the most troubling hallmarks of the family regulation system. As compared with other children, Black children are more likely to be reported to the family regulation system, agencies are more likely to investigate their cases, and they are more likely to be removed from their homes and placed in foster care (Children's Bureau, 2016). Once in foster care, Black children remain for longer, are less likely to be adopted, and are less likely to return home (Children's Bureau, 2021b; Golden & Macomber, 2009).

There is uncertainty about the precise causes and mechanisms that contribute to the disproportionality and the disparate outcomes for Black children, but several nonexclusive explanations are likely (Annie E. Casey Foundation, 2011; Children's Bureau, 2021b; Sedlk, 2010; Sedlak et al., 2010; Wildeman et al., 2014). First, before controlling for various factors, there is evidence that Black children experience higher rates of maltreatment than white children. These varying rates of maltreatment are largely explained by differences among families, including socioeconomic status (SES) and parental employment. These factors, especially low SES, are strong predictors for child maltreatment (Sedlak et al., 2010). Once researchers control for these and similar factors, the racial differences in maltreatment largely, although not completely, disappear (Sedlak et al., 2010). Second, child maltreatment is more common in disadvantaged areas, particularly areas with high concentrations of poverty, low levels of social integration, low rates of employment, and low levels of services (Annie E. Casey Foundation, 2011). Black families are more likely to live in these geographic areas. Third, Black families are more likely to live in neighborhoods without the kinds of resources that enable parents to keep children safely in their homes.

After a family has become involved with the family regulation system, the dearth of resources makes removal of the child more likely. Once children are removed, there is evidence that Black parents receive fewer resources that facilitate reunification and that children receive fewer services while in care, notably mental health services (Annie E. Casey Foundation, 2011). Finally, there is mixed evidence that racial bias plays a role in the decisions of key players in the family regulation system (Annie E. Casey Foundation, 2011). A particular focus is on the decisions that bring families into the family regulation system: decisions by community and mandated reporters about which children to report for a case of suspected maltreatment as well as the decisions of caseworkers about which incidents to investigate and confirm and when to seek the removal of a child from a home. Some studies have found differences by the race of the decision maker or the race of the child, but other studies have not (Annie E. Casey Foundation; Bowman et al., 2009; Font, et al., 2012; Lane et al., 2002).

Native American children are also disproportionately represented in the family regulation system and have worse outcomes. Native American children are placed in foster care at more than twice the rate of white children: 13 children for every 1,000 Native American children, as compared with five children for every 1,000 white children (Center for the Study of Social Policy & Annie E. Casey Foundation, 2011; Sedlak et al., 2010). Many of the same factors are at work, with the additional history of deliberate state efforts to break up Native American families. As the legislative history of the Indian Child Welfare Act describes, in the 1970s, at least 25% of all Native American children were removed from their homes, and the majority were placed with non-Native foster or adoptive families, or in boarding schools (S. Hrg. 98-952 Oversight of the Indian Child Welfare Act of 1978 (1984); Select Committee on Indian Affairs, 1977). This removal rate was five to 25 times the rate of removal for non-Native children (MacEachron et al., 1996). Boarding schools were created as a federal effort to weaken the relationship between Native American children and their parents (Marc, 2017). For example, as part of the "outing system," Native American children in boarding schools were placed with white families during vacations instead of being sent home (Marc, 2017). In 1958, the Indian Adoption Project (IAP) was federally introduced to place Native American children for adoption when their parents were found to be unsuitable (Marc, 2017). Congressional hearings in the 1970s found that child welfare agencies, encouraged by the IAP (Marc, 2017), placed Native American children in non-Native settings where they were completely disconnected from Native American culture and traditions (Select Committee on Indian Affairs, 1977). These decisions for removal were made primarily by non-Native social workers, who lacked cultural competency training (MacEachron et al., 1996).

Since its passage in 1978, the Indian Child Welfare Act has provided statutory protections for Native American children and families, including a higher bar for the removal of children and procedural protections to promote tribal decision making (25 U.S.C. §§ 1901-1963). There are not specific legal protections for Black children, however.

The Early Child Welfare System

The modern family regulation system is rooted in the Progressive Era. In contrast to the historical understanding that parents had complete control of their children (Blackstone, n.d.), Progressive Era reformers transformed the state's relationship to children and families. Beginning in the mid-19th century, states began to pass laws prohibiting child abuse, and by the early decades of the 20th century, a child protection network had been constructed that included public and private agencies, juvenile courts, and government probation officers (Gordon, 1988; Grossberg, 2003; Pleck, 1987). Reformers focused on poor and immigrant children, whose behavior, or that of their parents, the reformers perceived as evidence that parents were failing to raise their children to be law-abiding American citizens (Billingsley & Giovannoni, 1972; Platt, 1969/2009). Although there were cases of physical abuse, many of the problems, such as lack of medical care, limited adult supervision, and poor living conditions, were the product of poverty, not necessarily parental indifference.

This system continued until the early 1960s, when Henry Kempe, a pediatrician, and several colleagues identified what they called "battered-child syndrome"—the finding that children's injuries, often multiple broken bones, were not accidents and instead were the result of intentional acts by parents and other caregivers (Kempe et al., 1962, p. 23). This work dramatically increased public recognition of child abuse and led to the enactment of state laws creating child abuse hotlines and mandatory reporting laws.

Federal Involvement

In 1974, Congress enacted the first federal law addressing child maltreatment: the Child Abuse Prevention and Treatment Act (CAPTA). This law, which emphasized the removal of children from their homes, authorized grants to states to address child abuse and neglect on the condition that states adopt certain procedures to respond to allegations of child maltreatment and adopt specified definitions of child abuse and neglect. To win support for federal legislation, members of Congress led by Senator Mondale framed child abuse as an issue of pathological parenting. This enabled the quick passage of CAPTA but ignored the strong correlation between poverty and child maltreatment. By focusing on parental deficits rather than economic inequality, Senator Mondale gained support from conservatives who did not support welfare programs (Guggenheim, 2005). The federal Children's Bureau underscored this understanding of child maltreatment, aiding the media portrayal of child abuse as a disease or syndrome (Nelson, 2000). With this framing, it is perhaps unsurprising that CAPTA emphasized the removal of children from their homes and placement in foster care.

In the 1980s, however, federal legislation swung in the direction of family preservation. In response to significant and widely shared concerns about the high rates of removal of children and extended stays in foster care, Congress enacted the Adoption Assistance and Child Welfare Act of 1980 (AACWA; Guggenheim, 2005). This law was a sea change from prior policy and emphasized the goal of keeping children at home but also returning children to their families as soon as possible if they had been placed in foster care. As a condition of receiving federal child welfare funds, AACWA required states to adopt legislation allowing the removal of children only where "the removal from the home was the result of a judicial determination . . . that continuation therein would be contrary to the welfare of such child and . . . that reasonable efforts" to keep the child in the home had been made (42 U.S.C. § 672(a)(1); 42 U.S.C. § 671(a)(15)). The new standard thus emphasized the importance of family preservation efforts.

Crucially, AACWA changed the funding structure for foster care. Rather than reimbursing states only for the cost of foster care, which created an incentive for removal, AACWA authorized funds for services to prevent the removal of children and speed the return of children in foster care back to their homes. Subsequent legislation, notably the Family Preservation and Family Support Act of 1993, authorized additional funding for these services as well as broader family support efforts, which are intended to keep families out of the family regulation system entirely (42 U.S.C. § 629).

The promises of AACWA, however, never materialized. Instead, the foster care population soared through the 1980s and 1990s, with more children entering foster care, staying longer, and experiencing multiple placements (Green Book, 2012, Table 11-4; Guggenheim, 2005). There are numerous explanations for these trends, including the increasing use of crack cocaine and the failure of Congress to authorize, and states to provide, sufficient funds for preservation and reunification services. Indeed, studies from the late 1980s found that states often did not provide preservation services, and that courts either ignored the reasonable-efforts requirement or simply rubber-stamped the state's assertion that it had provided services (National Council of Juvenile & Family Court Judges, 1987).

The increases in placement and the extended stays in foster care set the stage for the next major wave of foster care reform. In 1997, Congress enacted the Adoption and Safe Families Act (ASFA), which dramatically altered the child welfare landscape. Both Congress and the Clinton administration had found that the child welfare system was not serving the interests of children because family preservation efforts were keeping some children in dangerous homes, and the problem of "foster care drift" (the term used to describe both long stays in foster care and placement in multiple homes) was getting worse (Gordon, 1999). Acting on the belief that children would be better served by promoting adoption rather than family preservation, Congress sought to move children to permanent homes more quickly and to make child safety, rather than family preservation, the paramount concern of the child welfare system (42 U.S.C. § 671(a)(15)(A); Golden & Macomber, 2009).

The centerpiece of ASFA is a clear-cut standard that set a time limit on family reunification efforts. As a condition of receiving federal funds, states had to enact laws limiting a child's stay in foster care. If a child had been in care for 15 of the most recent 22 months, the state was obligated to petition the court to terminate parental rights, with some exceptions. Congress required states to conduct a permanency hearing within 12 months (shortened from 18 months) of a child entering foster care and created greater incentives for adoption by giving subsidies to adoptive families. ASFA also broadened the focus of existing family preservation funding, which diluted the focus on family preservation and reunification. Calling the new program Promoting Safe and Stable Families, Congress expanded the scope of the funding stream to include services to promote and support adoption and adoptive families.

As the opioid crisis created another influx of foster children in the 2010s, Congress adopted legislation again prioritizing family preservation. The Family First Prevention Services Act of 2017 provides direct support to children and their families, with the goal of avoiding foster care placement. The act gives states access to federal funds for mental health services and drug treatment, in addition to parenting and kinship navigator programs (House of Representatives, 2018), with the goal of providing sufficient support so that children need not be removed.

Impact of Federal Laws

ASFA resulted in considerable changes. Even though states often invoke one of the exceptions to the time limit (Golden & Macomber, 2009), ASFA's time limit has had a substantial impact on speeding children to permanent placements. Beginning with the median stay in foster care, in the first year after ASFA was enacted (before the provisions had a chance to take effect), the median stay for children in foster care was 20.5 months (Children's Bureau, 2006). By 2019, the median stay in foster care had declined to 13.3 months (Children's Bureau, 2020).

The percentage and speed of adoptions have also increased. Of the children who exited foster care in 2019, 26% were adopted (Children's Bureau, 2020; Mnookin, 1975), as compared with only 15% in 1998 (Children's Bureau, 2006; Golden & Macomber, 2009). ASFA's emphasis on adoption has also translated into faster adoptions for more children. Of the children adopted in 1998, 84% had spent at least 2 years in foster care, as compared with 71% in 2005 (Golden & Macomber, 2009). Additionally, the time between the termination of parental rights and adoption has also shortened since ASFA, from more than 12 months in 1998 (Children's Bureau, 2006) to an average of 8.9 months in 2019 (Children's Bureau, 2020). Adoption rates, however, differ by race. Even though fewer Black children are entering foster care today (Children's Bureau, 2020), the adoption rate for Black children has declined considerably, while the adoption rates of Latinx and white children have increased (Golden & Macomber, 2009).

One of the biggest successes in permanency is the increased use of guardianship. This permanency option is typically used when a child is in kinship foster care and the child is unlikely to return to the custody of the parent. A guardianship allows the relative caring for the child to obtain permanent custody of the child and the foster care placement to end but without terminating parental rights. This is a much-needed permanency option for older children who may not want to be adopted, and for kinship caregivers who may not want to adopt, often because they do not want the termination of parental rights (Children's Bureau, 2011; Godsoe, 2013a). In 2019, 11% of all children leaving foster care were placed with guardians (Children's Bureau, 2020), as compared with only 2% in 1998 (Children's Bureau, 2006). One of the reasons for the greater use of guardianships is the Fostering Connections to Success

Act of 2008, which permits states to use federal child welfare funds to subsidize guardianships when the guardian is a relative, making guardianship a more viable option for these families.

Despite some potential benefits (e.g., more expedient cases), shorter stays in foster care and higher numbers of children being adopted or placed in guardianship have come at the cost of family reunification. That is, although children are now in foster care for shorter periods and are more likely to be adopted or placed in a guardianship, they are also less likely to return home. In 1998, 60% of the children leaving foster care returned home to their parents (Children's Bureau, 2006). In 2019, only 47% of the children leaving foster care were reunified with their families (Children's Bureau, 2020).

* * *

As this brief description should make clear, the various swings in legal rules and policies reflect debates about how best to protect children and promote their development: remove children from their homes and place them in alternative care (an approach that emphasizes the risks of child abuse and neglect) or keep children in their homes with supports in place (an approach that emphasizes the risks of removal and foster care). As the next section shows, legal scholars have long debated this tension between competing interests in child development.

Scholarly Debates
Legal Standards
In the 1970s, two legal scholars, Robert Mnookin and Michael Wald, articulated concerns about the family regulation system that continue to resonate today. Mnookin and Wald argued that the legal standards then in place could not identify families truly in need of intervention, did not sufficiently account for the dangers inherent in the removal of children from their homes, and did not move children through the system expeditiously (Mnookin, 1975; Wald, 1975, 1976). As a result, too many children were removed from their homes unnecessarily and then left to languish in the limbo of foster care.

These critiques led to many of the reforms described previously, including the requirement that child welfare agencies provide services to keep children at home rather than simply removing children, and the requirement that states adopt a time limit on family reunification efforts. Despite these changes to the standards governing child welfare, the reforms have had mixed success in changing actual practice on the ground. Determinacy on the front end—accurately identifying which children should be removed from their homes—remains challenging, and efforts to focus on family preservation have had only a modest impact on keeping children at home (Huntington, 2014). By contrast, determinacy on the back end—moving more children out of foster care—is easier to achieve. As described earlier, ASFA's time limit on reunification efforts has had the intended effect of shortening stays in foster care. This determinacy, however, has come at the cost of family reunification, with fewer children returning home—47% of children instead of 60% (Huntington, 2014). Whether this tradeoff is an improvement over the old system, where children spent more time in foster care but were also more likely to return home, is a matter of considerable controversy. But a more expeditious timeline puts considerable pressure on parents to make the required changes in time to regain custody.

Concerns About the Focus of the Child Welfare System
Legal scholars identify two significant shortcomings of the family regulation system. First, scholars argue that, although many families face significant challenges, the family regulation system does little to address these problems proactively or directly. Rather than supporting

families before problems arise, the system prioritizes crisis intervention. Dorothy Roberts (2022, 2005), for example, contrasts the current system, with its paltry support for families and its emphasis on removal, with the principles espoused by Black advocates for child welfare at the end of the 19th century. As Roberts describes, after the Civil War, Black women—who were barred from the reform movement of the time—created their own groups to address the well-being of children. Instead of focusing on a particular case of abuse or neglect, this movement supported, rather than penalized, mothers, believing that assisting mothers would assist the children (Roberts, 2005). Martin Guggenheim and other scholars have made similar arguments about the need to shrink the family regulation system and help parents, rather than remove their children (Guggenheim, 2005, 2009; Huntington, 2007).

Much of this work is based on the reality that the family regulation system largely addresses child neglect, rather than child abuse. Physical neglect is the primary reason children are removed from their homes: 63% of children in foster care in 2019 had a finding of physical neglect, as compared with only 13% of children with a finding of physical abuse; sexual abuse is even less likely to surface in the family regulation system (4%; Children's Bureau, 2020). One of the recurring questions, then, is whether foster care placement is the right response to physical neglect, which is strongly correlated with poverty (Drake & Jonson-Reid, 2013). A national study of child maltreatment found that children in low-SES households are seven times more likely to be neglected than children in other households (Sedlak et al., 2010). (There is also a correlation between SES status and abuse—with children in low-SES households three times more likely to experience abuse than other children.)

Most scholars emphasize the need to address poverty. Barbara Bennett Woodhouse, for example, contends that prevention efforts should focus on the relationship between parent and child as well as the context for that relationship (Woodhouse 2005). In her view, prevention should encompass an examination of the systems surrounding a family, including a child's peer group, neighborhood, and school. Woodhouse terms this approach an "environmentalist paradigm," contending that the current framework has been partially to blame for the failure to find effective solutions for reforming the family regulation system. A child's development depends on all these systems, and therefore, according to Woodhouse, child welfare should examine and support these systems, in addition to supporting the family.

Other scholars contend that although general antipoverty measures will have some effect on rates of child abuse and neglect, more targeted programs are also needed. For example, Garrison (2005, p. 618) has argued that "the link between poverty and child maltreatment is indirect and poorly understood" and that the connection between poverty and foster care placement rates, although correlated, is nonlinear. Garrison agrees that poverty reduction has a role to play in the prevention of child abuse and neglect but concludes that it is not a silver bullet. Instead, she favors such targeted programs as early childhood education that also serve the needs of parents (Garrison, 2005).

Not all legal scholars agree that the family regulation system should do more to support parents. Mirroring legal policy debates, some scholars argue that the family regulation system *should* emphasize the removal of children from their homes. Bartholet and Dwyer (1999, 2018) are the two leading proponents of this position, arguing that the system is too protective of the biological connection between parents and children and has too little regard for children's safety and well-being. For these scholars, the state should intervene more readily, moving children into adoptive homes more quickly and at a younger age.

Scholars' second concern about the family regulation system is the significant overrepresentation of Black and Native American families in the family regulation system and the worse outcomes the children experience once they are removed from their homes (Cleveland

& Quas, 2020). Roberts (2022, 2002) has offered one of the most sustained and influential critiques of racial inequality in the child welfare system, with a particular focus on the devastating impact of the family regulation system on Black families. Other scholars have written about the impact of the family regulation system on parents with disabilities (Kay, 2015), as well as the continuing need to address the overrepresentation of Native American children in the family regulation system (Krakoff, 2017).

Over the years, advocates have achieved some positive reforms, but there has been little fundamental change addressing either concern. The family regulation system continues to operate largely as a regime of crisis intervention, and racial disproportionality and disparities are still a hallmark of the system, reflecting and reinforcing inequality for Black and Native American families.

Future Directions

As this chapter has made clear, the abundant research on child development is clearly relevant to the family regulation system and the ongoing policy debates. The research strongly supports the understanding that parent–child relationships are essential to healthy child development, that child abuse and neglect can be highly detrimental to children, and that removal from the home also poses substantial risks to child development.

Determining the precise policies that should flow from these findings, however, is a fraught endeavor, because the research can be deployed in support of different, sometimes competing, policies. As noted earlier, some scholars use the research to argue that the family regulation system should do more to remove very young children from questionable caregiving situations. This leads to legal approaches like the ASFA, which emphasizes removal and termination, with short time limits for parents to address the issues underlying the abuse or neglect. In this line of argument, there is a mismatch between the timeline of child development and the timeline of a parent struggling with multiple issues. To take just one example, parental substance abuse is a common reason for removal of a child from a home (Children's Bureau, 2020), and yet when a parent undergoes treatment for substance abuse, relapse is an expected and normal part of recovery, potentially prolonging the period when the child may need to be in foster care (McLellan et al., 2000). For many families, the short timeframe imposed by current law and the challenges of addressing the issues underlying the removal of a child do not lend themselves to family reunification, as evidenced by the decreasing number of children returning home.

Rather than engage in the seemingly unresolvable debate about child removal versus family preservation, it is time to rethink the goals and possibilities of the family regulation system. As other scholars and I have argued, the system should work harder and earlier to keep children out of foster care altogether. In other words, rather than focusing so much attention on families at the brink of a crisis or immediately afterward, we should more directly address the conditions that lead to child abuse and neglect, particularly limited social and financial resources. There will always be some need for a child welfare system, but rather than try so hard to fix the system, we should reduce the need for state intervention.

A Different Path Forward

In thinking about how to reform the family regulation system and truly promote child development, the American Law Institute's new *Restatement of the Law, Children and the Law* provides a blueprint for action. The *Restatement*—which offers comprehensive coverage of the legal regulation of children, addressing legal issues facing children in families, schools, the justice system, and society—reflects both doctrinal changes and broader shifts in the legal system.

Beginning with doctrine, the *Restatement* recognizes the pivotal role of parental rights, which are rooted in the Constitution and form a bulwark against unnecessary state intervention. As the *Restatement* clarifies, parental rights limit state involvement to circumstances where parents pose a serious threat to a child's physical or mental health. State intervention is not authorized absent this heightened level of harm. This relatively high threshold recognizes that, although abuse and neglect clearly harm children, state intervention can also harm families and children. The *Restatement* is built on the understanding that the state's goal is to assist parents to provide adequate care to their children, not to remove children from their homes if other assistance suffices.

As noted previously, physical neglect is the most common basis for state intervention through the family regulation system, and therefore the legal definition has far-reaching consequences. The *Restatement* defines physical neglect as follows: "In a civil child-protection proceeding, a child is physically neglected when the child suffers serious physical harm or is exposed to a substantial risk of serious physical harm as a result of the failure of a parent, guardian, or custodian to exercise a minimum degree of care in providing for the physical needs of a child" (American Law Institute, Section 2.24(b)). The *Restatement*'s definition of physical neglect thus clarifies that state intervention is not authorized if a parent is minimally competent and able to meet the basic health and safety needs of the child. This definition of physical neglect balances the twin goals of protecting children from harm while respecting family integrity. The state can intervene only when a parent's conduct results in serious harm or a substantial risk of serious harm. Intervention is not warranted when a parent's care is merely suboptimal or does not conform to mainstream parenting practices. The definition thus recognizes that state intervention imposes its own costs on children and families. The definition also respects diverse parenting choices and practices, which is particularly important because of the history of discrimination against racial, ethnic, and religious minority parents in the United States. And by limiting state intervention to a relatively narrow set of cases, the definition reinforces the goal of keeping children in their homes, if this can be accomplished without substantial risk to the child.

The *Restatement* also recognizes that when a parent lacks financial means, it is difficult to provide adequately for the basic needs of a child. One goal of limiting physical neglect to circumstances where a parent is not minimally competent and able to meet the basic health and safety needs is to differentiate a parent who, with social welfare support from the state, would exercise a minimum degree of care from a parent who, even with financial support, fails to meet the minimum standard of care. Accordingly, the definition notes that courts should consider a parent's conduct but also a parent's financial resources.

Moving to broader shifts in the legal regulation of children, the *Restatement* has uncovered what Scott (the chief reporter for the *Restatement*) and I (an associate reporter) call the child well-being framework (Huntington & Scott, 2020). In this framework, the goal of legal regulation is the promotion of child well-being. In most areas of legal regulation, lawmakers seek to further children's well-being by paying attention to three factors. First, lawmakers increasingly rely on research about child and adolescent development as well as empirical evidence documenting the effectiveness of policy interventions. This body of knowledge makes it possible to advance child well-being with sophistication and effect. Second, lawmakers and the public have begun to recognize that policies promoting child well-being also promote social welfare, which strengthens and broadens support for contemporary regulation. Finally, lawmakers increasingly recognize the imperative of addressing racial and class inequality in the regulation of children and families.

These core elements provide a blueprint for reforming the family regulation system. Beginning with the first element (reliance on research), reform efforts must focus on evidence-based policies that protect children from maltreatment. Broad-based efforts that strengthen the parent–child relationship and address the risk factors for child abuse and neglect—including poverty, parental youth, single parenthood, domestic violence, substance abuse, and mental health—are effective at reducing the rate of maltreatment (Child Welfare Information Gateway, 2017); and more targeted programs that teach parenting skills and provide support for parents also have some success (Child Welfare Information Gateway, 2017; Wald, 2014). Any strategy to prevent child abuse and neglect must be multifaceted and draw on this substantial research to guide investments.

To strengthen families, there is a mechanism that is already part of the current child welfare system. One of the permissible expenditures for funds from the Promoting Safe and Stable Families Act is for "family support services." In contrast to family preservation programs, which are intended for specific families facing imminent risk of foster care placement, family support programs are intended to serve an entire community to strengthen families to avoid crises. These programs offer services such as parenting education, social support, case management and referral services, center-based early childhood education, adult education, and so on (Layzer et al., 2001). With the exception of center-based early childhood education, most of the programs work with parents rather than directly with children, reflecting the belief that helping parents helps children. There is considerable evidence that these efforts—which focus on helping parents—are effective at improving children's cognitive development, children's social and emotional development, parenting attitudes and knowledge, parenting behavior, and family functioning (Layzer et al., 2001).

These investments shift the focus from a reactive child welfare system toward a proactive system that nurtures family functioning early on, long before a family mistreats a child. This approach differs from family preservation because it does not begin work when a family reaches a crisis. Instead, the work starts at the point of family formation, seeking to strengthen the family to avoid a crisis entirely. This new approach should not be part of the child welfare system at all but instead integrated into broader policies about children and families. One concrete example is the Nurse–Family Partnership, which arranges for a public health nurse to visit a low-income, first-time parent during pregnancy and for the first 2 years of a child's life. The nurse works closely with the mother to improve prenatal health, help the new parents learn how to care for the child, and address the family's economic stability by helping the parents develop and accomplish goals relating to staying in school and finding work, as well as helping the parents plan subsequent pregnancies. Multiple studies have found a wide range of benefits for children and parents alike (Olds, 2002).

Turning to the second element of the framework (recognition of social welfare benefits), Medicaid expansion under the Patient Protection and Affordable Care Act is a good example of a social welfare program that enjoys widespread support from the public, strengthens families, and can help prevent abuse and neglect. Medicaid expansion did not dramatically increase the number of children receiving health care because most low-income children were already covered. But it does benefit children and promotes their well-being by supporting parents. Research demonstrates that Medicaid expansion improves parental access to mental health services and substance abuse treatment, two conditions linked to child abuse and neglect as well as poor family functioning generally (Children's Bureau, 2017). Further, Medicaid expansion has improved the finances of low-income families (Cross-Call, 2018), increased employment rates (Gavin, 2017; Ohio Department of Medicaid, 2018), and promoted housing stability (Gallagher et al., 2019), all of which benefit children. Medicaid expansion has been shown to be cost-effective, increasing public support (Cross-Call, 2018; Volger, 2014; Wen et al., 2017). Despite initial resistance in politically conservative states, all but 12 states have now expanded

Medicaid, including several states adopting the expansion through ballot initiatives (Status of State Action on the Medicaid Expansion Decision, n.d.).

The final prong of the child well-being framework (racial and economic inequality) is the most unrealized. Lawmakers largely are not combatting the structural inequalities that influence child outcomes (Dowd, 2018), and yet doing so is critical for reducing racial disproportionality and disparities in the family regulation system. As Nancy Dowd has explained, reversing structural inequality will require a broad-based approach to family well-being, including prenatal care, paid parental leave, universal health care, subsidized child care, efforts to make neighborhoods safer, a decreased reliance on incarceration, and much more (Dowd, 2018).

Even with an effective prevention program in place, there will still be some need for foster care. In these cases, it is essential to develop more realistic goals for children and parents. This means accepting the dual reality that some parents face significant challenges, and that there is not an adoptive home for every child, especially older children. One promising way forward is to continue to expand guardianships. As described earlier, guardianship is a good option for older children and children in care with relatives because it provides a permanent home for the child without terminating parental rights (Godsoe, 2013b). Guardianship programs recognize that family members' lives are complex and that a child and parent often maintain a connection even though it is inappropriate to return the child to the parent's custody. There is room for much innovation on this front, and guardianships may be a way around the unforgiving math of the current legal framework.

In all these ways, the child well-being framework can help reorient the family regulation system toward prevention.

Conclusion

The family regulation system presents a considerable challenge for child development and child well-being. Child abuse and neglect clearly harm children, but the means of intervening also present serious risks to children. The risks are especially acute for the families who are disproportionately involved in the family regulation system. There are no easy answers, but the stakes are clear, and there is some hope in following paths such as the one charted by the *Restatement of the Law, Children and the Law*.

References

(n.d.). https://www.childtrends.org/indicators/foster-care
105 P.L. 89, 111 Stat. 2115 (1997). *Adoption and Safe Families Act (ASFA) of 1997*.
110 P.L. 351, 122 Stat. 3949.
25 U.S.C. § 1911(a)-(b).
25 U.S.C. § 1914.
25 U.S.C. § 1915(a).
25 U.S.C. § 1920.
25 U.S.C. § 1921.
25 U.S.C. §§ 1901 1963.
42 U.S.C. § 625(a).
42 U.S.C. § 629.
42 U.S.C. § 629
42 U.S.C. § 629b(a)(4)–(5).
42 U.S.C. § 671(a)(15).
42 U.S.C. § 671(a)(15)(A).
42 U.S.C. § 671(a)(15)(D)(i)–(iii).
42 U.S.C. § 671(a)(28).
42 U.S.C. § 672(a)(1).
42 U.S.C. § 673(d).

42 U.S.C. § 673b.
42 U.S.C. § 675(5)I.
42 U.S.C. § 675(5)(E)
93 P.L. 247, 88 Stat. 4 (1974).
Ainsworth, M. D. (1967). *Infancy in Uganda: Infant care and the growth of love*. Johns Hopkins Press.
Ainsworth, M. D., & Bowlby, J. (1965). *Child care and the growth of love* (2nd ed.; Margery Fry, Ed.). Penguin Books.
Ainsworth, M. D. S., Blehar, M. C., Waters, E., & Wall, S. (1978). *Patterns of attachment: A psychological study of the strange situation*. Erlbaum.
American Law Institute. (n.d.). *Restatement of the law - - Children and the law*. § 2.24(b) & intro. note.
Baer, J. C., & Martinez, C. D. (2006). Child maltreatment and insecure attachment: A meta-analysis. *Journal of Reproductive and Infant Psychology, 24*, 187.
Bartholet, E. (1999). *Nobody's children: Abuse and neglect, foster drift, and the adoption alternative*. Beacon Press.
Billingsley, A., & Giovannoni, J. (1972). *Children of the storm: Black children and American child welfare*. Harcourt, Brace, Jovanovich.
Blackstone, W. (n.d.). *Commentaries*. 452.
Bowlby, J. (1969). *Attachment*. Basic Books.
Bowlby, J. (1973). *Separation: Anxiety and anger*. Basic Books.
Bowlby, J. (1980) *Attachment and Loss*. Basic Books.
Bowman, A., Hofer, L., O'Rourke, C., & Read, L. (2009). *Racial disproportionality in Wisconsin's child welfare system*. Department of Children & Family, University of Wisconsin.
Carlson, E. A. (1998). A prospective longitudinal study of attachment disorganization/disorientation. *Child Development, 69*, 1107.
Annie E. Casey Foundation. (2011). *Disparities and disproportionality in child welfare: Analysis of the research*.
Child Welfare Information Gateway. (2021). *Child welfare practice to address racial disproportionality and disparity*. U.S. Department of Health and Human Services, Administration for Children and Families, Children's Bureau.
Children's Bureau. (2006). *The AFCARS report final estimates for FY 1998–FY 2002*. U.S. Department of Health & Human Services, Administration for Children and Families, Administration on Children, Youth and Families. https://www.acf.hhs.gov/sites/default/files/documents/cb/afcarsreport12.pdf
Children's Bureau. (2011). *Subsidized guardianship: Child welfare waiver demonstrations*. U.S. Department of Health & Human Services. https://www.acf.hhs.gov/sites/default/files/cb/subsidized.pdf
Children's Bureau. (2016). *Racial disproportionately and disparity in child welfare*. U.S. Department of Health & Human Services.
Children's Bureau. (2017). *Child maltreatment prevention: Past, present, and future*. Child Welfare Information Gateway. https://www.childwelfare.gov/pubPDFs/cm_prevention.pdf
Children's Bureau. (2020). *No. 27, The AFCARS report 2*. U.S. Department of Health & Human Services.
Children's Bureau. (2021a). *Child maltreatment 2019*. U.S. Department of Health & Human Services, Administration of Children, Youth and Families, Children's Bureau.
Children's Bureau. (2021b). *Foster Care Statistics FY 2019*. Retrieved from Child Welfare Info. Gateway, U.S. Department of Health & Human Services. https://www.childwelfare.gov/pubs/factsheets/foster.pdf
Cicchetti, D. (2004). An odyssey of discovery: Lessons learned through three decades of research on child maltreatment. *American Psychologist, 59*(8), 731–741.
Cleveland, K., & Quas, J. A. (2020). Juvenile dependency court: The role of race in decisions, outcomes, and participant experiences. In M. Stevenson, B. L. Bottoms, & K. Burke (Eds.), *The legacy of race for children: Psychology, public policy, and law* (pp. 71–90) Oxford University Press.
Coan, J. (2018). Toward a neuroscience of attachment. In J. Cassidy & P. R. Shaver (Eds.), *Handbook of attachment: Theory, research and clinical implications* (3rd ed.) (pp. 242–272). Guilford Press.
Cross-Call, J. (2018, October 9). *Medicaid expansion continues to benefit state budges, contrary to critics' claims*. Center on Budget and Policy Priorities. https://www.cbpp.org/healedicaidaid-expansion-continues-to-benefit-state-budgets-contrary-to-critics-claims
Dong, M., Giles, W. H., Felitti, V. J., Dube, S. R., Williams, J. E., Chapman, D. P., & Anda, R. F. (2004). Insights into causal pathways for ischemic heart disease: Adverse Childhood Experiences Study. *American Heart Association, 110*, 1761, 1765–1766.
Dowd, N. E. (2018). *Reimagining equality: A new deal for children of color*. New York University Press.
Doyle, J. J., Jr. (2013). Causal effects of foster care: An instrumental-variables approach. *Child & Youth Services Review, 35*, 1143–1144, 1147–1149.
Drake, B., & Jonson-Reid, M. (2013). Poverty and child maltreatment. In J. E. Korbin & R. Krugman (Eds.), *Handbook of child maltreatment* (pp. 131–148). Springer.

Dwyer, J. G. (2018). *Liberal child welfare policy and its destruction of Black lives*. Routledge.
Felitti, J. V., Anda, R. F., Nordenberg, D., Williamson, D. F., Spitz, A. M., Edwards, V., Koss, M. P., Marks, J. S. (1998). Relationship of childhood abuse and household dysfunction to many of the leading causes of death in adults: The Adverse Childhood Experiences (ACE) Study. *American Journal of Preventative Medicine, 14*, 245, 249–250, 252–253.
Finkelhor, D. (1991). The scope of the problem. In Murray, K. & Gough, D. (Eds.), *Intervening child sexual abuse* (p. 12).
Font, S. A., Berger, L., & Slack, K. (2012). Examining racial disproportionality in child protective services case decisions. *Child. & Youth Services Review, 34*(11), 2188–2200.
Fraley, R. C., & Roisman, G. I. (2019). The development of adult attachment styles: Four lessons. *Current Opinion in Psychology, 25*, 26–30.
Gallagher, E. A., Radhakrishnan, G., & Grinstein-Weiss, M. (2019). The effect of health insurance on home payment delinquency: Evidence from ACA marketplace subsidies. *Journal of Public Economics, 67*.
Garrison, M. (2005). Reforming child protection: A public health perspective. *Virginia Journal of Social Policy & Law, 590*, 617–619.
Gauthier, Y., Fortin, G., & Jéliu, G. (2004). Clinical application of attachment theory in permanency planning for children in foster care: The importance of continuity of care. *Infant Mental Health Journal, 25*(4), 379–396.
Gavin, K. (2017, June 27). *Medicaid expansion helped enrollees do better at work or in job searches*. MHealth Lab. https://labblog.uofmhealth.org/industry-edicaidaid-expansion-helped-enrollees-do-better-at-work-or-job-searches
Godsoe, C. (2013a). Parsing parenthood. *Lews & Clarke Law Review, 17*, 113, 145–148.
Godsoe, C. (2013b). Permanency puzzle. *Michigan State Law Review, 2013*, 1113.
Golden, O., & Macomber, J. (2009). The Adoption and Safe Families Act (ASFA). In O. Golden, & J. Macomber (Eds.), *Intentions and results: A look back at the Adoption and Safe Families Act* (pp. 16–20, 26–28, 61). Urban Institute, Center for the Study of Social Policy.
Gordon, L. (1988). *Heroes of their own lives: The politics and history of family violence: Boston 1880–1960*. University of Illinois Press
Gordon, R. M. (1999). Drifting through Byzantium: The promise and failure of the Adoption and Safe Families Act of 1997. *Minnesota Law Review, 83*, 637, 646–650.
Grossberg, M. (2003). A protected childhood: The emergence of child protection in America. In W. Gamber, M. Grossberg, H. Hartog, W. Gamber, M. Grossberg, & H. Hartog (Eds.), *American public life and the historical imagination* (p. 213). University of Notre Dame Press.
Guggenheim, M. (2005). *What's wrong with children's rights*. Harvard University Press.
House of Representatives. (2018). *Family First Prevention Services Act of 2017, Pub. L. No. 115-123*, 132 Stat. 64. https://www.congress.gov/115/bills/hr253/BILLS-115hr253ih.pdf
Huntington, C. (2007). Mutual dependency in child welfare. *Notre Dame Law Review, 82*, 1485–1536
Huntington, C. (2014). The child welfare system and the limits of determinacy. *Law & Contemporary Problems, 76*, 221.
Huntington, C., & Scott, E. (2020). Conceptualizing legal childhood in the twenty-first century. *Michigan Law Review, 118*, 1371–1457.
Kaiser Family Foundation. (n.d.-a). *Health insurance coverage of children 0–18*. https://www.kff.org/other/state-indicator/children-0-18
Kaiser Family Foundation. (n.d.-b). *Status of state action on the Medicaid expansion decision*. https://www.kff.org/health-reform/state-indicator/state-activity-around-expanding-medicaid-under-the-affordable-care-act
Kay, J. D. (2015). Representing parents with disabilities. In M. Guggenheim, & V. S. Sankaran (Eds.), *Representing parents in child welfare cases: Advice and guidance for family defenders* (pp. 253–268). American Bar Association.
Kempe, H., Silverman, F. N., Steele, B. F., Droegemueller, W., & Silver, H. K. (1962). The battered-child syndrome. *Journal of the American Medical Association, 181*, 17–23.
Krakoff, S. (2017). They were here first: American Indian tribes, race, and the constitutional minimum. *Stanford Law Review, 69*, 491–548.
Lane, W. G., Rubin, D. M., Christian, C. W., & Monteith, R. (2002). Racial differences in the evaluation of pediatric fractures for physical abuse. *Journal of American Medicine Association, 13*, 1603.
Layzer, J. I., Goodson, B. D., Bernstein, L., & Price, C. (2001). *National evaluation of family support programs: The meta analysis*. ABT Associates, U.S. Department of Health & Human Services.
MacEachron, A. E., Gustavsson, N. S., Cross, S., & Lewis, A. (1996). The effectiveness of the Indian Child Welfare Act of 1978. *Social Service Review, 70*, 454–460.
Marc, M. (2017). Factors and events leading to the passage of the Indian Child Welfare Act. In E. Smith, & L. Merkel-Holguin (Eds.), *A history of child welfare* (pp. 257–275). Routledge.

McLellan, T., Lewis, D. C., O'Brien, C. P., & Kleber, H. D. (2000). Drug dependence, a chronic medical illness. *Journal of the American Medical Association, 13*, 1689.

Mnookin, R. H. (1975). Child-custody adjudication: Judicial functions in the face of indeterminancy. *Law & Contemporary Problems, 39*, 226, 275n.217.

National Council of Juvenile & Family Court Judges. (1987). *Making reasonable efforts: Steps for keeping families together.*

National Scientific Council on the Developing Child. (2005). *Excessive stress disrupts the architecture of the developing brain* [Working Paper No. 3]. https://www.developingchild.harvard.edu

National Scientific Council on the Developing Child. (2008). *Establishing a level foundation for life: Mental health begins in early childhood* [Working Paper No. 6]. https://www.developingchild.harvard.edu

National Scientific Council on the Developing Child. (2010). *Early experiences can alter gene expression and affect long-term development* [Working Paper No. 10]. https://www.developingchild.harvard.edu

National Scientific Council on the Developing Child. (2011). *Building the brain's "air traffic control" system: How early experiences shape the development of executive function* [Working Paper No. 11]. https://www.developingchild.harvard.edu

Nelson, B. (2000). *Making an issue of child abuse: Political agenda setting for social problems.* University of Chicago Press.

Nickerson, A., Bryant, R., Aderka, I., Hinton, D., & Hofmann, S. (2013). The impacts of parental loss and adverse parenting on mental health: Findings from the National Comorbidity Survey Replication. *Psychological Trauma, 5*, 119–127.

Ohio Department of Medicaid. (2018). *2018 Ohio Medicaid Group VIII assessment: A follow-up to the 2016 Group VIII assessment.* httpedicaidaid.ohio.gov/Portals/0/Resources/Reports/Annual/Group-VIII-Final-Report.pdf

Olds, D. (2002). Prenatal and infancy home visiting by nurses: From randomized trials to community replication. *Prevention Science, 3* (7), 153–173.

Penzerro, R., & Lein, L. (1995). Burning their bridges: Disordered attachment and foster care discharge. *Child Welfare, 74*, 351–366.

Platt, A. M. (2009). *The child savers: The invention of delinquency.* Rutgers University Press. (Original work published 1969)

Pleck, E. (2004). *Domestic tyranny: The making of American social policy against family violence from colonial times to the present.* University of Illinois Press.

Restatement of the Law- - Children and the Law part I, ch. 1, intro. note. (Tentative Draft No. 1, 2018). Am. L. Inst.

Roberts, D., (2022). *Torn Apart: How the Child Welfare System Destroys Black Families--and How Abolition Can Build a Safer World.* Basic Books.

Roberts, D. (2002). *Shattered bonds: The color of child welfare.* Basic Books.

Roberts, D. E. (2005). Black club women and child welfare: Lessons for modern reform. *Florida State University Law Review, 32*, 957–958.

S. Hrg. 98-952 Oversight of the Indian Child Welfare Act of 1978 (1984).

Sedlak, A. J. (2010). *Supplementary analysis of race differences in child maltreatment rates in the NIS-4.* U.S. Department of Health & Human Services.

Sedlak, A., Mattenburg, J., Basena, J., Petta, I., McPherson, K., Greene, A., & Li, S. (2010). *Fourth National Incidence Study of Child Abuse and Neglect (NIS-4): Report to Congress.* U.S. Department of Health & Human Services.

Select Committee on Indian Affairs. (1977). *Indian Child Welfare Act of 1977 (Part A).*

Shaver, P. R., Mikulincer, M., & Feeney, B. C. (2009). What's love got to do with it? Insecurity and anger in attachment relationships. *Virginia Journal of Social Policy & Law, 16*, 491.

Shonkoff, J. P., & Bales, S. N. (2011). Science does not speak for itself: Translating child development research for the public and its policymakers. *Child Development, 82*, 17, 23–24.

Sroufe, A. L. (2005). Attachment and development - A prospective, longitudinal study from birth to adulthood. *Attachment and Human Development, 7*, 349.

Staff of the House Committee on Ways & Means, 112th Congress. (2012). *Green Book: Background data and material within the jurisdiction of the Committee on Ways and Means.* http://greenbook.waysandmeans.house.gov/sites/greenbook.waysandmeans.house.gov/files/2012/CW%20Table11-4_FC-Entering_Served_Exiting_Incare_82-11%20RM-ES.pdf

Tough, P. (2011, March 14). The poverty clinic. *The New Yorker.*

U.S. Department of Health & Human Services, Administration for Children and Families, Administration of Children, Youth and Families, Children's Bureau. (2021). *Child Maltreatment 2019.*

Villegas, S., & Pecora, P. (2012). Mental health outcomes for adults in family foster care as children: An analysis by ethnicity. *Children and Youth Services Review, 34*, 1448–1458.

Volger, J. (2017, November 14). *Access to health care and criminal behavior: Short-run evidence from the ACA Medicaid expansions.*

Wald, M. S. (1975). State intervention on behalf of "neglected" children: A search for realistic standards. *Stanford Law Review, 27,* 985.

Wald, M. S. (1976). State intervention on behalf of "neglected" children: Standards for removal of children from their homes, monitoring the status of children in foster care, and termination of parental rights. *Stanford Law Review, 28,* 625.

Wald, M. S. (2014). Beyond child protection: Helping all families provide adequate parenting. In K. McCartney, Y. Hirokazu, L. B. Forcier, G. Miller, & M. Edelman (Eds.), *Improving the odds for America's children: Future directions in policy and practice* (pp. 138–146). Harvard Education Press.

Wen, H., Hockenberry, J. M., & Cummings, J. R. (2017). The effect of Medicaid expansion on crime reduction: Evidence from HIFA-waiver expansions. *Journal of Public Economics, 154,* 67.

Wildeman, C., Emanuel, N., Leventhal, J., Putnam-Hornstein, E., Waldfogel, J., & Lee, H. (2014). The prevalence of confirmed maltreatment among US children, 2004–2011. *JAMA Pediatrics, 168,* 706, 709.

Woodhouse, B. B. (2005). Egogenerism: An environmentalist approach to protecting endangered children. *Virginia Journal of Social Policy & Law, 409,* 411–426.

A Developmental Perspective on Unaccompanied Migrant Youth in the U.S. Immigration Legal System

Kalina M. Brabeck, Deborah Gonzalez, Sarah Rendón García, and Adrian Pendergast

Abstract

This chapter focuses on a subset of immigrant youth—unaccompanied youth who enter the United States without a caregiver and without legal status—and their experiences as they navigate the U.S. immigration system. The chapter considers (a) how these youth's developmental capacities and limitations shape their experiences within the U.S. legal system, including detention and deportation proceedings, and (b) how participation in the legal system shapes the youth's development. It summarizes legal issues affecting migrant youth, including child detention, the Flores settlement, and the Trafficking Victim Protection Reauthorization Act; youth's experiences in Office of Refugee Resettlement custody; available forms of relief for migrant youth; and youth's lack of right to counsel in deportation proceedings. It also examines the effects of development on youth's detention, understanding of and participation in the legal system, and testimony in immigration proceedings. The chapter concludes that the U.S. legal system fails to consider development science in its policies and practices with migrant youth.

Key Words: immigrant youth, unaccompanied migrant youth, immigration legal system, detention and deportation, youth development

Immigrant children and youth represent an increasingly large percentage of the U.S. population under age 18. In 1990, 13.4% of all U.S. children lived in immigrant families; this percentage rose twofold to 25.8% in 2019 (Migration Policy Institute, n.d.). Three subsets of children and youth living in these immigrant families are impacted in significant and notable ways by the U.S. immigration legal system: (a) the 1.1 million unauthorized youth who entered the United States with unauthorized parents (U.S. Office of Refugee Resettlement (ORR)], 2021), (b) the 4.1 million U.S.-born citizen children of unauthorized immigrant parents who reside in mixed-status families (American Immigration Council, 2021, and (c) unaccompanied youth[1] who entered the United States without a caregiver and without legal status (Zayas et al., 2017). While each of these three groups of youth is impacted by immigration policies and enforcement (for a review, see Barajas Gonzalez et al., 2021), this chapter focuses

---

[1] The term "unaccompanied minor" refers to a minor youth who enters the U.S. unaccompanied by a parent or legal guardian. The legal term is "unaccompanied alien child."

on the latter subset of immigrant youth—unaccompanied youth—and their experiences as they navigate the U.S. immigration system.

In this chapter, we consider (a) how these youth's developmental capacities and limitations shape their experiences within the U.S. legal system, including detention and deportation proceedings, and (b) how participation in the legal (and often health and human services) system shapes the youth's development. Given that the vast majority of unaccompanied youth—88%—are between the ages of 13 and 17 (U.S. Office of Refugee Resettlement [ORR], 2021), we primarily use the term "youth" (synonymous with "adolescent") in this chapter. When referring specifically to research with children ages 12 and under, we use the term "children." When both groups are included in scholarship, we specify "children and youth."

The number of unaccompanied youth entering the United States between 2000 and 2007 remained steady, with a yearly average of approximately 6,700 youth. However, the number of unaccompanied youth crossing the Mexican–U.S. border began to increase in 2009 and has largely continued increasing ever since: Numbers rose from approximately 20,000 in 2009 to 75,000 in 2019 (Congressional Research Service, 2021. While the number of unaccompanied youth crossing the border decreased somewhat in 2020, there was a 64% increase from January 2020 to January 2021, with 47,642 apprehensions in year to date (March) of 2021 (U.S. Customs & Border Protection, 2021). The vast majority of these youth come from Guatemala, Honduras, and El Salvador.

As of May 31, 2021, there were approximately 20,332 unaccompanied youth in the care of HHS, staying an average length of 35 days in an Office of Refugee Resettlement (ORR) "shelter"[2] (U.S. ORR, 2021). Among these youth in ORR facilities, 69% are male. The vast majority—88%—are over the age of 13, but the population includes "tender age" children (2% under age 6 and 10% ages 6–12). Upon discharge from ORR custody, 42% of the youth are released within the United States to a parent or legal guardian, 52% are released to a close relative (e.g., sibling, aunt, uncle, grandparent, first cousin), and 6% are released to a distant relative or unrelated adult (U.S. ORR, 2021). Youth released to a close relative may be in the "care" of a first cousin only a few years their senior (Frankel et al., 2021).

Unaccompanied youth experience an array of stressful, adverse, and potentially traumatic events before, during, and after reaching the United States (for a review, see Berger Cardoso et al., 2019). Many youth's decisions to migrate are motivated by experiences of poverty, violence, and persecution in their home countries (Stinchcomb & Hershberg, 2014). During migration, they are vulnerable to physical deprivation, assault, sexual abuse, and accidental injuries (Aldarondo & Becker, 2011). After arrival in the United States, they confront acculturative stress, social dislocation, discrimination and racism, underresourced schools and neighborhoods, and the constant fear of deportation (Berger Cardoso et al., 2019). Many youth experience significant interruptions in schooling that make it difficult for them to persist in U.S. schools (Frankel et al., 2021). Youth released to a parent (just over 40%; U.S. ORR, 2021) must navigate complicated reunifications. These reunifications are often affected by the extended periods of separation and the resulting consequences for parent–child attachment and upended family roles and processes (Berger Cardoso et al., 2021).

Despite the multiple challenges these youth face and their clearly identified need for support, the vast majority of youth do not receive postrelease services to ensure the safety of their

---

[2] While the government uses the term "shelter" to refer to these facilities, anthropologist Lauren Heidbrink (2014) points out that youth themselves refer to them as detention and spaces where they are treated like criminals: Their freedom is curtailed and their actions surveilled and sometimes used against them in immigration court. Therefore, we place the term "shelter" in quotations.

placement and to help them integrate into the United States after they are released from ORR custody (Grace & Roth, 2015). In light of these stressors and the lack of available supports, it is unsurprising that in a convenience sample of unaccompanied youth, roughly 60% met the criteria for posttraumatic stress disorder (PTSD), 30% met the criteria for a depressive disorder, and 30% reported suicidal ideation in the past year (Berger Cardoso, 2018). Amidst these many challenges, unaccompanied youth must navigate a complex legal system that generally treats them—in particular during deportation proceedings—without consideration of their developmental capacities and limitations. We next outline the legal process, from detention to deportation, that unaccompanied youth experience.

The Legal Process for Unaccompanied Migrant Youth: From Detention to Deportation Hearings

Child Detention

Immigrant children arrive, either with caregivers or without, in the United States either at a port of entry[3] or at a point in the border that is not designated by the DHS to be an authorized point of entry. While there are many different reasons that immigrant youth come to the United States (including seeking family reunification and fleeing violence, abuse, and poverty; Berger Cardoso et al., 2019), once they arrive without proper legal documents, they are treated uniformly: The youth are detained by U.S. Border Patrol (USBP) or Customs Border Protection (CBP) and immediately processed and placed into deportation proceedings, with some exceptions for children from contiguous countries.

Upon their arrest, unaccompanied youth are first placed in large warehouses that are divided by tall chain-linked fences meant to give the appearance of separate rooms, which separate the youth by age group and sex (Axios, 2018). They remain in these warehouses until they can be processed for transfer to the ORR, which is an arm of the HHS. Within these chain-link-fenced rooms, the youth are grouped together and typically sleep on the floor with only an aluminum blanket. These conditions have not substantively changed in the context of the COVID-19 pandemic nor under the Biden administration. Groups of youth are now divided by plastic tarps instead of chain-link "walls" and are given masks, but they have no way to socially distance (BBC, 2021). During their time in detention with the USBP or CBP, the youth are not provided any medical care or education (Congressional Research Service, 2021). In essence, the purpose of their stay is to allow the USBP or CBP to determine the youth's age and process them for deportation proceedings (DHS, 2010).

Once this process is complete, Immigration and Customs Enforcement (ICE) transfers the youth to the ORR, where they are housed in a "shelter" while the ORR can find a caregiver, or sponsor, to take the youth into custody. The caregiver can be a parent, family member, or family friend. In some instances, the youth may be transferred to a licensed state facility. The benefit of being transferred to ORR custody is that, once in ORR custody, the ORR "shelter" must provide that youth with medical care, education, food, clothing, and other necessities. While in the shelter and while receiving services, youth are *technically* free to leave. However, in reality, should they decide to walk out of the facility for any reason, the staff at the shelter facilities, according to ORR policy, are ordered to call local law enforcement for the return of the youth. Upon return, the youth is placed in a "staff security facility" that provides for more supervision with "services to control problem behavior and prevent escape" (ORR, 2021).

---

[3] A port of entry is a point in the border line that has been designated by the DHS to be an area where migrants can enter the United States and be inspected by a border protection agent.

Immigrant youth are understandably fearful of redetention; therefore, unlike any other youth who may leave their home to visit a friend, attend school, or go to a park, such youth are detained and their actions are restricted in the "shelters" in which they are housed until they can be released to the designated caregiver.

The History of Child Detention

Standards for detaining immigrant youth were established in 1997 when the Flores settlement agreement was signed. Prior to Flores, in 1985, two nonprofit organizations sued the former Immigration Naturalization Service (INS) to challenge their practices relating to the treatment and detention of children and youth. The nonprofits, which represented a class of unaccompanied youth detained by the INS, alleged that the INS detained unaccompanied youth and strip-searched them at the time of detention and again after every nonattorney visit.[4] In addition to being strip-searched, the unaccompanied youth were detained with adult migrants in detention facilities and had no access to an education, medical care, or an attorney to help them navigate the complex immigration system (Olivas, 1990). In the late 1980s and early 1990s, many detention facilities were built in remote areas where migrants—adult and child alike—had little to no access to phones, legal representation, or resources to help them with their deportation cases. In essence, migrant youth were (and in large part still are) treated as if they had the same mental capacity of understanding and acumen as adults (Olivas, 1990).

As a result of the litigation in 1985, in 1997, the former INS (today DHS) entered into an agreement to provide protections to youth who arrive at U.S. borders unaccompanied by an adult. Pursuant to the Flores settlement, youth are to be detained in the least restrictive setting appropriate to their age and special needs. DHS must provide the youth with proper food and water, medical assistance in emergencies, toilets and sinks, adequate temperature control and ventilation, adequate supervision to protect them from other youth and adults, and separation from unrelated adults (DHS, 2010). Additionally, the agreement called for the release of the children without delay to a parent, family member, family friend, or licensed program facility while their cases are being processed (Human Rights First, 2016).

Pursuant to the Flores settlement and the subsequent passing of the Trafficking Victim Protection Reauthorization Act, also known as the Wilberforce Act or the TVPRA,[5] ICE and CBP are required to release any unaccompanied or accompanied youth arriving at the border within 72 hours of apprehension into the custody of the ORR. The ORR, and its network of state licensed child "shelters," is tasked with providing housing, education, mental and medical care, case management, socialization, and recreation for youth. The ORR is further required to search for a suitable sponsor who can take custody and physical placement of the youth for the duration of the proceedings. Finally, the ORR must "develop a plan" to secure legal representation for the youth; however, the agency is not actually responsible for securing legal representation (Congressional Research Office, 2021. In practice, prior to release, the youth receive a Know Your Rights presentation and legal screening by the social worker in charge of the youth. The social worker in turn reaches out to pro bono counsel in the area of the youth's intended residence and connects the youth's sponsor with an attorney who may or may not be able to take on the case (Migration Policy Institute, 2021).

While youth are in ORR care, one of the primary roles of case management workers is to make efforts to find the person with whom youth were intended to be united upon entry to

---

[4] *Flores v. Meese*, 681 F.Supp. 665, 666 (C.D.C.A. 1988).
[5] 8 USC 1232 § 235 – TVPRA – Treatment of Children From Contiguous and Non-contiguous Countries.

the United States If there was no individual intended for reunification, the youth will remain in ORR care for the duration of removal proceedings. The intended caregiver is required to submit fingerprints and a background check, which can be a deterrent if the caregiver is themselves unauthorized and risks exposing their own immigration status to government officials (ORR, 2021). Thus, many youth remain in ORR "shelters" for long periods of time as their case or preparation for deportation proceeds.

Unaccompanied Youth in Immigration Proceedings
Although the Flores settlement agreement allowed for small improvements in the detention of unaccompanied youth, it did nothing to help these children navigate the deportation process. Unlike Australia, Canada, and many EU countries, and in contrast to the U.S. juvenile law, immigration courts do not grant children the right to government-sponsored counsel (Huynh, 2021). The result is that youth and children—including very young children—must either access pro bono lawyers, find resources to pay for a private lawyer, or represent themselves. Although there is case law that carves out some protections for immigrants who are mentally incompetent to assist in their representation, there is no such precedent and/or protections available for youth.[6] From a legal standpoint, the moment the CBP or USBP detains the youth, the process begins with the determination of whether the youth fits within the legal definition of an unaccompanied alien child (UAC). The designation of whether a child is a UAC grants the child various benefits that are not afforded to adults, such as the protections under the Flores settlement and not being removed from the United States immediately (with the exception of children from contiguous countries). If the youth does qualify as a UAC, then the only special protections granted relate to detention, as previously described. The legal standards or requirements relating to the removal proceedings are the same for children and youth as they are for adults. As mentioned previously, children from contiguous countries, such as Mexico, are not afforded the protections under the Flores settlement, except for protections afforded under the law related to fear of persecution and victims of trafficking.

Accessing an attorney is most difficult for nondetained youth who have been released to sponsors and do not have access to pro bono lawyers at ORR "shelters," who often visit to give Know Your Rights workshops (Grace & Roth, 2015; Huynh, 2021). For youth released to sponsors, few child welfare professionals (e.g., case managers, juvenile judges) understand the pathways to legal status available to immigrant youth and can help them pursue these options (Heidbrink, 2014). Often the youth, forced to represent themselves, are issued removal orders with little notice of when their case will be heard (American Immigration Council, 2016). These youth (12% of whom are children under age 12; U.S. ORR, 2021) must understand the charges against them and laws pertaining to the conditions under which they can remain in the United States. Then they need to translate that understanding into a coherent explanation to the judge, while a government attorney, well versed and trained in U.S. immigration law, argues for deportation. Treated the same as adults, children and youth are required to attend every hearing, secure legal representation at their own expense or defend themselves before the immigration judge, change their address with the court, respond to legal civil immigration violations, and meet any and all burdens of proof related to any application the youth may be making with the immigration court.

---

[6] Matter of M-A-M-, 25 I&N Dec. 474 (BIA 2011): "Aliens in immigration proceedings are presumed to be competent and, if there are no indicia of incompetency in a case, no further inquiry regarding competency is required." "If there are indicia of incompetency, the Immigration Judge must make further inquiry to determine whether the alien is competent for purposes of immigration proceedings."

The commencement of the unaccompanied youth's removal proceedings is not dependent on the youth's release from ORR custody nor the securing of legal representation, but rather on when ICE serves the notice to appear (NTA), the charging document, with the immigration court. The NTA informs the youth of the alleged civil immigration charges pending against them by way of citing the Immigration Nationality Act. The NTA thereby informs the youth that they are either *removable* or *inadmissible*, both terms with complex legal definitions. The NTA informs (or should inform) the youth of the place, date, and time of the removal proceedings. It further informs the youth of their obligations (e.g., to attend every hearing, to alert the immigration court about any changes of address) and of their rights (e.g., to admit or deny the legal allegations made against them, to seek legal counsel, and to provide evidence). The NTA further informs the youth of their right to appeal an immigration judge's decision and of the consequences of failing to appear at an immigration hearing (Immigration Legal Resource Center, 2020).

Upon the filing of the NTA with the immigration court, removal proceedings commence. Jurisdiction is determined by the location in which the youth is physically residing.[7] Once jurisdiction is attached, the immigration court schedules a master calendar hearing. A master calendar hearing is a preliminary hearing where the immigration judge advises youth (like adults) regarding the right to an attorney, the duty to change the address with the court and to appear at all hearings, and the right to respond to the allegations on the NTA (Department of Justice, n.d.). If the unaccompanied youth has the cognitive capacities to respond to the allegations on the NTA and file an application for relief with the immigration Judge, the case will then be set for an individual calendar hearing. This requires the youth to be fluent in English and to be familiar with the court's practice manual and rules of practice to ensure that any evidence the youth wishes to present is properly filed with the court and properly served upon the Office of Chief Counsel for DHS. Unlike the youth, DHS is always represented by a government attorney in immigration court.

The individual calendar hearing is an evidentiary hearing wherein the youth must present any evidence in support of the application for relief, understand all the elements of the law, and meet the appropriate burden of proof to win their case. Moreover, the youth must present the evidence, such as testimony and relevant documents, in accordance with the practice manual and the practice of the court in which the hearing is taking place. In some instances, because of the date of the NTA having been issued, removal proceedings may be well on their way while the unaccompanied youth remains in ORR custody and prior to the youth obtaining legal representation. If this occurs, then the unaccompanied youth must appear in court alone because failure to appear at any immigration court hearing will result in an automatic deportation order (U.S. Department of Justice, 2021).

There are very few forms of relief from deportation for newly arrived children and youth. The most common forms of relief are asylum and special immigrant juvenile (SIJ) status. In instances in which children or youth have been trafficked into the United States they may be eligible for a T visa. These forms of relief pose heavy burdens on children and youth to prove. Asylum requires that applicants prove that they (i.e., children or youth) have themselves been *persecuted on account of race, nationality, religion, political opinion, or membership in a social group*.[8] SIJ relief requires applicants to first seek a court order from the juvenile court having jurisdiction over children or youth indicating that one or both parents have either abandoned,

---

[7] See 8 CFR § 1003.41 – jurisdiction over removal proceeding with the immigration court commence upon the filing of the NTA.

[8] INA § 208; 8 USC § 1158.

abused, or neglected the children or youth. Once the state court order is obtained, only then can children and youth request status from the U.S. Citizenship and Immigration Service (USCIS) as an SIJ. If this status is granted by the USCIS, children and youth can then seek adjustment of status to that of a lawful permanent resident with the immigration court.[9]

T visas require that applicants prove that they were victims of trafficking or attempted trafficking. They must prove that they are physically in the United States directly because of the trafficking, that they have complied and will continue to comply with all reasonable requests for assistance by law enforcement relating to the investigation or prosecution of the traffickers, and that they will suffer extreme hardship if removed from the United States.[10] Prior to applying for a T visa, the applicants must obtain certification by the law enforcement agency investigating or prosecuting that they have provided assistance to the law enforcement agency. T visas are limited in number; only 5,000 visas per year may be granted regardless of applicants' age.

As is evident even in this brief description, and as with most immigration forms of relief, securing asylum, SIJ status, and T visas is incredibly complex. The process is difficult and confusing and places significant burdens of proof on the applicant to provide extensive evidence supporting their claims and requests. Given the complexity of the legal process and potential forms of relief, it is unsurprising that studies show that immigrant children who are represented by an attorney are more likely to both appear in court and win their cases. In 2014, the Transactional Records Access Clearinghouse (TRAC, 2014)[11] studied how many juvenile cases had been filed with the immigration court between 2005 and 2014 as well as how many of those juveniles were represented by an attorney and the likelihood of success in their cases with and without an attorney. TRAC's studies showed that only 31% of unaccompanied youth in removal proceedings were represented by an attorney. Of the youth who were represented by an attorney, 48% were successful in their removal case and were allowed to remain in the United States, while only 28% of the youth represented by an attorney were ordered to be removed and 26% of the youth were granted voluntary departure. In contrast, 77% of unrepresented youth were ordered to be removed from the United States, and only 10% of the unrepresented youth won their cases and were allowed to stay, with the remaining 13% being granted voluntary departure (TRAC, 2014). Moreover, studies show that 95% of youth represented by legal counsel appear in court to respond to removal proceedings, while only 33% of those not represented by legal counsel appear at their hearings (American Immigration Council, 2016). Thus, immigrant youth who are represented by an attorney are not only more likely to appear in court but also more likely to have their legal rights observed and more likely to be successful in court.

Insights From Developmental Research on Youth's Participation in Immigration Proceedings

The process of allowing immigrant youth to represent themselves assumes that they are (a) able to adequately understand the complex legal process outlined previously (including legal jargon, options for relief, court procedures and expectations, the different roles of professionals involved, etc.) and (b) able to adequately convey how their experiences relate to the various forms of relief available to them (e.g., their "credible fear" of returning to their home country

---

[9] INA § 101(a)(27)(J); 8 USC § 1101(a)(27)(J).

[10] Survivors of Trafficking and Violence Protection Act of 2000 (VTVPA); INA § 101(a)(15)(T); 8 CFR § 214.11.

[11] TRAC is a data-gathering, data research, and data distribution organization at Syracuse University.

and membership to a "protected social class" in the case of asylum). Research summarized next confirms that these assumptions fail to take into consideration children and youth's unique developmental capacities and vulnerabilities.

Developmental Perspective on Child/Youth Detention in ORR "Shelters"

In their research with detained children, both unaccompanied youth and children separated from caregivers at the border under the Trump administration's zero-tolerance policy, Roth and colleagues (2019) find that tender-age children (under age 12) have special developmental needs that tax the ORR "shelter" system, including physical touch, holding, physical space that can accommodate naps, developing mobile skills, exploration of their environments, play-based learning, and, for younger children, diaper changing. These accommodations are challenging for detention facilities, "shelters," and foster placements and require extensive resources. Younger children, whose verbal skills are still developing, often cannot articulate their needs, answer intake questions, or communicate the experiences they have endured. Thus, well-meaning caseworkers are often without critical information, for example, regarding children's health status, family structure, or trauma history, to adequately care for them (Roth et al., 2019). Linguistic and cultural barriers compound this, particularly for Indigenous Mayan youth from Central America (in particular, Guatemala).

Adolescents experience detention, which, pursuant to Flores, positions them as vulnerable entities in need of protection, at a point in development that is marked by a growing desire for agency and autonomy. These normative developmental processes are particularly relevant for unaccompanied youth, who have assumed adultlike roles and tasks in migrating to the United States without a caregiver. In her ethnographic study of five adolescent unaccompanied youth in the U.S. legal system, Heidbrink (2014) demonstrated how government paperwork, institutions, and policies served to undermine and erase the youth's agency and personhood. The reasons motivating youth's migration were ignored, their preferences for family reunification were often unheeded, and their attempts to communicate with others (e.g., via the Internet) were punished. Heidbrink (2014) further documented how unaccompanied youth themselves experience institutional care in ORR "shelters" as violence. Rather than describing the housing as safe places of protection, the youth themselves described them as detention facilities and prisonlike spaces where they were treated like criminals. Their freedom was restricted, their schedules dictated, and their actions and communications surveilled and recorded, and sometimes used against them in immigration court. Youth were given limited roles and information about their custodial arrangements, upcoming court dates, or impending deportations. Detention thereby undermined these youth's normative tasks of establishing identity and exercising agency. More broadly, for children and youth, the time spent in detention may feel especially protracted and like something to be terminated at all costs, even if that means giving up on potential legal relief in the future (Lustig, 2010).

Unaccompanied Youth and Self-Representation in Court

As described previously, unlike the detention process, children and youth are granted no special considerations in deportation proceedings. Although the immigration law system does not distinguish between adults and children in its rules concerning right to self-representation, developmental science confirms that children and youth are not "small adults." Children and youth's cognitive development impacts their ability to meaningfully comprehend the legal process, legal jargon, and the roles of the various adults involved in their case (Huynh, 2021; Juffer, 2016). Such is the case for all children and youth involved in criminal and juvenile proceedings (see Woolard, this volume; Viljoen et al., this volume). For immigrant youth, general developmental limitations are compounded by linguistic and cultural barriers (Huynh, 2021). Moreover, as described earlier, the immigration court system is particularly complex. Because of the concerns regarding a minor's ability to competently represent themselves, the American Academy of Pediatrics policy has recommended that no child or youth, under any circumstances, should be required to represent themselves in immigration proceedings (Pantell & AAP Committee on Psychosocial Aspects of Child and Family Health, 2017).

In a seminal study relevant to the expectation that children can sufficiently understand the legal process in order to competently represent themselves, Cooper et al. (2010) studied children's understanding of the legal system. Young children (under age 8) had minimal ability to define legal terms and identify the roles of adults involved in legal proceedings. Specifically, 21% of children ages 4–7 failed to provide any correct information of legal terms, and 74% provided two or fewer correct responses (the only familiar term, correctly identified by 65% of children, was "police"). While older children had better legal knowledge, only three out of 165 children aged 11–14 gave five or more correct definitions (out of a total seven questions), and 20% provided zero correct answers. Thus, consistent with previous research (e.g., Crawford & Bull, 2007), even adolescents struggled with understanding the process, roles, and definitions. In addition, other legal terms are more nebulous in immigration settings. For instance, because of 287(g) agreements that empower local police to enforce immigration policies (Ayón, 2016), police and ICE officials or other ORR and immigration staff may be conflated by youth or perceived as the same.

Quas and colleagues (2009) examined maltreated children's (ages 4–15) understanding of dependency hearings that they had just attended. Consistent with Cooper et al. (2010), while children's understanding improved with age, the majority evidenced limited understanding of what actually happened during their hearings, even though the hearings had just occurred and the children were present. One third of the children interviewed provided zero accurate information about what happened, and only one third of older children over age 12 could provide accurate information (Quas et al., 2009). Notably, unlike many immigrant children, children in dependency cases *have* legal representation and interact with professionals whose jobs mandate that they facilitate children's understanding (social workers, foster parents, investigators, court-appointed special advocates, guardians ad litem, lawyers, and judges); yet these children still struggled with terms and confusion (Quas et al., 2009). Similarly, over half the children in a study by Block and colleagues (2010) of dependent children's knowledge of recent proceedings responded "no" when asked whether they understood what was happening in their legal cases.

In adolescents, investigations often focus on legally relevant understanding in juvenile suspects. Viljoen and Roesch (2005), for example, examined the relationship between legal capacities (e.g., understanding Miranda rights, competency to stand trial) and cognitive development among 152 youth ages 11–17. The authors found that legal capacities increased with age, but also were mediated by cognitive development, in particular verbal ability. Youth's legal capacities were also negatively associated with attentional or hyperactive difficulties, little time with attorneys, and impoverished backgrounds.

Even those unaccompanied youth fortunate enough to have attorneys generally have little or no time with them, experience poverty, and may have attentional challenges related to PTSD, anxiety, and depression stemming from trauma (Barrera-Valencia et al., 2017). Thus, while older adolescents may have some better understanding of the process and their rights than children, adolescents still lack sufficient understanding, particularly if they are challenged with limited legal counsel, poverty, limited education, little English fluency, and mental health challenges related to trauma and adverse experiences. Drawing on developmental science and citing the Fifth Amendment's due process clause and the Immigration and Nationality Act's provision requiring a "full and fair hearing" before an immigration judge, the American Immigration Council and partners filed a lawsuit in 2014 seeking the right to appointed counsel for unrepresented children in immigration cases; their plaintiffs included children as young as age 1 (American Immigration Council, 2021).

Developmental Perspective on Child Testimony

Children and youth's ability to act as their own "star witness" and testify is also limited by development. For example, our ability to recall and contextualize the events of our lives evolves throughout childhood, as does our ability to distinguish between our own thoughts and the thoughts of others (Pantell & AAP Committee on Psychosocial Aspects of Child and Family Health, 2017). Children's ability to recall and understand their experiences improves with maturation. Indeed, research confirms that young children remember fewer details about their experiences than older children and adults (Eisen et al., 2002; Lamb et al., 2003). Children's memory for the events in their lives—autobiographical memory—is influenced by their developments in mnemonic processes (including ability to locate events in context and time), autonoetic awareness (the awareness of one's existence in a particular space and time), and narrative skills (the ability to organize and recount their experiences in comprehensible ways; Middleton, 2017). While these capacities emerge early in childhood (e.g., autonoetic awareness emerges between ages 4 and 6; narrative skills for past experiences emerge around age 3), they grow over childhood as the brain matures, making older children more reliable and detailed narrators than younger children (Patricia, 2007). Younger children demonstrate higher levels of memory inaccuracies, including difficulty accurately relating temporal attributes of events (e.g., last week could mean anytime in the future to a preschool-age child; Orbach & Lamb, 2001) and susceptibility to adult influence (Eisen et al., 2007). Experiencing themselves as powerless and dependent upon adults and seeking to avoid punishment, children may be overly compliant and susceptible to suggestion and intimidation by authority figures, including government attorneys and judges (Lamb & Sim, 2013; Leichtman & Ceci, 1995). This may be exacerbated by cultural norms of children being respectful and deferent toward adults, norms common in many Latinx and Asian communities (Calzada et al., 2010).

Further contributing to difficulties children have in testifying on their own behalf is the reality that children are often being asked to recount traumatic experiences, which may be the basis for their claims for relief. While highly emotional events are more likely to be encoded and available for later retrieval, protective responses to trauma—including shifts in attention, dissociation, and avoidance—can make it more difficult to narrate traumatic memories in a sequential and detailed manner (Goodman et al., 2009). Among children who demonstrate dissociative tendencies, elevated cortisol levels and PTSD symptoms are associated with greater memory errors for nonarousing events (Eisen et al., 2007). Moreover, even though the disorganized and at times limited ways that trauma is often recounted are documented empirically in the fields of psychology and traumatology, inconsistent or disorganized and limited disclosures can be exploited by government attorneys as "proof" of malingering or unreliable testimony. Moreover, past traumatic experiences can be triggered by the adversarial nature of the immigration court process, where youth lack power and agency, don't know what will happen next, and experience fear and helplessness reminiscent of prior trauma (Huynh, 2021).

Because of their emerging developmental capacities, children and youth seeking asylum or other forms of relief often have difficulty meeting the burden of proof for their available legal options. Some may struggle to distinguish which information is important to convey to support their claim. Younger children may not identify an experience as "trauma" or "hardship" if that experience (e.g., domestic abuse, poverty, persecution) has always been a part of their lives. Children may struggle to articulate their fear and convey their experiences in a manner that adults can understand, particularly when those experiences involve trauma and adversity (Juffer, 2016). Therapists working with children exposed to adversity and trauma frequently use nonverbal forms of expression (e.g., play, artwork) as a way of increasing children's comfort and with recognition that children do not recount traumatic experiences in the same verbal way that adults do (Desmond et al., 2015). In her ethnographic study of youth in immigration courts, Huynh (2021) observed, "The judge asked one last time and the boy responded he was not afraid and would like to return to Guatemala. It was evident that the child's initial reaction to the question of being fearful was a resounding yes, but when asked to articulate his fears, he did not know how to respond and proceeded to deny being afraid" (p. 626). This example reflects how confusion and deference to adults may lead unaccompanied youth to inadvertently undermine their claims. Cultural norms around stoicism, emotional restraint, and stigma around mental health issues may compound this.

Immigrant children's ability to articulate and convey their experiences in support of their claim is further complicated by language barriers, cultural unfamiliarity with the U.S. legal system, and limited or interrupted education. In addition, one way that claimants may demonstrate that their home government cannot protect them is by showing that they have reported to authorities. However, children and youth are unlikely to report to authorities for many reasons, including lack of transportation, lack of information, and fear of being punished by powerful adults (Juffer, 2016). Additionally, youth are unlikely to understand what a "protected social class" is, let alone prove their belonging to and persecution on the basis of such a group.

The failure of immigration judges to take into account children's development may also affect the accuracy of the child's testimony. In their review article, Brown and Lamb (2015) identify how different types of questioning influence children's accuracy. For example, broad, open-ended questions ("Tell me about why you came to the United States") and those that ask for elaboration of previously shared information ("You mentioned there was a gang in your neighborhood. Can you tell me more about that?") are associated with greater accuracy and fewer inconsistencies when compared with closed-ended questions ("How many people were in this gang?"). Even preschool children, who need additional structure and specificity, respond well to open-ended questions (e.g., "What happened when you lived with your aunt?" versus "Isn't it true that your aunt took care of you because your parents were in the United States?"). In addition, asking children open-ended recall questions ("Tell me about your childhood in Honduras") results in more accurate reporting than does asking closed-ended recognition questions, especially those that contain tags ("Isn't it true that you never told anyone you were being harassed by gang members?"; Lamb et al., 2007; Orbach & Lamb, 2001). Using age-appropriate language; constructing simple, straightforward questions; and trying to establish rapport with children further enhance the accuracy of children's testimony (Lamb & Sim, 2013).

Because of the recognition of the powerful influence of question type on children's testimonial accuracy, the Eunice Shriver National Institutes on Child Development (NICHD) created a protocol for forensic interviewing of children (see Slonecker et al., this volume). This protocol consists of three phases: rapport building and setting expectations/ground rules, substantive questioning guided by best practices, and closure through discussion of a neutral topic (Brown & Lamb, 2015). In immigration court, children are not adequately prepared, are at the mercy of various adults whom they don't know and don't trust, are linguistically and culturally lost, are rushed through, and are subjected to rapid, insensitive, and closed-ended questions from government attorneys who are unlikely to have any training or knowledge of best practice interviewing approaches (Huynh, 2021). This has consequences, not only for children's well-being, but also for their competency to recount their experiences and needs in their own defense: "Adults have a profound impact in shaping what children include in their accounts, and can easily undermine children's competency when they are describing the past and telling us what they know" (Brown & Lamb, 2015, p. 253).

Adolescents in Court

The majority of unaccompanied youth representing themselves in court are adolescents. As previously noted, older children tend to be better at accurately recalling and communicating their experiences than younger children (Lamb & Sim, 2013). They also have comparatively better understanding of the legal process and legal jargon than younger children, although this is still limited and not equivalent to that of adults, particularly given the linguistic, cultural, and educational barriers experienced by immigrant youth (Cooper et al., 2010). However, adolescents' unique developmental vulnerabilities affect their participation in their legal process in other ways. Between the ages of 11 and 15, youth begin to engage in logical thinking and problem solving, marking the transition from "concrete operational" to "formal operational" thinking (Piaget, 1952). However, as summarized by Lamb and Sim (2013), adolescents' ability to apply these cognitive skills to understand risk and probability does not translate into their ability to apply risk–benefit analyses to make decisions (see Woolard, this volume). Adolescents' prefrontal cortices are underdeveloped compared with adults, and adolescents are susceptible to overvaluing short-term gains over long-term rewards to impulsive and risky behavior, particularly when in the presence of peers (Steinberg, 2008). Developmental science has led researchers and legal scholars to argue for adolescents—including their capacity for rehabilitation—being treated differently from adults within the juvenile justice system (Terrell v. Ohio, 2018; Steinberg, 2017). There is no such comparable consideration of how development affects adolescents in the immigration legal system. For example, their propensity toward impulsivity, in combination with overvaluing short-term gains, may lead unaccompanied youth to accept voluntary departure even when they have a viable claim for asylum or another form of relief.

The Consequences of Detention and Deportation Proceedings for Youth's Development

Just as youth's development affects their participation in immigration court proceedings, the legal system—from arrest, to detention, to deportation proceedings—in turn impacts youth development. The consequences of detention and participation in deportation proceedings for youth's social emotional development will be considered next.

The Impact of Child Detention on Development

While the majority of existing research examines the impact of parental detention on children's development, a nascent body of international evidence documents how immigration and children's detention affect children's social, emotional, and physical development. Children who are detained due to migration experience traumas and/or stressors prior to and during migration (for a review see Berger Cardoso et al., 2019). These prior experiences are then combined with the challenges of being detained in a facility with heightened security measures, which together have a significant impact on children's development. Lorek et al. (2009) used semi-structured clinical interviews and standardized self-report questionnaires to assess the mental health of 24 children in a British detention center. All of the children who completed the psychological assessment reported symptoms of depression and anxiety; this included poor appetite, emotional symptoms, and behavioral difficulties. Among the 24 children, 11 also expressed fear of the detention center and asked their interviewer to explain why they were in prison. Consistent with self-report, parent-reported measures showed similar social–emotional and behavioral changes in their children since detention (Lorek et al., 2009).

Von Werthern et al. (2018) found similar adverse effects on the mental health of adults, adolescents, and children in immigration detention across the world in their review of 26 studies on immigration detention, 10 of which focused specifically on detained children and families. The authors reported a high prevalence of at least one psychiatric disorder, as well as sleeping and eating problems, among detained children. Their review included two studies comparing children and youth, ranging from age 4 to 15, in detention contexts compared those who were not. Detained children had higher levels of mental health challenges, such as anxiety, depression, and PTSD (Zwi et al., 2018; Rojas-Flores et al, 2017.

More recently, Maclean et al. (2019) found that detained immigrant children, especially those who had been separated from their mothers, experienced significant psychological distress. The researchers studied more than 425 children between the ages of 4 and 17 years old through interviews with their mothers, using the Parent-Report Strengths and Difficulties Questionnaire. In addition, 150 participants older than age 9 completed the UCLA Post-Traumatic Stress Disorder Reaction Index (PTSD-RI). The aim of the study was to assess the mental health of children who had been detained for over 2 months in the United States during 2018. Results indicated elevated scores for emotional, peer, and total difficulties among detained youth. Compared to older children, younger children between the ages of 4 and 8 years old displayed higher rates of behavioral challenges, including hyperactivity.

The impact of child detention is not limited to the presence of mental health problems. Changes in family structures in the context of migration or family separation also have consequences on children's social and emotional development. Wood (2018) highlights how children and youth can perceive detention and family separation on a continuum of lack of safety or threat. The profound impact of children's perceived fear on their development is then compounded by the additional threat to attachment when detention separates children from their primary caregivers. Wood (2018) describes children's response to this separation in "three fluid phases" that can predict their reaction to reunification, depending on which stage of separation they were in. Separation starts with an acute phase in the short term and results in passive compliance in the long term, the latter signifying that children have detached themselves from their caregiver and potentially developed the belief of abandonment. An important contextual factor in determining the impact of child detention on well-being is the amount of time children are detained. Wood (2018) shows how children in detention for longer durations display chronic long-term impacts on relationships beyond those with their caregivers. These findings are relevant not only to the children and youth separated from caregivers at the border under the Trump administration's zero-tolerance policy but also to unaccompanied youth, who continue under the Biden administration to experience the stress of detention on top of family separation and disrupted attachment, as well as potentially other traumatic exposures before and during migration (Berger Cardoso et al., 2021).

Dudley et al. (2012) present similar data on the long-term consequences on asylum-seeking children's mental health and the duration of detention. Their review of existing evidence from several countries focuses on both accompanied and unaccompanied detained child asylum seekers. Evidence from child detention in Australia suggests that poorer mental health and developmental disorders stem from children's loss of caregiving relationships and the harsh environments they experience in detention. Across the studies reviewed, Dudley et al. (2012) find high levels of psychiatric symptoms, including PTSD, self-harm, suicidal behaviors, and physical impairments, among children of all ages. They found that these incidences increase with longer detention periods but are present even for children detained for short periods of time. In addition to highlighting findings pointing to the causal relationship between children detained and psychological disorders, Dudley and colleagues (2012) conclude, "Detention creates new mental disorders, and exacerbates existing ones" (p. 286). The authors note that postdetention, previously detained children often do not have access to stable caregiving relationships, which lowers children's chances of healthy adjustment. Ultimately, Dudley et al. (2012) call for several changes across policy, research, and clinical practice, including improving the experience of asylum-seeking children during their detention and application process by centering psychological safety and trauma-informed practices. The previously described Flores settlement in the United States did establish new standards for the conditions of child detention, but the experience of child detention in the United States continues to fall short of centering the psychological safety of detained children and youth.

As previously explained, unaccompanied youth in the United States who are released from ORR custody to a sponsor must navigate a complicated legal system, often without legal representation. Their court cases carry extremely high stakes; if unsuccessful, they may be returned to unsafe environments, again separated from family with whom they recently reunited, and/or face crippling debts incurred during migration (Heidbrink, 2019). In addition to the extreme stress of not knowing whether they can safely stay in the United States, youth's participation in the complex and non-child-centered courtroom is an additional stressor.

Immigration Courtrooms: Children and Youth Navigating Adult Spaces

In her ethnographic study of children proceeding through the Executive Office for Immigration Review (EOIR), Huynh (2021) describes the ways in which immigration courts, which can be confusing and intimidating spaces for adults, are even more so for children. The physical spaces are not designed with children in mind: They are crowded, windowless, chaotic, clinical, and adversarial (Huynh, 2021). The immense backlog of immigration cases (in FY 2023, there was a backlog of 2,097,244 cases; TRAC, 2023) means that rooms are overfilled with confused and anxious people looking for the right room and waiting sometimes up to 30 minutes just to take the elevator (Huynh, 2021). Judges, responsible for moving cases along, have to act quickly, sometimes spending only 3 minutes per case and hearing multiple cases at once.

In addition to attorneys, judges, and friends of the court, there are multiple other adults that the child may interact with—social workers, shelter staff, sponsors, and interpreters—and sorting out the different roles is confusing. Youth—many of whom have experienced considerable interpersonal trauma—are asked to "trust" adults they have only just met. Even those who have an attorney to represent them often meet the attorney minutes before their case is meant to be heard. All of this is occurring outside the child's native language and often without the presence of a stable, supportive caregiver. While having an interpreter is considered part of the "fairness" of the hearing (U.S. Citizenship and Immigration Services, 1987), technical problems; linguistic nuances; lack of availability for less common languages, including Mayan languages prevalent among unaccompanied youth from Guatemala; and interpreters' unconscious bias create challenges to interpretation (Berk-Seligson, 2017). Limited understanding of legal jargon and processes and the uncertainty and unpredictability of the process amplify the anxiety, fear, and distress that immigrant youth experience in the courtroom (Huynh, 2021).

"Retraumatization" refers to a situation, event, or experience that resembles the initial dynamics of a traumatic event and results in similar affective, cognitive, and behavioral responses. The adversarial and intimidating nature of the court proceedings—lawyers who badger with questions, judges who appear in black robes, long wait times with uncertain outcomes, lack of understanding of what is happening, and lack of power and agency in what is happening to them—is experienced as retraumatizing to youth who enter the system having already endured adverse and traumatic experiences that motivated their migration in the first place (Juffer, 2016; Terrio, 2015). In addition to creating challenges to testimony, as described earlier, unaccompanied youth participating in immigration court cases may experience exacerbation of mental health symptoms, notably PTSD, because of the ways in which court processes and interactions trigger prior trauma (Juffer, 2016).

Threatening or Vulnerable? Agentic or Dependent?

The treatment of children and youth within the U.S. immigration legal system is deeply ambivalent. On the one hand, immigrant children and youth are treated as "small adults": They are arrested, held in detention, and required to represent themselves with virtually no consideration of how their developmental capacities affect their ability to participate in the high-stakes hearings that will determine their fate, or how that very participation will impact their development (Juffer, 2016). Immigration judges, unlike family court or juvenile delinquency judges, may not consider the best interest of the child, their unique developmental capacities and vulnerabilities, or their competency to represent themselves in court when deciding their fates (Terrio, 2015). On the other hand, while children are given more responsibility than they developmentally can carry, they also are treated as lacking in agency and autonomy. Citizen children cannot, for example, petition for an adult family member (e.g., go through the legal process to bring them to the United States with legal status) until they reach age 21 (Terrio, 2015). Their experiences motivating their migration and their wishes for family reunification are often minimized or ignored (Heidbrink, 2014). ORR "shelters" position unaccompanied youth as vulnerable victims, dependent on the welfare state for care and protection, which reflects a Western-situated notion of childhood that emphasizes children's dependency and vulnerability over their autonomy and agency (Heidbrink, 2014).

Similarly, U.S. immigration policy and proceedings position immigrant youth in some ways as vulnerable dependents, who need protection, and in other ways as threats to national security and sovereignty, who must therefore be controlled and expelled (Bhabba, 2014; Juffer, 2016; Menjívar & Kanstroom, 2013). Juffer (2016) notes that unaccompanied youth present a particular paradox: They at once seem to be more agentic youth who are less defined by their parents and make arduous journeys without caretakers, and also more vulnerable as they lack adult protection and most have faced traumatic and adverse experiences in their country and during migration (Juffer, 2016). Although the Flores settlement provides some allowance based on the presumed vulnerability of these youth, these allowances only extend through detention and do not apply to deportation proceedings, wherein children and youth are treated as though they hold all the competency and agency as do adults. Reflecting this view, in a 2016 statement widely disparaged by legal and developmental scholars, an immigration judge informed the *Washington Post*, "I've taught immigration law literally to 3-year-olds and 4-year-olds. . . . It takes a lot of time. It takes a lot of patience. They get it. It's not the most efficient, but it can be done."

The United Nations Convention on the Rights of the Child (UNCRC, 1989), which has been ratified by all nations except the United States, obligates that the child's best interests be the primary consideration in all matters affecting the child: "In all actions concerning children, whether undertaken by public or private social welfare institutions, courts of law, administrative authorities or legislative bodies, the best interests of the child shall be a primary consideration" (art. 3, para. 1). Children are understood as both vulnerable persons requiring protections *and* autonomous persons possessing agency (Bhabba, 2006). Legal scholars argue that the obligation to protect immigrant children in immigration proceedings is grounded in constitutional values of due process and equality, the best interest of the child principle from U.S. family law, and the standards in international human rights law, including the UNCRC (Carr, 2009; Estin, 2018; Wolozin, 2015). Building on the UNCRC, Thronson (2002) argues that children both possess rights pertaining to any human being *and* may claim special assistance to exercising those rights because of their age. While children are seen as autonomous beings with basic human rights, just like adults, they are also understood to be different from adults, and therefore in need of special protections. Thronson (2002) argues, "This unthinking abandonment of children to adult status serves to silence children by not providing them with the means to assure that their voices are heard" (p. 1002).

Conclusion

While U.S. immigration law may be ambivalent regarding whether immigrant children and youth are dependents in need of protection or potential threats as capable as adults, developmental science is clear that, while cognitive capabilities increase with age, both children and youth lack the competence to understand the complex immigration legal system, let alone represent themselves throughout it. Despite this evidence, there is a clear lack of developmental consideration in immigration court: Children are subject to the same criteria, evidentiary requirements, and burden-of-proof standards as adults (Terrio, 2015). Many unaccompanied youth—up to 40%—have legitimate claims that would lead to legal status if they could navigate the complex web of immigration laws and avenues (Chen & Gill, 2015). Moreover, participating in the non-child-friendly legal system—from detention to deportation proceedings—not only carries high stakes but also can negatively impact the development of children and youth.

One possible and most basic solution would be to apply "due process" and "the best interest of the child" as guiding principles in the treatment of unaccompanied youth after release from detention. This would at least guarantee unaccompanied youth an attorney or guardians ad litem, to ensure that they are properly defended and their rights are not violated. Transforming immigration courtrooms to be more child-friendly spaces, adopting NICHD recommendations for child questioning, and educating court-involved staff (lawyers, judges, etc.) about the effects of trauma and the possibilities of retraumatization may also improve children and youth's experiences moving through the system (Huynh, 2021). Finally, expanding avenues for relief that specifically respond to the vulnerability of children and youth, for example, SIJ status, can provide protections for youth's unique vulnerabilities and also support their agency in seeking a safe and productive life.

References

Aldarondo, E., & Becker, R. (2011). Promoting the well-being of unaccompanied immigrant minors. In L. P. Bukj & L. M. Piedra (Eds.), *Creating infrastructure for Latino mental health* (pp. 195–214). Springer.

American Immigration Council. (2016). *Children in immigration court: Over 95 percent represented by an attorney in court.* https://www.americanimmigrationcouncil.org/sites/defualt/files/research/children_in_immigration_court_0.pdf

American Immigration Council. (2021). *U.S. citizen children impacted by immigration enforcement* [Fact sheet]. https://www.americanimmigrationcouncil.org/research/us-citizen-children-impacted-immigration-enforcement

Axios. (2021). *What it's like for children being held in immigration facilities.* https://www.axios.com/inside-border-facility-detention-centers-migrant-children-us-mexico-0c5ea20e-623a-4546-b0d1-10bde69b2901.html

Ayón, C. (2016). Talking to Latino children about race, inequality, and discrimination: Raising families in an anti-immigrant political environment. *Journal of the Society for Social Work & Research, 7*(3), 449–477. https://www.journals.uschicago.edu/doi/pdfplus/10.1086/686929

Barajas-Gonzalez, R. G., Ayón, C., Brabeck, K., Rojas-Flores, L., & Valdéz, C. R. (2021). An ecological expansion of the adverse childhood experiences (ACEs) framework to include threat and deprivation associated with

U.S. immigration policies and enforcement practices: An examination of the Latinx immigrant experience. *Social Sciences & Medicine, 282*, 1–9.

Barrera-Valencia, M., Calderon-Delgado, L., Trejos-Castillo, E., & O'Boyle, M. (2017). Cognitive profiles of Post-Traumatic Stress Disorder and depression in children and adolescents. *International Journal of Clinical and Health Psychology, 17*(3), 242–250.

BBC. (2021). *Child migrants: First photos emerge of Biden-era detention centres*. https://www.bbc.com/news/world-us-canada-56491941

Berger Cardoso, J. B. (2018). Running to stand still: Trauma symptoms, coping strategies, and substance use behaviors in unaccompanied migrant youth. *Child and Youth Services Review, 92*, 143–152.

Berger Cardoso, J., Brabeck, K., Bjugstad, A., Hernandez, J., Prosperi, N., Venta, A., & Sharp, C. (2021). "*Una monera de dos caras*": Central American and Mexican immigrant mothers and youth's experiences of separation and reunification (pp. 55–84). In J. E. Glick, V. King, & S. M. McHale (Eds.), *Causes and consequences of parent-child separations: Pathways to resilience*. Springer.

Berger Cardoso, J. B., Brabeck, K., Stinchcomb, D., Heidbrink, L., Price, O. A., Gil-Garcia, O. F., Crea, T. M., & Zayas, L. H. (2019). Integration of unaccompanied migrant youth in the United States: A call for research. *Ethnic & Migration Studies, 45*(2), 173–292.

Berk-Seligson, S. (2017). *The bilingual courtroom: Court interpreters in the judicial process*. University of Chicago Press.

Bhabba, J. (2006). The child: What sort of human? *PMLA, 121*(5), 1526–1535.

Block, S. D., Oran, H., Oran, D., Baumrind, N., & Goodman, G. S. (2010). Abused and neglected children in court: Knowledge and attitudes. *Child Abuse and Neglect, 34*(9), 659–670.

Brown, D. A., & Lamb, M. (2015). Can children be useful witnesses? It depends on how they are questioned. *Child Development Perspectives, 9*(4), 930–955.

Calzada, E. J., Fernandez, Y., & Cortes, D. E. (2010). Incorporating the cultural value of *respeto* into a framework of Latino parenting. *Cultural Diversity and Ethnic Minority Psychology, 16*(1), 77–96.

Carr, B. (2009). Incorporating a "best interests of the child" approach to immigration law and procedure. *Yale Human Rights and Development Law Journal, 12*(1), 1–40.

Chen, A., & Gil, J. (2015). Unaccompanied children and the U.S. immigration system: Challenges and reforms. *Journal of International Affairs, 68*(2), 115–133.

Congressional Research Service. (2021). *Unaccompanied alien children: An overview*. https://sgp.fas.org/crs/homesec/R43599.pdf

Cooper, A., Wallin, A. R., Quas, J. A., & Lyon, T. D. (2010). Maltreated and nonmaltreated children's knowledge of the juvenile dependency court system. *Child Maltreatment, 15*(3), 255–260.

Crawford, E., & Bull, R. (2007). Teenagers' difficulties with key words regarding the criminal court process. *Psychology, Crime & Law, 12*(6), 653–667.

Desmond, K.J., Kindsvatter, A., Stahl, S., & Smith, H. (2015). Using creative techniques with children who have experienced trauma. *Journal of Creativity in Mental Health, 10*(4), 439–455.

Dudley, M., Steel, Z., Mares, S., & Newman, L. (2012). Children and young people in immigration detention. *Current Opinion in Psychiatry, 25*(4), 285–292.

Eisen, M. L., Goodman, G. S., Qin, J., & Crayton, J. (2007). Maltreated children's memory: Accuracy suggestibility, and psychopathology. *Developmental Psychology, 43*(6), 1275–1294.

Eisen, M. L., Qin, J., Goodman, G. S., & Davis, S. L. (2002). Memory and suggestibility in maltreated children: Age, stress arousal, dissociation, and psychopathology. *Journal of Experimental Child Psychology, 83*(3), 167–212.

Estin, A. L. (2018). Child migrants and child welfare: Toward a best interests approach. *Washington University Global Studies Law Review*, 589 (Paper Number 18-13). https://openscholarship.wustl.edu/law_globalstudied/vol17/iss3/5

Flores v. Meese, 681 F.Supp. 665, 666 (C.D.C.A. 1988).

Frankel, K. K., Brabeck, K. M., & Rendón García, S. A. (2021). Understanding unaccompanied immigrant youth's experiences in US schools: An interdisciplinary perspective. *Journal of Education for Students Placed at Risk, 27*, 27–58.

Goodman, G. S., Quas, J., & Ogle, C. M. (2009). Child maltreatment and memory. *Annual Review of Psychology, 51*, 325–351.

Grace, B. L., & Roth, B. J. (2015). *Post-release: Linking unaccompanied immigrant children to family and community*. University of South Carolina.

Heidbrink, L. (2014). *Migrant youth, transnational families and the state: Care and contested interests*. University of Pennsylvania Press.

Heidbrink, L., (2019). The coercive power of debt: Migration and deportation of indeigenous Guatemalan youth. *The Journal of Latin American and Carribeean Anthropology, 24*(1), 263–281.

Human Rights First. (2016). *The Flores settlement and family incarceration: A brief history and next steps.* https://www.humanrightsfirst.org/resource/flores-settlement-brief-history-and-next-steps

Huynh, J. (2021). *La charla*: Documenting the experience of unaccompanied minors in immigration court. *Journal of Ethnic and Migration Studies, 47*(3), 616–630.

Immigrant Legal Resource Center. (2020). *The notice to appear: Practice advisory.* https://www.ilrc.org/sites/default/files/resources/nta_practice_advisory.pdf

Juffer, J. (2016). Can the child subject speak? Precarious subjects at the US-Mexico border. *Feminist Frontiers, 281*(1), 94–120.

Lamb, M. E., Orbach, Y., Hershkowitz, I., Horowitz, D., & Abbott, C. B. (2007). Does the type of prompt affect the accuracy of information provided by alleged victims of abuse in forensic interviews? *Applied Cognitive Psychology, 21*(9), 117–113.

Lamb, M. E., & Sim, M. P. (2013). Developmental Factors Affecting Children in Legal Contexts. *Youth Justice, 13*(2), 131–144. https://doi.org/10.1177/1473225413492055

Lamb, M. E., Sternberg, K. J., Orbach, Y., Esplin, P. W., Steward, H., & Mitchell, S. (2003). Age differences in young children's responses to open-ended invitations in the course of forensic interviews. *Journal of Consulting and Clinical Psychology, 71*(5), 926–934.

Leichtman, M. D., & Ceci, S. J. (1995). The effects of stereotypes and suggestions on preschoolers' reports. *Developmental Psychology, 31*(4), 568–578.

Lorek, A., Ehntholt, K., Nesbitt, A., Wey, E., Githinji, C., Rossor, E., & Wickramasinghe, R. (2009). The mental health and physical health difficulties of children held within a British immigration center: A pilot study. *Child Abuse and Neglect, 33,* 573–585.

Lustig, S. L. (2010). An ecological framework for the refugee experience: What is the impact on child development? In G. W. Evans & T. D. Wachs (Eds), *Chaos and its influence on children's development: An ecological perspective* (pp. 239–251). Washington, DC: American Psychological Association.

MacLean, S. A., Agyeman, P. O., Walther, J., Singer, E. K., Baranowski, K. A., & Katz, C. L. (2019). Mental health of children held at a United States immigration detention center. *Social Science & Medicine, 230,* 303–308.

Menjívar, C., & Kanstroom, D. (Eds.). (2013). *Constructing immigrant "illegality": Critiques, experiences, and responses.* Cambridge University Press.

Middleton, J. (2017). Memory development and trauma in preschool children: Implications for forensic interviewing professionals—A review of the literature. *Forensic Research & Criminology International Journal, 4*(1), 1–6.

Migration Policy Institute. (n.d.). *Children in U.S. immigrant families by age group and state, 1990 versus 2019.* https://www.migrationpolicy.org/programs/data-hub/charts/children-immigrant-families

Migration Policy Institute. (2021). *Strengthening services for unaccompanied children in U.S. communities.* https://www.migrationpolicy.org/research/services- unaccompanied-children-us-communities

Olivas, M. (1990). Unaccompanied refugee children: Detention, due process, and disgrace. *Stanford Law & Policy Review, 2,* 159–166.

Orbach, Y., & Lamb, M. E. (2001). The relationship between within-interview contradictions and eliciting interview utterances. *Child Abuse and Neglect, 25*(3), 323–333.

Pantell, R. H., & AAP Committee on Psychosocial Aspects of Child and Family Health. (2017). The child witness in the courtroom. *Pediatrics, 139*(3), 1–9.

Patricia, J. B. (2007). *Remembering the times of our lives: Memory in infancy and beyond.* Psychology Press.

Piaget, J. (1952). *The origins of intelligence in children.* W. W. Norton & Co.

Quas, J. A., Wallin, A. R., Horwitz, B., Davis, E., & Lyon, T. D. (2009). Maltreated children's understanding of and emotional reactions to dependency court involvement. *Behavioral Sciences & the Law, 27*(1), 97–117.

Rojas-Flores, L., Clements, M. L., Hwang Koo, J., & London, J. (2017). Trauma and psychological distress in Latino citizen children following parental detention and deportation. *Psychological Trauma: Theory, Research, Practice, and Policy, 9*(3), 352.

Roth, B. J., Crea, T. M., Jani, J., Underwood, D., Hasson, R. G., III, Evans, K., & Zuch, M. (2019). Detached and afraid: U.S. immigration policy and the practice of forcibly separating parents and young children at the border. *Child Welfare, 96*(5), 29–49.

Steinberg, L. (2008). A social neuroscience perspective on adolescent risk-taking. *Developmental Review, 28*(1), 78–106.

Steinberg, L. (2017). Adolescent brain science and juvenile justice policymaking. *Psychology, Public Policy, and Law, 23*(4), 410–420.

Stinchcomb, D., & Hershberg, E. (2014). *Unaccompanied migrant children from Central America: Context, causes, and responses.* American University Center for Latin American & Latino. https://ssrn.com/abstract=2524001

Terrell v. State of Ohio (2018). https://www.supremecourt.gov/search.aspx?filename=/docket/docketfiles/html/public/18-5239.html

Terrio, S. J. (2015). *Whose child am I?: Unaccompanied, undocumented children in U.S. immigration custody*. University of California Press.

Thronson, D. (2002). Kids will be kids? Reconsidering conceptions of children's rights underlying immigration law. *Ohio State Law Journal, 63*, 979–1016.

Transactional Records Access Clearinghouse (TRAC). (2014). *New data on unaccompanied children in immigration court*. https://trac.syr.edu/immigration/reports/359/

Transactional Records Access Clearninghouse (TRAC). (2023). *Historical immigration courtlog backing tool*. https://trac.syr.edu/phptools/immigration/court_backlog/

United Nations. (1989). *Convention on the rights of the child*. https://www.ohchr.org/en/instruments-mechanisms/instruments/convention-rights-child

U.S. Citizenship and Immigration Services. (1987). *Interim decision #3032*. https://www.uscis.gov/ilink/docView/INT/HTML/INT/0-0-0-65/0-0-0-3848.html

U.S. Customs & Border Control. (2021). *CPB enforcement statistcs fiscal year 2021*. https://www.cbp.gov/newsroom/stats/cbp-enforcement-statistics-fy2021

U.S. Department of Homeland Security (DHS). (2010). *CBP's handling of unaccompanied alien children*. CBP's%20handling%20of%20unaccompanied%20minors%20-%20CTRL%20F.pdf

U.S. Department of Justice. (2021). *Practice manual chapter 4, subsection 4.15—Master calendar hearing*. https://www.justice.gov/eoir/eoir-policy-manual/4/15

U.S. Office of Refugee Resettlement (ORR). (2021). *Children entering the United States unaccompanied: Section 1, placement in ORR care provider facilities*. https://www.acf.hhs.gov/orr/policy-guidance/children-entering-united-states-unaccompanied-section-1

Viljoen, J. L., & Roesch, R. (2005). Competence to waive interrogation rights and adjunctive competence in adolescent defendants: Cognitive development, attorney contact, and psychological symptoms. *Law and Human Behavior, 29*(6), 723–742.

von Werthern, M., Robjant, K., Chui, Z., Schon, R., Ottisova, L., Mason, C., & Katona, C. (2018). The impact of immigration detention on mental health: a systematic review. *BMC Psychiatry, 18*(1), 1–19.

Wolozin, B. (2015). Doing what's best: Determining best interest for children impacted by immigration proceedings. *Drake Law Review, 64*, 141–188.

Wood, L. C. (2018). Impact of punitive immigration policies, parent-child separation and child detention on the mental health and development of children. *BMJ Paediatrics Open, 2*(1), e000338.

Zayas, L., Brabeck, K. M., Heffron, L. C., Dreby, J., Calzada, E., Parra-Cardona, J., Dettlaff, A. J., Heidbrink, L., Perreira, K. M., & Yoshikawa, H. (2017). Charting directions for research on immigrant children affected by undocumented status. *Hispanic Journal of Behavioral Sciences, 39*, 412–435.

Zwi, K., Mares, S., Nathanson, D., Tay, A. K., & Silove, D. (2018). The impact of detention on the social-emotional wellbeing of children seeking asylum: A comparison with community-based children. *European Child & Adolescent Psychiatry, 27*(4), 411–422.

CHAPTER 9

Adoption

Jesús Palacios, David M. Brodzinsky, and Harold D. Grotevant

Abstract

Adoption as a means of creating or expanding a family has undergone some remarkable changes in the past half century, resulting in considerable diversity in the constellation and dynamics of adoptive family life. These changes have been fueled by several societal forces including new adoption laws and regulations, research findings from emerging developmental science, and advocacy efforts by key adoption stakeholders. The current chapter explores the synergistic connections between these forces, and specifically between adoption placement practices, adoption law, and developmental science. The first section explores how adoption has been utilized by researchers to study age-old questions about human development, including the role of early experience on later development, recovery from adversity, critical periods in development, and contextual factors that impede or facilitate recovery from adversity. The second section explores the emergence of diversity in adoption in terms of the characteristics of children being adopted and the adults who are adopting them, which has been influenced by changes in adoption law and supported by empirical research challenging narrowly held views about the type of family that best supports children's needs. The third section examines more closely several examples of how developmental research has contributed to the emergence of diversity in adoptive family life, influencing decision making by adoption policymakers, agency administrators, and the court. The rich synergistic exchange between adoption practice, the law, and developmental science supports a more refined view of human development and a better understanding of how best to support adoptive family members.

Key Words: adoption, family diversity, early adversity, identity, adoption law, policy and practice

Adoption is the transfer of parental responsibilities for a child from the birth parents to those who legally assume the rights and obligations inherent to parenthood. The adopted child becomes a permanent member of the adoptive family, with the rights and obligations inherent to filiation. In one form or another, adoption has been practiced across time and cultures, with societies formalizing the practice through laws, regulations, and policies. Over time, developmental researchers, as well as those from other disciplines, discovered adoption as a fruitful area of study (see, for instance, Palacios & Brodzinsky, 2010). In turn, research findings have exerted their influence on the regulation and practice of adoption. This chapter explores the rich interconnections between the scientific study of human development and the regulation and practice of adoption. In keeping with the goals of this Handbook, the chapter illustrates how developmental science and the law have interacted and shaped one another and impacted adoptive family life.

The chapter is divided into three main sections. The first one explores some of the contributions of adoption research to the understanding of human development. Adoption represents a variation of the typical circumstances where parents protect, stimulate, and favor children's development. With exposure to different types of adversities during significant parts of children's early life and later placement with families selected for their motivation and capabilities, the "adoption design" (Palacios, 2018) has enriched the exploration of some classic questions in developmental research: for example, the influence of early experiences on the developmental trajectory later in life, the recovery after initial adversities, the existence of critical/sensitive developmental periods, and the contextual influences under which recovery is most likely to occur. Research findings on these matters will be summarized in this first section, as well as those pertaining to a key component of adopted persons' developmental profile: the construction of adoption identity.

The second section takes the perspective of the legal and practice regulation of adoption, with particular reference to the influence of some of the adoption research summarized previously. The diversity that characterizes contemporary adoptions is the main focus of this section, including diversity as defined by adoptees' characteristics, the characteristics of those who adopt them, and different adoption arrangements. This diversity is regulated by law and practice, changes across time and jurisdictions, and reflects the progress in understanding of adoption, but, more broadly, of family and parent–child relationships.

Finally, the third section explores the rich contribution of developmental science to adoption law and practice. A renewed concept of family, the recognition of the richness of family diversity, and the use of developmental science to support changes in family and adoption laws are good examples of this contribution. Moreover, two major models of human development, the ecological model and the lifespan perspective, have enriched and continue to enrich the understanding and practice of adoption.

Contributions of Adoption Research to Understanding of Human Development

Since its initial emergence as a scientific discipline, several questions have been at the heart of developmental psychology: What is the long-term impact of early experience? How plastic is children's development in response to variations in their environment? Is there a critical age after which recovery from early adversity is not possible or is more limited? Can later experiences overcome the negative consequences of early adversity? Experiments with human offspring have always been strictly limited for obvious ethical considerations, since it is unthinkable to purposely maltreat children of different ages and in different degrees to observe the developmental consequences in terms of timing and content. Also, in typical human circumstances, the initial rearing environment continues exerting its influence in later years, making it impossible to separate early from later experiences. These obstacles are largely overcome by the existence of contemporary children's adoption.

Although some babies are placed at birth or soon after birth with parental consent and no exposure to abuse or neglect, most children adopted these days enter their new ideally loving, protective, and stimulating families after experiencing significant levels of neglect and/or maltreatment from previous dysfunctional families or the privations of orphanage life. For example, in FY2019, 93% of the children adopted in the United States with public agency involvement were eligible for an adoption subsidy that helps adoptive families access support for their children's special needs (medical care, special equipment, therapy, tutoring programs; Children's Bureau, 2020). For the same year, 74% of the children adopted internationally by U.S. families were above the age of 3 years at placement, with 54% above the age of 5 years

(Children's Bureau, 2020), with similar characteristics noted in other countries (see Jurviste et al., 2016, for adoption demography in the European Union). Most children in intercountry adoption experienced rearing in collective care environments in the institutions of their country of origin before being adopted. Thus, most adopted children have experienced both early adversity and significant relational discontinuity prior to being placed in families assessed by social service agencies as suitable in terms of parental motivation, attitudes, and capabilities. Developmental researchers have taken ample advantage of this "natural" opportunity, studying developmental processes both while in adverse circumstances (maltreatment, institutional life) and after entering their new families (adoption). Adoption research informs social service practice, but also developmental science.

Adoption as a Context for Children's Recovery After Early Adversity

Neglect, abuse, and institutional rearing deny children early experiences crucial for healthy development. Positive and contingent interactions with caregivers provide the context for the development of neural circuits in the brain (Tottenham, 2020). If this stimulation is not present and the rearing context is neglectful or threatening for a significant length of time, normal development becomes compromised, given the critical importance of infancy and early childhood for later growth and development. The experience of child maltreatment initiates a probabilistic path involving the chronic dysregulation of normal developmental progress, with a cascade of problems in physical, neurobiological, cognitive, and socioemotional processes (Cicchetti, 2013). We first need to analyze the negative consequences of abuse, neglect, and institutional life on the health and development of the growing child before referring to adoption as a context for recovery after early adversity.

THE DEVELOPMENTAL CONSEQUENCES OF EARLY ADVERSITY

The consequences of early adversity depend on numerous factors, such as degree and nature of adversity, age at which adversity is experienced, age at adoption, and an array of individual traits, from genetic characteristics to vulnerability/resilience in the face of adverse circumstances. Although individual trajectories vary from child to child, research has uncovered some of the typical consequences of exposure to early adversity (see Brodzinsky et al., 2022; Gunnar & Reid, 2019; Palacios et al., 2019, for more detailed syntheses; see Stacks et al., this volume, for a discussion of the effects of exposure to harm, such as drug use, prenatally and in early infancy).

Children's *physical development* is altered by lack of appropriate nutrition, poor medical monitoring and care, interaction with indifferent or exhausted adults, and structural caregiving deficiencies characteristic of inadequate institutional settings, experiences that often follow preexisting problems such as poor prenatal care and maternal compromised health and wellbeing. Consequently, growth is frequently impaired, with linear growth, weight gain, and head circumference diminished through complex interactions between undernutrition, inflammation, and lack of nurture (Johnson & Gunnar, 2011).

As summarized by Brodzinsky et al. (2022), the consequences of early adversity on the *brain structure and functions* result in marked reductions of total brain volume, in gray matter (involved in sensory perception and motoric responses, speech, memory, impulse control, and emotions), and in regions such as the frontal cortex and hippocampus, as well as alterations in brain wiring. Similarly, abuse and threat characteristic of child maltreatment have a profound impact in brain regions such as the amygdala, with increased vigilance and reactivity that also affect the connectivity of the amygdala to other brain regions (Demers et al., 2018).

Early deprivation and trauma also have a negative impact on *executive functioning* (EF), which comprises important skills normally acquired through repeated interactions with contingent caregivers in nurturing environments. When these are lacking, normal functioning of EF components can be impaired, including problems in sustained attention, working memory, cognitive flexibility, planning and control of behavioral responses, encoding of memories, and response to emotional stimuli. Alterations in the development of EF affect not only cognitive development but also perspective taking and theory of mind (Gunnar & Reid, 2019).

Language development, IQ, and academic performance are also compromised by early adversity. The first 3 years of life are a period of rapid language acquisition under the influence of interactions that start with nonverbal contingent communication and then introduce the complexities of language structure and content. Deprivation and abuse compromise neural systems responsible for speech and language, with negative consequences on receptive and expressive language and language pragmatics (Sylvestre et al., 2016). Similarly, IQ delays are well documented for both institutionalized (Van IJzendoorn et al., 2008) and maltreated children, with a dose–response relationship between timing and duration of maltreatment and impaired cognition (Young-Southward et al., 2020). As would be expected, EF problems, cognitive and linguistic deficits, and exposure to violence are linked to decreased educational success (Sheridan & McLaughlin, 2016).

For young children growing up in abusive and/or neglectful families, as well as in collective institutional care, *attachment problems* come as no surprise. The formation of secure attachment relationships, a key component of infants' development, provides long-term benefits for later emotional, social, and behavioral adjustment (Groh et al., 2017). Young children exposed to adverse relational experiences are not offered the possibility to acquire focused attachment behaviors directed toward preferred caregivers, fail to seek and respond to comforting when distressed, show reduced social and emotional reciprocity, and exhibit disturbed emotion regulation, which taken together characterize reactive attachment disorder (Zeanah & Gleason, 2015). Research also indicates that exposure to neglect, abuse, and severely inadequate caregiving increases the lifetime risk for different psychopathological conditions, such as depression, anxiety disorders, posttraumatic stress disorder, and internalizing and externalizing symptoms (Cicchetti & Doyle, 2016).

Although the aforementioned deficits have been described by developmental domain, they are deeply interrelated. For instance, a secure attachment relationship supports the development of many aspects of healthy child functioning, including EF skills (Bernier et al., 2010). In turn, EF skills support the top-down regulation of other brain functions (Zelazo, 2020). Deficits in EF skills that emerge early in life are considered transdiagnostic indicators of risks for psychopathology (Wade et al., 2020) and are involved in a developmental cascade leading to relational problems and failures to achieve the developmental tasks of adolescence and emerging adulthood, resulting in affective disorders (Golm et al., 2020).

The radical change in rearing circumstances involved in adoption does not reset children's counter to zero, as if their lives were starting anew. From that moment on, their developmental trajectory is an interweaving of their initial adverse experiences and their new positive relationships and experiences. Our attention now turns to the results of this integration, analyzing the possibilities and limits of developmental recovery after adoption.

POSTADOPTION DEVELOPMENTAL TRAJECTORIES

As the previous section on the impact of early adversity noted, the analysis of recovery needs to start with a consideration of adoptees' heterogeneity. As highlighted by Brodzinsky et al. (2022), there is no singular adoption experience. Besides their individual characteristics, adopted children enter their new families through different pathways, have different preplacement experiences, are adopted at different ages, grow up in different types of families, and have different postadoption experiences in their communities. The magnitude of the differences between cases can be illustrated with data from the English Romanian Adoption (ERA) study, a longitudinal research program following a group of children adopted by English families from very depriving Romanian orphanages (see later for more information on this study). In this research, while most children with longer exposure to deprivation had persistent problems from young childhood through early adulthood, a fifth of the adoptees with a longer deprivation experience were problem-free throughout all assessments (Sonuga-Barke et al., 2017).

Critical/Sensitive Periods
Before examining the details of this process, a reference needs to be made to another classic developmental question: Is there an age threshold after which recovery is compromised? Stated another way, is there a critical period for positive and negative experiences to leave a permanent imprint on the developmental trajectory? The study of children exposed during known periods of time to adversities such as profound deprivation and then to more positive experiences sheds light on this question and key developmental concept.

Two longitudinal studies following the early adversity–later enrichment paradigm are particularly relevant here. One is the ERA study referred to earlier, with an original sample of children removed from very depriving institutions at ages between a few weeks and 42 months and placed with advantaged and motivated adoptive parents. The other one is the Bucharest Early Intervention Project (BEIP), in which a group of children between 6 and 31 months of age were recruited from institutions in Bucharest and then randomized to either continue in institutional care or to be placed in a high-quality foster care program initially managed by the research clinical team and later transferred to the local authorities. Both the ERA and the BEIP studies have followed their participants from early childhood to young adulthood, using a variety of assessments including neurobiological, behavioral, and clinical tools. The timing issue is well illustrated in Sonuga-Barke et al. (2017) for ERA and in Nelson et al. (2019) for BEIP.

The ERA results are more in accordance with the classic critical period concept, being one of the very few adoption studies supporting this position. Researchers identified a deprivation-specific pattern (cognitive impairment, inattention–overactivity, disinhibited attachment, and autistic-like social behaviors) extending into early adulthood. Since virtually all the participants displaying these problems were adopted after the age of 6 months, the suggestion is that introducing enriched rearing conditions before that threshold facilitates more normal development (Sonuga-Barke et al., 2017).

The BEIP conclusions are more complex and nuanced (Nelson et al., 2019). In this sample, the main difference was between those exposed to enriched circumstances before or after 24 months. But, perhaps more importantly, both the deprivation effects and the subsequent recovery varied by domain. Some domains were apparently unaffected by exposure to adversity (face and emotion processing), other domains showed evidence of improved caregiving effects but not evidence of critical period (social competence, psychiatric disorders), and other domains had little improvement after placement in a stimulating family environment (some EF and attention deficit hyperactivity disorder). The idea of a developmental critical period is also compromised by the fact that within broad constructs such as IQ, language, and attachment, there seem to be different critical periods for different underlying processes (Nelson et al., 2019).

Thus, it is doubtful that there is one critical or sensitive period that determines when recovery after initial adversity is impossible or at least unlikely (Brodzinsky et al., 2022). Across and within domains there are cascades of different sensitive periods under the influence of multiple experiential and biological factors. Also, later acquisitions can compensate for skills that were not well established previously, although in other cases poor initial acquisitions impair the development of more advanced skills (Nelson & Gabard-Durnam, 2020). Not only is the timing of developmental acquisitions malleable, but also current evidence indicates that, with enriched stimulation, there is residual plasticity for functional modifications in children adopted beyond infancy, a possibility that extends into adolescence, as illustrated with a few examples. The stress system response is recalibrated in adolescence in the presence of significant improvements in the supportiveness of the environment (Gunnar et al., 2019). Also, high-quality caregiving in adolescence is associated with improvements in EF, as well as in internalizing and externalizing symptoms, with stronger associations during adolescence than in the preceding years (Colich et al., 2021). Finally, positive changes have been observed in adopted adolescents' attachment representations when the adoptive mothers have a secure state of mind, an association more evident in adolescence than in the preceding years (Pace et al., 2019). While some of these improvements are likely a function of high-quality parenting involving sensitivity/responsiveness, structure/limit setting, and consistency (Koss et al., 2020), others occur in response to specialized interventions, such as parent enrichment (Yarger et al., 2022).

Differential Plasticity

As a general rule, following placement, adopted children show substantial catch-up from their delays in all domains of development and outperform the children who remained in vulnerable families or in institutional care (Van IJzendoorn & Juffer, 2006), although adopted children still lag behind their nonadopted community-based peers in some domains. Typically, many of the negative consequences of early adversity are overcome after some time in the new family. However, understanding the timing and extent of children's recovery must also consider the quality of their postadoption environment. Despite being judged as suitable for adoptive parenthood by child welfare authorities, some adoptive parents do not adequately comprehend or accept the complexities associated with raising an adopted child, nor the extent of their child's problems. Other parents may not have available supports—familial, extrafamilial, and professional—to help them meet the challenges faced by the family and the child, or they may be reluctant or unable to use the available supports. In such circumstances, recovery from adversity is likely to be compromised and highly variable in terms of timing and completeness.

Developmental researchers use the term differential plasticity (Palacios et al., 2014) to refer to the fact that, even when a particular domain of functioning appears to be strongly affected by early adversity, some facets of those domains may be more plastic and responsive to improved conditions than others. Moreover, while the negative consequences of early adversity are synchronic, with a frequent pattern of global developmental delay at placement (Palacios et al., 2011), the process of recovery seems asynchronous, with some domains recovering more rapidly and more completely than others. Differential plasticity can be illustrated in various important biological and developmental domains.

Growth and brain recovery are good examples of differential plasticity. Once removed from adversity and placed in supportive families, growth rebounds to soon be within ranges typical for the child's age (Gunnar & Reid, 2019; van IJzendoorn et al., 2020). The exception to this is head size, which lags behind, but is in normal ranges by early adolescence (Johnson et al., 2018). Within the brain, after placement in supportive families, no significant improvement is observed in total gray matter, but white matter and its track integrity recover, which means that recovery for the brain may largely consist of being better able to effectively use the neural circuits that survive early adverse care (Bick et al., 2015; Brodzinsky et al., 2022; Sheridan et al., 2012).

Although IQ is significantly impaired by early deprivation, meta-analytical evidence shows that adopted children's IQs are typically within normal ranges (average, 104) within a year or so of adoption and may be as much as 20 points higher than the IQ of peers left behind in institutional care (van IJzendoorn & Juffer, 2005). However, although IQ is typically predictive of school performance, the school achievement of adopted children is often problematic, with significant percentages developing learning difficulties (van IJzendoorn & Juffer, 2005). Part of these school problems may be related to the differential plasticity also observed in the domain of language development. Research has indicated that while internationally adopted children acquire contextually based day-to-day language soon and efficiently, they experience difficulties with the more abstract language typical of the school context (Dalen, 2005).

Another reason for normal IQs not translating into good school achievement could be associated with the differential plasticity also observed in the EF domain. Successful recovery in some EF functions impaired by early adversity, such as rule acquisition or planning, contrasts with the fact that other functions, critically important for school performance, such as sustained attention, working memory, and inhibitory control, continue to be impaired long after adoption (Bick et al., 2015; Peñarrubia et al., 2020).

A final illustration of differential plasticity comes from the domain of attachment. Research has shown that a few years after adoption, secure attachment relationships can be observed in adopted children on par with their nonadopted peers (Román et al., 2012), although with a higher presence of disorganized patterns in those adopted at later ages (van den Dries, 2009). However, attachment mental representations of self and others seem to change more slowly in adopted children and are still compromised years after adoption, even after attachment behaviors have normalized (Román et al., 2012). Attachment behaviors reflect children's help and comfort seeking in times of distress, specifically from those individuals who have consistently been available, emotionally sensitive, and efficacious in supporting their children during distressing times. Although children can form positive attachment representations of these adults, these representations may be overshadowed by more global insecure attachment representations formed in troubled relationships with previous caregivers and experiences of separation and loss. Thus, although adopted children may manifest behaviors usually associated with secure attachments relatively soon after placement, their mental representations of self and others sometimes reflect continued emotional vulnerability (Raby & Dozier, 2019). In this case, changes toward more positive representations of self and others can continue into adulthood.

Postadoption Contexts for Development

Developmental research has consistently documented that family process factors such as parenting quality, the quality of parent–child relationships and of the relationship between the parents affect children's and adolescents' adjustment much more than does family structure (Lamb, 2012). Golombok and Tasker (2015) conclude that caregiver warmth, communication, and conflict management are better predictors of children's socioemotional development than the composition of the family or the biological links between its members. Adoption research has confirmed and reinforced these conclusions in at least two ways.

First, as indicated before, important domains of child development show marked improvements after children are placed in their adoptive families. Research has uncovered some of the characteristics associated with these positive changes. To mention just a few examples, parental predictability, stability, and contingent responding are associated with positive changes in both EF and attachment (Smith & Pollak, 2020). This responsive parental style encourages age-appropriate behavior and contributes to IQ improvements among late-adopted children (Helder et al., 2016). Research has also shown that sensitive adoptive parenting increases children's secure attachment (Barone et al., 2017) and that parents with more secure attachment representations promote more secure representations in their adopted children (Steele et al., 2008). Similarly, in open adoption arrangements, research has shown that although family structural openness and communication openness are positively correlated, communication openness predicts children's adjustment (Brodzinsky, 2006). Also, in open adoption arrangements, satisfaction with contact (process) is a better predictor of behavioral adjustment than the existence or type of contact (structure; Grotevant et al., 2011).

Second, adoption research has also made significant contributions to the analysis of family configurations and their impact on children's development. As an example, several studies comparing children's adjustment in families headed by gay and lesbian adoptive parents with those with heterosexual parents consistently show the importance of family processes over family type (e.g., Golombok et al., 2014). In fact, in their review of research on adoptive families headed by sexual minority parents, Farr and Vázquez (2020) reported that the variability in children's adjustment was better predicted by process factors, such as quality of parenting, family resources, and children's exposure to bias and discrimination, than by the sexual orientation of their parents. Adoption by lesbian and gay parents will be discussed later in this chapter.

Developmental Construction of Adoption Identity

Adoptive identity begins when children are first aware that they are adopted and attempt to attribute meaning to their family status. Yet, when most children are informed of their adoption—typically in the preschool years—they have little understanding of what it means (Brodzinsky, 2011; Brodzinsky et al., 1984). As they mature cognitively and gain experience in different social contexts, however, they slowly "make meaning" of their adoption.

The years of adolescence and emerging adulthood are particularly important in the development of adoptive identity, since young people now have the cognitive maturity to explore how being an adopted person fits with other aspects of their identity, some of which they have chosen (career path, religious or political values), and others of which they did not choose but must come to terms with (e.g., racial/ethnic identity; Grotevant, 1997; Grotevant & Von Korff, 2011). These developmental processes occur within social contexts ranging from the proximal influence of their immediate family to the distal influences of the broader society (Grotevant et al., 2000).

Identity development can be particularly complex for adopted persons, as there are often multiple intersecting aspects of identity (e.g., adoption, culture, race/ethnicity, gender, adoptive and birth family) that must be integrated. Ultimately, development of a coherent sense of identity allows individuals to create a functional narrative that links their past, present, and future (Grotevant & Von Korff, 2011) and contributes to a sense of meaning and well-being (Adler et al., 2016). Research on adoptive identity has clearly demonstrated that it is a lifelong process involving active construction and reconstruction on the part of the person. As with other aspects of identity, reconsideration may occur in response to age-related cognitive and physical changes, as well as changes in relationships, abilities, and social contexts. Although there are common challenges, each person's lifelong path toward adoptive identity is unique.

One of the most important insights adopted persons acquire is that adoption involves not only gaining a family but also losing one. Adoption-related loss constitutes a core psychological issue for most adopted individuals (Brodzinsky, 2011; Roszia & Maxon, 2019), not only because of its extensiveness, but also because of the complexities in coming to terms with this type of loss.

Adoption and Loss
Adoption is a multidimensional experience and inherently linked to loss (Brodzinsky, 2011; Pinderhughes & Brodzinsky, 2019). It involves not only the loss of biological family members but also, for many, the loss of previous nonbiological caregivers and supports (e.g., foster parents, foster siblings, friends, orphanage staff, teachers, coaches, therapists), many of whom represented important attachment figures. The loss of previous caregivers also means the loss of individuals who help the child "make meaning" of their early life, which can be an important issue in identity development. Sometimes children experience status loss associated with adoption-related stigma (i.e., the realization that others may view adoption as a "second best" family status) and adoption-related microaggressions (Garber & Grotevant, 2015). In addition, children sometimes feel as if they don't "fit" or "belong" in the family when they are a different race or ethnicity than their parents or are unlike them and their siblings in other characteristics (e.g., academic success, talents, personality traits). Children placed transracially or transculturally also can experience a loss of racial, cultural, and linguistic connections with their birth heritage, especially as they move into adolescence and spend more time reflecting on their identity. This process can lead to a sense of self that feels incomplete and therefore compromised (Grotevant, 1997; Grotevant & Von Korff, 2011).

Coping with adoption loss can be complicated too, for a variety of reasons (Brodzinsky, 2011; Pinderhughes & Brodzinsky, 2019). First, it is statistically a relatively uncommon family form, with only a very small percentage of children in most Western cultures being adopted. Thus, children recognize that few of their friends and those around them truly understand what they have experienced or are currently experiencing—which can foster feelings of being different from others. It is also an ambiguous type of loss. Birth family and others from the past are typically not physically present in the child's life, although they are very often psychologically present in their thoughts and feelings (Brodzinsky, 2014; Fravel et al., 1993, 2000). The reasons for separation from birth family can also be confusing for the child. Some are placed voluntarily by their birth parents, which can raise questions in the child about whether they were valued or wanted; others are removed from their birth family by the authorities, which can lead to questions about whether they come from people of value. In either case, children often experience myriad distressing feelings (e.g., sadness, anger, embarrassment, guilt) as they struggle to understand and cope with issues surrounding their adoption and integrate it into their emerging sense of self. And finally, adopted individuals often experience others not understanding and even minimizing the losses they have experienced, leading to disenfranchised grief (Doka, 2002). In the face of all these circumstances, the ability to cope with adoption grief and form a healthy sense of self can be compromised (Brodzinsky et al., 2022; Grotevant, 1997; Grotevant & Von Korff, 2011). The way individuals experience these complex aspects of adoptive identity development are quite variable, with some devoting little effort to examining them, others experiencing unsettled feelings, and others having a more positive and integrated experience (Grotevant et al., 2017).

Adoption Policy, Practice, and the Law
Adoption, as a child welfare practice and a means of family building, is founded in law, at the national level in some countries and at the state or provincial levels in others. These laws and regulatory statutes, which have changed over time, have impacted adoption policy and practice in numerous ways.

Although one might hope that the evidence obtained through research can be used to guide adoption policy in a straightforward way, policy is also shaped by numerous other forces, contributing to a very complex relation between adoption research and policy. To take the case of the United States as an example, there is little in the way of a unified national adoption policy. Adoption law is considered part of family law, and most adoption policies are made at the state level (e.g., specific regulations involving the child welfare system). There are some national laws; however, most of them require implementing legislation at the state level. Therefore, influencing "adoption policy" can involve fighting for a cause in 50 different states at once.

A good example is the quest for adoptees' access to their original birth certificates, which traditionally have been sealed and reissued showing their adoptive parents as their only parents. Legislation favoring opening of original birth certificates has passed in a number of states, but the arguments supporting the decision typically come down to statements of values (e.g., it is a human right to know one's origins versus it is the state's responsibility to protect the privacy of women who placed children for adoption by concealing their identity). Research has played a relatively minor role in settling this issue. But even if the transfer from research to policy and practice is not linear or immediate, research has an unquestionable influence. The current policies and practices on relevant issues such as open adoption, special needs adoption, transracial placements, and adoption by gay and lesbian persons, for instance, would not have been possible without research findings showing their positive influence on children and families. Some of these issues are discussed later. Moreover, besides the contribution to legal and policy matters, adoption research makes significant contributions to basic developmental science, as discussed earlier and again later in this chapter.

It is also the case that legal, regulatory, and policy changes have been influenced by the efforts of advocacy groups as well as other stakeholders who may have personal or financial interests in the outcome. Adult adoptees are also organizing and adding their collective voices to these debates based on their personal experiences (e.g., McGinnis, 2012). The input of developmental scientists must compete with these other interests. In short, there has been a complex and synergistic relationship between developmental science, adoption research, policy, practice, and the law. In this section, we explore some examples of these relationships.

Changes in Adoption Law, Practice, and the Emergence of Adoption Diversity

Although adoption was practiced in many ancient societies, it was first regulated by law in the Babylonian Code of Hammurabi around 1750 BC. Over the centuries, there has been considerable variation in the practice of adoption, with some cultures and societies supporting it and others not (Singley, 2018; Volkman, 2005). In some cases, adoption resembled current Western practices, with the child's ties to the biological family severed at the time of adoption. In other cases, such as in many Pacific Island cultures, the "adopted" child's ties to the biological family remained intact.

Modern adoption policy and practice in most Western countries, however, emerged in the early 20th century, in conjunction with the rise of social work and child welfare as professional disciplines and the introduction of organized adoption agencies (Marr et al., 2020). Unlike today, with its emphasis on the best interest of the child, earlier adoption policy and practice primarily served the needs of adults—namely, childless couples. For example, little information about the child's history and birth family was shared with adoptive parents, and practice principles emphasized the importance of maintaining secrecy and confidentiality in the adoption process. In fact, adoptive parents were encouraged to raise their children "as if" they were born to them. To support this goal, agencies attempted to match parents and children by skin color and other physical or psychological features (e.g., hair color, intelligence, expected height and physical appearance), following the dictum *Adoptio naturam imitatur* (Adoption imitates nature). In many cases, parents were even discouraged from telling their children about being adopted. Secrecy in earlier adoptions was also promoted by prevailing views about sexual morality and very real prejudice (e.g., in employment and housing) against women raising children outside of marriage.

During the past four decades, adoption policies and practices have changed significantly because of new laws and regulatory statutes, as well as the result of emerging developmental science focusing on the needs and well-being of children and the efforts of adoption advocacy groups. The policy changes were also influenced by the movements of the 1960s concerning the rights of women and other groups in society, signaling a change in the traditional patriarchal view of marriage and family. These changes have resulted in much greater diversity in adoptive family structure and family life, including greater transparency in sharing children's background information with adoptive parents and emerging support for contact (when appropriate) between the adoptive and birth families (Grotevant, 2020; Pinderhughes & Brodzinsky, 2019). Rather than having adoption attempt to imitate nature, contemporary practice supports adoption imitating society (i.e., greater diversity), with children entering their new families through different pathways (i.e., in the United States, private domestic placement, domestic child welfare placement, intercountry placement, and kinship placement), at different ages, with different preplacement experiences, and often with racial/ethnic/cultural backgrounds different from their adoptive parents. In the sections that follow, we explore some of these diverse adoptive family forms, including the laws, policies, and findings from developmental science that supported this diversity.

FOSTER CARE ADOPTION

Throughout most of the 20th century, adoptions in the United States and many other Western countries primarily involved domestically born, healthy, White infants being placed with White, married, infertile, but otherwise healthy, couples. At that time, there was a significant pool of prospective adoptive parents who were unable to conceive biologically and a significant pool of women who sought adoptive placements for their children because of the strong societal stigma against raising a child outside of marriage. There was relatively little diversity in adoptive families in terms of the demographic characteristics of parents and children. Relatively few older children, children of color, or those with medical or psychological problems were adopted. In fact, child welfare professionals considered these children to be "unadoptable" (Cole & Donley, 1990). Adoption from foster care or across racial lines was also relatively uncommon. Because of this pattern, large numbers of children too often lingered in foster care, sometimes until the age of majority, when they "aged out" of the system. Social scientists have documented the damage done to children when they linger in foster care and are unable to achieve permanency in a stable and nurturing family (Konijn et al., 2019), and especially when they continue in care until the age of majority (Howard & Berzin, 2011).

Today, while there are people who would like to expand their families through adoption, many fewer women are choosing to place their children for adoption. This decline is due in part to more flexible societal values about what constitutes a family, which have been continually evolving since the 1960s. In addition, in the United States, the passage of the Adoption Assistance and Child Welfare Act in 1980 changed the practice of adoption. For the first time, states, through federal funding, could provide financial subsidies and other supports for families willing to adopt children from foster care. This legislation subsequently was followed by the Multiethnic Placement Act of 1994, the Interethnic Adoption Provisions Act of 1996, and the Adoption and Safe Families Act of 1997. The cumulative effect of these legislative acts was a huge rise in adoptions from foster care and a growing diversity in the types of children being adopted (Berrick, 2021). From 2010 to 2019, for example, on average, over 55,000 children per year were adopted from the U.S. child welfare system (Children's Bureau, 2020). Most children adopted from foster care are beyond the infancy years and many have experienced histories of neglect and/or abuse. A sizable percentage are racial minority children, often placed transracially, and many have one or more special needs, including medical or psychological problems and/or being members of a sibling group. Foster care adoption far outpaces all other types of nonkinship adoptions in the United States. Child welfare and psychological research strongly supported the benefits of adoption for children in foster care compared to allowing them to linger in state care (Dozier et al., 2012). Moreover, research on domestic transracial adoption also suggests that these children do as well psychologically and academically as those placed with racially matched parents, although other research has pointed out some of the complications that can occur for these youngsters in terms of identity development (e.g., Lee, 2003).

Although adoption from foster care is common in the United States, especially by those parents who are already fostering the children, it is less so in other countries, where long-term foster care is preferred, or where children in foster care who become adoptable are moved to other families approved for adoption. The diversity from one country to another in adoption regulations and practice is well reflected in Pösö et al. (2021). Furthermore, the use of institutions as a care alternative for those children who cannot live with their biological families is also more common in many other countries, even though there is increasing pressure to promote deinstitutionalization based on its very negative consequences for development throughout the life cycle (van IJzendoorn et al., 2020).

INTERCOUNTRY ADOPTION

Growing diversity in the makeup of adoptive families has also been tied to the rise of intercountry adoption, which began after World War II and the Korean War, and increased substantially in most Western countries from the 1980s to 2004, followed by a steep decline. The Hague Convention on Protection of Children and Co-operation in Respect of Intercountry Adoption, approved in 1993 and now ratified by more than 101 countries, is the international regulatory accord outlining the agreed-upon principles and practices of intercountry adoption. This accord was intended to protect the rights and welfare of children, birth parents, and adoptive parents, including protection of children from abuse, abduction, and trafficking. The convention established practice safeguards such as the child being deemed adoptable by a competent judiciary authority in the country of origin, as well as giving priority to an adoption or kinship placement in the child's birth country. It also encouraged countries of origin to develop improved alternative domestic childcare models for those in need to reduce the number of out-of-country adoptive placements. Both receiving countries and countries of origin must ratify the convention, pass domestic adoption laws consistent with it, and identify a central domestic authority to oversee intercountry placements to be viewed as in compliance with the convention. For example, the United States signed the convention in 1994 but it was not entered into force through the passage of appropriate domestic law until 2008. Unfortunately, countries that have not signed or ratified the convention can continue to conduct intercountry adoption programs without complying with the safeguards outlined in the convention, a limitation of the accord that is of great concern to the critics of intercountry adoption.

In the United States, 22,991 intercountry adoptive placements occurred in 2004, but by 2019, that figure had dropped to less than 3,000 (Selman, 2021). Similar reductions in intercountry adoptions have been reported for virtually all other Western countries. A sizable percentage of these adoptions involve transracial/transethnic and transcultural placements, as well as children who have experienced early adversity in their lives (e.g., neglect, multiple caregivers, orphanage life), contributing to greater demographic diversity in adoptive family structure and greater parenting challenges for adoptive parents (see Pinderhughes & Brodzinsky, 2019).

The reasons underlying the decline in, and the controversy surrounding, intercountry adoptions are complex. Critics of intercountry adoption point to problems with child trafficking and other illegal or unethical practices as a basis for a receiving country to no longer work with a sending country, or a sending country deciding to close its intercountry adoption program. Other concerns about intercountry adoptions involve misunderstandings among birth parents about relinquishing their children for adoption, the commodification of children, and prioritizing the needs of affluent Western adoptive families over those from poorer non-Western birth families. Proponents of intercountry adoption, on the other hand, argue that the needs of children for stable, nurturing families should outweigh the concerns of critics, especially because many of these children live in poorly resourced orphanages or other types of institutional environments that undermine their psychological well-being. They also argue that the problems of child trafficking and other unethical practices such as bribing country-of-origin officials are relatively rare and are better dealt with through improved laws and law enforcement than imposing barriers to intercountry placements (see Bartholet & Smolin, 2012; Briggs, 2012; Marr et al., 2020; Selman, 2009, for different perspectives on intercountry adoption).

ADOPTION BY LESBIANS AND GAY MEN

Another important change in adoption relates to the increasing number of lesbians and gay men who have become adoptive parents. This has occurred in conjunction with changes in family and adoption law supporting marriage equality for same-sex couples and the eligibility of lesbians and gay men to foster and/or adopt children. In the United States, there has been a lengthy struggle to achieve marriage equality for same-sex couples (Eisenberg, 2021). Although the roots of this legal struggle date back primarily to the 1970s and 1980s when the first lawsuits were filed related to the civil rights of sexual minorities, the movement picked up steam in 1996 with the first same-sex marriage trial (*Baehr v. Miike*, 1996), which took place in Hawaii. Although the judge in the case ruled that Hawaii's prohibition of same-sex marriage violated the state constitution, and therefore sexual minority couples should be granted marriage licenses, the ruling was subsequently made unenforceable when Hawaii voters approved an amendment to the state constitution indicating that marriage was reserved only for different-sex couples. Of importance, however, was the use of psychological and sociological expert testimony drawing upon research indicating that children were not disadvantaged when they were raised in alternative family forms, including those with lesbian and gay parents.[1]

Advocates for marriage equality and the rights of sexual minority individuals continued working diligently following the Hawaii decision, with growing success when Massachusetts became the first state to legalize same-sex marriage in 2004, and with several other states soon following suit. Finally, in 2015, the U.S. Supreme Court, in the case of *Obergefell v. Hodges* (2015), struck down state prohibitions regarding same-sex marriage, legalizing it in all states, territories, and native tribes. And with the legalization of same-sex marriage came the right for

---

[1] The second author was one of the experts offering testimony in the case.

sexual minorities to apply and be assessed for adoption and fostering in a manner comparable to different-sex couples.[2] Despite this ruling, sexual minorities continue to experience challenges in adopting and fostering in several states because of "religious" exemption laws that allow state-funded agencies to reject qualified LGBT individuals based on religious beliefs (Farr & Vázquez, 2020). It should also be noted that within the United States, there are groups actively working to undermine the *Obergefell* court decision and rescind the rights to marriage and parenting conferred by the Supreme Court decision. This is an example of a case where the research evidence (that children can be successfully raised by same-sex parents) and value stances (same-sex marriages are evil and should not be tolerated) are in irreconcilable conflict.

In the United States, proportionally, same-sex couples are seven times more likely to be raising adopted children than heterosexual couples (S. K. Goldberg & Conron, 2018). The couples are also more likely to be interracial than different-sex couples (Gates, 2013) and more likely to consider and adopt children of color (Farr & Patterson, 2009; Gates et al., 2007; A. E. Goldberg, 2009), as well as those with developmental challenges and other special needs (Brooks & Goldberg, 2001; Matthews & Cramer, 2006). These patterns suggest that lesbians and gay men are important potential resources for children who might not otherwise be adopted, and these parents are clearly contributing to the growing diversity of adoptive families.

It is important to recognize that most adoptions in the United States by lesbians and gay men involve domestic placements, either voluntary placements of infants by birth parents or placements from the child welfare system (A. E. Goldberg et al., 2014). Intercountry adoption by sexual minorities is much more difficult since, apart from the United States and South Africa, which are both receiving and sending countries for intercountry placements, no other sending country has laws or policies that support the placement of children with nonheterosexual individuals or couples (Brodzinsky, 2016). In fact, same-gender sexual behavior is still criminalized in some sending countries, making it impossible for authorities to even consider placement with lesbians and gay men. Still, such placements do occur, not only in the United States, but also in other countries. Often this involves placement with a single parent who does not identify as being lesbian or gay in their adoption application. And if already in a same-sex relationship, the individual is likely not to acknowledge this reality to the authorities in the sending country, and sometimes even to the domestic authorities processing the adoption application. Although it is not uncommon for sympathetic domestic authorities to adopt a "don't ask, don't tell" strategy in working with sexual minorities who seek an intercountry adoption, such a strategy raises possible ethical violations of the sending countries' laws and cultural beliefs, as well as possible violations of the principles of the Hague Convention.

OPEN ADOPTION

Acceptance of the principle of "the best interest of the child" has also guided changes in adoption policies and practices that support contact between members of a child's adoptive and birth families (Siegel & Smith, 2012). Open adoption is broadly defined as an arrangement in which there is some form of contact between a child's birth and adoptive family members. The

---

[2] In addition to the United States, at least 28 other countries have laws supporting marriage between sexual minorities at this point in time, including Argentina, Australia, Austria, Belgium, Brazil, Canada, Colombia, Costa Rica, Denmark, Ecuador, Finland, France, Germany, Iceland, Ireland, Luxembourg, Malta, Mexico, the Netherlands, New Zealand, Norway, Portugal, South Africa, Spain, Sweden, Switzerland, Taiwan, the United Kingdom, and Uruguay (https://www.hrc.org/resources/marriage-equality-around-the-world). Not all countries, however, allow these individuals to adopt children.

contact can vary in terms of how it occurs or who is involved, and it may change over time as individuals, relationships, and circumstances change (Grotevant, 2020). In fact, adoption is increasingly being viewed as the creation of an adoptive kinship network, in which the child connects their families of adoption and birth (Grotevant & McRoy, 1998; Reitz & Watson, 1992). Even in the case of a closed adoption in which there is no contact, the child still has a psychological connection to birth relatives. The salience of this psychological connection may wax and wane over a lifetime.

In the case of open adoptions, contact may be facilitated in varied ways, including exchange of pictures, gifts, and letters; personal visits; and technologically mediated means including social media and video conferencing (Cashen et al., 2021). Direct contact in U.S. domestic infant adoptions is becoming more common, with approximately two thirds of such children having some form of contact with birth relatives (Vandivere et al., 2009). In contrast, closed adoptions are becoming more infrequent and difficult to maintain, since it is relatively easy to search for relatives using the Internet (Whitesel & Howard, 2013) or genetic testing services (Rosenbaum, 2018).

To understand what we know about contact after adoption, we must consider domestic infant adoptions, adoptions from foster care, and intercountry adoptions separately. Nevertheless, in all cases it is important to note that contact is dynamic and may change across time as individuals, relationships, and circumstances change (Grotevant et al., 2019).

Contact in Domestic Infant Adoptions

The Minnesota–Texas Adoption Research Project (MTARP: Grotevant & McRoy, 1998; Grotevant et al., 2013) has followed 190 adoptive families and 169 birth mothers in the United States over four times of measurement spanning 30 years. Approximately one third of the adoptions began with no contact or shared information, another third involved the sharing of nonidentifying information through the agency, and the other third had fully disclosed contact from the outset. Contact patterns changed over time depending on the interpersonal relationships and dynamics among the participants, particularly the adoptive and birth parents. Where mutually satisfying relationships developed in the context of positive communication, ability to maintain boundaries, and flexibility in day-to-day interaction, contact was often sustained. Where trusting relationships did not develop or were compromised, contact often decreased or stopped (Grotevant, 2009).

The evidence supporting the benefits of open adoption is straightforward in some ways and complex in others. Children and adolescents who are in open adoptions do indeed have more information about their families of origin and have the opportunity to be known by and loved by more relatives. However, relationships in complex families can be challenging, especially when the participants do not all agree about the type of relationship they would like to have. Contact with birth relatives per se was not found to be directly associated with adjustment outcomes for adopted adolescents and young adults (e.g., Ge et al., 2008; Von Korff et al., 2006); however, as discussed earlier, adoptive family members' satisfaction with contact arrangements did predict better adoptee adjustment (Grotevant et al., 2011). The effect of contact on adoptive identity development in adolescence and emerging adulthood was mediated by the occurrence of adoption-related conversation within the family. When contact was occurring, the adolescent and parents talked more about their involvement with birth relatives, stimulating thinking about the meaning of adoption and their own sense of adoptive identity. In closed adoptions, since little new information was available to discuss, the construction of adoptive identity seemed less dynamic (Von Korff & Grotevant, 2011).

Contact in Child Welfare Adoptions

Contact between children adopted from the public child welfare system (usually following foster care) and their birth relatives has been considered challenging, since the children had been removed from their families, typically because of maltreatment. The best interest of the child mandates protecting the child's safety, but research is also beginning to show that there can be benefits from contact (e.g., Neil et al., 2015) and that such contact is not uncommon (Brodzinsky & Goldberg, 2016; Vandivere et al., 2009) The arrangements must ensure the child's safety by preventing retraumatization, taking into consideration the birth parents' capacity to participate in positive ways. Even if birth parents are unable to participate, there are often grandparents, siblings, and other extended family members who could provide important ongoing connections for the child.

In countries such as the United Kingdom, domestic infant adoptions and intercountry adoptions are rare, and the majority of placements are made through the public child welfare system. In such cases, Neil and colleagues (2015) have found direct contact to be preferable to indirect letterbox contact, because the former allows children to develop a better sense of what their birth relatives are like as people and ultimately feel more at ease with their own adoption story. Neil (2009) found that contact worked better when the adoptive mother showed high levels of communicative openness and the birth relatives accepted the finality of the placement: "How the adults think about and manage contact is vital to the child's experience" (Neil, 2019, p. 3).

In the Australian state of New South Wales, most adoptive placements are from foster care, and arrangements involving direct contact are required by law (del Pozo de Bolger et al., 2018). Researchers and practitioners feel that there are three primary benefits to direct contact: reassurance (for the child, the birth parents, and the adoptive parents), identity, and continuity (Wright, 2018). Consistent with Neil's findings as well as with findings from infant adoptions, reports from New South Wales suggest that a positive experience requires that the adults acknowledge the child's simultaneous connections to their families of birth and adoption, and that the adults maintain appropriate boundaries, communicate effectively, and demonstrate mutual respect (del Pozo de Bolger et al., 2018).

In-depth research and follow-up in New South Wales have also been conducted by Barnardos, an Australian agency that has been providing support for placements from care for many years. In a recently published monograph, Ward et al. (2021) report detailed quantitative and qualitative data about the mandated open adoptions in their jurisdiction. Consistent with other ongoing research on contact, this study demonstrates that, although contact can be difficult, it is ultimately beneficial for most children; that the type and frequency of contact must be tailored to meet the needs of the adopted child; and that open adoption is less about the contact itself and more about the relationships that emerge from the contact.

The importance of individualization cannot be overstated. And, of course, individualization challenges policymaking because it does not easily lend itself to establishment of broad guidelines that work for all children and families. In addition, individualization often brings greater expense, because more professionals are needed to tailor individual plans and to help families deal with challenges they might encounter over time. Nevertheless, a clear consensus is emerging that the time and expense are worthwhile when one considers the positive lifelong impact on adopted children.

Contact in Intercountry Adoptions

Contact in intercountry adoptions is still rare but is becoming more frequent (Baden, 2013; Brodzinsky & Goldberg, 2017). Barriers to contact include significant physical distance as well as cultural, economic, and language differences between the adoptive and birth family members (e.g., Högbacka, 2016; Roby & Matsumura, 2002). In a study of children from Romania and Russia adopted to New Zealand, Scherman and Hawke (2010) identified the positive value in the child's having more and accurate information about birth relatives and the ability to establish personal relationships that can endure. On the other hand, difficult aspects included some of the barriers mentioned previously plus pain of separation, additional unanswered questions, and seeing birth relatives living in poverty.

Even though contact during childhood in intercountry adoption is rare, there are increasing numbers of adoptees who seek information about their birth cultures and birth relatives once they are adults. One study noted highly varied reactions of Korean adoptees to the cultural differences they encountered, including views about family roles and expectations, standards for beauty, and attitudes about secrecy in the adoption. Some felt a deep sense of belonging to their birth culture, whereas others felt estranged (Docan-Morgan, 2016). A rapidly growing set of first-person accounts and memoirs written by adults adopted across national and cultural lines adds richness and depth to the limited research literature on the topic (e.g., Chau & Ost-Vollmers, 2012; Trenka et al., 2006). The written materials are richly supplemented by documentary videos and films that bring the complexities of the international adoption experience to life from the perspective of the adult adoptee.

Practice Policies, Law, and Adoption Contact
As we have already noted, contact between adoptive families and birth families has become increasingly more common in many Western countries. Yet, this practice is not required by national or state regulations and laws, an exception being in New South Wales in Australia, where direct contact between families is required by law (see earlier). Rather, contact in adoption reflects emerging policy and practice changes by private and public adoption agencies. For example, in the United States in the 1970s, a small number of private agencies began experimenting with open adoption. Based upon their experiences, as well as emerging research supporting the benefits of contact between adoptive and birth families (see earlier), more and more agencies, including public agencies, began promoting this practice, not only in the United States, but also in other countries. In many cases, contact is facilitated by postadoption agreements between the adoptive and birth families at the time of placement. These agreements typically outline the nature, timing, and extent of contact. Although these agreements are legally enforceable in some U.S. states, they are not in others (Child Welfare Information Gateway, 2019). In states with enforceable agreements, parties can petition the court to seek compliance with or a modification of the agreement. In some states, courts require the parties to seek mediation to resolve postadoption contact disputes. Laws in other states, with unenforceable contact agreements, are silent on the issue of compliance. It is important to note that, in reaching a decision regarding the enforceability and/or modification of a postadoption agreement, courts often rely on the "best interests of the child" standard (Child Welfare Information Gateway, 2019; Seymore, 2019). It is rare, however, for the court to revoke the adoption because of noncompliance with a postadoption agreement (Seymore, 2019).

Contribution of Developmental Science to Adoption Law and Practice
The rise in adoption diversity, in terms of the type of individuals deemed suitable to adopt, as well as the type of children being adopted, has been affected by changes in law and statutory regulations; some of those changes, as well as changes in adoption policy and practice, have been directly influenced by developmental science. Parke (2013) has discussed the history and myth of the "ideal" family form—that is, the nuclear family composed of two married,

heterosexual parents, with biological children, residing together, father as the "breadwinner" and mother as the primary caregiver. He notes that, despite widespread cultural endorsement of this stereotype in most Western societies, history suggests that many families did not conform to this ideal and that developmental research has not supported the notion that children unduly suffer when they live in a variety of alternative family forms. In fact, he makes the point discussed earlier in this chapter that family structure is much less important for children's well-being than family processes (i.e., quality of parenting and parent–child relationships, parental mental health, family support and resources; see Golombok & Tasker, 2015, and Lamb, 2012, for additional discussions of this point).

This research finding has supported decisions by adoption policymakers and agency administrators and, in some cases, decisions by courts (see discussion earlier regarding adoption by sexual minority individuals) to allow adoption by individuals who in the past were deemed unsuitable to adopt simply because they did not conform to stereotypes about who could provide a stable and nurturing home for children—for example, single adults, older adults, disabled adults, foster parents, adults of a different race than the child, and sexual minority adults. Rather than focusing on these types of characteristics, contemporary home studies or what are also called "suitability studies" seek to identify prospective adoptive parents who can understand and meet the specific needs of children waiting to be adopted. Adoptive placement matching no longer focuses on whether potential adoptive parents and children look alike, but rather whether adoption applicants have the type of parenting qualities and emotional stability that allow them to understand the challenges that children previously faced; the skills to support children's recovery from adversity; the ability to foster secure parent–child attachment; the willingness to help children explore, understand, and cope with adoption issues; the readiness to support children's connection with their racial and cultural heritage and birth family (when appropriate); and the commitment to utilize support services when needed. Time and again, research has confirmed that these parenting qualities are more predictive of successful adoptive placement and the long-term well-being of adopted children than the specific family structure in which children live (see Pinderhughes & Brodzinsky, 2019, for a review of adoptive parenting).

An important use of development science in support of legal changes in family and adoption law, which also gave rise to greater adoption diversity, relates to efforts to support marriage equality. As noted earlier, expert witnesses for plaintiffs in the gay marriage trial in Hawaii in 1996 introduced psychological and sociological research indicating that children were not disadvantaged when they were raised in alternative family forms, including those with lesbians and gay parents. Furthermore, in one of the lower court cases from Michigan (*DeBoer v. Snyder*, 2014) that was consolidated with several other lower court cases heard by the Supreme Court leading to marriage equality in the United States (*Obergefell v. Hodges*, 2015), plaintiffs' experts[3] drew upon nearly 25 years of research on the topic showing a remarkably consistent pattern of findings. Specifically, expert testimony indicated that there was clear and convincing evidence showing that children raised by lesbians and gay men, including those who had been adopted, showed no meaningful differences in psychological and academic adjustment compared to their agemates with opposite-sex parents. Moreover, the experts also opined that research supported the conclusion that lesbians and gay men had comparable parenting skills and created caregiving environments that were just as nurturing and supportive

---

[3] The second author was one of the experts.

for their children as heterosexual parents. These findings proved to be persuasive and were incorporated into the judge's ruling that Michigan's prohibition of same-sex marriage was unconstitutional.

On a very different front, developmental research has driven important advances in the understanding of adoption, as well as in some aspects of its regulation and practice. Two major models of human development have been particularly important: the ecological model and the lifespan approach.

By enlarging the focus to consider the different contexts in which development takes place, the ecological model developed by Bronfenbrenner (2005) has helped to gain a better understanding of adoption, as well as to consider the layers of influence on the development of adopted persons (Palacios, 2009). The model suggests that the likelihood of adoption being internalized as a positive or destabilizing personal and family experience is tied to the interaction of multiple contextual factors, including the society or culture within which the adoption occurred (*macrosystem*); the proximal community and professional interventions that impact the adopted person indirectly through its influence on parents and other caregivers (*exosystem*); the environments in which the adoptee spends most of their time such as family, peer group, and school (*microsystem*); and the dynamic interplay among these microsystems (*mesosystem*) and the changes in the environments and the person over time (*chronosystem*). Moreover, the impact of each of these contextual factors is mediated by developmental factors, especially children's cognitive and social–cognitive development, through which they attribute meaning to their adoption experience. As Brodzinsky et al. (2022) have demonstrated, this ecological perspective has multiple implications related to the regulation and practice of adoption, social attitudes toward adoption, support services for adoptive kinship members, and understanding multiple levels of influence on the lived experience of adoptees.

As with developmental research in general, adoption research for many years focused on the development of adoptees during childhood and adolescence (Palacios & Brodzinsky, 2010). More recently, the lifespan perspective, already dominant in developmental science, has also reached adoption research. Although some pioneering work had already opened the focus to what happens beyond the early years (e.g., the work of Brodzinsky et al., 1992, on the experience of adoption across the lifespan), only more recently has empirical research begun to address more systematically the study of psychological development in adoptees in the years of emerging adulthood and beyond. A good example is the study of adoptive identity in the transition from adolescence to emerging adulthood (Grotevant et al., 2017), which shows patterns of continuity and change in identity construction, as well as its relationship to the psychological adjustment of adult adoptees. Another example is new research on adoptees becoming parents (and adopters becoming grandparents), a topic on which publications (Despax et al., 2021) and research programs (Neil, 2021) are beginning to appear, with initial data showing the resilience of many adoptees and the effectiveness of adoption in breaking the cycle of intergenerational transmission of adversity. The practice of adoption cannot ignore the lifelong journey that adoption represents for all those touched by it.

Conclusions and Implications

Since its emergence as a formal child welfare practice, adoption has undergone considerable change in most Western countries in terms of policies and practices. These changes have been guided by new laws and regulations that have been shaped by multiple forces including shifting societal values, domestic and international politics, economic factors, ethical issues, the advocacy efforts of key adoption stakeholders (e.g., adoption professionals, adopted individuals, adoptive parents, birth parents), and the findings offered by developmental science and by adoption research. The cumulative effect of these forces has been a radical alteration of adoptive family life. Where once it was a relatively homogeneous family form, predominately characterized by White married couples parenting healthy White children placed as babies, today, as noted previously, it is an extremely diverse and complex family form. In fact, it is safe to say that there is no such thing as a "typical adoptive family."

The heterogeneity of adopted persons and the diversity of adoptive family life have offered developmental scientists a unique opportunity to examine important questions about the role of early experience on developmental outcomes and the extent to which children can recover from early adversity when they are provided with a more enriched environment in which to grow up. For ethical reasons, it is virtually impossible to explore these types of questions through controlled research. As noted earlier, by studying adopted children and their families with diverse backgrounds and postadoption experiences, developmental scientists now have important insights into the way in which children are shaped by their early history and the extent and means by which developmental trajectories are altered when children are provided with more nurturing and enriching environments. Moreover, if research on human development has been a fundamental source of inspiration for adoption research, adoption research, in turn, is serving to improve our understanding not only of adopted persons but also, more generally, of human development, as this chapter has emphasized.

Finally, the legal regulation of adoption and its policy and practice must be geared to ensuring that all children who cannot be raised by their birth parents or relatives can access the stability and permanency that adoption provides, affording adoptees and adopters throughout their lives an adequate response to their multiple and sometimes complex needs. To the extent that they help us better understand the nature and development of those needs, as well as how best to support the potential for change and resilience in adopted persons, the interrelationships between developmental science and adoption research will continue to contribute to the regulation and practice of adoption, as well as to improving the lives of adopted persons and their families.

References

Adler, J. M., Lodi-Smith, J., Philippe, F. L., & Houle, I. (2016). The incremental validity of narrative identity in predicting well-being: A review of the field and recommendations for the future. *Personality and Social Psychology Review, 20*(2), 142–175.

Baden, A. (2019). Intercountry adoption: The beginning of the end. In H.D. Grotevant (Ed.) *Rudd Adoption Research Program Publication Series: The future of adoption* (pp. 1–5). University of Massachusetts Amherst. https://www.umass.edu/ruddchair/sites/default/files/rudd.baden.pdf

Baehr v. Miike, Circuit Court for the First Circuit, Hawaii No. 91-1394 (1996).

Barone, L., Lionetti, F., & Green, J. (2017). A matter of attachment? How adoptive parents foster post-institutionalized children's social and emotional adjustment. *Attachment and Human Development, 19*, 323–339.

Bartholet, E., & Smolin, D. (2012). The debate. In J. L. Gibbons & K. Smith Rotabi (Eds.), *Intercountry adoption: Policies, practices, and outcomes* (pp. 233–251). Ashgate Publishing.

Bernier, A., Carlson, S. M., & Whipple, N. (2010). From external regulation to self regulation: Early parenting precursors of young children's executive functioning. *Child Development, 81*, 326–339.

Berrick, J. D. (2021). Adoption from care: Policy and practice in the United States. In T. Pösö, M. Skivenes, & J. Thoburn (Eds.), *Adoption from care: International perspectives on children's rights, family preservation and state intervention* (pp. 67–83). Policy Press.

Bick, J., Zhu, T., Stamoulis, C., Fox, N. A., Zeanah, C., & Nelson, C. A. (2015). Effect of early institutionalization and foster care on long-term white matter development: A randomized clinical trial. *JAMA Pediatrics, 169*(3), 211–219.

Briggs, L. (2012). *Somebody's children: The politics of transracial and transnational adoption*. Duke University Press.

Brodzinsky, D. (2006). Family structural openness and communication openness as predictors in the adjustment of adopted children. *Adoption Quarterly, 9*(4), 1–18.

Brodzinsky, D. M. (2011). Children's understanding of adoption: Developmental and clinical implications. *Professional Psychology: Research and Practice, 42*(2), 200–207.

Brodzinsky, D. M. (2014). The role of birthparents in the life of the adoptive family: Real versus symbolic presence. In E. Scabini & G. Rossi (Eds.), *Allargare lo spazio familiare: Adozione e affido. Studi interdisciplinary sulla famiglia* (pp. 223–238). Vita e Pensiero. (Chapter published in English)

Brodzinsky, D. (2016). Adoption, international. In A. Goldberg (Ed.), *The SAGE encyclopedia of LGBTIQ studies* (Vol. 1, pp. 12–14). Sage Publications.

Brodzinsky, D. M., & Goldberg, A. E. (2016). Contact with birth family in adoptive families headed by lesbian, gay male, and heterosexual parents. *Children and Youth Services Review, 62*, 9–17.

Brodzinsky, D. M., & Goldberg, A. E. (2017). Contact with birth family in intercountry adoptions: Comparing families headed by sexual minority and heterosexual parents. *Children and Youth Services Review, 74*, 117–124.

Brodzinsky, D. M., Gunnar, M., & Palacios, J. (2022). Adoption and trauma: Risks, recovery, and the lived experience of adoption. *Child Abuse & Neglect, 130*, 105309.

Brodzinsky, D. M., Schechter, M. D., & Henig, R. M. (1992). *Being adopted: The lifelong search for self*. Doubleday.

Brodzinsky, D. M., Singer, L. M., & Braff, A. M. (1984). Children's understanding of adoption. *Child Development, 55*(3), 869–878.

Bronfenbrenner, U. (Ed.). (2005). *Making human beings human: Bioecological perspectives on human development*. Sage Publications.

Brooks, D., & Goldberg, S. (2001). Gay and lesbian adoption and foster placements: Can they meet the needs of waiting children. *Social Work, 46*(2), 142–158.

Cashen, K. K., Grotevant, H. D., Wyman Battalen, A., Sellers, C. M., & McRoy, R. G. (2021). Tech-mediated and traditional communication modes in adult adoptees' contact with birth parents. *Family Relations, 70*(1), 120–129.

Chau, A., & Ost-Vollmers, K. (Eds.). (2012). *Parenting as adoptees*. CQT Media and Publishing.

Child Welfare Information Gateway. (2019). *Postadoption contact agreements between birth and adoptive families*. U.S. Department of Health and Human Services, Children's Bureau.

Children's Bureau. (2020). *The AFCARS report, No. 27*. U.S. Department of Health and Human Services, Administration on Children, Youth and Families. https://www.acf.hhs.gov/sites/default/files/documents/cb/afcarsreport27.pdf

Cicchetti, D. (2013). Resilient functioning in maltreated children: Past, present, and future perspectives. *Journal of Child Psychology and Psychiatry, 54*(4), 402–422.

Cicchetti, D., & Doyle, C. (2016). Child maltreatment, attachment and psychopathology: Mediating relations. *World Psychiatry, 15*(2), 89–90.

Cole, E. S., & Donley, K. S. (1990). History, values, and placement policy issues in adoption. In D. Brodzinsky & M. Schechter (Eds.), *The psychology of adoption* (pp. 273–294). Oxford University Press.

Colich, N. L., Sheridan, M. A., Humphreys, K. L., Wade, M., Tibu, F., Nelson, C. A., Zeanah, C. H., Fox, N. A., & McLaughlin, K. A. (2021). Heightened sensitivity to the caregiving environment during adolescence: Implications for recovery following early-life adversity. *Journal of Child Psychology and Psychiatry, 62*(8), 937–948.

Dalen, M. (2005). International adoptions in Scandinavia: Research focus and main results. In D. M. Brodzinsky & J. Palacios (Eds.), *Psychological issues in adoption: Research and practice* (pp. 211–231). Praeger.

Deboer v. Snyder, 772 F.3d 388 (6th Cir.) (2014).

del Pozo de Bolger, A., Dunstan, D., & Kaltner, M. (2018). Open adoptions of children from foster care in New South Wales Australia: Adoption process and post-adoption contact. *Adoption Quarterly, 21*(2), 82–101.

Demers, L. A., McKenzie, K. J., Hunt, R. H., Cicchetti, D., Cowell, R. A., Rogosch, F. A., Toth, S. L., & Thomas, K. M. (2018). Separable effects of childhood maltreatment and adult adaptive functioning on amygdala connectivity during emotion processing. *Biological Psychiatry and Cognitive Neuroscience and Neuroimaging, 3*(2), 116–124.

Despax, J., Bouteyre, E., & Guiller, T. (2021). Comparison of adoptees' and nonadoptees' experience of parenthood and mediating role of dyadic coping. *Journal of Social and Personal Relationships, 38*(2), 544–563.

Docan-Morgan, S. (2016). Cultural differences and perceived belonging during Korean adoptees' reunions with birth families. *Adoption Quarterly, 19*(2), 99–118.

Doka, K. J. (2002). *Disenfranchised grief: New directions, challenges, and strategies for practice*. Research Press.

Dozier, M., Kaufman, J., Kobak, R., O'Connor, T. G., Sagi-Schwartz, A., Scott, S., Shauffer, C., Smetana, J., van IJzendoorn, M. H., & Zeanah, C. H. (2014). Consensus statement on group care for children and adolescents: A statement of policy of the American Orthopsychiatric Association. *American Journal of Orthopsychiatry, 84*(3), 219–225.

Eisenberg, S. (2021). *The engagement: America's quarter-century struggle over same-sex marriage*. Pantheon Books.

Farr, R. H., & Patterson, C. J. (2009). Transracial adoption by lesbian, gay, and heterosexual parents: Who completes transracial adoptions and with what results? *Adoption Quarterly, 12*(3–4), 187–204.

Farr, R. H., & Vázquez, C. P. (2020). Adoptive families headed by LGBTQ parents. In G. M. Wrobel, E. Helder, & E. Marr (Eds.), *The Routledge handbook of adoption* (pp.164–175). Routledge.

Fravel, D. L., Grotevant, H. D., Boss, P. G., & McRoy, R. G. (1993). Boundary ambiguity across levels of openness in adoption. In M. Crosbie-Burnett (Ed.), *Proceedings of the theory construction and research methodology workshop of the National Council on Family Relations* (pp. 1–28). National Council on Family Relations.

Fravel, D. L., McRoy, R. G., & Grotevant, H. D. (2000). Birthmother perceptions of the psychologically present adopted child: Adoption openness and boundary ambiguity. *Family Relations, 49*(4), 425–433.

Garber, K. J., & Grotevant, H. D. (2015). "You were adopted?!" Microaggressions toward adolescent adopted individuals in same-race families. *Counseling Psychologist, 43*(3), 435–462.

Gates, G. (2013). *LGB families and relationships: Analyses of the National Health Interview Survey*. Williams Institute. https://williamsinstitute.law.ucla.edu/publications/lgb-families-and-relationships/

Gates, G. J., Badgett, M. V. L., Macomber, J. E., & Chambers, K. (2007). *Adoption and foster care by gay and lesbian parents in the United States*. Williams Institute and the Urban Institute. https://www.urban.org/sites/default/files/publication/46401/411437-Adoption-and-Foster-Care-by-Lesbian-and-Gay-Parents-in-the-United-States.PDF

Ge, X., Natsuaki, M. N., Martin, D. M., Leve, L. D., Neiderhiser, J. M., Shaw, D. S., Villareal, G., Scaramella, L., Reid, J. B., & Reiss, D. (2008). Bridging the divide: Openness in adoption and postadoption psychosocial adjustment among birth and adoptive parents. *Journal of Family Psychology, 22*(4), 529–540.

Goldberg, A. E. (2009). Lesbian and heterosexual preadoptive couples' openness to transracial adoption. *American Journal of Orthopsychiatry, 79*, 103–117.

Goldberg, A. E., Gartrell, N. K., & Gates, G. (2014). *Research report on LGB-parent families*. Williams Institute.

Goldberg, S. K., & Conron, K. J. (2018). *How many same-sex couples in the US are raising children?* Williams Institute. https://williamsinstitute.law.ucla.edu/publications/same-sex-parents-us/

Golm, D., Maughan, B., Barker, E. D., Hill, J., Kennedy, M., Knights, N., Kreppner, J., Kumsta, R., Schlotz, W., Rutter, M., & Sonuga-Barke, E. J. S. (2020). Why does early childhood deprivation increase the risk for depression and anxiety in adulthood? A developmental cascade model. *Journal of Child Psychology and Psychiatry, 61*(9), 1043–1053.

Golombok, S., Mellish, L., Jennings, S., Casey, P., Tasker, F., & Lamb, M. E. (2014). Adoptive gay father families: Parent-child relationships and children's psychological adjustment. *Child Development, 85*(2), 456–468.

Golombok, S., & Tasker, F. (2015). Socio-emotional development in changing families. In M. E. Lamb (Ed.), *Handbook of child psychology, Vol. 3: Social, emotional, and personality development* (pp. 419–463). John Wiley & Sons.

Groh, A. M., Fearon, R. P., Van IJzendoorn, M. H., Bakermans-Kranenburg, M. J., & Roisman, G. I. (2017). Attachment in the early life course: Meta-analytic evidence for its role in socio-emotional development. *Child Development Perspectives, 11*(1), 70–76.

Grotevant, H. D. (1997). Coming to terms with adoption: The construction of identity from adolescence into adulthood. *Adoption Quarterly, 1*(1), 3–17.

Grotevant, H. D. (2009). Emotional distance regulation over the life course in adoptive kinship networks. In G. Wrobel & E. Neil (Eds.), *International advances in adoption research for practice* (pp. 295–316). Wiley.

Grotevant, H. D. (2020). Open adoption. In G. M. Wrobel, E. Helder, & E. Marr (Eds.), *Routledge handbook of adoption* (pp. 266–277). Routledge.

Grotevant, H. D., Dunbar, N., Kohler, J. K., & Esau, A. L. (2000). Adoptive identity: How contexts within and beyond the family shape developmental pathways. *Family Relations, 49*(4), 379–387.

Grotevant, H. D., Lo, A., Fiorenzo, L., & Dunbar, N. D. (2017). Adoptive identity and adjustment from adolescence to emerging adulthood: A person-centered approach. *Developmental Psychology, 53*(11), 2195–2204.

Grotevant, H. D., & McRoy, R. G. (1998). *Openness in adoption: Connecting families of birth and adoption*. Sage Publications.

Grotevant, H. D., McRoy, R. G., Wrobel, G. M., & Ayers-Lopez, S. (2013). Contact between adoptive and birth families: Perspectives from the Minnesota Texas Adoption Research Project. *Child Development Perspectives, 7*(3), 193–198.

Grotevant, H. D., Rueter, M., Von Korff, L., & Gonzalez, C. (2011). Post-adoption contact, adoption communicative openness, and satisfaction with contact as predictors of externalizing behavior in adolescence and emerging adulthood. *Journal of Child Psychology and Psychiatry, 52*(5), 529–536.

Grotevant, H. D., & Von Korff, L. (2011). Adoptive identity. In S. Schwartz, K. Luyckx, & V. L. Vignoles (Eds.), *Handbook of identity theory and research* (pp. 585–601). Springer.

Grotevant, H. D., Wrobel, G. M., Fiorenzo, L., Lo, A. Y. H., & McRoy, R. G. (2019). Trajectories of birth family contact in infant adoptions. *Journal of Family Psychology, 33*(1), 54–63.

Gunnar, M. R., DePasquale, C. E., Reid, B. M., Donzella, B., & Miller, B. S. (2019). Pubertal stress recalibration reverses the effects of early life stress in postinstitutionalized children. *Proceedings of the National Academy of Sciences, 116*(48), 23984–23988.

Gunnar, M. R., & Reid, B. M. (2019). Early deprivation revisited: Contemporary studies of the impact on young children institutional care. , *Annual Review of Developmental Psychology, 1*, 93–118.

Helder, E. J., Mulder, E., & Gunnoe, M. L. (2016). A longitudinal investigation of children internationally adopted at school age. *Child Neuropsychology, 22*(1), 39–64.

Högbacka, R. (2016). *Global families, inequality and transnational adoption: The de-kinning of first mothers*. Palgrave Macmillan.

Howard, J., & Berzin, S. (2011). *Never too old: Achieving permanency and sustaining connections in older youth in foster care: Policy and practice perspective*. Donaldson Adoption Institute.

Johnson, D. E., & Gunnar, M. R. (2011). Growth failure in institutionalized children. *Monographs of the Society for Research on Child Development, 76*(4), 92–126.

Johnson, D. E., Tang, A., Almas, A. N., Degnan, K. A., McLaughlin, K. A., Nelson, C. A., Fox, N. A., Zeanah, C. H., & Drury, S. S. (2018). Caregiving disruptions affect growth and pubertal development in early adolescence in institutionalized and fostered Romanian children: A randomized clinical trial. *Journal of Pediatrics, 203*, 345–353.

Jurviste, U., Sabbati, G., Shreeves, R., & Dimitrova-Stul, A. (2016). *Adoption of children in the European Union* [Briefing]. European Parliamentary Research Service.

Konijn, C., Admiraal, S., Baart, J., van Rooij, F., Stams, G-J., Colonnesi, C., Lindauer, R., & Assink, M. (2019). Foster care placement instability: A meta-analytic review. *Children and Youth Services Review, 96*, 483–499.

Koss, K. J., Lawler, J. M., & Gunnar, M. R. (2020). Early adversity and children's regulatory deficits: Does post-adoption parenting facilitate recovery in postinstitutionalized children? *Development & Psychopathology, 32*(3), 879–896.

Lamb, M. E. (2012). Mothers, fathers, families, and circumstances: Factors affecting children's adjustment. *Applied Developmental Science, 16*(2), 98–111.

Lee, R. M. (2003). The transracial adoption paradox: History, research, and counseling implications of cultural socialization. *Counseling Psychologist, 31*(6), 711–744.

Marr, E., Helder, E., & Wrobel, G. M. (2020). Historical and contemporary contexts of US adoptions: An overview. In G. M. Wrobel, E. Helder, & E. Marr (Eds.), *The Routledge handbook of adoption* (pp. 3–21). Routledge.

Matthews, J. C., & Cramer, E. P. (2006). Envisaging the adoption process to strengthen gay- and lesbian-headed families. Recommendations for adoption professionals. *Child Welfare, 85*(2), 317–340.

McGinnis, H. (2012). All grown up: Rise of the Korean adult adoptee movement and implications for practice. In J. L. Gibbons & K. S. Rotabi (Eds.), *Intercountry adoption: Policies, practices, and outcomes* (pp. 293–310). Ashgate Publishing.

Neil, E. (2009). The corresponding experiences of adoptive parents and birth relatives in open adoptions. In G. M. Wrobel & E. Neil (Eds.), *International advances in adoption research for practice*. (pp. 269–293). Wiley-Blackwell.

Neil, E. (2019). Planning and supporting birth family contact when children are adopted from care. In H.D. Grotevant (Ed.), *Rudd Adoption Research Program Publication Series: The future of adoption* (pp. 1–5). University of Massachusetts Amherst. https://www.umass.edu/ruddchair/sites/default/files/rudd.neil.pdf

Neil, E. (2021). *Studying adoptive families beyond childhood: What do we know about adoptive families when adoptees become parents?* [Keynote address]. Seventh International Conference on Adoption Research (ICAR7), Milan, Italy.

Neil, E., Beek, M., & Ward, E. (2015). *Contact after adoption: A longitudinal study of post adoption contact arrangements*. CoramBAAF.

Nelson, C. A., & Gabard-Durnam, L. J. (2020). Early adversity and critical periods: Neurodevelopmental consequences of violating the expectable environment. *Trends in Neuroscience, 43*(3), 133–143.

Nelson, C. A., Zeanah, C. H., & Fox, N. A. (2019). How early experience shapes human development: The case of psychosocial deprivation. *Neural Plasticity, 14*, 1–12.

Obergefell v. Hodges, 576 U.S. 644 (2015).

Pace, C. S., Di Folco, S., Guerriero, V., & Muzi, S. (2019). Late-adopted children grown up: A long-term longitudinal study on attachment patterns of adolescent adoptees and their adoptive mothers. *Attachment & Human Development, 21*(4), 372–388.

Palacios, J. (2009). The ecology of adoption. In E. Neil (Ed.), *International advances in adoption research for practice* (pp. 71–94). Wiley-Blackwell.

Palacios, J. (2018). Adoption design. In M. Bornstein (Ed.), *The Sage encyclopedia of lifespan human development* (pp. 45–48). Sage Publications.

Palacios, J., Adroher, S., Brodzinsky, D., Grotevant, H., Johnson, D., Juffer, F., Martinez-Mora, L., Muhamedrahimov, R., Selwyn, J., Simmonds, J., & Tarren-Sweeney, M. (2019). Adoption in the service of child protection: An international interdisciplinary perspective. *Psychology, Public Policy, and Law, 25*(2), 57–72.

Palacios, J., & Brodzinsky, D. M. (2010). Adoption research: Trends, topics, outcomes. *International Journal of Behavioral Development, 34*(3), 270–284.

Palacios, J., Román, M., & Camacho, C. (2011). Growth and development in internationally adopted children: Extent and timing of recovery after early adversity. *Child: Care, Health & Development, 37*(2), 282–288.

Palacios, J., Román, M., Moreno, C., León, E., & Peñarrubia, M. (2014). Differential plasticity in the recovery of adopted children after early adversity. *Child Development Perspectives, 8*(3), 169–174.

Parke, R. D. (2013). *Future families: Diverse forms, rich possibilities.* John Wiley & Sons.

Peñarrubia, M., Palacios, J., & Román, M. (2020). Executive function and early adversity in internationally adopted children. *Children and Youth Services Review, 108*, 104587.

Pinderhughes, E. E., & Brodzinsky, D. M. (2019). Parenting in adoptive families. In M. H. Bornstein (Ed.), *Handbook of parenting, Vol 1: Children and parenting* (3rd ed., pp. 322–367). Routledge.

Pösö, T., Skivenes, M., & Thoburn, J. (2021). *Adoption from care: International perspectives on children's rights, family preservation and State intervention.* Policy Press.

Raby, K. L., & Dozier, M. (2019). Attachment across the lifespan: Insights from adoptive families. *Current Opinion in Psychology, 25*, 81–85.

Reitz, M., & Watson, K. W. (1992). *Adoption and the family system: Strategies for treatment.* Guilford Press.

Roby, J. L., & Matsumura, S. (2002). If I give you my child, aren't we family? A study of birthmothers participating in Marshall Islands-US adoptions. *Adoption Quarterly, 5*(4), 7–31.

Román, M., Palacios, J., Moreno, C., & López, A. (2012). Attachment representations in internationally adopted children. *Attachment & Human Development, 14*(6), 585–600.

Rosenbaum, S. I. (2018, August 4). The twilight of closed adoptions. *Boston Globe.* https://www.bostonglobe.com/ideas/2018/08/04/the-twilight-closed-adoptions/1Iu4c5da4W5qNbIPn5IEmL/story.html?event=event12

Roszia, S., & Maxon, A. D. (2019). *Seven core issues in adoption and permanency: A comprehensive guide to promoting understanding and healing in adoption, foster care, kinship families, and third-party reproduction.* Jessica Kingsley Publishers.

Scherman, R., & Hawke, W. (2010, July). *Openness and intercountry adoption* [Paper presentation]. Third International Conference on Adoption Research (ICAR3), Leiden, The Netherlands.

Selman, P. (2009). The movement of children for international adoption: Developments and trends in receiving states and states of origin, 1998–2004. In D. Marre & L. Briggs (Eds.), *International adoption: Global inequalities and the circulation of children* (pp. 320–351). New York University Press.

Selman, P. (2021). *Global statistics for intercountry adoption: Receiving states and states of origin 2000–2019.* https://assets.hcch.net/docs/a8fe9f19-23e6-40c2-855e-388e112bf1f5.pdf

Seymore, M. L. (2019). Adopting civil damages: wrongful family separation in adoption. *Washington & Lee Law Review, 77*, 895–962. https://scholarship.law.tamu.edu/facscholar/1309

Sheridan, M. A., Fox, N. A., Zeanah, C. H., McLaughlin, K. A., & Nelson, C. A. (2012). Variation in neural development as a result of exposure to institutionalization early in childhood. *Proceedings of the National Academy of Sciences, 109*(32), 12927–12932.

Sheridan, M. A., & McLaughlin, K. A. (2016). Neurobiological models of the impact of adversity on education. *Current Opinion in Behavioral Sciences, 10*, 108–113.

Siegel, D. H., & Smith, S. L. (2012). *Openness in adoption: From secrecy and stigma to knowledge and connections.* Donaldson Adoption Institute. http://adoptioninstitute.org/publications/2012_03_OpennessInAdoption.pdf

Singley, C. J. (2018). Adoption: Cultures of Ambivalence Past, Present—and Future?. *Adoption & Culture, 6*(1), 50–73.

Smith K. E., Pollak S. D. (2021). Rethinking concepts and categories for understanding the neurodevelopmental effects of childhood adversity. *Perspectives on Psychological Science, 16*(1), 67–93.

Sonuga-Barke, E. J. S., Kennedy, M., Kumsta, R., Knights, N., Golm, D., Rutter, M., Maughan, B., Schlotz, W., & Kreppner, J. (2017). Child-to-adult neurodevelopmental and mental health trajectories after early life deprivation: The young adult follow-up of the longitudinal English and Romanian Adoptees study. *Lancet, 389*, 1539–1548.

Steele, M., Hodges, J., Kanuik, J., Steele, H., Hillman, S., & Asquit, K. (2008). Forecasting outcomes in previously maltreated children: The use of the AAI in a longitudinal adoption study. In H. Steele & M. Steele (Eds.), *Clinical applications of the Adult Attachment Interview* (pp. 427–451). Guildford Press.

Sylvestre, A., Bussières, È.-L., & Bouchard, C. (2016). Language problems among abused and neglected children: A meta-analytic review. *Child Maltreatment, 21*(1), 47–58.

Tottenham, N. (2020). Early adversity and the neotenous human brain. *Biological Psychiatry, 87*(4), 350–358.

Trenka, J. J., Oparah, J. C., & Shin, S. Y. (Eds.). (2006). *Outsiders within: Writing on transracial adoption*. South End Press.

van den Dries, L., Juffer, F., van IJzendoorn, M. H., & Bakermans-Kranenburg, M. J. (2009). Fostering security? A meta-analysis of attachment in adopted children. *Children and Youth Services Review*, *31*(3), 410–421.

van IJzendoorn, M. H., Bakermans-Kranenburg, M. J., Duschinsky, R., Fox, N. A., Goldman, P. S., Gunnar, M. R., Johnson, D. E., Nelson, C. A., Reijman, S., Skinner, G. C. M., Zeanah, C. H., & Sonuga-Barke, E. J. S. (2020). Institutionalisation and deinstitutionalisation of children 1: A systematic and integrative review of evidence regarding effects on development. *Lancet Psychiatry*, *7*(8), 703–720.

van IJzendoorn, M., & Juffer, F. (2005). Adoption is a successful natural intervention enhancing children's IQ and school performance. *Current Directions in Psychological Science*, *14*(6), 326–330.

van IJzendoorn, M. H., & Juffer, F. (2006). The Emanuel Miller Memorial Lecture 2006: Adoption as intervention. Meta-analytic evidence of massive catch-up and plasticity in physical, socio-emotional, and cognitive development. *Journal of Child Psychology and Psychiatry*, *47*(12), 1228–1245.

van IJzendoorn, M. H., Luijk, M. P. C. M., & Juffer, F. (2008). IQ of children growing up in children's homes: A meta-analysis on IQ delays in orphanages. *Merrill-Palmer Quarterly*, *54*(3), 341–366.

Vandivere, S., Malm, K., & Radel, L. (2009). *Adoption USA: A chartbook based on the 2007 National Survey of Adoptive Parents*. U.S. Department of Health and Human Services, Office of the Assistant Secretary for Planning and Evaluation. https://aspe.hhs.gov/system/files/pdf/75911/index.pdf

Volkman, T. S. (Ed.). (2005). *Cultures of transnational adoption*. Duke University Press.

Von Korff, L., & Grotevant, H. D. (2011). Contact in adoption and adoptive identity formation: The mediating role of family conversation. *Journal of Family Psychology*, *25*(3), 393–401.

Von Korff, L., Grotevant, H. D., & McRoy, R. G. (2006). Openness arrangements and psychological adjustment in adolescent adoptees. *Journal of Family Psychology*, *20*(3), 531–534.

Wade, M., Zeanah, C. H., Fox, N. A., & Nelson, C. A. (2020). Global deficits in executive functioning are transdiagnostic mediators between severe childhood neglect and psychopathology in adolescence. *Psychological Medicine*, *50*(10), 1687–1694.

Ward, H., Moggach, L., Tregeagle, S., & Trivedi, H. (2021) *Outcomes of open adoption from care: An Australian contribution to an international debate*. Palgrave Macmillan.

Whitesel, A., & Howard, J. A. (2013). *Untangling the web II: A research-based roadmap for reform*. Donaldson Adoption Institute. https://www.adoptioninstitute.org/wp-content/uploads/2013/12/2013_12_UntanglingtheWeb2.pdf

Wright, A. C. (2018, March). *Permanency reforms in NSW child protection* [Presentation]. SCWK4003 – Violence Against Women and Children, Sydney, Australia.

Yarger, H. A., Lind, T., Raby, K. L., Zajac, L., Wallin, A., & Dozie, M. (2022). Intervening with Attachment and Biobehavioral Catch-Up to reduce behavior problems among children adopted internationally: Evidence from a randomized controlled trial. *Child Maltreatment*, *27*(3), 478–489.

Young-Southward, G., Eaton, C., O'Connor, R., & Minnis, H. (2020). Investigating the causal relationship between maltreatment and cognition in children: A systematic review. *Child Abuse & Neglect*, *107*, 104603.

Zeanah, C. H., & Gleason, M. M. (2015). Attachment disorders in early childhood—Clinical presentation, causes, correlates, and treatment. *Journal of Child Psychology and Psychiatry*, *56*(3), 207–222.

Zelazo, P. D. (2020). Executive function and psychopathology: Neurodevelopmental perspective. *Annual Review of Clinical Psychology, 16*, 431–454.

CHAPTER 10

The Promise and Problems of Policy-Minded Developmental Research: Recognizing Our Implicit Value Judgments and the Limits of Our Research

Thomas D. Lyon and Michael E. Lamb

Abstract
Children come into contact with the legal system for myriad reasons, including as suspected victims of maltreatment, in divorce cases when custody is at issue, as unaccompanied minors in immigration hearings, or as suspected offenders of crime. Considerable scientific research has been devoted to identifying how this involvement may adversely affect children and how the system might be altered to reduce those effects. In order to maximize the value of this research, it is imperative that scientists recognize both the value judgments that sometimes underlie their work and how their work's focus on outcomes often clashes with a legal focus on rights. This recognition, along with a clear articulation of the limitations of the direct policy implications of the work, will lead to stronger legal-oriented research with children. .

Key Words: children, child protection, immigration, juvenile court, dependency, maltreatment, adoption, divorce, criminal court, family court

The chapters in this section of the book document the diverse ways in which children can become entangled in the legal system and, in so doing, how different issues have risen to prominence in each of those domains. For purposes of this discussion, we can distinguish among chapters that highlight the distinct roles of infants and young children who are drawn into the legal system because they are victims of parental maltreatment (Stacks et al.; Huntington; Palacios et al.); chapters that focus on children old enough to serve as witnesses in legal proceedings, most often in criminal court (Slonecker et al.; Enriquez et al.); chapters that focus on children who are viewed as offenders against the law (Frick et al.; Brabeck et al.); and finally a chapter focusing on children whose parents' separation makes them unwitting pawns of judicial decisions in divorce custody disputes (Fabricius et al.).

In what follows, we discuss the issues that arise in each of these chapters, emphasizing several themes: (a) the importance of recognizing the value judgments that sometimes underlie research, (b) the ways in which researchers' focus on outcomes often clashes with a legal focus on rights, and (c) the need for researchers to acknowledge the limitations of their findings when making policy prescriptions. These themes are interrelated, because researchers are accustomed to thinking of their work as fact based rather than value laden but must confront values when they argue that their research has implications for public policy, particularly when they acknowledge uncertainty.

Early Maltreatment, and Parental Rights Versus Children's Welfare (Stacks et al., Huntington, Palacios et al.)

It is clear from the three chapters on abuse victims that maltreatment has serious and enduring adverse effects on children's developmental trajectories and outcomes. Over the last two or three decades, we have become increasingly aware (as detailed by Stacks et al.) of the many ways in which maltreatment can harm children, not only by way of visible wounds, but also by way of profound damage at the neural level, which can amplify and potentiate psychological injuries. Indeed, for some children, the damage begins in utero, attributable either to substances ingested by the mother or to circulating stress hormones triggered by domestic violence and other daily stresses. Such findings speak to the desirability of early intervention, including when it involves the removal of the child from the care of those whose care is deficient.

Most advantaged societies have developed legal procedures that allow public agencies to intervene in efforts to ameliorate or prevent the effects of child maltreatment. (Readers of the Stacks et al. and Huntington chapters could be forgiven for thinking that the problems have only developed and been addressed in the United States!) In the United States and other countries, attempts to protect children clash with legal principles that parents have the right to raise their children and that their autonomy and responsibility should be infringed upon as little as possible and only as a last resort. The urgency perceived by those who counsel prompt intervention thus contrasts with legal presumptions regarding the importance of the parents' roles and responsibilities, leading to what are seen as less drastic interventions, such as parent training and substance abuse counseling, that leave the children at home but are seldom adequately funded or widely enough available despite their potential (Huntington). Many of those children initially left at home are eventually removed from their parents' care, often, critics would argue, after suffering further harmful treatment at the hands of their parents because of the delayed action.

Attachment theory has clear relevance to analysis of the competing arguments: The theory underscores the importance to children's current and long-term well-being of remaining in the uninterrupted care of sensitively responsive parents (Forslund et al., 2022). This implies that children should be placed or left in the care of parents psychologically able to provide continuing care of high quality achieved either by strengthening the resources of the family of origin or by removing the child as early as possible for placement in the care of foster or adoptive parents.

Although those principles have been widely embraced by courts and child welfare authorities, children's experiences seldom match these recommendations. One key impediment to prompt intervention is the fact that the vast majority of removals from home occur in response to chronic neglect, rather than active forms of maltreatment, which might prompt greater revulsion and urgency on the part of the officials who must sanction any removal of children from their parents' care. The desire to give parents a chance, perhaps with the support of social services, typically means that removal from the parents is delayed longer than would be ideal from the perspective of attachment theory. In addition, agencies must routinely grapple with a shortage of qualified and skilled foster parents, most children are returned at least temporarily to the care of their parents, and even when that does not happen, children often spend time with several different foster families, leaving permanency a distant unrealized goal.

As Palacios et al. point out, by the time children have the opportunity for permanent placement in an adoptive family, many have been seriously damaged by extended experiences of abuse and repeated relationship disruption. Fortunately, there is solid evidence that many of those adverse effects can be reversed or ameliorated, with the magnitude of the reversal greater the earlier children are adopted; in reality, other than those who are removed from their parents' care at birth, the majority of adopted children are not placed early enough to benefit as much as they might (Palacios et al., 2019).

The difficulties encountered in early intervention illustrate the challenges in applying research findings to policymaking. First, one must attempt to balance outcomes with rights. Policy recommendations inherently involve implicit value judgments about the relative importance of parental rights and children's welfare (or, indeed, the relative importance of the parents' rights to raise children as they see fit and the children's rights to an abuse-free childhood). Researchers can measure outcomes but do not have any tools with which to assess when outcomes should or should not trump rights. As such, when they make policy prescriptions, they are likely to overlook or underestimate the importance of considerations that are difficult to measure but integral to legal policymaking.

Furthermore, it is not just parents' or children's rights that are at stake. An additional rights issue concerns racial inequalities in child protection (Huntington,; D. Roberts, 2022; Stacks et al.,). Even if racial disparities can be explained by differences in factors that reliably predict negative outcomes (an issue currently being debated), to the extent that those factors (e.g., extreme poverty, drug abuse) are themselves accentuated by racism, interventions arguably perpetuate racism. This is particularly so when neglect is preventable but society is unwilling to adequately fund prevention, leaving children and their families subject to coercive interventions that only occur after harmful effects are manifest.

Researchers cannot easily avoid these challenges by claiming that they are solely focused on improved outcomes. Even the most aggressive advocates of children's welfare are likely to stop short of policies that would entail radical denial of parental rights. Consider two examples. Few contemporary researchers would ever advocate sterilization as a means of preventing child maltreatment. No matter how many children one loses to child protection, one has the right to bear more children. As a result, foreseeable harms cannot be avoided. Similarly, it would be hard to find a researcher who would advocate that private parties should be able to forcibly adopt children on the grounds that they would provide better care than the biological parents. Without such interventions, however, many children fail to achieve their potential due to their parents' suboptimal care. Once researchers acknowledge that there should be limits to state intervention, they must confront their value judgments about what those limits should be, balancing their intuitions about rights with their knowledge about outcomes.

A second challenge faced by those applying research to policy concerns the imperfections of intervention in the real world. It is simple to argue that removal from a neglectful home promotes nurturance and positive attachment when placement is safe and permanent. But, as noted earlier, when placement is itself poorly monitored, placements are temporary, and parents usually regain custody, it is harder to claim that removal inevitably leads to attachment security and enhanced child well-being.

These problems may seem specific to child protection, but they raise more general issues with the application of research to practice. New intervention programs routinely appear superior to old programs, leading to regular and confusing changes in the policies being recommended. Furthermore, many new programs are initially tested using simple designs that fail to elucidate methodological limitations. Typically, a group of enthusiastic experts work with a similarly motivated group of volunteers who obtain positive outcomes. Regression to the mean guarantees that with a simple pre–post design, the worse off improve. Dropouts accentuate the selection effect: Only the enthusiastic enroll, and only the most enthusiastic stay enrolled, leading to an exaggerated sense of effectiveness. Brief follow-up assessments make it impossible to determine whether those apparent effects will be enduring or only temporary.

With promising results in hand, however, the programs are promoted and offered to a larger and more diverse group of participants. New workers, many more familiar with the "old" programs, are told they must do something new, and program participation is made mandatory. To the extent that expertise is required for delivering the new intervention or enthusiasm is necessary for benefiting from it, average outcomes decline. Expansion makes it difficult to monitor adherence or to modify implementation to account for local differences in special needs. With larger numbers of participants and greater funding, researchers are able to perform more sophisticated assessments of program efficacy. These assessments control for methodological flaws in smaller scale studies that often exaggerate positive effects. It soon becomes clear that the advantages associated with the new approach to intervention have been overestimated, and the cycle continues (Al-Ubaydli et al., 2021).

Child Witnesses, and False Allegations Versus False Denials (Slonecker et al., Enriquez et al.)

The legal interventions discussed in the first trio of chapters (Stacks et al., Huntington, and Palacios et al.) all involve what are variously called family or dependency courts, where the child's best interests are considered paramount, decisions can be made applying a "preponderance of the evidence" or "clear and convincing" standards of proof, and the child's testimony is only infrequently required. In contrast, when child maltreatment leads to criminal charges, the allegations must be proven beyond a reasonable doubt, and children are much more likely to be called to testify. These children are at the center of the chapters by Slonecker et al. and Enriquez et al. Since several widely publicized multivictim cases in the 1980s and 1990s, a large number of studies have focused on factors affecting the quality and reliability of children's testimony, which is often critical to successful prosecution for those cases taken to court.

Some of the research reviewed by Slonecker et al. focused on children's suggestibility and other factors that diminish their reliability; other studies, including our own, have sought to show how limitations and potential weaknesses can be overcome by employing developmentally appropriate interviewing practices that elicit testimony or information of higher quality (Lamb et al., 2018; Lyon et al., 2019) and are associated with higher rates of successful prosecution (Pipe et al., 2013). The suggestibility research has spurred the development of demonstrably more effective investigative interviewing practices in many countries, including the United States.

Slonecker and colleagues do an admirable job examining individual differences in memory performance and suggestibility (e.g., stress, attachment, intelligence). Theoretically, individual difference research is important, in part because it can help elucidate mechanisms underlying development. From an applied perspective, however, its relevance for legal proceedings is limited. It is difficult to move from studies identifying individual differences to measures capable of distinguishing between accurate and inaccurate witnesses. Even were this possible, those measures would be viewed with skepticism in the U.S. legal system, where assessments of the likelihood that particular witnesses should be believed are strongly disfavored, on the grounds that this is a jury function (Meixner, 2012). In some other countries, individualized assessment of witnesses is permissible, but the focus has been on the quality of the statements rather than characteristics of the individual (see, e.g., the enormous literature on Criteria-Based Content Analysis Oberlader et al., 2021). At any rate, Slonecker and colleagues argued that the results are mixed or that the statistical associations are complicated, such that simple assertions—for example, that stress improves/impairs memory—are impossible.

There is one individual difference that courts universally care a lot about: age. Age is easy to measure and has long had legal significance. It is also a factor familiar to developmentalists. Ceci and Bruck's (1993) classic review of 100 years of research on suggestibility emphasized the large and consistent age effects across studies. Through their review and a series of highly influential demonstrations of preschool children's suggestibility (see, e.g., Ceci et al., 1994), they helped to explain how bizarre allegations of ritualistic sexual abuse could emerge through persistent suggestive questioning of large numbers of young children. At the same time, research on basic development has demonstrated profound changes in young children's ability to monitor the sources of their knowledge and distinguish between what they believe and what they remember (K. P. Roberts & Blades, 2000).

It is a truism that if younger children are much more suggestible than older children, then older children are much less suggestible than younger children. This should be encouraging to legal practitioners, who recognize that preschool children only rarely testify in court (Evans & Lyon, 2012). It should also be the focus of researchers when reviewing research: The age range should always be noted, particularly when studies focus exclusively on preschool children. Perhaps because age differences seem obvious, Slonecker and colleagues are quick to point to research finding reverse age trends. However, the context in which these effects occur (false recognition of strong associates of words on to-be-remembered lists) and the way in which false memories are calculated (by excluding response biases due to guessing; Brainerd et al., 2006) prove the point that in the most legally relevant contexts, older children are less susceptible to suggestion than younger children.

When it comes to deliberate misrepresentation, older children are clearly much more capable than young children, and this has implications for the other side of the allegation coin: false denials of abuse. Experimental work has demonstrated that, whereas the youngest children have difficulty in keeping transgressions a secret, at least when directly confronted, children in their early grade school years and older are both adept at withholding information and denying wrongdoing (Williams et al., 2020). Social factors are also of obvious importance, including parents' influences on children's motivations to conceal wrongdoing, which only wanes as children mature into adolescence. Parents can relatively easily induce secrecy and even recantation (Gordon et al., 2014; Malloy & Mugno, 2016).

Curiously, researchers discussing false denials of abuse largely ignore experimental work helping us to identify basic mechanisms that underlie children's performance in real-world contexts. External validity is always an important concern, and disclosure of abuse is clearly more serious than the transgressions examined in deception research or the false reports created in suggestibility research, but the experimental findings can and should be considered alongside findings obtained in field studies, especially because observational research on disclosure has unique methodological challenges. Researchers have argued that false denials of abuse are uncommon because most children recruited from forensic samples disclose abuse and the rates of disclosure are higher in studies in which the abuse was substantiated. But just as selection effects easily undermine intervention research, they also undermine attempts to understand abuse disclosure.

The fact that most children in studies of children questioned about sexual abuse disclose abuse says more about how abuse is suspected than it says about sexually abused children's willingness to disclose: Most children are questioned about sexual abuse because they disclosed. The fact that disclosure rates are higher among substantiated cases says more about the substantiation of abuse than it says about sexually abused children's willingness to disclose: Substantiation is heavily dependent on disclosure (Lyon et al., 2020). When there is external evidence of abuse, which both reduces the likelihood of false allegations and makes detection and substantiation of abuse without disclosure more likely, large percentages of children deny abuse (especially by family members) when questioned, even when interviewers use the supportive techniques built into the Revised National Institute of Child Health and Human Development (NICHD) Protocol (Hershkowitz et al., 2014; Hershkowitz & Lamb, 2020).

High rates of nondisclosure do not justify suggestive questioning, because suggestive questioning can elicit false reports. Rather, such rates lead to the conclusion that initial denials and recantations of abuse have limited probative value in assessing the truthfulness of abuse disclosures. Along with delayed disclosure (London et al., 2008), these are components of the misleadingly named "child sexual abuse accommodation syndrome" that receive some empirical support (Hershkowitz et al., 2014; Lyon et al., 2020; Malloy et al., 2007). Moreover, denials can justify additional interviewing when there are strong reasons to suspect abuse and the repeated interviews avoid suggestion (Blasbalg et al., 2021; Hershkowitz et al., 2021).

What makes researchers' recommendations for interviewing practice complicated by value judgments is that some types of questioning increase true reports but also increase false reports (e.g., body diagrams: Dickinson & Poole, 2017). This should come as no surprise; the trade-offs between sensitivity and specificity have long been understood by researchers studying the differences between recognition and recall memory. Generally speaking, recognition has greater sensitivity than recall but lower specificity, thus increasing true positives but also increasing false positives (Ceci & Bruck, 1993). Whether questioning approaches that increase both true and false disclosures are ever justified requires a balancing of costs and benefits. Some researchers tend to worry about false allegations, and other researchers tend to worry about false denials. Both can point to the devastating consequences of mistakes for children and their families.

In order to avoid injecting their value judgments into their recommendations, researchers strive to identify interviewing methods that increase both sensitivity and specificity. The sensitivity of recall questions can be maximized through narrative practice (Brown et al., 2013), and the specificity of recognition questions can be maximized by pairing affirmative responses with requests for elaboration (Stolzenberg et al., 2017). Moreover, because younger children routinely provide unelaborated responses to recognition questions, and often exhibit a "no" bias, recognition questions can actually reduce sensitivity compared to carefully phrased "wh-" questions eliciting elaboration of children's prior responses (Henderson et al., 2023). Interviewing innovations can thus help us avoid value trade-offs.

Enriquez et al. focus not on the quality or accuracy of testimony but on the stress and difficulties occasioned when children must testify, often after long delays, in the face of considerable anxiety and competing pressures from family members while being challenged about their accuracy and honesty. Courts in the United States may learn from the reforms that have been introduced in the United Kingdom (and in particular in England and Wales) over the last 30 years (Spencer & Lamb, 2012).[1] For decades, video-recorded investigative interviews by specialist interviewers have been shown in court as the central part of the child's "evidence in chief." After the recording is shown, the child can be asked further questions by the prosecution and must be made available for cross-examination by counsel for the defendant. To

---

[1] Scotland has a legal system and tradition that are distinct from those in England and Wales. As a result, the reforms discussed here have proceeded on different time scales and with some different terminology in England and Wales, as opposed to Scotland. Northern Ireland has its own system.

minimize memory decay during the long delays that typify criminal prosecutions, and to allow victims to begin therapeutic interventions sooner than if they had to await the conclusion of criminal proceedings, U.K. courts recently began video-recording cross-examinations so that all of the child victim's testimony could be completed earlier than would otherwise be the case. Perhaps most importantly, judges are now required to hold Ground Rules Hearings (GRHs) with counsel before children are questioned in courtroom proceedings and all counsel are advised to have attended training focused on permissible questioning strategies. In the GRHs, agreement is reached about the ways in which questions can be formulated and asked, with judges encouraged to intervene if counsel violates those rules. The guidance on how to ask questions in court is summarized in the *20 Principles of Questioning* (2022; Slonecker et al. appear to misunderstand this as guidance for forensic interviewers). Counsel or judges can also request the involvement of intermediaries to facilitate the formulation of questions appropriate to the needs of vulnerable witnesses.

To date, there has been no systematic research on the extent to which these reforms have actually made involvement in court proceedings less stressful for children, though there is evidence that the developmental appropriateness of lawyers' questions has improved (e.g., Henderson, Andrews, & Lamb, 2019). Somewhat surprisingly (like many observers, we expected that video-recorded testimony would be less effective than "live" testimony), there is no evidence that rates of conviction have changed with the increasing use of recorded testimony and there have been no successful appeals against conviction on the grounds that defendants were denied fair trials because of the various reforms described earlier. Enriquez et al. make a strong case for a variety of reforms to U.S. practices and procedures to achieve the same kinds of benefits for young victim witnesses.

The enthusiastic response to legal reforms in the United Kingdom contrasts with the tepid response to more modest reforms in the United States, such as the use of remote testimony (via closed-circuit television), which has received some judicial support but appears to be rare in practice (Cross & Whitcomb, 2017; Goodman et al., 1999). In part this is due to prosecutorial worries about the potentially reduced impact of remote testimony, limited court resources, and the legal prerequisites imposed on the practice by the U.S. Supreme Court in *Maryland v. Craig* (1990), which require showing that without the special measures, the child witness would suffer such extreme emotional distress from testifying in the courtroom that she would be unable to communicate.

In part, however, the United States' modest reforms reflect the tension noted previously between a focus on outcomes and a focus on rights. The U.S. Supreme Court has moved toward an "originalist" approach to interpreting constitutional rights and has declared that criminal defendants' rights to confront their accuser require live in-person testimony because that was standard practice in England at the time the Bill of Rights was ratified (*Crawford v. Washington*, 2004). Although *Crawford* did not consider and therefore did not overrule *Craig*, it overruled the precedent upon which *Craig* was founded, a precedent that had adopted what the court now dismissively calls a "functionalist" approach to interpreting confrontation rights. That approach reasoned that since the purpose of confrontation is to increase the accuracy of evidence, procedures that preserve accuracy but dispense with live confrontation are permissible.

Craig's approach to confrontation rights is thus at odds with the Supreme Court's originalist approach to interpreting the Constitution. Researchers may reasonably complain that outcomes are more important than the preservation of archaic procedures, but if they wish to influence legal decision making, they must grapple with the value-based belief that lay perceptions of fairness are as important as scientific judgments about the accuracy of outcomes.

One strategy for adapting to the Supreme Court's value judgments about fair procedures is to recognize that, just as factual statements often contain hidden value judgments, value judgments often contain factual assumptions, and those assumptions are subject to empirical test. This is illustrated by the U.S. Supreme Court's cases assessing children's complaints of abuse subsequent to *Crawford*. The court recognized that the statements of children can be afforded special treatment under the Constitution (*Ohio v. Clark*, 2015). Consistent with its originalist approach, the court based its reasoning in large part on historical evidence that at the time the Bill of Rights was ratified, when children were too young to testify, their hearsay was freely admitted (citing Lyon & LaMagna, 2007). However, there was still room for social scientists to exert some influence. In *Crawford*, the court had held that the kind of hearsay that would violate defendants' confrontation rights were statements intended to substitute for trial testimony. In order to square its reasoning about history with its reasoning about the type of hearsay that should be excluded, the court in *Clark* cited psychological research that young children do not allege abuse with the expectation that their statements will be used in court (Lawrence et al., 2015).

Unfortunately, the U.S. Supreme Court's approach makes it difficult to argue for the constitutionality of video-recorded testimony. The purpose of video-recorded testimony is to substitute for trial testimony, and this is precisely what the Supreme Court has held offends the Constitution. Ironically, other elements of good investigative practice also increase the likelihood that the child's statements will be held inadmissible without the child's in-court testimony, including recording of interviews, structured questioning, and eliciting a promise to tell the truth. This is because as the interviews become more formal, lower courts are more likely to view them as substitutes for testimony (Lyon & Dente, 2012).

However, other reforms are possible. With slight modifications, U.S. courts could adopt the intermediate solution that has long been the practice in the United Kingdom, in which a videotaped interview is played at trial but supplemented with additional questions from the prosecution and cross-examination by the defense. The prosecution would lead with preliminary questioning of the child and then lay the foundation for admission of a pretrial interview (under standard hearsay exceptions, such as that for recorded recollections). The interview would then be played in court, and additional live examination would follow. The defendants' rights to confrontation would not be violated because the defendant would have the opportunity to question the child in court.

With respect to the questions asked in court, the U.S. Supreme Court has recognized that limits can be placed on courtroom questioning when the purpose is to ensure that the testimony is relevant and not misleading (*Holmes v. South Carolina*, 2006). The states can prohibit developmentally inappropriate questioning, an approach that has already received some statutory support (Cal. Evid. Code Section 765(b), 2022). Prosecutors could file pretrial motions outlining the types of questions that should be restricted on cross-examination.

Although overtly difficult questioning may be regulated, the remaining challenge is that courtroom practitioners are unlikely to recognize many forms of miscommunication. Indeed, research on miscommunications in court has often found that prosecutors are just as likely as defense attorneys to confuse children (Evans et al., 2017), and it is difficult to train lay adults to identify ambiguities (Wylie et al., 2021). Ultimately, the courts may need to move to more radical solutions, such as a ban on all yes/no questions and forced-choice questions without special leave from the court.

Child Offenders, and Punishment Versus Leniency (Frick et al., Brabeck et al.)

In their chapters, Frick et al. and Brabeck et al. shift focus to children whose involvement in the legal system hinges on their being viewed as offenders or law breakers. Frick et al. discuss youths who become engaged in law breaking as juveniles. Much of the literature on juvenile offenders has noted the distinction between those whose delinquency begins early and those whose entry into the system is delayed. There is considerable evidence that the early offenders are more likely to display callous–unemotional (CU) traits in childhood, lack empathy, engage in more violence, and continue criminal activities into adulthood, whereas the late offenders tend to have shorter and less serious criminal careers and the potential to become productive law-abiding adults. Preventive intervention is most likely to be effective, but it is unclear how this could be done legally and effectively, save perhaps by offering better universal mental health services to children so that those with worrisome traits (CU traits, emotional reactivity) can be identified early and offered interventions.

Frick and colleagues argue that different types of juvenile offenders should be offered tailored interventions. Adolescent-onset offenders are most likely showing signs of adolescent rebelliousness, which is least likely to lead to adult criminality, except through the criminogenic effects of harsh legal intervention. They are therefore best suited for diversion. Offenders whose behavioral problems emerged in childhood should be separated into two groups: those with CU traits and those with difficulties in regulating their emotions. Offenders with CU traits tend to be the most violent, and evidence for successful treatment is spotty (Wilkinson et al., 2016). Frick and colleagues highlight one successful intervention reducing CU traits, but as they warn, the study has questionable implications for intervention with adolescent offenders: The children were only 3–6 years old (Kimonis et al., 2019).

As long as the juvenile justice system emphasizes rehabilitation over punishment, research identifying typologies of adolescent offending can have the desired effects, counseling leniency with both adolescent-onset offenders and, perhaps in light of more recent findings, childhood-onset offenders whose behavioral problems stem from emotional dysregulation. Indeed, within the last 20 years, researchers studying adolescent neurological development have had some luck in convincing the Supreme Court that differences between adolescents and adults justify differential treatment, leading to the abolition of capital punishment for crimes committed by juveniles (*Roper v. Simmons*, 2005), mandatory life sentences without the possibility of parole (LWOP) (*Montgomery v. Louisiana*, 2016), and LWOP sentences for crimes short of murder (*Graham v. Florida*, 2010). A number of states have banned LWOP for juveniles altogether, and many hoped that the Supreme Court might eventually do so, as well as extend leniency upwards to young adults, given findings that neurological development continues into the 20s (Jouet, 2021).

The problem is that longer term trends reflect a shift toward more punitive reactions to adolescent offenders, including increasing numbers of transfers of youths to adult court and declines in the number of resources made available to provide the mental health and educational facilities that offending youths desperately need. Moreover, the changing composition of the Supreme Court within the last few years has already led to signs of retreat from leniency (see *Jones v. Mississippi*, 2021, an opinion by Justice Kavanaugh that the dissent asserted "guts" *Montgomery*).

In states preserving the LWOP option, courts need little coaxing to find the necessary evidence of "permanent incorrigibility" (*Montgomery v. Louisiana*, 2016, p. 209; Duncan, 2022). In this climate, identification of childhood-onset CU offenders may make matters worse. The

Supreme Court's lenience toward adolescent offenders was based on adolescents' impulsiveness, susceptibility to peer influence, and hope for rehabilitation (Steinberg, 2017). But as Frick and colleagues note, adolescent offenders with CU traits exhibit more planning, are less susceptible to peer influence, and are more likely to continue offending into their adulthood.

Brabeck et al. describe in some detail a rather different kind of "law-breaking" youth—those (mostly between 13 and 17 years of age) who have entered the country as unaccompanied minors. Many of them have escaped extreme poverty and have had long and traumatic journeys prior to entering the country, yet in the short run they are placed in detention facilities with inadequate health care and no educational resources. Many are then released to parents or relatives pending resolution of their petitions, but of course their undocumented status means that they are ineligible for most of the services they need. They are also not entitled to legal representation and must often represent themselves in proceedings held in a language they do not understand. Not surprisingly, the majority lose their cases and are deported. For many, though, the cycle has only begun, as they often make additional efforts to reenter the country as soon as they can.

Brabeck and colleagues present a compelling argument for better treatment of unaccompanied minors. It is impossible to argue that they would not benefit from legal representation, given the legal complexities of seeking asylum and other forms of relief; the barriers to understanding due to language, immaturity, and trauma; and the frequency with which they have valid claims for relief because of mistreatment in their home countries. Our continued neglect of their needs bespeaks a value judgment that their claims are secondary to society's interest in limiting immigration. This trade-off is perhaps best illustrated by the fact that, regardless of the number of trafficking victims in the United States, and regardless of their cooperation with law enforcement in prosecuting their traffickers, no more than 5,000 can obtain relief from deportation in any year. This suggests that researchers arguing for reforms should also confront assumptions about the costs of increased immigration to society and marshal empirical evidence documenting the benefits of liberalized immigration policies.

Joint Custody and Parents' Rights in a Different Context (Fabricius)
The final and perhaps numerically largest group of children and youth in the legal system are those whose parents separate, creating a need for formal assignment of responsibility for the children's future care. Although most separating parents sooner or later agree between themselves with whom the children will live, courts are frequently asked to make decisions regarding the amounts of child support owed by nonresident parents and in some cases must decide how responsibility for the children's day-to-day care should be divided. Fabricius focuses on the latter issues, reviewing evidence showing that, on average, children do better psychologically when they spend meaningful amounts of time with both of their parents. Informed by that evidence, Fabricius has promoted a rebuttable presumption in Arizona law that children of divorcing parents should spend equal amounts of time with both of their parents, drawing on the same principles of attachment theory that have been so difficult to honor in the child welfare decision making discussed in the chapters by Stacks et al., Huntington, and Palacios et al.

Such reforms of course contrast with the application of the approximation rule in many states, whereby future childcare responsibilities are divided roughly as they were before the separation. To date, there are not sufficient data to indicate whether one or the other approach offers superior outcomes (although on average children do better psychologically when they have meaningful postseparation relationships with both parents: Lamb, 2021), but the continuing appeal of these competing legal rules underscores the role of ideology and values when making decisions about children and the law.

Conclusion

Policy-minded research in developmental psychology is satisfying because of the real improvements that it can bring to the lives of youth and their families. At the same time, precisely because research can have profound effects on people's lives, applied researchers should assess the value judgments underlying their work, recognize that competing rights are often at stake in policy debates, and acknowledge the limitations of their findings. Doing so will improve the integrity and quality of applied research.

References

20 Principles of questioning. (2022). https://www.icca.ac.uk › wp-content › uploads › 2022 › 03 › 20-Principles-of-Questioning.

Al-Ubaydli, O., Lee, M. S., List, J. A., Mackevicius, C. L., & Suskind, D. (2021). How can experiments play a greater role in public policy? Twelve proposals from an economic model of scaling. *Behavioural Public Policy*, 5(1), 2–49.

Blasbalg., U, Hershkowitz, I., Lamb, M. E., & Karni-Visel, Y. (2021). Adherence to the Revised NICHD Protocol recommendations for conducting repeated supportive interviews is associated with the likelihood that children will allege abuse. *Psychology, Public Policy, and Law*, 27, 209–220.

Brainerd, C. J., Forrest, T. J., Karibian, D., & Reyna, V. F. (2006). Development of the false-memory illusion. *Developmental Psychology*, 42(5), 962–979.

Brown, D. A., Lamb, M. E., Lewis, C., Pipe, M. E., Orbach, Y., & Wolfman, M. (2013). The NICHD investigative interview protocol: An analogue study. *Journal of Experimental Psychology: Applied*, 19(4), 367–382.

Ceci, S. J., & Bruck, M. (1993). Suggestibility of the child witness: A historical review and synthesis. *Psychological Bulletin*, 113(3), 403–439.

Ceci, S. J., Huffman, M. L. C., Smith, E., & Loftus, E. F. (1994). Repeatedly thinking about a non-event: Source misattributions among preschoolers. *Consciousness and Cognition*, 3(3–4), 388–407.

Crawford v. Washington, 541 U.S. 36 (2004).

Cross, T. P., & Whitcomb, D. (2017). The practice of prosecuting child maltreatment: Results of an online survey of prosecutors. *Child Abuse & Neglect*, 69, 20–28.

Dickinson, J. J., & Poole, D. A. (2017). The influence of disclosure history and body diagrams on children's reports of inappropriate touching: Evidence from a new analog paradigm. *Law and Human Behavior*, 41(1), 1–12.

Duncan, H. (2022). Youth always matters: Replacing Eighth Amendment pseudoscience with an age-based ban on juvenile life without parole. *Yale Law Journal*, 131(6), 1936–2019.

Evans, A. D., & Lyon, T. D. (2012). Assessing children's competency to take the oath in court: The influence of question type on children's accuracy. *Law & Human Behavior*, 36, 195–205.

Evans, A. D., Stolzenberg, S. N., & Lyon, T. D. (2017). Pragmatic failure and referential ambiguity when attorneys ask child witnesses "Do you know/remember" questions. *Psychology, Public Policy, & Law*, 23, 191–199.

Forslund, T., Granqvist, P., van IJzendoorn, M. H., Sagi-Schwartz, A., Glaser, D., Steele, M., Hammarlund, M., Schuengel, C., Bakermans-Kranenburg, M. J., Steele, H., Shaver, P. R., Lux, U., Simmonds, J., Jacobvitz, D., Groh, A. M., Bernard, K., Cyr, C., Hazen, N. L., Foster, S . . . Duschinsky, R. (2022). Attachment goes to court: Child protection and custody issues. *Attachment and Human Development*, 24, 1–52.

Goodman, G. S., Quas, J. A., Bulkley, J., & Shapiro, C. (1999). Innovations for child witnesses: A national survey. *Psychology, Public Policy, and Law*, 5(2), 255–281.

Gordon, H. M., Lyon, T. D., & Lee, K. (2014) Social and cognitive factors associated with children's secret-keeping for a parent. *Child Development*, 85, 2374–2388.

Graham v. Florida, 560 U.S. 48 (2010).

Henderson, H. M., Andrews, S. J., & Lamb, M. E. (2019). Examining children in English High Courts with and without implementation of reforms authorized in Section 28 of the Youth Justice and Criminal Evidence Act. *Applied Cognitive Psychology*, 33, 252–264.

Henderson, H. M., Lamb, M. E., & Rafferty, A. F. (2019). The discussion of ground rules issues in pretrial preparation for vulnerable witnesses in English Crown Courts. *Criminal Law Review*, 7, 599–610.

Henderson, H. M., Lundon, G. M., & Lyon, T. D. (2023). Suppositional wh- questions about perceptions, conversations, and actions are more productive than paired yes-no questions when questioning maltreated children. *Child Maltreatment*, 28, 55–65.

Hershkowitz, I., & Lamb, M. E. (2020). Allegation rates and credibility assessment in forensic interviews of alleged child abuse victims: Comparing the Revised and Standard NICHD Protocols. *Psychology, Public Policy, and Law, 26*, 176–184.

Hershkowitz, I., Lamb, M. E., Blasbalg, U., & Karni-Visel, Y. (2021). The dynamics of two-session interviews with suspected victims of abuse who are reluctant to make allegations. *Development and Psychopathology, 33*, 739–747.

Hershkowitz, I., Lamb, M. E., & Katz, C. (2014). Allegation rates in forensic child abuse investigations: Comparing the revised and standard NICHD protocols. *Psychology, Public Policy, & Law, 20*, 336–344.

Holmes v. South Carolina, 547 U.S. 319 (2006).

Jones v. Mississippi, 141 S.Ct. 1307 (2021).

Jouet, M. (2021). Juveniles are not so different: The punishment of juveniles and adults at the crossroads. *Federal Sentencing Reporter, 33*, 278–284.

Kimonis, E. R., Fleming, G., Briggs, N., Brouwer-French, L., Frick, P. J., Hawes, D. J., . . . Dadds, M. (2019). Parent-Child Interaction Therapy adapted for preschoolers with callous-unemotional traits: An open trial pilot study. *Journal of Clinical Child & Adolescent Psychology, 48*(Suppl 1), S347–S361.

Lamb, M. E. (2021). An attachment theory approach to parental separation and child custody. In R. A. Thompson, J. A. Simpson, & L. Berlin (Eds.), *Attachment: The fundamental questions* (pp. 357–364). Guilford Press.

Lamb, M. E., Brown, D. A., Hershkowitz, I., Orbach, Y., & Esplin, P. W. (2018). *Tell me what happened* (2nd ed.). Wiley.

Lawrence, J. A., Levin, D. B., Brady, K. L., Jhai, M., & Lyon, T. D. (2015). Ohio v. Clark: Brief of Amicus Curiae American Professional Society on the Abuse of Children in Support of Petitioner. *Psychology, Public Policy, and Law, 21*(4), 365–373.

London, K., Bruck, M., Wright, D. B., & Ceci, S. J. (2008). Review of the contemporary literature on how children report sexual abuse to others: Findings, methodological issues, and implications for forensic interviewers. *Memory, 16*, 29–47.

Lyon, T. D., & Dente, J. A. (2012). Child witnesses and the Confrontation Clause. *Journal of Criminal Law & Criminology, 102*, 1181–1232.

Lyon, T. D., & LaMagna, R. (2007). The history of children's hearsay: From Old Bailey to post-*Davis*. *Indiana Law Journal, 82*, 1029–1058.

Lyon, T.D., McWilliams, K., & Williams, S. (2019). Child witnesses. In N. Brewer & A. B. Douglass (Eds.), *Psychological science and the law* (pp. 157–181). New York: Guilford.

Lyon, T. D., Williams, S., & Stolzenberg, S. N. (2020). Understanding expert testimony on child sexual abuse denial after New Jersey v. J.L.G.: Ground truth, disclosure suspicion bias, and disclosure substantiation bias. *Behavioral Sciences & the Law, 38*, 630–647.

Malloy, L. C., Lyon, T. D., & Quas, J. A. (2007). Filial dependency and recantation of child sexual abuse allegations. *Journal of the American Academy of Child & Adolescent Psychiatry, 46*, 162–170.

Malloy, L. C., & Mugno, A. P. (2016). Children's recantation of adult wrongdoing: An experimental investigation. *Journal of Experimental Child Psychology, 145*, 11–21.

Maryland v. Craig, 497 U.S. 836 (1990).

Meixner, J. B. (2012). Liar, liar, jury's the trier? The future of neuroscience-based credibility assessment in the court. *Northwestern University Law Review, 106*(3), 1451–1488.

Montgomery v. Louisiana, 136 S.Ct. 718 (2016).

Oberlader, V. A., Quinten, L., Banse, R., Volbert, R., Schmidt, A. F., & Schönbrodt, F. D. (2021). Validity of content-based techniques for credibility assessment—How telling is an extended meta-analysis taking research bias into account? *Applied Cognitive Psychology, 35*(2), 393–410.

Ohio v. Clark, 576 U.S. 237 (2015).

Palacios, J., Adroher, S., Brodzinsky, D. M., Grotevant, H. D., Johnson, D. E., Juffer, F., Martinez-Mora, L., Muhamedrahimov, R. J., Selwyn, J., Simmonds, J., & Tarren-Sweeney, M. (2019). Adoption in the service of child protection: An international, interdisciplinary perspective. *Psychology, Public Policy, & Law, 25*(2), 57–72.

Roberts, D. (2022). *Torn apart: How the child welfare system destroys black families and how abolition can build a safer world*. Basic Books.

Roberts, K. P., & Blades, M. (Eds.). (2000). *Children's source monitoring*. Psychology Press.

Roper v. Simmons, 543 U.S. 551 (2005).

Spencer, J. R., & Lamb, M. E. (Eds.). (2012). *Children and cross-examination: Time to change the rules?* Hart Publishing.

Steinberg, L. (2017). Adolescent brain science and juvenile justice policymaking. *Psychology, Public Policy, and Law, 23*(4), 410–420.

Stolzenberg, S. N., McWilliams, K., & Lyon, T. D. (2017). The effects of the hypothetical putative confession and negatively-valenced yes/no questions on maltreated and non-maltreated children's disclosure of a minor transgression. *Child Maltreatment, 22*, 167–173.

Wilkinson, S., Waller, R., & Viding, E. (2016). Practitioner review: Involving young people with callous unemotional traits in treatment—does it work? A systematic review. *Journal of Child Psychology and Psychiatry, 57*(5), 552–565.

Williams, S., McWilliams, K., & Lyon, T.D. (2020). Children's concealment of a minor transgression: The role of age, maltreatment, and executive functioning. *Journal of Experimental Child Psychology, 191*, 104664.

Wylie, B. E., Gongola, J., Lyon, T. D., & Evans, A. D. (2021). The difficulty of teaching adults to recognize referential ambiguity in children's testimony: The influence of explicit instruction and sample questions. *Applied Cognitive Psychology, 35*, 1297–1307.

CHAPTER 11

Risky and Antisocial Behavior in Adolescence

Michelle E. Manasse and Cesar J. Rebellon

Abstract

This chapter provides an interdisciplinary review of research concerning risky and antisocial behavior during the adolescent years. In particular, it summarizes and integrates existing research concerning two fundamental issues. First, it describes the developmental factors that contribute to the general tendency for risky and antisocial behavior to increase during adolescence. Second, it describes potential sources of interpersonal variation in risky and antisocial behavior during this stage of the life course. For both issues, the chapter discusses research bearing on the ways in which biological factors, family dynamics, the peer group, and the broader community collectively influence risky and antisocial behavior, paying special attention to the ways in which these factors interact to amplify or suppress one another's influences.

Key Words: adolescence, adolescent development, age-crime curve, antisocial behavior, life course, lifespan development, risk taking

Adolescence is characterized by an increase in a variety of risk-taking behaviors, including substance use, which can impair judgment or endanger long-term health; unsafe sexual practices, which can result in disease or unwanted pregnancy; reckless driving, which can cause accidental injury or death; and various forms of delinquency, such as physical violence or theft, which can result in victim retaliation or juvenile justice processing (Curry & Youngblade, 2006; Willoughby et al., 2013). Research suggests not only that the prevalence of such behaviors increases during adolescence but also that individuals who engage in one type of risky behavior are disproportionately likely to engage in a wide range of others (Gottfredson & Hirschi, 1990; Hirschi & Gottfredson, 1994). Multiple types of risky behavior may therefore be conceptually related, each reflecting an underlying "pattern of decision making that favors the selection of courses of action with uncertain and possibly harmful consequences" (Ernst et al., 2006, p. 299).

Conventional wisdom has observed for hundreds of years that age is related to risky and antisocial behavior (Walsh, 2009a). Over the past several decades, however, researchers have generated a wealth of new knowledge concerning the complex ways in which biological and social mechanisms interact to account for the general adolescent tendency toward risky behavior and for interpersonal variation in risky behavior among adolescents of the same age. The present chapter provides an interdisciplinary overview of such research. The first section concerns the degree to which an increase in adolescent risk taking is consistent across time and place, the ways in which normal physiological development contributes to this consistency, and the ways in which genetic variation may interact with preadolescent social environments to generate interpersonal differences in trajectories of risky behavior. The second section concerns the ways in which family environments contribute to risky and antisocial behavior during adolescence, as well as the ways in which these environments may interact with physiological development to amplify or dampen individuals' relative involvement in risky behavior. The third section describes the ways in which peer relationships become increasingly important during adolescence, as well as the ways in which they may contribute to risky and antisocial behavior. Finally, the concluding section describes a variety of mechanisms through which community-level factors play a role in adolescent behavior.

Physiological Influences on Risky and Antisocial Behavior in Adolescence

The Adolescent Peak in Risky and Antisocial Behavior

Among the most stable patterns in the study of antisocial behavior is the relationship between antisocial behavior and age (Braithwaite, 1989; Farrington, 1986; Farrington et al., 2013; Hirschi & Gottfredson, 1983; Moffitt, 1993; Piquero et al., 2003; Sweeten et al., 2013). Across both official and self-report data, a consistent pattern emerges: antisocial behavior increases rapidly after the onset of puberty, peaks in late adolescence/early adulthood, and declines over time beginning in late adolescence/early adulthood. In fact, findings of an adolescent peak in antisocial behavior are so robust that in 1913 Charles Goring coined it a "law of nature" (in Gottfredson & Hirschi, 1990, p. 124) and, more recently, Hirschi and Gottfredson (1983) have argued that the relationship between age and antisocial behavior is invariant across all social and cultural conditions. Indeed, adolescents continue to consistently show the highest propensity to take risks among all age groups, regardless of cultural variation (Duell et al., 2018).

Although Hirschi and Gottfredson (1983) observe the lawlike nature of the adolescent peak in antisocial behavior, they acknowledge that it "cannot be accounted for by any variables or combination of variables currently available to criminology" (p. 554). While sociological explanations can account for the influence of social groups on behavior and, thus, variations across populations, such explanations inevitably beg the question of what differentiates the period of adolescence from other life stages to account for adolescents' increased likelihood of antisocial behavior across time and culture. A truly invariant relationship between adolescence and antisocial behavior can only be explained by something that is similarly constant across all societies and cultures, suggesting that the biological changes intrinsic to adolescent development may account for a significant proportion of adolescents' unique propensity for antisocial and risk-taking behaviors.

Physiological Contributors to the Adolescent Peak in Risky and Antisocial Behavior

Puberty marks the beginning of the developmental period of adolescence, during which the body experiences a cascade of physiological changes designed to prepare juveniles for the competitive demands of adulthood:

> Adolescents must bond and mate with their own generation and explore their place in the world. . . . [T]here is much to learn about being an adult, and adolescence is a time to experiment with a variety of social skills before having to put them into practice in earnest. (Walsh, 2009a, p. 157)

Although modern society often negatively equates adolescence to a period of rebellion against social norms, and even a tendency toward self-destruction, evolutionary theorists characterize the hormonal and neurological changes of adolescence as fundamental to the process of asserting independence from the home environment and gaining adaptive advantage within adult domains.

The biological changes of adolescence begin at the onset of puberty with the activation of the hypothalamic–pituitary–gonadal axis, stimulating the release of growth hormones during sleep (Walsh, 2009a). This sudden influx of hormones initiates reproductive development and results in observable physical changes for adolescents (e.g., growth and the development of secondary sexual characteristics), but it also elicits some of the behavioral changes that characterize adolescence. In particular, a surge in testosterone levels drives adolescents to seek out novel, stimulating experiences and increasingly prioritize the peer relationships that provide access to potential romantic and/or sexual connections (Felson & Haynie, 2002; Kanazawa, 2009); Steinberg et al., 2008; Walsh, 2009a). Higher levels of testosterone have been linked consistently to heightened sensation seeking (Zuckerman, 2007), perhaps because higher testosterone levels lessen the experience of fear (van Honk et al., 2005), and although both male and female adolescents experience an increase in testosterone, male levels far exceed that of females, rendering juvenile males particularly

susceptible to thrill-seeking and dominant/aggressive behaviors (Walsh, 2009a). It is also important to note, however, that while adolescence is characterized by a dramatic increase in hormones, testosterone levels also vary significantly across the life course and in response to environmental conditions (Booth et al., 2006; Mazur, 2005).

While adolescence is widely associated with raging hormones, the period of adolescent development also brings significant neurological changes. The balance of neurotransmitters—the chemical messengers that carry signals between neurons—shifts, such that adolescents begin to produce more of the excitatory transmitters, dopamine and glutamate, while production of the inhibitory transmitters, gamma-aminobutyric acid and serotonin, drops (Collins, 2004; Walker, 2002). The prefrontal cortex, responsible for executive control functions, also undergoes a period of substantial restructuring beginning in early adolescence and extending into early adulthood (Giedd, 2004; Sowell et al., 2004; Steinberg, 2005; Walsh, 2009a):

> Studies have pointed both to significant growth and significant change in multiple regions of the prefrontal cortex throughout the course of adolescence, especially with respect to processes of myelination and synaptic pruning (both of which increase the efficiency of information processing). These changes are believed to undergird improvements in various aspects of executive functioning, including long-term planning, metacognition, self-evaluation, self-regulation and the coordination of affect and cognition. (Steinberg, 2005, p. 70)

Research utilizing functional magnetic resonance imaging (fMRI) further shows that adolescents, when compared to children/adults, have a higher ratio of nucleus accumbens activity relative to activity in regions of the prefrontal cortex (Eshel et al., 2007; Galvan et al., 2006); this fluctuation further heightens reward-seeking behaviors and impulsivity among adolescents (Walsh, 2009a, 2019).

According to Steinberg's (2010) dual systems model of adolescent risk taking, this complex cascade of physiological changes renders adolescents particularly susceptible to risky behavior through effects on two interconnected systems: the "socioemotional system" and the "cognitive control system." First, adolescent development leads to a surge of chemical activity (i.e., hormones and neurotransmitters) within the limbic system, priming the socioemotional network to be more responsive to stimulation and short-term rewards. However, the development of the cognitive control system, a far more gradual process of synaptic pruning and myelination, tends to lag behind, limiting self-regulation and impulse control. "The temporal gap between the arousal of the socioemotional system, which is an early adolescent development, and the full maturation of the cognitive control system, which occurs later, creates a period of heightened vulnerability to risk-taking during middle adolescence" (Steinberg, 2010, p. 216). As a heightened socioemotional system interacts with an immature cognitive control system, "the developments of early adolescence may well create a situation in which one is starting an engine without yet having a skilled driver behind the wheel" (Steinberg, 2005, p. 70).

Variation in Trajectories of Risky and Antisocial Development
While antisocial behavior peaks in adolescence and is quite commonplace among adolescents, with a relatively small population of "abstainers" (Barnes et al., 2011; Moffitt, 1993; Owens & Slocum, 2012), research has revealed distinct developmental trajectories of antisocial behavior (Laub & Sampson, 2003; Loeber & Stouthamer-Loeber, 1998; Moffitt, 1993; Moffitt et al., 1996; Nagin et al., 1995). Early onset/life course persistent (LCP) and adolescence limited (AL) are two of the most commonly discussed trajectories (Moffitt, 1993, 2003). On the one hand, the large majority of people—AL individuals—only participate in antisocial behaviors during adolescence, and on the other, there is a small group of individuals—LCP individuals—who experience high continuity in antisocial behavior across their life course (see also Narvey & Piquero, this volume).

Although the group of individuals following an LCP trajectory of antisocial behavior is small at approximately 5%–10% of the population (Gottfredson & Hirschi, 1990; Laub & Sampson, 2003; Moffitt & Caspi, 2001), Moffitt (1993, 2003) argues that LCP individuals experience an earlier onset of antisocial behavior and engage in a higher volume of more serious, and often more violent, acts. According to Moffitt, the continuity of antisocial behavior among LCP individuals originates in multiple biological risk factors that interact with environmental risk factors, particularly in the home environment, to foster the development of an antisocial personality/behavioral style in childhood. LCP individuals may find it difficult to get along with others, follow rules, or obey authority figures, thereby constraining access to prosocial peer networks and limiting educational success and work opportunities. Deficits beginning in childhood are therefore amplified during adolescence and continue into midlife, contributing to problematic outcomes in adulthood, including criminal behavior, substance abuse, work and/or family conflict, and poor physical and/or mental health (Moffitt, 1993, 2003).

Moffitt (1993, 2003) argues that the antisocial behavior of AL individuals follows a distinct trajectory from that of the LCP individuals because each group has distinct motivations for violating normative social expectations. While the AL individuals make up a significantly larger portion of the population than LCP individuals, the antisocial behavior of AL individuals is unlikely to involve serious and/or violent crime. According to Moffitt, the antisocial behavior of the AL individuals originates with a maturity gap experienced during adolescence, when adolescents' biological (e.g., reproductive) maturity exceeds their access to adult privileges and autonomy. Deviant and/or delinquent acts allow adolescents languishing in the maturity gap a method of asserting personal autonomy, accessing adult domains (e.g., smoking, drinking, sexual activity), and gaining social status. Yet, as AL individuals transition into early adulthood and the maturity gap diminishes, antisocial behaviors no longer provide the same benefit and in fact may become detrimental to emerging adult roles and responsibilities. According to Moffitt's theory, "LCP antisocial behavior is rare, persistent, pervasive, and pathological, whereas AL antisocial behavior is common, relatively transient, situational, and near normative" (Moffitt, 2018, p. 177).

A significant body of research supports Moffitt's theory that there exist different types of offenders with distinctive offending etiologies (Barnes & Beaver, 2010; Blokland et al.,

2005; Galambos et al., 2003; Piquero & Brezina, 2001; Tibbetts & Piquero, 1999), yet further research has also identified additional trajectories of antisocial behavior. Some research suggests that Moffitt's two-trajectory model obscures gender differences; antisocial females may be more likely to experience an adolescence-delayed-onset trajectory (Fontaine et al., 2009; Silverthorn & Frick, 1999). This population of antisocial females has similar risk factors to early-onset/life-course males, although their antisocial behavior does not emerge until adolescence. Nonetheless, like LCP males, females following the adolescence-delayed-onset trajectory show continuity in antisocial behavior from adolescence into adulthood as well as an increased risk of substance abuse and mental health disorders as adults. Individuals following a childhood-limited trajectory (Moffitt et al., 1996; C. L. Odgers et al., 2008; Raine et al., 2005) also have similar biological and environmental risk factors to LCP individuals and, like LCP individuals, manifest high levels of antisocial behavior in childhood. Yet, despite this early onset, childhood-limited individuals also desist from antisocial behavior early, failing to manifest it during adulthood or even the high-risk period of adolescence. Still, childhood-limited individuals, especially males, are likely to experience financial issues, social isolation, and mental illness as adults (Moffitt et al., 2002; C. L. Odgers et al., 2008).

Genetic and Epigenetic Influences on Interpersonal Differences

While the physiological changes of adolescent development are essentially universal, adolescents' behavioral responses to these hormonal and neurological changes are influenced by genetic and environmental factors. The potential influence of genetics on antisocial behavior has long been a contentious issue, as early biological arguments (e.g., Lombroso, 1876) rested upon deterministic claims that have been subsequently disproven, prompting resistance to biological paradigms in the decades that followed. However, as the scientific understanding of genetics has developed and our ability to measure a wide range of physiological variables has advanced, more recent research has revealed that genetic factors have a significant influence on yet do not *determine* antisocial behavior; the ultimate effect of genetic factors depends largely on the environment in which individuals live.

There is no gene "for" any human behavior, including antisocial acts; however, a genetic predisposition to particular traits can increase the likelihood of antisocial behavior, dependent on how those traits are triggered and/or suppressed by an individual's environment. Behavioral geneticists provide information on the genetic underpinnings of human traits/behavior by examining heritability coefficients, which calculate how much of the variation seen in particular traits can be attributed to genetic variation, as opposed to environmental influences. Heritability coefficients for specific traits related to antisocial behavior generally fall in the .20 to .80 range (Walsh, 2009b), while heritability coefficients for antisocial behavior itself fall between .40 and .58 (Miles & Carey, 1997; Moffitt, 2005; Rhee & Waldman, 2002; Viding et al., 2008). As such, while genetic factors play an essential role in antisocial behavior, environmental factors are similarly essential, accounting for between 40% and 60% of the variance in antisocial behavior, although heritability studies cannot identify precisely *which* genetic or environmental factors account for this influence.

Antisocial behavior is therefore caused by both genetic and environmental factors, and the relationship between genetics and environment is complex. Gene–environment correlation (rGE) refers to the tendency of individuals to select and produce their environment based on genetic factors. Children are likely to be exposed to environments that match their genetic predispositions due to shared characteristics with their parents (passive rGE), individuals also tend to self-select into environments that match their genetic predispositions (active rGE), and certain genetic traits tend to elicit particular responses from others in the environment (evocative rGE; Brendgen, 2012; Walsh, 2009b, 2019). In addition, gene–environment interactions (G×E) refer to differential sensitivity to environmental risk factors, for example, the likelihood of developing depression in response to traumatic life events. Genes therefore influence both differential *exposure* to environmental risk factors via active/passive/evocative rGE and differential *susceptibility* to environmental risk factors via G×E; in real-world scenarios, it is difficult to distinguish between these processes (Walsh, 2009b, 2019).

One mechanism through which such biosocial factors contribute to antisocial behavior is through variation in personality traits, which refer to relatively stable ways of interacting with the world across life domains (Blackburn, 1993; Caspi et al., 1994). Differences in personality and/or temperament are largely due to genes that control physiological arousal patterns, though these patterns are further influenced by one's environment and resulting experiences (Rothbart et al., 2000). rGE means that temperamental differences among adolescents can affect their access to prosocial relationships and opportunities. An irritable or aggressive teen, for example, may struggle to get along with others, thereby potentially reducing parent–child attachment, eliciting parent–child conflict, and limiting positive interactions with peers and authority figures in school and/or their community.

Although many individual traits have been linked to an increased likelihood of antisocial behavior (e.g., see Andrews & Bonta, 2006; DeLisi & Vaughn, 2015; Jolliffe & Farrington, 2010; Jones et al., 2011; J. D. Miller & Lynam, 2001), research suggests that individual traits conducive to antisocial behavior tend to co-occur within individuals; these clusters of related traits are considered "supertraits." Two supertraits consistently linked to antisocial behavior are constraint and negative emotionality (Andrews & Bonta, 2006; Caspi et al., 1994; DeLisi & Vaughn, 2015; L. Ellis & Walsh, 2000; Jones et al., 2011; J. D. Miller & Lynam, 2001). Adolescents are particularly at risk for antisocial behavior when they are low in constraint—impulsive, sensation seeking, and insensitive to others—while also high in negative emotionality, that is, likely to experience strong negative emotions in response to life events, externalize blame, and respond to stress and/or conflict in an aggressive manner (Caspi et al., 1994). For example, a teen who is both low in constraint and high in negative emotionality may be particularly likely to perceive threats from others and struggle to resist impulses to lash out, thereby contributing to acts of aggression and/or violence.

Cognitive traits, like personality traits, are also highly heritable, and deficits in verbal IQ, information processing, and executive function have been linked to a higher likelihood of antisocial behavior. Low scores on verbal IQ, which supports communication, problem solving, and abstract reasoning, are associated with antisocial behavior from childhood through adulthood, though low verbal IQ appears to particularly characterize adolescent antisocial populations (Archwamety & Katsiyannis, 2000; Isen, 2010). Antisocial behavior in adolescence may also result from problems in processing emotional information and deficits in executive function, both of which are largely controlled by the prefrontal cortex (Harty et al., 2009; E. K. Miller & Cohen, 2001), which is undergoing major restructuring during adolescent development. Executive function refers to cognitive processes that help us strategize, focus attention, and manage/remember multiple tasks; these skills are essential to filter distractions, plan/complete projects, and achieve long-term goals. The significance of executive functioning may further account for the robust association between antisocial behavior and diagnoses of attention-deficit/hyperactivity disorder (ADHD), which is defined, in part, through deficits in executive function. In separate meta-analyses, Morgan and Lilienfeld (2000) found that the effect size for executive function deficits in adolescent antisocial populations was in the medium to large range, while L. Ellis and Walsh (2000) found that 99 out of 100 studies identified a positive relationship between ADHD and various antisocial behaviors, including violence, property crimes, and drug abuse.

At the same time, the nature of one's social environment exerts a significant effect on the expression of prosocial versus antisocial traits:

> Disadvantaged environments suppress the expression of genes associated with prosocial traits such as IQ and permit the expression of genes associated with antisocial traits such as aggression. Advantaged environments operate on the genes in the opposite direction.... In the case of aggression, it means a stronger genetic "dose" is required for its expression in advantaged environments precisely because the environmental controls mitigating against its expression are so strong. (Walsh, 2009b, pp. 34–35)

Indeed, in their study examining 403 genetic variants from 39 genes shown to be linked to aggression in animal studies, Liu et al. (2015) find that the genetic risk for aggression and/or violence among adolescents is highly dependent upon environmental context. Under conditions of low social control, the genetic risk of aggression was amplified, while the genetic risk was suppressed among adolescents in conditions of moderate/high social control. Similarly, research on the gene that codes for monoamine oxidase A (MAOA)—an enzyme that regulates neurotransmitters—suggests that the genotype for low-activity MAOA interacts with childhood abuse to predict antisocial behavior (Caspi et al., 2002; Derringer et al., 2010; Kim-Cohen et al., 2006; Kolla et al., 2014); this, as well as additional G×E studies examining the effect of aversive home environments, will be discussed in more detail later.

The still-developing science of epigenetics may ultimately help to clarify the complex interaction between genes and environment. Epigenetics refers to changes in gene activity that occur without changes in the DNA sequence itself and assumes plasticity of the genome in response to environmental challenges. Although only limited studies have been conducted with human samples, early research suggests that epigenetic alterations may not only influence antisocial behaviors but also be heritable and thus transmitted through generations of offspring (Walsh, 2009b, 2019). For example, in a study by Serpeloni and colleagues (2017), not only did women suffering repeated domestic violence during pregnancy personally experience epigenetic effects of that prenatal stress, but also these same genetic changes were inherited and expressed in their grandchildren (Serpeloni et al., 2017).

Family Influences on Risky and Antisocial Behavior in Adolescence

While the biological changes occurring during adolescent development in addition to certain genetic predispositions may dramatically increase adolescents' likelihood to engage in antisocial behavior, the larger family environment fundamentally shapes the manifestation of these risk factors. As noted earlier, individual genetic factors of adolescents and/or their parents—such as the MAOA enzyme or personality traits—influence the environment an adolescent will experience through active, passive, and evocative rGE and further influence how susceptible an adolescent will be to environmental risk factors (G×E). Depending on the broader environmental context, particular experiences within the family may also function as either a protective or a risk factor in the development of antisocial behavior:

> For example, the lack of care-giver warmth may, on its own, modestly increase the likelihood of youth antisocial behavior. However, in the presence of other risk factors (e.g., gang membership, drug use, low impulse control), warm relationships between care-giver and child likely reduce the influence of these factors while the lack of warmth may significantly amplify the impact of those risk factors in generating antisocial behavior. (Derzon, 2010, p. 290)

Existing research highlights major risk factors within the family environment, including exposure to family conflict and/or abuse, interaction with antisocial
models, and insufficient parental supervision/attachment.

Family Environments and Trajectories of Risky and Antisocial Behavior

The hormonal and neurological changes that mark normal adolescent development create a predilection for sensation seeking and risk taking, making some level of participation in antisocial behavior, such as status offenses (e.g., skipping school, drinking alcohol) or minor delinquency (e.g., simple assault, shoplifting) so common among adolescents as to be essentially normative. The prevalence of antisocial behavior among adolescents may therefore reflect its adaptive role as a learning base to assert personal autonomy and establish a distinct identity from their family of origin (Moffitt, 1993, 2006; Walsh 2009a). Nonetheless, antisocial behavior among AL individuals may be exacerbated by the family's inability to accept and/or satisfy an adolescent's growing need for independence, control, and participation. Limited research on AL patterns of offending lends some support to Moffitt's (1993, 2006) claim that the "maturity gap" between biological and social maturity motivates the adolescent surge in antisocial behavior. Adolescents who mature earlier (Beaver & Wright, 2005; Felson & Haynie, 2002; Haynie, 2003; Piquero & Brezina, 2001) and desire more personal freedom (Agnew, 1984) are more likely to engage in antisocial behavior. However, parenting practices significantly influence AL participation in antisocial acts. Haynie (2003) found that while pubertal development was positively associated with both minor and serious delinquency for females, parental permissiveness largely mediated this relationship. Using a direct measure of the maturity gap (parental permissiveness score subtracted from a pubertal development scale), Barnes and Beaver (2010) find that the maturity gap predicted minor antisocial acts, but not serious crime, among males, though again the effect was gendered and did not hold for females.

Although this AL trajectory is considered the most common pattern of antisocial behavior, a smaller group of adolescents begin engaging in antisocial behaviors during childhood and will continue into adulthood (see Frick et al., this volume). Considered LCP "offenders," their deviance during adolescence—which tends to be both higher volume and more serious than that of the AL individuals—is part of a persistent trajectory that began prior to adolescent development. Moffitt (1993, 2006) argues that the early onset of antisocial behavior and subsequent pattern of deviance during adolescence reflect an interaction between a child's biological vulnerabilities and poor social environments. As discussed earlier, passive rGE entails an association between a child's inherited genotype and the environment in which parents raise that child. Connolly (2020), for example, argues that "Parents create household environments and relationships with their children based on their emotional and behavioral propensities, which they also pass down to their children via biological/genetic transmission and reinforce through socialization" (p. 6). For example, since individuals with antisocial personalities often romantically partner with other antisocial individuals (Galbaud du Fort et al., 1998; Krueger et al., 1998), their children will likely be faced with a "double whammy" of genetic and environmental risk factors, especially as the parents of "high risk" children may lack the cognitive abilities or disciplinary practices to effectively manage the misbehavior of their children.

Although Moffitt's concept of a poor social environment is not synonymous with low socioeconomic status (SES), she does argue that biological vulnerabilities are likely to be perpetuated by economically disadvantaged environments, both because biological deficits will increase vulnerability to the criminogenic aspects of impoverished environments and because parents in such environments may lack the time and/or financial resources to support high-risk children (Moffitt, 1993; Moffitt et al., 1994; Tibbetts & Piquero, 2006). For example,

Jaffee et al. (2006) found that parents who had been diagnosed with conduct disorder in adolescence provided risky caregiving environments for their children, characterized by both economic disadvantage (e.g., unemployment, single parenthood, and low socioeconomic status) and family conflict and suboptimal parenting practices (both of which will be discussed in more detail later).

Parents certainly influence the environments their children experience, but children's behavior also affects the parenting they receive through evocative rGE. Consistently aggressive or impulsive children may elicit more negative and/or hostile parenting practices, which subsequently contributes to childhood and/or adolescent antisocial behavior (Elam et al., 2017; Kiff et al., 2011; Latzman et al., 2009; Prinzie et al., 2004). A meta-analysis conducted by Klahr and Burt (2014) found that child-driven evocative rGE accounts for a moderate proportion (approximately 40%) of the variance in negative parenting practices, but also identified gender differences, such that mothers were more influenced by evocative rGE. As such, parents faced with behaviorally "difficult" children (i.e., children who cannot be soothed or those manifesting highly aggressive and/or impulsive behavior) may feel that they are unable to effectively address their child's problematic behavior and may withdraw from the parenting role (Racz & McMahon, 2011). For example, research suggests low-birthweight infants negatively influence the behavior of their caretakers (Tinsley & Parke, 1983), and higher levels of impulsivity among children are both concurrently and longitudinally associated with lower levels of parental monitoring during early adolescence (Neumann et al., 2010).

Family Conflict, Abuse, and Interpersonal Variation in Risky and Antisocial Behavior

Among the negative social environments shown to contribute to LCP antisocial behavior are those characterized by childhood abuse and family conflict (Caspi & Elder, 1988; Jaffee et al., 2015; Moffitt, 2006; Verona & Sachs-Ericsson, 2005). LCP individuals may be differentially exposed to such aversive family experiences, due to passive and evocative rGE processes, as discussed previously. The complexity of gene–environment interplay also means that children with biological risk factors may be more susceptible to conduct problems in response to abuse in the family environment (i.e., G×E). Particular genes appear to make juveniles with early-onset antisocial behavior more sensitive to negative social influences, such as abuse, when compared to AL individuals (Eley et al., 2003; Hoeve et al., 2014; Painter & Scannapieco, 2013; Taylor et al., 2000). Specifically, among the most consistent findings of interaction between genetic and environmental risks involves the MAOA enzyme and early traumatic experiences, particularly abuse. Childhood maltreatment increased the risk for a range of antisocial outcomes among juveniles who possessed the low-activity MAOA variant but did not predict antisocial behavior among abused children who did not possess higher genetic risk (Caspi et al., 2002; Foley et al., 2004; Jaffee et al., 2005; Kim-Cohen et al., 2006; Nilsson et al., 2006; Widom & Brzustowicz, 2006), suggesting such G×E interactions may be a mechanism by which antisocial behavior, such as violence, is transmitted across generations within families (Jaffee et al., 2015).

However, additional research suggests that a learning mechanism may also contribute to intergenerational transmission of antisocial behavior within families. Children may learn to engage in aggressive behavior, particularly in response to stress and/or conflict, through observations of their parents' behavior and the reinforcement and/or punishment they receive for their own aggressive acts (Conger et al., 2003; Jaffee, 2009; Patterson, 1998). In fact, exposure to violence in the home during the period of adolescent development when the socioemotional system is functioning in high gear alongside a dampened cognitive control system may intensify the effect of exposure to violence on adolescents' attitudes toward violence. For example, Peckins and colleagues (2018) find that boys who had greater exposure to domestic violence in their home endorsed stronger pro-violence attitudes at age 15, which predicted subsequent risk for antisocial behavior at age 17. This risk appears to be further exacerbated by G×E interaction as the relationship between pro-violence attitudes and antisocial behavior was significantly stronger among boys with heightened cortisol levels.

Parenting Practices and Interpersonal Variation in Risky and Antisocial Behavior
Another central aspect of family environment that exerts an influence on adolescent antisocial behavior is the level of monitoring/supervision parents apply to their children. Seminal work by Gottfredson and Hirschi (1990) suggests that parental attachment to their children and the extent to which they monitor their children and respond appropriately to deviance will determine children's ultimate level of self-control. Therefore, if caregivers fail to effectively supervise their children and punish problematic behaviors, their children may struggle to delay gratification, perceive the consequences of their actions, or deal with conflict in a prosocial manner (Gottfredson & Hirschi, 1990). A meta-analysis by Cullen et al. (2008) supports Gottfredson and Hirschi's contention that less effective parenting strategies are associated with lower levels of self-control. An earlier meta-analysis by Pratt and Cullen (2000) indicates that self-control is both among the strongest correlates of antisocial behavior and the most general, with its effects enduring regardless of how self-control is operationalized, and across race, even when controlling for other theoretical causes of antisocial behavior.

In practice, parental supervision levels also matter because parents have the ability to limit their adolescents' opportunities to engage in antisocial behavior. In homes with high levels of parental monitoring, parents know where their child is, who they are with, what they are doing, and when they will be home; these questions are particularly salient as adolescents become increasingly independent and participate in more activities outside the direct supervision of their parents and/or other adults. Indeed, adolescents who spend more time without adult supervision are more likely to engage in antisocial behavior (Osgood & Anderson, 2004). Research further suggests that juveniles' willingness to disclose their activities to their parents and parental monitoring of such information moderate the relationships between low self-control and antisocial behavior (Hay & Forrest, 2008; LaGrange & Silverman, 1999). Specifically, Kuhn and Laird (2013) find:

> Opportunity restrictions attenuated the association between low self-control and antisocial behavior such that low self-control was less strongly associated with antisocial behavior when youth experienced less antisocial peer involvement, less unsupervised time, more parental solicitation, and more family rules than when youth experienced more antisocial peer involvement, more unsupervised time, less parental solicitation, and fewer family rules. (p. 813)

In addition to parental supervision, the level of attachment/warmth between parents and children affects engagement in antisocial behavior during adolescence. Multiple studies suggest that intergenerational transmission of antisocial behavior is influenced by problematic parenting practices, such as low levels of supervision (Capaldi & Patterson, 1991) and low parental warmth (Thornberry et al., 2003). For example, Okuda et al. (2019) find that while sensation seeking was a strong predictor of antisocial behavior and high parental monitoring mitigated the relationship between sensation seeking and antisocial behavior, low levels of parental warmth were associated with antisocial behavior, even when controlling for a tendency toward sensation seeking. In fact, regardless of adolescents' predisposition to sensation seeking, parental warmth was more predictive of antisocial behavior than was a tendency toward sensation seeking (Okuna et al., 2019).

Peer Influences on Risky and Antisocial Behavior in Adolescence

In addition to the range of physiological changes associated with puberty, adolescence likewise ushers in important changes in the social worlds of adolescents. Of particular importance, adolescence is a period in the life course during which youth not only seek increasing autonomy from parents but also become more interested in spending time with, and seeking status among, peers (LaFontana & Cillessen, 2010; Moffitt, 1993). However, whereas peer status in childhood tends to equate largely with *sociometric popularity*, or being liked, other forms of status appear to become increasingly distinguishable and salient in early adolescence (Cillessen & Mayeux, 2004; Pouwels et al., 2018). First, adolescents become increasingly concerned with *perceived popularity*, reflecting the degree to which they are "well-known, socially-central, and emulated" (Cillessen & Rose, 2005, p. 102). Second, they become increasingly concerned with *dominance*, which "represents an individual's ability to control social and material resources within the peer group" (Closson & Hymel, 2016, p. 1837; see also Hawley, 1999, 2014). Notwithstanding puberty's direct biological influences on risk taking and antisocial behavior, sociological research suggests multiple ways in which adolescents' increasing concern with peer association and various forms of status can itself amplify their tendency toward risky behavior.

Routine Activities and Unstructured Peer Socializing During Adolescence

Most fundamentally, spending more unstructured and unsupervised time among peers may expose adolescents to *routine activities* and situations that present new opportunities for risky or antisocial behavior. Osgood et al. (1996), for example, conducted seminal research demonstrating that as high school seniors in the United States engage in more unstructured and unsupervised social activity among peers, their involvement in a range of criminal and risky behaviors tends to increase. These results did not appear attributable to stable, preexisting interpersonal differences among sample youth but did suggest that differences in unstructured and unsupervised socializing could account for a substantial proportion of the well-documented correlation between risky behavior and such demographic variables as age and sex.

Although Osgood et al.'s (1996) results come exclusively from U.S. respondents, research using a variety of samples outside the United States provides further evidence consistent with their general findings, shedding further light on the relationship between adolescents' routine activities and risky behavior. Limited research, for example, suggests that cultures allowing higher amounts of unstructured and unsupervised socializing among juveniles tend to exhibit higher rates of adolescent risk taking (Schlegel & Barry, 1991). More recently, research using a sample of adolescents from Sweden finds that long-term societal decreases in unstructured and unsupervised socializing among juveniles are associated with corresponding decreases in delinquency rates (Svensson & Oberwittler, 2021). Perhaps most notably, however, Hoeben and Weerman (2016) recently used data from a sample of adolescents in The Hague to explore what underlying mechanisms might explain the link between routine activities among peers and risky behavior. In addition to replicating Osgood et al.'s (1996) general findings, their results suggest that unsupervised time among peers may increase risky behavior partly by exposing juveniles to tempting opportunities, social pressure, and tolerance of risk, much of which they would not encounter in the absence of peers or in the presence of adult supervision.

The Influence of Popularity on Risky and Antisocial Behavior in Adolescence

In addition to researching the various ways in which routine activities among peers may influence risky behavior, scholars of adolescence have likewise examined whether achieving various types of popularity may contribute to risky behavior. On the one hand, sociometric popularity, which reflects how much adolescents are liked by their peers, might logically be expected to increase an adolescent's access to a wider variety of social interactions. These interactions, in turn, may lead well-liked individuals to receive more invitations to parties or other informal gatherings. In keeping with the "routine activities" paradigm described earlier (e.g., Osgood et al., 1996), such gatherings may expose well-liked individuals to greater opportunities for such behaviors as the consumption of illicit substances or involvement in risky sexual behavior, as well as to the other mechanisms that Hoeben and Weerman (2016) investigated in their study. On the other hand, insofar as one adolescent's achievement of perceived popularity or social dominance diminishes the relative social rank or influence of another, competition for these types of popularity may engender verbal aggression, bullying, or physical violence aimed at protecting these forms of popularity (Caravita & Cillessen, 2012; Cillessen & Mayeux, 2004). To the degree that the salience of perceived popularity and social dominance increasingly eclipse that of being well liked as children enter adolescence (Adler & Adler, 1998; Cillessen & Rose, 2005; Closson & Hymel, 2016), achieving these types of popularity might logically be predicted to promote the aforementioned types of antisocial behavior.

Research concerning these predictions tends to yield at least partially supportive results. For example, even as some studies find sociometric popularity to be inversely correlated with aggressive or hostile forms of antisocial behaviors, they often find sociometric popularity to be positively correlated with nonviolent forms of risky behavior including the use of chemical substances and nonviolent forms of antisocial behavior like minor property crime (e.g., Balsa et al., 2010; Coie et al., 1982; Luthar & D'Avanzo, 1999; Michell & Amos, 1997; Miller-Johnson et al., 2003). In contrast, research finds perceived popularity and social dominance among adolescents to be positively associated not only with nonviolent forms of risky behavior like the use of chemical substances but also with hostile and aggressive behaviors such as bullying and physical violence (e.g., Prinstein & Cillessen, 2003; Rose et al., 2004). Likewise, among studies incorporating a longitudinal component, results tend to be consistent with the notion that at least part of the bivariate association between popularity and risky or antisocial behavior reflects the influence of the former on the latter (e.g., Allen et al., 2005; Cillessen & Mayeux, 2004; Mayeux & Cillessen, 2008; Pouwels et al., 2018; Sandstrom & Cillessen, 2006; Valente et al., 2005).

Association With Delinquent and Antisocial Peers

Perhaps the most fundamental reason that routine activities and popularity among peers contribute to risky and antisocial behavior, however, involves the degree to which they increase the probability of exposure to delinquent or antisocial peers. Over the course of nearly a century, some of the most influential scholars in multiple disciplines have argued that one of the primary causes of risky and antisocial behavior is exposure to, association with, and imitation of risk-taking and antisocial behavioral models (e.g., Akers, 2009; Bandura, 1973; Sutherland, 1947). Although these scholars studied a range of behaviors among a range of different age groups, their essential predictions are of clear relevance to risky and antisocial behavior during adolescence, in large part because of the unique importance of the peer group during this stage of the life course. Innumerable studies have therefore examined whether adolescents reporting a higher prevalence of antisocial behavior among their peers are themselves disproportionately prone to the same behaviors. Results almost inevitably show not only that they are but also that the correlation between personal and peer behavior is consistently among the largest in the existing research literature concerning the predictors of risky and antisocial behavior (Pratt et al., 2010). Research focusing specifically on the correlation between personal and peer behavior among gang members suggests similar conclusions (Maxon, 2011).

Despite the consistent finding that antisocial behavior tends to be much more common among adolescents with antisocial friends and gang affiliations, critics (e.g., Gottfredson & Hirschi, 1990) have called into question the appropriate interpretation of such results. First, studies using cross-sectional designs preclude researchers from discerning whether such results reflect the influence of antisocial friends and gang members on respondents' own risky and antisocial behavior, the influence of respondents' own behavioral predilections on the types of peers with whom they choose to associate, or the independent influence of common environmental circumstances on multiple adolescents' behavioral trajectories. Second, among longitudinal studies that attempt to overcome the limits of cross-sectional designs, it remains possible that respondent perceptions of peer behavior are inaccurate, reflecting their unconscious projection of personal behavioral tendencies onto their peers. Over the past two decades, researchers have increasingly applied a range of methodological innovations to explore these possibilities empirically. For example, some researchers have incorporated survey measures of peer behavior derived directly from respondents' peers rather than relying on respondents' potentially inaccurate perceptions of peers (e.g., Haynie, 2001; Rebellon & Modecki, 2014), and some such researchers have likewise incorporated longitudinal designs with which to model the potentially reciprocal relationship between personal and peer behavior (e.g., Young et al., 2014). Other researchers have conducted random-assignment experiments examining whether confederates who provide behavioral models of cheating or stealing in laboratory settings can induce these behaviors in participants (e.g., Paternoster et al., 2013). On balance, the results of studies like these suggest that exposure to risk-taking or antisocial peers may lead adolescents to imitate such behavior, but that the magnitude of peer effects is not nearly as strong as earlier research implied.

Risky and Antisocial Behavior as Status Seeking Among Adolescents

In addition to suggesting that popularity may promote antisocial behavior by increasing exposure to risky environments or delinquent peers, some scholarship suggests that risky behavior may reciprocally contribute to popularity. From an evolutionary perspective (e.g., B. J. Ellis et al., 2012), adolescent risk taking among peers may reflect a fundamental aspect of human social development, whereby puberty heightens adolescents' attempts to demonstrate their value among peers in exchange for the social influence and dominance they increasingly crave. According to this perspective, successful risk taking may signal to peer audiences and prospective romantic partners not only that an adolescent possesses abilities or talents of potential benefit to the broader peer group but also that they are not afraid of using them in the pursuit of collective goals. Apart from merely being *liked* among peers, adolescents capable of stealing alcohol from their parents' house may achieve a measure of increasingly coveted *influence* among the peers with whom they share their prize, but only if they are willing to take the risk. Apart from merely being *liked* among peers, adolescents capable of protecting those peers from an assailant's physical assault may achieve a measure of increasingly coveted influence among the peers to whom they render aid, as well as a measure of increasingly coveted *dominance* over a bested assailant, but only if they are willing to partake in ostensibly antisocial behavior vis-à-vis the assailant (see also Rebellon, 2006; Rebellon et al., 2019).

Collectively, two strands of research suggest preliminary support for the evolutionary perspective presented earlier. First, Gardner and Steinberg (2005) conducted a seminal laboratory experiment demonstrating that adolescents were significantly more likely to take risks in the presence of peers, but that adults were equally likely to take risks regardless of the presence of peers. Further research has replicated this finding with anonymous and nonanonymous peer audiences, and some of these replications have used fMRI scans to demonstrate that the presence of peers activates portions of adolescents' limbic system, including the ventral striatum and the orbitofrontal cortex, responsible for the anticipation of reward (Albert et al., 2013; Chein et al., 2011; Weigard et al., 2014). Building on Gardner and Steinberg's (2005) general approach, O'Brien et al. (2011) demonstrated that the presence of peer audiences increased adolescent preferences for immediate but smaller economic rewards versus larger but delayed economic rewards. On the basis of these findings, O'Brien et al. (2011) speculate that "peer presence may function at the neurobiological level to sensitize adolescents and youths (more so than adults) to the value of immediate rewards" (p. 751; see also Steinberg, 2008).

At the same time, however, O'Brien et al. (2011) acknowledge "the possibility that peer presence also (or instead) influences adolescents' choices through other mechanisms" beyond its influence on the salience of economic or physical reward (p. 751). In particular, they suggest that adolescents in a peer context may choose short-term or risky options to impress peers and elevate their social status (see also Rebellon, 2006). This second interpretation is consistent with the evolutionary perspective presented previously and is bolstered by research suggesting that a portion of the previously discussed correlation between risk taking and popularity may reflect the influence of the former on the latter rather than exclusively reflecting the reverse. Research, for example, suggests that behaviors like substance use and aggression, as well as a general tendency toward risk taking, may contribute to popularity under at least some circumstances (Abel et al., 2002; Kreager, 2007; Mayeux & Cillessen, 2008; Rebellon, 2006; Rebellon et al., 2019; Rose et al., 2004). Given that perceived popularity and social dominance become more salient in early adolescence, it may be that the effect of peer audiences on adolescent risk taking does indeed reflect a general adolescent desire to impress peers, based on their lived experience observing that risk taking can increase these forms of coveted popularity during adolescence. This may further explain why, notwithstanding their cognitive immaturity, research suggests that chronically deviant juveniles intentionally foster reputations as rule breakers despite being aware of such behavior's potentially negative consequences. In sum, risky or antisocial behavior may not simply reflect adolescents' inability to understand negative consequences but may likewise reflect their higher concern with gaining or consolidating the peer status that they increasingly desire (Campbell, 1993; Caravita & Cillessen, 2012; P. Odgers et al., 1996; Rebellon, 2006; Rebellon et al., 2019; Reicher & Emler, 1985.

The Influence of Community Context on Risky and Antisocial Behavior in Adolescence

The community context within which adolescents live will also affect their social development and engagement in antisocial behavior through a variety of mechanisms. Structural disadvantage (e.g., neighborhood poverty levels) has been consistently linked to higher levels of antisocial behavior, particularly serious crime (DeCoster et al., 2006; Leventhal & Brooks-Gunn, 2000; Zimmerman & Messner, 2010), with research suggesting this pattern is due to lower levels of informal social control (Bursik & Grasmick, 1999; Sampson & Groves, 1989; Sampson et al., 1997) and higher levels of strain (Antunes & Manasse, 2021) among residents of disadvantaged communities. Children growing up within impoverished communities are likely to experience weak social institutions (e.g., underfunded schools) and suboptimal parenting practices (e.g., more unsupervised peer socializing) as well as more exposure to criminogenic strains (e.g., community violence). When considering the effect of community-level factors on adolescent behavior, however, it is essential to remember that some individuals will be more vulnerable to external influences in the community than others (Oberwittler, 2007). Normal adolescent development creates a period of heightened vulnerability to risk taking

(Steinberg, 2005, 2010), and genetic susceptibility to antisocial behavior may be exacerbated by exposure to the risk factors endemic to disadvantaged environments (Walsh, 2009b).

Although many antisocial acts are no more common in economically disadvantaged communities than in middle- or upper-class communities (e.g., drug use), the adversities associated with growing up in poverty have been linked to increased engagement in serious and/or violent delinquency (Bjerk, 2007; Fergusson et al., 2004; Jarjoura et al., 2002). For example, Jarjoura et al. (2002) find that living below the poverty line during the first 5 years of life was related to an increased likelihood of adolescent delinquency; family poverty measured in early adolescence was further linked to higher levels of concurrent delinquency. Similarly, Fergusson et al. (2004) found that youth born into low-SES families engaged in delinquent acts at three times the rate of youth born into high-SES families. The intergenerational stability of poverty may therefore account for some of the transmission of antisocial behavior within families (Thornberry et al., 2003), as the consequences of poverty can undermine family stability and effective parenting practices. A significant body of research suggests that weak emotional attachment between parents/children and ineffective parenting strategies (e.g., low supervision, harsh discipline) mediate the relationship between community structural characteristics and antisocial behavior (Berti & Pivetti, 2019; Fergusson et al., 2004; Sampson & Laub, 1994; Weatherburn & Lind, 2006), though this effect seems to be especially salient for boys (Weatherburn & Lind, 2006).

In fact, Sheidow and colleagues (2001) suggest that parenting practices and parent–child attachment may be especially salient for youth living in highly disadvantaged neighborhoods, in part due to the risk of exposure to violence within high-crime communities:

> Parents who supervise within the home, restrict unfettered access to the community, and refrain from harsh discipline can not only attenuate instances of [exposure to violence in the community], they also reduce youth unstructured socializing and association with deviant peers. (Antunes & Ahlin, 2017, p. 173)

The more time adolescents spend in unsupervised interactions with their peers, the more likely they are to be exposed to violence within their communities (Richards et al., 2004), and adolescents who personally experience and/or witness violence in their communities are significantly more likely to engage in antisocial behaviors themselves (Barr et al., 2012; Farrell & Sullivan, 2004; Gorman-Smith et al., 2004; Leventhal & Brooks-Gunn, 2000; Spano et al., 2009). Particular strategies of supervision and discipline utilized by parents may also be influenced by neighborhood conditions. For example, Maimon and Browning (2010) found that higher levels of informal social control and mutual trust between residents (i.e., collective efficacy) significantly limited the amount of time adolescents spent engaging in unstructured socializing with their peers, which subsequently reduced engagement in violence. Additional research suggests that parents who perceive there to be more crime/disorder in their neighborhoods are likely to impose more rules on their children (Byrnes et al., 2011; Rankin & Quane, 2002; Zubieri, 2016).

Community-level social processes also depend upon adolescents' school environment, which can be a powerful agent of socialization through the reinforcement of prosocial behavior and punishment of antisocial conduct. Impoverished communities tend to have underfunded schools, and indeed high levels of student poverty are associated with problematic organizational characteristics, such as difficulty recruiting and retaining high-quality teachers/staff (Simon & Johnson, 2015). Underfunded schools within impoverished communities, then, are more likely to struggle to provide a consistent and warm educational climate and promote student engagement, which can hamper both students' attachment to school and their academic achievement (Berg & Cornell, 2016; Lacour & Tissington, 2011; Ronfeldt et al., 2013; Willms, 2010; Wood et al., 2017). Students' positive attachment to school is associated with lower levels of substance use and other forms of delinquency during adolescence (Crosnoe et al., 2002; Savolainen et al., 2011; Shochet et al., 2006), while poor academic achievement is associated with higher levels of antisocial behavior/delinquency over time (Hoffmann et al., 2013; Savolainen et al., 2011). As noted previously, problematic school environments may exacerbate preexisting risk factors among individual adolescents in disadvantaged communities. For example, low academic performance and attachment to school have been shown to mediate a significant proportion of the effects of learning difficulties and childhood antisocial behavior on later adolescent antisocial behavior (Herrenkohl et al., 2001; Savolainen et al., 2011). Common school discipline tactics may also be counterproductive, as school suspension and expulsion have been shown to exacerbate rather than lessen future risky and/or antisocial behavior among adolescents (Gerlinger et al., 2021; Hemphill et al., 2006; see also Fine et al., this volume).

Conclusion

Research suggests consistent support for the notion that age is related to risky and antisocial behavior across time and place. In particular, such behavior tends to increase throughout adolescence, peak in late adolescence/early adulthood, and decrease over time throughout the remainder of the life course. Over the past several decades, research has begun to unveil an array of physiological mechanisms that collectively appear to account for the adolescent increase in risky and antisocial behavior. Among these are changes in hormone levels, changes in neurotransmitter levels, and the acceleration of development in certain regions of the brain. At the same time, even as these types of physiological changes appear to account for the seemingly universal increase in risky and antisocial behavior that characterizes adolescence, there exists substantial interpersonal variation in the degree to which different individuals increase or decrease their risky and antisocial behavior throughout adolescence and early adulthood. Research over the course of the past several decades suggests that this interpersonal variation appears related to the interaction of genetics with a range of environmental variables reflecting adolescent social experiences in their families, among their peers, and within their communities. Collectively, this research suggests that risky and antisocial behavior during adolescence stems largely from physiological factors unique to this developmental period of human development, but that the influence of these physiological factors can be amplified or suppressed by environmental factors amenable to social interventions.

References

Abel, G., Plumridge, L., & Graham, P. (2002). Peers, networks or relationships: Strategies for understanding social dynamics as determinants of smoking behaviour. *Drugs: Education, Prevention and Policy, 9*(4), 325–338.

Adler, P. A., & Adler, P. (1998). *Peer power: Preadolescent culture and identity.* Rutgers University Press.

Agnew, R. (1984). Autonomy and delinquency. *Sociological Perspectives, 27*(2), 219–240. https://doi.org/10.2307%2F1389019

Akers, R. L. (2009). *Social learning and social structure: A general theory of crime and deviance.* Transaction.

Albert, D., Chein, J., & Steinberg, L. (2013). The teenage brain: Peer influences on adolescent decision making. *Current Directions in Psychological Science, 22*(2), 114–120.

Allen, J. P., Porter, M. R., McCarland, F. C., Marsh, P., & McElhaney, K. B. (2005). The two faces of adolescents' success with peers: Adolescent popularity, social adaptation, and deviant behavior. *Child Development, 76,* 747–760.

Andrews, D. A., & Bonta, J. (2006). *The psychology of criminal conduct* (4th ed.). Anderson.

Antunes, M. J., & Ahlin, E. M. (2017). Youth exposure to violence in the community: Towards a theoretical framework for explaining risk and protective factors. *Aggression and Violent Behavior, 34,* 166–177. https://psycnet.apa.org/doi/10.1016/j.avb.2017.01.015

Antunes, M. J., & Manasse, M. (2021). Social disorganization and strain: Macro and micro implications for youth violence. *Journal of Research in Crime & Delinquency*. https://doi.org/10.1177%2F00224278211004667

Archwamety, T., & Katsiyannis, A. (2000). Academic remediation, parole violations, and recidivism rates among delinquent youths. *Remedial and Special Education*, *21*(3), 161–170.

Balsa, A. I., Homer, J. F., French, M. T., & Norton, E. C. (2010). Alcohol use and popularity: Social payoffs from conforming to peers' behavior. *Journal of Research on Adolescence*, *21*(3), 559–568.

Bandura, A. (1973). *Aggression: A social learning analysis*. Prentice-Hall.

Barnes, J. C., & Beaver, K. M. (2010). An empirical examination of adolescence-limited offending: A direct test of Moffitt's maturity gap thesis. *Journal of Criminal Justice*, *38*(6), 1176–1185. https://psycnet.apa.org/doi/10.1016/j.jcrimjus.2010.09.006

Barnes, J. C., Beaver, K. M., & Piquero, A. R. (2011). A test of Moffitt's hypotheses of delinquency abstention. *Criminal Justice and Behavior*, *38*(7), 690–709. https://psycnet.apa.org/doi/10.1177/0093854811405282

Barr, S. C., Hanson, R., Begle, A. M., Kilpatrick, D. G., Saunders, B., Resnick, H., & Amstadter, A. (2012). Examining the moderating role of family cohesion on the relationship between witnessed community violence and delinquency in a national sample of adolescents. *Journal of Interpersonal Violence*, *27*(2), 239–262. https://dx.doi.org/10.1177%2F0886260511416477

Beaver, K. M., & Wright, J. P. (2005). Biosocial development and delinquent involvement. *Youth Violence and Juvenile Justice*, *3*(2), 168–192. https://doi.org/10.1177/1541204004273318

Berg, J. K., & Cornell, D. (2016). Authoritative school climate, aggression toward teachers, and teacher distress in middle school. *School Psychology Quarterly*, *31*(1), 122–139. https://psycnet.apa.org/doi/10.1037/spq0000132

Berti, C., &. Pivetti, M. (2019). Childhood economic disadvantage and antisocial behavior: Intervening factors and pathways. *Children and Youth Services Review*, *97*, 120–126.

Bjerk, D. (2007). Measuring the relationship between youth criminal participation and household economic resources. *Journal of Quantitative Criminology*, *23*, 23–39.

Blackburn, R. (1993). *The psychology of criminal conduct*. John Wiley and Sons.

Blokland, A. A. J., Nagin, D., & Nieuwbeerta, P. (2005). Life span offending trajectories of a Dutch conviction cohort. *Criminology*, *43*(4), 919–954. https://doi.org/10.1111/j.1745-9125.2005.00029.x

Booth, A., Granger, D., Mazur, M., & Kivligan, K. (2006). Testosterone and social behavior. *Social Forces*, *85*(1), 167–191.

Braithwaite, J. (1989). *Crime, shame and reintegration*. Cambridge University Press.

Brendgen, M. (2012). Genetics and peer relations: A review. *Journal of Research on Adolescence*, *22*(3), 419–437.

Bursik, R. J., & Grasmick, H. G. (1999). *Neighborhoods and crime*. Lexington Books.

Byrnes, H. F., Miller, B. A., Chen, M.-J., & Grube, J. W. (2011). The roles of mothers' neighborhood perceptions and specific monitoring strategies in youth's problem behavior. *Journal of Youth and Adolescence*, *40*(3), 347–360. https://psycnet.apa.org/doi/10.1007/s10964-010-9538-1

Campbell, A. (1993). *Men, women and aggression*. New York: Basic Books.

Capaldi, D. M., & Patterson, G. R. (1991). Relation of parental transitions to boys' adjustment problems: I. A linear hypothesis. II. Mothers at risk for transitions and unskilled parenting. *Developmental Psychology*, *27*(3), 489–504. https://doi.org/10.1037/0012-1649.27.3.489

Caravita, S. C. S., & Cillessen, A. H. N. (2012). Agentic or communal? Associations between interpersonal goals, popularity and bullying in middle childhood and early adolescence. *Social Development*, *21*(2), 376–395.

Caspi, A., & Elder, G. H. J. (1988). Emergent family patterns: The intergenerational construction of problem behaviour and relationships. In R. A. Hinde & J. Stevenson-Hinde (Eds.), *Relationships within families: Mutual influences* (pp. 218–240). Clarendon Press.

Caspi, A., McClay, J., Moffitt, T. E., Mill, J., Martin, J., Craig, I. W., Taylor, A., & Poulton, R. (2002). Role of genotype in the cycle of violence in maltreated children. *Science*, *297*(5582), 851–854.

Caspi, A., Moffitt, T. E., Silva, P. A., Stouthamer-Loeber, M., Krueger, R. F., & Schmutte, P. S. (1994). Are some people crime-prone: The personality-crime relationships across countries, genders, races, and methods. *Criminology*, *32*(2), 163–195. https://doi.org/10.1111/j.1745-9125.1994.tb01151.x

Chein, J., Albert, D., O'Brien, L., Uckert, K., & Steinberg, L. (2011). Peers increase adolescent risk taking by enhancing activity in the brain's reward circuitry. *Developmental Science*, *14*(2), F1–F10.

Cillessen, A. H. N., & Mayeux, L. (2004). From censure to reinforcement: Developmental changes in the association between aggression and social status. *Child Development*, *75*(1), 147–163.

Cillessen, A. H. N., & Rose, A. J. (2005). Understanding popularity in the peer system. *Current Directions in Psychological Science*, *14*(2), 102–105.

Closson, L. M., & Hymel, S. (2016). Status differences in target-specific prosocial behavior and aggression. *Journal of Youth & Adolescence*, *45*(9), 1836–1848.

Coie, J. D., Dodge, K. A., & Coppotelli, H. (1982). Dimensions and types of social status: A cross-age perspective. *Developmental Psychology, 18*(4), 557–570.

Collins, R. (2004). Onset and desistance in criminal careers: Neurobiology and the age-crime relationship. *Journal of Offender Rehabilitation, 39*(3), 1–19.

Conger, R. D., Neppl, T., Kim, K. J., & Scaramella, L. (2003). Angry and aggressive behaviors across three generations: A prospective, longitudinal study of parents and children. *Journal of Abnormal Child Psychology, 31*(2), 143–160.

Connolly, E. J. (2020). Further evaluating the relationship between adverse childhood experiences, antisocial behavior, and violent victimization: A sibling-comparison analysis. *Youth Violence and Juvenile Justice, 18*(1), 3–23. https://doi.org/10.1177%2F1541204019833145

Crosnoe, R., Erickson, K. G., & Dornbusch, S. M. (2002). Protective functions of family relationships and school factors on the deviant behavior of adolescent boys and girls: Reducing the impact of risky friendships. *Youth & Society, 33*(4), 515–544. https://psycnet.apa.org/doi/10.1177/0044118X02033004002

Cullen, F. T., Unnever, J. D., Wright, J. P., & Beaver, K. M. (2008). Parenting and self-control. In E. Goode (Ed.), *Out of control: Assessing the general theory of crime* (pp 61-74). Stanford University Press.

Curry, L. A., & Youngblade, L. M. (2006). Negative affect, risk perception, and adolescent risk behavior. *Journal of Applied Developmental Psychology, 27*(5), 468–485.

DeCoster, S., Heimer, K., & Wittrock, S. M. (2006). Neighborhood disadvantage, social capital, street context, and youth violence. *Sociological Quarterly, 47*(4), 723–753. https://psycnet.apa.org/doi/10.1111/j.1533-8525.2006.00064.x

DeLisi, M., & Vaughn, M. G. (2015). Temperament as a biosocial construct for understanding antisocial behavior. In M. DeLisi & M. G. Vaughn (Eds.), *Criminological theory: Readings and retrospectives* (pp. 331-335). McGraw Hill.

Derringer, J., Krueger, R. F., Irons, D. E., & Iacono, W. G. (2010). Harsh discipline, childhood sexual assault, and MAOA genotype: An investigation of main and interactive effects on diverse clinical externalizing outcomes. *Behavioral Genetics, 40*(5), 639–648. https://psycnet.apa.org/doi/10.1007/s10519-010-9358-9

Derzon, J. H. (2010). The correspondence of family features with problem, aggressive, criminal, and violent behavior: A meta-analysis. Journal of Experimental Criminology, 6(3), 263–292.

Duell, N., Steinberg, L., Icenogle, G., Chein, J., Chaudhary, N., DiGiunta, L., Dodge, K. A., Fanti, K. A., Lansford, J. E., Oburu, P., Pastorelli, C., Skinner, A. T., Sorbring, E., Tapanya, S., Uribe Tirado, L. M., Alampay, L. P., Al-Hassan, S. M., Takash, H. M. S., Bacchini, D., & Chang, L. (2018). Age patterns in risk-taking across the world. *Journal of Youth & Adolescence, 47*(5), 1052–1072.

Elam, K. K., Chassin, L., Eisenberg, N., & Spinrad, T. L. (2017). Marital stress and children's externalizing behavior as predictors of mothers' and fathers' parenting. *Development and Psychopathology, 29*(1), 1–14. https://doi.org/10.1017/S0954579416001322

Eley, T. C., Lichtenstein, P., & Moffitt, T. E. (2003). A longitudinal behavioral genetic analysis of the etiology of aggressive and nonaggressive antisocial behavior. *Development and Psychopathology, 15*(2), 383–402. https://doi.org/10.1017/s095457940300021x

Ellis, B. J., DelGiudice, M., Dishion, T. J., Figueredo, A. J., Gray, P., Griskevicius, V., Hawley, P. H., Jacobs, W. J., James, J., Volk, A. A., & Wilson, D. S. (2012). The evolutionary basis of risky adolescent behavior: Implications for science, policy, and practice. *Developmental Psychology, 48*(3), 598–623. https://doi.org/10.1037/a0026220

Ellis, L., & Walsh, A. (2000). *Criminology: A global perspective*. Allyn & Bacon.

Ernst, M., Pine, D. S., & Hardin, M. (2006). Triadic model of the neurobiology of motivated behavior in adolescence. *Psychological Medicine, 36*(3), 299–312.

Eshel, N., Nelson, E., Blair, R., Pine, D., & Ernst, M. (2007). Neural substrates of choice selection in adults and adolescents: Development of the ventrolateral prefrontal and anterior cingulate cortices. *Neuropsychologia, 45*(6), 1270–1279. https://dx.doi.org/10.1016%2Fj.neuropsychologia.2006.10.004

Farrell, A. D., & Sullivan, T. N. (2004). Impact of witnessing violence on growth curves for problem behaviors among early adolescents in urban and rural settings. *Journal of Community Psychology, 32*(5), 505–525.

Farrington, D. P. (1986). Age and crime. In M. Tonry & N. Morris (Eds.), *Crime and justice: An annual review of research* (Vol. 7, pp. 189–250). University of Chicago Press.

Farrington, D. P., Piquero, A. R., & Jennings, W. G. (2013). *Offending from childhood to late middle age: Recent results from the Cambridge study in delinquent development*. Springer.

Felson, R., & Haynie, D. (2002). Pubertal development, social factors, and delinquency among adolescent boys. *Criminology, 40*(4), 967–988.

Fergusson, D., Swain-Campbell, N., & Horwood, J. (2004). How does childhood economic disadvantage lead to crime? Journal of Child Psychology and Psychiatry, 45(5), 956–966.

Foley, D. L., Eaves, L. J., Wormley, B., Silberg, J. L., Maes, H. H., & Riley, B. (2004). Childhood adversity, monoamine oxidase A genotype, and risk for conduct disorder. *Archives of General Psychiatry*, *61*(7), 738–744.

Fontaine, N., Carbonneau, R., Vitaro, F., Barker, E. D., & Tremblay, R. E. (2009). Research review: A critical review of studies on the developmental trajectories of antisocial behavior in females. *Journal of Child Psychology and Psychiatry*, *50*(4), 363–385.

Galambos, N., Barker, E., & Tilton-Weaver, L. (2003). Who gets caught at maturity gap? A study of pseudomature, immature, and mature adolescents. *International Journal of Behavioral Development*, *27*(3), 253–263.

Galbaud du Fort, G., Bland, R. C., Newman, S. C., & Boothroyd, L. J. (1998). Spouse similarity for lifetime psychiatric history in the general population. *Psychological Medicine*, *28*(4), 789–803.

Galvan, A., Hare, T., Parra, C., Penn, J., Voss, H., Glover, G., & Casey, B. J. (2006). Earlier development of the accumbens relative to orbitofrontal cortex might underlie risk-taking behavior in adolescents. *Journal of Neuroscience*, *26*(25), 6885–6892.

Gardner, M., & Steinberg, L. (2005). Peer influence on risk taking, risk preference, and risky decision making in adolescence and adulthood: An experimental study. *Developmental Psychology*, *41*(4), 625–635.

Gerlinger, J., Viano, S., Gardella, J. H., Fisher, B. W., Curran, F. C., & Higgins, E. M. (2021). Exclusionary school discipline and delinquent outcomes: A meta-analysis. *Journal of Youth and Adolescence*, *50*(8), 1493–1509.

Giedd, J. (2004). Structural magnetic resonance imagining of the adolescent brain. *Annals of the New York Academy of Science*, *1021*, 77–85.

Gorman-Smith, D., Henry, D. B., & Tolan, P. H. (2004). Exposure to community violence and violence perpetration: the protective effects of family functioning. *Journal of Clinical and Child Adolescent Psychology*, *33*(3), 439–449.

Gottfredson, M. R., & Hirschi, T. (1990). *A general theory of crime*. Stanford University Press.

Harty, S. C., Miller, C. J., Newcorn, J. H., & Halperin, J. M. (2009). Adolescent with childhood ADHD and comorbid disruptive behavior disorders: Aggression, anger, and hostility. *Child Psychiatry and Human Development*, *40*(1), 85–97.

Hawley, P. H. (1999). The ontogenesis of social dominance: A strategy-based evolutionary perspective. *Developmental Review*, *19*(1), 97–132.

Hawley, P. H. (2014). The duality of human nature: Coercion and prosociality in youths' hierarchy ascension and social success. *Current Directions in Psychological Science*, *23*(6), 433–438.

Hay, C., & Forrest, W. (2008). Self-control theory and the concept of opportunity: The case for a more systematic union. *Criminology*, *46*(4), 1039–1072. https://doi.org/10.1111/j.1745-9125.2008.00135.x

Haynie, D. L. (2001). Delinquent peers revisited: Does network structure matter? *American Journal of Sociology*, *106*(4), 1013–1057.

Haynie, D. L. (2003). Contexts of risk? Explaining the link between girls' pubertal development and their delinquency involvement. *Social Forces*, *82*(1), 355–397. https://doi.org/10.1353/sof.2003.0093

Hemphill, S. A., Toumbourou, J. W., Herrenkohl, T. I., McMorris, B. J., & Catalano, R. F. (2006). The effect of school suspensions and arrests on subsequent adolescent antisocial behavior in Australia and the United States. *Journal of Adolescent Health*, *39*(5), 736–744.

Herrenkohl, T. I., Guo, J., Kosterman, R., Hawkins, J. D., Catalano, R. F., & Smith, B. H. (2001). Early adolescent predictors of youth violence as mediators of childhood risks. *Journal of Early Adolescence*, *21*(4), 447–469.

Hirschi, T., & Gottfredson, M. R. (1983). Age and the explanation of crime. *American Journal of Sociology*, *89*(3), 552–584.

Hirschi, T., & Gottfredson, M. R. (1994). The generality of deviance. In T. Hirschi & M. R. Gottfredson (Eds.), *The generality of deviance* (pp. 1–22). Transaction Publishers.

Hoeben, E. M., & Weerman, F. M. (2016). Why is involvement in unstructured socializing related to adolescent delinquency? *Criminology: An Interdisciplinary Journal*, *54*(2), 242–281.

Hoeve, M., Colins, O. F., Mulder, E. A., Loeber, R., Stams, G. J. J. M., & Vermeiren, R. R. (2014). Trauma and mental health problems in adolescent males: Differences between childhood-onset and adolescent-onset offenders. *Criminal Justice & Behavior*, *42*(7), 685–702.

Hoffmann, J. P., Erickson, L. D., & Spence, K. R. (2013). Modeling the association between academic achievement and delinquency: An application of interactional theory. Criminology, *51*(3), 629–660.

Isen, J. (2010). A meta-analytic assessment of Wechsler's P>V sign in antisocial populations. *Clinical Psychology Review*, *30*(4), 423–435.

Jaffee, S. R., Belsky, J., Harrington, H., Caspi, A., & Moffitt, T. E. (2006). When parents have a history of conduct disorder: How is the care-giving environment affected? *Journal of Abnormal Psychology*, *115*(2), 309–319. https://psycnet.apa.org/doi/10.1037/0021-843X.115.2.309

Jaffee, S. R., Caspi, A., Moffitt, T. E., Dodge, K. A., Rutter, M., Taylor, A., & Tully, L. A. (2005). Nature nurture: Genetic vulnerabilities interact with child maltreatment to promote conduct problems. *Development and Psychopathology, 17*(1), 67–84.

Jarjoura, G. R., Triplett, R. A., & Brinker, G. P. (2002). Growing up poor: Examining the link between persistent childhood poverty and delinquency. *Journal of Quantitative Criminology, 18*(2), 159–187.

Jolliffe, D., & Farrington, D. P. (2010). Individual differences and offending. In E. McLaughlin & T. Newburn (Eds.), *The Sage handbook of criminological theory* (pp. 40–55). Sage.

Jones, S. E., Miller, J. D., & Lyman, D. R. (2011). Personality, antisocial behavior, and aggression: A meta-analytic review. *Journal of Criminal Justice, 39*(4), 329–337.

Kanazawa, S. (2009). Evolutionary psychology and crime. In A. Walsh & K. M. Beaver (Eds.), *Biosocial criminology: New directions in theory and research* (pp. 90–110). Routledge.

Kiff, C. J., Lengua, L. J., & Salewski, M. (2011). Nature and nurturing: Parenting in the context of child temperament. *Clinical Child and Family Psychology Review, 14*(3), 251–301. https://dx.doi.org/10.1007%2Fs10567-011-0093-4

Kim-Cohen, J., Caspi, A., Taylor, A., Williams, B., Newcombe, R., Craig, I. W., & Moffitt, T. E. (2006). MAOA, maltreatment, and gene–environment interaction predicting children's mental health: New evidence and a meta-analysis. *Molecular Psychiatry, 11*(10), 903–913.

Klahr, A. M., & Burt, S. A. (2014). Elucidating the etiology of individual differences in parenting: A meta-analysis of behavioral genetic research. *Psychological Bulletin, 140*(2), 544–586.

Kolla, N. J., Attard, S., Craig, G., Blackwood, N., & Hodgins, S. (2014). Monoamine oxidase A alleles in violent offenders with antisocial personality disorder: High activity associated with proactive aggression. *Criminal Behavior and Mental Health, 24*(5), 368–372. https://doi.org/10.1002/cbm.1917

Kreager, D. A. (2007). When it's good to be "bad": Violence and adolescent peer acceptance. *Criminology, 45*, 893–923.

Krueger, R. F., Moffitt, T. E., Caspi, A., Bleske, A., & Silva, P. A. (1998). Assortative mating for antisocial behavior: Developmental and methodological implications. *Behavior Genetics, 28*(3), 173–186.

Kuhn E. S., Laird R. D. (2013). Parent and peer restrictions of opportunities attenuate the link between low self-control and antisocial behavior. Social Development, 22, 813–830.

Lacour, M., & Tissington, L. D. (2011). The effects of poverty on academic achievement. *Educational Research and Reviews, 6*(7), 522–527.

LaFontana, K. M., & Cillessen, A. H. N. (2010). Developmental changes in the priority of perceived status in childhood and adolescence. *Social Development, 19*(1), 130–147.

LaGrange, T., & Silverman, R. (1999). Low self-control and opportunity: Testing the general theory of crime as an explanation for gender differences in delinquency. *Criminology, 37*(1), 41–72. https://doi.org/10.1111/j.1745-9125.1999.tb00479.x

Latzman, R. D., Elkovitch, N., & Clark, L. A. (2009). Predicting parenting practices from maternal and adolescent sons' personality. *Journal of Research in Personality, 43*(5), 847–855.

Laub, J. H., & Sampson, R. J. (2003). *Shared beginnings, divergent lives: Delinquent boys to age 70*. Harvard University Press.

Leventhal, T., & Brooks-Gunn, J. (2000). The neighborhoods they live in: The effects of neighborhood residence on child and adolescent outcomes. *Psychological Bulletin, 126*(2), 309–327. https://psycnet.apa.org/doi/10.1037/0033-2909.126.2.309

Liu H, Li Y, Guo G. (2015). Gene by social-environment interaction for youth delinquency and violence: Thirty-nine aggression-related genes. *Social Forces, 93*(3), 881–903.

Loeber, R., & Stouthamer-Loeber, M. (1998). Development of juvenile aggression and violence: Some common misconceptions and controversies. *American Psychologist, 53*(2), 242–259. https://psycnet.apa.org/doi/10.1037/0003-066X.53.2.242

Lombroso, C. (1876). *Criminal man*. Hoepli.

Luthar, S. S., & D'Avanzo, K. (1999). Contextual factors in substance use: A study of suburban and inner-city adolescents. *Development and Psychopathology, 11*(4), 845–867.

Maimon, D., & Browning, C. R. (2010). Unstructured socializing, collective efficacy, and violent behavior among urban youth. *Criminology, 48*(2), 443–474.

Maxon, C. (2011). Street gangs. In J. Q. Wilson & J. Petersilia (Eds.), *Crime and public policy* (pp. 158–182). Oxford University Press.

Mayeux, L., & Cillessen, A. H. (2008). It's not just being popular, it's knowing it too: The role of self-perceptions of status in the associations between peer status and aggression. *Social Development, 17*(4), 871–888.

Mazur, A. (2005). *Biosociology of dominance and deference*. Rowman & Littlefield.

Michell, L., & Amos, A. (1997). Girls, pecking order and smoking. *Social Science & Medicine, 44*(12), 1861–1869.

Miles, D., & Carey, G. (1997). Genetic and environmental architecture of human aggression. *Journal of Personality and Social Psychology, 72*(1), 207–217.

Miller, E. K., & Cohen, J. D. (2001). An integrative theory of prefrontal cortex function. *Annual Review of Neuroscience, 24*(1), 167–202.

Miller, J. D., & Lynam, D. (2001). Structural models of personality and their relation to antisocial behavior: A meta-analytic review. *Criminology, 39*(4), 765–798. https://doi.org/10.1111/j.1745-9125.2001.tb00940.x

Miller-Johnson, S., Costanzo, P. R., Coie, J. D., Rose, M. R., Browne, D. C., & Johnson, C. (2003). Peer social structure and risk-taking behaviors among African American early adolescents. *Journal of Youth and Adolescence, 32*(5), 375–384.

Moffitt, T. E. (1993). "Life-course-persistent" and "adolescence-limited" antisocial behavior: A developmental taxonomy. *Psychological Review, 100*(4), 674–701. https://psycnet.apa.org/doi/10.1037/0033-295X.100.4.674

Moffitt, T. E. (2003). Life-course-persistent and adolescence-limited antisocial behavior: A 10- year research review and a research agenda. In B. B. Lahey, T. E. Moffitt, & A. Caspi (Eds.), *Causes of conduct disorder and juvenile delinquency* (pp. 49–75). Guilford Press.

Moffitt, T. E. (2005). The new look of behavioral genetics in developmental psychopathology: Gene-environment interplay in antisocial behaviors. *Psychological Bulletin, 131*(4), 533–554.

Moffitt, T. E. (2006). A review of research on the taxonomy of life-course persistent versus adolescence-limited antisocial behavior. In F. T. Cullen, J. P. Wright, & K. R. Blevins (Eds.), *Taking stock: The status of criminological theory* (pp. 277–312). Transaction Publishers.

Moffitt, T. E., & Caspi, A. (2001). Childhood predictors differentiate life-course persistent and adolescence-limited antisocial pathways among males and females. *Development and Psychopathology, 13*(2), 355–375. https://doi.org/10.1017/s0954579401002097

Moffitt, T. E., Caspi, A., Dickson, N., Silva, P. A., & Stanton, W. (1996). Childhood-onset versus adolescent-onset antisocial conduct in males: Natural history from 3 to 18. *Development and Psychopathology, 8*(2), 399–424. https://psycnet.apa.org/doi/10.1017/S0954579400007161

Moffitt, T. E., Lynam, D., & Silva, P. A. (1994). Neuropsychological tests predicting persistent male delinquency. *Criminology, 32*(2), 277–300. https://doi.org/10.1111/j.1745-9125.1994.tb01155.x

Moffitt, T. E., Caspi, A., Harrington, H., Milne, B. J. (2002). Males on the life-course-persistent and adolescence-limited antisocial pathways: follow-up at age 26 years. *Development Psychopathology, 14*(1), 179–207.

Moffitt, T. E. (2018). Male antisocial behaviour in adolescence and beyond. *Nature Human Behaviour, 2*, 177–186.

Morgan, A. B., & Lilienfeld, S. O. (2000). A meta-analytic review of the relationship between antisocial behavior and neuropsychological measures of executive function. *Clinical Psychology Review, 20*(1), 113–136.

Nagin, D. S., Farrington, D. P., & Moffitt, T. E. (1995). Life-course trajectories of different types of offenders. *Criminology, 33*(1), 111–139. https://doi.org/10.1111/j.1745-9125.1995.tb01173.x

Neumann, A., Barker, E. D., Koot, H. M., & Maughan, B. (2010). The role of contextual risk, impulsivity, and parental knowledge in the development of adolescent antisocial behavior. *Journal of Abnormal Psychology, 119*(3), 534–545. https://psycnet.apa.org/doi/10.1037/a0019860

Nilsson, K. W., Sjoberg, R. L., Damberg, M., Leppert, J., Ohrvik, J., Alm, P. O., Lindstrom, L., & Oreland, L. (2006). Role of monoamine oxidase A genotype and psychosocial factors in male adolescent criminal activity. *Biological Psychiatry, 59*(2), 121–127.

Oberwittler, D. (2007). The effects of neighborhood poverty on adolescent problem behaviors: A multi-level analysis differentiated by gender and ethnicity. *Housing Studies, 22*(5), 781–803.

O'Brien, L., Albert, D., Chein, J., & Steinberg, L. (2011). Adolescents prefer more immediate rewards when in the presence of their peers. *Journal of Research on Adolescence, 21*(4), 747–753

Odgers, C. L., Moffitt, T. E., Broadbent, J. M., Dickson, N., Hancox, R. J., Harrington, H., Poulton, R., Sears, M. R., Thomson, W. M., & Caspi, A. (2008). Female and male antisocial trajectories: From childhood origins to adult outcomes. *Development and Psychopathology, 20*(2), 673–716.

Odgers, P., Houghton, S., & Douglas, G. (1996). Reputation enhancement theory and adolescent substance use. *Journal of Child Psychology and Psychiatry, 37*(8), 1015–1022.

Okuda, M., Martins, S. S., Wall, M. M., Chen, C., Santaella-Tenorio, J., Ramos-Olazagasti, M., Wei, C., Canino, G., Bird, H. R., & Duarte, C. S. (2019). Do parenting behaviors modify the way sensation seeking influences antisocial behaviors? *Journal of Child Psychology Psychiatry, 60*(2), 169–177.

Osgood, D. W., & Anderson, A. L. (2004). Unstructured socializing and rates of delinquency. *Criminology, 42*(3), 519–549.

Osgood, D. W., Wilson, J. K., O'Malley, P. M., Bachman, J. G., & Johnson, L. D. (1996). Routine activities and individual deviant behavior. *American Sociological Review, 61*(4), 635–655.

Owens, J. G., & Slocum, L. (2012). Abstainers in adolescence and adulthood: Exploring the correlates of abstention using Moffitt's developmental taxonomy. *Crime and Delinquency, 61*(5), 690–718.

Painter, K., & Scannapieco, M. (2013). Child maltreatment: The neurobiological aspects of posttraumatic stress disorder. *Journal of Evidence-Based Social Work, 10*(4), 276–284.

Paternoster, R., McGloin, J. M., Nguyen, H., & Thomas, K. J. (2013). The causal impact of exposure to deviant peers: An experimental investigation. *Journal of Research in Crime & Delinquency, 50*(4), 476–503.

Patterson, G. R. (1998). Continuities – A search for causal mechanisms: Comment on the special section. *Developmental Psychology, 34*(6), 1263–1268. https://psycnet.apa.org/doi/10.1037/0012-1649.34.6.1263

Peckins, M. K., Shaw, D. S., Waller, R., & Hyde, L. W. (2018). Intimate partner violence exposure predicts antisocial behavior via pro-violence attitudes among males with elevated levels of cortisol. *Social Development, 27*(4), 761–776.

Piquero, A. R., & Brezina, T. (2001). Testing Moffitt's account of adolescence-limited delinquency. *Criminology, 39*(2), 353–370.

Piquero, A. R., Farrington, D. P., & Blumstein, A. (2003). The criminal career paradigm. In M. Tonry (Ed.), *Crime and justice: A review of research* (Vol. 30, pp. 359–506). University of Chicago Press.

Pouwels, J. L., Lansu, T. A. M., & Cillessen, A. H. N. (2018). A developmental perspective on popularity and the group process of bullying. *Aggression and Violent Behavior, 43*, 64–70.

Pratt, T. C., & Cullen, F. T. (2000). The empirical status of Gottfredson and Hirschi's general theory of crime: A meta-analysis. *Criminology, 38*(9), 931–964. https://doi.org/10.1111/j.1745-9125.2000.tb00911.x

Pratt, T. C., Cullen, F. T., Sellers, C. S., Winfree, L. T., Jr., Madensen, T. D., Daigle, L. E., Fearn, N. E., & Gau, J. M. (2010). The empirical status of social learning theory: A meta-analysis. *Justice Quarterly, 27*(6), 765–802.

Prinstein, M. J., & Cillessen, A. H. N. (2003). Forms and functions of adolescent peer aggression associated with high levels of peer status. *Merrill-Palmer Quarterly, 49*(3), 310–342.

Prinzie, P., Onghena, P., Hellinckx, W., Grietens, H., Ghesquière, P., & Colpin, H. (2004). Parent and child personality characteristics as predictors of negative discipline and externalizing problem behaviour in children. *European Journal of Personality, 18*(2), 73–102. https://doi.org/10.1002/per.501

Racz, S. J., & McMahon, R. J. (2011). The relationship between parental knowledge and monitoring and child and adolescent conduct problems: A 10-year update. *Clinical Child and Family Psychology Review, 14*(4), 377–398.

Raine, A., Moffitt, T. E., Caspi, A., Loeber, R., Stouthamer-Loeber, M., & Lynam, D. (2005). Neurocognitive impairments in boys on the life-course persistent antisocial path. *Journal of Abnormal Psychology, 114*(1), 38–49.

Rankin, B. M., & Quane, J. M. (2002). Social contexts and urban adolescent outcomes: The interrelated effects of neighborhoods, families, and peers on African American youth. *Social Problems, 49*(1), 79–100.

Rebellon, C. J. (2006). Do adolescents engage in delinquency to attract the social attention of peers? An extension and longitudinal test of the social reinforcement hypothesis. *Journal of Research in Crime and Delinquency, 43*(4), 387–411.

Rebellon, C. J., & Modecki, K. L. (2014). Accounting for projection bias in models of delinquent peer influence: The utility and limits of latent variable approaches. *Journal of Quantitative Criminology, 30*(2), 163–186.

Rebellon, C. J., Trinkner, R., Van Gundy, K. T., & Cohn, E. S. (2019) No guts, no glory: The influence of risk-taking on adolescent popularity. *Deviant Behavior, 40*(12), 1464–1479.

Reicher, S., & Emler, N. (1985). Delinquent behaviour and attitudes to formal authority. *British Journal of Social Psychology, 24*(3), 161–168.

Rhee, S., & Waldman, I. (2002). Genetic and environmental influence on antisocial behavior: A meta-analysis of twin and adoption studies. *Psychological Bulletin, 128*(3), 490–529.

Richards, M. H., Larson, R., Miller, B. V., Luo, Z., Sims, B., Parrella, D. P., & McCauley, C. (2004). Risky and protective contexts and exposure to violence in urban African American young adolescents. *Journal of Clinical Child and Adolescent Psychology, 33*(1), 138–148.

Ronfeldt, M., Loeb, S., & Wyckoff, J. (2013). How teacher turnover harms student achievement. *American Educational Research Journal, 50*(1), 4–36.

Rose, A. J., Swenson, L. P., & Waller, E. M. (2004). Overt and relational aggression and perceived popularity: Developmental differences in concurrent and prospective relations. *Developmental Psychology, 40*(3), 378–387.

Rothbart, M., Ahadi, A., & Evans, D. (2000). Temperament and personality: Origins and outcomes. *Journal of Personality and Social Psychology, 78*(1), 122–135.

Sampson, R. J., & Groves, W. B. (1989). Community structure and crime: Testing social- disorganization theory. *American Journal of Sociology, 94*(4), 774–802.

Sandstrom, M. J., & Cillessen, A. H. N. (2006). Likable versus popular: Distinct implications for adolescent adjustment. *International Journal of Behavioral Development, 30*(4), 305–314.

Sampson, R. J., & Laub, J. H. (1994). Urban poverty and the family context of delinquency: A new look at structure and process in a classic study. *Child Development, 65*(2), 523–540.

Sampson, R. J., Raudenbush, S. W., & Earls, F. (1997). Neighborhoods and violent crime: A multilevel study of collective efficacy. *Science, 277*(5328), 918–924.

Savolainen, J., Hughes, L. A., Mason, W. A., Hurtig, T. M., Taanila, A. M., Ebeling, H., Moilanen, I. K., & Kivivuori, J. (2011). Antisocial propensity, adolescent school outcomes, and the risk of criminal conviction. *Journal of Research on Adolescence, 22*(1), 54–64. https://doi.org/10.1111/j.1532-7795.2011.00754.x

Schlegel, A., & Barry, H. (1991). *Adolescence: An anthropological inquiry*. Free Press.

Serpeloni, F., Radtke, K. M., Assis, S. G. A., Henning, F., Nätt, D., & Elbert, T. (2017). Grandmaternal stress during pregnancy and DNA methylation of the third generation: An epigenome-wide association study. *Translational Psychiatry, 7*(8), e1202.

Sheidow, A. J., Gorman-Smith, D., Tolan, P. H., & Henry, D. B. (2001). Family and community characteristics: Risk factors for violence exposure in inner-city youth. *Journal of Community Psychology, 29*(3), 345–360.

Shochet, I. M., Dadds, M. R., Ham, D., & Montague, R. (2006). School connectedness is an underemphasized parameter in adolescent mental health: Results of a community prediction study. *Journal of Clinical Child and Adolescent Psychology, 35*(2), 170–179.

Silverthorn, P., & Frick, P. J. (1999). Developmental pathways to antisocial behavior: The delayed-onset pathway in girls. *Development and Psychopathology, 11*(1), 101–126. https://psycnet.apa.org/doi/10.1017/S0954579499001972

Simon, N., & Johnson, S. M. (2015). Teacher turnover in high-poverty schools: What we know and can do. *Teachers College Record, 117*(3), 1–35.

Sowell, E., Thompson, P., & Toga, A. (2004). Mapping changes in the human cortex throughout the span of life. *Neuroscientist, 10*(4), 372–392. https://doi.org/10.1177/1073858404263960

Spano, R., Vazsonyi, A. T., & Bolland, J. (2009). Does parenting mediate the effects of exposure to violence on violent behavior? An ecological–transactional model of community violence. *Journal of Adolescence, 32*(5), 1321–1341.

Steinberg, L. (2005). Cognitive and affective development in adolescence. *Trends in Cognitive Sciences, 9*(2), 69–74.

Steinberg, L. (2008). A social neuroscience perspective on adolescent risk taking. *Developmental Review, 28*(1), 78–106.

Steinberg, L. (2010). A dual systems model of adolescent risk-taking. *Developmental Psychobiology, 52*(3), 216–224.

Steinberg, L., Albert, D., Cauffman, E., Banich, M., Graham, S., & Woolard, J. (2008). Age differences in sensation seeking and impulsivity as indexed by behavior and self-report: Evidence for a dual systems model. *Developmental Psychology, 44*(6), 1764–1778. https://psycnet.apa.org/doi/10.1037/a0012955

Sutherland, E. H. (1947). *The principles of criminology*. Lippincott.

Svensson, R., & Oberwittler, D. (2021). Changing routine activities and the decline of youth crime: A repeated cross-sectional analysis of self-reported delinquency in Sweden, 1999–2017. *Criminology, 59*, 351–386.

Sweeten, G., Piquero, A. R., & Steinberg, L. (2013). Age and the explanation of crime, revisited. *Journal of Youth and Adolescence, 42*(6), 921–938.

Taylor, J., Iacono, W. G., & McGue, M. (2000). Evidence for a genetic etiology of early-onset delinquency. *Journal of Abnormal Psychology, 109*(4), 634–643. https://doi.org/10.1037/0021-843X.109.4.634

Thornberry, T. P., Freeman-Gallant, A., Lizotte, A. J., Krohn, M. D., & Smith, C. A. (2003). Linked lives: The intergenerational transmission of antisocial behavior. *Journal of Abnormal Child Psychology, 31*(2), 171–184. https://doi.org/10.1023/a:1022574208366

Tibbetts, S. G., & Piquero, A. R. (2006). The influence of gender, low birth weight, and disadvantaged environment in predicting early onset of offending: A test of Moffitt's interactional hypothesis. *Criminology, 37*(4), 843–878. https://doi.org/10.1111/j.1745-9125.1999.tb00507.x

Tinsley, B. R., & Parke, R. D. (1983). The person-environment relationship: Lessons from families with preterm infants. In D. Magnuson & V. R. Allen (Eds.), *Human development: An interactional perspective* (pp. 93–110). Academic Press.

Valente, T. W., Unger, J., & Johnson, A. C. (2005). Do popular students smoke? The association between popularity and smoking among middle school students. *Journal of Adolescent Health, 37*(4), 323–329.

Van Honk, J., Peper, J., & Schutter, D. (2005). Testosterone reduces unconscious fear but not consciously experienced anxiety: Implications for the disorders of fear and anxiety. *Biological Psychiatry, 58*(3), 218–225. https://doi.org/10.1016/j.biopsych.2005.04.003

Verona, E., & Sachs-Ericsson, N. (2005). The intergenerational transmission of externalizing behaviors in adult participants: The mediating role of childhood abuse. *Journal of Consulting and Clinical Psychology, 73*(6), 1135–1145. https://doi.org/10.1037/0022-006X.73.6.1135

Viding, E. F., Larsson, H., & Jones, A. P. (2008). Quantitative genetic studies of antisocial behavior. *Philosophical Transactions of the Royal Society B, 363*(1503), 2519–2527. https://doi.org/10.1098/rstb.2008.0037

Walker, E. (2002). Adolescent neurodevelopment and psychopathology. *Current Directions in Psychological Science, 11*(1), 24–28.

Walsh, A. (2009a). Crazy by design: A biosocial approach to the age-crime curve. In A. Walsh & K. M. Beaver (Eds.), *Biosocial criminology: New directions in theory and research* (pp. 154–175). Routledge.

Walsh, A. (2009b). Criminal behavior from heritability to epigenetics: How genetics clarifies the role of the environment. In A. Walsh & K. M. Beaver (Eds.), *Biosocial criminology: New directions in theory and research* (pp. 29–49). Routledge.

Walsh, A. (2019). *Sensitivity reinforcement theory: A metatheory for biosocial criminology*. Routledge.

Weatherburn, D., & Lind, B. (2006). What mediates the macro-level effects of economic and social stress on crime? *Australian and New Zealand Journal of Criminology, 39*(3), 384–397. https://doi.org/10.1375/acri.39.3.384

Weigard, A., Chein, J., Albert, D., Smith, A., & Steinberg, L. (2014). Effects of anonymous peer observation on adolescents' preference for immediate rewards. *Developmental Science, 17*(1), 71–78.

Widom, C. S., & Brzustowicz, L. M. (2006). MAOA and the "cycle of violence": Childhood abuse and neglect, MAOA genotype, and risk for violent and antisocial behavior. *Biological Psychiatry, 60*(7), 684–689.

Willms, J. D. (2010). School composition and contextual effects on student outcomes. *Teachers College Record, 112*(4), 1008–1037.

Willoughby, T., Good, M., Adachi, P. J. C., Hamza, C., & Tavernier, R. (2013). Examining the link between adolescent brain development and risk taking from a social-developmental perspective. *Brain and Cognition, 83*(3), 315–323.

Wood, L., Kiperman, S., Esch, R. C., Leroux, A. J., & Truscott, S. D. (2017). Predicting dropout using student- and school-level factors: An ecological perspective. *School Psychology Quarterly, 32*(1), 35–49. https://psycnet.apa.org/doi/10.1037/spq0000152

Young, J. T. N., Rebellon, C. J., Barnes, J. C., & Weerman, F. M. (2014). Unpacking the black box of peer similarity in deviance: Understanding the mechanisms linking personal behavior, peer behavior, and perceptions. *Criminology, 52*(1), 60–86.

Zimmerman, G. M., & Messner, S. F. (2010). Neighborhood context and the gender gap in adolescent violent crime. *American Sociological Review, 75*(6), 958–980. https://doi.org/10.1177/0003122410386688

Zuberi, A. (2016). Neighborhoods and parenting: Assessing the influence of neighborhood quality on the parental monitoring of youth. *Youth & Society, 48*(5), 599–627.

Zuckerman, M. (2007). Sensation seeking and risky behavior. *American Psychological Association*. https://doi.org/10.1037/11555-000

CHAPTER 12

Adolescent Victims and Witnesses: Disclosures, Memory, and Suggestibility

Joshua Wyman, Rachel Dianiska, Hayden Henderson, and Lindsay C. Malloy

Abstract

Adolescence is a developmental window characterized by growth, change, and vulnerability in multiple domains. Several developmental characteristics of adolescence, both cognitive and socioemotional in nature, increase the likelihood adolescents will come into contact with the legal system as victims and witnesses and also shape the statements that adolescents provide in legal contexts. This chapter describes how several facets of adolescents' cognitive (e.g., executive functioning) and socioemotional (e.g., susceptibility to peer influence) development influence their disclosures, memory, and suggestibility. It reviews the current state of knowledge concerning what is known about adolescents' *willingness* to share their legally relevant experiences with others (i.e., issues related disclosure) and their *ability* to do so (i.e., issues related to memory and suggestibility). The chapter closes by discussing recommendations for policy and practice alongside novel or emerging issues regarding adolescents' involvement in the legal system as victims and witnesses that warrant additional scientific inquiry.

Key Words: adolescence, memory, suggestibility, disclosure, victims, witnesses, testimony

As a discipline, developmental psychology has a rich history of asking and answering important applied questions that concern and affect the lives of children and families in multiple domains (e.g., education, medicine, mental health, nursing). Since the 1980s in particular, many of these questions have been raised at the intersection of developmental psychology and the law in relation to young victims' and witnesses' capacities and limitations, as well as how best to facilitate their effective participation in the legal system. The scientific and practical interest in how youth experience and function within the various legal systems (e.g., criminal, civil, dependency) has undeniably advanced knowledge regarding youths' participation and performance in the legal system, while also advancing basic science and theory concerning children's memory, suggestibility, and disclosure of traumatic experiences. Furthermore, this research has resulted in significant changes to policies and laws that fundamentally alter justice for legally involved youth (see Owen-Kostelnik et al., 2006; Steinberg, 2009, for reviews).

Despite the significant progress that has been made in research and public policy concerning youths' involvement in the legal system, important questions remain about multiple aspects of their legal participation, especially in some of the less well-studied subsets of adolescent populations. The overarching purpose of the current chapter is to review research concerning the disclosures, memory, and suggestibility of adolescent victims and witnesses. Our focus is twofold: (a) reviewing what we know about adolescents' *willingness* to share their legally relevant experiences with others (i.e., issues related to disclosure) and (b) reviewing what we know about adolescents' *ability* to share their legally relevant experiences with others (i.e., issues related to memory and suggestibility). Although we will at times touch on issues of relevance to adolescent suspects and defendants (e.g., the role of peer influence in admissions of guilt), research concerning that subset of legally involved adolescents will be covered comprehensively in other chapters in this volume (see Cleary & Crane and Zottoli et al.). In addition, our chapter does not provide an exhaustive review of the literature on adolescent victims and witnesses; instead, we discuss several areas in which developmental characteristics and processes shape the statements that adolescents provide as victims and witnesses in legal settings. We do so with an eye toward outlining what is known in this area and what unanswered questions need to be addressed.

Much of the work on how adolescents function within the legal system has been devoted to understanding juveniles suspected of committing a crime rather than having witnessed or experienced a crime, the latter of whom are also faced with important roles to play in legal contexts. However, the developmental and contextual factors that affect adolescent witnesses and victims have received far less research attention. Instead, much of the work on youthful victims and witnesses has focused on younger children, with a disproportionate amount of work conducted on preschool-aged children despite very young children's relatively infrequent likelihood of extensive legal involvement (e.g., providing testimony; Brewer et al., 1997; Hershkowitz et al., 2005; Stroud et al., 2000). The minimal attention focused specifically on adolescent victims and witnesses is particularly noteworthy given that adolescents make up the second largest group likely to experience violent crime, behind only 18–24-year-old young adults (Morgan & Truman, 2019), and are more likely to testify as victims or witnesses than younger youth (Chong & Connolly, 2015; Walsh et al., 2010). Furthermore, 23% of maltreatment victims are between 12 and 17 years of age, a percentage that increases substantially for certain types of sexual victimization (e.g., 72% of sex-trafficking victims are adolescents; U.S. Department of Health and Human Services, 2020). As such, understanding reporting abilities in adolescent victims and witnesses is important and needed.

Although youth—like adults—may experience or witness multiple types of crimes, it is most common for youth, across childhood and adolescence, to become involved in the legal system (i.e., criminal or dependency court) because they have experienced maltreatment or witnessed family violence. In particular, in the United States and United Kingdom, sexual abuse is the most common reason for criminal court involvement (e.g., Goodman et al., 1999; Plotnikoff & Woolfson, 2009). Thus, much of the research that we review in this chapter concerns how adolescents disclose and narrate about sexual abuse or victimization.

Hallmark Features of Adolescent Development

Before discussing what is known about adolescent victims' and witnesses' disclosures, memory, and suggestibility, it is useful to discuss several hallmark features of adolescence, a developmental window characterized by rapid and significant changes in biological processes, cognitive abilities, social relationships, and motivational and emotional functioning (see Boyer, 2006). We do not discuss each and every notable characteristic of adolescence, but rather highlight a handful that are particularly important for adolescent victims and witnesses, distinguishing those that fall within the broader areas of cognitive and socioemotional development. We highlight how these characteristics influence whether, with whom, and how much of adolescents' experiences they share with others, especially legal authorities. Put another way, this chapter focuses on answering the question, "How does adolescent development influence what victims and witnesses say (and what they do not say) in legal contexts?" Finally, we discuss recommendations for policy and practice, alongside novel or emerging issues regarding adolescents' involvement in the legal system as victims and witnesses that warrant additional scientific inquiry.

Cognitive Development
During adolescence, there is significant maturation of important cognitive, memory, and language functions of relevance to adolescents' participation in the legal system as victims and witnesses, who will likely be asked to share memories of their experiences with others in interviews. This often requires, among other skills, remembering experiences over long periods of time, reasoning about what to say and to whom, narrating about their experiences in a coherent manner, and inhibiting responses to leading or suggestive questions. Thus, the development of executive functioning is key.

According to the dual systems model, the maturation of cognitive control and socioemotional systems of the brain occur at different timepoints. This temporary unevenness has an impact on adolescent behavior and risk (see Steinberg, 2009, for a review). Inceglo et al. (2019) conducted a large study of 10–30-year-olds from 11 countries. They found that adolescents' peak cognitive capacity preceded their psychosocial maturity, meaning their abilities that rely on "cold cognition" reached adult levels during their mid-teenage years, whereas their abilities that rely on "hot cognition" did not reach similar levels until adulthood. Cold cognition refers to abilities employed during deliberation in the absence of high levels of emotion, while hot cognition involves engaging mental processes during emotionally charged times (Icenogle et al., 2019). Within the legal system, adolescents may use hot cognition during interrogations to make impulsive and/or uninformed decisions (e.g., falsely confessing to a crime) when feeling stressed or pressured. Conversely, cold cognition is more likely to be used when the adolescent is given time and support to make informed legal decisions, such as when consulting with supportive adults (e.g., parents and their attorney) about whether to plead guilty to a crime.

The cognitive control systems of the brain consist of the lateral prefrontal and parietal cortices, which support higher order executive functions (Steinberg, 2007). These executive functions (EFs), including attention, impulse control, emotional regulation, planning, organization, mental flexibility, and working memory, are critical for adolescent decision making, behavior, and eyewitness testimony. They also improve significantly during adolescence, albeit some cognitive abilities—namely those related to cold cognition—improve more rapidly than others (Icenogle et al., 2019; Shulman et al., 2016). Adolescents with lower EF, particularly with respect to impulse control, not only are more at risk of engaging in impulsive and risk-taking behaviors that can lead to involvement in the juvenile justice system as suspects or defendants (Cauffman et al., 2017) but also may be at increased risk of victimization. For example, adolescents with lower levels of EF are at a greater risk of experiencing physical and emotional abuse by their peers (Kloosterman et al., 2014) and parents (Kirke-Smith et al., 2014), as well as witnessing crimes committed by others (Op den Kelder et al., 2018). That is, youth with impulse control deficits are more at risk of being involved in risky or unsafe situations (Cauffman et al., 2017), such as violent peer interactions, that can result in them witnessing or participating in criminal activity. Youth with deficits in EF, such as those diagnosed with attention-deficit/hyperactivity disorder (ADHD), are also more likely to have parents who have EF challenges and psychopathology; consequently, parental psychopathology increases a youth's risk for witnessing intimate partner violence (Lugo-Candelas et al., 2021).

Thus, adolescents' relative *lack* of impulse control, compared to adults, may lead to their exposure to crime and violence in the first place.

Experiencing trauma, including being a victim or witness to a crime, can also have a significant impact on brain development. Exposure to trauma can result in decreased volume in brain regions responsible for memory and EF (e.g., the hippocampus, anterior cingulate cortex, and prefrontal cortex), as well as increased amygdala activity that can cause heightened stress response and emotional responsivity commonly seen in victims of trauma (see Bolsinger et al., 2018, for a review). Traumatic events can also cause a reduction of neurotransmitters important for managing stress and anxiety (gamma-aminobutyric acid [GABA]), as well as learning and memory (glutamate) in the subcortical areas of the brain (Sheth et al., 2019). These neurological consequences of victimization and trauma can potentially impact adolescent capacities as eyewitnesses. For example, individuals diagnosed with posttraumatic stress disorder (PTSD) can display reduced memory functioning (Brewin et al., 2007), which can impair their ability to accurately recall some events while concurrently enhancing their memory for events directly linked to the PTSD. Potentially traumatic memories may also be remembered more vividly than nontraumatic experiences. However, the presence of elevated emotions and stress can impact adolescents' ability to produce organized narratives regarding these experiences (Berntsen et al., 2003). Although both children and adolescents may struggle to produce organized narratives under such circumstances, it may be easier to overlook the effects of emotional arousal and stress on adolescents and to expect more from them than children.

In sum, adolescents are more cognitively advanced than children, demonstrating more sophisticated executive functioning and reasoning skills (see Best & Miller, 2010, for a review). However, there is continued maturation of narrative abilities, language pragmatics, memory, and executive functioning skills during the adolescent years (Craik & Bialystok, 2006) in ways that have implications for their capacities and limitations as eyewitnesses. Perhaps most notably, adolescents demonstrate immaturity in executive functioning compared to adults, particularly with respect to impulse control, attention, and long-term planning, that can increase their vulnerability to being involved in the legal system and their subsequent ability to share information in a coherent manner once they are immersed in the legal system.

Socioemotional Development

Although in some ways adolescent cognitive development, especially in relation to cold cognition, approaches or is even on par with that of adults', adolescents' socioemotional development reveals a different story. Socioemotional processes, such as perspective taking, that may affect adolescent victims' and witnesses' disclosure decisions (e.g., whether, when, and to whom to reveal abuse) and emotional interpretations of specific situations (i.e., hot cognition reasoning and decision making) do not fully mature until young adulthood (Van der Graaff et al., 2014), although they are considerably more advanced in adolescents than in younger children (Humphrey & Dumontheil, 2016; Lemaigre et al., 2017).

One socioemotional process that is a key focus in adolescence is self-identity, which is often pursued through exploratory behavior and peer relationships. As captured in classic (e.g., Erikson's psychosocial model of personality development; Erikson, 1968) and contemporary theories (e.g., Luyckx et al., 2006), adolescents engage in more exploratory behaviors for the purpose of developing their own personal identity, beliefs, and goals. These exploratory behaviors may include increased interactions with friends instead of family; changes in their roles and responsibilities (e.g., getting their first job, caring for younger siblings, managing personal finances); and exploring different religious, political, or sexual views and experiences. Some exploratory behaviors can also be attributed to hormonal changes (e.g., increased production of testosterone and estrogen), maturation of the limbic and paralimbic systems of the brain, and increased dopaminergic activity in the socioemotional systems of the brain at the time of puberty (Steinberg, 2009). These hormonal and neurobiological changes during adolescence have been linked to increased sensation seeking and emotionally driven behaviors that typically involve an individual seeking a particular emotional feeling or outcome (e.g., pleasure, reward, or removal of pain; Steinberg, 2009). This may help explain why adolescents may engage in emotionally charged events such as drug and alcohol use, risky sexual activity, careless driving, truancy, and behaviors that result in unintentional injuries or violence. According to the dual systems model, behavior typically becomes more planned and rational in late adolescence as traits such as impulse control and resistance to peer pressure improve (Icenogle et al., 2019); this coincides with a reduction in the frequency of risky behavior by late adolescence and early adulthood (Piquero, 2007).

Another key socioemotional process that becomes increasingly salient in adolescence is an orientation toward peer relationships and away from the family unit (Steinberg, 2009). During childhood, the parents are the primary reference group regarding behavioral norms and expectations. However, adolescents are more likely to derive their behavioral norms from their peers given the adolescents' increased desire to be valued by those peers (Albert et al., 2013). Research indicates that susceptibility to peer influence increases through childhood as adolescents begin to separate themselves from familial control, peaking around the age of 14, and then declines slowly throughout high school (Steinberg & Scott, 2003). Thus, adolescents' behavior can be highly influenced by the presence and expectations of their peers, even in situations where adolescents identify a behavior or action as immoral, illegal, and/or dangerous.

Social acceptance by one's peers is a good indicator of adjustment (Brown & Larson, 2009), and research shows that the development of adolescents' identity is positively associated with attachment to peers and a better quality of relationship with peers (Ragelienė, 2016). This separation from caregivers and emphasis toward peer relationships increases both protective factors and risk factors regarding youth involvement with the legal system. That is, while peers may offer valuable support after experiencing maltreatment (e.g., peers are frequently disclosure recipients; Crisma et al., 2004; Fehler-Cabral et al., 2013), particularly in instances where adolescents are afraid to disclose to adults (Fehler-Cabral et al., 2013), peer influence may also increase the likelihood that adolescents will be exposed to future trauma (Steinberg, 2009). Adolescents take more risks and make poorer decisions with their peers than when they are alone (Albert et al., 2013; Allen & Brown, 2008; Gardner & Steinberg, 2005), and they often fail to disclose this information to parents because of concern of disapproval or punishment (e.g., drinking alcohol, going to a party where alcohol is served; Yau et al., 2009). Risky behavior valued by peers, such as fighting or drinking, may place adolescents in dangerous predicaments where they are more likely to experience victimization, particularly because adolescents engage in more sensation-seeking behaviors than younger children and adults (Steinberg, 2009).

Another feature of adolescence that is closely related to identity formation and peer relationships is one's desire for autonomy. As Steinberg (2005, p. 69, emphasis added) describes, "Adolescence is characterized by an increased need to regulate affect and behavior in accordance with long-term goals and consequences, *often at a distance from the adults who provided regulatory structure and guidance during childhood*." Adolescent "autonomy" is multidimensional and has been operationalized in many ways, including individuation and detachment from their parents, decreased susceptibility to peer pressure, and the development of "psychosocial maturity" and "self-reliance" (Steinberg & Silverberg, 1986). Research demonstrates that adolescents do develop autonomy as they get older, they grow less susceptible to parental influence (Berndt, 1979) and more susceptible to peer influence (Steinberg & Silverberg, 1986), and they become more capable of making their own decisions (Steinberg & Cauffman, 2017). However, a hallmark of healthy and autonomous decision making is not only making decisions *independently* but also recognizing when to turn to advice from more experienced sources. In attempts to be independent, adolescents may underestimate the importance of seeking advice (Steinberg & Cauffman, 2017), such as failing to solicit assistance when they commit a crime or when they or someone they know has been victimized. In fact, research demonstrates that many adolescents disclose victimization only to peers and fail to tell their parents (Schonbucher et al., 2012), which increases their risk of the victimization continuing. Adolescents' desire for autonomy and individuation from their caregivers may also manifest as oppositionality, rebellion, or rejection of parental advice (Steinberg & Cauffman, 2017). These behavioral manifestations could subsequently increase adolescent victims' reluctance to seek help from caregivers, particularly if their victimization occurred in a risky situation or if they feel responsible for what happened (e.g., because of their exploratory or rebellious behavior).

In sum, adolescents' unique socioemotional characteristics, including a focus on exploration, peers, and autonomy, are likely to contribute to increased interactions with the legal system as offenders, victims, and witnesses. It is imperative that the criminal justice system continue to recognize the developmental differences between children, adolescents, and adults so that special consideration can be given to the vulnerable adolescent age group, particularly for situations involving hot cognition.

Adolescents' Disclosures

Adolescents, like children and adults, may be questioned about events that they have experienced or witnessed, with their testimony being potentially crucial for solving cases, prosecuting offenders, facilitating treatment and other services, and promoting justice. In these interviews, adolescents must decide whether and to whom to disclose and how much to share; thus, adolescents' *willingness* to share their experiences with others, much more so than their ability to remember or report them completely and accurately, is of crucial concern. Despite considerable attention devoted to the disclosure of abuse among young children in forensic settings, far less attention has been focused on *adolescent* abuse disclosure in forensic settings as well as adolescent disclosure of other negative experiences (e.g., other types of victimization, witnessing crimes). However, there are multiple reasons, and some empirical evidence, to suggest that adolescents are at best minimally forthcoming to adults about their experiences and are at significant risk of nondisclosure when questioned forensically about events that they experienced or witnessed (Johnson, 2014). Such reluctance to disclose their experiences may be even more common among adolescents who are less trusting of adults, along with those with a history of maltreatment, who are at an elevated risk for subsequent victimization (Foshee et al., 2004) and involvement in delinquent activities (Mersky & Reynolds, 2007; Ryan & Testa, 2005).

In general, adolescents are often unwilling to disclose or discuss novel or risky behaviors in which they have engaged (e.g., alcohol or drug use), when asked by adults. For example, when adolescents' reports of how frequently they engage in sexual activity are compared to parents' reports on their adolescents' behavior, the adolescents report much more frequent activity than their parents do (Jaccard et al., 1998). Perhaps unsurprisingly, similar discrepancies emerge between adolescents' and parents' reports of adolescents' exposure to other high-risk experiences or behaviors (e.g., sexual assault, gun or weapon violence, motor vehicle accidents; Johnson, 2014). The tendency to withhold information extends beyond parent–child conversations. Many adolescents are not forthcoming with any adults when it comes to disclosing victimization that they have experienced. This may be especially true when considering adolescents who have experienced sexual abuse, and particularly the types of abuse more common among adolescents than children, such as experiences motivated by manipulation via online or offline perpetrators. Leander et al. (2008), for instance, found that among 68 adolescents (ages 11–19) who had been victims of Internet-initiated sexual abuse, only three (4%) disclosed to someone before the crime was discovered. The remaining 65 disclosed only after the police formally questioned them, with many of these adolescents remaining evasive even when external evidence was presented to them. Katz (2013) reported a similar trend in forensic interviews of adolescents victimized online by adults; not one adolescent disclosed prior to the abuse being discovered indirectly via online evidence (e.g., chats, images).

Research demonstrates that the majority of child sexual abuse victims either delay disclosure or never disclose during childhood, and even fewer cases are reported to the authorities (London et al., 2008; Lyon, 2009; McElvaney, 2015). Unlike with younger children in which sexual abuse is often discovered spontaneously or accidentally (Campis et al., 2003; Nagel et al., 1997), adolescents delay disclosure longer (Alaggia et al., 2017; Goodman-Brown et al., 2003; Hershkowitz et al., 2007; Lemaigre et al., 2017) and are more likely to disclose intentionally compared to younger children (Campis et al., 2003; Nagel et al., 1997). When adolescent victims do tell, they most often disclose to a friend (Hershkowitz et al., 2007; Priebe & Svedin, 2008; Schaeffer et al., 2011; Schonbucher et al., 2012) rather than an adult, the latter of whom is more common with child victims. In one field study examining children's and adolescents' sexual abuse disclosure recipients, 10–13-year-olds were twice as likely to mention telling their peers than 5–9-year-olds (Malloy et al., 2013).

Because adolescents are better at avoiding accidental disclosure and delaying disclosure—at least in part due to their more advanced executive functioning skills compared to younger children—adolescents may be better able to evade detection, and consequently, many victims are identified only because they *choose* to disclose eventually. For example, unlike other sexually abused adolescents who are more likely to intentionally disclose (Azzopardi et al., 2019), child sexual exploitation and abuse (CSEA) victims rarely self-report their victimization (Farrell et al., 2019). This means that such victims are accidentally or proactively identified by the police, such as during traffic stops, during sting operations, or in the course of other criminal investigations (Farrell et al., 2019). This is problematic as research demonstrates that a reliable predictor of sexual abuse disclosure is a prior disclosure (Azzopardi et al., 2019). In many CSEA cases, victims have never truly disclosed. Thus, they may not be ready to talk about it, making them a particularly reluctant population of victims (Henderson et al., 2021; Lindholm et al., 2015; Nogalska et al., 2021).

Features of Adolescent Development That Affect Their Disclosures

When considering why adolescents do not disclose or delay their disclosure of victimization, or limit their disclosures only to certain recipients, reasons include facets of the experiences themselves. Yet, reasons also include sources of influence reflective of typical adolescent development, including their reasoning about disclosure outcomes, their affiliation with peers, and their desire for autonomy.

Cognitive development. Regarding their reasoning about disclosure outcomes, in accordance with their more advanced cognitive and executive functioning skills, adolescents are better able than children to reason about the potential consequences of sharing information with others, such as disclosing that they engaged in risky behavior or have associated with peers who engaged in such behavior. This reasoning extends to contexts involving sexual abuse. As children get older, their sensitivity toward others' mental states also increases, meaning adolescents will be more attuned to how their disclosure could affect those around them (Lemaigre et al., 2017). Indeed, expectations of the negative consequences associated with disclosing sexual abuse tend to increase with age (Malloy et al., 2011, 2014, 2016), at least among children and adolescents. Many adolescents report delaying disclosure due to concern about negative consequences (e.g., disbelief, loss of familial support; Goodman-Brown et al., 2003; Lemaigre et al., 2017; Shalhoub-Kevorkian, 2005). Leach et al. (2016) found that adolescents who alleged abuse against suspects with a history of violent offending were less likely to disclose abuse in forensic interviews than other youth, perhaps because they considered the alleged perpetrator's prior violence and what it could mean if they disclosed.

Some victims are particularly reluctant to disclose to caregivers, even if they have a good relationship with them, because they fear they will be blamed or disbelieved, or they will be forced to report the abuses to authorities before they are ready (Crisma et al., 2004). And adolescents' concerns may at times be justified, as research shows that disclosure experiences may involve a combination of productive and hurtful responses from disclosure recipients (Fehler-Cabral et al., 2013; Malloy et al., 2007, 2013). Related to their increased ability to understand and reason about the potential consequences of disclosure with age is adolescents' consideration of who is the most appropriate or preferred recipient of their disclosure. Experimental research using hypothetical vignettes reveals that even 4–5-year-olds consider the identity of possible disclosure recipients when making decisions about disclosing adults' wrongdoing (Lyon et al., 2010; Malloy et al., 2014). However, the ability to reason about the differential effects of disclosing to particular individuals in more sophisticated ways improves with age.

Adolescents have numerous concerns to weigh when considering disclosing sexual abuse and are more equipped cognitively and socioemotionally to do so than children, with potentially different disclosure patterns emerging as a result. That is, while adolescents tend to take longer to disclose abuse, they are less likely than children to recant their claims of abuse (Malloy et al., 2007). Adolescents likely reason in more sophisticated ways about the consequences *before* disclosing, whereas children learn of the consequences only after they tell, prompting them to more often take back their claims. More research on abuse recantation among adolescents specifically and the factors that predict recantation is warranted, as well as in-depth studies of nondisclosures, including what triggers and facilitates disclosure, so that we can learn how to identify and intervene on behalf of adolescent victims.

Socioemotional development. Peer alliance appears to play a role in shaping adolescents' disclosure decisions. When adolescents do disclose negative experiences like abuse, they often select a peer or friend rather than an adult (e.g., Schaeffer et al., 2011). With age, children develop larger and more diverse social networks, especially those outside the home, and this provides them with more disclosure recipient options. Adolescents' growing affiliation toward and trust in peers, whose support may be especially valuable when discussing negative experiences (Manay & Collin-Vézina, 2021; Ungar et al., 2009), may also lead to these peers being preferred disclosure recipients. Or, adolescents may tell peers first as a way of "testing" others' reactions to their disclosures, trusting peers more than parents or other adults.

Disclosure to peers may be unlikely to lead to intervention, perhaps because victims request that peers keep the abuse secret from others or because peers are not aware of how to intervene. As children get older, they consider secrecy to be an increasingly valuable component of friendship (Rotenberg, 1991). This may help explain Malloy et al.'s (2013) field study of sexual abuse disclosures, which found that older youth had more "dead-end" disclosures (i.e., disclosures that did not lead to official reports), likely a result of older youth often choosing to tell their peers or friends initially. Adolescents' commitment to their peers is likely to be weighed heavily when deciding whether to tell someone else information that they gained in confidence. The same commitment that motivates adolescents to keep a peer's disclosure a secret from others could also extend to situations in which the peer was the perpetrator of a crime, such as with dating violence or date rape. Despite such occurring fairly often in teens (Young et al., 2009), disclosure to authorities is rare. Adolescents may also be afraid of causing problems for telling on their peers or friends (Hershkowitz et al., 2007).

Adolescents may be reluctant to disclose traumatic experiences out of a desire to be autonomous. Disclosing that they have been victimized may undermine their beliefs about their own autonomy or their desire to be seen as an autonomous individual by others, especially if that victimization was perpetrated by someone that they knew or trusted, as often occurs (Anderson et al., 1993; Giroux et al., 2018). They may, for instance, be experimenting with risky behaviors and practicing increased autonomy of decisions and behaviors and then take responsibility for the negative consequences of their behaviors, even if they have been manipulated or coerced into the behaviors. CSEA victims in particular likely have a strong need for autonomy, having had to survive very difficult circumstances with no or minimal support from others. This may increase the likelihood that they do not see themselves as victims (Anderson et al., 2014), but instead as independent agents making their own decisions. If victims believe they behaved consensually, they may think that there is "nothing to disclose" (Reid, 2016) and will fail to access services or cooperate in an investigation. Alternatively, they may not feel fully responsible but still feel complicit in the illegal behavior and thus fear punishment, such as incarceration (Farrell et al., 2019; Lavoie et al., 2019), and for that reason are still reluctant to seek help.

Many victims of child sexual abuse feel complicit in abuse and experience shame or self-blame, all of which contribute to nondisclosure (Hershkowitz et al., 2007). These feelings may be exacerbated for adolescents who are more likely than younger children to perceive that they are engaged in consensual activity or who may be closer in age to perpetrators. They may feel as though they made the decision to be involved with a particular perpetrator and perceive that they have a bond with that perpetrator, which reduces their willingness to tell (Katz, 2013; Leander et al., 2008). For CSEA victims in particular, they may feel love or loyalty for their exploiter, or they may be completely reliant on them for basic needs (Anderson et al., 2014; Reid, 2016), and thus, they may prefer to protect their exploiter rather than cooperate with an investigation (Reid, 2016).

Summary. Multiple factors influence adolescents' disclosure decisions, some of which include normative developmental processes common to adolescence, both cognitive and socioemotional in nature. As highlighted in this chapter, adolescents' reasoning skills, allegiance to peers, and desire for autonomy are key (but certainly not the only) factors that can affect adolescents' willingness to disclose their own victimization, other crimes, or negative events that they have witnessed. These developmental characteristics and processes may be particularly salient for youth who have experienced certain kinds of victimization (e.g., CSEA victims) and affect not just whether adolescents disclose but also who they tell. Peer disclosure recipients for sensitive disclosures may be chosen for several reasons, such as adolescents' enhanced rapport, comfort discussing such topics with a same-aged peer, and the perception that they share common experiences. At least for some adolescents, though, peers may be preferred recipients for sensitive disclosures precisely *because* the disclosure is not expected to lead to any formal intervention. Altogether, there is still much to learn about the role of peers in adolescents' legal involvement as victims and witnesses.

Adolescents' Memory and Suggestibility

We must consider not only adolescents' willingness to share their experiences but also their abilities to do so and how these abilities are potentially affected by the hallmark features of adolescent development that we have discussed. For an adolescent to share details of their own victimization or an event that they have witnessed in a forensic interview or courtroom setting, various skills are required including those related to memory, language, reasoning, narration, and more. In many ways, and with few exceptions, children's memory improves with age and their suggestibility decreases with age (see Malloy & Quas, 2009, for a review). By adolescence, there is far less concern about adolescents not demonstrating the basic memory and communication skills that can hinder young children's testimony. However, adolescents, like children and adults, may struggle to provide complete details of their experiences and can be susceptible to suggestion and false reports. In some situations (referred to as "developmental reversals"), adolescents may be even more suggestible than children (see Brainerd et al., 2008, for a review). Yet, it is important to note at the outset of this section that comparatively little work has focused on adolescents', rather than children's, memory and suggestibility.

In general, research indicates that adolescents typically produce eyewitness reports that are longer and more detailed than those of school-aged children, but less so than the reports of adults. For example, in Jack et al. (2014), adolescents provided more details in their free-recall reports than children about a witnessed event, but fewer details than young adults. Similarly, adolescents gave fewer perpetrator descriptors (e.g., facial features) than adults when recalling a video of a staged theft, but were similarly accurate with respect to perpetrator identification (Sheahan et al., 2017). These results suggest a linear development of eyewitness memory, at least in terms of the quantity of information reported in free recall. While adolescent recall accuracy of autobiographical memories seems to be somewhat comparable to that of adults, they may not recall the same quantity of information as adults (see Given-Wilson et al., 2017, for a review). However, it is not known whether adolescents in these studies perhaps remembered as much information as adults but were less motivated than adults to share these details with the interviewers.

Adolescents, like children and adults, may also provide false reports. Some of these may be intentionally false, such as when they lie to protect a friend from getting into trouble (e.g., Warr, 1993) or when they falsely confess to a crime or act of wrongdoing to protect someone else (Malloy et al., 2014; Pimentel et al., 2015). Others, though, may be unintentional, such as false memories, wherein adolescents provide inaccurate information that they believe to be true, or perhaps just suggested reports, wherein adolescents acquiesce to suggestions from others.

Much of the forensic work with adolescents has focused on their suggestibility as relevant to the suspect context. Adolescent suspects appear to be more vulnerable than adult suspects to interrogative suggestibility and misinformation (e.g., Gudjonsson & Singh, 1984; Lee, 2004; Loftus et al., 1992). That is, adolescents are more likely than adults to produce eyewitness information that is influenced or informed by secondary sources (e.g., leading questions or disapproval given by the interrogator), instead of solely their own recollections. In Richardson et al. (1995), for example, juvenile offenders performed worse than adult offenders on the Gudjonsson Suggestibility Scale (GSS). The GSS measures individual differences in interrogative suggestibility, such as the impact of leading questions and negative or critical feedback, on the quality and accuracy of eyewitness reports. In their study (and others; e.g., Singh & Gudjonsson, 1992), juveniles were more likely than adults to change their answers about a fictional mugging in response to leading questions and negative interviewer feedback. These results are consistent with more recent research (Haney-Caron et al., 2018), whereby adolescents residing in juvenile justice facilities, particularly those under the age of 15, were more likely to admit that they would falsely confess to a transgression in response to specific interrogative strategies (e.g., misleading or coercive questioning tactics) compared to adults who were matched in terms of mental age.

When it comes to suggestibility, adolescents' performance again most often falls in between children's and adults' suggestibility (Coxon & Valentine, 1997; Gudjonsson et al., 2016; Haney-Canon et al., 2018; Richardson et al., 1995; Singh & Gudjonsson, 1992). However, a phenomenon known as "developmental reversals" has been uncovered in which adolescents demonstrate greater susceptibility to false memories than younger children (e.g., Brainerd et al., 2018; see Brainerd et al., 2008, for a review). Typically, these studies involve participants listening to lists of words that have semantic similarities (e.g., "hungry" and "food") to other words that are not read out to them (e.g., "eating"). Using the Deese Roediger McDermott (DRM) paradigm (Roediger & McDermott, 1995), several studies have found that adolescents were more likely than younger children to falsely report hearing words that had not been read to them (see Brainerd et al., 2008). These developmental reversals for false memories are explained by the fact that adolescents are more likely to recall gist representations of the meanings of the information or events (e.g., recalling "keyboard" instead of "piano"), while children are more likely to rely on verbatim memory to recall the specific words that were read to them. Adolescents and adults, with their greater knowledge and life experience compared to children, are more likely than children to make semantic connections among the to-be-remembered words or events and thus have "false alarms" to semantically related items.

Features of Adolescent Development That Affect Their Memory and Suggestibility

As discussed next, there are several ways in which the hallmark features of adolescents' cognitive and socioemotional development help explain the findings that have emerged regarding adolescents' memory and suggestibility and how they, as a group, compare with children and adults.

Cognitive development. Adolescents' executive functioning skills are certainly relevant to the eyewitness memory and suggestibility literature (Icenogle et al., 2019; Shulman et al., 2016; Yurgelun-Todd, 2007). Impulse control is important for helping adolescent victims and witnesses to inhibit inaccurate, impulsive, or unplanned responses to interviewer questions and suggestions. Relative to adults, adolescents' weaknesses in impulse control (Stevens et al., 2007) can lead to increased memory contradictions and errors if they are not able to effectively monitor the accuracy of the information they are giving. These relative weaknesses also help explain why adolescents are more susceptible than adults to giving suggestive answers in response to leading questions (Gudjonsson & Singh, 1984; Lee, 2004; Loftus et al., 1992). Resisting misinformation requires higher order critical thinking and reasoning skills (e.g., knowing what information is true versus false), self-confidence in one's memory, inhibition, and active behavioral resistance, all of which may be less well developed in adolescents compared to adults.

Attention is another aspect of executive functioning with implications for adolescents' memory and suggestibility. Compared to adults, adolescents may not attend to and encode event-related information as well (see Blakemore & Choudhury, 2006, for a review). As a result, they may not recall important details (e.g., perpetrator facial features) because they were simply not attending well enough. This may help explain why adolescents produce fewer details than adults when recalling their prior experiences (Jack et al., 2014; Sheahan et al., 2017). At the same time, though, memory and language are better developed in adolescents than children (Craik & Bialystok, 2006), which facilitates adolescents' improved eyewitness memory recall. For example, improvements in working memory during adolescence facilitate better organization and sequencing of information in memory compared to children (Swanson, 1999), which can enhance the cohesiveness of adolescents' eyewitness narratives (VanMeter et al., 2023).

Adolescents may be less suggestible than children in part because of their more sophisticated metamemory, especially meta-suggestibility, skills. Meta-suggestibility, or the awareness of factors (e.g., suggestive questions) or situations (e.g., peer influence) that impair one's memory, increases with age during childhood and adolescence. In London et al. (2011), for instance, 91% of the 12–13-year-olds and only 30% of the 6–7-year-olds were able to identify some reasons that a hypothetical child made a false report about being assaulted, such as that the interviewer placed social pressure on the child interviewee to allege the assault. Overall, meta-suggestibility improved with age among the 6–13-year-old participants. Other research indicates that improvements in metamemory continue into adulthood (Ghetti et al., 2008).

Socioemotional development. Socioemotional processes, such as empathy and perspective taking (Van der Graaff et al., 2014), along with social and moral reasoning (Chiasson et al., 2016), also have implications for adolescents' memory and suggestibility. These processes may enhance recall given that the eyewitness needs to be aware of what information the interviewer requires, as well as how well the interviewer comprehends the information being provided. This can facilitate a "good" interview, whereby there is a reciprocal understanding and a mutual obligation to be clear. However, adolescents' more sophisticated socioemotional development compared to children may have some disadvantages in a forensic interview. Namely, adolescent victims and witnesses may be suspicious of adults' motives when they are questioned, leading them to be more resistant to an interviewer's strategic attempts to, for instance, build rapport or provide them with preinterview instructions. One means of combating disclosure reluctance when children are asked about a collaborative wrongdoing is to employ a putative confession instruction, by which the interviewer tells the child that the suspect has already told them "everything that happened" and "wants [the child] to tell the truth." Evans and Lyon (2019) found that the putative confession was not as effective in eliciting true disclosures among 11–12-year-olds than younger children, potentially due to the older youths' greater sophistication in interpreting and reasoning about the putative confession (e.g., questioning of what the interviewer means by "everything").

Adolescents' enhanced desire for peer approval and peer affiliation may provide several opportunities for their reports to be contaminated by others. For example, witness "coaching" is a concern for law enforcement. Particularly in CSEA cases, the adolescent may be "coached" by the perpetrator, accomplices, and/or other victims to produce a false report to protect the perpetrator. This can lead to the adolescent intentionally or unintentionally reporting the information given by others, instead of their own recollections. McGuire et al. (2011) found evidence of "memory conformity" among adolescents and young adults who were presented with postevent information from peers and other witnesses. In their study, adolescents and young adults incorporated true and false cowitness information into their memory recollections of a videotaped robbery; this resulted in a poorer recollection performance of the staged robbery compared to those who were not provided with this postevent information. Interestingly, at least in this study, adolescents were not significantly more likely to demonstrate memory conformity than adults. Other research, however, indicates that peer influence may taint the reports of adolescents more so than the reports of adults. Pimentel et al. (2015), for example, found that adolescents (ages 14–17) were more likely than adults (ages 18 and over) to lie and falsely take responsibility for an act of wrongdoing (i.e., a cheating incident) in order to protect a same-aged peer.

For events involving multiple witnesses, adolescents may seek out information from others, especially friends or peers, to inform their own interpretations of the event. In cases where the information given by others differs from their own recollections, they may knowingly or unknowingly incorporate this information into their memories of the event. As they mature and develop greater autonomy, they may become less dependent on the memories of others and rely more heavily on their own recollections, though as noted memory conformity remains an issue even for adults (McGuire et al., 2011).

Summary. In sum, adolescents' memory and resistance to suggestion improve with age. While they are typically better witnesses than children, they still provide fewer details and may be less accurate than adults. One caveat to this, however, involves developmental reversals, whereby adolescents may be more prone to suggestion than children. Regarding memory conformity, adolescents may be more vulnerable than adults; however, research presents conflicting results. As mentioned, cognitive and socioemotional development affect adolescents' ability to accurately recall and answer questions about their experiences.

Implications for Practice, Policy, and Future Research

Adolescence is a unique period of human development characterized by growth, change, and vulnerability in multiple domains. The developmental characteristics of adolescents covered in this chapter, falling into both cognitive and socioemotional domains, increase the likelihood that adolescents will be exposed to crime, especially violent crime, and exploitation. The same characteristics may also affect adolescents' willingness to share their experiences and ability to do so effectively in legal contexts. Next, we review practice and policy recommendations as well as critical future directions for research concerning adolescent victims and witnesses.

Adolescent-Specific Investigative Interviewing Protocols

A vital need is for more direct empirical attention on designing and testing interviewing methods specifically for questioning adolescent victims and witnesses about their experiences. In general, and in contrast with the relative lack of developmental modifications to interrogation practices used to question adolescent suspects (see Cleary & Crane, this volume), questioning practices have been altered significantly when interviewing young victims and witnesses. The latter practices (e.g., National Institute of Child Health and Human Development [NICHD] Investigative Interview Protocol; Lamb et al., 2018), though, have not regularly been tested on adolescent-age populations and have not taken their developmental needs into consideration. For example, the NICHD Protocol, while shown to increase the quality of children's reports and interviewers' questions (Lamb et al., 2007), is typically used with youth up until age 14. At the same time, other forensic interviewing recommendations, such as those outlined in the American Professional Society on the Abuse of Children (APSAC) *Handbook on Child Maltreatment* (Klika & Conte, 2017), do not tailor recommendations to adolescent victims and witnesses specifically. In fact, there are no empirically based adolescent-specific investigative interviewing protocols.

Although many recommendations, such as relying on open-ended invitations to talk (e.g., "Tell me everything you remember from the beginning to the end as best as you can"), following up with cued invitations (e.g., "You said X. Tell me more about X"), and avoiding leading or suggestive questions are likely important regardless of victim/witness age, others may be more age dependent (e.g., using ground rules, as discussed next). Furthermore, interviewing strategies that work for adults may not be as effective for adolescents. In adults, for example, using the Cognitive Interview (CI) leads to large gains in correct information obtained from a witness compared to control interviews *without* significantly impacting the overall accuracy of one's statement (Memon et al., 2010). Although the benefits of the CI have been examined with adults and young children (e.g., 4–9-year-olds; Holliday, 2003), few studies have specifically examined the efficacy of the CI when used with adolescents. Of those that have, gains in statement details are often smaller for adolescents compared to adults (Jack et al., 2014). More research is needed to understand which interview protocols, or components of interview protocols, are particularly effective with adolescent victims and witnesses.

Ground Rules

By the 1990s, many best practice guidelines for interviewing children instructed interviewers to establish certain "ground rules" at the outset of the interview (e.g., Memorandum of Good Practice, Home Office, 1992), and such ground rules are a formal part of some investigative interview protocols. For example, in the NICHD Protocol, interviewers set the ground rules at the outset of the interview during what is known as the "presubstantive phase." These rules are intended to explain children's role in the interview, set the conversational expectations, and provide them with the language necessary to navigate certain aspects of the interviews (e.g., that the interviewer is naïve to the original event, that they can say "I don't know" or "I don't understand" if they do not know the information requested or need clarification of an interviewer's question). Interviewers may also elicit a promise to tell the truth or have a discussion about honesty in this interview section, before substantive issues are discussed (Lyon & Dorado, 2008; Quas et al., 2018).

The relatively limited research on ground rules suggests that using such rules with children is beneficial to their cooperation and performance (see Brubacher et al., 2015, for a review). However, most of this research has not considered adolescent development, or failed to include adolescents at all. It is plausible that some ground rules would benefit adolescents (e.g., that it's okay to say "I don't know") but that other rules (e.g., emphasizing the interviewer's naivety) may be unnecessary and perhaps seem patronizing to adolescents, thus undermining trust and rapport between the interviewer and adolescent. This is an important question for future studies. Recent research suggests that older children (10–12 years), compared to younger children (4–5 years), may be more likely to receive ground rules instructions yet *less* likely to be given an opportunity to practice the ground rules (Fessinger et al., 2021). Whether adolescents *need* the practice to correctly implement the rules in interviews, and how interviewers and others (e.g., judges, jurors) react to adolescents' use of the ground rules when recounting their experiences are also important questions for future research.

Rapport Building

Interviewing guidelines widely recommend building rapport with victims and witnesses at the start of an interview, regardless of age (Fisher & Geiselman, 1992; Lamb et al., 2018; Lyon, 2014). The NICHD Protocol and Ten Step Investigative Interview, for instance, include a portion of the interview devoted to open-ended questioning to elicit information about personal experiences, which is followed by a request for a statement describing a recent, personally salient event (such as a holiday or birthday; i.e., "narrative practice"). In combination with ground rules, this portion of the interview is intended to teach children what is expected of them and how to provide narratives about their experience in response to open-ended invitations.

Suspected child victims who have established a positive and supportive rapport with interviewers provide more detailed, informative, and potentially more accurate eyewitness reports (see Saywitz et al., 2019, for a meta-analytic review). Rapport building with adult victims has similarly been shown to increase the amount of detail provided (Meissner, 2021). Yet, while much research has demonstrated the effectiveness of rapport in facilitating disclosure from both children and adults (see Lamb et al., 2007; Lavoie et al., 2021; Gabbert et al., 2020; Vallano & Schreiber-Compo, 2015), few studies have examined the efficacy of these techniques specifically with adolescents. More often, studies have tested how holistic interviewing approaches that include rapport building, such as the CI, influence reporting with samples that include adolescent-age participants.

For some techniques, like open-ended questioning, rapport building can increase the amount of correct information recalled. Sauerland et al. (2018) examined the effect of various rapport-building methods on the amount and accuracy of information elicited about a witnessed event. Interviewers built rapport with children, adolescents, and adults by asking either no personal questions, a few closed-ended personal questions, or a few open-ended personal questions prior to eliciting a free narrative about a previously witnessed video clip depicting the theft of a wallet. Compared to neutral or closed-ended rapport conditions, rapport that involved open-ended personal questions led to more correct details elicited by adolescents. The overall accuracy rate, however, was not affected by participant age or the type of rapport.

Field studies that have included children and adolescents (ages 3–18) further support the efficacy of narrative practice rapport building. Narrative practice involves familiarizing the eyewitness with the process of providing elaborate responses by asking them to narrate a neutral event (e.g., what they did yesterday) via open-ended questioning. As such, they learn to talk about themselves and practice narrating about personal details prior to being asked about a critical event, such as suspected sexual abuse. In addition to typical age-related increases in detail, narrative practice forensic interviews result in increased productivity in terms of both words spoken during the substantive phase of the interview ($d = 0.59$; Hamilton et al., 2016) and more abuse-specific details ($d = 0.64$; Anderson et al., 2014) in the statements of children and youth (ages 3–18) when compared to traditional interview formats. Furthermore, interviewers who offer support to the witness (e.g., providing unconditional positive feedback and maintaining eye contact) elicit more informative responses from children and adolescents up through 15 years of age (Teoh & Lamb, 2013), and there is a positive relationship between the amount of interviewer utterances to build rapport and the richness and informativeness of statements given by children and adolescents (Leander et al., 2009).

Rapport can be established in a number of ways, such as by discussing common interests or engaging in a cooperative activity, yet research is scant concerning how best to build rapport with adolescents in particular. A key component of rapport with adults, for example, is self-disclosure by an interviewer, which leads to mutual trust and enhanced disclosures (Dianiska et al., 2021). However, it remains unknown whether, given their adult authority status, an interviewer's self-disclosure would increase adolescent–interviewer rapport. This method may be especially unlikely to have the desired effect with CSEA victims who are typically less trusting of adults and reluctant to talk about their experiences. CSEA victims often come from marginalized groups who have poor relationships with police, which may increase distrust and reluctance (Farrell et al., 2019). Furthermore, when questioned by police, CSEA victims are often treated as criminals or delinquents rather than victims (Farrell et al., 2019; Lavoie et al., 2019; Wilson & Dalton, 2008), and even when officers do employ supportive tactics, these are still associated with increased reluctance (Nogalska et al., 2021). It is imperative that future research develop and test rapport-building approaches that capitalize on our knowledge of adolescent development and do not take a "one size fits all" approach with youth, whether that is children versus adults or CSEA victims versus other adolescent victims.

Individual Differences
Not only should future research focus on individual differences in adolescent victims and witnesses, but also recommendations for practice and policy should be mindful of such differences. Individual differences play a role in who experiences legal involvement as a victim or witness; in adolescents' disclosures, memory, and suggestibility; and in how their testimony is perceived by others. For example, children and adolescents diagnosed with an intellectual disability are more at risk for being victims of abuse and neglect compared to their typically-developing peers (Jones et al., 2012). CSEA victims are also more likely to have developmental disabilities (Reid, 2016). Youth with developmental disabilities are more likely to experience cognitive deficits with respect to language, memory, reasoning, problem solving, perspective taking, and judgment (American Psychiatric Association, 2013), which can impact their abilities to understand their legal rights and produce credible testimonies (see Wyman et al., 2018, for a review). While some work indicates that individuals with intellectual disabilities are more likely to provide false or suggested eyewitness reports than typically-developing individuals (see Griego et al., 2019, for a meta-analytic review), other research demonstrates that even young children with intellectual disabilities, especially mild disabilities, can provide reliable testimony about events that they have experienced or witnessed (Brown et al., 2012; Cederborg & Lamb, 2008).

Yet, generally speaking, adolescents with cognitive and developmental deficits are at a greater risk for having their testimony perceived as less credible than that of their typically-developing peers (Henry et al., 2011). This finding is coupled with the fact that many professionals who are most often involved in the investigation of these crimes, including police, child protective services, and forensic interviewers, report having inadequate training and procedures for servicing youth with intellectual disabilities (Taylor et al., 2016). Thus, it is crucial that interviewing protocols and interviewer training programs are tailored to the needs of youth with specific characteristics and disabilities, especially adolescent-aged youth, on whom limited knowledge is available.

Other individual differences are also worth considering, in terms of both future research needs and practice recommendations. For example, LGBTQ youth experience significantly higher rates of victimization at school (e.g., online and offline bullying, assault, homophobia, theft; see Myers et al., 2020, for a meta-analytic review), at home (physical and sexual abuse; Baams, 2018), and in their communities (e.g., sex trafficking; Xian et al., 2017) compared to heterosexual and cisgender youth. Rapport-building or interviewing strategies that consider their LGBTQ identity may be especially important in encouraging disclosures from this group of adolescents. Adolescents with ADHD are more likely to have deficits in important areas of executive functioning (e.g., attention, impulse control, and cognitive flexibility; Craig et al., 2016), and thus, may be more vulnerable to giving suggestive answers in response to leading interview questions (e.g., Gudjonsson & Young, 2021). These few examples highlight the complex array of characteristics, even with adolescents, that shape their willingness and ability to disclose information to legal authorities. Future research should consider not just how adolescents may have different needs as victims and witnesses than children and adults, but also how adolescents with particular characteristics may benefit from different kinds of support or interviewing strategies.

Reluctant Victims
Research suggests that adolescent victims who choose *not* to disclose are a particularly reluctant population (Henderson et al., 2021; Katz, 2013; Leander, 2010; Lindholm et al., 2015), and it is critical that these reluctant victims are identified and protected from further harm. Research

must explore the possibility that risk factors (e.g., presence/absence of an unsupportive caregiver) and protective factors (e.g., presence/absence of close peer relationships) differ in cases involving adolescent nondisclosers compared to children or adults who may be reluctant to disclose their experiences. For example, in Goodman-Brown et al. (2003), abuse characteristics (i.e., perpetrator relationship) differed between families that chose to participate in their study compared to those who chose not to participate, demonstrating the effects of a sampling bias on a small scale. Many researchers have noted that child sexual abuse victims who have not disclosed are rarely represented in research, and consequently, most research samples are not representative of child sexual abuse victims generally (Lemaigre et al., 2017; Lyon, 2009; Olafson & Lederman, 2006). Put more concretely, "reluctance is understated because reluctance makes itself invisible" (Lyon, 2009, p. 27).

Because adolescents are more likely to delay disclosure and less likely to "leak" disclosure than younger children, it is imperative that research begins to identify and examine adolescent nondisclosing victims so that better techniques for intervening and overcoming their reluctance can be developed. It is plausible that strategies that help overcome reluctance in children will not be similarly effective with adolescents. For example, pre-interview instructions that the suspect has already told the interviewer everything that happened (Lyon et al., 2014) have had positive effects on disclosure reluctance in some circumstances. This technique, described earlier in the chapter as "the putative confession," appears to be differentially effective based on the age of the child (Evans & Lyon, 2019). While it increased true disclosures of an adult's wrongdoing among 4–9-year-olds (i.e., the adult had caused a laptop to crash and then coached the children to lie about it), it did not work similarly for 11–12-year-olds.

Conclusions

Given adolescents' gradual tendency to engage in riskier behavior and to spend more time with peers rather than parents, it is perhaps unsurprising that adolescents inevitably are immersed in the juvenile and criminal justice system and are, at times, questioned about their experiences being victimized or witnessing crime. And, as we have reviewed in this chapter, the same developmental characteristics that affect adolescent suspects and defendants (see Cleary & Crane and Zottoli et al., this volume) shape adolescent witnesses and victims. Not only are these developmental characteristics, both cognitive and socioemotional in nature, important to consider when evaluating adolescent victims' and witnesses' responses and functioning once they are immersed in the legal system, but they are also crucial to understand as efforts are made to facilitate their participation. In this chapter, we have provided much-needed insight to address this vital question: How does adolescent development influence what they say (and do not say) in legal contexts as victims and witnesses? We have also, though, highlighted several new or emerging questions that warrant further scientific inquiry and the attention of practitioners and public policymakers in regard to adolescent victims and witnesses. Scientists and practitioners who study and work at the intersection of developmental psychology and law should work together to address these critical questions. We hope that this future work will lead to the development and refinement of methods for interview preparation (i.e., ground rules, rapport building) and interviewing that have the unique developmental characteristics of adolescents in mind.

References

Alaggia, R., Collin-Vézina, D., & Lateef, R. (2017). Facilitators and barriers to child sexual abuse (CSA) disclosures: A research update (2000-2016). *Trauma, Violence, & Abuse, 20*(2), 260-283.

Albert, D., Chein, J., & Steinberg, L. (2013). The teenage brain: Peer influences on adolescent decision making. *Current Directions in Psychological Science, 22*, 114-120.

Allen, J. P., & Brown, B. B. (2008). Adolescents, peers, and motor vehicles: the perfect storm? *American Journal of Preventive Medicine, 35*, S289-S293.

American Psychiatric Association. (2013). *Diagnostic and statistical manual of mental disorders (5th ed.)*. Arlington, VA: American Psychiatric Publishing.

Anderson, G. D., Anderson, J. N., & Gilgun, J. F. (2014). The influence of narrative practice techniques on child behaviors in forensic interviews. *Journal of Child sexual Abuse, 23*(6), 615-634.

Anderson, V. R., Kulig, T. C., & Sullivan, C. J. (2019). Estimating the prevalence of human trafficking in Ohio, 2014–2016. *American Journal of Public Health, 109*(10), 1396-1399.

Anderson, J., Martin, J., Mullen, P., Romans, S., & Herbison, P. (1993). Prevalence of Childhood Sexual Abuse Experiences in a Community Sample of Women. *Journal of the American Academy of Child & Adolescent Psychiatry, 32*, 911–919.

Azzopardi, C., Eirich, R., Rash, C. L., MacDonald, S., & Madigan, S. (2019). A meta-analysis of the prevalence of child sexual abuse disclosure in forensic settings. *Child Abuse & Neglect, 93*, 291-304.

Baams, L. (2018). Sexual orientation disparities: Starting in childhood and observable in adolescence? *Journal of Adolescent Health, 64*, 145-146.

Berndt, T. J. (1979). Developmental changes in conformity to peers and parents. *Developmental Psychology, 15*, 608–616.

Berntsen, D., Willert, M., & Rubin, D. C. (2003). Splintered memories or vivid landmarks? Qualities and organization of traumatic memories with and without PTSD. *Applied Cognitive Psychology, 17*, 675-693.

Blakemore, S. J., & Choudhury, S. (2006). Development of the adolescent brain: Implications for executive function and social cognition. *Journal of Child Psychology and Psychiatry, 47*, 296-312.

Bolsinger, J., Seifritz, E., Kleim, B., & Manoliu, A. (2018). Neuroimaging correlates of resilience to traumatic events: A comprehensive review. *Frontiers in Psychiatry, 9*.

Boyer, T. W. (2006). The development of risk-taking: A multi-perspective review. *Developmental Review, 26*, 291-345.

Brainerd, C. J., Holliday, R. E., Reyna, V. F., Yang, Y., & Toglia, M. P. (2010). Developmental reversals in false memory: Effects of emotional valence and arousal. *Journal of Experimental Child Psychology, 107*, 137-154.

Brainerd, C. J., Reyna, V. F., & Ceci, S. J. (2008). *Developmental reversals in false memory: A review of data and theory. Psychological Bulletin, 134*, 343.

Brainerd, C. J., Reyna, V. F., & Holliday, R. E. (2018). Developmental reversals in false memory: Development is complementary, not compensatory. *Developmental Psychology, 54*, 1773.

Brewer, K. D., Rowe, D. M., & Brewer, D. D. (1997). Factors Related to Prosecution of Child Sexual Abuse Cases. *Journal of Child Sexual Abuse, 6*, 91–111.

Brewin, C. R., Kleiner, J. S., Vasterling, J. J., & Field, A. P. (2007). Memory for emotionally neutral information in posttraumatic stress disorder: A meta-analytic investigation. *Journal of Abnormal Psychology, 116*, 448–463.

Brown, B. B., & Larson, J. (2009). Peer relationships in adolescence. In R. M. Lerner & L. Steinberg (Eds.), *Handbook of adolescent psychology: Contextual influences on adolescent development* (pp. 74–103). John Wiley & Sons, Inc.

Brown, D. A., Lewis, C. N., Lamb, M. E., & Stephens, E. (2012). The influences of delay and severity of intellectual disability on event memory in children. *Journal of Consulting and Clinical Psychology, 80*, 829–841.

Brubacher, S. P., Poole, D. A., & Dickinson, J. J. (2015). The use of ground rules in investigative interviews with children: A synthesis and call for research. *Developmental Review, 36*, 15-33.

Campis, L. B., Hebden-Curtis, J., & Demaso, D. R. (1993). Developmental differences in detection and disclosure of sexual abuse. *Journal of the American Academy of Child & Adolescent Psychiatry, 32*(5), 920-924.

Cauffman, E., Fine, A., Thomas, A. G., & Monahan, K. C. (2017). Trajectories of violent behavior among females and males. *Child Development, 88*, 41-54.

Cederborg, A. C., La Rooy, D., & Lamb, M. E. (2008). Repeated interviews with children who have intellectual disabilities. *Journal of Applied Research in Intellectual Disabilities, 21*, 103–113.

Chiasson, V., Vera-Estay, E., Lalonde, G., Dooley, J. J., & Beauchamp, M. H. (2017). Assessing social cognition: age-related changes in moral reasoning in childhood and adolescence. *The Clinical Neuropsychologist, 31*(3), 515-530.

Chong, K., & Connolly, D. A. (2015). Testifying through the ages: An examination of current psychological issues on the use of testimonial supports by child, adolescent, and adult witnesses in Canada. *Canadian Psychology/Psychologie Canadienne, 56*, 108–117.

Coxon, P., & Valentine, T. (1997). The effects of the age of eyewitnesses on the accuracy and suggestibility of their testimony. *Applied Cognitive Psychology: The Official Journal of the Society for Applied Research in Memory and Cognition, 11*, 415-430.

Craig, F., Margari, F., Legrottaglie, A. R., Palumbi, R., de Giambattista, C., & Margari, L. (2016). A review of executive function deficits in autism spectrum disorder and attention-deficit/hyperactivity disorder. *Neuropsychiatric disease and treatment, 12,* 1191–1202.

Craik, F. I., & Bialystok, E. (2006). Cognition through the lifespan: Mechanisms of change. *Trends in Cognitive Sciences, 10,* 131-138.

Crisma, M., Bascelli, E., Paci, D., & Romito, P. (2004). Adolescents who experienced sexual abuse: Fears, needs and impediments to disclosure. *Child Abuse & Neglect, 28,* 1035-1048.

Dianiska, R. E., Swanner, J. K., Brimbal, L., & Meissner, C. A. (2021). Using disclosure, common ground, and verification to build rapport and elicit information. *Psychology, Public Policy, and Law, 27,* 341–353.

Erikson, E. H. (1968). *Identity: Youth and crisis.* New York: Norton.

Evans, A. D., & Lyon, T. D. (2019). The effects of the putative confession and evidence presentation on maltreated and non-maltreated 9-to 12-year-olds' disclosures of a minor transgression. *Journal of Experimental Child Psychology, 188,* 104674.

Farrell, A., Dank, M., de Vries, I., Kafafian, M., Hughes, A., & Lockwood, S. (2019). Failing victims? Challenges of the police response to human trafficking. *Criminology & Public Policy, 18*(3), 649-673.

Fehler-Cabral, G., & Campbell, R. (2013). Adolescent sexual assault disclosure: The impact of peers, families, and schools. *American Journal of Community Psychology, 52,* 73-83.

Fessinger, M. B., McWilliams, K., Bakth, F. N., & Lyon, T. D. (2021). Setting the ground rules: use and practice of ground rules in child forensic interviews. *Child Maltreatment, 26,* 126-132.

Fisher, R. P., & Geiselman, R. E. (1992). *Memory enhancing techniques for investigative interviewing: The cognitive interview.* Charles C Thomas Publisher.

Foshee, V. A., Benefield, T. S., Ennett, S. T., Bauman, K. E., & Suchindran, C. (2004). Longitudinal predictors of serious physical and sexual dating violence victimization during adolescence. *Preventive Medicine, 39,* 1007-1016.

Gabbert, F., Hope, L., Luther, K., Wright, G., Ng, M., & Oxburgh, G. (2021). Exploring the use of rapport in professional information-gathering contexts by systematically mapping the evidence base. *Applied Cognitive Psychology, 35*(2), 329-341.

Gardner, M., & Steinberg, L. (2005). Peer influence on risk taking, risk preference, and risky decision making in adolescence and adulthood: An experimental study. *Developmental Psychology, 41,* 625–635.

Ghetti, S., Lyons, K. E., Lazzarin, F., & Cornoldi, C. (2008). The development of metamemory monitoring during retrieval: The case of memory strength and memory absence. *Journal of Experimental Child Psychology, 99,* 157-181.

Giroux, M. E., Chong, K., Coburn, P. I., & Connolly, D. A. (2018). Differences in child sexual abuse cases involving child versus adolescent complainants. *Child Abuse & Neglect, 79,* 224–233.

Given-Wilson, Z., Hodes, M., & Herlihy, J. (2018). A review of adolescent autobiographical memory and the implications for assessment of unaccompanied minors' refugee determinations. *Clinical Child Psychology and Psychiatry, 23,* 209-222.

Goodman, G. S., Quas, J. A., Bulkley, J., & Shapiro, C. (1999). Innovations for child witnesses: A national survey. *Psychology, Public Policy, and Law, 5,* 255-281.

Goodman-Brown, T. B., Edelstein, R. S., Goodman, G. S., Jones, D. P., & Gordon, D. S. (2003). Why children tell: A model of children's disclosure of sexual abuse. *Child Abuse & Neglect, 27,* 525-540.

Griego, A. W., Datzman, J. N., Estrada, S. M., & Middlebrook, S. S. (2019). Suggestibility and false memories in relation to intellectual disability and autism spectrum disorder: a meta-analytic review. *Journal of Intellectual Disability Research, 63,* 1464-1474.

Gudjonsson, G. H., & Singh, K. K. (1984). Interrogative suggestibility and delinquent boys: An empirical validation study. *Personality and Individual Differences, 5,* 425-430.

Gudjonsson, G., Vagni, M., Maiorano, T., & Pajardi, D. (2016). Age and memory related changes in children's immediate and delayed suggestibility using the Gudjonsson Suggestibility Scale. *Personality and Individual Differences, 102,* 25-29.

Gudjonsson, G., & Young, S. (2021). An investigation of 'don't know' and 'direct explanation' response styles on the Gudjonsson Suggestibility Scale: A comparison of three different vulnerable adult groups. *Personality and Individual Differences, 168,* 110385.

Hamilton, G., Brubacher, S., & Powell, M. (2017). The effects of practice narratives in interviews with Australian Aboriginal children. *Investigative Interviewing: Research and Practice, 8*(1), 31-44.

Haney-Caron, E., Goldstein, N. E., & Mesiarik, C. (2018). Self-perceived likelihood of false confession: A comparison of justice-involved juveniles and adults. *Criminal Justice and Behavior, 45,* 1955-1976.

Henderson H., Cho S., Nogalska A., & Lyon T. D. (2021). Identifying novel forms of reluctance in commercially sexually exploited adolescents. *Child Abuse & Neglect, 115,* 104994.

Henry, L., Ridley, A., Perry, J., & Crane, L. (2011). Perceived credibility and eyewitness testimony of children with intellectual disabilities. *Journal of Intellectual Disability Research, 55*, 385-391.

Hershkowitz, I., Horowitz, D., & Lamb, M. E. (2005). Trends in children's disclosure of abuse in Israel: A national study. *Child Abuse & Neglect, 29*, 1203–1214.

Hershkowitz, I., Lanes, O., & Lamb, M. E. (2007). Exploring the disclosure of child sexual abuse with alleged victims and their parents. *Child Abuse & Neglect, 31*, 111-123.

Holliday, R. E. (2003). Reducing misinformation effects in children with cognitive interviews: Dissociating recollection and familiarity. *Child Development, 74*, 728-751.

Icenogle, G., Steinberg, L., Duell, N., Chein, J., Chang, L., Chaudhary, N., ... & Bacchini, D. (2019). Adolescents' cognitive capacity reaches adult levels prior to their psychosocial maturity: Evidence for a "maturity gap" in a multinational, cross-sectional sample. *Law & Human Behavior, 43*, 69.

Lee, K. (2004). Age, neuropsychological, and social cognitive measures as predictors of individual differences in susceptibility to the misinformation effect. *Applied Cognitive Psychology, 18*(8), 997-1019.

Loftus, E. F., Levidow, B., & Duensing, S. (1992). Who remembers best? Individual differences in memory for events that occurred in a science museum. *Applied Cognitive Psychology, 6*, 93-107.

London, K., Bruck, M., Poole, D. A., & Melnyk, L. (2011). The development of metasuggestibility in children. *Applied Cognitive Psychology, 25*, 146-155.

Jaccard, J., Dittus, P. J., & Gordon, V. V. (1998). Parent-adolescent congruency in reports of adolescent sexual behavior and in communications about sexual behavior. *Child Development, 69*, 247-261.

Jack, F., Leov, J., & Zajac, R. (2014). Age-related differences in the free-recall accounts of child, adolescent, and adult witnesses. *Applied Cognitive Psychology, 28*, 30-38.

Johnson, S.D. (2014). Comparing factors associated with maternal and adolescent reports of adolescent traumatic event exposure. *Family Process*, 53, 214–224.

Jones, L., Bellis, M. A., Wood, S., Hughes, K., McCoy, E., Eckley, L., ... & Officer, A. (2012). Prevalence and risk of violence against children with disabilities: a systematic review and meta-analysis of observational studies. *The Lancet, 380*, 899-907.

Katz, C. (2013). Internet-related child sexual abuse: What children tell us in their testimonies. *Children and Youth Services Review, 35*, 1536-1542.

Kirke-Smith, M., Henry, L., & Messer, D. (2014). Executive functioning: Developmental consequences on adolescents with histories of maltreatment. *British Journal of Developmental Psychology, 32*, 305-319.

Klika, B & Conte, J. (2017). *The APSAC handbook on child maltreatment: Fourth edition*. SAGE Publications.

Kloosterman, P. H., Kelley, E. A., Parker, J. D., & Craig, W. M. (2014). Executive functioning as a predictor of peer victimization in adolescents with and without an Autism Spectrum Disorder. *Research in Autism Spectrum Disorders, 8*, 244-254.

Kogan, S. M. (2004). Disclosing unwanted sexual experiences: Results from a national sample of adolescent women. *Child Abuse & Neglect, 28*, 147-165.

Lamb, M. E., Brown, D. A., Hershkowitz, I., Orbach, Y., & Esplin, P. W. (2018). *Tell me what happened: Questioning children about abuse*. John Wiley & Sons.

Lamb, M. E., Orbach, Y., Hershkowitz, I., Esplin, P. W., & Horowitz, D. (2007). A structured forensic interview protocol improves the quality and informativeness of investigative interviews with children: A review of research using the NICHD Investigative Interview Protocol. *Child Abuse & Neglect, 31*, 1201-1231.

Lavoie, J., Dickerson, K. L., Redlich, A. D., & Quas, J. A. (2019). Overcoming disclosure reluctance in youth victims of sex trafficking: New directions for research, policy, and practice. *Psychology, Public Policy, and Law, 25*, 225.

Lavoie, J., Wyman, J., Crossman, A. M., & Talwar, V. (2021). Meta-analysis of the effects of two interviewing practices on children's disclosures of sensitive information: Rapport practices and question type. *Child Abuse & Neglect, 113*, 104930.

Leach, C., Powell, M. B., Sharman, S. J., & Anglim, J. (2017). The relationship between children's age and disclosures of sexual abuse during forensic interviews. *Child Maltreatment, 22*(1), 79-88.

Leander, L. (2010). Police interviews with child sexual abuse victims: Patterns of reporting, avoidance and denial. *Child Abuse & Neglect, 34*, 192-205.

Leander, L., Christianson, S. Å., & Granhag, P. A. (2008). Internet-initiated sexual abuse: adolescent victims' reports about on-and off-line sexual activities. *Applied Cognitive Psychology, 22*, 1260-1274.

Leander, L., Granhag, P. A., & Christianson, S. Å. (2009). Children's reports of verbal sexual abuse: Effects of police officers' interviewing style. *Psychiatry, Psychology and Law, 16*, 340-354.

Lemaigre, C., Taylor, E. P., & Gittoes, C. (2017). Barriers and facilitators to disclosing sexual abuse in childhood and adolescence: A systematic review. *Child Abuse & Neglect, 70*, 39-52.

Lindholm, J., Cederborg, A. C., & Alm, C. (2015). Adolescent girls exploited in the sex trade: Informativeness and evasiveness in investigative interviews. *Police Practice and Research, 16,* 197-210.

London, K., Bruck, M., Wright, D. B., & Ceci, S. J. (2008). Review of the contemporary literature on how children report sexual abuse to others: Findings, methodological issues, and implications for forensic interviewers. *Memory, 16,* 29-47.

Lugo-Candelas, C., Corbeil, T., Wall, M., Posner, J., Bird, H., Canino, G., Fisher, P. W., Suglia, S. F., & Duarte, C. S. (2021). ADHD and risk for subsequent adverse childhood experiences: understanding the cycle of adversity. *Journal of Child Psychology and Psychiatry, and Allied Disciplines, 62*(8), 971–978.

Luyckx, K., Goossens, L., Soenens, B., & Beyers, W. (2006). Unpacking commitment and exploration: Preliminary validation of an integrative model of late adolescent identity formation. *Journal of Adolescence, 29,* 361-378.

Lyon, T. D. (2009). Abuse disclosure: What adults can tell. In B. L. Bottoms, C. J. Najdowski, & G. S. Goodman (Eds.), *Children as victims, witnesses, and offenders: Psychological science and the law* (pp. 19–35). Guilford Press.

Lyon, T. D. (2014). Interviewing children. *Annual Review of Law and Social Science, 10,* 73-89.

Lyon, T. D., Ahern, E. C., Malloy, L. C., & Quas, J. A. (2010). Children's reasoning about disclosing adult transgressions: Effects of maltreatment, child age, and adult identity. *Child Development, 81,* 1714-1728.

Lyon, T. D., & Dorado, J. S. (2008). Truth induction in young maltreated children: The effects of oath-taking and reassurance on true and false disclosures. *Child Abuse & Neglect, 32,* 738-748.

Malloy, L. C., Brubacher, S. P., & Lamb, M. E. (2011). Expected consequences of disclosure revealed in investigative interviews with suspected victims of child sexual abuse. *Applied Developmental Science, 15,* 8-19.

Malloy, L. C., Brubacher, S. P., & Lamb, M. E. (2013). "Because she's one who listens": Children discuss disclosure recipients in forensic interviews. *Child Maltreatment, 18,* 245-251.

Malloy, L. C., Lyon, T. D., & Quas, J. A. (2007). Filial dependency and recantation of child sexual abuse allegations. *Journal of the American Academy of Child & Adolescent Psychiatry, 46,* 162-170.

Malloy, L. C., Mugno, A. P., Rivard, J. R., Lyon, T. D., & Quas, J. A. (2016). Familial influences on recantation in substantiated child sexual abuse cases. *Child Maltreatment, 21,* 256-261.

Malloy, L. C., & Quas, J. A. (2009). Children's suggestibility: Areas of consensus and controversy. In K. Kuehnle & M. Connell (Eds.), *The evaluation of child sexual abuse allegations: A comprehensive guide to assessment and testimony* (pp. 267–297). John Wiley & Sons Inc.

Malloy, L. C., Quas, J. A., Lyon, T. D., & Ahern, E. C. (2014). Disclosing adult wrongdoing: Maltreated and non-maltreated children's expectations and preferences. *Journal of Experimental Child Psychology, 124,* 78-96.

Manay, N., & Collin-Vézina, D. (2021). Recipients of children's and adolescents' disclosures of childhood sexual abuse: A systematic review. *Child Abuse & Neglect, 116,* 104192.

McElvaney, R. (2015). Disclosure of child sexual abuse: Delays, non-disclosure and partial disclosure. What the research tells us and implications for practice. *Child Abuse Review, 24,* 159-169.

McGuire, K., London, K., & Wright, D. B. (2011). Peer influence on event reports among adolescents and young adults. *Memory, 19,* 674-683.

McGuire, K., London, K., & Wright, D. B. (2015). Developmental trends in false memory across adolescence and young adulthood: A comparison of DRM and memory conformity paradigms. *Applied Cognitive Psychology, 29,* 334-344.

Meissner, C. A. (2021). "What works?" Systematic reviews and meta-analyses of the investigative interviewing research literature. *Applied Cognitive Psychology, 35,* 322-328.

Memon, A., Meissner, C. A., & Fraser, J. (2010). The cognitive interview: A meta-analytic review and study space analysis of the past 25 years. *Psychology, Public Policy, and Law, 16,* 340.

Memorandum of Good Practice. (1992). London, England: Her Majesty's Stationery Office.

Mersky, J. P., & Reynolds, A. J. (2007). Child maltreatment and violent delinquency: Disentangling main effects and subgroup effects. *Child Maltreatment, 12,* 246-258.

Morgan, R., & Truman, J. (2020, September). *Criminal Victimization, 2019.* Bureau of Justice Statistics. Retrieved January 3, 2021 from https://www.bjs.gov/content/pub/pdf/cv19.pdf

Myers, W., Turanovic, J. J., Lloyd, K. M., & Pratt, T. C. (2020). The victimization of LGBTQ students at school: A meta-analysis. *Journal of School Violence, 19,* 421-432.

Nagel, D. E., Putnam, F. W., Noll, J. G., & Trickett, P. K. (1997). Disclosure patterns of sexual abuse and psychological functioning at a 1-year follow-up. *Child Abuse & Neglect, 21,* 137-147.

Nogalska, A., Henderson, H., Cho, S., & Lyon, T. D. (2021). Police interviewing behaviors and commercially sexually exploited adolescents' reluctance. *Psychology, Public Policy, and Law, 27,* 328-340.

Olafson, E., & Lederman, J. C. S. (2006). The state of the debate about children's disclosure patterns in child sexual abuse cases. *Juvenile and Family Court Journal, 57,* 27-40.

Op den Kelder, R., Van den Akker, A. L., Geurts, H. M., Lindauer, R. J., & Overbeek, G. (2018). Executive functions in trauma-exposed youth: A meta-analysis. *European Journal of Psychotraumatology, 9,* 1450595.

Owen-Kostelnik, J., Reppucci, N. D., & Meyer, J. R. (2006). Testimony and interrogation of minors: Assumptions about maturity and morality. *American Psychologist, 61,* 286-304.

Pimentel, P. S., Arndorfer, A., & Malloy, L. C. (2015). Taking the blame for someone else's wrongdoing: The effects of age and reciprocity. *Law and Human Behavior, 39*(3), 219-231.

Piquero, A. R., Farrington, D. P., & Blumstein, A. (2007). *Key issues in criminal career research: New analyses of the Cambridge Study in Delinquent Development.* Cambridge University Press.

Plotnikoff, J., & Woolfson, R. (2009). Measuring up? Evaluating implementation of government commitments to young witnesses in criminal proceedings. *London, UK: National Society for the Prevention of Cruelty to Children.*

Price, H. L., Evans, A. D., & Bruer, K. C. (2019). Transmission of children's disclosures of a transgression from peers to adults. *Applied Developmental Science, 25*(3), 228-239.

Priebe, G., & Svedin, C. G. (2008). Child sexual abuse is largely hidden from the adult society: An epidemiological study of adolescents' disclosures. *Child Abuse & Neglect, 32,* 1095-1108.

Quas, J. A., Stolzenberg, S. N., & Lyon, T. D. (2018). The effects of promising to tell the truth, the putative confession, and recall and recognition questions on maltreated and non-maltreated children's disclosure of a minor transgression. *Journal of Experimental Child Psychology, 166,* 266-279.

Ragelienė, T. (2016). Links of adolescents identity development and relationship with peers: A systematic literature review. *Journal of the Canadian Academy of Child and Adolescent Psychiatry, 25,* 97-105.

Reid, J. A. (2016). Entrapment and enmeshment schemes used by sex traffickers. *Sexual Abuse, 28,* 491-511.

Richardson, G., Gudjonsson, G. H., & Kelly, T. P. (1995). Interrogative suggestibility in an adolescent forensic population. *Journal of Adolescence, 18,* 211-216.

Richardson, W. S., Wilson, M. C., Nishikawa, J., & Hayward, R. S. (1995). The well-built clinical question: a key to evidence-based decisions. *ACP Journal Club, 123,* A12-A13.

Roediger, H. L., & McDermott, K. B. (1995). Creating false memories: Remembering words not presented in lists. *Journal of Experimental Psychology: Learning, Memory, and Cognition, 21,* 803.

Rotenberg, K. J. (1991). Children's interpersonal trust: An introduction. In K. J. Rotenberg (Ed.), *Children's interpersonal trust: Sensitivity to lying, deception, and promise violations* (pp. 1-4). New York: Springer.

Ryan, J. P., & Testa, M. F. (2005). Child maltreatment and juvenile delinquency: Investigating the role of placement and placement instability. *Children and Youth Services Review, 27,* 227-249.

Sauerland, M., Brackmann, M., & Otgaar, H. (2018) Rapport: Little effect on children's, adolescents', and adults' statement quantity, accuracy, and suggestibility. *Journal of Child Custody, 15,* 268-285.

Saywitz, K. J., Wells, C. R., Larson, R. P., & Hobbs, S. D. (2019). Effects of interviewer support on children's memory and suggestibility: Systematic review and meta-analyses of experimental research. *Trauma, Violence, & Abuse, 20,* 22-39.

Schaeffer, P., Leventhal, J. M., & Asnes, A. G. (2011). Children's disclosures of sexual abuse: Learning from direct inquiry. *Child Abuse & Neglect, 35,* 343-352.

Schönbucher, V., Maier, T., Mohler-Kuo, M., Schnyder, U., & Landolt, M. A. (2012). Disclosure of child sexual abuse by adolescents: A qualitative in-depth study. *Journal of Interpersonal Violence, 27,* 3486-3513.

Shalhoub-Kevorkian, N. (2005). Disclosure of child abuse in conflict areas. *Violence Against Women, 11,* 1263-1291.

Sheahan, C. L., Pica, E., Pozzulo, J. D., & Nastasa, C. (2017). Eyewitness recall and identification abilities of adolescent and young-adults. *Journal of Applied Developmental Psychology, 53,* 86-95.

Sheth, C., Prescot, A. P., Legarreta, M., Renshaw, P. F., McGlade, E., & Yurgelun-Todd, D. (2019). Reduced gamma-amino butyric acid (GABA) and glutamine in the anterior cingulate cortex (ACC) of veterans exposed to trauma. *Journal of Affective Disorders, 248,* 166-174.

Shulman, E. P., Smith, A. R., Silva, K., Icenogle, G., Duell, N., Chein, J., & Steinberg, L. (2016). The dual systems model: Review, reappraisal, and reaffirmation. *Developmental Cognitive Neuroscience, 17,* 103-117.

Singh, K., & Gudjonsson, G. (1992). The vulnerability of adolescent boys to interrogative pressure: An experimental study. *The Journal of Forensic Psychiatry, 3,* 167-170.

Steinberg, L. (2005). Cognitive and affective development in adolescence. *Trends in Cognitive Sciences, 9,* 69-74.

Steinberg, L. (2007). Risk taking in adolescence: New perspectives from brain and behavioral science. *Current Directions in Psychological Science, 16,* 55-59.

Steinberg, L. (2009). Adolescent development and juvenile justice. *Annual Review of Clinical Psychology, 5,* 459-485.

Steinberg, L., & Cauffman, E. (1996). Maturity of judgment in adolescence: Psychosocial factors in adolescent decision making. *Law and Human Behavior, 20*(3), 249-272.

Steinberg, L., & Scott, E. S. (2003). Less guilty by reason of adolescence: developmental immaturity, diminished responsibility, and the juvenile death penalty. *American Psychologist, 58,* 1009.

Steinberg, L., & Silverberg, S. B. (1986). The vicissitudes of autonomy in early adolescence. *Child Development, 57*, 841-851.

Stevens, M. C., Kiehl, K. A., Pearlson, G. D., & Calhoun, V. D. (2007). Functional neural networks underlying response inhibition in adolescents and adults. *Behavioural Brain Research, 181*, 12-22.

Stroud, D. D., Martens, S. L., & Barker, J. (2000). Criminal investigation of child sexual abuse: A comparison of cases referred to the prosecutor to those not referred. *Child Abuse & Neglect, 24*, 689–700.

Swanson, H. L. (1999). What develops in working memory? A life span perspective. *Developmental Psychology, 35*, 986.

Taylor, J., Stalker, K., & Stewart, A. (2016). Disabled children and the child protection system: A cause for concern. *Child Abuse Review, 25*, 60-73.

Teoh, Y. S., & Lamb, M. (2013). Interviewer demeanor in forensic interviews of children. *Psychology, Crime & Law, 19*, 145-159.

Ungar, M., Tutty, L. M., McConnell, S., Barter, K., & Fairholm, J. (2009). What Canadian youth tell us about disclosing abuse. *Child Abuse & Neglect, 33*, 699-708.

U.S. Department of Health and Human Services. (2021). Child Maltreatment 2019. Retrieved from https://www.acf.hhs.gov/sites/default/files/documents/cb/cm2019.pdf

Vallano, J. P., & Schreiber Compo, N. (2015). Rapport-building with cooperative witnesses and criminal suspects: A theoretical and empirical review. *Psychology, Public Policy, and Law, 21*, 85.

Vanmeter, F., Henderson, H. M., Konovalov H., Blasbalg, U., & Karni-Visel, Y. (2023). Children's narrative coherence in 'Achieving Best Evidence' forensic interviews and courtroom testimony. *Psychology, Crime, & Law, 29*, 203-221.

Van der Graaff, J., Branje, S., De Wied, M., Hawk, S., Van Lier, P., & Meeus, W. (2014). Perspective taking and empathic concern in adolescence: Gender differences in developmental changes. *Developmental Psychology, 50*, 881-888.

Walsh, W. A., Jones, L. M., Cross, T. P., & Lippert, T. (2010). Prosecuting child sexual abuse: The importance of evidence type. *Crime & Delinquency, 56*, 436–454.

Warr, M. (1993). Age, peers, and delinquency. *Criminology, 31*, 17-40.

Wilson, J. M., & Dalton, E. (2008). Human trafficking in the heartland: Variation in law enforcement awareness and response. *Journal of Contemporary Criminal Justice, 24*, 296-313.

Wyman, J., Lavoie, J., & Talwar, V. (2018). Best practices for interviewing children with intellectual disabilities in maltreatment cases. *Exceptionality, 27*, 167-184.

Xian, K., Chock, S., & Dwiggins, D. (2017). LGBTQ youth and vulnerability to sex trafficking. In *Human trafficking is a public health issue* (pp. 141-152). Springer, Cham.

Yau, J. P., Tasopoulos-Chan, M., & Smetana, J. G. (2009). Disclosure to parents about everyday activities among American adolescents from Mexican, Chinese, and European backgrounds. *Child Development, 80*(5), 1481-1498.

Young, A. M., Grey, M., & Boyd, C. J. (2009). Adolescents' experiences of sexual assault by peers: Prevalence and nature of victimization occurring within and outside of school. *Journal of Youth and Adolescence, 38*, 1072-1083.

Yurgelun-Todd, D. (2007). Emotional and cognitive changes during adolescence. *Current Opinion in Neurobiology, 17*, 251-257.

CHAPTER 13

Police Interviewing and Interrogation of Adolescent Suspects

Hayley M. D. Cleary and Megan G. Crane

Abstract
Custodial police interrogations are high-stakes social interactions that can result in serious legal consequences for adolescent suspects. Psychological research on youths' immature judgment and susceptibility to influence reveals specific developmental vulnerabilities in the interrogation room. This chapter reviews scientific evidence regarding adolescents' Miranda rights comprehension, interrogative suggestibility, and propensity to comply with authority figures. It discusses case law and policy governing interrogation practices and the legal implications of adolescents' Miranda waivers and confessions. The chapter highlights the experiences of youth suspects of color as an especially disadvantaged group. It integrates contemporary law and developmental research around three key issues—Miranda, parent involvement in interrogations, and police use of coercion—to explore the interplay between developmental science and the law in juvenile interrogations. Finally, the chapter discusses the importance of legislative and policing reforms, including mandatory recording of all custodial interrogations, mandatory assistance of legal counsel, and prohibition of deception with adolescent suspects.

Key Words: adolescent, youth, juvenile, police, interrogation, development, law

Approximately 700,000 youth under age 18 are arrested in the United States every year (Puzzanchera, 2021). Some of those youth will be subjected to police questioning, either in custodial or in noncustodial settings. A custodial interrogation is when police question a suspect about involvement in an alleged crime and the suspect does not feel free to leave (*Thompson v. Keohane*, 1995). Additionally, some youth are "informally" questioned in non-custodial settings around their communities. Others are questioned by sworn police officers stationed in their schools. Still others encounter police via the child welfare, medical, or mental health systems. Some youth experience interrogation *before* they are formally arrested, while others are interrogated postarrest or never arrested at all. While it is difficult to estimate precisely how many adolescents face custodial interrogations each year, the breadth of police–youth contact that could lead to interrogation is considerable. According to Bureau of Justice Statistics data, 14% of 16–17-year-olds and 30% of 18–24-year-olds had contact with police in 2018 (Harrell & Davis, 2020).

This chapter outlines key developmental and legal principles at play when police officers question adolescent suspects about alleged criminal involvement. While police officers also question adolescents who are alleged crime victims or witnesses (see Malloy et al., this volume), we limit our discussion in this chapter to police interrogations of adolescent suspects. The stakes are high for these youth. Police interrogation is a gateway to prosecution, conviction, and incarceration. Adolescents who are convicted in adult court face the possibility of dire sentences, even life in prison (Zottoli et al., this volume). Incarceration in adult correctional facilities heightens risk of serious negative outcomes such as physical abuse, sexual assault, and suicide attempts (Mulvey & Schubert, 2012). Moreover, the interrogation experience alone could have long-term ramifications for youths' development. Adolescence is a critical period for legal socialization in which youth form stable attitudes about the legitimacy of legal actors and institutions (Tyler & Trinkner, 2017). Negative legal experiences in a high-stress setting such as custodial interrogation could shape adolescents' views about police and other legal authorities for years to come. Interrogation could potentially even trigger a trauma reaction among youth with a history of trauma symptoms (Cleary et al., 2021; Crane, 2017).

But what do juvenile interrogations look like? How do youth experience this interaction? Researchers have used different methodological approaches to peer behind the "veil of secrecy" and better understand juvenile interrogation processes and outcomes (Kassin et al., 2010, p. 25). The most direct (but logistically challenging) approach is to analyze actual interrogations of youth via electronically recorded interrogations. These observational studies, though few, suggest that youth frequently waive their Miranda rights and experience a wide variety of high-pressure interrogation tactics—for example, accusing the suspect repeatedly, expressing certainty in the suspect's guilt, or holding suspects alone in the interrogation room (Cleary, 2014; Feld, 2013a). Youths' self-reported interrogation experiences corroborate this finding (Arndorfer et al., 2015; Malloy et al., 2014). While particular interrogation characteristics vary widely, the goal of all accusatory custodial interrogations is the same: elicit a confession. Police interrogation is a carefully orchestrated, psychologically manipulative process designed to change the suspect's cost–benefit analysis (Kassin et al., 2010). Interrogators are trained to increase the perceived "cost" of denying involvement in the crime (e.g., by implying that the pressure will only increase) and decrease the "cost" of giving a confession (e.g., by implying lesser consequences); this, in turn, increases the benefit of confessing by ending the interrogative pressure.

Police themselves report using a wide variety of interrogation techniques, including coercive techniques, with adolescent suspects (Cleary & Warner, 2016; Reppucci et al., 2010). While police officials often recognize that many of these tactics carry risks when used with youth, many nonetheless report that they use the same tactics with adolescent suspects they use with adults. For example, police engage in both maximization (e.g., heightening suspect anxiety) and minimization (e.g., de-emphasizing crime seriousness) with child and adolescent suspects (Feld, 2013b; Meyer & Reppucci, 2007). They report lying to youth and using false evidence ploys (Cleary & Warner, 2016; Feld, 2013b). Police also utilize behavioral analysis techniques that purportedly indicate a suspect's deception (Cleary & Warner, 2016; Meyer & Reppucci, 2007), despite large error rates in behavioral lie detection (Driskell, 2012). Behavioral lie detection may be particularly unreliable for adolescent suspects since many purported cues of deception such as slouching, covering one's mouth or face, and gaze aversion (Inbau et al., 2013) are common traits or behaviors of adolescents.

Participants in, and outcomes of, juvenile interrogations can also vary widely. Both observational and self-report studies suggest adolescents infrequently receive support from legal counsel or helpful parents (Cleary, 2014; Feld, 2013a; Viljoen et al., 2005). Juvenile interrogations may conclude with the youth denying the charge, partially admitting involvement, or proffering a full confession (Cleary, 2014; Feld, 2013a). Youth who self-report confessing to police give both true and false confessions (Gudjonsson et al., 2006; Malloy et al., 2014). Once police obtain a confession, case law demonstrates it is extremely difficult to convince a judge or jury that the confession was false and/or coerced. Moreover, suspects who partially or fully confess are more likely to plead guilty, obviating any later opportunity to hear their case in court (Redlich et al., 2018).

Courts have long recognized that custodial interrogations are inherently coercive interactions and have implemented certain procedural safeguards to protect criminal suspects' constitutional rights. State legislatures have also enacted procedural reforms to improve interrogation processes and outcomes. The next section reviews constitutional law doctrines governing custodial interrogations and admissibility of suspect statements, whether by an adult or a minor, and then examines Supreme Court precedent regarding juvenile interrogations in particular.

Constitutional Law Governing Interrogations and Suspect Statements

The U.S. Supreme Court adopted protective measures in *Miranda v. Arizona* (1966) to safeguard suspects against self-incrimination. Under *Miranda*, incriminating statements made during custodial interrogation are inadmissible unless the suspect is first advised that they have the right to remain silent, that their statements may be used against them as evidence, that they have the right to consult with an attorney and have an attorney present during the interrogation, and that they have the right to have an attorney provided at no cost if they cannot afford one (*Miranda v. Arizona*, 1966). These well-established Miranda warnings are intended to protect suspects from inherently coercive custodial settings and must necessarily precede a custodial interrogation. If a suspect chooses to waive their constitutional rights and consent to custodial questioning, they must do so knowingly, voluntarily, and intelligently (*Miranda v. Arizona*, 1966).

Because *Miranda* concerns the coercive nature of a custodial interrogation, it only applies when an individual is in custody. Custody is determined by an objective test: Given the circumstances, would a reasonable person have felt free to terminate the interrogation and leave (*Stansbury v. California*, 1994; *Thompson v. Keohane*, 1995; *Yarborough v. Alvarado*, 2004)? Courts and police officers alike are required to examine all the circumstances surrounding the interrogation and evaluate how a "reasonable person" in the suspect's position would perceive their freedom to leave (*Thompson v. Keohane*, 1995). The U.S. Supreme Court in *Yarborough* (2004) maintained that custody determinations are an "objective" test and that neither the interrogating officer's nor the suspect's perceptions are material to the determination.

When a suspect provides an incriminating statement to police, their statement also must be voluntary in order to be constitutionally admitted as evidence at trial. The due process clause of the Fourteenth Amendment to the U.S. Constitution bars the use of an involuntary confession against a criminal defendant. Courts employ a "totality of the circumstances" test to determine whether a statement is involuntary, requiring judges to weigh both police conduct in the interrogation and traits of the individual suspect (*Schneckloth v. Bustamonte*, 1973). With regard to police conduct, courts consider factors such as the location and length of the interrogation; the number of officers present; whether the suspect was informed of their constitutional rights; whether the suspect was provided food, water, or the opportunity to sleep; whether police used any force; and whether police made any threats or promises. With regard to the individual suspect, courts consider factors such as the suspect's age, IQ, any mental illness, language abilities, education history, and prior experience with law enforcement (see also *Fare v. Michael C.*, 1979). The voluntariness test is supposed to operate as a sliding scale; the more vulnerable the suspect, the less coercion should be required for a finding of involuntariness (*Miller v. Fenton*, 1985).

Interrogation Law as Applied to Youth
The U.S. Supreme Court explicitly held that age is a relevant factor when determining whether a child is in custody for Miranda purposes (*J.D.B. v. North Carolina*, 2011). *J.D.B.* reflected the court's recognition that custodial pressures can be intense enough to generate false confessions. The court recognized that the risk of coercion is even greater for juvenile suspects, holding that "in some circumstances, a child's age would affect how a reasonable person in the suspect's position would perceive his or her freedom to leave" (*J.D.B. v. North Carolina*, 2011, p. 272). The court understood that evaluating circumstances through the eyes of a child would lead to different conclusions compared to the eyes of an adult. The court explained that the custody analysis remains an objective test, even accounting for the child's age, because youth age should be objectively apparent to the questioning officer.

In *J.D.B.*, the court relied upon and revitalized a long-standing body of case law recognizing that children are different from adults in ways that are practically and constitutionally relevant. Justice Sotomayor, writing for the majority, noted:

> A child's age is far more than a chronological fact. It is a fact that generates commonsense conclusions about behavior and perception. Such conclusions apply broadly to children as a class. And, they are self-evident to anyone who was a child once himself, including any police officer or judge. Time and again, this Court has drawn these commonsense conclusions for itself. We have observed that children generally are less mature and responsible than adults; they often lack the experience, perspective, and judgment to recognize and avoid choices that could be detrimental to them; that they are more vulnerable or susceptible to . . . outside pressures than adults; and so on. (*J.D.B. v. North Carolina*, 2011, p. 272)

This holding reinforces decades of precedent recognizing the unique legal and factual issues involved with interrogations of juvenile suspects (e.g., *Haley v. Ohio*, 1948). More recently, the U.S. Supreme Court renewed its understanding of these principles in a quartet of decisions outlawing the death penalty and mandatory life without parole sentences for juveniles (*Graham v. Florida*, 2010; *Miller v. Alabama*, 2012; *Montgomery v. Louisiana*, 2016; *Roper v. Simmons*, 2005; see Zottoli et al., this volume). Indeed, all of these decisions recognize the fundamental truth that "kids are different" from adults in ways that make them uniquely vulnerable during the pressure cooker of interrogation. Just as the U.S. Supreme Court has found that developmental immaturity makes youth inherently less culpable for their actions, these traits also make them more likely to involuntarily and falsely confess during police interrogations (Birckhead, 2008; Guggenheim & Hertz, 2012).

Special Care for Youth Interrogations: A Reasonable Juvenile Standard
The Supreme Court has held that "admissions and cautions of juveniles require special caution" and that courts must take "the greatest care . . . to assure that the [juvenile]'s admission was voluntary, in the sense not only that it was not coerced or suggested, but also that it was not the product of ignorance of rights or adolescent fantasy, fright, or despair" (*In re Gault*, 1967, p. 56). *J.D.B. v. North Carolina* (2011) provided the framework of a reasonable juvenile. *J.D.B.* explicitly requires factfinders to ask whether a reasonable child would have felt free to leave when evaluating whether a suspect was in custody. From a developmental perspective, there is no reason to limit the reasonable juvenile lens to custody analyses. All constitutional questions regarding youth interrogations, including the validity of a Miranda waiver and the voluntariness of a statement, should be approached and evaluated through the lens of a reasonable juvenile, which may vary even within the developmental period of adolescence (e.g., whether the youth is 13 years old versus 17 years old). What does it mean to view a youth's

interrogation through the eyes of a child? A California appellate court provides a model example of heightened judicial scrutiny of a juvenile confession.

In re Elias V. (2015) involved a 13-year-old boy who confessed to inappropriately touching his friend's 3-year-old sister during a 20-minute school-based interrogation by a detective with his school principal present. A trial court found Elias's confession voluntary because the interrogation was short and the detective was kind to him. However, an appellate court reversed the decision and explicitly called out the interrogating detective for using classic manipulation techniques. The appellate court held that a proper assessment of Elias's confession required putting oneself in the shoes of the 13-year-old and asking how he would perceive the conduct of the police interrogators (*In re Elias V.*, 2015). Thus, the suspect's adolescence informed the analysis of all of the legal issues in question, even those that initially appeared to relate only to police conduct. For example, the court concluded that "the aggressive, deceptive, and unduly suggestive tactics [the detective] employed would have been particularly intimidating" given that "Elias was a young adolescent" who was not "particularly sophisticated" and "had no prior confrontations with police" (*In re Elias V.*, 2015, p. 591). The court further concluded that the "use of deceptive techniques [was] significantly more indicative of involuntariness where, as here, the subject is a 13-year-old adolescent" (p. 593). Finally, the court also recognized that an adolescent is more suggestible and inclined to adopt a contaminated confession based on facts fed to him by the interrogator. As a result, the court considered the unreliable statements as a relevant factor in the involuntariness of the ultimate confession.

Unfortunately, judicial opinions like *Elias V.* are rare, for two primary reasons. First, the constitutionality of youth interrogation and juveniles' confession statements is not consistently litigated in juvenile court and rarely is appealed. Pretrial motions, such as a motion to suppress a confession as violating Miranda and/or involuntary, are rarely filed in juvenile courts across the country. Even when filed, they are often boilerplate and easily denied (Drizin & Luloff, 2007). Second, while there is a robust legal foundation for the principle that youth need special care in the interrogation room, this principle is infrequently applied in practice in a meaningful way. More often, courts account for youthfulness as a single factor in the totality of circumstances analysis for Miranda waivers and voluntariness. In order for "special care" to be meaningful, each of the factors in the totality of the circumstances analysis, both for Miranda waivers and voluntariness of statements, must be evaluated through the lens and experience of a reasonable juvenile of a similar developmental age. This inherently requires courts to consider the unique features of this developmental period.

Developmental Principles Relevant to Juvenile Interrogations

Police interrogation is, by design, a process of social influence (*J.D.B. v. North Carolina*, 2011; Kassin et al., 2010). While youths' developmental immaturity was intuited by earlier courts (*Gallegos v. Colorado*, 1962; *Haley v. Ohio*, 1948), it is now scientifically established that adolescents are uniquely vulnerable to influence in the interrogation context (see Cleary, 2017; Owen-Kostelnik et al., 2006, for reviews). For example, adolescents are more suggestible than adults, more likely to comply with requests from authority figures, more likely to waive their Miranda rights, and more susceptible to coerced and false confessions (see, generally, Kassin et al., 2010). Much of youths' vulnerability stems from their ongoing neurobiological development. Adolescence is a period of rapid neurological growth and maturation in which brain structures continue to mature and functionally integrate across systems (National Academies of Sciences, Engineering, and Medicine, 2019). The adolescent brain is primed for reward sensitivity before the cortical systems involved in executive functioning and impulse control have fully matured, which curtails adolescents' ability to regulate their emotions and behavior.

In this chapter, we highlight developmental principles specifically relevant to the interrogation context.

Youths' Miranda Comprehension and Awareness of Police Practices

As described previously, valid juvenile Miranda waivers must be knowing, intelligent, and voluntary (*In re Gault*, 1967; *Miranda v. Arizona*, 1966). These legal terms encompass a complex array of psychological constructs. The Miranda warnings themselves are not a single concept but rather distinct rights that could be (mis)understood individually or collectively (Zelle et al., 2015). Grisso (1980) adapted these legal terms into psychological constructs that could be systematically investigated and empirically validated. He conceptualized "knowing" with a term called *understanding*, meaning the youth has basic comprehension of the words and phrases used in Miranda language. He conceptualized "intelligent" as *appreciation*, meaning the youth grasps how rights function in context and can apply that knowledge to their own legal situation. In the decades following Grisso's (1981) seminal work, extensive research has confirmed that youth have difficulty with both understanding and appreciation of the Miranda warnings. For example, in one study of community youth, 26% of 16–17-year-olds demonstrated impaired Miranda understanding on a global comprehension measure, and as many as 70% of 11–13-year-olds showed impairment (Woolard et al., 2008). In a later study with 12–19-year-olds in detention facilities, 88% demonstrated comprehension deficits (Zelle et al., 2015). Across studies and sample types, youth who are younger and have lower IQs (particularly verbal IQ), lower academic achievement, and higher levels of interrogative suggestibility perform consistently worse than their counterparts on standardized, validated measures of Miranda understanding (McLachlan et al., 2011; Redlich et al., 2003; Woolard et al., 2008; Zelle et al., 2015). Moreover, several studies reported that justice-involved youth (and indeed, many adults) hold common misperceptions about their constitutional rights—for example, that remaining silent can be used against you in court or that court-appointed attorneys are required to disclose everything to the judge (Grisso, 1981; Rogers et al., 2014).

Whereas courts have struggled to define the concept of "intelligent" waiver (see, generally, Goldstein et al., 2015), psychologists contend that a basic factual understanding of constitutional rights and language is not enough; for a waiver to be intelligent, suspects must grasp the significance and potential implications of ceding those rights. Grisso's early work found that youth under 16 years showed substantially impaired Miranda appreciation, and later research confirms youths' appreciation is far inferior to adults' (Grisso, 1981). Youth fare worse on measures of appreciation than understanding and have particular difficulty grasping the right to silence (Goldstein et al., 2018; Viljoen et al., 2007). Youth also misunderstand the role of attorneys and/or conflate attorneys with other legal system actors such as social workers (Zelle et al., 2015). Across studies, youth consistently fail to fully grasp the notion of the right to silence as fundamental and irrevocable, instead conceptualizing it as a conditional privilege that, for example, can be taken away by a judge (Goldstein et al., 2003, 2018). Moreover, the "simplified" juvenile-specific Miranda warnings some police jurisdictions use have been found to be no more readable than typical adult versions and may even be more linguistically complex, further hindering youths' comprehension (Goldstein et al., 2012; Rogers et al., 2007). Finally, police often downplay or routinize the Miranda warnings with juvenile suspects, likely undermining youths' ability to appreciate the consequences of waiving them (Cleary & Vidal, 2016; Sim & Lamb, 2018).

Given youths' Miranda comprehension and appreciation difficulties and police tactics to minimize Miranda's importance, it comes as no surprise that most youth appear to waive their Miranda rights (Cleary & Vidal, 2016; Feld, 2013a). Thus, researchers have begun exploring youths' knowledge of police interrogation practices, testing the premise that valid Miranda waivers offer little protection if adolescent suspects do not understand what they are likely to face in an interrogation. These studies examined youths' knowledge about the "ground rules" of juvenile interrogations—for example, Do police have to tell parents when their children are considered suspects? Can police lie to suspects during questioning? Although few in number, studies to date reveal considerable gaps in youths' knowledge about the parameters of acceptable interrogation practices. In one study with 170 adolescents ages 11–17 years, about half of youth incorrectly believed that police must wait for parents to arrive at the police station before questioning a minor, and about half incorrectly believed police are not allowed to lie to suspects (Woolard et al., 2008). One third of youth did not know suspects can stop answering questions after having already started. Another study with 98 youth detained in a juvenile correctional facility found that youth averaged about 59% accuracy on a measure of factual understanding of police interrogation practices (Vidal et al., 2017).

Despite the reality that Miranda is failing to protect youth's rights, youth rarely win on this issue. Miranda issues are often not even raised in juvenile court, either because the youth does not have counsel (because they waived their right to be represented by counsel) or the youth pled guilty. Even if a youth has counsel and does not plead guilty, pretrial motions are rarely filed on Miranda grounds in juvenile court (Drizin & Luloff, 2007).

Interrogative Suggestibility

"Suggestibility" refers to a general vulnerability to outside influence. In the police interrogation context, scholars define "interrogative suggestibility" as the tendency to change one's narrative account of events in response to misleading information or perceived pressure during formal questioning (Gudjonsson, 2003). This construct is critical for evaluations of voluntariness in both Miranda waivers and confessions. This vulnerability is conceptualized as a product of both cognitive limitations and social influence. That is, suspects may display heightened suggestibility due to preexisting, chronic conditions (such as age or mental impairment) or in response to acute situational forces inherent in the interrogation itself (such as distress, fatigue, sleep deprivation, or social isolation; Davis & Leo, 2013). Researchers have devised ways to measure interrogative suggestibility in the context of police interrogations. The Gudjonsson Suggestibility Scales measure two components of interrogative suggestibility: yield and shift (see Gudjonsson, 2018, for a historical overview). *Yield*—the tendency to give in to leading questions—relates to a constellation of cognitive abilities such as memory and information processing abilities. *Shift*—the tendency to change one's statements in response to negative feedback—is rooted in the psychology of social learning and reinforcement and emphasizes the role of social pressures. Negative feedback refers to statements that explicitly or implicitly communicate the interrogators' dissatisfaction with an answer (see, generally, Gudjonsson, 2018).

In adult populations, interrogative suggestibility correlates with a broad array of personality traits and states (Gudjonsson, 2003). Low IQ, memory problems, anxiety, and a personal history of negative life events appear most strongly correlated with suggestibility (Gudjonsson, 2018). While fewer studies have examined interrogative suggestibility among adolescents compared to adults or young children, research generally shows adolescents are more suggestible than adults. Adolescents appear especially susceptible to negative feedback and are more likely to change their statements in response to it (Redlich et al., 2003; Richardson et al., 1995; Singh & Gudjonsson, 1992). Intellectual functioning (as measured via IQ scales or a proxy) consistently emerges as an important predictor of suggestibility in adolescents (McLachlan et al., 2011; Muris et al., 2004). Interrogative suggestibility in adolescents negatively correlates with competence to stand trial as well as Miranda rights comprehension (McLachlan et al., 2011;

Redlich et al., 2003). Importantly, suggestibility is correlated with the tendency to make false statements in both adolescents and adults (Otgaar et al., 2021; Redlich & Goodman, 2003).

Perceptions of and Compliance With Authority

Suggestibility is conceptually distinct from, but related to, acquiescence and compliance in the interrogation context. Gudjonsson (2003) defined acquiescence as an individual tendency to "answer questions in the affirmative irrespective of the content" (p. 377) and noted that, unlike suggestibility, acquiescence does not involve questions that specifically suggest an expected answer. Gudjonsson (2003) defined compliance as an individual tendency to "go along with propositions, requests or instructions, for some immediate instrumental gain," often to avoid conflict or please authority figures (p. 370). As defined in this context, suggestibility indicates that the suspect has internally accepted the interrogator's suggestion, whereas compliance does not necessarily (Gudjonsson, 2013).

To understand adolescent compliance in legal settings such as a police interrogation, we must first examine how adolescents function in society more broadly. Adolescents are socialized to obey rules, follow instructions, and observe social norms and standards (Steinberg, 2014). This socialization begins in early childhood and evolves as adolescents gradually develop autonomy and identity. Adolescents encounter authority figures daily, from parents and adult relatives to teachers and school administrators. These authority figures establish rules—often without adolescents' input—and hold the power to enforce those rules and administer punishment for rule violations. Adolescents internalize these rule-related social norms in part through legal socialization, a process that includes not only laws and legal norms but also nonlegal institutions such as families and schools (Tapp & Levine, 1974; Trinkner & Cohn, 2014).

Cleary (2017) discussed multiple ways in which adolescents' subordinate social status could manifest in the interrogation room and systematically induce compliance behaviors. Adolescent suspects' social location is critical to understanding their perceptions of, and compliance with, interrogators. Adolescent suspects are first and foremost *adolescents*—required to attend school, prohibited from purchasing alcohol, expected to obey household rules, and generally restricted in their movement and decisional autonomy. Adolescent suspects are then socially located as *suspects*—accused of committing a crime, often questioned in a socially controlled setting (police station), restrained in their movement (either physically or psychologically), and subjected to sometimes stressful and accusatory questioning. Already, the *adolescent* and *suspect* roles are conflated to dually disadvantage youth in this situation. Moreover, interrogators possess detailed knowledge about suspects' legal rights and the parameters of permissible interrogation practices that adolescents (and many adults) do not (Cleary & Warner, 2017; Woolard et al., 2008). Framed in empirical terms, we might expect main effects for both adolescent (compared to adult) status and suspect (compared to victim or witness) status. Moreover, we might also expect an interaction, such that suspects who are adolescents face compounded disadvantage. As Villalobos and Davis (2016) noted, "Simple compliance with demands of higher power individuals is among the basic dynamics of power in social interaction (perhaps including acquiescence with demands to confess)" (p. 12). Juveniles in the interrogation room occupy a lower power position on account of their adolescence *and* their suspect status.

Recent developmental research suggests adolescent compliance is not a global construct but rather is specific to particular issues or domains in adolescents' daily lives (e.g., prudential issues such as health and safety versus personal issues such as dating or friends; Darling et al., 2007; Thomas et al., 2018, 2020). Behavioral research indicates adolescents are more likely to comply or obey rules in some domains more than others, highlighting the importance of context. This comports with developmental neuroscience evidence showing that adolescents' judgment and decision making are affected by environmental cues (National Academies of Sciences, Engineering, and Medicine, 2019). Notably, adolescents are more sensitive to incentives and social reinforcement from peers and are more impulsive in response to positive rewards than both children and adults (Casey, 2015). It is no surprise, then, that adolescents demonstrate compliance-related behaviors in situations involving a variety of legal authority figures, as reported in both vignette and laboratory studies (Grisso et al., 2003; Moreira & Cardoso, 2020; Redlich & Goodman, 2003). The custodial interrogation context inherently creates social, legal, and psychological pressure to comply with interrogators' requests or demands. Interrogators' use of psychologically manipulative interrogation tactics can create additional incentive for adolescent suspects to seek the "reward" of relief from interrogative pressures. In particular, interrogators' promises of leniency (perceived or actual) are powerful drivers of confession decision making even in adults (Kassin et al., 2010; Redlich et al., 2020), and adolescents' neurobiological developmental stage renders them particularly vulnerable to acquiescence.

Legal Perceptions and Experiences Among Youth of Color

The vulnerabilities described should universally apply to all adolescents, simply by virtue of their ongoing development and social position. Certain subgroups of youth face even greater challenges. People of color are systematically and cumulatively disadvantaged in the circumstances that lead to interrogation, as well as the interrogation experience itself, which is theorized to increase vulnerability to police coercion (Villalobos & Davis, 2016). Abundant social psychological and developmental research highlights how racial and ethnic stereotypes, stereotype threat, cultural differences, and linguistic challenges can influence power dynamics in the interrogation room and impact both youth suspects' and interrogators' perceptions and behavior (see, generally, Stevenson et al., 2020). In this section we examine these issues in turn, first from adolescents' perspective and then from interrogators' perspective.

Youth of color, particularly Black youth, are systematically overrepresented in legal system contacts as well as the socioeconomic conditions that predict system contact (Blandon-Gitlin et al., 2020). Youth of color are more likely to experience poverty and residential segregation, which are associated with increased police presence in their communities (Glaser, 2014). Moreover, youth of color experience staggeringly disproportionate school-based disciplinary outcomes and referral to law enforcement compared to their White peers (Riddle & Sinclair, 2019), fueling a school-to-prison pipeline that increases both the frequency and seriousness of their law enforcement encounters. Increased police monitoring in both communities and schools leads to greater suspicion and more opportunities for police contact. A recent study reported that Black youth who had experienced contact with police before the eighth grade were 11 times more likely to be arrested at age 20 than White youth (McGlynn-Wright et al., 2022).

Inside the interrogation room, emerging evidence suggests that stereotype threat is a real concern for suspects of color, including adolescent suspects. Stereotype threat is the fear of being judged according to a stereotype associated with one's identity (Steele & Aronson, 1995). The stereotype associating Blackness with criminality is deeply entrenched in American culture (Welch, 2007), a form of racism that is often internalized by Black individuals (David et al., 2019). Similar cultural stereotypes associate Latinx people with criminal activity and violence (Unnever & Cullen, 2012). People of color are very aware that racial stereotypes exist, even as children (McKown & Weinstein, 2003; Wasserberg, 2014). Stereotype threat is emotionally and cognitively taxing; extensive research shows that priming racial stereotypes increases anxiety and physiological arousal, depletes cognitive resources, and ultimately impacts both physical performance and behavior (Major & O'Brien, 2005). Interrogation scholars theorize that stereotype threat increases vulnerability to coercion among suspects of color; their increased fear and anxiety, as well as attempts to self-regulate that fear and anxiety, induce behaviors that interrogators can misinterpret as deception. This is important because misattributing guilt to suspects who are actually innocent paves the way toward false confessions and wrongful convictions (Leo & Drizin, 2010), in part because interrogators may apply greater interrogative pressure when they presume the suspect is guilty as opposed to innocent (Kassin et al., 2003).

Stereotype threat in hypothetical interrogations is empirically demonstrated in adult populations (Najdowski et al., 2015) but has not yet been tested with adolescent suspects. However, stereotype threat more broadly (e.g., in academic settings) is widely demonstrated among adolescents of color (see Blandon-Gitlin et al., 2020, for a review). Moreover, the cognitive and emotional mechanisms through which stereotype threat impacts judgments and behaviors are likely to be exacerbated even further by youths' developmental stage. Davis and Leo (2012) proposed a theoretical model of situational suggestibility in which psychologically manipulative interrogation techniques can deplete suspects' abilities and motivation to resist persuasion. This "interrogation-related regulatory decline" occurs when various processes of cognitive and emotional control decompose—for example, attentional focus, working memory, emotional regulation, or the ongoing ability to prioritize long-term goals over short-term impulses (Davis & Leo, 2012). The powerful social forces at play during police interrogation can dysregulate even psychologically healthy adults and increase the likelihood of both true and false confessions. Adolescents are even more vulnerable because the brain structures that govern impulse control, judgment, and emotional regulation are not fully developed until early adulthood (National Academies of Sciences, Engineering, and Medicine, 2019).

On the law enforcement side, individual biases, cultural issues, and institutional racism create conditions that profoundly disadvantage youth suspects of color (Haney Caron & Fountain, 2021). At an individual level, police officers, like the general public, hold stereotypes associating people of color with crime (Eberhardt et al., 2004). Police exhibit racial bias against Black and Latinx people in many types of police encounters, including stop-and-frisk decisions, arrests, and use of force (see, generally, Burke et al., 2020). At a systems level, Black adolescents are more likely to be detained and arrested than White youth for the same crimes and are arrested at younger ages (Lau et al., 2018; Puzzancherra, 2021). American law enforcement has a long-standing history of racial profiling and overpolicing Black communities (Glaser, 2014). All these conditions increase the likelihood that youth of color are targeted for custodial interrogations (Blandon-Gitlin et al., 2020).

Inside the interrogation room, youth of color are more vulnerable to "adultification" than White youth. Adultification—being perceived as older and more mature than the child's actual age—affects Black youth in academic, medical, and legal settings (e.g., Baetzel et al., 2019; Epstein et al., 2017; Nanda, 2012). Authority figures are less likely to recognize Black adolescents' developmental immaturity, despite abundant evidence that youth of color and White youth experience similar developmental trajectories and behavioral patterns (Woolard & Henning, 2020). In legal contexts, Black youth are viewed as more culpable, more threatening, less amenable to treatment, and more deserving of punishment than their White counterparts (Graham & Lowery, 2004; Todd et al., 2016). In a series of studies examining the dehumanization of Black people (i.e., by priming an implicit association with apes), police officer participants rated Black felony suspects as significantly older than Latinx and White felony suspects—about 4½ years older (Goff et al., 2014). The more participants implicitly dehumanized Black youth, the more they perceived Black youth as older and more culpable than same-aged White youth. These findings were not relegated to hypothetical scenarios or attitudes; officers' dehumanization of Black youth also predicted their actual use of force against Black children, as evidenced by personnel records.

Key Policy and Practice Questions Concerning Juvenile Interrogations

As new studies emerge, policymakers and legal system professionals must make difficult decisions about whether and how to incorporate developmental research into evolving legal standards and practice. In some ways, recent reforms reflect increasing recognition of youths' unique vulnerabilities in the interrogation room. In other ways, law, policy, and police practice still lag behind the science. This section examines pressing policy and practice issues concerning police interrogation of adolescent suspects. We examine these issues from different policy and practice perspectives and examine the role of empirical research in effecting evidence-based change.

Does Miranda Serve Its Intended Function for Youth?

Kassin and colleagues (2019) recently argued—in reference to adult suspects—that "after more than a half-century, it is clear that *Miranda v. Arizona* (1966) has failed to fulfill its promise" to buffer criminal suspects from interrogative pressures (p. 120). Given adolescents' developmentally driven vulnerabilities and interrogators' training and practice of questioning youth as adults, we must critically examine whether Miranda warnings truly protect youth from what lies ahead. The law requires adolescent suspects' Miranda waivers to be knowing, intelligent, and voluntary (*In re Gault*, 1967). If adolescents do not adequately comprehend Miranda language (*knowing*), cannot fully grasp the downstream consequences of waiving their rights (*intelligent*), and experience endogenous and exogenous pressures to comply with adults (*voluntary*), then Miranda alone cannot guarantee adolescent suspects the due process protections to which they are constitutionally entitled.

One approach to remediation is to utilize juvenile-specific Miranda warnings whose language and content are tailored specifically for younger suspects. For example, "you have the right to remain silent" becomes "you don't have to talk to me," or "if you cannot afford an attorney, one will be appointed for you" becomes "if you cannot pay for a lawyer, the court will get you one for free." Juvenile-specific warnings also include information about the role of parents or guardians in the process. While these modifications may seem reasonable, juvenile-specific warnings tend to be longer, more grammatically complex, and harder to read than generalized warnings (Eastwood et al., 2015; Rogers et al., 2008). Adolescents struggle to recall and comprehend even the modified warnings (Eastwood et al., 2015; Freedman et al., 2014). Recent attempts to simplify Miranda waiver forms have focused on emphasizing youths' decisional autonomy (i.e., to talk or not to talk, to have an adult present or not; Eastwood et al., 2016). While admirable, emphasizing the fact of youths' choice does not communicate to adolescents the *implications* of their choices—the critical information they need to make an informed decision.

This is important because, at least anecdotally, courts routinely fail to robustly protect adolescents' Miranda rights. We see this in context of invoking one's right to counsel, where courts require the same degree of precision from adolescents trying to request an attorney as they require from adults. In an extreme case from Louisiana, a young man brought in on sexual assault charges spoke in colloquialism, saying to police, "If y'all think I did it, I know that I didn't do it so why don't you just give me a lawyer dog 'cause this is not what's up" (*State of Louisiana v. Demesme*, 2017, pp. 1206–1207). The court concluded in a concurrence opinion that the suspect did not clearly invoke his right to an attorney, because it was ambiguous whether he was asking for a dog, opining: "The defendant's ambiguous and equivocal reference to a 'lawyer dog' does not constitute an invocation of counsel that warrants termination of the interview" (*Louisiana v. Demesme*, 2017, pp. 1206–1207).

We also see Miranda's failure to adequately protect youth in the waiver context. Courts rarely invalidate adolescents' Miranda waivers (Maykut, 1994). This is particularly concerning in the context of implied waivers—that is, when suspects do not expressly waive their right to silence but their words or actions imply they are willing to talk (e.g., *North Carolina v. Butler*, 1979). Courts allow implied waivers from adolescents, just like adults, raising serious questions about whether youth understand exactly what they are communicating. For example, a California appellate court upheld the Miranda waiver of a 17-year-old who answered "yes" to whether he understood each right but was never expressly asked if he waived these rights (*People v. Steve M.*, 2019). Given research on adolescents' limited understanding for and appreciation of their constitutional rights, it would be prudent to carve out adolescent exceptions to some of the more rigid Miranda rules. For example, courts could (a) require less specificity and unambiguity to find an invocation; (b) prohibit implied waivers from youth; and (c) allow requests for a parent, family member, probation officer, or caseworker to serve as invocation of Fifth Amendment rights.

Are Parents Adequate Protectors of Youths' Interrogation Rights?

As early as 1962, the U.S. Supreme Court indicated that the assessment of the voluntariness of a youth's statement should take into account the presence or absence of a parent or other concerned adult during the interrogation (*Gallegos v. Colorado*, 1962). Soon after, the court again reiterated its assumption that parents could protect their children's rights in the interrogation room (*In re Gault*, 1967). Today, there is an uptick in state legislation that would increase parents' involvement in their adolescents' custodial interrogations. For example, in 2020, Virginia required that youth who have been arrested must have contact with a parent, guardian, or legal custodian prior to interrogation (§ 16.1-247.1), and Maine requires parents to be present or to consent to the youth's interrogation (5 M.R.S.A. 3203-A(2-A)). Connecticut renders inadmissible any confession or statement by a youth under age 16 unless parents have been informed of the child's rights to silence and counsel (Sec. 46b-137, 2012). Such laws reflect a commonsense notion that parents know what is best for their children. They also inherently presume that parents are both willing and able to protect youths' best interests. However, empirical research and legal scholarship raise serious questions about parents' *ability* and their *willingness* to serve that protective role.

First, an established body of research on Miranda comprehension and emerging research on parents' practical interrogation knowledge cast doubt on parents' ability to navigate their child's legal encounters. Miranda studies with adult populations show that even adults sometimes fail to understand or appreciate all elements of the Miranda warnings. Adult community samples perform adequately under benign testing conditions, but in real-world settings or with justice-involved persons, many factors impede comprehension (Kassin et al., 2019). One study with a diverse sample of parents found that nearly one quarter scored in the impaired range (Woolard et al., 2008). This is significant because, as described previously, the Miranda warnings comprise conceptually distinct but equally important rights, and impairment on any single item could have serious legal implications. Additionally, parents do not fully understand the parameters of police interrogation practices once questioning commences. For example, parents are largely unaware that police can lie to suspects, and they overestimate the degree to which police must involve them in the process (Cleary & Warner, 2017; Woolard et al.,

2008). A recent study with a large multistate sample reported that overall, parents were only 57% accurate on a measure of Miranda and interrogation procedural knowledge (Warner & Cleary, 2022).

Police may also interfere with parents' ability to protect youths' interest. Police may (inadvertently or intentionally) exploit the parent–child relationship by using parents as a tool to elicit confession. Police may enlist parents' help in convincing reluctant youth to talk, taking advantage of the trust between parent and child; parents may even assume an interrogative role and "team up" with police to pressure youth into cooperating (Cleary, 2014; Feld, 2013a). Interrogation training paradigms and recordings of actual interrogations indicate that this can occur even when parents are not physically present during the interrogation. One well-known law enforcement training program offers "themes" for interrogators to use with juvenile suspects (e.g., fear of disappointing one's parents; Inbau et al., 2013).

Policies requiring parent notification or involvement in juvenile interrogations do not account for the notion that parents are also expected to steer their children's moral compass. Parents are integral to adolescents' socialization (Steinberg, 2014), and case law is replete with examples of parents urging their children to "tell the truth" during custodial interrogations (Farber, 2004). But socializing youth to obey laws and take responsibility for their actions is antithetical to protecting youths' legal best interest in a custodial interrogation and the fundamental right against self-incrimination. Thus, policies that require parental notification or involvement place parents in a difficult position. As Farber (2004) noted, "A parent should not be forced to decide between teaching a child a moral lesson and protecting them from grave legal consequences" (p. 1307).

Second, even if parents possess the capacity to successfully advocate for youth during interrogations, there is reason to question the assumption they are always willing to do so. Police–youth encounters are rife with potential conflicts of interest (Drizin & Luloff, 2007). Sometimes parents are the victim of the alleged crime (e.g., the youth is accused of stealing money or assaulting the parent). The parent may be a codefendant or even the actual complainant. There may be family conflicts of interest, such as an adolescent accused of assaulting a sibling, the parent's other child (Farber, 2004). The parent may desire to protect the adolescent suspect but worry about social or financial repercussions of legal involvement, such as paying court fees, providing transportation to treatment or probation meetings, or facing social humiliation or shame (see Cleary, 2022). Alternately, parents sometimes look to the justice system for intervention and support in difficult situations. Frequent parent–child conflict, multiple delinquency petitions, a history of violence, or a general inability to "control" the youth may lead desperate parents to actually welcome law enforcement involvement (Farber, 2004).

Self-report data, though limited, also cast doubt on parents' willingness to protect youth in custodial interrogations. In one study with incarcerated youth, only two of 18 youth whose parents were present during the interrogation reported that their parent advised them to deny the offense; the remainder reported their parents wanted them to confess (10 of 18) or "tell the truth" (six of 18; Viljoen et al., 2005). Not a single youth reported that their parent advised them to exercise their right to remain silent. In a vignette study with middle-class parents, one third of parents recommended that the hypothetical youth confess, and slightly more than half recommended the youth obtain a lawyer. Notably, the parents who recommended remaining silent and/or obtaining a lawyer appeared to view silence as temporary (i.e., remaining silent only until a lawyer could help the youth "tell his side of the story"; Grisso & Ring, 1979). In the only study to our knowledge to examine parent advice in actual youth arrest cases ($N = 390$), more than 70% said absolutely nothing to their children regarding Miranda

(Grisso, 1980). Seventeen percent of parents told their children to waive their right and talk to police. Only 6% advised their child to remain silent, and another 6% wanted their child to make up their own mind.

Thus, empirical research to date suggests that even the most expansive state statutes providing a role for parents in youth interrogations are not sufficient to guarantee that youths' rights are protected and that they are buffered against intentional or unintentional police coercion. Available data, though limited, indicate that only the presence of an attorney—not a parent or other appropriate adult—can prevent youth from providing incriminating information to police (Cleary, 2017, 2022).

Should Police Be Allowed to Use Deception With Adolescent Suspects?

American police culture highly values confessions, and many interrogators are willing to go to extreme lengths to obtain one. Historically, police interrogators routinely used physical coercion and violence to get confessions (Leo, 2008). In 1936, the U.S. Supreme Court invalidated a confession obtained via torture in *Brown v. Mississippi* (1936), marking the end of the systemic use of physical violence in the interrogation room. Modern interrogation techniques focus entirely on psychological coercion, and controversial psychological tactics are still permitted. Deception—including lies, trickery, and false evidence—is a somewhat common tool in modern interrogation (Cleary & Warner, 2016; Kassin et al., 2007). In 1969, the U.S. Supreme Court blessed the use of deceptive interrogation tactics (*Frazier v. Cupp*, 1969). Today, many police agencies consider deception an acceptable, even necessary tool for interrogation. Since *Frazier*, courts have consistently signed off on deception, usually false evidence ploys, ranging from generalized bluff tactics (e.g., "We have all the evidence we need to show you're guilty") to very specific lies (e.g., "We have an eyewitness who identified you," "We have DNA evidence proving you committed the crime"). For adolescents, interrogators may lie about parents' statements or wishes (e.g., "Your mother wants you to just tell us the truth; she wants you to help us so you can go home to her").

Developmental neuroscience and youth-focused interrogation research converge on the notion that youth are ill-equipped to withstand police deception. Adolescents struggle to make rational judgments under stress and are vulnerable to outside influence, especially from authority figures. Moreover, youth (and many adults) are largely unaware that police are even allowed to lie (Woolard et al., 2008). This misconception is an enormous barrier to successfully navigating custodial interrogation that surely colors youths' interpretations of interrogating officers' speech and behavior. Youth are especially vulnerable to false evidence ploys—a tactic whereby police confront suspects with fabricated "evidence" suggesting they committed the crime (e.g., fingerprints, eyewitness testimony) to elicit a confession. In one laboratory study, 73% of 12–13-year-olds and 88% of 15–16-year-olds signed a statement admitting responsibility for an act they did not commit after being presented with false "evidence" of their guilt (Redlich & Goodman, 2003).

Indeed, it appears that police often interrogate youth the same way they interrogate adults, including use of deception. In one study of police interrogation training using a national sample of police, 85% of officers were trained to use deceit with adult suspects and 70% were trained to use deceit with juvenile suspects (Cleary & Warner, 2016). The majority of respondents reported being specifically trained to use false evidence ploys with adults (73%) and juveniles (57%). Moreover, police reported actually using these techniques with both adult and adolescent suspects; mean scores for using deceit were 2.85 (adults) and 2.54 (juveniles) on a 5-point scale (where 1 = *never*, 3 = *sometimes*, and 5 = *always*). In another study with a large urban police department, 34% of police reported using deceit with suspects ages

14–17 and 45% used deceit with children under 14 years old (Meyer & Reppucci, 2007). A follow-up study with 10 police agencies across the nation ($N = 1,828$ officers) confirmed these findings; 25% of officers who had interrogated juveniles in the past year reported using false evidence ploys with youth suspects (Reppucci et al., 2010).

There is a movement to ban deception in the interrogation room, particularly for youth, now that the existence of false confessions is beyond dispute. In 2021, Illinois became the first state to ban deception in juvenile interrogations by statute (Public Act 102-0101); Oregon quickly followed (SB418A). Six states (CA, CT, DE, IL, OR, UT) now prohibit police from lying to adolescent suspects. Some law enforcement agencies and officers embrace the change, but others are resistant to let go of deception. For example, Reid & Associates, purveyors of the Reid technique of interrogations, maintains that deception is only one tool in the interrogation toolbox and interrogators are trained to use it wisely, safely, and effectively (Inbau et al., 2013). Conversely, the Chicago-based interrogation training firm Wicklander-Zulawski recently disavowed the use of deception, testifying to the Oregon legislature that "the use of deception in effort to get a subject to tell us the truth seems contradictory, unethical, and unnecessary," and explained that deception can contaminate a confession and compromise its reliability (Thompson, 2021, p. 1). Wicklander-Zulawski actually abandoned the entire Reid technique in 2018, recognizing that its confrontational approach carried too high a risk of false confession.

Implications for Practice, Policy, and Research

Today, it is clear that adolescents are vulnerable during police interrogation because of their developmental immaturity and subsequent vulnerability to legally permissible, yet inherently coercive, interrogation tactics. The totality of developmental psychological research and interrogation science supports several important reforms.

First, we join the chorus of researchers (e.g., Kassin et al., 2010), law enforcement professionals (http://www.w-z.com), and attorneys (http://www.innocenceproject.org; http://www.nacdl.org) who have called—loudly and repeatedly—for states to require law enforcement agencies to record custodial interrogations with all suspects in their entirety. At the time of this writing, 31 states require some form of electronic recording via legislative mandate or state supreme court order. Recording reveals what actually occurs during Miranda warning administrations and in interrogations and permits triers of fact to make informed judgments about reliability and voluntariness. Recording enables confession experts to identify individual and situational factors that are empirically associated with youth vulnerability, coercion, or false confessions. Expert analysis may particularly benefit youth suspects of color, for whom racially biased policing and stereotype threat may increase the likelihood of interrogation and the stress experienced during interrogation (Blandon-Gitlin et al., 2020). Importantly, the camera should be turned on before participants even enter the room and should remain on, without interruption, until participants leave the room for the last time. Recordings that begin after Miranda administration or only include the (sometimes rehearsed) final confession statement do not accurately represent the full interaction and could ultimately be more damaging to youth in court.

Nonetheless, recording mandates are not a panacea for protecting youth. Instead, existing recording mandates are proof positive that additional protections are necessary because youths' vulnerability to coercion and exploitation is now plainly evident. While some states enacted parent notification requirements or encourage parent involvement in Miranda waiver decisions, such protections are inadequate for the many reasons discussed earlier. Given Miranda's failure to adequately protect youth and parents' inability to bridge the gap, adolescent suspects should be entitled to mandatory assistance of counsel for custodial interrogations. Assistance of counsel is already required in California, where all juveniles now have a nonwaivable right to consult with counsel before custodial interrogation (CA Welf. & Inst. Code Section 625.6), and in Illinois, where youth ages 15 and younger must be represented by counsel during custodial interrogations (Illinois Public Act 99-0882). Other jurisdictions may be resistant to this remedy, citing lack of resources or logistical barriers (e.g., noted in August & Henderson, 2021). However, it is increasingly clear that existing reforms consistently fail to adequately protect youths' rights.

Law enforcement can also reform their questioning strategies to reduce coercion. As a threshold matter, law enforcement should stop using behavioral analysis when questioning adolescents because many purported cues of deception are traits universal to adolescents, creating an unacceptably high risk of adolescents being mischaracterized as guilty and/or deceptive and thus triggering a custodial interrogation. Next, interrogators should stop using deception with adolescent suspects. Youth as a class do not possess the cognitive, social, or experiential sophistication necessary to recognize or withstand police deception. Prohibiting deception would create the dual benefits of better protecting youths' rights and enabling police to elicit more accurate and reliable information.

Second, interrogators should stop recruiting parents—intentionally or inadvertently—as collaborators in extracting confessions. Parents are not legally trained, practically informed, and/or socially positioned to protect their child's legal rights and best interests during custodial interrogations. This too speaks to the need for mandatory assistance of counsel; only a legally trained, nonfamily third party is adequately positioned to perform these functions. Some American attorneys support the U.K. model in which two supportive roles are present: an attorney to provide legal guidance and an "appropriate adult" for emotional support (August & Henderson, 2021). Research is needed to better understand whether this model fulfills the promise of protecting youths' rights, but the structure alone is a dramatic improvement over the fractured, flawed model that exists in U.S. juvenile interrogations.

Finally, attorneys must more often, and more robustly, raise potential issues in court, and courts must improve judicial analysis of adolescent interrogations and confessions to give teeth to the Supreme Court's decades-old mandate that youth warrant special care in the interrogation room. All legal analysis of youths' statements (including analysis of custody, Miranda waiver and/or invocation, and confession voluntariness) should be viewed through the lens of a reasonable juvenile. Attorneys should widely advocate for the reasonable juvenile standard and argue that certain rules should be applied differently when the suspect is an adolescent—for example, eliminating or lessening the requirement that Miranda invocations are unambiguous or the requirement for explicit requests for counsel. Attorneys could also advocate for prohibiting implicit Miranda waivers for youth. Attorneys should bolster their advocacy with the rich scientific research now available regarding the constitutionally relevant ways in which adolescents' brains and behavior are different. Finally, given adolescents' heightened suggestibility, courts should consider the reliability of adolescents' statements, even though it is not explicitly relevant under the constitutional voluntariness analysis. Pretrial reliability hearings in juvenile cases would be a strong first step but are not standard practice.

Researchers can bolster these empirically supported reforms and inspire new ones by conducting rigorous, well-designed studies on key topics of critical legal importance. We propose that stereotype threat in juvenile interrogations, adolescent perceptions of police coercion, and interrogation experiences of youth with particular challenges (e.g., intellectual or learning disabilities, trauma history) are key areas for future research. Also, recent legislation banning police deception in youth interrogations suggests that piecemeal reform (e.g., eliminating certain interrogation tactics from police practice) may be possible, inviting future research on other specific interrogation tactics that are particularly problematic with youth suspects. We call for studies specifically focused on the dangers of implied promises of leniency with youth suspects, implied threats, exploitation of the parent–child relationship, and certain minimization themes designed to exploit youth vulnerabilities (hormonal, emotional, or otherwise). We also argue that further research is necessary to demonstrate the significant risk of behavioral analysis resulting in the misclassification of innocent youth as guilty, leading directly to the coercive interrogation of an innocent youth, and paving the way for the wrongful conviction of an adolescent. It is also important to develop alternatives to traditional interrogation methods for youth, so we call for research on the efficacy of the cognitive interview, and other alternatives to Reid-style interrogations, as investigative tools. Additionally, given the uptick in legislation requiring parental involvement in the interrogation of youth, we argue that further research is required on the protectiveness, or lack thereof, of parental participation.

Finally, we call for researchers to work more directly with attorneys to develop legally relevant research questions. Legal professionals, especially defense attorneys, have firsthand experience with youths' interrogation-related vulnerabilities. Attorneys, in an ideal world, know their young clients well, and their clients trust them enough to shares the personal details of their experience in the interrogation room, as well as details about their background and current functioning that may have made them more vulnerable. Attorneys should conduct investigations, akin to a mitigation investigation, into the youth's background, personal records, and psychological functioning including detailed interviews of the client about the interrogation and with family/friends about the client's functioning and vulnerabilities. Thus, attorneys should possess valuable insights regarding their vulnerability in and experience of the interrogation and, more broadly, the criminal justice system. Attorneys also have front-row seats to the ways in which our juvenile and criminal court systems fail to recognize or reckon with the inherent vulnerabilities of adolescents in the interrogation room and fail to protect them from the consequences.

In sum, an enormous body of research from wide-ranging disciplines provides compelling evidence that adolescent suspects are set up to fail in custodial interrogations. Some literatures (e.g., developmental neuroscience) are quite robust, while others (e.g., stereotype threat in youth suspects of color) are emerging. Altogether, research on the interrogation process, its participants, and the cultures and contexts in which they occur clearly indicate that adolescent suspects' due process is at risk. Researchers are both well positioned and obligated to translate scientific findings regarding adolescent development into actionable best practices for questioning youth (Cleary, 2017). Social equity and justice demand that we continually seek out how and why interrogation disproportionately disadvantages vulnerable populations and support both policymakers and law enforcement professionals in developing evidence-based practices.

References

August, C. N., & Henderson, K. S. (2021). Juveniles in the interrogation room: Defense attorneys as a protective factor. *Psychology, Public Policy, and Law, 27*(2), 268–282.

Arndorfer, A., Malloy, L. C., & Cauffman, E. (2015). Interrogations, confessions, and adolescent offenders' perceptions of the legal system. *Law and Human Behavior, 39*(5), 503–513.

Baetzel, A., Brown, D. J., Koppera, P., Rentz, A., Thompson, A., & Christensen, R. (2019). Adultification of Black children in pediatric anesthesia. *Anesthesia & Analgesia, 129*(4), 1118–1123.

Blandon-Gitlin, I., Cleary, H., & Blair, A. (2020). Race and ethnicity as a compound risk factor in police interrogation of youth. In M. C. Stevenson, B. Bottoms, & K. Burke (Eds.), *The legacy of race for children: Psychology, public policy, and law* (pp. 169–188). Oxford University Press.

Birckhead, Tamar R., The Age of the Child: Interrogating Juveniles *After Roper v. Simmons*, 65 WASH. & LEE REV. 385 (2008)

Brown v. Mississippi, 297 U.S. 278 (1936),

Burke, K. C., Petty, T., Jones, T. M., Stevenson, M. C., Silberkleit, G., & Bottoms, B. L. (2020). Adults' perceptions of law-involved minority children and youth: Implications for researchers and professionals. In M. C. Stevenson, B. L. Bottoms, & K. Burke (Eds.), (2020). *The legacy of race for children: Psychology, public policy, and law* (pp. 189–210). Oxford University Press.

Casey, B. J. (2015). Beyond simple models of self-control to circuit-based accounts of adolescent behavior. *Annual Review of Psychology, 66*, 295–319.

Cleary, H. M. D. (2022). Ten reasons why parents aren't adequate protectors of youth in police interrogations. *The Champion, 46*(10), 20–32.

Cleary, H. M. D. (2014). Police interviewing and interrogation of juvenile suspects: A descriptive examination of actual cases. *Law and Human Behavior, 38*(3), 271–282.

Cleary, H. M. D. (2017). Applying the lessons of developmental psychology to the study of juvenile interrogations: New directions for research, policy, and practice. *Psychology, Public Policy, and Law, 23*(1), 118–130.

Cleary, H. M. D., Guarnera, L. A., Aaron, J., & Crane, M. (2021). How trauma may magnify risk of involuntary and false confessions among adolescents. *Wrongful Conviction Law Review, 21*(3), 173–204.

Cleary, H. M. D., & Vidal, S. (2016). Miranda in actual juvenile interrogations: Delivery, waiver, and readability. *Criminal Justice Review, 41*(1), 98–115.

Cleary, H. M. D., & Warner, T. C. (2016). Police training in interviewing and interrogation methods: A comparison of techniques used with adult and juvenile suspects. *Law and Human Behavior, 40*(3), 270–284.

Cleary, H. M. D., & Warner, T. C. (2017). Parents' knowledge and attitudes about youths' interrogation rights. *Psychology, Crime & Law, 23*(8), 777–793.

Crane, M. G. (2017). Childhood trauma's lurking presence in the juvenile interrogation room and the need for a trauma-informed voluntariness test for juvenile confessions. *South Dakota Law Review, 62*, 626–672.

Darling, N., Cumsille, P., & Loreto Martínez, B. (2007). Adolescents' as active agents in the socialization process: Legitimacy of parental authority and obligation to obey as predictors of obedience. *Journal of Adolescence, 30*(2), 297–311.

David, E. J. R., Schroeder, T. M., & Fernandez, J. (2019). Internalized racism: A systematic review of the psychological literature on racism's most insidious consequence. *Journal of Social Issues, 75*, 1057–1086.

Davis, D., & Leo, R. A. (2012). Interrogation-related regulatory decline: Ego depletion, failures of self-regulation, and the decision to confess. *Psychology Public Policy and Law, 18*(4), 673–704.

Davis, D., & Leo, R. A. (2013). Acute suggestibility in police interrogation: Self-regulation failure as a primary mechanism of vulnerability. In A. M. Ridley, F. Gabbert, & D. J. La Rooy (Eds.), *Suggestibility in legal contexts: Psychological research and forensic implications* (pp. 171–195). Wiley-Blackwell.

Driskell, J. E. (2012). Effectiveness of deception detection training: A meta-analysis. *Psychology, Crime, and Law, 18*(8), 713–731.

Drizin, S. A., & Luloff, G. (2007). Are juvenile courts a breeding ground for wrongful convictions? *Northern Kentucky Law Review, 34*, 257–322.

Eastwood, J., Snook, B., & Luther, K. (2015). Measuring the reading complexity and oral comprehension of Canadian youth waiver forms. *Crime & Delinquency, 61*(6), 798–828.

Eastwood, J., Snook, B., Luther, K., & Freedman, S. (2016). Engineering comprehensible youth interrogation rights. *New Criminal Law Review: An International and Interdisciplinary Journal, 19*(1), 42–62.

Eberhardt, J. L., Goff, P. A., Purdie, V. J., & Davies, P. G. (2004). Seeing Black: Race, crime, and visual processing. *Journal of Personality and Social Psychology, 87*(6), 876–893.

Epstein, R., Blake, J., & González, T. (2017). Girlhood interrupted: The erasure of Black girls' childhood. Available at SSRN: https://ssrn.com/abstract=3000695 or http://dx.doi.org/10.2139/ssrn.3000695

Farber, H. B. (2004). The role of the parent/guardian in juvenile custodial interrogations: Friend or foe? *American Criminal Law Review, 41*, 1277–1312.

Fare v. Michael C., 442 U.S. 707 (1979).

Feld, B. C. (2013a). *Kids, cops, and confessions: Inside the interrogation room*. New York University Press.

Feld, B. C. (2013b). Real interrogation: What actually happens when cops question kids. *Law and Society Review, 47*(1), 1–36.

Frazier v. Cupp, 394 U.S. 731 (1969).

Freedman, S., Eastwood, J., Snook, B., & Luther, K. (2014). Safeguarding youth interrogation rights: The effect of grade level and reading complexity of youth waiver forms on the comprehension of legal rights: Youth comprehension of legal rights. *Applied Cognitive Psychology, 28*(3), 427–431.

Gallegos v. Colorado, 370 U.S. 49 (1962).

Glaser, J. (2014). *Suspect race: Causes and consequences of racial profiling*. New York: Oxford University Press.

Goff, P. A., Jackson, M. C., Di Leone, B. A. L., Culotta, C. M., & DiTomasso, N. A. (2014). The essence of innocence: Consequences of dehumanizing Black children. *Journal of Personality and Social Psychology, 106*(4), 526–545.

Goldstein, N. E. S., Condie, L. O., Kalbeitzer, R., Osman, D., & Geier, J. L. (2003). Juvenile offenders' Miranda rights comprehension and self-reported likelihood of offering false confessions. *Assessment, 10*(4), 359–369.

Goldstein, N. E. S., Haney-Caron, E., Levick, M., & Whiteman, D. (2018). Waving good-bye to waiver: A developmental argument against youths' waiver of Miranda rights. *NYU Journal of Legislation and Public Policy, 21*(1), 1–67.

Goldstein, N. E. S., Kelly, S. M., Peterson, L., Brogan, L., Zelle, H., & Romaine, C. R. (2015). Evaluation of Miranda waiver capacity. In K. Heilbrun, D. DeMatteo, & N. E. S. Goldstein (Eds.), *APA handbook of psychology and juvenile justice* (pp. 467–488). American Psychological Association.

Goldstein, N. E. S., Messenheimer, S., Riggs-Romaine, C., & Zelle, H. (2012). Impact of juvenile suspects' linguistic abilities on Miranda understanding and appreciation. In P. Tiersma & L. Solan (Eds.), *Oxford handbook on language and law* (pp. 299–311). Oxford University Press.

Graham, S., & Lowery, B. S. (2004). Priming unconscious racial stereotypes about adolescent offenders. *Law and Human Behavior, 28*(5), 483–504.

Graham v. Florida, 560 U.S. 48 (2010).

Grisso, T. (1980). Juveniles' capacities to waive Miranda rights: An empirical analysis. *California Law Review, 68*, 1134–1166.

Grisso, T. (1981). *Juveniles' waiver of rights: Legal and psychological competence*. Plenum.

Grisso, T., & Ring, M. (1979). Parents' attitudes toward juveniles' rights in interrogation. *Criminal Justice and Behavior, 6*(3), 211–226.

Grisso, T., Steinberg, L., Woolard, J., Cauffman, E., Scott, E. S., Graham, S., Lexcen, F., Reppucci, N. D., & Schwartz, R. (2003). Juveniles' competence to stand trial: A comparison of adolescents' and adults' capacities as trial defendants. *Law and Human Behavior, 27*, 333–363.

Gudjonsson, G. H. (2003). *The psychology of interrogations and confessions: A handbook*. Wiley.

Gudjonsson, G. H. (2013). Interrogative suggestibility and compliance. In A. M. Ridley & D. J. La Rooy (Eds.), *Suggestibility in legal contexts: Psychological research and forensic implications* (pp. 45–61). John Wiley & Sons.

Gudjonsson, G. H. (2018). *The psychology of false confessions: Forty years of science and practice*. Wiley.

Gudjonsson, G. H., Sigurdsson, J. F., Asgeirsdottir, B. B., & Sigfusdottir, I. D. (2006). Custodial interrogation, false confession and individual differences: A national study among Icelandic youth. *Personality and Individual Differences, 41*, 49–59.

Guggenheim, Martin, & Hertz, Randy, *J.D.B.* and the Maturing of Juvenile Confession Suppression Law, 38 WASH. U. J. L. & POL'Y 109 (2012).

Haley v. Ohio, 332 U.S. 596 (1948).

Haney-Caron, E., & Fountain, E. (2021). Young, Black, and wrongfully charged: A cumulative disadvantage framework, *Dickinson Law Review, 125*(3), 653–726.

Harrell, E., & Davis, E. (2020, December). *Contacts between police and the public, 2018—Statistical tables*. U.S. Department of Justice, Bureau of Justice Statistics. https://bjs.ojp.gov/content/pub/pdf/cbpp18st.pdf

In re Elias V., 237 Cal. App. 4th 568 (2015).

In re Gault, 387 U.S. 1 (1967).

Inbau, F. E., Reid, J. E., Buckley, J. P., & Jayne, B. C. (2013). *Criminal interrogation and confessions* (5th ed.). Jones & Bartlett Learning.

J.D.B. v. North Carolina, 564 U.S. 261 (2011).

Kassin, S. M., Drizin, S. A., Grisso, T., Gudjonsson, G. H., Leo, R. A., & Redlich, A. D. (2010). Police-induced confessions: Risk factors and recommendations. *Law and Human Behavior, 34*(1), 3–38.

Kassin, S. M., Goldstein, C. C., & Savitsky, K. (2003). Behavioral confirmation in the interrogation room: On the dangers of presuming guilt. *Law and Human Behavior, 27*(2), 187–203.

Kassin, S. M., Leo, R. A., Meissner, C. A., Richman, K. D., Colwell, L. H., Leach, A.-M., & La Fon, D. (2007). Police interviewing and interrogation: A self-report survey of police practices and beliefs. *Law and Human Behavior, 31*(4), 381–400.

Kassin, S. M., Scherr, K. C., & Alceste, F. (2019). The right to remain silent: Realities and illusions. In R. Bull & I. Blandón-Gitlin (eds), *The Routledge international handbook of legal and investigative psychology* (pp. 2–19). Routledge.

Lau, K., Rosenman, M. B., Wiehe, S. E., Tu, W., & Aalsma, M. C. (2018). Race/ethnicity, and behavioral health status: First arrest and outcomes in a large sample of juvenile offenders. *Journal of Behavioral Health Services & Research, 45*(2), 237–251.

Leo, R. A. (2008). *Police interrogation and American justice*. Harvard University Press.
Leo, R. A., & Drizin, S. A. (2010). The three errors: Pathways to false confession and wrongful conviction. In G. D. Lassiter & C. A. Meissner (Eds.), *Police interrogations and false confessions: Current research, practice, and policy recommendations* (pp. 9–30). American Psychological Association.
Major, B., & O'Brien, L. T. (2005). The social psychology of stigma. *Annual Review of Psychology, 56*, 393–421.
Malloy, L. C., Shulman, E. P., & Cauffman, E. (2014). Interrogations, confessions, and guilty pleas among serious adolescent offenders. *Law and Human Behavior, 38*(2), 181–193.
Maykut, E. J. (1994). Who is advising our children: Custodial interrogation of juveniles in Florida. *Florida State University Law Review, 21*, 1345–1375.
McGlynn-Wright, A., Crutchfield, R. D., Skinner, M. L., & Haggerty, K. P. (2022). The usual, racialized, suspects: The consequence of police contacts with Black and White youth on adult arrest. *Social Problems, 69*(2), 299–315.
McKown, C., & Weinstein, R. S. (2003). The development and consequences of stereotype consciousness in middle childhood. *Child Development, 74*(2), 498–515.
McLachlan, K., Roesch, R., & Douglas, K. S. (2011). Examining the role of interrogative suggestibility in Miranda rights comprehension in adolescents. *Law and Human Behavior, 35*(3), 165–177.
Meyer, J. R., & Reppucci, N. D. (2007). Police practices and perceptions regarding juvenile interrogation and interrogative suggestibility. *Behavioral Sciences and the Law, 25*, 757–780.
Miller v. Alabama, 567 U.S. 460 (2012).
Miller v. Fenton, 474 U.S. 104 (1985).
Miranda v. Arizona, 384 U.S. 436 (1966).
Montgomery v. Louisiana, 577 U.S. 190 (2016).
Moreira, S., & Cardoso, C. (2020). Why young people obey private security guards? A scenario-based study. *Journal of Contemporary Criminal Justice, 36*(1), 144–160.
Mulvey, E. P., & Schubert, C. A. (2012, December). *Transfer of juveniles to adult court: effects of a broad policy in one court*. U.S. Department of Justice, Office of Justice Programs. https://ojjdp.ojp.gov/sites/g/files/xyckuh176/files/pubs/232932.pdf
Muris, P., Meesters, C., & Merckelbach, H. (2004). Correlates of the Gudjonsson Suggestibility Scale in delinquent adolescents. *Psychological Reports, 94*(1), 264–266.
Najdowski, C. J., Bottoms, B. L., & Goff, P. A. (2015). Stereotype threat and racial differences in citizens' experiences of police encounters. *Law and Human Behavior, 39*(5), 463–477.
Nanda, J. (2012). Blind discretion: Girls of color & delinquency in the juvenile justice system. 59 UCLA L. Rev. 1502. Available at SSRN: https://ssrn.com/abstract=3452907
National Academies of Sciences, Engineering, and Medicine. (2019). *The promise of adolescence: Realizing opportunity for all youth* (R. J. Bonnie & E. P. Backes, Eds.). National Academies Press.
North Carolina v. Butler, 441 U.S. 369 (1979).
Otgaar, H., Schell-Leugers, J. M., Howe, M. L., Vilar, A. D. L. F., Houben, S. T. L., & Merckelbach, H. (2021). The link between suggestibility, compliance, and false confessions: A review using experimental and field studies. *Applied Cognitive Psychology, 35*(2), 445–455. https://doi.org/10.1002/acp.3788
Owen-Kostelnik, J., Reppucci, N. D., & Meyer, J. R. (2006). Testimony and interrogation of minors: Assumptions about maturity and morality. *American Psychologist, 61*(4), 286–304.
People v. Steve M., 2019 WL 1649644, Ca. Ct. of Appeal, 2019.
Puzzanchera, C. (2021). *Juvenile arrests, 2019*. U.S. Department of Justice, Office of Justice Programs. https://ojjdp.ojp.gov/publications/juvenile-arrests-2019.pdf
Redlich, A. D., & Goodman, G. S. (2003). Taking responsibility for an act not committed: The influence of age and suggestibility. *Law and Human Behavior, 27*, 141–156.
Redlich, A. D., Shteynberg, R. V., & Nirider, L. H. (2020). Pragmatic implication in the interrogation room: A comparison of juveniles and adults. *Journal of Experimental Criminology, 16*(4), 555–564.
Redlich, A. D., Silverman, M., & Steiner, H. (2003). Pre-adjudicative and adjudicative competence in juveniles and young adults. *Behavioral Sciences & the Law, 21*(3), 393–410.
Redlich, A. D., Yan, S., Norris, R. J., & Bushway, S. D. (2018). The influence of confessions on guilty pleas and plea discounts. *Psychology, Public Policy, and Law, 24*(2), 147–157. https://doi.org/10.1037/law0000144
Reppucci, N. D., Meyer, J., & Kostelnik, J. (2010). Custodial interrogation of juveniles: Results of a national survey of police. In G. D. Lassiter & C. A. Meissner (Eds.), *Police interrogations and false confessions: Current research, practice, and policy recommendations* (pp. 67–80). American Psychological Association.
Richardson, G., Gudjonsson, G. H., & Kelly, T. P. (1995). Interrogative suggestibility in an adolescent forensic population. *Journal of Adolescence, 18*, 211–216.

Riddle, T., & Sinclair, S. (2019). Racial disparities in school-based disciplinary actions are associated with county-level rates of racial bias. *Proceedings of the National Academy of Sciences, 116*(17), 8255–8260.

Rogers, R., Harrison, K. S., Shuman, D. W., Sewell, K. W., & Hazelwood, L. L. (2007). An analysis of Miranda warnings and waivers: Comprehension and coverage. *Law and Human Behavior, 31*(2), 177–192.

Rogers, R., Hazelwood, L. L., Sewell, K. W., Shuman, D. W., & Blackwood, H. L. (2008). The comprehensibility and content of juvenile Miranda warnings. *Psychology, Public Policy, and Law, 14*(1), 63–87.

Rogers, R., Steadham, J. A., Fiduccia, C. E., Drogin, E. Y., & Robinson, E. V. (2014). Mired in Miranda misconceptions: A study of legally involved juveniles at different levels of psychosocial maturity. *Behavioral Sciences & the Law, 32*(1), 104–120.

Roper v. Simmons, 543 U.S. 551 (2005).

Schneckloth v. Bustamonte, 412 U.S. 218 (1973).

Sim, M. P. Y., & Lamb, M. E. (2018). An analysis of how the police "caution" is presented to juvenile suspects in England. *Psychology, Crime & Law, 24*(8), 851–872.

Singh, K., & Gudjonsson, G. (1992). The vulnerability of adolescent boys to interrogative pressure: An experimental study. *Journal of Forensic Psychiatry, 3*(1), 167–170.

Stansbury v. California, 511 U.S. 318 (1994).

State of Louisiana v. Desmese 228 So. 3d 1206 (2017).

Steele, C. M., & Aronson, J. (1995). Stereotype threat and the intellectual test performance of African Americans. *Journal of Personality and Social Psychology, 69*(5), 797.

Steinberg, L. (2014). *Age of opportunity: Lessons from the new science of adolescence*. Eamon Dolan/Houghton Mifflin Harcourt.

Stevenson, M. C., Bottoms, B. L., & Burke, K. C. (2020). *The legacy of race for children: Psychology, public policy, and law*. Oxford University Press.

Tapp, J., & Levine, F. J. (1974). Legal socialization: Strategies for an ethical legality. *Stanford Law Review, 27*(1), 1–72.

Thomas, K. J., Rodrigues, H., de Oliveira, R. T., & Mangino, A. (2020). What predicts pre-adolescent compliance with family rules? A longitudinal analysis of parental discipline, procedural justice, and legitimacy evaluations. *Journal of Youth and Adolescence, 49*, 936–950.

Thomas, K., Rodrigues, H., Morais Mizutani Gomes, A., Theodoro de Oliveira, R., Piccirillo, D., & Cardoso de Brito, R. (2018). Parental legitimacy, procedural justice and compliance with parental rules among Brazilian preadolescents. *International Journal of Child, Youth and Family Studies, 9*(3), 21–46.

Thompson, D. (2021, March). *Statement in support of SB 418*. https://olis.oregonlegislature.gov/liz/2021R1/Downloads/PublicTestimonyDocument/12114

Thompson v. Keohane, 516 U.S. 99 (1995).

Todd, A. R., Thiem, K. C., & Neel, R. (2016). Does seeing faces of young Black boys facilitate the identification of threatening stimuli? *Psychological Science, 27*(3), 384–393.

Trinkner, R., & Cohn, E. S. (2014). Putting the "social" back in legal socialization: Procedural justice, legitimacy, and cynicism in legal and nonlegal authorities. *Law and Human Behavior, 38*(6), 602–617.

Tyler, T. R., & Trinkner, R. (2017). *Why children follow rules: Legal socialization and the development of legitimacy*. Oxford University Press. https://doi.org/10.1093/acprof:oso/9780190644147.001.0001

Vidal, S., Cleary, H. M. D., Woolard, J. L., & Michel, J. (2017). Adolescents' legal socialization: Effects of interrogation and Miranda knowledge on legitimacy, cynicism, and procedural justice. *Youth Violence and Juvenile Justice, 15*(4), 419–440.

Viljoen, J. L., Klaver, J., & Roesch, R. (2005). Legal decisions of preadolescent and adolescent defendants: Predictors of confessions, pleas, communication with attorneys, and appeals. *Law and Human Behavior, 29*(3), 253–277.

Viljoen, J. L., Zapf, P. A., & Roesch, R. (2007). Adjudicative competence and comprehension of Miranda rights in adolescent defendants: A comparison of legal standards. *Behavioral Sciences and the Law, 25*, 1–19.

Villalobos, J. G., & Davis, D. (2016). Interrogation and the minority suspect: Pathways to true and false confession. In M. K. Miller & B. H. Bornstein (Eds.), *Advances in psychology and law* (pp. 1–41). Springer.

Unnever, J. D., & Cullen, F. T. (2012). White perceptions of whether African Americans and Hispanics are prone to violence and support for the death penalty. *Journal of Research in Crime and Delinquency, 49*(4), 519–544.

Warner, T. C., & Cleary, H. M. D. (2022). Parents' interrogation knowledge and situational decision-making in hypothetical juvenile interrogations. *Psychology, Public Policy, and Law, 28*(1), 78–91.

Wasserberg, M. J. (2014). Stereotype threat effects on African American children in an urban elementary school. *The Journal of Experimental Eeducation, 82*(4), 502–517.

Welch, K. (2007). Black criminal stereotypes and racial profiling. *Journal of Contemporary Criminal Justice, 23*(3), 276–288.

Woolard, J. L., Cleary, H. M. D., Harvell, S. A. S., & Chen, R. (2008). Examining adolescents' and their parents' conceptual and practical knowledge of police interrogation: A family dyad approach. *Journal of Youth and Adolescence, 37*(6), 685–698.

Woolard, J. L. & Henning, K. (2020). Racial minority youths' perceptions of the justice system: Life on the street. In M. C. Stevenson, B. Bottoms, & K. Burke (Eds.), *The legacy of race for children: Psychology, public policy, and law* (pp. 151–243). Oxford University Press.

Yarborough v. Alvarado, 541 U.S. 652 (2004).

Zelle, H., Romaine, C. L. R., & Goldstein, N. E. S. (2015). Juveniles' Miranda comprehension: Understanding, appreciation, and totality of circumstances factors. *Law and Human Behavior, 39*(3), 281–293.

CHAPTER 14

Youth in Juvenile and Criminal Court

Tina M. Zottoli, Tarika Daftary-Kapur, and Emily Haney-Caron

> **Abstract**
> This chapter describes the legal processes experienced by youth involved in the juvenile or criminal courts of the United States. The first part of the chapter traces the history of the U.S. juvenile justice system from its origination in the Progressive Era through to the present day, emphasizing system changes that have been important for social science research on the legal system. It then describes modern processes in both juvenile and criminal courts, highlighting differences between the two systems. Next, the chapter explores research and scholarship related to youth adjudicatory hearings and trials, youth plea bargaining, and outcomes for youth involved in the legal system. The chapter concludes with a brief summary and suggestions for future research.
>
> **Key Words:** youth, adolescence, juvenile courts, criminal courts, juvenile justice, juvenile legal system, criminal legal system, adolescent legal competencies, juvenile detention, juvenile law, juvenile sentencing

In the United States, there are two separate systems of justice for handling youth and adults accused of violating criminal laws. Each system relies on a different set of assumptions about the causes of criminal behavior and the purpose of state intervention (Zimring, 2005). Nevertheless, adolescents who violate criminal laws may find themselves under the jurisdiction of either an adult criminal court or a juvenile court. Whether a youth's case is heard in criminal court or juvenile court may be discretionary (i.e., decided by a judge or prosecutor) or mandatory (i.e., required by statute) and can depend on any of several factors, which vary from state to state, including the age of the youth accused of wrongdoing and the nature of the alleged offense (Griffin et al., 2011).

Juvenile courts function very differently from criminal courts in both procedure and process, and the dispositions for youth in juvenile court are typically intended to be rehabilitative and to entail fewer long-term repercussions (e.g., records are typically sealed; Zimring, 2005). As a result, the decisions that adolescents in juvenile court make with respect to their cases (e.g., whether to plead guilty) can have different long-term implications. At the same time, defendants in both criminal and juvenile court are protected by a number of due process and procedural rights, and the developmental immaturity of youth may necessitate additional or different safeguards than those commonly provided to adults for these rights to have real meaning for youth.

In this chapter, we first present a brief history of juvenile justice in the United States and an overview of juvenile and criminal court process. We then turn to a discussion of the research literatures on adolescent participation in juvenile court adjudicative hearings and criminal trials and on plea agreements involving adolescents. We end with a brief discussion of the outcomes associated with justice system involvement, particularly with respect to the criminal prosecution of youth. Throughout these discussions, we pay careful attention to the racialized history of juvenile justice in the United States and the disparate outcomes that historical and modern policies have had on minority, and especially Black, youth.

Before proceeding, we offer a note on terminology. First, throughout this chapter we use the terms "youth" or "adolescent" to refer to individuals between the ages of approximately 10 and 18 years. Although from the perspective of developmental science the period of adolescence extends beyond age 18 for most individuals (Sawyer et al., 2018), the United States historically has used 18 years of age as a bright dividing line between juvenile and criminal court jurisdiction. Second, although the term "juvenile" is often used interchangeably with "youth" or "adolescent" in scholarly works on system-involved youth, such usage can lead to confusion when criminal and juvenile systems are discussed in the same piece. To avoid any such confusion here, when we use the term "juvenile," we use it in its legal sense to refer to an individual whose case falls under the jurisdiction of a juvenile (or family) court, the age range for which varies among and within jurisdictions. As an example, in this chapter the term "juvenile defense attorney" refers specifically to an attorney representing youth in juvenile court. Finally, most readers will likely be aware that individual states, the federal government, the District of Columbia, and the U.S. territories each have their own legal systems, with unique features and policies. Unless we refer to a specific jurisdiction, when we write of the juvenile (or criminal) justice system and the juvenile (or criminal) court, the reader should note that we are describing the essential defining features that these systems share; state and even local jurisdictional differences are assumed.

A Brief History of Juvenile Justice in the United States

Space does not permit, and the aim of this chapter does not require, a complete treatment of the complex history of juvenile justice in the United States.[1] Rather, we present here a thumbnail sketch to orient the reader to the systems in which youth who are arrested for crimes may find themselves and to provide context for how the scientific research on adolescent development and legal competencies has shaped, and has been shaped by, juvenile and criminal justice policy and procedure. The founding principles of rehabilitation over punishment established in the first juvenile courts, an affirmation of due process rights some 60 years later, and the subsequent criminalization of the juvenile court provide an essential backdrop for understanding the experiences of youth today.

Early Roots and the Progressive Era

The juvenile justice system, as we might define it today, did not exist before the turn of the 20th century. From colonial times through the first 100 years or so of the nation's history, child discipline was, for the most part, a family affair (Olson-Raymer, 1983). For cases wherein a child committed a serious crime that warranted intervention by the state, prosecution and sentencing were generally (though not always) the same as they would be for an adult (Lawrence & Hemmens, 2008).

The early roots of a more formal juvenile justice system arose from the confluence of social, cultural, and technological changes of the 19th century that contributed to shifts in

---

[1] For comprehensive reviews see, for example, Feld (2017b), Krisberg (2018), and Ward (2012).

both urban population densities and demographic compositions, especially in the North. New industrial jobs brought rural dwellers to cities in search of work, and young people often came without parents; at the same time, immigration exploded, with a majority of newly arriving immigrants settling in cities (Krisberg, 2018). Urbanization brought with it poverty, crime, and an increase in the numbers of destitute youth (Lawrence & Hemmens, 2008). , and by the early 19th century, the belief that pauperism was causally linked to crime and delinquency was prevalent, especially among the privileged classes (Fox, 1969). It was against this backdrop that the earliest incarnation of a juvenile justice system developed.

Early reformers objected to placing youth in adult prisons and called for separate institutions for youth that were aimed at ameliorating poverty and immorality. *Houses of refuge*, the first of which was established in New York City in 1825, were founded to provide moral and practical education to youth who were delinquent or thought to be at risk for delinquency— so called "wayward youth" —(Pickett, 2018). However, the historical record suggests that these reforms were largely directed at children of European immigrants (Birckhead, 2017). Black and other non-White youth were placed in adult penal institutions at rates exceeding those of White children, and the children of slaves remained subject to plantation discipline (Birckhead, 2017; Ward, 2012). By the middle of the 19th century, Black youth were already overrepresented in the jails of cities with majority White populations, an effect that persists to the present day (e.g., Sterling, 2012). Moreover, among the few houses of refuge that did exist for Black youth, training was geared less toward academics or skilled work and more toward manual labor and service jobs, youth were held for long periods, and the facilities themselves were poor, suggesting a countervailing belief system that Black youth were not as worthy of, or amenable to, rehabilitative efforts as White children (Birckhead, 2017).

Other problems would eventually erode public support for the movement (Lawrence & Hemmens, 2008). For example, little distinction was made between youth who were engaged in serious offending and those who committed minor or noncriminal offending (e.g., street begging), leading the public to question whether youth benefited from being taken into state custody for such things. Problems that plagued adult prisons, such as overcrowding, also affected houses of refuge, and by the 1850s, institutional abuses had also become apparent (Pisciotta, 1982).

The failure of the houses of refuge, coupled with a nascent scientific understanding of adolescence as a unique period of development (e.g., Hall, 1904), ultimately gave way to the establishment of formal juvenile court systems in the United States. Coinciding with other Progressive Era reforms aimed at protecting children (e.g., child labor laws), and justified under the doctrine of *parens patriae* (i.e., the state as parent),[2] the first juvenile court in the United States was established in Cook County, Illinois, in 1899. Within a span of about 25 years, nearly every state had established its own juvenile court and the modern era of juvenile justice had begun (Schlossman & Kadish, 1983).

Operating under the twin assumptions that delinquency is a symptom of environmental and situational factors and that children, by virtue of unformed character, are more amenable to treatment than adults, the stated aim of these juvenile courts was to prioritize rehabilitation over punishment. As such, juvenile court processes were informal and dispositions were

---

[2] Literally translated from Latin as "parent of the country," the *parens patriae* doctrine legitimizes a paternal or protective role of a state over its citizens, such that orphans, dependent children, and persons deemed incompetent have a special protection from the state (Legal Information Institute, 2021). The juvenile court was thus justified by its proponents on the grounds that it is both the right and responsibility of the state to substitute its own control over children when the natural parents are unable or unwilling to (*In re Gault*, 1967).

individualized to the rehabilitative needs of the youth; little attention was paid to due process protections (Feld, 2020; Manfredi, 1998).

In practice, however, the informality of the juvenile court and the broad discretion afforded to judges contributed to variability and inconsistency in how youth were treated (Weithorn, 2006). In particular, decisions as to whether a youth should be system involved in the first place, subject to detention, or transferred to criminal court could vary considerably jurisdiction to jurisdiction, judge to judge, and case to case. Then, as now (e.g., Rachlinski et al., 2008), discretionary judgments were susceptible not only to arbitrariness but also to racial bias and discrimination. Accordingly, Black youth were more likely to come into the system at earlier ages, less likely to have their cases dismissed, and more likely to be detained than White youth (Birckhead, 2017).

It would take more than a half century before issues of due process and procedural fairness in the juvenile courts would come to the attention of the Supreme Court of the United States (SCOTUS). The backdrop was the civil rights movement of the 1950s and 1960s and the impetus that movement provided for the broad extension of due process and equal protection doctrines to historically disadvantaged or vulnerable groups, including criminal defendants (Debele, 1987; Feld, 2017b).

The Due Process Revolution and the Criminalization of the Juvenile Court

Between 1966 and 1970, and coinciding with a period of court history that expanded the due process rights of criminal defendants generally (e.g., *Gideon v. Wainwright*, 1963; *Miranda v. Arizona*, 1966), SCOTUS would decide a trio of cases that would fundamentally alter the workings of the juvenile court. The first of these cases, *Kent v. United States* (1966), formalized the process by which a youth could be transferred from juvenile to criminal court in the District of Columbia. Although the decision was based on statutory interpretation, it reflected the court's general concerns about the procedural arbitrariness of the juvenile courts. The next two decisions, *In re Gault* (1967) and *In re Winship* (1970), ushered in a new constitutional era for the juvenile court, conferring on youth in juvenile court the due process rights to counsel, notification of charges, confrontation of witnesses, protection of self-incrimination (*In re Gault*, 1967), and proof beyond reasonable doubt (*In re Winship*, 1970). In the words of Justice Fortas, who penned the opinions in *Kent* and *Gault*, functioning in a parental fashion was "not an invitation to procedural arbitrariness" (*Kent v. United States*, 1966, p. 554).

Undoubtedly the justices in the majorities viewed these reforms as consistent with the stated aim of the juvenile court to operate in the best interest of the child; nevertheless, the decisions also reflected uncertainty about the ability of the juvenile courts to effectuate the rehabilitative ideal on which was premised. Some scholars have argued that when viewed in retrospect, the due process transformation of the juvenile court, as well intentioned as it might have been, created the procedural mechanisms that set the stage for the subsequent criminalization of the juvenile court (Feld, 2017b; Manfredi, 1998). This next transformation of the juvenile court would come not through judges, but through lawmakers.

Beginning in the 1970s and continuing through the 1980s, crime rose in the United States (Juvenile Research and Statistics Association, 2000). This increase has been attributed largely to an uptick in the illegal drug trade and an increase in the availability of guns (Blumstein, 1995), though other factors (e.g., increasing criminalization; Gustafson, 2009) also played a role. A disproportionate amount of the serious and violent crime of this era was committed by young males in their teens and 20s—largely Black—whose communities had been devastated by the crack cocaine epidemic (Fryer et al., 2013). Coupled with several highly publicized cases (e.g., Willie Boskett in New York State; Hager, 2014), public opinion as to the effectiveness of the juvenile courts eroded (Bishop, 2006; Feld, 2017b). Although crime, including violent crime, would begin to drop off again by the early 1990s, the fear engendered by it would linger, as would the political utility of that fear (Henning, 2018). This was the era of the *superpredator*—a term coined by political scientist John DiLulio (1995) to describe youth who would commit violent crimes apparently without remorse. The idea, including its racist undertones, was seized upon by lawmakers and the media, ultimately justifying a legislative agenda toward harsher treatment of juveniles who committed crimes (Bogert, 2020; Henning, 2018)—including the mass incarceration of Black youth (Henning, 2018).

Between 1992 and 1997, legislatures in 47 states and the District of Columbia changed their laws in ways that contributed to more punitive juvenile courts and that substantially increased the numbers of youth restricted from juvenile court jurisdiction (Griffin et al., 1998; Snyder & Sickmund, 2006; Torbet et al., 1996).[3] These changes included lowering the maximum age for juvenile court jurisdiction and/or lowering the minimum age for transfer to adult court; automatically excluding youth from the jurisdiction of the juvenile court on the basis of the alleged offense and the age of the youth (i.e., statutory exclusion) or requiring the transfer of a youth from juvenile to criminal court (i.e., mandatory waiver); placing the discretion to file a case in juvenile or criminal court in the hands of the prosecutor (i.e., prosecutorial direct file); expanding sentencing options; and modifying or eliminating confidentiality requirements for some cases. These changes meant not only that many more system-involved youth were kept from the rehabilitative services of the juvenile system but also that they were exposed to severe criminal sanctions, including sentences of death and life without the possibility of parole (LWOP). This new reality prompted an expansion of research on adolescents prosecuted in criminal court.

The resulting literature, some of which we discuss later, exposed the detrimental effects of criminal adjudication and criminal detention on juveniles (e.g., Bishop, 2000) and revealed that youth were more likely than adults to have deficits in the capacities necessary to participate competently in their own defenses (e.g., Grisso et al., 2003). Moreover, society appeared to receive little benefit in exchange for the criminal adjudication of so many youth; for the most part, youth prosecuted as adults were no less likely—and in some instances were more likely—to recidivate than youth who remained in juvenile court, even accounting for the severity of charges (Fagan, 1996; Lanza-Kaduce et al., 2005; Myers, 2003).

The late 1990s also brought a rapid expansion of research in the fields of developmental psychology and cognitive neuroscience, which provided coherent psychosocial and biological explanations both for observed deficits in the legal competencies of adolescents and for developmental trajectories of antisocial behavior in youth and pathways to desistance. In time, public opinion supporting some of the harsher policies of the previous decade began to soften.

The Era of Developmental Science

From the turn of the 21st century through today, we have seen shifts in policy that were prompted by advances in the fields of developmental psychology and cognitive neuroscience beginning in the late 1990s (Feld, 2017b). Between 2005 and 2012, and relying in part on this science (e.g., Steinberg & Cauffman, 2003), SCOTUS held that the most serious of criminal sanctions—first the death penalty (*Roper v. Simmons*, 2005), then LWOP for nonhomicide offenses (*Graham v. Florida*, 2010), and ultimately mandatory LWOP for homicide offenses (*Miller v. Alabama*, 2012)—were unconstitutional for anyone under the age of 18 at the time

---

[3] For an edited volume providing a comprehensive review of legislative changes and their impacts, see Fagan and Zimring (2000).

of their offense. The *Miller* court emphasized that adolescence is marked by "transient rashness, proclivity for risk, and inability to assess consequences," and required courts to consider developmental factors when sentencing juvenile defendants (*Miller v. Alabama*, 2012, p. 471). Since *Miller*, over half of the states and the District of Columbia have eliminated LWOP sentences for adolescents entirely.

Other reforms at the state level include reduction in the use of detention, increased use of diversion programs, investment in community-based programming, provision of evidence-based interventions, and increased retention of youth in the juvenile system where they are more likely to have access to developmentally appropriate interventions (Bonnie, 2013). These changes have had a measurable impact. For example, in 1996, an estimated 200,000 youth were prosecuted in the nation's criminal courts (Woolard et al., 2005); in 2015, this number had dropped to an estimated 75,900 youth (Puzzanchera et al., 2018). Since 2005, the number of delinquency cases involving detention fell from just under 405,000 to just under 187,000, reflecting both a reduction in the use of detention *and* an overall reduction in the total number of youth involved in juvenile court proceedings (Office of Juvenile Justice and Delinquency Prevention, 2019).

In summary, the philosophy, policies, and procedures of juvenile justice in the United States have undergone several political transformations in the 120-plus years since the first formal juvenile court was established in 1899, with the most recent changes promoted in large part by advances in developmental psychology and cognitive neuroscience. As we turn to a discussion of modern juvenile and criminal justice processes, we will discuss in more detail the ways by which psychological science has helped, and continues to help, promote a more developmentally appropriate and culturally responsive system.

Modern Juvenile and Criminal Court Processes

Arguably the modern juvenile court is quite different from what it was at its inception. Nonetheless, the operating assumptions of the juvenile and criminal courts remain distinct (i.e., the juvenile court is predicated, in large part, on the rehabilitative potential for youth; the criminal courts are primarily concerned with retribution and deterrence). Juvenile court hearings, because they are quasi-civil (i.e., noncriminal) in nature, also allow for a level of informality in procedure that is not constitutionally possible in the criminal courts, even with the extension of the due process rights described earlier. For example, judges may solicit feedback from counselors and probation officers and permit the involvement of parents. As such, the experiences of youth in the juvenile and criminal courts are quite different.

Youth typically begin involvement with either system when they are referred by law enforcement, although referrals can come from other sources as well (e.g., schools, parents; Bonnie et al., 2013). Youth with more serious offenses may be subject to detention while their cases progress, with such a decision generally based on a finding that the youth poses a risk to the community if released or may fail to appear at future hearings. Although there are strict constitutional limitations on pretrial detention in criminal court (National Conference of State Legislatures, 2020), SCOTUS has approved a much wider set of detention criteria for juveniles (*Schall v. Martin*, 1984), including whether detention is in the best interest of the child's welfare. For detained youth, formal processing, delinquency adjudication, and, ultimately, incarceration are all more likely (Haney-Caron & Fountain, 2021) problems that may disproportionately impact youth of color and youth living in poverty who are detained at higher rates than White and more affluent youth (Rodriguez, 2010, 2013).[4]

---

[4] These disparities are not necessarily, or solely, attributable to racial bias on the part of judges. A number of other factors—themselves shaped by systemic racial inequities—may contribute to differential detention rates for

In many states, youth are first seen at juvenile court intake, which can be housed either within a probation department or within the prosecutor's office (Fairchild et al., 2019). At this stage, an intake officer may decide to dismiss the case if it lacks legal merit or is inconsistent with the goals of the juvenile justice system (Fairchild et al., 2019). Alternatively, a youth may be offered diversion, for which they agree to conditions such as restitution, community service, or mental health treatment in exchange for avoiding a delinquency petition and formal court processing (Bonnie et al., 2013). Diversion is commonly offered for lower level, first-time offenses (see Fountain et al., this volume, for a comprehensive discussion of alternative paths for juvenile justice–involved youth). Although diversion may also be offered to youth within the adult system, there may be fewer formal mechanisms for pretrial diversion when youth are processed as adults. Whereas close to half of cases that come into the juvenile system will be diverted or dismissed, most youth processed in the criminal justice system will be formally charged (Kirsberg, 2019).

For juvenile court youth whose cases are not dismissed or diverted, the next step is usually the filing of a delinquency petition with the court, which is the juvenile court equivalent of being charged with a crime. A delinquency petition typically alleges that the youth committed an act that would, were the youth an adult, meet the statutory elements of a criminal offense. This initiates formal court involvement, and at this point a youth will begin attending court hearings and may be offered a plea bargain by the prosecutor. A slight majority—55%—of cases seen at intake ultimately proceed to formal processing (Furdella & Puzzanchera, 2015). Here again, however, rates differ by race, such that Black and Indigenous youth are more likely to be formally processed than White youth (Peck & Jennings, 2016; Rodriguez, 2010).

As with criminal court cases, a large majority of juvenile court cases referred for formal processing are resolved through some form of plea agreement (National Juvenile Defender Center, n.d.). Youth who do not accept a plea offer instead have an adjudicatory (or delinquency) hearing, the juvenile court equivalent of a trial. Unlike defendants in criminal court, youth processed in juvenile court do not have a constitutional right to a jury trial, although juvenile jury trials are provided in some states in limited circumstances (Bonnie et al., 2013). Youth in juvenile court do, however, have constitutional rights to a speedy trial, to counsel, to cross-examination of witnesses, and to avoid self-incrimination (*In re Gault*, 1967), and the standard of proof at the adjudicatory hearing, like at a criminal trial, is that the youth's guilt of the alleged offenses must be proven beyond a reasonable doubt (*In re Winship*, 1970). Youth who plead guilty waive these rights and proceed directly to disposition (in the juvenile system) or sentencing (in the criminal system).

The dispositional hearing is the juvenile court equivalent of a sentencing hearing, at which the judge determines the sanctions and interventions that will be imposed on the youth. The most common disposition in juvenile court is probation, although youth may also be placed in a secure juvenile correctional facility or a residential treatment program, and may also be given fines or required to make restitution (Hockenberry & Puzzanchera, 2020). Because juvenile court dispositions are generally indeterminate, youth are commonly required to attend periodic review hearings. At these hearings, the judge determines whether the disposition imposed (e.g., probation, secure placement) continues to be appropriate, whether an

---

youth of color compared to White youth. For example, youth of color are more likely to have prior police contacts and prior legal system involvement, regardless of their offending behavior, than White youth (Feinstein, 2015; Padgaonkar et al., 2021; see Burke et al., this volume), which may weigh in favor of detention. Judges are also more likely to detain youth living in communities with structural disadvantages regardless of the charges faced because, for example, there may be few developmentally appropriate community resources available (Rodriguez, 2013).

alternative disposition is needed, or whether the youth's juvenile court involvement can conclude. Despite the serious implications of review hearings for the trajectory of a youth's system involvement, youth are not always represented by counsel during this postdisposition phase (Kokkalera et al., 2021). Whereas the disposition in the juvenile system is highly individualized, sentencing in criminal courts relies on a limited set of legal factors such as the seriousness of the current offense and the prior record of the individual. Many jurisdictions have rigid criminal court sentencing guidelines that do not allow the presiding judge much leeway in sentencing, thereby exposing convicted youth to extremely long prison sentences. Moreover, whereas delinquency records are often sealed, a criminal court conviction typically results in a criminal record that may carry with it a number of legal and extralegal collateral consequences (Butts & Mitchell, 2000).

Following disposition, a juvenile court youth may initiate an appeal if they believe there were deficiencies in the proceedings against them, though in practice appeals are exceedingly rare in the juvenile system (Drizin & Luloff, 2007; Feld, 2017b) and are almost never successful (Fedders, 2010). Youth convicted in criminal court can avail themselves of the same appellate avenues and rights as adult defendants. Notably, however, the acceptance of a plea offer, in either system, can substantially curtail appellate rights—and as discussed later in this chapter, the guilty plea is by far the most common means by which cases are resolved in both systems.

In summary, the juvenile justice system is, at least in part, predicated on the notion that youth are more amenable to treatment than adults and that the causes of criminal behavior in youth stem less from dispositional traits and more from factors of developmental immaturity and environmental influence. In contrast, in the criminal justice system the focus is on punishment, deterrence, and community protection; rehabilitation is secondary. Although defendants in both criminal and juvenile court are afforded a host of constitutional and procedural protections, defendants in juvenile court may also benefit from the informal nature of proceedings and individualized dispositions that take into account their specific criminogenic needs. Juvenile court youth are also generally protected from severe criminal sanctions available in criminal court, as well as the long-term impacts of a criminal record—benefits that are typically stripped from juveniles transferred to criminal court. In the following sections we discuss how developmental immaturity may affect the adjudicative process for youth involved in either court.

Youth Adjudicatory Hearings and Trials

At the adjudicatory hearing stage (in juvenile court) or the trial stage (in criminal court), youth must navigate a number of legal decisions as well as work with their attorney to develop an effective defense. Proceeding to trial (or pleading guilty) in criminal court requires, as a constitutional prerequisite, that a defendant be *competent*—that is, a defendant must have "sufficient present ability to consult with his lawyer with a reasonable degree of rational understanding" and a "rational as well as factual understanding of the proceedings against him" (*Dusky v. United States,* 1960). As typically operationalized in the psycholegal literature and in forensic assessment, a factual and rational understanding implies that one has not only a basic understanding of legal facts (e.g., role of court personnel and procedure) but also an appreciation of the legal process and potential outcomes for one's own personal situation, including a basic ability to engage in reasoned decision making related to such processes and outcomes (Bonnie, 1992). Likewise, sufficient capacity to assist counsel requires both a basic understanding of the attorney–client relationship and the ability to apply that knowledge to one's own case, as well as the ability to communicate and collaborate with one's attorney (Warren et al., 2016). The constitutional requirement that a defendant be competent recognizes that, for any of a defendant's other trial-related constitutional rights (e.g., right to trial, right to counsel, right against self-incrimination) to have meaning, they must be able to decide whether and how to exercise those rights (Scott & Grisso, 2005). Accordingly, defendants who, due to "mental disease or defect," do not meet this standard cannot be brought to trial (*Drope v. Missouri,* 1975).

Although *In re Gault* (1967) signaled the origin of a competence requirement in juvenile court (Cauffman & Steinberg, 2012), juvenile defense attorneys did not begin to regularly raise issues of competence to proceed until the 1990s as youth began to be transferred into the adult system with increasing frequency (Larson & Grisso, 2011). A lack of clarity persists regarding whether the standard for competence in juvenile court is the same as the criminal court standard articulated in *Dusky* (Scott & Grisso, 2005; Wingrove, 2007). As we noted earlier, the expressed rehabilitative purpose and less severe sanctions of the juvenile courts may mean that the level of understanding and functioning necessary to meaningfully participate in one's defense is reduced compared to criminal court (Feld, 2017a). Indeed, though research is limited, existing survey data suggest that judges and defense attorneys share this view that youth in juvenile court need somewhat lower levels of legal capacities to proceed than youth in adult court (Viljoen & Wingrove, 2007). Alternatively, given the developmental immaturity common among youth in the juvenile system, it can be argued that additional protections may be necessary to ensure their ability to meaningfully exercise trial-related rights.

Because the Supreme Court has never addressed the issue of adjudicatory competence in juvenile court, individual states have determined their own standards for juvenile court competence, which vary with respect to the level of functioning required (Warren et al., 2016). Additionally, whereas in criminal court a finding of incompetence is predicated on mental illness or cognitive/developmental disability, some states have added developmental immaturity as grounds for incompetence in juvenile court (Feld, 2017b). This shift recognizes that, for youth, mental illness and cognitive disability are not the only—or even the most common—causes of impaired understanding or capacity to reason about legal proceedings. However, legal professionals may view developmental immaturity as less important to a youth's competence than mental disorder or cognitive impairment, and there does not appear to be wide support among judges that developmental immaturity should be a basis for incompetence in juvenile court (Viljoen & Wingrove, 2007), though this has been changing gradually with time and varies by jurisdiction (Bryant et al., 2015). Presently, 15 states statutorily identify developmental immaturity as grounds for juvenile adjudicatory incompetence (Panza et al., 2020). In a recent survey of 27 juvenile court judges, more than half reported that adolescent development does not influence their decisions regarding adjudicative competence (Berryessa & Reeves, 2020); the others, however, said they both consider adolescent development in evaluating a youth's competency and attempt to tailor court procedures to make them developmentally appropriate for an individual youth (Berryessa & Reeves, 2020).

Allowing for a finding of incompetence based on developmental immaturity accounts for the reality that, to have a factual and rational understanding of court proceedings and to work effectively with an attorney, a number of developmental capacities are necessary (Wingrove, 2007). Specifically, one must be able to understand abstract and complex ideas, use that abstract knowledge to engage in a deliberative decision-making process, communicate effectively with legal actors, and engage in perspective taking to understand how to effectively respond to the defense attorney, prosecutor, and judge. Additionally, one must regulate challenging emotions to remain focused in court and in conversations with one's attorney, to attend to long- as well as short-term consequences, and to resist pressure from others (e.g., peers, family, attorney) to make independent decisions.

Importantly, as these capacities are still developing in childhood and adolescence, youth could not be expected to perform at the same level as adults in navigating the adjudicatory process (Cauffman & Steinberg, 2012). A large body of research on adolescent adjudicative competence confirms adolescents' developmental difficulties functioning at adult levels in this domain. Younger adolescents—under the age of 16—have lower levels of legal understanding and reasoning than adults and fail to fully grasp aspects of the legal system necessary to make decisions and participate in their defense (Cunningham, 2020; Ficke et al., 2006; Grisso et al., 2003; Redlich et al., 2003; Viljoen & Roesch, 2005). In one of the most robust studies to date on adolescent legal capacities, almost a third of legally involved and community-based 11–13-year-olds and nearly a fifth of 14–15-year-olds showed significant impairments in legal understanding, reasoning, or both, as measured by the MacArthur Competency Assessment Tool–Criminal Adjudication (Hoge et al., 1999), a standardized measure of capacities related to adjudicative competence; understanding and reasoning were more impaired in youth with lower intelligence test scores (Grisso et al., 2003). Psychosocial maturity, specifically future orientation (or a focus on longer term consequences when making decisions), explains part of the relationship between age and legal understanding and reasoning (Kivisto et al., 2011).

Despite these data and a long-standing concern of psycholegal scholars, there has been relatively little movement, at the statutory level, taking into account the impact of developmental immaturity on the competency of youth prosecuted in the criminal courts. While we are unaware of research documenting the extent to which individual judges might attend to developmental immaturity, we presume, based on our own anecdotal experiences, that at least some do. It is also reasonable to assume that the rationale of the SCOTUS decisions on sentencing of youth, described earlier (e.g., *Roper v. Simmons*, 2005), and related decisions on the capacities of youth as criminal defendants (e.g., *J.D.B. v. North Carolina*, 2011) have had an impact on other aspects of judicial decision making in cases involving youth.

A core element of adjudicative competency is the capacity to rationally consult with one's lawyer (*Dusky v. United States*, 1960). To work effectively with an attorney, a youth—either in juvenile or in criminal court—needs to understand the role of the defense attorney, trust in the attorney as their advocate, appreciate the protection provided by attorney–client privilege, and understand the ways in which an attorney provides benefit to the client (Fountain & Woolard, 2018). Unfortunately, there is a paucity of research on how youth relate to their attorneys and how they understand the attorney–client relationship. In a recent study that included criminal court youth, the vast majority reported trusting and getting along with their attorneys and believed their attorneys were good at their jobs (Zottoli et al., 2016). On the other hand, some youth may lack even the basic understanding that the defense attorney works for them and will advocate for them even if they are guilty, or may believe that what they tell their attorneys can be reported to their parents, the police, or the judge (Fountain & Woolard, 2017).

In a survey of over 200 juvenile defense attorneys, Viljoen et al. (2010) found that attorneys have questions about the competence of about 10% of the youth they represent due to limitations in youths' understanding of legal proceedings, failure to appreciate the seriousness of the proceedings, failure to weigh long-term consequences, and lack of participation in the defense process. However, these same attorneys reported only seeking a competence evaluation in about half of the cases in which they had concerns. Focusing specifically on the guilty plea context, NeMoyer et al. (2018) found that over 65% of the juvenile attorneys they surveyed had raised the issue of competency at least once; notably, however, just over 40% said that they had also declined to raise the issue for some clients, despite having concerns. These data suggest that many youths may proceed through delinquency adjudications despite not fully understanding the proceedings against them and/or being able to work effectively with their attorney (Feld, 2017a). Exacerbating the problem, many youth in the juvenile system waive their right to an attorney—likely often without comprehending what waiver of that right means (Feld, 2017a). This decision may stem from misconceptions as to the attorney's role or its importance, or because of an inability to pay fees; counsel provided to indigent youth often comes with administrative fees or even expectations of reimbursement (Feierman et al., 2018).

For youth who lack robust adjudicatory competence, defense attorneys report having difficulty gathering the information they need from their clients, struggling to communicate effectively with their clients, and having to take on a more directive role with youth than may be appropriate (Viljoen et al., 2010). Working effectively with youth requires that attorneys have some understanding of adolescent development, along with an interest in providing robust representation to youth. Attorneys may need to break down complex information into smaller pieces; repetition is often necessary and youth may need time to process information and formulate questions. Indeed, research suggests that youth who spend more time with their attorneys have a better understanding of legal processes than other youth (Viljoen & Roesch, 2005).

Unfortunately, for some defense attorneys and public defender offices, juvenile court is used as a way for new attorneys to develop lawyering skills before moving on to criminal court (Feld & Schaefer, 2010), meaning that attorneys working with youth may have the least training and experience. In most states, juvenile defenders are not required to complete any special training (Kokkalera et al., 2021). Lack of training on how to communicate effectively with youth might lead to misperceptions by some attorneys as to whether their clients have a factual and rational understanding of the juvenile court process. For example, Fountain and Woolard (2018) found that when attorneys in their sample believed that their clients understood their constitutional rights, these assumptions were often based on their (the attorneys) having explained the information, not on any specific indicators from the client, such as their client being able to explain things in their own words.

Lack of resources also contributes to poor representation in juvenile court. Defense attorneys commonly have extremely high caseloads and may not have the time or funds necessary to conduct a full investigation, file motions, or even regularly meet with their young clients (Drizin & Luloff, 2007; Fedders, 2010). Attorneys commonly do not meet with youth until court (Jones, 2004). These problems are not limited to the juvenile courts; caseloads of public defenders in criminal courts also typically exceed standards (Lefstein & Spangenberg, 2009). Across two separate samples of New York City youth charged in criminal court, most youth met with their attorneys only two or three times, and usually in conjunction with other court matters (Daftary-Kapur & Zottoli, 2014; Zottoli et al., 2016).

Youth of color—especially Black youth—may be disproportionately disadvantaged in attorney–client relationships. Youth of color are profoundly overrepresented in the juvenile and criminal justice systems, but a very large majority of attorneys are White (American Bar Association, 2020). Defense attorneys are not immune to implicit racial biases (Avery et al., 2020; Henning, 2017). Additionally, they may not recognize or fail to push back against biased language about their clients presented in court (Birckhead, 2017); such language can confirm or strengthen stereotypes and bias, potentially contributing to worse outcomes for Black youth (Birckhead, 2017). Extrapolating from research supporting an out-group empathy gap, Birckhead (2017) suggests that such issues could be exacerbated among White attorneys, who may view their Black clients less empathetically than their White clients and/or be less inclined to view Black clients as possibly innocent. These reasons, among others, may underlie research findings that Black youth are less likely to trust their attorneys or rely on their attorneys' recommendations, and may limit the information they choose to share with their attorneys (Schmidt et al., 2003; Viljoen & Roesch, 2005).

Guilty Pleas in Juvenile and Criminal Court

While the lion's share of research on the legal capacities of adolescents has focused on abilities centering on competency to proceed with trial, the vast majority of both criminal and juvenile court convictions (Devers, 2011; National Juvenile Defender Center, n.d.) follow not from a trial or delinquency hearing, in which one had an opportunity to confront witnesses and challenge evidence, but rather from a plea of guilty, by which one waives these, and other, rights.

Although the standard for adjudicative competency in criminal court subsumes the capacities necessary to waive one's rights and enter a guilty plea (*Godinez v. Moran*, 1993), waiver of these rights must be knowing, voluntary, and intelligent (*Boykin v. Alabama*, 1969; *Brady v. United States*, 1970). That is, to be convicted by guilty plea in criminal court, a defendant must have the *ability* to understand the plea process and the implications of a plea decision *and* must *actually* understand the process and implications of the decision (*Godinez v. Moran*, 1993; Redlich & Summer, 2012). Youth in juvenile court must similarly waive their right to an adjudicatory hearing before pleading guilty. Counsel must affirm on record that a juvenile is knowingly, voluntarily, and intelligently waiving their rights before a judge can accept the plea (Kaban & Quinlan, 2004). The judge is then tasked with the final determination as to whether the case facts support the claim that the juvenile's plea was made knowingly and voluntarily (Woolard et al., 2016). In some jurisdictions, judges must also confirm that the parent understands the rights the juvenile is waiving (Hertz et al., 2019).

Over the last decade a burgeoning psycholegal literature on guilty pleas in the United States has cast doubt on the ability of existing procedural safeguards to ensure the validity of guilty pleas (Redlich, 2016). Indeed, research on otherwise competent *adult* defendants who were convicted by guilty plea (i.e., their pleas were adjudged valid by a court) points to deficits in basic legal knowledge relevant to their plea decisions (Redlich & Summers, 2012; Zottoli & Daftary-Kapur, 2019). In light of the discussion of adjudicative competency in the previous section, it would be reasonable to expect the picture to be bleaker for youth.

A growing body of research has investigated several important questions regarding the guilty pleas of youth, including how youth make plea decisions, the extent to which youth understand the plea process and appreciate the outcomes that follow their decisions, and whether youth differ from adults in how they experience the plea process and make plea decisions (see Redlich et al., 2019, for a comprehensive review of studies published as of 2016; more recent papers include Fountain & Woolard, 2018; Helm et al., 2018; Zottoli & Daftary-Kapur, 2019). Converging data from field (e.g., Daftary-Kapur & Zottoli, 2014), experimental (e.g., Redlich & Shteynberg, 2016), and quasi-experimental (e.g., Grisso et al., 2003) research support the conclusion that many adolescents lack sufficient legal knowledge to enter a valid guilty plea; these studies also suggest that, compared to adults, youth may attend more to short-term benefits than long-term negative consequences and may consider fewer potential outcomes associated with their plea decisions.

In line with developmental science, changes in both legal understanding and factors considered when making plea decisions appear to track with age. Viljoen et al., (2005) interviewed detained juvenile defendants about their guilty plea decisions and found that older youth (ages 15–17) considered the evidence in their cases, whereas younger youth (ages 11–14) did not. Likewise, in studies utilizing hypothetical plea scenarios, adults have been found more likely than youth to consider the probability of acquittal in their plea decisions (Grisso et al., 2003) and more likely to endorse rationales for their plea decisions that reflect long-term consequences (Redlich & Shteynberg, 2016).

Studies directly comparing the plea decisions of similarly situated adults and youth are limited. A recent study that compared the plea knowledge and decision making of criminal court youth (n = 64) and adults (n = 56) who were convicted by plea in the same jurisdiction (New York City) found meaningful differences between the groups in their legal knowledge, the kinds of things they considered when making decisions, and their decision rationales (Zottoli & Daftary-Kapur, 2019). Whereas the majority of youth and adults understood the basic elements of a guilty plea, youth were less likely to recognize that pleas can result in a criminal record, and although all adult participants had a basic understanding of the trial process, just over a quarter of the youth possessed even a rudimentary understanding of the trial process and the rights that attached to defendants who go to trial. When asked to describe the factors they considered in making their plea decisions, consistent with findings from Grisso et al., (2003), the youth generated fewer total potential outcomes and were more likely than adults to generate outcomes that reflected immediate (those realized within a day) and short-term (those realized within a year) consequences (Zottoli & Daftary-Kapur, 2019).

The researchers also asked participants about the veracity of their guilty pleas. The majority of youth and adults reported that they were guilty as charged; however, a sizeable percentage of both youth (34.6%) and adults (19.6%) reported that their guilty pleas were false, and youth were more likely to make such claims (Zottoli & Daftary-Kapur, 2019). These rates are in keeping with a growing body of research suggesting both that plea bargaining plays a role in wrongful conviction (e.g., Dervan, 2012; Dervan & Edkins, 2013) and that adolescents might be more susceptible to entering false guilty pleas than adults (Helm & Reyna, 2018; Redlich & Shteynberg, 2016). For example, in a recent experiment there were no significant differences in the plea decisions of adolescent and young adult participants asked to assume the role of guilty defendants, but among those asked to assume innocence, adolescents were nearly 2.5 times more likely to plead guilty than adults (Redlich & Shteynberg, 2016). Helm and Reyna (2018) hypothesized that developmental differences in cognitive processing, as explained by fuzzy trace theory (Reyna, et al., 2005), might explain some of the differences in false guilty plea rates between youth and adults. Specifically, with all else being equal, adolescents are predicted to rely on verbatim processing (i.e., explicit numerical-level analysis) to a greater extent than adults, who tend to rely more on gist processing (i.e., meaning-level analysis). In a vignette-based study designed to test these ideas, "innocent" adolescents and college-aged students pleaded guilty significantly more often than post-college-aged adults; moreover, youth were influenced more by superficial incentives than adults (Helm et al., 2018). These data suggest there may be potential avenues for protecting against false guilty pleas that capitalize on developmental differences in cognitive processing.

Taken together, existing research gives reason to be concerned that at least some youth may be at risk to enter guilty pleas with insufficient knowledge and that developmental immaturities in perspective taking and limited experiential knowledge may affect the capacity of youth to generate and appreciate the full complement of potential consequences attached to their plea decisions (see Redlich et al., 2019). In addition, although data come from only a handful of studies in limited contexts, there is some evidence to suggest that youth may be more susceptible than adults to entering false guilty pleas.

Short of other legal interventions, attorneys are best positioned to assess for and mitigate deficiencies in their clients' legal knowledge and appreciation of potential consequences. However, as already noted, specific training in working with adolescent clients is rare and resources are often limited. As a result, youth in both criminal and juvenile courts typically meet infrequently with attorneys and often only when they are already set to appear in court (Daftary-Kapur & Zottoli, 2014; Jones, 2004; Zottoli et al., 2016). Since we have already discussed these issues in some detail earlier, here we simply note that meeting under these circumstances can make it difficult to convey complex information to clients—potentially contributing to the deficiencies in legal knowledge often reported in studies of adjudicated youth—and may exacerbate the potential that attorneys will not notice deficits in competency and legal knowledge in their clients. Another complicating factor for attorneys—though not one that is exclusive to cases involving youth—is that an interest in the child's adjudicative competency can compete with an interest in achieving the best practical outcome for the youth. Among the surveyed defense attorneys who had decided against raising a competency issue despite having concerns about their client's capacities to plead, NeMoyer et al. (2018) reported that about 15% said they wanted to avoid extending their client's time in detention and just under 10% thought raising the issue might lead to a less desirable plea agreement.

Role of Parents in the Plea Process
A unique feature of juvenile courts is that parents are often involved in the adjudicative process. Although parents do not have the legal authority to make a plea decision or enter a plea on their child's behalf (Etienne, 2018), jurisdictions vary with respect to how parents are incorporated into the plea decision process. Research on the role of parents in the juvenile court plea process is nascent, but there is some evidence to suggest that parents are often actively involved in advising their children how to plead (Pennington, 2017; Viljoen & Roesch, 2005). In some jurisdictions, parents may even be required to cosign their child's tender-of-plea form (Redlich & Bonventre, 2015). Fountain and Woolard (2021) interviewed attorneys from an urban, East Coast defenders' office about the role of parents in the plea negotiation process and found that overall attorneys favored including parents. The majority of attorneys reported that parents were involved in conversations about plea offers, attended hearings, and were an integral component of a successful plea agreement. Moreover, the attorneys explained that the judges wanted them to involve their clients' parents, recognizing that the success of any plea agreement is tied, at least in part, to ensuring that the terms do not unduly burden the parents who must provide necessary supports to their children over the length of the disposition (e.g., transporting youth). Whether such is recognized among juvenile courts generally is not known.

Dispositions and Sentencing in Juvenile and Criminal Court
In juvenile court, youth who are adjudicated delinquent at an adjudicatory hearing or who accept a plea offer receive a disposition, generally supervision in the community (i.e., probation) or out-of-home placement (i.e., confinement in a residential correctional or treatment facility). About two thirds of youth adjudicated delinquent receive probation, around a quarter receive some form of out-of-home placement, and the remainder receive some other sanction (e.g., fines, restitution; Hockenberry & Puzzanchera, 2020). A systematic review of over 20 studies revealed that youth may receive harsher dispositions when represented by counsel (Kokkalera et al., 2021). The authors suggest this counterintuitive finding stems from a host of factors related to accessibility and quality of counsel in juvenile court—for example, given the burden on the juvenile to prove indigence, judges may treat youth who waive counsel more leniently. Other potential factors noted by the authors include that attorneys might be appointed more frequently in serious cases and that some attorneys take on a working-group, as opposed to adversarial, role (Kokkalera et al., 2021).

Successfully navigating the dispositional stage may be challenging for youth in part because of court expectations inconsistent with youth developmental capacities. For example, youth on probation commonly have a large number of requirements with which they must simultaneously comply, including attending school, passing drug screenings, abiding by curfews, and completing community service (NeMoyer et al., 2014). Youth commonly struggle to successfully meet all of the expectations of probation. An archival analysis of probation cases by NeMoyer et al. (2014) revealed that approximately half of youth failed to comply with one or more probation requirements, which, in some cases, resulted in the judge revoking probation and instead placing the youth out of the home.

Black youth tend to receive more punitive dispositions from juvenile court judges (Rodriguez, 2010) and may be viewed by probation officers as more blameworthy and less deserving of therapeutic interventions than White youth (Bridges & Steen, 1998). Racial disparities in juvenile court dispositions track the racial bias that has permeated the system since the earliest incarnations of the juvenile court: White youth are seen as deserving of treatment and more likely to be given rehabilitative interventions, whereas Black youth are seen as more deserving of punishment and more likely to be given punitive dispositions (Haney-Caron & Fountain, 2021). Racial disparities may extend to other dispositions as well; for example, youth of color may be given higher fines and fees than their White counterparts or may receive fines and fees disproportionate to the family's ability to pay (Piquero & Jennings, 2017; Selbin, 2019; see Viljoen et al., this volume, for youth in detention and associated outcomes).

Youth sentenced in criminal court typically face the same sanctions as adults, which may include mandatory minimums. Mandatory minimums require judges to impose a predetermined minimum sentence, based solely on conviction charge and, sometimes, criminal history. They remove from the sentencing equation any consideration of the defendant's life circumstances or the context of the offense (see generally, Steiner, 2017).

Mandatory minimums, often criticized as disproportionate for adult defendants (e.g., Cullen, 2018), may be especially so for youth. These sentences were drafted with adults in mind. As such, their application to adolescents not only strips from a judge the freedom to consider the mitigating factors of youth, including that the vast majority of youth who commit crimes will not persist in criminal behavior beyond early adulthood, but also disregards the fact that the meaning and impact of long sentences vary as a function of the convicted person's age. This fact was recognized by the majority in *Graham v. Florida* (2010), the SCOTUS decision that abolished LWOP sentences for persons convicted of nonhomicide offenses committed before age 18. Writing for the majority, Justice Kennedy explained that "a juvenile offender will on average serve more years and a greater percentage of his life in prison than an adult offender. A 16-year-old and a 75-year-old each sentenced to life without parole receive the same punishment in name only" (*Graham v. Florida,* 2010, p. 19).

Although SCOTUS has abolished the most severe forms of criminal sanctions for youth (i.e., death, LWOP for nonhomicide offenses, and mandatory LWOP for homicide), there is considerable variability across the United States with respect to the kinds of sentences faced by youth. Although 25 states have banned LWOP sentences for youth, the remaining states still permit the sentence under discretionary schemes. Additionally, many states have yet to address the appropriateness of sentencing youth to "virtual" life sentences—sentences for a term of years that could exceed life expectancy. For example, in Tennessee, one must serve 51 years of a sentence of life *with* the possibility of parole before one is eligible for release (Sentencing Reform Act, 1989).[5]

There is little evidence to suggest these sentences serve anything other than a punitive purpose. Data on recently released "juvenile lifers" is particularly illustrative. In *Montgomery*

---

[5] As of this writing, the Tennessee legislature is considering a bill (SB0561/HB1532) to reduce time served before parole eligibility from 51 to 25 years; https://wapp.capitol.tn.gov/apps/BillInfo/Default.aspx?BillNumber=SB0561.

v. Louisiana (2016), SCOTUS held that the rule abolishing mandatory LWOP established in *Miller* applied retroactively. In so doing, the court invalidated the sentences of approximately 2,100 individuals across the United States (a group collectively referred to as "juvenile lifers"; e.g., Daftary-Kapur & Zottoli, 2020). Hundreds of these individuals have since been released with negligible risk to public safety. Philadelphia and Michigan had the largest concentration of juvenile lifers. Of the first 174 juvenile lifers released in Philadelphia, only two (1.14%) have been reconvicted of any offense, both of which were minor (Daftary-Kapur & Zottoli, 2020). Similarly, only one of the 142 juvenile lifers released in Michigan has been rearrested as of this writing (Samples, 2021).

On the other hand, the cost to incarcerate an adolescent for decades is substantial. Philadelphia is set to save an estimated $9.5 million over the first decade following the release of the first 174 former juvenile lifers (Daftary-Kapur & Zottoli, 2020). In light of these data and the SCOTUS decisions that precipitated them, mandatory minimums, especially as applied to youth, warrant revision. The Iowa Supreme Court appears to agree, recognizing that punishing a juvenile for "retributive purposes irrespective of an individualized analysis of the juvenile's categorically diminished culpability is an irrational exercise" (*State v. Lyle*, 2014, p. 399). To our knowledge, no other state court has expressed as strong a conclusion regarding mandatory sentencing for youth, though some states (e.g., California; Harris, n.d.) have begun to reconsider their criminal sentencing schemes as applied to youth.

Impact of Criminal Prosecution and Sentencing on Youth

Adult prosecution of youth is predicated on the assumption that the more severe sanctions available in the criminal courts deter crime, either among youth actually transferred (specific deterrence) or among youth who might otherwise offend (general deterrence), but as noted earlier in this chapter, the efficacy of juvenile transfer is debatable. A handful of reviews on transfer laws suggest that transferred youth may be more likely to reoffend, reoffend more quickly and at higher rates, and commit more serious offenses following release from prison than juveniles retained in the juvenile justice system (Bishop & Frazer, 2000; Howell, 1996; McGowan et al., 2007; Redding, 2010). For instance, Fagan (1996) compared outcomes for youth charged with robbery and burglary in New York, where they were excluded from juvenile court by statute, with youth charged with the same offenses in matched counties in New Jersey, where juvenile court jurisdiction extended up to age 18; youth in New York were rearrested more often and more quickly for serious offenses than their counterparts in New Jersey. Bishop et al. (1996) found similar results in Florida. The Task Force on Community Preventative Services of the Centers for Disease Control and Prevention found that transferring juveniles to the adult justice system generally increased rates of violent offending (Tonry, 2007).

Youth convicted in criminal court may suffer other long-term legal consequences. Depending on the laws of their state, a criminal conviction may subject a youth to criminal court jurisdiction for any subsequent offense committed as a juvenile, even if it would not have resulted in criminal prosecution had it been a first offense (i.e., once an adult, always an adult; Griffin et al., 2011); and felony convictions often result in a host of nonpenal collateral consequences such as restrictions on federal assistance, voting rights, and the ability to obtain certain professional licensures and employment (Council of State Governments, n.d.). Moreover, criminal convictions are usually public record, and persons with criminal convictions typically have to report their conviction in employment applications. Considering that Black youth are transferred to criminal court at rates disproportionate to their representation in the system (Thomas & Wilson, 2018), the downstream impacts of criminal convictions also serve to perpetuate racial disparities in socioeconomic attainment.

From a developmental standpoint, criminal prosecution of youth may be more disruptive than juvenile court adjudication, because criminal sanctions may interfere with acquisition of crucial educational, vocational, and social skills (Scott & Steinberg, 2008). Taylor (2015) examined the relationship between adult prosecution and educational outcomes. Although there was no significant impact on rates of attending and graduating college or obtaining a vocational certificate, prosecution in adult court was associated with significant reduction in annual income in adulthood, even after controlling for sentence length and other relevant factors expected to impact income (e.g., number of weeks worked per year, graduation from high school, graduation from college).

Finally, compared to youth held in juvenile detention centers, youth held in adult correctional facilities are seven times more likely to commit suicide, five times more likely to be sexually assaulted, twice as likely to be beaten by staff, and more likely to be attacked with a weapon (Bishop & Frazier, 2000; Chesney-Lind & Mauer, 2003; Forst et al., 1989).

While there has been a consistent decline in the number of youths housed in adult prison—the most recent estimate was 956 youth in 2016 down from a high of 9,485 in 1999 (Troilo, 2018)—only 18 of the 44 states that incarcerate youth as adults maintain designated housing units for youth (Hockenberry & Sladkey, 2018).

Conclusion and Future Directions

In this chapter we presented an overview of historical and modern perspectives on juvenile justice, and we examined, through the lens of developmental psychology, the experiences of adolescents involved in the juvenile and criminal courts, focusing in particular on issues pertaining to their capacities to meaningfully exercise their rights. We also discussed the negative impacts of detention and adult prosecution on developmental outcomes for youth. In doing so, we touched upon the ways in which systemic racism, present from the earliest incarnations of the juvenile justice system, has led to disparate outcomes for Black and other minority youth at all stages within the criminal and juvenile justice systems.

The last one and a half decades have brought about many developmentally necessary and scientifically supported reforms. Today, fewer youth find themselves the object of criminal prosecution and fewer youth are formally processed by the juvenile courts. Youth are also detained less frequently in both systems. We are also increasingly aware of the racialized history of juvenile (and criminal) justice in this country and the mechanisms by which systems perpetuate racial disparity.

Progress continues. Current empirically informed initiatives include increasing the age limit of juvenile court jurisdiction beyond 18 years and likewise raising age-limit restrictions for meting out the most serious of criminal sanctions. For example, at the time of this writing the state of Illinois is contemplating legislation to ban LWOP sentences for persons who were under the age of 21 at the time of their offense (HB1064), and the American Psychological Association is working on legislative advocacy aimed at extending the ban on the death penalty into early adulthood. There is much room for additional research to inform whether, where, and how we draw legal lines—which will always be arbitrary at the boundaries—to demarcate developmental stages for these and myriad other important legal questions. Space does not permit a detailed discussion here, but we point interested readers to Scott et al. (2016) for a thoughtful review and legal commentary on how we might understand young adulthood as a legally distinct, transitional stage, warranting special consideration with respect to criminal adjudication in some contexts.

Many other areas touched on in this chapter remain ripe for continued research. For example, despite a rapid acceleration in research related to plea bargaining in recent years, we still know much less about the plea experiences of youth than we do about the experiences of youth participating at trial or in delinquency hearings. Likewise, understanding the attorney–youth relationship and how parents/guardians affect outcomes for justice-involved youth remains understudied. Psychologists are also uniquely positioned to provide attorneys and judges with empirically supported guidance for communicating with youth and to help jurisdictions implement policies that mitigate against the impact of implicit bias. These represent but a few of the many opportunities for continued work.

To conclude, we highlight both the importance of empirically informed policy and the reality that science is but one of many factors that influence policymakers, and often it is not at the top. As scientists who study adolescent decision making and legal capacities, we are naturally pleased to note the gains made in recent years to implement more developmentally appropriate and culturally sensitive policies. Nonetheless, from the perspective of developmental science, we have much further to go. Moreover, we should not discount the fragility of recent gains. At the time of this writing, we are encountering an upsurge in racial animosity among some segments of society (Abramowitz & McCoy, 2019; Newman et al., 2021), and although there appears to remain some momentum for criminal justice reform within both major political parties, there have also been backlashes against policies aimed at reducing the criminal justice footprint (e.g., Balko, 2021). To ensure that the progress made over the last 15 or so years continues, psycholegal scholars must effectively communicate the ways in which society at large benefits in the long run from juvenile and criminal justice policies that are both developmentally sound and socially and economically equitable. Such is no easy task within a large and demographically, geographically, and politically diverse society.

References

Abramowitz, A., & McCoy, J. (2019). United States: Racial resentment, negative partisanship, and polarization in Trump's America. *Annals of the American Academy of Political and Social Science*, *681*(1), 137–156.

American Bar Association (2020). Profile of the legal profession. https://www.americanbar.org/content/dam/aba/administrative/news/2020/07/potlp2020.pdf

Avery, J. J., Starck, J., Zhong, Y., Avery, J. D., & Cooper, J. (2020). Is your own team against you? Implicit bias and interpersonal regard in criminal defense. *Journal of Social Psychology*, *161*(5), 543–559.

Balko, R. (2021). The bogus backlash against progressive prosecutors. Opinion. *Washington Post*. https://www.washingtonpost.com/opinions/2021/06/14/bogusbacklash-against-progressive-prosecutors/

Berryessa, C. M., & Reeves, J. (2020). The perceptions of juvenile judges regarding adolescent development in evaluating juvenile competency. *Journal of Criminal Law and Criminology*, *110*(3), 551–592.

Birckhead, T. (2017). The racialization of juvenile justice and the role of the defense attorney. *Boston College Law Review*, *58*(2), 379.

Bishop, D. M. (2006). Public opinion and juvenile justice policy: Myths and misconceptions. *Criminology and Public Policy*, *5*, 653–664.

Bishop, D. M. (2000). Juvenile offenders in the adult criminal justice system. *Crime and Justice*, *27*, 81–167.

Bishop, D. M., Frazier, C. E., Lanza-Kaduce, L., & Winner, L. (1996). The transfer of juveniles to criminal court: Does it make a difference? *Crime & Delinquency*, *42*(2), 171–191.

Bishop, D., & Frazier, C. (2000). Consequences of transfer. In J. Fagan & F. E. Zimring (Eds.), *The changing borders of juvenile justice: Transfer of adolescents to the criminal court* (pp. 227–276).

Blumstein, A. (1995). Youth violence, guns and the illicit drug industry. *Journal of Criminal Law and Criminology (1973-)*, *86*(1), 10–36.

Bogert, C. (2020). *Analysis: How the media created a "superpredator" myth that harmed a generation of Black youth*. https://www.nbcnews.com/news/us-news/analysis-how-media-created-superpredator-myth-harmed-generation-black-youth-n1248101

Bonnie, R. J. (1992). The competence of criminal defendants: Beyond Dusky and Drope. *University of Miami Law Review*, *47*, 539.

Bonnie, R. J., Johnson, R. L., Chemers, B. M., & Schuck, J. (2013). *Reforming juvenile justice: A developmental approach*. National Academies Press.

Boykin v. Alabama (1969), 395 U.S. 238

Brady v. United States (1970), 397 U.S. 742

Bridges, G., & Steen, S. (1998). Racial disparities in official assessments of juvenile offenders: Attributional stereotypes as mediating mecha- nisms. *American Sociological Review, 63*, 554–570.

Bryant, A., Matthews, G., & Wilhelmsen, B. (2015). Assessing the legitimacy of competence to stand trial in juvenile court: The practice of CST with and without statutory law. *Criminal Justice Policy Review, 26*(4), 371–399.

Butts, J.A., & Mitchell, O. (2000). *Brick by brick: Dismantling the border between juvenile and adult justice*. In C. M. Friel (Ed.), *Boundary changes in criminal justice organizations* (pp. 167–213). Washington, DC: U.S.

Cauffman, E., & Steinberg, L. (2012). Emerging findings from research on adolescent development and juvenile justice. *Victims & Offenders, 7*(4), 428–449.

Chesney-Lind, M., & Mauer, M. (Eds.). (2003). *Invisible punishment: The collateral consequences of mass imprisonment*. New Press.

Council of State Governments. (n.d.). *National inventory of the collateral consequences of conviction*. https://niccc.csgjusticecenter.org

Cullen, J. (2018). *Sentencing laws and how they contribute to mass incarceration*. Brennan Center for Justice. https://www.brennancenter.org/our-work/analysis-opinion/sentencing-laws-and-how they-contribute-mass-incarceration

Cunningham, K. A. (2020). Advances in juvenile adjudicative competence: A 10-year update. *Behavioral Sciences & the Law, 38*(4), 406–420.

Daftary-Kapur, T., & Zottoli, T. M. (2014). A first look at the plea deal experiences of juveniles charged in adult court. *International Journal of Forensic Mental Health, 13*(4), 323–336.

Daftary-Kapur, T., Zottoli, T. (2020). Resentencing of Juvenile Lifers: The Philadelphia Experience. https://www.msudecisionmakinglab.com/philadelphia-juvenile-lifers

Debele, G. A., & Debele, G. A. (1987). The due process revolution and the juvenile court: The matter of race in the historical evolution of doctrine. *Law & Inequality: A Journal of Theory and Practice, 5. 513 -548*.

Dervan, L. E. (2012). Bargained Justice: Plea-Bargaining's Innocence Problem and the Bradys Safety-Value. *Utah L. Rev.*, 51- 97.

Dervan, L. E., & Edkins, V. A. (2013). The innocent defendant's dilemma: an innovative empirical study of plea bargaining's innocence problem. Journal of Criminal Law and Criminology, *103*(1), 1–48.

Devers, L. (2011). Plea and charge bargaining. *Research summary, 1*, 1–6. https://fluxconsole.com/files/item/663/85127/PleaBargainingResearchSummary(1).pdf

DiLulio, J. (1995). The coming of the super-predators. *Washington Examiner*. https://www.washingtonexaminer.com/weekly-standard/the-coming-of-the-super-predators

Drizin, S. A., & Luloff, G. (2007). Are juvenile courts a breeding ground for wrongful convictions? *Northern Kentucky Law Review, 34*, 257–322.

Drope v. Missouri, 420 U.S. 162 (1975).

Dusky v. United States, 362 U.S. 402 (1960).

Etienne, M. (2018). Managing parents: Navigating parental rights in juvenile cases. *Conn. L. Rev., 50*, 61–90.

Fagan, J., & Zimring, F. E. (Eds.). (2000). *The changing borders of juvenile justice: Transfer of adolescents to the criminal court*. University of Chicago Press.

Fagan, J. (1996). The comparative advantage of juvenile versus criminal court sanctions on recidivism among adolescent felony offenders. *Law & Policy, 18*(1-2), 77–114.

Fairchild, A. J., Gupta-Kagan, J., & Andersen, T. S. (2019). Operationalizing intake: Variations in juvenile court intake procedures and their implications. *Children and Youth Services Review, 102*, 91–101.

Fedders, B. (2010). Losing hold of the guiding hand: Ineffective assistance of counsel in juvenile delinquency representation. *Lewis & Clark Law Review, 14*, 771–820.

Feierman, J., Mozaffar, N., Goldstein, N., & Haney-Caron, E. (2018). *The price of justice: The high cost of "free" counsel for youth in the juvenile justice system*. Juvenile Law Center.

Feinstein, R. (2015). A qualitative analysis of police interactions and disproportionate minority contact. *Journal of Ethnicity in Criminal Justice, 13*(2), 159–178.

Feld, B. C. (2017a). Competence and culpability: Delinquents in juvenile courts, youths in criminal courts. *Minnesota Law Review, 102*(2), 473–576.

Feld, B. C. (2020). Race, Politics, and the Criminalizing of Juvenile Justice: Changing Conceptions of Adolescents' Competence and Culpability. In *Criminal Justice Theory, Volume 26* (pp. 143–183). Routledge.

Feld, B. C. (2017b). *The evolution of the juvenile court*. New York University Press.

Feld, B. C., & Schaefer, S. (2010). The right to counsel in juvenile court: The conundrum of attorneys as an aggravating factor at disposition. *Justice Quarterly, 27*(5), 713–741.

Ficke, S. L., Hart, K. J., & Deardorff, P. A. (2006). The performance of incarcerated juveniles on the MacArthur Competence Assessment Tool-Criminal Adjudication (MacCAT-CA). *Journal of the American Academy of Psychiatry and the Law Online*, 34(3), 360–373.

Forst, M., Fagan, J., Vivona, S. T. (1989). Youth in prisons and Training School: Perceptions and Consequences of the Treatment-Custody Dichotomy. *Juvenile & Family Court Journal*, 40 (1), 1–14.

Fountain, E. N., & Woolard, J. L. (2018). How defense attorneys consult with juvenile clients about plea bargains. *Psychology, Public Policy, and Law*, 24(2), 192–203.

Fountain, E. N., & Woolard, J. (2021). Negotiating with parents: Attorney practices in the juvenile plea bargain process. *Law and Human Behavior*, 45(2), 112.

Fox, S. J. (1969). Juvenile justice reform: An historical perspective. *Stanford Law Review*, 22, 1187–1239.

Fryer, R. G., Heaton, P. S., Levitt, S. D., & Murphy, K. M. (2013). Measuring crack cocaine and its impact. *Economic Inquiry*, 51(3), 1651–1681.

Furdella, J., & Puzzanchera, C. (2015). *Delinquency cases in juvenile court, 2013*. Juvenile Offenders and Victims: National Report Series. Office of Juvenile Justice and Delinquency Prevention.

Gideon v. Wainwright 372 U.S. 335 (1963)

Godinez v. Moran, 509 U.S. 389 (1993)

Graham v. Florida, 560 U.S. 48 (2010).

Griffin, P., Addie, S., Adams, B., & Firestine, K. (2011). *Trying juveniles as adults: An analysis of state transfer laws and reporting*. Office of Juvenile Justice and Delinquency Prevention. https://www.ojp.gov/pdffiles1/ojjdp/232434.pdf

Griffin, P., Torbet, P., & Szymanski, L. (1998). *Trying juveniles as adults in criminal court: An analysis of state transfer provisions*. Office of Justice Programs, Office of Juvenile Justice and Delinquency Prevention.

Grisso, T., Steinberg, L., Woolard, J., Cauffman, E., Scott, E., Graham, S., Lexcen, F., Dickon Reppucci, N., &. Schwartz, R. (2003). Juveniles' competence to stand trial: A comparison of adolescents' and adults' capacities as trial defendants. *Law and Human Behavior*, 27(4), 333–363.

Gustafson, K. (2009). The criminalization of poverty. *Journal of Criminal Law and Criminology*, 99(3), 643–716.

Hager, E. (2014). *The Willie Bosket case: How children became adults in the eyes of the law*. Marhshall Project. https://www.themarshallproject.org/2014/12/29/the-willie-bosket-case

Hall, G. S. (1904). Adolescence in literature, biography, and history. In G. S. Hall, *Adolescence: Its psychology and its relations to physiology, anthropology, sociology sex, crime, religion and education* (Vol. I, pp. 513–589). D Appleton & Company.

Haney-Caron, E., & Fountain, E. (2021). Young, Black, and wrongfully charged: A cumulative disadvantage framework. *Dickinson Law Review*, 125, 653–726.

Harris, M. (n.d.). *California law gives youth sentences to life without parole another chance*. National Center for Youth Law. https://youthlaw.org/publication/california-law-gives-youth-sentenced-to-life-without-parole-another-chance/

Henning, K. (2017). Race, paternalism, and the right to counsel. *American Criminal Law Review*, 54, 649–694.

Henning, K. (2018). The challenge of race and crime in a free society: The racial divide in fifty years of juvenile justice reform. *George Washington Law Review*, 86, 1604–1666.

Helm, R. K., & Reyna, V. F. (2018). Cognitive, developmental, and neurobiological aspects of risk judgments. *Psychological Perspectives on Risk and Risk Analysis: Theory, Models, and Applications*, 83–108.

Helm, R. K., Reyna, V. F., Franz, A. A., & Novick, R. Z. (2018). Too young to plead? Risk, rationality, and plea bargaining's innocence problem in adolescents. *Psychology, Public Policy, and Law*, 24(2), 180.

Hertz, R., Guggenheim, M., & Amsterdam, A. G. (2019). *Trial manual for defense attorneys in juvenile cases*. National Juvenile Defender Center.

Hockenberry, S., & Puzzanchera, C. (2020). *Juvenile arrests, 2018*. Juvenile Justice Statistics National Report Series Bulletin. https://ojjdp.ojp.gov/sites/g/files/xyckuh176/files/media/document/254499.pdf

Hockenberry, S., & Sladky, A. (2018). *Juvenile residential facility census, 2018: Selected findings*. Office of Juvenile Justice and Delinquency Prevention. https://eric.ed.gov/?id=ED615791

Hoge, S. K., Bonnie, R. J., Poythress, N., & Monahan, J. (1999). *The MacArthur competence assessment tool—Criminal adjudication*. Odessa, FL: Psychological Assessment Resources.

House Bill 1064, 102nd General Assembly, Illinois (2021). https://www.ilga.gov/legislation/billstatus.asp?DocNum=1064&GAID=16&GA=102&DocTypeID=HB&LegID=129732&SessionID=110

Howell, J. (1996). Juvenile Transfers to the Criminal Justice System: State of the Art. *Law & Policy: Volume 18*(1–2), 17–60.

In re Gault, 387 U.S. 1 (1967).

In re Winship, 397 U.S. 358 (1970).

J.D.B. v. North Carolina, 564 U.S. 261 (2011).

Jones, J. B. (2004). Access to counsel. *Office of Juvenile Justice and Delinquency Prevention*. https://doi.org/10.1037/e381692004-001

Juvenile Research and Statistics Association. (2000). *Crime and justice atlas*. https://www.jrsa.org/projects/Historical.pdf

Kent v. United States, 383 U.S. 541 (1966).

Kivisto, A. J., Moore, T. M., Fite, P. A., & Seidner, B. G. (2011). Future orientation and competence to stand trial: The fragility of competence. *Journal of the American Academy of Psychiatry and the Law Online, 39*(3), 316–326.

Kokkalera, S. S., Tallas, A., & Goggin, K. (2021). Contextualizing the impact of legal representation on juvenile delinquency outcomes: A review of research and policy. *Juvenile and Family Court Journal, 72*(1), 47–71.

Kaban, B., & Quinlan, J. C. (2004). Rethinking a "knowing, intelligent and voluntary waiver" in Massachusetts' juvenile courts. *Journal of the Center for Families, Children, and the Courts, 5*, 35–55.

Krisberg, B. A. (2018). *Juvenile Justice and Delinquency*. SAGE.

Lanza-Kaduce, L., Lane, J., Bishop, D. M., & Frazier, C. E. (2005). Juvenile offenders and adult felony recidivism: The impact of transfer. *Journal of Crime and Justice, 28*(1), 59–77.

Larson, K. A., & Grisso, T. (2011). *Developing statutes for competence to stand trial in juvenile delinquency proceedings: A guide for lawmakers*. John D. and Catherine T. MacArthur Foundation.

Lawrence, R., & Hemmens, C. (2008). *Juvenile justice: A text/reader*. Sage.

Legal Information Institute. (2021). Wex. Parens patriae. https://www.law.cornell.edu/wex/parens_patriae

Manfredi, C. P. (1998). *The Supreme Court and juvenile justice*. Lawrence, Kan.: University Press of Kansas.

McGowan, A. (2007). Effects on violence of laws and policies facilitating the transfer of juveniles from the juvenile justice system to the adult justice system: A systematic review. *American Journal of Preventive Medicine, 32*(4), 7–28.

Miller v. Alabama, 567 U.S. 460 (2012).

Miranda v. Arizona 384 U.S. 436 (1966).

Montgomery v. Louisiana, 136 S. Ct. 718, 577 U.S. 190, 193 L. Ed. 2d 599 (2016).

Myers, D. L. (2003). The Recidivism of Violent Youths in Juvenile and Adult Court: A Consideration of Selection Bias. *Youth Violence and Juvenile Justice, 1*(1), 79–101.

National Juvenile Defender Center. (n.d.). *Pleas*. https://njdc.info/pleas/

National Conference of State Legislatures (2020), Statutory Framework of Pretrial Release. https://www.ncsl.org/civil-and criminal-justice/statutory-framework-of-pretrial-release

NeMoyer, A., Goldstein, N. E., McKitten, R. L., Prelic, A., Ebbecke, J., Foster, E., & Burkard, C. (2014). Predictors of juveniles' noncompliance with probation requirements. *Law and Human Behavior, 38*(6), 580–591.

NeMoyer, A., Kellye, S., Zelle, H., & Goldstein, N. E. (2018). Attorney perspectives on juvenile and adult clients' competence to plead guilty. *Psychology, Public Policy, and Law, 24*, 171–179.

Newman, B., Merolla, J. L., Shah, S., Lemi, D. C., Collingwood, L., & Ramakrishnan, S. K. (2021). The Trump effect: An experimental investigation of the emboldening effect of racially inflammatory elite communication. *British Journal of Political Science, 51*(3), 1138–1159.

Office of Juvenile Justice and Delinquency Prevention. (2019). *Statistical briefing book*. https://www.ojjdp.gov/ojstatbb/

Olson-Raymer, G. (1983). The role of the federal government in juvenile delinquency prevention: Historical and contemporary perspectives. *Journal of Criminal Law and Criminology, 74*(2), 578–600.

Padgaonkar, N. T., Baker, A. E., Dapretto, M., Galván, A., Frick, P. J., Steinberg, L., & Cauffman, E. (2021). Exploring disproportionate minority contact in the juvenile justice system over the year following first arrest. *Journal of Research on Adolescence, 31*(2), 317–334.

Panza, N. R., Deutsch, E., & Hamann, K. (2020). Statutes governing juvenile competency to stand trial proceedings: An analysis of consistency with best practice recommendations. *Psychology, Public Policy, and Law, 26*(3), 274–285.

Peck, J. H., & Jennings, W. G. (2016). A critical examination of "being Black" in the juvenile justice system. *Law and Human Behavior, 40*(3), 219–232.

Pennington, L. (2017). Socializing distrust of the justice system through the family in juvenile delinquency court. *Law & Policy, 39*(1), 27–47.

Pickett, J. T. (2018). Using behavioral economics to advance deterrence research and improve crime policy: Some illustrative experiments. *Crime & Delinquency, 64*(12), 1636–1659.

Piquero, A. R., & Jennings, W. G. (2017). Research note: Justice system–imposed financial penalties increase the likelihood of recidivism in a sample of adolescent offenders. *Youth Violence and Juvenile Justice, 15*(3), 325–340.

Pisciotta, A. W. (1982). Saving the children: The promise and practice of parens patriae, 1838–98. *Crime & Delinquency, 28*(3), 410–425.

Puzzanchera, C., Sickmund, M., & Sladky, A. (2018). *Youth younger than 18 prosecuted in criminal court: National estimate, 2015 cases*. Pittsburgh, PA: National Center for Juvenile Justice.

Rachlinski, J. J., Johnson, S. L., Wistrich, A. J., & Guthrie, C. (2008). Does unconscious racial bias affect trial judges? *Notre Dame Law Review, 84*, 1195.

Redlich, A. D. (2016). The validity of pleading guilty. *Advances in Psychology and Law, 2*, 1–26.

Redlich, A. D., & Bonventre, C. L. (2015). Content and comprehensibility of juvenile and adult tender-of-plea forms: Implications for knowing, intelligent, and voluntary guilty pleas. *Law and Human Behavior, 39*(2), 162.

Redlich, A. D., & Shteynberg, R. V. (2016). To plead or not to plead: A comparison of juvenile and adult true and false plea decisions. *Law and Human Behavior, 40*(6), 611.

Redlich, A. D., Zottoli, T., & Daftary-Kapur, T. (2019). Juvenile justice and plea bargaining. *A system of pleas: Social science's contribution to the real justice system*, 107–131.

Redlich, A. D., Silverman, M., & Steiner, H. (2003). Pre-adjudicative and adjudicative competence in juveniles and young adults. *Behavioral Sciences & the Law, 21*(3), 393–410.

Redding, R. E. (2010). Juvenile transfer laws: An effective deterrent to delinquency? *Juvenile Justice Bulletin*. https://www.ojp.gov/pdffiles1/ojjdp/220595.pdf

Roper v. Simmons, 543 U.S. 551 (2005).

Reyna, V. F., Adam, M. B., Poirier, K. M., LeCray, C. W., & Brainerd, C. J. (2005). Risky decision making in childhood and adolescence: A fuzzy-trace theory approach. In J. E. Jacobs, P. A. Klaczynski, J. E. Jacobs, & P. A. Klaczynski (Eds.), *The development of judgment and decision making in children and adolescents* (pp. 77–106). Lawrence Erlbaum Associates Publishers.

Rodriguez, N. (2010). The cumulative effect of race and ethnicity in juvenile court outcomes and why preadjudication detention matters. *Journal of Research in Crime and Delinquency, 47*(3), 391–413.

Rodriguez, N. (2013). Concentrated disadvantage and the incarceration of youth: Examining how context affects juvenile justice. *Journal of Research in Crime and Delinquency, 50*(2), 189–215.

Samples, S. (2021, August 9). *Crime by "juvenile lifers" after prison "very rare", state says*. UpMatters. https://www.upmatters.com/news/michigan-news/crime-by-juvenile-lifers-after-prison-very-rare-state-says/?mc_cid=17114948a5&mc_eid=0f32ce0632

Sawyer, S. M., Azzopardi, P. S., Wickremarathne, D., & Patton, G. C. (2018). The age of adolescence. *Lancet Child & Adolescent Health, 2*(3), 223–228.

Schall v Martin 467 U.S. 253 (1984).

Schlossman, S. L., & Kadish, S. (1983). Juvenile justice: History and philosophy. *Encyclopedia of Crime and Justice, 3*, 961–969.

Schmidt, M. G., Reppucci, N. D., & Woolard, J. L. (2003). Effectiveness of participation as a defendant: The attorney–juvenile client relationship. *Behavioral Sciences & the Law, 21*(2), 175–198.

Scott, E., & Grisso, T. (2005). Developmental incompetence, due process, and juvenile justice policy. *North Carolina Law Review, 83*, 101–147.

Scott, E. S., & Steinberg, L. (2008). Adolescent development and the regulation of youth crime. *The Future of Children, 18*(2), 15–33. https://doi.org/10.1353/foc.0.0011

Scott, E. S., Bonnie R. J., & Steinberg, L. (2016). Young adulthood as a transitional legal category: science, social change, and justice policy. *Fordham Law Review, 85*(2), Article 12, 641–666.

Selbin, J. (2019). Juvenile fee abolition in California: Early lessons and challenges for the debt-free justice movement. *North Carolina Law Review, 98*, 401–418.

Sentencing Reform Act, Tenn. Code Ann. § 40-35-501(h)(2) (1989, current through 2021).

Snyder, H. N., & Sickmund, M. (2006). *Juvenile offenders and victims: 2006 national report*. Office of Juvenile Justice and Delinquency Prevention.

State v. Lyle, 854 N.W.2d 378 (Iowa 2014).

Sterling, R (2012) Fundamental Unfairness: In re Gault and the Road Not Taken. *Maryland Law Review, 72*, Available at SSRN: https://ssrn.com/abstract=2079767

Steiner, E. (2017). *Mandatory minimums, maximum consequences*. Juvenile Law Center. https://jlc.org/news/mandatory-minimums-maximum-consequences

Summers, A. & Redlich, A.D. (2012). Voluntary, knowing, and intelligent pleas: Understanding the plea inquiry. *Psychology, Public Policy, and Law*, 18, 626–643.

Torbet, P., Gable, R., Montgomery, I., & Hurst, H. (1996). *State responses to serious & violent juvenile crime*. Office of the Juvenile Justice and Delinquency Prevention.

Taylor, M. (2015). Juvenile transfers to adult court: an examination of long-term outcomes of transferred and non-transferred juveniles. *Juvenile and Family Court Journal, 6*(4), 29–47.

Thomas, J. M., & Wilson, M. (2018). The color of juvenile transfer: policy & practice recommendation. *Social Justice Brief - NASW.*

Troilo, M. (2018). Locking up youth with adults: An update. *Prison Policy Initiative.*

Tonry, M. (2007). Treating juveniles as adult criminals: An iatrogenic violence prevention strategy if ever there was one. *American Journal of Preventive Medicine, 32*(4, Suppl1), S3–S4.

Viljoen, J. L., Klaver, J., & Roesch, R. (2005). Legal decisions of preadolescent and adolescent defendants: Predictors of confessions, pleas, communication with attorneys, and appeals. *Law and Human Behavior, 29*, 253–277.

Viljoen, J. L., McLachlan, K., Wingrove, T., & Penner, E. (2010). Defense attorneys' concerns about the competence of adolescent defendants. *Behavioral Sciences & the Law, 28*(5), 630–646.

Viljoen, J. L., & Roesch, R. (2005). Competence to waive interrogation rights and adjudicative competence in adolescent defendants: Cognitive development, attorney contact, and psychological symptoms. *Law and Human Behavior, 29*(6), 723–742.

Viljoen, J. L., & Wingrove, T. (2007). Adjudicative competence in adolescent defendants: Judges' and defense attorneys' views of legal standards for adolescents in juvenile and criminal court. *Psychology, Public Policy, and Law, 13*(3), 204.

Ward, G. K. (2012). *The Black child-savers.* University of Chicago Press.

Warren, J. I., Jackson, S. L., & Coburn, J. J. (2016). Evaluation and restoration of competency to stand trial. In K. Heilbrun, D. DeMatteo, & N. E. S. Goldstein (Eds.), *APA handbook of psychology and juvenile justice* (pp. 489–514). American Psychological Association.

Weithorn, L. A. (2006). The legal contexts of forensic assessment of children and families. In S. N. Sparta & G. P. Koocher (Eds.), *Forensic mental health assessment of children and adolescents* (pp. 11–29). Oxford University Press.

Wingrove, T. A. (2007). Is immaturity a legitimate source of incompetence to avoid standing trial in juvenile court. *Nebraska Law Review, 86*, 488–514.

Woolard, J. L., Henning, K., & Fountain, E. (2016). Power, process, and protection: Juveniles as defendants in the justice system. *Advances in Child Development and Behavior, 51*, 171–201.

Woolard, J. L., Odgers, C., Lanza-Kaduce, L., & Daglis, H. (2005). Juveniles within adult correctional settings: Legal pathways and developmental considerations. *International Journal of Forensic Mental Health, 4*(1), 1–18.

Zimring, F. (2005). *American juvenile justice.* Oxford University Press.

Zottoli, T. M., & Daftary-Kapur, T. (2019). Guilty pleas of youths and adults: Differences in legal knowledge and decision making. *Law and Human Behavior, 43*(2), 166–179.

Zottoli, T. M., Daftary-Kapur, T., Winters, G. M., & Hogan, C. (2016). Plea discounts, time pressures and false guilty pleas in youth and adults who pleaded guilty to felonies New York City. *Psychology, Public Policy and the Law, 22*(3), 250–259.

CHAPTER 15

Alternatives to Traditional Court Processing: Diversion and Specialty Courts

Erika Fountain, Christina Ducat, and Allison Lloyd

> **Abstract**
> Informal processing is essential to juvenile courts. It directs youth away from the formal legal system and the consequences of involvement. Many youth are informally processed and placed into diversionary programs or specialty courts, yet relatively little is known about their outcomes. Youth must admit guilt to be eligible for many programs, and failure to succeed can result in youth returning to the formal court process. As a result, scholars caution that while informal processing is intended to reduce the footprint of the juvenile courts, it may actually increase the number of justice-involved youth and racial disparities in juvenile court. This is likely due, at least in part, to the fact that youth considering diversion programs are often doing so without legal counsel. This chapter describes informal processing, diversion, and specialty courts, before discussing the potential benefits and risks to youth. Recommendations for practice, policy, and research are discussed.
>
> **Key Words:** juvenile justice, diversion, specialty courts, problem-solving courts, youth justice

The juvenile courts have transitioned through several eras of reform since their inception in 1899. Initially, juvenile courts were seen as providing "treatment without trial" (Sweet, 1991, p. 396), intended to provide delinquent youth rehabilitation rather than punitive sanctions in the adult system. These courts relied on the doctrine of *parens patriae* (or the state as parent), which provided the court justification to intervene by taking on a paternal role in lieu of parental correction (National Research Council & Institute of Medicine, 2001). This justified handling juvenile cases absent the due process protections provided to adults for several decades until youth were officially afforded due process rights by the court in the 1960s (*In re Gault*, 1967). This arguably made juvenile courts procedurally similar to criminal courts. Soon thereafter, in the 1980s and '90s, policy reform efforts expanded prosecutorial power, allowing greater charging discretion and leading to more punitive charging originally avoided by the juvenile courts (Gupta-Kagan, 2018). These reforms drove more and more youth to the criminal justice system, increasing the number of youth eligible for the most punitive sanctions. The most recent shifts toward less punitive action came with the rise of behavioral and developmental neuroscience support for treating youth differently from adults and emphasizing the importance of community support in youth rehabilitation. The Supreme Court, informed by this work, began to restrict the sentencing of youth, reigning in the more punitive aspects of earlier policy changes (see *Graham v. Florida*, 2010; *Miller v. Alabama*, 2012; *Roper v. Simmons*, 2005).

Throughout its history of reforms, the original tenant of juvenile courts—rehabilitation—has remained at the forefront of the public's mind as well as in state and local juvenile justice policies. Even while punitive reforms were being codified, public support for rehabilitative efforts remained high and policymakers continued to espouse the juvenile justice system's commitment to rehabilitation (Bishop, 2006). While policy changes pushed more youth to the criminal courts, legislation has continued to emphasize the rehabilitative objective of the juvenile justice system by, for example, creating specialty courts and other diversionary programs in an attempt to reduce the negative impact of system involvement on youth (Bishop, 2006).

This chapter explores those rehabilitative alternatives that provide certain youth with informal pathways through the juvenile court system (see also Gillespie et al., this volume, for alternative courts for emerging adults). First, we begin by describing informal processing of juvenile cases including how commonly cases are handled informally by the courts and which youth typically benefit from informal case processing. We then present an overview of the various forms of alternatives to traditional prosecution available at each stage of juvenile legal system contact from prearrest to the preadjudication phase before discussing the relevant risks and benefits. Finally, we discuss the potential implications of diverting youth away from traditional prosecution as well as directions for future research and policy.

Diverting youth away from traditional prosecution is not a new phenomenon. Indeed, it could be argued the original juvenile courts themselves were developed as a way to divert youth from the more punitive and destructive sanctions rendered in criminal courts (Hinshaw, 1993; Zimring, 2000). However, diversion—or handling cases outside of formal court processing and treating youth in community-based programs—became increasingly relied upon in the 1960s as a way to protect youth from the stigmatization of being labeled delinquent (Hinshaw, 1993). Diversion was seen as such an important and necessary tool for juvenile courts that the Juvenile Justice and Delinquency Prevention Act (JJDPA) of 1974 emphasized the use of diversionary programs to keep youth out of the traditional juvenile courts (JJDPA, 1974) to protect youth from the stigmatization of being labeled delinquent.

Informal processing of juvenile cases (i.e., not filing or withdrawing a delinquency petition) is an essential tenet of today's juvenile courts (Gupta-Kagan, 2018; Mears, 2011). Informally handling juvenile cases offers cost savings and more efficient case processing for the state (Cohen & Broderick, 2016) while ideally protecting youth from a lengthy set of consequences, both direct and collateral, such as commitment, access to public benefits, housing, education, driving privileges, and employment, among others (Henning, 2004; Janssen, 2018). Informal processing allows cases that may not benefit from intensive monitoring or intervention to be diverted or to gain access to needed services without a formal record of court involvement that could hinder positive youth development and transition to adulthood (Mears, 2011).

Rates of Informal Processing

In 2019, approximately 46% of all juvenile causes were handled informally by the courts. Of those cases that were informally processed, 40% were dismissed, 15% were placed on informal probation, and 44% were assigned some "other" outcome (typically diversion; Sickmund et al., 2021). While these youth were not adjudicated delinquent and therefore not subjected to disposition hearings, they agreed to informal probation or *other* consequences such as diversion programming or a voluntary referral to social service agencies, payment of restitution or other fines, community service, or others (Hockenberry & Puzzanchera, 2021). Even youth who are initially formally processed by the juvenile courts but who are ultimately not adjudicated delinquent may experience some form of informal probation or other voluntary disposition (20% of all formally processed youth; Hockenberry & Puzzanchera, 2021). While these sanctions are not the result of being adjudicated delinquent, they still may result in legal consequences if, for example, the youth fail to comply with the agreement. Unlike formal involvement, when a youth successfully completes informal probation or other sanctions, their case is dismissed. However, if they fail to meet the terms of the agreement, their case may be reconsidered for formal processing (Mears, 2011).

Of course, informal processing is not consistently applied across youth. Typically, younger youth (15 and younger), girls, and White youth are more likely to have their cases handled informally (Hockenberry & Puzzanchera, 2021). In 2019, White youth were less likely to have their cases formally processed compared to Black, Hispanic, American Indian, or Asian youth (Hockenberry & Puzzanchera, 2021). Black youth, in particular, are also more likely to be formally processed for certain crimes such as property and drug offenses, meaning they were more likely to be petitioned for those offenses than cases involving other racial groups (Hockenberry & Puzzanchera, 2021). While these data are the most recent, they represent continuing evidence of a broader trend (Mears, 2011). In general, less punitive diversionary practices are consistently more likely to benefit White youth, youth who are younger, and girls. Larger, urban jurisdictions that rely on more complex court systems are also more likely than smaller, more rural systems to formally process youths' cases. Thus, youth living in urban areas are also less likely to benefit from alternatives to traditional court processing (Dennis, 2017).

It is also important to note that cases that are handled informally are more likely to involve lower level offenses that may be more representative of normative adolescent misbehavior (Haney-Caron & Fountain, 2021; Henning, 2013). For example, in 2019, 53% of all simple assault cases were handled informally compared to only 28% of aggravated assault cases. Similar trends can be seen where more serious cases such as burglary and motor vehicle theft are more likely to be formally processed than cases involving larceny-theft, vandalism, or trespassing (Hockenberry & Puzzanchera, 2021). In other words, alternatives to traditional prosecution are mostly reserved for youth who may be engaging in lower level offenses that are more representative of typical adolescent misbehavior and that likely do not require legal intervention. Unfortunately, many of these lower level charges may be prone to subjectivity and racial bias (e.g., simple assault, obstruction of justice, etc.; Haney-Caron & Fountain, 2021), which may explain some of the racial disparities described previously (Gupta-Kagan, 2018). For example, in South Carolina, where 27% of the population is Black or African American (U.S. Census Bureau QuickFacts South Carolina, 2021), the charge of *disturbing schools* (i.e., a discretionary charge representing any willful or unnecessary obnoxious behavior or disruption or prevention of orderly conduct in school) was grossly disproportionately applied to Black youth (76% of youth charged with this offense) before being repealed in 2018 (Haney-Caron & Fountain, 2021). Because petitioning youth for minor youthful misbehavior can result in serious, long-term consequences including military enlistment prospects, denial of financial aid, or loss of housing (Dennis, 2017), Black youth, who are more likely to be denied the benefits of diversion, may be more likely to be harshly punished and criminalized for typical adolescent misbehavior and are more likely to experience the negative impacts of justice system contact (Haney-Caron & Fountain, 2021; Henning, 2013).

An Overview of Alternatives to Formal Processing

Informal processing bypasses the official filing of a petition in juvenile court; instead, youth are expected to admit guilt before voluntarily agreeing to informal probation or diversion programming (Mears et al., 2016). About a quarter of all youth referred to the juvenile courts are diverted (Schwalbe, 2011). Diversion can take many forms and occur at various stages of the juvenile justice process, ranging from prearrest diversionary practices such as warn-and-release programs and civil citation programs to comprehensive psychosocial programming and specialty courts, among others (Mears et al., 2016; J. V. Ray & Childs, 2015; Schwalbe, 2011). Alternative pathways can also begin before police encounters, for example, when calls to police are diverted to mental health first responders (e.g., CAHOOTS, or Crisis Assistance Helping Out on the Streets programs). While there have been more calls for pre-police involvement interventions as preventative measures (e.g., Akbar, 2020), the alternative pathways discussed here will focus on interventions for youth who have already had system contact with legal actors. Such interventions can begin with police contact (e.g., civil citation programs) or can be based in the courts, such as those that are prosecutor initiated (e.g., informal probation, deferred adjudication) or that rely on judicial intervention (e.g., specialty courts).

Prearrest or Police-Led Diversion

Whether a youth comes into contact with the juvenile court system is largely (if not entirely) based on how police use their discretion. Police are gatekeepers to the juvenile justice system, while intake officers and prosecutors have discretion in determining whether to dismiss, divert, or formally process a case (Mears et al., 2016). Warn-and-release policies are the least invasive forms of police-led diversion, essentially allowing youth to avoid arrest after cautioning from police (Wilson & Hoge, 2013). Wilson and Hoge (2013) found that for youth who are low-risk offenders, minimal interventions such as warn-and-release can be more effective at reducing reoffending than traditional court processing. These findings lend support to the notion that intervening with youth who may otherwise age out of normative adolescent misbehavior may produce iatrogenic effects. That is, increased or unnecessary interaction with the legal system may increase offending in youth who are low risk. Another form of police-led diversion, civil citation policies, shifts some of the power to divert youth into programming into the hands of police, essentially allowing police to make diversion decisions in the field (J. V. Ray & Childs, 2015). The ideal goal of civil citation programs is to divert low-risk youth away from the juvenile justice system at its earliest stages to protect them from any negative repercussions of having an arrest on record. In these cases, police are given the authority to determine whether to arrest a youth or issue a civil citation. Importantly, though, is the fact that youth must admit guilt to avoid arrest. If youth admit guilt, then, as with other diversion programs, they can be punished while uniquely avoiding an arrest record (Mears et al., 2016). If the youth does not admit guilt, or if they are noncompliant with the civil citation program requirements, they can still be arrested (Nadel et al., 2018).

The first known civil citation program for youth emerged in Miami-Dade County, Florida, in 2007 as an attempt to respond to the overwhelming number of youth being referred to juvenile court for misdemeanor or low-level offenses (Mears et al., 2016). By allowing officers to issue civil citations instead of arresting youth, the program hopes to reduce or eliminate official contact with the juvenile justice system for youth accused of committing first-time misdemeanor offenses. The approach was quickly adopted throughout the state, with several states including California, Delaware, Hawaii, and North Carolina implementing similar programs shortly thereafter (Mears et al., 2016; Nadel et al., 2018).

Civil citation programs may benefit youth in a number of ways, but they are not without certain risks. First and foremost, as with all diversion programs, the goal of civil citation is to help youth avoid the negative impact of juvenile justice system involvement while still holding them accountable for their misbehavior (Sullivan et al., 2010). Theoretically, additional benefits stem from the programming itself, which is intended to reduce recidivism while improving educational and other outcomes for youth (Mears et al., 2016). Additionally, these programs are thought to also benefit the state by reducing costs and overall caseloads, allowing the juvenile justice system to prioritize interventions for more serious cases. While these benefits may be realized, critics of diversionary programming caution that, if not implemented with fidelity, it may actually lead to a net widening and iatrogenic effects for youth. For instance, these policies effectively increase the amount of discretion police have over juvenile causes, which, given their increased prominence in youth spaces (Campos-Manzo et al., 2020), increases their ability to criminalize youthful misbehavior (Henning, 2013). For example, as policing school spaces became more common, police gained greater oversight and discretion to respond to youthful misbehavior that originally had not been referred to the juvenile justice system but had been handled in schools (Dennis, 2017). While civil citation programs were introduced as an alternative, less punitive option in counties where the inclusion of school resource officers led to an increase in juvenile justice referrals (Sullivan et al., 2010), some fear civil citations may be used as a supplement, as opposed to as an alternative option. Critics caution that the mere existence of civil citation programs may lead police to intervene by arresting or diverting cases where otherwise they would have done nothing (Mears et al., 2016). Where youth are diverted, this leads to increased monitoring of the youth, making it more likely that youthful indiscretions or misbehavior is "caught" and criminalized. Furthermore, failing to successfully complete the diversion program's requirements may also trigger an official case petition that otherwise would not have existed, thereby increasing the scope of the juvenile justice system.

Unfortunately, rigorous evaluations of civil citation programs are lacking. Methodologically, these evaluations are complicated, specifically because civil citation programs target youth's first-time contact with police, meaning there is often not a clear counterfactual to reference when estimating the effectiveness of citation (Mears et al., 2016). Is the citation program providing citations to youth who would have been otherwise arrested, or are cited youth those who might otherwise have been warned and released without incurring an official record? Early quasi-experimental studies examining juvenile justice referral rates before and after the implementation of civil citation programs show mixed results (Nadel et al., 2018; Sullivan et al., 2010). One review of Florida's civil citation program found that in its first year, while most youth were successfully completing program requirements, there was only a modest effect in reducing the rate of second referrals (Sullivan et al., 2010). Later evaluations of the program, though, suggest that cited youth recidivate less often (4%) than those completing postarrest diversion programming (12%; Caruthers, 2017). In its first year, the program showed no impact on reducing disproportionate minority contact in juvenile justice or on the number of school-based referrals to juvenile justice (Sullivan et al., 2010). Moreover, recent analyses find racial disparities such that Black youth are more likely to be arrested than White youth for citation-eligible offenses (Caruthers, 2017). A later analysis of Florida's civil citation program also produced mixed results, with some counties successfully diverting youth and others experiencing net widening (Nadel et al., 2018). Importantly, Nadel and colleagues (2018) found variability across Florida counties' fidelity to implementation, which they argue contributed to the mixed findings. In some instances, they found the civil citation achieved its intended effect of diverting arrests. However, there were some, albeit fewer, counties that experienced net-widening impacts of implementing the civil citation program (Nadel et al., 2018). These findings stress the importance of implementation fidelity in achieving the program's intended diversionary goals.

Court-Sponsored Diversion
Once youth have been arrested and referred to juvenile court, intake and/or juvenile court prosecutors review referrals to determine whether there is legal sufficiency to formally process the youth's case and if that would best serve the rehabilitative goals of the juvenile court (Backstrom & Walker, 2006; Gupta-Kagan, 2018). In the late 1980s and early 1990s, swift policy changes across the United States provided prosecutors with increased charging discretion that coincided with an increase in juvenile cases being formally processed. Before then, prosecutors were often overseeing cases that others (e.g., probation or intake officers) had decided to file (Gupta-Kagan, 2018). Today, the decision to divert youth or not largely rests with the prosecutor, with some exceptions. Prosecutors are largely involved in the decision to dismiss, divert, or petition youths, with some states balancing this power between prosecutors and intake officers. For example, many states give prosecutors absolute charging discretion, some states utilize intake officers to make recommendations to prosecutors, some authorize intake officers to divert youth with prosecutorial oversight of their decision, and very few authorize intake officers to make diversion decisions on their own (Gupta-Kagan, 2018).

Court-sponsored diversion can begin at various legal time points, take many forms, and rely on increasing levels of youth monitoring. Youths' cases can be diverted through informal processing or prefiling, but prosecutors may also offer diversion programs to youth postfiling, often referred to as *deferred adjudication.* Some scholars argue that deferred adjudication is not true diversion since it occurs once a youth has been petitioned by the court. Deferred adjudication serves primarily to reduce the extent to which youth penetrate the legal system but exposes them to the adversarial process just the same and relies on continued adjudication as a consequence of program failure (Henning, 2013). However, it is included in this chapter because inherent to deferred adjudication is the potential to avoid adjudication and gain subsequent dismissal of the petition. Postarrest diversion via informal processing (typically) assigns the youth to informal programming absent any official court action. In other words, the case is never petitioned, there is no adjudicatory hearing, there is no delinquency or disposition imposed, and the youth should avoid the collateral consequences associated with juvenile adjudication (of which there are several; Gupta-Kagan, 2018). While this allows the youth to avoid a formal petition, entrance to diversion programming often requires an admission of guilt, which eliminates any chances for case dismissal (Henning, 2013; Mears, 2011. Additionally, while there is no adjudication or disposition, informal sanctions associated with diversion are meant to be agreed to voluntarily by youth, and sometimes their parents or guardians, and failure to comply is not inconsequential (Mears, 2011).

Diversion programming takes many forms and can be sponsored by prosecutors' offices, probation, community-based providers, and others (Cocozza et al., 2005). Most diversion programming relies on two features: monitoring youth behavior and service provision. However, the level to which each program relies on monitoring and/or providing services can vary dramatically. Furthermore, the availability of diversion programming in a given community is largely affected by funding, the sociopolitical environment, the target population, and the services made available by the community-based organizations present, among other factors (Cocozza et al., 2005). Juvenile prosecutors' offices may design their own diversion programming for youth that can focus on anything from truancy intervention programs to alcohol or marijuana use and even theft (Backstrom & Walker, 2006). They may also rely on outside agencies or community-based programs to develop and implement diversion programs for youth, though in those cases prosecutors' offices maintain oversight of eligibility requirements and other guidelines for youth participating in those programs (National Juvenile Justice

Prosecution Center, 2016). In general, diversion programs vary widely and may include community service, dispute resolution, restorative justice programs, peer or teen courts, other specialty courts, community-based providers, case management programs, wraparound services, mentoring, individual-based treatment, or highly structured comprehensive family-based therapeutic interventions (e.g., multisystemic therapy or functional family therapy) among other varieties (Cocozza et al., 2005; Farrell et al., 2018).

A firm evidence base for diversion programing is lacking (Mears, 2011), and what exists provides mixed results. While established interventions such as multisystemic or functional family therapy have consistently shown their effectiveness, much of this work has evaluated the utility of these programs with youth at later stages of system involvement (Schwalbe et al., 2011). Fewer studies have focused on evaluating programs for diverted youth who may be qualitatively distinct from youth at deeper ends of juvenile justice processing and likely have differing needs (Schwalbe et al., 2011). This is concerning given that a quarter or more of justice-involved youth are diverted. Schwalbe and his colleagues (2011) conducted a meta-analysis reviewing experimental and quasi-experimental evaluations of diversion programs for youth. Their findings indicated that, in general, diversion programming was no better than warn-and-release practices *or* formal court processing when looking at their ability to prevent recidivism. However, when looking at specific types of diversion programming, the results begin to distinguish between program type. For example, while case management was a commonly evaluated program, there was no evidence to support its effectiveness. However, family-based treatment programs did lead to significant reductions in recidivism (Schwalbe et al., 2011). Their work also highlights the importance of treatment implementation with fidelity to program standards. For example, restorative justice programs were beneficial in reducing recidivism, but only when they were implemented with active involvement of the researchers. Therefore, not surprisingly, programs are more effective when they have higher quality implementation (Wilson & Hoge, 2013).

Specialty Youth Courts

Specialty courts provide an alternative to traditional justice processing and are intended to be better suited to handle unique circumstances (B. Ray, 2014). For example, juvenile court is arguably one of the first specialty courts and was meant to provide an alternative to the harsh sanctions of criminal justice while more appropriately responding to youth's specific needs. Family courts and drug courts are also examples of specialty courts. These courts proliferated in the mid-1990s in part to improve efficiencies but also as an attempt to reduce incarceration (Dennis, 2017). Specialty courts were intended to provide a form of "therapeutic justice" unavailable in traditional court processing (Winick, 2003). Miami-Dade County is responsible for instituting the first specialty court in 1989 when it created the United States' first drug court (Dennis, 2017). Since then, over 3,000 specialty courts have emerged, with 388 designated as specialty youth courts (National Drug Court Resource Center, 2021). Specialty youth courts are made up of courts intended to divert youth charged with low-level offenses from formal processing such as teen or peer courts, as well as youth versions of drug and mental health courts. If realized, the benefits of specialty courts could serve as a mechanism for diverting youth away from formal processing. However, legal scholars (e.g., Meekins, 2007; Thompson, 2002) have cautioned these courts may create ethical concerns for defense attorneys, especially around protecting juvenile clients' constitutional rights. Other critics have questioned whether the prevalence of specialty courts results from their cost savings as opposed to actual benefits for youth (Dennis, 2017). Unfortunately, research examining the effectiveness of specialty youth courts is somewhat limited (Madell et al., 2013).

Juvenile Drug Courts

Juvenile drug court (JDC) programs combine case management with community-based substance abuse treatment programming. JDC interventions are intensive; youth are subjected to biweekly status meetings, family assessments, random drug testing multiple times a week, intensive case management, and requirements for regular school attendance (Hiller & Saum, 2014). Program intensiveness reduces over the course of several phases, which can take approximately a minimum of a year to complete. Youth must meet certain requirements to advance to the next phase of processing, and fully completing these programs results in the dismissal of charges or record expungement. Noncompliance throughout the program can result in the imposition of additional sanctions such as increased status review meetings or community service (Hiller & Saum, 2014). One of the major concerns with JDCs is the high attrition or failure rate; across dozens of evaluations, an average of 46% of youth failed to complete drug court programming. These youth were primarily young boys of color (Hiller & Saum, 2014), suggesting these programs are less effective for some youth.

While adult drug courts have been evaluated numerous times, rigorous research on the effectiveness of JDCs is lacking (Hiller & Saum, 2014). An evaluation of nine JDC programs found that youth referred to drug courts had worse outcomes than those in traditional probation programs (Blair et al., 2015). The same team conducted a process evaluation at these sites and found inconsistent or low adherence to evidence-based practices. Blair and colleagues (2015) partially attributed the lack of positive outcomes to a failure at the implementation stage, which may have contributed to the program's effectiveness. Earlier studies are mixed. While some JDCs did reduce youth recidivism, those effects were small, statistically significant findings and may not have been due to the drug courts alone (Hiller & Saum, 2014). In fact, positive effects on youth recidivism were typically seen in programs that combined efforts with proven strategies such as multisystemic therapy. Still, other studies show that youth who participated in JDCs were similar to control youth on postprogram recidivism and drug use outcomes (Rodriguez & Webb, 2004). As such, there are still open questions about JDCs' utility and effectiveness among scholars (Hiller & Saum, 2014).

Juvenile Mental Health Courts

Juvenile mental health courts (JMHCs) were designed and implemented in response to the common concern among juvenile justice practitioners that there are incredibly high rates of justice-involved youth with mental health needs. These rates are particularly high among detained youth, with nearly 60% of detained youth meeting diagnostic criteria for one or more psychiatric, substance, or affective disorders (Teplin et al., 2002). While there are lower rates found among nondetained youth (20%–30%), this group still exhibits high mental health needs when compared to non-justice-involved youth (Hiller & Saum, 2014). Like adult mental health courts, JMHCs' focus is on providing mental health treatment to youth while also monitoring youth behavior through probation. They oversee youth at the pre- or postadjudication stage, meaning some are used as diversion from traditional court processing while many require a guilty plea to participate (Callahan et al., 2012). These specialty courts are similar to drug courts in that noncompliance is addressed by increasing sanctions. Many of these programs are housed within juvenile courts or probation departments, meaning rewards and sanctions are often justice related. For example, sanctions could include increasing the number of hearings the youth must attend, community service, or even placement in a residential facility (Callahan et al., 2012). Incentives or rewards for adherence may involve a reduction in hearings, relaxing curfew requirements, gift cards, and the dismissal of charges (Callahan et al., 2012). While modeled after adult mental health courts, youth versions very commonly also require parental buy-in and engagement in the program and commonly include family therapy in addition to outpatient mental health treatment and case management (Hiller & Saum, 2014).

Not unlike drug courts, there is limited research evaluating the effectiveness of JMHCs. Adult mental health courts have been shown to reduce rates of rearrest among adults (Steadman et al., 2011), but it is unclear whether the same effects would be realized for youth. A recent meta-analysis of adult mental health court and JMHC evaluations reported only four effect sizes of JMHCs compared to a sample of 34 for adult mental health courts in their analyses (Fox et al., 2021. While concerningly small, this actually represents an increase in research on JMHCs given that Hiller and Saum (2014) reported only one article examining outcome effects for JMHCs. Although the existing research suggests JMHCs may have positive outcomes on youth recidivism, more rigorous studies are needed to increase the reliability of these initial findings (Fox et al., 2021). JMHCs are operating absent rigorous evidence supporting their utility, but they have not proliferated as drug courts have. While there are over 450 adult mental health courts across the United States, there are only 56 that serve youth with mental health needs across 16 states (Treatment Court Locators, 2021). Scholars have raised concerns regarding the potential for net widening and the potential for coercion and due process violations as these programs continue to emerge throughout the country absent strong support for their effectiveness (Hiller & Saum, 2014).

Teen Courts

Teen courts, also known as youth, peer, or student courts, represent a unique alternative to traditional court processing for youth accused of status offenses or who have no prior contact with the juvenile courts. Most teen courts operate under a framework of restorative justice to restore the youth, victim, and community in a prosocial way (Hiller & Saum, 2014). Like other juvenile diversionary programs, parent engagement is not uncommon and parental consent is required for youth to participate. Teen courts serve as a diversion program for youth who are referred by police, schools, or court actors at various stages of legal system involvement. They may serve a true diversionary role (i.e., if referred prearrest) but are also often an option for informal, nonpetitioned, or deferred adjudication cases (Hiller & Saum, 2014). Teen (or peer) courts are often staffed by adolescent volunteers who may serve the role of judge and/or jury in deciding how cases should be solved. While not a true adjudicative process, as an admission of guilt is already required for youth referred to teen courts, the adolescent volunteers are charged with determining the appropriate sanctions. Cases are often minor, with courts often responding to charges such as shoplifting, disorderly conduct, alcohol and curfew violations, petty theft, or criminal mischief. Peer sentencing typically requires the youth to engage in community service, future teen court jury service, restitution or fines, education classes, writing an apology to the victim, family mediation, or tours of local jails (Hiller & Saum, 2014). If youth successfully complete their disposition agreement, they can avoid a formal delinquency. However, true to the strategies of most diversion programs, failure to comply with or complete teen sentencing within time constraints can result in a return to formal processing (Norris et al., 2011).

Not unlike other specialty courts, the effectiveness of teen courts is yet to be determined. A team conducting a systematic review of teen court evaluation studies warned that the lack of rigorous studies combined with the lack of consistent programming across teen courts (among other factors) made evaluating their effectiveness incredibly difficult (Gase et al., 2016). Programming across teen courts can vary substantially, whereby some versions rely on an adult judge and others allow teen judges to oversee hearings, and some use a tribunal-style hearing and others use a peer jury model (Hiller & Saum, 2014). Evaluations of teen court effectiveness, therefore, have proven difficult and have resulted in mixed findings. In Gase and colleagues' (2016) systematic review of teen court evaluations, they found that most studies, including randomized control trials, showed no significant reduction in recidivism compared to other forms of processing. While four of the 20 studies reviewed showed positive impacts, 10 found null effects on recidivism, and one found results favoring traditional processing; the remaining studies only presented descriptive statistics (Gase et al., 2016). Like other specialty courts, teen court effectiveness is unclear. However, as teen courts are proliferating across the country, there is an increasing need to understand whether they are beneficial to youth. Some of the concerns worth examining regard the voluntary nature of teen courts, whether peer juries capitalize on peer influence in a positive way or shame youth, and whether sanctioning youth and noncompliance have a net-widening effect.

Alternatives to Informal Court Processing for Justice-Involved Youth: Risks and Pitfalls

The potential benefits of informal processing cannot be overstated. Programs that direct youth away from the formal legal system are an essential tool in reducing the negative impact of formal system processing on youth, reducing the number of youths burdened by collateral consequences, keeping youth in their communities, maintaining education continuity, and reducing the criminalization of normative adolescent misbehavior. The decision to informally process youth is also an essential tool for reducing the existing racial disparities that have plagued the juvenile system since its inception (Henning, 2013; Ward, 2012). When diversion programs are successful, they provide cost savings to the court. Furthermore, successful programming provides evidence for the use of nonlegal interventions for youth such as functional family therapy and multisystemic therapy (Cocozza et al., 2005). Scholars caution, however, that some forms of diversion and informal processes carry costs along with these advantages. For example, scholars have remarked on several risks posed by informal processing such as the potential for net widening, increasing the existing racial, ethnic, and gender disparities in the juvenile legal system, as well as due process and developmental concerns (Haney-Caron & Fountain, 2021; Mears et al., 2016).

Racial and Ethnic Disparities in Informal Processing

Police officers, intake officers, probation officers, and prosecutors have considerable discretion to determine who is arrested, is diverted, is informally processed, or receives offers for deferred adjudication. Inherent in that discretion is an opportunity to correct existing racial disparities in our legal system (see Burke et al., this volume). Black youth in particular are more likely to be arrested (Haney-Caron & Fountain, 2021) and formally processed (Hockenberry & Puzzanchera, 2021). While discretion provides an opportunity to correct racial disparities, police are more likely to use their discretion to divert White youth but not non-White youth. An examination of youth eligible for prearrest diversion found that two thirds of White youth were diverted compared to only one third of non-White youth (Ericson & Eckberg, 2016). Intake officers are similarly biased against youth of color. A Department of Justice investigation revealed that Black youth are 2.4 times as likely as White youth to be referred to juvenile court (Gupta-Kagan, 2018). These two decision points alone contribute to concerning levels of racial disparity. When combined with the cumulative disadvantage associated with prior arrest and system involvement, these disparities set Black youth up for harsher sanctions and deeper system involvement (Haney-Caron & Fountain, 2021).

Racial disparities are of particular concern in informal processing and diversion. The greatest racial disparities can be found in the arrest and referral of lower level offenses that are often eligible for alternatives to formal processing. Black youth are more likely to be arrested and charged for lower level offenses that typically represent normative adolescent misbehavior (Henning, 2013). As a result, prosecutors who are tasked with deciding whether to dismiss, divert, or petition these youth often favor formally petitioning youth of color. Therefore, if informal processing does result in net benefits for youth, then those benefits are less likely to be experienced by youth of color. While racial disparities have been consistent throughout the juvenile justice system (Ward, 2012), some suggest that as prosecutors increasingly referred more youth and diverted fewer (e.g., in the 1980s and 1990s), those disparities widened (Gupta-Kagan, 2018).

The implicit bias inherent in legal decision making has not gone unnoticed, and diversion decision making is not immune. Researchers analyzing the observations made by probation officers found it was not uncommon for officers to describe the misbehavior of youth of color as resulting from personality flaws or defects (Bridges & Steen, 1998). Conversely, those same analyses revealed that White youth's misbehavior was often described as resulting from environmental issues or family hardship. Probation officers, who are sometimes tasked with intake decision making, use these assumptions about youthful misbehavior to inform their disposition recommendations. This often resulted in harsher sanctions for youth of color.

The Potential for Net Widening

Informal processing is also at risk of perpetuating two forms of net widening. On the one hand, net-widening critics worry that diversion alternatives funnel youth whose cases may have been otherwise dismissed into the juvenile justice system. Once there, those youth are put at risk of program failure, which often results in another form of net widening—harsher sanctions and deeper system involvement resulting from being identified as higher risk because of their prior involvement. While it is true that informal processing requires there to be legal sufficiency to divert the case, it is also the case that many petitioned cases (i.e., cases that are formally processed) are ultimately dismissed by a juvenile court judge. In fact, in 2019, 27% of petitioned cases were ultimately dismissed (Sickmund et al., 2021). Had any of those cases been informally processed instead, they may have never realized the opportunity for dismissal.

While diversion programming is typically seen as an informal form of juvenile justice involvement, it would be a mistake to assume that diversion evades intensive system control or power to further punish youth. While diversion is intended to be a minimally invasive form of system involvement, it can actually expose youth to harsher sanctions (Mears, 2011). As we describe previously, with each level of informal processing—prearrest, preadjudication, and postadjudication—several important factors exist that put youth at risk of later and greater system involvement. First, youth are very commonly expected to admit guilt or take responsibility for the offense they are being charged with to gain entrance to diversion programming (Callahan et al., 2012). From a rehabilitation standpoint, this makes sense as youth cannot be rehabilitated for something they haven't done. However, this admission eliminates any chance of a later dismissal if the next factor becomes relevant (Mears, 2011). Second, attending an informal program is not without formal consequences. If youth fail to meet the program's expectations or are noncompliant in any way, they can be arrested (prearrest diversion), returned to juvenile court for formal processing (preadjudication), or adjudicated delinquent (postadjudication; Henning, 2013; Mears, 2011). Once returned to the system, these youth are identified as being higher risk. Police now recognize these youth as needing additional oversight and will more heavily monitor them, and the courts will use failed diversion to justify harsher consequences (Henning, 2013). Therefore, if diversion fails and ultimately results in a youth returning to the system and facing harsher consequences, it does not successfully serve as a diversionary mechanism for that youth but actually increases the youth's exposure to greater legal involvement.

Informal processing is not necessarily a simple, minimally invasive experience for youth where success is all but guaranteed. In fact, some programs include various expectations that may place undue burdens on youth and their families. For example, JDCs require at times multiple drug tests a week in addition to expecting youth to attend daily school, have biweekly status hearings with the judge, and attend substance abuse treatment (Hiller & Saum, 2014). In another example, Mears (2011) reports that some youth and defense attorneys would prefer a short-term placement over informal probation. At times, the sheer number of constraints and expectations placed on youth and their families are too arduous to keep up with. Indeed, informal probation may be as intensive as formal probation, and youth may be spending anywhere from several months to several years under probation monitoring (Krisberg & Austin, 1993). Additionally, the imposition of fines or restitution payments as part of informal sanctioning can create additional barriers to success for youth and their families (Haney-Caron & Fountain, 2021). Studies have shown that economic sanctions make it difficult for youth to succeed and successfully exit the system (Feierman et al., 2016), thus extending and deepening their contact with juvenile courts. Therefore, while these sanctions are informal because they can lead to dismissal, they may be just as taxing as formal sanctions. Unfortunately, it is well documented that many youth struggle to comply and successfully complete programming requirements, and typically success rates are lower among youth of color (NeMoyer et al., 2014). Some may argue that these racial disparities can be attributed to the youth themselves, but scholars have increasingly drawn attention to the structural and systemic barriers that youth of color must uniquely face and overcome to succeed in justice programming (Bridges & Steen, 1998; Fountain & Mahmoudi, 2021; Smith et al., 2009).

Taken together, informal processing is not without serious consequences, programming assigned to youth can be intensive and difficult to complete, and the efficacy of such programming is unclear. Unlike adult programming, there is a dearth of research examining the efficacy of juvenile diversion programming and other informal dispositions. Additionally, because diversion can take various forms, lacking consensus on when diversion is effective and under what parameters is of great concern (Mears, 2011; Schwalbe et al., 2011). Evaluations that do exist are often site specific and don't generalize to broader diversion categories (Wright & Levine, 2021. It is also the case that variability and inconsistency in outcome measurement makes it difficult to perfectly compare effects across programs. Given the potential risks associated with failing to complete a diversion program, it is important to ensure youth are being placed in programs that will not create more harm. If the program's efficacy is in question, then program failure shouldn't be punished with harsher sanctions and increased system involvement.

"Treatment Without Trial": The Absence of Due Process in Informal Processing

The Supreme Court extended due process rights to youth in the 1960s to protect youth from the potential overreach of state involvement. However, over half a century later, youth advocates fear diversion may also be increasing the number of youth under state control without due process protections (Henning, 2013). Youth are not typically entitled to an attorney before a petition is filed. Some states do provide youth with attorneys at intake, but they are rare (Mears, 2011). While diversion is meant to be a voluntary agreement between the youth, their parent, and the intake officer or prosecutor, it requires youth to waive several important rights to be eligible. Namely, participating in juvenile diversion requires youth to admit guilt and waive the right to trial (Henning, 2013). As a result, youth are making waiver decisions without the assistance of counsel who could advise the youth on whether diversion is in their best legal interest (Mears, 2011). Others have noted the lack of judicial oversight over informal processing decisions and have argued that this could result in innocent youth, or those who should have been dismissed, being subjected to unnecessary interventions through diversion programming (Henning, 2013). Aside from the aforementioned risks associated with diversion, subjecting youth to interventions when they are not needed not only wastes system resources but also creates future delinquency (Mears, 2011).

Many of the same developmental concerns that plague later adjudicatory decision making are relevant here and support the need for assistance of counsel at earlier, preadjudicatory stages. Younger youth—those who are more likely to be informally processed—are more suggestible to the pressure of authority figures and are more likely to acquiesce to authority figures' recommendations than adults (Grisso et al., 2003). Further, adolescents and their parents, understandably, lack the requisite legal knowledge to discern whether certain decisions are in their best legal interest or whether their case may warrant dismissal (Cavanagh & Cauffman, 2017; Grisso et al., 2003). While not technically a plea bargain, agreeing to admit guilt in exchange for admittance to diversion programming is, in practice, very similar and requires similar decision-making capacities. It is commonly shown that in situations that pit immediate benefits against long-term consequences (such as confessing to police or accepting a plea bargain), youth are more likely to prioritize the immediate benefits of legal waiver decisions and discount the longer term or negative ramifications (Daftary-Kapur & Zottoli, 2014; Fountain & Woolard, 2018; Grisso et al., 2003). When youth are presented with an option that allows them to avoid an aversive and lengthy legal process while gaining the opportunity to have their case dismissed, they are likely to overlook, or undervalue, the likelihood and consequences of program failure. Certainly, most defendants—youth or adult—will appreciate the immediate benefit of reduced sanctions and dismissal. However, youth are uniquely prone to short-sighted decision making in stressful contexts and would make these decisions even when adults might be less likely to. It is important to stress, because certainly many adults accept plea bargains, that youth are uniquely vulnerable to short-sighted decision making (Daftary-Kapur & Zottoli, 2014; Grisso et al., 2003; Redlich & Shteynberg, 2016). Whenever youth are expected to admit guilt and waive their rights, defense attorneys are essential to the process. Attorneys can educate youth and their families on their options and the strength of their case, and provide an opportunity for youth to at least consider and weigh the alternatives.

The voluntary nature of the youth's decision to participate in programming comes into question without due process protections in place. Prearrest diversion—which is often ideal—functions completely outside any due process protections or judicial oversight (Hinshaw, 1993). Unlike police warn-and-release programs, civil citation programs that expect an admission of guilt to avoid arrest may be overly coercive, and innocent youth may feel they have no real choice other than to falsely confess and admit guilt. Youth who might benefit from informal court processing should be able to access and benefit from the assistance of counsel. This is made even more salient because most nonpetitioned cases represent younger youth and lower level or status offenses. Younger youth (15 and younger) are the most vulnerable to short-sighted decision making and lacking the necessary capacities to be competent to stand trial (Grisso et al., 2003). While these decisions are preadjudicatory, they likely require similar capacities. Furthermore, it is not unreasonable to assume that some diverted youth who were alleged to have committed lower level offenses may have had their cases dismissed. A defense attorney would be better positioned to evaluate the strength of the youth's case and any potential chance for dismissal. Armed with that knowledge, youth and their parents would be better able to make an informed decision. Providing youth with due process protections could potentially ameliorate some of the racial disparities and any net widening that results from diverting cases that are more appropriate for dismissal.

Implications and Future Directions

Having alternatives to traditional court processing for youth is an important and essential part of the juvenile justice system as continued reform efforts make the system truly rehabilitative. The juvenile courts have very clear reasons for why and how youth should become involved, but exiting the system is a more ambiguous, often cyclical, process. To truly be diversionary, alternatives must reduce the footprint of the juvenile courts. Measures, therefore, should be taken to ensure they lessen instead of unintentionally expand the state control of youth. The research outlined here supports several implications for juvenile justice practice and policy and presents several interesting questions for future research to grapple with.

Informal processing is mostly available to youth being punished for low-level, often relatively harmless, adolescent misbehavior. The state should use their discretion to "systemically limit the use of courts" to punish adolescent misbehavior (Henning, 2013, p. 460). Criminalizing normative adolescent misbehavior not only bloats the juvenile justice system but also may increase future delinquency (see Haney-Caron & Fountain, 2021). Most youth who engage in typical adolescent misbehavior, even when it extends to law breaking, will age out of misbehavior (Moffitt, 1993; see Manasse & Rebellon, this volume). Further, intervening with very low-risk offenders or providing too intensive services can increase recidivism (thereby creating delinquency; Bonta & Andrews, 2007). However, even for youth who might benefit from informal processing, measures can still be taken to ensure diversionary programs do not unnecessarily extend the juvenile justice's footprint. Sanctions for failing diversion programming should not be punitive or create formal court involvement. This is especially true when programs' effectiveness is still in question as it could be the case that program failure is attributable to the program itself. Furthermore, program failure should not result in youth being considered higher risk. Youth with prior court involvements often experience harsher sanctions (Haney-Caron & Fountain, 2021), and informal processing should not be considered true prior involvement. Finally, decriminalization or the least invasive option should be used whenever possible (Dennis, 2017). For example, warn-and-release programs should be used before civil citation programs to reduce the scope of the juvenile system.

Youth should have access to counsel at intake to ensure they are admitting guilt voluntarily. In general, youth should always be able to consult with an attorney when they are subject to agreements that include any form of sanction for program failure. This is especially true when those sanctions include arrest, formal processing, being adjudicated delinquent, or formal disposition. Youth may feel compelled to admit guilt, even when innocent (Redlich & Shteynberg, 2016), if they believe they have no real option or that it is in their best legal interest. Importantly, younger youth may not consider the strength of their cases when making decisions regarding how to proceed in legal contexts (Viljoen et al., 2005). Attorney protections may ensure that youth are aware of the strength of their case, their chances at dismissal, and the chances and consequences of program failure. Attorneys may be able to caution youth against options that are known to have high failure rates since dismissal is conditional on whether the youth is successful. While diversion decisions are distinct from plea bargain decision making, they follow similar processes such that youth must admit guilt and waive their right to trial in exchange for a preferred outcome. An important difference is that the benefit is conditional and not guaranteed. Therefore, future research should explore the developmental similarities between diversion, deferred adjudication, and plea bargain decision making among youth. Research should pay particular attention to how younger youth, those who are more likely to be informally processed, manage these decisions.

The inclusion of alternatives such as diversion and specialty courts is an acknowledgment that oftentimes misbehavior does not require prosecution. They additionally represent an understanding that traditional prosecution can be unduly harmful for youth whose misbehavior is representative of normative adolescent misconduct. While the intention behind many of these alternatives may be to offer youth a rehabilitative alternative to more punitive sanctions, it is unclear how often this objective is truly met. More research is needed into the effectiveness of youth-specific diversion programs and specialty courts to ensure the promotion of positive youth development while protecting youth from harsher system pathways.

References

Akbar, A. A. (2020). An abolitionist horizon for (police) reform. *California Law Review*, *108*(6), 1781–1846.

Backstrom, J. C., & Walker, G. L. (2006). The role of the prosecutor in juvenile justice: Advocacy in the courtroom and leadership in the community. *William Mitchell Law Review*, *32*(3), 963–988. http://open.mitchellhamline.edu/wmlr/vol32/iss3/6

Bishop, D. M. (2006). Public opinion and juvenile justice policy: Myths and misconceptions. *Criminology and Public Policy*, *5*(4), 653–664. https://bit.ly/2ZS9MwV

Blair, L., Sullivan, C., Latessa, E., & Sullivan, C. J. (2015). *Juvenile drug courts: A process, outcome, and impact evaluation*. Juvenile Justice Bulletin. https://ojjdp.ojp.gov/sites/g/files/xyckuh176/files/pubs/248406.pdf

Bonta, J., & Andrews, D. A. (2007). Risk-need-responsivity model for offender assessment and rehabilitation. *Rehabilitation*, *6*(1), 1–22. https://bit.ly/3bEePUo

Bridges, G. S., & Steen, S. (1998). Racial disparities in official assessments of juvenile offenders: Attributional stereotypes as mediating mechanisms. American sociological review, 554-570.

Callahan, L., Cocozza, J., Steadman, H. J., & Tillman, S. (2012). A national survey of US juvenile mental health courts. *Psychiatric Services*, *63*(2), 130–134.

Campos-Manzo, A. L., Flores, M., Pérez, D., Halpert, Z., & Zevallos, K. (2020). Unjustified: Youth of color navigating police presence across sociospatial environments. *Race and Justice*, *10*(3), 297–319.

Caruthers, D. (2017). *Stepping up: Florida's top juvenile civil citation efforts*. Caruthers Institute. https://bit.ly/3omhpoL

Cavanagh, C., & Cauffman, E. (2017). What they don't know can hurt them: Mothers' legal knowledge and youth re-offending. *Psychology, Public Policy, and Law*, *23*(2), 141–153.

Cocozza, J. J., Veysey, B. M., Chapin, D. A., Dembo, R., Walters, W., & Farina, S. (2005). Diversion from the juvenile justice system: The Miami-Dade juvenile assessment center post-arrest diversion program. *Substance Use & Misuse*, *40*(7), 935–951.

Cohen, D. M., & Broderick, S. (2016). *New prosecutorial perspectives: A framework for effective juvenile justice*. Texas Public Policy Foundation. https://bit.ly/3BB2g6N

Daftary-Kapur, T., & Zottoli, T. M. (2014). A first look at the plea deal experiences of juveniles tried in adult court. *International Journal of Forensic Mental Health*, *13*(4), 323–336.

Dennis, A. L. (2017). Decriminalizing childhood. *Fordham Urban Law Journal*, *45*(1), 1–44. https://ir.lawnet.fordham.edu/ulj/vol45/iss1/1

Ericson, R. D., & Eckberg, D. A. (2016). Racial disparity in juvenile diversion: The impact of focal concerns & organizational coupling. *Race and Justice*, *6*(1), 35–56.

Farrell, J., Betsinger, A., & Hammond, P. (2018). *Best practices in youth diversion*. Institute for Innovation & Implementation. https://bit.ly/3EJJaxk

Feierman, J., Goldstein, N., Haney-Caron, E., & Fairfax Columbo, J. (2016). *Debtors' prison for kids? The high cost of fines & fees in the juvenile justice system*. Juvenile Law Center. https://bit.ly/3wAaTNH

Fountain, E. N., & Mahmoudi, D. (2021). Mapping juvenile justice: Identifying existing structural barriers to accessing probation services. *American Journal of Community Psychology*, *67*(1–2), 116–129.

Fountain, E. N., & Woolard, J. L. (2018). How defense attorneys consult with juvenile clients about plea bargains. *Psychology, Public Policy, and Law*, *24*(2), 192–203.

Fox, B., Miley, L. N., Kortright, K. E., & Wetsman, R. J. (2021). Assessing the effect of mental health courts on adult and juvenile recidivism: A meta-analysis. *American Journal of Criminal Justice*, *46*(4), 644–664.

Gase, L. N., Schooley, T., DeFosset, A., Stoll, M. A., & Kuo, T. (2016). The impact of teen courts on youth outcomes: A systematic review. *Adolescent Research Review*, *1*(1), 51–67.

Graham v. Florida, 560 US 48 (2010).

Grisso, T., Steinberg, L., Woolard, J., Cauffman, E., Scott, E., Graham, S., Lexcen, F., Reppucci, N. D., & Schwartz, R. (2003). Juveniles' competence to stand trial: A comparison of adolescents' and adults' capacities as trial defendants. *Law and Human Behavior, 27*(4), 333–363.

Gupta-Kagan, J. (2018). Rethinking family-court prosecutors: Elected and agency prosecutors and prosecutorial discretion in juvenile delinquency and child protection cases. *University of Chicago Law Review, 85*(3), 743–825.

Haney-Caron, E., & Fountain, E. (2021). Young, black, and wrongfully charged: A Cumulative Disadvantage Framework. *Dickinson Law Review, 125*(3), 653–726. https://ideas.dickinsonlaw.psu.edu/dlr/vol125/iss3/3

Henning, K. (2004). Eroding confidentiality in delinquency proceedings: Should schools and public housing authorities be notified. *New York University Law Review, 79*(2), 520–611. https://scholarship.law.georgetown.edu/facpub/88

Henning, K. (2013). Criminalizing normal adolescent behavior in communities of color: The role of prosecutors in juvenile justice reform. *Cornell Law Review, 98*(2), 383–462. https://scholarship.law.georgetown.edu/facpub/1009

Hiller, M. L., & Saum, C. A. (2014). Juvenile drug courts, juvenile mental health courts, and teen courts. In A. R. Roberts, W. T. Church, & D. W. Springer (Eds.), *Juvenile justice source book: Past, present, and future* (2nd ed., pp. 215–240). Oxford University Press. https://bit.ly/3BNVPxm

Hinshaw, S. A., II (1993). Juvenile diversion: An alternative to juvenile court. *Journal of Dispute Resolution, 1993*(2), 305–321. https://scholarship.law.missouri.edu/jdr/vol1993/iss2/3

Hockenberry, S., & Puzzanchera, C. (2021). *Juvenile court statistics 2019.* National Center for Juvenile Justice. https://www.ojjdp.gov/ojstatbb/njcda/pdf/jcs2019.pdf

In re Gault, 387 U.S. 1 (1967).

Janssen, J. (2018). Collateral consequences for justice-involved youth: A model approach to reducing the number of collateral consequences. *Marquette Benefits and Social Welfare Law Review, 20*(1), 25–68. https://scholarship.law.marquette.edu/benefits/vol20/iss1/3

Juvenile Justice and Delinquency Prevention Act, P.L. 93-415, Sec. 223 (1974).

Krisberg, B., & Austin, J. F. (1993). *Reinventing juvenile justice* (Vol. 31). Sage Publications.

Madell, D., Thom, K., & McKenna, B. (2013). A systematic review of literature relating to problem-solving youth courts. *Psychiatry, Psychology and Law, 20*(3), 412–422.

Mears, D. P. (2011). The front end of the juvenile court: Intake and informal versus formal processing. In D. M. Bishop & B. C. Feld (Eds.), *The Oxford handbook of juvenile crime and juvenile justice* (pp. 574–605). Oxford University Press.

Mears, D. P., Kuch, J. J., Lindsey, A. M., Siennick, S. E., Pesta, G. B., Greenwald, M. A., & Blomberg, T. G. (2016). Juvenile court and contemporary diversion: Helpful, harmful, or both? *Criminology & Public Policy, 15*(3), 953–981.

Meekins, T. M. (2007). Risky business: Criminal specialty courts and the ethical obligations of the zealous criminal defender. *Berkeley Journal of Criminal Law, 12,* 75–126. https://www.bjcl.org/assets/files/12_1-BerkeleyJCrimL75.pdf

Miller v. Alabama, 567 U.S. 460 (2012)

Moffitt, T. E. (1993). Adolescence-limited and life-course-persistent antisocial behavior: A developmental taxonomy. *Psychological Review, 100*(4), 674–701.

Nadel, M. R., Pesta, G., Blomberg, T., Bales, W. D., & Greenwald, M. (2018). Civil citation: Diversion or net widening? *Journal of Research in Crime and Delinquency, 55*(2), 278–315.

National Drug Court Resource Center. (2021). *Treatment courts across the United States (2020).* National Drug Court Resource Center, University of North Carolina Wilmington.

National Juvenile Justice Prosecution Center. (2016). *Juvenile prosecution policy positions and guidelines.* https://bit.ly/3BGU1pJ

National Research Council & Institute of Medicine. (2001). *Juvenile crime, juvenile justice.* National Academies Press.

NeMoyer, A., Goldstein, N. E. S., McKitten, R. L., Prelic, A., Ebbecke, J., Foster, E., & Burkard, C. (2014). Predictors of juveniles' noncompliance with probation requirements. *Law and Human Behavior, 38*(6), 580–591.

Norris, M., Twill, S., & Kim, C. (2011). Smells like teen spirit: Evaluating a Midwestern teen court. *Crime & Delinquency, 57*(2), 199–221.

Ray, B. (2014). Problem-solving courts. In J. S. Albanese (Ed.), *The encyclopedia of criminology and criminal justice* (pp. 1–5). John Wiley & Sons.

Ray, J. V., & Childs, K. (2015). Juvenile diversion. In M. D. Krohn & J. Lane (Eds.), *The handbook of juvenile delinquency and juvenile justice* (pp. 422–438). Wiley Blackwell.

Redlich, A. D., & Shteynberg, R. V. (2016). To plead or not to plead: A comparison of juvenile and adult true and false plea decisions. *Law and Human Behavior, 40*(6), 611–625.

Rodriguez, N., & Webb, V. J. (2004). Multiple measures of juvenile drug court effectiveness: Results of a quasi-experimental design. *Crime & Delinquency, 50*(2), 292–314.

Roper v. Simmons, 543 U.S. 551 (2005)

Schwalbe, C. S., Gearing, R. E., MacKenzie, M. J., Brewer, K. B., & Ibrahim, R. (2011). A meta-analysis of experimental studies of diversion programs for juvenile offenders. *Clinical Psychology Review, 32*(1), 26–33.

Sickmund, M., Sladky, A., & Kang, W. (2021). *Easy access to juvenile court statistics: 1985–2019*. https://www.ojjdp.gov/ojstatbb/ezajcs/

Smith, H., Rodriguez, N., & Zatz, M. S. (2009). Race, ethnicity, class, and noncompliance with juvenile court supervision. *Annals of the American Academy of Political and Social Science, 623*(1), 108–120.

Steadman, H. J., Redlich, A., Callahan, L., Robbins, P. C., & Vesselinov, R. (2011). Effect of mental health courts on arrests and jail days: A multisite study. *Archives of General Psychiatry, 68*(2), 167–172.

Sullivan, C. J., Dollard, N., Sellers, B., & Mayo, J. (2010). Rebalancing response to school-based offenses: A civil citation program. *Youth Violence and Juvenile Justice, 8*(4), 279–294.

Sweet, R. J. (1991). Deinstitutionalization of status offenders: In perspective. *Pepperdine Law Review, 18*(2), 389–415. https://digitalcommons.pepperdine.edu/plr/vol18/iss2/8

Teplin, L. A., Abram, K. M., McClelland, G. M., Dulcan, M. K., & Mericle, A. A. (2002). Psychiatric disorders in youth in juvenile detention. *Archives of General Psychiatry, 59*(12), 1133–1143.

Thompson, A. C. (2002). Courting disorder: Some thoughts on community courts. *Washington University Journal of Law and Policy, 10*, 63–99. https://openscholarship.wustl.edu/law_journal_law_policy/vol10/iss1/5

Treatment Court Locators. (2021). https://www.samhsa.gov/gains-center/treatment-court-locator

U.S. Census Bureau QuickFacts South Carolina. (2021). *Race and Hispanic origin survey*. U.S. Census Bureau. https://www.census.gov/quickfacts

Viljoen, J. L., Klaver, J., & Roesch, R. (2005). Legal decisions of preadolescent and adolescent defendants: Predictors of confessions, pleas, communication with attorneys, and appeals. *Law and Human Behavior, 29*(3), 253–277.

Ward, G. K. (2012). *The Black child-savers: Racial democracy and juvenile justice*. University of Chicago Press.

Wilson, H. A., & Hoge, R. D. (2013). The effect of youth diversion programs on recidivism: A meta-analytic review. *Criminal Justice and Behavior, 40*(5), 497–518.

Winick, B. J. (2003). Therapeutic jurisprudence and problem-solving courts. *Fordham Urban Law Journal, 30*(3), 1055–1103. https://ir.lawnet.fordham.edu/ulj/vol30/iss3/14

Wright, R. F., & Levine, K. L. (2021). Models of prosecutor-led diversion programs in the United States and beyond. *Annual Review of Criminology, 4*, 331–351.

Zimring, F. E. (2000). The common thread: Diversion in juvenile justice. *California Law Review, 88*(6), 2477, 2479–2495. https://www.jstor.org/stable/3481221

Adolescent Incarceration: Rates, Impact, and Reform

Jodi L. Viljoen, Shanna M. Y. Li, Julia M. Schillaci-Ventura, and Dana M. Cochrane

Abstract

Adolescence is a period marked by heightened risk taking, including illegal behaviors. In response to such behaviors, thousands of adolescents around the world are held in custodial facilities every year. This chapter considers whether incarceration is an appropriate response to adolescent offending. Through a review of the literature, the chapter discusses past and present incarceration trends and examines the impacts of incarceration on recidivism, family and peer relationships, mental and physical health, psychosocial development, and victimization while in custody. It also highlights an overrepresentation of diverse groups within the justice system, including adolescents of color as well as adolescents who are transgender, gender nonconforming, and sexual minorities. Ultimately, although the quality of research is variable, the breadth of current research suggests that incarceration not only fails to reduce recidivism but also is linked to a number of additional adverse impacts. The chapter concludes by presenting strategies and initiatives aimed to reduce the incarceration of adolescents.

Key Words: adolescents, incarceration, reforms, recidivism, juvenile justice, mental health

Adolescence is widely recognized, by scholars and parents alike, to be a period of heightened risk taking (Steinberg et al., 2018). Adolescents are more likely than adults to engage in a variety of risky behaviors, including not only substance use and sexual risk taking but also offending and illegal behaviors (Chen & Jacobson, 2012; Piquero et al., 2015; see Manasse & Rebellon, this volume). This peak in risky and antisocial behavior can be traced to developmental processes (Cauffman & Steinberg, 2000). Compared to adults, adolescents are biologically predisposed to seek out novel and exciting experiences that offer immediate rewards and reinforcement (Shulman et al., 2016). They place less emphasis on long-term risks of behavior (Shulman et al., 2016), are more susceptible to peer influence (Albert et al., 2013), and are less able to control impulses (Steinberg, 2010).

As research has demonstrated, these factors help to explain the heightened rates of illegal behaviors that occur in the teenage years and early 20s (Monahan et al., 2013; Sweeten et al., 2013). As adolescents mature and gain temperance and perspective-taking abilities (Monahan et al., 2013), their offending often decreases or stops entirely (Moffitt et al., 2002). For instance, in the Pathways to Desistance Study, Mulvey et al. (2010) followed over 1,000 adolescents over a 3-year period. Even though all the adolescents in their sample had a history of serious offending, only 9% showed persistent high-level offending during the follow-up.

Given that adolescent offending is often temporary and linked to psychosocial immaturity, this raises questions about what constitutes appropriate penalties for adolescents who engage in illegal behaviors. As the U.S. Supreme Court has recognized (e.g., *Montgomery v. Louisiana*, 2016; *Roper v. Simmons*, 2005), adolescents are less culpable for their behaviors than adults. Nevertheless, many adolescents who are arrested or adjudicated are incarcerated. Indeed, by conservative estimates, at least 410,00 children and adolescents throughout the world are held in pretrial detention and postadjudication custodial facilities in a year (United Nations, 2019, p. 249).

This begs the question: Is incarceration useful and effective in deterring adolescents from reoffending, or does it interfere with healthy and prosocial development? In this chapter, we examine this question. To start, we review the rates of adolescent incarceration, historically and currently, and highlight striking racial and ethnic disparities in incarceration rates. Next, we examine the impact of incarceration on adolescents' recidivism, family and peer relationships, school and work, mental and physical health, and psychosocial development. Throughout the chapter, we use "incarceration" as an umbrella term to capture pretrial detention and postadjudication custodial placements. We use the term "adolescents" to capture people between the ages of 10 and 19 years (World Health Organization, 1989).

Adolescent Incarceration Rates: History and Current Patterns

Although society has incarcerated adolescents who have committed crimes for hundreds of years, the type of institutions in which they have been held has evolved. In the 1700s, adolescents and younger children who committed crimes were placed in almshouses, alongside adults with various problems and medical conditions (Mallet & Tedor, 2018). However, in the 1800s, as society came to conceptualize adolescence as a distinct developmental period, progressive reformers spearheaded the creation of separate age-segregated facilities called houses of refuge that housed adolescents who had committed crimes as well as adolescents who were orphaned or neglected (Feld, 2017). Many of the adolescents were poor immigrants, and most were White. Black adolescents were placed in adult correctional facilities or in separate segregated facilities for adolescents (Ward, 2012).

In the mid-1800s, reformers began to create smaller, cottagelike facilities that were euphemistically referred to as reform schools (Feld, 2017). These reform schools were often built in rural areas to remove children from corrupting influences. Despite claims that reform schools provided a homelike environment, in reality, they were prisons, and "often brutal and disorderly ones" (Kett, 1977, p. 132). Black adolescents, particularly those in the South, were often held in adult correctional facilities or leased out for labor on chain gangs (Ward, 2012).

The turn of the century was marked by the creation of a separate court system for juveniles. The first juvenile court was built in 1899 in Cook County, Illinois (Mallet & Tedor, 2018), but other states quickly followed suit (Feld, 1999). Because the juvenile court system was welfare based and intended to help adolescents and children, procedural safeguards were considered unnecessary, and incarceration was viewed as rehabilitative rather than punitive (Webster et al., 2019). As a result, juveniles (aged 18 and younger) were frequently placed in custodial facilities. From the 1940s to 1960s, rates of placement in the United States increased from 100,000 to 400,000 juveniles (Mallet & Tedor, 2018). Many facilities were overcrowded with a lack of treatment services and medical care.

In 1967, the U.S. Supreme Court ruled that the lack of procedural safeguards for adolescents was unacceptable (*In re Gault*, 1967). Through a series of court cases, adolescents were granted various due process rights, including the right to legal counsel (*In re Gault*, 1967; *In re Winship*, 1970). This recognition of due process brought a temporary decrease in adolescent incarceration rates (Mallet & Tedor, 2018). However, by the 1990s, adolescent incarceration rates were again growing at a rapid pace, fueled by growing public concern about increases in adolescent violence and sensationalized media reports depicting a new class of "juvenile superpredators." From 1991 to 1999, the number of American adolescents in residential placements increased by 41% (S. N. Snyder & Sickmund, 2006). Adolescent incarceration rates in many other countries, such as Canada (Webster et al., 2019), England and Wales (Bateman, 2017), and Scotland (Scottish Government, 2017), also increased.

Since the early 2000s, adolescent incarceration rates in the United States and elsewhere (e.g., Canada) have decreased (Webster et al., 2019). In the United States, pretrial detention rates decreased 52% between 2005 and 2018 (Hockenberry & Puzzanchera, 2020). In addition, postadjudication out-of-home placements decreased from 150,800 juveniles in 2005 to 62,1000 juveniles in 2018. However, this downward trend appears to stem primarily from a decrease in adolescent arrests in the United States rather than from a decrease in the tendency to place adolescents who commit crimes (Hockenberry & Puzzanchera, 2020). In particular, from 2005 to 2018, the proportion of adjudicated juveniles who received out-of-home placements has remained stable at 26% to 28% (Hockenberry & Puzzanchera, 2020).

Despite the overall decreases in adolescent incarceration, racial and ethnic disparities in placements have persisted. In 2005, 31% of Black adolescents, 32% of Hispanic adolescents, and 24% of Indigenous adolescents who were adjudicated received out-of-home placements as compared to 24% of White adolescents in the United States (Hockenberry & Puzzanchera, 2020). In 2018, placement rates were 32% of Black and Hispanic adolescents and 27% of Indigenous adolescents, as compared to 23% of White adolescents. According to the United Nations Global Study on Children Deprived of Liberty, the United States continues to have the highest known adolescent imprisonment rate in the world (United Nations, 2019).

Impact of Adolescent Incarceration Rates
Recidivism
Although theories of deterrence speculate that adolescents who have been incarcerated will be deterred from reoffending to avoid being locked up again, scholars have hypothesized that incarceration might instead heighten reoffense risk (Nagin et al., 2009). More specifically, custodial facilities may serve as "schools for crime" by increasing exposure to delinquent peers and severing positive influences, such as with family relationships and education (Aizer & Doyle, 2015). In addition, police might also be more likely to closely monitor adolescents with prior contacts, and adolescents may come to view themselves as criminals, leading to a self-fulfilling prophecy (see Farrington & Murray, 2014).

However, testing whether incarceration helps prevent recidivism, or conversely, worsens it, is difficult because adolescents who are incarcerated typically have a more serious offense history and are higher risk for reoffending than those who are not incarcerated (Loughran et al., 2009). This means that to truly understand the link between incarceration and recidivism, researchers need to carefully control for confounds in their study design and analyses.

Most studies, including high-quality studies that control for confounds, have found that, at best, incarcerating adolescents fails to significantly reduce recidivism (Weatherburn et al., 2009) and, at worst, it has a weak criminogenic effect, leading to slightly higher recidivism rates (e.g., Aizer & Doyle, 2015; Bontrager Ryon et al., 2013; Kraus, 1974; Walker & Herting, 2020). As an example, Loughran et al. (2009) compared recidivism rates for a sample of serious adolescent offenders, some of whom were incarcerated and others who were placed on probation. Prior to analyzing their results, they tested whether incarcerated adolescents differed from adolescents on probation on 66 variables (e.g., number of prior offenses). As expected, incarcerated adolescents had more prior offenses and scored higher on many risk factors. However, even after statistically controlling for these differences, incarceration did not reduce recidivism rates, nor were long periods of incarceration more effective in reducing recidivism than shorter periods. In another study, Bontrager Ryon et al. (2013) examined 269 adolescents placed in residential facilities to a matched sample of adolescents on probation. After controlling for adolescents' risk level, adolescents who were placed in residential facilities had a 58% probability of reconviction, whereas adolescents on probation had a 42% probability of reconviction.

Conversely, a few studies have found that incarceration appears to reduce reoffending (Hjalmarsson, 2009). However, despite some heterogeneity in findings, all four meta-analyses that have examined links between incarceration of adolescents and adults and recidivism have reported that incarceration has a null effect (P. Smith et al., 2002; Villettaz et al., 2015) or a mildly criminogenic effect (Jonson, 2010; Petrich et al., 2020). These meta-analyses reinforce the conclusion that incarceration is ineffective in deterring reoffending.

Research suggests that incarceration could be especially harmful for adolescents compared to adults. In their meta-analysis, Petrich et al. (2020) found that studies with exclusively adolescent samples showed larger criminogenic effects for incarceration than did those composed wholly of adults. However, this association was no longer significant once other variables were considered. In addition, though policy and public stakeholders seem to expect that tougher sanctions—such as incarcerating adolescents in adult facilities—will reduce the likelihood of reoffending, research indicates otherwise. Compared to otherwise similar young adults in these facilities, adolescents detained in adult facilities are more likely to engage in prison misconduct and violence (Kuanliang et al., 2008). Indeed, one report from the U.S. Department of Justice indicated that, among all inmates released from adult facilities, adolescent offenders demonstrated the highest rates of rearrest, reconviction, and return to prison with a new sentence (Langan & Levin, 2002). Beyond being seemingly counterproductive, the available evidence indicates that placement in adult facilities may adversely impact the well-being of adolescent offenders.

Families

Compared to studies on recidivism, research examining the effects of adolescent incarceration on families is scarce. Much of the current research uses qualitative methods such as interviews as opposed to rigorous experimental designs with matched community samples. However, one quantitative study, which compared institutional and community samples, found that adults who had been incarcerated as adolescents were significantly more likely to view their parents as less caring and trusting than those who had not been incarcerated as adolescents (Lanctôt et al., 2007). Qualitative studies also suggest that incarceration may negatively impact family relationships. For instance, Adams and McCarthy (2020) noted that caregivers of incarcerated male youth, especially those who were racial and ethnic minorities, often experienced cultural shaming from family members as well as isolation and self-blame for their child's offending and incarceration. In another qualitative study, Sturges and Hanrahan (2011) interviewed mothers with children involved with the justice system, including incarcerated adolescents, and found that while some mothers describe having a "good" relationship, others expressed anger about their child's criminality and fears of safety upon their return from custody.

At the same time, incarceration has also been suggested to potentially improve or make family dynamics more manageable. For instance, McCarthy and Adams (2019) interviewed caregivers of incarcerated male youth and found that the temporary removal of youth from the family environment may, in some instances, provide a moment of respite, allowing for time to reflect, recover, and rebuild family relationships.

Nevertheless, family contact via visitation or phone calls has been associated with better institutional adjustment and school performance, higher odds of reentry plans, and declines in depressive symptoms and behavioral incidents (Agudelo, 2013; Monahan et al., 2011; Ruch & Yoder, 2018). In fact, parental visitation has been found to predict declines in depressive symptoms even if adolescents characterized parent–child relationships as negative (Monahan et al., 2011).

Unfortunately, many barriers are associated with visitation. Some institutions have restricted visitation hours and families that live far away may be less likely to visit due to the time and costs associated with travel, which may disproportionately affect low-income families (see Mikytuck & Woolard, 2019; Office of Juvenile Justice and Delinquency Prevention [OJJDP], 2013). Further, likely because of disadvantage and higher poverty rates among people of color (see Jargowsky, 2015), racial and ethnic minorities have also been found to receive fewer visitations compared to their White peers (e.g., Agudelo, 2013; Mikytuck & Woolard, 2019; Monahan et al., 2011).

Peers

Not only may incarceration impact family relationships, but it might also strain adolescents' prosocial peer relationships. When adolescents are involved in the criminal justice system, they are inherently labeled as an "adolescent offender" or "delinquent." These labels may stigmatize adolescents and, in turn, make it challenging to establish new positive peer relationships upon release (Mears & Travis, 2004; Rose & Clear, 2003). As labeling theory suggests (Lemert, 1951, 1967), adolescents may internalize these labels as part of their identity, which may increase their likelihood of engaging with fellow "delinquents" (Bernburg et al., 2006).

In addition to negatively impacting prosocial peer relationships, some scholars suggest that incarceration promotes relationships with antisocial peers. According to deviant peer contagion theory, when deviant adolescents are grouped together, they mutually reinforce deviant attitudes, values, and behaviors through socializing with each other (Dishion & Tipsord, 2011; Dodge et al., 2006). The strength of this iatrogenic effect, however, has been questioned. Through a review of 18 meta-analytic studies, Weiss et al. (2005) concluded that research findings in support of peer contagion effects may be overstated due to methodological issues and marginally significant effect sizes.

Yet, more recent and methodologically sound research has found that incarceration reinforces deviant peer associations. Little (2006) found that, regardless of baseline exposure to antisocial peers, incarcerated adolescents demonstrated a significantly faster rate of exposure to, and association with, antisocial peers compared to their nonincarcerated counterparts. Additionally, compared to a matched control group from a community sample of adolescents, Basto-Pereira et al. (2018) found that adolescents with a history of justice system involvement had a significantly greater number of delinquent friends. Peer contagion effects, however, may be moderated by factors such as self-control (Gardner et al., 2008) and peer rejection (J. Snyder et al., 2010).

The negative impact that incarceration appears to have on prosocial networks may continue into adulthood. A recent longitudinal study found that, compared to the general population and other at-risk populations (e.g., chronically mentally ill persons), the average social network size for adults who were incarcerated as adolescents was quite small ($M = 1.8$ members) and dense ($M = 0.8$; Zwecker et al., 2018). In other words, as adults, incarcerated adolescents have very small, tightly knit friend networks in which nearly every member knows another person within the group.

Lastly, incarceration may strengthen gang affiliations. Through within-individual analyses, a 7-year longitudinal study found evidence suggesting that, compared to being on the street, incarceration leads to a greater likelihood of adolescent gang participation (Pyrooz et al., 2017). Indeed, within correctional facilities, the usual reasons for leaving gangs (e.g., family ties, employment) are absent (Decker et al., 2014) and programs to facilitate gang disengagement are often not available (Burman, 2012).

School and Future Employment

In addition to straining prosocial relationships, incarceration may hinder an adolescent's ability to obtain, and succeed in, prosocial opportunities such as school and work. Schools can be hesitant to allow previously incarcerated adolescents to reenroll (Aizer & Doyle, 2015), and employers are often reluctant to hire workers with a history of criminal justice system involvement (Stoll & Bushway, 2008).

Though relevant research is limited, available studies point to the possibility that adolescent incarceration leads to educational disadvantages. For instance, incarceration may hinder the development of skills necessary to succeed academically (e.g., self-governance, responsibility; Dmitrieva et al., 2012; Steinberg et al., 2004). Perhaps consequently, one study found that, compared to a matched control group of community adolescents, adolescents with a history of justice system involvement displayed significantly lower school grade achievement (Basto-Pereira et al., 2018).

These academic difficulties may snowball into low graduation rates. Indeed, even after incrementally controlling for confounding variables (e.g., sex, poverty), incarcerated adolescents are unlikely to complete high school (Aizer & Doyle, 2015). Even a short period of incarceration (i.e., 1–2 months) can negatively impact the likelihood that an adolescent will return to high school upon release (Aizer & Doyle, 2015). These educational repercussions may extend beyond high school. One study found that, compared to otherwise similar adolescents without a criminal record, adolescents who are arrested are substantially less likely to enroll in a 4-year college program (Kirk & Sampson, 2013).

Although educational and vocational opportunities are available to adolescents during incarceration, these services are subpar compared to what the general adolescent population receives. Findings from a survey of juvenile correctional agencies in all 50 states indicate that only 13 states (26%) provide incarcerated adolescents with the same types of educational services available to adolescents in the community (e.g., postsecondary courses, credit recovery programs), and only nine states (18%) provide incarcerated adolescents with access to the same types of vocational services (e.g., vocational certification programs; Council of State Governments Justice Center, 2015).

Education-related disadvantages may cascade into difficulties with employment. Most research in this area, however, focuses on individuals who were incarcerated as adults. These findings may not generalize to those with a history of juvenile incarceration. For instance, whereas research generally finds the impact of adult incarceration on future employment to be short-lived (e.g., Western & Beckett, 1999), adolescent incarceration appears to have a long-term negative effect (e.g., Fagan & Freeman, 1999; Western, 2001). Specifically, Western (2001) found that, after 15 years, men who were incarcerated as juveniles continue to exhibit higher unemployment rates than their counterparts who never were incarcerated, whereas the impact of adult incarceration appears to decay within 4 or 5 years upon release. Indeed, compared to adults with no history of incarceration, research suggests that adults who were incarcerated as adolescents hold jobs for shorter periods of time (Lanctôt et al., 2007) and are more than twice as likely to receive public assistance (Gilman et al., 2015).

Mental Health

In addition to impacting relationships, school, and employment opportunities, incarceration may have immediate and long-term impacts on adolescents' mental health. Research has demonstrated that incarcerated adolescents have higher physical and mental health needs as compared to adolescents on probation or normative samples of adolescents (Lyons et al., 2001). This may be partly due to incarcerated adolescents having higher rates of poverty, trauma, adverse childhood experiences, and more barriers to health care access (Baglivio et al., 2014). However, incarceration itself may negatively impact adolescents' health. For instance, separation from family, friends, and outside health care access may exacerbate preexisting health conditions or trigger the onset of mental illness (Ng et al., 2011).

Consistent with this possibility, some research has concluded that incarceration might indeed be linked to long-term negative impacts on adolescents' mental health. For instance, Barnert and colleagues (2017) found that compared to people who had never been incarcerated, people who had custodial placements during adolescence had higher rates of depression and suicidal thoughts, as well as poorer general health. However, research is scarce and most studies do not account for the fact that incarcerated adolescents may have preexisting risk factors for mental health difficulties, such as poverty and other adverse life experiences.

However, Gilman et al. (2015) used propensity score matching to compare adolescents who had been incarcerated to a similar sample of adolescents who had never been incarcerated. They matched adolescents on offense history, substance use, impulsivity, socioeconomic status, parental and peer criminality, and numerous protective factors such as social support. Based on their results, adolescents with incarceration experiences were approximately two times more likely to develop alcohol abuse in adulthood. However, there were no significant differences between adolescents who had and who had not been incarcerated on rates of depression, anxiety, and drug abuse during adulthood. A further study that compared a non-justice-involved sample of adolescents to a sample who had been incarcerated found that in adulthood, the previously incarcerated sample reported higher depression scores and lower self-esteem scores (Lanctôt et al., 2007).

Although incarceration could lead to long-term mental health difficulties, at the same time, some researchers have noted that, in the short term, custodial placements may serve to stabilize adolescents with chaotic lives, providing routine, structure, and access to schooling and counseling as well as a break from substance use (Monahan et al., 2011). Consistent with the hypothesis that incarceration may provide short-term stabilization, several studies have found that mental health symptoms in prison generally improve over time for most individuals, with only small groups deteriorating (Brown & Ireland, 2006; Lennox, 2014; Monahan et al., 2011). For example, Brown and Ireland (2006) found that symptoms of both anxiety and depression significantly declined from admission to follow-up at 6 weeks. However, these studies examined mental health symptoms at admission to custodial placements rather than mental health symptoms prior to custody. This is an important distinction; mental health symptoms could temporarily spike at admittance, therefore creating the misleading impression that incarceration provides stabilization of mental health symptoms.

Furthermore, rather than having a consistent impact on all adolescents, the impact of incarceration on adolescents' mental health may vary by adolescent. Gonçalves et al. (2016) found that a negative perception of the correctional climate was the largest predictor of mental health symptoms with incremental validity over personal variables such as age and history of mental illness. The small group of adolescents who had a negative perception of the custodial climate were the most likely to experience deteriorating mental health.

In addition, adolescents who are detained in adult facilities appear to be more likely to show mental health difficulties than those in juvenile facilities. In one study, adolescents in adult facilities received higher average scores on each subscale (i.e., substance use, aggression, somatic complaints, suicide ideation, thought disturbances, traumatic experiences) of a well-validated symptom inventory (i.e., the Massachusetts Youth Screening Instrument-Version 2) compared to a matched sample of adolescents in juvenile correctional facilities (Murrie et al., 2009). In a similarly designed study, Ng et al. (2011) found that even after controlling for common predictors of depression (e.g., poverty, parental criminality), adolescents in adult placements were significantly more likely to experience depression than community-based adolescents or adolescents placed in juvenile facilities. Compared to their counterparts in juvenile facilities, adolescents in adult facilities also engage in more self-harm behaviors and are at a greater risk of suicide (Austin et al., 2000; Beyer, 1997; Woolard et al., 2005).

Another major concern for the mental well-being of incarcerated adolescents is solitary confinement, in which inmates are placed alone in a small cell for between 22 and 24 hours a day, with restricted contact with peers and staff and suspension of family visits. Materials such as books, radio, or TV are also limited, therefore creating an experience of both social and sensory isolation. Despite many voices decrying this practice, including President Obama, who issued a ban on solitary confinement for juveniles in federal institutions in 2016 due to their developmental vulnerability (Eilperin, 2016), solitary confinement practices remain common in more than 20 states (Kraner et al., 2016). Studies have found that disciplinary segregation can have detrimental effects on mental health in adults, including increased risk of mental illness and suicide (Grassian, 2006; Luigi et al., 2020). However, systematic, randomized controlled studies have not examined this in adolescents.

Nonetheless, experts argue there is no reason that the findings in adults would not also apply to adolescents, and given that adolescents are still developing, the effects are likely even worse (Cauffman et al., 2018). Indeed, initial research shows that segregation is associated with increased rates of self-harm in adolescents. For instance, Kaba et al. (2014) analyzed all incarcerations in the New York City jail system between 2010 and 2013. After controlling for history of mental illness, race, and gender, individuals who were placed in solitary confinement were more likely to self-harm, and this association was even stronger in adolescents as compared to adults. Based on the authors' clinical observations and discussions with study participants, self-harm was often used to escape or defer a period of solitary confinement, highlighting the desperation some persons in custody face to avoid the extreme isolation.

Physical Health

In terms of physical health outcomes, on the positive side, some research indicates that custodial placements are linked to higher vaccination among adolescents (Udell & Mohammed, 2018). However, researchers have found that adolescents who have been incarcerated are more likely to have long-term health problems than other adolescents (Barnert et al., 2017; Schnittker & John, 2007). In a study that tracked a nationally representative sample of adolescents for 21 years, Schnittker and John (2007) found that a history of any incarceration in adolescence increased the likelihood of severe health problems causing functional limitations preventing employment. They concluded that there were no cumulative effects of the amount of time in custody or number of times incarcerated. However, these studies failed to control for potentially confounding variables like social disadvantage. Studies in adults have also found that adults who have been incarcerated experience higher mortality rates than those who have not been incarcerated (Massoglia & Pridemore, 2015). However, again, studies have failed to control for potential confounds. As such, future studies should use methodology such as propensity score matching to create better comparison groups to help determine if incarceration is a cause or correlate of physical health problems.

The COVID-19 pandemic has exposed some of the vulnerabilities of incarcerating adolescents in close confines. As of September 1, 2021, over 5,000 detained children and adolescents in the United States had contracted COVID-19 (Segule, 2021). As these statistics only represent confirmed cases of COVID-19, this figure underestimates the true prevalence rate of COVID-19 among incarcerated adolescents. Overcrowding, lack of access to hygiene and personal protective equipment, and a daily influx of new detainees can bring infections into facilities (Barnert, 2020). Furthermore, Barnert (2020) argues that many incarcerated adolescents may have weakened immune systems due to the emotional stress of prison, compounded with further social isolation due to distancing measures. If an incarcerated adolescent develops symptoms of COVID-19, the social distancing protocols may resemble solitary confinement (Barnert, 2020). Furthermore, as of September 1, 2021, few states in the United States were reporting information on COVID-19 vaccination rates for incarcerated children and adolescents, and those that were reporting this information had low vaccination rates (Segule, 2021).

Psychosocial Development
Not only might incarceration interfere with mental and physical health, but also it could delay normal developmental processes, particularly with respect to psychosocial development. Psychosocial maturity is composed of three components: temperance (the ability to inhibit impulsive and aggressive behavior), perspective (the ability to anticipate future consequences and see things from other people's perspectives), and responsibility (the ability to function independently; Steinberg, 2008). For the optimal development of psychosocial maturity, adolescents need to be in an environment where they can learn and practice their psychosocial skills (Chung et al., 2008).

However, custodial settings place adolescents in the exclusive company of other deviant peers, who will likely be unable to model good judgment or other maturity (Chung et al., 2008). Further, the aims of many custodial settings may be the opposite of what would foster the successful development of psychosocial maturity (Chung et al., 2008). For example, incarcerated individuals are meant to obey the rules without questioning, even in instances where they do not make sense or are unfairly enforced (Kummerlowe & Flanagan, 1995). Adolescents in custody also adhere to restrictive and rigid routines (i.e., set sleep, meal, and study schedules). This does not help teach adolescents the skills to be able to organize their own schedule after they are released.

Although limited research has examined the relations between incarceration and psychosocial development, what does exist hints at more short-term effects, rather than significant long-term consequences. Dmitrieva et al. (2012) tracked psychosocial maturity development in 1,000 justice-involved adolescent males over a 7-year period. They compared adolescents who experienced a secure confinement stay to adolescents who remained supervised in the community for the duration of the study. Although adolescents who were incarcerated showed slower gains in global psychosocial maturity, as well as temperance and responsibility, the total amount of time spent in custody did not impact maturity levels. In addition, the negative effects were not cumulative, and the effect was short-lived—after adolescents were released from custody, their psychosocial maturity soon matched the adolescents who remained in the community.

In addition to examining psychosocial development in general, one specific aspect of psychosocial maturity that could be impacted by incarceration is impulsivity. Bollich-Ziegler et al. (2020) examined trajectories of self-control from the ages of 10 to 25 in a longitudinal study of over 7,000 people. They found that adolescents' self-control worsened during incarceration, whereas adolescents on probation and in the community showed increases in self-control during the same period. The authors speculated that, during incarceration, incarcerated peers might encourage and model impulsive behavior, which in turn could normalize these behaviors. It is unclear if incarcerated adolescents catch up to their peers in their self-control abilities after release from custody, as this was not examined.

Finally, some research has investigated the impact of incarceration on identity development, as it could be difficult to develop a prosocial identity against the backdrop of incarceration. McCuish et al. (2018) found that most adolescents entered custody with a positive self-perception, in line with previous research that justice-involved adolescents tend to be more egotistical than others (Le Blanc, 1997). Only a small minority showed positive changes in self-perception across their stay in custody, with the authors concluding that most adolescents made efforts to maintain their antisocial identity while incarcerated (McCuish et al., 2018).

Victimization
Another potential impact of incarceration on adolescents is a heightened risk for victimization. Victimization within custodial facilities is commonplace; findings from an OJJDP survey indicated that 46% of adolescents reported having personal property stolen, 10% had been robbed, 29% had been assaulted or threatened, and 4% had been forced into sexual activity while in custody (Sedlak et al., 2013). In addition, a report by the Bureau of Justice Statistics (BJS) also found that approximately 7% of adolescents experienced sexual victimization by peers and, of particular concern, facility staff during their stay in custody (E. L. Smith & Stroop, 2019). Likewise, staff may also contribute to violent victimization through direct (e.g., physical force) and indirect means (e.g., turning a blind eye; Peterson-Badali & Koegl, 2002).

As adolescents may be waived to adult justice systems, government initiatives (i.e., the Prison Rape Elimination Act [PREA], 2003) have focused on the sexual victimization of adolescents in adult facilities. In 2004, adolescents under the age of 18 made up 1% of adult jail inmates in the United States (S. N. Snyder & Sickmund, 2006). Yet, data from the BJS indicated that in 2005, adolescents under the age of 18 accounted for 21% of inmate-on-inmate sexual violence victims in adult jail facilities (Beck & Harrison, 2006). Early research estimated that sexual victimization of adolescents was approximately five times higher in adult versus juvenile placements (e.g., Beyer, 1997; Forst et al., 1989).

Subsequent research has not confirmed these estimates. Through the PREA, the BJS (2020) is responsible for collecting and reviewing prison rape statistics within American correctional facilities. Using self-report survey data from the BJS, Ahlin and Hummer (2019) found that while 6% of those aged 16–17 were victimized sexually in juvenile facilities, approximately 2% of their peers had experienced sexual victimization in adult facilities by inmates and staff. In addition, adolescents in juvenile facilities (10%) are more likely to experience sexual victimization than adults in prisons (4%) and jails (3%; BJS, 2020). However, in light of lower than expected rates of sexual victimization in adult facilities, it is important to consider the "culture of violence" (see Ahlin, 2019). The normalization of violence and other forms of victimization in these facilities may cause reluctancy in adolescents to report abuse or seek help. Indeed, interview data indicates that although adolescents in adult facilities report lower rates of assault and criminal victimization compared to adolescents in juvenile facilities, they are substantially more likely to be afraid for their safety (Fagan & Kupchik, 2011).

Victimization in custody appears to be associated with several risk factors. Prior victimization, especially having experienced multiple types of victimization (i.e., poly-victimization; Finkelhor et al., 2007), may heighten the risk of victimization in custody. Yoder et al. (2019) found that childhood poly-victimization among 7,073 adolescents predicted physical and sexual victimization during incarceration, as well as being robbed. In addition, the relationship between early victimization experiences and adolescents' victimization during incarceration was mediated or explained by adolescents' trauma symptoms. Thus, trauma from prior victimization may exacerbate one's vulnerability to victimization in custody.

Similarly, with 8,659 adolescents, Ahlin (2021) found that sexual victimization over the past year of incarceration was significantly higher with those who had prior experiences of sexual victimization. Consistent with the adult literature, adolescents who do not identify as heterosexual were also more likely to experience victimization in custody. Interestingly, whereas gang affiliation and spending more time in custody are protective factors for adult inmates' victimization risk, adolescents who were gang affiliated and who had longer stays were at greater risk for victimization.

Impacts on Diverse Populations
Racial and Ethnic Disparities

Incarceration creates a disproportionate burden on Black, Indigenous, and other people of color (BIPOC). As reviewed previously, incarceration, for the most part, has been associated with negative outcomes including recidivism; disruptions with prosocial relationships, education, and employment; problems with health and psychosocial development; and victimization. Given that racial and ethnic minorities, particularly those who are Black, Hispanic/Latinx, and Indigenous, are disproportionately incarcerated (e.g., OJJDP, 2021a, 2021b, 2021c), it follows that a larger number of BIPOC adolescents are exposed to the harms of incarceration (Mueller et al., 2020).

Some researchers have linked disparities with differential selection and processing wherein BIPOC are more likely to be *selected* due to profiling and increased police contact in low-socioeconomic and minority neighborhoods. They may also be more likely to be *processed* given police discretion and the potential for biases to influence arrest and subsequent court decisions (Piquero, 2008). For instance, using longitudinal data with 12,752 participants, Gase et al. (2016) found that after controlling for self-reported delinquency, Black respondents were still significantly more likely to have been arrested compared to their White peers. Similarly, a meta-analysis reported that Black individuals received harsher sentences than White individuals, even after accounting for offense severity and history (Mitchell, 2005). Thus, through an accumulation of disparate processing decisions at various contact points (e.g., arrest), disparities tend to become more pronounced as adolescents are processed deeper in the system (e.g., incarceration).

Another explanation, differential involvement, asserts that BIPOC commit a greater number of crimes, particularly violent offenses, resulting in a greater likelihood of incarceration (Piquero, 2008; see also Blumstein, 1982, 1993). However, because racial and ethnic minorities have been historically (and still are) oppressed and pushed into racialized neighborhoods that continue to be disproportionately affected by poverty and crime (see Jargowsky, 2015), differences in offending behaviors are likely rooted in social inequities. Notably, these explanations are not mutually exclusive (Piquero, 2008).

Limited research has focused on BIPOC adolescents' experiences in custody. However, Mueller et al. (2020) found that non-White adolescents had significantly more infractions, and those who had more infractions also had longer seclusion times and stays. While this suggests that non-White adolescents commit more infractions, it could also reflect differential treatment by staff such that non-White adolescents may be more likely to be reported for minor infractions. In contrast, more serious infractions may be less susceptible to discretion; Boessen and Cauffman (2016) reported no significant racial or ethnic differences with adolescent institutional offending.

Moreover, research with adult inmates suggests that racial and ethnic prejudices of the broader society are often reflected inside prisons (see Goetting, 1985). Indeed, one study that interviewed 73 Black adult inmates found that, despite most having experienced positive interactions in prison, all participants also reported having experienced racial discrimination by inmates and staff (Office of the Correctional Investigator, 2013). It is therefore likely that discrimination against BIPOC adolescents is similarly common both outside of and in custody. However, research on the experiences of incarcerated BIPOC adolescents is greatly needed.

Gender and Sexual Minority Adolescents

Whereas research identifying racial and ethnic disparities has been quite extensive, comparatively limited literature has focused on adolescents who are transgender and gender nonconforming (TGNC) as well as those who are sexual minorities. Specifically, people who are TGNC have gender identities, gender expressions, and/or gender roles that do not fully align with dominant gender norms of their assigned sex at birth (see American Psychological Association [APA], 2015a, 2015b). In addition, sexual minorities have sexual orientations that do not align with societal norms of heterosexuality, such as, but not limited to, people who identify as lesbian, gay, bisexual, questioning, and queer (see APA, 2012, 2015b).

While emerging research suggests a general overrepresentation of TGNC and sexual minority adolescents within juvenile justice populations (e.g., Irvine & Canfield, 2016), a recent systematic review and meta-analysis found disproportionate involvement with sexual minority girls in particular (i.e., 31% of girls in the justice system were sexual minorities versus 16% in the community; Jonnson et al., 2019). Studies also suggest that approximately 12%–20% of incarcerated adolescents are TGNC and/or sexual minorities (e.g., Belknap et al., 2014; Irvine, 2010; Irvine & Canfield, 2016; Majd et al., 2009; Wilson et al., 2017).

Like racial and ethnic disparity research, differential involvement and differential treatment may help to explain overrepresentation with TGNC and sexual minority adolescents (Poteat et al., 2016; see Piquero, 2008). For instance, compared to cisgender (i.e., gender identity aligns with sex assigned at birth; APA, 2015b) and heterosexual adolescents, TGNC and sexual minority adolescents are more likely to have experienced child abuse, homelessness, and involvement with child welfare (Irvine, 2010). In turn, these factors may contribute to survival crimes (e.g., theft) and status offenses (e.g., truancy; Irvine & Canfield, 2016), which results in differential involvement of offending behaviors.

Differential treatment may also contribute to overrepresentation through misconceptions and biases against people who are TGNC and sexual minorities. For instance, transgender, nonconforming, lesbian, gay, and bisexual girls who deviate from feminine social norms may be perceived as more "aggressive" or "dangerous" (Wilson et al., 2017). One study found that sexual minority adolescents, and especially lesbian, gay, and bisexual girls, were more likely than their heterosexual peers to receive harsher sanctions that were disproportionate to their transgressions (Himmelstein & Brückner, 2011). Moreover, because people who are TGNC, sexual minorities, and BIPOC may all experience differential treatment, it is important to consider the intersections of race/ethnicity, sexual orientation, and gender (Crenshaw, 1989). For example, one adolescent described being Black and gay in the justice system as a "double whammy" (Majd et al., 2009, p. 23). These compounded biases may lead to extra punitive sanctions and unfair treatment.

In addition, custodial facilities may be particularly hostile environments for TGNC and sexual minority adolescents. Based on interviews with justice professionals and adolescents, Majd et al. (2009) reported that TGNC and sexual minority adolescents are exposed to "egregious conditions" (p. 5), including a lack of supportive services and trained staff, victimization and harassment based on TGNC and sexual minority status, and excessive solitary confinement under the guise of protection. Further, as facilities are often segregated by biological sex, TGNC adolescents experience an increased risk of sexual victimization. They may also be prohibited from presenting in a way that fully aligns with their gender (Irvine & Canfield, 2016). As such, these conditions call for reform within custodial facilities as well as the need for appropriate alternatives to incarceration.

Strategies to Decrease Incarceration

Over the past decade, many policymakers and advocates had made a tremendous push to reduce adolescent incarceration. Incarceration is not only ineffective but also costly. The cost of incarcerating an adolescent is more than $588 per day, or $214,620 per year for a single adolescent (Justice Policy Institute, 2020).

Law and Policy Reform

Many states and jurisdictions have enacted legal and policy reforms that aim to reduce incarceration. In the United States, at least 400 juvenile justice bills have been enacted across the 50 states since 2018 (National Conference of State Legislatures, 2020a). These law and policy reforms have taken several forms. First, to avert unnecessary contacts with the justice system, many jurisdictions have enacted laws and policies that promote diversion. As an example, in Broward County, Florida, the school board, juvenile justice agencies, and law enforcement adopted an agreement to limit school referrals to court and curb the school-to-prison pipeline (National Conference of State Legislatures, 2018).

Second, once adolescents are in contact with the justice system, several states now stipulate that custodial placements cannot be given to adolescents with misdemeanor offenses or those who are low risk for reoffending (e.g., Arkansas, Georgia, Hawaii, Texas; National Conference of State Legislatures, 2018, 2020a). In Canada, judges can only impose custodial sentences if an adolescent has committed a violent offense and has previously been found guilty and failed to comply with a noncustodial sentence (Youth Criminal Justice Act, 2002).

Third, for adolescents who are placed in custody, some states have placed limitations on the length of time an adolescent can be held. For instance, in Utah, juveniles can be placed for up to 6 months unless they are charged with certain violent felonies (e.g., aggravated sexual assault; Utah House Bill 239, 2017). In addition, to curb the use of custody for adolescents who commit probation violations, some states have developed graduated approaches or placed limits on how long an adolescent can be detained (National Conference of State Legislatures, 2018, 2020a). For instance, in Virginia, juveniles can be detained for no longer than 7 days for violating a court order (Virginia House 1437, 2020).

Fourth, there has been a significant push to close juvenile justice facilities in the United States (Harvell et al., 2020). Given that rates of adolescents in custody have decreased substantially during the past two decades, many facilities were operating below capacity. Thus, many facilities have closed. In 2000, there were 3,047 juvenile justice facilities nationwide. By 2018, the number of facilities had decreased by more than half, falling to 1,510 facilities (Puzzanchera et al., 2020).

Finally, the Supreme Court of the United States abolished the use of life sentences without the possibility of parole for juveniles convicted of offenses other than homicide (*Graham v. Florida*, 2010). Further, the Supreme Court ruled that the *mandatory* use of life-without-parole sentences in juvenile homicide cases is unconstitutional (*Miller v. Alabama*, 2012; see also *Montgomery v. Louisiana*, 2016). However, more recently, the Supreme Court ruled that life-without-parole sentences can still be imposed on juveniles who have committed homicide even if the adolescent has not been found to be "permanently incorrigible" (*Jones v. Mississippi*, 2020). Thus, life-without-parole sentences have been restricted but not entirely abolished. The United States remains the only nation in the world that sentences adolescents to life without parole (Rovner, 2021).

Justice Reinvestment Initiatives

Another strategy that states have used to reduce incarceration rates is to reallocate money that would have been spent on incarceration toward the provision of community-based alternatives (Sabol & Baumann, 2020). These justice reinvestment initiatives often require counties to pay costs to incarcerate adolescents in state institutions, reimbursing counties for instead managing adolescents in the community, and/or provide funding for community-based programs (Petteruti et al., 2009).

As an example, Ohio launched the Reasoned and Equitable Community and Local Alternatives to the Incarceration of Minors (RECLAIM) initiative (Schweitzer et al., 2017). They later extended this initiative to the most populous counties with the highest adolescent incarceration rates (Targeted RECLAIM). To deter overuse of incarceration, counties must pay a fee for incarcerating adolescents in a state institution. In addition, if they do not reduce their admission rates, they receive a financial penalty. To encourage viable alternatives to incarceration, the RECLAIM initiative provides counties with funds to implement empirically supported interventions, such as the Thinking for a Change program (Bush et al., 1997), Aggression Replacement Training (Goldstein et al., 1998), or multisystemic therapy (Henggeler et al., 1998). Although research on the effectiveness of justice reinvestment initiatives is scarce, Schweitzer et al. (2017) found that adolescents in the Targeted RECLAIM program were 2.4 times less likely than a matched comparison group to be reincarcerated during the follow-up period.

Juvenile Detention Alternatives Initiative

Besides reducing postadjudication incarceration, some foundations and advocacy groups have focused on strategies to reduce pretrial detention. In the early 1990s, the Annie E. Casey Foundation (2017) launched the Juvenile Detention Alternatives Initiative (JDAI). By 2017, this initiative had expanded to include more than 300 jurisdictions in 39 states (Annie E. Casey Foundation, 2017). The JDAI emphasizes collaboration between various stakeholders (e.g., court, probation) as well as the collection and use of data to identify and address the factors that drive the overuse and detention. As part of the JDAI, sites adopt standardized risk assessment instruments to help identify and divert low-risk adolescents from detention (Steinhart, 2006). In addition, they are encouraged to adopt alternatives to detention such as day or evening reporting centers (Mendel, 2009).

In a recent report, annual detention admissions decreased by 49% across 164 JDAI sites (Annie E. Casey Foundation, 2017). Because that report did not include comparison groups, it does not provide insight into whether detention rates decreased above and beyond existing trends toward decreased detention. However, in an earlier study, Schwartz et al. (1991) compared the detention rates at the initial JDAI (Broward County, Florida) to the rest of

Florida. They found that although detention decreased throughout the state, it decreased more in Broward County (22% decrease in detention) than in the non-JDAI sites (6% decrease). Despite overall decreases in detention rates, the Annie E. Casey Foundation (2017) observed increases in racial and ethnic disparities at JDAI sites. However, research has also found an increase in disparities in other jurisdictions (see Hockenberry & Puzzanchera, 2020). As such, because of the lack of comparison groups, it is unclear whether the JDAI is linked to increases in disparities or if this instead reflects an overall trend. Other research has found that disparities decreased following the adoption of the JDAI (Feyerherm, 2000), or no changes in racial and ethnic disparities (Carlton et al., 2017; Maloney & Miller, 2015).

Community-Based Treatment

Many efforts to reduce adolescent incarceration, including the JDAI and RECLAIM, include an emphasis on community-based treatment as an alternative to incarceration. One of the most well-known approaches, multisystemic therapy (MST), was explicitly developed to help adolescents with serious criminal behavior remain in the community. Within this approach, a therapist meets regularly with adolescents and their families in the adolescent's home (Henggeler et al., 2009). The therapist is available 24 hours a day, 7 days a week. A meta-analysis showed that adolescents who completed MST compared to the usual services showed small but significant decreases in reoffending as well as decreases in out-of-home placements (van der Stouwe et al., 2014). In one study, these effects persisted for up to 22 years (Sawyer & Borduin, 2011). Furthermore, an economic analysis in the United States found that MST led to taxpayer savings of $49,443 per adolescent in direct costs, and $199,374 per adolescent once intangible factors, such as victim suffering, were considered (Klietz et al., 2010).

Several other community-based treatment approaches, including functional family therapy (Hartnett et al., 2017), cognitive behavioral therapy (Lipsey et al., 2007), dialectical behavioral therapy (Trupin et al., 2002), certain trauma-focused interventions (Ford et al., 2012), and multidimensional treatment foster care (Åström et al., 2020), also have research support. In addition, the risk–needs–responsivity (RNR) model (Bonta & Andrews, 2017) provides a set of guiding principles for rehabilitation efforts. According to this model, adolescents should receive interventions that target their criminogenic needs or modifiable risk factors, are commensurate with their risk level, and are tailored to their individual characteristics, such as their strengths and culture. Interventions that adhere to the RNR principles are more effective in reducing recidivism than those that do not ($r = .26$ versus $r = -.02$; Andrews & Bonta, 2010).

Risk Assessment Instruments

Initiatives to reduce adolescent incarceration, such as the JDAI and RECLAIM program, often incorporate the use of risk assessment instruments. The goal of these tools is to help identify adolescents who pose a low risk for reoffending so that these adolescents can be diverted from incarceration (Steinhart, 2006). Risk assessment instruments have gained widespread use in pretrial detention, probation, and custodial settings. In probation, for instance, 42 states had adopted a standardized risk assessment instrument on a statewide basis as of 2020, five use a regional assessment, and four use a local assessment (Juvenile Justice Geography, Policy, Practice & Statistics, 2020). In addition, some states have passed legislation mandating the use of tools. As an example, legislation in Louisiana stipulates that juveniles can only be placed in secure detention if this is deemed necessary based on a risk screening instrument (National Conference of State Legislatures, 2020b).

The use of risk assessment instruments has been found to help decrease incarceration rates. In a recent meta-analysis, the adoption of risk assessment tools was associated with small but significant decreases in pretrial detention rates and in overall rates of restrictive placements for adolescents and adults (Viljoen et al., 2019). However, many of the studies in this area have serious limitations. Furthermore, the impact of risk assessment tools on incarceration rates depends on a variety of factors, such as whether the tool has been administered successfully and professionals are using it consistently and as intended (Vincent et al., 2016). Even though the use of risk assessment tools may lead to decreases in overall incarceration rates, there are growing concerns that they may decrease incarceration rates more for White adolescents than for adolescents who are BIPOC, thereby exacerbating disparities (see Vincent & Viljoen, 2020). However, research is scarce. In one study, Feyerherm (2000) found that when a risk assessment instrument was adopted as part of the JDAI, adolescent detention rates decreased by 51% for White adolescents, 55% for Indigenous adolescents, and 57% for Black adolescents, indicating a decrease in disparities (see Viljoen et al., 2019). However, Maloney and Miller (2015) found that when a tool was adopted, detention decreased at similar rates for Black, Hispanic, and White adolescents, indicating that rates of disparities did not change.

Disproportionate Minority Contact Mandate
The widespread disparities in incarceration rates have led to some targeted efforts to reduce inequities experienced by adolescents who are BIPOC. In 1988, U.S. Congress passed an amendment to the Juvenile Justice and Delinquency Prevention Act targeted at reducing disproportionate minority confinement (DMC; Leiber & Fix, 2019). Over the years, this legislation has broadened to also include disproportionate minority contact that occurs at earlier phases within the justice system, such as disparities in arrests (Kempf-Leonard, 2007). As part of this federal DMC mandate, states are required to evaluate the extent of DMC in their state (e.g., the ratio of the percentage of Black adolescents who are confined to the percentage of White adolescents who are confined), identify the underlying reasons for DMC, and implement interventions to reduce DMC (Leiber & Fix, 2019). States are also required to evaluate and monitor efforts to reduce DMC. If a state fails to show a "good-faith effort" to comply with these requirements, then the federal government can withhold up to 20% of their formula grant funding (Leiber & Fix, 2019).

Although strategies vary by state, some of the commonly used strategies to reduce DMC are to facilitate collaborations between juvenile justice stakeholders (e.g., police, judges), shift juvenile justice culture away from punitive approaches, and create alternatives to detention, such as evening reporting centers (Spinney et al., 2014). Despite the DMC mandates, overrepresentation of Black adolescents did not fall from 2005 to 2015 at the national level in the United States (Leiber & Fix, 2019). However, several studies indicate that jurisdictions that adhere to DMC interventions have been more effective in reducing DMC than those that do not. In Pennsylvania, counties that adopted DMC interventions (e.g., DMC training for police, revised risk assessment instruments) showed greater decreases in the placement of Black and Hispanic adolescents in secure facilities than counties that did not (Donnelly, 2017). In Connecticut, Black–White disparities in detention decreased following the adoption of DMC interventions (e.g., police training), but Black–White disparities in postadjudication commitment did not significantly change, nor did disparities for Hispanic/Latinx adolescents (Zane, 2021). As such, DMC continues to be a serious problem in detention settings and the larger criminal justice system (see Najdowski et al, this volume).

Conclusions
Although some studies have concluded that incarceration might bring about certain isolated benefits, such as increased opportunities to receive vaccinations (Gaskin et al., 2015) and

temporary reprieve from volatile family environments (McCarthy & Adams, 2019), in general, incarceration appears to do more harm than good. Studies with matched comparison groups demonstrate that incarceration is not only ineffective in reducing crime (Loughran et al., 2009) but also linked to increased exposure to antisocial peers (Basto-Pereira et al., 2018), increased gang affiliations (Pyrooz et al., 2017), poorer academic performance (Basto-Pereira et al., 2018), and lower graduation rates (Aizer & Doyle, 2015). In addition, custodial centers can be unsafe for adolescents—many adolescents experience victimization while incarcerated, with especially high sexual victimization rates among adolescents who are sexual minorities (Ahlin, 2021).

Some of the negative effects of incarceration, such as delays in psychosocial development, might be temporary and adolescents may catch up to peers once they are released (Dmitrieva et al., 2012). However, other negative impacts appear to be long-lasting, carrying into adulthood. For example, people who have been incarcerated as adolescents are more likely to experience long-term unemployment (Western, 2001) and receive public assistance as an adult (Gilman et al., 2015). They are also more likely to meet criteria for alcohol abuse during adulthood (Gilman et al., 2015).

Given that incarceration is both ineffective and expensive, policymakers, advocates, and researchers have worked to reduce adolescent incarceration by developing and implementing alternatives to incarceration, such as the JDAI and community-based treatment programs. However, although incarceration rates have substantially fallen since the early 2000s (Hockenberry & Puzzanchera, 2020; Webster et al., 2019), numerous problems remain, including poor conditions in adolescent custodial facilities and persistent racial and ethnic disparities in incarceration rates. To tackle these issues, several lines of work are needed.

First, researchers need to conduct high-quality studies on the impact of incarceration on short-term and long-term outcomes on adolescents' relationships, school and work, health, and well-being. Many existing studies have failed to control for confounds or use appropriate comparison groups of adolescents, making it difficult to tease apart the impact of incarceration from preexisting risk factors for adverse outcomes. Without rigorous designs and careful attention to potential confounds, this body of research may be prone to biases and lack the level of credibility needed to facilitate justice reforms.

Second, researchers should evaluate whether existing efforts to reduce incarceration are effective. An enormous amount of time, money, and effort has gone into efforts such as justice reinvestment initiatives, but surprisingly little research has examined whether these approaches achieve their intended efforts. Researchers also need to carefully evaluate if such initiatives might have unintended consequences, such as leading to greater decreases in detention for White adolescents than BIPOC adolescents (Annie E. Casey Foundation, 2017).

Third, researchers and policymakers need to work to successfully implement initiatives that have been proven to be effective (Elliott et al., 2020). Some approaches have been widely implemented. For instance, MST has been implemented in 34 states and 15 countries (Multisystemic® Services, 2021). However, despite this, evidence-based programs constitute less than 10% of programs offered in states with a listing of known programs (Lipsey, 2018). Furthermore, even when agencies have adopted supported programs and practices, problems with fidelity can occur without careful monitoring (see Elliott et al., 2020).

Fourth, researchers and practitioners need to work to improve the conditions and treatment of adolescents who are placed in custodial facilities. Given that staff play an instrumental role in either worsening or improving the treatment of adolescents in custody, improving staff training and accountability is critical. Of concern, studies demonstrate that staff sometimes contribute to the victimization and mistreatment of adolescents in their care (e.g., Ahlin &

Hummer, 2019). Conversely, staff who are perceived as helpful and dependable by incarcerated adolescents can be beneficial for reducing adolescents' fears of victimization during their incarceration (Kupchik & Snyder, 2019). Training for custodial staff should include attention to gender and sexual diversity (Majd et al., 2009) and racial and ethnic diversity (Crosby, 2016).

Finally, one of the most pressing areas will be to reduce racial and ethnic disparities in arrest and incarceration rates. Despite concerning indicators that disparities are increasing, at this point, the best strategies for reducing disparities remain unclear (Leiber & Fix, 2019).

In sum, although in many ways current practices with respect to adolescent incarceration appear better than they were in the late 1990s and 2000s when incarceration rates soared, now is not the time for complacency. For the most part, the decreasing rates of adolescent incarceration rates in the United States stem from decreases in rates of adolescent crime rather than decreases in the relative proportion of adolescents who are incarcerated (Hockenberry & Puzzanchera, 2020). This means that the next time the public's fears of crime increase, all the work that has been done to bring down adolescent incarceration rates will be at risk of coming undone. To prevent this, researchers need to build a stronger research foundation to guide sound policy decisions.

References

Adams, M., & McCarthy, D. (2020). Race and parenting in the context of youth incarceration. *Ethnic and Racial Studies, 43*(16), 175–192. https://doi.org/10.1080/01419870.2019.1686161

Agudelo, S. V. (2013). *The impact of family visitation on incarcerated youths' behavior and school performance: Findings from the families as partners project.* VERA Institute of Justice. https://www.vera.org/publications/the-impact-of-family-visitation-on-incarcerated-youths-behavior-and-school-performance-findings-from-the-families-as-partners-project

Ahlin, E. M. (2019). Moving beyond prison rape: Assessing sexual victimization among youth in custody. *Aggression and Violent Behavior, 47*, 160–168. https://doi.org/10.1016/j.avb.2019.04.002

Ahlin, E. M. (2021). Risk factors of sexual assault and victimization among youth in custody. *Journal of Interpersonal Violence, 36*(3–4), 2164–2187. https://doi.org/10.1177%2F0886260518757226

Ahlin, E. M., & Hummer, D. (2019). Sexual victimization of juveniles incarcerated in jails and prisons: An exploratory study of prevalence and risk factors. *Victims and Offenders, 14*(7), 793–810. https://doi.org/10.1080/15564886.2019.1658675

Aizer, A., & Doyle, J., Jr. (2015). Juvenile incarceration, human capital, and future crime: Evidence from randomly assigned judges. *Quarterly Journal of Economics, 130*(2), 759–803. https://doi.org/10.1093/qje/qjv003

Albert, D., Chein, J., & Steinberg, L. (2013). The teenage brain: Peer influences on adolescent decision making. *Current Directions in Psychological Science, 22*(2), 114–120. https://doi.org/10.1177/0963721412471347

American Psychological Association (APA). (2012). Guidelines for psychological practice with lesbian, gay, and bisexual clients. *American Psychologist, 67*(1), 10–42. https://doi.org/10.1037/a0024659

American Psychological Association (APA). (2015a). Guidelines for psychological practice with transgender and gender nonconforming people. *American Psychologist, 70*(9), 832–864. https://doi.org/10.1037/a0039906

American Psychological Association (APA). (2015b). *Key terms and concepts in understanding gender diversity and sexual orientation among students.* https://www.apa.org/pi/lgbt/programs/safe-supportive/lgbt/key-terms.pdf

Andrews, D. A., & Bonta, J. (2010). Rehabilitating criminal justice policy and practice. *Psychology, Public Policy, and Law, 16*(1), 39–55. https://doi.org/10.1037/a0018362

Annie E. Casey Foundation. (2017). *Juvenile detention alternatives (JDAI at 25): Insights from the annual results report.* http://www.aecf.org/resources/jdai-at-25

Åström, T., Bergström, M., Håkansson, K., Jonsson, A. K., Munthe, C., Wirtberg, I., Wiss, J., & Sundell, K. (2020). Treatment foster care Oregon for delinquent adolescents: A systematic review and meta-analysis. *Research on Social Work Practice, 30*(4), 355–367. https://doi.org/10.1177/1049731519890394

Austin, J., Johnson, K. D., & Gregoriou, M. (2000). *Juveniles in adult prisons and jails: A national assessment* (Report No. NCJ 182503). Bureau of Justice Assistance, U.S. Department of Justice. https://www.ojp.gov/pdffiles1/bja/182503.pdf

Baglivio, M. T., Epps, N., Swartz, K., Huq, M. S., Sheer, A., & Hardt, N. S. (2014). The prevalence of adverse childhood experiences (ACE) in the lives of juvenile offenders. *Journal of Juvenile Justice, 3*(2), 1–23.

Barnert, E. S. (2020). COVID-19 and youth impacted by juvenile and adult criminal justice systems. *Pediatrics*, *146*(2), e20201299. https://doi.org/10.1542/peds.2020-1299

Barnert, E. S., Dudovitz, R., Nelson, B. B., Coker, T. R., Biely, C., Li, N., & Chung, P. J. (2017). How does incarcerating young people affect their adult health outcomes? *Pediatrics*, *139*(2), e20162624. https://doi.org/10.1542/peds.2016-2624

Basto-Pereira, M., Ribeiro, S., & Maia, Â. (2018). Needs and achievements of the juvenile justice system: Insights from two empirical studies with Portuguese young adults. *International Journal of Offender Therapy and Comparative Criminology*, *62*(7), 1787–1805. https://doi.org/10.1177/0306624X17690450

Bateman, T. (2017). *The state of youth justice 2017: An overview of trends and developments*. National Association for Youth Justice. http://uobrep.openrepository.com/uobrep/handle/10547/622241

Beck, A. J., & Harrison, P. M. (2006). *Sexual violence reported by correctional authorities, 2005* (Report No. NCJ 214646). Office of Justice Programs, U.S. Department of Justice. https://2009-2017.state.gov/documents/organization/150083.pdf

Belknap, J., Holsinger, K., & Little, J. S. (2014). Lesbian, gay, and bisexual youth incarcerated in delinquent facilities. In D. Peterson & V. Panfil (Eds.), *Handbook of LGBT communities, crime, and justice* (pp. 207–228). Springer. https://doi.org/10.1007/978-1-4614-9188-0_11

Bernburg, J. G., Krohn, M. D., & Rivera, C. J. (2006). Official labeling, criminal embeddedness, and subsequent delinquency. *Journal of Research in Crime and Delinquency*, *43*(1), 67–88. https://doi.org/10.1177/0022427805280068

Beyer, M. (1997). Experts for juveniles at risk of adult sentences. In P. Puritz, A. Capozello, & W. Shang (Eds.), *More than meets the eye: Rethinking assessment, competency and sentencing for a harsher era of juvenile justice* (pp. 1–22). American Bar Association, Juvenile Justice Center.

Blumstein, A. (1982). On the racial disproportionality of United States' prisons. *Journal of Criminal Law and Criminology*, *73*(3), 1259–1281. https://doi.org/10.2307/1143193

Blumstein, A. (1993). Racial disproportionality of U.S. prison populations revisited. *University of Colorado Law Review*, *64*(3), 743–760.

Boessen, A., & Cauffman, E. (2016). Moving from the neighborhood to the cellblock: The impact of youth's neighborhoods on prison misconduct. *Crime & Delinquency*, *62*(2), 200–288. https://doi.org/10.1177/0011128713478131

Bollich-Ziegler, K. L., Beck, E. D., Hill, P., & Jackson, J. J. (2020). *Do correctional facilities correct our youth?: Effects of incarceration and court-ordered community service on personality development*. Unpublished manuscript.

Bonta, J., & Andrews, D. A. (2017). *The psychology of criminal conduct* (6th ed.). Routledge.

Bontrager Ryon, S., Winokur Early, K., Hand, G., & Chapman, S. (2013). Juvenile justice interventions: System escalation and effective alternatives to residential placement. *Journal of Offender Rehabilitation*, *52*(5), 358–375. http://dx.doi.org/10.1080/10509674.2013.801385

Brown, S. L., & Ireland, C. A. (2006). Coping style and distress in newly incarcerated male adolescents. *Journal of Adolescent Health*, *38*(6), 656–661. https://doi.org/10.1016/j.jadohealth.2005.09.005

Bureau of Justice Statistics. (2020). *PREA data-collection activities, 2020*. https://bjs.ojp.gov/content/pub/pdf/pdca20.pdf

Burman, M. L. (2012). *Resocializing and repairing homies within the Texas prison system: A case study on security threat group management, administrative segregation, prison gang renunciation and safety for all* [Unpublished doctoral dissertation]. University of Texas at Austin.

Bush, J., Glick, B., & Taymans, J. (1997). *Thinking for a change: Integrated Cognitive Behavior Change Program*. National Institute of Justice.

Carlton, M., Orchowsky, S., & Iwama, J. (2017). Assessing DMC initiatives: A case study of two states. In N. Parson-Pollard (Ed.), *Disproportionate minority contact: Current issues and policies* (2nd ed., pp. 89–116). Carolina Academic Press.

Cauffman, E., Fine, A., Mahler, A., & Simmons, C. (2018). How developmental science influences juvenile justice reform. *University of California Irvine Law Review*, *8*(1), 21–40.

Cauffman, E., & Steinberg, L. (2000). (Im)maturity of judgment in adolescence: Why adolescents may be less culpable than adults. *Behavioral Sciences & the Law*, *18*(6), 741–760. https://doi.org/10.1002/bsl.416

Chen, P., & Jacobson, K. C. (2012). Developmental trajectories of substance use from early adolescence to young adulthood: Gender and racial/ethnic differences. *Journal of Adolescent Health*, *50*(2), 154–163. https://doi.org/10.1016/j.jadohealth.2011.05.013

Chung, H. L., Little, M., & Steinberg, L. (2008). The transition to adulthood for adolescents in the juvenile justice system: A developmental perspective. In D. W. Osgood, E. M. Foster, G. R. Ruth, & C. Flanagan (Eds.), *On your own without a net: The transition to adulthood for vulnerable populations* (pp. 68–91). University of Chicago Press.

Council of State Governments Justice Center. (2015). *Locked out: Improving educational and vocational outcomes for incarcerated youth*. https://csgjusticecenter.org/wp-content/uploads/2020/01/LOCKED_OUT_Improving_Educational_and_Vocational_Outcomes_for_Incarcerated_Youth.pdf

Crenshaw, K. (1989). Demarginalizing the intersection of race and sex: A Black feminist critique of antidiscrimination doctrine, feminist theory and antiracist politics. *University of Chicago Legal Forum, 1989*(1), 139–167. https://chicagounbound.uchicago.edu/uclf/vol1989/iss1/8

Crosby, S. D. (2016). Trauma-informed approaches to juvenile justice: A critical race perspective. *Juvenile and Family Court, 67*(1), 5–18. https://doi.org/10.1111/jfcj.12052

Decker, S. H., Pyrooz, D. C., & Moule, R. K. (2014). Disengagement from gangs as role transitions. *Journal of Research on Adolescence, 24*(2), 268–283. https://doi.org/10.1111/jora.12074

Dishion, T. J., & Tipsord, J. M. (2011). Peer contagion in child and adolescent social and emotional development. *Annual Review of Psychology, 62*(1), 189–214. https://doi.org/10.1146/annurev.psych.093008.100412

Dmitrieva, J., Monahan, K., Cauffman, E., & Steinberg, L. (2012). Arrested development: The effects of incarceration on the development of psychosocial maturity. *Development and Psychopathology, 24*(3), 1073–1090. https://doi.org/10.1017/S0954579412000545

Dodge, K. A., Dishion, T. J., & Lansford, J. E. (2006). Deviant peer influences in intervention and public policy for youth. *Social Policy Report, 20*(1), 1–20.

Donnelly, E. A. (2017). The Disproportionate Minority Contact Mandate: An examination of its impacts on juvenile justice processing outcomes (1997–2011). *Criminal Justice Policy Review, 28*(4), 347–369. https://doi.org/10.1177/0887403415585139

Eilperin, J. (2016, January 26). Obama bans solitary confinement for juveniles in federal prisons. *Washington Post*. https://www.washingtonpost.com/politics/obama-bans-solitary-confinement-for-juveniles-in-federal-prisons/2016/01/25/056e14b2-c3a2-11e5-9693-933a4d31bcc8_story.html

Elliott, D. S., Buckley, P. R., Gottfredson, D. C., Hawkins, J. D., & Tolan, P. H. (2020). Evidence-based juvenile justice programs and practices: A critical review. *Criminology & Public Policy, 19*(4), 1305–1328. https://doi.org/10.1111/1745-9133.12520

Fagan, J., & Freeman, R. B. (1999). Crime and work. In M. Tonry (Ed.), *Crime and justice: A review of research* (Vol. 25, pp. 225–290). University of Chicago Press. https://doi.org/10.1086/449290

Fagan, J., & Kupchik, A. (2011). Juvenile incarceration and the pains of imprisonment. *Duke Forum for Law and Social Change, 3*, 29–61. http://dx.doi.org/10.2139/ssrn.1772187

Farrington, D. P. & Murray, J. (Eds.). (2014). *Labeling theory: Empirical tests* (1st ed., Vol. 18). Routledge. https://doi.org/10.4324/9780203787656

Feld, B. C. (1999). *Bad kids: Race and the transformation of the juvenile court*. Oxford University Press.

Feld, B. C. (2017). *The evolution of the juvenile court: Race, politics, and the criminalizing of juvenile justice*. New York University Press.

Feyerherm, W. H. (2000). Detention reform and over-representation: A successful synergy. *Corrections Management Quarterly, 4*(1), 44–51.

Finkelhor, D., Ormrod, R. K., & Turner, H. A. (2007). Poly-victimization: A neglected component in child victimization. *Child Abuse & Neglect, 31*(1), 7–26. https://doi.org/10.1016/j.chiabu.2006.06.008

Ford, J. D., Steinberg, K. L., Hawke, J., Levine, J., & Zhang, W. (2012). Randomized trial comparison of emotion regulation and relational psychotherapies for PTSD with girls involved in delinquency. *Journal of Clinical Child and Adolescent Psychology, 41*(1), 27–37. https://doi.org/10.1080/15374416.2012.632343

Forst, M., Fagan, J., & Vivona, T. S. (1989). Youth in prisons and training schools: Perceptions and consequences of the treatment-custody dichotomy. *Juvenile and Family Court Journal, 40*(1), 1–14. https://doi.org/10.1111/j.1755-6988.1989.tb00634.x

Gardner, T. W., Dishion, T. J., & Connell, A. M. (2008). Adolescent self-regulation as resilience: Resistance to antisocial behavior within the deviant peer context. *Journal of Abnormal Child Psychology, 36*(2), 273–284. https://doi.org/10.1007/s10802-007-9176-6

Gase, L. N., Glenn, B. A., Gomez, L. M., Kuo, T., Inkelas, M., & Ponce, N. A. (2016). Understanding racial and ethnic disparities in arrest: The role of individual, home, school, and community characteristics. *Race and Social Problems, 8*(4), 296–312. https://doi.org/10.1007/s12552-016-9183-8

Gaskin, G. L., Glanz, J. M., Binswager, I. A., & Anoshiravani, A. (2015). Immunization coverage among juvenile justice detainees. *Journal of Correctional Health Care, 21*(3), 265–275. https://doi.org/10.1177/0885066615587790

Gilman, A. B., Hill, K. G., & Hawkins, J. D. (2015). When is a youth's debt to society paid? Examining the long-term consequences of juvenile incarceration for adult functioning. *Journal of Developmental and Life-Course Criminology, 1*(1), 33–47. https://doi.org/10.1007/s40865-015-0002-5

Goetting, A. (1985). Racism, sexism, and ageism in the prison community. *Federal Probation, 49*(3), 10–22.

Goldstein, A. P., Glick, B., & Gibbs, J. C. (1998). *Aggression replacement training: A comprehensive intervention for aggressive youth* (Rev. ed.). Research Press.

Gonçalves, L. C., Endrass, J., Rossegger, A., & Dirkzwager, A. J. (2016). A longitudinal study of mental health symptoms in young prisoners: Exploring the influence of personal factors and the correctional climate. *BMC Psychiatry, 16*(91), 91–101. https://doi.org/10.1186/s12888-016-0803-z

Graham v. Florida, 130 S. Ct. (2010).

Grassian, S. (2006). Psychiatric effects of solitary confinement. *Washington University Journal of Law & Policy, 22*, 325–383.

Hartnett, D., Carr, A., Hamilton, E., & O'Reilly, G. (2017). The effectiveness of functional family therapy for adolescent behavioral and substance misuse problems: A meta-analysis. *Family Process, 56*(3), 607–619. https://doi.org/10.1111/famp.12256

Harvell, S., Warnberg, C., Matei, A., & Mensing, E. (2020, March). *Closing youth prisons: Lessons from agency administrators.* Urban Institute Justice Policy Center. https://www.urban.org/sites/default/files/publication/101917/closing-youth-prisons-lessons-from-agency-administrators_1.pdf

Henggeler, S. W., Schoenwald, S. K., Borduin, C. M., Rowland, M. D., & Cunningham, P. B. (1998). *Multisystemic treatment of antisocial behavior in children and adolescents.* Guilford Press.

Henggeler, S. W., Schoenwald, S. K., Borduin, C. M., Rowland, M. D., & Cunningham, P. B. (2009). *Multisystemic therapy for antisocial behavior in children and adolescents* (2nd ed.). Guilford Press.

Himmelstein, K. E. W., & Brückner, H. (2011). Criminal-justice and school sanctions against nonheterosexual youth: A national longitudinal study. *Pediatrics, 127*(1), 40–57. https://doi.org/10.1542/peds.2009-2306

Hjalmarsson, R. (2009). Juvenile jails: A path to the straight and narrow or to hardened criminality? *Journal of Law and Economics, 52*(4), 779–809. https://doi.org/10.1086/596039

Hockenberry, S., & Puzzanchera, C. (2020). *Juvenile court statistics, 2018* (Report No. NCJ 254798). Office of Juvenile Justice and Delinquency Prevention, U.S. Department of Justice. https://ojjdp.ojp.gov/sites/g/files/xyckuh176/files/media/document/juvenile-court-statistics-2018.pdf?utm_source=govdelivery&utm_medium=email&utm_campaign=publications

In re Gault, 387 U.S. 1 (1967).

In re Winship, 397 U.S. 358 (1970).

Irvine, A. (2010). "We've had three of them": Addressing the invisibility of lesbian, gay, bisexual and gender nonconforming youths in the juvenile justice system. *Columbia Journal of Gender and Law, 19*(3), 675–701. https://doi.org/10.7916/cjgl.v19i3.2603

Irvine, A., & Canfield, A. (2016). The overrepresentation of lesbian, gay, bisexual, questioning, gender nonconforming and transgender youth within the child welfare to juvenile justice crossover population. *Journal of Gender, Social Policy & the Law, 24*(2), 243–261. http://digitalcommons.wcl.american.edu/jgspl/vol24/iss2/2

Jargowsky, P. A. (2015). *The architecture of segregation: Civil unrest, the concentration of poverty, and public policy.* Century Foundation. http://apps.tcf.org/architecture-of-segregation

Jones v. Mississippi, 140 S. Ct. 1293 (2020).

Jonnson, M. R., Bird, B. M., Li, S. M. Y., & Viljoen, J. L. (2019). The prevalence of sexual and gender minority youth in the justice system: A systemic review and meta-analysis. *Criminal Justice and Behavior, 46*(7), 999–1019. https://doi.org/10.1177%2F0093854819848803

Jonson, C. L. (2010). *The impact of imprisonment on offending: A meta-analysis* [Unpublished doctoral dissertation]. University of Cincinnati.

Justice Policy Institute. (2020). *Sticker shock: The cost of youth incarceration.* https://www.justicepolicy.org/uploads/justicpolicy/documents/Sticker_Shock_2020.pdf

Juvenile Justice Geography, Policy, Practice & Statistics. (2020). *Juvenile justice services. Risk assessment.* http://www.jjgps.org/juvenile-justice-services#risk-assessment?year=2020

Kaba, F., Lewis, A., Glowa-Kollisch, S., Hadler, J., Lee, D., Alper, H., Selling, D., MacDonald, R., Solimo, A., Parsons, A., & Venters, H. (2014). Solitary confinement and risk of self-harm among jail inmates. *American Journal of Public Health, 104*(3), 442–447. https://doi.org/10.2105/AJPH.2013.301742

Kempf-Leonard, K. (2007). Minority youths and juvenile justice: Disproportionate minority contact after nearly 20 years of reform efforts. *Youth Violence and Juvenile Justice, 5*(1), 71–87. https://doi.org/10.1177/1541204006295159

Kett, J. F. (1977). *Rites of passage: Adolescence in American 1790 to the present.* Basic Books.

Kirk, D. S., & Sampson, R. J. (2013). Juvenile arrest and collateral educational damage in the transition to adulthood. *Sociology of Education, 86*(1), 36–62. https://doi.org/10.1177/0038040712448862

Klietz, S. J., Borduin, C. M., & Schaeffer, C. M. (2010). Cost–benefit analysis of multisystemic therapy with serious and violent juvenile offenders. *Journal of Family Psychology, 24*(5), 657–666. https://doi.org/10.1037/a0020838

Kraner, N., Barrowclough, N., Weiss, C., & Fisch, J. (2016). *Jurisdiction survey of juvenile solitary confinement rules in juvenile justice systems*. Lowenstein Center for the Public Interest. https://lowenstein.com/media/2825/51-jurisdiction-survey-of-juvenile-solitary-confinement-rules-72616.pdf

Kraus, J. (1974). Comparison of corrective effects of probation and detention on male juvenile offenders. *British Journal of Criminology, 14*(1), 49–62. https://doi.org/10.1093/oxfordjournals.bjc.a046510

Kuanliang, A., Sorensen, J. R., & Cunningham, M. D. (2008). Juvenile inmates in an adult prison system: Rates of disciplinary misconduct and violence. *Criminal Justice and Behavior, 35*(9), 1186–1201. https://doi.org/10.1177/0093854808322744

Kummerlowe, C., & Flanagan, T. J. (1995). Coping with imprisonment. In T. J. Flanagan (Ed.), *Long-term imprisonment: Policy, science and correctional practice* (pp. 41–50). Sage Publications.

Kupchik, A., & Synder, R. B. (2019). Impact of juvenile inmates' perceptions and facility characteristics on victimization in juvenile correctional facilities. *Prison Journal, 89*(3), 265–285. https://doi.org/10.1177/0032885509339505

Lanctôt, N., Cernkovich, S. A., & Giordano, P. C. (2007). Delinquent behavior, official delinquency, and gender: Consequences for adulthood functioning and well-being. *Criminology, 45*(1), 131–157. https://doi.org/10.1111/j.1745-9125.2007.00074.x

Langan, P. A., & Levin, D. J. (2002). *Recidivism of prisoners released in 1994* (Report No. NCJ 193427). Bureau of Justice Statistics, U.S. Department of Justice. http://bjs.gov/content/pub/pdf/rpr94.pdf

Le Blanc, M. (1997). A generic control theory of the criminal phenomenon: The structural and the dynamical statements of an integrative multilayered control theory. In T. Thornberry (Ed.), *Developmental theories of crime and delinquency: advances in criminological theory* (Vol. 7., pp. 215–285). Transaction Press.

Leiber, M. J., & Fix, R. (2019). Reflections on the impact of race and ethnicity on juvenile court outcomes and efforts to enact change. *American Journal of Criminal Justice, 44*(4), 581–608. https://doi.org/10.1007/s12103-019-09479-3

Lemert, E. M. (1951). *Social pathology: A systematic approach to the theory of sociopathic behavior*. McGraw-Hill.

Lemert, E. M. (1967). *Human deviance, social problems, and social control*. Prentice-Hall.

Lennox, C. (2014). The health needs of young people in prison. *British Medical Bulletin, 112*(1), 17–25. https://doi.org/10.1093/bmb/ldu028

Lipsey, M. W. (2018). Effective use of the large body of research on the effectiveness of programs for juvenile offenders and the failure of the model programs approach. *Criminology & Public Policy, 17*(1), 189–198. https://doi.org/10.1111/1745-9133.12345

Lipsey, M. W., Landenberger, N. A., & Wilson, S. J. (2007). Effects of cognitive-behavioral programs for criminal offenders. *Campbell Systematic Reviews, 3*(1), 1–27. https://doi.org/10.4073/csr.2007.6

Little, M. (2006). *A social development model of incarceration on juvenile offenders' social network support, exposure to antisocial peers, aggressive offending and psychological adjustment* [Unpublished doctoral dissertation]. Temple University.

Loughran, T. A., Mulvey, E. P., Schubert, C. A., Fagan, J., Piquero, A. R., & Losova, S. H. (2009). Estimating a dose-response relationship between length of stay and future recidivism in serious juvenile offenders. *Criminology, 47*(3), 699–740. https://doi.org/10.1111/j.1745-9125.2009.00165.x

Luigi, M., Dellazizzo, L., Giguère, C. É., Goulet, M. H., & Dumais, A. (2020). Shedding light on "the hole": A systematic review and meta-analysis on adverse psychological effects and mortality following solitary confinement in correctional settings. *Frontiers in Psychiatry, 11*, 840. https://doi.org/10.3389/fpsyt.2020.00840

Lyons, J. S., Royce Baerger, D., Quigley, P., Erlich, J., & Griffin, E. (2001). Mental health service needs of juvenile offenders: A comparison of detention, incarceration, and treatment settings. *Children's Services: Social Policy, Research, and Practice, 4*(2), 69–85. https://doi.org/10.1207/S15326918CS0402_2

Majd, K., Marksamer, J., & Reyes, C. (2009). *Hidden injustice: Lesbian, gay, bisexual, and transgender youth in juvenile courts*. Legal Services for Children, National Juvenile Defender Center, and National Center for Lesbian Rights. https://www.nclrights.org/wp-content/uploads/2014/06/hidden_injustice.pdf

Mallet, C. A., & Tedor, M. F. (2018). *Juvenile delinquency: Pathways and prevention*. Sage.

Maloney, C., & Miller, J. (2015). The impact of a risk assessment instrument on juvenile detention decision-making: A check on "perceptual shorthand" and "going rates"? *Justice Quarterly, 32*(5), 900–927. https://doi.org/10.1080/07418825.2013.863961

Massoglia, M., & Pridemore, W. A. (2015). Incarceration and health. *Annual Review of Sociology, 41*, 291–310. https://doi.org/10.1146/annurev-soc-073014-112326

McCarthy, D., & Adams, M. (2019). Can family-prisoner relationships ever improve during incarceration? Examining the primary caregivers of incarcerated youth men. *British Journal of Criminology, 59*(2), 378–395. https://doi.org/10.1093/bjc/azy039

McCuish, E., Lussier, P., & Corrado, R. (2018). Incarceration as a turning point? The impact of custody experiences and identity change on community reentry. *Journal of Developmental and Life-Course Criminology, 4*(4), 427–448. https://doi.org/10.1007/s40865-018-0088-7

Mears, D. P., & Travis, J. (2004). Youth development and reentry. *Youth Violence and Juvenile Justice, 2*(1), 3–20. https://doi.org/10.1177/1541204003260044

Mendel, R. A. (2009). *Two decades of JDAI: A progress report.* Annie E. Casey Foundation. https://folio.iupui.edu/bitstream/handle/10244/396/JDAI_National_final_10_07_09.pdf

Mikytuck, A. M., & Woolard, J. L. (2019). Family contact in juvenile confinement facilities: Analysis of the likelihood of and barrier to contact. *Journal of Offender Rehabilitation, 58*(5), 371–397. https://doi.org/10.1080/10509674.2019.1615600

Miller v. Alabama, 132 S. Ct. 2455 (2012).

Mitchell, O. (2005). A meta-analysis of race and sentencing research: Explaining the inconsistencies. *Journal of Quantitative Criminology, 21*(4), 439–466. https://doi.org/10.1007/s10940-005-7362-7

Moffitt, T. E., Caspi, A., Harrington, H., & Milne, B. J. (2002). Males on the life-course-persistent and adolescence-limited antisocial pathways: Follow-up at age 26 years. *Development and Psychopathology, 14*(1), 179–207. https://doi.org/10.1017/S0954579402001104

Monahan, K. C., Goldweber, A., & Cauffman, E. (2011). The effects of visitation on incarcerated juvenile offenders: How contract with the outside impacts adjustment on the inside. *Law and Human Behavior, 35*(2), 143–151. https://doi.org/10.1007/s10979-010-9220-x

Monahan, K. C., Steinberg, L., Cauffman, E., & Mulvey, E. P. (2013). Psychosocial (im)maturity from adolescence to early adulthood: Distinguishing between adolescence-limited and persisting antisocial behavior. *Development and Psychopathology, 25*(4), 1093–1105. https://doi.org/10.1017/S0954579413000394

Montgomery v. Louisiana, 577 U.S. __ (2016).

Mueller, D. J., Sullivan, C. J., & McManus, H. D. (2020). Disproportionate experiences in custody? An examination of minority youths' outcomes in secure facilities. *Justice Quarterly, 37*(2), 332–357. https://doi.org/10.1080/07418825.2018.1528375

Multisystemic® Services. (2021, August). *Home page.* https://www.mstservices.com/

Mulvey, E. P., Steinberg, L., Piquero, A. R., Besana, M., Fagan, J., Schubert, C., & Cauffman, E. (2010). Trajectories of desistance and continuity in antisocial behavior following court adjudication among serious adolescent offenders. *Development and Psychopathology, 22*(2), 453–475. https://doi.org/10.1017%2FS0954579410000179

Murrie, D. C., Henderson, C. E., Vincent, G. M., Rockett, J. L., & Mundt, C. (2009). Psychiatric symptoms among juveniles incarcerated in adult prison. *Psychiatric Services, 60*(8), 1092–1097. https://doi.org/10.1176/appi.ps.60.8.1092

Nagin, D. S., Cullen, F. T., & Jonson, C. L. (2009). Imprisonment and reoffending. *Crime & Justice, 38*(1), 115–200. https://doi.org/10.1086/599202

National Conference of State Legislatures. (2018). *Principles of effective juvenile justice policy.* https://www.ncsl.org/Portals/1/Documents/cj/JJ_Principles_122017_31901.pdf

National Conference of State Legislatures. (2020a). *Principles of effective juvenile justice policy update.* https://www.ncsl.org/research/civil-and-criminal-justice/juvenile-justice-principles.aspx

National Conference of State Legislatures. (2020b). *Juvenile justice 2019 year-end report.* https://www.ncsl.org/research/civil-and-criminal-justice/juvenile-justice-2019-year-end-report.aspx

Ng, I. Y., Shen, X., Sim, H., Sarri, R. C., Stoffregen, E., & Shook, J. J. (2011). Incarcerating juveniles in adult prisons as a factor in depression. *Criminal Behaviour and Mental Health, 21*(1), 21–34. https://doi.org/10.1002/cbm.783

Office of Juvenile Justice and Delinquency Prevention (OJJDP). (2013). *Family listening sessions: Executive summary.* https://ojjdp.ojp.gov/sites/g/files/xyckuh176/files/pubs/241379.pdf

Office of Juvenile Justice and Delinquency Prevention (OJJDP). (2021a). *Racial and ethnic fairness: Juvenile commitment rates by race/ethnicity, 1997–2019.* https://www.ojjdp.gov/ojstatbb/special_topics/qa11803.asp?qaDate=2019

Office of Juvenile Justice and Delinquency Prevention (OJJDP). (2021b). *Racial and ethnic fairness: Juvenile detention rates by race/ethnicity, 1997–2019.* https://www.ojjdp.gov/ojstatbb/special_topics/qa11802.asp?qaDate=2019

Office of Juvenile Justice and Delinquency Prevention (OJJDP). (2021c). *Racial and ethnic fairness: Juvenile residential placement rates by race/ethnicity, 1997–2019.* https://www.ojjdp.gov/ojstatbb/special_topics/qa11801.asp?qaDate=2019

Office of the Correctional Investigator. (2013). *A case study of diversity in corrections: The Black inmate experience in federal penitentiaries.* https://www.oci-bec.gc.ca/cnt/rpt/pdf/oth-aut/oth-aut20131126-eng.pdf

Peterson-Badali, M., & Koegl, C. J. (2002). Juveniles' experiences of incarceration: The role of correctional staff in peer violence. *Journal of Criminal Justice, 30*(1), 41–49. https://doi.org/10.1016/S0047-2352(01)00121-0

Petrich, D. M., Pratt, T. C., Jonson, C. L., & Cullen, F. T. (2020). *A revolving door? A meta-analysis of the impact of custodial sanctions on reoffending* [Unpublished paper]. University of Cincinnati.

Petteruti, A., Velazquez, T., & Walsh, N. (2009). *The costs of confinement: Why good juvenile justice policies make good fiscal sense*. Justice Policy Institute.

Piquero, A. R. (2008). Disproportionate minority contact. *Future of Children, 18*(2), 59–79. https://doi.org/10.1353/foc.0.0013

Piquero, A. R., Gonzalez, J. R., & Jennings, W. G. (2015). Developmental trajectories and antisocial behavior over the life-course. In J. Morizot & L. Kazemian (Eds.), *The development of criminal and antisocial behavior: Theory, research and practical applications* (pp. 75–88). Springer. https://doi.org/10.1007/978-3-319-08720-7_6

Poteat, V. P., Scheer, J. R., & Chong, E. S. K. (2016). Sexual orientation-based disparities in school and juvenile justice discipline: A multiple group comparison of contributing factors. *Journal of Educational Psychology, 108*(2), 229–241. https://doi.org/10.1037/edu0000058

Prison Rape Elimination Act of 2003, 42 U.S.C. § 15601 (2003). https://www.govinfo.gov/content/pkg/STATUTE-117/pdf/STATUTE-117-Pg972.pdf

Puzzanchera, C., Hockenberry, S., Sladky, T. J., & Kang, W. (2020). *Juvenile residential facility census databook*. Office of Juvenile Justice and Delinquency Prevention. https://www.ojjdp.gov/ojstatbb/jrfcdb/

Pyrooz, D. C., Gartner, N., & Smith, M. (2017). Consequences of incarceration for gang membership: A longitudinal study of serious offenders in Philadelphia and Phoenix. *Criminology, 55*(2), 273–306. https://doi.org/10.1111/1745-9125.12135

Roper v. Simmons, 543 U.S. 551 (2005).

Rose, D. R., & Clear, T. R. (2003). Incarceration, reentry, and social capital: Social networks in the balance. In J. Travis & M. Waul (Eds.), *Prisoners once removed: The impact of incarceration and reentry on children, families, and communities* (pp. 313–341). Urban Institute Press.

Rovner, J. (2021, May 24). *Juvenile life without parole: An overview*. Sentencing Project. https://www.sentencingproject.org/publications/juvenile-life-without-parole/

Ruch, D. A., & Yoder, J. R. (2018). The effects of family contact on community reentry plan among incarcerated youths. *Victims & Offenders, 13*(5), 609–627. https://doi.org/10.1080/15564886.2017.1401571

Sabol, W. J., & Baumann, M. L. (2020). Justice reinvestment: Vision and practice. *Annual Review of Criminology, 3*(1), 317–339.

Sawyer, A. M., & Borduin, C. M. (2011). Effects of multisystemic therapy through midlife: A 21.9-year follow-up to a randomized clinical trial with serious and violent juvenile offenders. *Journal of Consulting and Clinical Psychology, 79*(5), 643–652. https://doi.org/10.1037/a0024862

Schnittker, J., & John, A. (2007). Enduring stigma: The long-term effects of incarceration on health. *Journal of Health and Social Behavior, 48*(2), 115–130. https://doi.org/10.1177/002214650704800202

Schwartz, I. M., Barton, W., & Orlando, F. (1991). Keeping kids out of secure detention: The misuse of juvenile detention has a profound impact on child welfare. *Public Welfare, 49*, 20–26.

Schweitzer, M., Labrecque, R. M., & Smith, P. (2017). Reinvesting in the lives of youth: A targeted approach to reducing recidivism. *Criminal Justice Policy Review, 28*(3), 207–219. https://doi.org/10.1177/0887403415579262

Scottish Government. (2017). *Preventing offending: Getting it right for children and young people: Progress report*. https://www.gov.scot/publications/youth-justice-strategy-preventing-offending-getting-right-children-young-people/documents/

Sedlak, A. J., McPherson, K. S., & Basena, M. (2013). *Nature and risk of victimization: Findings from the Survey of Youth in Residential Placement*. Office of Juvenile Justice and Delinquency Prevention, U.S. Department of Justice. https://www.njjn.org/uploads/digital-library/Nature-and-risk-of-victimization_OJJDP-Bulletin_June-2013.pdf

Segule, M. N. (2021, September 1). *The vaccine rollout is leaving incarcerated children behind*. UCLA Law COVID Behind Bars Data Project. https://uclacovidbehindbars.org/children-left-behind

Shulman, E. P., Smith, A. R., Silva, K., Icenogle, G., Duell, N., Chein, J., & Steinberg, L. (2016). The dual systems model: Review, reappraisal, and reaffirmation. *Developmental Cognitive Neuroscience, 17*, 103–117. https://doi.org/10.1016/j.dcn.2015.12.010

Smith, E. L., & Stroop, J. (2019). *Sexual victimization reported by youth in juvenile facilities, 2018*. Bureau of Justice Statistics, U.S. Department of Justice. https://bjs.ojp.gov/content/pub/pdf/svryjf18.pdf

Smith, P., Goggin, C., & Gendreau, P. (2002). *The effects of prison sentences and intermediate sanctions on recidivism: General effects and individual differences*. Solicitor General of Canada. https://www.publicsafety.gc.ca/cnt/rsrcs/pblctns/ffcts-prsn-sntncs/index-en.aspx#exe

Snyder, H. N., & Sickmund, M. (2006). *Juvenile offenders and victims: 2006 national report*. Office of Justice Programs, Office of Juvenile Justice and Delinquency Prevention, U.S. Department of Justice. https://www.ojjdp.gov/ojstatbb/nr2006/downloads/nr2006.pdf

Snyder, J., McEachern, A., Schrepferman, L., Just, C., Jenkins, M., Roberts, S., & Lofgreen, A. (2010). Contributions of peer deviancy training to the early development of conduct problems: Mediators and moderators. *Behavior Therapy, 41*(3), 317–328. https://doi.org/10.1016/j.beth.2009.05.001

Spinney, E., Cohen, M., Feyerherm, W., Stephenson, R., Yeide, M., & Hopps, M. (2014). *Case studies of nine jurisdictions that reduced disproportionate minority contact in their juvenile justice systems*. Office of Juvenile Justice and Delinquency Prevention, U.S. Department of Justice. https://www.ojp.gov/pdffiles1/ojjdp/grants/250301.pdf

Steinberg, L. (2008). A social neuroscience perspective on adolescent risk-taking. *Developmental Review, 28*(1), 78–106. https://doi.org/10.1016/j.dr.2007.08.002

Steinberg, L. (2010). A dual systems model of adolescent risk-taking. *Developmental Psychobiology, 52*(3), 216–224. https://doi.org/10.1002/dev.20445

Steinberg, L., Chung, H. L., & Little, M. (2004). Reentry of young offenders from the justice system: A developmental perspective. *Youth Violence and Juvenile Justice, 2*(1), 21–38. https://doi.org/10.1177/1541204003260045

Steinberg, L., Icenogle, G., Shulman, E. P., Breiner, K., Chein, J., Bacchini, D., Chang, L., Chaudhary, N., Di Giunta, L., Dodge, K. A., Fanti, K. A., Lansford, J. E., Malone, P. S., Oburu, P., Pastorelli, C., Skinner, A. T., Sorbring, E., Tapanya, S., Tirado, L. M. U., . . . Takash, H. M. S. (2018). Around the world, adolescence is a time of heightened sensation seeking and immature self-regulation. *Developmental Science, 21*(2), 1–13. https://doi.org/10.1111/desc.12532

Steinhart, D. (2006). *Juvenile detention risk assessment: A practice guide to juvenile detention reform*. Annie E. Casey Foundation. https://assets.aecf.org/m/resourceimg/aecf-juveniledetentionriskassessment1-2006.pdf

Stoll, M. A., & Bushway, S. D. (2008). Effect of criminal background checks on hiring ex-offenders. *Criminology & Public Policy, 7*(3), 371–404. https://doi.org/10.1111/j.1745-9133.2008.00516.x

Sturges, J. E., & Hanrahan, K. J. (2011). The effects of children's criminality on mothers of offenders. *Journal of Family Issues, 32*(8), 985–1006. https://doi.org/10.1177/0192513X10396805

Sweeten, G., Piquero, A. R., & Steinberg, L. (2013). Age and the explanation of crime, revisited. *Journal of Youth and Adolescence, 42*(6), 921–938. https://doi.org/10.1007/s10964-013-9926-4

Trupin, E. W., Stewart, D. G., Beach, B., & Boesky, L. (2002). Effectiveness of dialectical behaviour therapy program for incarcerated female juvenile offenders. *Child and Adolescent Mental Health, 7*(3), 121–127. https://doi.org/10.1111/1475-3588.00022

Udell, W. A., & Mohammed, S. (2018). The prevalence of physical health problems among youth in the juvenile justice system: A systematic review. *Journal of Health Disparities Research and Practice, 12*(3), 71–94.

United Nations. (2019). *United Nations global study on children deprived of liberty*. https://omnibook.com/view/e0623280-5656-42f8-9edf-5872f8f08562/page/1

Utah House Bill 239. (2017). http://le.utah.gov/~2017/bills/static/HB0239.html

van der Stouwe, T., Asscher, J. J., Stams, G. J., Deković, M., & van der Laan, P. H. (2014). The effectiveness of Multisystemic Therapy (MST): A meta-analysis. *Clinical Psychology Review, 34*(6), 468–481. https://doi.org/10.1016/j.cpr.2014.06.006

Viljoen, J. L., Jonnson, M. R., Cochrane, D. M., Vargen, L. M., & Vincent, G. M. (2019). Impact of risk assessment instruments on rates of pretrial detention, postconviction placements, and release: A systematic review and meta-analysis. *Law and Human Behavior, 43*(5), 397–420. https://doi.org/10.1037/lhb0000344

Villettaz, P., Gillieron, G., & Killias, M. (2015). The effects on re-offending of custodial vs. non-custodial sanctions: An updated systematic review of the state of knowledge. *Campbell Systematic Reviews, 11*(1), 1–92. https://doi.org/10.4073/csr.2015.1

Vincent, G. M., Guy, L. S., Perrault, R. T., & Gershenson, B. (2016). Risk assessment matters, but only when implemented well: A multisite study in juvenile probation. *Law and Human Behavior, 40*(6), 683–696. https://doi.org/10.1037/lhb0000214

Vincent, G. M., & Viljoen, J. L. (2020). Racist algorithms or systemic problems? Risk assessments and racial disparities. *Criminal Justice and Behavior, 47*(12), 1576–1584. https://doi.org/10.1177/0093854820954501

Virginia House 1437, an Act to amend and reenact Section 16.10292 of the Code of Virginia. (2020). https://custom.statenet.com/public/resources.cgi?id=ID:bill:VA2020000H1437&ciq=ncsl53&client_md=d233760aeb0a6afc0291050f50f27944&mode=current_text

Walker, S. C., & Herting, J. R. (2020). The impact of pretrial juvenile detention on 12-month recidivism: A matched comparison study. *Crime & Delinquency, 66*(13–14), 1865–1887. https://doi.org/10.1177/0011128720926115

Ward, G. K. (2012). *The Black child-savers: Racial democracy and juvenile justice*. University of Chicago Press.

Weatherburn, D., Vignaendra, S., & McGrath, A. (2009). *The specific deterrent effect of custodial penalties on juvenile re-offending*. Criminology Research Council. https://www.aic.gov.au/sites/default/files/2020-05/02_0405.pdf

Webster, C. M., Sprott, J. B., & Doob, A. N. (2019). The will to change: Lessons from Canada's successful decarceration of youth. *Law & Society Review, 53*(4), 1092–1131. https://doi.org/10.1111/lasr.12433

Weiss, B., Caron, A., Ball, S., Tapp, J., Johnson, M., & Weisz, J. R. (2005). Iatrogenic effects of group treatment for antisocial youths. *Journal of Consulting and Clinical Psychology, 73*(6), 1036–1044. https://doi.org/10.1037/0022-006X.73.6.1036

Western, B. (2001). Incarceration, unemployment, and inequality. *Focus, 21*(1), 3–36.

Western, B., & Beckett, K. (1999). How unregulated is the US labor market? The penal system as labor market institution. *American Journal of Sociology, 104*(4), 1030–1060. https://doi.org/10.1086/210135

Wilson, B. D. M., Jourdan, S. P., Meyer, I. H., Flores, A. R., Stemple, L., & Herman, J. L. (2017). Disproportionality and disparities among sexual minority youth in custody. *Journal of Youth and Adolescence, 46*(7), 1547–1561. https://doi.org/10.1007/s10964-017-0632-5

Woolard, J. L., Odgers, C., Lanza-Kaduce, L., & Daglis, H. (2005). Juveniles within adult correctional settings: Legal pathways and developmental considerations. *International Journal of Forensic Mental Health, 4*(1), 1–18. https://doi.org/10.1080/14999013.2005.10471209

World Health Organization. (1989). *The health of youth: Background document* (A42/Technical discussions/2).

Yoder, J. R., Hodge, A. I., Ruch, D., & Dillard, R. (2019). Effects of childhood polyvictimization on victimization in juvenile correctional facilities: The mediating role of trauma symptomatology. *Youth Violence and Juvenile Justice, 17*(2), 129–153. https://doi.org/10.1177%2F1541204018757038

Youth Criminal Justice Act (S.C. 2002. c. 1). https://laws-lois.justice.gc.ca/eng/acts/y-1.5/

Zane, S. N. (2021). Have racial and ethnic disparities in juvenile justice declined over time? An empirical assessment of the DMC mandate. *Youth Violence & Juvenile Justice, 19*(2), 163–185. https://doi.org/10.1177/1541204020962163

Zwecker, N. A., Harrison, A. J., Welty, L. J., Teplin, L. A., & Abram, K. M. (2018). Social support networks among delinquent youth: An 8-year follow-up study. *Journal of Offender Rehabilitation, 57*(7), 459–480. https://doi.org/10.1080/10509674.2018.1523821

CHAPTER 17

Rethinking the Age of Majority

Vivian Hamilton

Abstract

Young people today come of age in a cultural and economic milieu that prolongs their attainment of the traditional markers of adulthood. Their subjective conceptions of the transition to adulthood depart radically from the traditional conception, with its emphasis on discrete transition events (e.g., marriage and entry into the workforce). Instead, the modern transition to adulthood is a gradual process consisting of the acquisition of general capabilities, rather than the achievement of externally constructed events. The state-established age of legal majority stands in marked contrast to this gradual and prolonged process. Thus, the legal construction of adulthood is starkly at odds with its social and cultural constructions. This chapter argues that abandoning the presumptive age of legal majority in favor of context-specific rules advances the state's liberty-respecting ends and better aligns the legal and sociocultural constructions of adulthood. The developmental and behavioral sciences can and ought to supplement more traditional policymaking considerations.

Key Words: adolescents' rights, age of majority, legal majority, adulthood, transitions into adulthood

The near-universal U.S. age of majority is 18, but both here and abroad it has historically fluctuated, ranging from the midteens to the mid-20s. These fluctuations in the age of majority have generally accorded with changes in the capacities required of society's adult citizens, and the age by which individuals tend to attain those capacities. Historically, young people have crossed the legal—and social—threshold to adulthood upon gaining the capacities to (a) perform the types of work required of a given time and place, (b) bear arms and fight on behalf of the state, and/or (c) form and support a family.

The U.S. age of majority was lowered from 21 to 18, however, for reasons quite unrelated to capacity. Yet research across disciplines demonstrates that setting the age of majority at 18 fails to accord with the trajectory of individual development, the time necessary to acquire the skills and abilities demanded of individuals in the modern labor market and broader socioeconomic context, and even the social experiences of young people coming of age in modern American culture. The *legal* construction of adulthood is thus starkly at odds with the *social* meaning and experiences of adulthood.

Neither raising nor lowering the age of majority will be sufficient to redress its deficiencies. Instead, individuals predictably acquire different capabilities across the course of their development and exercise them with varying levels of competence in different contexts (Arshagouni, 2006). Thus, while 18 is a singularly inapt age at which to set majority across virtually every legal context to which it applies, in this chapter, I argue that no categorical age of majority can reliably capture the context-specific acquisition of various capacities.

The inadequacy of the categorical age of majority is reflected in the ever-growing number of exceptions to it. These exceptions aim to adapt rules to better conform to the needs of society and capacities (or incapacities) of young people. The exceptions have historically tended toward extending rights to individuals younger than the age of majority. Thus, young people will have exercised many of the rights technically reserved for adults—entering contracts, deciding medical treatment, even marrying—long before reaching adult status.

Increasingly, however, legal exceptions extend rules that once applied strictly to minors to individuals past the age of majority. In doing so, these exceptions to presumptive majority recognize that most young individuals will enter adulthood unready to assume some of the most significant attributes of their new status, such as the financial self-sufficiency intimated by adults' legal disentitlement to parental support. For most young adults, financial dependency will instead continue well into their adult years.

Scholars and jurists alike have critiqued the body of law affecting young people as lacking coherence (*Roper v. Simmons*, 2005). For example, Todres (2012) has argued that by approaching "the concept of maturity in a piecemeal and issue-specific fashion," the law has developed "a legal construct of maturity that is anything but consistent or coherent" (pp. 1109–1110). This chapter, however, diverges from earlier critiques in its call for dismantling altogether the age of majority and thus doing away with the conception of adulthood as a distinct legal status. The core commitments of the liberal democratic state require extending to individuals the right to exercise those self-regarding capacities of which they are capable. That end calls for adopting context-specific rules informed by insights from the social and developmental sciences, which can help explain the development of capabilities and their exercise in different contexts.

The age of majority is a construct that has quite lost any social or legal utility it may have once had, and it should thus be abandoned. The remainder of this chapter examines it, details its flaws, and proposes a principled and pragmatic alternative to it.

The Legally Constructed Status of Adulthood

In law, "status" denotes a group sharing some set of attributes that justifies its membership being governed by a common set of rules. Legal statuses can thus facilitate the efficient functioning of a complex society. "Corporation," "marriage," and "minor," for example, are all legal statuses defined and governed by distinct sets of legal rules. "Adult" is another.

Like the law generally, statuses shape and are shaped over time by social forces. Their meanings can be at once legally and socially constructed, and they thus evolve along with changing social circumstances.

Childhood and adulthood are also socially and legally constructed statuses whose meanings have varied dramatically over time and across cultures (Appell, 2009). Despite what may appear to be the inevitability of our current binary classification system, in which individuals are either minors or adults, the progression from childhood to adulthood is fluid and not readily amenable to biological definition (Scott, 2000). Instead, structural (e.g., legal and economic norms) and cultural (e.g., social norms) changes have influenced the course and timing of individuals' transitions to adulthood.

The Age of Majority: A Brief History

The age of majority has historically fluctuated depending on the capacities required of adults at different times and places. Even within a given society, it has occasionally varied according to the capacities required of different social roles that young individuals were destined to fill. In Medieval England, for example, the age of majority for English males destined for the military status of knighthood was 21, before which they would not have completed the training nor gained the strength required of them. However, young men destined for agricultural life attained adult status at the significantly younger age of 15, by which they would have gained the capacity to engage in farm work (James, 1960). Perhaps unsurprisingly, the age required for the elite status of knighthood was the age whose imprint would endure (James, 1960).

The immediate historical origins of the U.S. age of majority lie in the English common-law tradition (James, 1960). The American colonies would adopt age 21 as the near-universal age of majority (Stephenson, 2004). The U.S. age of majority remained unchanged from the country's founding well into the 20th century. Then, in 1942, wartime needs prompted Congress to lower the age of conscription from 21 to 18, a change that would eventually lead to the lowering of the age of majority generally (Cultice, 1992; Hamilton, 2012).

For a period of years following the lowering of the draft age to 18, the voting age (and the general age of majority) remained 21. The obligation of military service, however, has long been linked to the right to political participation (Amar, 2005; Keyssar, 2009). Thus, congressional debates to subject 18-year-olds to the draft were soon followed by proposals to also extend to 18-year-olds the right to vote (Cultice, 1992). These proposals led to the eventual passage of the 26th Amendment in 1971, lowering the voting age to 18 in both state and federal elections.

Eighteen has thus become firmly entrenched as the presumptive age of majority, replacing in just a few decades its centuries-old predecessor of 21. Its widespread adoption notably reflected a desire for a certain sort of consistency rather than a widely held consensus that young people reached maturity or generally attained adultlike capabilities before age 21.

Legal Effects of Majority: An Overview

Today, the legal age of majority reflects a presumption that typical individuals of that age are "mature enough to function in society as adults, to care for themselves, and to make their own self-interested decisions" (Scott, 2000, p. 559). Every state has adopted a legal age of majority through various legislative or judicial measures (Scott, 2000).

Common and statutory law frequently address more directly other age-related laws—both those that comport with the age of majority and those that act as exceptions to it. The following subparts briefly identify some of the more significant of the civil effects that attend the age of majority.

Disentitlement to parental and/or state support. There is a strong presumption that a young person's entitlement to parental support ends at majority, generally age 18 (National Conference of State Legislatures, 2015). A number of states allow the extension of support orders past 18 if a child is enrolled in but has not yet graduated from high school (National Conference of State Legislatures, 2015). For example, 24 states will allow the extension of support orders to age 19 if certain conditions are met; some other states permit extensions beyond 19.

Similarly, young people presumptively age out of foster care once they turn 18 or, in some states, 19 (Magyar, 2006). Currently, seven states provide for continuing foster care past age 18 when the young person is enrolled in some sort of educational or rehabilitative program. Four states give their courts discretion to determine whether to continue state custody past age 18 based on factors that can include the young person's best interests or need for services. And finally, another four states' statutes explicitly provide for retaining custody for the purpose of helping a young person successfully transition to independence. Dedicated federal funds exist to help states provide foster care only to individuals younger than 18 and 18-year-olds enrolled in high school who will likely graduate before their 19th birthdays.

By ending parental and state support obligations at majority, in just under half the states, the law treats those who are aged 18 and over, or who have completed a high school education, as capable of financial independence and responsible for their own financial support (Magyar, 2006). While a high school education may in previous decades have enabled financial security and self-sufficiency, today high school alone rarely suffices. In the modern economy, well-paying jobs providing the opportunity for middle-class living typically require postsecondary education or other trade-specific training. The legal effects of the age of majority operate to leave high school graduates without parental (or state) support before allowing them a sufficient opportunity to attain financial security. In doing so, the age of majority both disserves young people and ineffectively meets the workforce needs of the employers that drive the nation's economy.

Freedom from parental authority. During their children's minority, parents have not only a legally enforceable obligation to provide for the support of their children but also a constitutional right to the "custody and control" of their children (*Pierce v. Society of Sisters*, 1925; see also *Meyer v. Nebraska*, 1923).

Just as many aspects of the parent's authority tend to exist informally, its technical cessation once a child reaches the age of majority also tends to occur informally. However, two legal doctrines—invoked, ironically, when there is a failure or absence of presumptive parental authority—help delineate the contours of parental authority.

The first is the doctrine of emancipation, which confers upon a minor "the rights, duties, privileges, and responsibilities provided by the civil law to a person who has reached the age of majority under civil law" (Haw. Rev. Stat. § 577-25, 2015; Sanger & Willemsen, 1992). Generally, minors found to be living independently of their parents and supporting themselves may be declared emancipated (Sanger & Willemsen, 1992). The rights of emancipated minors typically allow them to enter contracts (such as lease agreements), receive certain forms of public assistance usually reserved to heads of household, and retain their own earnings. For example, a Wisconsin statute (Wis. Stat. § 48.987, 2015) provides that a self-supporting minor is entitled to their own earnings. Emancipation also relieves parents of the duty to support the minor child (Dean, 1994).

The second legal mechanism, the ungovernability action, permits parents to initiate a judicial action seeking to have a minor child found "ungovernable" (Kandel & Griffiths, 2003). A minor may be brought under court supervision if the minor is found to be a "habitual truant or is incorrigible, ungovernable, or habitually disobedient and beyond the lawful control of his or her parents, guardian or lawful custodian" (N.Y. Fam. Ct. Act § 732). State statutes adopt intentionally vague standards under which a young person's actions, albeit lawful but which violate the parents' mores and expectations, may justify a court's determination that the youth should be in the custody of a social services department for placement and treatment in a foster home or other institution (Kandel & Griffiths, 2003). These actions can include engaging in sexual relationships over parents' objections, being truant from school, violating curfews, and general disobedience.

Emancipated minors step into the shoes of their parents, exercising for themselves the authority that parents would normally exercise over them. Parents who successfully have a child adjudicated ungovernable allow the state, at least temporarily, to substitute parental control with its *parens patriae* power. Ungovernability actions illustrate the sort of authority parents are entitled to exercise over their children and with which children are expected to comply. Even if a child's actions stop short of criminal or delinquent behavior—such as general noncompliance with parents' wishes—the state may act to reinforce parental authority. Thus, both emancipation and ungovernability actions help illustrate the scope of parental authority.

Contract rights. On reaching the age of majority, individuals may disaffirm contracts entered during their minority (Perillo, 2002). The common law has for centuries provided minors this protection, known as the infancy defense or infancy doctrine (Williston & Lord, 1993). The infancy doctrine has historically existed to protect young people from squandering their wealth or from falling prey to unscrupulous adults who would take advantage of their inexperience in the marketplace (DiMatteo, 1995). Disaffirmance does not permit the rescinding individual to reap the benefit of the voided contract. Instead, each party generally must return to the other any consideration given (Perillo, 2002).

Common and statutory law have both created several exceptions to the infancy defense (DiMatteo, 1995; Perillo, 2002; Williston & Lord, 1993). One of these exceptions prevents the later disaffirmance of contracts that provide minors the "necessaries of life" (DiMatteo, 1995; Perillo, 2002; Williston & Lord, 1993). Thus, when minors purchase basic necessities, the exception aims to counteract one of the potential drawbacks of the infancy defense—merchants' unwillingness to conduct business with minors for fear of later disaffirmance (Mehler, 1963). Other statutorily created exceptions prohibit the disaffirmance of certain types of contracts where legislatures deemed that finality and certainty should outweigh the right of disaffirmance (DiMatteo, 1995). These exceptions commonly include insurance contracts, child support agreements, and student loans (DiMatteo, 1995; Perillo, 2002; Williston & Lord, 1993).

While the right to contract is regularly touted as one of the rights of adulthood, it is in reality a right that is regularly exercised by minors. The threat of disaffirmance does little to dissuade merchants or hinder minors from conducting business. Instead, minors are active and significant participants in the marketplace, as both consumers and sellers.

Minors' regular involvement in market transactions arguably renders the right to contract an almost irrelevant marker of the transition to adult status. Indeed, for decades, both scholars and jurists have been calling for the doctrine's overhaul or outright repeal (see *Kiefer v. Howe Motors*, 1968; DiMatteo, 1995; Mehler, 1963).

Critics of the infancy doctrine argue that adolescents have sufficient capacity to enter contracts to which they should be held. The doctrine may have the perverse effect of permitting market-savvy individuals to later disavow contracts that they were sufficiently capable of entering as minors (DiMatteo, 1995). More recently, commentators have pointed to the growing body of developmental research tending to confirm the cognitive capacity of adolescents to enter contracts (Glassman & Karno, 2009). For example, Cunningham (2006) noted the absence of "effort to change the infancy doctrine despite criticism from academics and even courts [and] despite the . . . widespread agreement among psychologists that children's cognitive abilities develop at a far earlier age than originally thought" (p. 292). To the extent the infancy doctrine flies in the face of social reality, provides unneeded protection to (at least a subset of) minors, and contravenes the core moral underpinning of contract law itself—the keeping of promises—it is ripe for revision (Cunningham, 2006; Hartman, 2000).

The right to full labor market participation. Federal and state laws impose restrictions on the types and hours of employment in which individuals younger than 18 may engage. Federal law, through the Fair Labor Standards Act (FLSA), curtails the employment of individuals younger than 16, but it imposes relatively few restrictions on the employment of those aged 16 and older. The FLSA instead leaves 16- and 17-year-olds largely free to engage in paid employment in nonhazardous occupations; for example, the act imposes no work restrictions on individuals aged 16 and older. Many states, however, have adopted measures that extend greater protections to older teens with the goal of preventing their paid work from interfering with their health or education. These measures generally impose limits on the number of hours 16- and 17-year-olds may work. Once workers reach age 18, they are no longer subject to these special protections.

The provisions of the FLSA and other labor regulations that free individuals from restrictions on their employment upon reaching the age of majority roughly correspond with the completion of high school. As noted, economic changes have made postsecondary education increasingly necessary to obtaining middle-class income. Due to increases in the costs of that education and parents' unwillingness or inability to provide ongoing financial support, more students today than in recent decades find it necessary to work either full or part time while enrolled in school (Gauthier & Furstenberg, 2005).

It is regrettable that the difficulty of financing postsecondary education requires many students to combine work and school, increasing the length of time required to complete their educations and obtain desirable employment. Ameliorating this difficulty might entail any number of policy revisions. Those efforts arguably ought not occur, however, by way of revisions to existing labor protections.

The right to political and civic participation. With few exceptions, individuals acquire the rights and duties of political and civic participation at age 18. The national voting age is 18 (Hamilton, 2012). States have the authority to set the voting age lower, but the 26th Amendment prevents their setting it higher. Some states permit 17-year-olds to vote in primary elections if they will turn 18 by the general election, but no state has chosen to allow individuals younger than 18 to vote. There has been a global move to lower the voting age, as well as scattered efforts in several U.S. states and municipalities to do so (Hamilton, 2012). Some municipalities, including Hyattsville, Greenbelt, and Takoma Park, all in Maryland, have enacted legislation lowering the voting age to 16 for local elections (Powers, 2013). Berkeley and Oakland, California, allow 16-year-olds to vote in school board elections.

The national age for draft eligibility and voluntary enlistment in any of the branches of the military absent parental consent is 18. Individuals who obtain parental consent may voluntarily enlist at 17. The age at which individuals become eligible to sit on federal juries is 18, lowered from 21 in 1972 by amendment to the federal Jury Selection and Service Act. In the states, there is only slightly more variation in the age of jury eligibility, and these closely track the states' respective ages of majority (National Conference of State Legislatures, 2015). Thus, the near-universal age at which individuals become eligible for jury service is 18 (in 46 states and the District of Columbia); the age for jury service eligibility is 19 in two states and 21 in two other states.

Although individuals acquire most rights to civic and political participation upon reaching the age of majority, it is not unusual for governments to impose separate age requirements on holders of various state and federal offices. Both federal and state constitutional provisions require individuals to meet higher age requirements in order to qualify to hold certain offices.

The right to medical and procreative choice. The authority to make medical decisions affecting minors presumptively rests with their parents (Hill, 2012; Mutcherson, 2005). Only upon reaching the age of majority are individuals categorically entitled to make their own medical decisions (Vukadinovich, 2004). Minors may consent to treatment in some circumstances, including in cases of emergency, in cases involving reproductive health care, and in cases involving mental health care (Hartman, 2002; Hill, 2012).

States may require minors to obtain parental consent prior to obtaining an abortion. But states must provide for an alternative bypass procedure where a neutral third party must consent to the abortion upon finding either that (a) the minor is sufficiently mature and informed to make the decision independently or (b) an abortion would be in her best interests (see *Bellotti v. Baird*, 1979, and *Planned Parenthood v. Danforth*, 1976; Guggenheim, 2002). Generally, emancipated minors and minors determined on an individualized basis to possess adequate maturity (pursuant to what is known as the "mature minor" doctrine) may also make their own medical decisions (Newman, 2001).

Exceptions to the Age of Majority

A survey of just a number of the legal exceptions to the presumptive age of majority, like the one that follows, leads to two conclusions about the age of majority itself. First, the proliferation of exceptions to it demonstrates that the age of majority insufficiently meets current social needs. That the exceptions alter legal consequences for individuals variously past the age of majority and those who have not yet attained it, moreover, suggests that perhaps no categorical age of majority can adequately meet social needs.

Second, the existence of exceptions that apply in specific legal contexts demonstrates that it is not unduly burdensome for lawmakers to engage in this sort of context-specific rulemaking. Stated differently, categorical rules like the age of majority serve useful purposes by eliminating uncertainty and advancing efficiency. Yet lawmaking that impacts young people has already begun to alter in order to better address, in comparison to the presumptive age of majority, the needs of society and capacities or incapacities of young people.

Giving sexual consent. Every state has established a minimum age at which individuals may consent to sex. Seven states have set the age of sexual consent at 18—the legal age of majority in those states. The remainder have set the age of consent below the age of majority (Drobac, 2004). The most common age adopted by states is 16, while four states have set the age of sexual consent at age 14 (Drobac, 2004; Todres, 2012).

Although sexual consent laws on occasion lead to the criminal prosecution of teenagers who engage in consensual sex, states have generally revised their laws so that only individuals who are significantly older than the minor below the age of consent are subject to prosecution (Glosser, 2004). Historically, statutory rape laws aimed to protect young women and restrict their sexual activity (Olsen, 1984). Today, the age of sexual consent and statutory rape laws that rely on the age differential between the victim and perpetrator reflect pragmatic responses to the prevalence of teenage sexual activity. Indeed, nearly half of all high school students surveyed in 2009 reported having engaged in sexual intercourse (Eaton, 2009).

The right to drive. Although car crashes kill more teens than any other cause, the United States grants drivers' licenses earlier than any other nation in the developed world (Hamilton, 2014). Every state issues licenses to individuals younger than 18, with most states setting the age of licensure at 16. A few states set the driving age at 14 or 15, and only one—New Jersey—has set it higher, at age 17 (Hamilton, 2014).

As reviewed by Hamilton (2014), the youngest drivers crash at the highest rates. Crash rates are consistently highest among 16-year-olds and decline substantially with each year of increasing age. Driving experience alone does not account for the different crash rates, and younger novice drivers have significantly higher crash rates than do older novices. This evidence has led most states to adopt graduated licensing systems that permit novice drivers to gain experience but impose on them restrictions (e.g., passenger limits and night-time driving restrictions) aimed at reducing their exposure to hazardous driving contexts (Hamilton, 2014).

The right to purchase, possess, and consume alcohol. Congress conditioned states' receipt of federal highway funds on their imposing a drinking age of 21 (e.g., see *South Dakota v. Dole*, 1987). In light of high rates of alcohol-related injuries and death, many states readily raised their drinking ages (Rosenthal, 1988). Some lawmakers argued against what they viewed as inconsistent and unfair treatment of young people aged 18 and older. They reasoned that young people who were subject to the draft and permitted to enlist voluntarily in the armed services ought not be denied the adult right to consume alcohol (Cunningham, 2006). While arguments against raising the drinking age above states' ages of majority failed, some scholars have suggested that the psychological research on adolescent and emerging adult capacity supports lowering the drinking age (Cunningham, 2006). As an increasing number of states legalize or decriminalize marijuana for adults (see https://www.ncsl.org/research/health/state-medical-marijuana-laws.aspx), these same arguments may be made in this emerging context.

Continued entitlement to parental support and benefits. The Dependent Coverage Mandate of the Affordable Care Act (ACA) expanded the availability of health insurance for young adults by allowing those aged 19–26 to remain covered as dependents under their parents' plans (Collins, 2012). Minors have long received medical coverage through their parents' employer-provided health plans. After age 18 or graduating from college, however, minors were reclassified as adults and lost their dependent status, along with the derivative health benefits that attended it (Collins, 2012). These young adults obtained health coverage only with difficulty, if at all (Collins, 2011). In 2010, only one in three young adults aged 19–25 had no health insurance (Cohen & Martinez, 2011; DeNavas-Walt, 2012). The effect of the Dependent Coverage Mandate was dramatic, and parents rushed to add their adult children to their health plans. In the year after its passage, parents had extended health insurance to 6.6 million young adults who had been ineligible for such coverage before the ACA's passage (Antwi, 2012; Cohen & Martinez, 2011). As of 2016, moreover, six states require or authorize insurers to cover young adults beyond age 26, with age cut-offs ranging from 29 to 31 (National Conference of State Legislatures, 2016). The Dependent Coverage Mandate extends to a wide swath of legal adults a benefit long associated with minor and dependent status. Its very title signals that this cohort of legal adults commonly remains reliant on others in significant respects. As such, they lack the independence that is one of the characteristic markers of adulthood, despite having formally attained that legal status.

Adulthood Deinstitutionalized
The nature of the transition to adulthood is not at all fixed or definite (Arnett, 2006). It is instead variable, not only with respect to its timing (whether it occurs earlier or later in a young person's life), but also with respect to its substance (those characteristics whose attainment marks adult status). Arguably the nature of the transition has contributed to a modern conception of adulthood itself as a status achieved only gradually and not dependent on the attainment of specific external events, such as marriage or the completion of education (Arnett, 2007).

Structural Influences on the Transition to Adulthood
Historians of society have identified five significant events that have, for more than a century, marked the transition from minority to adulthood for most young Americans: (a) marrying, (b) leaving their parents' homes, (c) establishing households of their own, (d) completing their educations or leaving school, and (e) entering the workforce (Modell et al., 1976). While a minority of the young population has always taken other paths to adulthood (e.g., never marrying or remaining resident with their parents), the dominance of this five-part pathway to adulthood has made it the modern "bedrock of social organization," channeling most Americans onto "paths to a narrowly conceived adulthood" (Stanger-Ross et al., 2005, p. 626).

Most young Americans thus experienced each of the five transition events along the course to adulthood. The timing of the events and the order in which they have tended to occur, however, have varied in important ways over time (Stanger-Ross et al., 2005). A whole range of interrelated social contexts have influenced these variations, with structural changes having particular salience for young people coming of age in the 20th and early 21st centuries. Scholars now characterize the transition to adulthood during this period of roughly 100 years not as a continuous evolution or trend, but as separable into three discrete but related eras.

Viewing the "dramatic shifts" in the path to adulthood in the historical context in which they transpired helps "serve to undermine a normative understanding of the transition to adulthood and to point, instead, to its deeply historical dynamics" (Stanger-Ross et al., 2005, p. 645). Young people's conceptions of the transition to adulthood emphasize the variable aspects of the pathway to adulthood and the variable meaning of adulthood itself.

Sociocultural Conceptions of Modern Adulthood

Psychologist Jeffrey Arnett conducted a series of studies across the United States to identify contemporary conceptions of adulthood among young people themselves (Arnett, 2004, 2006). The studies found that their conceptions depart radically from the traditional conception of the transition to adulthood. For one, young people rarely list any of the five transition events that have long defined the attainment of adult status. Instead, researchers have consistently found that individuals perceive the most significant markers of adulthood to be (a) accepting responsibility for oneself, (b) making independent decisions, and (c) attaining financial independence (Arnett, 2004, 2006).

Additionally, for the young people who participated in the studies, accepting responsibility for oneself connotes shouldering the responsibilities previously assumed by parents rather than expecting parents to deal with the consequences of one's actions (Arnett, 2004). Independent decision making to them connotes making important life decisions oneself, outside the influence of one's parents. And to be financially independent means no longer relying on one's parents to pay one's bills (Arnett, 2004).

As Arnett (2006) explains, individuals achieve each of the three markers gradually rather than experiencing them as the transition events, which people experience as "milestones that take place at a specific time and that a person clearly either has or has not reached" (p. 4) such as getting married or completing education. This absence of readily identifiable markers may contribute to what young people who have attained the age of legal majority consistently report with respect to their status: Despite having formally reached legal adult status, young people in the process of developing what they perceive to be the markers of adulthood report that they do not consider themselves adults. Instead, they feel as though they occupy a status somewhere between adolescence and full adulthood (Arnett, 2006).

Arnett (2000) has termed this in-between period "emerging adulthood," which he characterizes as a distinct developmental period spanning approximately ages 18–25 (see also Gillespie et al., this volume). He emphasizes that it is a status largely experienced by young people in wealthier, developed nations rather than a universal stage of development. Nonetheless, his theory of emerging adulthood finds additional empirical support in the developmental sciences. Indeed, there is now an empirical journal dedicated to the construct of emerging adulthood (https://journals.sagepub.com/home/eax), as well as the Society for the Study of Emerging Adulthood with a biennial conference (http://www.ssea.org/).

Cognitive and Socioemotional Development From Adolescence Through Emerging Adulthood

Developmental neuroscientists, aided by technological developments over the last decade that allow them to observe the brain as it performs different tasks, posit that the development of neural systems along different timelines can help explain adolescent risk taking and poor decision making despite adolescents' apparent cognitive abilities, as well as other aspects of adolescent behavior (Burnett et al., 2011; Casey et al., 2008).

The first neural system, referred to as the socioemotional system, involves social information processing and reward seeking and processing (Geier & Luna, 2009; Steinberg, 2008). Activity in neural reward systems peaks rapidly around the time of pubertal maturation (in early adolescence) and then declines (Geier & Luna, 2009; Nelson et al., 2012). It is this peak in activity, neuroscientists believe, that leads to heightened reward salience—that is, adolescents experience rewarding stimuli as even more rewarding than during either childhood or adulthood. This helps explain adolescent sensation-seeking behaviors in which they seek out new and highly stimulating experiences and willingly take risks in order to attain them (Steinberg, 2008).

The system referred to as the cognitive control system, involving abilities to intentionally coordinate and engage in goal-directed behavior, follows a different developmental trajectory. Its development is more gradual and linear than that of the socioemotional system (Gogtay & Thompson, 2010; Paus, 2005; Steinberg, 2008; Toga et al., 2006). Along with other structural changes in the brain, this developmental trajectory correlates with the steady improvement of basic cognitive processes into adolescence, with the maturation of basic cognitive processes largely complete by midadolescence (Luna et al., 2010; Steinberg, 2008).

In sum, adolescents' basic cognitive abilities tend to mature by age 16 and give them the increased capacity to learn, process information, reason, and make rational decisions. Self-regulatory capacities continue to develop, however, making adolescents susceptible to the confounding influence of their heightened sensitivity to reward (Steinberg, 2008). This heightened sensitivity, which peaks around midadolescence, inclines adolescents toward sensation seeking, risk taking, and impulsivity. Self-regulatory immaturity can dominate or overwhelm cognitive processes and drive adolescent behaviors, particularly in high-pressure contexts and those triggering heightened emotion (Luna et al., 2010; Steinberg, 2008).

Improved coordination of affect (the external expression of emotions) and cognition correlates with increased connectivity between regions of the brain involved in social and emotional information processing and those involved in cognitive processes (Luna et al., 2010; Steinberg, 2008). Thus, emotional regulation and impulse control both improve through adolescence and into the mid-20s. The continuation of developmental processes into the postadolescent period provides some neurobiological support that buttresses the behavioral case for categorizing "emerging adulthood" as a distinct period of development (Arnett, 2013).

Dismantling the Categorical Age of Majority

Informed by the preceding sections of this chapter, in this section I contend that the exceptions to the presumptive age of majority better address the needs of society and young people alike. I argue for the explicit adoption of a "rule comprising exceptions"—in other words, for the abandonment altogether of the presumptive age of legal majority in favor of context-specific rules. The state's commitment to individual liberty supports such an approach because it extends to individuals those rights which they have attained the capacity to exercise.

I also argue that other commitments, namely commitments to community, mitigate against the retention of adulthood as a categorical legal status. Finally, I provide guidance to lawmakers seeking to assess capacity in certain contexts, offering insights from behavioral decision research, and propose the adoption of a number of policy measures consistent with the policymaking approach advanced here.

Context-Specific Competence

Young people reliably attain different capabilities at distinct stages of development. Accordingly, across a range of policymaking contexts, a categorical rule will fail to take account either of context-specific capacities or of ongoing deficiencies. The core commitments of the liberal democratic state require it to account for context-specific capabilities (Byrnes, 2005). Further, the state's commitment to community (in tension with individual liberty but important nonetheless) provides further support for jettisoning adulthood as status.

Individual competence and core commitments of the liberal democratic state. Individual liberty is the core value of the liberal constitutional democratic state, and safeguarding its citizens' liberty is therefore the state's primary end (see Hamilton, 2010). The minimum entitlement of all citizens is the basic liberty to decide one's life course for oneself, and it is the state's duty to guarantee it. Those individuals whose capabilities in some respect remain immature have two basic categories of interests that the state should take account of in its decision making: welfare interests and autonomy interests (Hamilton, 2010). Their welfare interests pertain to their well-being, irrespective of any affirmative choice they make, including an interest in being protected from their own deficiencies. Their autonomy-related interests pertain to their exercising those specific liberties of which they are capable.

Simply put, lawmakers should work to become more cognizant of and responsive to young people's capacities and extend to them age- and context-specific liberties to make the self-regarding decisions of which they are capable (Dwyer, 2006; Hamilton, 2010). This decision-making process can indeed be a complex one, although the developmental and behavioral sciences can (and ought to) supplement the more traditional policymaking considerations.

Respected scholars (e.g., Scott, 2000) have argued against abandoning the age of majority as a categorical rule. Scott reasons that, although like all categorical rules it includes some level of imprecision, the age of majority serves society's purposes relatively well by advancing the goals of certainty and administrative efficiency. Moreover, to the extent it underestimates young persons' capacities in certain legal contexts (such as minors' competence to execute contracts) and delays their ability to exercise certain rights, the harms are generally slight, and temporary.

Although I agree with Scott's (2000) identification of the costs and benefits of the categorical rule, I would weigh them differently. Existing law, rife with exceptions to the age of majority, demonstrates that context-specific decision making poses no undue burden on lawmakers. The argument that failure to extend liberties despite individual capacity imposes minimal harm elides the primacy of the state's obligation to individual liberty. Where capacity exists, the justification for denying that liberty (or vesting it in a parent or guardian) disappears. Further, with respect to certain rights, delay itself can constitute denial. For example, the 16-year-old who would refuse surgery to correct a nonfatal congenital defect will be denied the right to do so if her parents consent to the procedure. For the young patient, acquiring the right to make her own medical decisions after reaching majority provides no relief from the earlier denial of that right.

Adult status, autonomy, and relationship. As discussed previously, young people in today's developed nations identify as markers of adulthood (a) accepting responsibility for oneself, (b) making independent decisions, and (c) attaining financial independence. At one level, this construction of adulthood is altogether unobjectionable. Most parents, after all, work to raise their children to be responsible, financially independent adults. At another level, this conception of adulthood is deeply troubling. Conspicuously absent from it are notions of obligation to community or family, or indeed any recognition of the role of ongoing connection and interdependence (Federle, 1993; Fineman, 2004). The current conception of adulthood instead emphasizes as normative the attainment of individual autonomy and independence. The absence of notions of community is particularly notable in light of the growing importance of ongoing familial support to young people coming of age today.

To the extent it expresses a societal expectation or norm of across-the-board independence (decisional, financial, etc.), the current conception of adulthood is out of step with the experiences of today's young people. To the extent that the law conveys a normative expectation that they are adults and thus ought to possess adult characteristics, their inability to have done so by the legally prescribed age may be both experienced and perceived as failure. Not attaining the characteristics of adulthood by the legal age of majority, however, merely reflects the particular social context—including the economic context—in which they are coming of age.

The state's affirmative duty to act for the purpose of expressing the importance of connection and interdependence is arguably quite limited. But doing so presents lawmakers with what seems a rare opportunity to advance individual liberty (by rejecting the categorical rule in favor of rules more tailored to individual capacities) while also expressing the importance of relationships and community.

Assessing Capacity: Lessons from Existing Law and Science

Categorical rules like an age of legal majority advance goals of administrative efficiency and certainty (Scott, 2000). The existence of a categorical rule spares the decision maker in a given case the task of making burdensome (and likely unreliable) individualized assessments of capacity. Yet, as argued earlier, lawmakers in the liberal state have a duty to assess the capacities of immature citizens in legal contexts (Hamilton, 2010).

In any given context, the interplay of various factors will influence capacity. It is possible to characterize age-related capacity as a function of (a) patterns of cognitive and socioemotional development; (b) the nature of the capacity being exercised (e.g., characteristics of the task to be performed or the decision to be made); (c) the context in which the capacity will be exercised; and (d) the broader social, cultural, and economic milieu. The interrelationship of factors in these categories shapes in predictable ways the typical individual's capacity, for example, to make a decision in a certain context or perform a given task. Identifying and accounting for the relevant aspects of these influences on the exercise of capacity can significantly improve policymakers' predictive power.

What, if anything, can brain science contribute to lawmaking or policymaking? It is now well known that developmental science has shed light on aspects of child and adolescent behavior that has important policymaking implications (Maroney, 2009; Steinberg, 2009). Perhaps the most widely touted of these has been lawmaking in the area of juvenile justice (Scott & Steinberg, 2008). Casual observation can—and has—led to erroneous generalizations about behavior. These mistaken generalizations in turn have led to misguided policymaking. For example, adolescent impulsivity and susceptibility to peer pressure in certain situations have led to the conclusion that they lack the capacity to make reliably mature voting decisions in elections or medical decisions in a doctor's office (Hamilton, 2012). Conversely, adolescents' ability to learn the mechanics of motor vehicle operation has led to the conclusion that they have the capacity to operate them competently (Hamilton, 2014). Both conclusions are wrong, and insights from the psychological and neurological sciences help to explain why.

Conclusion

Young people's conception of adulthood, and their experience of becoming adults, bears little resemblance to the legal construction of adulthood as status. Although they formally attain adult status upon reaching the legal age of majority, that formal marker has remarkably little meaning in young people's lives. What is now socially meaningful is the gradual attainment of the various indicia of adulthood—responsibility for oneself, autonomous decision making, and financial self-sufficiency.

I have argued in this chapter that the categorical age of majority contravenes a legal reality constructed by the proliferation of exceptions to it, young people's social experience and subjective constructive of the transition to adulthood, and the capacities gained (and deficiencies retained) over the predictable course of individual developmental processes. By retaining it, the state fails its foremost obligation to safeguard the basic liberties of its citizens. Legal consequences linked to the age of majority are best amended to attach to the specific age to which they pertain—whether or not that is the current age of majority.

I suggest further that the time may have come to jettison not only adulthood as legal status but also adulthood as social construct. Doing so presents the state with a rare opportunity to simultaneously safeguard individual autonomy rights through context-specific rulemaking and also advance the importance of community relationships and the interdependencies of citizens, even in liberal society.

References

Amar, A. R. (2005). *America's constitution: A biography*. Random House.
Appell, A. R. (2009). The pre-political child of child-centered jurisprudence. *Houston Law Review, 46*(3), 703–706.
Arnett, J. J. (2000). Emerging adulthood: A theory of development from the late teens through the twenties. *American Psychologist, 55*(5), 469–480. https://doi.org/10.1037/0003-066X.55.5.469
Arnett, J. J. (2004). *Emerging adulthood: The winding road from the late teens through the twenties*. Oxford University Press.
Arnett, J. J. (2006). Emerging adulthood: Understanding the new way of coming of age. In J. J. Arnett & J. L. Tanner (Eds.), *Emerging adults in America: Coming of age in the 21st century* (pp. 3–19). APA Books. https://doi.org/10.1037/11381-001
Arnett, J. J. (2007). Suffering, selfish, slackers? Myths and reality about emerging adults. *Journal of Youth and Adolescence, 36*(1), 23–29. https://doi.org/10.1007/s10964-006-9157-z
Arnett, J. J. (2013). *Adolescence and emerging adulthood: A cultural approach*. Pearson Education.
Arshagouni, P. (2006). But I'm an adult now . . . sort of: Adolescent consent in health care decision-making and the adolescent brain. *Journal of Health Care Law & Policy, 9*(2), 315–364.
Bellotti v. Baird, 443 U.S. 622 (1979).
Burnett, S., Sebastian, C., Kadosh, K. C., & Blakemore, S. J. (2011). The social brain in adolescence: Evidence from functional magnetic resonance imaging and behavioural studies. *Neuroscience & Biobehavioral Reviews, 35*(8), 1654–1664. https://doi.org/10.1016/j.neubiorev.2010.10.011
Byrnes, J. P. (2005). The development of self-regulated decision making. In J. Jacobs & P. Klaczynski (Eds.), *The development of judgment and decision-making in children and adolescence* (pp. 5–38). Erlbaum.
Casey, B. J., Jones, R. M., & Hare, T. A. (2008). The adolescent brain. *Annals of the New York Academy of Science, 1124*(1), 111–126. https://doi.org/10.1196/annals.1440.010
Collins, S. R. (2012). *Young, Uninsured, and in Debt: Why Young Adults Lack Health Insurance and How the Affordable Care Act Is Helping*. Commonwealth Fund (p. 2). http://www.commonwealthfund.org/<diff>/media/Files/Publications/Issue%20Brief/2012/Jun/1604_collins_young_uninsured_in_debt_v4.pdf
Collins, S. R. (2011), *Realizing Health Reform's Potential: How the Affordable Care Act Is Helping Young Adults Stay Covered*, Commonwealth Fund (p. 1), http://www.commonwealthfund.org/<diff>/media/files/publications/issue-brief/2011/may/1508_collins_how_aca_is_helping_young_adults_reform_brief_v5_corrected.pdf
Cultice, W. W. (1992). *Youth's battle for the ballot: A history of voting age in America*. Greenwood.
Cunningham, L. (2006). Question of capacity: Towards comprehensive and consistent vision of children and their status under law. *UC Davis Journal of Juvenile Law Policy, 10*(2), 275–378.
Dean, W. E. (1994). Ireland v. Ireland: Judicial emancipation of minors in Idaho: Protecting the best interests of the child or conferring a windfall upon the parent? *Idaho Law Review, 31*, 205–215.
DeNavas-Walt, C. (2012, September). *Income, poverty, and health insurance coverage in the United States: 2011*. U.S. Census Bureau. http://www.census.gov/prod/2012pubs/p60-243.pdf
DiMatteo, L. A. (1995). Deconstructing the myth of the "infancy law doctrine": From incapacity to accountability. *Ohio Northern University Law Review, 21*, 481–526.

Drobac, J. A. (2004). Sex and the workplace: "Consenting" adolescents and a conflict of laws. *Washington Law Review, 79*(2), 486–574.

Dwyer, J. G. (2006). *The relationship rights of children*. Cambridge University Press.

Eaton, D. K. (2009). Youth risk behavior surveillance-United States. Morbidity & Mortality Weekley Report, June 2010, 98 tbl.61.

Emancipation of Certain Minors. Haw. Rev. Stat. § 577-25, 2015.

Federle, K. H. (1993). On the road to reconceiving rights for children: A postfeminist analysis of the capacity principle. *DePaul Law Review, 42*, 1017–1019.

Fineman, M. A. (2004). *The autonomy myth: A theory of dependency*. New Press.

Gauthier, A. H., & Furstenberg, F. F. (2005). Historical trends in patterns of time use among young adults in developed countries. In R. A. Settersten (Ed.), *On the frontier of adulthood: Theory, research, and public policy* (pp. 150–176). University of Chicago Press.

Geier, C., & Luna, B. (2009). The maturation of incentive processing and cognitive control. *Pharmacology Biochemistry and Behavior, 93*(3), 212–221. https://doi.org/10.1016/j.pbb.2009.01.021

Glassman, M., & Karno, D. (2009). On establishing a housing right of contract for homeless youth in America. *Seattle Journal for Social Justice, 7*(2), 437–466.

Glosser, A. (2004). Statutory Rape: A Guide to State Laws and Reporting Requirements. *Department of Health & Human Services*, ES-1, 6 tbl.1, 6-8. http://aspe.hhs.gov/hsp/08/SR/StateLaws/report.pdf

Gogtay, N., & Thompson, P. M. (2010). Mapping gray matter development: Implications for typical development and vulnerability to psychopathology. *Brain and Cognition, 72*(1), 6–15. https://doi.org/10.1016/j.bandc.2009.08.009

Guggenheim, M. (2002). Minor rights: The adolescent abortion cases. *Hofstra Law Review, 30*(3), 589–646.

Hamilton, V. E. (2010). Immature citizens and the state. *BYU Law Review, 2010*(4), 1055–1148.

Hamilton, V. E. (2012). Democratic inclusion, cognitive development, and the age of electoral majority. *Brooklyn Law Review, 77*(4), 1447–1514.

Hamilton, V. E. (2014). Liberty without capacity: Why states should ban adolescent driving. *Georgia Law Review, 48*, 1019–1084.

Hartman, R. (2000). Adolescent autonomy: Clarifying an ageless conundrum. *Hastings Law Journal, 51*(6), 1265–1362.

Hartman, R. (2002). Coming of age: Devising legislation for adolescent medical decision-making. *American Journal of Law & Medicine, 28*(4), 409–454.

Hill, B. (2012). Medical decision making by and on behalf of adolescents: Reconsidering first principles. *Journal of Health Care Law & Policy, 15*(1), 37–74.

James, T. T. (1960). The age of majority. *American Journal of Legal History, 4*(1), 22–33.

Kandel, R., & Griffiths, A. (2003). Reconfiguring personhood: From ungovernability to parent adolescent autonomy conflict actions. *Syracuse Law Review, 53*(3), 995–1066.

Keyssar, A. (2009). *The right to vote: The contested history of democracy in the United States*. Basic Books. https://www.nypl.org/sites/default/files/keyssar_-_chapter_6_excerpt.pdf

Luna, B., Padmanabhan, A., & O'Hearn, K. (2010). What has fMRI told us about the development of cognitive control through adolescence? *Brain and Cognition, 72*(1), 101–113. https://doi.org/10.1016/j.bandc.2009.08.005

Magyar, K. A. (2006). Betwixt and between by being booted nonetheless: Developmental perspective on aging out of foster care. *Temple Law Review, 79*(2), 557–606.

Maroney, T. A. (2009). The false promise of adolescent brain science in juvenile justice. *Notre Dame Law Review, 85*(1), 89–176.

Mehler, I. M. (1963). Infant contractual responsibility: Time for reappraisal and realistic adjustment. *University of Kansas Law Review, 11*(3), 361–374.

Meyer v. Nebraska, 262 U.S. 390 (1923).

Modell, J., Furstenberg, F. F., Jr., & Hershberg, T. (1976). Social change and transitions to adulthood in historical perspective. *Journal of Family History, 1*(1), 7–32.

Mutcherson, K. M. (2005). Whose body is it anyway? An updated model of healthcare decision-making rights for adolescents. *Cornell Journal of Law and Public Policy, 14*(2), 251–326.

Antwi, Y. A., Effects of Federal Policy To Insure Young Adults: Evidence from the 2010 Affordable Care Act Dependent Coverage Mandate, (Nat'l Bureau of Econ. Research, Working Paper No. 18200, June 2012)

Cohen, R. A. & Martinez, M. E. (September 2011). *Health Insurance Coverage: Early Release of Estimates from the National Health Interview Survey*. CDC. http://www.cdc.gov/nchs/data/nhis/earlyrelease/insur201109.pdf

Kiefer v. Fred Howe Motors, Inc., 158 N.W.2d 288, 290 (Wis. 1968).

National Conference of State Legislatures. (2015, March). *Termination of support—Age of majority*. https://www.ncsl.org/research/human-services/termination-of-child-support-age-of-majority.aspx

National Conference of State Legislatures. (2016, November 11). *Dependent health coverage and age for healthcare benefits*. https://www.ncsl.org/research/health/dependent-health-coverage-state-implementation.aspx

Nelson, C. A., Thomas, K. M., & De Haan, M. (2012). *Neuroscience of cognitive development: The role of experience and the developing brain*. John Wiley & Sons.

Newman, A. (2001). Adolescent consent to routine medical and surgical treatment: A proposal to simplify the law of teenage medical decision-making. *Journal of Legal Medicine*, 22(4), 501–532. https://doi.org/10.1080/019476 40152750946

Olsen, F. (1984). Statutory rape: A feminist critique of rights analysis. *Texas Law Review*, 387, 390–401.

Paus, T. (2005). Mapping brain maturation and cognitive development during adolescence. *Trends in Cognitive Sciences*, 9(2), 60–68. https://doi.org/10.1016/j.tics.2004.12.008

Perillo, J. M. (2002). *Corbin on contracts* (7th rev. ed., § 27.6). LexisNexis.

Pierce v. Society of Sisters, 268 U.S. 510 (1925).

Planned Parenthood v. Danforth, 428 U.S. 52 (1976).

Powers, L. A. (2013, May 14). Takoma Park grants 16-year-olds right to vote. *Washington Post*. https://www.washingtonpost.com/local/takoma-park-grants-16-year-olds-right-to-vote/2013/05/14/b27c52c4-bccd-11e2-89c9-3be8095fe767_story.html

Roper v. Simmons, 543 U.S. 551 (2005).

Rosenthal, M. P. (1988). The minimum drinking age for young people: An observation. *Dickinson Law Review*, 92(3), 649–664.

Sanger, C., & Willemsen, E. (1992). Minor changes: Emancipating children in modern times. *University of Michigan Journal of Law Reform*, 25(2), 239–356.

Scott, E. S. (2000). The legal construction of adolescence. *Hofstra Law Review*, 29(2), 547–598.

Scott, E. S., & Steinberg, L. D. (2008). *Rethinking juvenile justice*. Harvard University Press. http://64.207.185.181/downloads/2010_12_01_RethinkingJuvenileJusticeSteinbergPresentation.pdf

South Dakota v. Dole, 483 U.S. 203 (1987).

Stanger-Ross, J., Collins, C., & Stern, M. J. (2005). Falling far from the tree: Transitions to adulthood and the social history of twentieth-century America. *Social Science History*, 29(4), 625–648. https://doi.org/10.1017/S01455 5320001333X

Steinberg, L. (2008). A social neuroscience perspective on adolescent risk-taking. *Developmental Review*, 28, 83.

Steinberg, L. (2009). Should the science of adolescent brain development inform public policy? *American Psychologist*, 64(8), 739–750. https://doi.org/10.1037/0003-066X.64.8.739

Steinberg, L. (2014). Should the science of adolescent brain development inform public policy? *Court Review*, 50(2), 70–77.

Stephenson, D. G. (2004). *The right to vote: Rights and liberties under the law*. ABC-CLIO.

Todres, J. (2012). Maturity. *Houston Law Review*, 48(5), 1107–1166.

Toga, A. W., Thompson, P. M., & Sowell, E. R. (2006). Mapping brain maturation. *Focus*, 29(3), 148–390. https://doi.org/10.1016/j.tins.2006.01.007

Vukadinovich, D. M. (2004). Minors' rights to consent to treatment: Navigating the complexity of state laws. *Journal of Health Law*, 37(4), 667.

Williston, S., & Lord, R. A. (1993). *A treatise on the law of contracts* (4th ed.). Baker, Voorhis.

CHAPTER 18

Schools and Juvenile Justice

Adam D. Fine, Kayleigh A. Stanek, and Andrea N. Montes

> **Abstract**
> School environments prioritize not just academic achievement but also youth development and socialization. However, the school environment can serve as a catalyst for involving youth in the juvenile justice system. In contemporary schools, students often have contact with legal actors, such as school resource officers or probation officers. Many schools also invest in policies and programs that involve bringing court actors into the school environment to respond to student misbehavior or to be a part of efforts to improve school safety. This chapter discusses the current state of the literature on how schools and the legal system interact, and their combined impact on students' well-being. Scholars have found that embedding legal actors within schools can disproportionately affect minority students and create a school-to-prison pipeline. Simultaneously, there is little evidence that these initiatives have improved school safety. It concludes with recommendations for advancing research, policy, and practice.
>
> **Key Words:** school safety, school delinquency, disparities, school resource officers, truancy, juvenile probation, school probation

In the United States, youth spend more of their waking time in school than anywhere else, making schools the primary place where youth development occurs. While schools can provide a positive environment for many students, it can also be the place where students first come into contact with the juvenile justice system (JJS). In an effort to maintain a safe school environment, and in response to school shootings across the nation, many school districts now have legal actors who work on their campuses. The goal of this chapter is to explore how schools and the legal system interact. In so doing, we also discuss how these well-intentioned efforts can sometimes cause harm.

The chapter opens with a discussion about the linkages between juvenile delinquency and school safety, including an exploration of key theoretical frameworks that explain the dynamic and contextual processes that may contribute to youth delinquency and, in turn, undermine school safety. The second section focuses on approaches often leveraged in an effort to improve or maintain school safety, including both traditional deterrence-based approaches, such as zero tolerance, and modern approaches, such as the Friendly Schools Project, the Emotional and Behavioral Health–Crisis Response and Prevention intervention, and restorative justice (RJ) programming. The third section discusses how the legal system has become embedded within schools. This discussion focuses on the employment of school resource officers (SROs) and juvenile probation officers (JPOs), as well as the use of school-based diversion programs such as teen court and truancy boards. The fourth section discusses some of the most problematic, iatrogenic outcomes of school safety initiatives. These include fueling the school-to-prison pipeline (STPP) and contributing to racial and ethnic disparities in juvenile justice outcomes. The final section offers suggestions for improving relations between schools and the legal system and recommends shifting to developmentally appropriate approaches that enhance school safety while reducing juvenile delinquency.

School Safety and Juvenile Delinquency

Youth, parents, school staff, and policymakers frequently express questions about whether their schools are safe. Indeed, parents report having serious concerns about their children's safety in schools, and parents' ratings of how safe their children are in school are declining. Leveraging Gallup data, Jones (2018) reported that in 2018, 35% of parents feared for their child's safety while at school, which was up from 24% in 2017 and was the highest since a peak in 1999. Among youth, concerns about safety may increase with age. The results of a 2015 Gallup Student Poll revealed that when compared to fifth graders, almost 50% fewer high schoolers felt safe in school (see a review by Calderon, 2016).

Beyond the moral and ethical imperatives associated with ensuring students feel safe in school, safety has myriad implications for youth outcomes, including that youth who feel unsafe in school are more likely to engage in delinquency. This situation creates a vicious cycle wherein youth who feel unsafe are more likely to engage in delinquency, and that delinquency in turn makes the school less safe. In an effort to better understand why youth engage in delinquency at school, a number of theoretical perspectives have emerged across multiple disciplines, each being followed by dozens of studies that test particular aspects of the theoretical perspective. In what follows, we provide introductions to three of the most widely supported and researched theoretical models that help explain the linkages between perceptions of school safety and delinquency.

Social Disorganization Theory

Juvenile delinquency, including violence, is not equally distributed across schools. It is an unfortunate reality that, like crime in neighborhoods, delinquency rates are substantially and consistently higher in some schools. Social disorganization theory (SDT; Shaw & McKay, 1942) begins with the premise that there is a nonrandom distribution of crime. It then explores the reasons that crime rates may be higher within certain communities. At its core, SDT posits that structural characteristics can explain neighborhood-level differences in the rates of crime, violence, or delinquency (Bellair, 2017; Kubrin & Mioduszewski, 2019; Shaw & McKay, 1942). As Kubrin and Mioduszewski (2019) explain, a main contribution of SDT is that it challenges the prevailing rational choice explanations of criminal behavior and instead points to social problems as one of crime's root determinants.

Traditionally, SDT has been applied to neighborhoods and communities, but its logic has recently been extended to school environments (Pusch, 2022). While only a handful of studies have tested SDT within the school setting, the research is largely supportive of the proposition that more disorganized schools tend to have higher rates of juvenile delinquency (Pusch, 2022). Consistent with the tenets of SDT, it is more difficult for students in schools with high rates of student mobility to form connections with other students, which in turn inhibits the development of social control (Pusch, 2022; Wilson, 2004). Indeed, the building of shared social norms among students is required to invoke social control and enhance student safety (Sampson et al., 1997; Zaykowski & Gunter, 2012). Studies find that students feel safer not only in schools where there are strong student–teacher bonds (Williams et al., 2018) but also when they are exposed to less violence (Adams & Mrug, 2019; Crosnoe et al., 2004; Waasdorp et al., 2011).

General Strain Theory

General strain theory (GST; Agnew, 1992) is another theoretical perspective that helps explain the linkages between school safety and delinquency. At its broadest level, GST proposes that individuals may respond to strenuous experiences by engaging in antisocial behavior or crime. Agnew (1992) argued that there are different types of strain including being exposed to negative or aversive stimuli, the removal (or even the mere threat of removal) of stimuli that the individual values, and the failure of the individual to achieve their goals. Within a school context, being exposed to physical or emotional violence, or the threat thereof, constitutes clear examples of possible strains on youth.

A second component of GST is the individual's perceptions of the strain. To the extent that the individual experiences strain and perceives that experience to be unfair, the individual becomes more likely to engage in antisocial behavior as a way of coping with the strain (Agnew, 2001). This component has become a key part of research examining how GST operates for youth. Researchers suggest that in line with expectations of GST, the extent to which a youth feels as though an aspect of their environment is unsafe or unfair is just as strongly associated with their likelihood of delinquency as are objective measures of strain (Moon & Morash, 2017; Wilcox et al., 2005). As a specific example, youths' perceptions of school disorder are associated with their likelihood of engaging in externalizing and delinquent behavior (Hurd et al., 2018).

A third component of GST posits that some factors, including social support, resources, and coping skills, may moderate or buffer the strain–delinquency relation. For instance, among youth who experience a similar strain such as bullying or violence, those who feel as though they can rely on positive, supportive networks or resources in the school may be better equipped to process or overcome the particular strain. Emotional support is a key protective factor. Indeed, research suggests that youth who perceive that the school's rules or teachers are unfair or unsupportive are more likely to engage in delinquency (James et al., 2020; Wynne & Joo, 2011). Conversely, the cycle of violence within juvenile detention institutions can be mitigated when youth believe that the staff care about them (C. Brown et al., 2019). Violence can also be mitigated when students believe that adults in their school support them (James et al., 2015, 2020).

Clearly, some aspects of GST are consistent with SDT. Both argue that structural factors and youths' perceptions of them can contribute to increased youth delinquency in schools, which, in turn, can undermine school safety. When students feel as though they do not belong in their school, they become more likely to engage in delinquency, violence, and misbehavior (Allen & Kern, 2017; Pusch, 2022). As such, it appears as though both personal and contextual features of the school environment impact youth behavior. Within the developmental literature, no theory captures this nexus of person–context–time better than the social–ecological model.

Social–Ecological Model

The social–ecological model (Bronfenbrenner, 1979, 1994, 2005), also called the bioecological model, suggests that there are four defining features that interact dynamically to influence development and behavior: (a) process, (b) person, (c) context, and (d) time. To Bronfenbrenner (2005), experience is a critical element of the model. While objective features of the context are scientifically relevant and do matter for producing change, experience—the way the individual subjectively perceives the properties of their environment—is even more vital. As Bronfenbrenner and Morris (2007) explain, "Human development takes place through processes of progressively more complex reciprocal interaction between an active, evolving biopsychological human organism and the persons, objects, and symbols in its immediate external environment" (p. 798). A unique feature of this model is that it is often perceived as a meta-theory, a theoretical perspective that can elegantly incorporate aspects of other theoretical models and frameworks at each level.

On the person level, there is a prevailing developmental perspective that views adolescent delinquency as somewhat normative (Cauffman et al., 2018). According to decades of research on the age–crime curve, adolescence is a critical time for both the initiation and desistance from delinquency, including in schools. The age–crime curve suggests that the relation between age and crime is curvilinear, with the likelihood of crime beginning to increase during adolescence and reaching its peak between the ages of 18 and 25 (Gottfredson & Hirschi, 1990; Stolzenberg & D'Alessio, 2008). In fact, over a million youth under the age of 18 are arrested each year (Hockenberry & Puzzanchera, 2020), and most of these youth age out of crime normatively. To help explain this pattern, researchers have proposed the dual systems model, wherein an adolescent's vulnerability to engaging in risky and often reckless misbehavior is explained at least in part by diverging developmental trends of two critical brain systems (for a review, see Shulman et al., 2016). The "socioemotional system" or incentive-processing system begins developing at earlier ages and amplifies adolescents' desires to engage in exciting and risky behavior. In contrast, the "cognitive control" system takes longer to develop and displays protracted growth into the 20s. Because this latter system is not fully developed until later ages, there is a developmentally normative mismatch between an early-maturing system driving an adolescent's affinity for exciting and risky behavior on the one hand and a later-maturing cognitive control system that is not yet strong enough to restrain an adolescent's impulses. Research indicates that this dual system is virtually ubiquitous across national contexts (Icenogle et al., 2019). While the dual systems theory is not an explicit part of the social–ecological model, it helps explain an individual's propensity to engage in misbehavior in school during the adolescent years at the person level.

The social–ecological model also includes the impact of context. SDT proposes that social disorganization may undermine feelings of safety and promote misbehavior. It is widely understood that students' interpersonal relationships with teachers and peers are important contextual influences that impact how youth feel about their school. Indeed, students who perceive school positively also tend to enjoy school more and have better relationships with their peers, whereas youth with negative perceptions of the school environment tend to report worse outcomes across domains. For instance, in their study of the Maryland Safe and Supportive Schools Survey (conducted in New York), Coyle and colleagues (2021) found that when students felt more social support from their teachers and peers, they also felt safer in their schools. When blended with the dual systems theory, the implications for youth delinquency in school are quite clear: Youth who have a developmentally normative mismatch between their cognitive control and socioemotional systems and who are placed in a disorganized school context where they do not feel supported may be more prone to engage in delinquency.

A defining feature of the social–ecological model is its proposition that relations are bidirectional (Bronfenbrenner, 1994, 2005); just as a context impacts a youth, the youth also impacts the context. From the social–ecological perspective, youth who feel unsafe in school may decrease their attendance and performance (Barrett et al., 2012). In addition, their social engagement with peers and teachers (O'Malley et al., 2012; Yuan & McNeely, 2018) and with others in the school (Nguyen et al., 2020) may be harmed. To the extent that youths' behaviors improve or worsen, so too might the school climate.

Beyond the dynamic relations between the individual and the direct school context, the social–ecological model also incorporates the influence of contexts interacting with each other, absent the individual, and with time (Bronfenbrenner, 1979, 2005). Specifically, it points to forces and contexts that impact each other and may eventually impact students. For instance, due to policy changes over time, a school may face budget constraints and may be forced to fire teachers, thereby impacting the student-to-teacher ratios that are critical for maintaining a safe school environment. As another example, budget cuts may reduce or eliminate mental health services that could prevent violence in the school environment (Cuellar et al., 2018), including having to choose between funding SRO positions over school psychologists or social workers. The social–ecological model thus provides critical insights into how the school context may impact the school environment and, in turn, youths' perceptions of safety.

The theoretical perspectives described in this section provide rich frameworks for understanding the link between school safety and youth delinquency. The discussion highlights that school safety is a concern not just because of the moral imperative of ensuring youth are safe and feel safe while in school, but also because school safety is theoretically and empirically linked to juvenile delinquency. Students engage in more delinquency when they perceive their schools to be unsafe and less cohesive (Loukas et al., 2010; O'Neill & Vogel, 2020; Rodney et al., 2005), and school violence is associated with youth exhibiting both internalizing and externalizing problem behaviors, including engaging in violence themselves (see Cardwell et al., 2021; Varela et al., 2021). The natural question that arises, then, is what are schools doing to make their students safer?

Developing Safer Schools: Interventions and Prevention Programs

Over the last four decades, several approaches for enhancing school safety have been promoted and tested. This section begins with a discussion about the traditional zero-tolerance and deterrence-based approaches, including describing how they can fuel the STPP. We then turn to promising alternatives that have emerged in recent years, including those rooted in RJ.

Zero Tolerance

Traditional models for enhancing school safety focus on leveraging deterrence-based approaches (Pesta, 2022), which primarily entail trying to reduce unwanted behavior by driving up the costs of engaging in it and reducing its perceived benefits. This rational choice perspective assumes that individuals, including youth, are rational actors who weigh the pros and cons of acting before engaging in a particular behavior. However, based on the dual systems theory (Cauffman et al., 2018; Shulman et al., 2016), it is developmentally normative for youth to not fully consider the consequences of their behavior before acting. Altogether, the evidence for universal deterrability is lacking and evidence instead indicates immense variability in how deterrable individual people are (Infante & Fine, 2021).

Among the deterrence-based approaches, zero-tolerance policies appear to be the most widespread within schools. In response to students feeling unsafe, and undoubtedly due to pressure from both parents and political forces, schools in the late 20th century began enacting harsher, more punitive disciplinary policies for misbehaving students. As described by the American Psychological Association (APA) Zero Tolerance Task Force (2008, p. 2), "Originally developed as an approach to drug enforcement, the term became widely adopted in schools in the early 1990s as a philosophy or policy that mandates the application of predetermined consequences, most often severe and punitive in nature, that are intended to be applied regardless of the seriousness of behavior, mitigating circumstances, or situational context." The report also indicated that parents widely supported the use of zero-tolerance policies, while simultaneously noting that the policies are often developmentally inappropriate.

There is almost no empirical support for using zero-tolerance approaches to improve safety. Evidence typically suggests zero-tolerance and deterrence-based policies more generally are ineffective and, in some instances, can actually *worsen* safety. For instance, using data from the 10,992 students and 1,132 schools represented in the National Educational Longitudinal Study, Way (2011) found that stricter school rules *increased* classroom disruptions. Fissel and colleagues (2019), using longitudinal data from the Rural Substance Abuse and Violence Project, found no evidence that school-level reactive practices and proactive strategies impacted in-school delinquency. In fact, despite the widespread public support of zero-tolerance policies, discussed in outlets such as the APA's 2008 report, and the approach's basis in the tenets of deterrence theory, those authors concluded that their results showed no empirical rationale for using harsh punishments, such as zero-tolerance policies, in schools. Many other researchers entirely discourage, or at least strongly question, the use of zero-tolerance policies in schools (Huang & Cornell, 2020; Sellers & Arrigo, 2018; Welch & Payne, 2018). Nonetheless, over the years, schools have increased their use of punitive forms of punishment (Losen & Skiba, 2010; Rocque & Snellings, 2018).

Zero-tolerance policies have also been linked to several adverse outcomes for youth. For example, they have been found to contribute to increases in exclusionary discipline, suspensions, and expulsions in schools, as well as increases in the use of juvenile justice referrals (Losen & Skiba, 2010). These types of disciplinary actions can stigmatize and ostracize students from their peers and schoolwork, which may further increase their likelihood of engaging in delinquent acts (Smokowski et al., 2020). In addition, research has shown how school discipline measures can contribute to juvenile justice involvement for many youth, particularly minority students (Pigott et al., 2018; Skiba et al., 2014). Not least, referrals to the JJS and other such punishments often do not address the root problems of the behavior in question.

At a macro level, zero-tolerance policies have contributed to the STPP. This theoretical pipeline represents the high number of youth, most of whom are racial or ethnic minorities, who experience exclusionary school punishments or harsh disciplinary actions that then make them more likely to enter the formal JJS (Christle et al., 2005; Skiba et al., 2014). It has been argued that increases in harsh discipline, zero-tolerance policies, and the placement of legal actors in schools (as discussed later) have created a new "disciplinology" that punishes youth for normal developmental behaviors that historically were handled by teachers or the schools themselves (S. J. Brown et al., 2020; Rocque & Snellings, 2018).

The reality is that once in this "pipeline," it is often difficult for students to find resources and other supports to get out (Rocque & Snellings, 2018). Becoming involved in the JJS or criminal justice system can have negative consequences for juveniles including limited educational and employment opportunities or inability to access government programs (i.e., food stamps, housing, etc.). These consequences can in turn increase their likelihood of reoffending (Smokowski et al., 2017). However, there are promising alternatives that have been shown to reduce juvenile delinquency without involving the JJS or compromising school safety.

Promising Alternatives to Zero Tolerance

A natural question arises after relying on zero tolerance for so many years: If not zero tolerance, then what? The empirical literature is rife with studies demonstrating that improving school environments yields better psychological, social, behavioral, and academic outcomes for students. While schools today struggle with implementing evidence-based programs to improve school safety and the broader school climate (VanLone et al., 2019), reviews of the literature do indicate quite clearly that well-designed school-based intervention programs can improve outcomes (Menesini & Salmivalli, 2017). Indeed, though some reviews yield mixed results (e.g., Della Cioppa et al., 2015), meta-analytic evidence and literature reviews demonstrate that school safety programs can be effective in diverse contexts and countries (Gaffney et al., 2019; Hawkins et al., 2012). Further, whole-school approaches (as compared to single-classroom programs or traditional forms of discipline) appear particularly effective when they incorporate socioecological strategies that account for the various developmental contexts in which youth are embedded (e.g., classroom, school, and home). Two programs stand out as particularly promising based on quality evaluations.

First, Cross and colleagues (2018) conducted a 3-year, randomized controlled trial of the Friendly Schools Project (FSP) among more than 3,000 secondary school students. The FSP intervention is an interesting case study because it uses the social–ecological approach (Bronfenbrenner, 1994). It considers cognitive and emotional development at the individual level, family engagement and peer interactions at the contextual level, and the broader societal conditions in which youth are embedded. In the FSP, intervention schools receive individualized training and resources to support students, and the intervention itself is designed to address classroom curriculum, school policies, and both social and physical environments within the school, including school–home–community links. The program yielded small, short-term effects across a range of outcomes, including student bullying, victimization, mental health symptomatology, and perceptions of school safety (see also Cross et al., 2019).

Second, Bohnenkamp and colleagues (2021) evaluated the Emotional and Behavioral Health–Crisis Response and Prevention (EBH-CRP) intervention. EBH-CRP aims to increase schools' competencies for preventing and responding to students' emotional and behavioral health (EBH) crises, which affect students' feelings of safety in their schools. The EBH-CRP model leverages multiple evidence-informed strategies that address EBH. As a bundled model, conclusions cannot be made about the effects of specific components, which include (a) universal prevention, (b) early identification, (c) service linkage to streamline referrals and use of EBH supports, (d) crisis response, and (e) postcrisis relapse prevention. However, in their study of 40 schools randomized into treatment and control groups, Bohnenkamp and colleagues (2021) found that the EBH-CRP intervention minimized the occurrence of several adverse outcomes, including suspensions, office discipline referrals, juvenile justice referrals, and bullying. Altogether, the results indicated that interventions such as the EBH-CRP can strengthen and streamline schools' existing EBH resources.

There are many other programs that are being currently evaluated or have proven results in nations outside of the United States. For instance, the Finnish KiVa program has been studied in both randomized controlled trials and nationwide dissemination studies. The research suggests that the program, which incorporates various levels of intervention, can effectively reduce bullying, especially in primary schools (Kärnä et al., 2011; Yeager et al., 2015).

Beyond the programs described, there are also promising approaches grounded in RJ (Braithwaite, 2020). RJ approaches begin with the recognition that crime harms people and communities. The person who perpetrated the offense learns to recognize and understand the harms they caused in part by engaging with and listening to the victim. The intention is to shame the offense, not the offender, and have the person who perpetrated the offense make amends and reintegrate back into the community (Church et al., 2021). In many cases, the intention is for that person to build stronger bonds than what existed in the first place.

Despite its increasing use in schools in the United States, a surprisingly limited amount of research has evaluated the effect of RJ programs on school safety. Even fewer have isolated the effects of the RJ program versus other components of the intervention or prevention program. For instance, Bonell and colleagues (2018) conducted a cluster-randomized study of the Learning Together Intervention (LTI) at the school level, including a comparison to standard practice (i.e., controls) over 3 years in secondary schools. The LTI incorporates staff training in restorative practices, a school action group, and a student curriculum focused on social and emotional skills. The results of their evaluation found that LTI improved psychological functioning, emotional well-being, and quality of life. Further, it reduced police contacts, substance use, and student bullying (Bonell et al., 2018). However, considering that the comprehensive program incorporated so many approaches simultaneously, the specific effect of RJ itself cannot be estimated.

Katic and colleagues (2020) recently completed a comprehensive review of RJ, but their study could only evaluate 10 articles. Overall, the majority of studies reported positive outcomes for school safety. Related work by Darling-Hammond and colleagues (2020) also found that RJ programs can improve school safety and reduce student misbehavior. In short, research on RJ appears promising. However, despite the advances made in this area of research, there is not yet a robust literature on the effects of RJ programming on school safety (see also Mas-Expósito et al., 2022).

Embedding the Legal System Within Schools

In their efforts to maintain a safe learning environment for youth, many schools have looked directly to the legal system and its actors. This has taken many forms including placing police officers or JPOs in schools to help respond to misbehavior and crime, as well as enacting school-based juvenile justice programs like teen courts and truancy diversion courts (see Fountain et al., this volume). Each of these results in legal actors becoming a member of the school community. In this section, we examine the literature on school–JJS partnerships, including embedding legal actors in schools and implementing school-based JJS programs.

Legal Actors Embedded in Schools
SCHOOL RESOURCE OFFICERS

In an effort to reduce victimization and crime within schools, school district administrators have employed law enforcement officers to patrol their campuses. The most common type of school-based officer is the SRO. The definition of "SRO" varies from place to place, but they are generally defined as a sworn officer who is assigned to work within schools and maintain safety (Theriot, 2009; Weiler & Cray, 2011). Though SROs were rare until the 1990s (Counts et al., 2018; Viano et al., 2021; Weiler & Cray, 2011), they are common on contemporary school campuses. Because SROs are not required to register with a national database and individual police departments and school systems are not required to report how many SROs they employ, data on the prevalence of SROs in schools are based on schools' self-reported data. With those caveats in mind, the National Center for Education Statistics estimates that in 2018, approximately 58% of schools had at least one sworn law enforcement official present, and 46.5% of public schools specifically reported having an SRO (see Table 11 in Diliberti et al., 2019).

It is common for SROs to serve in several, sometimes conflicting, capacities. One of the most common SRO approaches is the National Association of School Resource Officer's "triad model," which expects officers to simultaneously act as law enforcers, counselors, and law-related educators. In practice, how these roles are implemented varies across schools and officers. These diverse expectations can function as a "multitool" of SROs that allows them to fill whatever gaps or roles the school and youth need. However, the reality is that it can lead to frustration and conflict for both SROs and school personnel. SROs and school personnel frequently have differing opinions on how SROs should function in the school environment (Coon & Travis, 2012; Ghavami et al., 2021; Gill et al., 2016; Granot et al., 2021). This confusion is further exacerbated by the unique needs and resources of a school community and the particular philosophy of other school staff.

Proponents of using SROs believe that SROs can prevent school crime and violence, enhance students' perceptions of safety, connect students who have experienced trauma with services, and allow teachers to focus on educating and creating bonds with students (Coon & Travis, 2012; Curran et al., 2020; Gill et al., 2016). They also argue that SROs can act as positive role models for students, which may have the benefit of improving the relationship between law enforcement and the community (B. Brown & Benedict, 2002; Theriot, 2016; Turner & Beneke, 2020). Yet, despite these arguments, there is little evidence to suggest that SROs improve school safety (e.g., Na & Gottfredson, 2013). Researchers have instead identified adverse consequences of employing SROs. The use of SROs can increase the use of exclusionary discipline, contributing to the STPP, widening the net of social control through the use of referrals to the JJS, and having a disproportionate negative effect on minority students (Coon & Travis, 2012; Kupchik, 2009; Theriot, 2009; Turner & Beneke, 2020). SRO presence also may influence how misbehavior is handled by teachers and other school personnel (Montes et al., 2021). With an SRO present, teachers may feel more comfortable having the SRO handle the situation (Crutchfield et al., 2009; Gregory et al., 2017), thereby criminalizing misbehavior that they would have ordinarily handled without involving justice system personnel (Na & Gottfredson, 2013; Theriot, 2009). This evidence, as well as calls by the public to remove SROs from campuses, has prompted many school districts to eliminate these positions in their schools (S. Schwartz et al., 2021).

JUVENILE PROBATION OFFICERS

With the shift away from confinement for youth, probation became a highly desirable and more common legal sanction for youth who commit crimes (R. G. Schwartz, 2018). In fact, the majority (61%) of youth who go through the juvenile court are placed on probation and are able to remain in their communities (Hockenberry & Puzzanchera, 2020). Although the JJS was created to respond to the acknowledged differences between youth and adults, juvenile probation, much like adult probation, focuses primarily on monitoring and controlling the youth (R. G. Schwartz, 2018). Probation does allow youth to stay in their community and to connect with and receive community-based services. However, for some youth, probation can lead to future confinement or can deepen JJS involvement when minor forms of misbehavior and noncompliance with supervisory conditions are uncovered (Cauffman et al., 2021; Hafoka et al., 2017; R. G. Schwartz, 2018).

The primary legal actor youth interact with when on probation is their JPO. While SROs often interact with students who have engaged in delinquency at school, JPOs work with juveniles who have already been adjudicated delinquent or who have been diverted from formal court processing (Alarid et al., 2011a; Cauffman et al., 2021; Hafoka et al., 2017). JPOs' primary goals are to address the criminogenic needs of their clients, limit reoffending, and foster rehabilitation (Hafoka et al., 2017).

The underlying logic of employing school-based JPOs is that they can better serve the youth on their caseload by building stronger relationships with youth through more frequent contact; generating a better understanding of the youth and their needs and, in turn, responding with a more holistic approach; serving as a conduit to resources the youth needs both on campus and in the community; acting as an advocate for youth's academic needs; and coordinating the approach and services of the juvenile court and school (see, generally, Mears et al., 2019). As compared to community-based JPOs, school-based JPOs should theoretically have more opportunities to bond with youth, learn about the needs of the youth and their family, act as mentors, and, when needed, help the youth and their family connect to community resources. At a systems level, the logic is that the youth on probation may be the students who engage in the most misbehavior. Reducing their at-school misbehavior should then enhance school safety.

The risks of this approach are similar to the risks of employing SROs. Given school-based JPOs' abilities to surveil youth for a large proportion of the day, minor misbehavior and technical violations of probation may be more likely to be identified, and when that happens, the youth then is at risk of having additional court contact (Hafoka et al., 2017; R. G. Schwartz, 2018). There is also a risk that youth on probation will be labeled as "troublemakers" by their peers and school staff, thus stigmatizing the youth and potentially contributing to a greater likelihood of both being surveilled more closely and engaging in delinquency.

There have been many challenges to studying the effectiveness of placing JPOs on school campuses. In addition to JPOs being placed on only a limited number of campuses, the JPOs are often part of a larger program. For example, in one district, school-based JPOs were employed alongside case managers and counselors as a part of a larger, comprehensive delinquency prevention program (Mears et al., 2019). That renders isolating the effect of the school-based JPOs on in-school delinquency impossible. An additional challenge is that JPOs frequently work directly with SROs (e.g., Alarid et al., 2011b), making it difficult to disentangle the SRO effect from the JPO effect. There is no known study to date that has been able to overcome all of these challenges.

The literature suggests that there are considerable barriers to implementing a program with school-based JPOs. For instance, the state of Pennsylvania invested heavily in the use of school-based JPOs, yet some of their early evaluations indicated that "the lack of a clear job description that defines the roles and duties of school-based probation officers has caused problems when school administrators have expectations different from those of probation officers" (Torbet et al., 2001, p. 4). In addition, some programs have been designed so that youth have a community probation officer who handles their case outside of school and a school-based JPO who handles their case inside of school, which has caused role confusion and created tension when officers' approaches or philosophies were not aligned (Henderson et al., 2008). They also face some of the same implementation difficulties that SROs face, such as balancing the educational focus of the school and the punishment focus of the juvenile court (S. J. Brown et al., 2020).

School-Based Diversion Programs
Legal actors embedded in schools are becoming more common, but there are other ways in which the JJS interacts with school communities. One increasingly popular way is through the use of school-based diversion programs such as teen/youth courts and specialized truancy programs. These programs often serve as a "diversion" from the juvenile court system, providing youth, especially first-timers, the opportunity to stay out of the formal JJS (Bouchard & Wong, 2017). Given the increased risk for adverse outcomes for youth who enter the JJS (Radice, 2017; Siennick & Widdowson, 2020), these diversion programs aim to prevent further negative consequences and keep juveniles within their communities.

TEEN COURT

Contrary to adults, juveniles do not typically have the right to a trial by a jury of their peers. The vast majority of youth who go through the JJS are processed, sanctioned, and supervised by adults. However, teen court has emerged as a problem-solving "court" wherein a youth, typically a first-timer who is accused of committing a low-level offense, can be sentenced by a jury of same-aged peers. Teen courts are frequently housed within schools, and while the makeup of the teen court can vary by jurisdiction, with other models including peer jury, youth judge, or youth tribunal (National Association of Youth Courts, 2017), they typically consist of a youth or adult judge and youth defense and prosecuting attorneys, bailiff, and juries (Bouchard & Wong, 2017; Smokowski et al., 2017). Some of the youth on the other side of the bench are themselves justice involved and are required to participate as a part of their own adjudicatory experience. In the teen court process, youth follow typical court proceedings, help with decision making, and help determine the appropriate sanctions for the offender (DeFosset et al., 2017).

Participation in this diversion program is deemed "voluntary." However, youth are almost universally required to admit wrongdoing in order to be able to participate in the program (Smokowski et al., 2017), and while youth can opt out at any time, they will be referred back to the traditional JJS if they do (Bouchard & Wong, 2017). Given what is known about the detrimental effects of formal JJS involvement, teen court theoretically serves as a developmentally appropriate solution; the process is individualized and sanctions are designed to allow the juvenile to take responsibility for their actions while also repairing the harm felt by the community (Bouchard & Wong, 2017).

While there are many benefits to teen courts, there are also clear drawbacks. One major issue is the aspect of labeling of the juvenile by their peers. Although teen courts can avoid the "adjudicated delinquent" labeling that comes with being formally processed through the JJS, youth are still processed and labeled as "delinquent." Receiving such a label, especially by peers, may alter a youth's self-identity (Magidson & Kidd, 2021) and stigmatize them beyond the "courtroom" walls (Bouchard & Wong, 2017). In fact, considering teen courts often take place at schools, it is surprising that so little research has studied the effects of participating in a teen court on youths' attitudes toward school and their relationships with peers and teachers.

Additionally, teen courts may act as a form of net widening. Low-risk youth who ordinarily would have been sanctioned and dismissed may now face this more involved process that increases the amount of time they are exposed to the system (Bouchard & Wong, 2017). Teen courts may also unnecessarily involve youth who are unlikely to reoffend again but may face more severe consequences and be placed in the JJS if they do not complete the sanctions assigned by the teen court. For instance, they may receive community service hours that they ordinarily would not have received, and may have difficulty completing them due to transportation barriers. This could change the trajectory of a youth who otherwise would not have entered the JJS or faced the negative consequences associated with system involvement. Further, there is the question of coercion; youth can only participate if they admit wrongdoing (Smokowski et al., 2017), which may lead youth to falsely admit responsibility. Finally, there is the unexamined question of whether it constitutes unnecessary double processing. In many jurisdictions, youth can only enter teen court after having admitted guilt and having been adjudicated delinquent, which means they must have already gone through the formal juvenile court process and been adjudicated delinquent before then going through the teen court version of the same process. Whether teen court provides better outcomes for youth as compared to traditional community supervision or sanction-and-dismiss conditions remains an open question. Perhaps more saliently, whether teen courts should be housed in schools and whether they impact youths' views of schools are critical questions.

TRUANCY COURT

Truancy court constitutes a similar diversion program that is closely related to and often embedded within the school system. Truancy courts, also often called boards, focus on reducing youth's number of unexcused school days, given that chronic truancy is a risk factor for in-school and out-of-school delinquency and truancy itself is a violation of the law (Hendricks et al., 2010; Mazerolle et al., 2017; Shoenfelt & Huddleston, 2006). Indeed, school attendance is vital for improving students' academic performance, as well as social and behavioral development (Shoenfelt & Huddleston, 2006; Sutphen et al., 2010). While the exact number and definition can vary by state, chronic truancy is often defined as missing at least 10% of the school year (McNeely et al., 2019; Sutphen et al., 2010). However, because the definitions of truancy and "chronic" truancy can vary from state to state or school to school, there is no known nationwide prevalence estimate of this problem.

There are a number of ways truancy has been addressed by schools including individualized treatment, court interventions (both family and juvenile), police interventions, suspension, and, more recently, a hybrid model incorporating truancy courts with an individualized approach for students (Flannery et al., 2012; Haight et al., 2014). Truancy court is often held within school buildings or with school personnel serving on the court or acting as advisors (Byer & Kuhn, 2003; Hendricks et al., 2010). While various models exist, one prevailing model, popularized by Judge Joan Byer in Louisville, Kentucky, focuses on treating the "whole" child and assessing all risk factors in order to reduce truancy (Byer & Kuhn, 2003). The goal of programs based on Judge Byer's model is to target major risk factors for delinquency and truancy.

To reduce truancy, truancy courts and related intervention programs often take steps that become progressively more severe. An example is as follows: First, the school will call a parent meeting to learn more about the child's situation and see if the parents can help get their child to go to school (McNeely et al., 2019). Second, after continued absences, a hearing will typically be held with the student, their parents, a school administrator, and a county attorney to set up an attendance contract and a plan to get the child to school. During this hearing, the student is informally asked why they are having difficulties attending school and what solutions may help increase their attendance. At this hearing the student and/or their parents may be referred to certain services that may help address the underlying causes of the truancy, such as mental health issues or homelessness (McNeely et al., 2019). Third, if the student continues to miss school, a petition can be filed with the juvenile court.

With the introduction of law enforcement into schools, students may be more likely to come into contact with the JJS and its representatives. Further, certain students may be more prone to interactions with SROs or may be more likely to be referred to school-based programming such as teen court or truancy court. This increased supervision, monitoring, and control has disproportionate impacts on racial and ethnic minorities, which is the subject of the next section.

Racial and Ethnic Disparities

Similar to the adult criminal justice system, racial and ethnic minority youth are overrepresented in the JJS (Nicholson-Crotty et al., 2009; see Najdowski et al., this volume). In fact, they often make up the majority of those detained by the JJS even in jurisdictions where they are the minority (Leiber & Fix, 2019). These disparities in the JJS often start in school; in fact, large disparities exist in school discipline, exclusionary discipline, and juvenile justice referrals, which are most commonly experienced by racial and ethnic minority students (Crutchfield et al., 2009; Hirschfield, 2018; Nicholson-Crotty et al., 2009). Research indicates that even after accounting for schools' structural factors and students' characteristics, these disparities remain, with Black students being the most likely to experience school-based punishment (Nicholson-Crotty et al., 2009). For instance, even after accounting for student behavior, teachers are more likely to issue disciplinary referrals to students of color, particularly Black students (Bradshaw et al., 2010). Given this situation, it is vital that we understand why and how student–teacher interactions and teacher discretion contribute to disparities in discipline for minority students.

Teachers interact with students more than any other adult within the school and play a vital role in how students become involved with the JJS (Bradshaw et al., 2010; Hirschfield, 2018). This begins with how teachers decide to discipline a student. Currently, the majority of disciplinary consequences for students are discretionary, based on how teachers decide to respond to behavior. When behaviors are not explicitly right or wrong, such as voicing an opinion or talking back, implicit biases may lead to the criminalization of minority youth (Smolkowski et al., 2016). Research has shown that teachers and administrators are more likely to view minority students as having worse demeanors, being more argumentative, and having more negative attitudes compared to their White counterparts (Kupchik & Ellis, 2008; Skiba et al., 2000; Smolkowski et al., 2016), and behaviors exhibited by minority students are more likely to be interpreted as criminal or delinquent (Crutchfield et al., 2009; Kupchik & Ellis, 2008). It has been well established that racial disparities exist in teachers' use of exclusionary discipline and out-of-school suspensions (Losen & Gillespie, 2012; Smolkowski et al., 2016). Indeed, when teachers use their discretion, Black students and those belonging to other racial and ethnic minority groups are more likely to be subjected to harsh disciplinary actions, including exclusionary discipline (Gregory et al., 2017; Kupchik & Ellis, 2008; Skiba et al., 2000; Smolkowski et al., 2016). To make matters worse, schools with higher percentages of minority youth have increased their use of security measures such as cameras, metal detectors, and random locker searches (Kupchik & Ellis, 2008) that, in turn, increase the likelihood of youth coming into contact with law enforcement and JJS personnel (Crutchfield et al., 2009). Such schools are also more likely to have SROs (Kupchik & Ellis, 2008).

Collectively, these approaches form a system that funnels juveniles, many of whom belong to minoritized groups, into the JJS. It is important to note that even RJ programs, which are considered some of the most promising and progressive intervention and prevention programs for enhancing school safety and reducing juvenile delinquency, are quite limited in one key area: They do not typically address systemic, social–organizational structures that maintain racial inequity in school punishment (Schiff, 2018).

Where Do We Go From Here?

There have been considerable advances in understanding the role legal actors play in schools and ensuring that they do not contribute to the STPP. While there is still much to learn, we offer nine recommendations for moving forward.

First, school officials should avoid their punitive intuition that prompts them to favor either enacting or enhancing their zero-tolerance and deterrence-based approaches (Van Rooij & Fine, 2021). Instead, when faced with school safety issues, they should favor theoretically and empirically grounded practices that attack the root causes of student misbehavior and delinquency at school. Schools and legal systems should adopt evidence-based practices for handling discipline and improving school safety. Though "evidence" is typically interpreted to mean the results of outcome evaluations, it should also encompass evidence of need, as well as evidence that a particular approach can be implemented as intended (see, generally, Mears, 2010). As we discussed earlier, multiple promising approaches exist that promote positive development without compromising school safety.

Second, a greater emphasis should be placed on preparing legal actors for working with youth on school campuses. One way to do so may be to require them to participate in relevant trainings. A recent study by Strategies for Youth (2019) found that more than half of states do not require SROs to undergo training on how to work with youth, and even fewer states mandate training on combating biases. Giving officers the tools to effectively and positively engage with youth may improve their interactions with youth and in turn contribute to positive outcomes.

Third, any approach that places legal actors in schools should also have robust mechanisms for oversight and monitoring. What is clear from the research on SROs is that they take on a wide range of tasks and have considerable discretion in implementing their day-to-day duties (S. J. Brown et al., 2020). Such discretion is perhaps a good thing when an officer uses it to provide needed resources to a student and their family, for example. But it can lead to collateral consequences when this discretion results in typical youthful behavior being criminalized. Similarly, if principals and teachers are partnering with legal actors to ensure students' safety both on and off campus, that may be a sign of a successful partnership. However, if they are pressuring legal actors to handle disciplinary matters or to remove at-risk youth from schools, that is a harm to both students and the school community. Greater monitoring and oversight could help to minimize these potential harms while also identifying practices that lead to desirable outcomes.

Fourth, and in a similar vein, both scholars and on-the-ground staff need to invest in understanding whether interactions between staff members (e.g., principals, teachers, officers) influence how legal actors operate in schools (see, generally, Montes et al., 2021). For example, researchers have found that SROs can increase the likelihood of court contact for minor offenses (Na & Gottfredson, 2013). Though this finding in and of itself may warrant removing legal actors from schools, it also suggests a need for understanding the decision making that led to a student being arrested or referred to the juvenile court. If school staff commonly call on law enforcement to intervene when a student misbehaves, it suggests a need to hold school staff more accountable for how they respond to misbehavior. If it is in fact law enforcement officers prioritizing their "legal" roles, it suggests that when schools do employ these individuals, their contracts and memorandums of understanding need to clearly state their responsibilities and how they should implement their duties. In either instance, school communities would benefit from clarifying to all school and legal staff when legal actors should and should not intervene in incidents of misbehavior and what alternatives are available when legal intervention is not warranted.

Fifth, almost all of the empirical research on legal actors focuses on how or if their presence or actions lead to police or court contact. There remains a gap in our understanding of how these actors influence other outcomes. For example, the National Association of School Resource Officers (2012) trains officers to act as law enforcers, counselors, and educators, yet we know little about how SROs' counseling or educational initiatives influence youth or schools. A more comprehensive understanding of the impacts legal actors have on school communities will require a focus not just on legal outcomes but also on academic and social and emotional well-being outcomes. It will also require improving our understanding of how their presence and behavior impact school-level outcomes, such as climate, safety, and equity.

Sixth, schools must reduce racial and ethnic disparities in how they and the legal actors embedded within them respond to student misbehavior. After the killing of George Floyd and the ensuing civil protests against police brutality, many jurisdictions chose to remove police officers from their school campuses (Balingit et al., 2020). One of the underlying concerns that was the basis for this shift was that legal actors, police in particular, disproportionately target Black youth. It is not yet known what approaches, if any, will replace the use of officers in these jurisdictions. Schools or districts that are moving away from a reliance on legal actors for improving school safety should evaluate the potential short- and long-term consequences of any new practices, including the potential for racial and ethnic disparities to occur. Scholars can also contribute to these efforts. For example, scholars should be aiming to identify schools or districts where the gap in disparities is shrinking. What can be learned from these jurisdictions? What are the conditions that led to this reduction? What can further reduce the disparities that persist? How can such reductions be sustained and replicated?

Seventh, schools that continue to employ legal actors may need to reevaluate how these actors are used. Indeed, improving safety while also treating students fairly and not contributing to either racial and ethnic disparities or the STPP may mean reimagining the role of school police and other legal actors. Some schools are already taking this step by partnering with legal actors to encourage safe police-youth interactions, but not employing them to work full time on their campuses. One such example is the Team Kids Challenge, which promotes nonenforcement, nonsurveillance interactions between police and students where they team up on community service projects. This program has been found to enhance students' perceptions of police legitimacy (Fine et al., 2020) and their developmental assets (Fine et al., 2021), which are critical for youth thriving (Scales et al., 2000). For schools and communities that want to employ legal actors or encourage interactions between officers and youth, it is important that they use contracts or memorandums of understanding to explicitly define the roles these individuals should play when on campus (Coon & Travis, 2012; Devlin & Gottfredson, 2018), and also evaluate the effects on children.

Eighth, more broadly, schools and districts might consider reinvesting funds that are typically allocated toward employing police or other legal actors within the school into evidence-based approaches that improve school safety. Doing so might mean adopting a broader view of what it means to combat school safety issues. The underlying logic of using school police is that officers can deter violence, respond quickly when violence does occur, and secure the school's perimeter. Scholars and advocates argue, however, that a better approach may be to target the root causes of crime and to allocate resources toward students' mental health and social and emotional well-being (Greenberg et al., 2017). They argue that doing so will *prevent* school violence rather than be *responsive* to it. Considering that research has not found consistent evidence that school police prevent on-campus violence or shootings, these alternative approaches might be a better use of schools' limited resources (e.g., Na & Gottfredson, 2013). In addition, committing funds to an approach that has not been supported by evidence could mean diverting already limited resources away from needed services or interventions, such as social workers or school psychologists, which ultimately may harm efforts to improve safety. Not least, schools should consider their ability to properly implement SRO programs (e.g., adequately train the officers, have adequate oversight). If they are unable to do so, employing police may cause more harm than benefit.

Finally, one of parents' main concerns for their children's well-being in schools is gun violence. Fears over guns in schools has expanded the use of lockdown and active shooter drills (Musu et al., 2019). Indeed, recent research suggests that 96% of K–12 schools have implemented some sort of active threat protocol (Wang et al., 2020). While these may seem logical, the research tends to find that they can cause significant, unintended harm to youth (Limber & Kowalski, 2020), including making students even more fearful (Bonanno et al.,

2021). More research is needed on the potential for lockdown drills to have iatrogenic effects on schools and youth. Schools considering using these practices must also evaluate how the practice impacts their students and school community.

Conclusion

In the United States, youth spend the majority of their waking time in school, and schools are the primary place where youth development occurs. Given the amount of time spent within school walls, it is inevitable that some delinquency occurs; yet some students engage in more delinquency than others, and some schools experience higher rates of delinquency. Reasons for this were outlined in this chapter, creating a theoretical foundation for understanding delinquency and how that has shaped initiatives to deal with it. Though schools strive to provide a safe environment for students to learn and interact with one another, this chapter details how some well-intentioned efforts have caused harms, especially for racial and ethnic minorities. Some approaches that rely on bringing legal actors onto school campuses not only have failed to keep schools safe or make students feel safer but also have created conditions under which juvenile delinquency becomes more common. While there have been considerable advances in understanding the role legal actors play in schools and ensuring that they do not contribute to the STPP, there is much more to learn. The nine recommendations provided here are only the beginning.

References

Adams, J., & Mrug, S. (2019). Individual- and school-level predictors of violence perpetration, victimization, and perceived safety in middle and high schools. *Journal of School Violence, 18*, 468–482.

Agnew, R. (1992). Foundation for a general strain theory of crime and delinquency. *Criminology, 30*(1), 47–88.

Agnew, R. (2001). Building on the foundation of general strain theory: Specifying the types of strain most likely to lead to crime and delinquency. *Journal of Research in Crime and Delinquency, 38*(4), 319–361.

Alarid, L. F., Sims, B. A., & Ruiz, J. (2011a). Juvenile probation and police partnerships as loosely coupled systems: A qualitative analysis. *Youth Violence and Juvenile Justice, 9*(1), 79–95.

Alarid, L. F., Sims, B. A., & Ruiz, J. (2011b). School-based juvenile probation and police partnerships for truancy reduction. *Journal of Knowledge and Best Practices in Juvenile Justice and Psychology, 5*, 13–20.

Allen, K.-A., & Kern, M. L. (2017). *School belonging in adolescents: Theory, research and practice.* Springer.

American Psychological Association Zero Tolerance Task Force. (2008). Are zero tolerance policies effective in the schools?: An evidentiary review and recommendations. *American Psychologist, 63*(9), 852–862.

Balingit, M., Strauss, V., & Bellware, K. (2020, June 12). Fueled by protests, school districts across country cut ties with police. *Washington Post.* https://www.washingtonpost.com/education/2020/06/12/schools-police-george-floyd-protests/

Barrett, K. L., Jennings, W. G., & Lynch, M. J. (2012). The relation between youth fear and avoidance of crime in school and academic experiences. *Journal of School Violence, 11*(1), 1–20.

Bellair, P. (2017). Social disorganization theory. In *Oxford research encyclopedia of criminology and criminal justice.*

Bohnenkamp, J. H., Schaeffer, C. M., Siegal, R., Beason, T., Smith-Millman, M., & Hoover, S. (2021). Impact of a school-based, multi-tiered emotional and behavioral health crisis intervention on school safety and discipline. *Prevention Science, 22*(4), 492–503.

Bonanno, R., McConnaughey, S., & Mincin, J. (2021). *Children's experiences with school lockdown drills: A pilot study. Children & Schools, 43*(3), 175–185.

Bonell, C., Allen, E., Warren, E., McGowan, J., Bevilacqua, L., Jamal, F., Legood, R., Wiggins, M., Opondo, C., Mathiot, A., Sturgess, J., Fletcher, A., Sadique, Z., Elbourne, D., Christie, D., Bond, L., Scott, S., Viner, R. M. (2018). Initiating change in the school environment to reduce bullying and aggression: A cluster andomized controlled trial of the Learning Together (LT) intervention in English secondary schools. *The Lancet, 392*(10163), 2452–2464.

Bouchard, J., & Wong, J. S. (2017). A jury of their peers: A meta-analysis of the effects of teen court on recidivism. *Journal of Youth and Adolescence, 46*, 1472–1487.

Bradshaw, C. P., Mitchell, M. M., O'Brennan, L. M., & Leaf, P. J. (2010). Multilevel exploration of factors contributing to the overrepresentation of Black students in office disciplinary referrals. *Journal of Educational Psychology, 102*(2), 508–520.

Braithwaite, J. (2020). Restorative justice and reintegrative shaming. In Chouhy, C., Cochran, J. C., & Jonson, C. L. (Eds.) *Criminal justice theory* (pp. 281–308). Routledge.

Bronfenbrenner, U. (1979). *The ecology of human development: Experiments by nature and design.* Harvard Univeristy Press.

Bronfenbrenner, U. (1994). Ecological models of human development. In T. Husen & T. N. Postlethwaite (Eds.), *International encyclopedia of education* (2nd ed., Vol. 3, pp. 1643–1647). Pergamon Press/Elsevier Science.

Bronfenbrenner, U. (2005). *Making human beings human.* Sage.

Bronfenbrenner, U., & Morris, P. (2007). The bioecological model of human development. In R. M. Lerner & W. Damon (eds). *Handbook of Child Psychology*, Vol 1, 793–828.Wiley.

Brown, B., & Benedict, W. R. (2002). Perceptions of the police: Past findings, methodological issues, conceptual issues and police implication. *Policing International Journal of Police Strategies & Management, 25*(3), 543–580.

Brown, C., Fine, A., & Cauffman, E. (2019). Do positive perceptions of correctional staff mitigate institutional violence among youthful offenders? *Psychology, Public Policy, and Law, 25*(1), 38–45.

Brown, S. J., Mears, D. P., Collier, N. L., Montes, A. N., Pesta, G. B., & Siennick, S. E. (2020). Education versus punishment? Silo effects and the school-to-prison pipeline. *Journal of Research in Crime and Delinquency, 57*, 403–443.

Byer, J. L., & Kuhn, J. (2003). A model response to truancy prevention: The Louisville truancy court diversion project. *Juvenile and Family Court Journal, 54*(1), 59–67.

Calderon, V. (2016). *Foster a sense of safety in students by building engagement.* http://www.gallup.com/opinion/gallup/190301/foster-sense-safety-students-building-engagement.aspx?g_source=school%20safety&g_medium=search&g_campaign=tiles

Cardwell, S. M., Bennett, S., & Mazerolle, L. (2021). Bully victimization, truancy, and violent offending: Evidence from the ASEP Truancy Reduction Experiment. *Youth Violence and Juvenile Justice, 19*(1), 5–26.

Cauffman, E., Beardslee, J., Fine, A., Frick, P., & Steinberg, L. (2021). Crossroads in juvenile justice: The impact of initial processing decision on youth five years after first arrest. *Development & Psychopathology, 33*(2), 700–713.

Cauffman, E., Fine, A., Mahler, A., & Simmons, C. (2018). How developmental science influences juvenile justice reform. *University of California, Irvine Law Review, 8*, 21–40.

Church, A. S., Marcus, D. K., & Hamilton, Z. K. (2021). Community service outcomes in justice-involved youth: Comparing restorative community service to standard community service. *Criminal Justice and Behavior, 48*(9), 1243-1260.

Coon, J. K., & Travis, L. F. (2012). The role of police in public schools: A comparison of principal and police reports of activities in schools. *Police Practice & Research, 13*, 15–30.

Counts, J., Randall, K. N., Ryan, J. B., & Katsiyannis, A. (2018). School resource officers in public schools: A national review. *Education and Treatment of Children, 41*(4), 405–430.

Coyle, S., Weinreb, K. S., Davila, G., & Cuellar, M. (2021, May). *Relationships matter: The protective role of teacher and peer support in understanding school climate for victimized youth.* Child & Youth Care Forum.

Christle, C. A., Jolivette, K., Nelson, C. M. (2005). Breaking the school to prison pipeline: Identifying school risk and protective factors for youth delinquency. *Exceptionality, 13*, 69–88.

Crosnoe, R., Johnson, M. K., & Elder, G. H. (2004). Intergenerational bonding in school: The behavioral and contextual correlates of student–teacher relationships. *Sociology of Education, 77*(1), 60–81.

Cross, D., Runions, K. C., Shaw, T., Wong, J. W., Campbell, M., Pearce, N., . . . Resnicow, K. (2019). Friendly Schools universal bullying prevention intervention: Effectiveness with secondary school students. *International Journal of Bullying Prevention, 1*(1), 45–57.

Cross, D., Shaw, T., Epstein, M., Pearce, N., Barnes, A., Burns, S., . . . Runions, K. (2018). Impact of the Friendly Schools whole-school intervention on transition to secondary school and adolescent bullying behaviour. *European Journal of Education, 53*(4), 495–513.

Crutchfield, R. D., Skinner, M. L., Haggerty, K. P., McGlynn, A., & Catalano, R. F. (2009). Racial disparities in early criminal justice involvement. *Race and Social Problems, 1*, 218–230.

Cuellar, M. J., Elswick, S. E., & Theriot, M. T. (2018). School social workers' perceptions of school safety and security in today's schools: A survey of practitioners across the United States. *Journal of School Violence, 17*(3), 271–283.

Curran, F. C., Fisher, B. W., Viano, S. L., & Kupchik, A. (2020). *Understanding school safety and the use of school resource officers in understudied settings.* U.S. Department of Justice, Office of Justice Programs.

Darling-Hammond, S., Fronius, T. A., Sutherland, H., Guckenburg, S., Petrosino, A., & Hurley, N. (2020). Effectiveness of restorative justice in US K-12 schools: A review of quantitative research. *Contemporary School Psychology, 24*, 295–308.

DeFosset, A. R., Schooley, T. S., Abrams, L. S., Kuo, T., & Gase, L. N. (2017). Describing theoretical underpinnings in juvenile justice diversion: A case study explicating Teen Court program theory to guide research and practice. *Children and Youth Services Review, 73*, 419–429.

Della Cioppa, V., O'Neil, A., & Craig, W. (2015). Learning from traditional bullying interventions: A review of research on cyberbullying and best practice. *Aggression and Violent Behavior, 23*, 61–68.

Devlin, D., & Gottfredson, D. (2018). The roles of police officers in schools: Effects on recording and reporting of crime. *Youth Violence and Juvenile Justice, 16*, 208–223.

Diliberti, M., Jackson, M., Correa, S., & Padgett, Z. (2019). *Crime, violence, discipline, and safety in U.S. public school: Findings from the school survey on crime and safety: 2017–2018* (NCES 2019-061). National Center for Education Statistics.

Fine, A., Padilla, K., & Tapp, J. (2021). Can working collaboratively with law enforcement on community service promote positive youth development? *Police Practice and Research: An International Journal, 22*(7), 1739-1759.

Fine, A., Padilla, K., & Tom, K. (2020). Police legitimacy: Identifying developmental trends and whether youths' perceptions can be changed. *Journal of Experimental Criminology, 18*, 67-87.

Fissel, E. R., Wilcox, P., & Tillyer, M. S. (2019). School discipline policies, perceptions of justice, and in-school delinquency. *Crime & Delinquency, 65*(10), 1343–1370.

Flannery, K. B., Frank, J. L., & McGrath Kato, M. (2012). School disciplinary responses to truancy: Current practice and future directions. *Journal of School Violence, 11*(2), 118–137.

Gaffney, H., Ttofi, M. M., & Farrington, D. P. (2019). Evaluating the effectiveness of school-bullying prevention programs: An updated meta-analytical review. *Aggression and Violent Behavior, 45*, 111–133.

Ghavami, N., Thornton, B. E., & Graham, S. (2021). School police officers' roles: The influence of social, developmental and historical contexts. *Journal of Criminal Justice, 72*, 1–15.

Gill, C., Gottfredson, D., & Hutzell, K. (2016). Can school policing be trauma-informed? Lessons from Seattle. *Policing: An International Journal of Police Strategies & Management, 39*(3), 551–565.

Gottfredson, M. R., & Hirschi, T. (1990). *A general theory of crime*. Stanford University Press.

Granot, Y., Tyler, T. R., & Durkin, A. (2021). Legal socialization during adolescence: The emerging role of school resource officers. *Journal of Social Issues, 77*, 414-436.

Greenberg, M. T., Domitrovich, C. E., Weissburg, R. P., & Durlak, J. A. (2017). Social and emotional learning as a public health approach to education. *Future of Children, 27*, 13–32.

Gregory, A., Skiba, R. J., & Mediratta, K. (2017). Eliminating disparities in school discipline: A framework for intervention. *Review of Research in Education, 71*, 253–278.

Hafoka, M., Woo, Y., Hsieh, M., van Wormer, J., Stohr, M. K., & Hemmens, C. (2017). What legally prescribed functions tell us: Role differences between adult and juvenile probation officers. *Federal Probation, 81*(3), 32–47.

Haight, C. M., Chapman, G. V., Hendron, M., Loftis, R., & Kearney, C. A. (2014). Evaluation of a truancy diversion program at nine at-risk middle schools. *Psychology in the Schools, 51*(7), 779–787.

Hawkins, J. D., Oesterle, S., Brown, E. C., Monahan, K. C., Abbott, R. D., Arthur, M. W., & Catalano, R. F. (2012). Sustained decreases in risk exposure and youth problem behaviors after installation of the communities that care prevention system in a randomized trial. *Archives of Pediatrics & Adolescent Medicine, 166*(2), 141–148.

Henderson, M. L., Mathias-Humphrey, A., & McDermott, M. (2008). Barriers to effective program implementation: Rural school-based probation. *Federal Probation, 72*(1), 28–36.

Hendricks, M. E., Sale, E. W., Evans, C. J., McKinley, L., & Delozier Carter, S. (2010). Evaluation of a truancy court intervention in four middle schools. *Psychology in the Schools, 47*(2), 173–183.

Hirschfield, P. J. (2018). The role of schools in sustaining juvenile justice system inequality. *Future of Children, 28*(1), 11–35. https://www.jstor.org/stable/26641545

Hockenberry, S., & Puzzanchera, C. (2020). *Juvenile court statistics 2018*. National Center for Juvenile Justice. https://ojjdp.ojp.gov/sites/g/files/xyckuh176/files/media/document/juvenile-court-statistics-2018.pdf

Huang, F. L., & Cornell, D. G. (2020). Teacher support for zero tolerance is associated with higher suspension rates and lower feelings of safety. *School Psychology Review, 50*(2-3), 388-405.

Hurd, N. M., Hussain, S., & Bradshaw, C. P. (2018). School disorder, school connectedness, and psychosocial outcomes: Moderation by a supportive figure in the school. *Youth & Society, 50*(3), 328–350.

Icenogle, G., Steinberg, L., Duell, N., Chein, J., Chang, L., Chaudhary, N., . . . Bacchini, D. (2019). Adolescents' cognitive capacity reaches adult levels prior to their psychosocial maturity: Evidence for a "maturity gap" in a multinational, cross-sectional sample. *Law and Human Behavior, 43*(1), 69–85.

Infante, A., & Fine, A. (2021). Deterrability and moral judgment. In B. Van Rooij & D. Sokol (Eds.), *The Cambridge handbook of compliance* (Cambridge Law Handbooks, pp. 277–287). Cambridge University Press.

James, K., Bunch, J., & Clay-Warner, J. (2015). Perceived injustice and school violence: An application of general strain theory. *Youth Violence and Juvenile Justice, 13*(2), 169–189.

James, K., Watts, S. J., & Evans, S. Z. (2020). Fairness, social support, and school violence: Racial differences in the likelihood of fighting at school. *Crime & Delinquency, 66*(12), 1655–1677.

Jones, J. (2018). *More parents, children fearful for safety at school*. https://news.gallup.com/poll/241625/parents-children-fearful-safety-school.aspx

Kärnä, A., Voeten, M., Little, T., Alanen, E., Poskiparta, E., & Salmivalli, C. (2011). Effectiveness of the KiVa antibullying program: Grades 1–3 and 7–9. *Journal of Educational Psychology, 105*, 535–551.

Katic, B., Alba, L. A., & Johnson, A. H. (2020). A systematic evaluation of restorative justice practices: School violence prevention and response. *Journal of School Violence, 19*(4), 579–593.

Kubrin, C. E., & Mioduszewski, M. D. (2019). Social disorganization theory: Past, present and future. In M. D. Krohn, N. Hendrix, G. Penly Hall, & A. J. Lizotte (Eds) *Handbook on crime and deviance* (pp. 197–211). Springer.

Kupchik, A. (2009). Things are tough all over: Race, ethnicity, class and school discipline. *Punishment & Society, 11*, 291–317.

Kupchik, A., & Ellis, N. (2008). School discipline and security: Fair for all students? *Youth & Society, 39*(4), 549-574.

Leiber, M. J., & Fix, R. (2019). Reflections on the impact of race and ethnicity on juvenile court outcomes and efforts to enact change. *American Journal of Criminal Justice, 44*(4), 581–608.

Limber, S. P., & Kowalski, R. M. (2020). How schools often make a bad situation worse. *International Journal on Child Maltreatment: Research, Policy and Practice, 3*(2), 211–228.

Losen, D. J., & Gillespie, J. (2012). *Opportunities suspended: The disparate impact of disciplinary exclusion from school*. Center for Civil Rights Remedies at the Civil Rights Project at UCLA.

Losen, D. J., & Skiba, R. J. (2010). *Suspended education: Urban middle schools in crisis*. UCLA Civil Rights Project.

Loukas, A., Roalson, L. A., & Herrera, D. E. (2010). School connectedness buffers the effects of negative family relations and poor effortful control on early adolescent conduct problems. *Journal of Research on Adolescence, 20*(1), 13-22.

Magidson, M., & Kidd, T. (2021). Juvenile diversion and the family: How youth and parents experience diversion programming. *Criminal Justice and Behavior, 48*(11), 1576-1595.

Mas-Expósito, L., Krieger, V., Amador-Campos, J. A., Casañas, R., Albertí, M., & Lalucat-Jo, L. (2022). Implementation of whole school restorative approaches to promote positive youth development: Review of relevant literature and practice guidelines. *Education Sciences, 12*(3), 187.

Mazerolle, L., Bennett, S., Antrobus, E., & Eggins, E. (2017). The coproduction of truancy control: Results from a randomized trial of a police-schools partnership program. *Journal of Research in Crime and Delinquency, 54*(6), 791–823.

McNeely, C. A., Lee, W. F., Rosenbaum, J. E., Alemu, B., & Renner, L. M. (2019). Long-term effects of truancy diversion on school attendance: A quasi-experimental study with linked administrative data. *Prevention Science, 20*, 996–1008.

Mears, D. P. (2010). *American criminal justice policy: An evaluation approach to increasing accountability and effectiveness*. Cambridge University Press.

Mears, D., Montes, A., Siennick, S., Peta, G., Brown, S., & Collier, N. (2019). *The causal logic model of the Palm Beach County School Safety and Student Performance Program*. National Institute of Justice.

Menesini, E., & Salmivalli, C. (2017). Bullying in schools: The state of knowledge and effective interventions. *Psychology, Health & Medicine, 22*(Suppl 1), 240–253.

Montes, A. N., Mears, D. P., Collier, N. L., Pesta, G. B., Siennick, S. E., & Brown, S. J. (2021). Blurred and confused: The paradox of police in schools. *Policing: A Journal of Policy and Practice, 15*(2), 1546-1564.

Moon, B., & Morash, M. (2017). A test of general strain theory in South Korea: A focus on objective/subjective strains, negative emotions, and composite conditioning factors. *Crime & Delinquency, 63*(6), 731–756.

Musu, L., Zhang, A., Wang, K., Zhang, J., & Oudekerk, B. A. (2019). *Indicators of school crime and safety: 2018* (Report No. NCES 2019-047/NCJ 252571). U.S. Department of Education, National Center for Education Statistics, and U.S. Department of Justice, Bureau of Justice Statistics, Office of Justice Programs.

Na, C., & Gottfredson, D. C. (2013). Police officers in schools: Effects on school crime and the processing of offending behaviors. *Justice Quarterly, 30*(4), 619-650.

National Association of School Resource Officers. (2012). *To protect and educate: The school resource officer and the prevention of violence in schools*.

National Association of Youth Courts. (2017). *Youth courts: Facts & stats*. http://www.youthcourt.net/about/facts-and-stats

Nguyen, K., Yuan, Y., & McNeeley, S. (2020). School security measures, school environment, and avoidance behaviors. *Victims and Offenders, 15*(1), 43–59.

Nicholson-Crotty, S., Birchmeier, Z., & Valentine, D. (2009). Exploring the impact of school discipline on racial disproportion in the juvenile justice system. *Social Science Quarterly, 90*(4), 1003–1018.

O'Malley, M., Katz, K., Renshaw, T. L., & Furlong, M. J. (2012). Gauging the system: Trends in school climate measurement and intervention. In S. R. Jimerson, A. B. Nickerson, M. J. Mayer, & M. J. Furlong (Eds.), *Handbook of school violence and school safety: International research and practice* (pp. 317–329). Routledge.

O'Neill, J., & Vogel, M. (2020). School cohesion perception discrepancy and student delinquency. *Journal of Youth and Adolescence, 49*(7), 1492–1502.

Pesta, R. (2022). School punishment, deterrence, and race: A partial test of defiance theory. *Crime & Delinquency, 68*(3), 463-494.

Pigott, C., Stearns, A. E., & Khey, D. N. (2018). School resource officers and the school to prison pipeline: Discovering trends of expulsions in public schools. *American Journal of Criminal Justice, 43*, 120–138.

Pusch, N. (2022). Macro-level criminological perspectives and school delinquency: A meta-analysis. *Youth & Society, 54*(7), 1247-1279.

Radice, J. (2017). The juvenile record myth. *Georgetown Law Journal, 106*, 365–446.

Rocque, M., & Snellings, Q. (2018). The new disciplinology: Research, theory, and remaining puzzles on the school-to-prison pipeline. *Journal of Criminal Justice, 59*, 3–11.

Rodney, L. W., Johnson, D. L., & Srivastava, R. P. (2005). The impact of culturally relevant violence prevention models on school-age youth. *Journal of Primary Prevention, 26*(5), 439–454.

Sampson, R. J., Raudenbush, S. W., & Earls, F. (1997). Neighborhoods and violent crime: A multilevel study of collective efficacy. *Science, 277*, 918–924.

Scales, P. C., Benson, P. L., Leffert, N., & Blyth, D. A. (2000). Contribution of developmental assets to the prediction of thriving among adolescents. *Applied developmental science, 4*(1), 27-46.

Schiff, M. (2018). Can restorative justice disrupt the "school-to-prison pipeline"? *Contemporary Justice Review, 21*(2), 121–139.

Schwartz, R. G. (2018). A 21st century developmentally appropriate juvenile probation approach. *Juvenile and Family Court Journal, 69*(1), 41–54.

Schwartz, S., Sawchuk, S., Pendharkar, E., & Najarro, I (2021, June 4). *These districts defunded their school police. What happened next?* Education Week. https://www.edweek.org/leadership/these-districts-defunded-their-school-police-what-happened-next/2021/06

Sellers, B. G., & Arrigo, B. A. (2018). Zero tolerance, social control, and marginalized youth in US schools: A critical reappraisal of neoliberalism's theoretical foundations and epistemological assumptions. *Contemporary Justice Review, 21*(1), 60–79.

Shaw, C. R., & McKay, H. D. (1942). *Juvenile delinquency and urban areas*. University of Chicago Press.

Shoenfelt, E. L., & Huddleston, M. R. (2006). The truancy court diversion program of the family court, Warren circuit court division III, Bowling Green, Kentucky: An evaluation of impact on attendance and academic performance. *Family Court Review, 44*(4), 683–695.

Shulman, E. P., Smith, A. R., Silva, K., Icenogle, G., Duell, N., Chein, J., & Steinberg, L. (2016). The dual systems model: Review, reappraisal, and reaffirmation. *Developmental Cognitive Neuroscience, 17*, 103–117.

Siennick, S. E., & Widdowson, A. O. (2020). Juvenile arrest and later economic attainment: Strength and mechanisms of the relationship. *Journal of Quantitative Criminology, 38*, 23-50.

Skiba, R. J., Arredonod, M. I., & Williams, N. T. (2014). More than a metaphor: The contribution of exclusionary discipline to a school-to-prison pipeline. *Equity & Excellence in Education, 47*(4), 546–564.

Skiba, R. J., Michael, R. S., Nardo, A. C., & Peterson, R. (2000). *The color of discipline: Sources of racial and gender disproportionality in school punishment* (Rep. No. SRS1). Indiana Education Policy Center.

Smokowski, P. R., Evans, C. B. R., Rose, R., & Bacallao, M. (2020). A group randomized trial of school-based teen courts to address the school to prison pipeline, reduce aggression and violence, and enhance school safety in middle and high school students. *Journal of School Violence, 19*(4), 566–578.

Smokowski, P. R., Rose, R. A., Evans, C. B. R., Barbee, J., Cotter, K. L., & Bower, M. (2017). The impact of teen court on rural adolescents: Improved social relationships, psychological functioning, and school experiences. *Journal of Primary Prevention, 38*, 447–464.

Smolkowski, K., Girvan, E. J., McIntosh, K., Nese, R. N. T., & Horner, R. H. (2016). Vulnerable decision points for disproportionate office discipline referrals: Comparisons of discipline for African American and White elementary school students. *Behavioral Disorders, 41*(4), 178–195.

Stolzenberg, L., & D'Alessio, S. J. (2008). Co-offending and the age-crime curve. *Journal of Research in Crime and Delinquency, 45*(1), 65–86.

Strategies for Youth. (2019). *Two billion dollars later. States begin to regulate school resource officers in the nation's schools: A survey of state laws.*

Sutphen, R. D., Ford, J. P., & Flaherty, C. (2010). Truancy interventions: A review of the research literature. *Research on Social Work Practice, 20*(2), 161–171.

Theriot, M. T. (2009). School resource officers and the criminalization of student behavior. *Journal of Criminal Justice, 37*, 280–287. https://doi.org/10.1016/j.jcrimjus.2009.04.008

Theriot, M. T. (2016). The impact of school resource officer interaction on students' feelings about school and school police. *Crime & Delinquency, 62*(4), 446–469.

Torbet, P., Ricci, R., Brooks, C., & Zawacki, S. (2001). *Evaluation of Pennsylvania's school-based probation program.* National Center for Juvenile Justice.

Turner, E. O., & Beneke, A. J. (2020). "Softening" school resource officers: The extension of police presence in schools in an era of Black Lives Matter, school shootings, and rising inequality. *Race Ethnicity and Education, 23*(2), 221–240.

van Rooij, B., & Fine, A. (2021). *The behavioral code: The hidden ways law makes us better . . . or worse.* Beacon Press.

VanLone, J., Freeman, J., LaSalle, T., Gordon, L., Polk, T., & Rocha Neves, J. (2019). A practical guide to improving school climate in high schools. *Intervention in School and Clinic, 55*(1), 39–45.

Varela, J. J., Zimmerman, M. A., Ryan, A. M., Stoddard, S. A., & Heinze, J. E. (2021). School attachment and violent attitudes preventing future violent behavior among youth. *Journal of Interpersonal Violence, 36*(9–10), NP5407–NP5426.

Viano, S., Curran, F. C., & Fisher, B. (2021). Kindergarten cop: A case study of how a coalition between school districts and law enforcement led to school resource officers in elementary schools. *Educational Evaluation and Policy Analysis, 43*(2), 253–279. https://doi.org/10.3102%2F0162373721989290

Waasdorp, T. E., Pas, E. T., O'Brennan, L., & Bradshaw, C. (2011). A multilevel perspective on the climate of bullying: Discrepancies among students, school staff, and parents. *Journal of School Violence, 10*(2), 115–132.

Wang, K., Chen, Y., Zhang, J., & Oudekerk, B. A. (2020). *Indicators of school crime and safety: 2019* (Report No. NCES 2020-063/NCJ 254485). U.S. Department of Education, National Center for Education Statistics, and U.S. Department of Justice, Bureau of Justice Statistics, Office of Justice Programs.

Way, S. M. (2011). School discipline and disruptive classroom behavior: The moderating effects of student perceptions. *Sociological Quarterly, 52*, 346–375.

Weiler, S. C., & Cray, M. (2011). Police at school: A brief history and current status of school resource officers. *Clearing House, 84*, 160–163.

Welch, K., & Payne, A. A. (2018). Zero tolerance school policies. In J. Deakin, E. Taylor, & A. Kupchick (Eds.) *The Palgrave international handbook of school discipline, surveillance, and social control* (pp. 215–234). Palgrave Macmillan.

Wilcox, P., Augustine, M. C., Bryan, J. P., & Roberts, S. D. (2005). The "reality" of middle-school crime: Objective vs. subjective experiences among a sample of Kentucky youth. *Journal of School Violence, 4*(2), 3–28.

Williams, S., Schneider, M., Wornell, C., & Langhinrichsen-Rohling, J. (2018). Student's perceptions of school safety: It is not just about being bullied. *Journal of School Nursing, 34*(4), 319–330.

Wilson, D. (2004). The interface of school climate and school connectedness and relationships with aggression and victimization. *Journal of School Health, 74*, 293–300.

Wynne, S. L., & Joo, H. J. (2011). Predictors of school victimization: Individual, familial, and school factors. *Crime & Delinquency, 57*(3), 458–488.

Yeager, D. S., Fong, C. J., Lee, H. Y., & Espelage, D. L. (2015). Declines in efficacy of anti-bullying programs among older adolescents: Theory and a three-level meta-analysis. *Journal of Applied Developmental Psychology, 37*, 36–51.

Yuan, Y., & McNeeley, S. (2018). Fear of crime and behavioral adaptations: Testing the effects of fear of violence on unstructured socializing with peers. *Deviant Behavior, 39*(12), 1633–1646.

Zaykowski, H., & Gunter, W. (2012). Youth victimization: School climate or deviant lifestyles? *Journal of Interpersonal Violence, 27*, 431–452.

CHAPTER 19

Adolescents and Youth Justice: Framing the Developmental Research

Thomas Grisso

> **Abstract**
> This conclusion chapter uses issues raised in the *Adolescent* subsection to reflect on what types of research can best assist the youth justice system and youth who encounter it. After a brief historical note, the chapter uses three lenses to examine the value of the research the field has done thus far and to reveal worthwhile future research. The first lens reviews how translational studies of adolescent and youth justice contribute to discrete phases in the applied research enterprise. The second lens anticipates what will be needed to sustain the progress made thus far in the developmental era of youth justice reform. The third lens is determining whether there is an ideal model to which youth justice law and policy could aspire. The chapter closes with a reflection on how our research can best be done to improve its impact on law and legal practice.
>
> **Key Words:** adolescence and law, youth justice, translational research, developmental justice reform, evidence-based intervention, racial disparities

The eight chapters in this section on adolescence and the law demonstrate the breadth and depth of past research in developmental psychology addressing questions about youth who offend, the youth justice system, and their interactions. In broad terms, this research aims to help the youth justice system fulfill two major objectives in society. First, the system should be fair in its laws, legal processing, and adjudication of youth. This requires that law is informed about the developmental characteristics of adolescence relevant for shaping law, policy, and practices that are fair and just. Second, the system seeks positive effects on youth's futures, aiming at contributing to youth development and crime prevention. This objective requires developmental psychology's guidance on how the system can best respond to youth in its custody to reduce both offending and reoffending.

This commentary chapter uses issues raised in the preceding chapters in this section of the *Handbook* to reflect on what types of research can best assist the youth justice system and youth who encounter it. After a brief historical note, the chapter uses three lenses through which to examine the value of the research the field has done thus far, as well as to reveal worthwhile research we might do in the future. Each of the three lenses frames and focuses our attention somewhat differently. Using multiple lenses helps reveal which research in the preceding chapters is of special importance, as well as identifying what we have not been studying that would be worthwhile. The chapter closes with a reflection on *how* our research can best be done to improve its impact on law and legal practice.

Historical Context

Reading these chapters, one is struck by how far we have come in our assistance to youth justice since juvenile courts emerged early in the 20th century. Studies applying developmental psychology to law were few until the 1970s. There were three reasons for their appearance at that time: (a) U.S. society's midcentury civil rights movement that drew attention to children's rights, (b) the U.S. Supreme Court's recognition of adolescents' due process rights in juvenile court (e.g., *In re Gault*, 1967; *Kent v. U.S.*, 1966), and (c) the birth of an organized field of psychology and law in the 1970s (Grisso, 1991; Grisso & Brodsky, 2018).

Developmental psychologists of that era began discussing the potential for developmental studies of children and the law, exemplified in two edited volumes of treatises on the topic (Feshbach & Feshbach, 1978; Koocher, 1976). Soon thereafter, edited volumes (Melton et al., 1983; Reppucci et al., 1984) included examples of new research on adolescents' capacities to make legally relevant decisions: for example, to waive rights in interrogations (Grisso, 1981) and to make medical decisions (Weithorn & Campbell, 1982).

After modest progress during the next two decades, studies applying developmental psychology to questions in youth justice blossomed in the late 1990s and the following two decades—the studies most evident in the chapters in this section. At least two events fueled this surge of research. One was a remarkable increase in violent crime in the 1980s and 1990s that resulted in draconian get-tough laws and policies harmful to youth development, stimulating research to test and challenge the laws' presumptions. Another influence was the MacArthur Foundation's funding, beginning in 1997, of its Research Network on Adolescent Development and Juvenile Justice (John D. & Catherine T. MacArthur Foundation, n.d.; refer to https://www.macfound.org/networks/research-network-on-adolescent-development-juvenil). This team of psychologists, criminologists, and legal scholars, under the direction of Dr. Laurence Steinberg, performed developmentally informed behavioral studies on adolescents' psychosocial immaturity compared to adults and its legal relevance. The results eventually were merged with evolving findings from developmental neuroscience on adolescents' brain development. Chapters in this section repeatedly describe the impact of this research, forming a scientific basis for the U.S. Supreme Court's series of landmark decisions on adolescents' lesser culpability for purposes of sentencing (e.g., *Roper v. Simmons*, 2005).

As a wave of related studies emerged, the cumulative effect launched what is now called the "developmental era" in youth justice reform (National Research Council of the National Academies, 2013). Much of the science used in this reform is documented in these eight chapters, aiming to improve due process protection by taking account of youth's lesser capacities, developing alternatives to juvenile justice processing, and improving outcomes for youthful offenders.

Developmental psychology has not made these advances alone. Studying the adolescent–youth justice interaction has required that developmental psychologists employ theories, perspectives, and methods derived from other fields as well. In these chapters, one also finds—explicitly or in the shadows—clinical psychology (developmental psychopathology), social psychology, educational psychology, criminology, sociology, and legal scholarship. Such varied perspectives are necessary because basic research on adolescents' normative development does not necessarily define their behaviors in real-world circumstances. As emphasized by Bronfenbrenner (2005), a full understanding of adolescent behavior requires studying it in an ecological context: in the family environment, in schools and on the street, and, of course, in interaction with police, courts, and legal processing. Understanding these contexts requires borrowing from other areas of science to make our developmental psychological studies relevant for law.

Recognizing the prolific outpouring of research on adolescence and the law in recent decades, the chapters in this section also provide guidance for new issues and opportunities to inform and improve the law and legal process for adolescents. What further can we do?

The Basic and Translational Research Enterprise

Let us look at the research in these chapters not according to the chapters' topics, but through the lens of the research enterprise. The intention to do scientific research that can be applied for social good is explicit for developmental psychologists who focus on legal issues. The process of reaching applied objectives can be framed as an enterprise, beginning with basic studies of adolescents' development and proceeding through phases of research to make the basic science applicable to law and the youth justice system. One structure for framing this process in the biological and behavioral sciences organizes the research enterprise into several steps, beginning with *basic* research and proceeding through various stages of *translational* research (e.g., Khoury et al., 2007).

Translational research is, by definition, applied research. Beginning with theoretical and empirical guidance from basic biological or behavioral studies, translational research puts science to use for various benefits: in this case, to improve fairness and outcomes for adolescents in interaction with the youth justice system. Borrowing from the general translational research model provided by Khoury et al. (2007), Grisso et al. (2019) offered a way to frame our translational psychological studies of adolescence and youth justice. It uses the four classic types of translational research, "T1" through "T4," which are defined in the following discussion. Applying this model to the studies in this section's chapters, how do our current studies contribute to these phases in the applied research enterprise? And through that lens, what do we find that needs our further attention as researchers aiming to improve youth justice?

Basic Research

G. Stanley Hall, Piaget, Erikson, Kohlberg, Bronfenbrenner, and many others—these are the historic roots of our modern behavioral science showing how adolescents differ from adults. Recent basic behavioral science on psychosocial immaturity, repeatedly described in the preceding chapters, has been merged with developmental neuroscience findings to shape such concepts as the dual systems model of psychosocial development in adolescence (for a review see Steinberg & Icenogle, 2019). Refinements in basic research in these areas are ongoing: for example, behavioral and neuroscience studies of the continued development of adolescents into the early adult years (e.g., Cohen et al., 2016).

As we have seen in recent U.S. Supreme Court cases, basic developmental research can be "applied" to provide a theoretical logic for policy change. Alone, however, basic research providing developmental knowledge of youth's growth and capacities raises the question, "How do we know what kind of difference that makes in real-world contexts?" The following translational steps in the research enterprise borrow from basic scientific gains to address that question.

T1 Research: Translating Basic Science in a Legal Context

T1 translational research uses basic research findings to test hypotheses regarding the implications for behavior within social contexts—in this case, examining their relevance when applied in a sociolegal context. For example, can we test basic developmental findings to determine empirically whether they improve our understanding of reasons for youth's offending? Can they empirically account for why the youth justice system's responses to delinquency reduce, do not reduce, or exacerbate youth offending? Some majority of studies reported in this section's chapters are T1 research. For example, they describe applications of basic research to examine the legal competencies of adolescents, such as their vulnerabilities in interrogation (Cleary & Crane) and as witnesses (Wyman et al.), their lesser capacities for pleading and participation in trials (Zottoli et al.), and the developmental consequences of incarceration (Viljoen et al.).

Our T1 studies often weigh youth justice practices against the developmental needs and capacities of adolescents, and in so doing, often they locate problems. These problems sometimes include iatrogenic consequences, ineffective interventions, and disconnects between adolescents' capacities and their expected participation as defendants, as well as laws that sentence youth without adequate recognition of their lesser culpability compared to adults. Having located problems, our T1 research often leads to recommendations for change but does not necessarily provide solutions. For example, Fine et al. offer nine recommended modifications in school safety programs, but most of them would require decisions about how and with what methods such changes could be made. That requires T2 research, which is examined later in this discussion.

The preceding chapters cover considerable territory for T1 research in this field, but less in evidence here are lines of T1 research employing basic findings from *developmental psychopathology*. As Fountain et al. note, psychiatric and behavioral disorders are far more prevalent among justice-involved youths (e.g., Teplin et al., 2002). This has led to several areas of T1 research being underreported in these chapters, so a few examples are worth mention. (For more complete reviews see Grisso, 2004; Nagel et al., 2016.)

First, much T1 research has examined the youth justice system's inadequacies in meeting justice-involved youth's mental health needs and have called for solutions (Cocozza et al., 2010; Desai et al., 2006; Swank & Gagnon, 2016). How we should respond is not clear. Simply increasing mental health services in detention or corrections facilities might have negative net-widening effects, increasing rates of arrest of youth simply to provide them mental health services to which they may not otherwise have access. A second example is T1 research examining whether mental health disorders are an independent risk factor for violent or nonviolent offending. The answer appears to be "no" (e.g., Schubert et al., 2011), but the importance of treating them to improve outcomes may be significant (Nagel et al., 2016).

As a final example of the importance of developmental psychopathology for this field, the preceding chapters describe research showing that most youth who offend desist from offending as they reach young adulthood, but a small percentage are "life course persistent" (Farrington et al., 2013; Moffitt, 1993; referenced by Manasse & Rebellon, this volume). What those chapters do not mention is the substantial amount of T1 research that attempts to identify during adolescence youth who may be developing enduring antisocial character, including a search for early signs of psychopathy as a personality disorder (for a review see Vincent et al., 2016).

T2 Research: Evidence-Based Applications

Responding to T1 identification of areas in law in need of change, T2 research aims to develop evidence-based products, strategies or interventions that might improve application of science to real-world environments for society's benefit. Examples in the preceding chapters include references to developmentally informed assessment tools that can improve youth justice decisions about youth, models for diversion programs, and science-based methods for prosocial modification of youth's behaviors and environments. T2 research is demanding, requiring conceptual development of the product and demonstration of its evidence-based efficacy, as well as attention to its potential practical utility within the youth justice context.

Many T2 products are assessment tools designed to address specific problems in youth justice. As such, these tools can do more than improve measurement. When eventually they become embedded in youth justice practice, they can change the system's climate, perspective, and policies. For example, risk assessment tools like the Youth Level of Services/Case Management Inventory (Hoge & Andrews, 2010) can serve as guides for legal decisions about youth that minimize unnecessary incarceration of low-risk adolescents, as well as provide a template for matching the right case intervention with youth's individual needs (Hoge, 2016). Similarly, the Massachusetts Youth Screening Instrument (Grisso & Barnum, 2006), a 10-minute self-report questionnaire designed specifically for use by staff with every youth upon entrance to a detention or corrections facility, encourages staff awareness of the relevance of youth's mental health problems and increases detention facility referrals to clinicians who provide mental health services (Williams & Grisso, 2011).

The preceding chapters sometimes mention the need for more T2 research to move the system toward more developmentally appropriate practices, potentially reducing the problems identified in their T1 research. Here are a few T2 possibilities related to, but not specifically proposed in, the preceding chapters, and for which little work has yet been done.

DEVELOPMENTALLY INFORMED INTERVIEW PROTOCOLS

In the present context, interview protocols are guides for use by forensic clinicians or youth justice professionals (e.g., law enforcement or probation officers) when interviewing adolescents. Their purpose is to provide the system ways of questioning youth that give proper attention to their developmental differences from adults while gathering information essential to the legal process. Typically semistructured, such interview tools have several potential benefits when constructed with attention to youth's developmental capacities and vulnerabilities. They may promote more reliable information by reducing the effects of youth's susceptibility to suggestion. In addition, legal questioning that adjusts to cognitive and emotional characteristics of adolescence may promote positive legal socialization and reduce stress and trauma in youth's contacts with representatives of the legal system. The value of developmentally informed interview protocols is described by Wyman et al. pertaining to the questioning of young witnesses.

Cleary et al. offer substantial evidence regarding the negative effects of law enforcement questioning of adolescent suspects. Currently law enforcement officers typically are guided in their interrogations by coercive techniques originally designed for use with adult suspects and embedded in widely used interrogation manuals (e.g., Inbau et al., 2013). Can developmental psychologists create a youth interrogation model and manual, informed by our knowledge of adolescents' capacities and vulnerabilities, thus offering an evidence-based alternative to ordinary interrogation techniques? Can such efforts demonstrate that they elicit more reliable, less distorted information than current methods? Similarly, as noted by Zottoli et al., the process of pleading and plea bargains can be complex for defendants, especially less mature adolescents. Can we develop a semistructured interview protocol, developmentally informed, for use by defense attorneys to walk a youth through the alternatives and their consequences, perhaps simultaneously assessing the youth's grasp of the situation?

ASSESSMENT TOOLS

The preceding chapters say little about the work of clinical forensic psychologists who perform evaluations for the courts. In that role, they have considerable value as advisors to the court regarding the developmental characteristics of youth. Here are two examples of ways developmental researchers could assist them.

As noted by Zottoli et al., recognition of youth's right to competence to stand trial is challenging to the courts (and forensic examiners) when considered from a developmental perspective. The field has a semistructured, developmentally informed interview guide for examining adolescents' abilities relevant for competence to stand trial (Grisso, 2005), but it is neither a scored nor normed tool. Standardized, normed, and validated tools for trial competency have been developed for use with adults, but they have significant limitations when used with adolescents, especially because they are without adolescent norms. Creation of a developmentally informed tool of this type for adolescents is a worthwhile project for the future.

Several of the preceding chapters describe how basic and T1 research has studied psychosocial (im)maturity using theoretical models to conceptualize it. For example, one model is based on three aspects of psychosocial maturity: risk taking and impulsiveness (temperance), one's consideration of future consequences (perspective), and autonomous decision making (responsibility Cauffman & Steinberg, 2000; Steinberg & Cauffman, 1996). A variety of research measures have been used in basic and T1 research to test hypotheses about differences in these capacities between adolescents and adults (e.g., Cauffman & Steinberg, 2000; Monahan et al., 2009 reviewed by Kavanaugh & Grisso, 2021). However, most of these tools used in basic or T1 research are computer-assisted tasks and self-report questionnaires suitable primarily for administration in research laboratories. Moreover, they have not been normed and validated for broad adolescent populations. Thus, we need versions of these tools suitable for use by forensic psychologists evaluating young people in individual court cases. One can also imagine a psychosocial maturity instrument composed of several such tools. That such applied tools have not yet been developed is surprising and in need of remedy.

EVIDENCE-BASED INTERVENTIONS

Fountain et al. describe difficulties in evaluating the effectiveness of alternatives to youth justice processing (diversion programs and specialty courts). Part of the problem is that diversion programs, or specialty courts, are not uniform in their models, requirements, or procedures, varying in many ways across jurisdictions. Until we develop a manualized form of diversion—as some successful youth interventions have done (e.g., multisystemic therapy: Henggeler, 2016)—it will be difficult to meaningfully examine the degree to which diversion is successful in reducing recidivism.

Youth's competency to stand trial is discussed by Zottoli et al. but not the problem of restoration (remedial intervention) when youth are found not competent to proceed due to mental disorder, intellectual disability, or developmental immaturity. Although youth's right to be competent in juvenile court has been recognized for over two decades, programs to remediate youths found not competent have evolved only haphazardly in most states, without systematic attention to developmental factors associated with adolescence (Kruh et al., 2021; Viljoen & Grisso, 2007; Warren et al., 2016). Consequently, youth found incompetent to stand trial often face trial delays and uncertain outcomes. An evidence-based approach to remediating adolescents' legal incompetence to proceed is greatly needed. Fortunately, more systematic models are beginning to emerge, and there are claims that one (in Virginia) may soon reach evidence-based status (Warren et al., 2016).

T3 and T4 Research: Implementation and Effectiveness

T3 research examines ways to put T2 evidence-based practices into place in the youth justice system such that they will be implemented with fidelity. Can the tool or method be employed on the ground as designed and validated in T2 research? This type of research requires attention to logistics, training of those in the youth justice system who implement the method, and measures of quality control across time. T4 research then examines the effectiveness of the intervention: for example, outcomes such as reduction in recidivism or other positive youth outcomes. T2 research shows the method's efficacy, T3 shows its practicality for application, and T4 seeks to determine its effectiveness in real practice.

T3 and T4 research are essential to complete the applied developmental research enterprise. Yet their theoretical framework and empirical strategies are not essentially "developmental," drawing more from implementation science and evaluation research. Nevertheless, developmental psychologists might assist such research in various ways: for example, training youth justice staff to understand the developmental aspects of the intervention.

Sustaining the Developmental Reform

A second lens through which to view our research objectives is to anticipate what will be needed to sustain the progress made thus far in what has come to be called the "developmental reform" of youth justice (National Research Council of the National Academies, 2013). Developmental psychology has contributed significantly to this reform: for example, informing U.S. Supreme Court landmark decisions on adolescents' lesser culpability, promoting developmentally informed legislative changes in most states, and on-the-ground changes in policies and practices in juvenile courts and detention facilities (Cauffman et al., 2018). Due in part to these reforms, the arrest and incarceration of adolescent offenders have decreased by more than one half in the past 20 years (Annie E. Casey Foundation, 2021).

But can the pace of reform and its gains be sustained? Across the youth justice system's 120-year history, it has cycled through other reforms in response to changes in societal demands, crime rates, public attitudes, and political perspectives (Bernard & Kurlychek, 2010). Could the developmental reform movement be similarly challenged? And if so, what kinds of research might meet the challenge?

Recently Cavanagh and colleagues (2022) reported a multistage study that asked an expert panel of developmental, legal, and youth advocacy professionals to reach consensus about the greatest threats to developmental reform. In 2015, after a series of meetings, the expert panel reached a consensual forecast of 11 specific threats that might arise, ranking them by likelihood and the degree of damage they might do to the reform. Five years later, the same panel was asked to reach consensus on which of the threats they had forecasted had indeed emerged. One part of the panel's task was to identify areas of research that had potential to mitigate certain threats. Some of the areas of research they identified are especially aligned with the preceding chapters in this section.

Racial Disparities in Youth Justice

Several chapters in this section identify the importance of racial disparities in youth justice as a research target. The developmental reform in juvenile justice has not resolved this issue (Henning, 2018). Indeed, the expert panel in Cavanagh et al. (2022) identified racial disparities in arrest, system processing, and sentencing as among the most likely and potentially most damaging threats to the reform. The panel originally forecasted that the reduction in arrests and incarceration of youth, although a reform success, would disproportionately advantage White youth, which subsequent research has affirmed (e.g., Abrams et al., 2021). Panelists recommended two types of research to address the issue.

First, they welcomed research to develop and test focused interventions to reduce legal decision makers' racial biases at various intercepts in the youth justice system. Theories and strategies required for such research typically are in the territory of social or cognitive psychology, focusing on decision theory, implicit social attitudes, and stereotypes. Yet developmental psychologists can play a role in those studies, to the extent that stereotypes and biases being examined pertain to race, age, and related developmental characteristics.

A second recommendation, for which developmental researchers could play a larger part, focused on the development of assessment tools that can reduce racial bias in decision making when used by legal decision makers. Herein lies one of the more complex questions facing us in this area. As noted by the National Research Council of the National Academies (2013), one source of racial disproportionality in justice settings might be harmful social conditions that disproportionately affect childhood neurological and behavioral development for youth of color, leading to a greater risk of offending in adolescence. By itself, this is a call for basic and T1 developmental research on that question. Yet a greater complexity lies in the fact that many of the disproportionate and developmentally negative environmental conditions that we find might themselves be embedded in our tools used to assess risk of antisocial behavior. That is, risk factors and systemic developmental disadvantage may be conflated in ways that could contribute to racially disproportionate risk assessment results. More extensive review of research on this issue is offered by Vincent and Viljoen (2020).

Age of Juvenile Jurisdiction

In this volume, Hamilton describes laws pertaining to the age of majority and age of permission for various legal purposes. In addition to the issues Hamilton reviews, youth justice policy analysts currently are debating the appropriate ages for juvenile court jurisdiction. The panel in Cavanagh et al. (2022) identified this as a matter of opportunity but with potential to create substantial resistance that could challenge the broader efforts of the developmental reform. Therefore, they called for both basic and translational research to inform future considerations about age for juvenile court jurisdiction.

The debate on this point is on two fronts. One is the proper minimum age for juvenile court jurisdiction (Tolliver et al., 2021). Currently, about two thirds of the states have no minimum age for charging children with delinquencies, and all but two of the remainder allow delinquency filings for youth ages 6–10 (Juvenile Justice GPS, n.d.) To address this question, T1 research could translate basic research on children's development (e.g., the development of moral reasoning capacities, intentionality, and time perspective) to test hypotheses related to the law's notions of criminal culpability. Equally important might be research aimed at describing the probable ineffectiveness of legal sanctions for young children for reducing future offending.

At the other end of the youth age spectrum, the upper age of juvenile court jurisdiction has been shifting in recent years. In the 1990s, about one quarter of the states used 15 or 16 as the upper age for juvenile court jurisdiction; now almost all states set the upper age at the 18th birthday (Juvenile Justice GPS, n.d.). Developmental neuroscience research suggesting continued brain development into the early 20s has now fueled a movement in some states to raise the age higher (Cauffman et al., 2018), in one state to the 20th birthday (Vermont).

Such considerations could use further basic developmental research on similarities and differences between adolescents and young adults in their psychosocial functioning (e.g., Cohen et al., 2016; Steinberg & Icenogle, 2019). In addition, T1 developmental studies are needed to identify positive and potentially negative effects of creating an extended youth justice system that merges adolescents and young adults (consult also Gillespie et al., in this volume). For example, what are the positive or negative implications of older adolescents' tendency toward peer influence when in secure custody with young adults? Are older adolescents and young adults sufficiently similar that we can respond to them with similar intervention methods for reducing future offending?

Measuring "Success" in Youth Justice Interventions

Finally, preceding chapters demonstrate that when researchers (and society) measure the successes or failures of youth justice practices, the outcome criterion usually used is recidivism. The Cavanagh et al. (2022) expert panel identified this as a likely and potentially damaging threat to the reform when used as the sole measure of success. When this criterion predominates, and if crime rates rise, the publicly favored remedy may be incarceration. This ignores the other primary objective for a developmentally informed youth justice system: contributing to positive youth development for longer range gains. After a youth receives youth justice services, success in getting a job or remaining in school—or an increase in psychosocial maturity—is no less important as a measure of "success" than recidivism, although their influence on crime reduction may not be immediately evident. One potential strategy to confront this problem is to create a "success metric" that represents the second objective. Can we develop outcome measures that assess the system's effectiveness on criteria representing positive adolescent development?

Toward a Different Youth Justice Model

A final lens through which to view the potential relevance of our research for youth justice is to zoom out to the broadest question: Is there an ideal model to which youth justice law and policy could aspire? Zottoli et al. describe the history of U.S. youth justice, beginning with a rehabilitation model, then a due process model, and now a developmentally driven reform recognizing reduced culpability for adolescents who offend. Is the latest model the ideal?

A developmentally informed system is certainly an advance and, in many respects, warrants continuation as a framework for youth justice. Yet, as Slobogin and Fondacaro (2009) have articulated so well, youth justice reform that emphasizes the lesser culpability of adolescents, while providing some benefits, also contains a troubling flaw, precisely because culpability is its driving consideration. The post-*Gault* due process era provided the same rights in juvenile court as in criminal court. But in the context of a crime wave in the 1980s and 1990s, new laws "criminalized" youth's offending, such that the system's response to their offending was driven by a retributive (deserved punishment) objective typical of the criminal justice system. The developmental reform movement began when psychological and neuroscience research demonstrated a developmental reason for youth to be considered less culpable or blameworthy than adults for similar offenses. While this has resulted in somewhat reduced penalties for adolescents than for adults, Slobogin and Fondacaro point out that this apparent benefit is provided within a retributive framework that does nothing to reduce the criminalization of youth justice. Under a "lesser culpability" argument, society's response to adolescent offending is still driven by retribution objectives to punish the offense, merely a bit less so.

Slobogin and Fondacaro (2009), therefore, argue for a new model of youth justice that recognizes different, nonretributive responses to all offenses during adolescence. They propose a model that retains due process in juvenile court but rejects a retributive purpose (other than as an indicator of the maximum possible dispositional length) and instead offers a post-adjudication disposition driven by what they call the *individual prevention* objective. After adjudication, the system would employ developmentally informed evidence-based therapeutic methods known to reduce offending, with secure custody unrelated to notions of deserved punishment and imposed only on higher risk youth who need it to allow implementation of effective interventions that will lower the future risk of offending.

Slobogin and Fondacaro describe case law and legal theory that could support their individual prevention model, and today's diversion programs are an incrementally consistent shift in that direction. But the future of such a model is uncertain. Nonetheless, one can argue that it is a future to be pursued. In that light, what does pursuit of this future suggest about directions for developmental research on adolescents and the law? Here are three possibilities.

First, a logical place from which to launch a nonretributive model of youth justice is to seek to reduce or abolish the practice of transfer of youth for trial in criminal court (discussed by Zottoli et al.). The law of transfer (in some states called waiver) is deeply rooted in past and present youth justice in the United States (reviewed by Heilbrun et al., 2017; Reppucci et al., 2009). The legal mechanisms for transfer differ greatly across states, variously requiring judicial decisions, prosecutors' choices, and/or statutes requiring transfer for certain offenses (Fagan & Zimring, 2000). Transfer is one of the primary legal avenues toward retributive penalties for adolescents. Reducing or abolishing it could be assisted by redirecting psychology's evidence on youth's lesser culpability and legal competency, not merely seeking shorter retributive sentences but addressing the developmental inappropriateness of subjecting youth to adult retributive sentences altogether.

A second direction for research would examine more closely the impact of retributive and adultlike sanctions on adolescents from a crime prevention perspective. Viljoen et al. describe studies of the ineffectiveness, in crime prevention terms, of incarceration simply for retributive purposes; yet they point out that more research is needed to offer scientifically convincing evidence on this point. Helpful also would be more research on recidivism rates for youth transferred and sentenced in criminal court compared to similar youth retained in the youth justice system. Past studies have suggested poorer outcomes for transferred youth (for a review see Zottoli et al., this volume), but these studies have not always been able to control for the range of variables on which to form matched groups.

Finally, any argument for replacing a retributive response with an individual prevention model would require substantial assurance that evidence-based therapeutic methods can indeed reduce recidivism for a wide range of youthful offenders. This suggests a need for increased research on the value of evidence-based interventions with high-risk youth. In addition, improved risk assessment instruments (especially those that reduce disproportionate minority results) will be important for assignments to appropriate levels and types of intervention and to ensure public safety. The field has a good empirical foundation on which to build better research in these areas.

Concluding Comments: Having an Impact

This commentary has focused on *what* research this field should pursue, but *how* we do our research also is important. All our developmental psychological research on adolescents and the law is, of course, intended for use by the law, legal system, and legal practitioners who require scientific information about adolescents. The quality of the research is important for that objective, but even studies meeting the highest scientific standards require more to fulfill that purpose. They require *relevance, credibility*, and *accessibility* as judged by the legal professionals whom we intend to assist and influence.

The *relevance* of our research is enhanced when we involve legal scholars and practicing legal advocates at the time we design our studies. Once performed, our research findings must fit the legal context in which we hope they will be applied. Most of us are not fully prepared to make that judgment. We can learn law, of course, and gain some knowledge of the legal system to which our research applies. Yet most of us neither are lawyers nor work daily in the legal system. Consultation with law scholars and practicing legal advocates can help us frame our studies in legally relevant ways, greatly increasing the likelihood that our work, once done, will avoid barriers to its use by those who influence and practice law.

Concerning *credibility*, there is evidence that lawmakers who consult science to inform law are less likely to believe findings when they perceive ideological bias in a study's process or presentation (Bogenschneider & Bogenschneider, 2020). Most of us in this field walk a fine line between scientific neutrality and our objective to do research that may advocate for certain changes in the law. Often we are driven in part by our values concerning the welfare of adolescents. This is unavoidable and is no problem so long as we restrain our zeal. In part, this can be done by constructing our developmental studies as though we do not care how the study turns out or as though we wish to prove our beliefs are wrong (Grisso & Steinberg, 2005). Ironically, involving legal advocates when designing research (to increase its relevance) can itself threaten our credibility if it interferes with scientific integrity in designing the study. Perceived credibility also is harmed when we report our findings and their implications in ways that overinterpret our results or overstep our role. Excessive advocacy rhetoric and demands for change are not necessary and, indeed, can damage the credibility of our findings that support a possible legal interpretation or change in law.

Finally, this field's research findings must be *accessible* to legal professionals to have an impact on law and legal practice. Findings reported in our science journals are neither easy for them to find nor easy to read. Even seasoned legal advocates on the expert panel in the Cavanaugh et al. (2022) study described earlier admitted they were not well acquainted with newer scientific findings relevant for their youth advocacy. Lawmakers say they need better access to science and more concise descriptions than science journals provide (Bogenschneider & Bogenschneider, 2020). How best to do that has been a puzzle for some time (e.g., Grisso & Melton, 1987), but potentially successful strategies are possible given this era's information technology options. Ultimately, meeting this need requires a developmental psychology and law clearinghouse mechanism specifically for youth justice lawyers.

In closing, after exploring juvenile law and working with the juvenile courts during almost all its post-*Gault* years, one can observe that our youth justice system has some things in common with adolescents. Both are continuously evolving in search of a better future. Both are sometimes disappointing and short-sighted but often surprise us with signs of their potential. Both are sometimes frustrating, but both are amenable to change if appropriately assisted. The chapters in this section demonstrate what developmental psychology can contribute to the maturation of both adolescents and the youth justice system, given time and our patient guidance.

References

Abrams, L., Mizel, M., & Barnert, E. (2021). The criminalization of young children and overrepresentation of black youth in the juvenile justice system. *Race and Social Problems, 13*, 73–84.

Annie E. Casey Foundation. (2021). *Youth incarceration in the United States.* https://www.aecf.org/resources/youth-incarceration-in-the-united-states

Bernard, T., & Kurlychek, M. (2010). *The cycle of juvenile justice.* Oxford University Press.

Bogenschneider, K., & Bogenschneider, B. (2020). Empirical evidence from state legislators: How, when, and who uses research. *Psychology, Public Policy and Law, 4*, 413–424.

Bronfenbrenner, U. (2005). The bioecological theory of human development (2001). In U. Bronfenbrenner (Ed.), *Making human beings human: Bioecological perspectives on human development* (pp. 3–15). Sage Publications.

Cauffman, E., Fine, A., Mahler, A., & Simmons, C. (2018). How developmental science influences juvenile justice reform. *University of California-Irvine Law Review, 8*, 101–120.

Cauffman, E., & Steinberg, L. (2000). (Im)maturity of judgment in adolescence: Why adolescents may be less culpable than adults. *Behavioral Sciences & the Law, 18*, 741–760.

Cavanagh, C., Paruk, J., & Grisso, T. (2022) The developmental reform in juvenile justice: Its progress and vulnerability. *Psychology, Public Policy, and Law, 28*(2), 151–166. https://doi.org/10.1037/law0000326

Cocozza, J., Skowyra, K., & Shufelt, J. (2010). *Addressing the mental health needs of youth in contact with the juvenile justice system in systems of care communities.* Technical Assistance Partnership for Child and Family Mental Health. https://ncyoj.policyresearchinc.org/img/resources/Addressing-the-Mental-Health-Needs-of-Youth-468141.pdf

Cohen, A., Breiner, K., Steinberg, L., Bonnie, R., Scott, E. S., Taylor-Thompson, K., Rudolph, M., Chein, J., Richeson, J., Heller, A., Silverman, M., Dellarco, D., Fair, D., Galván, A., & Casey, B. (2016). When is an adolescent an adult?? Assessing cognitive control in emotional and nonemotional contexts. *Psychological Science, 27,* 549–562.

Desai, R., Goulet, J., Robbins, J., Chapman, J., Migdole, S., & Hoge, M. (2006). Mental health care in juvenile detention facilities: A review. *Journal of the American Academy of Psychiatry and the Law, 34,* 204–214.

Fagan, J., & Zimring, F. (Eds.) (000). *The changing borders of juvenile justice: Transfer of adolescents to the criminal court.* University of Chicago Press.

Farrington, D., Piquero, A., & Jennings, W. (2013). *Offending from childhood to late middle age: Recent results from the Cambridge study in delinquent development.* Springer.

Feshbach, N., & Feshbach, S. (Eds.). (1978). *The changing status of children: Rights and responsibilities.* Special Issue. *Journal of Social Issues, 34,* 168–178.

Grisso, T. (1981). *Juveniles' waiver of rights: Legal and psychological competence.* Plenum

Grisso, T. (1991). A developmental history of the American Psychology-Law Society. *Law and Human Behavior, 15,* 213–231.

Grisso, T. (2004). *Double jeopardy: Adolescent offenders with mental disorders.* University of Chicago Press.

Grisso, T. (2005). *Evaluating juveniles' adjudicative competence: A guide for clinical practice.* Professional Resource Press.

Grisso, T., & Barnum, R. (2006). *Massachusetts Youth Screening Instrument-Version 2: User's manual and technical report.* Professional Resource Press.

Grisso, T., & Brodsky, S. (Eds.). (2018). *The roots of modern psychology and law: A narrative history.* Oxford University Press.

Grisso, T., Fountain, E., NeMoyer, A., & Thornton, L. (2019). The role of translational psychological science in juvenile justice reform. *Translational Issues in Psychological Science, 5,* 13–20.

Grisso, T., & Melton, G. (1987). Getting child developmental research to legal practitioners. In G. Melton (Ed.), *Reforming the law: Impact of child developmental research* (pp. 146–176). Guilford.

Grisso, T., & Steinberg, L. (2005). Between a rock and a soft place: Developmental research and the child advocacy process. *Journal of Clinical Child and Adolescent Psychology, 34,* 619–627.

Heilbrun, K., DeMatteo, D., King, C., & Filone, S. (2017). *Evaluating juvenile transfer and disposition: Law, science, and practice.* Routledge.

Henggeler, S. (2016). Community-based interventions for juvenile offenders. In K. Heilbrun, D. DeMatteo, & N. Goldstein (Eds.), *APA handbook of psychology and juvenile justice* (pp. 575–596). American Psychological Association.

Henning, K. (2018). The challenge of race and crime in free society: The racial divide in fifty years of juvenile justice reform. *George Washington Law Review, 86,* 1604–1666.

Hoge, R. (2016). Risk, need, and responsivity in juveniles. In K. Heilbrun, D. DeMatteo, & N. Goldstein (Eds.), *APA handbook of psychology and juvenile justice* (pp. 170–196). American Psychological Association.

Hoge, R., & Andrews, D. (2010). *Youth Level of Services/Case Management Inventory 2.0 (YLS/CMI): Users' manual.* Multi-Health Systems.

In re Gault, 387 U.S. 1 (1967).

Inbau, F., Reid, J., Buckley, J., & Jayne, B. (2013). *Criminal interrogation and confessions* (5th ed.). Jones & Bartlett Learning.

John D. and Catherine T. MacArthur Foundation (n.d.). *Research Network on Adolescent Development and Juvenile Justice.* https://www.macfound.org/networks/research-network-on-adolescent-development-juvenil

Juvenile Justice GPS (n.d.). *Juvenile jurisdiction.* http://www.jjgps.org/

Kavanaugh, A., & Grisso, T. (2021). *Evaluations for sentencing of juveniles in criminal court.* Oxford University Press.

Kent v. U.S., 383 U.S. 541 (1966).

Khoury, M., Gwinn, M., Yoon, P., Dowling, N., Moore, C., & Bradley, L. (2007). The continuum of translation research in genomic medicine: How can we accelerate the appropriate integration of human genome discoveries into health care and disease prevention? *General Medicine, 9,* 665–674.

Koocher, G. (Ed.). (1976). *Children's rights and the mental health professions.* Wiley.

Kruh, I., Gowensmith, N., Alkema, A., Swenson, K., & Platt, D. (2021). Community-based remediation of juvenile competence to stand trial: A national survey. *International Journal of Forensic Mental Health, 21*(4), 321–333. https://doi.org/10.1080/14999013.2021.2007431

Melton, G., Koocher, G., & Saks, M. (Eds.). (1983). *Children's competence to consent.* Spectrum.

Moffitt, T. E. (1993). "Life-course-persistent" and "adolescence-limited" antisocial behavior: A developmental taxonomy. *Psychological Review, 10*, 674–701.

Monahan, K., Steinberg, L., Cauffman, E., & Mulvey, E. (2009). Trajectories of antisocial behavior and psychosocial maturity from adolescence to young adulthood. *Developmental Psychology, 45*, 1654–1668.

Nagel, A., Guamera, L., & Reppucci, N. D. (2016). Adolescent development, mental disorder, and decision making in delinquent youths. In K. Heilbrun, D. DeMatteo, & N. Goldstein (Eds.), *APA handbook of psychology and juvenile justice* (pp. 117–138). American Psychological Association.

National Research Council of the National Academies. (2013). *Reforming juvenile justice: A developmental approach*. National Academies Press.

Reppucci, N. D., Michel, J., & Kostelnik, J. (2009). Challenging juvenile transfer: Faulty assumptions and misguided policies. In B. Bottoms, C. Najdowski, & G. Goodman (Eds.), *Children as victims, witnesses, and offenders: Psychological science and the law* (pp. 295–312). Guilford Press.

Reppucci, N., Weithorn, L., Mulvey, E., & Monahan, J. (Eds.). (1984). *Children, mental health, and the law*. Sage Publications.

Roper v. Simmons, 125 U.S. 1183 (2005).

Schubert, C., Mulvey, E., & Glashen, C. (2011). Influence of mental health and substance use problems and criminogenic risk on outcomes in serious juvenile offenders. *Journal of the American Academy of Child and Adolescent Psychiatry, 50*, 25–37.

Slobogin, C., & Fondacaro, M. (2009). Juvenile justice: The fourth option. *Iowa Law Review, 9*, 1–62.

Steinberg, L., & Cauffman, E. (1996). Maturity of judgment in adolescence: Psychosocial factors in adolescent decision making. *Law and Human Behavior, 20*, 249–272.

Steinberg, L., & Icenogle, G. (2019). Using developmental science to distinguish adolescents and adults under the law. *Annual Review of Developmental Psychology, 1*, 21–40.

Swank, J., & Gagnon, J. (2016). Mental health services in juvenile correctional facilities: A national survey of clinical staff. *Journal of Child and Family Studies, 25*, 2862–2872.

Teplin, L., Abram, K., McClelland, G., Dulcan, M., & Mericle, A. (2002). Psychiatric disorders in youth in juvenile detention. *Archives of General Psychiatry, 59*, 1133–1143.

Tolliver, D., Abrams, L., & Barnert, E. (2021). Setting a U.S. national minimum age for juvenile justice jurisdiction. *Journal of the American Medical Association, Pediatrics, 175*, 665–666.

Viljoen, J., & Grisso, T. (2007). Prospects for remediating juveniles' adjudicative incompetence. *Psychology, Public Policy and Law, 13*, 87–114.

Vincent, G., Kimonis, E., & Clark, A. (2016). Juvenile psychopathy: Appropriate and inappropriate uses in legal proceedings. In K. Heilbrun, D. DeMatteo, & N. Goldstein (Eds.), *APA handbook of psychology and juvenile justice* (pp. 197–232). American Psychological Association.

Vincent, G., & Viljoen, J. (2020). Racist algorithms or systemic problems? Risk assessment and racial disparities. *Criminal Justice and Behavior, 47*, 1–9.

Warren, J., Jackson, S., & Coburn, J. (2016). Evaluation and restoration of competency to stand trial. In K. Heilbrun, D. DeMatteo, & N. Goldstein (Eds.), *APA handbook of psychology and juvenile justice* (pp. 489–514.) American Psychological Association.

Weithorn, L., & Campbell, S. (1982). The competency of children and adolescents to make informed treatment decisions. *Child Development, 53*, 1589–1598.

Williams, V., & Grisso, T. (2011). *Does mental health screening fulfill its purpose?* Models for Change Initiative. John D. & Catherine T. MacArthur Foundation. https://www.modelsforchange.net/publications/316

CHAPTER 20

Adult Development and the Law: Intersections, Interactions, and Influences

Allison D. Redlich and Jodi A. Quas

> **Abstract**
> In the second section of the *Oxford Handbook of Developmental Psychology and the Law*, leading scholars describe how young, middle-aged, and older adults' experiences with the justice system are complex and broad. For some, this includes contact with the criminal justice system, when, for example, younger or older adults are suspected of committing crimes or have potentially witnessed crimes. They must be questioned and possibly participate in criminal proceedings as a result. For others, this includes contact after criminal conviction. For example, mothers but also older adults may be living behind bars often with children or significant health needs that shape their legal experiences. For others, legal experiences focus on their rights as individuals to make decisions about themselves, their bodies, and their families and children. As the chapters highlight, there is enormous value in terms of both policy and practice to viewing legal involvement through the lens of lifespan development.
>
> **Key Words:** aging offenders, cognitive impairment, emerging adulthood, end-of-life decisions, parental incarceration, reproductive rights, social inequities, adult eyewitness testimony

Much of developmental science has focused on infancy through adolescence. Indeed, the developmental phases that humans experience in the first two decades of life are significant and fast-paced. Within the subfield of psychology and law, arguably the same pattern can be seen. For example, Wylie and colleagues (2018) analyzed the content of 40 years of *Law and Human Behavior* (the journal of the American Psychology–Law Society, Division 41 of the American Psychological Association), finding that less than 0.1% of studies included adults with a mean age of 65 years and older; in contrast, 11.6% included children aged 18 years and younger.

However, in the relatively recent past, scientists have turned their attention to later stages of development with the recognition that developmental periods after adolescence can be equally important as those in the first two or so decades of life. For example, a report from the National Academy of Sciences (Bonnie et al., 2015) strongly recommended that young adulthood (i.e., ages 18–26 years) be viewed as "a critical window of development and occasion for intervention" (p. 2). Indeed, this period, termed emerging adulthood, is now an established and well-studied lifespan stage (see Arnett, 2000, 2015), one that has numerous implications for the law and young adults involved in the legal systems. Likewise, as illustrated in a recent special issue of the *American Psychologist* (May–June, 2020; see Arnett et al., 2020), there is also a push to rethink and emphasize later phases of adult development as unique and important periods of the lifespan. For example, Mehta and colleagues (2020) put forth the stage of established adulthood (ages 30–45 years) arguing that this developmental period is distinct from "emerging adulthood and midlife in terms of physical health, well-being, cognitive development, and the career-and-care-crunch of competing work and family responsibilities" (p. 431). Adults are now more likely to remain single and child-free, and to live and remain healthier longer. Are these trends true of adults involved in the legal system? How does development during the emerging adulthood years affect "bright line" demarcations common to justice systems here and abroad? What are the implications of living healthier longer on death planning and future forecasting? These are examples of questions in which psycholegal scholars can unite development, beyond adolescence, and legal system involvement.

The *Adulthood* and *Aging* sections of the *Oxford Handbook on Developmental Psychology and the Law* include 10 chapters as well as a Conclusion chapter (Rodriguez & Waggoner, Chapter 31) tying the chapters together. These chapters were designed to address how developmental science and the law interact and shape one another across the lifespan, with a specific focus on developmental periods spanning from early through late adulthood.

Adulthood

In the section on *Adulthood*, seven different areas in which development in adulthood could influence—and be influenced by—participation in the legal system are reviewed. In previous subsections of this Handbook, we included chapters on risk and resiliency and pathways to deviant behavior among children (Frick et al., Chapter 3) and adolescents (Manasse & Rebellon, Chapter 11). As a complement, in the *Adulthood* subsection, we include "Understanding Deviancy in Adulthood," in which Narvey and Piquero (Chapter 21) describe adult-onset offenders who differ from adolescent-limited and life-course-persistent offenders. Although there are competing theories about whether a category of adult-onset offenders truly exists, Narvey and Piquero provide evidence suggesting that this group indeed exists and, as a result, increased attention should be focused on understanding these adults' risks and trajectories. Complementing the chapter on adult offenders is the contribution by Gillespie et al. (Chapter 22) on the experiences of emerging adults involved in the justice system. More specifically, Gillespie and colleagues describe a new type of court, young adult court, and other diversion programs aimed at adults in this developmental window. In reviewing developmental science for this age group, Gillespie et al. describe the "science to practice gap," namely that persons in this age range are simultaneously underdeveloped in their maturation and overrepresented in the legal system—a double-edged sword. The team also reviews the growing number of young adult courts in the United States, providing an important overview for researchers going forward.

Chapter 23 focuses on a different at-risk group, adults with developmental/intellectual disabilities, and their encounters with and experiences in the criminal justice system. Salekin and Wood provide a comprehensive review of adults with limited cognitive abilities, demonstrating that they are also overrepresented (relative to their prevalence in the general population) in the justice system, not only as defendants and perpetrators, but also as victims. Further, Salekin and Wood describe the potential consequences of cognitive deficits on the ability to waive Miranda rights, stand trial and plead guilty, and be considered legally culpable, as well as for providing reliable eyewitness identifications and confessions.

Whereas the first set of chapters in the *Adulthood* subsection focus on pathways into, and general experiences with, the criminal legal system, Chapter 24 is on experiences in carceral settings, namely women, pregnancy, and motherhood in prison. Shlafer et al. explain that nearly six in 10 incarcerated women have minor children, with 3%–4% of women entering prison pregnant. The authors review existing statutes surrounding motherhood and incarceration, discussing alternatives to incarceration, options before serving sentences, visitation and nursery programs while imprisoned, and reunification and reentry plans. Their review demonstrates, quite provocatively, that developmental science is and is not accounted for in laws and policies, highlighting the need for further intervention, legislation, and change.

In Chapter 25, Whelan and Goodwin step outside of the criminal justice arena. Their contribution provides an important and timely overview of reproductive health rights in the United States. More specifically, they focus on abortion, contraception, and pregnancy, demonstrating how reproductive health encompasses a broad array of key issues (such as the role of pharmacists in distributing contraception). In doing so, the authors highlight how laws, policies, and practices shape aspects of reproductive health and affect development, which then lays the foundation for suggestions for further research.

Burke et al. (Chapter 26) also address a timely issue facing our nation—racial disparities. The authors begin by using Bronfenbrenner's social–ecological model, applying it to the policing context and people of color specifically. In this manner, the authors address the broader social climate that can enable racialized policing of people of color (macrosystem); the institution and practice of policing and how these influence the interactions of law enforcement and people of color (exosystem); how such interactions with police can shape attitudes toward them (mesosystem); and how, in turn, these experiences can shape how people of color experience, navigate, learn, and develop in response to police discrimination (microsystem).

Lastly, LeBel and Ritchie (Chapter 27) provide a comprehensive overview of prisoner reentry across the life course. They focus on three phases that can affect the success of reentering society: before prison, the circumstances and events that may have contributed to the criminal act/lifestyle; in prison, the carceral environment and conditions that can shape future behavior and adjustment to life after release; and after prison, including potential turning points and challenges faced. In addition to examining recidivism postrelease, LeBel and Richie expand their review to include other consequential life course outcomes, such as employment, housing, family relationships/marriage, and health, all of which have critical implications for reform and practice to improve reentry for all those affected.

Aging

We included three important chapters in the *Aging* subsection of this Handbook. First, Chapter 28 is "Ethical Considerations and Ramifications of Advance Care Planning and End-of-Life Decision Making for Older Adults" by Teaster and Shealy. This chapter reviews the ethical and legal considerations of advance care planning and end-of-life decisions commonly confronted by older adults. Such planning and decisions necessarily entail psychological and legal issues. For example, Teaster and Shealy advocate for abolishing taboos around death and dying and increasing communications around these topics, while also calling for the enactment of stronger and more person-centered consent laws and the provision of more equitable health care. In their words, "End-of-life issues inevitably involve worth, dignity, self-determination, and quality of life. End-of-life circumstances also involve legalities, faith systems, money, advocacy, and politics. In some instances, end-of life issues also involve racism, ageism, and sexism." Clearly these issues and circumstances bring the interplay of psychology and the law, overlaid with developmental stage of older adulthood.

Brank's chapter (Chapter 29) concerns "Older Adults as Victims and Witnesses." Whereas there has been some research on eyewitness reporting in older adults, the overwhelming majority of research on eyewitness memory and suggestibility has been on children, adolescents, and young adults (see Slonecker et al., Chapter 4; Wyman et al., Chapter 12; Dickinson et al.,

2019). However, as Brank notes, in a span of less than 35 years, the number of adults aged 65 and older is expected to double. And given that older adults are at increased risk for certain forms of victimization (such as elder abuse), their chances of having to provide testimony rise. Brank provides an excellent overview of the issues inherent to older adults as victims and witnesses (including their actual and perceived capabilities), encouraging more research with this vastly understudied but growing population.

Finally, Wylie and Hubner (Chapter 30) focus on "Aging in the Criminal Justice System: A Call for Age-Focused Research, Policy, and Practice." Wylie and Hubner make a compelling case that although there is a dearth of research (particularly in the psychology and law field) on older adults as perpetrators of crime and their experiences in correctional institutions, the sheer number of such individuals is growing rapidly. Research, policy, and practice have not kept pace but inevitably need to.

Conclusion

In conclusion, the *Oxford Handbook on Developmental Psychology and Law* aimed to provide comprehensive and up-to-date reviews of topics quite familiar to psychology and law scholars (e.g., children's capabilities as victims/witnesses). At the same time, we aimed to introduce novel topics to these scholars, topics that have significant relevance to the interaction of psychology and law but have been largely ignored by the field. Arguably, the topics within Section II of the Handbook on *Adulthood* and *Aging* are where there is much room to grow. However, we just touch the surface. These areas, while important and timely, represent a mere fraction of the developmental issues inherent to the criminal and civil legal systems that could be addressed, and many of these are only beginning to account for the nuanced but highly influential ways that social inequities across individuals, due to a wide range of marginalization experiences, further shape development and legal experiences (see Chapter 31, Rodriguez & Waggoner, for a detailed discussion). Shifting the focus of developmental psychology and law toward the entire lifespan of development would prove beneficial to the scholars within the field, as well as to the millions of younger and older adults who come into contact with the criminal and civil legal systems every year.

References

Arnett, J. J. (2000). Emerging adulthood: A theory of development from the late teens through the twenties. *American Psychologist, 55*, 469–480.

Arnett, J. J. (2015). (Ed.). *The Oxford handbook of emerging adulthood.* Oxford University Press.

Arnett, J. J., Robinson, O., & Lachman, M. E. (2020). Rethinking adult development: Introduction to the special issue. *American Psychologist, 75*(4), 425–430.

Bonnie, R., Stroud, C., & Briener, H. (2015). (Eds.). *Investing in the health and well-being of young adults.* National Academies Press.

Dickinson, J. J., Compo, N. S., Carol, R. N., Schwartz, B. L., & McCauley, M. R. (2019). *Evidence-based investigative interviewing.* Routledge.

Mehta, C. M., Arnett, J. J., Palmer, C. G., & Nelson, L. J. (2020). Established adulthood: A new conception of ages 30 to 45. *American Psychologist, 75*(4), 431–444.

Wylie, L. E., Hazen, K. P., Hoetger, L. A., Haby, J. A., & Brank, E. M. (2018). Four decades of the journal Law and Human Behavior: A content analysis. *Scientometrics, 115*(2), 655–693.

CHAPTER 21

Understanding Deviancy in Adulthood

Chelsey S. Narvey and Alex R. Piquero[1]

Abstract
The current chapter provides an overview of the present state of research on adult deviancy, with a specific focus on adult criminal offending. The chapter outlines the relationship between age and crime, providing an understanding of the age–crime curve. Additionally, it reviews two main theories that discuss this relationship, comparing and contrasting their central tenets. Based on these theoretical foundations, the current state of the literature regarding onset of criminal offending is presented, providing two differing sets of opinions: one, that adult-onset criminality does not exist, but instead that these individuals had been engaging in offending behavior throughout the life course; two, that adult-onset offending does indeed exist and can be explained. Lastly, the chapter discusses implications for research, policy, and practice.

Key Words: adult offending, adult deviancy, adult onset, life course persistent, age–crime curve

Criminological research is ripe with studies that focus on understanding deviant behavior, with a prominent focus on the teenage years. It is well established and widely recognized that adolescents commit most crime and are most likely to engage in risk-taking behavior (e.g., see Manesse & Rebellon, this volume). Epidemiological research evaluating adolescent risk taking has demonstrated that risky behavior is one of the leading causes of youth morbidity and mortality worldwide (World Health Organization, 2021), and researchers around the globe have cited adolescent risk-taking behavior (i.e., cigarette smoking, drinking, unprotected sex, etc.) as a public health issue (Willoughby et al., 2013; Xing et al., 2006). This can be explained, at least in part, by findings that suggest that adolescents typically demonstrate an increased propensity for or inclination toward deviant and risky behavior (Eisner, 2002; Lotrean et al., 2010; Steinberg, 2008; Willoughby et al., 2013). Cross-nationally, deviant behavior tends to increase in frequency throughout adolescence until its eventual decline as one ages into their 20s (Eisner, 2002), so much so that age has been identified as one of the brute facts of criminal activity (Fuller et al., 2015; Hirschi & Gottfredson, 1983; Piquero et al., 2003; Plant et al., 2009; Willoughby et al., 2013).

Within criminology, much of the focus has been on the patterns of age–crime distributions across various factors such as time, space, and type of offense, as well as pathways into

---

[1] All analyses and conclusions presented here are those of the authors and should not be attributed to the Bureau of Justice Statistics or the U.S. Department of Justice.

offending and the subsequent "aging out" of criminal behavior. Age–crime trends generally depict crime increasing in early adolescence, reaching a peak in the late teens to early adulthood, and then declining thereafter (Britt, 1992; D'Unger et al., 1998; Farrington, 1986; Greenberg, 1985; Lauritsen, 1998; Lipsey & Derzon, 1998; Piquero et al., 2003; Quetelet, 1984; Sampson & Laub, 2003; Steffensmeier et al., 1989).

Several theories within psychology center their explanations of crime, deviancy, and risk around this relationship. Neuroscientific research that has recently focused on adolescent brain development has demonstrated the differences in youth versus adult brains. Within adolescents, the brain centers responsible for processing reward develop more rapidly than those responsible for managing cognitive control, leading youth to have an increased sensitivity to the potential rewards that risk-taking behavior might provide them, combined with a decreased ability to use the cognitive capacity required in self-regulation and decision making (Casey et al., 2011). From a biopsychosocial perspective, this helps to explain why the propensity for risk taking is higher in adolescence and tapers as individuals enter into adulthood (see, e.g., Monahan et al., 2015).

This relationship between crime, deviance, and age has also been a concerted focus within criminological theories, especially those that focus on development across the life course. One of the most well researched of these is Moffitt's (1993) developmental taxonomy, which suggests that individuals fall into one of three categories: adolescent-limited offenders, life-course-persistent offenders, or abstainers. A large body of literature has tested Moffitt's theory focusing specifically on adolescent-limited offenders. Less is known, however, about those who either (a) continue to offend into adulthood or, even more scarcely, (b) start to offend in adulthood. This remains the case within most criminological research, where the field is saturated with studies that make use of youth samples but is limited in its research that focuses on adult populations.

This gap in the research led Cullen (2011) to coin the term "adolescent-limited criminology," detailing the fact that most research on the causes and correlates of criminal offending draws on samples of adolescents and young adults. Cullen cited the need for more research that used samples of older adults in order to understand the etiology of deviant behavior among this population. This need is not only due to the lack of research but also because scholars in the early part of the last two decades suspected possible increases in crime committed by adults and the elderly (Feldmeyer & Steffensmeier, 2007; Kunz, 2014). Some noted that older persons were committing more crime (Marquart et al., 2000), and others looked at prison and jail data to infer that individuals committing crimes seemed to be older and more violent (Kuhlmann & Ruddell, 2005). Moreover, recent decades have been marked with an increase in the proportion of elderly persons within the population and changes in the demographic makeup of society at large, with more individuals tending to live longer, healthier, and more mobile lives well into old age (Kunz, 2014). However, some elderly individuals also experience high levels of poverty and an increase in homelessness, with many living on the streets (Federal Interagency Forum on Aging-Related Statistics, 2008). Still, some life course scholars are hesitant to support the notion that elderly crime might rise. For one, the age–crime curve has been consistent throughout time and place and across crime type (Tittle et al., 2003). Also, the improved economic and social welfare of the aging population in recent years should make them *less*, not more, likely to engage in crime (Hardy & Hazelrigg, 1999; Holden & Hatcher, 2006). Lastly, researchers in the 1970s and 1980s also made claims about the future rise of elderly crime that went underresearched and underappreciated (Bachand, 1984; Feinberg, 1984).

Although scarce in comparison to adolescent-focused research, there has been a growing body of research dedicated to elder adults in the last several years. Older Americans have recently become the fastest growing age group in the U.S. population, leading to an increase in studies that focus on the intersection of aging with several factors, including but not limited to the economy, health care, and politics (Schulz et al., 2006). This expansion of research on the elderly has also extended into the field of criminology, with several studies focusing on patterns of crime in adults (Farrington, 1986; Feldmeyer & Steffensmeier, 2007; Goodman et al., 2005), but much more of this work focuses on victimization in large part because of their assumed vulnerability (e.g., see Brank, this volume). Additionally, research has examined the ways in which childhood and adolescent risk factors extend into adulthood (Donaldson et al., 2016; Dubow et al., 2016; Reavis et al., 2013). On this score, recent evidence has demonstrated that adverse childhood experiences can have long-lasting consequences that reach into the adult years (DeLisi & Beauregard, 2018; Levenson & Socia, 2016). Childhood trauma can disrupt developmental pathways that typically lead to prosocial behaviors across the life course (Carrion & Wong, 2012; McLean, 2016), thus increasing the likelihood of risky and deviant behavior in adulthood. Research has also determined that for some, behavior, personality traits, and experiences in adolescent years can affect later crime involvement in adulthood (Dubow et al., 2016). Additionally, a large body of criminological research highlights the important effects of parental childrearing on offspring socialization and self-control, and, indirectly, on the relationship to subsequent antisocial and criminal behavior over the life course (Gottfredson & Hirschi, 1990; Moffitt, 1993).

This chapter presents an up-to-date overview of the current state of the literature on adult offenders. We aim to provide readers with an overview of the factors associated with individuals who persist in their offending from adolescence to adulthood as well as those individuals who have onset in adulthood. To provide some background context for readers who may not be intimately familiar with the basic criminological literature, we begin with a detailed overview of the age–crime curve. We then present a summary of the factors associated with adult offending. Next, we review the theories that consider adult offending, specifically chronic offending across the life course. We also review the research on adult-onset offending, presenting recent research that supports the notion that adult onset is not trivial. In doing so, we provide readers with a synthesis of the current state of the literature on the topic of adult antisocial behavior. Lastly, we discuss the implications for research, policy, and practice and present ideas for future areas of research.

The Relationship Between Age and Crime
The Age–Crime Curve
There is widespread agreement within the criminological community that age is inversely related to risk taking, antisocial and deviant behavior, and criminal offending. This relationship, known as the age–crime curve, has been a lasting theme within criminology, dating back to the early work of Quetelet (1831) in France. It was further researched with the Glueck studies of the 1930s and 1940s (Glueck & Glueck, 1930), where focus started to shift to the analysis of an individual's criminal career and the many factors that could be associated with offending over the life course. Since then, the age–crime curve has garnered attention from many criminologists (Blumstein et al., 1988a, 1988b; DeLisi, 2015; Farrington, 1986; Farrington et al., 2013; Gottfredson & Hirschi, 1986, 1987; Hirschi & Gottfredson, 1983; Jennings et al., 2016). Generally, the term refers to the fact that "the prevalence of offending in populations increases from late childhood, peaks during mid to late adolescence, and then decreases in adulthood" (Loeber, 2012, p. 11). It describes an aggregate distribution that begins to rise during early adolescence, peaks in mid- to late adolescence, and then precipitously declines in early adulthood. For the most part, this relationship seemingly applies to all

populations and most crime types (though violence tends to peak somewhat later). It seems that despite variability in many of the other variables related to crime (i.e., economic status, race, sex, marital status, education, etc.), youth commit more crime than do their adult counterparts. This relationship is strong, is resilient, and has been stable across time (Steffensmeier & Streifel, 1991), so much so that criminologists have stated that "age is everywhere correlated with crime. Its effects on crime do not depend on other demographic correlates of crime" (Hirschi & Gottfredson, 1983, p. 581).

As we have noted, crime peaks in adolescence and declines thereafter. The reasons for this are not difficult to understand—adolescents are less patient and are less willing and able to delay gratification (Steinberg et al., 2009). Additionally, modern society presents adolescents with some level of freedom and less supervision and responsibilities, increasing the time they spend with friends and away from responsible guardians. This can leave them with less legitimate coping mechanisms and an increased ability to solve problems or find thrill through deviant behavior (Agnew, 2003; Akers & Jennings, 2019). As they mature, however, individuals are better able to envision the future and in particular the long-term consequences of their actions that coincide with their improved coping skills and their interest and need in maintaining more positive relationships (Rocque, 2015; Warr, 1998). Unlike teens, adults have developed the ability to delay gratification and begin to take responsibility for their actions. This explains why, generally, adolescents and teens commit more crime than adults. However, this does not mean that adults completely abstain from crime. Individuals over the age of 18, what is typically considered the "adult" cut-off point, still do engage in criminal activity and risky behavior, though to a lesser extent or at a much lower rate. While it is expected that most teens will engage in some level of deviance during their adolescent years, the same is not expected of adults. Therefore, predicting adult deviant and/or antisocial behavior is somewhat more challenging. In the ensuing section, we briefly review the literature on this topic.

Predicting Adult Antisocial Behavior
Research across several domains (psychology, neurobiology, criminology, sociology, etc.) has explored the antecedents of adult antisocial and criminal behavior. Findings generally demonstrate a link to childhood development, specifically to adverse experiences early in life and early signs of antisocial behavior. Consistent with Moffitt's developmental taxonomy (described in more detail later), most adults who engage in antisocial and deviant behavior demonstrated signs of this early in the life course. Systematic reviews of early risk factors have demonstrated that individuals who engage in crime and delinquent behavior as adults tend to have a greater number of risk factors in childhood, and the magnitude of these risk factors is stronger as well (Farrington et al., 2017). In fact, research has even questioned the concept of adult-onset offending, demonstrating that most individuals who are first convicted as adults have clear histories of childhood conduct problems or disorders and potential juvenile offending that merely went undetected by police and official records (Beckley et al., 2016). This suggests that much of adult risky and antisocial behavior can be tied to early development and childhood experiences that may lie dormant or manifest differently or later in the life course. Recently, nationally representative research has demonstrated that those who engage in offending well into adulthood generally came from low-socioeconomic-status (SES) families as children, lacked maternal closeness, had a history of more harsh discipline in early years, and had poor, unhealthy child–parent communication (Keijsers et al., 2012). Research has confirmed that children who grow up in lower SES households are at increased risk of being more aggressive during childhood and to engage in violent offending in adulthood (Dubow et al., 2016).

Crime data have shown that most individuals who engage in criminal offending commit one single act and upon arrest tend to discontinue in their deviant or antisocial behaviors (e.g., Wolfgang et al., 1972). Most adolescents will naturally desist from crime, even without formal criminal justice intervention or any intervention from authorities. Others, however, continue to commit offenses—some a few less serious crimes, and others more serious. A small group of these persistent offenders, in fact, account for a majority of all criminal offenses and they typically continue to offend into adulthood. Within the criminological literature, these persons are referred to as career criminals (or chronic offenders; Wolfgang et al., 1972). Although the original research that discovered the differences in these groups of offenders relied on a birth cohort of individuals followed to late adolescence, it nonetheless launched further research into the chronic offender, and into criminal chronicity more generally (see Jolliffe et al., 2017, for a review). In recent years, criminological theorists have begun to explore the concept of the criminal career, and several independent though interrelated theories have emerged. The first focuses on changes in criminal offending throughout the life course caused by experiences and life events. The second promotes the view that a stable trait or individual characteristic makes certain people more likely to commit crime. The third and final concept suggests that there are a variety of different pathways into different types of criminal careers, and that there are different types and classes of offenders. Understanding these theories, and how they theorize adult offending behavior, is a central piece of this chapter. Specifically, we will focus on the theories that (a) explore different paths of offending and (b) explain adult offending through the idea of a latent trait that exists across the life course, as proposed by Gottfredson and Hirschi (1990). We will then present the research that supports a different class of offenders—those that only begin to engage in criminal behavior once already in adulthood, referred to as adult-onset offenders.

Theoretical Understanding of Adult Risky Behavior

As criminologists began to explore the concept of criminal career offending and further research risky and antisocial behavior later on in the life course, several unique—though interrelated—theories were proposed. One of these is Moffitt's developmental taxonomy, which outlines two distinct pathways to antisocial and criminal behavior over the life course. In contrast to Moffitt's taxonomy, a competing framework suggests that much human development—including criminal behavior—is guided by a latent trait that remains relatively stable across the life course. One of the main criminological theories, the theory of self-control, adopts this view. Both of these theories will be briefly explained next.

Moffitt's Developmental Taxonomy

Moffitt's developmental taxonomy theory suggests that there are two groups of offenders: adolescent limited (AL) and life course persistent (LCP). A tertiary group who are hypothesized to refrain from antisocial behavior are considered abstainers. The two offender groups have unique pathways to offending and trajectories of criminal activity. Moffitt argued that individuals who offend can be separated into these two groups based largely on age of onset of antisocial behavior, how long the behavior persists, and the correlates associated with the offending pathways exhibited by the two groups.

More specifically, AL offenders typically begin to engage in delinquent acts during adolescence, and their time spent offending is mainly limited to the adolescent years. Moffitt suggests that roughly 90% of juveniles can be considered AL offenders, whereas the remaining minority of approximately 5%–10% are what she considers to be LCP offenders (DeLisi & Piquero, 2011), the focal group of this chapter (as their behavior commences in childhood and persists into adulthood). LCP offenders typically begin showing signs of antisocial behavior early in the life course, continue to engage in delinquent acts throughout adolescence, and do not desist during adulthood. These offenders are assumed to possess neuropsychological deficits and to have come from difficult family environments and upbringings (McGloin et al., 2006; Tibbetts & Piquero, 1999). These offenders do not "age out" of crime like most juveniles do, but rather continue to engage in some form of antisocial behavior throughout the life course. Research has supported the patterns of persistence that Moffitt's theory highlights, demonstrating that LCP offenders generally engage in offending behavior more frequently and conduct a larger variety of deviant acts (Donker et al., 2003). Additionally, these individuals will exhibit more mental health issues and are typically more impulsive, well into adulthood (Mazerolle et al., 2000; Vermeiren, 2003). Some research has shown that individual traits, rather than environment, exhibit a stronger effect on those who continue to offend into adulthood (Wikström & Loeber, 2000).

Moffitt hypothesizes that the genesis of LCP offending resides in the interaction between individual and environmental/societal factors. She anticipates that LCP offenders experience neurological deficits including poor attention, hyperactivity, and decreased self-regulation skills that are all evident early in childhood, as well as familial and social disadvantages that are unable to help children overcome these deficits. Specifically, Moffitt proposes that LCP offending behavior originates with early childhood neurodevelopmental impairments. She suggests that these problems lead to a host of cognitive problems and deficits. Given this, the lowered self-control inhibits their appropriate socialization and effective development, making them more likely to engage in criminal activity. In addition to their decreased neurological development and its negative consequences, Moffitt also suggests that these children typically are also raised in disadvantaged familial and neighborhood environments. This combination then lays the foundation for risky and antisocial behavior throughout one's life course. She explains (Moffitt, 2018, p. 20):

> LCP originates early in life, when the difficult behavior of a high-risk child is exacerbated by a high-risk social environment. According to the theory, the child's risk emerges from inherited or acquired neuropsychological problems, initially manifested as difficult temperament, cognitive deficits, or hyperactivity. The environment's risk comprises factors such as disrupted family attachment bonds, inadequate parents, maltreatment, and poverty. The environmental risk domain expands beyond the family as the child ages, to include poor relationships with other people, such as peers and teachers. Opportunities to learn prosocial skills are missed. Over the first two decades of development, accumulating transactions between the individual and the environment incrementally construct a disordered personality with hallmark features of violent aggression and a broad repertoire of antisocial behaviors persisting to midlife. Antisocial behavior that is life-course persistent infiltrates multiple adult life domains, including illegal activities, substance misuse, problems with employment, and victimization of intimate partners and children. This cumulative infiltration gradually diminishes the possibility of reform, accounting for the persistence of LCP behavior.

A large body of research has supported this theory (see Moffitt, 2018, for a review). Prospective longitudinal studies across several countries have followed a number of different cohorts to test the theory, some even including follow-up periods into their 50s and 70s (Bergman & Andershed, 2009; Farrington et al., 2013; Huesmann et al., 2009; Pulkkinen et al., 2009). One, the Cambridge Study in Delinquent Development (CSDD), followed over 400 males in London from age 8 to 56. The study used both official records and self-report interviews to measure delinquent behavior. In testing the taxonomy using this sample, Farrington and colleagues (2013) found evidence supporting two different groups: one AL group that peaked during younger years, and a second group that exhibited more chronic offending that offended later into adulthood, an LCP group. Additionally, they found that the LCP group had poorer midlife outcomes across several domains and were still being convicted up to the age of 56. Other research has also found that men up to age 51 who had a history of childhood abuse and neglect were more likely to be in the chronic high-rate offending group (Widom et al., 2018). Additionally, Blokland and colleagues (2005) found that a small group of LCP offenders in the Netherlands were still being convicted into their 70s.

Research has evinced support for Moffitt's idea that there exist two groups of offenders that exhibit different behavior. Still, other theorists present similar though unique ideas of what best explains offending, with the most common being Gottfredson and Hirschi's (1990) general theory of crime (GTC) and its key correlate of low self-control (LSC). Similar to Moffitt (1993), Gottfredson and Hirschi also propose that the most serious and chronic offenders have their origins in poor parenting practices that result in ineffective socialization (and hence poor self-control) and that their problem behavior begins early in childhood. They diverge, however, in the idea of different groups.

A Latent Trait Theory: Gottfredson and Hirschi's Theory of Low Self-Control

As aforementioned, a second, though related, school of thought supports the idea that an individual trait is the strongest contributor to risky and deviant behavior across the life course, including into adulthood. In 1990, Gottfredson and Hirschi introduced their GTC with its key correlate of LSC. In so doing, they argued that their theory could be applied to all criminal activity, as well as acts analogous to crime, across all demographic groups and cultures. Gottfredson and Hirschi (1990) defined self-control as "the differential tendency of people to avoid criminal acts whatever the circumstances in which they find themselves" (p. 87). They suggested that all people are born with the innate desire to seek immediate pleasure and therefore need to be taught self-control. The theory hypothesizes that individuals acquire self-control to the extent that their parents effectively socialize them in early childhood by (a) monitoring their child's behavior, (b) recognizing deviant behavior when it occurs, and (c) responding to deviant behavior by appropriately punishing their child. Parents who engage in all three of these socialization practices demonstrate attachment, supervision, and discipline, which Gottfredson and Hirschi (1990) claim are the three most important family variables that determine one's level of self-control. According to them, low self-control is produced by the absence of nurturance, discipline, and training. Once one's level of self-control is established early in life, the GTC expects that it is relatively stable (between persons) over the life course and is relatively unaffected by other variables or institutions. LSC is characterized by six characteristics: (a) volatile temper, (b) risk seeking, (c) self-centered orientation, (d) impulsivity, (e) preference for simple tasks, and (f) prioritization of physical (over mental) activities, all of which tend to coalesce within persons and therefore tend to conform to a single, unidimensional latent trait (Grasmick et al., 1993). Based on these tenets, Gottfredson and Hirschi (1990) suggest that low self-control combined with the opportunity to commit crime is a (perhaps *the*) primary cause of criminal behavior. Therefore, their theory explains the age–crime curve through opportunity, suggesting that the *propensity* to commit crime remains stable throughout the life course, and it is the change in opportunity to commit crime that explains the decline we see in adulthood. The theory has garnered support through the years, including when examined in adult populations (Burton et al., 1999; DeLisi & Vaughn, 2008; Pratt & Cullen, 2000; Vazsonyi et al., 2017).

These two theories, though unique, share several similar tenets and one main underlying idea: that adult offending is explained through early behavior in childhood and that the

Table 21.1 Age-Specific Risk Factors for Understanding Offending Behavior		
Offending Behavior	Age of Onset	Risk Factors
Moffitt's Life Course Persistent	Antisocial behavior evident in early childhood and persists across the life course	Individual cognitive deficiencies and problems, typically combined with poor environments
Moffitt's Adolescent Limited	First offense usually occurs in late adolescence or early teen years and desists by adulthood	Peer influence Biological maturity
Gottfredson and Hirschi's Criminal and Analogous Behavior	No specific age of onset	Lack of self-control, usually developed by ages 8–12
Adult Onset	First offense occurs after the age of 18	Episodic events that lead to deviant forms of coping

only reasons we see offending in adulthood is a continuation of those who have the most risk of offending in childhood and adolescence. Both theories convey that adult-onset offending is rare, if existent at all. However, recent research suggests otherwise, indicating that there do indeed exist individuals who begin their offending behavior later on in life. This body of research will be presented and reviewed in the next section and is visually summarized in Table 21.1.

Adult-Onset Offending

The onset of crime, referred to as the first or initial time that an individual engages in a criminal act, is an important piece in understanding criminal careers as it provides some level of insight into why people engage in offending behaviors. Generally, most individuals' criminal onset occurs in adolescence or the teenage years, and most research on the topic focuses on samples in this age group (Farrington et al., 1990; Moffitt, 1993). Recently, however, scholars have called for more research exploring the phenomenon of late-onset offending in adulthood, suggesting that this understudied population presents a significant gap in the criminological literature deserving of sustained research attention (DeLisi & Piquero, 2011). In the last several decades, researchers have documented evidence of adult-onset offending (Zara & Farrington, 2009). Recent estimates based on projections of lifetime conviction risks suggest that at least 25% of first convictions will occur after the age of 30 (Skardhamar, 2014). Several large-scale studies have presented the results from dozens of research projects that used adult samples. First, Eggleston and Laub (2002) present a summary of 15 longitudinal studies that used official data. Based on the findings of these studies, they concluded that an average of 52.4% of juvenile delinquents went on to commit an adult offense, yet only 49.8% on average of the adult offenders were made up of these persistent offenders. They also found that a large portion of the adult offenders were nondelinquent as juveniles, stating that "the average percentage of nondelinquents who began offending in adulthood was 17.9 percent, yet these nondelinquents comprised 50.2 percent of the adult offender population, on average" (Eggleston & Laub, 2002, p. 604). They conclude that the adult-onset offender is worthy of systematic observation and further research, an endeavor that others have pursued. More recently, Beckley and colleagues (2016) updated Eggleston and Laub's (2002) research, adding research from 1998 into 2014. They present 35 studies using 25 unique data sets, 19 of which were from the United States. They found that percentages of adult-onset offending varied widely, ranging from 6% to 87%. Similarly, van Koppen (2018) presented 28 longitudinal studies that used official data with samples of individuals over the age of 18. All 28 of these studies found some evidence for adult-onset offending, though the numbers again varied widely—from 9% to 72% of all offenders across these studies. van Koppen (2018) concluded that an average of 39% (with a median of 38%) of the offenders had an adult onset, based on official data.

It is important to bear in mind that data from official sources should be interpreted with caution, as age of onset is typically overestimated when using official numbers (Farrington, 1989; Jolliffe et al., 2017; Sohoni et al., 2014; Theobald & Farrington, 2011). In all of the aforementioned studies, age of onset is determined by first encounter with the law. Therefore, the adult-onset offenders observed in these studies may have an actual history of delinquent behavior prior to adulthood that had either gone undetected or had never led to an arrest or a conviction. Therefore, there remains the possibility that official adult-onset offenders have unofficial histories of offending, thus skewing the true numbers and overestimating their existence.

Still, there is some suggestion that other factors might lead to an *under*estimation of age of onset. van Koppen (2018) presents two: First, the probability of being arrested is not distributed equally across age. That is, older offenders are less likely to be apprehended due to the nature of the crimes they are more likely to commit. McGee and Farrington (2010) found that older individuals who engaged in criminal offending tended to commit crimes that had a lower likelihood of detection than younger offenders. This might be explained, at least in part, by the fact that different age groups receive different levels of supervision and official control by authorities. Younger individuals in general (offenders and nonoffenders) are more likely to be supervised by official and nonofficial authorities, including police, teachers, parents, neighbors, and other community members (Charette & van Koppen, 2016). These differences lead to an effect of age on the likelihood of arrest, with youth being more likely to be arrested, thus underestimating the true proportion of adult-onset offenders based on official data. A second reason one might suspect an underestimation in age of onset is due to the nature of longitudinal studies. Typically, study samples only follow persons up to a certain age, and usually not into mid- to late adulthood. For example, if one study only follows individuals up until age 25, there is no way to observe onset after that time period. This, in turn, lowers the proportion of adult-onset offenders that is detected. Therefore, the longer the period of time for which individuals are followed, the more likely that the proportion of adult-onset offenders might increase in number.

These discrepancies in the determination of true onset age are clearly described by Zara and Farrington (2009, 2010). Using official record data from the CSDD, they identified three different groups of individuals. First, there were 38 late starters in the sample, defined as those whose first conviction occurred after the age of 21 (an even more conservative estimate than the often used adulthood cut-off age of 18). In contrast, there were 129 persons whose first conviction occurred before the age of 21, labeled as early starters. Lastly, there were 236 nonoffenders. Therefore, approximately 23% of the sample were adult-onset offenders. The benefit of the CSDD is that it also included self-report data. Therefore, official records could be cross-checked against potential early delinquent history that had gone undetected for each group discovered. In doing so, Zara and Farrington determined that of the 38 late starters, 8% ($n = 3$) had self-reported criminal behavior prior to the age of 21—measured as an offense that had gone undetected in official data. Additionally, for those who were considered nonoffenders based on official data, 7% ($n = 16$) self-reported that they had committed offenses in adulthood—again, behavior that had gone undetected by official records. Based on these numbers, van Koppen (2018, p. 99) adjusted for self-reported offending and presents the following:

> Adjusted for self-reported offending, 51 men had an adult onset (38 + 16 − 3), 140 had an early onset (129 + 8 + 3), and 212 never offended (236 − 16 − 8). Both the group of adult-onset and early-onset offenders became larger after adding information obtained from individuals themselves. Based on a combination of official and self-reported offenses, 26.7% of the offenders had an adult onset. This shows that, at least in this study, the underestimation of adult-onset offending due to official non-offenders committing crimes in adulthood is larger than the overestimation of adult-onset offending due to undetected crimes before age 18 by official adult-onset offenders.

Certainly, early-onset offenders exist in much larger numbers than do adult-onset offenders. Additionally, it is likely that most adults who engage in antisocial behavior have done so throughout their life course (and likely had not been detected). However, this does not negate the possibility that adult-onset offending exists, as some research has shown. Additional studies have contributed to this finding using both official and self-reported measures of offending. Using a sample of 321 persons followed up until age 25, Lay and colleagues (2005) determined that 45% of the 93 offenders in the sample were either convicted or self-reported offending only as adults. Underlying the issues with relying solely on official records, they also demonstrated that considering official data alone would have presented them with an adult-onset sample of only 12 persons, or 13%.

Adult-onset offenders also tend to differ from youthful offenders in a number of different ways (Loeber & Farrington, 2012). First, they usually commit less crime than their younger counterparts. In one study based in Queensland, adult-onset offenders made up slightly over half of the sample but only accounted for one quarter of the total offenses (Thompson et al., 2014). Research using the CSDD has also shown that adult-onset offenders committed an average of two crimes, compared to an average of six for those who began offending at an early age (Zara & Farrington, 2013).

It is generally agreed upon that there exists a negative correlation between age of onset and criminal career length; that is, criminal career length will decrease as age of onset increases (McGee & Farrington, 2010; Zara & Farrington, 2013). This might be due, at least in part, to the types of crimes that adult-onset offenders typically commit. Research has determined that different crimes might have different ages of onset (Harris, 2011; Loeber, 1988). Typically, crimes such as shoplifting, burglary, and vandalism are unique to juveniles, whereas robbery, drug trafficking, and rape typically first occur when an offender is already in adulthood (Harris, 2011; McGee & Farrington, 2010). Adult-onset offenders are more likely to engage in sex offending, stealing from their place of employment, vandalism, fraud, and carrying weapons. On the other hand, they are less likely to engage in robbery, burglary, minor drug offenses, and vehicle thefts (Sapouna, 2017).

The differences in the types of offenses committed also draw attention to differences in the seriousness of the crimes of adult-onset offenders (Piquero et al., 2007). Here, evidence has been mixed. Some studies have found that adult-onset offenders tend to commit less serious crimes (Beckley et al., 2016; Carrington et al., 2005). In a large-scale study using 54,498 individuals, Thompson and colleagues (2014) determined that more than half of their sample were adult-onset offenders. Of these persons, only 10% had ever committed a serious offense and 43% had only committed minor offenses. However, other research has demonstrated the opposite; in earlier work, Wolfgang and colleagues (1987) observed that adult-onset offenders were committing more serious crimes than their youthful counterparts. The seriousness of these offenses may also differ across crime-type mixture. Generally, offenders diversify in the types of crimes they commit. However, as they age they tend to engage in crimes that have some form of self-benefit, such as theft and fraud (Farrington, 2014; Piquero et al., 1999). Crime specialization is generally low in juvenile offenders but tends to increase with age (Farrington, 2014; McGloin et al., 2006; Piquero et al., 1999). Some research has theorized that specialization might increase in adult-onset offenders due to their minimal experience with offending and limited established routines that include opportunity to commit crimes (Catalano et al., 2017).

Finally, it has also been determined that adult-onset offenders tend to recidivate less than those with an early onset. Some research has even determined that adult-onset offenders were six times less likely to recidivate than those who had an earlier onset (McGee & Farrington, 2010). Additionally, Zara (2012) found that half as many late-onset offenders reoffended within the CSDD sample compared to early-onset offenders (40% compared to 80%, respectively). These results have been generalized to other samples as well. For example, 57% of adult-onset offenders in the Queensland Longitudinal Dataset only offended once, and 19% offended only twice, with only 9% of the adult-onset offenders committing more than five crimes (Thompson et al., 2014).

Taken together, this research yields several findings. First, there is clear evidence for the existence of the adult-onset offender. Second, these offenders generally differ in their behavior than do early-onset offenders. Typically, juvenile-onset offenders engage in the most serious criminal careers across the life course (van Koppen, 2018). These two findings raise the question of whether a unique theory for adult-onset behavior is warranted. This question has been explored, and researchers have concluded that the rarity of the event negates the need for this, explaining that there is room for the explanation of adult-onset offending in the current mainstream criminological theories that already exist (Beckley et al., 2016). Additionally, recent research that explored both official records and self-reported offending behavior determined that there exists significant overlap; that is, "official records and self-reports tended to identify the same people as the most persistent offenders, and the same people as the most prosocial ones" (Zara & Farrington, 2020, p. 363). This has been supported by prior research as well, dating back several decades (Huizinga & Elliott, 1986; Loeber et al., 2016; Prinzie et al., 2016).

Understanding adult risky and antisocial behavior is important for several reasons, and being able to differentiate the behaviors exhibited between these two groups of individuals helps to not only advance research but also contribute to policy, programming, prevention, and appropriate interventions. While research has demonstrated certain risk factors that might be present in early childhood and throughout adolescence, predicting later antisocial behavior is not an exact science and is often fraught with overprediction (e.g., Laub & Sampson, 2006; Sampson, 2009). Attempting to predict who will engage in deviant behavior or in criminal acts involves risk assessment; its goal is to identify those who are at a high or increased risk of either reoffending or acting violently (Gottfredson & Moriarty, 2006). In the ensuing section, this will be discussed in further detail. We will begin by outlining the implications of this chapter for future research and provide what we hope are useful ideas worthy of further exploration. We will then go on to explain why this work matters for policy and present some initial thoughts and examples of what has potential to prevent adult antisocial behavior.

Implications for Research, Policy, and Practice
Research
Criminological research is ripe with studies that focus on adolescent and juvenile offending. The large majority of criminological theories center around the adolescent time period and the

correlates and patterning of antisocial behavior. Less work, however, has paid close attention to adult offending and in particular adult onset. As noted, in the last several decades, a call for more focus on this group has been expressed and some researchers have begun to further explore the adult offending/offender phenomenon. Most, however, have focused specifically on criminal offending. Much less work has looked at antisocial and risky behavior in adulthood more generally (i.e., risky sexual behavior, seatbelt wearing, etc.). These behaviors also warrant further attention, as they might provide more insight into the continuum of deviant behaviors that exists for adults, and the unique differences that exist between older persons that place them in different places on this scale.

Additionally, recent work in psychology has discovered that human brains continue to develop up until the age of 25 (Arnett, 2000; see Cauffman et al., this volume). This, combined with societal and lifestyle changes of young adults, might warrant further research using a later age cut-off point for "adulthood." While the law typically considers anyone above the age of 18 as an adult, and some research has used age 21 as an adult cut-off, future studies might want to explore whether there is even less prevalence of late-onset offending in those over the age of 25 years, and if there exist even more differences between the types of crimes that those with an age of onset between the ages of 18 and 25 commit versus those who are 25 and older. From a policy standpoint, if research indicates that individuals have a second developmental growth opportunity between ages 18 and 25, this might be an opportune time for intervention and at the very least a different type of police response (e.g., diversion). Young offender courts serve as one potential example of this, which provide developmentally appropriate responses to emerging adults in the system. Currently, at least four states in the United States are considering this. In 2018, Connecticut, Illinois, Massachusetts, and Vermont legislatures considered bills that would extend the adult cut-off age beyond 18 years. Countries outside of the United States are also implementing some of these changes. For example, Germany uses youth courts and youth corrections, where those under the age of 18 cannot be tried in an adult court. The Netherlands has begun extending youth sanctions and uses a flexible model, where adult sanctions can be applied to juveniles, but the case remains in the juvenile justice system; this means that a youth court judge still resides over the case and youth court procedures are followed throughout the entirety of the trial. Lastly, Croatia has established special procedures for responding to youth and has begun assessing maturity of the offender in their criminal justice response (see Matthews et al., 2018, for a full review).

Moreover, while research has begun to emerge that evaluates risk factors for later antisocial behavior, the work is still limited. In Jolliffe and colleagues' (2017) recent systematic review of early risk factors for AL offenders, LCP offenders, and late-onset offenders, the team only discovered seven longitudinal studies that explored the topic of adult-onset offending. This demonstrates the need for more research that follows individuals across the lifespan and can explore the unique risk factors that exist between groups, especially into later years. This is especially true given the effect that this can have on policy.

Policy and Practice

Understanding why people commit crime is central to building appropriate responses to antisocial behavior. From a policy perspective, differentiating between types of offenders helps to better discern why different people commit crime. Given what is known about best practices for criminal justice response, exploring unique individual differences helps to reduce future offending. The risk–needs–responsivity model has demonstrated that unique, individually tailored responses to the specific needs of a person are most effective in reducing the likelihood that they will offend again (Andrews & Bonta, 2010). Therefore, the way we would respond to an AL offender, an LCP offender, or a late-onset offender may differ. For example, if a first-time offender was convicted of an offense but would never carry out another one (or at the least there is good reason/predictability to believe that they would not), the best response may be no additional criminal justice system official intervention (McAra & McVie, 2010). On the other hand, however, the best and most cost-effective response to someone likely to continue offending might be a tailored and structured number of interventions that specifically address the unique risk factors that increase their likelihood of reoffending (Welsh & Farrington, 2007). Knowing this, it becomes clear why understanding the specific needs of each person is critical for intervention.

Additionally, being able to best identify the risk of someone being a potential LCP offender as early on as possible is vital to appropriate criminal justice response and is an important policy issue that holds both social and financial implications. In fact, research by Cohen and Piquero (2009) estimated the costs of individual crimes and discovered that the value of savings of deterring a 14-year-old high-risk juvenile offender from continuing to commit crime across the life course ranged from $2.6 million to $5.3 million; deterring a high-risk youth at birth would save between $2.6 million and $4.4 million. Further research has demonstrated that the cost of LCP offending ranges anywhere from "two and a half to ten times more than the costs of high adolescence peaked offending, very low-rate chronic offending, and low adolescence peaked offending, respectively" (Piquero et al., 2013, p. 54). This, combined with the fact that LCP offenders commit most violent crime (Piquero et al., 2012), underscores the need for intervention and policy that specifically targets the risk that these offenders face. Research has demonstrated that these risks are unique to LCP offenders and differ significantly from those who offend only during adolescence or from those who have a late onset of offending behavior. Zara and Farrington (2013) found that early-onset, LCP offending is best predicted by antisocial behavior and family risk and moderately affected by socioeconomic risk measures. In their study, late-onset offending, however, was predicted more by internalizing problems later in life.

More recently, Jolliffe and colleagues (2017) conducted a systematic review of the literature that has undertaken research using the Pittsburgh Youth Study and the CSDD. They also found that LCP offenders presented with a greater number of risk factors and found that their magnitude was greater than for AL and late-onset offenders. In fact, they discovered that late-onset offenders had the least amount and magnitude of risk factors across all groups. Specifically, they noted that LCP offenders were "more likely to lack guilt, report parental stress, have poor parental communication and poor parental supervision compared with AL offenders" (Jolliffe et al., 2017, p. 22). Moore and colleagues (2017) studied a sample of over 20,000 Americans and discovered that compared to AL offenders, LCP offenders had risk factors such as low childhood SES, lack of maternal closeness, and a history of harsh discipline.

Taken together, these findings suggest that early and late onset of offending warrant separate considerations with respect to policy responses and need unique risk assessment processes and reactions. Additionally, they highlight the need for psychological factors to be included in risk assessment as doing so will both improve the ability to predict potential future offending and better inform prevention policies, programs, and interventions. Evidently, most of the resources and funding should be put into programming that focuses on reducing risks for would-be LCP offenders.

Research has found increasing evidence for many childhood risk factors that LCP offenders evince, and there has been congruence in these findings whether or not LCP offending is measured using official data or self-reports. This is important as it "increases confidence that they predict LCP offending behavior rather than biasing factors" (Zara & Farrington,

2020, p. 364). Therefore, including these factors in childhood risk assessment tools could help improve the ability to determine who might go on to offend throughout their life course, and may improve decision making regarding appropriate response. Policymakers should consider adopting multisystemic treatment efforts for at-risk youth, which include personal, social, educational, and family services.

Research has found support for several different programs that target these elements and that aim to increase protective factors and decrease risks (see Farrington, 2015, for a larger review). For one, Stop Now and Plan (SNAP), a cognitive–behavioral child skills training program, targets high impulsivity in young children, typically under the age of 12 (Augimeri et al., 2011). Evaluations of this program have found that children who went through SNAP had significantly decreased scores on the Delinquency and Aggression subscales of the Child Behavior Checklist pre- to postintervention as compared to the control group, and that this persisted over time (Augimeri et al., 2007). Second, preschool intellectual enrichment programs have worked to improve school achievement later on in life, which can protect against criminal behavior (Schweinhart et al., 1993). Additionally, parental programs that increase warmth, communication, and appropriate discipline have demonstrated promising results. Some examples include parental management training (Sanders et al., 2012) and nurse home visitation programs, which have long-term benefits and are cost-effective (Olds, 2006; Olds et al., 2003). Meta-analyses of these early family/parent training programs continue to show support for their implementation (Piquero et al., 2009, 2016). Lastly, comprehensive programs exist that involve a wide range of prevention strategies, including Communities That Care (a program that uses community resources to address deviant behavior such as aggression and/or drug use in youth).

Appropriate responses for adult-onset offenders are not as clear-cut as those for adolescent-onset offenders, since research tends to support that this is caused by time-specific, episodic events as opposed to dormant developmental issues. Nonetheless, stress management that helps adults cope in appropriate, prosocial ways can be improved.

Conclusion

Criminological research has dedicated a breadth of research to understanding what leads people to commit crime. Most of this research has focused on juvenile offending populations, but the literature has shifted in recent years to include those that (a) show signs of risk early in life and (b) only begin offending once already in adulthood. The research on these topics has demonstrated unique, individual-level differences across these populations, both in why they offend and in the types of offending behavior they engage in, highlighting the need for further research and a deeper understanding of these groups. Key distinctions have been found between LCP, AL, and adult-onset offenders.

As the field progresses forward, a deeper understanding of these differences is warranted, especially for adult-onset offenders. If these individuals are likely to be affected by occasional stressful life events, then future research should evaluate these triggers. For example, the COVID-19 pandemic might have led to a structural shift in the proportion of adult-onset offenders. Research has demonstrated that the pandemic affected rates of domestic violence in the country, a behavior typically engaged in by adults (Piquero et al., 2020). Future research should evaluate whether some of this increase was due to a change in first-offense domestic violence perpetrators. Additionally, lockdowns and job losses increased levels of stress, anxiety, and deviant coping—as evinced in the uptick of alcohol use and sales as well as opioid use and abuse throughout the pandemic (Haley & Saitz, 2020; Pollard et al., 2020). This may have also resulted in changes in other types of criminal offending.

Future prevention efforts should also ensure they differentiate by risk based on type of offender. The programs aimed at preventing LCP offending will differ from those aimed at preventing adult-onset offending. Changes in societal norms and the growing understanding of the maturing adult brain should also be considered in both prevention and criminal justice response. Additionally, the United States can look to other countries that have adopted age-specific and development-focused correctional policies and practices, such as Germany, the Netherlands, and Croatia.

The purpose of this chapter was to provide an overview of adult risky and antisocial behavior, with a specific focus on adult criminality. Though rare in comparison to juvenile crime, adult offending is not nonexistent. This chapter highlighted the growing body of evidence surrounding adult offending, including offending behavior that persists across the life course and offending behavior that just begins in adulthood. The main theories that explain offending behavior well into later life were presented, and evidence in support of their propositions was highlighted. Additionally, the chapter reviewed the differing opinions on whether adult-onset offending truly exists, concluding that it is present enough to warrant further research. Lastly, the research presented is tied to policy and programming, as well as ideas for future studies that can advance the field with respect to adult offending behaviors. As the body of research on adult offending continues to grow in both breadth and depth on this topic, this chapter can be used as a guide and resource for those who wish to explore this population of individuals further.

References

Agnew, R. (2003). An integrated theory of the adolescent peak in offending. *Youth & Society*, *34*(3), 263–299.

Akers, R. L., & Jennings, W. G. (2019). The social learning theory of crime and deviance. In *Handbook on crime and deviance* (pp. 113–129). Springer.

Andrews, D. A., & Bonta, J. (2010). *The psychology of criminal conduct*. Routledge.

Arnett, J. J. (2000). Emerging adulthood: A theory of development from the late teens through the twenties. *American Psychologist*, *55*(5), 469.

Augimeri, L. K., Farrington, D. P., Koegl, C. J., & Day, D. M. (2007). The SNAP™ Under 12 Outreach Project: Effects of a community based program for children with conduct problems. *Journal of Child and Family Studies*, *16*(6), 799–807.

Augimeri, L. K., Walsh, M., & Slater, N. (2011). Rolling out SNAP® an evidence-based intervention: A summary of implementation, evaluation, and research. *International Journal of Child, Youth and Family Studies*, *2*(2.1), 330–352.

Bachand, D. J. (1984). *The elderly offender: an exploratory study with implications for continuing education of law enforcement personnel* [Doctoral dissertation, University of Michigan].

Beckley, A. L., Caspi, A., Harrington, H., Houts, R. M., Mcgee, T. R., Morgan, N., Schroeder, F., Ramrakha, S., Poulton, R., & Moffitt, T. E. (2016). Adult-onset offenders: Is a tailored theory warranted? *Journal of Criminal Justice*, *46*, 64–81.

Bergman, L. R., & Andershed, A. K. (2009). Predictors and outcomes of persistent or age-limited registered criminal behavior: A 30-year longitudinal study of a Swedish urban population. *Aggressive Behavior: Official Journal of the International Society for Research on Aggression*, *35*(2), 164–178.

Blokland, A. A., Nagin, D., & Nieuwbeerta, P. (2005). Life span offending trajectories of a Dutch conviction cohort. *Criminology*, *43*(4), 919–954.

Blumstein, A., Cohen, J., & Farrington, D. P. (1988a). Criminal career research: Its value for criminology. *Criminology*, *26*(1), 1–35.

Blumstein, A., Cohen, J., & Farrington, D. P. (1988b). Longitudinal and criminal career research: Further clarifications. *Criminology*, *26*, 57.

Britt, C. L. (1992). Constancy and change in the US age distribution of crime: A test of the "invariance hypothesis." *Journal of Quantitative Criminology*, *8*(2), 175–187.

Burton, V. S., Jr., Evans, T. D., Cullen, F. T., Olivares, K. M., & Dunaway, R. G. (1999). Age, self-control, and adults' offending behaviors: A research note assessing a general theory of crime. *Journal of Criminal Justice*, *27*(1), 45–54.

Carrington, P. J., Matarazzo, A., & DeSouza, P. (2005). *Court careers of a Canadian birth cohort*. Statistics Canada, Canadian Centre for Justice Statistics.

Carrion, V. G., & Wong, S. S. (2012). Can traumatic stress alter the brain? Understanding the implications of early trauma on brain development and learning. *Journal of Adolescent Health*, 51(2), S23–S28.

Casey, B. J., Hare, T. A., & Galván, A. (2011). Risky and impulsive components of adolescent decision making. *Decision Making, Affect, and Learning: Attention and Performance*, 23, 425.

Catalano, R. F., Jisuk, P., Harachi, T. W., Haggerty, K. P., Abbott, R. D., & Hawkins, J. D. (2017). Mediating the effects of poverty, gender, individual characteristics, and external constraints on antisocial behavior: A test of the social development model and implications for developmental life-course theory. In D. P. Farrington (Ed.), *Integrated developmental and life-course theories of offending* (pp. 93–124). Routledge.

Charette, Y., & van Koppen, V. (2016). A capture-recapture model to estimate the effects of extra-legal disparities on crime funnel selectivity and punishment avoidance. *Security Journal*, 29(4), 561–583.

Cohen, M. A., & Piquero, A. R. (2009). New evidence on the monetary value of saving a high risk youth. *Journal of Quantitative Criminology*, 25(1), 25–49.

Cullen, F. T. (2011). Beyond adolescence-limited criminology: Choosing our future—the American Society of Criminology 2010 Sutherland address. *Criminology*, 49(2), 287–330.

D'Unger, A. V., Land, K. C., McCall, P. L., & Nagin, D. S. (1998). How many latent classes of delinquent/criminal careers? Results from mixed Poisson regression analyses. *American Journal of Sociology*, 103(6), 1593–1630.

DeLisi, M. (2015). Age–crime curve and criminal career patterns. In J. Morizot & L. Kazemian (Eds.), *The development of criminal and antisocial behavior* (pp. 51–63). Springer.

DeLisi, M., & Beauregard, E. (2018). Adverse childhood experiences and criminal extremity: New evidence for sexual homicide. *Journal of Forensic Sciences*, 63(2), 484–489.

DeLisi, M., & Piquero, A. R. (2011). New frontiers in criminal careers research, 2000–2011: A state-of-the-art review. *Journal of Criminal Justice*, 39(4), 289–301.

DeLisi, M., & Vaughn, M. G. (2008). The Gottfredson–Hirschi critiques revisited: Reconciling self-control theory, criminal careers, and career criminals. *International Journal of Offender Therapy and Comparative Criminology*, 52(5), 520–537.

Donaldson, C. D., Handren, L. M., & Crano, W. D. (2016). The enduring impact of parents' monitoring, warmth, expectancies, and alcohol use on their children's future binge drinking and arrests: A longitudinal analysis. *Prevention Science*, 17, 606–614.

Donker, A. G., Smeenk, W. H., van der Laan, P. H., & Verhulst, F. C. (2003). Individual stability of antisocial behavior from childhood to adulthood: Testing the stability postulate of Moffitt's developmental theory. *Criminology*, 41(3), 593–609.

Dubow, E. F., Huesmann, L. R., Boxer, P., & Smith, C. (2016). Childhood and adolescent risk and protective factors for violence in adulthood. *Journal of Criminal Justice*, 45, 26–31.

Eggleston, E. P., & Laub, J. H. (2002). The onset of adult offending: A neglected dimension of the criminal career. *Journal of Criminal Justice*, 30(6), 603–622.

Eisner, M. (2002). Crime, problem drinking, and drug use: Patterns of problem behavior in cross-national perspective. *Annals of the American Academy of Political and Social Science*, 580, 201–225.

Farrington, D. P. (1986). Age and crime. *Crime and Justice*, 7, 189–250.

Farrington, D. P. (1989). Early predictors of adolescent aggression and adult violence. *Violence and Victims*, 4(2), 79–100.

Farrington, D. P. (2014). Integrated cognitive antisocial potential theory. In D. G. Bruinsma & D. Weisburd (Eds.), *Encyclopedia of criminal justice and criminology* (pp. 2552–2564). Springer.

Farrington, D. P. (2015). The developmental evidence base: Prevention. In D. A. Crighton & G. J. Towl (Eds.), *Forensic psychology* (2nd ed., pp. 141–159). Wiley.

Farrington, D. P., Gaffney, H., & Ttofi, M. M. (2017). Systematic reviews of explanatory risk factors for violence, offending, and delinquency. *Aggression and Violent Behavior*, 33, 24–36.

Farrington, D. P., Loeber, R., Elliott, D. S., Hawkins, J. D., Kandel, D. B., Klein, M. W., McCord, J., Rowe, D. C., & Tremblay, R. E. (1990). Advancing knowledge about the onset of delinquency and crime. In B. B. Lahey & A. E. Kazdin, (Eds.), *Advances in clinical child psychology* (pp. 283–342).

Farrington, D. P., Piquero, A. R., & Jennings, W. G. (2013). *Offending from childhood to late middle age: Recent results from the Cambridge study in delinquent development*. Springer Science & Business Media.

Federal Interagency Forum on Aging-Related Statistics. (2008). *Older Americans 2008: Key indicators of well-being*. Centers for Disease Control and Prevention.

Feinberg, J. (1984). *Offense to others* (Vol. 2). Oxford University Press on Demand.

Feldmeyer, B., & Steffensmeier, D. (2007). Elder crime: Patterns and current trends, 1980–2004. *Research on Aging, 29*(4), 297–322.

Fuller, E., Clifton, S., Field, N., Mercer, C. H., Prah, P., Macdowall, W., Mitchelle, K., Sonnenberg, P., Johnson, A. M., & Wellings, K. (2015). *Natsal-3: Key findings from Scotland*. National Center for Social Science Research. http://natcen.ac.uk/media/997277/NatSal-Scotland.pdf

Glueck, S. S., & Glueck, E. T. (1930). *Five hundred criminal careers*. Knopf.

Goodman, S., Steffensmeier, D. J., & Ulmer, J. T. (2005). *Confessions of a dying thief: Understanding criminal careers and illegal enterprise*. Aldine Transaction.

Gottfredson, M., & Hirschi, T. (1986). The true value of lambda would appear to be zero: An essay on career criminals, criminal careers, selective incapacitation, cohort studies, and related topics. *Criminology, 24*(2), 213–234.

Gottfredson, M., & Hirschi, T. (1987). The methodological adequacy of longitudinal research on crime. *Criminology, 25*(3), 581–614.

Gottfredson, M. R., & Hirschi, T. (1990). *A general theory of crime*. Stanford University Press.

Gottfredson, S. D., & Moriarty, L. J. (2006). Statistical risk assessment: Old problems and new applications. *Crime & Delinquency, 52*(1), 178–200.

Grasmick, H. G., Tittle, C. R., Bursik, R. J., Jr., & Arneklev, B. J. (1993). Testing the core empirical implications of Gottfredson and Hirschi's general theory of crime. *Journal of Research in Crime and Delinquency, 30*(1), 5–29.

Greenberg, D. F. (1985). Age, crime, and social explanation. *American Journal of Sociology, 91*(1), 1–21.

Haley, D. F., & Saitz, R. (2020). The opioid epidemic during the COVID-19 pandemic. *JAMA, 324*(16), 1615–1617. https://doi.org/10.1001/jama.2020.18543

Hardy, M. A., & Hazelrigg, L. E. (1999). Fueling the politics of age: On economic hardship across the life course: Comment on Mirowsky & Ross. *American Sociological Review, 64*(4), 570–576.

Harris, P. M. (2011). The first-time adult-onset offender: Findings from a community corrections cohort. *International Journal of Offender Therapy and Comparative Criminology, 55*(6), 949–981.

Hirschi, T., & Gottfredson, M. R. (1983). Age and the explanation of crime. *American Journal of Sociology, 89*, 552–584.

Holden, K., & Hatcher, C. (2006). Economic status of the aged. In R. H. Binstock, L. K. George, S. J. Cutler, J. Hendricks, & J. H. Schulz (Eds.), *Handbook of aging and the social sciences* (pp. 219–237). Academic Press.

Huesmann, L. R., Dubow, E. F., & Boxer, P. (2009). Continuity of aggression from childhood to early adulthood as a predictor of life outcomes: Implications for the adolescent-limited and life-course-persistent models. *Aggressive Behavior: Official Journal of the International Society for Research on Aggression, 35*(2), 136–149.

Huizinga, D., & Elliott, D. S. (1986). Reassessing the reliability and validity of self-report delinquency measures. *Journal of Quantitative Criminology, 2*(4), 293–327.

Jennings, W. G., Loeber, R., Pardini, D. A., Piquero, A. R., & Farrington, D. P. (2016). *Offending from childhood to young adulthood: Recent results from the Pittsburgh Youth Study*. Springer International Publishing.

Jolliffe, D., Farrington, D. P., Piquero, A. R., Loeber, R., & Hill, K. G. (2017). Systematic review of early risk factors for life-course-persistent, adolescence-limited, and late-onset offenders in prospective longitudinal studies. *Aggression and Violent Behavior, 33*, 15–23.

Keijsers, L., Branje, S., Hawk, S. T., Schwartz, S. J., Frijns, T., Koot, H. M., van Lier, P., & Meeus, W. (2012). Forbidden friends as forbidden fruit: Parental supervision of friendships, contact with deviant peers, and adolescent delinquency. *Child Development, 83*(2), 651–666.

Kuhlmann, R., & Ruddell, R. (2005). Elderly jail inmates. *Californian Journal of Health Promotion, 3*(2), 49–60.

Kunz, F. (2014). *Kriminalität älterer Menschen: Beschreibung und Erklärung auf der Basis von Selbstberichtsdaten*. Duncker & Humblot.

Laub, J. H., & Sampson, R. J. (2006). *Shared beginnings, divergent lives: Delinquent boys to age 70*. Harvard University Press.

Lauritsen, J. L. (1998). The age-crime debate: Assessing the limits of longitudinal self-report data. *Social Forces, 77*(1), 127–154.

Lay, B., Ihle, W., Esser, G., & Schmidt, M. H. (2005). Juvenile-episodic, continued or adult-onset delinquency? Risk conditions analysed in a cohort of children followed up to the age of 25 years. *European Journal of Criminology, 2*(1), 39–66.

Levenson, J. S., & Socia, K. M. (2016). Adverse childhood experiences and arrest patterns in a sample of sexual offenders. *Journal of Interpersonal Violence, 31*(10), 1883–1911.

Lipsey, M., & Derzon, J. (1998). Predictors of violent or serious delinquency in adolescence and early adulthood: A synthesis of longitudinal research. In R. Loeber & D. P. Farrington (Eds.), *Serious and violent juvenile offenders: Risk factors and successful interventions* (pp. 86–105).

Loeber, R. (1988). Natural histories of conduct problems, delinquency, and associated substance use. In R. B. Lahey & A. E. Kazdin (Eds.), *Advances in clinical child psychology* (pp. 73–124). Springer.

Loeber, R. (2012). Does the study of the age-crime curve have a future. *The future of criminology*, 11–19.

Loeber, R., & Farrington, D. P. (Eds.). (2012). *From juvenile delinquency to adult crime: Criminal careers, justice policy, and prevention*. Oxford University Press.

Loeber, R., Slot, W., & Stouthamer-Loeber, M. (2016). A cumulative developmental model of risk and promotive factors. In R. Loeber (Ed.), *Tomorrow's criminals* (pp. 151–180). Routledge.

Lotrean, L. M., Laza, V., Ionut, C., & de Vries, H. (2010). Assessment of health risk behaviours and their interrelationships among young people from two counties of Romania. *Journal of Public Health*, 18, 403–411.

Marquart, J. W., Merianos, D. E., & Doucet, G. (2000). The health-related concerns of older prisoners: Implications for policy. *Ageing & Society*, 20(1), 79–96.

Matthews, S., Schiraldi, V., & Chester, L. (2018). Youth justice in Europe: Experience of Germany, the Netherlands, and Croatia in providing developmentally appropriate responses to emerging adults in the criminal justice system. *Justice Evaluation Journal*, 1(1), 59–81.

Mazerolle, P., Brame, R., Paternoster, R., Piquero, A., & Dean, C. (2000). Onset age, persistence, and offending versatility: Comparisons across gender. *Criminology*, 38(4), 1143–1172.

McAra, L., & McVie, S. (2010). Youth crime and justice: Key messages from the Edinburgh Study of Youth Transitions and Crime. *Criminology & Criminal Justice*, 10(2), 179–209.

McGee, T. R., & Farrington, D. P. (2010). Are there any true adult-onset offenders? *British Journal of Criminology*, 50(3), 530–549.

McGloin, J. M., Pratt, T. C., & Piquero, A. R. (2006). A life-course analysis of the criminogenic effects of maternal cigarette smoking during pregnancy: A research note on the mediating impact of neuropsychological deficit. *Journal of Research in Crime and Delinquency*, 43(4), 412–426.

McLean, S. (2016). *The effect of trauma on the brain development of children*. CFCA Practice Resource. Australian Institute of Family Studies.

Moffitt, T. E. (1993). Adolescence-limited and life-course-persistent antisocial behavior: A developmental taxonomy. *Psychological Review*, 100(4), 674.

Moffitt, T. E. (2018). Male antisocial behaviour in adolescence and beyond. *Nature Human Behavior*, 2, 177–186.

Monahan, K., Steinberg, L., & Piquero, A. R. (2015). Juvenile justice policy and practice: A developmental perspective. *Crime and Justice*, 44(1), 577–619.

Moore, A. A., Silberg, J. L., Roberson-Nay, R., & Mezuk, B. (2017). Life course persistent and adolescence limited conduct disorder in a nationally representative US sample: Prevalence, predictors, and outcomes. *Social Psychiatry and Psychiatric Epidemiology*, 52(4), 435–443.

Olds, D. L. (2006). The nurse–family partnership: An evidence-based preventive intervention. *Infant Mental Health Journal*, 27(1), 5–25.

Olds, D. L., Hill, P. L., O'Brien, R., Racine, D., & Moritz, P. (2003). Taking preventive intervention to scale: The nurse-family partnership. *Cognitive and Behavioral Practice*, 10(4), 278–290.

Piquero, A. R., Farrington, D. P., & Blumstein, A. (2003). The criminal career paradigm: Background and recent developments. In M. Tonry (Ed.), *Crime and justice: A review of research* (Vol. 30, pp. 359–506). University of Chicago Press.

Piquero, A. R., Farrington, D. P., & Blumstein, A. (2007). *Key issues in criminal career research: New analyses of the Cambridge Study in Delinquent Development*. Cambridge University Press.

Piquero, A. R., Farrington, D. P., Welsh, B. C., Tremblay, R., & Jennings, W. G. (2009). Effects of early family/parent training programs on antisocial behavior and delinquency. *Journal of Experimental Criminology*, 5, 83–120.

Piquero, A. R., Jennings, W. G., & Barnes, J. C. (2012). Violence in criminal careers: A review of the literature from a developmental life-course perspective. *Aggression and Violent Behavior*, 17(3), 171–179.

Piquero, A. R., Jennings, W. G., Diamond, B., Farrington, D. P., Tremblay, R. E., Welsh, B. C., & Gonzalez, J. M. R. (2016). A meta-analysis update on the effects of early family/parent training programs on antisocial behavior and delinquency. *Journal of Experimental Criminology*, 12, 229–248.

Piquero, A. R., Jennings, W. G., & Farrington, D. (2013). The monetary costs of crime to middle adulthood: Findings from the Cambridge study in delinquent development. *Journal of Research in Crime and Delinquency*, 50(1), 53–74.

Piquero, A., Paternoster, R., Mazerolle, P., Brame, R., & Dean, C. W. (1999). Onset age and offense specialization. *Journal of Research in Crime and Delinquency*, 36(3), 275–299.

Piquero, A. R., Riddell, J. R., Bishopp, S. A., Narvey, C., Reid, J. A., & Piquero, N. L. (2020). Staying home, staying safe? A short-term analysis of COVID-19 on Dallas domestic violence. *American Journal of Criminal Justice*, 45(4), 601–635.

Plant, M. A., Plant, M. L., Miller, P., Gmel, G., & Kuntsche, S. (2009). The social consequences of binge drinking: A comparison of young adults in six European countries. *Journal of Addictive Diseases, 28*, 294–308.

Pollard, M. S., Tucker, J. S., & Green, H. D. (2020). Changes in adult alcohol use and consequences during the COVID-19 pandemic in the US. *JAMA Network Open, 3*(9), e2022942.

Pratt, T. C., & Cullen, F. T. (2000). The empirical status of Gottfredson and Hirschi's general theory of crime: A meta-analysis. *Criminology, 38*(3), 931–964.

Prinzie, P., Stams, G. J., & Hoeve, M. (2016). Family processes and parent and child personality characteristics. In R. Loeber (Ed.), *Tomorrow's criminals* (pp. 109–120). Routledge.

Pulkkinen, L., Lyyra, A. L., & Kokko, K. (2009). Life success of males on nonoffender, adolescence-limited, persistent, and adult-onset antisocial pathways: Follow-up from age 8 to 42. *Aggressive Behavior: Official Journal of the International Society for Research on Aggression, 35*(2), 117–135.

Quetelet, A. (1831). *Research on the propensity to crime of different ages*. (S. F. Test Sylvester, Trans.). Anderson Publishing Co.

Quetelet, A. (1984). *Adolphe Quetelet's research on the propensity for crime at different ages*. Anderson Publishing Company.

Reavis, J. A., Looman, J., Franco, K. A., & Rojas, B. (2013). Adverse childhood experiences and adult criminality: How long must we live before we possess our own lives? *Permanente Journal, 17*(2), 44.

Rocque, M. (2015). The lost concept: The (re) emerging link between maturation and desistance from crime. *Criminology & Criminal Justice, 15*(3), 340–360.

Sampson, R. J., & Laub, J. H. (2003). Life-course desisters? Trajectories of crime among delinquent boys followed to age 70. *Criminology, 41*(3), 555–592.

Sanders, M. R., Baker, S., & Turner, K. M. (2012). A randomized controlled trial evaluating the efficacy of Triple P Online with parents of children with early-onset conduct problems. *Behaviour Research and Therapy, 50*(11), 675–684.

Sapouna, M. (2017). Adult-onset offending: A neglected reality? Findings from a contemporary British general population cohort. *International Journal of Offender Therapy and Comparative Criminology, 61*(12), 1392–1408.

Schulz, J. H., Borowski, A., Binstock, R. H., George, L. K., Cutler, S. J., & Hendricks, J. (2006). *Handbook of aging and the social sciences*.

Schweinhart, L. J., Mcnair, S., Barnes, H., & Larner, A. M. (1993). Observing young children inaction to assess their development: The High/Scope Child Observation Record study. *Educational and Psychological Measurement, 53*(2), 445–455.

Skardhamar, T. (2014). Lifetime conviction risk—A synthetic cohort approach. *Journal of Scandinavian Studies in Criminology and Crime Prevention, 15*(1), 96–101.

Sohoni, T., Paternoster, R., McGloin, J. M., & Bachman, R. (2014). "Hen's teeth and horse's toes": The adult onset offender in criminology. *Journal of Crime and Justice, 37*(2), 155–172.

Steffensmeier, D. J., Allan, E. A., Harer, M. D., & Streifel, C. (1989). Age and the distribution of crime. *American Journal of Sociology, 94*(4), 803–831.

Steffensmeier, D., & Streifel, C. (1991). Age, gender, and crime across three historical periods: 1935, 1960, and 1985. *Social Forces, 69*(3), 869–894.

Steinberg, L., Graham, S., O'Brien, L., Woolard, J., Cauffman, E., & Banich, M. (2009). Age differences in future orientation and delay discounting. *Child Development, 80*(1), 28–44.

Steinberg, L. (2008). A neurobehavioral perspective on adolescent risk-taking. *Developmental Review, 28*(1), 78–106.

Theobald, D., & Farrington, D. P. (2011). Why do the crime-reducing effects of marriage vary with age? *British Journal of Criminology, 51*(1), 136–158.

Thompson, C., Stewart, A., & Allard, T. (2014). Examining adult-onset offending: A case for adult cautioning. *Trends and Issues in Crime and Criminal Justice*, no. 488, 1–8.

Tibbetts, S. G., & Piquero, A. R. (1999). The influence of gender, low birth weight, and disadvantaged environment in predicting early onset of offending: A test of Moffitt's interactional hypothesis. *Criminology, 37*(4), 843–878.

Tittle, C. R., Ward, D. A., & Grasmick, H. G. (2003). Gender, age, and crime/deviance: A challenge to self-control theory. *Journal of research in crime and delinquency, 40*(4), 426–453.

van Koppen, M. V. (2018). Criminal career dimensions of juvenile- and adult-onset offenders. *Journal of Developmental and Life-Course Criminology, 4*(1), 92–119.

Vazsonyi, A. T., Mikuška, J., & Kelley, E. L. (2017). It's time: A meta-analysis on the self-control-deviance link. *Journal of Criminal Justice, 48*, 48–63.

Vermeiren, R. (2003). Psychopathology and delinquency in adolescents: A descriptive and developmental perspective. *Clinical Psychology Review*, *23*(2), 277–318.

Warr, M. (1998). Life-course transitions and desistance from crime. *Criminology*, *36*(2), 183–216.

Welsh, B. C., & Farrington, D. P. (2007). Saving children from a life of crime: Toward a national strategy for early prevention. *Victims and Offenders*, *2*(1), 1–20.

Widom, C. S., Fisher, J. H., Nagin, D. S., & Piquero, A. R. (2018). A prospective examination of criminal career trajectories in abused and neglected males and females followed up into middle adulthood. *Journal of Quantitative Criminology*, *34*(3), 831–852.

Wikström, P. O. H., & Loeber, R. (2000). Do disadvantaged neighborhoods cause well-adjusted children to become adolescent delinquents? A study of male juvenile serious offending, individual risk and protective factors, and neighborhood context. *Criminology*, *38*(4), 1109–1142.

Willoughby, T., Good, M., Adachi, P. J. C., Hamza, C., & Tavernier, R. (2013). Examining the link between adolescent brain development and risk taking from a social-developmental perspective. *Brain and Cognition*, *83*, 315–323.

Wolfgang, M. E., Figlio, R. M., & Sellin, T. (1972). *Delinquency in a birth cohort*. University of Chicago Press.

Wolfgang, M. E., Figlio, R. M., & Sellin, T. (1987). *Delinquency in a birth cohort*. University of Chicago Press.

World Health Organization. (2021). *Adolescent and young adult health*. https://www.who.int/news-room/fact-sheets/detail/adolescents-health-risks-and-solutions

Xing, Y., Ji, C., & Zhang, L. (2006). Relationship of binge drinking and other health-compromising behaviors among urban adolescents in China. *Journal of Adolescent Health*, *39*, 495–500.

Zara, G. (2012). Adult onset offending. In R. Loeber & B. C. Welsh (Eds.), *The future of criminology* (pp. 85–93). Oxford University Press.

Zara, G., & Farrington, D. P. (2009). Childhood and adolescent predictors of late onset criminal careers. *Journal of Youth and Adolescence*, *38*(3), 287–300.

Zara, G., & Farrington, D. P. (2010). A longitudinal analysis of early risk factors for adult-onset offending: What predicts a delayed criminal career? *Criminal Behaviour and Mental Health*, *20*(4), 257–273.

Zara, G., & Farrington, D. P. (2013). Assessment of risk for juvenile compared with adult criminal onset implications for policy, prevention, and intervention. *Psychology, Public Policy, & Law*, *19*, 235–249.

Zara, G., & Farrington, D. P. (2020). Childhood risk factors for self-reported versus official life-course-persistent, adolescence-limited, and late-onset offending. *Criminal Justice and Behavior*, *47*(3), 352–368.

CHAPTER 22

Transitioning to Adulthood in the Legal System: The Creation of Young Adult Courts

Marie L. Gillespie, Nicholas S. Riano, and Elizabeth Cauffman

Abstract

Transition-age youth, or those between the ages of 18 and 25, represent a unique population that warrants differential treatment in the legal system due to rapid psychosocial changes. This chapter addresses the developmental science that underlies distinctions inherent to this age group and explains the current representation of young adults in the legal system. The chapter provides an overview of diversion programs designed to incorporate developmental research, which are being increasingly implemented in the United States. It highlights a case study of a novel young adult court in Southern California, which aims to reduce the collateral consequences of felony convictions. The chapter concludes with policy implications and future directions in both research and practice to improve the lives of young adults in the legal system.

Key Words: transition-age youth, young adult court, diversion program, developmental neuroscience, translational science, decision making, felony convictions

The criminal legal system is often characterized as dealing in absolutes, with very little room for nuance within population-level guidelines and regulations. For example, adjudications at trial are determined to be either guilty or not guilty, and individuals are considered either children or adults in the eyes of the law—a change that happens overnight on one's 18th birthday. While much attention has been rightfully afforded to children impacted by the legal system, the normative developmental process of the transition to adulthood has long been unrecognized. As such, it is important to narrowly define this developmental stage. Emerging adults, or transition-age youth (TAY), can encompass a broad range of ages: Some agencies and scholars consider the age of transition to begin at 16, and others extend the end of this period to age 30. For the purposes of this chapter, and to remain consistent with the predominance of neurodevelopmental research, we define TAY as those aged 18–25.

In this chapter, we discuss how TAY have been (and currently are) perceived and systemically managed by legal entities. We address the developmental science underlying the distinctions inherent to this age group and explain the current representation of young adults in the legal system. Further, we describe the science-to-practice paradigm shift exemplified by the changing laws that govern young adults and describe diversion programs that are being increasingly implemented throughout the United States. To this end, we showcase the current state of diversion research for this age group by detailing a novel young adult court program in Southern California. Finally, we conclude with a discussion of policy implications and future directions in research and practice. We also provide information on graduate and other higher education programs that focus on the treatment of young adults in the legal system. Before one can understand or appreciate the creation of a young adult court, it is first important to know the history of the legal system and how adolescents and young adults have been treated over the years.

A Brief History of Juvenile Justice in the United States

In the early 20th century, progressive ideologies helped decouple the ways that juveniles and adults were treated within the legal system, with the hope that younger individuals could be rehabilitated more effectively (Jenkins, 2017). This compassionate approach to juvenile crime included the establishment of an 1899 court in Chicago dedicated solely to serving children. The late 19th century marked a surge in industrialization across the United States, as well as a rapidly increasing immigrant population. Most immigrants resided in segregated housing around urban industrial centers, while wealthier families moved into newly emerging suburbs. While progressive ideologies encouraged the view of childhood as a period with unique developmental needs, immigrant parents could not afford long-lasting child dependency. This resulted in a juvenile system that systematically discriminated between "our children" and "other people's children" (i.e., immigrants; Feld, 2017). As a result of these social and structural changes, hundreds of predominantly immigrant youth who had committed minor infractions were arrested and jailed alongside those who had committed serious crimes. To combat this, a group of female activists led by Julia Lathrop and Lucy Flower advocated for children's rights. This group is credited with conceiving the world's first juvenile/rehabilitative court, then named the "parental court" (Tanenhaus, 2002).

For approximately 80 years, the rehabilitative model of the juvenile justice system prevailed. However, the emergence of the "tough on crime" movement of the late 1980s, which quickly gained momentum under the Reagan administration, shifted the legal treatment of juveniles from idealistic, rehabilitative methods to more punitive ones. As a result, these policies nearly reverted the aims and goals of juvenile courts to the punitive nature of the adult courts they were meant to replace. For example, "superpredators" became a common term used by politicians and the media (Steinberg, 2000), often when referring to youth of color (Finley & Schindler, 1999), which served to blur the public's distinction between juveniles and adults. This shift in public bias largely persisted until the landmark U.S. Supreme Court decision banning the death penalty for juveniles (*Roper v. Simmons*, 2005), and later abolishing mandatory life sentences without the possibility of parole for juveniles (*Miller v. Alabama*, 2012). Even still, many states allow juveniles to be tried as adults under certain circumstances: Children as young as 12 have been tried as adults for first-degree murder (Axelrod, 2015).

Although children and adults have been adjudicated separately since 1899 (Tanenhaus, 2002), the first courts designed to process *emerging adults* or TAY were only recently established (i.e., The 2004 Douglas County Young Adult Court; Nebraska Supreme Court: Administrative Office of the Courts and Probation, 2020). While we do not argue that TAY should be viewed by the legal system through the same lens as juveniles, there is scientific evidence supporting separate, developmentally tailored legal approaches to young adults that uniquely distinguish TAY from both juveniles *and* adults. However, current neuroscientific research does not drive policy and practice efforts within the criminal legal system in the United States. For example, Pennsylvania is still in the process of resentencing youth to adhere to *Montgomery v. Louisiana*, the 2016 Supreme Court decision that asserted that *Miller* should be applied retroactively to cases decided prior to 2012 (*Montgomery v. Louisiana*, 2016). The 1979 case of Avis Lee in Pennsylvania illustrates the punitive stance of the legal system toward those who have reached the age of majority. When she was 18, Lee agreed to serve as a lookout during a robbery. When the victim resisted, Lee's codefendant shot and killed him. Lee was subsequently convicted of second-degree felony murder, despite trying to help the victim, and was sentenced to life in prison without the possibility of parole. After years of public outcry and five denied petitions, Lee's sentence was commuted in 2021 by Pennsylvania Governor Tom Wolf—after she spent 41 years in prison (Abolitionist Law Center, 2019; Melamed, 2021). Cases such as these have been appealed on the basis of salient neuroscience research, which demonstrates that even youth over the age of 18 exhibit immature neural networks responsible for impulse control and decision-making.

Emerging Adults in the Legal System
While special considerations for juveniles have existed for over a century, applying evidence-based considerations couched in developmental neuroscience to this population is a burgeoning concept. Despite recent progress, the law has been slow to recognize emerging adulthood as a separate and sensitive temporal period. Rather than extend considerations and leniency for juveniles after 18, several states routinely treat 16- and 17-year-olds as adults when accused of a crime. In fact, research has shown that there is an increase in punishment severity when a defendant becomes an "adult," above and beyond the general effect of aging (Hjalmarsson, 2009). This means that although TAY may continue to have the immaturity and impulsivity that are characteristic of adolescence, they now face more severe jail and/or prison sentences. Notably, TAY have the highest rates of recidivism when compared to other age groups: Nearly 80% of TAY are rearrested within a few years of being released (Carson & Golinelli, 2013). Longitudinal data from state prisons show consistent findings: 90% of TAY who were incarcerated were rearrested within 10 years of their release, compared to recidivism rates of 75%–85% for those who were older (Antenangeli & Durose, 2021).

Though a publicly available and unified repository of demographic information for all TAY impacted by the legal system does not exist, estimates compiled from several sources paint a grim picture. In 2016, TAY accounted for about 29% of those incarcerated in jails and prisons (Justice Policy Institute, 2016) and represented 25% of all arrests (Fair and Just Prosecution, 2019), while composing only about 10% of the U.S. population. However, it is important to note that the percentage of TAY in jails is much higher than those in prison. As of December 31, 2019, there were about 121,500 young adults aged 18–24 with sentences of 1 year or longer being held in state and federal prisons across the United States, representing about 8.8% of the total prison population (Bureau of Justice Statistics, 2019). Consistent with the general incarcerated U.S. population, emerging adults in state and federal prisons are predominately male (93.5%), and young adults of color are overrepresented (males: 41.5% Black, 26% Latinx; females: 22.8% Black, 24.1% Latinx; Bureau of Justice Statistics, 2019). Additionally, racial disparities exist when comparing the percentages of TAY incarcerated in state and federal prisons to all incarcerated individuals, such that racial disparities among TAY are more pronounced than those found in the general incarcerated population. For instance, while Black males represent 31.5% of all prisoners in the United States, Black TAY males represent nearly 40% of TAY prisoners. This trend is also observed for Latinx males: While they represent 21.9% of all prisoners in the United States, Latinx TAY males represent 24.3% of all TAY prisoners (Bureau of Justice Statistics, 2019).

The majority of incarcerated TAY are housed in county jails, whereby they tend to serve shorter sentences for lower-level offenses compared to TAY in state and federal prisons (Bureau of Justice Statistics, 2019; Justice Policy Institute, 2016). Two explanations may illuminate this stark contextual difference: racial disparities in arrests resulting from less severe offenses, and the greater impulsivity underlying TAY offending may lead to more minor offenses and shorter sentences (i.e., jail time).

Racial and Socioeconomic Disparities in Transition-Age Youth Arrests

First, people of color have been historically marginalized in U.S. society, and these incarceration statistics may be due in part to the disadvantages faced by TAY of color (see generally Burke et al., this volume). Beyond the scope of this chapter, there is long-standing research on the intergenerational cycle of incarceration that disproportionately impacts families of color (Maruschak et al., 2021; Wakefield & Wildeman, 2013). Additionally, widespread consequences faced by youth of color include further disparities in poverty rates, barriers to educational attainment, and decreased social supports (Gaston, 2016; Shaw, 2016). These inequities contribute to the overrepresentation of people of color in the criminal legal system (Gramlich, 2018). Additionally, predominantly Black schools are more likely to have zero-tolerance discipline policies and a large on-campus law enforcement presence compared to predominantly White schools, increasing students' chances of arrest (Robles-Ramamurthy & Watson, 2019).

Research has shown that one of the most robust predictors of arrest is a previous arrest, and youth who hold a negative perception of the criminal legal system are more likely to engage in criminal activity (Fine et al., 2017). Thus, because children of color are more likely to have negative experiences with the criminal legal system (e.g., parental incarceration, police harassment) and are more likely to suffer the ramifications of a heavily policed school environment, several factors compound the likelihood that they will be arrested during their lifetime. These racial disparities increase as young adults age, greatly affecting the likelihood of arrest and incarceration of TAY.

Houselessness may also compound these disparities: Living in a lower income bracket increases the likelihood that TAY of color will experience houselessness, and indeed, the rate of unhoused young adults is increasing (Heerde et al., 2021). Unhoused individuals are 11 times more likely to be arrested (Bailey et al., 2020), particularly for need-based crimes such as theft of food items (McCarthy & Hagan, 1992). Research has also suggested that the increased likelihood of arrest may be due to police profiling and discrimination (O'Grady & Gaetz, 2004). As law enforcement becomes more punitive, the criminalization of inevitable aspects of being houseless, such as sleeping in a public place, may be a factor in the increased rates of arrest for TAY.

Impulsivity and Risk Taking

Another factor that may explain the discrepancy between rates of TAY in jails and prisons is that risk taking and impulsive behavior are primary characteristics of young adults (Casey et al., 2020), indicating that TAY are likely committing more crimes that warrant jail stays compared to lengthier prison sentences. In fact, the Office of Juvenile Justice and Delinquency Prevention (OJJDP) reports such disparities in TAY charge types. Although they composed fewer than 20% of all arrests in 2019, young adults aged 18–24 were nonetheless overrepresented for certain key impulse-related offenses, such as liquor law violations (46% of all arrests), robbery (31% of all arrests), and weapons possession (27% of all arrests; OJJDP Statistical Briefing Book, 2019). Moreover, the most common type of violent offending is simple assault, which accounts for almost two thirds of all violent crime (Morgan & Truman, 2020). This charge can be conceptualized as an impulsive, youth-based crime contextually rooted in interpersonal conflict (e.g., peer fighting). Beyond the fact that TAY are overrepresented in the criminal legal system, continued neurological development into the mid-20s indicates that emerging adults warrant differential treatment compared to other age groups when they do commit crimes.

Science-to-Practice Gap: Underdeveloped and Overrepresented

As illustrated by the previous arrest data, adolescence and emerging adulthood are periods in which individuals are more prone to risky behavior. This timeframe marks the highest rates of preventable deaths from unintentional accidents and injuries (Kann et al., 2018). Moreover, rates of substance use tend to be the highest among this age group (Center for Behavioral Health Statistics and Quality, 2019), which explains the higher incidence of drug-related offending and subsequent incarceration (Perker & Chester, 2018, 2021). Consequently, several factors underlie this intense surge, and subsequent decline, in risk-taking behavior over time.

A wealth of research suggests that the overrepresentation of young people in the criminal legal system is undergirded by their underdeveloped brain networks, particularly those governing sensation and reward seeking, emotion regulation, and self-control (Casey et al., 2020). Further, neurological and developmental research supports the legal distinction between TAY and older adults. Brain imaging studies, as well as brain autopsies, have confirmed that the prefrontal cortex continues to mature into the mid-20s (Casey et al., 2020; Cauffman & Steinberg, 2012; Simmonds et al., 2017). This is especially salient when assessing TAY criminal culpability, as the prefrontal cortex is responsible for skills such as executive functioning (e.g., planning, goal setting) and self-control (Diamond, 2013). But aren't young adults cognitively capable of understanding the consequences of their actions? While youth—including teens—perform as well as adults in some simple cognitive tasks, their capacity for self-regulation, especially in emotionally and socially heightened situations (e.g., when stressed or being watched by peers), does not reach maturity until much later (Cohen et al., 2016). Steinberg and colleagues administered a cognitive battery (e.g., memory and verbal fluency tasks) and psychosocial self-report questionnaires (e.g., sensation seeking and risk perception, peer influences on decision making) to over 900 individuals aged 10–30. Results showed that while intellectual ability reached its peak at age 16–17, psychosocial maturity did not catch up to those levels until age 26 (Steinberg et al., 2009). This is sometimes referred to as the "maturity gap" between cognitive and psychosocial development in young adults (Icenogle et al., 2019), which spans from mid-adolescence until about age 25 (see Figure 22.1).

Despite clear indications of continued brain maturation into the mid-20s, TAY remain an understudied group. Limited existing studies have found variation in the cognitive capacities of TAY in response to social influences, and TAY simultaneously differ from and share features with adolescents and older adults (Weigard et al., 2014). Thus, growing evidence suggests that emerging adulthood is a *unique and sensitive period* during which individuals can process cognitive tasks as well as adults but are still susceptible to diminished cognitive capacity. Additionally, emotionally and socially heightened situations are conducive to risk taking and impulsive behaviors, which in turn could be linked to criminality (Lantz, 2020; Rowan et al., 2021).

Much of TAY offending can be attributed to heightened *reward sensitivity* and a diminished ability to foresee the consequences of one's actions, compounding the effects of the maturity gap. A desire to engage in reward-seeking behavior is potent before age 30, often at the expense of considering potentially harmful consequences. Both behavioral investigations (Cauffman et al., 2010; Davidow et al., 2016) and neuroimaging studies (van Duijvenvoorde et al., 2016; Van Leijenhorst et al., 2010) have found that young people learn faster than older adults when rewarded for correct or appropriate responses (Shulman et al., 2016).

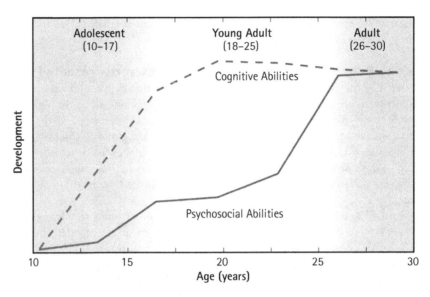

Figure 22.1 Maturity age gap in psychological and cognitive abilities. Figure adapted from Icenogle et al. (2019) and Casey et al. (2020).

Consequently, young adults' increased risk taking and desire for novel and intense feelings leave them more vulnerable to committing illegal acts.

Luckily, this inclination toward risky behavior and sensation seeking is transient: Developmental science provides that most individuals will "age out" of a propensity for antisocial behavior. As the scientific body of knowledge about TAY and their specific needs continues to grow, one thing is certain: There is no scientific basis, nor any developmental tenet, that supports a harsh demarcation necessitating differential treatment before and after one's 18th birthday. This age was likely selected to align with other phasic changes, such as the right to vote, purchase alcohol, get married, and join the military, behaviors that certainly reflect the important decisions of adulthood (Lai, 2013). While it is important that TAY face consequences for their illegal acts, the criminal legal system should also consider the developmental framework that may have led youth to commit a crime, and the capacity for change within that individual, highlighted by their age. Indeed, young adults' sensitivity to rewards also implies that they are more amenable to change and rehabilitation than older adults (Cauffman et al., 2018; Steinberg, 2014; Steinberg & Cauffman, 1999). Although neurobiological immaturity is often studied in the context of offending behaviors, it also reflects greater *plasticity*, or the ability to "rewire" neural connections and networks in response to environmental input (Frankenhuis & Walasek, 2020). Therefore, diversion programs specifically designed for this age group warrant further attention and rigorous scientific evaluation.

What we know about TAY from the neurodevelopmental research can be summed up into several key points: These emerging adults (a) are still developing the parts of their brains responsible for planning, self-control, and comprehension of the future consequences of their actions well into their mid-20s; (b) are strongly influenced by peers and more likely to act impulsively around others and in emotionally heightened situations compared to older adults; (c) are highly sensitive to and influenced by rewards (more so than punishment); and (d) are therefore also highly amenable to change and likely to benefit from interventions. TAY are therefore vulnerable to situations that would lead to legal system involvement due to sensation-seeking behavior (e.g., substance use, aggression) and poor executive functions (e.g., poor capacity to consider future consequences). In addition, TAY are in their last period of brain plasticity whereby interventions can effectively lead to lasting behavior change.

A Multiplicity of Harms: How Felonies Lead to Failing Trajectories

One of the most detrimental consequences of being arrested after the age of majority is that the legal outcome can result in a felony conviction. The "felon" label, uniquely provided to those who are legal adults, carries tremendous and potentially lifelong financial, social, and personal burdens. Having a felony conviction produces myriad collateral consequences, of which the effects are considerably worse for TAY of color (Goldman et al., 2019; Pettit & Gutierrez, 2018; Stewart & Uggen, 2020; Wheelock, 2005).

A felony conviction can mean losing the right to vote and being denied gainful employment in the public sector, occupational licenses, welfare assistance, and public housing (Chesney-Lind & Mauer, 2003; Love et al., 2013; Travis, 2005). Convicted felons are also prohibited from serving in the armed forces, exerting rights under the Second Amendment, and serving on a jury (Persons Not Qualified, 2010; Qualifications for Jury Service, 2018; Student Eligibility, 2018; U.S. Const. amend. XIV, 1868; Unlawful Acts, 2018). Nationwide, there are more than 44,000 collateral consequences tied to a felony conviction (Berson, 2013; U.S. Department of Justice: Office of Justice Programs, n.d.; see Figure 22.2). In California alone, the National Inventory of Collateral Consequences of Conviction estimates 700 collateral consequences (U.S. Department of Justice: Office of Justice Programs, n.d.). For example, in the state of California, the charge of felony theft is the difference between stealing property worth $950 versus $949.99. As such, a single penny can dictate whether a TAY is denied employment, public housing, and educational opportunities. This disruption to the acquisition of human and social capital can lead to significant inequities among young adults exposed to the criminal legal system (Augustyn & Loughran, 2017).

During a time when emerging adults are establishing their independence and building the foundations upon which they hope to become financially and socially successful, harsh and

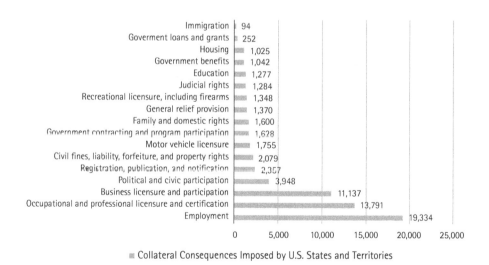

Figure 22.2 Collateral consequences of felony convictions. Adapted from the United States Commission on Civil Rights (2019). For a full explanation of each category, see the National Inventory of the Collateral Consequences of Conviction Inventories website, https://www.usccr.gov/files/pubs/2019/06-13-Collateral-Consequences.pdf

developmentally inappropriate legal sanctions can have lasting adverse impact on employment and legal earnings (Fagan & Freeman, 1999; Pager, 2003; Ward & Tittle, 1993). In addition, people of color are significantly more likely to be adjudicated for drug offenses that disqualify them from access to financial aid and education scholarships (e.g., Pell Grants) while simultaneously representing those with the greatest unmet need for financial assistance to acquire higher education (Wheelock & Uggen, 2006). Grimly exemplifying how the ripple effects of felony convictions can perpetuate legal racial inequities, a Government Accountability Office report (Wheelock, 2005) found that approximately 20,000 students were denied Pell Grants and 30,000 applicants were denied student loans due to felony drug convictions. Of note, higher school dropout rates directly affect financial prospects; those without a high school diploma earn an income *half that of those* with a bachelor's degree (McFarland et al., 2017). With respect to civic engagement, in 2020, it was found that one in 16 Black adults could not vote due to their felony records, starkly highlighting the racial disparities embedded within felony disfranchisement in the United States (Chung, 2021).

During the critical period when most youth attain the education that serves as the foundation for subsequent future achievements and sustaining income, it makes sense that justice-involved TAY deprived of educational funding exhibit poor adjustment (Steinberg et al., 2004; William T. Grant Commission on Work Family and Citizenship, 1988). Moreover, the current cohort of young adults in the United States is markedly different than previous generations in terms of economic inequality and barriers to social mobility (Institute of Medicine & National Research Council, 2015). Life milestones, such as financial maturity and building a family, are attained at a slower rate (Berlin et al., 2010). Involvement with the legal system can therefore intensify the challenges faced by TAY, particularly as society expects this age group to assume their adult roles and accept associated responsibilities at a disproportionate rate to which they are able.

Ironically, we deny young adults with a felony conviction the very resources that would reduce the likelihood of reoffending and that would facilitate healthy, prosocial reintegration with society. For example, finding quality employment is one of the strongest predictors of desistance from crime, but people with a felony conviction have severely limited access to stable employment (Agan & Starr, 2017; Sampson & Laub, 1995; Schmitt & Warner, 2010). Fortunately, there appears to be widespread bipartisan support for criminal justice reform to specifically address these harmful repercussions (U.S. Commission for Civil Rights, 2019, and several corporations have advanced job opportunities to individuals with felonies in adherence of the 2012 Equal Employment Opportunity Commission's guidance (U.S. Equal Employment Opportunity Commission, 2012). This push for legislative growth is likely a result of the approximately $65 billion in work output lost to limited employment opportunities (Schmitt & Warner, 2010).

Overall, while there is no question that those who commit crimes need to be held accountable, research has demonstrated that incarceration and harsh legal sanctions may worsen normative developmental challenges during the transition to adulthood, compounding the obstacles toward housing, health care, education, employment, and prosocial relationships. Thus, there is a great need for a new, developmentally appropriate approach to social justice for this vulnerable age group.

Narrowing the Gap: Diversion Programs for Transition-Age Youth

The stated goals of the criminal legal system attempt to balance the needs and interests of society with the rehabilitation and reform of the person who has committed the crime. To that end, courts often approach the administration of justice through either a punishment-oriented or rehabilitative lens. The punitive approach to justice seeks to punish a person and remove them from society through formal legal processing and incarceration. Conversely, the rehabilitative approach seeks to reduce recidivism by providing services and supports to address the underlying cause of criminal behavior. This social justice approach, also known as *informal processing or diversion*, has been both empirically and anecdotally validated as a highly successful and as the preferred method for reducing future crime among youth in the justice system (Cauffman et al., 2021).

Diversion programs are often specifically tailored to the population they serve. As such, diversion programs for adults, young adults, and adolescents may appear drastically different in their scope and implementation, and vary depending on the nature of the offense. For example, various drug courts seek to treat addiction as a public health concern rather than a criminal issue, and often provide counseling and addiction recovery support in lieu of incarceration. Mental health courts similarly dispense with formal adjudication and instead provide psychological or psychiatric services to those who have committed crimes and are impacted by mental illness and/or addiction. Given the punitive model permeating through the U.S. criminal legal system, it is not surprising that the courts have been even less forgiving of emerging adults compared to juveniles. Nonetheless, a paradigm shift is on the horizon. Most states now allow juvenile courts to continue exercising jurisdiction over adjudicated youth even after they turn 18 (Office of Juvenile Justice and Delinquency Prevention, 2019). Moreover, at least 28 states have implemented some policies that specifically address TAY within the adult legal system, such as young adult courts, diversion programs, reduced sentencing options, and separate jail and prison facilities (see Figure 22.3). However, most of the programs discussed subsequently—including the drug and mental health courts described previously—are limited to individuals who have no prior convictions or have committed low-level or nonviolent offenses. Thus, justice-involved TAY who do not meet these strict requirements may be denied

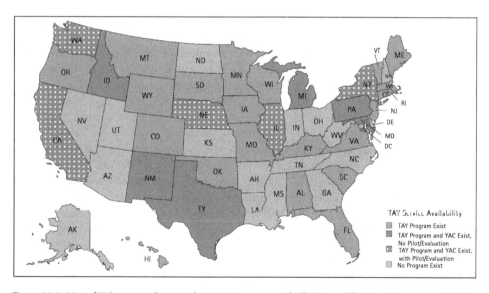

Figure 22.3 Map of U.S. states with criminal justice programs specifically designed for transition-age youth (TAY), including young adult courts (YACs), and states that include pilot programs and/or evaluations. Note: This figure was created in October 2021 and may not be a comprehensive list of policies nationwide, as laws consistently change. Furthermore, the criteria for policies vary widely from state to state, with some states applying program eligibility to those under the age of 25, and other states only applying them to those up to age 19.

access to rehabilitative programs that have been designed to specifically meet the distinct needs of young adults.

Diversion Program Typology

Diversion programs are often categorized based on the legal processing point at which they are implemented and can be conceptualized as such: prearrest, pretrial, posttrial, and correctional based. Although the latter two categories indicate that interventions are provided *after* one has been adjudicated, these can still be understood as diversion programs—they aim to divert youth from jail or prison, thus altering life-course-persistent trajectories of criminal behavior.

Prearrest programs seek to provide services and supports to at-risk individuals before a crime has been committed, to reduce the incidence of criminal activity in a certain geographic area or among a certain age cohort. Other variations include interventions that occur before a crime has been adjudicated. One example of a prearrest program aimed at those over 18 years of age was implemented in Pinellas County, Florida, which granted law enforcement the ability to give out "notice of referrals" in lieu of arrests. In this program, judges are able to divert individuals who committed certain misdemeanor offenses so as to avoid creating or adding to a felony criminal record. The program can be repeated up to three times if individuals do not have a misdemeanor conviction in the previous 2 years or a felony conviction in the previous 5 years, and the program involves completing community service hours to avoid filing charges (Russo, Pelletier, & Sullivan, 2016).

Pretrial programs (sometimes referred to as postarrest diversion programs) intervene after a crime has been committed and a person has been charged, but before sentencing occurs. Justice-involved TAY receive individualized support through specialized services, and upon successful completion of these programs, charges are often either reduced or dropped entirely. One example of a pretrial/postarrest diversion program is the Eastern District of New York Special Options Services (U.S. Pretrial Services Agency—Eastern District of New York, 2000), which provides TAY defendants with services and skills training on topics such as parenting, anger and stress management, and health care. Youth who successfully complete the program are eligible to have their charges reduced or dismissed.

Posttrial diversion programs seek to provide avenues for expunging a criminal record for those who have already completed a sentence. The Intensive Supervision Service in Columbia, South Carolina, best exemplifies this type of diversion: youth aged 17–25 who are sentenced under the Youthful Offender Act (Youthful Offender Act, SC, 2016) who have no previous convictions can apply for record expungement of their nonviolent offenses if they have no additional convictions in the 5 years after they complete their sentence. Moreover, the South Carolina Department of Corrections created the Division of Young Offender Parole and Reentry Services under the Youthful Offender Act, which oversees institution- and community-based services for TAY (South Carolina Department of Corrections, 2007). In line with developmental science, the definition of what constitutes a youthful offender in South Carolina under the Youthful Offender Act was changed from younger than 17 to younger than 25 in 2010.

Finally, ***correctional-based programs*** provide services for those serving a sentence within a facility. Successful completion of such programs, which include developmentally appropriate services, often results in additional facility privileges and/or reduced sentence time. Although it is more common for facilities to reserve one specialized housing unit to young adults, such as Mountain View's highly structured TAY prison program in Maine (Maine Department of Corrections, 2014), other states have adopted a facility-wide approach. For example, Pennsylvania's State Correctional Institute—Pine Grove is a facility that is entirely dedicated to their Young Adult Offender Program, which, according to their website, is managed "as a therapeutic community providing this unique population the opportunity to mature in a nurturing environment" since 2001 (Pennsylvania Department of Corrections, 2001).

Diversion Outcome Research

The results of diversion programs have been widely studied, and positive outcomes from these interventions are well documented. The current body of literature focuses largely on the effectiveness of diversion for individuals under 18 years of age; diversion programs for TAY are as of yet understudied. Several general themes emerge from these juvenile investigations, which could feasibly be applied to emerging adults and are briefly included in this chapter:

1. Diversion is superior to formal processing for reducing reoffending.
2. The type and quality of diversion programs matter.
3. Racial disparities exist in both the access to and effectiveness of diversion programs

Diversion Versus Formal System Involvement. A meta-analysis of 45 published and unpublished articles on youth aged 12–18 who have low to moderate reoffending risk levels demonstrated that those who were diverted were significantly less likely to reoffend than those processed through formal legal channels (Wilson & Hoge, 2013). Specifically, recidivism rates for youth involved in a diversion program were about 32%, whereas formally processed youth recidivated at about 41%. These findings persisted regardless of the type of diversion program (caution programs, warnings, structured treatment, and services).

Another meta-analysis included 29 studies that either randomized or quasi-randomized youth aged 17 and under to different legal system interventions and found that formal processing was *never* related to better youth outcomes or crime deterrence, based on aggregate effect sizes (Petrosino et al., 2010). In fact, formal legal processing was generally related to higher rates of recidivism than diversion with services or community release.

Finally, a landmark quasi-experimental study of over 1,200 male youth demonstrated that 13-17 year old boys who were diverted were less likely than those formally processed to be rearrested, to be incarcerated, engage in aggressive and/or violent offending, and affiliate with delinquent peers up to 5 years after a first arrest (Cauffman et al., 2021). Again, formal processing was never related to better outcomes in any of the tested domains throughout young adulthood. Although juvenile-based diversion outcomes are encouraging, it is clear that significantly more longitudinal and robust research is needed to investigate the impact of diversion programs geared toward TAY who are initially diverted between age 18 and the mid-20s.

Type and Quality of Diversion Programs. The most promising diversion programs for youth often involve a psychotherapy or family skills-building component and/or focus on restorative justice (i.e., repairing harm caused by crime by taking responsibility and through various methods of victim outreach and community service). No matter how well designed, the success of any diversion program hinges on appropriate implementation, including provider adherence to treatment protocols and youth engagement toward completion. For example, juveniles aged 12–17 years enrolled in drug court who completed multisystemic therapy showed significant reductions in behavior problems and alcohol use over time, but only when their therapists were highly adherent to the treatment principles, which incorporate ecologically valid components and family engagement (Gillespie et al., 2017). Additionally, diverted youth aged 13–17 assigned to receive functional family therapy (FFT) had fewer adjudicated felony offenses in the year posttreatment compared to youth processed through the traditional legal route *only if* the therapist adhered to treatment protocols; youth whose therapists were nonadherent were more likely to recidivate (Sexton & Turner, 2010). Another study demonstrated that FFT diversion reduced recidivism among youth 18–19 years old *only if* the program was fully completed; starting the program but not finishing it was not related to any reduction in recidivism (Kretschmar et al., 2018).

Racial Disparities in Diversion Research. Unfortunately, youth of color are less likely to be diverted compared to White youth, and even when youth of color are diverted, those intervention programs are rarely designed to be culturally competent. A study of several police departments assessing the likelihood that officers would choose to divert eligible youth aged 10–17 found race-based mediation effects with respect to the defendant. Generally, police departments chose to charge (rather than divert) most eligible youth encountered. Notably, a smaller proportion of youth of color eligible for diversion were actually diverted by police (37%), compared to eligible White youth who were diverted (45%; Ericson & Eckberg, 2016). This study also examined prosecutorial discretion in diversion and charging decisions—prosecutors diverted only 25% of eligible cases and were more likely to charge youth of color and divert White youth in theft-related offenses.

Even among youth of color who are diverted, successes may be diminished due to the nature of the program. A meta-analysis of 21 studies found that diversion programs for youth aged 12–18 were less effective for youth of color, highlighting the well-established racial disparities in overpolicing and repeat police contact (Gelman et al., 2007; Wong et al., 2016). Researchers have also found that a lack of cultural competency among FFT therapists, specifically, may have contributed to low success rates for youth of color aged 18–19 participating in these diversion programs (Kretschmar et al., 2018).

Positive Life Outcomes. In addition to deterring future offending, diversion programs report positive life outcomes for participants as well. According to Cauffman and colleagues (2021), young adults aged 18–22 who participated in a diversion program were more likely to be enrolled in school, graduate from high school or equivalent, and have higher perceptions of opportunities than formally processed youth.

Most diversion effectiveness literature encompasses an age-heterogenous sample of juvenile and young adult populations, and thus there is a dearth of information on diversion programs for TAY. Even still, several themes from the juvenile diversion literature likely apply to diversion success for emerging adults as well—such as the importance of well-designed and well-implemented treatment programs that address salient racial/cultural intervention factors. Future research in this area should focus on the TAY population, as the unique needs of this age group (e.g., providing employment and career assistance, parenting programs) may require nuances within diversion programs to ensure their success.

Current Transition-Age Youth Diversion Programs in the United States

Several diversion programs for TAY exist in the United States, with several more in the early implementation stages. Table 22.1 provides an overview of select operational programs and includes eligibility criteria and points of intervention. Up-to-date, comprehensive lists of programs are beyond the scope of the present chapter and may be found elsewhere (e.g., Stein et al., 2017; U.S. District Court: Eastern District of New York, 2015).

Current Limitations of Diversion Programs

Pre- and posttrial diversion programs such as those detailed previously are not available to TAY defendants in all jurisdictions. Even where such programs are provided, eligibility criteria and age cut-offs vary widely. Moreover, the point of intervention varies among such programs; some are designed to adjust sentencing decisions for young adults, while

Table 22.1 Select Operational Transition-Age Youth Diversion Programs in the United States (by Diversion Typology and by Date Founded)

Name	Location	Founded	Eligibility Criteria	Ages
Prearrest Interventions				
Pinellas Adult Pre-Arrest Diversion (APAD) Program	Pinellas County, FL	2016	No prior misdemeanor conviction in the past 2 years, no prior felony conviction in the past 5 years. Must not have gone through program in the past 3 months or have gone through the program more than three times. Select offenses only	18+
Pretrial/Postarrest Interventions				
Youthful Offender Program*	Polk County, IA	1995	First-time felony offenders without gang involvement	16–22
Special Options Services[a]	Eastern District, NY	2000	Nonviolent offenses only, limited criminal history with no prior violent offenses	18–24
Deferred Sentencing Program	U.S. District Court, RI	2015	Case-by-case basis; nonviolent offenses only	"Youthful Offenders"
Young Adult Opportunity Program[a]	Southern District, NY	2015–2017	Limited criminal history; no prior charges or convictions of violent crime, firearm or sex offenses, crimes against children; no other pending cases or warrants	18–25
PATH Program[a]	Long Beach, CA	2016	Minor offenses only	16–24
Achieve Inspire Motivate (AIM) Court	Dallas County, TX	2016	Nonviolent felony charges only, no prior convictions or probations	17–24
Posttrial Interventions				
San Francisco TAY Unit	San Francisco, CA	2009	Must be indicated as "high at risk or in risk" and reside in neighborhoods designated by police as "hot zones"	18–25
CHOICE	Boston, MA	2010	Available to those on administrative and supervised probation only	18–26
Intensive Supervision Service[a]	Columbia, SC	2011–2012	No prior convictions; nonviolent, Class D felonies or lesser only	<25

(*continued*)

Table 22.1 Continued

Name	Location	Founded	Eligibility Criteria	Ages
Sentencing Planner Program[a]	San Francisco, CA	2012	N/A—sentencing planners make recommendations on a case-by-case basis	18–25
RETHINK Program	Santa Rosa, CA	2012	Misdemeanors and some low-level felony offenses only	18–25
Young Adult Initiative	District of Columbia	2013	Individuals in transitional housing unit and sex offender unit are not eligible	<25
Justice Reinvestment Program	Multnomah County, OR	2014	Those who face a presumptive prison sentence	18–25
Young Adult Justice Initiative	Brooklyn, NY	2016	Misdemeanor offenses only	16–24
Hennepin County TAY Unit[a]	Hennepin County, MN	2021	Currently targets those on probation	18–21
Correctional-Based Interventions				
Young Adult Offender Program, Pennsylvania State Correctional Institution—Pine Grove[b]	Indiana, PA	2001	Those that committed murder, attempted murder, rape, robbery, kidnapping, involuntary deviate sexual intercourse, and aggravated assault between the ages of 15 and 17 years old charged as adults	<21
Mountain View Young Adult Offender Program	Charleston, ME	2014	Prisoners classified as minimum, medium, or community custody, who committed first-time offense in the adult prison system. Must indicate moderate, high, or maximum risk/needs, and have between 9 months and 5 years of sentence remaining	18–25
Pine Hills Youth Correctional Facility[a]	Miles City, MT	2016	Male, low to medium risk TAY only. No history of violent or sexual crimes	18–25
Transitional-Age Youth (TAY) Housing Module; Road to Reentry Study[a]	Orange County, CA	2021	Male, low to medium risk TAY	18–25

[a] Indicates an intervention that included a pilot or formal evaluation component, to the best of our knowledge.

[b] https://pappc.org/docs/vol-62%20no-1.pdf

others provide pathways to reduced or dismissed charges, and fewer still aim to prevent the onset of offending (prearrest) or reoffending after incarceration (reentry programs). Finally, the availability of postrelease reentry programs for TAY is scarce, but key examples might provide guidelines for novel program implementation. For example, the Youthful Offender System within the Colorado Department of Corrections provides orientation, prerelease education, and postrelease supervision services for young adults up to age 19 who are preparing to complete their sentence (Colorado Department of Corrections, 2021). Though this program does not provide services encompassing the broad TAY age range, it is a promising start to reentry programs for young adults. Overall, there is little consistency within diversion programs for TAY, and the success and outcomes of these programs are largely unknown.

Specialized Transition-Age Youth Diversion: The Young Adult Court

One unique form of diversion for TAY is the young adult court (YAC), a specialized judicial entity designed solely to process those between the ages of 18 and 25. It exists separately from juvenile court; its defendants are typically over the age of 18 and would otherwise be processed in the formal adult criminal legal system.

Mission, Aims, and Purpose. Like other uniquely designed collaborative courts, YACs exist to serve TAY—a neurodevelopmentally distinct subpopulation. YACs bridge accountability with opportunity as they encourage the reduction of criminal behavior while simultaneously promoting the successful transition to adulthood. By acknowledging the developmental and prevention science that surrounds the continuing development of TAY, these courts balance accountability with service provision to avoid the long-term social damage associated with punitive sanctioning. This is accomplished via dedicated judges, close partnerships with other legal and community stakeholders, and frequent, supportive contact with defendants.

Common Components. YACs typically assess the reoffending risk for each defendant and provide case management services and treatment options that address the needs of each individual. Similar to other specialty courts, common services include intensive case management, drug monitoring, referrals for substance use treatment, counseling and therapy services, life skills training, housing support, and academic support, in addition to probation and court supervision. Upon successful conclusion of the program, the court will often reduce or dismiss the felony charge that prompted court entry. This is key, as it allows those who successfully complete the court program to avoid the stigmatization and diminished ability for societal engagement that are associated with being labeled a felon. Avoiding this permanent marker affords young adults unfettered access to employment and educational opportunities.

Current Young Adult Courts in the United States

Several YACs are currently operational in the United States; a selection of these courts is presented in Table 22.2. In 2016, an analysis of legal responses to young adult offending found that YACs represented only six of the 56 types of operational programs for TAY (Hayek, 2016). Although several additional courts emerged in the years since the 2016 report, these courts remain uncommon, and most YAC program outcomes are anecdotal. Additionally, the YAC concept is not limited to the United States—a handful of such programs exist internationally as well. Two notable examples are the Young Adult Court of Porirua, New Zealand, and the Manchester Youth Justice service operating within the Manchester and Salford Magistrates Court in Greater Manchester, United Kingdom.

Table 22.2 Operational Young Adult Courts in the United States (by Foundation Date)

Location	Founded	Eligibility	Ages
Douglas County, NE[a]	2004	Must plead guilty to a felony and agree to restitution	18–24
Lockport City, NY	2009	Nonviolent, low-level offenses only	16–21
Bonneville County, ID	2012	Felony or misdemeanor charges referred by the drug court	18–24
Kalamazoo County, MI	2013	First-time misdemeanor youth sentenced to probation	17–20
King County, WA[b]	2014	Drug-related cases only (a young adult subsidiary of the King County Drug Court)	18–25
San Francisco County, CA[a]	2015	Prioritizes serious misdemeanors and felonies. Excludes some driving under the influence, gang affiliation, domestic violence, sex offense, and gun-related charges	18–24
Brooklyn, NY[a]	2016	Misdemeanor offenses only. Domestic violence, sex crimes, and driving while intoxicated charges are deemed ineligible	16–24
Midtown Manhattan, NY[a]	2016	Misdemeanor offenses only	18–20
Delaware County, PA[c]	2016	Young adults charged with a first-time felony marijuana drug offense	18–25
Dallas County, TX	2016	Misdemeanors and select felonies only	17–25
Cook County, IL[a]	2017	Nonviolent misdemeanors and felonies only	18–26
Bernalillo County, NM	2017	Arrested in Bernalillo County, facing criminal charges, exhibit need for specialty services and treatment	18–25
Orange County, CA[a]	2018	Males; first-time felony offenses for nonviolent crimes	18–25
Prince Frederick, MD	2021	No prior felony criminal record, minor offenses only. Excludes violent offenses, driving under the influence, firearms violations, and domestic offenses	18–25

[a] Indicates an intervention that included a pilot or formal evaluation component, to the best of our knowledge.

[b] https://kingcounty.gov/~/media/courts/Clerk/drugCourt/documents/Young-Adult-Track-Guidelines.ashx?la=en

[c] https://delcopa.gov/courts/specialtycourts/youngoffendercourt.html

Limitations of Current Young Adult Court Implementation

As demonstrated, YACs exhibit relatively poor adoption across the United States (see Figure 22.3 for U.S. map), and the few that do exist are vastly disparate in terms of eligibility criteria, age range, and program features. As a result, it is very difficult to benchmark the success of these programs in general—most rely on anecdotal evidence to tout their success (or failure), and therefore outcomes have yet to be rigorously studied, and longitudinal data is largely nonexistent. However, an effort to robustly research the outcomes of a YAC is currently underway in Orange County, California. Specifically, the present authors and researchers from the University of California, Irvine are conducting a randomized controlled trial of the Orange County Young Adult Court (OC YAC: https://www.occourts.org/directory/collaborative-courts) to determine potential differences in outcomes among those who are randomly assigned to participate in the court versus those participating in "treatment as usual" who are processed as they typically would be through the legal system. Young adults who plead in through the OC YAC are provided intensive case management services that provide youth health and wellness, life skills and employment, housing, and education. Youth are also supervised by a probation officer trained in the developmental framework underlying TAY behavior and motivations. The informational brochure provided to attorneys and potential clients is provided in Figure 22.4.

Collaboration

The court is overwhelmingly collaborative, involving a diverse group of agencies such as the superior court; the Orange County District Attorney's Office, Public Defender's Office, Alternate Defender's Office, and Probation Department; various health care agencies; the Orangewood Foundation and Community Action Partnership of Orange County; and several other community providers.

Referrals for potentially eligible cases are submitted to the OC YAC team (i.e., judge, defense attorney, case manager, probation officer, and deputy district attorney) from respective agencies in Orange County. Defendants are then deemed eligible or ineligible per the legal criteria outlined by the court and clients are found suitable or not suitable via social worker assessments (e.g., have sufficient motivation to engage in the program as described to them, adequate cognitive capacity to benefit from services). For example, if a client is found to suffer from significant mental health problems (e.g., schizophrenia) and/or severe addiction, these TAY may be referred to more appropriate collaborative courts suiting their needs and abilities. Participants enter a guilty plea for the crime with which they are charged, and they meet with the YAC OC presiding judge, district attorney, and their lawyer to create an individualized action plan for progressing through the court.

The YAC team collaborates approximately every other week during case conferencing prior to court and discusses the youth's identified goals and related improvements and treatment barriers. In the subsequent court meeting, the judge provides commensurate rewards (e.g., public verbal praise and encouragement, certificates) and appropriate sanctions (e.g., GPS monitoring, increased supervision, mandatory addiction recovery courses) all aiming to redirect the youth toward success. Exemplifying the collaborative nature of this program, the judge consults with the treatment team and developmental researchers on how to best approach a youth struggling to meet their goal and balances punitive and reward-based approaches to optimally motivate the youth.

Participants advance through four incentivized, graduated levels of the program, which incrementally move TAY toward addressing criminogenic, educational, employment, and housing needs while rewarding success and implementing the aforementioned corrective measures when necessary. Figure 22.5 represents the four program phases presented to participants in their orientation handbook. Youth and case managers collaborate to complete "phase-up petitions" whereby achievements, barriers, and goals are outlined. Using developmentally appropriate scaffolding approaches, youth are guided to first start by identifying realistic steps (Phase 1) and gradually expand to exhibiting future orientation (e.g., "Some challenges or difficulties I might encounter in Phase 4 are . . . and I will deal with them by . . ."). After completion of the four phases of the program, the youth is recommended for graduation, at

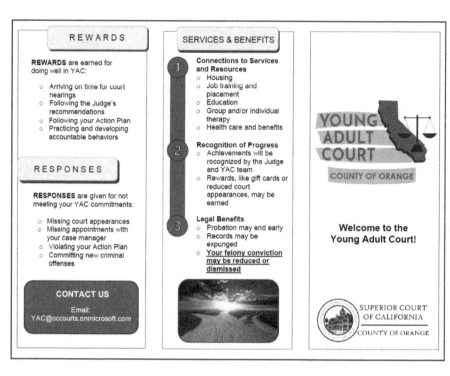

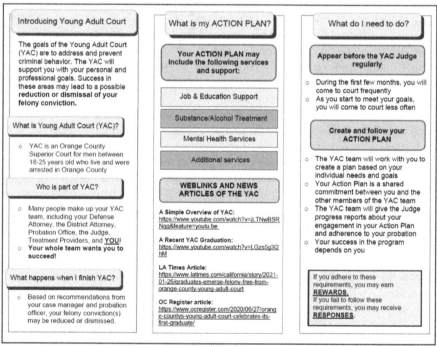

Figure 22.4 Young Adult Court of Orange County informational brochure.

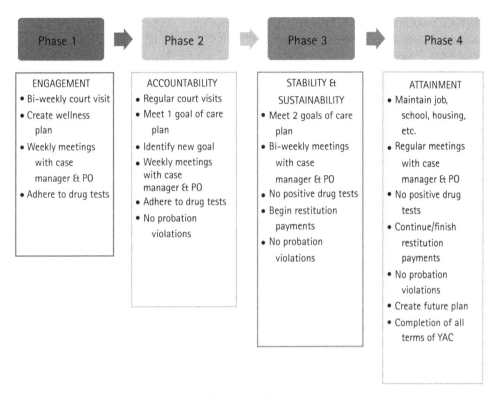

Figure 22.5 Four phases of the Orange County Young Adult Court Program.

which time the initial felony charge is dismissed or reduced to a misdemeanor by the presiding judge, rendering them felony conviction free. Youth are required to remain in the program for a minimum of 18 months to be considered for graduation. The entire process involves considerable scaffolding, with the goal of empowering each TAY to be self-sufficient and productive members of society through a collaborative framework. For example, one youth graduating from the program may have 3 consecutive months of negative drug tests; attended the majority of scheduled court dates and probation meetings; attained stable housing and employment; enrolled in educational/vocational courses; regularly attended counseling, addiction recovery groups, and/or medical appointments; successfully applied for financial assistance and maintained a personal budget, obtained a driver's license; and/or paid off any restitution owed to the courts.

While the findings from the University of California, Irvine study are not yet available, the randomized controlled trial of the YAC in Orange County is positioned to provide important data on how the criminal justice system can hold young adults accountable while providing resources that reduce recidivism and promote success at later ages. Additionally, this evaluation will represent the first rigorous empirical consideration of the impact of YACs in the country, which, as noted, is greatly needed. Specifically, the findings will provide an important start to identifying a lever for change in justice system policies that improve outcomes for young adults.

Policy Implications and Future Directions

Neuroscience and behavioral researchers have made great efforts to unfold and explain the many factors implicated in decision making—how, why, and when youth are vulnerable to risk taking, reward seeking, impulsivity, peer influences, and myriad underlying socioeconomic factors in relation to making day-to-day life choices. Despite these advances, the law has evidenced great difficulty in the management of young adults. For instance, U.S. Supreme Court Justice Antonin Scalia argued that researchers cannot have their cake and eat it too—we cannot advocate for youth to have decisions over their own bodies (e.g., abortion rights) and simultaneously state that they should not be held accountable under the death penalty for other decisions (e.g., criminal activity). Much work is still needed to bridge these gaps and advance scientific findings.

"Raise the Age" and Other Efforts

Although the current state of affairs on how the majority of jurisdictions process TAY through the legal system is counterproductive, several task forces have been created to address the developmental disparities noted in this chapter. "Raise the Age" efforts to expand the age at which youth are adjudicated through juvenile courts in New York, Connecticut, and Illinois have led to decreases in fiscal spending and rearrests for youth impacted by those legislations (Kenmore, 2019; Lindell & Goodjoint, 2020). These three states have now introduced bills to further raise the age of juvenile adjudication to 21. Youthful offender statutes, as previously mentioned, are growing increasingly common for TAY processed in the adult legal system, with states like New Jersey defining those aged 18–30 as warranting distinct treatment, and with South Carolina defining age at conviction rather than the more standard delineation of age at the time of the crime. Further, sentencing guidelines now overwhelmingly take into account TAY-based developmental science and consider age as a mitigating factor, and the American Bar Association supports death penalty bans for those under the age of 21 (Death Penalty Information Center, 2018). In 2017, California became the only state to grant parole eligibility to individuals serving life sentences who were 25 years old or younger at the time of their offense, thereby directly applying *Miller v. Alabama* to TAY (Cal. Penal Code § 3051).

Although robust research initiatives like the ones detailed for the OC YAC are scant, randomized controlled trials of diversion programs for TAY are emerging across the United States. For example, the Transformative Justice program is a pretrial diversion program for youth aged 17–24 charged with a first-time nonviolent felony offense and was established in 2019 (Lone Star Justice Alliance, 2021). Like the OC YAC, a randomized trial examines the impact of a multidisciplinary team approach to providing mental health, housing, and employment resources to young adults—research is still underway at Texas A&M University. Lastly, guidance on developing effective and scientifically grounded diversion programs for TAY was recently released by Mathematica Policy Research (Stein et al., 2017). Authors listed interdisciplinary collaboration, acquisition of funding, and program evaluation as essential components of youth diversion program development. As research becomes more applied and deliberately incorporates community-based collaborations that speak to service providers and lawmakers, the science-to-practice gap regarding TAY-based diversion will increasingly close.

The confluence of neurodevelopmental findings, the detrimental consequences of legal involvement on young adults, and the challenging sociopolitical climate in which TAY live evinces a clear need for policymakers, stakeholders, and researchers to collaboratively develop and expand upon innovative, developmentally based solutions for TAY. Young adults are empowered with considerable capacity to change, grow, improve, and learn (Cauffman & Steinberg, 2000; Steinberg, 2014). Shifting the legal lens toward a developmental approach takes time, collaboration, resources, and proof of efficacy. One way in which the field can move more quickly toward racial and developmental equity for youth involved in the justice system is for students to focus their research efforts toward rigorously investigating these topics. Many graduate programs have specific focus areas on youth development and the law, including those in the areas of psychology, public policy, neuroscience, criminology and law, social ecology, and human development, to name a few. Guidance on finding an appropriate program can be found nested within professional organizations, such as American Psychology–Law Society (https://www.apls-students.org and https://www.apadivisions.org/division-41/education/students)—Division 41 of the American Psychological Association (APA). The APA also compiles and maintains a list of developmental psychology graduate programs. In addition, the Society for Research on Adolescence is an excellent resource for discovering emerging research on topics of youth development in legal contexts (https://www.s-r-a.org). Lastly, we provide a list of important works published recently on these topics, which we highly recommend for those interested in furthering their knowledge base and deepening understanding of these concepts.

For the developmental science: Casey, B., Taylor-Thompson, K., Rubien-Thomas, E., Robbins, M., & Baskin-Sommers, A. (2020). Healthy development as a human right: Insights from developmental neuroscience for youth justice. *Annual Review of Law and Social Science*, *16*, 203–222.

For an overview of the Supreme Court cases impacting youth: McDonald, S. (2018). *The influence of brain development research on the response to young adult males 18–24 years of age in the criminal justice system* (Publication No. 19 163-DOC-01). Massachusetts Department of Corrections. https://www.mass.gov/doc/the-influence-of-brain-development-research-on-the-responseto-young-adult-males/download

For description of emerging programs for justice-involved TAY: Lindell, K., & Goodjoint, K. (2020). *Rethinking justice for emerging adults: Spotlight on the Great Lakes region*. https://jlc.org/sites/default/files/attachments/2020-09/JLC-Emerging-Adults-9-2.pdf

For guidance on developing young adult diversion programs: Stein, J., Bodenlos, K., Yanez, A., Lacoe, J., & Berk, J. (2017). *Detour to opportunity: A guide on young adult diversion from the criminal justice system*. https://wdr.doleta.gov/research/FullText_Documents/Detour%20to%20Opportunity%20-%20A%20Guide%20on%20Young%20Adult%20Diversion%20from%20the%20Criminal%20Justice%20System.pdf

References

Abolitionist Law Center. (2019). *The fight to free Avis Lee continues despite the denial of appeal by the Pennsylvania Supreme Court*. https://abolitionistlawcenter.org/tag/avis-lee/

Agan, A., & Starr, S. (2017). The effect of criminal records on access to employment. *American Economic Review*, *107*(5), 560–564.

Antenangeli, L., & Durose, M. R. (2021). *Recidivism of prisoners released in 24 states in 2008: A 10-year follow-up period (2008–2018)*. US Department of Justice, Office of Justice Programs, Bureau of Justice Statistics.

Axelrod, T. (2015). Youngest children ever to be tried as adults for 1st-degree murder to be released soon. *ABC News*. Retrieved July 23, 2021, from *https://abcnews.go.com/US/youngest-children-adults-1st-degree-murder-released/story?id=32644967*

Augustyn, M. B., & Loughran, T. A. (2017). Juvenile waiver as a mechanism of social stratification: A focus on human capital. *Criminology*, *55*(2), 405–437.

Bailey, M., Crew, E., & Reeve, M. (2020). *No access to justice: Breaking the cycle of homelessness and jail*. Vera Institute of Justice. https://www.vera.org/downloads/publications/no-access-to-justice.pdf

Berlin, G., Furstenberg F, Jr., & Waters, M. C. (2010). The transition to adulthood: introducing the issue. *The Future of Children*, *20*(1), 3–18.

Berson, S. B. (2013). Beyond the sentence-understanding collateral consequences. *National Institute of Justice Journal*, *272*, 25–28.

Bureau of Justice Statistics. (2019). *Number of sentenced state and federal prisoners per 100,000 U.S. residents of corresponding sex, race, Hispanic origin, and age groups, December 31, 2018*. Princeton University.

Carson, E. A., & Golinelli, D. (2013). *Prisoners in 2012: Trends in admissions and releases, 1991–2012*. Bureau of Justice Statistics.

Casey, B. J., Taylor-Thompson, K., Rubien Thomas, E., Robbins, M., & Baskin-Sommers, A. (2020). Healthy development as a human right: Insights from developmental neuroscience for youth justice. *Annual Review of Law and Social Science, 16,* 203–222.

Cauffman, E., Beardslee, J., Fine, A., Frick, P. J., & Steinberg, L. (2021). Crossroads in juvenile justice: The impact of initial processing decision on youth 5 years after first arrest. *Development and Psychopathology, 33*(2), 700–713.

Cauffman, E., Fine, A., Mahler, A., & Simmons, C. (2018). How developmental science influences juvenile justice reform. *UC Irvine Law Review, 8,* 21.

Cauffman, E., Shulman, E. P., Steinberg, L., Claus, E., Banich, M. T., Graham, S., & Woolard, J. (2010). Age differences in affective decision making as indexed by performance on the Iowa Gambling Task. *Developmental Psychology, 46*(1), 193.

Cauffman, E., & Steinberg, L. (2000). (Im)maturity of judgment in adolescence: Why adolescents may be less culpable than adults. *Behavioral Sciences & the Law, 18*(6), 741–760.

Cauffman, E., & Steinberg, L. (2012). Emerging findings from research on adolescent development and juvenile justice. *Victims & Offenders, 7*(4), 428–449.

Center for Behavioral Health Statistics and Quality. (2019). *National Survey on Drug Use and Health: 2018 public use file and codebook*. https://www.samhsa.gov/data/sites/default/files/reports/rpt29395/2019NSDUHMethodsSummDefs/2019NSDUHMethodsSummDefs082120.htm

Chesney-Lind, M., & Mauer, M. (Eds.). (2003). *Invisible punishment: The collateral consequences of mass imprisonment*. New Press.

Chung, J. (2021). *Voting rights in the era of mass incarceration: A primer*. The Sentencing Project, 28. https://www.sentencingproject.org/publications/felony-disenfranchisement-a-primer/

Cohen, A. O., Breiner, K., Steinberg, L., Bonnie, R. J., Scott, E. S., Taylor-Thompson, K., Rudolph, M. D., Chein, J., Richeson, J. A., Heller, A. S., Silverman, M. R., Dellarco, D. V., Fair, D. A., Galván, A., & Casey, B. J. (2016). When is an adolescent an adult? Assessing cognitive control in emotional and nonemotional contexts. *Psychological Science, 27*(4), 549–562.

United States Commission on Civil Rights (2019). *Collateral consequences: The crossroads of punishment, redemption, and the effects on communities*. Briefing report. Washington, DC: Author. Retrieved from https://www.usccr.gov/files/pubs/2019/06-13-Collateral-Consequences.pdf

Colorado Department of Corrections. (2021). *Youthful Offender System*. https://cdoc.colorado.gov/facilities/pueblo-campus/youthful-offender-system

Davidow, J. Y., Foerde, K., Galván, A., & Shohamy, D. (2016). An upside to reward sensitivity: The hippocampus supports enhanced reinforcement learning in adolescence. *Neuron, 92*(1), 93–99.

Death Penalty Information Center. (2018). *American Bar Association resolution: Ban death penalty for offenders age 21 or younger*. https://deathpenaltyinfo.org/news/american-bar-association-resolution-ban-death-penalty-for-offenders-age-21-or-younger

Diamond, A. (2013). Executive functions. *Annual Review of Psychology, 64,* 135–168.

Ericson, R. D., & Eckberg, D. A. (2016). Racial disparity in juvenile diversion: The impact of focal concerns and organizational coupling. *Race and Justice, 6*(1), 35–56.

Fagan, J., & Freeman, R. B. (1999). Crime and work. *Crime and Justice, 25,* 225–290.

Fair and Just Prosecution. (2019). *Juvenile and young adult issues*. https://fairandjustprosecution.org/issues/juvenile-and-young-adult-issues/

Feld, B. C. (2017). *The evolution of the juvenile court*. New York University Press.

Fine, A., Cavanagh, C., Donley, S., Frick, P. J., Steinberg, L., & Cauffman, E. (2017). Is the effect of justice system attitudes on recidivism stable after youths' first arrest? Race and legal socialization among first-time youth offenders. *Law and Human Behavior, 41*(2), 146.

Finley, M., & Schindler, M. (1999). Punitive juvenile justice policies and the impact on minority youth. *Federal Probation, 63,* 11.

Frankenhuis, W. E., & Walasek, N. (2020). Modeling the evolution of sensitive periods. *Developmental Cognitive Neuroscience, 41,* 100715.

Gaston, S. (2016). The long-term effects of parental incarceration: Does parental incarceration in childhood or adolescence predict depressive symptoms in adulthood? *Criminal Justice and Behavior, 43*(8), 1056–1075.

Gelman, A., Fagan, J., & Kiss, A. (2007). An analysis of the New York City police department's "stop-and-frisk" policy in the context of claims of racial bias. *Journal of the American Statistical Association, 102*(479), 813–823.

Gillespie, M. L., Huey, S. J., Jr., & Cunningham, P. B. (2017). Predictive validity of an observer-rated adherence protocol for multisystemic therapy with juvenile drug offenders. *Journal of Substance Abuse Treatment, 76*, 1–10.

Goldman, B., Cooper, D., & Kugler, T. (2019). Crime and punishment: A realistic group conflict approach to racial discrimination in hiring convicted felons. *International Journal of Conflict Management, 30*(1), 2-23.

Gramlich, J. (2018). *The gap between the number of blacks and whites in prison is shrinking.* Pew Research Center.

Hayek, C. (2016). *Environmental scan of developmentally appropriate criminal justice responses to justice-involved young adults.* National Institute of Justice.

Heerde, J. A., Bailey, J. A., Toumbourou, J. W., Rowland, B., & Catalano, R. F. (2021). Adolescent antecedents of young adult homelessness: A cross-national path analysis. *Prevention Science, 23*(1), 85-95.

Hjalmarsson, R. (2009). Crime and expected punishment: Changes in perceptions at the age of criminal majority. *American Law and Economics Review, 11*(1), 209–248.

Icenogle, G., Steinberg, L., Duell, N., Chein, J., Chang, L., Chaudhary, N., Di Giunta, L., Dodge, K. A., Fanti, K. A., & Lansford, J. E. (2019). Adolescents' cognitive capacity reaches adult levels prior to their psychosocial maturity: Evidence for a "maturity gap" in a multinational, cross-sectional sample. *Law and Human Behavior, 43*(1), 69.

Institute of Medicine & National Research Council. (2015). *Investing in the health and well-being of young adults.*

Jenkins, E. D. (2017). Adjudicating the young adult: Could specialized courts provide superior treatment to this emerging classification? *Howard Law Journal, 61*, 455.

Justice Policy Institute. (2016). *Improving approaches to serving young adults in the justice system.* https://justicepolicy.org/wp-content/uploads/justicepolicy/documents/jpi_young_adults_final.pdf

Kann, L., McManus, T., Harris, W. A., Shanklin, S. L., Flint, K. H., Queen, B., Lowry, R., Chyen, D., Whittle, L., Thornton, J., Lim, C., Bradford, D., Yamakawa, Y., Leon, M., Brener, N., & Ethier, K. A. (2018). Youth risk behavior surveillance—United States, 2017. *MMWR Surveillance Summaries, 67*(8), 1–114.

Kenmore, A. (2019). *As New York raises the age, youth arrests fall.* The Imprint. https://imprintnews.org/featured/new-york-raises-age-youth-arrests-fall/36630

Kretschmar, J. M., Tossone, K., Butcher, F., & Marsh, B. (2018). Examining the impact of a juvenile justice diversion program for youth with behavioral health concerns on early adulthood recidivism. *Children and Youth Services Review, 91*, 168–176.

Lai, J. (2013, April 23). *Old enough to vote, old enough to smoke?* Slate. https://slate.com/news-and-politics/2013/04/new-york-minimum-smoking-age-why-are-young-people-considered-adults-at-18.html

Lantz, B. (2020). Co-offending group composition and violence: The impact of sex, age, and group size on co-offending violence. *Crime & Delinquency, 66*(1), 93–122.

Lindell, K., & Goodjoint, K. (2020). *Rethinking justice for emerging adults: Spotlight on the Great Lakes region.* Juvenile Law Center. https://jlc.org/sites/default/files/attachments/2020-09/JLC-Emerging-Adults-9-2.pdf

Lone Star Justice Alliance. (2021). *Transformative justice.* https://www.lonestarjusticealliance.org/transformative-justice.html

Love, M. C., Roberts, J., & Klingele, C. M. (2013). Collateral consequences of criminal convictions: Law, policy and practice. Thompson Reuters Westlaw/NACDL Press, American University, WCL Research Paper No. 2014-48.

Maine Department of Corrections (2014). *Mountain View Young Adult Offender Program.* https://www.law.umich.edu/special/policyclearinghouse/Documents/Maine%20Mountain%20View%20Young%20Adult%20Handbook.pdf

Maruschak, L. M., Bronson, J., & Alper, M. (2021). *Parents in prison and their minor children.* Bureau of Justice Statistics.

McCarthy, B., & Hagan, J. (1992). Mean streets: The theoretical significance of situational delinquency among homeless youths. *American Journal of Sociology, 98*(3), 597–627.

McFarland, J., Hussar, B., De Brey, C., Snyder, T., Wang, X., Wilkinson-Flicker, S., Gebrekristos, S., Zhang, J., Rathbun, A., & Barmer, A. (2017). *The condition of education 2017* (NCES 2017-144). National Center for Education Statistics.

Melamed, S. (2021). "They don't deserve to die in prison": Gov. Wolf grants clemency to 13 lifers. *Philadelphia Inquirer.* https://www.inquirer.com/news/commutation-pennsylvania-gov-wolf-fetterman-board-pardons-evans-horton-brothers-20210211.html

Miller v. Alabama, 132 S. Ct. 2455 (2012).

Montgomery v. Louisiana, 577 U.S., 14-280 (2016).

Morgan, R., & Truman, J. (2020). *Criminal victimization, 2019.* U.S. Department of Justice, Office of Justice Programs, Bureau of Justice Statistics.

O'Grady, B., & Gaetz, S. (2004). Homelessness, gender and subsistence: The case of Toronto street youth. *Journal of Youth Studies, 7*(4), 397–416.

Office of Juvenile Justice and Delinquency Prevention. (2019). *Juvenile justice system structure & process: Jurisdictional boundaries*. https://www.ojjdp.gov/ojstatbb/structure_process/qa04106.asp

OJJDP Statistical Briefing Book. (2019). *Estimated number of arrests by offense and age group, 2019*. https://www.ojjdp.gov/ojstatbb/crime/ucr.asp?table_in=1

Pager, D. (2003). The mark of a criminal record. *American Journal of Sociology, 108*(5), 937–975.

Pennsylvania Department of Corrections. (2001). *SCI Pine Grove*. https://www.cor.pa.gov/Facilities/StatePrisons/Pages/Pine-Grove.aspx

Perker, S. S., & Chester, L. (2018). *Combating the crisis: Using justice reform to address the drug epidemic among emerging adults* (Emerging Adult Justice in Massachusetts). Columbia University Justice Lab. https://justicelab.columbia.edu/sites/default/files/content/CombatingTheCrisis.pdf

Perker, S. S., & Chester, L. E. (2021). The justice system and young adults with substance use disorders. *Pediatrics, 147*(Suppl 2), S249–S258.

Persons not qualified, 10 U.S.C. § 504 (2010).

Petrosino, A., Turpin-Petrosino, C., & Guckenburg, S. (2010). Formal system processing of juveniles: Effects on delinquency. *Campbell Systematic Reviews, 6*(1), 1–88.

Pettit, B., & Gutierrez, C. (2018). Mass incarceration and racial inequality. *American Journal of Economics and Sociology, 77*(3–4), 1153–1182.

Qualifications for jury service, 28 U.S.C. § 1865(b)(5) (2018).

Robles-Ramamurthy, B., & Watson, C. (2019). Examining racial disparities in juvenile justice. *Journal of the American Academy of Psychiatry and the Law, 47*(1), 48–52.

Roper v. Simmons, 543 U.S. 551 (2005).

Rowan, Z. R., Kan, E., Frick, P. J., & Cauffman, E. (2021). Not (entirely) guilty: The role of co-offenders in diffusing responsibility for crime. *Journal of Research in Crime and Delinquency, 59*(4), 415–448.

Law Offices of Russo, Pelletier, & Sullivan. (2016). *The Pinellas Adult Pre-Arrest Diversion (APAD) program*.

Sampson, R. J., & Laub, J. H. (1995). *Crime in the making: Pathways and turning points through life*. Harvard University Press.

Schmitt, J., & Warner, K. (2010). *Ex-offenders and the labor market*. Center for Economic and Policy Research. https://cepr.net/documents/publications/ex-offenders-2010-11.pdf

Sexton, T., & Turner, C. W. (2010). The effectiveness of functional family therapy for youth with behavioral problems in a community practice setting. *Journal of Family Psychology, 24*(3), 339–348.

Shaw, M. (2016). The racial implications of the effects of parental incarceration on intergenerational mobility. *Sociology Compass, 10*(12), 1102–1109.

Shulman, E. P., Smith, A. R., Silva, K., Icenogle, G., Duell, N., Chein, J., & Steinberg, L. (2016). The dual systems model: Review, reappraisal, and reaffirmation. *Developmental Cognitive Neuroscience, 17*, 103–117.

Simmonds, D. J., Hallquist, M. N., & Luna, B. (2017). Protracted development of executive and mnemonic brain systems underlying working memory in adolescence: A longitudinal fMRI study. *Neuroimage, 157*, 695–704.

South Carolina Department of Corrections. (2007). *Young offender parole & reentry services*. http://doc.sc.gov/programs/yoprs.html#:~:text=The%20Division%20of%20Young%20Offender%20Parole%20and%20Reentry,of%20conviction%20and%20have%20no%20previous%20YOA%20convictions.

Stein, J., Bodenlos, K., Yanez, A., Lacoe, J., & Berk, J. (2017). *Detour to opportunity: A guide on young adult diversion from the criminal justice system*. Mathematica Policy Research. https://www.mathematica.org/download-media?MediaItemId={199F00F7-CC1E-48AF-B624-7725D27EDEDD}

Steinberg, L. (2000). The juvenile psychopath: Fads, fictions, and facts. *Perspectives on Crime & Justice, 5*, 35.

Steinberg, L. (2014). *Age of opportunity: Lessons from the new science of adolescence*. Houghton Mifflin Harcourt.

Steinberg, L., & Cauffman, E. (1999). A developmental perspective on serious juvenile crime: When should juveniles be treated as adults. *Federal Probation, 63*, 52–57.

Steinberg, L., Chung, H. L., & Little, M. (2004). Reentry of young offenders from the justice system: A developmental perspective. *Youth Violence and Juvenile Justice, 2*(1), 21–38.

Steinberg, L., Graham, S., O'Brien, L., Woolard, J., Cauffman, E., & Banich, M. (2009). Age differences in future orientation and delay discounting. *Child Development, 80*(1), 28–44.

Stewart, R., & Uggen, C. (2020). Criminal records and college admissions: A modified experimental audit. *Criminology, 58*(1), 156–188.

Student eligibility, 20 U.S.C. § 1091(r) (2018).

Tanenhaus, D. S. (2002). The evolution of juvenile courts in the early twentieth century: Beyond the myth of immaculate construction. In Tanenhaus, D. S., Rosenheim, M. K., Zimring, F. E., & Dohrn, B. *A century of juvenile justice* (pp. 42–73). University of Chicago Press.

Travis, J. (2005). *But they all come back: Facing the challenges of prisoner reentry*. Urban Institute.

Unlawful acts, 18 U.S.C. § 922(g)(1) (2018).

U.S. Const. amend. XIV, § 2. (1868)

U.S. Department of Justice: Office of Justice Programs (n.d.). *National Inventory of Collateral Consequences of Conviction*. Accessed January 15, 2022, https://niccc.nationalreentryresourcecenter.org/

U.S. District Court: Eastern District of New York. (2015). *Alternatives to incarceration in the Eastern District of New York*. https://img.nyed.uscourts.gov/files/local_rules/ATI.EDNY_.SecondReport.Aug2015.pdf

U.S. Equal Employment Opportunity Commission. (2012). *Enforcement guidance on the consideration of arrest and conviction records in employment decisions under Title VII of the Civil Rights Act*. https://www.eeoc.gov/laws/guidance/arrest_conviction.cfm.

U.S. Pretrial Services Agency—Eastern District of New York. (2000). *Special Options Services*. https://www.nyept.uscourts.gov/special-options-services

van Duijvenvoorde, A. C., Achterberg, M., Braams, B. R., Peters, S., & Crone, E. A. (2016). Testing a dual-systems model of adolescent brain development using resting-state connectivity analyses. *Neuroimage, 124*, 409–420.

Van Leijenhorst, L., Moor, B. G., de Macks, Z. A. O., Rombouts, S. A., Westenberg, P. M., & Crone, E. A. (2010). Adolescent risky decision-making: Neurocognitive development of reward and control regions. *Neuroimage, 51*(1), 345–355.

Wakefield, S., & Wildeman, C. (2013). *Children of the prison boom: Mass incarceration and the future of American inequality*. Oxford University Press.

Ward, D. A., & Tittle, C. R. (1993). Deterrence or labeling: The effects of informal sanctions. *Deviant Behavior, 14*(1), 43–64.

Weigard, A., Chein, J., Albert, D., Smith, A., & Steinberg, L. (2014). Effects of anonymous peer observation on adolescents' preference for immediate rewards. *Developmental Science, 17*(1), 71–78.

Wheelock, D. (2005). Collateral consequences and racial inequality: Felon status restrictions as a system of disadvantage. *Journal of Contemporary Criminal Justice, 21*(1), 82–90.

Wheelock, D., & Uggen, C. (2006). *Race, poverty and punishment: The impact of criminal sanctions on racial, ethnic, and socioeconomic inequality*. National Poverty Center.

William T. Grant Commission on Work Family and Citizenship. (1988). *The forgotten half: Pathways to success for America's youth and young families*.

Wilson, H. A., & Hoge, R. D. (2013). The effect of youth diversion programs on recidivism: A meta-analytic review. *Criminal Justice and Behavior, 40*(5), 497–518.

Wong, J. S., Bouchard, J., Gravel, J., Bouchard, M., & Morselli, C. (2016). Can at-risk youth be diverted from crime? A meta-analysis of restorative diversion programs. *Criminal Justice and Behavior, 43*(10), 1310–1329.

Youthful Offender Act, SC, 164 § 1090 et seq. (2016). https://www.scstatehouse.gov/code/t24c019.php

CHAPTER 23

Adults With Developmental Disabilities in the Criminal Justice System

Karen L. Salekin and Mary E. Wood

Abstract
Individuals with developmental disabilities, especially intellectual disability, present with characteristic deficits in their intellectual functioning and social–interpersonal skills that place them at a unique disadvantage at nearly every stage of the criminal justice process, from initial involvement in criminal conduct and/or victimization through sentencing. The current chapter reviews the literature regarding the ways in which these deficits interact with criminal justice involvement, including adjudicative competence, capacity to waive Miranda rights, and culpability. This review culminates with a discussion of potential solutions to improve the identification of individuals with developmental disabilities in the criminal justice system, as well as ways to reduce the potential detrimental impact of their deficits in an adversarial system.

Key Words: intellectual disability, autism, psycholegal abilities, competence to proceed, Miranda waiver, culpability

Individuals with developmental disabilities are at a particular disadvantage across multiple stages of the criminal justice system, from initial police encounters through sentencing. Indeed, characteristic intellectual and social–emotional deficits commensurate with intellectual disability (ID), for example, result in unique challenges, thereby raising concerns about the integrity and fairness of proceedings for this population. These concerns are further exacerbated by evidence that individuals with developmental disabilities may be overrepresented, yet underidentified, in this system. The present chapter will review currently available data regarding prevalence rates within the criminal justice system, discuss the ways in which typical deficits interfere with participation in the adjudicative process, and conclude with a review of potential solutions to address these concerns. The content of this chapter is primarily related to individuals with ID in the criminal justice system. Research related to individuals with autism spectrum disorder (ASD) is provided where available.

Defining Intellectual and Developmental Disabilities
Since its inception in 1876, the American Association on Intellectual and Developmental Disabilities (AAIDD) has been at the forefront of public policy, research, classification, and best practice for people with intellectual and developmental disabilities. In 2021, the AAIDD published the 12th edition of their manual, titled *Intellectual Disability: Definition, Diagnosis, Classification and Systems of Support*, in which the authors provide a systematic approach to

naming, defining, diagnosing, classifying, and planning supports for people with IDs (AAIDD, 2021). This manual was developed to meet the needs of diverse groups of individuals involved in the lives of individuals with ID, including those who come in contact via the criminal justice system.

Unlike the AAIDD, the American Psychiatric Association (APA) does not specialize in intellectual and developmental disabilities. In contrast, the organization has identified, classified, and put forth diagnostic criteria for hundreds of disorders that span the gamut of mental health concerns (*Diagnostic and Statistical Manual of Mental Disorders*, 5th ed. [DSM-5]; APA, 2013). In their classification system, intellectual and developmental disabilities are located under the overarching category of neurodevelopmental disorders, which encompass disorders that are known to originate during the developmental period. Within this category are six primary subcategories, under which are 13 disorders (not including identifiers such as "other" or "unspecified"); important details such as diagnostic features, prevalence, development and course, differential diagnosis, and diagnostic markers, among others, are provided for each disorder.

Using the DSM-5 criteria as an example, ID is identified in the following manner (APA, 2013, p. 33):

A. Deficits in intellectual functions, such as reasoning, problem solving, planning, abstract thinking, judgment, academic learning, and learning from experience, confirmed by both clinical assessment and individualized, standardized intelligence testing.
B. Deficits in adaptive functioning that result in failure to meet developmental and sociocultural standards for personal independence and social responsibility. Without ongoing support, the adaptive deficits limit functioning in one or more activities of daily life, such as communication, social participation, and independent living, across multiple environments, such as home, school, work, and community.
C. Onset of intellectual and adaptive deficits during the developmental period.

Of note, ID is the only disorder that has been provided constitutional protection via the Supreme Court of the United States (SCOTUS).

The protection afforded to individuals with ID was established in *Atkins v. Virginia* (2002), at which time SCOTUS categorically barred individuals with ID from execution. In making their determination, SCOTUS leaned heavily on the cognitive impairments associated with this disorder. As noted in the majority opinion:

> Mentally retarded persons frequently know the difference between right and wrong and are competent to stand trial, but, by definition, they have diminished capacities to understand and process information, to communicate, to abstract from mistakes and learn from experience, to engage in logical reasoning, to control impulses, and to understand others' reactions. (*Atkins v. Virginia*, 2002, pg. 13)

In addition to the above, the court made reference to the overarching issue of how the cognitive and behavioral characteristics place defendants at greater risk for execution

> because of the possibility that they will unwittingly confess to crimes they did not commit, their lesser ability to give their counsel meaningful assistance, and the fact that they are typically poor witnesses and that their demeanor may create an unwarranted impression of lack of remorse for their crimes. (*Atkins v. Virginia*, 2002, pg. 16)

It is clear that the justices in the majority recognized that individuals with ID are ill equipped to navigate the criminal justice system. Unfortunately, this mandated protection comes at the end of a long and arduous process, and only for those convicted of the most serious crimes (i.e., those identified as "death worthy").

Similar to ID, ASD is a lifelong neurodevelopmental disorder that originates during early childhood years. The disorder is characterized by deficits in social communication and interactions, as well as restricted and repetitive patterns of behavior, interests, or activities (APA, 2013). Areas of deficits are numerous and expressed in ways unique to each individual. Some of the commonly known deficits are (a) socioemotional reciprocity; (b) nonverbal communication used for social interaction; (c) problems developing, maintaining, and understanding relationships; (d) stereotyped or repetitive motor movements; (e) insistence of sameness, inflexible adherence to routine, or ritualized patterns of verbal and nonverbal behavior; (f) restricted, fixated, and abnormally intense interests; and (g) hyper- or hyporeactivity to sensory input or unusual interest in sensory aspects of the environment (APA, 2013, p. 50). Deficits associated with ASD interfere with functioning in multiple domains (e.g., educational, occupational) and may not become apparent until later in life. Due to the heterogeneity of symptoms and severity, the impact of ASD on daily functioning is person specific.

Prevalence of Developmental Disabilities in the Criminal Justice System

Estimates of the prevalence rate for developmental disabilities in the criminal justice system are highly variable, which has largely been credited to research design and methodological limitations (Lindsay, 2002; MacEachron, 1979; Taylor & Lindsay, 2018). For example, studies with less stringent inclusion criteria (e.g., inclusion of individuals in the borderline intellectual functioning range) raise concerns about representativeness and generalizability, as well as overestimates of prevalence. In contrast, studies with more strict criteria (e.g., requiring a documented diagnosis confirmed by recent standardized testing) run the risk of excluding individuals with ID, resulting in underestimates of true prevalence. The context from which study samples were drawn is also crucial to consider, as prevalence rates differ depending on the stage of the adjudicative process (i.e., pretrial versus postconviction; inmates versus probationers; Hayes, 2002; Lindsay, 2002). Other reasons for this variability include source of the sample, gender, psychometric test used, and differences in functional age for diagnostic inclusion (Hayes, 2018).

Despite the previously noted caveats, research regarding individuals with ID in the criminal justice system has shown that individuals with ID are overrepresented, both in the United States and internationally, relative to prevalence rates in the general population (i.e., approximately 1%; AAIDD, 2021; APA, 2013; Maulik et al., 2011). Estimates in correctional settings have ranged anywhere from less than 1% to as high as 45% (though the upper limit is more frequently at or below 20%; Day, 1993; Hayes, 1996; Lindsay, 2002; Noble & Conley, 1992). In one of the earlier studies from the United States, Denkowski and Denkowski (1985) surveyed administrators from each of the states' adult corrections system regarding prevalence rates of ID in their inmate population, as well as details of the diagnostic procedure in place. Results indicated that 36 systems reported routine screening for ID, and the average prevalence rate was higher among those utilizing group-administered intelligence testing as part of that process (i.e., 6.2%) versus an individually administered, comprehensive assessment (i.e., the Wechsler scales; 2%). These results were generally consistent with epidemiological reports from several states that suggested prevalence rates of ID between 0.5% and 19% in U.S. prisons (Noble & Conley, 1992). Outside the United States, Cocker and colleagues (2007) estimated that the prevalence rate among pretrial detainees in Canada was 19%, whereas Fazel and colleagues (2008) summarized the characteristics of nearly 12,000 prisoners across four different countries, reporting that between 0.5% and 1.5% of this population was diagnosed with ID. A recent study from the United Kingdom found a 9% prevalence rate of ID in a sample of male inmates; of these individuals, 40% were identified as having comorbid attention-deficit/hyperactivity disorder (ADHD), and 0.01% identified as having both ASD and ID (Young et al., 2018).

Prevalence rates of ID in forensic settings outside of the prison system (i.e., individuals who have been court ordered to undergo forensic mental health evaluations and/or treatment as part of the adjudicative process) have been found to represent a relatively small but meaningful group of individuals. Results from multiple studies have identified prevalence rates that range from 2% to 11% across samples of defendants referred for competence-to-stand-trial evaluations (Bonnie, 1990; Brookbanks & Freckelton, 2018; Stafford & Wygant, 2005; Warren et al., 2006). In general, estimated prevalence rates have been higher in forensic inpatient settings relative to samples drawn from evaluation referrals.

Although prevalence rates are generally higher in inpatient settings, the rates vary greatly. On the low end, Colwell and Gianesini (2011) found that 7% of individuals discharged following a period of inpatient restoration treatment were diagnosed with ID, whereas Woodbury-Smith and colleagues (2018) found that approximately one in five forensic beds (19%) was filled by an individual with ID. Although Stinson and Robbins (2014) reported that 47% of the patient population in a secure forensic hospital in the midwestern United States were reported to have either an ID or cognitive impairment, this estimate included individuals with a broad range of impairments including traumatic brain injury (TBI), fetal alcohol syndrome (FAS), and borderline intellectual functioning (BIF), for example. The prevalence estimate dropped to 15% when only the mild and moderate ID groups were included, a rate that is more consistent with other studies. In a more recent study, Mosotho and colleagues (2020) identified 120 males who had been diagnosed with ID and admitted to a forensic unit in South Africa over a 10-year period (2006–2016), the majority of whom had been diagnosed with mild ID (70.8%), though the prevalence rate is unknown because the overall number of admissions was not reported.

Fewer studies have investigated the prevalence rate of ASD in the criminal justice system, with most suggesting the same or lower prevalence rates relative to other groups, though the results have similarly been mixed with variable estimates across studies (Haw et al., 2013; King & Murphy, 2014; Lindsay et al., 2014; Lunsky et al., 2012; Rutten et al., 2017; Yu et al., 2020). While Brewer and Young (2018) reported that individuals with ASD are overrepresented in the criminal justice system, the results of a recent, large epidemiological study of young adults (ages 17–23) in the southeastern United States suggested that individuals with ASD were not overrepresented in either the juvenile or criminal justice systems (Yu et al., 2020). With respect to the forensic system, Helverschou and colleagues (2015) identified 48 individuals with ASD who underwent forensic evaluations in a 10-year period in Norway, while Lindsay and colleagues (2014) found that the rate of referral to a forensic ID service across multiple sites in England and Scotland was consistent with the expected rate of ASD in that population (10%). Young and colleagues (2018) identified 8.5% of male prisoners as having ASD; 63% of these individuals had comorbid ADHD, and as previously mentioned, an extremely small percentage (i.e., 0.01%) were identified as having both ASD and ID.

While there is evidence to suggest that individuals with ID and/or other developmental disabilities may be overrepresented in the criminal justice and associated forensic systems, there are several caveats in this area of research that are important to highlight. First and foremost, identifying individuals with developmental disabilities is difficult and complex, especially in the criminal justice system. Indeed, there are rarely obvious indicia of ID and/or ASD (e.g., physical characteristics, distinct symptoms) such that it is considered an "invisible disability." While some associated characteristics or features may be apparent to others (e.g., communication difficulties and/or concreteness of thought), it is unlikely that detection would be possible on the basis of observation/interaction alone. This becomes even less probable in highly structured settings such as jails and prisons, as functional impairments can be less pronounced given the artificial context and degree of structural supports (i.e., reduced demands of the environment serve to mask impairments).

Identification of individuals with ID in the criminal justice system is further complicated by the personality variables such as the "cloak of competence" where individuals with ID deliberately attempt to mask their deficits to avoid detection (Edgerton, 1972). Indeed, often credited to the stigma associated with having a disability, individuals with ID may engage in compensatory behaviors or strategies, including acquiescing and/or feigning comprehension of directives (Appelbaum, 1994), effectively reducing the likelihood of being identified as having a disability. Altogether, these caveats raise considerable concern about underidentification of individuals with developmental disabilities, especially ID, in the criminal justice system, thus producing systematic underestimates with respect to prevalence.

Pathways Into the Criminal Justice System

Of arguably greater importance than estimates of prevalence, however, is understanding the pathways through which individuals with ID/ASD become involved in the criminal justice system, as well as the associated characteristics and/or risk factors that may be unique to this population. A variety of explanations for the apparent overrepresentation of individuals with ID in the criminal justice system have been offered, including those that focus on characteristics of the defendant (i.e., susceptibility hypothesis; for a review, see Lindsay & Taylor, 2018) and/or contextual influences (e.g., psychosocial disadvantage; Hayes, 2018), whereas Appelbaum and Appelbaum (1994) consider reduced appreciation of consequences and/or a failure to utilize alternative supports as potentially explanatory.

In addition to being overrepresented as defendants or perpetrators in the criminal justice system, individuals with ID are subject to victimization at alarming rates (e.g., Baladerian et al., 2013, review; Dion et al., 2018; Harrell, 2017; Hickson &, Khemka, 2016; L. Jones et al., 2012; Petersilia, 2001; Pfeffer, 2016). A 2010 survey published by the U.S. Department of Justice clearly demonstrated that the extent of victimization of individuals with ID is extremely high (Harrell & Rand, 2010), with 730,000 nonfatal violent crimes and 1.8 million property crimes having been experienced by community-dwelling individuals 12 years old and older during 2008 alone. Of particular concern is that the types of nonfatal violent crimes not only are physically and emotionally devastating but also can easily eventuate in death (i.e., rape, sexual assault, robbery, and aggravated and simple assault). Fogden and colleagues posited that there is a relationship between the interpersonal functioning and cognitive capabilities of individuals with ID and their exposure to dangerous situations, with more frequent exposure increasing the risk of victimization. These researchers also noted that people who engage in criminal conduct are likely to have been victims of abuse (Fogden et al., 2016).

Although the results of early studies suggested a significant relationship between intelligence and criminal behavior, subsequent research has indicated this relationship is weaker and less consistent than initially reported, and more recent conceptualizations of criminality favor contextual and environmental influences rather than disability (Lindsay & Taylor, 2018). Of interest, the results of previous studies suggest that the risk factors associated with criminal justice involvement in nondisabled offender populations are also predictive of offending among individuals with ID (e.g., youthfulness, male gender, psychosocial disadvantage; Fitzgerald et al., 2011; J. Jones, 2007; Lindsay et al., 2004). In addition, there is evidence that variables including impoverished relationships, exposure to violence, and adverse childhood experiences relate to offending in individuals with ID, as they do with the larger population of offenders (Lindsay et al., 2004; Wheeler et al., 2014). In response to these findings, scholars have argued that future research should instead focus on understanding the nature and circumstances of offending, as well as both static and dynamic risk factors (J. Jones, 2007; Wheeler et al., 2014).

With respect to offending, research has sought to determine whether defendants with ID/ASD are more likely to commit certain types of crimes, as well to determine the relative rate of offending compared to their nondisabled peers. Although methodological issues continue to limit conclusive opinions to some of these questions (especially the relative rate of offending compared to the larger population; Lindsay, 2002; Taylor & Lindsay, 2018), some general findings merit discussion. Several studies have suggested a higher prevalence rate of ID among samples of arsonists, with estimates ranging from approximately 3% to 15% (Bradford & Dimock, 1986; Leong & Silva, 1999; Puri et al., 1995; Rix, 1997; Simpson & Hogg, 2001). In addition, various studies have suggested that individuals with ID are overrepresented among sex offenders and that these offenses are more likely to include younger male victims and less likely to involve serious violence and/or harm, though the role of impulsivity has been somewhat inconsistent (Blanchard et al., 1999; Day, 1993; Gleaser & Deane, 1999; Hayes, 1993; Parry & Lindsay, 2003; Simpson & Hogg, 2001; Walker & McCabe, 1973).

While some have suggested that individuals with ASD may be more likely to commit offenses due to sensory preoccupations, poor social awareness, or theory of mind deficits (e.g., stalking, fire setting), this has not consistently borne out in subsequent research. Indeed, several studies have failed to identify unique offending patterns for individuals with ASD relative to other groups (Haw et al., 2013; Lindsey et al., 2014; Yu et al., 2021). In contrast, Freckelton (2013) reported that offenders with ASD disproportionately commit offenses including arson, sexual offenses, and stalking, for example. Within the population of offenders with ASD, Gunasekaran and Chaplin (2012) reported offending differences between lower and higher functioning individuals, and Higgs and Carter (2015) found that sex offenders with ASD were older and more likely to have ID compared to violent offenders.

Of concern, there is some evidence to suggest that the shift from inpatient and/or residential placement to community outpatient settings (often referred to as the deinstitutionalization movement) may be one contributor to increasing prevalence rates of developmental disabilities, especially ID, in the criminal justice system. The most direct evidence of this is from a study in the United Kingdom that evidenced a significant increase in court referrals and concomitant reduction in community referrals for a community service program for individuals with ID over a 20-year period (Lindsay, Haut, & Steptoe, 2011). Other studies have focused on outcomes following police response to crisis situations, as police have considerable discretion in determining how to respond to these calls, which may include informal resolution at the scene, transfer/admission to a hospital for further assessment and/or stabilization, or arrest.

Lunsky and colleagues (2012) reviewed the responses of service agencies to crisis situations for 751 individuals with ID in Canada, approximately 17% of whom had a history of legal involvement. Compared to those without a history of legal involvement, the subset of individuals with a history of legal issues were younger and more likely to be male, to reside in an independent or minimally supportive environment (relative to a group home), to have higher cognitive functioning, and to be diagnosed with a substance use disorder. These individuals were also less likely to be diagnosed with ASD. The majority of the crisis situations involved physical aggression, which was more likely among individuals with lower cognitive functioning and those residing in minimally supported environments (relative to group homes). Although prior legal involvement was not predictive of physical aggression, it was a significant predictor of police involvement, leading the authors to question whether context, rather than the offense and/or level of risk, explained the involvement of police in crisis situations.

In a similar study, Raina and colleagues (2013) examined the factors associated with outcomes following police response to crisis situations in a sample of 138 adults with ID in Canada. Over half of the crises involved physical aggression, and 12% were in the context of suicidal behavior. The majority of cases (55%) resulted in transport to the hospital emergency room, approximately 10% resulted in arrest, and the remainder were informally resolved at the scene. Consistent with the findings of Lunsky and colleagues (2012), those with a history of forensic involvement were more likely to be arrested and less likely to be taken to the hospital than those without this history. In addition, physical aggression and independent living were associated with a higher likelihood of arrest, leading the authors to speculate about the role of the *combination* of factors in explaining police response and ultimate arrest (i.e., prior forensic involvement combined with the context of the situation and availability of residential supports; Raina et al., 2013). Although additional research is needed, these studies raise some concern that criminal justice involvement may reflect the need for a higher level of care and/or stigma associated with prior legal involvement rather than criminogenic risk necessitating incarceration.

Potential Consequences of Cognitive Deficits in the Criminal Justice System

Broadly speaking, individuals with developmental disabilities present with a broad range of cognitive abilities and deficits. In light of this breadth and variability, Greenspan and Woods (2014) made the argument that ID should be considered a disorder of thinking or reasoning (i.e., "the ability to flexibly deal with problems") rather than a disorder of learning disability, as the latter focuses more on the acquisition of knowledge rather than how it is applied. Case law has highlighted the importance of intact cognitive functioning as it pertains to criminal justice involvement. Indeed, intellectual functioning is a critical component in relation to a number of psycholegal capacities (e.g., competence to stand trial, competence to waive Miranda rights, criminal responsibility, eyewitness testimony, competence to testify), as well as criminal culpability (e.g., *Atkins v. Virginia,* 2002; criminal responsibility). The following sections highlight some of the ways in which intellectual deficits associated with ID and/or ASD impact participation in the criminal justice process across various contexts, with the caveat that the examples herein are not exhaustive, as the population of individuals with developmental disabilities is diverse and heterogenous in terms of deficits, strengths, and presentation. Beyond this, these issues are highly context dependent and therefore unique to each case. In other words, "the functional capabilities of most defendants with [ID] depend as much upon the demands and supports of the environment as they do upon the innate abilities of the individual" (Applebaum, 1994, p. 323).

Capacity to Waive Miranda

The landmark case *Miranda v. Arizona* (1966) established procedural safeguards during interrogations with police, requiring that police inform suspects of their constitutional rights to remain silent and have an attorney present, for example, as well as the potential consequences of waiving those rights. The compendium of cases addressing the oft-cited Miranda warnings have consistently emphasized the need for waivers of these rights to be "knowing, intelligent, and voluntary." The requirement that this decision be made knowingly and intelligently clearly emphasizes the importance of intellectual ability in waiving these rights, which is consistent with research documenting a positive relationship between IQ and comprehension of Miranda rights (Fulero & Everington, 2004; Grisso, 1998).

The analysis of whether a defendant's waiver of rights was made knowingly and intelligently requires determination as to whether the individual has the ability to know and understand the rights (i.e., "knowing"), but also whether the decision represented a reasoned choice among alternatives in light of the consequences (i.e., "intelligent"); the latter capacity clearly represents a more complex decision-making process. At the time of arrest, the suspect must be able to comprehend the words that compose the Miranda warnings presented to them (e.g., the meaning of the word "right"), which are most often above their capacity to both read and comprehend (Baroff, 1996; Rogers, 2008). In contrast, making of an "intelligent" waiver requires that the defendant understand the implications of their choice, such as the potentially detrimental consequences of self-incrimination; this type of forward thinking and weighing of choices has been shown to be impaired among individuals with intellectual deficits (Clare & Gudjonsson, 1995; Fulero & Everington, 1995).

Previous research has consistently indicated that individuals with ID have difficulty comprehending their Miranda rights (e.g., Cloud et al., 2002; Erickson et al., 2020; Everington & Fulero, 1999; Fulero & Everington, 1995, 2004; Grisso, 1998; O'Connell et al., 2005). These concerns were clearly demonstrated in Cloud et al. (2002), where only one quarter of the sample of offenders with ID understood the right to remain silent. Furthermore, they didn't understand the context of the interrogation procedure, the legal consequences of confessing, or the meaning of the words let alone the sentences. Similarly, O'Connell and colleagues (2005) found that half of their sample of individuals with ID earned scores of zero on all five warnings on a commonly used Miranda comprehension instrument, compared to less than 1% of the general population. Moreover, when their knowledge was assessed using recognition format, only 2% of the participants earned scores above chance level, in comparison to 75% of the normative sample. Using three scales of the Standardized Assessment of Miranda Abilities (SAMA; Rogers et al., 2012), Erickson and colleagues found that individuals with mild to moderate ID demonstrated a marked lack of comprehension of the Miranda warnings, as well as substantial failure to recall warnings after they had been presented. Specifically, 36% of the sample was unable to recall even one of the warnings, and as noted by Winningham and colleagues (2018), the inability to remember a minimum of two components is indicative of substantial impairment in Miranda abilities.

Perhaps the greatest impediment to comprehending Miranda rights is the complexity of the warning, both in language and in content, and particularly so when it exceeds the capabilities of the individual (see, e.g., Greenfield et al., 2001; Rogers et al., 2007, 2008, 2010, 2011). As noted in Rogers (2008), a mere 20.9% of the warnings are written below a sixth-grade level, with the vast majority written at between the range of sixth and eighth grade; perhaps of greater concern is that 2.2% of the warnings require at least some college education. In addition, Rogers and colleagues (2013) found that there exists a lot of misconceptions as to the meaning of the warning. For example, 31% of pretrial defendants and 26.3% of college students believed that the right to silence can be used against you, and 61.3% of the sample did not know how explicit the request for an attorney must be. Of note, research has demonstrated that adolescents and cognitively impaired adults show significant impairment in the comprehension of these rights (e.g., Grisso, 1981; for a review, see Rogers et al., 2014; Zelle et al., 2015).

Competence to Stand Trial

In *Dusky v. United States* (1960), the U.S. Supreme Court ruled that a defendant must possess a "sufficient present ability to consult with his [or her] lawyer with a reasonable degree of rational understanding" and a "rational as well as factual understanding of the proceedings against him [or her]" to be considered competent to proceed with the charge(s) against them, and subsequent case law has further clarified this standard and related issues (e.g., *Godinez v. Moran*, 1993; *Pate v. Robinson*, 1966; *Sell v. United States*, 2003). Evaluations of competence to stand trial (CST; also referred to as competence to proceed and/or adjudicative competence) are the most frequently conducted forensic mental health evaluations (Melton et al. 2018), and in recent years, referral rates have been consistently rising (Gowensmith, 2019; Heilbrun et al., 2019). The typical referral for a CST evaluation and associated restoration treatment is an individual diagnosed with a psychotic disorder who is experiencing symptoms that interfere with competence-related abilities (Warren et al., 2006), which is consistent with the fact that psychiatric medications are the most commonly utilized method of competence restoration treatment (Heilbrun et al., 2019; Zapf, 2013).

The *Dusky* standard, which is used in most jurisdictions in the United States, is often conceptualized as a three-pronged test: (a) factual understanding, (b) rational understanding, and (c) ability to consult counsel. While the importance of cognition is clear, it is notable that these abilities extend beyond the basic acquisition/retention of knowledge to include the capacity to conceptualize abstract concepts, strategically consider various options, and apply information about the process to their own case, for example (Ostermeyer et al., 2018). The importance of cognition is supported by a retrospective examination of the association between clinical judgments of competence and neuropsychological test performance, in which Nestor and colleagues (1999) found that defendants recommended as competent scored higher on measures of intelligence, attention, and memory. Given the relative weight accorded to underlying cognitive capacities in this inquiry, it makes conceptual sense that individuals with developmental disabilities would present with competence-related deficits, which is consistent with previous research that suggests individuals with ID represent between 2% and 10% of competence evaluation referrals (Bonnie, 1990; Stafford & Wygant, 2005; Warren et al., 2006), with a base rate of incompetence ranging from 12% to 90% (Cochran et al., 2001; Everington & Dunn, 1995; Mosotho et al., 2020) and lower restoration rates among those with lower levels of cognitive functioning (Anderson & Hewitt, 2002; Mikolajewski et al., 2017; Miller, 2003; Warren et al., 2013).

It is important to note that defendants with developmental disabilities such as ID and ASD present with unique competence-related deficits relative to their counterparts, which warrant special consideration during both the assessment and treatment processes (Applebaum, 1994; Brown et al., 2017; Wood et al., 2019). Indeed, defendants with ID are significantly more likely to present with impaired factual understanding, which serves as the foundation upon which more complex abilities are built (Rosenfeld & Wall, 1998; Warren et al., 2006). For this reason, some scholars have argued that treatment should be conceptualized as competence *attainment* (versus *restoration*) with this population, reflecting the greater focus on foundational skills and knowledge acquisition at the outset (Anderson & Hewitt, 2002; Ellis & Luckasson, 1985). These arguments are supported by the fact that prior research has consistently indicated that defendants with intellectual/cognitive deficits (i.e., ID) are significantly less likely to be restored than their counterparts (Anderson & Hewitt, 2002; Mossman, 2007). Wall and colleagues (2003) developed a competency training program for defendants with ID, which required modifying the content, structure, and delivery such that they were compatible with the capabilities of individuals with ID (e.g., simplified language, one-on-one instruction, repetition). While it is one of the only programs that has been developed for individuals with ID, restoration (or attainment) rates remain lower relative to other groups of defendants (Wall & Christopher, 2012), and there remain questions as to its effectiveness, especially considering the resource-intensive nature of the program (Schouten, 2003; Zapf, 2013).

For the previously stated reasons, the competence inquiry largely centers on a defendant's underlying cognitive/intellectual ability, which is a prominent area of weakness for individuals with developmental disabilities. Although full-scale IQ (FSIQ) scores (i.e., composite scores considered to reflect general cognitive ability) have historically been considered the most prominent feature in diagnosing ID (Tassé et al., 2016), these estimates provide little meaningful information about an individual's level of functioning and/or underlying capacity.

Individuals with the same FSIQ score may present with vastly different strengths and weaknesses, for which a more detailed assessment is crucial. Consider, for example, the following competence-related abilities identified by Zapf and Roesch (2009) in the *Best Practices in Forensic Mental Health Assessment* series for competence evaluations: (a) capacity to comprehend and appreciate the charges or allegations, (b) capacity to engage in reasoned choice of legal strategies and options (i.e., plausible appraisal of likely outcome, comprehension of the implications of a guilty plea or plea bargain), and (c) capacity to testify relevantly (i.e., capacity to track oral questions and respond appropriately). With respect to the latter of these abilities, for example, Gudjonsson et al. (2000) found that intellectual ability was related to the capacity to testify as a witness among individuals with ID, and Kebbell et al. (2004) found that the testimonial accounts of witnesses with ID were significantly shorter, and they were significantly more likely to agree to leading questions than matched counterparts without ID.

Several authors have reviewed some of the characteristic features and deficits seen in defendants with ID, the majority of which would fall under the overarching umbrella of "intellectual deficits." Applebaum (1994), for example, noted that problem-solving and reasoning deficits tend to be the most problematic, and he noted that defendants with ID are often concrete in their reasoning, are rigid in their thinking, and struggle to learn from prior mistakes, all of which have the potential to interfere with an individual's ability to participate in the adjudicative process effectively. The same year, Applebaum and Applebaum (1994) reviewed a variety of "clues" that a defendant may have ID and discussed the interplay with competence-related abilities. These "clues" were categorized into three broad domains: (a) cognition (e.g., concreteness), (b) communication (e.g., poor comprehension of questions), and (c) connotation (e.g., impulsivity). The authors also provided examples of ways to tailor the assessment to the defendant's unique needs (e.g., avoid leading questions due to acquiescence bias, repeat concepts to aid retention, and build rapport given heightened vulnerabilities), which have consistently been echoed by others (Applebaum & Applebaum, 1994; Salekin et al., 2010; Wall & Christopher, 2012; Wood et al., 2019).

It is important to note that although these "clues" are important to consider, there remain persistent concerns about the underidentification of defendants with ID in the criminal justice system overall, but also in identifying those who may require a competence evaluation. As mentioned, the term "cloak of competence" was coined to reflect the fact that individuals with ID oftentimes go to great lengths to mask their deficits (e.g., "cooperation without comprehension"; Applebaum, 1994), leading Ellis and Luckasson (1989) to argue that individuals with training and professional experience in special education should be involved in the criminal justice process. Consistent with these concerns, Everington (1989) found that defendants with a dual diagnosis (rather than ID alone) were more likely to be referred for a competency evaluation, even though this was not associated with the outcome, suggesting that defendants who are not diagnosed with another disorder/condition may go undetected. In the same study, defendants with ID suffered worse postarrest outcomes (i.e., lengthier incarcerations) relative to their nondisabled counterparts, raising concerns about the broader impact on this subset of defendants on the basis of their disability.

Culpability

In addition to interfering with various psycholegal capacities, intellectual deficits are relevant to considerations of the degree of culpability an individual may possess for an offense. Of particular relevance is the landmark case *Atkins v. Virginia* (2002), in which SCOTUS categorically excluded individuals with ID from capital punishment. It was noted that the number of states that had already prohibited executions of offenders with ID "provides powerful evidence that today our society views mentally retarded offenders as categorically less culpable than the average criminal" (*Atkins v. Virginia*, 2002, p. 11). The court cited myriad deficits that served to reduce the culpability of offenders with ID, including "diminished capacities to understand and process information, to communicate, to abstract from mistakes and learn from experience, to engage in logical reasoning, to control impulses, and to understand others' reactions" (*Atkins v. Virginia*, 2002, p. 13). Although narrowly limited to the capital context, the decision in *Atkins* clearly outlined the ways in which deficits associated with ID systematically reduce individuals' level of culpability for an alleged offense.

As described throughout, intellectual deficits may manifest as impaired decision-making abilities, reduced flexibility (i.e., cognitive rigidity), and/or slowed processing of information. In some individuals, this pattern of impairments may result in looking to others for clues about how to behave (i.e., other-directedness) and, when combined with the social skills deficits described elsewhere (e.g., suggestibility, naiveté), increase the risk of involvement in criminal conduct, with an arguably reduced degree of culpability.

Several authors have addressed issues of criminal responsibility for individuals with ASD, describing it as "a complex issue, which requires careful consideration along criminological, philosophical and biological grounds, in the same way that similar arguments of responsibility have been approached among individuals with psychopathy" (Woodbury-Smith & Dein, 2014, p. 2378). In this discussion, it was noted that theory of mind deficits, emotion regulation deficits, and difficulty interpreting cues may be relevant to consider, concluding that "decisions regarding culpability [may] need to be based on cognitive strengths and vulnerabilities rather than diagnosis" (Woodbury-Smith & Dein, 2014, p. 2739).

Katz and Zemishlany (2006) presented three cases in which symptoms of Asperger syndrome (AS) were relevant to a defendant's criminal intent or *mens rea*. In these examples, all three individuals misinterpreted social situations to some degree, combined with an inability to appreciate others' point of view. The authors concluded that the social judgment of AS "is deficient to a degree that inhibits their ability to understand that what they were doing was wrong" (Katz & Zemishlany, 2006, p. 172). Two cases out of New Zealand provided similar examples wherein the judge considered features associated with ASD as contributing to a lack of understanding of appropriate sexual behavior (e.g., reduced capacity for relationships and difficulty perceiving others' feelings) and/or a failure to express remorse (e.g., cognitive rigidity and egocentrism). In contrast, among individuals with ASD undergoing forensic evaluations in Norway, there were rarely clear connections between the offense and relevant symptoms (Helverschou et al., 2015).

Social Skills Deficits and Involvement in the Criminal Justice System

Dispositional factors influence legal outcomes at multiple stages of the judicial process, beginning at the time of arrest and carrying through until the end of the judicial process. At times, involvement in the criminal justice system continues through postconviction proceedings, with some individuals facing the possibility of execution. For a multitude of reasons, dispositional factors identified in people with ID and/or ASD render them particularly vulnerable to external influences such as police tactics, substituted judgment (decisions made by others), and stress (Cloud et al., 2002; Davis & Leo, 2014; Drizin & Leo, 2004; Ellis & Luckasson, 1985; Everington & Fulero, 1999; Perske, 2000, 2005). Dispositional factors such as suggestibility, confabulation, acquiescence, gullibility, and naivety are commonplace among individuals with ID, all of which, particularly in combination, result in poor judgment and decision making. Within the forensic realm, these characteristics increase the likelihood of conviction (Beail, 2002; Clare & Gudjonsson, 1993; Gudjonsson & Henry, 2003; Perske, 1994; Milne et al., 2002).

There are contrasting views as to the meaning of the term "suggestibility" in a forensic context. Gudjonsson and Clark (1986) conceptualized it as an interpersonal process and defined interrogative suggestibility as "the extent to which, within a closed social interaction, people come to accept messages communicated during formal questioning, as the result of which their subsequent behavioural response is affected" (p. 84). Similarly, Powers et al. (1979), defined suggestibility as "the extent to which they [people] come to accept a piece of post-event information and incorporate it into their recollection" (p. 339). Both of these definitions have proven to be helpful in terms of understanding the impact of memory processes and suggestibility within the legal arena. Confabulation is a type of memory error in which gaps in memory are unconsciously filled with contrived, misinterpreted, or distorted information (French et al., 2009). Those higher in suggestibility are more prone to confabulation; hence the self-report of individuals with ID may be in error, which is concerning during police interviews and interrogations, as well as when communicating with attorneys or testifying in court (Gudjonsson, 2003; Gudjonsson & Clare, 1995). These individuals are more likely to take on the views of others or incorporate their statements into their own, resulting in tainted memories and inaccurate written or oral accounts of events.

In contrast to suggestibility, which occurs outside of consciousness, acquiescence is an action carried out by an individual for a particular purpose. As noted by both Rapley and Antaki (1996) and Finlay and Lyons (2002), acquiescence is difficult to define. According to Finlay and Lyons (2002), acquiescence is not a unitary construct and can reflect a situational pull (e.g., the desire to please, sense of submissiveness, or concealing one's lack of knowledge or inability to comprehend) but can also be a response to questions that are too complex for that individual to grasp. Acquiescence has been defined as the act "of being willing to do what someone wants and to accept their opinions, even if you are not sure that they are right" (https://www.oxfordlearnersdictionaries.com/us/definition/american_english/acquiescence). In contrast, from a psychometric perspective, acquiescing has been defined as the tendency to agree with, or say yes to, statements or questions, regardless of the content of the items (Block, 1965; Couch & Keniston, 1960). Different samples, methods, and procedures produce a somewhat confusing view of the factors that feed into acquiescence, though it is well known that individuals with ID acquiesce at a higher rate than do their typically developing peers (see, e.g., Clare & Gudjonsson, 1995; Heal & Sigelman, 1995; Matikka & Vesela, 1997).

According to Greenspan and colleagues (2001), credulity (i.e., the tendency to believe a highly questionable statement despite very little evidence) is the source of gullibility, or "a vulnerability to being tricked or manipulated, despite scanty evidence" (p. 102). The authors noted that gullible outcomes are influenced by situational (e.g., availability of supports) and dispositional factors (i.e., desire to please). Wrapped into the construct of gullibility are personality characteristics such as naiveté and the tendency to emulate and to trust others, the latter having both positive and negative effects on social functioning for individuals with ID. Later, Greenspan (2008) discussed gullibility within the context of "induced socially foolish action" (p. 147) According to Greenspan, foolish action refers to "behavior that has a high likelihood of backfiring, sometimes with disastrous consequences, because of a failure to attend to risk that are obvious to most people" (p. 149). Moreover, he identified that induced socially foolish action is expressed in the form of gullibility and "occurs in the context of manipulation by one or more other persons, in which one agrees to a course of action that is not in one's interest, on the basis of false information or encouragement" (p. 149).

According to Lexico.com, nNaiveté is a state or action caused by, or relating to, a person's lack of knowledge, "experience, wisdom or judgment" (https://www.lexico.com/en/definition/naive) and, similar to gullibility, interferes with social functioning. It is an interpersonal trait that leaves a person vulnerable to exploitation (illegal and legal) and embarrassment. In a legal setting, naive individuals can easily be tricked into believing false statements, which can result in severely negative consequences for an individual involved in the judicial system.

Keeping in mind these five psychosocial factors, it is easy to envision how these traits can result in deleterious and dangerous consequences within the legal system. As previously stated, these factors weigh heavily on the ability of an individual to navigate the criminal justice system. For instance, in situations where an individual is a victim, eyewitness, or both, interactions with supportive others are likely to occur, and these interactions can impact the reliability and validity of information provided to police. In situations where the individual is a suspect or defendant, supportive others are not available prior to defense counsel being appointed; instead, the individual is alone and interacting with law enforcement, who are doing their best to obtain incriminating evidence. Further, once incarcerated, exploitation and sexual abuse are commonplace. A review of these areas of concern is provided later.

Memory, Intellectual Disability, and Eyewitness Identification

The research on the malleability of memory has been conducted with children, youth, and adults, and the results have clearly shown that memories change from the point of experience to the time of recall. Postevent experiences (e.g., speaking with other observers) can impair the memory of the original event, and the impairment occurs quickly and individuals become more confident of the accuracy of their memory over time (Ceci & Bruck, 1995; Kassin, 1985; Wells & Murry, 1983; Yarmey & Jones, 1993). Loftus, among others, refers to this process as the "misinformation effect," which she defined as "the impairment in memory for the past that arises after exposure to misleading information" (Loftus, 2005, p. 1). Furthermore, the acceptance of the altered memory as real is known as "misinformation acceptance." Both processes have been studied for many years and supported around the globe (Ceci et al., 1987; Gibling & Davis, 1988; Loftus, 1975, 1979).

The misinformation effect has primarily been studied using children as the primary source of data within the laboratory setting. The overarching findings are that children are influenced by both individual characteristics (e.g., suggestibility, cognitive functioning, confabulation, temperament) and situational factors (e.g., complexity of questions asked, repeated questioning/interviewing, leading questions; Ceci & Bruck, 1993; Chae et al., 2018). A classic study conducted by Ceci and colleagues demonstrated that a preschool child's recollection of events can be quickly manipulated and result in a complete fabrication of an event that never occurred (the mousetrap referenced in Ceci et al., 1994).

As noted earlier, misinformation interferes with accuracy to the degree that the resulting memory does not reflect the truth but instead reflects the information fed to the individual by an external source (see, e.g., Loftus et al., 1978; Loftus & Pickrell, 1995; Pickrell et al.,

2017). Exposure to misleading information can arise in multiple ways for individuals with ID in the criminal justice system. For eyewitnesses and victims, the sources may be multiple, such as media, discussions with other eyewitnesses, and interviews with law enforcement, among many (Loftus, 2005). Bruck and colleagues authored the amicus brief for *State v. Michaels* and in it provided detailed information on the multiple problems with reports of sexual abuse (Bruck et al., 1995).

Despite concerns about the ecological validity of the experimental evidence of tainted memories (Yuille & Cooper, 2012), there are case examples that demonstrate the impact of some of the previously noted variables (e.g., the sighting of John Doe 2 at the Oklahoma City Bombing, Memon & Wright, 1999; the case of A. J. Hutto, which garnered national attention, American Broadcast System, 2010). In the latter case, there was ample evidence of taint throughout the investigation of events, including interview techniques, concerns related to ability to view the scene, and alleged motivation, among others. In addition to external factors, A. J. had known individual factors such as age (6 years) and the stress resulting from the loss of his sister and the arrest of his mother.

Research exists to show that children's reporting of events isn't always wrong but that bringing out accurate information requires the use of appropriate interviewing techniques, control of nonverbal communication, and appropriate interview conditions, external factors that are extremely important for children with ID (Agnew & Powell, 2004; Henry et al., 2011; Michel et al., 2000; Pozzulo & Lindsay, 1998). Though it has been posited that individuals with ID do not make competent witnesses (Milne et al., 2001; Perske, 1994), available research suggests that these individuals may make good witnesses, but accuracy is highly dependent on the type of questioning (see Kebbel & Hatton, 1999, for a review; McNulty et al., 1995; Terne & Yuille, 2008; Valenti-Hein & Schwartz, 1993). An example of support for this belief is the finding that children provide less information in response to free recall questions/requests than their age-matched, typically developing peers, but the information they do provide is just as accurate (Agnew & Powell, 2004; Gordon et al., 1994; Henry & Gudjonsson, 1999, 2003). Though yet to be studied, the similarity between adults with their peers, matched on age, scholastic functioning, peer relations, suggestibility, response to leading questions, etc., these authors feel confident in the belief that research findings for child eyewitnesses will be highly similar to adults with ID.

Griego and colleagues (2019) conducted a meta-analytic review of research that utilized samples of individuals with ID or ASD (adult and children) in relation to memory distortions, in this case suggestibility and false memories. The authors conducted a thorough search for studies that met their stringent criteria (one of which was the use of a clinically diagnosed sample and a nonclinical control sample) and came up with 36 possibilities, which, after review, dwindled down to 11 studies. The results showed a significant trend that indicated that individuals diagnosed with ID showed increased false memories and were more suggestible than the nonclinical control sample. In contrast, the trend (also significant) was in the opposite direction for individuals with ASD, showing that they had "superior memory" in comparison to their control sample, as well as decreased suggestibility. The authors noted that a limitation of the review was that the sample of individuals with ASD were higher functioning adults with average or above-average intelligence. Another limitation was that only five of the 11 studies included adult participants, once again showing the dearth of studies that are directly applicable to adults in the criminal justice system.

Terne and Yuille (2008) conducted a study of leading questions with a sample of adults with ID and found that this group demonstrated higher levels of suggestibility when faced with one of the two leading questions, but that they were just as accurate in identification as the college-age control sample, and that individuals with ID produced fewer action and descriptive details than the control sample. These authors concluded that adults with ID can make good witnesses, but they must be interviewed in a nonleading manner (Heal & Sigelman, 1995; Matikka & Vesela, 1997). As has been the consistent trend, these results are akin to those found for children (Klemfuss & Ceci, 2013; Odegard et al., 2010).

Using a similar method to Terne and Yuille (2008), Wilcock and Henry (2013) found that in contrast to typically developing adults, those with ID performed more poorly regardless of whether the perpetrator was present in the photo lineup. These individuals were also more confident in their accuracy and were less likely to understand the purpose of the lineup as well as some of the instructions. These findings are partially consistent with those of Erickson and Issacs (2003), who found that individuals with ID were equally accurate in making identifications when the perpetrator was present but more apt to make a false identification when the photo lineup contained an innocent suspect.

Waiver of Miranda Rights and Custodial Interrogation

The decision to waive Miranda rights is one that requires understanding of the meaning of the rights provided, having the ability to weigh the pros and cons of doing so, and making a decision based on accurate information that is in a person's best interests. While cognitive ability plays a large role in making this decision, equally important are dispositional characteristics that factor into interpersonal communications. As previously noted, individuals with ID demonstrate many dispositional characteristics that impede their ability to successfully navigate this situation. Traits such as compliance to authority (Blair, 2007; Gudjonsson, 2003), heightened suggestibility (Gudjonsson, 2003, 2010), acquiescence (Matikka & Vesela, 1997), and a desire to please almost ensure that individuals with ID will speak to law enforcement (see, e.g., the case of Medell Banks; Herbert, 2002).

From the time of first contact, people with ID face heightened risks of self-incrimination, falsely confessing, and subsequently having those confessions used against them. For a person under suspicion, their initial impression is critical, as it determines whether police proceed to interrogation. As noted by Kassin (2015), once a person becomes a suspect, there is a strong presumption of guilt, which, in turn, predisposes to an inclination to ask confirmatory questions, use persuasive tactics, and seek confessions (Hill et al., 2008; Kassin et al., 2003). To the knowledge of these authors, research has yet to be carried out regarding the perceptions of risk that individuals with ID might have in relation to contact with law enforcement; however, a study such as this has been conducted with individuals with ASD.

The results of a small survey indicate that individuals with ASD are concerned about interacting with police and the ways in which their appearance and behaviors may misinterpreted to their disadvantage (Salerno-Ferraro & Schuller, 2020). The results demonstrated that there were a number of areas of concern, the most significant being police misinterpreting the disorder and the typical characteristics associated with it. For example, participants reported concern that aversion of eye contact would be interpreted as deceit or guilt, fidgeting or stimming interpreted as anxiety or guilt, and communication issues (e.g., remaining silent, not being able to respond quickly) as indicative of guilt. These respondents also reported that the sensory overload that would originate from the situation, such as flashing lights, noise, and physical touching, would result in behaviors that would have a strong and extremely negative impact on the situation. These general concerns and resultant dissatisfaction with police contact were also found by Crane and colleagues (2016).

Though counterintuitive, innocence has been found to put arrestees at risk for self-incrimination, which may rise to the level of a full confession (Kassin, 2005). The entry point is upon first contact with officers and at that moment people have no reason to feel the need for concern because they have not done anything wrong (Kassin, 2005; Kassin & Norwick, 2004). Due to the individual factors previously identified, the issue of being innocent is of great concern for this population. Once the waiver has been made and interrogation begins, response styles such as yay-saying (i.e., acquiesce), nay-saying, and the tendency to answer either/or questions by agreeing with the last option presented will put into question the veracity of the information obtained.

It is after making the decision to waive one's Miranda rights that the problems begin. The process of interrogation involves interacting with a law enforcement officer and either telling or retelling a crime for which a person is suspected of having committed. Unlike the interview process for an eyewitness, the process of interrogation is designed to elicit a confession, not to garner information to aid in the investigation (see, e.g., Kassin, 2007, 2017; Kassin et al., 2018; for a review see Kassin et al., 2010; Leo, 2008). The process begins with the belief that the suspect is guilty, and under this assumption law enforcement will do what they are legally permitted to do in order to obtain that confession. As decided in the landmark case of *Frazier v. Cupp* (1969), police are permitted to lie to suspects, with few limitations. For example, police can falsely inform a suspect that they have evidence against them, and they use tactics such as minimizing the suspect's role in the crime and stressing the importance of cooperation. In addition to police tactics, the process is generally carried out in a stark and unwelcoming environment.

As noted, during the discussion of eyewitness testimony, the structure and style of questioning greatly impact responses of people with ID. The combination of leading and complex questions that tend to be lengthy are particularly problematic when coupled with characteristics such as acquiescence, gullibility, naiveté, and suggestibility (Davis & Leo, 2014; Heal & Sigelman, 1995; Matikka & Vesela, 1997; Scherr et al., 2020). An example of the impact of suggestibility was found by O'Connell and colleagues (2005), who evaluated the impact of "friendly feedback" on responses during questioning; they expected this would result in changing responses, which was exactly the case. In their discussion, the authors identified heightened suggestibility of the participants as one reason for their findings but also noted that it was possible that decisions were also influenced by the desire to please authority figures. In addition to finding that individuals diagnosed with ID have significantly lower Miranda abilities than the general population, Erickson and colleagues (2020) found that adults with ID demonstrated greater acquiescence scores on the SAMA.

Leo (1996) observed 175 police interrogations, in which 78.29% of suspects waived their rights. The tactics most often used during the interrogations were appealing to the suspect's self-interest and confronting the suspect with existing evidence of guilt. There were a number of other techniques employed less often such as undermining the suspect's confidence in their denial of guilt, identifying contradictions in their story of what happened, and appealing to the importance of cooperation. It can easily be seen how these tactics would overwhelm individuals with ID; all five advantaged law enforcement because of the characteristics of suggestibility, compliance, desire to please, and naiveté. Schatz (2018) noted that as of June 2, 2017, there were 245 individuals who falsely confessed, and of those, approximately 25% (~61) of individuals exhibited some indica of intellectual disability.

Competence to Stand Trial and Competence to Plead Guilty

As previously mentioned, the standard for competence to stand trial was set forth in the case of *Dusky v. United States* (1960). As written, the ruling would suggest that competence is mostly based on intellect and reasoning ability, then personality characteristics. However, the need to work with their attorney requires more than just cognitive functioning; it also requires reciprocal interaction, which is where dispositional factors can interfere with case outcomes. To date, research regarding the impact that dispositional traits have on competence to stand trial does not exist. However, since both ID and ASD are associated with problems in social functioning, there is no reason to believe that these deficits would not impact the attorney–client relationship.

In light of the absence of research, it can only be surmised that all five of the dispositional factors associated with ID (i.e., suggestibility, confabulation, acquiescence, gullibility, and naiveté) could have a negative impact on the trial of a defendant with ID. For example, the defendant may blindly follow the lead of an incompetent attorney; the tendencies of trusting others, acquiescing to authority, naiveté, and gullibility may be the most influential, though this won't be known until research becomes available. Another example would be the defendant who tried very hard to communicate accurate information to their attorney but whose accounts were tainted by interviewing practices that resulted in errors in recall, distortion of accounts, and/or recalling events that never occurred. Though data does not exist to support or refute this statement, there is little likelihood that attorneys know enough about interviewing individuals with ID to know how to prevent this taint from occurring. Consider the case of a defendant with ASD who expresses lack of eye contact, repetitive and unusual movements, a need for consistency, and an inability to tolerate highly stimulating environments. Not only might this interaction be novel or frightening to an attorney, but also it might result in them not wanting to work with this person yet keeping them on their caseload for financial reasons. Moreover, this interaction would likely be frightening to the defendant and result in an impaired relationship from the outset.

Given the detriment of these factors throughout the adjudicative process, it is imperative for defense counsel to understand how these individuals may present, as well as the factors that should raise concerns regarding a developmental disability. Arguably, there has been more attention paid to individuals with mental illness in the criminal justice system, and thus it might be that attorneys are only looking for signs and symptoms that cannot be ignored, such as bizarre auditory or visual hallucinations or expressed beliefs in aliens or that their soul has been snatched by their pet. These are not the types of things to be looking for when working with individuals who have a developmental disorder.

The transition from competence to stand trial to plea bargaining is not a difficult one because the standard is the same. In the landmark case *Godinez v. Moran* (1993), SCOTUS held that the competence to plead guilty and the competence to waive counsel were the same as those delineated in *Dusky* regardless of the case or the needs of the individual. In the words of the justices:

> The competency standard for pleading guilty or waiving the right to counsel is the same as the competency standard for standing trial: whether the defendant has "sufficient present ability to consult with his lawyer with a reasonable degree of rational understanding" and a "rational as well as factual understanding of the proceedings against him," *Dusky* v. *United States,* 362 U. S. 402 *(per curiam).* There is no reason for the competency standard for either of those decisions to be higher than that for standing trial. The decision to plead guilty, though profound, is no more complicated than the sum total of decisions that a defendant may have to make during the course of a trial, such as whether to testify, whether to waive a jury trial, and whether to cross-examine witnesses for the prosecution. Nor does the decision to waive counsel require an appreciably higher level of mental functioning than the decision to waive other constitutional rights (*Godinez v. Moran,* 1993, pg. 389).

As noted by Scherr and colleagues (2020), dispositional and situational factors play a role in decision making during the plea-bargaining process. As of September 26, 2021, there have been 2,857 innocent individuals exonerated in the United States; 592 entered guilty pleas (an increased identification of 94 individuals over the course of 2 years; see Scherr et al., 2020), and of those, 13% (77) falsely confessed (National Registry of Exonerations, 2021). Guilty pleas are known to be the most common disposition, occurring in approximately 95% of convictions (Pastore & Maguire, 2003), and can have profound ramifications. The decision to accept a plea may be cognitively sound or be negatively influenced by factors internal and external to the individual. At-risk populations, such as juveniles and individuals with mental health issues, have self-reported rates of false guilty pleas up to two times higher (e.g., 27% of juveniles and 37% of offenders with mental health problems, respectively; Redlich et al., 2010; Zottoli et al., 2016).

The plea-bargaining process involves a number of important actions that require comprehension, reasoning, and rational decision making, as well as social and interpersonal skills that are typical for one's chronological age. While there is no expectation that a defendant will make such a decision on their own (thought they could), they should have an attorney who is competently able to carry out some of the basic tasks related to plea bargaining. At minimum, the attorney should explain the strengths and weaknesses of the defendant's case, the likelihood of conviction, and the terms of the plea agreement (e.g., the charge, the possible sentences, the difficulty in getting a plea agreement vacated). Instances in which attorneys have been brought forward on ineffective assistance of counsel (IAC) charges in relation to plea bargaining are rare, but a couple of cases highlight the importance of a defendant having counsel prepared to do their job and represent their client to the best of their abilities. In a case where the client has ID, the previously noted "at minimum tasks" for the attorney are much more challenging.

A case example is given to highlight the need for "more than adequate" counsel in cases where a defendant has a developmental disability: the case of Medell Banks, who was charged with capital murder for the death of a baby that more likely than not never existed (Herbert, 2002). Medell was an individual with ID who denied his guilt but who, upon the advice of counsel, accepted a plea of manslaughter with a sentence of 15 years; the counsel who represented him had never tried a capital case because he was a Social Security attorney and had never studied criminal law. It was actually the trial counsel themselves who brought an ineffective assistance of counsel (IAC) claim against himself – which is unheard of - and the appellate court granted a motion for the withdrawal of Medell's guilty plea. The difference at his trial was that lead counsel was skilled in both criminal law and ID; he was successful at negotiating a new plea deal that was in line with Medell's best interests, a guilty plea to a misdemeanor charge of tampering with evidence. Though it is very likely that Medell didn't understand the plea-bargaining process the first time, the second time came with the awareness of the previous outcome and the successful communication of all the relevant information to Medell, who had an IQ of 57. Given space limitations, the case of Robert Johnson cannot be covered; however, a detailed overview of the case and the issues related to plea bargaining, ID, and IAC in the case of Robert Johnson is available in the petition for a writ of certiorari in the Supreme Court of Missouri (Johnson v. Missouri, 2019).

Summary and Recommendations

Individuals with developmental disabilities, especially ID and ASD, present with distinct intellectual and social skills deficits that render them uniquely vulnerable at virtually every stage of involvement with the criminal justice system. Indeed, impaired reasoning and decision making, concreteness of thought, cognitive rigidity and inflexibility, and comprehension difficulties raise considerable concern regarding various psycholegal capacities (e.g., adjudicative competence, Miranda waiver), whereas suggestibility, naiveté, and acquiescence heighten the risks associated with false confessions and involvement in crime, for example. Unfortunately, several factors contribute to the systematic underidentification of individuals with developmental disabilities in the criminal justice system (e.g., cloak of competence, invisibility of developmental disabilities), which are of considerable concern given that their detrimental impact is heightened if the individual is not identified as someone with a disability and for whom greater scrutiny and/or assistance may be needed.

Identification and Screening Efforts
Due to the myriad concerns regarding the risks associated with the systematic underidentification of individuals with developmental disabilities in the criminal justice system, various scholars have argued for the implementation of methods designed to identify and screen for developmental disabilities in criminal justice settings. For example, several scholars (Everington & Luckasson, 1989; Fulero & Everington, 2004) have advocated for special education professionals to aid in identifying individuals with disabilities, whereas Close and Walker (2010) argued for the participation of a forensic special educator who is knowledgeable about developmental disabilities and who could function as a "knowledgeable ally." Others have argued for the implementation of broad screening efforts to identify individuals with disabilities in the criminal justice system. The Hayes Ability Screening Index (Hayes, 2000), for example, is one of the more widely used instruments. Mason and Murphy (2002) reported that a screening tool correctly identified 87% of their sample of individuals with ID in the United Kingdom. In another study, Close and Walker (2010) provided a "Checklist of Indicators" for law enforcement to identify individuals with disabilities. More recently, Murphy et al. (2017) reviewed various screening instruments that have been developed for this purpose, including the Learning Disability Screening Questionnaire (McKenzie & Paxton, 2006). Despite the apparent need for screening, however, Scheyett and colleagues (2009) reported that few jails in North Carolina were utilizing screening practices.

Accommodations and Reduced Threshold for Scrutiny
In addition to better detection and identification of individuals with disabilities in the criminal justice system, modifications and accommodations are imperative to ensure effective participation in the adjudicative process. Examples include modified interview guidelines, adapted treatment modalities, and distinct procedures (see, e.g., Applebaum & Applebaum, 1994; Gudjonsson & Joyce, 2011; Wall et al., 2003; Wall & Christopher, 2012; Wood et al., 2019). Given the myriad difficulties that uniquely interfere with effective identification and assessment of deficits in this population (i.e., cloak of competence, acquiescence, suggestibility), there is also a need for heightened scrutiny when interacting with defendants with a known (or suspected) history of developmental disabilities (Everington & Fulero, 1999).

Balancing Autonomy and Vulnerability in an Adversarial System
As described throughout, individuals with developmental disabilities present with a broad range of deficits that increase their vulnerability in the criminal justice system, which is further complicated by the adversarial nature of the system and the presumption of autonomy. In addition, there is considerable value bestowed upon an individual's right to make their own decisions in American society, which must be balanced against the need to protect an individual from the potential for harm that may result from this vulnerability. In recent years, supported decision-making (SDS) arrangements have started to replace the traditional all-or-nothing

view of capacity inherent in guardianship, allowing for individuals with a disability to maintain power to make decisions, but with the assistance of an advisor of their choosing. Relevant to this context, the United Nations endorsed SDS in their recognition that some individuals with disabilities may need support in the area of legal capacities, which has applicability to the involvement of individuals with developmental disabilities in the criminal justice system as victims, witnesses, and/or defendants (Dinerstein, 2017). Consistent with the notion of SDS, in an investigation of the experiences of 27 adults with developmental disabilities in the criminal justice system in the United States, Sarrett and Ucar (2021) reported that confusion was widespread, leading some participants to suggest the involvement of a support person.

Conclusion

As described throughout, individuals with developmental disabilities, namely ID and ASD, face unique challenges when interfacing with the criminal justice system. Concerns regarding adequate and effective participation in the adjudicative process exist across all phases, beginning with initial encounters with police and carrying through to the sentencing phase. The situation is particularly troubling since individuals with developmental disabilities are overrepresented in the criminal justice system yet underidentified due to the invisibility of their disability and dispositional factors that facilitate their passing through the system unnoticed (e.g., cloak of competence, acquiescence). For these reasons, efforts to aid in the identification of this population during the adjudicative process, as well as widespread education regarding typical areas of concern (i.e., awareness of when/how these deficits may impede their involvement), are recommended as a means of mitigating these problems. Further research is needed regarding the utility of these methods to address this problem, which should be weighed against the associated concerns regarding threats to autonomy.

References

Agnew, S. E., & Powell, M. B. (2004). The effect of intellectual disability on children's recall of an event across different question types. *Law and Human Behavior, 28*(3), 273–294.

American Association on Intellectual and Developmental Disabilities (AAIDD). (2021). *Intellectual disability: Definition, diagnosis, classification, and systems of supports* (12th ed.).

American Broadcast Company. (2010). *What did A. J. see?* https://www.youtube.com/watch?v=J55d73OiMKs; https://www.youtube.com/watch?v=tTbu757A3I8; https://www.youtube.com/watch?v=N_DbjO_e9ps

American Psychiatric Association (APA). (2013). *Diagnostic and statistical manual of mental disorders* (5th ed.). https://doi.org/10.1176/appi.books.9780890425596

Anderson, S. D., & Hewitt, J. (2002). The effect of competency restoration training on defendants with mental retardation found not competent to proceed. *Law and Human Behavior, 26*, 343–351.

Appelbaum, K. L. (1994). Assessment of criminal-justice-related competencies in defendants with mental retardation. *Journal of Psychiatry and Law, 22 (3)*, 311–327.

Appelbaum, K. L., & Appelbaum, P. S. (1994). Criminal-justice-related competencies in defendants with mental retardation. *Journal of Psychiatry & Law, 22(4)*, 483–503.

Atkins v. Virginia, 536 U.S. 304 (2002). https://www.oyez.org/cases/2001/00-8452

Baladerian, N. J., Coleman, T. F., & Stream, J. (2013). *Abuse of people with disabilities: Victims and their families speak out.* Spectrum Institute: Disability and Abuse Project. https://ncvc.dspacedirect.org/handle/20.500.11990/998

Baroff, G. S. (1996). The mentally retarded offender.

Beail, N. (2002). Interrogative suggestibility, memory and intellectual disability. *Journal of Applied Research in Intellectual Disabilities, 15*(2), 129–137.

Blair, J. P. (2007). The roles of interrogation, perception, and individual differences in producing compliant false confessions. *Psychology, Crime & Law, 13*(2), 173–186.

Blanchard, R., Watson, M. S., Choy, A., Dickey, R., Klassen, P., Kuban, M., & Ferren, D. J. (1999). Pedophiles: Mental retardation, maternal age, and sexual orientation. *Archives of Sexual Behavior, 28*(2), 111–127.

Block, J. (1965). *The challenge of response sets: Unconfounding meaning, acquiescence, and social desirability in the MMPI.* Appleton-Century-Crofts.

Bonnie, R. J. (1990). The competence of criminal defendants with mental retardation to participate in their own defense. *Journal of Criminal Law & Criminology, 81*, 419–446.

Bradford, J., & Dimock, J. (1986). A comparative study of adolescents and adults who willfully set fires. *Psychiatric Journal of the University of Ottawa, 11*(4), 228–234.

Brewer, N., & Young, R. L. (2018). *Crime and autism spectrum disorder: Myths and mechanisms*. Jessica Kingsley Publishers.

Brookbanks, W., & Freckelton, I. (2018). Legal issues concerning offenders with intellectual and developmental disabilities. In W. R. Lindsay & J. L. Taylor (Eds.), *The Wiley handbook on offenders with intellectual and developmental disabilities: Research, training, and practice* (pp. 56–85). John Wiley & Sons Ltd.: Hoboken, NJ.

Brown, J. M., Haun, J., Zapf, P. A., & Brown, N. N. (2017). Fetal Alcohol Spectrum Disorders (FASD) and competency to stand trial (CST): Suggestions for a "best practices" approach to forensic evaluation. *International Journal of Law and Psychiatry, 52*, 19–27.

Bruck, M., Ceci, S. J., & Rosenthal, R. (1995). Amicus brief for the case of State of New Jersey v. Michaels presented by Committee of Concerned Social Scientists. *Psychology, Public Policy, and Law, 1*, 272–322.

Ceci, S. J., & Bruck, M. (1993). Suggestibility of the child witness: A historical review and synthesis. *Psychological Bulletin, 113*, 403–439.

Ceci, S. J., & Bruck, M. (1995). *Jeopardy in the courtroom: A scientific analysis of children's testimony*. American Psychological Association.

Ceci, S. J., Loftus, E. F., Leichtman, M., & Bruck, M. (1994). The possible role of source misattributions in the creation of false beliefs among preschoolers. *International Journal of Clinical & Experimental Hypnosis, 42*, 304–320.

Chae, Y., Hobbs, S. D., & Bederian-Gardner, D. (2018). Eyewitness memory abilities in typically developing children. In J. Johnson, G. Goodman, & P. C. Mundy (Eds.), *The Wiley handbook of memory, autism spectrum disorder, and the law* (pp. 179–195). Wiley Blackwell.

Clare, I. C. H., & Gudjonsson, G. H. (1993). Interrogative suggestibility, confabulation, and acquiescence in people with learning disabilities (mental handicap): Implications for reliability during police interrogations. *British Journal of Clinical Psychology, 32*, 295–301.

Clare, I. C. H., & Gudjonsson, G. H. (1995). The vulnerability of suspects with intellectual disabilities during police interviews: A review and experimental study of decision-making. *Mental Handicap Research, 8*, 110–128.

Close, D. W., & Walker, H. M. (2010). Navigating the criminal justice system for youth and adults with developmental disabilities: Role of the forensic special educator. *Journal of Behavior Analysis of Offender and Victim Treatment and Prevention, 2*(2), 74–103.

Cloud, M., Shepherd, G. B., Berkoff, A. N., & Shur, J. V. (2002). Words without meaning: The Constitution, confessions, and mentally retarded suspects. *University of Chicago Law Review, 69*, 495–624.

Cochrane, R. E., Grisso, T., & Frederick, R. I. (2001). The relationship between criminal charges, diagnoses, and psycholegal opinions among federal pretrial defendants. *Behavioral Sciences & the Law, 19*(4), 565–582.

Cocker, A. G., Cote, G., Toupin, J., & St-Onge, B. (2007). Rate and characteristics of men with an intellectual disability in pre-trial detention. *Journal of Intellectual & Developmental Disability, 32*, 143–152.

Colwell, L. H., & Gianesini, J. (2011). Demographic, criminogenic, and psychiatric factors that predict competency restoration. *Journal of the American Academy of Psychiatry and the Law, 39*, 297–306.

Couch, A., & Keniston, K. (1960). Yeasayers and naysayers: Agreeing response set as a personality variable. *Journal of Abnormal and Social Psychology, 60*(2), 151–174.

Crane, L., Maras, K. L., Hawken, T., Mulcahy, S., & Memon, S. (2016). Experiences of autism spectrum disorder and policing in England and Wales: Surveying police and the autism community. *Journal of Autism and Developmental Disorders, 46*, 2028–2041.

Davis, D., & Leo, R. A. (2014). The problem of interrogation-induced false confessions. Sources of failure in prevention. In S. J. Horowitz & M. L. Goldstein (Eds.), *Handbook of forensic sociology and psychology*.

Day, K. (1993). Crime and mental retardation: A review. In K. Howells & C. R. Hollin (Eds.), *Clinical approaches to the mentally disordered offender* (pp. 48–56). Wiley.

Denkowski, G. C., & Denkoswki, K. M. (1985). The mentally retarded offender in the system prison system: Identification, prevalence, adjustment, and rehabilitation. *Criminal Justice and Behavior, 12*, 55–70.

Dinerstein, R. (2017). Supported decision making and competency in the criminal justice system. In *Competency of individuals with intellectual and developmental disabilities in the criminal justice system: A call to action for the criminal justice community* (pp. 29–31). The Arc National Center on Criminal Justice and Disability.

Dion, J., Paquette, G., Tremblay, K. N., Collin-Vézina, D., & Chabot, M. (2018). Child maltreatment among children with intellectual disability in the Canadian Incidence Study. *American Journal on Intellectual and Developmental Disabilities, 123*, 176–188.

Dusky v. United States, 362 U.S. 402 (1960). https://www.oyez.org/cases/1959/504%20MISC

Drizin, S. A., & Leo, R. A. (2004). The problem of false confessions in the post-DNA world. *North Carolina Law Review, 82*, 891–1003.

Edgerton, R. (1972). *The cloak of competence: Stigma in the lives of the mentally retarded.* University of California Press.

Ellis, J., & Luckasson, R. (1985). Mentally retarded criminal defendants. *George Washington Law Review, 53*, 414–492.

Erickson, K., & Issacs, B. (2003). Eyewitness identification accuracy: A comparison of adults with and those without intellectual disability. *Mental Retardation, 41*(3), 161–173.

Erickson, S. L., Salekin, K. L., Johnson, L. N., & Doran, S. C. (2020). The predictive power of intelligence: Miranda abilities of individuals with intellectual disability. *Law and Human Behavior, 44*, 60–70.

Everington, C. (1989). Demographic variables associated with competence to stand trial referral and evaluation of criminal defendants with mental retardation. *Journal of Psychiatry and Law, 17*(4), 627–640.

Everington, C., & Dunn, C. (1995). A second validation study of the Competence Assessment for Standing Trial for Defendants with Mental Retardation (CAST-MR). *Criminal Justice and Behavior, 22*(1), 44–59.

Everington, C., & Fulero, S. M. (1999). Competence to confess: Measuring understanding and suggestibility of defendants with mental retardation. *Mental Retardation, 37*, 212–220.

Everington, C., & Luckasson, R. (1989). Addressing the needs of the criminal defendant with mental retardation: The special educator as a resource to the criminal justice system. *Education and Training in Mental Retardation, 24*, 193–200. http://www.jstor.org/stable/2387482

Fazel, S., Xenitidis, K., & Powell, J. (2008). The prevalence of intellectual disabilities among 12000 prisoners—A systematic review. *International Journal of Law and Psychiatry, 31*, 369–373.

Finlay, W. M. L., & Lyons, E. (2002). Acquiescence in interviews with people with mental retardation. *Intellectual and Developmental Disabilities, 40*(1), 14–29.

Fitzgerald, S., Gray, N. S., Taylor, J., & Snowden, R. J. (2011). Risk factors for recidivism in offenders with intellectual disabilities. *Psychology, Crime & Law, 17*, 43–58.

Fogden, B. C., Thomas, D. M., Daffern, M., & Ogloff, J. R. P. (2016). Crime and victimization in people with intellectual disability: A case linkage study. *BMC Psychiatry, 16*, 170-179.

Frazier v. Cupp, 394 U.S. 731 (1969). https://www.oyez.org/cases/1968/643

Freckelton, I. (2013). Autism spectrum disorder: Forensic issues and challenges for mental health professionals and courts. *Journal of Applied Research in Intellectual Disabilities, 26*, 420-434.

French, L., Garry, M., & Loftus, E. F. (2009). False memories: A kind of confabulation in non-clinical subjects. In W. Hirstein, *Confabulation: Views from neuroscience, psychiatry, psychology and philosophy* (pp. 33-66). Oxford University Press.

Fulero, S. M., & Everington, C. (1995). Assessing competency to waive *Miranda* rights in defendants with mental retardation. *Law and Human Behavior, 19*, 533–543.

Fulero, S. M., & Everington, C. (2004). Mental retardation, competency to waive Miranda rights, and false confessions. In G. D. Lassiter (Ed.), *Interrogations, confessions, and entrapment* (pp. 163–179). Kluwer Academic/Plenum Publishers.

Gibling, F., & Davies, G. (1988). Reinstatement of context following exposure to post-event information. *British Journal of Psychology, 79*, 129–141.

Gleaser, W., & Deane, K. (1999). Normalisation in an abnormal world: a study of prisoners with intellectual disability. *International Journal of Offender Therapy and Comparative Criminology, 43*, 338–356.

Godinez v. Moran, 509 U.S. 389 (1993). https://supreme.justia.com/cases/federal/us/509/389/#tab-opinion-1959315

Gordon, B. N., Jens, K. G., Hollings, R., & Watson, T. E. (1994). Remembering activities performed versus those imagined: Implications for testimony of children with mental retardation. *Journal of Clinical Child Psychology, 23*(3), 239–248.

Gowensmith, W. N. (2019). Resolution or resignation: The role of forensic mental health professionals amidst the competency services crisis. *Psychology, Public Policy, and Law, 25*(1), 1–14.

Greenfield, D. P., Dougherty, E. J., Jackson, R. M., Podboy, J. W., & Zimmerman, M. L. (2001). Retrospective evaluation of Miranda reading levels and waiver competency. *American Journal of Forensic Psychology, 19*, 75–86.

Greenspan, S. (2008). Foolish action in adults with intellectual disabilities: The forgotten problem of risk-unawareness. In L. M. Glidden (Ed.), *International review of research in mental retardation* (pp. 147–119). Elsevier.

Greenspan, S., Loughlin, G., & Black, R. (2001). Credulity and gullibility in persons with mental retardation. In L. M. Glidden (Ed.), *International review of research in mental retardation* (pp. 101–135). Academic Press.

Greenspan, S., & Woods, G. W. (2014). Intellectual disability as a disorder of reasoning and judgement: The gradual move away from intelligence quotient-ceilings. *Current Opinion in Psychiatry, 27*(2), 110–116.

Griego, A. W., Datzman, J. N., Estrada, S. M., & Middlebrook, S. S. (2019). Suggestibility and false memories in relation to intellectual disability and autism spectrum disorders: A meta-analytic review. *Journal of Intellectual Disability Research, 63*(12), 1464–1474.

Grisso, T. (1981). Juveniles' comprehension of Miranda warnings. *Juveniles' Waiver of Rights: Legal and Psychological Competence*, 59–93.

Grisso, T. (1998). *Instruments for assessing understanding and appreciation of Miranda rights*. Professional Resource Press.

Gudjonsson, G. H. (2003). *The psychology of interrogations and confessions: A handbook*. John Wiley & Sons.

Gudjonsson, G. H. (2010). Interrogative suggestibility and false confessions. In J. M. Brown & E. A. Campbell (Eds.), *The Cambridge handbook of forensic psychology* (pp. 202–207). Cambridge University Press.

Gudjonsson, G. H., & Clark, N. K. (1986). Suggestibility in police interrogation: A social psychological model. *Social Behaviour, 1*(2), 83–104.

Gudjonsson, G. H., & Clare, I. C. (1995). The relationship between confabulation and intellectual ability, memory, interrogative suggestibility and acquiescence. *Personality and Individual Differences, 19*(3), 333–338.

Gudjonsson, G. H., & Henry, L. (2003). Child and adolescent witnesses with intellectual disability: The importance of suggestibility. *Legal and Criminological Psychology, 8*(2), 241–252.

Gudjonsson, G. H., & Joyce, T. (2011). Interviewing adults with intellectual disabilities. *Advances in Mental Health and Intellectual Disabilities, 5*, 16–21.

Gudjonsson, G. H., Murphy, G. H., & Clare, I. C. H. (2000). Assessing the capacity of people with intellectual disabilities to be witnesses in court. *Psychological Medicine, 30*, 307–314.

Gunasekaran, S., & Chaplin, E. (2012). Autism spectrum disorders and offending. *Advances in Mental Health and Intellectual Disabilities, 6*, 306–313.

Harrell, E. (2017). *Crimes against persons with disabilities, 2009–2015 statistical tables* (NCJ Publication No. 250632). Bureau of Justice Statistics, U.S. Department of Justice. https://www.bjs.gov/content/ pub/pdf/capd0915st.pdf

Harrell, E., & Rand, M. (2010). *Crime against people with disabilities, 2008* (NCJ Publication No. 231328). Bureau of Justice Statistics, U.S. Department of Justice. https://bjs.ojp.gov/content/pub/pdf/capd08.pdf

Haw, C., Radley, J., & Cooke, L. (2013). Characteristics of male autistic spectrum patients in low security: Are they different from non-autistic low secure patients? *Journal of Intellectual Disabilities and Offending Behaviour, 4*, 24–42.

Hayes, S. C. (1993). *People with an intellectual disability and the criminal justice system: Appearances before local courts* (Research Report No. 4). NSW Law Reform Commission.

Hayes, S. C. (1996). *People with an intellectual disability and the criminal justice system: Two rural courts* (Research Report No. 5). NSW Law Reform Commission.

Hayes, S. C. (2000). *Hayes Ability Screening Index (HASI) manual*. University of Sydney Department of Behavioral Sciences in Medicine.

Hayes, S. C. (2002). Early intervention of early incarceration? Using a screening test for intellectual disability in the criminal justice system. *Journal of Applied Research in Intellectual Disabilities, 15*, 120–128.

Hayes, S. (2018). Criminal behavior and intellectual and developmental disabilities. In W. R. Lindsay & J. L. Taylor (Eds.), *The Wiley handbook on offenders with intellectual and developmental disabilities: Research, training, and practice* (pp. 21–37). John Wiley & Sons.

Heal, L. W., & Sigelman, C. K. (1995). Response bias in interviews of individuals with limited mental ability. *Journal of Intellectual Disability Research, 39*(4), 331–340.

Heilbrun, K., Giallella, C., Wright, H. J., DeMatteo, D., Griffin, P. A., Locklair, B., & Desai, A. (2019). Treatment of restoration of competent to stand trial: Critical analysis and policy recommendations. *Psychology, Public Policy, and Law, 25*(4), 266–283.

Helverschou, S. B., Rasmussen, K., Steindal, K., Sondanaa, E., Nilsson, B., & Nottestad, J. A. (2015). Offending profiles of individuals with autism spectrum disorder: A study of all individuals with autism spectrum disorder examined by the forensic psychiatric service in Norway between 2000 and 2010. *Autism, 19*, 850–858.

Henry, L. A., Gudjonsson, G. H. (1999). Eyewitness memory and suggestibility in children with mental retardation. *American Journal of Mental Retardation, 104*(6), 491–508.

Henry, L. A., & Gudjonsson, G. H. (2003). Eyewitness memory, suggestibility, and repeated recall sessions in children with mild and moderate intellectual disabilities. *Law and Human Behavior, 27*(5), 481–505.

Henry, L. A., Ridley, A., Perry, J., & Crane, L. (2011). Perceived credibility and eyewitness testimony of children with intellectual disabilities. *Journal of Intellectual Disability Research, 55*(4), 385–391.

Herbert, B. (2002, August 15). An imaginary homicide. *New York Times*. https://www.nytimes.com/2002/08/15/opinion/an-imaginary-homicide.html/

Hickson, L., & Khemka, I. (2016). Prevention of maltreatment of adults with intellectual and developmental disabilities. In J. R. Lutzker, K. Guastaferro, & M. B. Benka-Coker (Eds.), *Maltreatment of people with intellectual and developmental disabilities* (pp. 233–261). American Association on Intellectual and Developmental Disabilities.

Higgs, T., & Carter, A. J. (2015). Autism spectrum disorder and sexual offending: Responsivity in forensic interventions. *Aggression and Violent Behavior, 22*, 112-119.

Hill, C., Memon, A., & McGeorge, P. (2008). The role of confirmation bias in suspect interviews: A systematic evaluation. *Legal and Criminological Psychology, 13*(2), 357–371.
https://www.lexico.com/en/definition/naive
https://www.oxfordlearnersdictionaries.com/us/definition/american_english/acquiescence
Jones, J. (2007). Persons with intellectual disabilities in the criminal justice system: Review of issues. *International Journal of Offender Therapy and Comparative Criminology, 51*(6), 723–733.
Jones, L., Bellis, M. A., Wood, S., Hughes, K., McCoy, E., Eckley, L., Bates, G., Mikton, C., Shakespeare, T., & Officer, A. (2012). Prevalence and risk of violence against children with disabilities: A systematic review and meta-analysis of observational studies. *The Lancet, 380*, 899–907.
Kassin, S. M. (1985). Eyewitness identification: Retrospective self-awareness and the accuracy-confidence correlation. *Journal of Personality and Social Psychology, 49*(4), 878–893.
Kassin, S. M. (2005). On the psychology of confessions: Does innocence put innocents at risk? *American Psychologist, 60*(3), 215–228.
Kassin, S. M. (2007). Internalized false confessions. In M. P. Toglia, J. D. Read, D. F. Ross, & R. C. L. Lindsay (Eds.), *The handbook of eyewitness psychology, Vol. 1. Memory for events* (pp. 175–192). Lawrence Erlbaum Associates Publishers.
Kassin, S. M. (2015). The social psychology of false confessions. *Social Issues and Policy Review, 9*(1), 25–51.
Kassin, S. M. (2017). False confessions: How can psychology so basic be so counterintuitive? *American Psychologist, 72*(9), 951–964.
Kassin, S. M., Drizin, S. A., Grisso, T., Gudjonsson, G. H., Leo, R. A., & Redlich, A. D. (2010). Police-induced confessions: Risk factors and recommendations. *Law and Human Behavior, 34*, 3–38.
Kassin, S. M., Goldstein, C. C., & Savitsky, K. (2003). Behavioral confirmation in the interrogation room: On the dangers of presuming guilt. *Law and Human Behavior, 27*(2), 187–203.
Kassin, S. M., & Norwick, R. J. (2004). Why suspects waive their Miranda rights: The power of innocence. *Law and Human Behavior, 28*, 211–221.
Kassin, S. M., Redlich, A. D., Alceste, F., & Luke, T. J. (2018). On the general acceptance of confessions research: Opinions of the scientific community. *American Psychologist, 73*(1), 63.
Katz, N., & Zemishlany, Z. (2006). Criminal responsibility in Asperger's syndrome. *Israel Journal of Psychiatry Related Sciences, 43*, 166–173.
Kebbell, M. R., & Hatton, C. (1999). People with mental retardation as witnesses in court: A review. *Mental Retardation, 37*, 179–187.
Kebbell, M. R., Hatton, C., & Johnson, S. D. (2004). Witnesses with intellectual disabilities in court: What questions are asked and what influence do they have? *Legal and Criminological Psychology, 9*, 23–35.
King, C., & Murphy, G. H. (2014). A systematic review of people with autism spectrum disorder and the criminal justice system. *Journal of Autism and Developmental Disorders, 44*(11), 2717–2733.
Klemfuss, J. Z., & Ceci, S. J. (2013). The law and science of children's testimonial competency. In R. E. Holliday & T. A. Marche (Eds.), *Child forensic psychology: Victim and eyewitness memory* (pp. 179–208). Palgrave Macmillan/Springer Nature.
Leo, R. A. (1996). Miranda's revenge: Police interrogation as a confidence game. *Law & Society Review, 30*(2), 259–288.
Leo, R. A. (2008). *Police interrogation and American justice*. Harvard University Press.
Leong, G. B., & Silva, J. A. (1999). Revisiting arson from an outpatient forensic perspective. *Journal of Forensic Sciences, 44*(3), 558–563.
Lindsay, W. R. (2002). Integration of recent reviews on offenders with disabilities. *Journal of Applied Research in Intellectual Disabilities, 15*(2), 111–119.
Lindsay, W. R., Carson, D., O'Brien, G., Holland, A. J., Taylor, J. L., Wheeler, J. R., & Steptoe, L. (2014). A comparison of referrals with and without autism spectrum disorder to forensic intellectual disability services. *Psychiatry, Psychology and Law, 21*(6), 947–954.
Lindsay, W., Haut, F., & Steptoe, L. (2011). Referral patterns for offenders with intellectual disability: A 20-year study. *Journal of Forensic Psychiatry & Psychology, 22*(4), 513–517.
Lindsay, W. R., & Taylor, J. L. (2018). Historical and theoretical approaches to offending in people with intellectual and developmental disabilities. In W. R. Lindsay & J. L. Taylor (Eds.), *The Wiley handbook on offenders with intellectual and developmental disabilities: Research, training, and practice* (pp. 1–20). John Wiley & Sons.
Lindsay, W. R., Taylor, J. L., & Sturmey, P. (2004). Natural histories and theories of offending in people with developmental disabilities. In W. R. Lindsay, J. L. Taylor, & P. Sturney (Eds.), *Offenders with developmental disabilities* (pp. 3–21). John Wiley & Sons.
Loftus, E. F. (1975). Leading questions and the eyewitness report. *Cognitive Psychology, 7*(4), 560–572.

Loftus, E. F. (1979). *Eyewitness testimony*. Harvard University Press.
Loftus, E. F. (2005). Planting misinformation in the human mind: A 30-year investigation of the malleability of memory. *Learning and Memory, 12*(4), 361–366.
Loftus, E. F., Miller, D. G., & Burns, H. J. (1978). Semantic integration of verbal information into a visual memory. *Journal of Experimental Psychology: Human Learning and Memory, 4*(1), 19–31.
Loftus, E. F., & Pickrell, J. E. (1995). The formation of false memories. *Psychiatric Annals, 25*(12), 720–725.
Lunsky, Y., Raina, R., & Jones, J. (2012). Relationship between prior legal involvement and current crisis for adults with intellectual disability. *Journal of Intellectual & Developmental Disability, 37*(2), 163–168.
MacEachron, A. E. (1979). Mentally retarded offenders: Prevalence and characteristics. *American Journal of Mental Deficiency, 84*(2), 165–176.
Mason, J., & Murphy, G. (2002). Intellectual disability amongst people on probation: Prevalence and outcome. *Journal of Intellectual Disability Research, 46*(3), 230–238.
Matikka, L. A., & Vesela, H. T. (1997). Acquiescence in quality-of-life interviews with adults who have mental retardation. *Mental Retardation, 35*(2), 331–340.
Maulik, P. K., Mascarenhas, M. N., Mathers, C. D., Dua, T., & Saxena, S. (2011). Prevalence of intellectual disability: A meta-analysis of population-based studies. *Research in Developmental Disabilities, 32*(2), 419–436.
McKenzie, K., & Paxton, L. (2006). Promoting access to services: The development of a new screening tool. *Learning Disability Practice, 9*(6), 17–21.
McNulty, C., Kissi-Deborah, R., & Newsom-Davies, I. (1995). Police involvement with clients having intellectual abilities: A pilot study in South London. *Mental Handicap Research, 8*(2), 129–136.
Melton, G. B., Petrila, J., Poythress, N. G., Slobogin, C., Lyons, P. M., Jr., & Otto, R. K. (Eds.). (2018). *Psychological evaluations for the courts: A handbook for mental health professionals and lawyers* (3rd ed.). Guilford Press.
Memon, A., & Wright, D. B. (1999). Eyewitness testimony and the Oklahoma bombing. *The Psychologist, 12*(6), 292–295.
Michel, M. K., Gordon, B. N., Ornstein, P. A., & Simpson, M. A. (2000). The abilities of children with mental retardation to remember personal experiences: Implications for testimony. *Journal of Clinical Child Psychology, 29*(3), 453–463.
Mikolajewski, A. J., Manguno-Mire, G. M., Coffman, K. L., Deland, S. M., Thompson, J. W., & Thompson, J. J. (2017). Patient characteristics and outcomes related to successful outpatient competency restoration. *Behavioral Sciences & the Law, 35*(3), 225–238.
Miller, R. D. (2003). Hospitalization of criminal defendants for evaluation of competence to stand trial or for restoration of competence: Clinical and legal issues. *Behavioral Sciences and the Law, 21*(3), 369–391.
Milne, R., & Bull, R. (2001). Interviewing witnesses with learning disabilities for legal purposes. *British Journal of Learning Disabilities, 29*(3), 93–97.
Milne, R., Clare, I. C. H., & Bull, R. (2002). Interrogative suggestibility among witnesses with mild intellectual disabilities: The use of an adaptation of the GSS. *Journal of Applied Research in Intellectual Disabilities, 15*(1), 8–17.
Miranda v. Arizona, 384 U.S. 436 (1966). https://www.oyez.org/cases/1965/759
Mosotho, N. L., Bambo, D., Mkhombo, T., Mgidlana, C., Motsumi, N., Matlhabe, T., Joubert, G. & Le Roux, H. E. (2020). Demographic, clinical and forensic profiling of alleged offenders diagnosed with an intellectual disability. *Journal of Forensic Psychology Research and Practice, 20*(4), 362–376.
Mossman, D. (2007). Predicting restorability of incompetent criminal defendants. *Journal of the American Academy of Psychiatry and the Law, 35*(1), 34–43.
Murphy, G. H., Gardner, J., & Freeman, M. J. (2017). Screening prisoners for intellectual disabilities in three English prisons. *Journal of Applied Research in Intellectual Disabilities, 30*(1), 198–204.
National Registry of Exonerations. (2021). % Exonerations by Contributing Factor. https://www.law.umich.edu/special/exoneration/Pages/detaillist.aspx
Nestor, P. G., Daggett, D., Haycock, J., & Price, M. (1999). Competence to stand trial: A neuropsychological inquiry. *Law and Human Behavior, 23*(4), 397–412.
Noble, J. H., & Conley, R. W. (1992). Toward an epidemiology of relevant attributes. In R. W. Conley, R. Luckasson, & G. N. Bouthilet (Eds.), *The criminal justice system and mental retardation. Defendants and victims* (pp. 17–53). Paul H. Brookes.
O'Connell, M. J., Garmoe, W., & Goldstein, N. E. S. (2005). *Miranda* comprehension in adults with mental retardation and the effects of feedback style on suggestibility. *Law and Human Behavior, 29*, 359–369.
Odegard, T. N., Cooper, C. M., Holliday, R. E., & Ceci, S. J. (2010). Interviewing child victims: Advances in the scientific understanding of child eyewitnesses. In J. M. Lampinen & K. Sexton-Radek (Eds.), *Protecting children from violence: Evidence-based interventions* (pp. 105–127). Psychology Press.

Ostermeyer, B., Anacker, L., Perdue, J., Saxton, A., & Noffsinger, S. (2018). Examining decision-making: Understanding civil and criminal competencies. *Psychiatric Annals*, *48*(2), 79–85.

Parry, C. J., & Lindsay, W. R. (2003). Impulsiveness as a factor in sexual offending by people with mild intellectual disability. *Journal of Intellectual Disability Research*, *47*(6), 483–487.

Pastore, A., & Maguire, K. (2003). *Sourcebook of criminal justice statistics: 2002*. U.S. Government Printing Office.

Pate v. Robinson, 383 U.S. 375, 386 (1966). https://www.oyez.org/cases/1965/382

Perske, R. (1994). Thoughts on the police interrogation of individuals with mental retardation. *Mental Retardation*, *32*(5), 377–380.

Perske, R. (2000). Deception in the interrogation room: Sometimes tragic for persons with mental retardation and other developmental disabilities. *Mental Retardation*, *38*(6), 532–537.

Perske, R. (2005). Search for persons with intellectual disabilities who confessed to serious crimes they did not commit. *Mental Retardation*, *43*(1), 58–65.

Petersilia, J. R. (2001). Crime victims with developmental disabilities: A review essay. *Criminal Justice and Behavior*, *28*(6), 655–694.

Pickrell, J. E., McDonald, D., Bernstein, D. M., & Loftus, E. F. (2017). Misinformation effect. In E. F. Loftus (Ed.), *Cognitive illusions: Intriguing phenomena in thinking, judgment and memory* (2nd ed., pp. 406–423). Routledge/Taylor & Francis Group.

Powers, P. A., Andriks, J. L., & Loftus, E. F. (1979). Eyewitness accounts of females and males. *Journal of Applied Psychology*, *64*(3), 339–347.

Pozzulo, J. D., & Lindsay, R. C. L. (1998). Identification accuracy of children versus adults: A meta-analysis. *Law and Human Behavior*, *22*(5), 549–570.

Puri, B. K., Baxter, R., & Cordess, C. C. (1995). Characteristics of firesetters: A study and proposed multiaxial psychiatric classification. *British Journal of Psychiatry*, *166*(3), 393–396.

Raina, P., Arenovich, T., Jones, J., & Lunsky, Y. (2013). Pathways into the criminal justice system for individuals with intellectual disability. *Journal of Applied Research in Intellectual Disabilities*, *26*(5), 404–409.

Rapley, M., & Antaki, C. (1996). A conversation analysis of the "acquiescence" of people with learning disabilities. *Journal of Community & Social Psychology*, *6*(3), 207–227.

Redlich, A. D., Summers, A., & Hoover, S. (2010). Self-reported false confessions and false guilty pleas among offenders with mental illness. *Law & Human Behavior*, *34*(1), 79–90.

Rix, K. B. (1997). Fit to be interviewed by the police? *Advances in Psychiatric Treatment*, *3*, 33–40.

Robert Johnson v. State of Missouri (2019). https://www.supremecourt.gov/DocketPDF/19/19-7153/127052/20191230152806678_Petition.pdf

Rogers, R. (2008). A little knowledge is a dangerous thing . . . Emerging Miranda research and professional roles. *American Psychologist*, *63*(8), 776–787.

Rogers, R., Fiduccia, C. E., Drogin, E. Y., Steadham, J. A., Clark, J. W., & Cramer, R. J. (2013). General knowledge and misknowledge of *Miranda* rights: Are effective Miranda advisements still necessary? *Psychology, Public Policy, and Law*, *19*(4), 432–442.

Rogers, R., Harrison, K. S., Shuman, D. W., Sewell, K. W., & Hazelwood, L. L. (2007). An analysis of Miranda warnings and waivers: Comprehension and coverage. *Law and Human Behavior*, *31*(2), 177–192.

Rogers, R., Hazelwood, L. L., Sewell, K. W., Harrison, K. S., & Shuman, D. W. (2008). The language of *Miranda* warnings in American jurisdictions: A replication and vocabulary analysis. *Law and Human Behavior*, *32*(2), 124–136.

Rogers, R., Rogstad, J. E., Gillard, N. D., Drogin, E. Y., Blackwood, H. L., & Shuman, D. W. (2010). "Everyone knows their Miranda rights": Implicit assumptions and countervailing evidence. *Psychology, Public Policy, and the Law*, *16*(3), 300–318.

Rogers, R., Rogstad, J. E., Steadham, J. A, & Drogin, E. Y. (2011). In plain English: Avoiding recognized problems with *Miranda* comprehension. *Psychology, Public Policy, and the Law*, *17*(2), 264–285.

Rogers, R., Steadham, J. A., Fiduccia, C. E., Drogin, E. Y., & Robinson, E. V. (2014). Mired in Miranda misconceptions: A study of legally involved juveniles at different levels of maturity, *Behavioral Sciences & the Law*, *32*(1), 104–120.

Rosenfeld, B., & Wall, A. (1998). Psychopathology and competence to stand trial. *Criminal Justice and Behavior*, *25*(4), 443–462.

Rutten, A. X., Vermeiren, R. J. M., & Nieuwenhuizen, C. V. (2017). Autism in adult and juvenile delinquents: A literature review. *Child and Adolescent Psychiatry and Mental Health*, *11*, 45-57.

Salekin, K. L., Olley, J. G., & Hedge, K. (2010). Offenders with intellectual disability: Characteristics, prevalence, and issues in forensic assessment. *Journal of Mental Health Research in Intellectual Disabilities*, *3*(2), 98–116.

Salerno-Ferraro, A. C., & Schuller, R. A. (2020). Perspectives from the ASD community on police interactions: Challenges & recommendations. *Research in Developmental Disabilities*, *105*, 103732.

Sarrett, J. C., & Ucar, A. (2021). Beliefs about and perspectives of the criminal justice system of people with intellectual and developmental disabilities: A qualitative study. *Social Sciences & Humanities Open, 3*, 100122.

Schatz, S. J. (2018). Interrogated with intellectual disabilities: The risk of a false confession. *Stanford Law Review, 70*, 643–690.

Scherr, K. C., Redlich, A. D., & Kassin, S. M. (2020). Cumulative disadvantage: A psychological framework for understanding how innocence can lead to confession, wrongful conviction, and beyond. *Perspectives on Psychological Science, 15*(2), 353–383.

Scheyett, A., Vaughn, J., & Taylor, M. F. (2009). Screening and access to services for individuals with serious mental illnesses in jails. *Community Mental Health Journal, 45*(6), 439–446.

Schouten, R. (2003). Commentary: Training for competence—Form or substance? *Journal of the American Academy of Psychiatry and the Law, 31*(2), 202–204.

Sell v. United States, 123 S. Ct. 2174, 2179 (2003).

Simpson, M. K., & Hogg, J. (2001). Patterns of offending among people with intellectual disability: A systematic review. Part I: Methodology and prevalence data. *Journal of Intellectual Disability Research, 45*(5), 384–396.

Stafford, K. P., & Wygant, D. B. (2005). The role of competency to stand trial in mental health courts. *Behavioral Sciences and the Law, 23*(2), 245–258.

State v. Michaels, 136 N.J. 299, 642 A.2d 1372 (1994).

Stinson, J. D., & Robbins, S. B. (2014). Characteristics of people with intellectual disabilities in a secure U.S. forensic hospital. *Journal of Mental Health Research in Intellectual Disabilities, 7*(4), 337–358.

Tassé, M. J., Luckasson, R., & Schalock, R. L. (2016). The relation between intellectual functioning and adaptive behavior in the diagnosis of intellectual disability. *Intellectual and Developmental Disabilities, 54*(6), 381–390. https://doi.org/10.1352/1934-9556-54.6.381

Taylor, J. L., & Lindsay, W. R. (2018). Offenders with intellectual and developmental disabilities: Future directions for research and practice. In W. R. Lindsay & J. L. Taylor (Eds.), *The Wiley handbook on offenders with intellectual and developmental disabilities: Research, training, and practice* (pp. 453–471). John Wiley & Sons.

Terne, M., & Yuille, J. C. (2008). Eyewitness memory and eyewitness identification performance in adults with intellectual disabilities. *Journal of Applied Research in Intellectual Disabilities, 21*(6), 519–531.

Valenti-Hein, D. C., & Schwartz, L. D. (1993). Witness competency in people with mental retardation: Implications for prosecution of sexual abuse. *Sexuality and Disability, 11*(4), 287–294.

Wall, B. W., & Christopher, P. P. (2012). A training program for defendants with intellectual disabilities who are found incompetent to stand trial. *Journal of the American Academy of Psychiatry & the Law, 40*(3), 366–373.

Wall, B. W., Krupp, B. H., & Guilmette, T. (2003). Restoration of competency to stand trial: A training program for persons with mental retardation. *Journal of the American Academy of Psychiatry and the Law, 31*(2), 189–201.

Walker, N., & McCabe, S. (1973). *Crime and insanity in England*. Edinburgh University.

Warren, J. I., Chauhan, P., Kois, L., Dibble, A., & Knighton, J. (2013). Factors influencing 2,260 opinions of defendants' restorability to adjudicative competency. *Psychology, Public Policy, and Law, 19*(4), 498–508.

Warren, J. I., Murrie, D. C., Stejskal, W., Colwell, L. H., Morris, J., Chauhan, P., & Dietz, P. (2006). Opinion formation in evaluating the adjudicative competence and restorability of criminal defendants: A review of 8,000 evaluations. *Behavioral Sciences & the Law, 24*(2), 113–132.

Wells, G. L., & Murray, D. M. (1983). What can psychology say about Neil v. Biggers criteria for judging eyewitness identification accuracy? *Journal of Applied Psychology, 68*(3), 347–362.

Wheeler, J. R., Clare, I. C. H., & Holland, A. J. (2014). What can social and environmental factors tell us about the risk of offending by people with intellectual disabilities? *Psychology, Crime & Law, 20*(7), 635–658.

Wilcock, R., & Henry, L. (2013). The performance of eyewitness with intellectual disability on photographic lineups. *International Journal of Disability, Development, and Education, 60*(1), 44–52.

Winningham, D. B., Rogers, R., Drogin, E. Y., & Velsor, S. F. (2018). Missing out on Miranda: Investigating Miranda comprehension and waiver decisions in adult inpatients. *International Journal of Law and Psychiatry, 61*, 81–89.

Wood, M. E., Lawson, K. M., Anderson, J. L., Kinney, D. I., Nitch, S., & Glassmire, D. M. (2019). Reasonable accommodations for meeting the unique needs of defendants with intellectual disability. *Journal of the American Academy of Psychiatry and the Law, 47*(3), 1–19.

Woodbury-Smith, M., & Dein, K. (2014). Autism spectrum disorder (ASD) and unlawful behaviour: Where do we go from here? *Journal of Autism and Developmental Disorders, 44*(11), 2734–2741.

Woodbury-Smith, M., Furimsky, I., & Chaimowitz, G. (2018). Point prevalence of adults with intellectual developmental disorder in forensic psychiatric inpatient services in Ontario, Canada. *International Journal of Risk and Recovery, 1*(1), 4–11.

Yarmey, A. D., & Jones, H. P. T. (1983). Is the study of eyewitness identification a matter of common sense? In S. Lloyd-Bostock & B. Clifford (Eds.), *Evaluating witness evidence* (pp. 13-40). Wiley.

Young, S., Gonzalez, R. A., Mullens, H., Mutch, L., Mulet-Lambert, I., & Gidjonsson, G. H. (2018). Neurodevelopmental disorders in prison inmates: Comorbidity and combined associations with psychiatric and behavioural disturbance. *Psychiatry Research, 261*(12), 109–115.

Yu, Y., Bradley, C. C., Boan, A. D., Charles, J. M., & Carpenter, L. A. (2021). Young adults with autism spectrum disorder and the criminal justice system. *Journal of Autism and Developmental Disorders, 51*(10), 3624–3636.

Yuille, J. C., & Cooper, B. S. (2012). Challenging the eyewitness expert. In D. Faust (Ed.), *Coping with psychiatric and psychological testimony: Based on the original work by Jay Ziskin* (pp. 685–695). Oxford University Press.

Zapf, P. (2013). *Standardizing protocols for treatment to restore competency to stand trial: Interventions and clinically appropriate time periods* (Document No. 13-01-1901). Washington State Institute for Public Policy.

Zapf, P., & Roesch, R. (2009). *Evaluation of competence to stand trial*. Oxford University Press.

Zelle, H., Romaine, C. L. R., & Goldstein, N. E. S. (2015). Juveniles' *Miranda* comprehension: Understanding, appreciation, and totality of circumstances factors. *Law and Human Behavior, 39*(3), 281–293.

Zottoli, T. M., Daftary-Kapur, T., Winters, G. M., & Hogan, C. (2016). Plea discounts, time-pressures and false guilty pleas in youth and adults who pleaded guilty to felonies in New York City. *Psychology, Public Policy, and Law, 22*(3), 250–259.

CHAPTER 24

Pregnancy and Parenting in Prison

Rebecca J. Shlafer, Joanna Woolman, and Mariann A. Howland

> **Abstract**
> The majority of women involved in the criminal legal system are mothers, and approximately 3% to 4% of women entering prison are pregnant. This chapter explores how developmental science and the law interact and shape the experiences of pregnant women and mothers involved in the criminal legal system and their children before, during, and after incarceration. It considers how several areas of law, including criminal law, family law, and child welfare, coalesce to impact parents and children. The chapter attends closely to relevant principles of developmental science, including sensitive windows of development early in life and the salience of parent–child attachment relationships. The chapter concludes that, with a few exceptions, policies and laws often fail to address the unique needs of parents who are incarcerated and their children. This leaves much room for developmental science to be translated into evidence-based policies and practices to support these families.
>
> **Key Words:** pregnancy, parent, incarceration, child welfare, parent-child attachment

Over the past 30 years, unprecedented numbers of women[1] in the United States have been incarcerated. The majority of incarcerated women are of reproductive age (Carson, 2020), and most are mothers with minor children (Maruschak et al., 2021). Estimates indicate that approximately 3%–4% of women admitted to U.S. jails and prisons are pregnant (Sufrin et al., 2019, 2020). Pregnancy and the postpartum period represent sensitive windows of development not only for children but also for parents. The transition to parenthood involves significant changes in biological, psychological, and social systems (Davis & Narayan, 2020; Glynn et al., 2018; Kim, 2016), and it is important to understand the ways in which involvement in the criminal legal system interacts with these developmental processes. Beyond their direct and current involvement with the criminal legal system, many incarcerated pregnant women and mothers have experienced varied and ongoing interactions with other aspects of the law, including their own and their children's involvement in juvenile and family courts. In this chapter, we explore how developmental science and the law interact for pregnant women and mothers who are incarcerated. We first review key data on pregnant women and parents

---

[1] Throughout this chapter, the terms "women" and "pregnant women" are used. We acknowledge that not everyone who is incarcerated in a women's prison identifies as a woman. Further, we acknowledge that pregnancy can overlap with multiple gender identities and that not all people who are pregnant or have the capacity for pregnancy identify as women.

in prison (with an explicit focus in many places on maternal incarceration, as we explain later) and then consider the intersections between developmental science and the law before, during, and after incarceration.

Maternal Incarceration in the United States

The number of people in prisons and jails in the United States has increased by a staggering 500% during the last four decades (Sentencing Project, 2021). In 2016, 47% of people in state prisons and 57% of people in federal prisons reported having at least one minor child, with 1.5 million children estimated to have a parent in prison (Maruschak et al., 2021). This trend has been driven in large part by an increase in the number of women who are incarcerated, due primarily to changes in state and federal policies, including harsher drug sentencing laws (Sentencing Project, 2021). The number of women incarcerated has risen by more than 700% in the last 40 years (Sentencing Project, 2021), with approximately 222,000 women incarcerated in prisons and jails in 2019 (Sentencing Project, 2020; Zheng & Minton, 2021). In addition, large numbers of women are under criminal justice supervision in the community, with an estimated 885,000 women on probation and 114,140 women on parole in 2018–2019 (Sentencing Project, 2020).

Approximately 75% of women who are incarcerated are of reproductive age (Carson, 2020), and 58% report having minor children, with the majority (64%) of mothers living with at least one of their children prior to incarceration (Glaze & Maruschak, 2010; Maruschak et al., 2021). Nationally, limited data are available about pregnant women who are incarcerated (Bronson & Sufrin, 2019). Jails and prisons do not systematically track pregnancy rates; however, national estimates indicate that approximately 3%–4% of women are pregnant when entering jail or prison (Sufrin et al., 2019, 2020). Sufrin and colleagues have estimated that approximately 1,300 women give birth while in custody each year (Sufrin et al., 2019).

Women involved in the criminal legal system often present with multiple, intersecting, marginalized identities. Mass incarceration in the United States has disproportionately affected women of color and women from low-income communities (American Civil Liberties Union, 2005; Sentencing Project, 2020). In 2019, the imprisonment rate per 100,000 was 83 for Black women, 63 for Hispanic women, and 48 for White women (Carson, 2020). Racial disparities are evident throughout the criminal justice system, including in policing, arrests, sentence lengths, and solitary confinement (Kovera, 2019; Sawyer, 2020). In addition, women involved in the criminal legal system are more likely to have histories of poverty, trauma, serious mental illness, and substance dependence compared to their female peers who are not involved in the criminal legal system and compared to incarcerated men (Fazel et al., 2006; Fazel & Danesh, 2002; Grella et al., 2013). Compared to fathers in state prisons, mothers in state prisons are more likely to report homelessness prior to incarceration, past physical or sexual abuse, and current medical and mental health problems (Glaze & Maruschak, 2010).

In this chapter, we will focus on women and mothers for several reasons. First, women in state and federal prisons are more likely to be parents with minor children, compared to men (58% versus 47%, respectively; Maruschak et al., 2021). Mothers in prison are also more likely than fathers in prison to have lived with their minor children and to have provided most of the daily care for them prior to incarceration (Glaze & Maruschak, 2010). In addition, data from the Bureau of Justice Statistics indicate that when fathers were incarcerated, approximately 90% reported that their children were living with their nonincarcerated mothers, while only 37% of mothers in prison reported that their children lived with the other parent (Glaze & Maruschak, 2010). Cumulatively, these statistics suggest that children often experience greater disruption in their caregiving and living arrangements when mothers compared to fathers are incarcerated.

This chapter will consider how developmental science and different aspects of the law interact and shape the experiences of pregnant women and mothers involved in the criminal legal system and their children. Throughout the chapter, we refer to "statutes," which include current laws that are enforced in states. Typically when we discuss statutes, we are including information about state laws that impact individuals as a result of their direct actions (e.g., criminal penalties for driving under the influence of alcohol). We also refer to "policies" or "policy." When we discuss policy, we are also talking about laws in some instances—but our policy focus includes statutes (both state and federal) and also governmental or agency policies or procedures (which are not codified in state statutes). We think it is important to recognize that laws impact individuals and shift public policy, which in turn impacts families, communities, systems, and funding for direct services.

Legal Intersections When Parents Go to Prison

Several areas of law—including criminal law, family law, and child welfare law—coalesce to impact parents before, during, and after they are incarcerated. As a preliminary matter, the legal presumption of parentage in most states is maternal or through marriage. To establish parentage and then custody or visitation, unmarried fathers or nonbinary parents need to sign an initial recognition of parentage (or in some states sign the child's birth certificate) and also file a petition to establish custody. Only a biological mother or married father has initial custody and parental rights to a child. For some fathers or nonbinary parents, establishing custody can be challenging, particularly if the child is born in prison. Notably, having access to the child and mother immediately after birth to sign and notarize these documents often doesn't happen for women separated from their families and partners while in prison.

Parents facing the possibility of going to prison have serious legal considerations relating to the care and custody of their children that are often urgent and complex. There are significant legal consequences for many parents who are incarcerated—mainly the risk of losing either custody or parental rights of their children. And those who are reentering after prison may seek to restore their parental rights or seek custody or contact with their children after prison. Here, we consider how various laws and policies intersect with developmental science before, during, and after a parent's incarceration (Figure 24.1).

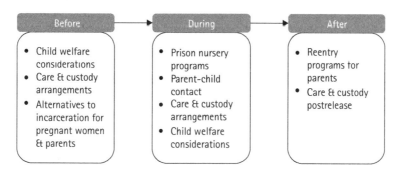

Figure 24.1 Developmental and Legal Considerations for Pregnant and Parenting People Before, During, and After Incarceration.

Legal Considerations Before a Parent Is Incarcerated

When mothers are convicted of crimes and faced with a criminal sentence, there are two primary systems that they must navigate—the criminal justice system and the child welfare system (Schumacher, 2017). Despite many women being simultaneously caught up in both systems, the two systems operate surprisingly separately, making the navigation of each even more challenging (Schumacher, 2017). For example, when a woman is facing criminal charges and her child has been removed from her care, in many states there is no clear path on which case should proceed. For example, in Minnesota, a woman could be navigating both the child welfare and criminal justice systems at the same time, putting her rights to remain silent and to confront her accusers in the criminal case at risk as she tries to cooperate with the state in the child welfare case. She is often left in a difficult and risky situation as she tries to meet federal child welfare timelines to reunify with her child while at the same time protecting her due process rights in the criminal case. This may be particularly challenging for mothers with infants and young children, as states often expedite child welfare timelines for children under a certain age. Federal timelines require filing a permanency petition within 11 months of a child being removed from their home. However, some states like Minnesota have added a 6-month review on permanency, which means that if a parent is not engaging in services or regularly visiting their child (both common with parents in prison), the state can move to permanency at the 6-month mark. These timelines and the implications for incarcerated parents are discussed in more detail later.

The Adoption Assistance and Child Welfare Act (Adoption Assistance and Child Welfare Act, 1980) was passed in 1980. For the first time, federal child welfare timelines were created and mandated for states. These timelines were created to address concern about young children lingering in foster care for years and mandated that children only remain in foster care for a limited time before finding a permanent home (Adoption Assistance and Child Welfare Act, 1980; Ross, 2004).

There are strategic decisions that need to be made when a mother is involved in both systems, because the outcomes and interventions in one system impact the other and ultimately affect not only the mother but also her children. The same trend of intersecting systems is less common with men who go to prison, primarily because men are less often the primary caregivers of their children (Glaze & Maruschak, 2010). When a father is facing incarceration, there is often another primary female caregiver available to take the children (Glaze & Maruschak, 2010). However, there are serious gaps in services for men who are incarcerated and seeking to have visitation and connection with their children (Lewis, 2004), which we discuss in more detail later.

Some women who are going to prison do not have child protection involvement; they are the lucky ones. However, these women (and men who are primary custodians) still must navigate finding a safe home for their children when they are in prison. This is where family law often comes into play in the lives of parents going to prison. There are two legal strategies that can be used to avoid child protection involvement prior to a mother entering prison. These include a delegation of parental authority (DOPA), which can be done without court intervention, and a voluntary transfer of legal custody (which does need court intervention).

A DOPA (Clausen Booth, 2002) allows parent(s) to give a chosen caregiver permission to care for the child for a limited amount of time. A separate DOPA is needed for each individual child (Lewis, 2004). This designated caregiver is called an "attorney-in-fact" (Education for Justice, n.d.). Typically, a DOPA agreement gives caregivers permission to take a child to medical appointments; seek physical, mental, and oral health care for the child; enroll the child in school; and consult with professionals in the child's life (e.g., teachers, doctors, therapists;

Clausen Booth, 2002). The power a DOPA grants is limited, as a DOPA can be revoked at any time, and parents retain all their legal rights and responsibility and can take their child back at any time (Clausen Booth, 2002). Parents may delegate temporary authority over a child's care, custody, or property to another for a period not exceeding 1 year (Education for Justice, n.d.). Thus, a DOPA is not a permanent option and is separate and distinct from a transfer of custody (see later). Besides being over 18, there are no specific requirements or a citizenship requirement. For these and other reasons, DOPA agreements are commonly used when parents are facing deportation or short periods of incarceration (Education for Justice, n.d.). States differ in the length of time that DOPAs remain in effect. In Minnesota, for example, DOPAs are valid for a maximum of 1 year (Delegation of Power by Parent or Guardian, 2020). In some other states such as Arizona and California, DOPAs are limited to 6 months rather than 1 year.

DOPAs make sense in situations where time spent in jail or prison is relatively short and it is anticipated that the parent will be able to return to their home and parenting duties. For example, a DOPA is a great option for pregnant women who deliver in custody and anticipate being incarcerated for only a short period of time following the infant's birth. In this way, an alternative caregiver can make appointments for well-child visits, get routine vaccinations, etc., which are particularly important during this developmental period. For situations where a parent may be facing significantly longer time in prison, the second option—a voluntary transfer of legal custody—may be a better choice for providing stability and care for children, in particular children who are young and still developing primary attachment relationships. For example, putting a plan in place to allow young infants to bond with a caregiver during their first year is important. In some cases, it may make sense to transfer custody of the infant to a relative to ensure the consistency of care and attachment needed at that important development stage. A transfer of legal custody provides more stability because it cannot be undone simply by a parent deciding to revoke it (like a DOPA); it is a legal determination made by a court that is often very challenging to modify or undo.

Unlike DOPAs, a transfer of legal custody requires a petition to the court and court oversight. Transfers of legal custody therefore take significantly more time to complete than the signing of a DOPA. They are a much more permanent legal option for parents seeking relief prior to a prison sentence. In some states, there are time barriers to petitioning the court for a transfer of legal custody (e.g., you have to wait 2 years from the date of a final order for custody to modify it, unless there is some showing of child endangerment; see Modification of Order, 2020). A petition or request to the court for a modification or transfer of legal custody is typically governed by a set of factors relating to a child's developmental needs. These factors vary from state to state but often include the ability of a parent or caregiver custodian to be able to meet the medical, educational, physical, and emotional needs of the child. Additionally, such factors as supporting the child's heritage or culture are also important. Some states also include the ability of caregivers to keep siblings connected.

Alternatives to Incarceration for Pregnant People and Mothers

In line with developmental science, a few states have laws that aim to keep parents and their children together in order to prevent the separation that would result from a period of incarceration. These laws provide judges with discretion to sentence a pregnant person or parent to probation or some other community-based alternative instead of confinement to jail or prison. We explore several examples next.

The state of Wisconsin has a law (Mother–Young Child Care Program, 2015) permitting pregnant women or those with a child under 1 year of age to participate in a program as an alternative to revocation of probation, extended supervision, or parole. The program is offered through a private, nonprofit organization and is required to (a) place individuals in the least restrictive environment; (b) provide a stable, safe, and stimulating environment for the child; (c) provide services with the goal of achieving a stable mother–child relationship; and (d) prepare each mother to be able to live in a safe, lawful, and stable manner in the community upon parole, extended supervision, or discharge.

Other states have laws that outline alternatives to incarceration for primary caregivers. Rigorous evaluation of these programs is limited, but they are reported to have positive outcomes for parents and children. For example, in 2010, the Oklahoma legislature established a pilot diversion program for primary caregivers convicted of nonviolent offenses (Pilot Diversion Program, 2020). The law directs the Department of Corrections to "develop a community-based diversion program that provides comprehensive and gender-specific services (p. 111)" for individuals convicted of nonviolent offenses who are primary caregivers to minor children. One diversion program that grew out of this legislation, ReMerge, offers comprehensive wrap-around services for mothers and their families, including safe and sober housing, material resources, transportation, access to physical and mental health care, parenting and practical skills training, and education and employment support. According to their website (ReMerge, n.d.), since launching in 2011, the program has graduated 154 mothers of 383 children from their programs. ReMerge indicates that women graduating from their program have safe and stable housing, are reunified with their minor children, are set up for stable employment, and are eligible to have their charges dismissed.

In 2015, Oregon established the Family Sentencing Alternative Pilot Program (Relating to Offenders with Minor Children, 2015). This program allows eligible parents who are facing prison sentences for nonviolent offenses to be diverted from prison and instead participate in intensive supervision, treatment, and programming to meet their needs as parents. A January 2021 report (Oregon Department of Corrections and Department of Human Services–Child Welfare, 2021) describes preliminary evidence of positive outcomes from the program's first 5 years, which served 212 primary caregivers of 391 minor children. Specifically, children of parents in the program were reported to have shorter average stays in foster care than children in foster care with parents in prison (706 days versus 1,066 days), and participation in the program was associated with lower rates of recidivating or revocation events.

Collectively, these state laws recognize key principles of developmental science, including the developmental salience of infancy and early childhood in the lifespan and the importance of the parent–child relationship for child development and the well-being of both children and parents. In addition, with the expressed goal of not separating mothers and their infants, the Wisconsin law recognizes the importance of attachment, bonding, and breastfeeding for infant health and development, as well as for maternal health and well-being.

In recent years, two states have considered other policy options for pregnant people. In New Mexico, for example, a 2019 law (Pregnant and Lactating Inmate Options, 2019) provides for judicial discretion for the release of individuals who are pregnant or lactating. Under the statute, "a person who is due to give birth may be granted release from incarceration in prison or jail prior to the presumptive birth date of the child and for up to eighteen months after the birth of the child (p. 1)." A similar law in Minnesota (Private Employment of Inmates or Specialized Programming for Pregnant Inmates of State Correctional Institutions in Community, 2021) permits the commissioner of corrections to conditionally release pregnant people and those who have given birth within the previous 8 months. Under the statute, individuals may be released to community-based programming for the purpose of participation in prenatal or postnatal care programming and to promote mother-child bonding in addition to other programming requirements as established by the commissioner, including evidence-based parenting skills programming; working at paid employment; seeking employment; or participating in vocational training, an educational program, or chemical dependency or mental health treatment services.

Legal Considerations During a Parent's Incarceration
Prison Nursery Programs

Despite changes in laws in some states and the aforementioned programs, the overwhelming majority of people who give birth while serving time in state or federal prisons are separated from their newborns in the immediate postpartum period, typically within 2–3 days of birth. Women in eight states may apply to live with their newborns in prison nursery programs, although there are often few spots and strict eligibility criteria, limiting the number of people who participate (see Goshin et al., 2017, for a review). Prison nurseries are rare in the United States relative to other countries (Law Library of Congress, U.S. Global Legal Research Directorate, 2014); however, research with mother–infant dyads in the prison nursery program at the Bedford Hills Correctional Facility in New York has demonstrated positive developmental and behavioral outcomes. Byrne's research found that infants who lived with their mothers in prison demonstrated age-appropriate developmental trajectories, attachment patterns comparable to low-risk community samples (Byrne et al., 2010), and significantly lower internalizing behaviors during preschool when compared to a group of children separated from their mothers by incarceration (Goshin, Byrne, & Blanchard-Lewis, 2014). In addition, mothers who participated in the prison nursery programs in New York and Nebraska were less likely to recidivate (Carlson, 2009; Goshin, Byrne, & Henninger, 2014).

Maintaining the Parent–Child Relationship During Incarceration

As described previously, there are very few options that allow pregnant and parenting people to avoid being separated from their children during a period of incarceration. As such, visiting and other forms of contact (e.g., phone calls, letters) become critically important ways that parents and children stay connected during a period of incarceration. Eighty-six percent of mothers and 83% of fathers in state or federal prison report some parent–child contact, but only 37% of mothers and 35% of fathers report receiving an in-person visit from their children (Bureau of Justice Statistics, 2021). Most parent–child contact is through telephone calls and letters (Bureau of Justice Statistics, 2021).

For incarcerated parents who are also involved in the child welfare system or family court, maintenance of the parent–child relationship through visits, phone calls, and letters during incarceration may have important legal implications for parents' contact and reunification with children postrelease. Most states have enacted policies that create a presumption for parental visitation during a child protection case (see Olmsted County Child & Family Services Division-Rochester, Minnesota, 2005). Courts have routinely held that incarceration alone may not be the sole basis to deny visitation or reunification efforts between a parent and child (*Hennepin County Welfare Department v. Staat,* 1970; Matter of Welfare of MDO, 1990). However, there are significant legal barriers and prison policies that prevent parents in prison getting visits with their children.

Although the U.S. Supreme Court has held that people in prison have a fundamental right to access the courts (*Ex Parte Hull*, 1949; *Johnson v. Avery*, 1969), some parents in prison are not able to appear or participate in hearings in their child protection case. Therefore, they are not able to advocate directly to the court for visits or other services that would aid in maintaining their relationship with their children. Parents are often not transported to court hearings or, in some cases, allowed to participate via telephone. Fundamentally, lack of access to a court proceeding where a request for visitation could be made is a critical reason that visitation does not occur.

Additionally, many parents in prison do not have regular access to or communication with their legal representation for their child protection cases (if they have legal representation that is court appointed at all). This stems from the fact that it is generally hard to communicate with people who are incarcerated. Coordinating phone calls and visitation at some prisons also remains challenging. However, lack of attorney engagement or correspondence is also a direct result of poor practice and overworked public sector attorneys who handle these cases (Gerber et al., 2019). Without vigorous legal advocacy, many parents who are incarcerated do not have a voice in their dependency case. Finally, many county agencies and some judges are unfamiliar with the policies and procedures at prisons in their state. This leaves many parents who are incarcerated without access to support from their caseworker or the court to enforce requests for visitation.

Even when the legal barriers have been navigated, there are additional barriers to parent–child contact and communication during a parent's incarceration. When determining where a person will be incarcerated, prison administrators prioritize security and rarely consider proximity to children (Beyer et al., 2010). And, because states have fewer women's prisons than men's, mothers are generally incarcerated in prisons that are farther away from their children than are fathers (Casey-Acevedo & Bakken, 2002; Greenfeld & Snell, 1999; Mignon & Ransford, 2012). This distance often creates considerable barriers for families who wish to visit, particularly considering the time and resources (e.g., reliable transportation, money for gas) needed to visit.

Furthermore, visiting rules and environments are rarely created with children's developmental needs in mind. Jail and prison policies (e.g., type of visit, allotted visit length, who can visit) vastly differ between states and even counties within the same state (Shlafer et al., 2015). Shlafer and colleagues (2015) surveyed the largest prison and jail in the most populous county in each state to describe visiting policies between children and their parents. The majority of jails (60%) offered barrier visits (stations in which conversation with the parent occurs via holes in a partition, through Plexiglas, or phone hook-up); 20% provided on-site video visits; 16% used off-site video visits; and 14% offered face-to-face visits without a barrier, otherwise known as contact visits (Shlafer et al., 2015). In contrast, most prisons offered contact visits, although physical touching or holding children is often limited or prohibited, and parents and visitors must follow strict rules that are often not developmentally appropriate (e.g., not allowed to use the restroom during the visit, children are not permitted to switch from sitting on the parent's lap and then the caregiver's lap). Furthermore, visiting environments are often drab with little stimulation for children and few opportunities for high-quality parent–child interaction.

Some scholars and advocates have expressed concerns about visits, especially when children are unable to touch their parents and must interact through a phone or barrier (e.g., Arditti et al., 2003; Dallaire et al., 2015). Others have described concerns about security procedures (e.g., metal detectors, frisking) that can be frightening for children (e.g., Dallaire et al., 2012) and long wait times that make the visit physically and emotionally difficult for children (Poehlmann-Tynan, 2015; Poehlmann-Tynan et al., 2017). Yet, studies have broadly highlighted that any form of visits with parents who are incarcerated is important for children's emotional and behavioral well-being, development, and attachment to their parent (Hindt et al., 2020; Maldonado, 2006; Poehlmann et al., 2010; Poehlmann-Tynan, 2015;

Poehlmann-Tynan et al., 2017; Shlafer & Poehlmann, 2010). Given these conflicting narratives and the limitations of the current scientific literature, Poehlmann and colleagues (2010) concluded that the effects of parent–child contact likely depend on the quality of visits. Given the legal importance of visits for parents involved in the child welfare system (described more later), jails and prisons should do more to create developmentally appropriate, family-friendly environments that support parent–child relationships.

Impact of Federal Child Welfare Permanency Timelines on Incarcerated Parents

The Adoption and Safe Families Act (AFSA, 1997) sets forth federally mandated child welfare timelines that states must adopt in order to receive Title IV-E funding (the funding that the federal government allocates to states for the cost of foster care among other things). ASFA requires that children removed from the care of their parents who have spent 15 of the last 22 months in substitute care must move to permanency (a final legal resolution to their child protection case). The urgency of the timelines codified in ASFA stems from child developmental research that supports children finding permanent homes quickly and not languishing in foster care (ASFA, 1997; Ross, 2004).

There is inherent tension in the federal timelines between child development and the perceived urgency to reach permanency, and parental health and well-being. Like previous child welfare statutes, ASFA was designed around child development principles, including consideration of "(1) the child's need for parental continuity—an adult who serves as the child's 'psychological parent,' (2) the importance of instilling in the child the feeling of being safe, protected and loved, and (3) the child's compressed sense of time and the concomitant urgency of resolution" (Ross, 2004; p. 173). These needs are often in direct conflict with the time and resources that parents need to achieve stability in their mental health and appropriate and effective treatment for their substance use disorders. For many parents, adequately addressing a substance use disorder is not something that occurs within an 11-month timeline. Similarly, co-occurring disorder treatments also typically require more than a year to successfully complete.

These rigorous timelines prevent many incarcerated parents from having any chance to retain custody of children or their parental rights because many prison sentences are longer than the timeframe specified by ASFA. There are limited legal exceptions to the barriers, and often parental incarceration is not included (Ross, 2004). In half of the states, like Iowa, there is an explicit connection between the termination of parental rights and a parent's absence due to incarceration. The Iowa law states that termination is appropriate when the parent has been imprisoned and is unlikely to be released from prison for a period of more than 5 years (Schumacher, 2017).

Reasonable Efforts at Reunification Must Be Provided to Most Parents Who Are Incarcerated

"Reasonable efforts" refers to activities of state social services agencies that aim to provide the assistance and services needed to preserve and reunify families. The federal Title IV-E program requires states to make reasonable efforts to preserve and reunify families. Generally, these efforts consist of accessible, available, and culturally appropriate services that are designed to improve the capacity of families to provide safe and stable homes for their children. Reasonable efforts also refer to the activities of caseworkers, including safety checks and home visits, that are performed on an ongoing basis to ensure that parents and other family members are participating in needed services and are making progress on case plan goals.

Many parents in prison face challenges in receiving services required by the reasonable efforts of the agency to reunify them with their children. For example, parents involved in child welfare cases are often ordered to complete chemical dependency treatment, parenting skills courses or therapy, family therapy, individual therapy, a mental health evaluation, and regular drug testing. Most of these specialized services, however, are not available to parents in prison. For example, many prisons do not offer treatment to people serving sentences of less than 1 year. In Minnesota, for example, women who are serving fewer than 6 months in prison are not eligible for extensive and comprehensive drug treatment. As already described, visitation, which is required on most case plans (and is certainly required as part of a county's provision of reasonable efforts), is challenging in many prison settings. The COVID-19 pandemic caused even further delays in visitation and some county social services, with considerable disruptions to people who are incarcerated and their families (Children's Bureau, n.d.; Dallaire et al., 2021).

There are some circumstances under which reasonable efforts are not required for termination; these circumstances often impact parents who are incarcerated. Notably, reasonable efforts are not required in cases where there has been a determination of egregious harm, a parent has abandoned a child, or a parent has been convicted of a serious crime (Duty to Ensure Placement Prevention and Family Reunification; Reasonable Efforts, 2020).

Terminating Parental Rights When Parents Are Incarcerated

Incarceration alone is not a per se basis to terminate a parent's parental rights (*Matter of the Children of Vasquez*, 2003). Instead, county agencies seeking termination (and ultimately judges making termination decisions) must make an individualized determination showing that a parent's incarceration is directly related to their unfitness to parent (Termination of Parental Rights, 2020). However, abandonment is a basis for termination under many statutes, and in some cases incarceration for an extended period of time may constitute abandonment. Additionally, the federal timelines requiring the filing of termination of parental rights petition if a child has been in care for 15 out of the last 22 months lead to termination filings of incarcerated parents. Many factors weigh into this calculus including the type of crime, length of time of potential prison term, services available to the parent and child during the period of incarceration, and age and developmental needs of the child.

Many parents facing prison time and in prison serving time have open child welfare cases and are negatively affected by the child welfare system (Duty to Ensure Placement Prevention and Family Reunification; Reasonable Efforts, 2020). Every state has a process to remove children from parental care based on abuse or neglect, and all states include abandonment and reference to criminal activity and its impact on parenting in some capacity on their list of removal factors (Lewis, 2004). Additionally, all 50 states provide for the involuntary termination of parental rights by statute. In order to both remove children from their parents and terminate the parental rights of a parent, due process protections provided by the 14th Amendment must be complied with (*Mathews v. Eldridge*, 1976; U.S. Const. Amend. XIV).

Parents' interest in raising their children is a fundamental right (*Troxel v. Granville*, 2000; *Wisconsin v. Yoder*, 1972). Although there is a fundamental right to parent protected by the U.S. Constitution, there is no fundamental right to counsel for parents facing termination (*Lassiter v. Dep't of Social Services*, 1981). In this case, the U.S. Supreme Court declined to provide constitutionally mandated legal representation to parents facing the termination of their parental rights. This decision has had dire consequences on the legal rights and access to representation of parents who are incarcerated (in particular for noncustodial fathers). Most states provide statutorily mandated counsel for custodial parents facing the termination of their parental rights (National Coalition for a Civil Right to Counsel, n.d.). There are only four states that do not mandate the right to counsel for custodial parents in child welfare cases. Minnesota recently joined the list of states that do provide a right to counsel in state statute with the passage of HF 312 (Appointment of Counsel, 2021).

Legal Considerations for Parents Leaving Prison

In this next section, we consider the intersections of the law and developmental science when parents are reentering their family systems following a period of incarceration. Parents may seek custody or contact with their children after prison. Some parents may also seek to restore their parental rights following a period of incarceration. For parents leaving prison, there are often limited options for reestablishing relationships with their children if they have lost either their parental rights (through the child welfare system) or custody (through the family court process) while in prison. Some parents may have a chance of actually regaining custody of their children; however, most parents leaving prison need to start with seeking supervised visitation with their children to reestablish the relationship that was diminished or severed during prison.

For parents who signed a DOPA (discussed earlier), they simply need to revoke the DOPA in writing. This allows the parent to regain the ability to care for the day-to-day needs of their child. This process is administratively simple and requires no court intervention. For parents who lost custody through a court process as a result of going to prison, regaining full custody of a child after leaving prison is an uphill battle. In some states, there are strict requirements limiting parents' ability to come into court to modify custody determinations for a period of years after a final order (see Annulment; When to Bring, 2020). Similarly, some states require a showing of endangerment to undo a permanent custody determination (see Annulment; When to Bring, 2020).

In most circumstances, parents will be seeking the right to have access to or visitation with their child after leaving prison. There are factors that the courts consider when making a decision about whether noncustodial parent visitation is in the best interest of a child. These factors include whether the parent can provide for the educational, physical, and emotional well-being of the child; whether the parent is sober; whether the parent has stable housing; and in some cases, whether the parent's criminal parole will allow for contact with children. Some criminal sentences prevent contact with children both while in prison and after due to the nature of the crime (typically criminal sexual conduct and assault crimes include these restrictions). For parents with a conviction that requires registration on a sexual offender registry, it can be nearly impossible to get legally sanctioned contact with their children.

Recognizing the needs of parents who are leaving prison, some states have enacted laws to address this issue. For example, a 2010 Oklahoma law (Pilot Diversion Program, 2020) directs the Department of Corrections to create a pilot reentry program that includes "a comprehensive, gender-specific reentry plan for inmates who upon release from custody will be the primary caregiver of minor children (p. 111)." In addition, the pilot program sought to modify existing reentry programs and services and to develop new programs and services to address the needs of parents being released from prison, including parenting education, life skills, social support, and employment.

Reestablishment of Parental Rights Following a Parent's Release From Prison

Some incarcerated parents lose their parental rights while they are in prison. This is because for parents who are in prison for more than a year, they are not able to complete the court-required services or case plans needed to reunify with their children or because their state has a law that allows termination due to parental abandonment (which could mean the parent is in prison in some contexts). Historically there have been no real legal avenues for these parents to reestablish their parental rights or to reestablish relationships with their children after being in prison. However, some states have passed innovative laws that allow parents to petition the court to reestablish parental rights. These laws provide hope and a mechanism for parents leaving prison who have lost their rights to try to get them back.

Hawaii was the first state to recognize the legal need of orphaned children and the potential value of reestablishing parental rights (Taylor Adams, 2010). Other states including California, Nevada, Illinois, and Minnesota have passed legislation to allow for parents to reestablish their parental rights (Taylor Adams, 2010). The Hawaii statute may be the most child centered. It provides that at any time following the expiration of one year from the termination order, the parent or child-placing agency may move the court to set aside the judgment if the child has not been adopted or placed in a prospective adoptive home (Family Court; Findings and Judgment, 2013). In reviewing the request, the court considers the current circumstances of the child and parent and determines whether those circumstances and the child's best interests justify the continuance of the termination of rights (Family Court; Findings and Judgment, 2013; Taylor Adams, 2010). Conversely, Minnesota's statute to reestablish parental rights requires that parents who seek this remedy must wait 4 years after a final order terminating parental rights. This lengthy timeline requirement prevents many parents from seeking this remedy because many children are ultimately adopted during this time (Reestablishment of the Legal Parent and Child Relationship, 2020).

Conclusion

This chapter considered how developmental science and different aspects of the law interact and shape the experiences of pregnant women and mothers involved in the criminal legal system and their children. Several areas of law coalesce to impact parents in complicated ways before, during, and after they are incarcerated. Although some aspects of the law have specifically considered the unique needs of pregnant and parenting people in prisons and jails (e.g., alternatives to incarceration), most often, incarcerated parents find themselves at the crossroads of policies and laws that do not address their needs or the developmental needs of their children. A growing body of evidence has documented the developmental outcomes of children affected by incarceration; yet, more work needs to be done to translate this research into evidence-based policy to support the needs of children and families affected by incarceration.

References

Adoption and Safe Families Act of 1997, Pub. L. No. H.R.867 (1997). https://www.congress.gov/bill/105th-congress/house-bill/867
Adoption Assistance and Child Welfare Act of 1980, Pub. L. No. 96–272 (1980). https://www.congress.gov/bill/96th-congress/house-bill/3434
American Civil Liberties Union. (2005). *Caught in the net: Impact of drug policies on women and families.* https://www.aclu.org/caught-net-impact-drug-policies-women-and-families
Annulment; When to bring, MN Stat § 518.05 (2020). https://www.revisor.mn.gov/statutes/cite/518.05
Appointment of counsel, MN Stat § 260C.163, Subd. 3 (2021). https://www.revisor.mn.gov/statutes/cite/260C.163
Arditti, J. A., Lambert-Shute, J., & Joest, K. (2003). Saturday morning at the jail: Implications of incarceration for families and children. *Family Relations, 52*(3), 195–204.
Beyer, M., Blumenthal-Guigui, R., & Krupat, T. (2010). Strengthening parent-child relationships: Visit coaching with children and their incarcerated parents. In Y. R. Harris, J. A. Graham, & G. J. O. Carpenter (Eds.), *Children of incarcerated parents: Theoretical, development, and clinical issues* (pp. 187–214). Springer Publishing Co.
Bronson, J., & Sufrin, C. (2019). Pregnant women in prison and jail don't count: Data gaps on maternal health and incarceration. *Public Health Reports, 134*(1 Suppl), 57S–62S.

Bureau of Justice Statistics. (2021). *Survey of prison inmates, United States, 2016*. Inter-university Consortium for Political and Social Research [distributor].

Byrne, M. W., Goshin, L. S., & Joestl, S. S. (2010). Intergenerational transmission of attachment for infants raised in a prison nursery. *Attachment & Human Development*, *12*(4), 375–393.

Carlson, J. R. (2009). Prison nurseries: A pathway to crime-free futures. *Corrections Compendium*, *34*(1), 17–24.

Carson, E. A. (2020). *Prisoners in 2019*. Bureau of Justice Statistics. https://bjs.ojp.gov/content/pub/pdf/p19.pdf

Casey-Acevedo, K., & Bakken, T. (2002). Visiting women in prison: Who visits and who cares. *Journal of Offender Rehabilitation*, *34*(3), 67–83.

Children's Bureau. (n.d.). *Creatively achieving permanency for children in foster care during COVID-19*. https://www.childwelfare.gov/topics/adoption/allinadoptionchallenge/blog/covid/

Clausen Booth, C. (2002). *First steps: Getting started raising relatives' children*. Minnesota Kinship Caregivers Association. https://www.scottcountymn.gov/DocumentCenter/View/120/First-Steps---Getting-Started-Raising-Relative-Children-PDF?bidId=

Dallaire, D. H., Ciccone, A., & Wilson, L. C. (2012). The family drawings of at-risk children: Concurrent relations with contact with incarcerated parents, caregiver behavior, and stress. *Attachment & Human Development*, *14*(2), 161–183.

Dallaire, D. H., Shlafer, R. J., Goshin, L. S., Hollihan, A., Poehlmann-Tynan, J., Eddy, J. M., & Adalist-Estrin, A. (2021). COVID-19 and prison policies related to communication with family members. *Psychology, Public Policy, and Law*, *27*(2), 231–241.

Dallaire, D., Zeman, J., & Thrash, T. (2015). Differential effects of type of children's contact with their jailed mothers and children's behavior problems. In J. Poehlmann-Tynan (Ed.), *Children's contact with incarcerated parents: Implications for policy and intervention* (pp. 23–38). Springer International Publishing.

Davis, E. P., & Narayan, A. J. (2020). Pregnancy as a period of risk, adaptation, and resilience for mothers and infants. *Development and Psychopathology*, *32*(5), 1625–1639.

Delegation of power by parent or guardian, MN Stat § 524.5–211 (2020). https://www.revisor.mn.gov/statutes/cite/524.5-211

Duty to ensure placement prevention and family reunification; Reasonable efforts, MN Stat § 260.012 (2020). https://www.revisor.mn.gov/statutes/cite/260.012

Education for Justice. (n.d.). *Delegation of parental authority (DOPA)—Do it yourself*. https://www.lawhelpmn.org/self-help-library/legal-resource/delegation-parental-authority-dopa-do-it-yourself

Ex parte Hull, § 312 U.S. 546 (1949). https://www.loc.gov/item/usrep312546/

Family court; Findings and judgment, HI Rev Stat § 571–63 (2013). https://www.capitol.hawaii.gov/hrs/isysquery/7a99cb92-fa78-4e14-9d48-413df4b24064/2/doc/#hit1

Fazel, S., Bains, P., & Doll, H. (2006). Substance abuse and dependence in prisoners: A systematic review. *Addiction*, *101*(2), 181–191.

Fazel, S., & Danesh, J. (2002). Serious mental disorder in 23 000 prisoners: A systematic review of 62 surveys. *The Lancet*, *359*(9306), 545–550.

Gerber, L. A., Pang, Y. C., Ross, T., Guggenheim, M., Pecora, P. J., & Miller, J. (2019). Effects of an interdisciplinary approach to parental representation in child welfare. *Children and Youth Services Review*, *102*, 42–55.

Glaze, L. E., & Maruschak, L. M. (2010). *Parents in prison and their minor children*. Bureau of Justice Statistics. https://bjs.ojp.gov/content/pub/pdf/pptmc.pdf

Glynn, L. M., Howland, M. A., & Fox, M. (2018). Maternal programming: Application of a developmental psychopathology perspective. *Development and Psychopathology*, *30*(3), 905–919.

Goshin, L. S., Arditti, J. A., Dallaire, D. H., Shlafer, R. J., & Hollihan, A. (2017). An international human rights perspective on maternal criminal justice involvement in the United States. *Psychology, Public Policy, and Law*, *23*(1), 53–67.

Goshin, L. S., Byrne, M. W., & Blanchard-Lewis, B. (2014). Preschool outcomes of children who lived as infants in a prison nursery. *Prison Journal*, *94*(2), 139–158.

Goshin, L. S., Byrne, M. W., & Henninger, A. M. (2014). Recidivism after release from a prison nursery program. *Public Health Nursing*, *31*(2), 109–117.

Greenfeld, L. A., & Snell, T. L. (1999). *Women offenders*. Bureau of Justice Statistics. https://bjs.ojp.gov/content/pub/pdf/wo.pdf

Grella, C. E., Lovinger, K., & Warda, U. S. (2013). Relationships among trauma exposure, familial characteristics, and PTSD: A case-control study of women in prison and in the general population. *Women & Criminal Justice*, *23*(1), 63–79.

Hennepin County Welfare Department v. Staat, 178 N. W. (2d) 709 (1970). https://cite.case.law/minn/287/501/

Hindt, L. A., Leon, S. C., & Lurigio, A. J. (2020). Visits with fathers involved in the criminal justice system and behavioral outcomes among children in foster care. *Children and Youth Services Review, 118*, 105371.

Johnson v. Avery, 393 U.S. 483 (1969). https://www.loc.gov/item/usrep393483/

Kim, P. (2016). Human maternal brain plasticity: Adaptation to parenting. *New Directions for Child and Adolescent Development, 2016*(153), 47–58.

Kovera, M. B. (2019). Racial disparities in the criminal justice system: Prevalence, causes, and a search for solutions. *Journal of Social Issues, 75*(4), 1139–1164.

Lassiter v. Dep't of Social Services, 452 US 18 (1981). https://www.loc.gov/item/usrep452018/

Law Library of Congress, U.S. Global Legal Research Directorate. (2014). *Laws on children residing with parents in prison*. Law Library of Congress, Global Legal Research Center. https://www.loc.gov/item/2015296887

Lewis, P. (2004). Behind the glass wall: Barriers that incarcerated parents face regarding the care, custody and control of their children. *American Academy of Matrimonial Lawyers, 19*, 97.

Maldonado, S. (2006). Recidivism and paternal engagement. *Family Law Quarterly, 40*(2), 191–211.

Maruschak, L. M., Bronson, J., & Alper, M. (2021). *Parents in prison and their minor children*. Bureau of Justice Statistics. https://bjs.ojp.gov/content/pub/pdf/pptmcspi16st.pdf

Mathews v. Eldridge, 424 U.S. 319 (1976). https://www.loc.gov/item/usrep424319/

Matter of the children of Vasquez, 658 N.W.2d 249 (2003). https://casetext.com/case/matter-of-the-children-of-vasquez

Matter of Welfare of MDO, 462 N.W.2d 370 (1990). https://www.courtlistener.com/opinion/2212288/matter-of-welfare-of-mdo/?q=cites%3A1893659

Mignon, S., & Ransford, P. (2012). Mothers in prison: Maintaining connections with children. *Social Work in Public Health, 27*, 69–88.

Modification of order, MN Stat § 518.18 (2020). https://www.revisor.mn.gov/statutes/cite/518.18

Mother–young child care program, WI Stat § 301.049 (2015). https://docs.legis.wisconsin.gov/statutes/statutes/301/049

National Coalition for a Civil Right to Counsel. (n.d.). *Status map*. http://www.civilrighttocounsel.org/map

Olmsted County Child & Family Services Division- Rochester, Minnesota. (2005). *Visitation/family access guidelines*. https://www.dhs.state.mn.us/main/groups/county_access/documents/pub/dhs_id_048528.pdf

Oregon Department of Corrections and Oregon Department of Human Services–Child Welfare (2021). *Family Sentencing Alternative Pilot Program report to the Senate and House Committees on Judiciary*. https://www.oregonlegislature.gov/citizen_engagement/Reports/Joint%20Family%20Sentencing%20Alternative%20Pilot%20Project%20Report%201_1_2021.pdf

Pilot diversion program, 57 OK Stat § 57–510.8b (2020). https://oksenate.gov/sites/default/files/2019-12/os57.pdf

Poehlmann, J., Dallaire, D., Loper, A. B., & Shear, L. D. (2010). Children's contact with their incarcerated parents: Research findings and recommendations. *American Psychologist, 65*(6), 575–598.

Poehlmann-Tynan, J. (2015). Children's contact with incarcerated parents: Summary and recommendations. In Barbara H. Fiese (Ed.). *Children's contact with incarcerated parents: Implications for policy and intervention* (pp. 83–92). Springer.

Poehlmann-Tynan, J., Burnson, C., Runion, H., & Weymouth, L. A. (2017). Attachment in young children with incarcerated fathers. *Development and Psychopathology, 29*(2), 389–404.

Pregnant and lactating inmate options, NM SB192 (2019). https://legiscan.com/NM/text/SB192/2019

Private employment of inmates or specialized programming for pregnant inmates of state correctional institutions in community, MN Stat § 244.065 (2021). https://www.revisor.mn.gov/laws/2021/0/Session+Law/Chapter/17/

Reestablishment of the legal parent and child relationship, MN Stat § 260C.329 (2020). https://www.revisor.mn.gov/statutes/2020/cite/260C.329

Relating to offenders with minor children, OR House Bill 3503 (2015). https://olis.oregonlegislature.gov/liz/2015R1/Downloads/MeasureDocument/HB3503/A-Engrossed

ReMerge (n.d.) *About us*. https://www.remergeok.org/about-us

Ross, C. (2004). The tyranny of time: Vulnerable children, bad mothers, and statutory deadlines in parental termination proceedings. *Virginia Journal of Social Policy and Law, 11*, 176–228.

Sawyer, W. (2020). *Visualizing the racial disparities in mass incarceration*. https://www.prisonpolicy.org/blog/2020/07/27/disparities/

Schumacher, E. (2017). A tale of two systems: Single mothers and the troublesome lack of interaction between the criminal justice and child welfare systems in Iowa. *Journal of Gender, Race, and Justice, 21*(1), 261–279.

Sentencing Project. (2020). *Incarcerated women and girls*. https://www.sentencingproject.org/publications/incarcerated-women-and-girls/

Sentencing Project. (2021). *Trends in U.S. corrections*. https://www.sentencingproject.org/wp-content/uploads/2021/07/Trends-in-US-Corrections.pdf

Shlafer, R. J., Loper, A. B., & Schillmoeller, L. (2015). Introduction and literature review: Is parent–child contact during parental incarceration beneficial? In J. Poehlmann-Tynan (Ed.), *Children's contact with incarcerated parents: Implications for policy and intervention* (pp. 1–21). Springer International Publishing.

Shlafer, R. J., & Poehlmann, J. (2010). Attachment and caregiving relationships in families affected by parental incarceration. *Attachment & Human Development, 12*(4), 395–415.

Sufrin, C., Beal, L., Clarke, J., Jones, R., & Mosher, W. D. (2019). Pregnancy outcomes in US prisons, 2016–2017. *American Journal of Public Health, 109*(5), 799–805.

Sufrin, C., Jones, R. K., Mosher, W. D., & Beal, L. (2020). Pregnancy prevalence and outcomes in U.S. jails. *Obstetrics & Gynecology, 135*(5), 1177–1183. https://journals.lww.com/greenjournal/Fulltext/2020/05000/Pregnancy_Prevalence_and_Outcomes_in_U_S__Jails.24.aspx

Taylor Adams, L. (2010). Resurrecting parents of legal orphans: Un-terminating parental rights. *Virginia Journal of Social Policy and the Law, 17*(318), 2010.

Termination of parental rights, MN Stat § 260C.301 (2020). https://www.revisor.mn.gov/statutes/cite/260C.301

Troxel v. Granville, 530 U.S. 57 (2000). https://www.loc.gov/item/usrep530057/

U.S. Const. Amend. XIV. https://constitution.congress.gov/browse/amendment-14/#:~:text=No%20State%20shall%20make%20or,equal%20protection%20of%20the%20laws

Wisconsin v. Yoder, 406 U.S. 205 (1972). https://www.loc.gov/item/usrep406205/

Zheng, Z., & Minton, T. D. (2021). *Jail inmates in 2019*. Bureau of Justice Statistics. https://bjs.ojp.gov/content/pub/pdf/ji19.pdf

CHAPTER 25

The Impact of Reproductive Rights on Women's Development

Allison M. Whelan and Michele Bratcher Goodwin

> **Abstract**
> Reproductive health, an essential element of women's overall health, shapes and influences physical, mental, and socioeconomic development and well-being. Further, the decision of whether, when, and how to build a family and birth a child can profoundly affect short- and long-term adult development and well-being. As a result, laws, policies, and practices that influence reproductive health may positively influence or undermine a woman's development, depending on whether they facilitate or restrict access to care. As the United States leads industrialized nations in maternal mortality and morbidity, examining the impacts of reproductive rights on women's development represents an urgent concern. This chapter focuses primarily on abortion, contraception, and pregnancy to demonstrate how reproductive health encompasses a broad array of important issues. It reviews relevant laws, policies, and practices that shape aspects of reproductive health and describes their effects on various facets of development. It concludes by discussing the implications of the current evidence and offering suggestions for further research.
>
> **Key Words:** reproductive rights, abortion, contraception, pregnancy, adult development

Reproductive health is a key component of women's overall physical, mental, and socioeconomic development and well-being (Office of Disease Prevention and Health Promotion, 2021; World Health Organization, 2021). Thus, reproductive laws, policies, and practices that facilitate access to reproductive health care are essential to healthy adult development and well-being. Much is written about the importance of overall health on healthy adult development—of which reproductive health is just one component—but less is written about how law and, more specifically, reproductive rights and justice influence adult development either positively or negatively, especially pregnancy. This chapter aims to fill those gaps.

This chapter focuses on women's adult development, including that of transgender and nonbinary persons, and reflects to the importance of meaningful reproductive health services for individuals of all gender identities. Indeed, women are not the only persons capable of becoming pregnant (e.g., transgender men and nonbinary individuals) or in need of reproductive health care and therefore affected by laws, policies, and practices that impact reproductive health. As such, this chapter recognizes reproductive health on a spectrum, inclusive of all women, persons capable of becoming pregnant, and persons whose lives may be affected by reproductive laws, judicial decision making, and justice.

Reproductive justice represents a "pivotal problem" of the 21st century (Goodwin & Whelan, 2015), with reproductive rights increasingly under attack in the United States and throughout the world (Davies & Harman, 2020). For example, the U.S. Supreme Court's June 2022 decision in *Dobbs v. Jackson Woman's Health Organization*, which overturned *Roe v. Wade* and *Planned Parenthood v. Casey*, reflects one of the latest and most glaring attacks on access to reproductive health care. The contemporary landscape is troubling because "deciding if, when, and how to become a parent is a significant developmental milestone in the adult life course" (Athan, 2020, p. 445).

Indeed, "theories, anecdotes, and the opinions of laypersons are nearly unanimous: People who become parents and are involved in the raising of children are transformed and follow a different developmental trajectory from people who do not engage in parent roles" (Palkovitz et al., 2003, p. 307). Pregnancy, childbirth, and parenting have significant physical, psychological, economic, and other effects on people's lives. Women in particular spend much of their adolescent and adult lives managing reproduction, whether menses, birth control, pregnancies, perimenopause, or menopause. Women are cognizant about the management of their reproduction and the benefits, as well as the social and economic pitfalls, that incur with parenthood, despite laws that impose burdens on their reproductive rights in the form of abortion bans and restrictions, such as "informed consent" and "waiting period" provisions that delay women's ability to terminate a pregnancy. According to the Guttmacher Institute (2019a), American women spend an average of three decades—more than three quarters of their reproductive lives—trying to avoid pregnancy.

Notwithstanding efforts to manage their reproduction, approximately half of all pregnancies in the United States each year are unintended (Centers for Disease Control and Prevention, 2023; Guttmacher Institute, 2019a; Office of Disease Prevention and Health Promotion, n.d.; United Health Foundation, 2021a). As defined by the Guttmacher Institute (2019a) and the Centers for Disease Control and Prevention (2021), an "unintended pregnancy" occurs when (a) pregnancy is wanted later in life but not at the time the current pregnancy occurred (i.e., a "mistimed" pregnancy) or (b) pregnancy is not wanted at the time of the current pregnancy or later in life (i.e., an "unwanted" pregnancy).

In fact, roughly 5% of reproductive-age women experience an unintended pregnancy each year in the United States. This rate is significantly higher than peer nations (Guttmacher Institute, 2019a). In 2011 (the most recent data available), approximately 18% of all pregnancies in the United States were *unwanted*, defined as a pregnancy that occurred when the woman did not want the pregnancy at the time or at any time in the future. This amounted to nearly 1.1 million of the total 6.1 million pregnancies that year. Forty-two percent of unintended pregnancies in 2011 ended in abortion, and 58% ended in birth (Guttmacher Institute, 2019a).

Considering these and other data discussed throughout this chapter, laws, policies, and practices that impact whether and when a person births and/or parents can have profound short- and long-term effects on adult development and well-being. This chapter proceeds by reviewing relevant laws, policies, and practices that impact reproductive health care, with a focus on the United States. It then describes the pertinent developmental issues, including a synthesis of relevant scholarship, which informs how the described laws, policies, and practices affect women's adult development. The chapter concludes by discussing the implications of the current evidence and offering suggestions for further research.

Review of Laws, Policies, and Practices

This section examines laws, policies, and practices related to the ability to control one's reproduction, with a focus on access to abortion and contraception in the United States. This discussion captures an important aspect of contemporary controversies and debates, mindful that landscape is constantly changing and that myriad laws, policies, and practices not covered in this chapter impact reproductive rights and women's development. Additionally, other laws not covered here affect other periods of development, such as those governing sexual education and minors' rights to access reproductive health care without parental consent, which can have a significant impact on adolescent development. In reading this chapter, it is important to acknowledge that historically marginalized and vulnerable populations, including women of color, are the populations most burdened by a number of crises related to reproduction (Davis, 2020). As a result, the impact of laws, policies, and practices related to reproductive magnify for these populations.

Laws, Policies, and Practices That Impact Access to Abortion

Many federal and state laws, policies, and practices impact access to abortion. In effect, they either facilitate or restrict access to abortion. In light of the U.S. Supreme Court's 2022 ruling in *Dobbs*, the U.S. landscape of reproductive health care is in a constant state of flux.

FEDERAL LAWS, POLICIES, AND PRACTICES

Pivotal U.S. Supreme Court Cases

In 1973, the U.S. Supreme Court decriminalized abortion rights in its landmark 7–2 decision in *Roe v. Wade,* and further honed its jurisprudence in *Planned Parenthood of Southeastern Pennsylvania v. Casey* (1992), which affirmed "the right of the woman to choose to have an abortion before viability and to obtain it without undue interference from the State" (p. 846). Most recently, the Supreme Court gutted fifty years of precedent when it overturned *Roe* and *Casey* in *Dobbs v. Jackson Women's Health Organization*.

In *Roe,* the court struck down several Texas laws that criminalized abortion except when necessary to save the life of the mother. *Roe* established a three-part framework, in which the woman's right to abortion and the state's right to protect potential life shift. According to the court's framework, a woman's right to abortion is strongest during the first trimester, a period during which the state may not regulate abortion. During the second trimester, the state may promote its interest in the health of the pregnant person by regulating abortion in ways that reasonably relate to maternal health. Postviability, the state may promote its interest in potential human life by regulating, or even proscribing, abortion except when necessary to preserve the life or health of the mother.

Nearly 20 years later in *Casey,* the court reaffirmed *Roe* but abandoned the three-part framework, replacing it with a new standard that asks whether abortion restrictions place an "undue burden" on the woman seeking an abortion. Restrictions that place an undue burden are unconstitutional.

More recently, in *Whole Woman's Health v. Hellerstedt* (2016), the court reaffirmed *Casey* and in the process struck down two targeted restrictions on abortion providers (TRAP) laws. TRAP laws, which are designed to shut down abortion providers by imposing various penalties and costs, such as unnecessary building requirements and hospital relationship/admitting privilege mandates (Planned Parenthood, n.d.-a), represent an important strategy of the antiabortion movement. *Hellerstedt* centered on two Texas laws. One required abortion providers to obtain admitting privileges at local hospitals located within 30 miles of their clinic. The second required any abortion facility to satisfy minimum safety standards for ambulatory surgical centers (e.g., specifications relating to the size of the nursing staff, building dimensions, and other building requirements). The court struck down both laws, explaining that neither promoted patient health and safety but rather imposed undue burdens on a woman's right to seek a previability abortion. Four years later, in *June Medical Services L.L.C. v. Russo* (2020), the court struck down a similar admitting privileges requirement in a Louisiana law.

However, the court's shifting demographic resulted in a conservative majority opposed to abortion rights. The addition of conservative justice Amy Coney Barrett to the court, which established a strong 6–3 conservative majority, raised fears that this would "cement a more dramatic downfall for abortion rights" (Boonin, 2020). These fears have now materialized with he Supreme Court's decision in *Dobbs* to overturn *Roe* and *Casey*. The court's decision in *Dobbs*, however, did not materialize out of thin air. There were myriad warning that the court appeared willing to reconsider, and potentially overhaul, its abortion jurisprudence, as illustrated by its decision in *Whole Woman's Health v. Jackson* (2021) to let stand a 2021 Texas antiabortion law (Texas Heartbeat Act, 2021), which barred abortions after about 6 weeks of pregnancy—a time at which many pregnant people will be unaware of their pregnancies—and provides a private right of enforcement.

The Hyde Amendment

First adopted in 1976, the Hyde Amendment prohibits the use of federal funds for abortion except in cases of rape or incest or if the pregnancy is determined to endanger the woman's life (Public Law No. 94-439, 1976). This law dramatically limits abortion coverage under Medicaid and other federal programs and has a disparate impact on low-income women, as well as women of color (National Women's Law Center, 2017). This is important because unintended pregnancies are highest among low-income women, Black women, and Latina women, who are also more likely to rely on Medicaid (Guttmacher Institute, 2019a; National Women's Law Center, 2017).

President Joseph Biden has consistently sought to remove the Hyde Amendment provision from his budget proposals, in keeping with his campaign promise. In fact, his budget proposal for fiscal year 2022 was the first time in nearly 30 years that a president proposed a budget without the Hyde Amendment (Rinkunas, 2021). President Biden's attempts have yet to be successful, as legislators in favor of its removal have reluctantly reintroduced the Hyde Amendment to strike legislative deals and appease conservative lawmakers during negotiations (Martinez, 2022).

Medication Abortion

Women in the United States gained access to medication abortion in 2000, when the U.S. Food and Drug Administration (FDA) approved the use of mifepristone in a regimen with misoprostol for the termination of intrauterine pregnancy (Mifeprex, 2019). Mifepristone, sold under the brand name Mifeprex and in generic form, has long been subject to various federal and state restrictions. Yet over time, many of the federal restrictions fell away, in line with the opinions of leading medical authorities, who long argued that the were burdensome and medically unnecessary (*American College of Obstetricians and Gynecologists v. U.S. Food and Drug Administration*, 2020).

At the time of this writing, there are numerous cases working their way through the courts focused on medication abortion. Two cases garnering much attention involve conflicting rulings issued by two separate federal court judges. The first, *Alliance for Hippocratic Medicine v. FDA*, was issued on April 7, 2023, by Judge Matthew Kacsmaryk in the U.S. District Court for the Northern District of Texas. Judge Kacsmaryk issued a preliminary injunction that suspended the FDA's 23-year approval of mifepristone. He also endorsed the view that a previously dormant, 150-year old law —the Comstock Act—"plainly forecloses mail-order abortion" (p. 38).

The Biden Administration appealed this ruling to the Fifth Circuit Court of Appeals. In a 2-1 decision, the U.S. Court of Appeals for the Fifth Circuit blocked the part of Judge Kacsmaryk's ruling that overturned the FDA's 2000 approval but allowed the re-imposition of restrictions on mifepristone previously lifted by the FDA. This includes limiting mifepristone's approved use to seven weeks' gestation, instead of ten weeks, and requiring that patients pick up the medication in person (i.e., prohibiting the use of mail pharmacies). The Biden Administration again appealed, this time to the U.S. Supreme Court, which temporarily blocked the decisions of both lower courts, returning the case to the Fifth Circuit. The Supreme Court ruled that access to mifepristone will remain unchanged for the duration of the lawsuit, which is expected to make its way back to the Supreme Court (Center for Reproductive Rights, 2023).

The second, and conflicting, ruling was issued that same day—April 7, 2023—in the U.S. District Court in the Eastern District of Washington by Judge Thomas O. Rice. This case—*Washington v. FDA*—was filed by eighteen Attorneys General from seventeen states and the District of Columbia and challenges the FDA's decision to impose restrictions on the dispensing and prescribing of mifepristone through what is known as a Rick Evaluation and Mitigation Strategy (REMS). Essentially, this case is the mirror image of the Texas case, arguing that the FDA must *remove* restrictions rather than reimpose restrictions or ban the drug. In this case, the court ordered the FDA to maintain the current availability of mifepristone in the seventeen states and D.C.

Despite the back-and-forth nature of the courts' actions, the Supreme Court's recent ruling means that, for now, access to mifepristone remains unchanged and the drug is still considered approved by the FDA. Under federal regulations, mifepristone thus remains available through 70 days' gestation, including through th use of retail and mail pharmacies. The drug remains subject to certain federal restrictions, including requiring prescribers and dispensing pharmacies to obtain special certifications (U.S. Food and Drug Administration, 2021). And importantly, as discussed later, many states now impose, or are considering imposing, additional restrictions or even bans on medication abortion. Thus, while the FDA's decisions to gradually ease the restrictions on mifepristone represent important milestones, ongoing court cases and state-level bans and restrictions remain a formidable hurdle to medication abortion access.

Mexico City Policy

U.S. laws and policies also impact reproductive rights and reproductive health throughout the world. The Mexico City Policy, often referred to as the "global gag rule," has been instated by every Republican president since Ronald Reagan. By contrast, the Clinton, Obama, and Biden administrations all rescinded the policy. To receive U.S. governmental global family planning funding under the original policy, foreign nongovernmental organizations (NGOs) were required to certify that they would not "perform or actively promote abortion as a method of family planning" using funds from any source (including non-U.S. funds; Kaiser Family Foundation, 2021, White House Office of Policy Development, 1984, p. 578). The Trump administration expanded the policy so that it applied to most U.S. bilateral global health assistance, including funding for HIV under the president's Emergency Plan for AIDS Relief (PEPFAR), maternal and child health, malaria, nutrition, and other programs. The Trump administration also sought to further tighten restrictions to reach other areas of U.S. development assistance beyond global health and other non-U.S. funding streams (Kaiser Family Foundation, 2021).

STATE LAWS, POLICIES, AND PRACTICES

As a result of *Dobbs*, states are now the primary abortion battleground in the United States. Motivated by the strengthening conservative majority of the U.S. Supreme Court, 2021 marked the first time that states enacted more than one hundred abortion restrictions in a single year (Nash, 2021). Yet the push to curtail abortion rights began at least a decade prior.

For example, between 2011 and 2013 alone, more abortion restrictions were enacted than the previous decade combined (Boonstra & Nash, 2014).

Increasingly, states designed laws to challenge *Roe* and the constitutional right to an abortion explicitly, such as through "trigger laws," which were designed to take effect automatically or through quick state action if the Supreme Court overturned *Roe*—as it has now done in *Dobbs*. Many states now ban abortion with increasingly limited exceptions, while others retain laws that chip away at abortion rights or make abortion more difficult to access. These include TRAP laws, informed consent/counseling requirements, waiting periods, restrictions on medication abortion, and insurance restrictions (American Civil Liberties Union, n.d., Whelan & Goodwin, 2022).

By design, TRAP laws shut down abortion providers by imposing costly and burdensome regulations, such as facility requirements and hospital relationship/admitting privilege requirements. Proponents of TRAP laws suggest these laws protect and promote women's health. Yet leading medical organizations, including the American Medical Association and American College of Obstetricians and Gynecologists, oppose these laws because, in practice, they have the opposite effect by blocking access to safe abortions (Whelan & Goodwin, 2022).

As described earlier, the Supreme Court's 1992 decision in *Casey* upheld *Roe*, yet also set the stage for mandatory counseling and waiting periods, ranging from 18 to 72 hours, which make accessing abortion unnecessarily time-consuming, difficult, and costly. In large part, however, the counseling requirements are duplicative, medically unnecessary, and sometimes even mandate the provision of scientifically questionable information. Mandatory waiting periods are particularly problematic when the initial counseling must be done in person, thus requiring patients to make two potentially lengthy trips to obtain an abortion (Whelan & Goodwin, 2022.

And while medication abortion was frequently perceived as a silver lining, particularly after the FDA's decision to relax some of the federal restrictions, states, as noted above, are increasingly banning or severely restricting access to medication abortion. take different approaches on medication abortion. Many states ban, or are considering banning, the dispensing of mifepristone through the mail, along with other restrictions beyond those required by the FDA, such as reducing the gestational limit to less than the FDA-approved 70 days, allowing only physicians to prescribe the drug, and requiring patients to take the medication in the presence of a physician (Guttmacher Institute, 2021a, 2021b).

States also restrict access to abortion by limiting insurance coverage, such as by banning or limiting covered provided by all private insurance plans, plans offered through health insurance exchanges, or plans offered to public employees. These restrictions, combined with those imposed by the federal Hyde Amendment, can make the cost of an abortion prohibitive (Whelan & Goodwin, 2022).

In addition to restrictions and requirements imposed on the procedure itself, 46 states have enacted "conscience laws" that allow certain health care providers and health care institutions to refuse to provide abortion services (Guttmacher Institute, 2021c). These laws "provide[] the means and legal protection to individuals and institutions (professing sincerely held religious beliefs) to refuse to provide, assist, or otherwise facilitate" services relating to abortion, sterilization, or contraception (Goodwin & Whelan, 2016, p. 1312).

Laws, Policies, and Practices That Impact Access to Contraception
FEDERAL LAWS, POLICIES, AND PRACTICES

Pivotal U.S. Supreme Court Cases
In *Griswold v. Connecticut* (1965), a pivotal reproductive rights case related to contraception, the U.S. Supreme Court struck down a state prohibition against the prescription, sale, or use

of contraceptives to or by married couples. The court held that the U.S. Constitution guarantees a right to privacy when married individuals make decisions about intimate personal matters such as childbearing. Seven years later, in *Eisenstadt v. Baird* (1972), the Supreme Court struck down a state law that permitted married persons to obtain contraceptives but prohibited unmarried persons from obtaining contraceptives, thus establishing the right of unmarried individuals to obtain contraceptives.

Federal Laws and Policies

The contraceptive coverage guarantee under the Affordable Care Act (ACA) applies to most private health plans nationwide. The federal guarantee requires coverage of FDA-approved methods of contraception used by women, along with related counseling and services. Plans must cover these services without cost-sharing requirements such as deductibles and copays (Guttmacher Institute, 2021d; Healthcare.gov, n.d.).

The ACA's initial "Preventive Care Guidelines," incorporated by the Departments of Health and Human Services, Labor, and the Treasury, granted the Health Resources and Services Administration discretion to exempt religious employers, such as churches, from providing contraceptive coverage. The breadth of these exemptions expanded over time, and in October 2017, the Trump administration issued regulations that provide sweeping religious and moral exemptions to the ACA's contraceptive coverage guarantee (42 C.F.R. § 147.131, 2018; 42 C.F.R. § 147.132, 2018). In July 2020, the Supreme Court upheld the Trump administration's legal authority to issue these regulations (*Little Sisters of the Poor v. Pennsylvania*, 2020). In August 2021, the Biden administration indicated an intent to initiate rulemaking to amend the Trump administration's final regulations (U.S. Department of Health and Human Services et al., 2021). In January 2023, the Biden Administration proposed a rule that would curtail the Trump-era restrictions (Firth, 2023). As of this writing, the rule has not been finalized.

On July 13, 2023, the FDA took a major step toward increasing access to birth control by approving the first over-the-counter daily oral contraceptive. As of this writing, however, it is unknown how much the nonprescription pill will cost or whether it will be covered by insurance. The full impact of the FDA's decision thus remains to be seen (Gupta, 2023).

In addition to regular, long-term contraception options such as birth control pills and long-acting reversible contraception (LARC) methods (e.g., intrauterine devices IUDs]), emergency contraception is available to prevent pregnancy after unprotected sex. One of the available FDA-approved emergency contraceptives, Plan B One-Step, is available over the counter without a prescription for women and girls of any age. The drug is sold under various names and can typically be found in retail drugstores. It is most effective when taken within 72 hours of unprotected sex (Planned Parenthood, 2013, 2021).

STATE LAWS, POLICIES, AND PRACTICES

In response to the ACA contraception coverage mandate, some states amended and expanded their insurance requirements to match or exceed the federal guarantee, such as requiring coverage for contraception that is available over the counter without a prescription, allowing women to receive an extended supply of contraception at one time (e.g., a 1-year supply rather than a 1- or 3-month supply), or requiring coverage of male sterilization without out-of-pocket costs (Guttmacher Institute, 2021d).

Twelve states, such as Arizona, Mississippi, and Tennessee, however, have conscience laws that allow certain health care providers and health care institutions to refuse to comply with the contraceptive mandate and allow them to refuse to provide services related to contraception, including emergency contraception (Guttmacher Institute, 2021c). For example, such laws may allow pharmacists and other health care providers to refuse to dispense or prescribe contraception or emergency contraception (Goodwin & Whelan, 2016).

States take different approaches to emergency contraception. Some state laws facilitate access to emergency contraception, such as requiring hospital emergency rooms to provide emergency contraception–related services to sexual assault victims and allowing pharmacists to dispense emergency contraception without a prescription under certain conditions. Other states restrict access, such as by excluding emergency contraception from their contraceptive coverage mandates and allowing pharmacists and pharmacies to refuse to dispense emergency contraception (Guttmacher Institute, 2021e).

Coercive/Compulsory Laws, Policies, and Practices

In addition to laws, policies, and practices that facilitate or restrict access to abortion and contraception, there are laws, policies, and practices that coerce or force contraception, sterilization, and/or abortion in certain situations. Even when the law specifically prohibits such practices, they nevertheless continue to occur throughout the world.

It is misguided to believe these practices no longer occur in the United States. There is a long history of forced contraception and sterilization in the United States, particularly of women of color or those otherwise deemed "unfit" for reproduction. These practices, including the forced contraception and sterilization of the intellectually disabled, were legally blessed by the 1927 Supreme Court decision in *Buck v. Bell*, which has never been overturned (*Buck v. Bell*, 1927; Whelan, 2021).

These practices are now less common in the United States, but they still occur. A whistleblower's revelations in 2020 brought these issues back into the spotlight. In September 2020, Dawn Wooten, a licensed practical nurse employed by the Irwin County Detention Center (ICDC) in Georgia, alleged, among other things, that some women detainees at ICDC received hysterectomies without their full understanding or consent (Project South et al., 2020). Nearly 1 year later, in June 2021, Britney Spears revealed that she was denied the right to have her IUD removed and have another child under the conditions of her conservatorship. As revealed by Spears during a court hearing:

> I want to be able to get married and have a baby. . . . I was told right now in the conservatorship, I'm not able to get married or have a baby. I have (an) IUD inside of (me) right now, so I don't get pregnant. I wanted to take the IUD out, so I can start trying to have another baby, but this so-called team won't let me go to the doctor to take it out because they don't want me to have any more children. (Oliver, 2021)

Spears's experience sparked broader public discussion about how her experience reflects that of many women with disabilities and perceived disabilities.

Such practices are also common, and sometimes more extreme, throughout the world. For example, China recently announced a three-child policy, a major change from its decades-old one-child, then two-child, policy. Under these policies, many women feel forced, or are forced, to get an abortion if they already have more children than the policy allows (Goldman, 2021; Liu, 2020). One family planning official in China reported that she was responsible for authorizing over 1,500 forced abortions, around a third of which were during late-term pregnancies (Fong, 2016). These policies impact women and the physical, mental, and social development of the children born outside of the plan without official permission (Johnson, 2016, pp. 90–92).

Furthermore, according to an investigation by the Associated Press (2020), the Chinese government regularly subjects minority women to pregnancy checks, forced IUDs, sterilizations, and abortions. This has happened to hundreds of thousands of women. According to the Associated Press, these measures are supported by mass detention, which is used as a threat and a punishment for failure to comply. In fact, "having too many children is a major reason people are sent to detention camps . . . with the parents of three or more ripped away from their families unless they can pay huge fines" (Associated Press, 2020). In other countries, women face similar practices and women with HIV are forced or coerced into being sterilized or having an abortion (Barot, 2012; Scott, n.d.).

The myriad laws, policies, and practices discussed in this section that relate to reproductive health all have the potential to impact women's development and well-being, which is discussed further in the following section.

Developmental Issues and Synthesis of Current Scholarship and Debate

A woman's physical, mental, and socioeconomic development and well-being are all affected by laws, policies, and practices that impact access to reproductive health care. Pregnancy and the process of giving birth "represent[] a profound life change" (Askren & Bloom, 1999, p. 395). Thus, access to comprehensive reproductive health care that enables women to make autonomous decisions about whether and when to birth is an important component of women's adult development. Contraception, for example, "has myriad health, social, and economic benefits" (Guttmacher Institute, 2021d), and "policies that expand access to abortion and other reproductive health care not only enhance women's reproductive autonomy, but have economic benefits as well" (Institute for Women's Policy Research, 2019, p. 5). Taken together, the research discussed in this section indicates that laws, policies, and practices that impact women's ability to control whether and when to birth impose many short- and long-term effects on physical, mental/emotional, and socioeconomic development. Yet far too often, women are denied this control, particularly low-income women and women of color. Indeed, "[s]ystemic racism and reproductive oppression have, over centuries, denied bodily autonomy to Black girls and women and led to disproportionately adverse sexual and reproductive health outcomes" (Wulah, Abdi & Sanders, 2023).

Physical Health and Development

As this chapter demonstrates, laws and policies that promote or restrict access to reproductive health care affect women's physical health and development. For example, the laws described previously that restrict access to contraception or abortion—which result in women carrying unintended pregnancies to term—may negatively impact women's physical development. On the other hand, laws that facilitate access to contraception or abortion—which enable women to control their reproduction, but which may also have certain risks—may have an overall positive effect on women's physical development. Having an abortion, taking contraceptives, carrying a pregnancy to term, and raising a child can all influence a woman's physical health and development. These issues are addressed in the following sections.

ABORTION

Like all medical procedures, there are risks associated with abortion, but it is generally considered safe for most women (American College of Obstetricians and Gynecologists, 2020; Kukielka, 2020; Sajadi-Ernazarova & Martinez, 2021). The World Health Organization has compared the safety of abortion to a penicillin shot (World Health Organization, 2012, p. 49), and other research shows that a pregnancy is 14 times more likely to result in maternal morbidity than an abortion (Raymond & Grimes, 2012). And in some situations, abortion is necessary to preserve a woman's health or save a woman's life (American College of Obstetricians and Gynecologists, 2019a).

One of the most recent comprehensive studies on the consequences of abortion versus an unwanted pregnancy is the Turnaway Study. The Turnaway Study is the largest study to date examining women's experiences with abortion and unwanted pregnancy in the United States, and aimed to describe the physical, mental, and socioeconomic consequences of having an abortion compared to carrying an unwanted pregnancy to term after being denied an abortion. The study was led by a team of scientists at Advancing New Standards for Reproductive Health (ANSIRH), a program within the University of California San Francisco (UCSF) Bixby Center for Global Reproductive Health, part of UCSF's Department of Obstetrics, Gynecology, and Reproductive Sciences (ANSIRH, n.d.).

Prior research on the effects of abortion focused heavily on the mental health consequences of abortion, ignoring such conditions associated with pregnancy generally, and childbirth. Studies that centered on mental health often suffered from methodological limitations. For example, prior studies used inappropriate comparison groups, such as comparing women who obtain abortions with those who continue their pregnancies by choice, rather than comparing women who select abortions with women who continue their pregnancies not by choice but because, for example, they were denied or unable to access an abortion (ANSIRH, n.d.). In contrast, the Turnaway Study's research team interviewed nearly 1,000 women who sought an abortion in the United States. Some women in their research cohort received abortions because they were under the gestational limit of the relevant clinic, whereas some women were "turned away" and carried to term because they were past the gestational limit of the clinic (ANSIRH, 2020).

In short, and as discussed further throughout this chapter, the Turnaway Study found no evidence that abortion harms women. For every outcome analyzed, women who received an abortion were either the same or, more frequently, better off than women who were denied an abortion:

> [The former's] physical health was better. Their employment and financial situations were better. Their mental health was initially better and eventually the same. They had more aspirational plans for the coming year. They had a greater chance of having a wanted pregnancy and being in a good romantic relationship years down the road. And the children they already had were better off, too. (Foster, 2020, p. 21)

By contrast, women who carried unwanted pregnancies to term frequently experienced complications from delivery and, over the next 5 years, increased chronic head and joint pain and hypertension. They were more likely to self-report poor health, experience increased anxiety and loss of life satisfaction in the short term, and suffer economic hardships. Further, women with violent partners found it difficult to remove themselves from the relationship after the birth (Foster, 2020). Another key takeaway from the Turnaway Study is that women are "able to foresee consequences [e.g., about abortion and childbirth] and make decisions that are best for their lives and families" (Foster, 2020, p. 21). Other research, some of which is discussed in this section, supports the findings of the Turnaway Study.

Estimates suggest that the abortion-related complication rate is approximately 2%, with most complications considered "minor," such as pain, bleeding, infection, and postanesthesia complications. Other less common "major" complications may include uterine atony and subsequent hemorrhage, uterine perforation, injuries to adjacent organs, cervical laceration, failed abortion, septic abortion, and disseminated intravascular coagulation (Sajadi-Ernazarova & Martinez, 2021; Upadhyay, Desai, et al., 2015).

Deaths associated with legal abortion are rare. According to data collected by the U.S. Centers for Disease Control and Prevention, two abortion-related deaths occurred in 2018, the most recent year for which data were available (Kortsmit et al., 2021). An analysis by Zane and her colleagues (2015) found that from 1998 to 2010, out of approximately 16.1 million abortions, 108 women died, resulting in a morality rate of 0.7 deaths per 100,000 procedures overall. To put this in perspective, the U.S. maternal mortality ratio for 2021 was 32.9 maternal deaths per 100,000 live births (Hoyert, 2023). The weight of the evidence has also failed to uncover links between abortion and a number of other reproductive and pregnancy-related health risks, such as secondary infertility, ectopic pregnancy, spontaneous abortion and stillbirth, pre-eclampsia, chronic and gestational hypertension, placenta previa and accreta, and breast cancer (National Academies of Sciences, Engineering, and Medicine, 2018, pp. 129–158).

Abortion opponents cite adoption as a "moral alternative" to abortion. While this may be one option, advancing a pregnancy to term and then placing a child for adoption may significantly impact a woman's development, including her physical health. Askren and Bloom's (1999) metanalysis of English-language studies published from 1978 through 1994 about the postrelinquishment experience of birth mothers is informative on this point, and more recent research supports their findings (Madden et al., 2018). As described further in the following section on mental health, women who place a child for adoption may feel intense grief. Physically, if the intense grief reaction is prolonged, it can manifest itself in psychosomatic symptoms and secondary illness, including gynecologic infections, frequent or severe headaches, somatic symptoms, and sexual difficulties (Askren & Bloom, 1999).

Furthermore, results from the Turnaway Study suggest that most women denied an abortion choose parenting rather than adoption. Thus, messaging that presents adoption as a direct contrast to abortion presents a "false dichotomy," as most birth mothers and women seeking abortions are not interested in adoption (Sisson et al., 2017, p. 136). Research also suggests that women who consider abortion do not weigh it against adoption, but rather consider adoption only when abortion is inaccessible or unavailable (Sisson et al., 2017).

CONTRACEPTION

Many different types of contraceptives are available, including oral contraceptives (e.g., combination oral contraceptives that contain both estrogen and progestin, and progestin-only oral contraceptives) and LARC methods (e.g., copper or hormonal IUDs). Like all drugs and devices, contraceptives have risks. Given the myriad options, however, some form of contraceptive is generally considered safe for most women (American College of Obstetricians and Gynecologists, 2017, 2019b; Planned Parenthood, n.d.-b, , n.d.-c).

The primary purpose of contraception is to prevent pregnancy, but there are many other potential benefits. For example, if all women had access to the contraception they wanted, worldwide maternal mortality would decrease by 25%. This means that meeting 100% of the needs for contraception would prevent over 76,000 maternal deaths worldwide each year (Darroch, 2018, Table 18). Furthermore, certain contraceptive methods may reduce the risk of some types of cancer; treat various menstrual-related symptoms and disorders; and prevent or lessen other conditions such as bone thinning, iron deficiency, and serious infections in the ovaries, fallopian tubes, and uterus (Kaunitz, 2021; Kavanaugh & Anderson, 2013; Planned Parenthood, n.d.-b).

PREGNANCY AND CHILDBIRTH

Pregnancy and childbirth can profoundly destabilize a woman's physical health (Centers for Disease Control and Prevention, 2020a). Pregnancy causes significant physical changes that "can exacerbate underlying or preexisting conditions, like renal or cardiac disease, and can severely compromise health or even cause death" (American College of Obstetricians and Gynecologists, 2019a). Moreover, the actual process of giving birth "encompasses much pain, emotional stress, vulnerability, possible physical injury or death, and permanent role change" (Askren & Bloom, 1999, p. 395).

Women in the United States suffer the highest maternal mortality rate among industrialized nations. As maternal mortality rates declined worldwide in 2017, the World Health Organization reported that the United States and the Dominican Republic were the only two countries to report a significant increase in their maternal mortality ratios since 2000 (Commonwealth Fund, 2020). The most recently available U.S. maternal mortality rate for 2021 was 32.9 maternal deaths per 100,000 live births, significantly higher than the 2020 rate of 23.8. This translated to 1,205 maternal deaths in 2021. Furthermore, the racial disparities are stark. The maternal mortality rate for non-Hispanic Black women (69.9) was 2.6 times the rate for non-Hispanic White women (26.6) (Hoyert, 2023).

Importantly, in states most hostile to abortion and other reproductive rights, maternal mortality rates remain the highest when compared to rates across all U.S. states. Of the states reporting maternal mortality data for 2021, Mississippi had the highest rate (82.5) (USA Facts, 2023).

In studies comparing women who received an abortion with women who were denied an abortion, the women denied abortions who gave birth self-reported more chronic pain and rated their overall health worse compared to those who received an abortion. In the short term, women giving birth after being denied an abortion experienced more potentially life-threatening complications such as eclampsia and postpartum hemorrhage (Gerdts et al., 2015; Ralph, Schwarz, et al., 2019).

Taken together, the weight of the evidence suggests that women who use contraception and/or receive abortions to avoid unwanted pregnancies are no worse off physically than women who give birth after wanted pregnancies. On the contrary, the data suggest that women who avoid unwanted pregnancies are typically better off physically than women who give birth after wanted pregnancies.

Mental Health and Development

Reproductive health affects mental health in myriad ways. The mental health effects related to decisions about reproduction (e.g., obtaining or being denied an abortion, carrying a pregnancy to term, placing a child for adoption, raising a child, etc.) can include anxiety, depression, denial, anger, guilt, remorse, loss of life satisfaction, loss of self-esteem, and shame (American Psychological Association, 2018; Askren & Bloom, 1999; Foster, 2020; Madden et al., 2018). Research shows that "successful fertility regulation heightens adaptive capacities and coping capabilities. Good conceptive control makes for good family health and thus good mental health" (David, 1994, p. 345).

Much of the literature on reproductive rights and mental health centers on debates about the impact of abortion on a woman's mental health. It is difficult to draw definitive conclusions from the research, as many researchers note that studies frequently suffer from methodological problems, such as inappropriate comparison groups, inadequate controls, and erroneous conclusions (Biggs et al., 2017; Charles et al., 2008; Madden et al., 2018; Reardon, 2018; Steinberg & Finer, 2012). Drawing conclusions also proves difficult due to the wide variety of findings and inconsistent results.

Even so, an increasing body of evidence suggests that while some women experience and are at greater risk of experiencing negative mental health outcomes after an abortion, receiving an abortion generally does not increase a woman's risk for various negative mental outcomes. For example, after reviewing the literature, Charles and her colleagues (2008) concluded that

> the highest quality studies had findings that were mostly neutral, suggesting few, if any, differences between aborters and their respective comparison groups in terms of mental health sequelae. Conversely, studies with the most flawed methodology consistently found negative mental health sequelae of abortion. (pp. 449–450)

The American Psychological Association (APA) states that although some women may experience stress after an abortion, "having an abortion does not increase a woman's risk for depression, anxiety, or post-traumatic stress disorder" (APA, 2018). According to an APA task force report in 2008, which reviewed the scientific literature, the relative risk of mental health problems after a single elective abortion during the first trimester is no greater than carrying the pregnancy to term (APA, 2018; Major et al., 2008). And among women who experience mental health problems, many of the issues may be related to co-occurring risk factors that predispose them to both unwanted pregnancies and mental health problems (APA, 2018).

The APA cites a publication from the Turnaway Study, which found no evidence that abortion has a negative effect on mental health or well-being. On the contrary, the study found that being denied an abortion is associated with increased anxiety, stress, and lower self-esteem shortly after the denial. Over time, the Turnaway Study found that these outcomes generally improve and that women denied an abortion have similar mental health outcomes compared to women who were able to get an abortion (Biggs et al., 2017). Further, throughout the course of a 5-year study, over 95% of women felt that abortion was the right decision for them. Relief was the most commonly felt emotion at all times over the course of the study (Rocca et al., 2020). Perceived abortion stigma at the time of seeking an abortion, however, was associated with negative psychological outcomes years later (Biggs et al., 2020).

As noted previously, abortion opponents may point to adoption as an alternative to abortion. When considering the mental health consequences of abortion, the psychological stressors associated with an unintended pregnancy, birth, and thereafter placing the child for adoption or raising the child must also be considered, as unwanted pregnancies and subsequent births also affect mental health (Bahk et al., 2015; Barton et al., 2017; Foster, 2020). In contrast to myriad studies on mental health consequences of abortion, "we know relatively little about the ramifications for the well-being of women who continue unplanned pregnancies to term," despite the fact that "having a child and raising that child are key events in the life course" (Herd et al., 2016, p. 421).

Consensus exists among adoption researchers that many women who place a child for adoption feel intense grief, loss, remorse, guilt, and isolation, and may experience lifelong emotional and interpersonal consequences (Askren & Bloom, 1999; Madden et al., 2018). In fact, according to Askren and Bloom (1999), mothers who relinquish their child for adoption experience more grief symptoms than mothers who experience the death of a child.

More generally, it is estimated that one in eight women experiences postpartum depression, such as feeling sad, pessimistic, or angry; crying more frequently; having difficulty sleeping; feeling disconnected from their babies; and worrying about hurting their babies. In addition to the immediate and short-term safety concerns for the child, postpartum depression can have long-term consequences for the child, including impaired mental and motor development, behavioral issues, poor self-regulation, and low self-esteem (United Health Foundation, 2021b). Importantly, studies suggest that women experiencing unintended pregnancies may be at greater risk for postpartum depression than those with intended pregnancies (Barton et al., 2017; Cheng et al., 2009; Mercier et al., 2019). Furthermore, structural racism in the U.S. health care system results in significant inequities in the diagnosis of perinatal and maternal mental health disorders as well as access to treatment (Matthews et al., 2021). Thus, a common theme continues: women of color face particular and outsized burdens with respect to their reproductive health, with potentially devastating developmental consequences.

The various and often contradictory findings about abortion, unintended pregnancy, adoption, parenting, and mental health make it difficult to draw definitive conclusions about these issues. Even so, it is clear that laws, policies, and practices that either facilitate or restrict access to reproductive health care can have both negative and positive effects on women's mental health. Given the ongoing debate and need for further study, laws, policies, and practices should facilitate, rather than restrict, a woman's choice, allowing her to weigh the potential risks and benefits based on her own circumstances.

Socioeconomic Development and Well-Being

Deciding whether and when to have a child involves numerous socioeconomic factors and considerations. This chapter takes a broad view of what is encompassed by the term "socioeconomic," including economics, education, interpersonal relationships, and social equality. A growing body of research suggests that laws, policies, and practices that enable women to control whether and when to birth have many social and economic benefits (Bernstein & Jones, 2019; Casey, 2010; Sonfield et al., 2013).

ECONOMICS AND EDUCATION

Bringing a pregnancy to term and then raising a child is a costly undertaking in the United States. According to the U.S. Department of Agriculture, the 2015 estimated cost to raise a child from birth to age 17 in a two-child, middle-income, married-couple family (defined as pretax income of $59,200–$107,400) was $233,610. For the lowest income couples (pretax income of less than $59,200), the estimated cost was $174,690. And for the highest income couples (pretax income of more than $107,400), the estimated cost was $372,210 (Lino et al., 2017). Given these costs, research suggests that being denied an abortion leads to economic insecurity for women and their families, which lasts a number of years after the denial (Foster, Biggs, Ralph, et al., 2018). Pregnant women who consider, but do not have, an abortion have considerable health and social service needs (e.g., food stamps; Special Supplemental Nutrition Program for Women, Infants, and Children; and housing assistance), and children born to women who were denied an abortion are more likely to live in homes without enough money for basic living expenses (Berglas et al., 2019; Foster, Biggs, Raifman, et al., 2018).

According to Susan Cohen (2004), former vice president for public policy at the Guttmacher Institute, "[a] mistimed or unwanted birth . . . can drastically limit a woman's life options and undermine family well-being, thus seriously hampering social and economic development" (p. 5). Indeed, women who lack control over their reproduction have "considerable difficulty" completing their education and maintaining gainful employment (David, 1994, p. 343; Bernstein & Jones, 2019). A review of the evidence amassed by Bernstein and Jones (2019) suggests that although results can vary by subgroups, access to contraceptives improves women's higher education rates, increases the number of women in the workforce, results in substantially higher earnings for women by their 30s and 40s, and reduces the probability that a woman will live in poverty. In fact, the mere knowledge that contraception is accessible can affect economic outcomes. According to Bernstein and Jones (2019), "Prior to ever using contraception, the knowledge that she will have the future ability to control whether and when to have a child can shape a young women's aspirations and life plans . . . [which] can impact her investment in education and her career choice" (p. 9).

With respect to abortion, the Turnaway Study found that over the course of 5 years, there was no association between having a child after being denied an abortion and graduating, leaving, or returning to school. That said, being denied an abortion does have some impact on education, as women who sought and received an abortion completed more advanced degrees than those who raised a child after being denied an abortion (Ralph, Mauldon, et al., 2019). Further, unplanned pregnancies may reduce labor participation (Nuevo-Chiquero, 2014; Yazdkhasti et al., 2015), which, in turn, impacts a woman's income and poverty status. Women who have an abortion are also more likely to have—and achieve—positive 1-year plans compared to women who seek but are denied an abortion (Upadhyay, Biggs, & Foster, 2015).

For women who cannot access or afford an abortion, affordable contraception becomes even more important. As discussed in previously, although the ACA and many state laws require coverage of certain contraceptives, laws allowing exemptions for employers, insurers, and providers based on religious or moral beliefs threaten a woman's ability to obtain affordable birth control, thus increasing her chances of an unintended pregnancy and potential need for an abortion. These exemptions are problematic because "the legal right to contraception is not sufficient—for women to see economic benefits of contraception, it needs to be accessible" (Bernstein & Jones 2019, p. 22).

SOCIAL EQUALITY

The consequences of an unintended pregnancy can be particularly life-altering for vulnerable women, imposing significant constraints in the lives of women of color and further exacerbating racial and economic inequality. Low-income women are more likely to experience an unintended pregnancy but are less likely to be able to access and/or afford an abortion or contraception. The rate of unintended pregnancy among women with incomes less than 100% of the federal poverty level was 112 per 1,000 in 2011, more than five times the rate among women with incomes of at least 200% of the federal poverty level (Guttmacher Institute, 2019a).

Out-of-pocket costs for abortion or contraception have a greater impact on the most vulnerable, such as low-income women and women of color, who are disproportionately likely to have an abortion (Guttmacher Institute, 2019b). A low-income person's ability to afford an abortion is complicated, in part, by the Hyde Amendment's ban on federal funding for abortions except in certain limited situations. Accessible and affordable abortions are essential because

> a right to abortion without access is a right in name only. . . . [R]estrictions like Hyde can place often insurmountable barriers to access abortion, while perpetuating racial and economic inequality. . . . Black, Latino, and LGBTQ people are disproportionately likely to have low incomes and get insurance through Medicaid, thereby facing the coverage ban. (Rinkunas, 2021)

Further, state laws that reduce funding to family planning services, which "inherently target the lower-income women eligible for these programs," reduce access to abortion and contraception, resulting in an increased number of unintended pregnancies that have potential downstream economic effects for women, their families, and society in general (Bernstein & Jones, 2019, p. 24).

INTERPERSONAL RELATIONSHIPS

A woman's ability to control whether and when to have a child can impact interpersonal relationships. For example, both married and unmarried couples experiencing unintended pregnancies have less stable relationships than those experiencing intended pregnancies (Guzzo &

Hayford, 2012, 2014; Lichter et al., 2016; Maddow-Zimet et al., 2016; Palkovitz et al., 2003; Stykes & Guzzo, 2020). Children change relationship dynamics and introduce new stressors to a relationship, and research indicates that transitioning to parenthood reduces relationship quality. Furthermore, unintended pregnancies, relationship dynamics, and well-being are linked (Stykes & Guzzo, 2020).

Unintended pregnancies are more common among unmarried women. As a result, this group is the focus of most studies relating to the topic, but married women also experience and are affected by unintended or mistimed pregnancies. Stykes and Guzzo (2020), for example, found that couples in which both parents intended the birth reported the highest levels of marital stability, whereas couples in which either the woman did not intend the birth or neither parent intended the birth reported the greatest instability. The authors also found that when a married woman believes that her partner did not intend the birth, there is a higher risk of marital instability, regardless of whether the woman intended the birth.

Separately, there is a relationship between reproductive health care and intimate partner violence, which includes sexual, physical, emotional, and economic abuse. Restricting access to family planning and abortion can keep women physically and financially vulnerable to their abusers because control over a woman's sexual and reproductive life is often one component of abuse (Hall et al., 2014; National Women's Law Center, 2013). Intimate partner violence can have many negative—and even deadly—consequences for women and their children, including physical complications, economic instability, and mental health consequences (Centers for Disease Control and Prevention, 2020b).

Intimate partner violence is associated with pregnancy in several ways. For one, intimate partner violence can contribute to higher rates of unintended pregnancy. Second, the violence itself may commence, or increase in frequency or severity, with the onset of pregnancy. Finally, the effects may be additive across pregnancies, with a woman's odds of experiencing intimate partner violence increasing approximately 11% with each additional pregnancy (Gee et al., 2009; National Domestic Violence Hotline, n.d.). Intimate partner violence is also related to other social equality issues, as low-income women and women of color are more likely to be victims of intimate partner violence (National Women's Law Center, 2013).

The Supreme Court acknowledged the relationship between access to reproductive health care and intimate partner violence in the now-overturned *Planned Parenthood of Southeastern Pennsylvania v. Casey* (1992). In striking down a spousal notification law, the Supreme Court recognized that

> for the great many women who are victims of abuse inflicted by their husbands, or whose children are the victims of such abuse, a spousal notice requirement enables the husband to wield an effective veto over his wife's decision. Whether the prospect of notification itself deters such women from seeking abortions, or whether the husband, through physical force or psychological pressure or economic coercion, prevents his wife from obtaining an abortion until it is too late, the notice requirement will often be tantamount to the veto found unconstitutional in [*Planned Parenthood of Central Missouri v.*] *Danforth*. (*Planned Parenthood of Southeastern Pennsylvania v. Casey*, 1992, p. 897)

In *Danforth*, the court held unconstitutional a law that required a married woman to obtain her husband's consent before undergoing an abortion (*Planned Parenthood of Central Missouri v. Danforth*, 1976).

Because abusers frequently attempt to control their victims' sexual and reproductive health, contraceptive use may be difficult for women experiencing intimate partner violence to navigate and control. Thus, access to affordable contraception not dependent on partner involvement is critical for women at risk of intimate partner violence. Such options include progesterone injections, contraceptive implants, or intrauterine contraceptives. Affordability is also key, because many women at risk of abuse report skipping birth control because they could not afford it (Gee et al., 2009).

Access to abortion is also critical in instances of intimate partner violence. The literature shows that some women cite intimate partner violence as a reason for wanting an abortion (Hall et al., 2014). Studies also suggest that among women seeking an abortion, having an abortion is associated with a reduction over time in physical violence from the man involved in the pregnancy. In contrast, carrying the pregnancy to term is not. Women who have an abortion may be more likely and able to end their relationships with their violent partners, whereas those who carry a pregnancy to term are more likely to have sustained contact with the partner and remain in the relationship for a longer period of time (Mauldon et al., 2015; Roberts et al., 2014). A woman's risk of further violence and ability to extricate herself from the abusive relationship, however, are likely influenced by her ability to not inform her abuser about the abortion.

Other Consequences

This chapter focuses on the impact of reproductive laws, policies, and practices on women's adult development. That said, it is important to acknowledge that reproductive laws, policies, and practices also shape the health and well-being of children, families, and society.

More research is needed, but studies suggest that children benefit when women gain control over whether and when they have children. Unintended pregnancies increase the risk of problems for women and infants, in part because women who do not intend pregnancies may delay obtaining prenatal care or engage in behavior inconsistent with promoting a healthy pregnancy (Centers for Disease Control and Prevention, 2021). Research suggests that unintended pregnancies are associated with an increased risk of impaired child development and poor maternal–child relationships (de La Rochebrochard & Joshi, 2013). Henry P. David (1994, 2006), for example, studied the effect of "compulsory childbearing" on 220 children born between 1961 and 1963 to women in Prague twice denied an abortion for the same pregnancy compared to a control group of 220 children born to women who had purposely discontinued contraception or had accepted unplanned pregnancies. The children were followed from approximately age 9 to 35. In short, "all the differences in psychosocial development were consistently in disfavour of the subjects born from unwanted pregnancies," increasing the children's risk for negative psychosocial development and mental well-being (David, 2006, p. 187).

Researchers also associate unintended pregnancies with poorer prenatal and postnatal behaviors, such as less prenatal care and breastfeeding, a more authoritarian parenting style, and a less effective home learning environment (Centers for Disease Control and Prevention, 2021; de La Rochebrochard & Joshi, 2013). Each of these, in turn, potentially impacts children's development, both in childhood and later in life. This research suggests increased mental health problems and lower self-esteem among teenagers and young adults born after an unplanned pregnancy (de La Rochebrochard & Joshi, 2013). Further study is needed to understand whether the association of an unplanned pregnancy with child development represents a causal pathway or whether it can be attributed to other factors, such as the mother's sociodemographic characteristics that make her more likely to experience an unintended pregnancy (Su, 2017).

Research also shows that access to subsidized contraception reduces childhood poverty in the short term and adult poverty a generation later (Bernstein & Jones, 2019). The Turnaway

Study found that children born to women denied abortions were more likely to live in lower income households, live below the federal poverty level, and live in homes that do not have enough money to pay for basic living expenses, compared to children of women who received an abortion and then had subsequent children within 5 years (Foster et al., 2019; Foster, Biggs, et al., 2018). The Turnaway Study also found that children born to women denied an abortion were more likely to experience poor maternal bonding. The authors concluded that these findings suggest that access to abortion allows women to choose to have children when they have more financial and emotional resources to devote to them (Foster, Biggs, et al., 2018).

In addition to affecting the child born from an unintended pregnancy, unintended pregnancies can also affect existing children. In fact, one reason women report seeking abortions is so they can care for their existing children (Biggs et al., 2013; Foster et al., 2019). The Turnaway Study compared the youngest existing children under the age of 5 of women denied abortions to those of women who received an abortion, and found that from 6 months to 4.5 years after their mothers sought abortions, existing children of women denied abortions had lower mean child development scores than children whose mothers received an abortion (Foster et al., 2019).

Unintended pregnancies, which researchers consider a "major health problem" in the United States, contribute to societal challenges (American College of Obstetrics and Gynecology, 2015; Centers for Disease Control and Prevention, 2016). Preventing unintended pregnancies could potentially save the U.S. government billions of dollars each year (Centers for Disease Control and Prevention, 2016; Sonfield & Kost, 2015; Trussel et al., 2013). Access to reproductive health care that allows women to control whether and when to have a child gives women more choices to pursue higher education and participate in the labor force (Joint Economic Committee, 2020). This, in turn, can benefit the U.S. economy through higher labor force participation and greater numbers of women with disposable incomes.

Conclusion

In this chapter, we sought to highlight salient issues related to pregnancy, abortion, and contraception. Even with its breadth and scope, we are nonetheless mindful of the rapidly changing legal landscape of reproductive health, rights, and justice, including states' enactment of laws restricting abortion rights, rollbacks and threats to contraceptive care access, and worrying trends related to maternal morbidity and mortality. Altogether, we predict continued, troubling attacks on reproductive liberties that will likely result in poor health outcomes for women, LGBTQ+ populations, and any children they may bear.

Consistently, and over decades, research weighs in favor of facilitating, rather than restricting, women's reproductive decision making. As a normative matter, at a minimum this should include access to affordable (a) contraception (including emergency contraception), (b) abortion (including medication abortion), (c) prenatal care, and (d) postnatal maternal and child health care. Moreover, enhancing reproductive decision making for the most vulnerable women improves their well-being.

Even while future research could further probe the causal relationships between restricting reproductive rights and consequences to mental, physical, and socioeconomic health and well-being, certain key findings that emerge from recent studies offer a compelling start. For example, future research could build on the Turnaway Study by using a larger sample size and following the women for a longer period of time after they receive or are denied an abortion. A similar study could also be performed to assess the impact of access to contraception. Other research could compare women living in states deemed "hostile" to reproductive rights (e.g., Texas) with those in states deemed "sanctuaries" (e.g., California). Such research could avoid pitfalls in prior studies by controlling for confounding factors and including proper comparison groups. Finally, we recommend that future research, practice, and policymaking take into account historical and contemporary patterns of systemic discrimination, centering on race, sex, disability, and LGBTQ+ justice.

References

42 C.F.R. § 147.131 (2018). https://www.ecfr.gov/cgi-bin/text-idx?node=pt45.1.147&rgn=div5#se45.2.147_1131

42 C.F.R. § 147.132 (2018). https://www.ecfr.gov/cgi-bin/text-idx?node=pt45.1.147&rgn=div5#se45.2.147_1132

Advancing New Standards for Reproductive Health (ANSIRH). (n.d.). *The Turnaway Study*. https://www.ansirh.org/research/ongoing/turnaway-study.

Advancing New Standards for Reproductive Health (ANSIRH). (2020). *Introduction to the Turnaway Study*. https://www.ansirh.org/sites/default/files/publications/files/turnawaystudyannotatedbibliography.pdf

Alliance for Hippocratice Medicine v. FDA, Case No. 2:22-cv-00223-Z (N.D. Tex. April 7, 2023)/

American Civil Liberties Union. (n.d.). *Government-mandated delays before abortion*. https://www.aclu.org/other/government-mandated-delays-abortion

American College of Obstetricians and Gynecologists. (2015, reaffirmed 2018). *Committee Opinion No. 642: Increasing access to contraceptive implants and intrauterine devices to reduce unintended pregnancy*. https://www.acog.org/-/media/project/acog/acogorg/clinical/files/committee-opinion/articles/2015/10/increasing-access-to-contraceptive-implants-and-intrauterine-devices-to-reduce-unintended-pregnancy.pdf

American College of Obstetricians and Gynecologists. (2017). Long-acting reversible contraception: Implants and intrauterine devices. *Obstetrics & Gynecology, 130*(5), e.251–e269.

American College of Obstetricians and Gynecologists. (2019a). *Abortion can be medically necessary*. https://www.acog.org/news/news-releases/2019/09/abortion-can-be-medically-necessary

American College of Obstetricians and Gynecologists. (2019b). Over-the-counter access to hormonal contraception. *Obstetrics & Gynecology, 134*(4), e96–e105.

American College of Obstetricians and Gynecologists. (2020). Medication abortion up to 70 days of gestation. *Obstetrics & Gynecology, 136*(4), e31–e47.

American College of Obstetricians and Gynecologists v. U.S. Food and Drug Administration, Complaint, case no. 8:20-cv-01320 (D. Md.) (2020).

American Psychological Association (APA). (2018). *Abortion and mental health*. https://www.apa.org/pi/women/programs/abortion

Askren, H. A., & Bloom, K. C. (1999). Postadoptive reactions of the relinquishing mother: A review. *Journal of Obstetric, Gynecologic & Neonatal Nursing, 28*(4), 395–400.

Associated Press. (2020, June 29). *China cuts Uighur births with IUDs, abortion, sterilization*. https://apnews.com/article/ap-top-news-international-news-weekend-reads-china-health-269b3de1af34e17c1941a514f78d764c

Athan, A. M. (2020). Reproductive identity: An emerging concept. *American Psychologist, 75*(4), 445–456.

Bahk, J., Yun, S. C., Kim, Y., & Khang, Y. H. (2015). Impact of unintended pregnancy on maternal mental health: A causal analysis using follow up data of the Panel Study on Korean Children (PSKC). *BMC Pregnancy and Childbirth, 15*(85), 1–12.

Barot, S. (2012). Governmental coercion in reproductive decision making: See it both ways. *Guttmacher Policy Review, 15*(4), 7–12. https://www.guttmacher.org/sites/default/files/article_files/gpr150407.pdf

Barton, K., Redshaw, M., Quigly, M. A., & Carson, C. (2017). Unplanned pregnancy and subsequent psychological distress in partnered women: A cross-sectional study of the role of relationship quality and wider social support. *BMC Pregnancy and Childbirth, 17*(44), 1–9.

Berglas, N. F., Kimport, K., Williams, V., Mark, K., & Roberts, S. C. M. (2019). The health and social service needs of pregnant women who consider but do not have abortions. *Women's Health Issues, 29*(5), 364–369.

Bernstein, A., & Jones, K. M. (2019). *The economic effect of contraceptive access: A review of the evidence*. Institute for Women's Policy. https://iwpr.org/wp-content/uploads/2020/07/B381_Contraception-Access_Final.pdf

Biggs, M. A., Brown, K., & Foster, D. G. (2020). Perceived abortion stigma and psychological well-being over five years after receiving or being denied an abortion. *PLOS One, 15*(1).

Biggs, M. A., Gould, H., & Foster, D. G. (2013). Understanding why women seek abortions in the US. *BMC Women's Health, 13*(29), 1–13.

Biggs, M. A., Upadhyay, U. D., & McCulloch, C. E. (2017). Women's mental health and well-being 5 years after receiving or being denied an abortion. *JAMA Psychiatry, 74*(2), 169–178.

Boonin, S. (2020, October 21). The confirmation of Amy Coney Barrett—and the end of *Roe* as we know it. *Ms. Magazine*. https://msmagazine.com/2020/10/21/amy-coney-barrett-roe-v-wade-june-medical-services/

Boonstra, H. & Nash. E. A surge of state abortion restrictions puts providers—and the women they serve—in the crosshairs. *Guttmacher Policy Review*, 17, 9–15.

Buck v. Bell, 274 U.S. 200 (1927).

Casey, P. R. (2010). Abortion among young women and subsequent life outcomes. *Best Practice & Research Clinical Obstetrics and Gynaecology*, 24, 491–502.

Center for Reproductive Rights (2023). *Alliance for Hippocratic Medicine v. FDA*. https://reproductiverights.org/case/alliance-for-hippocratic-medicine-v-fda/

Centers for Disease Control and Prevention. (2016). *At a glance 2016: Women's reproductive health*. https://www.cdc.gov/chronicdisease/resources/publications/aag/pdf/2016/aag-reproductive-health.pdf

Centers for Disease Control and Prevention. (2020a). *Pregnancy complications*. https://www.cdc.gov/reproductivehealth/maternalinfanthealth/pregnancy-complications.html

Centers for Disease Control and Prevention. (2020b). *Preventing intimate partner violence*. https://www.cdc.gov/violenceprevention/pdf/ipv/IPV-factsheet_2020_508.pdf

Centers for Disease Control and Prevention. (2023). *Unintended pregnancy*. https://www.cdc.gov/reproductivehealth/contraception/unintendedpregnancy/index.htm

Charles, V. E., Polis, C. B., Sridhara, S. K., & Blum, R. W. (2008). Abortion and long-term mental health outcomes: A systematic review of the evidence. *Contraception*, 78(6), 436–450.

Cheng, D., Schwarz, E. B., Douglas, E., & Horon, I. (2009). Unintended pregnancy and associated maternal preconception, prenatal, and postpartum behaviors. *Contraception*, 79, 194–198.

Cohen, S. A. (2004). The broad benefits of investing in sexual and reproductive health. *Guttmacher Report on Public Policy*, 7(1), 5–8. https://www.guttmacher.org/sites/default/files/article_files/gr070105.pdf

Commonwealth Fund. (2020, December 16). *Maternal mortality in the United States: A primer*. https://www.commonwealthfund.org/publications/issue-brief-report/2020/dec/maternal-mortality-united-states-primer

Darroch, J. E. (2018). *Adding it up: Investing in contraception and maternal and newborn health, 2017*. Guttmacher Institute. https://www.guttmacher.org/sites/default/files/report_pdf/adding-it-up-2017-estimation-methodology.pdf

David, H. P. (1994). Reproductive rights and reproductive behavior: Clash or convergence of private values and public policies? *American Psychologist*, 49(4), 343–349.

David, H. P. (2006). Born unwanted, 35 years later: The Prague study. *Reproductive Health Matters*, 14(7), 181–190.

Davies, S. E., & Harman, S. (2020). Securing reproductive health: A matter of international peace and security. *International Studies Quarterly*, 64(2), 277–284.

Davis, D.-A. (2020). Reproducing while Black: The crisis of Black maternal health, obstetric racism, and assisted reproductive technology. *Reproductive Biomedicine and Society Online*, 11, 56–64.

De La Rochebrochard, E., & Joshi, H. (2013). Children born after unplanned pregnancies and cognitive development at 3 years: Social differentials in the United Kingdom Millennium Cohort. *American Journal of Epidemiology*, 178(6), 910–920.

Dobbs. v. Jackson Women's Health Organization, 142 S. Ct. 2228 (2022).

Eisenstadt v. Baird, 405 U.S. 438 (1972).

Firth, S. (2023, January 30). Biden administration targets Trump-era exemptions to birth control coverage. *MedPage Today*. https://www.medpagetoday.com/publichealthpolicy/healthpolicy/102885

Fong, M. (2016). *One child: The story of China's most radical experiment*. Houghton Mifflin Harcourt.

Foster, D. G. (2020). *The turn away study: Ten years, a thousand women, and the consequences of having—or being denied—an abortion*. Scribner.

Foster, D. G., Biggs, M. A., Raifman, S., Gipson, J., Kimport, K., & Rocca, C. H. (2018). Comparison of health, development, maternal bonding, and poverty among children born after denial of abortion vs pregnancies subsequent to an abortion. *JAMA Pediatrics*, 172(11), 1053–1060.

Foster, D. G., Biggs, M. A., Ralph, L., Gerdts, C., Roberts, S., & Glymour, M. M. (2018). Socioeconomic outcomes of women who receive and women who are denied wanted abortions in the United States. *American Journal of Public Health*, 108(3), 407–413.

Foster, D. G., Raifman, S. E., Gipson, J. D., Rocca, C. H., & Biggs, M. A. (2019). Effects of carrying an unwanted pregnancy to term on women's existing children. *Journal of Pediatrics*, 205, 183–189.e1.

Gee, R. E., Mitra, N., Wan, F., Chavkin, D. E., & Long, J. A. (2009). Power over parity: Intimate partner violence and issues of fertility control. *American Journal of Obstetrics & Gynecology*, 201(2), 148e1–7.

Gerdts, C., Dobkin, L., Foster, D. G., & Schwarz, E. B. (2015). Side effects, physical health consequences, and mortality associated with abortion and birth after an unwanted pregnancy. *Women's Health Issues*, 26(1), 55–59.

Goldman, R. (2021, May 31). From one child to three: How China's family planning policies have evolved. *New York Times*. https://www.nytimes.com/2021/05/31/world/asia/china-child-policy.html

Goodwin, M., & Whelan, A. (2015). Reproduction and the rule of law in Latin America. *Fordham Law Review*, *83*(5), 2577–2604.

Goodwin, M., & Whelan, A. (2016). Constitutional exceptionalism. *University of Illinois Law Review*, *2016*(4), 1287–1330.

Griswold v. Connecticut, 381 U.S. 479 (1965).

Gupta, A.H. (July 13, 2023). A birth control pill will soon be available without a prescription. Here's what to know. *New York Times*. https://www.nytimes.com/2023/05/10/well/live/birth-control-pill-otc.html

Guttmacher Institute. (2019a). *Unintended pregnancies in the United States*. https://www.guttmacher.org/fact-sheet/unintended-pregnancy-united-states#

Guttmacher Institute. (2019b). *Induced abortion in the United States*. https://www.guttmacher.org/sites/default/files/factsheet/fb_induced_abortion.pdf

Guttmacher Institute. (2021a). *Medication abortion*. https://www.guttmacher.org/evidence-you-can-use/medication-abortion

Guttmacher Institute. (2021b). *Medication abortion*. https://www.guttmacher.org/state-policy/explore/medication-abortion

Guttmacher Institute. (2021c). *Refusing to provide health services*. https://www.guttmacher.org/state-policy/explore/refusing-provide-health-services

Guttmacher Institute. (2021d). *Insurance coverage of contraceptives*. https://www.guttmacher.org/state-policy/explore/insurance-coverage-contraceptives

Guttmacher Institute. (2021e). *Emergency contraception*. https://www.guttmacher.org/state-policy/explore/emergency-contraception

Guzzo, K. B., & Hayford, S. R. (2012). Unintended fertility and the stability of coresidential relationships. *Social Science Research*, *41*(5), 1138–1151.

Guzzo, K. B., & Hayford, S. R. (2014). Fertility and the stability of cohabiting unions: Variation by intendedness. *Journal of Family Issues*, *35*(4), 547–576.

Hall, M., Chappell, L. C., Parnell, B. L., Seed, P. T., & Bewley, S. (2014). Associations between intimate partner violence and termination of pregnancy: A systematic review and meta-analysis. *PLOS Medicine*, *11*(1).

Healthcare.gov. (n.d.). *Birth control benefits*. https://www.healthcare.gov/coverage/birth-control-benefits/

Herd, P., Higgins, J., Sicinski, K., & Merkurieva, I. (2016). The implications of unintended pregnancies for mental health in later life. *American Journal of Public Health*, *106*(3), 421–429.

Hoyert, D. L. (2023). Maternal mortality rates in the United States, 2021. *NCHS Health E-Stats*. https://www.cdc.gov/nchs/data/hestat/maternal-mortality/2021/maternal-mortality-rates-2021.pdf

Institute for Women's Policy Research. (2019). *The economic effects of abortion access: A review of the evidence*. https://iwpr.org/wp-content/uploads/2020/07/B377_Abortion-Access-Fact-Sheet_final.pdf

Johnson, K. J. (2016). *China's hidden children*. University of Chicago Press.

Joint Economic Committee. (2020). *The economic benefits of birth control and access to family planning*. https://www.jec.senate.gov/public/_cache/files/bb400414-8dee-4e39-abd3-c2460fd30e7d/the-economic-benefits-of-birth-control-and-access-to-family-planning.pdf

June Medical Services L.L.C. v. Russo, 140 S.Ct. 2103 (2020).

Kaiser Family Foundation. (2021, January 28). *The Mexico City Policy: An explainer*. https://www.kff.org/global-health-policy/fact-sheet/mexico-city-policy-explainer/

Kaunitz, A. M. (2021). *The importance of contraception*. The Global Library of Women's Medicine's Welfare of Women Global Health Programme. https://www.glowm.com/section-view/heading/The%20Importance%20of%20Contraception/item/373#.YOR84mhKiUl.

Kavanaugh, M. L., & Anderson, R. M. (2013). *Contraception and beyond: The health benefits of services provided at family planning centers*. Guttmacher Institute. https://www.guttmacher.org/sites/default/files/report_pdf/health-benefits.pdf

Kortsmit, K., Jatlaoui, T. C., Mandel, M. G., Reeves, J. A., Clark, E., Pagano, H. P., Nguyen, A., Petersen, E., & Whiteman, M. K. (2021). Abortion surveillance—United States, 2019. *Morbidity and Mortality Weekly Report*, *70*(9), 1–29. https://www.cdc.gov/mmwr/volumes/69/ss/pdfs/ss6907a1-H.pdf

Kukielka, E. (2020). Patient safety events submitted by abortion facilities in Pennsylvania 2017–2019. *Patient Safety Journal*, *2*(4), 62–71.

Lichter, D. T., Michelmore, K., Turner, R. N., & Sassler, S. (2016). Pathways to a stable union? Pregnancy and childbearing among cohabiting and married couples. *Population Research Policy Review*, *35*, 377–399.

Lino, M., Kuczynski, K., Rodriguez, R., & Schap, T. (2017). *Expenditures on children by families, 2015*. Miscellaneous Publication No. 1528-2015. U.S. Department of Agriculture, Center for Nutrition Policy and Promotion. https://fns-prod.azureedge.net/sites/default/files/crc2015_March2017.pdf

Little Sisters of the Poor v. Pennsylvania, 140 S.Ct. 2367 (2020).

Liu, Y. (2020, February). *Speaking the unspoken and unspeakable: Living with the aftermath of sibling abortion under China's one-child policy.* Proceedings of the European Congress of Qualitative Inquiry, Malta. https://dora.dmu.ac.uk/handle/2086/19694

Madden, E. E., Ryan, S., Aguiniga, D. M., Killian, M., & Romanchik, B. (2018). The relationship between time and birth mother satisfaction with relinquishment. *Families in Society: The Journal of Contemporary Social Services, 99*(2), 170–183.

Maddow–Zimet, I., Lindberg, L., Kost, K., & Lincoln, A. (2016). Are pregnancy intentions associated with transitions into and out of marriage? *Perspectives on Sexual and Reproductive Health, 48*(1), 35–43.

Major, B., Appelbaum, M., Beckman, L., Dutton, M. A., Felipe Russo, N., & West, C. (2008). *Report of the APA task force on mental health and abortion.* American Psychological Association. https://www.apa.org/pi/women/programs/abortion/mental-health.pdf

Martinez, A. (2022, Apr. 6). Biden's proposed budget left out the Hyde Amendment, and advocates hope it stays that way. *Prism.* https://prismreports.org/2022/04/06/biden-2023-budget-hyde-amendment/

Matthews, K., Morgan, I., Davis, K., Estriplet, T., Perez, S., & Crear-Perry, J.A. (2021). Pathways to equitable and antiracist maternal mental health care: Insights from Black women stakeholders. *Health Affairs, 40*(1), 1597-1604.

Mauldon, J., Foster, D. G., & Roberts, S. C. M. (2015). Effect of abortion vs. carrying to term on a woman's relationship with the man involved in the pregnancy. *Perspectives on Sexual and Reproductive Health, 47*(1), 11–18.

Mercier, R. J., Garret, J., Thorp, J., & Siega-Riz, A. M. (2019). Pregnancy intention and postpartum depression: Secondary data analysis from a prospective cohort. *BJOG, 120*(9), 1116–1122.

Mifeprex. (2019). *Full prescribing information.* https://www.accessdata.fda.gov/drugsatfda_docs/label/2019/020687s022lbl.pdf

Nash, E. (2021, October 4). *For the first time ever, U.S. states enacted more than 100 abortion restrictions in a single year.* Guttmacher Institute. https://www.guttmacher.org/article/2021/10/first-time-ever-us-states-enacted-more-100-abortion-restrictions-single-year

National Academies of Sciences, Engineering, and Medicine. (2018). *The safety and quality of abortion care in the United States.* National Academies Press.

National Domestic Violence Hotline. (n.d.). *Pregnancy and abuse: How to stay safe for your 9 months.* https://www.thehotline.org/resources/pregnancy-and-abuse-how-to-stay-safe-for-your-9-months/

National Women's Law Center. (2013). *If you really care about preventing domestic and sexual violence, you should care about reproductive justice!* https://www.nwlc.org/sites/default/files/pdfs/intimate_partner_violence_repro_justice_10-25-13.pdf

National Women's Law Center (2017). *The Hyde Amendment creates an unacceptable barrier to women getting abortions.* https://nwlc.org/resource/hyde-amendment-creates-unacceptable-barrier-women-getting-abortions/

Nuevo-Chiquero, A. (2014). The labor effects of unplanned childbearing. *Labour Economics, 29,* 91–101.

Office of Disease Prevention and Health Promotion. (n.d.). *Reduce the proportion of unintended pregnancies—FP-01.* https://health.gov/healthypeople/objectives-and-data/browse-objectives/family-planning/reduce-proportion-unintended-pregnancies-fp-01

Office of Disease Prevention and Health Promotion. (2021). *Reproductive and sexual health.* https://www.healthypeople.gov/2020/leading-health-indicators/2020-lhi-topics/Reproductive-and-Sexual-Health/determinants

Ohio, H. Bill 480 (2021).

Oliver, D. (2021, June 24). Britney Spears forced IUD sparks important conversations about disability, reproductive rights. *USA Today.* https://www.usatoday.com/story/life/health-wellness/2021/06/24/britney-spears-conservatorship-forced-iud-and-disability-reproductive-rights/5333756001/

Ollstein, A. M. & Scholtes, J. (2022, February 15). *Dems, despite their control, all but concede on federal abortion spending.* Politico. https://www.politico.com/news/2022/02/15/ban-federal-funds-abortion-democrats-00008761

Palkovitz, R., Marks, L. D., Appleby, D. W., & Holmes, E. K. (2003). Parenting and adult development: Contexts, processes, and products of intergenerational relationships. In L. Kuczynski (Ed.), *Handbook of dynamics in parent-child relations* (pp. 307–324). Sage Publications.

Planned Parenthood. (n.d.-a). *What are TRAP laws?* https://www.plannedparenthoodaction.org/issues/abortion/trap-laws

Planned Parenthood. (n.d.-b). *How safe is the birth control pill?* https://www.plannedparenthood.org/learn/birth-control/birth-control-pill/how-safe-is-the-birth-control-pill

Planned Parenthood. (n.d.-c). *IUD.* https://www.plannedparenthood.org/learn/birth-control/iud

Planned Parenthood. (2013). *Do I have to take "the morning-after pill" the morning after I have sex? Or can I take it right away?* https://www.plannedparenthood.org/learn/teens/ask-experts/do-i-have-to-take-the-morning-after-pill-the-morning-after-i-have-sex-or-can-i-take-it-right-away

Planned Parenthood. (2021). *Can I buy emergency contraception if I'm 16?* https://www.plannedparenthood.org/learn/teens/ask-experts/can-i-buy-emergency-contraception-if-im-16

Planned Parenthood of Central Missouri v. Danforth, 428 U.S. 52 (1976).

Planned Parenthood of Southeastern Pennsylvania v. Casey, 505 U.S. 833 (1992).

Project South, Georgia Detention Watch, Georgia Latino Alliance for Human Rights, & South Georgia Immigrant Support Network (2020, September 14). *[Letter to Joseph V. Cuffari, Cameron Quinn, Thomas P. Giles, and David Paulk].* https://projectsouth.org/wp-content/uploads/2020/09/OIG-ICDC-Complaint-1.pdf

Public Law No. 94-439, 90 Stat. 1418 (September 30, 1976).

Ralph, L. J., Mauldon, J., Biggs, M. A., & Foster, D. G. (2019). A prospective cohort study of the effect of receiving versus being denied an abortion on educational attainment. *Women's Health Issues, 29*(6), 455–464.

Ralph, L. J., Schwarz, E. B., Grossman, D., & Foster, D. G. (2019). Self-reported physical health of women who did and did not terminate pregnancy after seeking abortion services: A cohort study. *Annals of Internal Medicine, 171*(4), 238–247.

Raymond, E. G., & Grimes, D. A. (2012). The comparative safety of legal induced abortion and childbirth in the United States. *Obstetrics & Gynecology, 119* (2 Pt 1), 215–219.

Reardon, D. C. (2018). The abortion and mental health controversy: A comprehensive literature review of common ground agreements, disagreements, actionable recommendations, and research opportunities. *SAGE Open Med, 6*, 1–38.

Rinkunas, S. (2021, May 28). Joe Biden stakes out position against discriminatory abortion rule. *The Guardian.* https://www.theguardian.com/world/2021/may/28/joe-biden-abortion-hyde-amendment-budget.

Roberts, S. C. M., Biggs, M. A., Chibber, K. S., Gould, H., Rocca, C. H., & Foster, D. G. (2014). Risk of violence from the man involved in the pregnancy after receiving or being denied an abortion. *BMC Medicine, 12*(144).

Rocca, C. H., Samari, G., Foster, D. G., Gould, H., & Kimport, K. (2020). Emotions and decision rightness over five years following an abortion: An examination of decision difficulty and abortion stigma. *Social Sciences & Medicine, 248*, 112704.

Roe v. Wade, 410 U.S. 113 (1973).

Sajadi–Ernazarova, K. R., & Martinez, C. L. (2021). *Abortion complications.* StatPearls. https://pubmed.ncbi.nlm.nih.gov/28613544/

Scott, L. (n.d.). *Forced sterilization and abortion: A global human rights problem.* amfAR. https://www.amfar.org/forced-sterilization-and-abortion-a-global-human-rights-problem/

Sisson, G., Ralph, L., Gould, H., & Foster, D. G. (2017). Adoption decision making among women seeking abortion. *Women's Health Issues, 27*(2), 136–144.

Sonfield, A., Hasstedt, K., Kavanaugh, M. L., & Anderson, R. (2013). *The social and economic benefits of women's ability to determine whether and when to have children.* Guttmacher Institute. https://www.guttmacher.org/sites/default/files/report_pdf/social-economic-benefits.pdf

Sonfield, A., & Kost, K. (2015). *Public costs from unintended pregnancies and the role of public insurance programs in paying for pregnancy-related care: National and state estimates for 2010.* Guttmacher Institute. https://www.guttmacher.org/sites/default/files/report_pdf/public-costs-of-up-2010.pdf

Steinberg, J. R., & Finer, L. B. (2012). Coleman, Coyle, Shuping, and Rue make false statements and draw erroneous conclusions in analyses of abortion and mental health using the National Comorbidity Survey. *Journal of Psychiatric Research, 46*(3), 407–409.

Stykes, J. B., & Guzzo, K. B. (2020). Unintended childbearing and marital instability: An emphasis on couples' intentions. *Journal of Divorce & Remarriage, 61*(7), 504–524.

Su, J. H. (2017). Unintended birth and children's long-term mental health. *Journal of Health and Social Behavior, 58*(3), 357–370.

Texas Heartbeat Act, S. bill 8 (2021).

Trussel, J., Henry, N., Hassan, F., Prezloso, A., Law, A., & Filonenko, A. (2013). Burden of unintended pregnancy in the United States: Potential savings with increased use of long-acting reversible contraception. *Contraception, 87*(2), 154–161.

United Health Foundation. (2021a). *America's health rankings: Unintended pregnancy.* https://www.americashealthrankings.org/explore/health-of-women-and-children/measure/unintended_pregnancy/state/U.S

United Health Foundation. (2021b). *America's health rankings: Postpartum depression.* https://www.americashealthrankings.org/explore/health-of-women-and-children/measure/postpartum_depression/state/ALL

Upadhyay, U. D., Biggs, M. A., & Foster, D. G. (2015). The effect of abortion on having and achieving aspirational one-year plans. *BMC Women's Health, 15.*

Upadhyay, U. D., Desai, S., Zlidar, V., Weitz, T. A., Grossman, D., Anderson, P., & Taylor, D. (2015). Incidence of emergency department visits and complications after abortion. *Obstetrics & Gynecology, 125*(1), 175–183.

USA Facts (May 15, 2023). Which states have the highest maternal mortality rates? https://usafacts.org/articles/which-states-have-the-highest-maternal-mortality-rates/

U.S. Department of Health and Human Services, U.S. Department of Labor, & U.S. Department of the Treasury. (2021, August 16). *FAQs about Affordable Care Act implementation Part 48*. https://www.dol.gov/sites/dolgov/files/EBSA/about-ebsa/our-activities/resource-center/faqs/aca-part-48.pdf

U.S. Food and Drug Administration. (2021). *Questions & answers on Mifeprex*. https://www.fda.gov/drugs/postmarket-drug-safety-information-patients-and-providers/questions-and-answers-mifeprex

Washington et al. v. FDA, Case No. 1:23-CV-3026-TOR (E.D. Wash. April 7, 2023).

Whelan, A. M. (2021). Unequal representation: Women in clinical research. *Cornell Law Review Online, 106*(3), 87–128.

Whelan, A. M. & Goodwin, M. (2022). Abortion rights and disability equality: A new constitutional battleground. *Washington & Lee Law Review, 79*(3), 965–1005.

White House Office of Policy Development. (1984). U.S. policy statement for the International Conference on Population. *Population and Development Review, 10*(3), 574–579.

Whole Woman's Health v. Hellerstedt, 136 S.Ct. 2292 (2016).

Whole Woman's Health v. Jackson, No. 21-463, 2021 WL 5855551 (2021).

World Health Organization. (2012). *Safe abortion: Technical and policy guidance for health systems*.

World Health Organization. (2021). *Sexual health*. https://www.who.int/health-topics/sexual-health#tab=tab_1

Wulah, A., Abdi, F.M., & Sanders, M. (2023). *Promoting Black girls' and women's sexual and reproductive health requires acknowledging their history and experiences*. https://www.childtrends.org/publications/promoting-black-girls-and-womens-sexual-and-reproductive-health-requires-acknowledging-their-history-and-experiences

Yazdkhasti, M., Pourezza, A., Pirak, A., & Abdi, F. (2015). Unintended pregnancy and its adverse social and economic consequences on health system: A narrative review article. *Iran Journal of Public Health, 44*(1), 12–21.

Zane, S., Creanga, A. A., Berg, C. J., Pazol, K., Suchdev, D. B., Jamieson, D. J., & Callaghan, W. M. (2015). Abortion-related mortality in the United States: 1998-2010. *Obstetrics and Gynecology, 126*(2), 258–265.

CHAPTER 26

Racial Disparities in Policing: Psychological Consequences Over the Lifespan

Kelly C. Burke, Cynthia J. Najdowski, and Margaret C. Stevenson

Abstract

This chapter reviews the psychological consequences of racialized policing for people of color over the course of their lives, organizing the review within Bronfenbrenner's social-ecological model and emerging science on racial, legal, and racial-legal socialization. First, the chapter considers the broader social climate that criminalizes and punishes people of color, and thereby generates racialized policing (macrosystem). Then, it turns to the institution and practice of policing and how this influences the way people of color come to think about their relationships with police (exosystem). Next, the chapter examines how vicarious experiences with police shape attitudes toward police (mesosystem), and how direct experiences and personal history factors influence how people of color experience, navigate, learn, and develop in response to police discrimination (microsystem). Finally, the chapter explores the cumulative effects of racialized policing on life outcomes and the evidence of coping and resilience among people of color, ending with implications for policy and practice.

Key Words: race, ethnicity, policing, bias, discrimination, development, racial socialization, legal socialization, social-ecological model

---

I can conceive of no Negro native to this country who has not, by the age of puberty, been irreparably scarred by the conditions of his life. . . . the wonder is not that so many are ruined but that so many survive.

—*James Baldwin*, Notes of a Native Son

The United States is raw with racial strife. One of the most disturbing problems of our time is the biased and discriminatory policing of people of color. On May 25, 2020, George Floyd, an unarmed Black man, was stopped by Minneapolis police on suspicion of using a counterfeit $20 bill. What should have been a "routine" encounter turned to horror and became the catalyst for a global uprising. Former officer Derek Chauvin, a White man, kneeled on Floyd's neck for more than 9 minutes while three other officers did nothing to intervene, ultimately killing Floyd (Cobb, 2021). Despite lockdowns and health concerns associated with the COVID-19 pandemic, the murder sparked massive protests around the world. While awaiting the jury's decision following Chauvin's April 2021 murder trial, individuals across the

United States came together, braced to either celebrate Chauvin's conviction or demonstrate against his acquittal. Meanwhile, a "Blue Lives Matter" or "Back the Blue" countermovement also evolved, calling for people to support police and pushing for policies that require more severe punishment for those who harm law enforcement or resist arrest (see, e.g., Valencia, 2020). These events made it indisputable that many people experience great angst and concern about racially biased and discriminatory policing and are no longer willing to tolerate it, and also that a substantial proportion of the population is opposed to this movement. This point in time represents a significant opportunity for a racial reckoning for policing and the U.S. criminal legal system more broadly, but it remains to be seen whether calls for the eradication of racism and transformative change will be heeded.

There is a long, interconnected history between policing (and the criminal legal system) and mistreatment of people of color, dating back to colonization and slavery (for reviews, see Braga et al., 2019; Cunneen & Tauri, 2019; Hinton & Cook, 2021; National Academies of Sciences, Engineering, and Medicine, 2018; Willis-Esqueda, 2020). Structural and systemic issues within policing (e.g., zero-tolerance policies; overpolicing "high crime" neighborhoods; "broken windows" policing; stop, question, and frisk policies) and individual officer-level factors (e.g., explicit and implicit bias) disproportionately disadvantage people of color and contribute to racial inequities throughout the criminal legal system (e.g., Braga et al., 2019; Fagan et al., 2010; Hall et al., 2016; Rios, 2011; Spencer et al., 2016; Swencionis & Goff, 2017). What are the psychological consequences of these disparities for people of color over the course of their lives?

Drawing upon the literatures from criminology and social, developmental, and clinical psychology, we first review evidence of burdensome and disparate policing of people of color. Second, we use Bronfenbrenner's (1977, 1979) social–ecological model and emerging science on racial, legal, and racial–legal socialization (e.g., Hughes et al., 2006) to understand how discriminatory policing affects people of color across the lifespan. Our social–ecological analysis incorporates historical and societal-level factors that generate and sustain racialized criminalization and punishment; institutional factors within policing that contribute to discrimination and shape how people of color come to think about and understand their relationships with police; social and physical environments that influence these relationships; and factors that influence how people of color actually experience and respond to police encounters. Finally, we explore the cumulative negative effects of racially discriminatory policing on people of color, including socioeconomic (im)mobility and future experiences within the criminal legal system, as well as evidence of coping and resilience among people of color. We conclude with a discussion of implications for policy and practice.

Of note, our review emphasizes Black people's experiences with policing during youth and adulthood. The focus on Black people's experiences reflects the state of the field, however, and we have been intentionally inclusive of the limited body of existing research relevant to other racial and ethnic groups who are disproportionately affected by policing. We also describe the few studies that have examined the developmental effects of racialized policing on people of color. The sparseness of work done on these issues to date highlights a need for more researchers to attend to the experiences of all people of color, to do so through an intersectional lens, and to understand psychological consequences across different developmental stages and throughout the lifespan.

Evidence That Policing Is Racially Biased and Discriminatory

Compared to White people, people of color face disproportionately negative treatment in the criminal legal system (e.g., Cunneen & Tauri, 2019; Kovera, 2019; Stevenson et al., 2020).

Some disparities in punishment originate even before individuals come into contact with the criminal legal system, during their early school experiences. Children of color are more likely to be suspended, expelled, and subjected to other harsh disciplinary measures, despite exhibiting similar forms of misbehavior as White children (Malik, 2017; Petras et al., 2011; Skiba et al., 2011; U.S. Department of Education, Office for Civil Rights, 2014). This is concerning because experiencing school discipline is related to an increased likelihood of future involvement with the criminal legal system (Christle et al., 2007; Zinsser & Wanless, 2020; see Fine et al., this volume), a link that has been termed the "school-to-prison pipeline." Indeed, teachers and school administrators appear to play a role in facilitating disproportionately negative interactions between Black children and police within schools. As evidence, one study showed these groups exhibited more support for expulsion and also arrest when a student involved in a hypothetical school fight and subjected to police force was portrayed as Black rather than White (Watson & Stevenson, 2022). These experimental results line up with data showing that, in a sample of eighth graders, Black students reported experiencing more instances of school discipline and, in turn, more contact with police as compared to White students (Crutchfield et al., 2012). Black youth are also disproportionately more likely to be arrested for youth-perpetrated school violence than are White youth (Hullenaar et al., 2021).

Unfortunately, the path to criminal legal involvement can begin as early as preschool for children of color, setting the stage for numerous negative outcomes, such as impaired socioemotional development and academic achievement, as well as children spending more time with crime-involved peers in the community, and increased delinquency and police involvement (Arcia, 2006; Christle et al., 2007; Greenwood et al., 2002; Lee et al., 2011; Shollenberger, 2015; Zinsser & Wanless, 2020). As youth move into middle and high school, they are met with other policies, such as the increased use of school resource officers and measures that serve to criminalize school misbehavior (e.g., metal detectors), which promote suspensions and expulsions, relate to problematic behavior (e.g., increased truancy), and contribute to racial disparities (American Psychological Association Zero Tolerance Task Force, 2008; Granot et al., 2021; National Center for Education Statistics, 2018; Petteruti, 2011). In fact, as more and more schools employ police as school resource officers (U.S. Department of Education, 2021), children's first experiences with the police increasingly occur within the school setting. Further, in general, students are more likely to be arrested if they attend a school with versus without a school resource officer; this is especially the case for Black and Latinx students (Hudson & Ruth, 2018; Nance, 2016).

In addition to experiencing greater contact with police through schools, compared to White youth in community settings, Black youth are more likely to be detained and arrested, and arrested at younger ages, even after statistically controlling for offense severity and other factors (e.g., Hsia et al., 2004; Lau et al., 2018; Nguyen & Reuter, 2012; U.S. Department of Justice, Office of Juvenile Justice and Delinquency Prevention, 2019; Wordes et al., 1994). Police officers are also less likely to process youth of color through diversion programs focused on rehabilitation (e.g., Bishop et al., 2010; Ericson & Eckberg, 2016). A considerable amount of research indicates that police also stop, question, frisk, search, handcuff, detain, and arrest Black and Latinx adults—particularly young Black men—more often than they do White adults (e.g., Fagan & Davies, 2000; Goel et al., 2016; Goff et al., 2016; Hetey et al., 2016; Levchak, 2021; Pierson et al., 2020; for reviews, see Braga et al., 2019; Kahn & Martin, 2016; Kovera, 2019). This is despite a lack of racial differences in the rate at which individuals engage in criminal activity, barring serious violent crime (Braga et al., 2019); even after accounting for potential confounds like crime level among racial groups or within neighborhoods, offense severity, community complaints, precinct characteristics, civilian behavior, sociodemographic factors; and despite evidence that police are less likely to find contraband when they search Black rather than White adults (Ayres & Borowsky, 2008; Baumgartner et al., 2018; Beckett et al., 2006; Fagan et al., 2016; Gelman et al., 2007). Moreover, Black and Latinx adults are more likely to experience both threats of force and actual use of force compared to White individuals (Goff et al., 2016; Harrell & Davis, 2020; Kramer & Remster, 2018; Levchak, 2017, 2021; Morrow et al., 2017; Ross et al., 2021; Scott et al., 2017). Even more concerning, over the lifespan, Black boys and men are at the greatest risk of dying from police use of force, followed by Alaska Native/American Indian men and women, Black women, and Latino men, all of whom are at greater risk of being killed by police relative to their White counterparts (Edwards et al., 2019). Yet, among victims of fatal police shootings, Black individuals are less likely to be armed than White individuals (Nix et al., 2017).

Whereas racial disparities in police treatment tend to be greatest among younger men (e.g., Scheb et al., 2009; Tillyer & Engel, 2013), they tend to be less prominent among older adults. Some research has even shown no disparities at later developmental stages. For instance, discretionary searches conducted during traffic stops have been found to occur at a similar rate for older Black and White men (Rosenfeld et al., 2012). Yet, in other regards, unequal treatment based on race affects even older people of color. For instance, in a vignette study, police officer participants were more likely to suspect a Black versus White man, regardless of whether he was described as being in his 20s or 40s (S. W. Phillips, 2020). Also, although police stops decrease for all racial and ethnic groups beginning in early adulthood, police still tend to stop older Black men more often than older White men (Figures & Legewie, 2019). Likewise, overall, the risk of being killed by police is greatest between the ages of 20 and 35 and thereafter decreases over the lifespan. Nonetheless, on average Black men continue to face greater risk of experiencing a fatal police encounter than White men until around 60–70 years of age, after which point disparities begin to level off (Edwards et al., 2019).

In sum, negative and burdensome policing plagues people of color throughout most of their lives, beginning as early as preschool and fading only during late adulthood. What effects does racially disparate policing have on the psychological development and well-being of people of color?

Consequences of Racially Disproportionate Policing: Application of the Social–Ecological Developmental Framework

In this section, we turn our attention to the causes of racially disparate policing and consequences of mistreatment for people of color across the lifespan. Where research has examined development, we organize our discussion by beginning with early childhood effects and continuing through the course of life to consider what is (and is not) known about older people of color who have spent decades bearing this burden. In doing so, we integrate and organize knowledge about the numerous ways that policing is racialized and how bias and discrimination affect people of color in line with Bronfenbrenner's (1977, 1979) social–ecological model of human development.

Specifically, the social–ecological model conceives of the developing person in relation to a set of interconnected social contexts that vary in degree of proximity to the person, with more proximal contexts embedded within more distal ones, and across which the person has different roles, relationships, and activities. First, at the outermost level of these nested environments is the macrosystem. The macrosystem relates to the basic social organization of one's culture, as developed through historical, sociopolitical, and cultural pressures. The focus at this level is on understanding how people accommodate new information and experiences into their schemas or cognitive frameworks for thought and behavior across different contexts. Within the macrosystem is the exosystem. This level includes the formal and informal social structures that indirectly influence development through their impact on the more proximal settings of the mesosystem and microsystem. The mesosystem accounts for the potential for events in one immediate setting to influence thoughts, behavior, and development in other immediate settings. It comprises relations between proximal microsystem settings, such as family, peers, school, and neighborhood. Finally, the most immediate level at which learning occurs is the microsystem. This is the environment nearest to the developing person and with which the person directly interacts. The social–ecological model accounts for reciprocal and interactive effects between the person, other people, and features of immediate and distal contexts.

With this framework in mind, we begin with a wide view of race and policing, emphasizing first the importance of the macrosystem—the broader sociopolitical and cultural climate that criminalizes and punishes people of color, and thereby generates racialized policing, as well as how this climate is reflected and sustained by policing practices. We then work our way through the settings as they increase in proximity to the person. Specifically, we conceptualize the exosystem as the institution and practice of policing; the mesosystem as the relations between police and other immediate settings in which people learn and develop—vicarious experiences with police shared within families, peer groups, schools, and communities; and the microsystem as the direct interactions people have with police officers as well as individual difference and personal history factors that influence how people of color experience, navigate, learn, and develop in response to police bias and discrimination within each level (see Figure 26.1). Where appropriate, we also integrate theory on racial, legal, and racial–legal socialization—how children learn and acquire knowledge about their racial group and identity (Anderson & Stevenson, 2019; Hughes et al., 2006) and their own legal values and attitudes (Tyler & Trinkner, 2018), and how children of color develop attitudes toward the legal system as a function of direct and vicarious experiences with police (e.g., Whitaker & Snell, 2016), respectively. Within our application of the social–ecological framework, we also unpack the mental health consequences of racially biased and discriminatory policing for people of color across different systems and life stages.

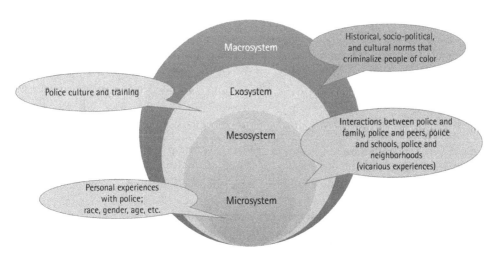

Figure 26.1 A social–ecological model of policing and development.

The Macrosystem: Policing at the Societal Level
We examine first the macrosystem by considering broad societal factors that help create a climate in which aggressive policing and mistreatment of people of color are encouraged. These factors include historical, sociopolitical, and cultural norms that support criminalization and punishment of people of color. Racial attitudes and stereotypes that psychologists have identified as contributors to contemporary instances of prejudice and discrimination emerged at least as early as the 1600s: Colonialists disparaged Africans, depicting them as apelike savages, and some of the earliest laws criminalized African and Indigenous people's resistance to slavery and colonization. Their actions were painted as violent, aggressive, and fierce, when they were actually dire attempts to gain freedom and flee from oppression and cruelty (Kendi, 2016). Thus, at its inception, policing in the United States was rooted in perpetuating the subjugation and oppression of African and Indigenous people (e.g., via the Fugitive Slave Act of 1850; see Cunneen & Tauri, 2019; Hinton & Cook, 2021; Rucker & Richeson, 2021; Willis-Esqueda, 2020). Even after enslaved Black people were emancipated through the Civil War, laws known as Black Codes were enacted during the Reconstruction era that criminalized Black people for any number of social conditions (e.g., homelessness, unemployment) and so-called offenses (e.g., interracial marriage), thus moving Black people into the criminal legal system so they could be exploited for labor via convict leasing (Davis, 2005; Du Bois, 1935).

The consequences of this history are manifest in the racial disparities in police treatment and disproportionate incarceration of people of color that have existed for hundreds of years, and that continue today. This is because macrosystem forces exert an influence on the way that people of color are perceived by others, further shaping and reinforcing societal-level beliefs and discriminatory policing. Consider, for example, that by the late 1800s, mass criminalization and incarceration of Black individuals were already taking place (Hinton & Cook, 2021). In turn, data indicating that Black individuals were overrepresented in the criminal legal system were utilized to support stereotypes associating them with violence and criminality. Notwithstanding others' strong assertions that the overrepresentation of Black individuals in the criminal legal system "picture[s] only the *apparent* and not the *real* criminality of the Negro" (Sellin, 1928, p. 53, emphasis in original), these data were used to legitimize and support Jim Crow and other discriminatory laws and policies (Muhammad, 2019). The criminal legal system further developed over time to disadvantage Black people via the wars on crime and drugs (e.g., Alexander, 2010; Chavez-Dueñas et al., 2019; Muhammad, 2019). Thus, as Hinton and Cook (2021, p. 269) noted, "Considered an objective truth and a statistically irrefutable fact, notions of [B]lack criminality justified both structural and everyday racism." As a result, Black people today are the recipients of heightened police attention and aggressive intervention in the form of surveillance, stops, searches, arrests, and use of force. Although Black people are most disproportionately affected by racialized policing, policing practices that are based on structural racism ensnare members of other racial and ethnic groups too, including poor White people (Davis, 2005).

Another historical factor is the trend to enact policy that derides and criminalizes immigrants of color, which then contributes to disparities in who is policed and how (Díaz, 2011; Gonzales & Chaves, 2012; K. R. Johnson, 1998, 2009; Menjívar et al., 2018; Urbina & Álvarez, 2016; Willis-Esqueda, 2020). U.S. immigration law and policy generally favor White immigrant people and discriminate against immigrant people of color. Consider, for example, the Naturalization Act of 1790, which restricted naturalization to "free White persons"; the Immigration Act of 1924, which prohibited immigration from Asia; and Executive Order No. 13769, which in 2017 banned immigration from predominately Muslim countries. Such policies have harmed immigrants of color not only directly but also indirectly by fostering negative stereotypes, prejudice, and discrimination within society (for review, see Thronson & Thronson, 2020), including stereotypes that depict Latinx people as criminals (Levy et al., 1998; Marin, 1984; Santana & Smith, 2001; Welch et al., 2011). This relates to policing both because officers are sometimes charged with enforcing immigration law (see, e.g., Goff et al., 2013), and because they may adopt anti-immigrant attitudes or negative beliefs that translate into discriminatory treatment of racial and ethnic immigrant groups (e.g., Farris & Hollman, 2017).

MACROSYSTEM-LEVEL IMPACTS ON DEVELOPMENT AND WELL-BEING

Effects on the development of people of color at this level include learning societal beliefs that portray people of color as deserving of disproportionate police attention and mistreatment. There is some evidence that the media perpetuates the transmission and reinforcement of such stereotypes from generation to generation. Myriad studies document consistent race-based stereotypical representations within various media outlets (for a review, see Mastro, 2009) including the news (e.g., Dixon, 2008), YouTube (Kopacz & Lawton, 2013), and television programming (Wilson et al., 2012). For instance, a content analysis of 1,699 advertisements from 1992 to 1994 revealed that Black men were portrayed as significantly more aggressive than their White counterparts (Coltrane & Messineo, 2000). Although the media portrayal of Black people has shifted for the better over time—as compared to virtually exclusively negative portrayals prior to the 1980s (Greenberg et al., 2002)—content analyses of more recent media suggest that Black people still may be more likely than their White counterparts to be portrayed as criminals (for review, see Signorielli, 2010; but see Glascock, 2003; Mastro & Behm-Morawitz, 2005), aggressive, and thuglike (Tyree, 2011). Of importance, substantial evidence reveals that media exposure to negative racial stereotypes predicts negative intergroup attitudes, stereotype endorsement, and behaviors and shapes social policy support (for a review, see Mastro, 2009). For instance, one study showed that greater exposure to crime news predicted greater perceived culpability of a Black suspect but not a White suspect, and greater exposure to the overrepresentation of Black people as criminals on television news predicted increased beliefs that Black people are violent (Dixon, 2008). Another study revealed that 94% of participants were consciously aware of stereotypes associating Black individuals with violence (Goff et al., 2008, Study 4).

Another insidious consequence of cultural transmissions of anti-Black stereotypes is that the Black-ape association historically present in media depictions of Black people (e.g., the film "King Kong") continues to be alive in the minds of many people today (Goff et al., 2008). Centuries after the first African slaves were brought to North America, there is evidence that early colonists' stereotypes associating Black individuals with apelike imagery persist at the implicit (unconscious) level. Goff et al. (2008, Study 4) found that although only 9% of White men participants were consciously aware of the historical portrayal of Black individuals as apes, they were more quick to associate Black individuals with ape-related words compared to feline-related words. The media's role in perpetuating ape-related dehumanization of Black individuals has been linked to startlingly negative outcomes: Black individuals convicted of a capital crime were significantly more likely to be sentenced to death when newspaper articles used more (vs. less) ape-related adjectives to describe them (Goff et al., 2008, Study 6).

Of importance, Black people are aware of cultural anti-Black stereotypes (e.g., Kreuger, 1996). They report being perceived as violent by White people (Sigelman & Tuch, 1997) and as criminals by strangers (Cheryan & Monin, 2005). Negative representations of people of color have the potential to become internalized. In support, a cross-sectional content analysis of prime-time television shows revealed that positive media representations of Black and Latinx people increased warm ingroup feelings among these groups, but negative media representations diminished Black and Latinx people's warm ingroup feelings (Tukachinsky et al., 2017).

Evidence also suggests that, compared to their White counterparts, youth and adults of color are exposed to police abuse of people of color more frequently via mass media (First et al., 2020; Novich & Zduniak, 2021). This exposure is traumatizing, generating fear of victimization for themselves and loved ones, posttraumatic stress disorder (PTSD), anxiety, depression, and anger (Bryant-Davis et al., 2017; First et al., 2020; Galovski et al., 2016; Lipscomb et al., 2019; Novich & Zduniak, 2021; Staggers-Hakim, 2016; Tynes et al., 2019). For instance, a nationally representative study involving Black and Latinx youth found that greater frequency of viewing traumatic race-related events online—specifically, more instances of someone of the same race or ethnicity being beaten, arrested, detained, or shot by law enforcement—was related to experiencing significantly more symptoms of depression and PTSD (Tynes et al., 2019). Black adolescent boys also have reported that national cases involving police abuse of people of color create fear about what could happen to them in potential police encounters (Staggers-Hakim, 2016).

Of course, adults of color are not immune to trauma stemming from media exposure to police violence. In the week following the release of video footage of George Floyd's murder, the percentage of Black adults who displayed clinically significant levels of anxiety or depressive symptoms increased by 5%, exceeding levels for every other racial or ethnic group in the United States (Fowers & Won, 2020). Lipscomb and colleagues (2019) interviewed Black adults to understand how they were affected by viewing video or reading about the fatal police shooting of Stephen Clark, an unarmed 22-year-old Black man holding his cellphone. Respondents indicated that social media exposure to this incident created anger, sadness, feelings of injustice, and increased vigilance and dissociation. One respondent explained:

> It's a shame that a man can be gunned down in his own backyard for no reason. I've seen videos where police made an extra effort to de-escalate a situation, but it seems overwhelmingly Black males are not given that courtesy. It feels like we are being hunted. There is no justice for the men who lost their lives over trivial circumstances. The police are taking the law into their own hands and carrying out death sentences out on the streets. (Lipscomb et al., 2019, p. 16)

The media effects we reviewed reflect the macrosystem-level problems that contribute to racialized policing as well as the aggressive and violent policing of people of color itself. The result is that people of color are socialized into a context that devalues them, which puts people of color at risk of internalizing lower racial esteem or self-worth and experiencing psychological trauma. As we review next, the sociopolitical, cultural, and psychological tendencies that dehumanize Black people and associate them with crime are also sustained as they trickle down from the macrosystem to the exosystem context, where racism is supported by the subculture of policing; the mesosystem context, where police disproportionately interact with and mistreat family members and peers of people of color; and the microsystem context, where people of color are viewed through the lens of police officers' conscious or unconscious negative racial stereotypes and attitudes, situational conditions exacerbate officers' reliance on stereotypes and attitudes, and people of color experience interactions with police officers in psychologically distinct ways because of their expectations and actual experiences of racial bias and discrimination.

The Exosystem: Policing as an Institution and in Practice
Although the criminalization of people of color is rooted in colonization and slavery, racially biased policing continued over the years even as laws and policies evolved. Of importance, the

broader climate has influenced how policing developed over time. In particular, the wars on crime and drugs that became central to policing beginning in the 1960s fostered the militarization of policing and an accompanying "warrior mindset" (Stoughton, 2016). How do these features of the exosystem contribute to racial disparities in policing, and how do they affect people of color? In this section, we discuss how the subculture of policing itself is oriented toward aggressive policing directed disproportionately at people of color relative to White people.

Although not all officers are socialized into police culture the same way, and although police culture has changed in recent years (e.g., with some officers kneeling in solidarity with protestors who rose up in the summer following George Floyd's murder; Silverman, 2020) and will likely continue to do so moving forward, police training and culture can instill

> a bone-deep commitment to survive a bad situation no matter the odds or difficulty, to not give up even when it is mentally and physically easier to do so. . . . [It] represents an attitude that officers should display in the most physically dangerous and psychologically precarious situations. (Stoughton, 2014, p. 226).

The rationale for training officers with this warrior mindset is that policing can be extremely dangerous and officers must be resilient while protecting civilians and themselves. As Stoughton explains, however, over the years this mindset expanded from being applied only in perilous situations into a generalized mentality that promotes an adversarial, aggressive style of policing as the default method for handling all situations. From their first day in the academy, officers are trained to assert their authority; they "learn to treat every individual they interact with as an armed threat and every situation, as a deadly force encounter in the making. *Every* individual, *every* situation—no exceptions" (Stoughton, 2014, p. 228, emphasis in original).

As such, the warrior mentality creates a value system that informs how some officers perceive their duty, how they approach interactions with civilians, and ultimately how they behave (Stoughton, 2016). It discourages cooperative policing, teaching officers that "even acting friendly can make [officers] a target" (Stoughton, 2014, p. 229), and instead encourages officers to distance themselves emotionally from civilians and act aggressively (Stoughton, 2016). Thus, some argue that there is a "warrior problem" in policing that contributes to poor police–civilian relations and harms cooperative, community-oriented policing (President's Task Force on 21st Century Policing, 2015; for reviews, see Stoughton, 2014, 2016). Indeed, officers who are more versus less oriented toward a warrior mentality are less likely to prioritize communication during hypothetical encounters, more likely to prioritize physical control, and more likely to report favorable attitudes toward force misconduct (McLean et al., 2020). In contrast, those who are more rather than less oriented toward a guardian mentality—which emphasizes empathy, cooperation, patience, and respect (Stoughton, 2016)—are more likely to prioritize communication and less likely to report favorable attitudes toward force misconduct.

Of special concern, Rahr and Rice (2015) argue that the military-style bootcamp of police training reinforces power differentials in police encounters—recruits are expected to obey their superiors without question and any rule breaking is punished via verbal reprimands or physical consequences (e.g., push-ups). They explain:

> Upon graduation, we send our newly trained recruits out into the community—they finally have power. Despite the way they were treated during their training, we expect them to treat the powerless people they encounter in the community with dignity and respect. . . . Why are we then surprised when some officers treat both suspects and citizens with the disdain and detachment they saw modeled by those in power at the academy? (Rahr & Rice, 2015, p. 5)

Because the warrior mentality occurs within the broader U.S. sociocultural context where people of color are discriminated against and dehumanized, it has the potential to amplify power differences between state actors and those who are marginalized within society. That is, it may promote the mindset—explicitly or implicitly—that police are guardians of the non-marginalized (e.g., White people) and warriors against the marginalized (e.g., people of color). As a result, this may contribute to aggressive policing practices targeted largely at people of color, in turn fueling discriminatory impacts.

Indeed, recent research shows that, although the guardian and warrior mentalities are distinct from one another, they are not orthogonal—officers can have both mentalities (McLean et al., 2020). Yet, there is also evidence that the mindset an officer adopts in a given situation may differ depending on the context and the race and ethnicity of the individuals with whom they interact. For example, with respect to perceptions of gun violence, J. Carlson (2020) found that police chiefs discussed gang- and drug-related gun violence involving perpetrators of color and victims of color as an issue of racialized perpetration, often conflating the victims of such violence with the perpetrators. In that context, chiefs adopted a warrior mindset such that police were warriors who needed to catch bad guys of color and contain violence. In contrast, chiefs discussed active shooting events—which are more likely to involve White perpetrators and victims—from the viewpoint of White victimhood, such that police were guardians who needed to save and protect White people from violence. J. Carlson (2020) concluded that the mindsets are activated in ways that lead police to think and act as though they are warriors against Black and Latinx criminals and guardians of White victims.

EXOSYSTEM-LEVEL IMPACTS ON DEVELOPMENT AND WELL-BEING

As a result of the interactions between the macrosystem (historical and societal beliefs and attitudes toward people of color, e.g., the Black criminal stereotype) and the exosystem (the warrior mindset and military-style training that emphasizes obedience to authority), people of color are overpoliced, more aggressively policed, and underserved relative to White people. This has a number of concrete consequences.

One issue is that the overpolicing of people of color translates into disproportionate attention to their actual crimes relative to their White counterparts' crimes. As just one example, the New York City Police Department's (NYPD) discriminatory policies (*Floyd v. City of New York*, 2013) led to officers unconstitutionally stopping, questioning, and frisking thousands of Black and Latinx civilians (New York Civil Liberties Union, 2013). Notably, however, White civilians were more likely to be caught with contraband. This suggests that White people's crimes were disproportionately less likely to be detected than those committed by Black people, generating a condition of relative leniency for White people in New York City at the time. At the same time, 90% of Black individuals who were stopped by NYPD officers in 2012 were not arrested nor did they receive a summons (New York Civil Liberties Union, 2013). Thus, overpolicing also results in unwarranted suspicion and investigation of people of color who are actually innocent (see Najdowski, 2014), which in turn can presumably contribute to false accusations and wrongful convictions. In support, the National Registry of Exonerations (2013) reported that over a 25-year timeframe, 47% of wrongful convictions that resulted in exonerations involved Black individuals, despite the fact that Black people represented only 13% of the U.S. population (Rastogi et al., 2011). Both types of miscarriage of justice—when White people are not suspected of crimes they actually committed and when people of color are suspected of crimes of which they are actually innocent—contribute to the appearance of racial disparities in criminal activity. This further fuels dehumanization of people of color and stereotypes that link them to crime, and thereby contributes to continued discrimination in laws, policies, and policing (e.g., Muhammad, 2019).

Because people of color are overpoliced, they are disproportionately likely to experience negative police encounters stemming from "warrior mentality" training. Indeed, aggressive strategies are used more commonly to police communities of color (Braga et al., 2019) and during White-on-Black police–civilian interactions. For instance, Dixon et al. (2008) analyzed police car video recordings and found that White officers were less respectful, less approachable, and more dismissive toward Black (relative to White) drivers during routine stops (see also Camp et al., 2021).

Considering all of this, the warrior mindset may socialize people of color to have a corresponding "us versus them" mentality toward police. It is unsurprising that children and young adults of all races believe that police behave especially disrespectfully and aggressively toward youth of color (Carr et al., 2007). In general, Black, followed by Latinx, youth have more negative attitudes than White youth toward police officers and the criminal legal system as a whole (e.g., A. D. Fine et al., 2017; Hurst et al., 2000; D. Johnson et al., 2017; Solis et al., 2009; Taylor et al., 2001; Wu et al., 2015). Youth of color report more cynicism toward the legal system and perceive their interactions with police to be more unfair and less legitimate than White youth. They also report less trust in the police and greater dissatisfaction with police encounters, and they perceive themselves to be "symbolic assailants in the eyes of police" (Brunson & Miller, 2006a, p. 613; see also A. D. Fine & Cauffman, 2015; Geistman & Smith, 2007; Hagan et al., 2005; Wu et al., 2015). Moreover, compared to White adults, Black adults report lower confidence in police (this is particularly true among Black people under the age of 55; Gilberstadt, 2020; Peck, 2015), are more likely to believe that Black people receive unfair treatment from the police (Hagan & Albonetti, 1982), and are more likely to perceive that racial profiling is a widespread issue (D. K. Carlson, 2004; Ludwig, 2003). These effects tend to emerge even when analyses control for individuals' personal direct contacts with police (Brick et al., 2009), suggesting they are influenced by broader contextual factors.

Furthermore, despite being overpoliced, Black youth and adults also feel underprotected and underserved, perceiving that police officers do not care about their victimization or about serious crime in their communities (Boehme et al., 2022; Brunson & Gau, 2014; Brunson & Wade, 2019; Brunson & Weitzer, 2009; Gau & Brunson, 2010; Jacoby et al., 2018; Smith Lee & Robinson, 2019). Thus, the proactive policing and warrior frameworks potentially play a role not only in driving police officers to have more negative beliefs about people of color but also in causing people of color to have more negative beliefs about police.

The Mesosystem: Relations Between Police and Immediate Settings

The mesosystem level involves the mechanisms by which people of color are affected by police mistreatment of other people with whom they have social relationships in various immediate settings, such as in their homes, schools, workplaces, and neighborhoods. This level also addresses the characteristics of these settings (e.g., neighborhood poverty, residential segregation, instability) that relate to reactions to being mistreated by police. How does policing in the social and physical environments where people live, learn, work, and play affect people of color?

To begin, most parents of color engage in cultural or racial socialization by communicating with their children in ways designed to increase children's awareness about racial discrimination (see Hughes et al., 2006, for a review). Parents may prepare their children of color for racial bias by providing instructions for managing bias, giving guidance on coping with discrimination, and/or promoting mistrust (i.e., recommending wariness during interracial interactions; Hughes & Johnson, 2001). For instance, studies have found that 95% of Black parents reported discussing racial discrimination with their children (Frabutt et al., 2002), and approximately half of Black adults recalled experiencing parental preparation for bias (Thompson, 1994; see also Hughes et al., 2006). Although parent self-report survey data reveal low frequencies of communications involving promotion of mistrust (for a review, see Hughes et al., 2006), intensive interviews with Black parents reveal that approximately one third emphasize distrust and avoidance regarding interactions with White people (Hughes & DuMont, 2002).

As theory would suggest, Black parents' experiences with discrimination emerge as predictors of racial socialization of their children, particularly of preparation for bias (Hughes et al., 2006). Children's experiences with racial discrimination also appear to trigger parental discussions regarding bias preparation (White-Johnson et al., 2010). Racial socialization also depends on characteristics of the children themselves. For instance, parents' bias preparation and promotion of mistrust generally increase as children age and increase in cognitive maturity (Hughes et al., 2006). There is also some evidence that Black boys are more likely to be exposed to preparation for bias than are Black girls (Hughes et al., 2006). Many parents who belong to various racial and ethnic groups (e.g., Latinx, Afro-Caribbean, etc.) report communicating with their children in ways designed to increase children's awareness about racial discrimination, and such bias preparation is especially prevalent among Black parents (Biafora et al., 1993; Hughes, 2003; Hughes & Chen, 1999; Phinney & Chavira, 1995). Of note, although White parents typically do not engage in explicit racial socialization, they may do so implicitly by instilling a colorblind ideology that conveys to their children that Whiteness affords no privileges and that the color of one's skin is irrelevant to societal outcomes (Ferguson et al., 2022).

In addition to racial socialization, children experience legal socialization, which refers to the processes by which individuals develop and understand their own legal values and attitudes. Legal socialization is theorized to be shaped by various contexts of authority across the lifespan, including family, school, and the criminal legal system (Tyler & Trinkner, 2018). For instance, school resource officers can play a role in students' legal socialization—the less procedurally just students perceive their school resource officers to be, the less legitimate they perceive local police to be and the weaker their sense of identification and belonging with their school community (Granot et al., 2021).

Drawing upon curriculum theory, Meares and Prowse (2021) explained that individuals learn through schooling and social policy that one of the functions of the state, particularly the police, is to provide security to its citizens. Yet, this overt curriculum often contradicts the hidden curriculum that people of color learn about through family, school, and neighborhoods, as well as through their own contacts with police (which we discuss later). This means that there is a subcomponent of both racial socialization and legal socialization that focuses on developing a race-based understanding of legal institutions. Such racial–legal socialization is facilitated by racial and ethnic minority parents communicating beliefs and attitudes to their children as well as negative vicarious experiences with the police among families and peers of color that children witness or learn about.

Specifically, within Black families, there exists an intergenerational transmission of the realities of police violence and racism and expectations for interactions with police (Brunson & Weitzer, 2011). Just as Black parents engage in preparation for bias and promotion of mistrust within interracial interactions in general (Anderson & Stevenson, 2019; Hughes et al., 2006), Black families also communicate with children specifically about racist police brutality with the goal of promoting norms for interacting with the police in ways that will keep children safe (Pickett et al., 2022; A. J. Thomas & Blackmon, 2015; Whitaker & Snell, 2016). Black youth learn that they will be stereotyped by police, learn to anticipate hostile behavior from police (for a review, see Woolard & Henning, 2020), and eventually come to perceive aggressive policing as the norm (Brunson, 2007). The education and warnings children of color receive from their family and peers promote hypervigilant behavior that is depicted as required to keep safe during police interactions. They are socialized to interact with police so as to avoid any possibility of being perceived as a threat—they are taught by family to always be respectful, never resist, be compliant, never make sudden movements, and keep hands in clear sight (Brunson & Weitzer, 2011; Woolard & Henning, 2020). This form of racial–legal socialization communicated by Black parents to their children has been coined "the talk" (Whitaker & Snell, 2016).

Indeed, the collective experiences of police brutality within Black communities is a powerful component of racial–legal socialization because Black youth more frequently hear about police violence perpetrated against others than experience it directly (Hurst et al., 2000; Weitzer & Tuch, 2002), and Black people are more likely than White people to witness some form of racial profiling or police violence in their social environments (e.g., Bor et al., 2018; Weitzer & Tuch, 2002).

MESOSYSTEM LEVEL IMPACTS ON DEVELOPMENT AND WELL-BEING

Through the racial–legal socialization process, parents' attitudes toward the police are transmitted to youth (e.g., Brunson & Weitzer, 2011). That is, even if youth have never experienced police mistreatment firsthand, vicarious experiences shape their attitudes toward and trust in police (e.g., Brunson & Weitzer, 2011; Hurst et al., 2000; Jones-Brown, 2000). In support, Cavanagh and Cauffman (2019) explored mothers' and their delinquent youths' attitudes toward police over a 3-year period. Mothers' attitudes had a stronger influence on shaping their sons' attitudes over time than did the sons' own personal contacts with police. As in Black youth, Black adults' negative vicarious experiences (i.e., hearing about others' experiences interacting with the police) can play a bigger role in generating negative attitudes toward the police than their own negative direct experiences (Rosenbaum et al., 2005).

Racial–legal socialization also creates fear and worry for many people of color. For example, as the number of police officers in schools increases, Black children's feelings of safety decrease (Lacoe, 2015), and youth and adults of color feel like they live in occupied territories and restrict their mobility to avoid harassment (Balto, 2019; Braga et al., 2019; Fader, 2021; Rios, 2011; Wallace, 2018). The feeling of being under constant surveillance and threat that people of color experience when their neighborhoods are overpoliced can harm the community's mental and physical health (Shmool et al., 2015; for review, see Bandes et al., 2019). In addition, a loss of confidence in law enforcement's duty to protect one's community can lead people of color to fear becoming victims of crime, distance themselves and disengage from police in an effort to maintain their autonomy and protect themselves physically (e.g., Solis et al., 2009; Weaver et al., 2019, 2020), and reduce their willingness to cooperate with police (e.g., by serving as a witness) and to seek help from police (Braga et al., 2019; Mazerolle et al., 2013; Solis et al., 2009; Sunshine & Tyler, 2003; Tyler, 2017; Tyler & Huo, 2002), which can further contribute to community violence and instability (Bandes et al., 2019; Epp et al., 2014; Kahn & Martin, 2016).

As noted, Black individuals who vicariously witness instances of police brutality and discrimination against people of color also experience adverse mental health effects such as anxiety, depression, and anger, along with physical health problems like hypertension and cardiovascular disease (e.g., Alang et al., 2017; Aymer, 2016; Bor et al., 2018; McFarland et al.,

2019; for reviews, see Bandes et al., 2019; Bryant-Davis et al., 2017; Dukes & Kahn, 2017; Simckes et al., 2021). Further, Black youth are more negatively impacted by vicarious experiences with police than are White youth (McFarland et al., 2019). Similarly, among a sample of adults who lived near Ferguson, Missouri, in the wake of the police-involved death of Michael Brown, Black adults reported higher and more clinically significant levels of posttraumatic stress and depressive symptomology than did White adults (Galovski et al., 2016). Also, Bor et al.'s (2018) study of a nationally representative sample revealed that among Black, but not White, adults, each vicarious experience of a police-involved killing of at least one unarmed Black person in their state in the prior 3 months was correlated with significantly more poor mental health days (i.e., days on which they experienced depression, stress, or emotional problems). The significance of this problem is underscored by the fact that 49% of Black adults had experienced vicarious police violence against an unarmed Black person.

Because people of color are disproportionately more likely to experience police contact, arrest, and incarceration than are White individuals, the consequences of these experiences also are disproportionately more likely to affect children and families of color. Indeed, Black, Latinx, American Indian/Alaskan, and multiracial children are more likely to have a parent incarcerated than are White children (Federal Interagency Forum on Child and Family Statistics, 2017; Glaze & Maruschak, 2008). Parental incarceration can disrupt family structure and dynamics, leading to family separation and, in turn, negative mental health, socio-emotional, cognitive, and behavioral consequences for children and families (Miller & Crain, 2020; Uggen & McElrath, 2014; Western & Wildeman, 2009). Even after statistically controlling for factors associated with parental incarceration (e.g., parent mental health, substance use, poverty), children of incarcerated parents are more likely to exhibit anxiety, depression, aggression, worse academic performance, learning disabilities, developmental delays, delinquent behavior, and increased risk for involvement in the juvenile justice system (Adalist-Estrin, 2018; Kampfner, 1995; Miller & Bank, 2013; Miller et al., 2013; Poehlmann, 2005; Turney, 2014; for a meta-analytic review, see Murray et al., 2012). Parental incarceration also harms relationships with extended family, peers, and the community (Christian, 2009; S. D. Phillips & Erkanli, 2007); creates economic difficulties; puts children at greater risk of exposure to parents' substance use and mental health issues and to violence in the home and community (DeHart & Altshulter, 2009; Miller, 2014; Miller & Bank, 2013; S. D. Phillips & Erkanli, 2007); and is associated with physical health disorders (DeHart et al., 2018).

The Microsystem: Direct Interactions and Personal Factors

The final, most proximal level of the social–ecological model is the microsystem, which considers direct interpersonal interactions with police officers. We first review officer- and situational-level factors that contribute to racialized policing; although many policing practices appear racially neutral on the surface, they invite bias and are discriminatory in effect (e.g., no-knock warrants; Almendarez, 2021; Mencarini et al., 2020; Sack, 2017). Then, we turn to the ways in which people of color are affected as a result of their own personal experiences with police bias, as well as the biological and personal history factors (e.g., age, gender, past police encounters) that affect reactions to being a victim of police mistreatment. Finally, we consider how the broader macrosystem context influences and shapes the ways in which people of color experience and interpret their direct encounters with police.

OFFICER-LEVEL RISK FACTORS FOR RACIALIZED POLICING

Bronfenbrenner and Morris (1998) theorized that, within the immediate settings of the microsystem, a person's race is a stimulus—a demand characteristic—that influences others' expectations and influences how interactions unfold. Indeed, there is concern that police officers are predisposed to react to people differently and discriminatorily based on the color of their skin. This is important to consider as police officers tend to report higher levels of social dominance orientation and right-wing authoritarianism (Gatto et al., 2010; Sidanius et al., 1994)—tendencies associated with support for hierarchical inequalities between social groups and to be socially conservative, submissive to authority figures, and aggressive toward people who are viewed as deviating from norms, respectively, and which are each generally associated with prejudice and dehumanization of marginalized social groups (Costello & Hodson, 2011; Kteily et al., 2015; Osborne et al., 2021). In police officers, these tendencies are related to more frequent use of force (e.g., Swencionis et al., 2021; for discussion, see Hall et al., 2016). Socialization into police culture also contributes to the development of dispositional characteristics that promote explicit (i.e., intentional and conscious) forms of prejudice (Gatto et al., 2010; Teahan, 1975), perhaps in connection to the subcultural norms reviewed previously that promote the warrior mindset, power differentials, and hierarchy maintenance (as an example of how the mesosystem and microsystem may interact). Of concern, surveys of nationally representative samples indicate that police professionals, particularly White men officers, endorse more anti-Black attitudes and stereotypes than do nonpolice professionals, even after controlling for variables like education and political ideology (LeCount, 2017; Roscigno & Preito-Hodge, 2021).

Even so, it is important to acknowledge that many law enforcement officers are well intentioned, nonprejudiced, and not motivated to start their encounters with people of color in biased or discriminatory ways. Nonetheless, there are implicit (i.e., automatic and nonconscious) cognitive associations and stereotypes that also contribute to biased and discriminatory policing. When individuals are primed with cues—like Black skin—that activate negative racial stereotypes, these stereotypes can guide information processing and influence decision making in a biased manner, often without people realizing it (S. M. Andersen et al., 2007; Eberhardt et al., 2004; Hunt, 2015). In the United States, racial stereotypes associate Black and Latinx individuals, particularly boys and men, with gang membership and criminality (e.g., Esbensen & Carson, 2012; Marin, 1984; Santana & Smith, 2001; Welch et al., 2011). Thus, as a result of officers' knowledge of negative stereotypes about people of color, even those who are low in explicit racial prejudice can be susceptible to implicit, subtle forms of bias. Indeed, police officers, like laypeople, are more likely to associate Black than White people with negative concepts, crime, and weapons (J. P. Andersen et al., 2023; Eberhardt et al., 2004; James et al., 2016).

Unfortunately, whether explicit or implicit, anti-Black attitudes and stereotypes affect officers' perceptions and judgments in ways that translate into harsher treatment of Black people as compared to non-Black people. In support, Graham and Lowery (2004, Study 1) subliminally primed police officers with either neutral words or words that were stereotypically related to Black people, and then had officers read a vignette about a juvenile offender whose race was not mentioned. Officers who had been primed with the stereotypical words perceived the juvenile as more culpable, mature, violent, bad, and deserving of punishment, even when analyses controlled for the officers' overt racial prejudice. In another study, the more that police officers implicitly dehumanized Black people (by associating stereotypically Black names with apes), the more likely they were to perceive Black boys as older and more culpable (i.e., less innocent; Goff et al., 2014). Greater implicit dehumanization of Black youth also related to greater actual use of force (per police personnel records) against Black versus non-Black youth, even after controlling for officers' explicit and implicit levels of racial prejudice. Like youth, adults of color are at risk of adverse outcomes resulting from police officers' implicit racial attitudes and stereotypes. For instance, Black people who look more stereotypically Black (i.e., have darker skin, fuller lips, and broader noses) are at greater risk of being shot (Kahn & Davies, 2011), whereas the more White a suspect looks, the less force officers use against them (Kahn et al., 2016).

In addition to implicit and explicit biases, social identity threats can also explain racially disparate police treatment. Social identity threat occurs when a person experiences a challenge or threat of negative judgment and treatment arising from negative cultural stereotypes and beliefs about a social identity that they hold and value (Steele, 2010). The source of the threat lies at the cultural level, but the threat is experienced when cues in the immediate setting make cultural-level stereotypes and beliefs salient, exemplifying how the macrosystem and microsystem are interconnected and interactive, in line with the social–ecological model (Bronfenbrenner, 1979). Two studies have demonstrated that police officers, regardless of their racial or ethnic identity, feel social identity threat related to concern that community members may judge them as stereotypical racist police officers (McCarthy et al., 2021; Trinkner et al., 2019). In both studies, the more concerned officers were about being judged as racist, the less confident they felt in the legitimacy of their authority and, in turn, the less they supported procedurally just, fair policing and the more they supported coercive policing strategies (e.g., using excessive force). It would seem that police officers would be most likely to experience this threat—and thus, to police coercively—when interacting with community members of color (but see Burke, 2023 who found no effects of civilian race on officers' self-reported levels of stereotype threat).

SITUATIONAL-LEVEL RISK FACTORS FOR RACIALIZED POLICING

Of importance, the broader climate also influences how policing is practiced on the ground. In particular, the wars on crime and drugs that became central to policing beginning in the 1960s fostered the institutionalization of proactive policing policies, including broken windows and zero-tolerance policing, overpolicing of "high crime" neighborhoods, stop and frisk, and quality-of-life policing (Bass, 2001; Braga et al., 2019; Murch, 2015). At issue is that proactive policing gives officers wide latitude to determine which laws to enforce when against whom (Hinton & Cook, 2021). When disputes arise over an officer's decision, the "reasonable officer standard" applies. This deems it constitutional for police to use their powers (e.g., whether to use force) if another officer in the same situation would consider the same decision to be reasonable (*Graham v. Connor*, 1989). It also takes into consideration that police often make split-second decisions under "tense, uncertain, and rapidly evolving" conditions (*Graham v. Connor*, 1989, p. 397). Unfortunately, however, multitasking, time pressure, and stress increase the likelihood that officers will employ stereotypes and similar heuristics to simplify cognitive tasks and facilitate rapid judgments and decision making (Kahneman, 2011; Macrae et al., 1994). They also have the effect of reducing people's cognitive resources and ability to exert control over bias and discrimination (Bodenhausen, 1990; Correll et al., 2002; Govorun & Payne, 2006; Ito et al., 2015; Ma et al., 2013; Payne, 2005; Singh et al., 2020). This is especially concerning in light of the fact that when information, motives, and situations are ambiguous—as they typically are when police officers encounter unfamiliar people and environments—stereotypic associations and attitudes are more likely to shape interpretations and decisions (e.g., Dovidio & Gaertner, 2000; Kunda & Sherman-Williams, 1993).

MICROSYSTEM-LEVEL IMPACTS ON DEVELOPMENT AND WELL-BEING

Only a handful of studies have explored how youths' attitudes toward police and the criminal legal system develop over time; however, those that have indicate the important roles that race and ethnicity, age, and contact with police and the criminal legal system play in shaping these attitudes. Overall, the developmental trajectory of perceptions of police legitimacy appears to follow an upward U-shape, such that youth perceive the police as less and less legitimate throughout adolescence (13–18 years old) and then begin to develop more favorable perceptions from late adolescence to early adulthood (19–22 years old). However, this trajectory varies as a function of race and ethnicity (A. D. Fine, Amemiya, et al., 2021; A. D. Fine & Cauffman, 2015; see also A. D. Fine et al., 2017; McLean et al., 2019). During adolescence, White youths' perceptions of police tend to become less favorable to a greater extent than Latino youths' perceptions; however, perceptions become more favorable for both groups moving into early adulthood, with White youth having higher perceptions by the time they reach 22. In contrast, Black youths' perceptions differ most notably from the other two groups, becoming more negative and staying more negative over time, with perceptions of police only slightly improving during early adulthood (A. D. Fine, Amemiya, et al., 2021). A. D. Fine and Cauffman's (2015) findings suggest that these observed differences may be explained by contact with police and the criminal legal system. Specifically, they found that greater police contact (i.e., an increased likelihood of being picked up by a police officer) and an increased probability of being rearrested worsened Black and White youths' perceptions of the legitimacy of the criminal legal system as they transitioned into early adulthood. For Latino youth, however, neither contact with police nor rearrest predicted perceptions of legitimacy. A. D. Fine and Cauffman (2015) note that because Black youth were significantly more likely to be picked up by police and rearrested than were Latino and White youth (despite no differences in levels of self-reported offending), greater police and legal system contact, particularly negative contact, might explain why they have the most negative perceptions of legitimacy.

To explain the racial and ethnic differences in perceptions of police legitimacy, A. D. Fine, Amemiya, and colleagues (2021) drew on conflict perspective (Hagan et al., 2005) and the expanded nigrescence model (Cross & Vandiver, 2001; Worrell et al., 2001) to theorize about Black youths' negative perceptions of police legitimacy. They proposed that for Black youth, negative interactions with police may contribute to racial consciousness, in turn shaping identity development. Negative encounters may lead Black youth to believe (or confirm their belief) that they are perceived more negatively by the police than are youth from other racial and ethnic groups, particularly White youth. As a result, Black youth may reject the majority culture in which police operate on behalf of the majority racial group and develop poorer perceptions of police legitimacy. Although A. D. Fine, Amemiya, and colleagues (2021) only theorized about the role of racial and ethnic identity development in explaining their results, research by Lee and colleagues (2010) demonstrated that it does indeed shape how Black adolescents perceive the police. Specifically, among Black youth, stronger ethnic identity was associated with higher perceptions of police discrimination, yet it also was associated with higher perceptions of police legitimacy. Although seemingly contradictory, from a developmental perspective, the authors explain that the cognitive and psychosocial maturity that accompanies ethnic identity development may have allowed Black youth to be more conscious of police discrimination, but also may have allowed them to recognize the police as a legitimate authority in society (see also Lee et al., 2011). Alternatively, results could be explained by the strength of respondents' American identity—individuals who identify more highly with their American identity perceive the police to be more legitimate, and this effect holds among Black and Latinx individuals (the relation is weaker for Asian and Pacific Islander individuals; Wolfe & McLean, 2021).

Unfortunately, however, people of color may identify less strongly with their American identity compared to their White counterparts. Despite their knowledge of policing's overt function to "protect and serve" civilians, as reviewed, many people of color experience mistreatment and are underserved (Meares & Prowse, 2021; Weaver et al., 2019): Black, Latinx, and other people of color are more likely than White people to believe that police officers treated them unfairly during their interactions (Hagan & Albanetti, 1982; Hagan et al., 2005; Ludwig, 2003). The contradiction between knowledge regarding what police are supposed to do and what is actually experienced shapes how people of color perceive and respond to police. Indeed, youth and adults of color who experience aggressive and discriminatory policing report more negative attitudes toward police than do their White counterparts, including perceiving that racial profiling is widespread (D. K. Carlson, 2004; Ludwig, 2003) and trusting the police less (e.g., Nadal et al., 2017; Solis et al., 2009; Weitzer & Tuch, 2005, 2006). Procedurally just policing (i.e., treating civilians with dignity, respect, neutrality, and voice; Lind & Tyler, 1988; Tyler & Lind, 1992) signals to civilians that they are valued and respected in society (Sunshine & Tyler, 2003). As Bradford and colleagues (2014, p. 531) note, however, "Policing is about exclusion as well as inclusion, and to be excluded is to be deemed as less than a full citizen." When people of color experience negative police encounters and mistreatment, they not only perceive the police to be less legitimate and come to have less trust in police but also identify less strongly with their citizen identity (Bradford et al., 2014; see also Bradford, 2014).

This line of theorizing and research illustrates the ways in which the social–ecological model accounts for how various levels are nested within each other and have reciprocal relations with each other. Youth of color expect to be stereotyped as criminals (as discussed in more detail in the next section on stereotype threat), and when they actually experience negative encounters with police, it confirms their expectations. This, in turn, has effects that expand beyond the borders of the microsystem to change their relationship to policing as an institution and the state as a macro-level force. The study by Cavanagh and Cauffman (2019) that was discussed previously also showed that when delinquent boys were rearrested during the 3-year observation period, their mothers' attitudes toward police became more negative, further demonstrating reciprocal relations between microsystem factors (youth rearrests) and mesosystem factors (mothers' attitudes toward police).

Even more troubling than how negative contact with police shapes attitude development is how negative contact harms mental health and well-being (for review, see Jindal et al., 2021). Among Black and Latino youth, experiencing proactive policing is associated with greater delinquency (even after controlling for prior delinquency), and this association is partially explained by greater psychological distress (Del Toro et al., 2019). Of concern, the younger youth are, the greater these effects. Personal contact with police is also linked to poorer health among Latinx youth compared to White youth (McFarland et al., 2019). Moreover, even after controlling for illegal behavior, contact with police in childhood significantly predicts the likelihood that Black, but not White, youth will later be arrested in adulthood, suggesting that Black youth are more at risk of "secondary sanctioning" (McGlynn-Wright et al., 2022). Relatedly, Black youth who report greater perceived discrimination at the societal level and on the part of police are more likely to be arrested or jailed by the time they are 24–25 years old, even after statistically controlling for other factors such as previous delinquent behavior (Gibbons et al., 2020). Of interest, police contact is associated with poorer future orientation—how successful youth predict they will be as an adult—for White, but not Black, youth, perhaps because contact with police has become a normative expectation for Black youth (Testa et al., 2022). Although perceptions of police do not appear to differ as a function of gender (e.g., Nadal et al., 2017), there are notable gender differences in the sources of anxiety and fear that people of color face when it comes to police violence. Whereas Black and Latino boys and men are concerned with physical mistreatment and harassment by police,

Black and Latina girls and women report concerns about sexual misconduct and a lack of responsiveness by police (Brunson & Miller, 2006b; Solis et al., 2009). Of importance, compared to White individuals, people of color are also more likely to experience police violence directly, and directly experiencing police violence is associated with greater risk of PTSD, psychotic experiences, suicidal ideation, and attempting suicide (e.g., DeVylder et al., 2018; for review, see Bryant-Davis et al., 2017). Frequent and aggressive police contact also can serve as a reminder to people of color of the stigma and prejudice they face, and as a result can contribute to poorer self-esteem and internalized racism (e.g., Solis et al., 2009; for review, see Bandes et al., 2019).

Of note, the potential consequences of direct experiences with police extend far beyond the first point of contact (for reviews, see Kahn & Martin, 2016; Simckes et al., 2021). The adverse mental health effects stemming from negative police contact can be compounded in jail and prison, where mental health and substance abuse resources are limited to begin with, and culturally responsive components are lacking (e.g., Fader, 2013; Primm et al., 2005). Upon reentry to society, people of color contend not only with stigma and prejudice associated with the color of their skin but also that associated with their criminal history, the latter of which is likely itself a consequence of the social control policies responsible for the disproportionate mass incarceration of people of color (Gotsch, 2018; Harrison & Beck, 2006; Lofstrom & Raphael, 2016; Shepherd & Willis-Esqueda, 2018). As a result, people of color face a host of additional obstacles when they leave jail or prison (e.g., barriers to public housing, food assistance, employment and health benefits, higher education, voting, jury duty, citizenship). These obstacles can contribute to greater risk for substance use and abuse, financial disadvantage, recidivism, and reincarceration (Demarco et al., 2021; Iguchi et al., 2002, 2005; Kalt, 2003; Pager, 2003). Wrongfully convicted individuals who are eventually exonerated also suffer from negative mental health consequences—including anxiety, depression, and PTSD—as well as relationship and adjustment issues (Brooks & Greenberg, 2021; Wildeman et al., 2011). Furthermore, Black men who have been incarcerated suffer from the detrimental consequences of social identity threat in the context of education: Compared to nonincarcerated Black men, they are more likely to expect educators to stereotype them on the basis of their intellectual ability, which in turn is associated with them having poorer beliefs regarding the utility of education and lower motivation to pursue education (Murphy et al., 2020). The consequences of incarceration can therefore have direct, negative effects at the microsystem level, as well as reciprocal effects at the mesosystem (e.g., with respect to children of incarcerated parents) and at other levels of the social–ecological model. For example, restricting the right to serve on a jury can limit racially diverse jury pools (Segal, 2010; Wheelock, 2011), contributing to the criminalization of people of color at the macro level.

MICROSYSTEM-LEVEL IMPACTS RESULTING FROM THE BROADER MACROSYSTEM CONTEXT

There is a growing body of evidence that macro-level factors also influence people of color to experience police encounters in psychologically different ways as compared to White people. In this section we consider evidence that, just as police officers experience social identity threat (e.g., Trinkner et al., 2019), so do people of color when racialized stereotypes and beliefs become salient in police encounters. We also consider how the historic and sociopolitical context generates different psychological experiences of police encounters as they unfold.

Stereotype threat in police encounters. People of color experience social identity threat as concern of being judged and treated unfairly by police before encounters even begin because of stereotypes depicting them as prone to crime. That is, Black and Latinx people feel this so-called "stereotype threat" in police encounters (Najdowski, 2018; Najdowski et al., 2012,

2015). Evidence for this phenomenon was first found in two studies conducted by Najdowski and colleagues (2015). First, the researchers asked Black and White undergraduate participants to report how they feel when interacting with police officers in general. Black students were significantly more likely than White students to agree with statements like "I worry that police officers might stereotype me as a criminal because of my race" and "I worry that police officers' perceptions of me might be affected by my race." In line with other work showing that stereotypes about crime are both racialized and gendered (e.g., Coles & Pasek, 2020; Ghavami & Peplau, 2013; Goff et al., 2008; Purdie-Vaughns & Eibach, 2008; E. L. Thomas et al., 2014), Najdowski et al. (2015) also found that, on average, Black men, but not Black women, reported experiencing stereotype threat in police encounters. The researchers next invited Black and White men to imagine what it would be like if they were walking down the street at night carrying a backpack and a police officer exited a store just ahead of them, stopped, and then watched them. The hypothetical encounter activated the stereotype of Black criminality and made it cognitively accessible for significantly more Black men than White men (27% versus 3%). For example, one Black participant reported, "I would think that the officer is racially profiling me and is probably thinking that I stole one of the items in my bookbag" (Najdowski et al., 2015, p. 469). Black men also were significantly more likely than White men to anticipate feeling stereotype threat in the encounter, as well as concern that the officer might accuse them of doing something wrong.

Najdowski (2018) extended this line of work by engaging Black and White men in an elaborate staged encounter with a White confederate acting as a security officer. Each participant was left alone in the laboratory and then confronted by the confederate officer, who stated that he was investigating a report about a stolen tablet computer and asked the participant questions about the tablet he was using. Black men were significantly more concerned than White men were that the officer would be influenced by racial stereotypes and suspect them of having committed a crime, with one out of two Black men agreeing they would experience stereotype threat compared to only one in 20 White men. Thus, the racial differences Najdowski et al. (2015) found in expected feelings of stereotype threat in abstract police encounters and in a specific hypothetical encounter generalized to a realistic encounter with a White security officer.

Of importance, although the studies reviewed thus far compared experiences and reactions to stereotype threat among Black and White men, Najdowski et al. (2012) compared the White participants from Najdowski et al. (2015) to a different sample of Latinx participants. Their results showed that Latinx men and women are also concerned that police officers will stereotype them as criminals on the basis of their ethnicity. Specifically, 57% of Latinx men and women agreed they feel stereotype threat in police encounters in general, and 48% of Latinx men agreed they would feel stereotype threat in a specific hypothetical police encounter; significantly fewer of their White counterparts similarly agreed (11% and 7%, respectively). It remains to be seen whether other people of color also experience feelings of stereotype threat during their interactions with police officers.

All of this is concerning because stereotype threat could have detrimental consequences in the context of police encounters. Ironically, stereotype threat and its psychological correlates produce nonverbal behaviors that are the same as those that police commonly perceive as indicative of deception or guilt (e.g., Akehurst et al., 1996; Mann & Vrij, 2006; Vrij et al., 2006; Vrij & Semin, 1996; for review, see Najdowski, 2011) and that police are trained to look for as preattack indicators in civilians' behavior (Kahn et al., 2018). Specifically, Najdowski et al. (2015, Study 2) found that the more Black men expected they would feel stereotype threat in the hypothetical police encounter they were asked to imagine, the more they anticipated they would engage in self-regulatory efforts (e.g., cognitively monitor the situation and their behavior for risk of being stereotyped), and, in turn, the more they anticipated that they would "look nervous," "try to avoid looking nervous," "avoid making eye contact," or "freeze up" (p. 468). In contrast, White men's feelings of stereotype threat had neither a direct effect on anticipated self-regulatory efforts nor an indirect effect on anticipated suspicious behavior. In addition, in Najdowski's (2018) staged encounter study, participants were unknowingly videotaped during the encounter and independent observers rated how nervous they appeared. Analyses showed that Black men appeared more nervous than did White men. Moreover, this effect was partially explained by Black men's greater feelings of stereotype threat during the encounter. Thus, the racial difference in internal psychological state manifested in observable behavior; expecting to be judged and treated unfairly due to the negative stereotype of Black criminality led Black men to behave differently—more "suspiciously"—than White men in an encounter with a police-type figure.

These findings are of immense practical significance. Police often use a person's behavior in their decision making about how an interaction should unfold, including whether they should make an arrest or not (e.g., Stroshine et al., 2008). Indeed, more than half of street stops made by NYPD officers in 2012 were justified on the basis of civilians' "furtive movements," and this reason was cited more often when stops involved Black rather than White civilians (Najdowski, 2014). It is also important to note that stereotype threat is likely to increase people of color's risk of being subjected to police scrutiny and contacts regardless of whether they are actually guilty; none of the participants in the studies conducted by Najdowski and her colleagues had committed any crimes, mock or otherwise (Najdowski, 2014; Najdowski et al., 2012, 2015). Moreover, stereotype threat effects may accumulate throughout the criminal legal system, including in interrogations, where they may translate into disparities in false confessions (see Najdowski, 2011), and in courtrooms, where they may produce wrongful convictions.

It is not yet clear at what age people of color begin to experience stereotype threat in police contexts. Of interest, children as young as age 3 appear to have full capacity to experience self-conscious, evaluative emotions (Lewis, 2007), and children's ability to infer others' stereotypes (i.e., "stereotype consciousness") increases drastically from age 6 to 10 (McKown & Weinstein, 2003). Moreover, Black and Latinx children are even more aware of group stereotypes than those from nonracially marginalized groups at all ages (McKown & Weinstein, 2003). Considering these findings, it is possible that young children of color might be susceptible to the negative effects of stereotype threat during police encounters. Future research might explore this question and consider impacts across the lifespan and throughout different contexts where police may be encountered, including school, work, and community settings.

Racial differences in perceived freedom during police encounters. Voluntariness to consent to a police search or seizure is examined in light of whether a "reasonable person" in the same situation would feel free to leave or refuse a search (e.g., *Florida v. Bostick*, 1991). Legal scholars have argued that the reasonable person test should take race into account (e.g., Carbado, 2002; Robinson, 2008). Indeed, individuals have beliefs about "how to be" (Markus & Kitayama, 2003, p. 4), and these models of agency can vary between people from different backgrounds (Snibbe & Markus, 2005). Given the unique abuses that Black citizens have experienced at the hands of the state, from before the founding of the United States to the police violence that has dominated media headlines in recent years, it is likely that Black and White people have different models of agency for interactions with police officers. In particular, Black people, particularly boys and men, may feel more under the control of the state and less able to assert their freedom in police encounters as compared to their White counterparts.

It is important to test this hypothesis because Black people are more likely than White people to be stopped by police (Engel & Johnson, 2006). To the extent that Black people feel compelled to interact with police or comply with their demands, their psychological and behavioral reactions could increase their risk of wrongful arrest (Najdowski et al., 2015). Moreover, even though searches of Black and White people yield similar rates of contraband (see Engel & Johnson, 2006), if Black people feel less free to refuse a search than do White people, they will be disproportionately likely to be arrested. Finally, when stops and searches produce evidence of illegal activity, consent reduces the range of defenses available to citizens during later stages of criminal legal processing. Thus, racial differences in perceived freedom in police encounters can have a constellation of consequences that, in concert, create racial disparities in criminal legal outcomes.

Thus, Najdowski and colleagues (2023) conducted a study to determine the degree of racial differences in response to imagining the state has control of one's liberty related to police officers' access to their bodily location, time, possessions, etc. They predicted that, compared to White people, Black people would view a "reasonable person" as being less able to deny state control and assert freedom in a variety of police encounters. They asked Black and White individuals to imagine whether "a reasonable person" would feel as though they have the right and ability to deny consent in a variety of hypothetical police encounters modeled from actual Supreme Court cases dealing with Fourth Amendment issues of consent to search and seizure (e.g., *Florida v. Bostick*, 1991; *Schneckloth v. Bustamonte*, 1973; *United States v. Mendenhall*, 1980). Results showed that Black and White participants reported similar levels of perceived state control and freedom when imagining a police officer approaching a person on the street or in their vehicle or requesting information, identifying material, or data. On average, both Black and White participants believed a reasonable person would feel somewhat free to say no to a police officer who, for example, instructed the person to empty their pockets, stop at a highway checkpoint, or step out of their vehicle; moderately free to say no if the officer asked for the person's citizenship status or fingerprints; and very free to say no to an officer's request for the person's Internet browsing or GPS history. In contrast, however, racial differences emerged in perceptions of a reasonable person's feeling of being free to walk away from an encounter with a police officer in a public setting or to say no to the officer's request to various kinds of searches. For example, compared to White participants, Black participants reported that a reasonable person would feel less free to walk away if a police officer enters a store and starts asking other customers questions. Black participants also perceived that a reasonable person would feel less free to say no to a police officer's request to search the person's bag or the trunk of the person's car or to conduct a strip search or body cavity search. On average, all participants believed that if a person said no to any of the police officer's requests or walked/drove away from the encounter, it was somewhat likely that the officer would make the person carry out the request or stop them from leaving, arrest the person, or use physical force against the person. Even so, Black participants were significantly more likely than White participants to expect the police officer to make an arrest or use force in response to a reasonable person's noncompliance.

The researchers also asked participants to report how free they think a reasonable White person and a reasonable Black person each would feel in response to a police officer's effort to stop or search them. Overall, participants perceived that a reasonable White person would be significantly more free to say no to a police officer or to leave an encounter than would a reasonable Black person. However, this effect was especially large among Black participants who, compared to White participants, perceived both a reasonable White person as more free and a reasonable Black person as less free.

Najdowski et al.'s (2023) study took a first step in understanding how different racial groups perceive agency and freedom in encounters with state agents. Future tests of the research question under more realistic conditions are needed now. Also, the research highlighted the need for the development of interventions to help narrow the gap between Blacks' and Whites' perceived agency and freedom in police encounters. Such racial differences in perceived agency, control, and freedom could explain documented racial differences in tendencies to yield civil liberties in police encounters (e.g., consent to have one's body or property searched; Northwestern University Center for Public Safety, 2008). Further, if different groups experience agency differently in the context of interactions with representatives of the state, the meaning of many laws that rely on the "reasonable person" standard is fundamentally altered. Results undergird calls (e.g., Robinson, 2008) for identity-sensitive legal theory that considers the experiences of a "reasonable Black person."

Cumulative Consequences of Racialized Policing and Evidence of Resilience

In this section, we consider the cumulative consequences of racialized policing for people of color across the span of their lives, as well as evidence of coping and resilience in the face of racialized policing. In particular, we consider whether racial and racial–legal socialization may help buffer the negative effects of racialized policing on people of color.

To begin, people of color confront racism at every level of the social–ecological model, and as a result, they have to contend with repeated racial stress, which has cumulative traumatic effects not only on themselves but also on their communities and future generations. As Comas-Díaz et al. (2019, p. 1) explain, although racial trauma shares similarities to PTSD, it differs because it "involves ongoing individual and collective injuries due to exposure and re-exposure to race-based stress." Indeed, a wealth of research indicates that historical, vicarious, and direct experiences of racism, real or perceived, are associated with a host of negative mental and physical health issues among people of color, such as internalized racism and dehumanization, depression, anxiety, and hypertension (e.g., Bryant-Davis, 2007; Bryant-Davis & Ocampo, 2006; Chou et al., 2012; Cokley et al., 2011 Comas-Díaz et al., 2019; Pieterse et al., 2012; Saleem et al., 2020; U.S. Department of Health and Human Services, 2000; Williams & Williams-Morris, 2000). Likewise, Bryant-Davis and colleagues (2017) explain that negative interactions with police historically, vicariously, and directly can create cumulative racial trauma for people of color across the lifespan.

It is important to note also, however, that negative experiences with the police are not limited to negative outcomes. In many ways, people of color are resilient even in the face of negative interactions with police. Negative experiences with the police also can function to create a sense of community and commonality among Black communities and in turn motivate collective action to combat police oppression (Weaver et al., 2020; see also Meares & Prowse, 2021). This is evident in the community activism and the Black Lives Matter movement that erupted in response to racially disparate criminal legal responses to killings of people of color by civilians and police officers, as well as examples of researchers, activists, and communities of color uniting in solidarity to provide evidence of discriminatory policing practices and instigate change (e.g., see Stoudt & Torre, 2014; for review see M. Fine & Cross, 2016). By sharing their negative experiences with others, people of color can resist the status quo or "master narrative" and, in doing so, inspire changes to macrosystem factors (e.g., cultural norms; Syed & McClean, 2023).

Also, as reviewed previously, exposure to racially charged incidents involving the police can create added stress and trauma for Black youth and can reinforce Black parents' fear for their children's safety and the importance of preparing their children for police encounters (A.

J. Thomas & Blackmon, 2015). Moreover, although witnessing police bias and discrimination can be traumatizing, without learning about it and being prepared to address it, youth of color may come to blame themselves for victimization or internalize the racism they experience. However, parents' and other family members' racial socialization of their children, particularly when it is preemptive (Derlan & Umaña-Taylor, 2015) and involves messages of pride and empowerment (Winchester et al., 2022), affords youth psychological protection from racial trauma and is associated with a host of positive youth outcomes, including psychological well-being, self-esteem, academic success, and positive racial identity (see Anderson & Stevenson, 2019, for a review). In general, racial socialization practices are theorized to help children of color develop positive racial identities, learn how to cope effectively with the trauma and stress that result from direct or indirect exposure to discrimination and prejudice, and navigate society successfully. Thus, in the wake of the 2020 police-involved deaths of people of color, Metzger and colleagues developed a racial trauma guide (see University of Georgia, Department of Psychology, Franklin College of Arts and Sciences, n.d.) to assist families in speaking to their children of color about recent events involving police, encouraging parents to use these events as an opening to teach children effective coping skills, such as using role play to practice how to respond to racial discrimination and coping collectively by, for example, civic engagement and activism (see also Association of Black Psychologists, 2016; Jones et al., 2020). Although racial–legal socialization research suggests that youth of color are socialized to have negative attitudes toward legal authorities, it is important to explore the possible adaptive nature of such attitudes. Just as racial socialization has been shown to buffer children and adults from stress associated with racial discrimination (Anderson & Stevenson, 2019), racial–legal socialization might similarly protect youth of color from racially biased policing by preparing people of color to manage those experiences more safely. For instance, Black individuals' past experiences navigating interracial interactions may buffer them against the depleting effects associated with engaging in interracial interactions because they have greater familiarity with the situation, which puts less strain on their regulatory resources (S. E. Johnson & Richeson, 2009). Although fear of being racially discriminated against by a police officer has been shown to have some iatrogenic effects (Najdowski et al., 2015), it is important for future research to test the parameters of this effect and explore the possible protective factors associated with racial–legal socialization.

This also highlights the importance of teaching about race and racism at home and in schools, for youth of color and, especially, for White youth. Moreover, as early as preschool, children begin to show evidence of racial bias in their attitudes and expectations of others (for review, see Waxman, 2021). And White people may lack awareness of the realities of racism in society while simultaneously remaining blind to the privileges afforded to them merely because of the color of their skin. In turn, neither will understand the problem as a systemic issue. Indeed, following George Floyd's murder, Ferguson et al. (2022) found that the majority of White parents remained silent on the topic when it came to discussing it with their children. Unfortunately, such practices can have deleterious effects by continuing a cycle that perpetuates and reinforces racism. Yet, White children whose parents discuss race with them are more aware of systemic racism. By learning and talking about racism from an early age, youth of all races and ethnicities can come to understand it as a systemic issue and be better equipped to mobilize to eradicate structural and institutional racism (Ferguson et al., 2022).

Implications for Policy and Practice

We now turn to implications for policy and practice at each level of the social–ecological model, because for truly meaningful change to occur, reform will require intervention at each level. Before doing so, however, a word of caution is warranted—the evidence supporting various interventions and programs for police reform is limited (Peeples, 2020). We therefore urgently encourage social scientists and police departments to work together to test the effectiveness and limitations of potential solutions. Indeed, scientists are generally trained to approach and develop implications and applications of science cautiously, conservatively, and critically. Eberhardt (2020), however, argues that such cautious slowness and aspiration of an unattainable scientific benchmark have the potential to impede immediate, beneficial, and necessary progress toward interventions that can and should be developed and informed by existing empirical research (see also Goff & Rau, 2020). Therefore, although we urge social scientists to continue to conduct much-needed future collaborative research, we hope that they will simultaneously apply existing and cutting-edge research to the development of policing interventions.

Macrosystem Implications
Policing exists within the broader sociocultural fabric of the United States. As such, it would be naïve not to acknowledge the reality that broader, macro-level issues—such as society's dehumanization of people of color and stereotypical associations that are embedded within the fabric of the country—are critical to reform efforts. Racial disparities must be addressed in other areas, including, for example, housing, employment, health, and homelessness. As noted legal scholar Tracey Meares points out:

> It's impossible to point to one specific problem and say, "That's it—that's the issue." . . . Our communities lack the resources to deal with their social problems. And our response has been to deploy armed first responders to address the issue way down the chain from the source. (Karma, 2020, para. 53)

Legal reforms are also required—it will be important to reform laws that fail to hold police officers accountable for their actions, such as qualified immunity, whereby "government officials performing discretionary functions generally are shielded from liability for civil damages insofar as their conduct does not violate 'clearly established' statutory or constitutional rights of which a reasonable person would have known" (*Harlow v. Fitzgerald*, 1982, p. 801).

Reform also must occur in Americans'—particularly White Americans'—actions and behaviors. In the wake of the 2020 police-involved deaths of people of color, macro-level changes supporting police reform appeared to be looming. Americans witnessed with their own eyes video recordings of police abusing and even murdering people of color. Outrage peaked following George Floyd's murder. The overall trend indicated increasing support for the Black Lives Matter movement and police reform, suggesting increasing awareness of the systemic racism that permeates U.S. society and the potential for transformative change. Yet, in the weeks following Floyd's murder, stark differences in Black and White Americans' views of policing reemerged—whereas Black Americans' opinions stayed the same, White Americans' support for reform subsided (Blake, 2020). This suggests that White people's support for reform may be largely reactionary—increasing in response to high-profile events and then ebbing. In contrast, Black people's support persists, because every day they live with the knowledge and trauma of racial disparities in police abuse.

Exosystem Implications
Implications at the exosystem level involve transforming police culture away from a philosophy that perpetuates social hierarchies and power differentials (i.e., the warrior mindset) and toward a culture that emphasizes empathy, cooperation, and respect for civilians of *all* races

and ethnicities (i.e., the guardian mindset; President's Task Force on 21st Century Policing, 2015; Stoughton, 2016). As described previously, much of police training and culture focuses on a military-style model. Yet, officers spend the majority of their time engaging in nonviolent and noncriminal activities (e.g., Asher & Horwitz, 2020) and would be better off receiving training in interpersonal communication, conflict resolution, and de-escalation skills (Karma, 2020; Peeples, 2020). Departments also can create special units with special training to respond to incidents involving the homeless or individuals suffering from mental illness (see, e.g., Najdowski & Goff, 2022). Others also suggest the need for state and/or national registries to track police officers' disciplinary history, the same way that states track doctors' performance history. Doing so could help prevent the rehiring of officers who have been fired for misconduct at other departments (Peeples, 2020).

Mesosystem Implications

At the mesosystem level, it is crucial to build positive relationships between the police and the community. It is also important for communities of color to be involved in the reform process. This will not only provide people of color with a voice in the process (consistent with procedural justice [Lind & Tyler, 1988], and democratic principles generally) but also offer the opportunity for police and communities of color to cooperate and work with each other toward a common goal—two central components of creating positive intergroup contact (Allport, 1954). Results from randomized control trials demonstrate that community-oriented policing programs that provide the opportunity for individuals to interact with police in a positive, prosocial, nonenforcement context can improve both youths' and adults' perceptions of police (A. D. Fine, Padilla, et al., 2022; Peyton et al., 2019). As another example, "Coffee with a Cop" is a program developed by the Hawthorne Police Department in California to break down barriers between police and civilians and encourage positive interpersonal interactions. Furthermore, educating officers about the sociocultural and historical factors that contribute to crime in communities of color could help officers better understand and appreciate the systemic racism that plagues these communities and, in turn, reduce reliance on stereotypes and aggressive policing tactics (see Bonam et al., 2019, for an example of how this type of intervention can raise White adults' awareness of systemic racism).

In addition, implementing diversion programs in schools would be beneficial. Goldstein et al. (2021) assessed outcomes from 2,301 Philadelphia public school students (76% of whom were Black) over the span of 5 years, enabling them to explore the impact of the implementation of a novel diversion program designed to divert children who perpetrate minor offenses from arrest and toward community-based services. Compared to arrest rates among youth prior to the implementation of the diversion program, the arrest rates of youth following the implementation of the diversion program were significantly lower, as were their recidivism rates. Once the researchers matched the diverted and nondiverted samples by race, gender, and age, however, there was no significant effect of diversion program availability and recidivism rates, suggesting that the program's positive effects for reducing racial disparities in the school-to-prison pipeline might be restricted to arrest rates. Nonetheless, this program is not worse than formal processing at deterring future crime, and if it can prevent children from having a record, that is highly beneficial. Importantly, however, there also have been calls and initiatives to reduce the number of school resource officers in schools or eliminate them altogether from those who point out that their presence in that setting naturally increases youth arrest rates because student misbehavior that was once handled internally by a school is instead outsourced to school officers and criminalized (Pigott et al., 2018; see also Fine et al., this volume).

Importantly, to achieve change, we must also address the "Whiteness pandemic" in America: "socialization into the centuries-old culture of Whiteness— involving colorblindness, passivity, and fragility—that perpetrates and perpetuates U.S. racism" (Ferguson et al., 2022, p. 344. It is crucial that White America abandons its colorblind ideology and instead commits to an antiracist ideology that acknowledges the realities of White privilege and racism that exist in society. Such changes must begin by educating children from an early age about these realities. As Ferguson et al. (2022, p. 359) explain, "These discussions have long been essential parenting in Black families, and while they may be new and awkward for White parents, they are equally essential to breaking patterns of racialized power structures and systemic harm" (see also Perry et al., 2022).

Microsystem Implications

Microsystem implications consist of targeting individual processes among officers, including programs targeted at officers' attitudes and behaviors. For instance, training officers about adolescent development can improve officers' attitudes and interactions with youth (LaMotte et al., 2010). Other police training programs teach officers about implicit and explicit racial bias, how to be aware of biases, and how to combat them (for reviews, see Dukes & Kahn, 2017; Kahn & Martin, 2016; but see Worden et al., 2020, for limited behavioral effects of implicit bias training). Examples include the Perspectives on Profiling curriculum (Museum of Tolerance, n.d.) and trainings developed by the Center for Policing Equity and Fair and Impartial Policing. Many programs rely on training police in the principles of procedural justice, which is a promising avenue to police reform as such training has the potential to improve officers' attitudes and behaviors during civilian encounters and minimize civilian complaints and police use of force (e.g., Antrobus et al., 2019; Mazerolle et al., 2013; President's Task Force on 21st Century Policing, 2015; Wood et al., 2020). Moreover, greater perceived procedural justice is associated with less legal cynicism and higher perceptions of police legitimacy among youth, which are associated with a lower likelihood of reoffending as well as lower belief in the "code of the street" (i.e., a street code that encourages violence to handle conflict and protect oneself from victimization; Cavanagh et al., 2020; A. D. Fine, Moule et al., 2022). Likewise, racial disparities in schools can be mitigated by requiring procedural justice training for school resource officers. Students who perceive their school resource officers to act in a more (versus less) procedurally just manner report greater academic success and a stronger sense of belonging with their school (Granot et al., 2021), and these relations are particularly strong among students of color. Yet, there is limited research exploring whether procedural justice training mitigates racially discriminatory policing (but see Epp et al., 2014), reflecting an important direction for future research.

In addition to targeting individual officer processes, it is also necessary to address situational factors and, in particular, discretionary practices that exacerbate racial profiling and disproportionately target people of color (e.g., broken windows and zero-tolerance policing, overpolicing of "high crime" neighborhoods, stop and frisk; Braga et al., 2019; Woolard & Henning, 2020). This will not only help reduce racial disparities in policing but also curb downstream consequences that result from police contact (e.g., mass incarceration). For instance, a simple but promising method that decreases racial disparities in stops and searches is having officers complete a justification form that includes the question, "Is this intelligence-led?" (Oakland Police Department, n.d.). Approaches such as these and others (e.g., strict criteria specifying when officers can or cannot engage in pursuit) that remove race from the decision-making process can potentially help to reduce reliance on implicit biases (see Goff & Rau, 2020). Department policies limiting the length of officers' shifts would also be beneficial, as fatigue and cognitive depletion impair police officers' ability to inhibit stereotypes and biases and to de-escalate situations (James, 2018; Ma et al., 2013; Staller et al., 2018).

Finally, to develop sound policy interventions, we need new research to focus on the gaps in current knowledge. As noted previously, most studies have compared Black and White perspectives; Latinx views are underrepresented and Asian American and Indigenous Peoples' views are virtually invisible in this literature (but see, e.g., Goff et al., 2008). It is necessary to examine relations between police and other racial and ethnic groups (Weitzer, 2014). It is also necessary to acknowledge that racial and ethnic groups are not monolithic, and subgroups may differ in their attitudes toward and experiences with police, and they may also differ as a function of other intersectional identities (e.g., immigrant generation status; Piquero et al., 2016). How do the intersections of race, ethnicity, gender, sexual orientation, socioeconomic status, and immigration status interact to shape individuals' reactions to police mistreatment? Future research into methods to reduce racially disparate policing, improve relations between police and the community, and address the consequences of police mistreatment will require a deeper understanding not only of the ways in which intersectional identities shape how police respond to civilians but also of the unique ways in which individuals with intersectional identities are affected by their interactions with police. For instance, some evidence suggests that intersecting identities can influence police officers' perceptions and decisions: Black transgender women report that police profile them as sex workers yet fail to take them seriously (and sometimes even arrest them) when they report domestic violence victimization (Carpenter & Marshall, 2017). Because such experiences are likely to involve multifaceted forms of discrimination, it is necessary to explore multifaceted interventions that are sensitive to these experiences.

Researchers also need to consider how the different levels of the social–ecological model intersect with and influence each other. Focusing solely on individual, micro-level factors (as is common in psychology) will not suffice because police officers, like laypeople, are raised in the same macro-level society that fosters reliance on racial stereotypes and prejudices, and that are exacerbated by situational risk factors (e.g., ambiguity) associated with the job. Researchers must take a multifaceted and multisystem approach to studying issues of racialized policing. Doing so will offer a more nuanced understanding of how people of color are impacted by racialized policing, which in turn will provide better insight into the systemic changes required for meaningful change to occur (see Najdowski & Goff, 2022).

In a related vein, there is limited research examining the psychological consequences of racialized policing within a developmental life course framework. This is necessary for understanding how childhood, adolescent, and adult experiences with police interact to shape the attitudes, experiences, and well-being of people of color. There are only a handful of studies that take a longitudinal approach to this issue, and those that do typically involve youth and young adults (e.g., A. D. Fine et al., 2017, 2021). Yet there is a troubling lack of research exploring the experiences of older adults of color and how their early and later life experiences with police influence their life outcomes. Such studies are necessary for better understanding individual difference, personal history, and other unique factors that are relevant to the way people of color experience and respond to police at various stages of development. For instance, at what age do people of color begin to experience stereotype threat? This has important implications for the presence of school resource officers: If police officers trigger young children to feel anxiety and fear over being stereotyped as criminals, how might their presence in schools negatively impact their educational development? How might school resource officers' stereotype endorsement affect their perceptions of youth (e.g., as more suspicious) as well as their reactions (e.g., increased likelihood for arrest) and further contribute to the school-to-prison pipeline?

As M. Fine and Cross (2016) emphasize, it is also important that psychological research study not just how people of color are negatively influenced by police mistreatment but also how they demonstrate resilience in the face of it. For instance, researchers should explore the ways in which racial–legal socialization might protect people of color from the deleterious effect of police mistreatment, and how communities of color unite to actively combat the discrimination that they experience.

Conclusion

In this chapter, we have explored the psychological consequences of racially disparate policing for people of color across the lifespan, integrating our review around Bronfenbrenner's (1977, 1979) social–ecological model (see Figure 26.1). The consequences are rooted in historical and cultural factors at the broadest level of society, the practices and institution of policing, vicariously experiencing police interactions with other people of color, and people's own direct interactions with police. Racial disparities in policing shape how people of color learn about police, perceive police, and experience police encounters, and also contribute to mental health issues and trauma that have cumulative, negative effects across generations. Ending racial disparities in policing will require intervention at every level of the social–ecological model. We hope that this review of the scientific literature and other related reviews inspire psychologists to either begin or continue the messier and harder work required of stepping out of the laboratory and into the real world by developing and implementing interventions. This work is necessary, is long overdue, and has the potential to improve the quality of life across the lifespan and even save lives.

Acknowledgments

The authors would like to thank the undergraduate research team at the University at Albany's PULSE Lab for providing excellent library support.

References

Adalist-Estrin, A. N. N. (2018). Responding to the need of children and families of the incarcerated: Twelve guiding principles. In L. Gordon (Ed.), *Contemporary research and analysis on the children of prisoners: Invisible children* (pp. 100–115). Cambridge Scholars Publishing.

Akehurst, L., Köhnken, G., Vrij, A., & Bull, R. (1996). Lay persons' and police officers' beliefs regarding deceptive behaviour. *Applied Cognitive Psychology, 10*(6), 461–471.

Alang, S., McAlpine, D., McCreedy, E., & Hardeman, R. (2017). Police brutality and Black health: Setting the agenda for public health scholars. *American Journal of Public Health, 107*(5), 662–665.

Alexander, M. (2010). *The new Jim Crow: Mass incarceration in the age of colorblindness*. New Press.

Allport, G. W. (1954). *The nature of prejudice*. Addison-Wesley

Almendarez, J. (2021, February 17). *No-knock warrants: Black Cincinnatians more often the focus as use decreases overall.* Cincinnati Public Radio. https://www.wvxu.org/local-news/2021-02-17/no-knock-warrants-black-cincinnatians-more-often-the-focus-as-use-decreases-overall

American Psychological Association Zero Tolerance Task Force. (2008). Are zero tolerance policies effective in the schools?: An evidentiary review and recommendations. *American Psychologist, 63*(9), 852–862.

Andersen, J. P., Di Nota, P. M., Boychuk, E. C., Schimmack, U., & Collins, P. I. (2023). Racial bias and lethal force errors among Canadian police officers. *Canadian Journal of Behavioural Science, 55*(2), 130-141.

Andersen, S. M., Moskowitz, G. B., Blair, I. V., & Nosek, B. A. (2007). Automatic thought. In A. W. Kruglanski & E. T. Higgins (Eds.), *Social psychology: Handbook of basic principles* (pp. 138–175). Guilford Press.

Anderson, R. E., & Stevenson, H. C. (2019). RECASTing racial stress and trauma: Theorizing the healing potential of racial socialization in families. *American Psychologist, 74*(1), 63–75.

Antrobus, E., Thompson, I., & Ariel, B. (2019). Procedural justice training for police recruits: Results of a randomized controlled trial. *Journal of Experimental Criminology, 15*, 29–53.

Arcia, E. (2006). Achievement and enrollment status of suspended students: Outcomes in a large, multicultural school district. *Education and Urban Society, 38*(3), 359–369.

Asher, J., & Horwitz, B. (2020, June 19). How do the police actually spend their time? *New York Times*. https://www.nytimes.com/2020/06/19/upshot/unrest-police-time-violent-crime.html

Association of Black Psychologists. (2016, July). *Familycare, communitycare, and selfcare tool kit: Healing in the face of cultural trauma*. https://d3i6fh83elv35t.cloudfront.net/newshour/app/uploads/2016/07/07-20-16-EEC-Trauma-Response-Community-and-SelfCare-TookKit-1.pdf

Aymer, S. R. (2016). "I can't breathe": A case study—Helping Black men cope with race-related trauma stemming from police killing and brutality. *Journal of Human Behavior in the Social Environment*, 26(3–4), 367–376.

Ayres, I., & Borowsky, J. (2008). *A study of racially disparate outcomes in the Los Angeles Police Department*. https://www.aclusocal.org/sites/default/files/wp-content/uploads/2015/09/11837125-LAPD-Racial-Profiling-Report-ACLU.pdf

Baldwin, J. (1955). *Notes of a native son*. Beacon Press.

Balto, S. (2019). *Occupied territory: Policing Black Chicago from red summer to Black power*. UNC Press Books.

Bandes, S. A., Pryor, M., Kerrison, E. M., & Goff, P. A. (2019). The mismeasure of Terry stops: Assessing the psychological and emotional harms of stop and frisk to individuals and communities. *Behavioral Sciences & the Law*, 37(2), 176–194.

Bass, S. (2001). Policing space, policing race: Social control imperatives and police discretionary decisions. *Social Justice*, 28(1), 156–176.

Baumgartner, F. R., Epp, D. A., & Shoub, K. (2018). *Suspect citizens: What 20 million traffic stops tell us about policing and race*. Cambridge University Press.

Beckett, K., Nyrop, K., & Pfingst, L. (2006). Race, drugs, and policing: Understanding disparities in drug delivery arrests. *Criminology*, 44(1), 105–137.

Biafora, F. A., Jr., Warheit, G. J., Zimmerman, R. S., Gil, A. G., Apospori, E., Taylor, D., & Vega, W. A. (1993). Racial mistrust and deviant behaviors among ethnically diverse Black adolescent boys *Journal of Applied Social Psychology*, 23(11), 891–910.

Bishop, D. M., Leiber, M., & Johnson, J. (2010). Contexts of decision making in the juvenile justice system: An organizational approach to understanding minority overrepresentation. *Youth Violence and Juvenile Justice*, 8(3), 213–233.

Blake, A. (2020, August 29). A slip in support for Black Lives Matter? *Washington Post*. https://www.washingtonpost.com/politics/2020/08/29/slip-support-black-lives-matter/

Bodenhausen, G. V. (1990). Stereotypes as judgmental heuristics: Evidence of circadian variations in discrimination. *Psychological Science*, 1(5), 319–322.

Boehme, H. M., Cann, D., & Isom, D. A. (2022). Citizens' perceptions of over- and under-policing: A look at race, ethnicity, and community characteristics. *Crime & Delinquency*, 68(1), 123–154.

Bonam, C. M., Nair Das, V., Coleman, B. R., & Salter, P. (2019). Ignoring history, denying racism: Mounting evidence for the Marley hypothesis and epistemologies of ignorance. *Social Psychological and Personality Science*, 10(2), 257–265.

Bor, J., Venkataramani, A. S., Williams, D. R., & Tsai, A. C. (2018). Police killings and their spillover effects on the mental health of Black Americans: A population-based, quasi-experimental study. *The Lancet*, 392(10144), 302–310.

Bradford, B. (2014). Policing and social identity: Procedural justice, inclusion and cooperation between police and public. *Policing and Society*, 24(1), 22–43.

Bradford, B., Murphy, K., & Jackson, J. (2014). Officers as mirrors: Policing, procedural justice and the (re)production of social identity. *British Journal of Criminology*, 54(4), 527–550.

Braga, A. A., Brunson, R. K., & Drakulich, K. M. (2019). Race, place, and effective policing. *Annual Review of Sociology*, 45(1), 535–555.

Brick, B. T., Taylor, T. J., & Esbensen, F. A. (2009). Juvenile attitudes towards the police: The importance of subcultural involvement and community ties. *Journal of Criminal Justice*, 37(5), 488–495.

Bronfenbrenner, U. (1977). Toward an experimental ecology of human development. *American Psychologist*, 32(7), 513–531.

Bronfenbrenner, U. (1979). *The ecology of human development: Experiments by nature and design*. Harvard University Press.

Bronfenbrenner, U., & Morris, P. A. (1998). The ecology of developmental processes. In W. Damon & R. M. Lerner (Eds.), *Handbook of child psychology: Theoretical models of human development* (pp. 993–1028). John Wiley & Sons.

Brooks, S. K., & Greenberg, N. (2021). Psychological impact of being wrongfully accused of criminal offences: A systematic literature review. *Medicine, Science and the Law*, 61(1), 44-54.

Brunson, R. K. (2007). "Police don't like Black people": African-American young men's accumulated police experiences. *Criminology & Public Policy*, 6(1), 71–101.

Brunson, R. K., & Gau, J. M. (2014). Race, place, and policing the inner-city. In M. D. Reisig & R. J. Kane (Eds.), *The Oxford handbook of police and policing* (pp. 362–382). Oxford University Press.

Brunson, R. K., & Miller, J. (2006a). Young Black men and urban policing in the United States. *British Journal of Criminology, 46*(4), 613–640.

Brunson, R. K., & Miller, J. (2006b). Gender, race, and urban policing: The experience of African American youths. *Gender & Society, 20*(4), 531–552.

Brunson, R. K., & Wade, B. A. (2019). "Oh hell no, we don't talk to police": Insights on the lack of cooperation in police investigations of urban gun violence. *Criminology & Public Policy, 18*(3), 623–648.

Brunson, R. K., & Weitzer, R. (2009). Police relations with Black and White youths in different urban neighborhoods. *Urban Affairs Review, 44*(6), 858–885.

Brunson, R. K., & Weitzer, R. (2011). Negotiating unwelcome police encounters: The intergenerational transmission of conduct norms. *Journal of Contemporary Ethnography, 40*(4), 425–456.

Bryant-Davis, T. (2007). Healing requires recognition: The case for race-based traumatic stress. *Counseling Psychologist, 35*(1), 135–143.

Bryant-Davis, T., Adams, T., Alejandre, A., & Gray, A. A. (2017). The trauma lens of police violence against racial and ethnic minorities. *Journal of Social Issues, 73*(4), 852–871.

Bryant-Davis, T., & Ocampo, C. (2006). A therapeutic approach to the treatment of racist-incident-based trauma. *Journal of Emotional Abuse, 6*(4), 1–22.

Burke, K. C. (2023, March). *The psychological mechanisms involved in police officer decision making during interactions with Black and White civilians.* [Data blitz.] American Psychology-Law Society Conference, Philadelphia, PA, United States.

Camp, N. P., Voigt, R., Jurafsky, D., & Eberhardt, J. L. (2021). The thin blue waveform: Racial disparities in officer prosody undermine institutional trust in the police. *Journal of Personality and Social Psychology, 121*(6), 1157–1171.

Carbado, D. W. (2002). (E)racing the Fourth Amendment. *Michigan Law Review, 100*(5), 946–1044.

Carlson, D. K. (2004, July 20). *Racial profiling seen as pervasive, unjust.* Gallup. http://www.gallup.com/poll/12406/Racial-ProfilingSeen-Pervasive-Unjust.aspx

Carlson, J. (2020). Police warriors and police guardians: Race, masculinity, and the construction of gun violence. *Social Problems, 67*(3), 399–417.

Carpenter, L. F., & Marshall, R. B. (2017). Walking while trans: Profiling of transgender women by law enforcement, and the problem of proof. *William & Mary Journal of Race, Gender, & Social Justice, 24*(1), 5–38.

Carr, P. J., Napolitano, L., & Keating, J. (2007). We never call the cops and here is why: A qualitative examination of legal cynicism in three Philadelphia neighborhoods. *Criminology, 45*(2), 445–480.

Cavanagh, C., & Cauffman, E. (2019). The role of rearrests in juvenile offenders' and their mothers' attitudes toward police. *Law and Human Behavior, 43*(3), 220–231.

Cavanagh, C., Fine, A., & Cauffman, E. (2020). How do adolescents develop legal cynicism? A test of legal socialization mechanisms among youth involved in the justice system. *Justice Quarterly,* 1–19.

Chavez-Dueñas, N. Y., Adames, H. Y., Perez-Chavez, J. G., & Salas, S. P. (2019). Healing ethno-racial trauma in Latinx immigrant communities: Cultivating hope, resistance, and action. *American Psychologist, 74*(1), 49–62.

Cheryan, S., & Monin, B. (2005). "Where are you really from?": Asian Americans and identity denial. *Journal of Personality and Social Psychology, 89*(5), 717–730.

Chou, T., Asnaani, A., & Hofmann, S. G. (2012). Perception of racial discrimination and psychopathology across three US ethnic minority groups. *Cultural Diversity and Ethnic Minority Psychology, 18*(1), 74–81.

Christian, S. (2009). *Children of incarcerated parents.* National Conference of State Legislatures.

Christle, C. A., Jolivette, K., & Nelson, C. M. (2007). School characteristics related to high school dropout rates. *Remedial and Special Education, 28*(6), 325–339.

Cobb, J. (2021, July 5). Derek Chauvin's trial and George Floyd's city. *New Yorker.* https://www.newyorker.com/magazine/2021/07/12/derek-chauvins-trial-and-george-floyds-city

Cokley, K., Hall-Clark, B., & Hicks, D. (2011). Ethnic minority-majority status and mental health: The mediating role of perceived discrimination. *Journal of Mental Health Counseling, 33*(3), 243–263.

Coles, S. M., & Pasek, J. (2020). Intersectional invisibility revisited: How group prototypes lead to the erasure and exclusion of Black women. *Translational Issues in Psychological Science, 6*(4), 314–324.

Coltrane, S., & Messineo, M. (2000). The perpetuation of subtle prejudice: Race and gender imagery in 1990s television advertising. *Sex Roles, 42*(5), 363–389.

Comas-Díaz, L., Hall, G. N., & Neville, H. A. (2019). Racial trauma: Theory, research, and healing: Introduction to the special issue. *American Psychologist, 74*(1), 1–5.

Correll, J., Park, B., Judd, C. M., & Wittenbrink, B. (2002). The police officer's dilemma: Using ethnicity to disambiguate potentially threatening individuals. *Journal of Personality and Social Psychology, 83*(6), 1314–1329.

Costello, K., & Hodson, G. (2011). Social dominance-based threat reactions to immigrants in need of assistance. *European Journal of Social Psychology, 41*(2), 220–231.

Cross, W. E., Jr., & Vandiver, B. J. (2001). Nigrescence theory and measurement: Introducing the Cross Racial Identity Scale (CRIS). In J. G. Ponterotto, J. M. Casas, L. A. Suzuki, & C. M. Alexander (Eds.), *Handbook of multicultural counseling* (2nd ed., pp. 371–393). Sage.

Crutchfield, R. D., Skinner, M. L., Haggerty, K. P., McGlynn, A., & Catalano, R. F. (2012). Racial disparity in police contacts. *Race and Justice, 2*(3), 179–202.

Cunneen, C., & Tauri, J. M. (2019). Indigenous peoples, criminology, and criminal justice. *Annual Review of Criminology, 2,* 359–381.

Davis, A. (2005). *Abolition democracy: Beyond empire, prisons, and torture.* Seven Stories Press.

DeHart, D. D., & Altshulter, S. J. (2009). Violence exposure among children of incarcerated mothers. *Child and Adolescent Social Work Journal, 26*(5), 467–479.

DeHart, D. D., Shapiro, C., & Clone, S. (2018). "The pill line is longer than the chow line": Impact of incarceration on prisoners and their families. *Prison Journal, 98*(2), 188–212.

Del Toro, J., Lloyd, T., Buchanan, K. S., Robins, S. J., Bencharit, L. Z., Smiedt, M. G., Reddy, K. S., Pougetg, E. R., Kerrison, E. M., & Goff, P. A. (2019). The criminogenic and psychological effects of police stops on adolescent Black and Latino boys. *Proceedings of the National Academy of Sciences, 116*(17), 8261–8268.

DeMarco, L. M., Dwyer, R. E., & Haynie, D. L. (2021). The accumulation of disadvantage: Criminal justice contact, credit, and debt in the transition to adulthood. *Criminology, 59*(3), 545–580.

Derlan, C. L., & Umaña-Taylor, A. J. (2015). Brief report: Contextual predictors of African American adolescents' ethnic-racial identity affirmation-belonging and resistance to peer pressure. *Journal of Adolescence, 41,* 1–6.

DeVylder, J. E., Jun, H., Fedina, L., Coleman, D., Anglin, D., Cogburn, C., Link, B., & Barth, R. P. (2018). Association of exposure to police violence with prevalence of mental health symptoms among urban residents in the United States. *JAMA Network Open, 1*(7), e184945. 10.1001/jamanetworkopen.2018.4945

Díaz, J. (2011). Immigration policy, criminalization and the growth of the immigration industrial complex: Restriction, expulsion, and eradication of the undocumented in the US. *Western Criminology Review, 12*(2), 35–54.

Dixon, T. L. (2008). Crime news and racialized beliefs: Understanding the relationship between local news viewing and perceptions of African Americans and crime. *Journal of Communication, 58*(1), 106–125.

Dixon, T. L., Schell, T. L., Giles, H., & Drogos, K. L. (2008). The influence of race in police–civilian interactions: A content analysis of videotaped interactions taken during Cincinnati police traffic stops. *Journal of Communication, 58*(3), 530–549.

Dovidio, J. F., & Gaertner, S. L. (2000). Aversive racism and selection decisions: 1989 and 1999. *Psychological Science, 11*(4), 315–319.

Du Bois, W. E. B. (Ed.). (1935). *Black Reconstruction in America: Toward a history of the part which black folk played in the attempt to reconstruct democracy in America, 1860–1880.* Routledge.

Dukes, K. N., & Kahn, K. B. (2017). What social science research says about police violence against racial and ethnic minorities: Understanding the antecedents and consequences—An introduction. *Journal of Social Issues, 73*(4), 690–700.

Eberhardt, J. L. (2020). *Biased: Uncovering the hidden prejudice that shapes what we see, think, and do.* Penguin Books.

Eberhardt, J. L., Goff, P. A., Purdie, V. J., & Davies, P. G. (2004). Seeing Black: Race, crime, and visual processing. *Journal of Personality and Social Psychology, 87*(6), 876–893.

Edwards, F., Lee, H., & Esposito, M. (2019). Risk of being killed by police use of force in the United States by age, race–ethnicity, and sex. *Proceedings of the National Academy of Sciences, 116*(34), 16793–16798.

Engel, R. S., & Johnson, R. (2006). Toward a better understanding of racial and ethnic disparities in search and seizure rates. *Journal of Criminal Justice, 34*(6), 605–617.

Epp, C. R., Maynard-Moody, S., & Haider-Markel, D. P. (2014). *Pulled over: How police stops define race and citizenship.* University of Chicago Press.

Ericson, R. D., & Eckberg, D. A. (2016). Racial disparity in juvenile diversion: The impact of focal concerns and organizational coupling. *Race and Justice, 6*(1), 35–56.

Esbensen, F. A., & Carson, D. C. (2012). Who are the gangsters? An examination of the age, race/ethnicity, sex, and immigration status of self-reported gang members in a seven-city study of American youth. *Journal of Contemporary Criminal Justice, 28*(4), 465–481.

Executive Order No. 13769, 3 C. F. R. 8977-8982 (2017).

Fader, J. J. (2013). *Falling back.* Rutgers University Press.

Fader, J. J. (2021). "I don't have time for drama": Managing risk and uncertainty through network avoidance. *Criminology, 59*(2), 291–317.

Fagan, J. A., Braga, A. A., Brunson, R. K., & Pattavina, A. (2016). Stops and stares: Street stops, surveillance, and race in the new policing. *Fordham Urban Law Journal, 43*, 539–614.

Fagan, J. A., & Davies, G. (2000). Street stops and broken windows: Terry, race, and disorder in New York City. *Fordham Urban Law Journal, 28*(2), 457–504.

Fagan, J. A., Geller, A., Davies, G., & West, V. (2010). Street stops and broken windows revisited. In S. K. Rice & M. D. White (Eds.), *Race, ethnicity, and policing* (pp. 309–348). New York University Press.

Farris, E. M., & Holman, M. R. (2017). All politics is local? County sheriffs and localized policies of immigration enforcement. *Political Research Quarterly, 70*(1), 142–154.

Federal Interagency Forum on Child and Family Statistics. (2017). *America's children: Key national indicators of child well-being, 2017*. U.S. Government Printing Office.

Ferguson, G. M., Eales, L., Gillespie, S., & Leneman, K. (2022). The Whiteness pandemic behind the racism pandemic: Familial Whiteness socialization in Minneapolis following #GeorgeFloyd's murder. *American Psychologist 77*(3), 344–361.

Figures, K. D., & Legewie, J. (2019). Visualizing police exposure by race, gender, and age in New York City. *Socius, 5*, 1-2.

Fine, A. D., Amemiya, J., Frick, P., Steinberg, L., & Cauffman, E. (2021). Perceptions of police legitimacy and bias from ages 13 to 22 among Black, Latino, and White justice-involved youth. *Law and Human Behavior, 45*(3), 243–255.

Fine, A. D., & Cauffman, E. (2015). Race and justice system attitude formation during the transition to adulthood. *Journal of Developmental and Life-Course Criminology, 1*(4), 325–349.

Fine, A. D., Cavanagh, C., Donley, S., Frick, P. J., Steinberg, L., & Cauffman, E. (2017). Is the effect of justice system attitudes on recidivism stable after youths' first arrest? Race and legal socialization among first-time youth offenders. *Law and Human Behavior, 41*(2), 146–158.

Fine, A. D., Moule, R., Trinkner, R., Frick, P. J., Steinberg, L., & Cauffman, E. (2022). Legal socialization and individual belief in the code of the streets: A theoretical integration and longitudinal test. *Justice Quarterly, 39*(6), 1310-1331).

Fine, A. D., Padilla, K. E., & Tom, K. E. (2022). Police legitimacy: Identifying developmental trends and whether youths' perceptions can be changed. *Journal of Experimental Criminology, 18*, 67-87.

Fine, M., & Cross, W. E., Jr. (2016). Critical race, psychology, and social policy: Refusing damage, cataloging oppression, and documenting desire. In A. N. Alvarez, C. T. H. Liang, & H. A. Neville (Eds.), *The cost of racism for people of color: Contextualizing experiences of discrimination* (pp. 273–294). American Psychological Association.

First, J. M., Danforth, L., Frisby, C. M., Warner, B. R., Ferguson, M. W., Jr., & Houston, J. B. (2020). Posttraumatic stress related to the killing of Michael Brown and resulting civil unrest in Ferguson, Missouri: Roles of protest engagement, media use, race, and resilience. *Journal of the Society for Social Work and Research, 11*(3), 369–391.

Florida v. Bostick, 501 U.S. 429 (1991).

Floyd v. City of New York, 08 Civ. 2274 (SAS), U.S. Dist. LEXIS 113205, (S.D.N.Y., August 12, 2013).

Fowers, A., & Wan, W. (2020, June 12). Depression and anxiety spiked among Black Americans after George Floyd's death. *Washington Post*. https://www.washingtonpost.com/health/2020/06/12/mental-health-george-floyd-census/

Frabutt, J. M., Walker, A. M., & MacKinnon-Lewis, C. (2002). Racial socialization messages and the quality of mother/child interactions in African American families. *Journal of Early Adolescence, 22*(2), 200–217.

Galovski, T. E., Peterson, Z. D., Beagley, M. C., Strasshofer, D. R., Held, P., & Fletcher, T. D. (2016). Exposure to violence during Ferguson protests: Mental health effects for law enforcement and community members. *Journal of Traumatic Stress, 29*(4), 283–292.

Gatto, J., Dambrun, M., Kerbrat, C., & De Oliveira, P. (2010). Prejudice in the police. On the processes underlying the effects of selection and group socialisation. *European Journal of Social Psychology, 40*(2), 252–269.

Gau, J. M., & Brunson, R. K. (2010). Procedural justice and order maintenance policing: A study of inner-city young men's perceptions of police legitimacy. *Justice Quarterly, 27*(2), 255–279.

Geistman, J., & Smith, B. W. (2007). Juvenile attitudes toward police: A national study. *Journal of Crime and Justice, 30*(2), 27–51.

Gelman, A., Fagan, J., & Kiss, A. (2007). An analysis of the New York City police department's "stop-and-frisk" policy in the context of claims of racial bias. *Journal of the American Statistical Association, 102*(479), 813–823.

Ghavami, N., & Peplau, L. A. (2013). An intersectional analysis of gender and ethnic stereotypes: Testing three hypotheses. *Psychology of Women Quarterly, 37*(1), 113–127.

Gibbons, F. X., Fleischli, M. E., Gerrard, M., Simons, R. L., Weng, C.-Y., & Gibson, L. P. (2020). The impact of early racial discrimination on illegal behavior, arrest, and incarceration among African Americans. *American Psychologist, 75*(7), 952–968.

Gilberstadt, H. (2020, June 5). *A month before George Floyd's death, Black and White Americans differed sharply in confidence in the police*. Pew Research Center. https://www.pewresearch.org/fact-tank/2020/06/05/a-month-before-george-floyds-death-black-and-white-americans-differed-sharply-in-confidence-in-the-police/

Glascock, J. (2003). Gender, race, and aggression in newer TV networks' primetime programming. *Communication Quarterly*, *51*(1), 90–100.

Glaze, L. E., & Maruschak, L. M. (2008). *Parents in prison and their minor children*. U.S. Department of Justice: Office of Justice Programs. https://bjs.ojp.gov/content/pub/pdf/pptmc.pdf

Goel, S., Rao, J. M., & Shroff, R. (2016). Precinct or prejudice? Understanding racial disparities in New York City's stop-and-frisk policy. *Annals of Applied Statistics*, *10*(1), 365–394.

Goff, P. A., Epstein, L. M., & Reddy, K. S. (2013). Crossing the line of legitimacy: The impact of cross-deputization policy on crime reporting. *Psychology, Public Policy, and Law*, *19*(2), 250–258.

Goff, P. A., Jackson, M. C., Leone, D., Lewis, B. A., Culotta, C. M., & DiTomasso, N. A. (2014). The essence of innocence: Consequences of dehumanizing Black children. *Journal of Personality and Social Psychology*, *106*(4), 526–545.

Goff, P. A., Lloyd, T., Geller, A., Raphael, S., & Glaser, J. (2016). *The science of justice: Race, arrests, and police use of force*. Center for Policing Equity. https://policingequity.org/images/pdfs-doc/CPE_SoJ_Race-Arrests-UoF_2016-07-08-1130.pdf

Goff, P. A., & Rau, H. (2020). Predicting bad policing: Theorizing burdensome and racially disparate policing through the lenses of social psychology and routine activities. *Annals of the American Academy of Political and Social Science*, *687*(1), 67–88.

Goff, P. A., Thomas, M. A., & Jackson, M. C. (2008). "Ain't I a woman?": Towards an intersectional approach to person perception and group-based harms. *Sex Roles*, *59*(5), 392–403.

Goldstein, N. E. S., Kreimer, R., Guo, S., Le, T., Cole, L. M., NeMoyer, A., Burke, S., Kikuchi, G., Thomas, K., & Zhang, F. (2021). Preventing school-based arrest and recidivism through prearrest diversion: Outcomes of the Philadelphia police school diversion program. *Law and Human Behavior*, *45*(2), 165–178.

Gonzales, R. G., & Chavez, L. R. (2012). "Awakening to a nightmare," abjectivity and illegality in the lives of undocumented 1.5-generation Latino immigrants in the United States. *Current Anthropology*, *53*(3), 255–281.

Gotsch, K. (2018). Families and mass incarceration. In T. LaLiberte, K. Barry, & K. Walthour (Eds.), *CW360: Criminal Justice Involvement of Families in Child Welfare* (p. 7). Center for Advanced Studies in Child Welfare, University of Minnesota. https://cascw.umn.edu/wp-content/uploads/2018/04/CW360_Spring2018_WebTemp.pdf

Govorun, O., & Payne, B. K. (2006). Ego—depletion and prejudice: Separating automatic and controlled components. *Social Cognition*, *24*(2), 111–136.

Graham v. Connor, 490 U.S. 386 (1989).

Graham, S., & Lowery, B. S. (2004). Priming unconscious racial stereotypes about adolescent offenders. *Law and Human Behavior*, *28*(5), 483–504.

Granot, Y., Tyler, T. R., & Durkin, A. (2021). Legal socialization during adolescence: The emerging role of school resource officers. *Journal of Social Issues*, *77*(2), 414–436.

Greenberg, B. S., Mastro, D., & Brand, J. E. (2002). Minorities and the mass media: Television into the 21st century. In J. Bryant, D. Zillmann, J. Bryant, & M. B. Oliver (Eds.), *Media effects: Advances in theory and research* (pp. 343–362). Routledge.

Greenwood, C. R., Horton, B. T., & Utley, C. A. (2002). Academic engagement: Current perspectives on research and practice. *School Psychology Review*, *31*(3), 328–350.

Hagan, J., & Albonetti, C. (1982). Race, class, and the perception of criminal injustice in America. *American Journal of Sociology*, *88*(2), 329–355.

Hagan, J., Shedd, C., & Payne, M. R. (2005). Race, ethnicity, and youth perceptions of criminal injustice. *American Sociological Review*, *70*(3), 381–407.

Hall, A. V., Hall, E. V., & Perry, J. L. (2016). Black and blue: Exploring racial bias and law enforcement in the killings of unarmed Black male civilians. *American Psychologist*, *71*(3), 175–186.

Harlow v. Fitzgerald, 457 U.S. 800 (1982).

Harrell, E., & Davis, E. (2020). *Contacts between police and the public, 2018*. U.S. Department of Justice, Office of Justice Programs. https://bjs.ojp.gov/content/pub/pdf/cbpp18st.pdf

Harrison, P. M., & Beck, A. J. (2006). *Prison and jail inmates at midyear 2005*. U.S. Department of Justice, Bureau of Justice Statistics. https://bjs.ojp.gov/library/publications/prison-and-jail-inmates-midyear-2005

Hetey, R., Monin, B., Maitreyi, A., & Eberhardt, J. (2016). *Data for change: A statistical analysis of police stops, searches, handcuffings, and arrests in Oakland, California*. Stanford University Social Psychological Answers to Real-World Questions. https://sparq.stanford.edu/data-change-0

Hinton, E., & Cook, D. (2021). The mass criminalization of Black Americans: A historical overview. *Annual Review of Criminology*, *4*, 261–286.

Hsia, H. M., Bridges, G. S., & McHale, R. (2004). *Disproportionate minority confinement: 2002 update*. U.S. Department of Justice, Office of Justice Programs, Office of Juvenile Justice and Delinquency Prevention.

Hudson, C. S., & Ruth, L. (2018). *The Latino-White education gap in Connecticut: Indicators of inequality in access and outcomes*. Connecticut Voices for Children. https://ctvoices.org/publication/the-latino-white-education-gap-in-connecticut-indicators-of-inequality-in-access-and-outcomes/

Hughes, D. L. (2003). Correlates of African American and Latino parents' messages to children about ethnicity and race: A comparative study of racial socialization. *American Journal of Community Psychology, 31*(1–2), 15–33.

Hughes, D. L., & Chen, L. (1999). The nature of parents' race-related communications to children: A developmental perspective. In L. Balter & C. S. Tamis-LeMonda (Eds.), *Child psychology: A handbook of contemporary issues* (pp. 467–490). Psychology Press.

Hughes, D. L., & DuMont, K. (2002). Using focus groups to facilitate culturally anchored research. In T. A. Revenson, A. R. D'Augelli, S. E. French, D. L. Hughes, D. Livert, E. Seidman, M. Shinn, & H. Yoshikawa (Eds.), *Ecological research to promote social change* (pp. 257–289). Springer.

Hughes, D. L., & Johnson, D. (2001). Correlates in children's experiences of parents' racial socialization behaviors. *Journal of Marriage and Family, 63*(4), 981–995.

Hughes, D. L., Rodriguez, J., Smith, E. P., Johnson, D. J., Stevenson, H. C., & Spicer, P. (2006). Parents' ethnic-racial socialization practices: A review of research and directions for future study. *Developmental Psychology, 42*(5), 747–770.

Hullenaar, K. L., Kurpiel, A., & Ruback, R. B. (2021). Youth violent offending in school and out: Reporting, arrest, and the school-to-prison pipeline. *Justice Quarterly, 38*(7), 1–23.

Hunt, J. S. (2015). Race in the justice system. In B. L. Cutler & P. A. Zapf (Eds.), *APA handbook of forensic psychology: Criminal investigation, adjudication, and sentencing outcomes* (Vol. 2, pp. 125–161). American Psychological Association.

Hurst, Y. G., Frank, J., & Browning, S. L. (2000). The attitudes of juveniles toward the police: A comparison of Black and White youth. *Policing: An International Journal of Police Strategies & Management, 23*(1), 37–53.

Iguchi, M. Y., Bell, J., Ramchand, R. N., & Fain, T. (2005). How criminal system racial disparities may translate into health disparities. *Journal of Health Care for the Poor and Underserved, 16*(4), 48–56.

Iguchi, M. Y., London, J. A., Forge, N. G., Hickman, L., Fain, T., & Riehman, K. (2002). Elements of well-being affected by criminalizing the drug user. *Public Health Reports, 117*(Suppl 1), S146–S150.

Immigration Act of 1924, Pub. L. No. 68–139, 43 Stat. 153 (1924).

Ito, T. A., Friedman, N. P., Bartholow, B. D., Correll, J., Loersch, C., Altamirano, L. J., & Miyake, A. (2015). Toward a comprehensive understanding of executive cognitive function in implicit racial bias. *Journal of Personality and Social Psychology, 108*(2), 187–218.

Jacoby, S. F., Richmond, T. S., Holena, D. N., & Kaufman, E. J. (2018). A safe haven for the injured? Urban trauma care at the intersection of healthcare, law enforcement, and race. *Social Science & Medicine, 199*, 115–122.

James, L. (2018). The stability of implicit racial bias in police officers. *Police Quarterly, 21*(1), 30–52.

James, L., James, S. M., & Vila, B. J. (2016). The reverse racism effect: Are cops more hesitant to shoot Black than White suspects? *Criminology & Public Policy, 15*(2), 457–479.

Jindal, M., Mistry, K. B., Trent, M., McRae, A., & Thornton, R. L. (2021). Police exposures and the health and well-being of Black youth in the US: A systematic review. *JAMA Pediatrics, 176*(1), 78–88.

Johnson, D., Wilson, D. B., Maguire, E. R., & Lowrey-Kinberg, B. V. (2017) Race and perceptions of police: Experimental results on the impact of procedural (in)justice. *Justice Quarterly, 34*(7), 1184–1212.

Johnson, K. R. (1998). Race, the immigration laws, and domestic race relations: A "magic mirror" into the heart of darkness. *Indiana Law Journal, 73*(4), 1111–1159.

Johnson, K. R. (2009). The intersection of race and class in U.S. immigration law and enforcement. *Law & Contemporary Problems, 72*, 1–36.

Johnson, S. E., & Richeson, J. A. (2009). Solo status revisited: Examining racial group differences in the self-regulatory consequences of self-presenting as a racial solo. *Journal of Experimental Social Psychology, 45*(4), 1032–1035.

Jones, S. C., Anderson, R. E., Gaskin-Wasson, A. L., Sawyer, B. A., Applewhite, K., & Metzger, I. W. (2020). From "crib to coffin": Navigating coping from racism-related stress throughout the lifespan of Black Americans. *American Journal of Orthopsychiatry, 90*(2), 267-282.

Jones-Brown, D. D. (2000). Debunking the myth of officer friendly: How African American males experience community policing. *Journal of Contemporary Criminal Justice, 16*(2), 209–229.

Kahn, K. B., & Davies, P. G. (2011). Differentially dangerous? Phenotypic racial stereotypicality increases implicit bias among ingroup and outgroup members. *Group Processes & Intergroup Relations, 14*(4), 569–580.

Kahn, K. B., Goff, P. A., Lee, J. K., & Motamed, D. (2016). Protecting whiteness: White phenotypic racial stereotypicality reduces police use of force. *Social Psychological and Personality Science, 7*(5), 403–411.

Kahn, K. B., & Martin, K. D. (2016). Policing and race: Disparate treatment, perceptions, and policy responses. *Social Issues and Policy Review*, *10*(1), 82–121.

Kahn, K. B., McMahon, J. M., & Stewart, G. (2018) Misinterpreting danger? Stereotype threat, pre-attack indicators, and police-citizen interactions. *Journal of Police and Criminal Psychology*, *33*, 45–54.

Kahneman, D. (2011). *Thinking, fast and slow*. Macmillan.

Kalt, B. C. (2003). The exclusion of felons from jury service. *American University Law Review*, *53*, 65–190.

Kampfner, C. J. (1995). Post-traumatic stress reactions in children of imprisoned mothers. In K. Gabel & D. Johnston (Eds.), *Children of incarcerated parents* (pp. 89–102). Lexington Books.

Karma, R. (2020, July 31). *We train police to be warriors — and then send them out to be social workers*. Vox. https://www.vox.com/2020/7/31/21334190/what-police-do-defund-abolish-police-reform-training

Kendi, I. X. (2016). *Stamped from the beginning: The definitive history of racist ideas in America*. Nation Books.

Kopacz, M. A., & Lawton, B. L. (2013). Talking about the YouTube Indians: Images of Native Americans and viewer comments on a viral video site. *Howard Journal of Communications*, *24*(1), 17–37.

Kovera, M. B. (2019). Racial disparities in the criminal justice system: Prevalence, causes, and a search for solutions. *Journal of Social Issues*, *75*(4), 1139–1164.

Kramer, R., & Remster, B. (2018). Stop, frisk, and assault? Racial disparities in police use of force during investigatory stops. *Law & Society Review*, *52*(4), 960–993.

Kreuger, J. (1996). Personal beliefs and cultural stereotypes about race characteristics. *Journal of Personality and Social Psychology*, *71*, 536-548.

Kteily, N., Bruneau, E., Waytz, A., & Cotterill, S. (2015). The ascent of man: Theoretical and empirical evidence for blatant dehumanization. *Journal of Personality and Social Psychology*, *109*(5), 901–931.

Kunda, Z., & Sherman-Williams, B. (1993). Stereotypes and the construal of individuating information. *Personality and Social Psychology Bulletin*, *19*(1), 90-99.

Lacoe, J. R. (2015). Unequally safe: The race gap in school safety. *Youth Violence and Juvenile Justice*, *13*(2), 143–168.

LaMotte, V., Ouellette, K., Sanderson, J., Anderson, S. A., Kosutic, I., Griggs, J., & Garcia, M. (2010). Effective police interactions with youth: A program evaluation. *Police Quarterly*, *13*(2), 161–179.

Lau, K. S., Rosenman, M. B., Wiehe, S. E., Tu, W., & Aalsma, M. C. (2018). Race/ethnicity, and behavioral health status: First arrest and outcomes in a large sample of juvenile offenders. *Journal of Behavioral Health Services & Research*, *45*(2), 237–251.

LeCount, R. J. (2017). More Black than blue? Comparing the racial attitudes of police to citizens. *Sociological Forum*, *32*(S1), 1051-1072.

Lee, J. M., Steinberg, L., & Piquero, A. R. (2010). Ethnic identity and attitudes toward the police among African American juvenile offenders. *Journal of Criminal Justice*, *38*(4), 781–789.

Lee, J. M., Steinberg, L., Piquero, A. R., & Knight, G. P. (2011). Identity-linked perceptions of the police among African American juvenile offenders: A developmental perspective. *Journal of Youth and Adolescence*, *40*(1), 23–37.

Levchak, P. J. (2017). Do precinct characteristics influence stop-and-frisk in New York City? A multi-level analysis of post-stop outcomes. *Justice Quarterly*, *34*(3), 377–406.

Levchak, P. J. (2021). Stop-and-frisk in New York City: Estimating racial disparities in post-stop outcomes. *Journal of Criminal Justice*, *73*, 101784.

Levy, S. R., Stroessner, S. J., & Dweck, C. S. (1998). Stereotype formation and endorsement: The role of implicit theories. *Journal of Personality and Social Psychology*, *74*(6), 1421–1436.

Lewis, M. (2007). Self-conscious emotional development. In J. L. Tracy, R. W. Robins, & J. P. Tangney (Eds.), *The self-conscious emotions: Theory and research* (pp. 134–149). Guilford Press.

Lind, E., & Tyler, T. (1988). *The social psychology of procedural justice*. Plenum Press.

Lipscomb, A. E., Emeka, M., Bracy, I., Stevenson, V., Lira, A., Gomez, Y. B., & Riggins, J. (2019). Black male hunting! A phenomenological study exploring the secondary impact of police induced trauma on the Black man's psyche in the United States. *Journal of Sociology*, *7*(1), 11–18.

Lofstrom, M., & Raphael, S. (2016). Crime, the criminal justice system, and socioeconomic inequality. *Journal of Economic Perspectives*, *30*(2), 103–126.

Ludwig, J. (2003, May 13). *Americans see racial profiling as widespread*. Gallup. http://www.gallup.com/poll/8389/Americans-SeeRacial-Profiling-Widespread.aspx

Ma, D. S., Correll, J., Wittenbrink, B., Bar-Anan, Y., Sriram, N., & Nosek, B. A. (2013). When fatigue turns deadly: The association between fatigue and racial bias in the decision to shoot. *Basic and Applied Social Psychology*, *35*(6), 515–524.

Macrae, C. N., Milne, A. B., & Bodenhausen, G. V. (1994). Stereotypes as energy-saving devices: A peek inside the cognitive toolbox. *Journal of Personality and Social Psychology*, *66*(1), 37–47.

Malik, R. (2017). *New data reveal 250 preschoolers are suspended or expelled every day*. Center for American Progress. https://www.americanprogress.org/issues/early-childhood/news/2017/11/06/442280/new-data-reveal-250-preschoolers-suspended-expelled-every-day/

Mann, S., & Vrij, A. (2006). Police officers' judgements of veracity, tenseness, cognitive load and attempted behavioural control in real-life police interviews. *Psychology, Crime & Law, 12*(3), 307–319.

Marin, G. (1984). Stereotyping Hispanics: The differential effect of research method, label, and degree of contact. *International Journal of Intercultural Relations, 8*(1), 17–27.

Markus, H. R., & Kitayama, S. (2003). Models of agency: Sociocultural diversity in the construction of action. In V. Murphy-Berman & J. J. Berman (Eds.), *Cross-cultural differences in perspectives on the self* (pp. 18–74). University of Nebraska Press.

Mastro, D. E. (2009). Racial/ethnic stereotyping and the media. In R. L. Nabi & M. B. Oliver (Eds.), *The SAGE handbook of media processes and effects* (pp. 377–391). Sage Publications.

Mastro, D. E., & Behm-Morawitz, E. (2005). Latino representation on primetime television. *Journalism & Mass Communication Quarterly, 82*(1), 110–130.

Mazerolle, L., Antrobus, E., Bennett, S., & Tyler, T. R. (2013). Shaping citizen perceptions of police legitimacy: A randomized field trial of procedural justice. *Criminology, 51*(1), 33–63.

McCarthy, M., Trinkner, R., & Goff, P. A. (2021). The threat of appearing racist: Stereotype threat and support for coercion among Australian police officers. *Criminal Justice and Behavior, 48*(6), 1–15.

McFarland, M. J., Geller, A., & McFarland, C. (2019). Police contact and health among urban adolescents: The role of perceived injustice. *Social Science & Medicine, 238*, 112487.

McGlynn-Wright, A., Crutchfield, R. D., Skinner, M. L., & Haggerty, K. P. (2022). The usual, racialized, suspects: The consequence of police contacts with Black and White youth on adult arrest. *Social Problems, 69*(2), 299-315.

McKown, C., & Weinstein, R. S. (2003). The development and consequences of stereotype consciousness in middle childhood. *Child Development, 74*(2), 498–515.

McLean, K., Wolfe, S. E., & Pratt, T. C. (2019). Legitimacy and the life course: An age-graded examination of changes in legitimacy attitudes over time. *Journal of Research in Crime and Delinquency, 56*(1), 42–83.

McLean, K., Wolfe, S. E., Rojek, J., Alpert, G. P., & Smith, M. R. (2020). Police officers as warriors or guardians: Empirical reality or intriguing rhetoric? *Justice Quarterly, 37*(6), 1096–1118.

Meares, T. L., & Prowse, G. (2021). Policing as a public good: Reflecting on the term "to protect and serve" as dialogues of abolition. *Florida Law Review, 73*(1), 1-30

Mencarini, M., Costello, D., & Duvall, T. (2020, November 29). Louisville police's "no-knock" warrants most often targeted Black residents in the West End. *Courier Journal*. https://www.courier-journal.com/story/news/local/breonna-taylor/2020/11/29/louisville-police-no-knock-warrants-usually-targeted-black-residents/6069189002/

Menjívar, C., Gómez Cervantes, A., & Alvord, D. (2018). The expansion of "crimmigration," mass detention, and deportation. *Sociology Compass, 12*(4), e12573.

Miller, K. M. (2014). Maternal criminal justice involvement and co-occurring mental health and substance abuse problems: Examining moderation of sex and race on children's mental health. *Children and Youth Services Review, 37*, 71–80.

Miller, K. M., & Bank, L. (2013). Moderating effects of race on internalizing and externalizing behaviors among children of criminal justice and child welfare involved mothers. *Children and Youth Services Review, 35*(3), 472–481.

Miller, K. M., & Crain, C. (2020). The impact of parental criminal justice involvement on children of color. In M. C. Stevenson, B. L. Bottoms, & K. C. Burke (Eds.), *The legacy of racism for children: Psychology, law, and public policy* (pp. 111–128). Oxford University Press.

Miller, K. M., Orellana, E. R., Johnson, A. B., Krase, K., & Anderson-Nathe, B. (2013). Maternal criminal justice and child welfare involvement: Associations between risk exposures and childhood mental health. *Social Work Research, 37*(4), 1–12.

Morrow, W. J., White, M. D., & Fradella, H. F. (2017). After the stop: Exploring the racial/ethnic disparities in police use of force during Terry stops. *Police Quarterly, 20*(4), 367–396.

Muhammad, K. G. (2019). *The condemnation of Blackness: Race, crime, and the making of modern urban America, with a new preface*. Harvard University Press.

Murch, D. (2015). Crack in Los Angeles: Crisis, militarization, and Black response to the late twentieth-century War on Drugs. *Journal of American History, 102*(1), 162–173.

Murphy, M. C., Carter, E. R., Emerson, K. T., & Cheryan, S. (2020). The long reach of prejudiced places? Stereotype expectations and motivation to pursue education among previously- and never-incarcerated black men. *Self and Identity, 19*(4), 456–472.

Murray, J., Farrington, D. P., & Sekol, I. (2012). Children's antisocial behavior, mental health, drug use, and educational performance after parental incarceration: A systematic review and meta-analysis. *Psychological Bulletin, 138*(2), 175–210.

Museum of Tolerance. (n.d.). *Perspectives on profiling*. https://www.museumoftolerance.com/for-professionals/programs-workshops/tools-for-tolerance-for-law-enforcement-and-criminal-justice/racial-profiling/perspectives-on-profiling.html

Nadal, K. L., Davidoff, K. C., Allicock, N., Serpe, C. R., & Erazo, T. (2017). Perceptions of police, racial profiling, and psychological outcomes: A mixed methodological study. *Journal of Social Issues, 73*(4), 808–830.

Najdowski, C. J. (2011). Stereotype threat in criminal interrogations: Why innocent Black suspects are at risk for confessing falsely. *Psychology, Public Policy, and Law, 17*(4), 562–591.

Najdowski, C. J. (2014). Interactions between African Americans and police officers: How cultural stereotypes create a wrongful conviction pipeline for African Americans. In A. D. Redlich, J. R. Acker, R. J. Norris, & C. L. Bonventre (Eds.), *Examining wrongful convictions: Stepping back, moving forward* (pp. 55–70). Carolina Academic Press.

Najdowski, C. J. (2018, March). *Investigating racial stereotypes as a factor contributing to miscarriages of justice*. [Invited address in acceptance of the Saleem Shah Early Career Award.] American Psychology-Law Society Conference, Memphis, TN, United States.

Najdowski, C. J., Anderson, M., Matyasovszky, G. A., Bernstein, K. M., & Solomon, P. A. (2023). *Racial differences in perceptions of agency and freedom in police encounters*. Manuscript in preparation.

Najdowski, C. J., Bottoms, B. L., & Goff, P. A. (2015). Stereotype threat and racial differences in citizens' experiences of police encounters. *Law and Human Behavior, 39*, 463–477.

Najdowski, C. J., Bottoms, B. L., Goff, P. A., & Spanton, J. (2012, March 14–17). *Do Hispanics experience stereotype threat in police encounters?* [Poster presentation.] American Psychology-Law Society Conference, San Juan, Puerto Rico.

Najdowski, C. J., & Goff, P. A. (2022). Towards a psychological science of abolition democracy: Insights for improving theory and research on race and public safety. *Social Issues and Policy Review, 16*(1), 33–78.

Nance, J. P. (2016). Students, police, and the school-to-prison pipeline. *Washington University Law Review, 93*, 919–987.

National Academies of Sciences, Engineering, and Medicine. (2018). *Proactive policing: Effects on crime and communities*. National Academies Press.

National Center for Education Statistics. (2018). *Safety and security practices at public schools*. https://nces.ed.gov/programs/coe/indicator/a19

National Registry of Exonerations. (2013). *Exonerations in 2013*. https://www.law.umich.edu/special/exoneration/documents/exonerations_in_2013_report.pdf

Naturalization Act of 1790, Pub. L. No. 1–31, 1 Stat. 103 (1790).

New York Civil Liberties Union. (2013). *NYPD stop-and-frisk activity in 2012*. http://www.nyclu.org/files/publications/2012_Report_NYCLU_0.pdf

Nguyen, H., & Reuter, P. (2012). How risky is marijuana possession? Considering the role of age, race, and gender. *Crime & Delinquency, 58*(6), 879–910.

Nix, J., Campbell, B. A., Byers, E. H., & Alpert, G. P. (2017). A bird's eye view of civilians killed by police in 2015: Further evidence of implicit bias. *Criminology & Public Policy, 16*(1), 309–340.

Northwestern University Center for Public Safety. (2008). *Traffic stops statistics study: 2007 annual report*.

Novich, M., & Zduniak, A. (2021). Violence trending: How socially transmitted content of police misconduct impacts reactions toward police among American youth. In J. Bailey, A. Flynn, & N. Henry (Eds.), *The Emerald international handbook of technology facilitated violence and abuse* (pp. 271-288). Emerald Publishing Limited.

Oakland Police Department. (n.d.). *2016–2018 racial impact report*. https://cao-94612.s3.amazonaws.com/documents/OPD-Racial-Impact-Report-2016-2018-Final-16Apr19.pdf

Osborne, D., Satherley, N., Little, T. D., & Sibley, C. G. (2021). Authoritarianism and social dominance predict annual increases in generalized prejudice. *Social Psychological and Personality Science, 12*(7), 1136–1145.

Pager, D. (2003). The mark of a criminal record. *American Journal of Sociology, 108*(5), 937–975.

Payne, B. K. (2005). Conceptualizing control in social cognition: How executive functioning modulates the expression of automatic stereotyping. *Journal of Personality and Social Psychology, 89*(4), 488–503.

Peck, J. H. (2015). Minority perceptions of the police: A state-of-the-art review. *Policing: An International Journal of Police Strategies & Management, 38*(1), 173–203.

Peeples, L. (2020). Brutality and racial bias: What the data say. *Nature, 583*(7814), 22–24. https://www.nature.com/articles/d41586-020-01846-z

Perry, S., Skinner-Dorkenoo, A., Abaied, J., & Waters, S. (2022). Applying what evidence we have: Support for having race conversations in White US families. *Perspectives on Psychological Science, 17*(3), 895–900.

Petras, H., Masyn, K. E., Buckley, J. A., Ialongo, N. S., & Kellam, S. (2011). Who is most at risk for school removal? A multilevel discrete-time survival analysis of individual- and context-level influences. *Journal of Educational Psychology, 103*(1), 223–237.

Petteruti, A. (2011). *Education under arrest: The case against police in schools* (Vol. 1). Justice Policy Institute. https://www.ojp.gov/ncjrs/virtual-library/abstracts/education-under-arrest-case-against-police-schools

Peyton, K., Sierra-Arévalo, M., & Rand, D. G. (2019). A field experiment on community policing and police legitimacy. *Proceedings of the National Academy of Sciences, 116*(40), 19894–19898.

Phillips, S. D., & Erkanli, A. (2007). Differences in patterns of maternal arrest and the parent, family and child problems encountered in working with families. *Children and Youth Services Review, 30*(2), 157–172.

Phillips, S. W. (2020). The formation of suspicion: A vignette study. *International Journal of Police Science & Management, 22*(3), 274–284.

Phinney, J. S., & Chavira, V. (1995). Parental ethnic socialization and adolescent coping with problems related to ethnicity. *Journal of Research on Adolescence, 5*(1), 31–53.

Pickett, J., Graham, A., & Cullen, F. (2022). The American racial divide in fear of the police. *Criminology, 60*(2), 291-320.

Pierson, E., Simoiu, C., Overgoor, J., Corbett-Davies, S., Jenson, D., Shoemaker, A., Ramachandran, V., Barghouty, P., Phillips, C., Shroff, R., & Goel, S. (2020). A large-scale analysis of racial disparities in police stops across the United States. *Nature Human Behaviour, 4*(7), 736–745.

Pieterse, A. L., Todd, N. R., Neville, H. A., & Carter, R. T. (2012). Perceived racism and mental health among Black American adults: A meta-analytic review. *Journal of Counseling Psychology, 59*(1), 1–9.

Pigott, C., Stearns, A. E., & Khey, D. N. (2018). School resource officers and the school to prison pipeline: Discovering trends of expulsions in public schools. *American Journal of Criminal Justice, 43*(1), 120–138.

Piquero, A. R., Bersani, B. E., Loughran, T. A., & Fagan, J. (2016). Longitudinal patterns of legal socialization in first-generation immigrants, second-generation immigrants, and native-born serious youthful offenders. *Crime & Delinquency, 62*(11), 1403–1425.

Poehlmann, J. (2005). Representations of attachment relationships in children of incarcerated mothers. *Child Development, 76*(3), 679–696.

President's Task Force on 21st Century Policing. (2015). *Final report of the President's Task Force on 21st Century Policing*. Office of Community Oriented Policing Services, U.S. Department of Justice.

Primm, A. B., Osher, F. C., & Gomez, M. B. (2005). Race and ethnicity, mental health services and cultural competence in the criminal justice system: Are we ready to change? *Community Mental Health Journal, 41*(5), 557–569.

Purdie-Vaughns, V., & Eibach, R. P. (2008). Intersectional invisibility: The distinctive advantages and disadvantages of multiple subordinate-group identities. *Sex Roles, 59*(5), 377–391.

Rahr, S., & Rice, S. K. (2015). *From warriors to guardians: Recommitting American police culture to democratic ideals* (NCJ 248654). New Perspectives in Policing Bulletin. U.S. Department of Justice, National Institute of Justice.

Rastogi, S., Johnson, T. D., Hoeffel, E. M., & Drewery, M. P. (2011). *The Black population: 2010*. U.S. Census Bureau. https://www.census.gov/prod/cen2010/briefs/c2010br-06.pdf

Rios, V. M. (2011). *Punished: Policing the lives of Black and Latino boys*. New York University Press.

Robinson, R. K. (2008). Perceptual segregation. *Columbia Law Review, 108*(5), 1093–1180.

Roscigno, V. J., & Preito-Hodge, K. (2021). Racist cops, vested "blue" interests, or both? Evidence from four decades of the General Social Survey. *Socius, 7*, 1-13, 2378023120980913.

Rosenbaum, D. P., Schuck, A. M., Costello, S. K., Hawkins, D. F., & Ring, M. K. (2005). Attitudes toward the police: The effects of direct and vicarious experience. *Police Quarterly, 8*(3), 343–365.

Rosenfeld, R., Rojek, J., & Decker, S. (2012). Age matters: Race differences in police searches of young and older male drivers. *Journal of Research in Crime and Delinquency, 49*(1), 31–55.

Ross, C. T., Winterhalder, B., & McElreath, R. (2021). Racial disparities in police use of deadly force against unarmed individuals persist after appropriately benchmarking shooting data on violent crime rates. *Social Psychological and Personality Science, 12*(3), 323–332.

Rucker, J. M., & Richeson, J. A. (2021). Toward an understanding of structural racism: Implications for criminal justice. *Science, 374*(6565), 286–290.

Sack, K. (2017, March 18). Door-busting drug raids leave a trail of blood. *New York Times*. https://www.nytimes.com/interactive/2017/03/18/us/forced-entry-warrant-drug-raid.html

Saleem, F. T., Anderson, R. E., & Williams, M. (2020). Addressing the "myth" of racial trauma: Developmental and ecological considerations for youth of color. *Clinical Child and Family Psychology Review, 23*(1), 1–14.

Santana, M. C., & Smith, R. F. (2001). News coverage of Hispanics surpasses expectations. *Newspaper Research Journal, 22*(2), 94–104.

Scheb, J. M., Lyons, W., & Wagers, K. A. (2009). Race, gender, and age discrepancies in police motor vehicle stops in Knoxville, Tennessee: Evidence of racially biased policing? *Police Practice and Research: An International Journal*, *10*(1), 75–87.

Schneckloth v. Bustamonte, 412 U.S. 218 (1973).

Scott, K., Ma, D. S., Sadler, M. S., & Correll, J. (2017). A social scientific approach toward understanding racial disparities in police shooting: Data from the Department of Justice (1980–2000). *Journal of Social Issues*, *73*(4), 701–722.

Segal, P. Z. (2010). A more inclusive democracy: Challenging felon jury exclusion in New York. *City University of New York Law Review*, *13*(2), 313–385.

Sellin, T. (1928). The Negro criminal: A statistical note. *Annals of the American Academy of Political and Social Science*, *140*, 52–64.

Shepherd, S. M., & Willis-Esqueda, C. (2018). Indigenous perspectives on violence risk assessment: A thematic analysis. *Punishment & Society*, *20*(5), 599–627.

Shmool, J. L., Yonas, M. A., Newman, O. D., Kubzansky, L. D., Joseph, E., Parks, A., Callaway, C., Chubb, L. G., Shepard, P., & Clougherty, J. E. (2015). Identifying perceived neighborhood stressors across diverse communities in New York City. *American Journal of Community Psychology*, *56*(1), 145–155.

Shollenberger, T. L. (2015). Racial disparities in-school suspension and subsequent outcomes. In D. J. Losen (Ed.), *Closing the school discipline gap: Equitable remedies for excessive exclusion* (pp. 31–44). Teachers College Press.

Sidanius, J., Liu, J. H., Shaw, J. S., & Pratto, F. (1994). Social dominance orientation, hierarchy attenuators and hierarchy enhancers: Social dominance theory and the criminal justice system. *Journal of Applied Social Psychology*, *24*(4), 338–366.

Sigelman, L., & Tuch, S. A. (1997). Metastereotypes: Blacks' perceptions of Whites' stereotypes of Blacks. *Public Opinion Quarterly*, *61*(1), 87–101. http://www.jstor.org/stable/2749513.

Signorielli, N. (2010). Research ethics in content analysis. In A. Jordan, D. Kunkel, J. Manganello, & M. Fishbein (Eds.), *Media messages and public health: A decisions approach to content analysis* (pp. 106–114). Routledge.

Silverman, H. (2020, June 2). *Police officers are joining protesters for prayers and hugs in several US cities*. CNN. https://www.cnn.com/2020/06/02/us/police-protesters-together/index.html

Simckes, M., Willits, D., McFarland, M., McFarland, C., Rowhani-Rahbar, A., & Hajat, A. (2021). The adverse effects of policing on population health: A conceptual model. *Social Science & Medicine*, *281*, 1–9.

Singh, B., Axt, J., Hudson, S. M., Mellinger, C. L., Wittenbrink, B., & Correll, J. (2020). When practice fails to reduce racial bias in the decision to shoot: The case of cognitive load. *Social Cognition*, *38*(6), 555–570.

Skiba, R. J., Horner, R. H., Chung, C. G., Rausch, M. K., May, S. L., & Tobin, T. (2011). Race is not neutral: A national investigation of African American and Latino disproportionality in school discipline. *School Psychology Review*, *40*(1), 85–107.

Smith Lee, J. R., & Robinson, M. A. (2019). "That's my number one fear in life. It's the police": Examining young Black men's exposures to trauma and loss resulting from police violence and police killings. *Journal of Black Psychology*, *45*(3), 143–184.

Snibbe, A. C., & Markus, H. R. (2005). You can't always get what you want: Educational attainment, agency, and choice. *Journal of Personality and Social Psychology*, *88*(4), 703–720.

Solis, C., Portillos, E. L., & Brunson, R. K. (2009). Latino youths' experiences with and perceptions of involuntary police encounters. *Annals of the American Academy of Political and Social Science*, *623*(1), 39–51.

Spencer, K. B., Charbonneau, A. K., & Glaser, J. (2016). Implicit bias and policing. *Social and Personality Psychology Compass*, *10*(1), 50–63.

Staggers-Hakim, R. (2016). The nation's unprotected children and the ghost of Mike Brown, or the impact of national police killings on the health and social development of African American boys. *Journal of Human Behavior in the Social Environment*, *26*(3–4), 390–399.

Staller, M. S., Christiansen, P., Zaiser, B., Körner, S., & Cole, J. C. (2018). Do they aggress earlier? Investigating the effects of ego depletion on police officers' use of force behavior. *Journal of Police and Criminal Psychology*, *33*, 332–344.

Steele, C. M. (2010). *Whistling Vivaldi: How stereotypes affect us and what we can do*. WW Norton & Company.

Stevenson, M. C., Bottoms, B. L., & Burke, K. C. (Eds.). (2020). *The legacy of racism for children: Psychology, law, and public policy*. Oxford University Press.

Stoudt, B. G., & Torre, M. E. (2014). *The Morris Justice Project: Participatory action research*. Sage Publications.

Stoughton, S. W. (2014). Law enforcement's warrior problem. *Harvard Law Review Forum*, *128*, 225–234.

Stoughton, S. W. (2016). Principled policing: Warrior cops and guardian officers. *Wake Forest Law Review*, *51*, 611–676.

Stroshine, M., Alpert, G., & Dunham, R. (2008). The influence of "working rules" on police suspicion and discretionary decision making. *Police Quarterly*, *11*(3), 315–337.

Sunshine, J., & Tyler, T. R. (2003). The role of procedural justice and legitimacy in shaping public support for policing. *Law & Society Review, 37*(3), 513–548.

Swencionis, J. K., & Goff, P. A. (2017). The psychological science of racial bias and policing. *Psychology, Public Policy, and Law, 23*(4), 398–409.

Swencionis, J. K., Pouget, E. R., & Goff, P. A. (2021). Hierarchy maintenance policing: Social dominance and police use of force. *Proceedings of the National Academy of Sciences, 118*(18), e2007693118.

Syed, M., & McLean, K. C. (2023). Master narrative methodology: A primer for conducting structural-psychological research. *Cultural Diversity and Ethnic Minority Psychology, 29*(1), 53–63.

Taylor, T. J., Turner, K. B., Esbensen, F. A., & Winfree, L. T., Jr. (2001). Coppin' an attitude: Attitudinal differences among juveniles toward police. *Journal of Criminal Justice, 29*(4), 295–305.

Teahan, J. E. (1975). A longitudinal study of attitude shifts among Black and White police officers. *Journal of Social Issues, 31*(1), 47–56.

Testa, A., Turney, K., Jackson, D. B., & Jaynes, C. M. (2022). Police contact and future orientation from adolescence to young adulthood: Findings from the Pathways to Desistance Study. *Criminology, 60*(2), 263-290.

Thomas, A. J., & Blackmon, S. K. M. (2015). The influence of the Trayvon Martin shooting on racial socialization practices of African American parents. *Journal of Black Psychology, 41*(1), 75–89.

Thomas, E. L., Dovidio, J. F., & West, T. V. (2014). Lost in the categorical shuffle: Evidence for the social non-prototypicality of Black women. *Cultural Diversity and Ethnic Minority Psychology, 20*(3), 370–376.

Thompson, V. L. S. (1994). Socialization to race and its relationship to racial identification among African Americans. *Journal of Black Psychology, 20*(2), 175–188.

Thronson, V. T., & Thronson, D. B. (2020). Child immigration: Barriers predicated on national origin and racial identity. In M. C. Stevenson, B. L. Bottoms, & K. C. Burke (Eds.), *The legacy of racism for children: Psychology, law, and public policy* (pp. 211–226). Oxford.

Tillyer, R., & Engel, R. S. (2013). The impact of drivers' race, gender, and age during traffic stops: Assessing interaction terms and the social conditioning model. *Crime & Delinquency, 59*(3), 369–395.

Trinkner, R., Kerrison, E. M., & Goff, P. A. (2019). The force of fear: Police stereotype threat, self-legitimacy, and support for excessive force. *Law and Human Behavior, 43*(5), 421–435.

Tukachinsky, R., Mastro, D., & Yarchi, M. (2017). The effect of prime time television ethnic/racial stereotypes on Latino and Black Americans: A longitudinal national level study. *Journal of Broadcasting & Electronic Media, 61*(3), 538–556.

Turney, K. (2014). Stress proliferation across generations? Examining the relationship between parental incarceration and childhood health. *Journal of Health and Social Behavior, 55*(3), 302–319.

Tyler, T. R. (2017). Procedural justice and policing: A rush to judgment? *Annual Review of Law and Social Science, 13*, 29–53.

Tyler, T. R., & Huo, Y. (2002). *Trust in the law: Encouraging public cooperation with the police and courts.* Russell Sage Foundation.

Tyler, T. R., & Lind, E. A. (1992). A relational model of authority in groups. In M. P. Zanna (Ed.), *Advances in experimental social psychology* (pp. 115–191). Elsevier.

Tyler, T. R., & Trinkner, R. (2018). *Why children follow rules: Legal socialization and the development of legitimacy.* Oxford University Press.

Tynes, B. M., Willis, H. A., Stewart, A. M., & Hamilton, M. W. (2019). Race-related traumatic events online and mental health among adolescents of color. *Journal of Adolescent Health, 65*(3), 371–377.

Tyree, T. (2011). African American stereotypes in reality television. *Howard Journal of Communications, 22*(4), 394–413.

Uggen, C., & McElrath, S. (2014). Parental incarceration: What we know and where we need to go. *Journal of Criminal Law and Criminology, 104*(3), 597–604. https://www.jstor.org/stable/44113401

United States v. Mendenhall, 446 U.S. 544 (1980).

University of Georgia, Department of Psychology, Franklin College of Arts and Sciences. (n.d.). *Coping with racial trauma.* https://www.psychology.uga.edu/coping-racial-trauma

Urbina, M. G., & Álvarez, S. E. (2016). Neoliberalism, criminal justice and Latinos: The contours of neoliberal economic thought and policy on criminalization. *Latino Studies, 14*(1), 33–58.

U.S. Department of Education. (2021). *Report on indicators of school crime and safety: 2020.* https://nces.ed.gov/pubs2021/2021092.pdf

U.S. Department of Education, Office for Civil Rights. (2014). *Annual report to Congress: Fiscal years 2012 and 2013.*

U.S. Department of Health and Human Services. (2000). *Executive summary: Mental health: Culture, race and ethnicity: A supplement to mental health: A report of the surgeon general.* https://www.ncbi.nlm.nih.gov/books/NBK44249/#A1210

U.S. Department of Justice, Office of Juvenile Justice and Delinquency Prevention. (2019). *Juvenile arrest rates by race, 1980–2019*. https://www.ojjdp.gov/ojstatbb/special_topics/qa11502.asp?qaDate=2019

Valencia, M. J. (2020, November 1). How "Blue Lives Matter" trend has emerged as the identity politics of the right. *Boston Globe*. https://www.bostonglobe.com/2020/11/01/metro/how-blue-lives-matter-trend-has-emerged-identity-politics-right/

Vrij, A., Akehurst, L., & Knight, S. (2006). Police officers', social workers', teachers' and the general public's beliefs about deception in children, adolescents and adults. *Legal and Criminological Psychology, 11*(2), 297–312.

Vrij, A., & Semin, G. R. (1996). Lie experts' beliefs about nonverbal indicators of deception. *Journal of Nonverbal Behavior, 20*(1), 65–80.

Wallace, D. (2018). Safe routes to school? Black Caribbean youth negotiating police surveillance in London and New York City. *Harvard Educational Review, 88*(3), 261–286.

Watson, A. R. A., & Stevenson, M. C. (2022). Teachers' and administrators' perceptions of police-to-student encounters: The impact of student race, police legitimacy, and legal authoritarianism. *Race and Justice, 12*(4), 736–754.

Waxman, S. R. (2021). Racial awareness and bias begin early: Developmental entry points, challenges, and a call to action. *Perspectives on Psychological Science, 16*(5), 893–902.

Weaver, V., Prowse, G., & Piston, S. (2019). Too much knowledge, too little power: An assessment of political knowledge in highly policed communities. *Journal of Politics, 81*(3), 1153–1166.

Weaver, V., Prowse, G., & Piston, S. (2020). Withdrawing and drawing in: Political discourse in policed communities. *Journal of Race, Ethnicity and Politics, 5*(3), 604–647.

Weitzer, R. (2014). The puzzling neglect of Hispanic Americans in research on police–citizen relations. *Ethnic and Racial Studies, 37*(11), 1995–2013.

Weitzer, R., & Tuch, S. A. (2002). Perceptions of racial profiling: Race, class, and personal experience. *Criminology, 40*(2), 435–456.

Weitzer, R., & Tuch, S. A. (2005). Racially biased policing: Determinants of citizen perceptions. *Social Forces, 83*(3), 1009–1030.

Weitzer, R., & Tuch, S. A. (2006). *Race and policing in America: Conflict and reform*. Cambridge University Press.

Welch, K., Payne, A. A., Chiricos, T., & Gertz, M. (2011). The typification of Hispanics as criminals and support for punitive crime control policies. *Social Science Research, 40*(3), 822–840.

Western, B., & Wildeman, C. (2009). The Black family and mass incarceration. *Annals of the American Academy of Political and Social Science, 621*(1), 221–242.

Wheelock, D. (2011). A jury of one's "peers": The racial impact of felon jury exclusion in Georgia. *Justice System Journal, 32*(3), 335–359.

Whitaker, T. R., & Snell, C. L. (2016). Parenting while powerless: Consequences of "the talk." *Journal of Human Behavior in the Social Environment, 26*(3–4), 303–309.

White-Johnson, R. L., Ford, K. R., & Sellers, R. M. (2010). Parental racial socialization profiles: Association with demographic factors, racial discrimination, childhood socialization, and racial identity. *Cultural Diversity and Ethnic Minority Psychology, 16*(2), 237–247.

Wildeman, J., Costelloe, M., & Schehr, R. (2011). Experiencing wrongful and unlawful conviction. *Journal of Offender Rehabilitation, 50*(7), 411–432.

Williams, D. R., & Williams-Morris, R. (2000). Racism and mental health: The African American experience. *Ethnicity & Health, 5*(3–4), 243–268.

Willis-Esqueda, C. (2020). Bad characters and desperados: Latinxs and causal explanations for legal system bias. *UCLA Law Review, 67*, 1204–1222.

Wilson, C. C., II, Gutiérrez, F., & Chao, L. (2012). *Racism, sexism, and the media: Multicultural issues into the new communications age*. Sage Publications.

Winchester, L. B., Jones, S. C. T., Allen, K., Hope, E., & Cryer-Coupet, Q. (2022). Let's talk: The impact of gendered racial socialization on black adolescent girls' mental health. *Cultural Diversity and Ethnic Minority Psychology, 28*(2), 171–181.

Wolfe, S. E., & McLean, K. (2021). Is it un-American to view the police as illegitimate? The role of national identity in the legal socialization process. *Journal of Social Issues, 77*(2), 577–599.

Wood, G., Tyler, T. R., & Papachristos, A. V. (2020). Procedural justice training reduces police use of force and complaints against officers. *Proceedings of the National Academy of Sciences, 117*(18), 9815–9821.

Woolard, J. L., & Henning, K. (2020). Racial minority youths' perceptions of the justice system: Life on the street. In M. C. Stevenson, B. L. Bottoms, & K. C. Burke (Eds.), *The legacy of racism for children: Psychology, law, and public policy* (pp. 151–168). Oxford University Press.

Worden, R. E., McLean, S. J., Engel, R. S., Cochran, H., Corsaro, N., Reynolds, D., Najdowski, C. J., & Isaza, G. T. (2020). *The impacts of implicit bias awareness training in the NYPD*. John F. Finn Institute.

Wordes, M., Bynum, T. S., & Corley, C. J. (1994). Locking up youth: The impact of race on detention decisions. *Journal of Research in Crime and Delinquency, 31*(2), 149–165.

Worrell, F. C., Cross, W. E., Jr., & Vandiver, B. J. (2001). Nigrescence theory: Current status and challenges for the future. *Journal of Multicultural Counseling and Development, 29*(3), 201–210.

Wu, Y., Lake, R., & Cao, L. (2015). Race, social bonds, and juvenile attitudes toward the police. *Justice Quarterly, 32*(3), 445–470.

Zinsser, K. M., & Wanless, S. B. (2020). Racial disproportionality in the school-to-prison pipeline. In M. C. Stevenson, B. L. Bottoms, & K. C. Burke (Eds.), *The legacy of racism for children: Psychology, law, and public policy* (pp. 129–150). Oxford University Press.

CHAPTER 27

Prisoner Reentry and the Life Course

Thomas P. LeBel and Matt Richie

> **Abstract**
> This chapter addresses prisoner reentry and the life course. It focuses on three distinct phases or timeframes: what happened in the life course for many individuals before arriving at the prison gate, events that take place while incarcerated, and what transpires after release from prison. Although recidivism (rearrest, conviction, return to prison) is discussed, the chapter also examines other important life course events or outcomes such as employment, housing, family relationships/marriage, and health. Other factors that make achieving a successful life (maximizing one's potential) difficult for formerly incarcerated persons are described such as the stigma of incarceration and the collateral (legal) consequences of a felony conviction. The chapter concludes by discussing directions for future research.
>
> **Key Words:** prisoner reentry, prison, life course, turning point, stigma, collateral consequences, wounded healer, advocacy

This chapter addresses prisoner reentry and the life course. We focus on three distinct phases or timeframes: what happened in the life course for many individuals before arriving at the prison gate, events that take place while incarcerated, and what transpires after release from prison (see Gaes, 2016, for a similar schema). Although we discuss recidivism (rearrest, conviction, return to prison), we also examine other important life course events or outcomes such as employment, housing, and marriage (De Giorgi, 2017; Mears et al., 2013). We also focus on factors that make achieving a successful life (maximizing one's potential) for formerly incarcerated persons difficult: the stigma of incarceration and the collateral consequences of a felony conviction.

First, it is important to explain the scope of the issue we will be discussing. There are 1.43 million men and women incarcerated in state and federal prisons (Carson, 2020). In 2019 alone, 608,000 sentenced prisoners were released from state and federal prisons (Carson, 2020, p. 15). Consequently, prisoner reentry has become a major concern for states and the federal government (Travis et al., 2014). It is a well-known fact that many individuals returning to the community from prison will have further contact with the criminal justice system (i.e., recidivate). A study of prisoners released in 34 states in 2012 found that 71% were arrested and nearly half (46%) were returned to prison within 5 years (Durose & Antenangeli, 2021; see also Visher et al., 2017). Importantly, in a previous recidivism study involving 30 states, almost half (47%) of the persons with no arrest within 3 years of release had an arrest during years 4 through 9 (Alper & Durose, 2018). Moreover, Alper and Durose (2018) report that nearly one in four (24%) of all released individuals in 2005 were arrested during the ninth year. These recidivism findings suggest that more extensive longitudinal research and life course follow-up is needed.

Maruna et al. (2004; see also Visher & Travis, 2003) state, "Reintegration is both an event and a process. Narrowly speaking, re-entry comes the day a prisoner is released from confinement.... More broadly, re-entry is also a long-term process, one that actually starts prior to release and continues well afterwards" (p. 5).

Using this definition, prisoner reentry includes many processes that begin before the individual is sent to prison, experiences while incarcerated, issues faced at the moment of release and during the first months out, and encounters during the re/integration process of the first few years in the community (Irwin, 1970; Mears et al., 2015; Visher & Travis, 2003). Most research involving formerly incarcerated persons examines the first few years postrelease and tends to concentrate on the factors related to recidivism (Harding et al., 2019; Mears et al., 2013; Visher & La Vigne, 2021; Western, 2018). Thus, due to the lack of long-term follow-up, little is known about the life experiences of formerly incarcerated persons 3 or more years after release from prison (Kazemian & Walker, 2019; Mears et al., 2013).

Maruna and colleagues (2004) initially theorized desistance as a two-stage process. Primary desistance was the stoppage of criminal behavior for those who become habitual offenders. In some sense, many offenders achieve primary desistance several times throughout the life course because there are temporary stoppages in criminal behavior. As such, primary desistance is an important benchmark, but Maruna and colleagues (2004) argue that if individuals are to remain crime free beyond these temporary stoppages, they must engage in secondary desistance. Secondary desistance is defined as a cognitive shift away from their former criminal selves and toward a more prosocial self and someone who engages in more appropriate adult roles (employee, partner, parent, volunteer, etc.). It is through secondary desistance that individuals can not only increase the length of the temporary stoppages in criminal behavior but also repair their criminal identity and move toward a more prosocial identity and life.

In recent years, an additional stage in the desistance process (tertiary desistance) has been added, which fits well with a life course perspective. Anderson and McNeill (2019) "define desistance broadly as a process of human development (inevitably occurring in and affected by particular social contexts) that involves moving away from crime and toward social integration and participation" (p. 600). Essentially, tertiary desistance requires others and society to see past the prior misdeeds of the individuals attempting to desist from crime.

Weaver asserts that "the study of desistance is distinct in criminology, in seeking to explain why people cease and sustain cessation from offending, rather than why they offend" (Weaver, 2019, p. 641). However, other desistance researchers examine the factors that make it difficult for individuals formerly involved with crime to "stay straight" and lead a satisfying law-abiding life (Bushway, 2020; Halsey et al., 2017; Maruna, 2001; Nugent & Schinkel, 2016; Patton & Farrall, 2021). Importantly, for the purposes of this chapter, "desistance is a social process as much as a personal one" (Honeywell, 2019, p. 123; McNeill, 2014). Moreover, Honeywell (2019, p. 125) asserts that "desistance is in fact an unending trajectory as individuals continually strive towards acceptance within society."

Although we will discuss many characteristics of individuals experiencing reentry to the community and its aftermath, due to space constraints we do not specifically focus on race/ethnicity, women, youth/young adults, or persons with convictions for sexual offenses. In the sections to follow we examine the following: characteristics of individuals before entering prison; the impact of serving time in prison; prisoner reentry as a potential turning point;

reentry challenges (including employment, housing, family relationships and marriage, and health concerns); the harsh reality of life after prison; the stigma of incarceration in prison; and the collateral consequences of a felony conviction. The penultimate section provides a somewhat optimistic life course outcome by describing one way forward for formerly incarcerated persons: becoming a professional ex-, wounded healer, or advocate. We then end the chapter by discussing directions for future research.

Before Arriving at the Prison Gate: Important Characteristics of People in Prison

In looking at the backgrounds and characteristics of incarcerated persons, one can see many are "off-time" in regard to life course milestones, and also that they have experienced a great deal of "challenges of correlated adversity" (Western, 2018, p. 176). Pettit and Western (2004, p. 154) describe a common progression to adult status involving "moving from school to work, then to marriage, to establishing a home and becoming a parent." However, individuals who have been arrested, and especially those who have been incarcerated, are more likely to report being "off-time" for these common behavioral signposts of adulthood status (Massoglia & Uggen, 2010, p. 569). Sampson and Laub (1997; Laub et al., 2019), well-regarded life course theorists and researchers, argue that there is often substantial stability (state dependence) over time for those experiencing hardships early in life. They describe state dependence (and cumulative disadvantage) as prior delinquent behavior's accruing effect on weakening bonds to conventional institutions in society (such as formal education, employment, and marriage; Laub et al., 2019; Sampson & Laub, 1997). Similarly, Wheelock and Uggen (2010, p. 261) argue that incarceration "sustains and exacerbates" inequalities and disadvantages, and that nearly half of incarcerated persons likely have incomes below the poverty line prior to their incarceration. Essentially, the negative consequences of delinquency and incarceration can knife off future opportunities to leading a conventional and successful life.

Wakefield and Uggen (2010, p. 393) succinctly state that "prisons tend to house those with the least human capital, financial capital, and social capital." This lack of capital is evident when examining the formal education and employment history of incarcerated and recently released persons. Using data from the National Former Prisoner Survey, Couloute (2018a) reports that about a quarter of persons on parole supervision did not have a high school diploma or GED. Moreover, the majority (three fourths) of formerly incarcerated people who did not have a high school diploma earn a GED while incarcerated (Coulette, 2018a; Harding et al., 2019). Thus, having only a GED or no educational credential at all represents the majority (58%) of formerly incarcerated persons. Research conducted by Western and Wildeman (2009, p. 231) indicates that Black men born between 1975 and 1979 who did not graduate from high school had a 70% chance of serving time in prison by age 35. Importantly, regardless of educational credentials, Mizrahi and colleagues (2016) report that more than 60% of persons incarcerated in prison are functionally illiterate.

Bushway and Apel (2012) note that formal employment in the year before incarceration is also nonnormative, with less than one third working. Likewise, Harding and colleagues (2019, p. 218) found that only about 17% indicated having any employment in the formal labor market in the year before entering prison. Looney and Turner (2018) delineate how about half of the persons in prison report having no income from formal work in the 3 years prior to their incarceration. Later, we discuss how formal employment remains a significant barrier after release from prison.

Individuals serving time in prison have extensive histories of substance use, mental health disorders, chronic health conditions, and disabilities (Mallik-Kane & Visher, 2008; Western,

2018). An analysis of the 2016 Survey of Prison Inmates (SPI), a nationally representative self-report survey of the adult incarcerated population, found that among those not incarcerated for the entire 12 months prior to admission to prison, nearly half (49%) of state prisoners met the *Diagnostic and Statistical Manual of Mental Disorders,* fourth edition (DSM-IV, American Psychiatric Association, 2000) criteria for substance use disorder (for drug use and/or alcohol use; Maruschak et al., 2021a). Data from the "Returning Home" studies also emphasized that regular illicit drug use and alcohol consumption were common before being incarcerated (Visher & La Vigne, 2021).

Based on information gleaned from self-report, nearly half (43%) of state prisoners detailed being told by a mental health professional that they had a mental health disorder or condition (major depressive disorder, bipolar disorder, anxiety disorder, posttraumatic stress disorder [PTSD], personality disorder, or schizophrenia/other psychotic disorder; Maruschak et al., 2021b). Meanwhile, about four in 10 state prisoners reported currently having a chronic condition such as cancer, high blood pressure, stroke, diabetes, arthritis, asthma, cirrhosis of the liver, and heart- or kidney-related problems (Maruschak et al., 2021c; see also Visher & La Vigne, 2021). Moreover, about 17% of state prisoners reported ever having an infectious disease such as tuberculosis, hepatitis B, hepatitis C, HIV/AIDS, and sexually transmitted diseases (see also Massoglia & Pridemore, 2015). Nearly four in 10 state prisoners (40%) reported having a disability (e.g., cognitive, ambulatory, vision, hearing, independent living, and self-care). More than one fourth (26%) of state prisoners reported that at some point in their lives a doctor, psychologist, or teacher had told them that they had an attention-deficit disorder (Maruschak et al., 2021d; Mizrahi et al., 2016). In addition, one fourth (25%) of state prisoners reported having ever attended special education classes, while 15% had been told that they had a learning disability.

Many people in prison and individuals who have recently reentered the community report having experienced interpersonal trauma (physical, sexual, and/or crime related) of some sort before their incarceration (Harding et al., 2019; Western, 2018). Research with incarcerated women and youth, in particular, indicates that the vast majority experienced physical and/or sexual abuse as children and often as adults as well (Beck et al., 2010; Green et al., 2005; Sedlak & McPherson, 2010). Bernstein (2014, p. 153), for example, reports that "walking onto a juvenile unit is like entering a trauma ward, an emotional MASH unit where the gore is no less visceral for being interior." Notably, the majority of adult males also report experiences of trauma before incarceration, especially physical and crime-related trauma (Carlson et al., 2010; Komarovskaya et al., 2011; Maschi et al., 2015).

The prison (and reentry) population is getting older. At year-end 2019, an estimated 44% of sentenced prisoners in the United States were age 40 or older (Carson, 2020, p. 15). In New York State, the average age of incarcerated individuals on January 1, 2019, was 39 years old (Division of Program Planning, Research and Evaluation, 2020). Similarly, in California, the average male prisoner is now almost 40 years old, and between 2000 and 2017, the share of prisoners aged 50 or older more than quintupled, from 4% to 23% (Harris et al., 2019). Of course, as noted by Shapland and colleagues (2016, p. 288), "it is . . . important to bear in mind that chronological age is not the same as developmental age" . . . but we should also "pay greater attention to data about both physiological and psychological maturity." However, because the prison population is now essentially middle-aged (average of approximately 40 years old), one can see that many persons are drastically off-time for many important life course milestones, such as having a career with a living wage. Next, we discuss the impact prison itself is thought to have on attaining positive life outcomes.

The Impact of Prison

As discussed in the previous section, many people "entering prison will already be 'off-time'" (Pettit & Western, 2004, p. 155). However, as suggested by Harding and colleagues (2019, p. 222), it is important to examine "what role prison plays in structuring an individual's sequence of future life events." Other researchers have also argued that imprisonment may be an important turning point in the life course (Pettit & Western, 2004) or "critical life event" (Mears et al., 2013, p. 324). Based on the literature, the predominant view is that serving time in prison has a detrimental impact on one's life chances, or that it keeps individuals in a marginal status (Dennison & Demuth, 2018; Haney, 2012; Pettit & Western, 2004; Remster, 2019; Western, 2018). In discussing the negative impact of time spent in prison, Zamble and Porporino (1988, p. 153) talk of becoming "frozen developmentally." For example, Grounds (2005) reports that all of the exonerees in his study felt that time had stopped while they were incarcerated, and one man explained that "I'm thirty-five but I'm twenty in my head" (p. 46).

Nearly 50 years ago, Connett (1973, p. 113), a formerly incarcerated person, succinctly summarized the impact of serving time in prison by stating that "it seems certain they create in many feelings of dependence, inadequacy, unworthiness, guilt, self-hatred, insecurity, frustration, alienation, fear, apathy, rage, and confusion." Haney (2012, p. 2) articulates three important Ds of incarceration that can have a damaging psychological impact: "danger, dehumanization, and deprivation." Listwan and colleagues (2012, 2013) found that prisoners who scored higher on a coercion index, based on victimization experiences (especially violent) and perceptions of the prison environment as threatening and hostile, were more likely to be rearrested or reimprisoned after release. Other studies have also reported that victimization in prison is related to depression, anxiety, and/or posttraumatic stress symptoms (including anger) following release (Schappell et al., 2016; Wolff & Shi, 2009; Zweig et al., 2015). Zweig and colleagues (2015) analyzed data from the multisite evaluation of the Serious and Violent Offender Reentry Initiative to assess the impact of victimization on a variety of reentry outcomes. Zweig and colleagues' (2015) analyses determined that prisoners who are physically assaulted or threatened have negative emotional reactions including hostility and depression, and that these emotional reactions increase recidivism (especially violent criminal behavior) and substance use up to 15 months postrelease. Additionally, because this study is longitudinal in nature, it can specify that victimization experiences in prison preceded and potentially caused these negative effects. Haney (2003) argues that in adapting to survive these pains of living in prison, "many people are permanently changed" (p. 38).

As explained earlier, many persons enter prison reporting having had an infectious disease of some sort (Maruschak et al., 2021c). However, the prison environment itself places incarcerated persons at greater risk of acquiring additional infectious diseases (Massoglia & Pridemore, 2015). In a white paper published in early 2021, Wang and colleagues (2021) indicate that nearly one in five persons incarcerated in prison had tested positive for COVID-19, which is an infection rate about five times higher than the general population. Moreover, the age-adjusted mortality rate from COVID-19 was three times higher for the prison population than the general population (Wang et al., 2021). Thus, the carceral environment can have harmful effects on both physical and mental health (Massoglia & Pridemore, 2015; Schnittker et al., 2012).

Kazemian and Travis (2015, p. 370) posit that the "effects of incarceration extend beyond the prison walls." Irwin (1985) explains how incarceration keeps people detached from society because it "tends to maintain people in a rabble status or convert them to it" (p. 45). Using data from the National Longitudinal Study of Adolescent to Adult Health, Dennison and Demuth (2018) found that incarceration has negative consequences on achieved socioeconomic status

(SES; formal education and occupational status), especially for those who had higher SES (based on parental factors) before involvement in the criminal justice system. Dennison and Demuth (2018, p. 19) conclude that criminal justice "system involvement inevitably destroys human capital, undermines future life chances, and ultimately promotes a 'rabble' class."

Patterson (2013) identified a linear relationship between time served and life expectancy such that for each year in prison, an incarcerated person can expect to lose 2 years off their life expectancy. Similarly, Pridemore (2014) found that men who had been incarcerated were more than twice as likely to die prematurely. Importantly, he noted that formerly incarcerated men were more likely than those never incarcerated to die from a drug overdose, infectious diseases, and homicide. Binswanger and colleagues (2016) determined that independent risk factors for overdose mortality postrelease include substance use disorder (and especially problems with opiates/sedatives), injection drug use, panic disorder, and psychiatric prescriptions before release.

Haney (2003, p. 45; see also Kupers, 2005; Liem, 2016) argues that "for some prisoners, incarceration is so stark and psychologically painful that it represents a form of trauma severe enough to produce posttraumatic stress reactions in the free world." Gorski (2010, paragraph 4) asserts that "Post Incarceration Syndrome (PICS)" is "caused by being subjected to prolonged incarceration in environments of punishment with few opportunities for education, job training, or rehabilitation." Liem and Kunst (2013; Liem, 2016) suggest that PICS constitutes a discrete subtype of PTSD that results from long-term imprisonment. Based on in-depth interviews with 25 released "lifers" who had served an average of 19 years in prison, they concluded that their narratives indicated a specific conglomeration of symptoms including each of the four characteristic PTSD feature clusters (intrusion, hyperarousal, persistent avoidance, and emotional numbing; Liem & Kunst, 2013, p. 335; Grounds, 2005). Schnittker (2014) found that former prisoners were much more likely to report avoidant or anxious styles indicating more discomfort in getting close with others or "avoiding other people altogether" (p. 133). These findings led Schnittker (2014) to conclude that "the lasting damage of incarceration rests with how it reshapes beliefs, perceptions, and mindsets" (p. 135). To conclude, a growing and consistent body of evidence suggests that incarceration in prison has a negative impact and reduces a person's life chances.

Although much of the summarized research fits a "doom and gloom" theme, there is some research indicating that individuals may make positive steps toward change while incarcerated that can improve their life chances after release (Aresti et al., 2010; Giordano et al., 2002; Honeywell, 2019; Irwin, 2009; Kazemian, 2020; Maruna et al., 2003; McNeill, 2016). However, Kazemian (2020, p. 150) concludes that achieving positive growth in prison "requires extraordinary agency and motivation." In a similar vein, Harding and colleagues (2019) argue that "prison can serve as a turning point away from crime and substance abuse only when an individual has the social and material resources to capitalize on the moment of optimism at release" (p. 227). Of course, prison administrators can be encouraged to provide more opportunities for personal growth that may improve life chances postrelease (Kazemian, 2020; Maruna et al., 2003; Visher et al., 2017).

Prisoner Reentry as a Turning Point?

Irwin (2005, p. 202, n.3) asserts in his many years of research that he was "consistently reassured that *most* persons passing through the prison make up their mind to attempt to live a noncriminal life and stay out of prison." Moreover, research indicates that most persons involved with the criminal justice system have essentially the same goals and aspirations as the law-abiding public such as owning a home, establishing a career, and owning a car (Austin &

Irwin, 2000; Burnett, 1992; Erickson et al., 1973; Helfgott, 1997; Irwin, 1970; Matthews, 2021; Petersilia, 2003; Visher & O'Connell, 2012). However, research also suggests that for many returning prisoners, these expectations for "conventional" material success are unrealistic (Bucklen & Zajac, 2009; Erickson et al., 1973; Irwin, 1970) and need to be scaled back (Lin, 2000; Nugent & Schinkel, 2016). These observations are consistently supported in field research; at the point of release, most incarcerated persons express a strong desire and willingness to "go straight" (Burnett, 1992; Visher & Courtney, 2007). Petersilia (2003, p. 14; Boman & Mowen, 2018; Harding et al., 2019) argues that "if we fail to take advantage of this mindset, we miss one of the few potential turning points to successfully intervene in offenders' lives."

It is often asserted that released prisoners can "make it if they so desire" (Petersilia, 2003, p. 8) or "if [they] don't give up" (Irwin, 2005, p. 178). Essentially, despite the structural challenges formerly incarcerated persons face, most still subscribe to Horatio Alger's "rags to riches" story, in that with hard work and skills, "a former prisoner that wants to can 'make it' in a law-abiding way in society" (LeBel et al., 2017, p. 282; see also De Giorgi, 2017; Matthews, 2021; McNamee & Miller, 2014). Ironically, the optimism of being able to make it is strongly held by incarcerated and formerly incarcerated persons themselves, and has been consistently supported in research (Burnett, 1992; LeBel et al., 2015; Visher & Courtney, 2007). Research from the Urban Institute's Returning Home study consistently finds that prior to release, about three fourths of respondents expected it to be "pretty easy" or "very easy" to stay out of prison following release (Visher & Courtney, 2007). Many researchers note that the belief in one's ability to "go straight" or one's sense of self-efficacy, self-confidence, optimism, or hope may be a necessary, if not sufficient, condition for an individual to be able to succeed after prison and desist from crime more generally (LeBel et al., 2008; Maruna, 2001; Nelson et al., 1999; O'Brien, 2001; Visher & O'Connell, 2012).

LeBel and colleagues (2008; see also Harding et al., 2019; Kazemian, 2020; Visher & Courtney, 2007) found that soon-to-be-released prisoners' positive mindset was a significant predictor of postimprisonment outcomes. In particular, one's sense of self-efficacy (hope) contributed positively to the reintegration process. Similarly, Woldgabreal et al. (2016) found that persons under community supervision with higher positive psychological states (PPSs; self-efficacy, optimism, and hope) had lower rates of recidivism. Hope can impact a person's likelihood of selecting into and taking advantage of positive social opportunities, like employment or marital attachment; it can also help a person weather life's disappointments or inevitable setbacks in such areas (LeBel et al., 2008; O'Brien, 2001). Importantly, the quality of a person's actual reentry plan in regard to housing, employment, social support, and health concerns (substance use, physical, and mental) appears to be critical to postrelease success across a variety of domains (see Dickson et al., 2013; Kazemian, 2020; Polaschek & Yesberg, 2015; Visher et al., 2017).

Maruna (2001, p. 55) argues that "the situation facing recidivist offenders is something like a brick wall. It is surmountable but is enough of an obstacle to make most turn around and 'head back.'" Sociocognitive research with formerly incarcerated persons suggests that long-term, persistent offenders tend to lack feelings of agency, experiencing their lives as being largely determined for them in a fatalistic mindset that Maruna (2001) refers to as being "doomed to deviance." The negative impact of this belief system also gains credibility from Maruna's (2001, p. 9) finding that "the active offenders . . . seemed fairly accurate in their assessments of their situation (dire), their chances of achieving success in the 'straight' world (minimal), and their place in mainstream society ('need not apply')."

Maruna (2004) posits that the understanding that one's outcomes are due to external, stable, and uncontrollable factors may be partly responsible for former prisoners' continued involvement in crime. In contrast, hope requires both the "will and the ways," the desire for a particular outcome, and also the perceived ability and means of achieving the outcome (Burnett & Maruna, 2004, p. 395; LeBel et al., 2008).

In reality, one's sense of hope or optimism for the future may be "overwhelmed by the challenges of reentry" (Harding et al., 2019, p. 226; Nugent & Schinkel, 2016; Patton & Farrall, 2021). According to Irwin (2005, p. 174) "Most prisoners step into the outside world with a small bundle of stuff under their arm, a little bit of money, perhaps their $200 'gate' money, and that's all." In fact, in some states, the situation could be even more bleak with less money in hand at release (La Vigne et al., 2009).

Patton and Farrall (2021, p. 227) suggest that the collective pains of desistance, or dire structural and social circumstances, constitute a form of "negative desistance capital." Some of these pains of desistance include goal frustration and goal failure, isolation, stigma and rejection/exclusion, and hopelessness (Nugent & Schinkel, 2016; Patton & Farrall, 2021). Based on these obstacles, some people returning from prison may have in a sense "given up" or lost (or lacked) hope on remaining arrest free and/or going straight (LeBel et al., 2008; Maruna, 2001; Visher & O'Connell, 2012), and resigned themselves to either a life of involvement with the criminal justice system or perhaps living on the margins of society. This idea supports Halsey and colleagues' (2017) assertion that "the phenomenon in need of explanation is not a 'will to crime' or 'repeat offending' but rather, dissipation of the will to desist, grounded in a sense of moral exclusion" (p. 13).

Reentry Challenges

Based on the background and characteristics of incarcerated persons, many scholars have concluded that the vast majority returning to the community have never been "meaningfully integrated in the first place" (Kazemian, 2020, p. 200; see also Fader, 2013; Graham & McNeill, 2017; Irwin, 1985; Western, 2018). For example, Graham and McNeill (2017) use the term "re/integration" in recognition of this baleful notion. Individuals released from prison must overcome many challenges in order to succeed after prison including problems with employment, housing, reestablishing family relationships, and health-related concerns (see LeBel & Maruna, 2012, for a more detailed review of the obstacles in transitioning from prison to the community; Apel & Ramakers, 2019; Kirk, 2019; Leverentz, 2014; Massoglia & Pridemore, 2015; Travis et al., 2014). Harding et al. (2019, p. 224), for example, argue that many of the sources of social control, such as steady employment, independent housing, and marriage, "are simply not available to contemporary returning prisoners—even those motivated to desist." Giordano's (2014) follow-up with criminal justice system–involved individuals now in their 30s indicates that few had access to what she referred to as a "respectability package" (a combination of full-time employment, a good marriage, and children; Giordano et al., 2002). In fact, only 17% had achieved both marriage and full-time employment (Giordano, 2014). This finding is an indication of being off-time for important life course milestones, as well as the difficulty of getting back on track for those involved in the criminal justice system at any level. It is important to keep in mind that these challenges/barriers, and others, are interrelated in the lives of formerly incarcerated persons (Burnett, 1992; Remster, 2019). Next we discuss these challenges in more detail.

Employment

According to Laub and colleagues (2019, p. 314), the cumulative disadvantage accrued by engaging in criminal behavior is "likely felt hardest when discussing employment." In fact, Couloute and Kopf's (2018) research indicates that formerly incarcerated persons are unemployed at a rate of 27.3%, which is higher than the total U.S. unemployment rate during the Great Depression. An even higher percentage of formerly incarcerated persons do not have a job when one accounts for those not looking for work. A decent job can be a source of noncriminal contacts and also reinforce "legitimate" goals and values that promote the adoption of a law-abiding lifestyle. Sampson and Laub (1993), however, argue that employment "by itself" does not support desistance; rather, "employment coupled with job stability, commitment to work, and mutual ties binding workers and employers' reduces criminality" (p. 146). Moreover, Irwin (2009) argues that "doing good involves having a job with a 'living wage,' security, and job satisfaction" (p. 132).

For those returning from prison, obtaining and maintaining a job is likely the first, and most important, step required to move up the economic and social ladder (see Harding et al., 2014). When incarcerated persons and parolees are asked to express their needs, employment and job training are typically at, or near, the top of the list (Erickson et al., 1973; Nelson et al., 1999; Visher & Lattimore, 2007). However, many returning prisoners have low levels of formal education, lack employment skills, and have limited work experience (Harding et al., 2019; Petersilia, 2003). Moreover, a person's race/ethnicity has a significant negative effect on obtaining even low-wage employment, equal to or greater than the impact of having a criminal record (Decker et al., 2015; Pager, 2007; Pager et al., 2009). Pager (2007, p. 101) notes that "while being black or having a criminal record each represent a strike against the [job] applicant, with two strikes, you're out." Because of these barriers, some individuals have taken to starting their own businesses and becoming entrepreneurs. Unfortunately, their criminal past often prohibits these self-employment ventures from providing gainful employment or the experience necessary to gain other jobs (Matthews, 2021; see the Collateral Consequences section later).

Extant research indicates that obtaining and maintaining stable full-time employment for formerly incarcerated persons is a task easier said than done. Consequently, as Western (2018, p. 84; Sugie, 2018) writes, "A poverty-level income in a minimum-wage job is often a best-case scenario for this population," or "final destination" (Matthews, 2021, p. 25). This sort of short-term "survival work" influenced Sugie (2018; see also De Giorgi, 2017; Harding et al., 2019; Western, 2018) to conclude that "in the long term, foraging portends a bleak future. . . . Foraging jobs do not promote skill building that can be leveraged into a career" (p. 1457). Unfortunately, many returning prisoners also appear to be frustrated and unhappy because they have few options besides low-paying and "dead end" jobs (Visher et al., 2008).

Halushka (2020) provides insight into how individuals released from prison (several years before being interviewed) navigate this reality, writing that formerly incarcerated persons "aged-out of crime" by learning how to become "professionally poor" (p. 234). Their situation consists of navigating and recycling between low-wage jobs, public assistance, and transitional housing programs, often years after release from prison. Halushka (2020) notes that the men in the sample learned how to navigate these systems and survive but that no matter how proficient they were at overcoming certain obstacles, they were never able to establish themselves as financially stable. Other scholars have found evidence of this reality and emphasize the theme of survival, whether it be panhandling to make ends meet even when employed (De Giorgi, 2017) or participating in the underground economy, mainly small hustles in "the drug game" (Fader, 2013, p. 220). All this being the case, it is not surprising that formerly incarcerated persons have significantly lower rates of wealth accumulation, which impacts not only the individuals themselves but also their families and children (Maroto, 2015; Zaw et al., 2016).

Housing and Neighborhood Context

Obtaining and sustaining safe and secure housing is a challenge for many formerly incarcerated persons. Most persons returning home from prison will initially move in with family (Clark, 2015; Nelson et al., 1999; Solomon et al., 2006). However, approximately 10% of released individuals will experience homelessness at the time of their release or shortly after (Greenberg & Rosenheck, 2008). A substantial minority also return initially to transitional housing, work release centers, or temporary emergency shelters (Clark, 2015). For example, perhaps 8%–15% (Remster, 2019; Sugie, 2018) will live in shelters at or soon after release from prison. Couloute (2018b) argues that housing insecurity (living in a rooming house, hotel, or motel) provides a more realistic measurement of the number of formerly incarcerated people lacking access to permanent housing. She found that the rate of housing insecurity was nearly three times greater than the homelessness rate. Moreover, Remster (2019, p. 459) finds that those who utilize shelters continue to do so multiple times over 7 years postrelease. Western (2018; Harding et al., 2019) notes that in the first couple of years postrelease almost no formerly incarcerated persons were able to secure independent housing. Thus, for a substantial minority of persons reentering the community, housing insecurity is a long-term outcome.

Research consistently points to the fact that neighborhoods and residential context matter for a wide variety of social, health, behavioral, and economic reasons (Sampson, 2012; Sharkey & Faber, 2014). The geographic concentration of returning prisoners in inner-city minority neighborhoods has become an important topic of interest for prisoner reentry researchers (Sampson & Loeffler, 2010; Travis et al., 2014). The reality of reentry is that at least half of released prisoners return to their old neighborhood (La Vigne et al., 2009; Yahner & Visher, 2008) or to a similarly disadvantaged community with high rates of crime and relatively few services and support systems to promote successful reintegration (Clear, 2007; Harding et al., 2013; Travis et al., 2014). Released prisoners themselves certainly appear to recognize that their chances of success are diminished by returning to the same old neighborhood as many report that drug dealing is a major problem, that it is difficult to avoid crime, and that their neighborhood is not a good place to find a job (Brooks et al., 2008; La Vigne et al., 2009; Visher & Courtney, 2007). Additionally, prisoners who return to more disadvantaged and disorganized neighborhoods recidivate at a greater rate (Kubrin & Stewart, 2006; Yahner & Visher, 2008; see also Kirk, 2012). Kubrin and Stewart (2006, p. 189) argue that "by ignoring community context, we are likely setting up ex-inmates for failure."

Housing difficulties are largely due to formerly incarcerated persons' exclusion from public and private housing markets (Equal Rights Center, 2016; Thacher, 2008; U.S. Commission on Civil Rights, 2019). Additionally, housing application requirements such as expensive security deposits, credit checks, and professional references often prohibit individuals with a criminal record from obtaining safe and affordable housing (Couloute, 2018b; U.S. Commission on Civil Rights, 2019). This reality forces these individuals into substandard housing conditions in disadvantaged neighborhoods with high crime rates (Desmond, 2016). Serving time in prison thus seems to have a detrimental impact on the quality of housing as those who recently returned home often report living in less healthy conditions than before their imprisonment (Weijters & More, 2015). This finding suggests a downward housing trajectory or spiral of sorts, at least initially upon return to the community.

When individuals cannot secure safe and affordable housing, other barriers to reentry intensify (Geller & Curtis, 2011). Individuals who struggle finding housing are more likely to have a substance abuse issue, a mental health condition, or both (Greenberg & Rosenheck, 2008). Without adequate housing, employment becomes harder to obtain (Fries et al., 2014; Tran-Leung, 2015). Research consistently finds that residential instability increases the likelihood of recidivism (Clark, 2015; Lutze et al., 2014; Steiner et al., 2015; Visher & Courtney, 2007). In particular, periods of homelessness significantly increase the risk of recidivism, including return to prison for parole revocations (Lutze et al., 2014; Metraux & Culhane, 2004; Steiner et al., 2015; Tran-Leung, 2015). Similarly, Clark (2015) determined that rearrest rates were highest for persons released directly to emergency shelters or motels, whereas revocation rates were highest for those released to correctional-based transitional housing.

Despite these barriers associated with housing, there are programs that have been found to alleviate these issues for individuals experiencing homelessness. Programs that provide housing and supportive services for individuals have shown to be effective in reducing recidivism (Lutze et al., 2014; Tsai & Rosenheck, 2012). By providing "housing first" and support without unnecessary restrictions on these services, the barriers to reentry can become easier to overcome (Tsemberis, 2010).

Family Relationships and Marriage
Strong social bonds to conventional society are thought to be important for successful prisoner reintegration (Petersilia, 2003; Western et al., 2015; Wolff & Draine, 2004), with the strength and quality of one's family relationships being of central importance (Boman & Mowen, 2017; Harding et al., 2014; Visher et al., 2009). Returning prisoners consistently report receiving high levels of both material (housing, food, money, clothing) and emotional (encouragement, acceptance, a person to talk to, etc.) support from their families, often exceeding their prerelease expectations (La Vigne et al., 2009). After release, many released prisoners felt that family support had been an important factor in avoiding a return to prison (Harding et al., 2019; Visher & La Vigne, 2021). In fact, Visher and Courtney (2007) report that over the first year after release, the largest percentage of returning prisoners identified family support as the *most important thing* that had kept them out of prison. Similarly, Harding and colleagues' (2019; see also Boman & Mowen, 2018; Western, 2018) research indicates that better relationships with family (romantic partners, parents, children, and other close relations) provides important informal social controls that assist formerly incarcerated persons in remaining in the community and successfully pursuing life goals.

Marriage has long been a key factor in producing better outcomes for desistance from crime. However, Petersilia (2003) cites that only 17% of prisoners are married. A meta-analysis of 58 studies found that individuals who are married are typically less likely to reoffend, especially when the strength of the relationship is considered (Skardhamar et al., 2015). Additionally, formerly incarcerated persons with social support from romantic partners (and family members) were at increased odds to experience upward economic mobility (Harding et al., 2014) and reduced substance use (Visher et al., 2009). These relationships also allow individuals to redefine themselves in a more prosocial light (family man, good provider, good father or mother, etc.). Having a prosocial partner is not only a way to avoid recidivism but also clearly a method to improve the lives of these individuals.

Unfortunately, marriage and family relationships are impacted by crime. Barnes and colleagues (2014) found that individuals involved in crime are less likely to get married. Meanwhile, Bersani and DiPietro (2016) determined that the dissolution of marriage (divorce) tends to increase offending and recidivism for men. Additionally, peer criminality may have a larger impact on an individual's criminal behavior when compared to the support from family—meaning that attachment to deviant peers and their lifestyle may be more impactful than familial support (Boman & Mowen, 2018). Essentially, if former prisoners can establish a relationship with a partner (and/or have family members) with social capital, the odds of reoffending go down. However, this situation is far from reality for many formerly incarcerated persons. As such, attempts to redevelop prosocial bonds and social capital appear to be critical for successful reintegration (Harding et al., 2019; Travis et al., 2014; Wolff & Draine, 2004).

Health Concerns (Substance Use, Mental Illness, Chronic Conditions)

By examining different types of substance abuse (drug, alcohol, and both), Dowden and Brown (2002) found that it plays a critical role in recidivism research. In fact, they are so confident in their findings that they argue that "drug abuse may be the strongest single predictor of recidivism" (Dowden & Brown, 2002, p. 261). More recent studies support this view, as Western (2018; see also Harding et al., 2019; Visher & La Vigne, 2021) found that drug and/or alcohol use played a significant role in return to prison, employment and income instability, and/or homelessness and housing insecurity. Importantly, individuals returning home recognize their drug use as a primary factor in many of their legal and social problems (La Vigne et al., 2004). When formerly incarcerated persons recidivate, the greatest percentage recognizes that drug use influenced their return to prison (Brooks et al., 2008; Visher & Courtney, 2007).

Western (2018) describes "human frailty" of persons returning to the community from prison as "the correlated adversity of mental illness, drug use, and disability" (p. 59). Other researchers have also found that mental health issues are often associated with alcohol and substance abuse and can make employment and housing more difficult to obtain and maintain, which ultimately affects recidivism (Fries et al., 2014; Mallik-Kane & Visher, 2008). Likewise, evidence suggests that having a co-occurring disorder (substance use and mental health) is linked to recidivism (Fries et al., 2014; Wilson et al., 2011). Thus, dealing with health-related concerns is an important factor in the life course after imprisonment (Massoglia & Pridemore, 2015).

The Harsh Reality of Life After Prison

For many, "going straight" after prison may be experienced as "'an endurance test with little to no reward" (Nugent & Schinkel, 2016, p. 13; see also De Giorgi, 2017; Patton & Farrall, 2021). In fact, many persons returning back to the community from prison will end up living "a menial and lonely existence" (Nugent & Schinkel, 2016, p. 570). Western (2018, p. 60) advances the idea that "the people we ask to make the largest changes in their lives often have the least capacity to do so." Irwin (2005, p. 191) argues that even though "most parolees *eventually* stay out of prison," neither formerly incarcerated persons nor the general public would consider this a successful outcome. Austin and Irwin (2000, p. 156; Irwin, 2005, p. 197) compound this negative prognosis by estimating that more than 25% of released prisoners "eventually end up on the streets, where they live out a short life of dereliction, alcoholism, and drug abuse." Unfortunately, this sort of marginal existence is likely the long-term outcome for many people released from prison. Harding and colleagues (2014) examined the "trajectories of well-being" for 22 released prisoners over a 2–3-year period. They report that nearly two thirds of these individuals (14/22, 63.6%) suffered from either continual hardship indicating "transitioning between extreme *desperation* and *survival* when they were not in custody" or "a vacillation between periods of *stability* and *survival*" (Harding et al., 2014, p. 450). Similarly, other researchers often find that many of the released persons they interviewed are struggling to find safe and affordable housing and avoid homelessness, find employment with a living wage, and deal with their physical and mental health conditions (De Giorgi, 2017; Miller, 2021; Western, 2018).

The Stigma of Incarceration in Prison

It is now generally understood that formerly incarcerated persons are stigmatized and discriminated against in society (see, e.g., LeBel, 2012a; Petersilia, 2003; Travis et al., 2014). Petersilia (2003, p. 19), for example, suggests that the plight of felons is best summed up as such: "A criminal conviction—no matter how trivial or how long ago it occurred—scars one for life." Moreover, Irwin (2005), based on 40 years of research with incarcerated and formerly incarcerated individuals, argues that "doing good" in a postprison lifestyle is "very difficult for ex-convicts to achieve because of their debilitating prison experiences and their ex-convict stigma" (p. 192).

Researchers have pointed out that formerly incarcerated persons have multiple stigmatized identities and suffer from double or triple stigma as a former prisoner and because of other personal characteristics such as their race (Pager, 2007), past substance use (van Olphen et al., 2009), and/or a mental disorder (Mallik-Kane & Visher, 2008). The findings from LeBel's (2012b; Tobin-Tyler & Brockmann, 2017; Western, 2018) research reveals that discrimination based on one's status as a former prisoner is only one obstacle men and women face, and must overcome, upon reentry to the community. To assess perceptions of discrimination, respondents were asked, "[Do] you believe that you have been discriminated against?" and were then supplied with a list of 10 reasons. Most (79.4%) identified at least one reason for discrimination, and almost half (46.6%) reported three reasons or more. More respondents reported discrimination for being a former prisoner (65.3%) than for any other reason. Discrimination for race or ethnicity was the second most frequently reported reason (48.0%), followed closely by past drug or alcohol use (47.5%; see Link et al., 1997; Luoma et al., 2007) and lack of money or being poor (35.3%; see Hansen et al., 2014). A substantial minority of formerly incarcerated persons also reported experiencing discrimination because of their gender, religious beliefs, HIV-positive status, and a diagnosed mental disorder (Link et al., 1989). Tobin-Tyler and Brockmann (2017, p. 546) assert that "these overlapping and mutually reinforcing characteristics are each stigmatizing conditions independent of criminal justice involvement."

With the proliferation of criminal registries and the increased use of background checks (see Denver et al., 2017; Lageson & Maruna, 2018; Solomon, 2012), it has become much harder for former prisoners to keep their past hidden (i.e., to remain merely discreditable and not discredited; Goffman, 1963) in our information-driven society. For example, Lageson and Maruna (2018, p. 117) assert that "by far the biggest change in the labeling dynamics of the past two decades . . . has been the remarkable proliferation of criminal records across easily searchable electronic databases (Jacobs, 2015)." Umez and Gaines (2021) note that background checks and/or conviction disclosure requirements on applications may deter persons with criminal convictions from seeking many jobs. There has been an increase in criminal background screening in admission to college (Stewart & Uggen, 2020; Weissman et al., 2015). Recently, Stewart and Uggen (2020) found that 72% of universities still inquire about criminal history. Having to disclose a felony conviction appears to increase the attrition rate for completing the application process (Stewart & Uggen, 2020; Weissman et al., 2015). Essentially, online criminal records "make the issue of stigma both more urgent and more intractable" (Lageson & Maruna, 2018, p. 114).

There is increasing acknowledgment that not only being labeled an "ex-con" but also the perception that one is stigmatized by society may make prisoner reintegration more difficult (LeBel, 2012a; Owens, 2009; Winnick & Bodkin, 2009). Many researchers have assessed perceptions of "ex-con" stigma from the perspective of currently or formerly incarcerated persons (Gunnison & Helfgott, 2013; Halsey et al., 2017; Harding, 2003; Irwin, 1970, 2005; LeBel,

2012a, 2012b; Munn, 2012; Winnick & Bodkin, 2009). Research has consistently found that stigmatized individuals attempt to "pass" as normal (Goffman, 1963) or more generally strive to keep their stigmatized status a secret from others (e.g., Jones et al., 1984). According to Irwin (1970, p. 137), "Most ex-convicts can 'pass' with ease" if they so desire. In several qualitative studies of formerly incarcerated persons, "passing" behavior or concealment of one's criminal past and incarceration history was found to be the most often used stigma management strategy (Harding, 2003; Munn, 2012). LeBel's (2016) research with formerly incarcerated persons found that those with higher scores for concealment had lower self-esteem and were less satisfied with their lives. These findings suggest that the greater use of concealment in one's personal life and in filling out applications might have a potentially harmful impact on facilitating the successful reentry and reintegration of a substantial number of formerly incarcerated persons. Munn (2012) found that some of the formerly incarcerated men in her study "maintain both spatial and social/emotional distance" from others to "evade judgement" (p. 168; Nugent & Schinkel, 2016). This sort of avoidant strategy is similar to Irwin's (2005, p. 198) description of the postprison lifestyle of "drifting on the edge" or "laying low."

A major consequence of being labeled a criminal involves the exclusion of labeled individuals from conventional opportunities (Sampson & Laub, 1997). In a study of formerly incarcerated persons in New York State, LeBel (2012a) found that many reported experiences of personal rejection in their lifetime because of their status as a former prisoner for several important activities and events. The most commonly reported rejection experiences involved employment and housing. For employment, 52.1% reported that rejection occurred at least sometimes; almost one quarter (23.9%) indicated this occurred often or very often. Similarly, the majority (71%) of male formerly incarcerated persons in the Returning Home study felt that their criminal record had negatively affected their job search (Visher et al., 2008). For housing, 42.7% reported that rejection occurred at least sometimes; almost one quarter (21.6%) indicated this occurred often or very often (LeBel, 2012a). These somewhat low numbers reporting experiences of rejection may be partly a result of avoiding situations where these types of discrimination can occur.

Importantly, stigma appears to have real and long-term consequences, as research results reveal that soon-to-be released prisoners' perception of "social prejudice against ex-convicts" predicts recidivism (LeBel et al., 2008), and that stronger perceptions of being personally stigmatized because of one's status as a former prisoner are negatively related to believing that "a former prisoner that wants to can 'make it' in a law-abiding way in society" and to self-esteem (see LeBel, 2012b; LeBel et al., 2015). LeBel and colleagues (2015) examined perceptions of the stability of stigmatization in a study involving formerly incarcerated persons who were asked to respond with their level of agreement to the statement, "Society will never fully accept that former prisoners have paid their debt to society." They found that formerly incarcerated persons receiving reentry services were very pessimistic, and that the majority (56%) agreed or strongly agreed that one's debt to society can never be paid. An important examination of the long-term psychological effects of stigma is provided in Farrall and colleagues' (2014) longitudinal study of probationers. They noted that a key component of "interviewees' emotional trajectories was that of frustration—of the feeling that one's future was being unnecessarily impeded because of what one had done in the past" (p. 282). For those 10–13 years postconviction, "intermittent reminders of their past returned to haunt them in the course of trying to achieve normal objectives" (Farrall et al., 2014, p. 211; see also Gunnison & Helfgott, 2013, p. 140). Thus, perhaps the most damaging long-term psychological effects of having a felony record and/or serving time in prison is the perception that stigmatization based on one's criminal past will never end.

Collateral Consequences of a Felony Conviction

It is well documented that former prisoners suffer from many collateral consequences or "civil disabilities" such as statutory restrictions placed on public and private employment, eligibility for public assistance/benefits, public housing, voting, financial aid to attend college, firearm ownership, criminal registration, and the like (American Bar Association, 2018; Travis, 2002; Umez & Gaines, 2021). Travis (2002) refers to these restrictions as "invisible punishments," while Miller and Stuart (2017) discuss how these restrictions represent the consequences of "carceral citizenship." Uggen and Stewart (2015) refer to these collateral consequences of punishment as "piling on," and in general, these civil disabilities can severely limit the life chances of persons with felony convictions. O'Hear (2019, p. 230) suggests that "collateral consequences may prove to be the sanctions that are the most significant to many defendants over the long run," while the American Bar Association (2018, p. 9) notes that they "might have lifetime effect" for persons with criminal records.

A database titled the National Inventory of Collateral Consequences of Conviction (NICCC) catalogs and describes over 40,000 collateral consequences imposed by statutory and regulatory provisions from all 50 states. The NICCC is operated by the American Institutes for Research as part of the National Reentry Resource Center (Umez & Gaines, 2021). The average number of active collateral consequences in each state is estimated to be approximately 1,700, with close to 950 of these listed as federal consequences that apply throughout the United States (Umez & Gaines, 2021, p. 3). Recently, Love and Schlussel (2020a, p. 1) have documented extensive state-level activity in "reducing barriers faced by people with criminal records in the workplace, at the ballot box, and in many other areas of daily life." In fact, the vast majority of states (43) enacted laws in 2019 reducing some form of collateral consequences (Love & Schlussel, 2020a; Umez & Gaines, 2021).

A substantial majority (72%) of all collateral consequences catalogued in the NICCC limit employment (Umez & Gaines, 2021, p. 6). These employment-related collateral consequences include more than 10,000 limitations in each of three distinct categories: on hiring and retaining workers; on occupational and professional licenses, and on business licensure and participation (Umez & Gaines, 2021; Umez & Pirius, 2018). Laws frequently bar employers from hiring formerly incarcerated persons (convicted felons) in many sectors of the economy including jobs involving child care, elder care, health care, and financial services (Love & Schlussel, 2020b; Umez & Gaines, 2021). According to Umez and Pirius (2018), licensed workers now make up nearly 25% of all employed Americans. Unfortunately, many of these consequences impact some of the most in-demand job fields or industries: health care; public employment; education and schools; and adult care, nursing homes, and residential care facilities (Umez & Gaines, 2021, p. 12). The limitations on business licensure and participation include "self-employed" contract positions including driving for Uber or Lyft, transportation services that are now commonplace in most metropolitan areas.

Importantly, nearly half (44%) of employment-related consequences are mandatory, while the vast majority (83%) have a lifetime or undefined ("indefinite") duration or effect (Umez & Gaines, 2021). A conviction for "any felony" triggers about half of all mandatory employment-related consequences listed in the NICCC (Umez & Gaines, 2021). O'Hear (2019, p. 165) posits that "a conviction for a violent crime increasingly seems even more momentous—pushing the person into a veritable third-class citizenship." He reports that persons convicted of a violent crime are subject to an additional 600 categorical violence consequences (CVCs) that impact all stages of the criminal process from preconviction to reentry to the community from prison. In particular, persons with violent convictions may be more restricted from obtaining employment (occupational licenses) involving working directly with children, the elderly, or persons with disabilities (O'Hear, 2019, p. 212). Moreover, O'Hear (2019, p. 229) notes that these collateral consequences are often applied retroactively to old violent convictions.

Whittle (2018) examined the collateral sanction/consequences literature published between 1995 and 2014 assessing the effects of certain types of sanctions on recidivism. Whittle (2018) reports that the majority of research finds that some collateral sanctions, such as public assistance and housing, increase recidivism, while most other types do not appear to significantly impact recidivism. She concludes that "at least for some sanctions, recidivism may be an unintended consequence of collateral sanction policies" (Whittle, 2018, p. 518).

There are several ways to decrease collateral consequences, including ban-the-box measures (Avery, 2019), certificates of rehabilitation or relief (COR; Love & Schussel, 2020b; McCann et al., 2021), and record sealing and expungement (Jacobs, 2015). The ban-the-box movement was initiated to provide greater opportunity for persons with criminal convictions to get over the first hurdle of having to acknowledge their criminal past on public-sector job applications. Avery (2019) reports that 35 states and more than 150 cities and counties have adopted ban-the-box policies. Some jurisdictions (state, local, and federal) have extended policies involving these fair-chance laws to private employers and government contractors (Love & Schlussel, 2020a). These laws often require employers to consider if and how criminal convictions are related to the job, how long ago the conviction occurred, and evidence of rehabilitation (Avery, 2019). Although focused almost exclusively on employment, a similar "ban-the-box" initiative is needed for housing as formerly incarcerated persons also face many barriers in obtaining safe and secure accommodations. Federal law allows local housing authorities to consider criminal convictions, and some offenses (i.e., drug and sex) can disqualify formerly incarcerated persons from living in public housing (Jacobs, 2015).

According to Umez and Gaines (2021, p. 18), certificates of relief or rehabilitation convert mandatory collateral consequences into discretionary ones. CORs thus provide a formerly incarcerated person with the right not to be automatically denied employment or licensure solely based on their criminal record. However, McCann and colleagues (2021) report that only about one third (16) of states currently have CORs. Garretson (2016) argues that to make the use of certificates of rehabilitation more effective moving forward, "legislation must exist with a strong education component, an expectation of use, and be utilized with legislation that gives certificates teeth" (p. 41).

A standard topic in corrections textbooks is the "principle of least eligibility," which is defined as "the doctrine that prisoners ought to receive no goods or services in excess of those available to people who have lived within the law" (Clear et al., 2016, p. 356). For example, Matthews (2021, p. 40; Garland et al., 2013) found that people in the community indicated "formerly incarcerated individuals might only be entitled to a second-class American Dream" and should not expect to receive standard financial indicators of success such as owning a home or car. However, some recent research indicates that the American public may be more receptive to limiting collateral consequences that negatively impact employment, as well as others "found to have no useful purpose" (Burton et al., 2020). In particular, Burton and colleagues (2020, p. 26) report that nearly two thirds of the general public think that ban-the-box is a "good idea," while more than 70% want collateral sanctions eliminated unless they can be "shown to reduce crime." Overall, implementing ban-the-box measures and certificates of rehabilitation can improve employment opportunities and life chances of formerly incarcerated persons as research indicates that a person with a 7-year-old felony conviction is no more likely to receive another conviction than a person who has never been convicted of a crime (Blumstein & Nakamura, 2009; Kurlychek et al., 2006). Basically, the actual structural impediments to desistance and successful reintegration are extensive and need to be lessened and removed for formerly incarcerated persons to have a more realistic opportunity to succeed (Farrall et al., 2014; Healy, 2013; LeBel et al., 2008; Patton & Farrall, 2021).

One Way Forward: Becoming a Professional Ex-, Wounded Healer, or Advocate

As noted previously, obtaining and maintaining employment with a living wage is difficult for many people returning home from prison. Researchers now recognize a strategy or orientation among formerly incarcerated persons (and people recovering from substance misuse) involving becoming a "professional ex-" (Brown, 1991) or a "wounded healer" (Honeywell, 2019; LeBel, 2007; Maruna, 2001; Smith, 2021; White, 2000). Brown (1991) asserts that it is important to consider how one might "adopt a legitimate career premised upon an identity that embraces one's deviant history" (p. 220). Similarly, Maruna (2001) argues that "the desisting self-narrative frequently involves reworking a delinquent history into a source of wisdom to be drawn from while acting as a drug counselor, youth worker, community volunteer, or mutual-help group member" (p. 117). Although it is likely impossible to measure the true extent of the wounded healer or professional ex- phenomenon as it relates to formerly incarcerated persons, it appears that a substantial number attempt to exit the "convict role" by helping others in a formal capacity.

Miller and Stuart (2017, p. 542) assert that "many organizations have enacted 'felon friendly policies' in the face of labor market exclusion." For many of the individuals choosing the wounded healer or professional ex- path, opportunities for employment are most available in the prisoner reentry service field (Miller & Stuart, 2017). Irwin (2005, p. 178) noted that "most of the program staff themselves, often the directors, are ex-convicts. . . . This type of career is very popular among prisoners and ex-prisoners." Moreover, LeBel and colleagues (2015) report that several staff members at programs providing reentry services expressed that "this is the only job where my criminal record is viewed as an asset." In fact, a majority (58.2%) of the clients "plan to pursue a career" where they can give back and help other people in some capacity (LeBel et al., 2015; see also Irwin, 2005; Maruna, 2001).

LeBel and colleagues (2015) examined if, how, and why formerly incarcerated staff members of prisoner reentry programs differ from the clients. As compared to the clients, formerly incarcerated staff members had served more prison time, were significantly older, had completed some college or more, and were more likely to be currently married. Thus, they appeared to be more "on-time" in regard to life course milestones than the clients currently receiving reentry services. Having a staff position as a professional ex- was positively related to perceiving less personal stigma, having more prosocial attitudes/beliefs, using active coping strategies such as advocacy, self-esteem, satisfaction with life, and having more positive relationships with family members (LeBel et al., 2015). Moreover, staff members were much less likely to forecast that they will get arrested in the next 3 years. Therefore, the professional exes appear to have undergone a remarkable change in their self-identities and worldviews and convey a strong sense of meaning and purpose in their lives (LeBel et al., 2015; Maruna, 2001).

Unfortunately, many of these professional ex- positions do not pay well. For example, LeBel and colleagues (2015) report that few (19.2%) staff members reported income of more than $2,500 dollars per month despite the fact that the vast majority (86.2%) were working full time. This finding suggests that formerly incarcerated persons might be stuck in low-paying positions due to few other viable options for employment, the lack of credentials or skills for promotion, or a "razor wire ceiling" of sorts keeping them from moving up into supervisory positions (LeBel et al., 2015; Miller & Stuart, 2017; Nixon, 2017; Umez &

Gaines, 2021, p. 13). Perhaps in the long run, the way to be the most successful after identifying as a wounded healer is allowing oneself to move on from that role.

Maruna and LeBel (2009; see also LeBel, 2009; Smith, 2021) have discussed going a "third mile" as moving beyond the helping roles of the professional ex-/wounded healer to engaging in more direct activism and advocacy efforts to reform the criminal justice system in myriad ways. They argue that this is a natural next step in efforts toward destigmatization of formerly incarcerated persons. Of course, it is important to keep in mind that only a relatively small cadre of individuals participate in "third mile" forms of activism (Maruna & LeBel, 2009; Smith, 2021). Many of these organizations (JustLeadershipUSA [JLUSA], 2023; All of Us or None, 2021) specifically employ formerly incarcerated persons to engage in community organizing, public speaking, and prison reform actions (Martin, 2017; Nixon, 2017; Smith, 2021). Similar to those formerly incarcerated persons working for agencies providing social services, those engaged in paid advocacy/activism positions can be considered "high-achieving" in regard to their formal education, social support, housing situation, and employment skills more generally (Smith, 2021, p. 54).

Glenn Martin, the founder of JLUSA, argues that "criminal justice reformers will need to engage and employ the leadership of the world's most formidable experts on incarceration and criminal justice—the incarcerated themselves" (Martin, 2017, p. 51; see also Nixon, 2017; Smith, 2021). JLUSA, for example, attempts to accomplish reforms in the criminal justice system through advocacy campaigns, leadership training, and member engagement. The JLUSA website states that " [w]e amplify the power of people who have been directly impacted by the criminal legal system to self-organize and empower their communities to dismantle racist and oppressive systems in their communities to build a just U.S." (*JLUSA, 2023*).

LeBel's (2009) quantitative research provides some support of the benefits of involvement in advocacy for formerly incarcerated persons. His survey research found that an advocacy orientation is positively correlated with one's psychological well-being and, in particular, satisfaction with life as a whole. He found a strong negative correlation between one's advocacy orientation and criminal attitudes and behavior, indicating that this strategy may help to maintain a person's prosocial identity and facilitate ongoing desistance from crime. These findings suggest that involvement in advocacy-related activities might have potential in facilitating the successful reintegration of some formerly incarcerated persons.

Future Research and Conclusions

There is a great need to better utilize a "life course perspective" to examine the important events that occur before, during, and after incarceration (Mears et al., 2013). Reentry and reintegration are long-term processes with many ups and downs even for those "doing good" (Irwin, 2005, p. 192; Maruna et al., 2004). As Schnittker (2014, p. 136) argues, "The psychological consequences of incarceration are easy to overlook," and so is the seemingly never-ending struggle to overcome the stigma of a criminal past (LeBel, 2012a). As a society, we need to abandon the old definition of successful reentry, meaning that an individual managed to avoid arrest or conviction for a new crime (Halushka, 2020; Western, 2018). By assessing the quality of life (socioeconomic viability, physical and mental well-being, and civic integration) for individuals, we can better understand the messy nature of prisoner reentry (De Giorgi, 2017). Of course, this is no small task.

Moving forward, longitudinal research, using longer assessment timeframes and combining qualitative, quantitative, and more interdisciplinary and ethnographic work, is needed to provide a more in-depth understanding of the life course for persons who have been incarcerated (Fader, 2013; Halushka, 2020; Kazemian & Travis, 2015; Liem & Kunst, 2013). Fader's (2013) collection of narratives diagramming the chaotic lives of young men provides in-depth information as to how these individuals navigated life after incarceration but also provides a window into various ups and downs that many experience. The study of desistance and prisoner reentry is strengthened not only by the number of years we "track" people but also by the detailed life histories of the individuals experiencing these processes. By favoring depth over breadth, we can better understand some of the more hidden aspects to prisoner reentry such as treatment heterogeneity, stigma management strategies, and the impact of collateral consequences (Gaes, 2016; LeBel, 2012a, Whittle, 2018). Moreover, as suggested by Gunnison and Helfgott (2013, p. 145; see also Grounds, 2005; Halushka, 2020; Remster, 2019), "examining the differences in the postprison life experiences of ex-offenders as they move further out in the survival curve" is essential.

Graham and McNeill (2017) argue that tertiary desistance (obtaining a sense of belonging in the community) may be out of reach for many individuals because of the stigma a criminal conviction carries. The successful re/integration of formerly incarcerated persons requires addressing stigma and discrimination (collateral consequences) in mainstream society to give them a realistic "second chance" at becoming law-abiding, tax-paying citizens. This will involve education of the public in the harm of current practices of exclusion as well as fostering the idea that former prisoners, through the consistent display of prosocial behavior, can earn their way back to full citizenship status. In effect, this would recognize formerly incarcerated persons' "debt to society" as fully paid and give them official permission to legally move on from the past (Lageson & Maruna, 2018; Maruna, 2001). For this to occur, communities in America will need to halt the accumulation of stigmatizing laws and reduce the dissemination of discrediting information to the public. Without a momentous reduction in the structural obstacles that hinder re/integration of incarcerated persons, many in our society will remain outsiders for the rest of their lives.

References

All of Us or None. (2021). *About AOUON*. https://prisonerswithchildren.org/about-aouon/

Alper, M., & Durose, M. R. (2018). *2018 update on prisoner recidivism: A 9-year follow-up period* (NCJ 250975). U.S. Department of Justice, Office of Justice Programs, Bureau of Justice Statistics.

American Bar Association. (2018). *Collateral consequences of criminal convictions judicial bench book: The National Inventory of Collateral Consequences of Criminal Convictions*.

American Psychiatric Association (2020). *Diagnostic and statistical manual of mental disorders*, text revision (4th ed).

Anderson, S., & McNeill, F. (2019). Desistance and cognitive transformation. In D.P. Farrington, L. Kazemian, & A.R. Piquero (Eds.), *The Oxford handbook of developmental and life-course criminology* (pp. 600–623). Oxford University Press.

Apel, R., & Ramakers, A. (2019). Impact of incarceration on employment prospects. In B. M. Huebner & N. Frost (Eds.), *ASC Division on Corrections and Sentencing handbook, Vol. 3: The handbook on the consequences of sentencing and punishment decisions* (pp. 85–104). Routledge.

Aresti, A., Eatough, V., & Brooks-Gordon, B. (2010). Doing time after time: An interpretative phenomenological analysis of reformed ex-prisoners' experiences of self-change, identity and career opportunities. *Psychology, Crime & Law, 16*(3), 169–190.

Austin, J., & Irwin, J. (2000). *It's about time: America's imprisonment binge* (3rd ed.). Wadsworth.

Avery, B. (2019). *Ban the box: U.S. cities, counties, and states adopt fair hiring policies*. National Employment Law Project.

Barnes, J. C., Golden, K., Mancini, C., Boutwell, B. B., Beaver, K. M., & Diamond, B. (2014). Marriage and involvement in crime: A consideration of reciprocal effects in a nationally representative sample. *Justice Quarterly, 31*(2), 229–256.

Beck, A. J., Harrison, P. M., & Guerino, P. (2010). *Special report: Sexual victimization in juvenile facilities reported by youth, 2008–2009*. U.S. Department of Justice, Bureau of Justice Statistics.

Bernstein, N. (2014). *Burning down the house: The end of juvenile prison*. New Press.

Bersani, B. E., & DiPietro, S. M. (2016). Examining the salience of marriage to offending for black and Hispanic men. *Justice Quarterly, 33*(3), 510–537.

Binswanger, I. A., Stern, M. F., Yamashita, T. E., Mueller, S. R., Baggett, T. P., & Blatchford, P. J. (2016). Clinical risk factors for death after release from prison in Washington State: A nested case–control study. *Addiction, 111*(3), 499–510.

Blumstein, A., & Nakamura, K. (2009). Redemption in the presence of widespread criminal background checks. *Criminology, 42*(2), 327–359.

Boman, J. H., IV, & Mowen, T. J. (2017). Building the ties that bind, breaking the ties that don't: Family support, criminal peers, and reentry success. *Criminology & Public Policy, 16*, 753–774.

Boman, J. H., IV, & Mowen, T. J. (2018). The role of turning points in establishing baseline differences between people in developmental and life-course criminology. *Criminology, 56*(1), 191–224.

Brooks, L. E., Solomon, A. L., Kohl, R., Osborne, J. W. L., Reid, J., McDonald, S. M., & Hoover, S. M. (2008). *Reincarcerated: The experiences of men returning to Massachusetts prisons*. Urban Institute.

Brown, J. D. (1991). The professional ex-: An alternative for exiting the deviant career. *Sociological Quarterly, 32*, 219–230.

Bucklen, K. B., & Zajac, G. (2009). But some of them don't come back (to prison!): Resource deprivation and thinking errors as determinants of parole success and failure. *Prison Journal, 89*(3), 239–264.

Burnett, R. (1992). *The dynamics of recidivism: Summary report*. University of Oxford, Centre for Criminological Research.

Burnett, R., & Maruna, S. (2004). So "prison works", does it? The criminal careers of 130 men released from prison under home secretary, Michael Howard. *Howard Journal, 43*(4), 390–404.

Burton, A. L., Burton, V. S., Jr., Cullen, F. T., Pickett, J. T., Butler, L. C., & Thielo, A. J. (2020). Beyond the new Jim Crow: Public support for removing and regulating collateral consequences. *Federal Probation, 84*(3), 19–33.

Bushway, S. (2020). What if people decide to desist? Implications for policy. In B. Orrell (Ed.), *Rethinking reentry* (pp. 140–162). American Enterprise Institute (AEI).

Bushway, S. D., & Apel, R. (2012). A signaling perspective on employment-based reentry programming. *Criminology and Public Policy, 11*(1), 21–50.

Carlson, B. E., Shafer, M. S., & Duffee, D. E. (2010). Traumatic histories and stressful life events of incarcerated parents II: Gender and ethnic differences in substance abuse and service needs. *Prison Journal, 90*(4), 494–515.

Carson, E. A. (2020). *Prisoners in 2019* (Bulletin, NCJ 255115). U.S. Department of Justice, Office of Justice Programs, Bureau of Justice Statistics.

Clark, V. A. (2015). *The effect of community context and post-release housing placements on recidivism*. Minnesota Department of Corrections.

Clear, T. R. (2007). *Imprisoning communities: How mass incarceration makes disadvantaged neighborhoods worse*. Oxford University Press.

Clear, T. R., Reisig, M. D., & Cole, G. F. (2016). *American corrections*. Cengage Learning.

Connett, A. V. (1973). Epilogue. In R. J. Erickson, W. J. Crow, L. A. Zurcher, & A. V. Connett (Eds.), *Paroled but not free* (pp. 106–116). Behavioral Publications.

Couloute, L. (2018a). *Getting back on course: Educational exclusion and attainment among formerly incarcerated people*. Prison Policy Initiative. https://www.prisonpolicy.org/reports/education.html

Couloute, L. (2018b). *Nowhere to go: Homelessness among formerly incarcerated people*. Prison Policy Initiative. https://www.prisonpolicy.org/reports/housing.html

Couloute, L., & Kopf, D. (2018). *Out of prison & out of work: Unemployment among formerly incarcerated people*. Prison Policy Initiative. https://www.prisonpolicy.org/reports/outofwork.html

De Giorgi, A. (2017). Back to nothing: Prisoner reentry and neoliberal neglect. *Social Justice, 44*(1), 83–120.

Decker, S. H., Ortiz, N., Spohn, C., & Hedberg, E. (2015). Criminal stigma, race, and ethnicity: The consequences of imprisonment for employment. *Journal of Criminal Justice, 43*(2), 108–121.

Dennison, C. R., & Demuth, S. (2018). The more you have the more you lose: Criminal justice involvement, ascribed socioeconomic status, and achieved SES. *Social Problems, 65*, 191–210.

Denver, M., Siwach, G., & Bushway, S. D. (2017). A new look at the employment and recidivism relationship through the lens of a criminal background check. *Criminology, 55*(1), 174–204.

Desmond, M. (2016). *Evicted: Poverty and profit in the American city*. Crown.

Dickson, S. R., Polaschek, D. L. L., & Casey, A. R. (2013). Can the quality of high-risk violent prisoners' release plans predict recidivism following intensive rehabilitation? A comparison with risk assessment instruments. *Psychology, Crime & Law, 19*, 371–389.

Division of Program Planning, Research and Evaluation. (2020). *Under custody report: Profile of under custody population as of January 1, 2019*. New York State Corrections and Community Supervision.

Dowden, C., & Brown, S. L. (2002). The role of substance abuse factors in predicting recidivism: A meta-analysis. *Psychology, Crime, & Law, 8*(3), 243–264.

Durose, M. R., & Antenangeli, L. (2021). *Recidivism of prisoners released in 34 states in 2012: A 5-year follow-up period (2012–2017)* (Special report, NCJ 255947). U.S. Department of Justice, Office of Justice Programs, Bureau of Justice Statistics.

Equal Rights Center. (2016). *Unlocking discrimination: A DC area testing investigation about racial discrimination and criminal records screening policies in housing.* equalrightscenter.org/site/DocServer/Unlocking_Discrimination_Web.pdf?docID=2722

Erickson, R. J., Crow, W. J., Zurcher, L. A., & Connett, A. V. (1973). *Paroled but not free*. Behavioral.

Fader, J. (2013). *Falling back: Incarceration and transitions to adulthood among urban youth*. Rutgers University Press.

Farrall, S., Hunter, B., Sharpe, G., & Calverley, A. (2014). *Criminal careers in transition: The social context of desistance from crime*. Oxford University Press.

Fries, L., Fedock, G., & Kubiak, S. P. (2014). Role of gender, substance use, and serious mental illness in anticipated post jail homelessness. *Social Work Research, 38*(2), 107–116.

Gaes, G. G. (2016). Does a prison term prevent or promote more crime? In T. G. Blomberg, J. M. Brancale, K. M. Beaver, & W. D. Bales (Eds.), *Advancing criminology and criminal justice policy* (pp. 282–296). Routledge.

Garland, B., Wodahl, E., & Schuhmann, R. (2013). Value conflict and public opinion toward prisoner reentry initiatives. *Criminal Justice Policy Review, 24*(1), 27–48.

Garretson, H. J. (2016). Legislating forgiveness: A study of post-conviction certificates as policy to address the employment consequences of a conviction. *Boston University Public Interest Law Journal, 25*(1), 1–41.

Geller, A., & Curtis, M. A. (2011) A sort of homecoming: Incarceration and the housing security of urban men. *Social Science Research, 40*(1), 1196–1213.

Giordano, P. C. (2014). Gender, crime, and desistance: Toward a theory of cognitive transformation. In J. A. Humphrey & P. Cordella (Eds.), *Effective interventions in the lives of criminal offenders* (pp. 41–62). Springer.

Giordano, P. C., Cernkovich, S. A., & Rudolph, J. L. (2002). Gender, crime and desistance: Toward a theory of cognitive transformation. *American Journal of Sociology, 107*, 990–1064.

Goffman, E. (1963). *Stigma: On the management of spoiled identity*. Prentice-Hall.

Gorski, T. T. (2010). *Post incarceration syndrome and relapse*. https://itj-gorski.blogspot.com/2010/11/post-incarceration-syndrome-pics-and.html

Graham, H., & McNeill, F. (2017). Desistance: Envisioning futures. In P. Carlen & L. A. França (Eds.), *Alternative criminologies* (pp. 433–451). Routledge.

Green, B. L., Miranda, J., Daroowalla, A., & Siddique, J. (2005). Trauma exposure, mental health functioning, and program needs of women in jail. *Crime & Delinquency, 51*(1), 133–151.

Greenberg, G. A., & Rosenheck, R. A. (2008). Homeless in the state and federal prison population. *Criminal Behavior and Mental Health, 18*, 88–103.

Grounds, A. T. (2005). Understanding the effects of wrongful imprisonment. *Crime and Justice, 32*, 1–58.

Gunnison, E., & Helfgott, J. B. (2013). *Offender reentry: Beyond crime & punishment*. Lynne Rienner Publishers.

Halsey, M., Armstrong, R., & Wright, S. (2017). "F*ck it!": Matza and the mood of fatalism in the desistance process. *British Journal of Criminology, 57*(5), 1041–1060.

Halushka, J. M. (2020). The runaround: Punishment, welfare, and poverty survival after prison. *Social Problems, 67*(2), 233–250.

Haney, C. (2003). The psychological impact of incarceration: Implications for post-prison adjustment. In J. Travis & M. Waul (Eds.), *Prisoners once removed: The impact of incarceration and reentry on children, families, and communities* (pp. 33–66). Urban Institute Press.

Haney, C. (2012). Prison effects in the era of mass incarceration. *Prison Journal*. doi:10.1177/0032885512448604

Hansen, H., Bourgois, P., & Drucker, E. (2014). Pathologizing poverty: New forms of structural stigma under welfare reform. *Social Science & Medicine, 103*, 76–83.

Harding, D. J. (2003). Jean Valjean's dilemma: The management of ex-convict identity in the search for employment. *Deviant Behavior, 24*, 571–595.

Harding, D. J., Morenoff, J. D., & Herbert, C. (2013). Home is hard to find: Neighborhoods, institutions, and the residential trajectories of returning prisoners. *Annals of the American Academy of Political and Social Science, 647*, 214–236.

Harding, D. J., Morenoff, J. D., & Wyse, J. J. B. (2019). *On the outside: Prisoner reentry and reintegration*. University of Chicago Press.

Harding, D. J., Wyse, J. J. B., Dobson, C., & Morenoff, J. D. (2014). Making ends meet after prison. *Journal of Policy Analysis and Management, 33*(2), 440–470.

Harris, H., Goss, J., Hayes, J., & Gumbs, A. (2019). *California's prison population*. Public Policy Institute of California.

Healy, D. (2013). Changing fate? Agency and the desistance process. *Theoretical Criminology, 17*(4), 557–574.

Helfgott, J. B. (1997). Ex-offender needs versus community opportunity in Seattle, Washington. *Federal Probation*, *61*, 12–24.

Honeywell, D. (2019). Components of identity transformations within the desistance process. In D. Best & C. Colman (Eds.), *Strengths-based approaches to crime and substance use: From drugs and crime to desistance and recovery* (pp. 123–139). Routledge.

Irwin, J. (1970). *The felon*. Prentice Hall.

Irwin, J. (1985). *The jail: Managing the underclass in American society*. University of California Press.

Irwin, J. (2005). *The warehouse prison: Disposal of the new dangerous class*. Roxbury Publishing Company.

Irwin, J. (2009). *Lifers: Seeking redemption in prison*. Routledge.

Jacobs, J. B. (2015). *The eternal criminal record*. Harvard University Press.

Jones, E. E., Farina, A., Hastorf, A. H., Markus, H., Miller, D. T., & Scott, R. A. (1984). *Social stigma: The psychology of marked relationships*. Erlbaum.

JustLeadershipUSA. (2023). *About us*. https://jlusa.org/about/

Kazemian, L. (2020). *Positive growth and redemption in prison: Finding light behind bars and beyond*. Routledge.

Kazemian, L., & Travis, J. (2015). Imperative for inclusion of long termers and lifers in research and policy. *Criminology & Public Policy*, *14*(2), 355–395.

Kazemian, L., & Walker, A. (2019). Effects of incarceration. In D. P. Farrington, L. Kazemian, & A. R. Piquero (Eds.), *The Oxford handbook of developmental and life-course criminology* (pp. 576–599). Oxford University Press.

Kirk, D. S. (2012). Residential change as a turning point in the life course of crime: Desistance or temporary cessation? *Criminology*, *50*(2), 329–358.

Kirk, D. S. (2019). The collateral consequences of incarceration for housing. In B. M. Huebner & N. Frost (Eds.), *ASC Division on Corrections and Sentencing handbook, Vol. 3: The handbook on the consequences of sentencing and punishment decisions* (pp. 53–68). Routledge.

Komarovskaya, I. A., Loper, A. B., Warren, J., & Jackson, S. (2011). Exploring gender differences in trauma exposure and the emergence of symptoms of PTSD among incarcerated men and women. *Journal of Forensic Psychiatry & Psychology*, *22*(3), 395–410.

Kubrin, C. E., & Stewart, E. A. (2006). Predicting who reoffends: The neglected role of neighborhood context in recidivism studies. *Criminology*, *44*(1), 165–195.

Kupers, T. A. (2005). Posttraumatic stress disorder in prisoners. In S. Stojkovic (Ed.), *Managing special populations in jails and prisons* (pp. 10-1–10-21). Civic Research Institute.

Kurlychek, M., Brame, R., & Bushway, S. D. (2006). Scarlet letters and recidivism: Does an old criminal record predict future offending? *Criminology & Public Policy*, *3*, 64–83.

La Vigne, N. G., Shollenberger, T. L., & Debus, S. A. (2009). *One year out: Tracking the experiences of male prisoners returning to Houston, Texas*. Urban Institute.

La Vigne, N. G., Visher, C., & Castro, J. (2004). *Chicago prisoners' experiences returning home*. Urban Institute.

Lageson, S., & Maruna, S. (2018). Digital degradation: Stigma management in the internet age. *Punishment & Society*, *20*(1), 113–133.

Laub, J. H., Rowan, Z. R., & Sampson, R. J. (2019). The age-graded theory of informal social control. In D. P. Farrington, L. Kazemian, & A. R. Piquero (Eds.), *The Oxford handbook of developmental and life-course criminology* (pp. 295–322). Oxford University Press.

LeBel, T. P. (2007). An examination of the impact of formerly incarcerated persons helping others. *Journal of Offender Rehabilitation*, *46*(1/2), 1–24.

LeBel, T. P. (2009). Formerly incarcerated persons' use of advocacy/activism as a coping orientation in the reintegration process. In B. M. Veysey, J. Christian, & D. J. Martinez (Eds.), *How offenders transform their lives* (pp. 165–187). Willan.

LeBel, T. P. (2012a). Invisible stripes? Formerly incarcerated persons' perceptions of stigma. *Deviant Behavior*, *33*, 89–107.

LeBel, T. P. (2012b). "If one doesn't get you another one will": Formerly incarcerated persons' perceptions of discrimination. *Prison Journal*, *92*(1), 63–87.

LeBel, T. P. (2016, April 15). *To tell or not to tell? Formerly incarcerated persons' use of concealment as a stigma management strategy* [Invited paper and presentation]. Prisoner Reentry and Reintegration Workshop, Rutgers University, Newark, NJ, United States.

LeBel, T. P., Burnett, R., Maruna, S., & Bushway, S. (2008). The "chicken and egg" of subjective and social factors in desistance from crime. *European Journal of Criminology*, *5*(2), 130–158.

LeBel, T. P., & Maruna, S. (2012). Life on the outside: Transitioning from prison to the community. In J. Petersilia & K. Reitz (Eds.), *The Oxford handbook of sentencing and corrections* (pp. 657–683). Oxford University Press.

LeBel, T. P., Richie, M., & Maruna, S. (2015). Helping others as a response to reconcile a criminal past: The role of the wounded healer in prisoner reentry programs. *Criminal Justice and Behavior, 42*(1), 108–120.

LeBel, T. P., Richie, M., & Maruna, S. (2017). Can released prisoners "make it"? Examining formerly incarcerated persons' belief in upward mobility and the "American dream." In S. Stojkovic (Ed.), *Prisoner reentry: Critical issues and policy directions* (pp. 245–305). Palgrave Macmillan.

Leverentz, A. (2014). *The ex-prisoner's dilemma: How women negotiate competing narratives of reentry and desistance.* Rutgers University Press.

Liem, M. (2016). *After life imprisonment: Reentry in the era of mass incarceration.* New York University Press.

Liem, M., & Kunst, M. (2013). Is there a recognizable post-incarceration syndrome among released "lifers"? *International Journal of Law and Psychiatry, 36*(3–4), 333–337.

Lin, A. C. (2000). *Reform in the making: The implementation of social policy in prison.* Princeton University Press.

Link, B. G., Cullen, F. T., Struening, E., Shrout, P., & Dohrenwend, B. P. (1989). A modified labeling theory approach in the area of the mental disorders: An empirical assessment. *American Sociological Review, 54*, 400–423.

Link, B. G., Struening, E. L., Rahav, M., Phelan, J. C., & Nuttbrock, L. (1997). On stigma and its consequences: Evidence from a longitudinal study of men with dual diagnosis of mental illness and substance abuse. *Journal of Health and Social Behavior, 38*, 177–190.

Listwan, S. J., Hanley, D., & Colvin, M. (2012). *The prison experience and reentry: Examining the impact of victimization on coming home* (Doc. No. 238083). National Institute of Justice.

Listwan, S. J., Sullivan, C. J., Agnew, R., Cullen, F. T., & Colvin, M. (2013). The pains of imprisonment revisited: The impact of strain on inmate recidivism. *Justice Quarterly, 30*, 144–168.

Looney, A., & Turner, N. (2018). *Work and opportunity before and after incarceration.* Brookings Institution.

Love, M., & Schlussel, D. (2020a). *Pathways to reintegration: Criminal record reforms in 2019.* Collateral Consequences Resource Center. https://ccresourcecenter.org/wp-content/uploads/2020/02/Pathways-to-Reintegration_Criminal-Record-Reforms-in-2019.pdf

Love, M., & Schlussel, D. (2020b). *The many roads to reintegration: A 50-state report on laws restoring rights and opportunities after arrest or conviction.* Collateral Consequences Resource Center. https://ccresourcecenter.org/the-many-roads-to-reintegration/

Luoma, J. B., Twohig, M. P., Waltz, T., Hayes, S. C., Roget, N., Padilla, M., & Fisher, G. (2007). An investigation of stigma in individuals receiving treatment for substance abuse. *Addictive Behaviors, 32*, 1331–1346.

Lutze, F. E., Rosky, J. W., & Hamilton, Z. K. (2014). A multisite outcome evaluation of Washington State's Reentry Housing Program for high-risk offenders. *Criminal Justice and Behavior, 41*(4), 471–491.

Mallik-Kane, K., & Visher, C. A. (2008). *Health and prisoner reentry: How physical, mental, and substance abuse conditions shape the process of reintegration.* Urban Institute.

Maroto, M. L. (2015). The absorbing status of incarceration and its relationship with wealth accumulation. *Journal of Quantitative Criminology, 31*, 207–236.

Martin, G. E. (2017). From moment to movement: The urgency for formerly incarcerated individuals to lead decarceration efforts. In M. W. Epperson & C. Pettus-Davis (Eds.), *Smart decarceration: Achieving criminal justice transformation in the 21st century* (pp. 44–52). Oxford University Press.

Maruna, S. (2001). *Making good: How ex-convicts reform and reclaim their lives.* American Psychological Association.

Maruna, S. (2004). Desistance from crime and explanatory style: A new direction in the psychology of reform. *Journal of Contemporary Criminal Justice, 20*(2), 184–200.

Maruna, S., Immarigeon, R., & LeBel, T. P. (2004). Ex-offender reintegration: Theory and practice. In S. Maruna & R. Immarigeon (Eds.), *After crime and punishment: Pathways to offender reintegration* (pp. 3–26). Willan.

Maruna, S., & LeBel, T. (2009). Strengths-based approaches to reentry: Extra mileage toward reintegration and destigmatization. *Japanese Journal of Sociological Criminology, 34*, 58–80.

Maruna, S., LeBel, T. P., & Lanier, C. (2003). Generativity behind bars: Some "redemptive truth" about prison society. In E. de St. Aubin, D. McAdams, & T. Kim (Eds.), *The generative society: Caring for future generations* (pp. 131–151). American Psychological Association.

Maruschak, L. A., Bronson, J., & Alper, M. (2021a). *Alcohol and drug use and treatment reported by prisoners* (Survey of Prison Inmates, 2016, statistical tables, NCJ 252641). U.S. Department of Justice, Office of Justice Programs, Bureau of Justice Statistics.

Maruschak, L. A., Bronson, J., & Alper, M. (2021b). *Indicators of mental health problems reported by prisoners* (Survey of Prison Inmates, 2016, statistical tables, NCJ 252643). U.S. Department of Justice, Office of Justice Programs, Bureau of Justice Statistics.

Maruschak, L. A., Bronson, J., & Alper, M. (2021c). *Medical problems reported by prisoners* (Survey of Prison Inmates, 2016, statistical tables, NCJ 252644). U.S. Department of Justice, Office of Justice Programs, Bureau of Justice Statistics.

Maruschak, L. A., Bronson, J., & Alper, M. (2021d). *Disabilities reported by prisoners* (Survey of Prison Inmates, 2016, statistical tables, NCJ 252642). U.S. Department of Justice, Office of Justice Programs, Bureau of Justice Statistics.

Maschi, T., Viola, D., Morgen, K., & Koskinen, L. (2015). Trauma, stress, grief, loss, and separation among older adults in prison: The protective role of coping resources on physical and mental well-being. *Journal of Crime and Justice, 38*(1), 113–136.

Massoglia, M., & Pridemore, W. A. (2015). Incarceration and health. *Annual Review of Sociology, 41*, 291–310.

Massoglia, M., & Uggen, C. (2010). Settling down and aging out: Toward an interactionist theory of desistance and the transition to adulthood. *American Journal of Sociology, 116*(2), 543–582.

Matthews, E. (2021). *Reentry and the American Dream: People returning to the community share the same dream but lack the same access* [Research paper]. American University School of Public Affairs. https://ssrn.com/abstract=3803660

McCann, W., Kowalski, M. A., Hemmens, C., & Stohr, M. K. (2021). An analysis of certificates of rehabilitation in the United States. *Corrections, 6*(1), 18–44.

McNamee, S. J., & Miller, R. K. (2014). *The meritocracy myth* (3rd ed.). Rowman and Littlefield.

McNeill, F. (2014). Punishment as rehabilitation. In G. Bruinsma & D. Weisburd (Eds.), *Encyclopedia of criminology and criminal justice* (pp. 4195–4206). Springer.

McNeill, F. (2016). Desistance and criminal justice in Scotland. In H. Croall, G. Mooney, & M. Munro (Eds.), *Crime, justice and society in Scotland* (pp. 200–216). Routledge.

Mears, D. P., Cochran, J. C., & Cullen, F. T. (2015). Incarceration heterogeneity and its implications for assessing the effectiveness of imprisonment on recidivism. *Criminal Justice Policy Review, 26*(7), 691–712.

Mears, D. P., Cochran, J. C., & Siennick, S. E. (2013). Life-course perspectives and prisoner reentry. In C. L. Gibson & M. D. Krohn (Eds.), *Handbook of life-course criminology: Emerging trends and directions for future research* (pp. 317–333). Springer-Verlag.

Metraux, S., & Culhane, D. P. (2004). Homeless shelter use and reincarceration following prison release. *Criminology & Public Policy, 3*, 139–160.

Miller, R. J. (2021). *Halfway home: Race, punishment, and the afterlife of mass incarceration*. Little, Brown and Company.

Miller, R. J., & Stuart, F. (2017). Carceral citizenship: Race, rights and responsibility in the age of mass supervision. *Theoretical Criminology, 21*(4), 532–548.

Mizrahi, J. L., Jeffers, J., Ellis, E. B., & Pauli, P. (2016). *Disability and criminal justice reform: Keys to success*. RespectAbility.

Munn, M. (2012). The mark of criminality: Rejections and reversals, disclosure and distance: Stigma and the ex-prisoner. In S. Hannem & C. Bruckert (Eds.), *Stigma revisited: Implications of the mark* (pp. 147–169). University of Ottawa Press.

Nelson, M., Deess, P., & Allen, C. (1999). *The first month out: Post-incarceration experiences in New York City*. Vera Institute of Justice.

Nixon, V. D. (2017). Learning to lead in the decarceration movement. In M. W. Epperson & C. Pettus-Davis (Eds.), *Smart decarceration: Achieving criminal justice transformation in the 21st century* (pp. 90–100). Oxford University Press.

Nugent, B., & Schinkel, M. (2016). The pains of desistance. *Criminology & Criminal Justice, 16*, 568–584.

O'Brien, P. (2001). *Making it in the "free world."* SUNY Press.

O'Hear, M. (2019). Third-class citizenship: The escalating legal consequences of committing a "violent" crime. *Journal of Criminal Law & Criminology, 109*(2), 165–235.

Owens, C.D., Jr. (2009). Social symbols, stigma, and the labor market experiences of former prisoners. *Journal of Correctional Education, 60*(4), 316–342.

Pager, D. (2007). *Marked: Race, crime, and finding work in an era of mass incarceration*. University of Chicago Press.

Pager, D., Western, B., & Sugie, N. (2009). Sequencing disadvantage: Barriers to employment facing young Black and White men with criminal records. *Annals of the American Academy of Political and Social Science, 623*, 195–213.

Patterson, E. J. (2013). The dose-response of time served in prison on mortality: New York State, 1989–2003. *American Journal of Public Health, 103*(3), 523–528.

Patton, D., & Farrall, S. (2021). Desistance: A utopian perspective. *Howard Journal, 60*(2), 209–231.

Petersilia, J. (2003). *When prisoners come home: Parole and prisoner reentry*. Oxford University Press.

Pettit, B., & Western, B. (2004). Mass imprisonment and the life course: Race and class inequality in U.S. incarceration. *American Sociological Review, 69*, 151–169.

Polaschek, D. L. L., & Yesberg, J. A. (2015). Desistance in high-risk prisoners: Pre-release self-reported desistance commitment and perceptions of change predict 12-month survival. *Practice: The New Zealand Corrections Journal, 3*(1), 24–29.

Pridemore, W. A. (2014). The mortality penalty of incarceration: Evidence from a population-based case-control study. *Journal of Health and Social Behavior, 55*(2), 215–233.

Remster, B. (2019). A life course analysis of homeless shelter use among the formerly incarcerated. *Justice Quarterly, 36*(3), 437–465.

Sampson, R. J. (2012). *Great American city: Chicago and the enduring neighborhood effect.* University of Chicago Press.

Sampson, R. J., & Laub, J. H. (1993). *Crime in the making.* Harvard University Press.

Sampson, R. J., & Laub, J. H. (1997). A life-course theory of cumulative disadvantage and the stability of delinquency. In T. P. Thornberry (Ed.), *Developmental theories of crime and delinquency: Advances in criminological theory* (pp. 133–161). Transaction Publishers.

Sampson, R. J., & Loeffler, C. (2010). Punishment's place: The local concentration of mass incarceration. *Daedalus, 139*, 20–31.

Schappell, A., Docherty, M., & Boxer, P. (2016). Violence and victimization during incarceration: Relations to psychosocial adjustment during reentry to the community. *Violence and Victims, 31*(2), 361–378.

Schnittker, J. (2014). The psychological dimensions and social consequences of incarceration. *Annals of the American Academy of Political and Social Science, 651*(1), 122–138.

Schnittker, J., Massoglia, M., & Uggen, C. (2012). Out and down: Incarceration and psychiatric disorders. *Journal of Health and Social Behavior, 5*, 448–464.

Sedlak, A. J., & McPherson, K. S. (2010). *Conditions of confinement: Findings from the Survey of Youth in Residential Treatment (Juvenile Justice Bulletin).* U.S. Department of Justice, Office of Justice Programs, Office of Juvenile Justice and Delinquency Prevention.

Shapland, J., Farrall, S., & Bottoms, A. (2016). Diversity or congruence? Sketching the future: An afterword. In J. Shapland, S. Farrall, & A. Bottoms (Eds.), *Global perspectives on desistance: Reviewing what we know and looking to the future* (pp. 282–293). Routledge.

Sharkey, P., & Faber, J. W. (2014). Where, when, why, and for whom do residential contexts matter? Moving away from the dichotomous understanding of neighborhood effects. *Annual Review of Sociology, 40*(1), 559–579.

Skardhamar, T., Savolainen, J., Aase, K. N., & Lyngstad, T. H. (2015). Does marriage reduce crime? A systematic review of research. *Crime and Justice, 44*(1), 385–446.

Smith, J. M. (2021). The formerly incarcerated, advocacy, activism, and community reintegration. *Contemporary Justice Review, 24*(1), 43–63.

Solomon, A. L. (2012). In search of a job: Criminal records as barriers to employment. *NIJ Journal, 270*, 42–51.

Solomon, A., Visher, C., La Vigne, N., & Osbourne, J. (2006). *Understanding the challenges of prisoner reentry: Research findings from the Urban Institute's prisoner reentry portfolio.* Urban Institute.

Steiner, B, Makarios, M. D., & Travis, L. E., III. (2015). Examining the effects of residential situations and residential mobility on offender recidivism. *Crime and Delinquency, 61*, 375–401.

Stewart, R., & Uggen, C. (2020). Criminal records and college admissions: A modified experimental audit. *Criminology, 58*(1), 156–188.

Sugie, N. F. (2018). Work as foraging: A smartphone study of job search and employment after prison. *American Journal of Sociology, 123*(5), 1453–1491.

Thacher, D. (2008). The rise of criminal background screening in rental housing. *Law & Social Inquiry, 33*, 5–30.

Tobin-Tyler, E., & Brockmann, B. (2017). Returning home: Incarceration, reentry, stigma and the perpetuation of racial and socioeconomic health inequity. *Journal of Law, Medicine & Ethics, 45*(4), 545–557.

Tran-Leung, M. C. (2015). *When discretion means denial. A national perspective on criminal records barriers to federally subsidized housing.* Sargent Shriver National Center on Poverty Law.

Travis, J. (2002). Invisible punishment: An instrument of social exclusion. In M. Mauer & M. Chesney-Lind (Eds.), *Invisible punishment: The collateral consequences of mass imprisonment* (pp. 15–36). New Press.

Travis, J., Western, B., & Redburn, S. (Eds.). (2014). *The growth of incarceration in the United States: Exploring causes and consequences.* National Academies Press.

Tsai, J., & Rosenheck, R. A. (2012). Incarceration among chronically homeless adults: Clinical correlates and outcomes. *Journal of Forensic Psychology Practice, 12*, 307–324.

Tsemberis, S. (2010). Housing first: Ending homelessness, promoting recovery, and reducing costs. In I. G. Ellen & B. O'Flaherty (Eds.), *How to house the homeless* (pp. 37–56). Russell Sage Foundation.

Uggen, C., & Stewart, R. (2015). Piling on: Collateral consequences and community supervision. *Minnesota Law Review, 99*, 1871–1910.

Umez, C., & Gaines, J. (2021). *After the sentence, more consequences: A national report of barriers to work.* Council of State Governments Justice Center.

Umez, C., & Pirius, R. (2018). *Barriers to work: Improving employment in licensed occupations for individuals with criminal records.* National Conference of State Legislatures (NCSL).

U.S. Commission on Civil Rights. (2019). *Collateral consequences: The crossroads of punishment, redemption, and the effects on communities.* U.S. Commission on Civil Rights.

van Olphen, J., Eliason, M. J., Freudenberg, N., & Barnes, M. (2009). Nowhere to go: How stigma limits the options of female drug users after release from jail. *Substance Abuse Treatment, Prevention, & Policy, 4*, 1–10.

Visher, C. A., & Courtney, S. M. E. (2007). *One year out: Experiences of prisoners returning to Cleveland*. Urban Institute.

Visher, C., Debus, S., & Yahner, J. (2008). *Employment after prison: A longitudinal study of releasees in three states*. Urban Institute.

Visher, C. A., Knight, C. R., Chalfin, A., & Roman, J. K. (2009). *The impact of marital and relationship status on social outcomes for returning prisoners*. Urban Institute.

Visher, C. A., & La Vigne, N. (2021). Returning home: A pathbreaking study of prisoner reentry and its challenges. In P. K. Lattimore, B. M. Huebner, & F. S. Taxman (Eds.), *ASC Division on Corrections and Sentencing handbook, Vol. 5: Handbook on moving corrections and sentencing forward: Building on the record* (pp. 278–298). Routledge.

Visher, C. A., & Lattimore, P. K. (2007). Major study examines prisoners and their reentry needs (NCJ 219609). *NIJ Journal, 258*, 30–33.

Visher, C. A., Lattimore, P. K., Barrick, K., & Tueller, S. (2017). Evaluating the long-term effects of prisoner reentry services on recidivism: What types of services matter? *Justice Quarterly, 34*(1), 136–165.

Visher, C. A., & O'Connell, D. J. (2012). Incarceration and inmates' self perceptions about returning home. *Journal of Criminal Justice, 40*, 386–393.

Visher, C. A., & Travis, J. (2003). Transitions from prison to community: Understanding individual pathways. *Annual Review of Sociology, 29*, 89–113.

Wakefield, S., & Uggen, C. (2010). Incarceration and stratification. *Annual Review of Sociology, 36*, 387–406.

Wang, E., Brinkley-Rubinstein, L., Puglisi, L., & Western, B. (2021). Recommendations for prioritization and distribution of COVID-19 vaccine in prisons and jails. *Correctional Health Care Report, 22*(2), 35–38.

Weaver, B. (2019). Understanding desistance: A critical review of theories of desistance. *Psychology, Crime & Law, 25*(6), 641–658.

Weijters, G., & More, A. (2015). Comparing income and housing of former prisoners after imprisonment with their situation before imprisonment. *European Journal on Criminal Policy and Research, 21*, 35–48.

Weissman, M., Rosenthal, A., Warth, P., Wolf, E., & Messina-Yauchzy, M. (2015). *The use of criminal history records in college admissions: Reconsidered*. Center for Community Alternatives. http://www.communityalternatives.org/pdf/Reconsidered-criminal-hist-recs-in-college-admissions.pdf

Western, B. (2018). *Homeward: Life in the year after prison*. Russell Sage Foundation.

Western, B., Braga, A. A., Davis, J., & Sirois, C. (2015). Stress and hardship after prison. *American Journal of Sociology, 120*(5), 1512–1547.

Western, B., & Wildeman, C. (2009). The black family and mass incarceration. *Annals of the American Academy of Political and Social Science, 621*, 221–242.

Wheelock, D., & Uggen, C. (2010). Punishment, crime, and poverty. In A. C. Lin & D. R. Harris (Eds.), *The colors of poverty: Why racial and ethnic disparities persist* (pp. 261–292). Russell Sage Foundation.

White, W. L. (2000). The history of recovered people as wounded healers: II. The era of professionalization and specialization. *Alcoholism Treatment Quarterly, 18*(2), 1–25.

Whittle, T. N. (2018). Felony collateral sanctions effects on recidivism: A literature review. *Criminal Justice Policy Review, 29*, 505–524.

Wilson, A. B., Draine, J., Hadley, T., Metraux, S., & Evans, A. (2011). Examining the impact of mental illness and substance use on recidivism in a county jail. *International Journal of Law and Psychiatry, 34*, 264–268.

Winnick, T. A., & Bodkin, M. (2009). Stigma, secrecy, and race: An empirical examination of black and white incarcerated men. *American Journal of Criminal Justice, 34*(1/2), 131–150.

Woldgabreal, Y. A., Day, A., & Ward, T. (2016). Linking positive psychology to offender supervision outcomes: The mediating role of psychological flexibility, general self-efficacy, optimism, and hope. *Criminal Justice and Behavior, 43*(6), 1–25.

Wolff, N., & Draine, J. (2004). The dynamics of social capital of prisoners and community reentry: Ties that bind? *Journal of Correctional Health Care, 10*(3), 457–490.

Wolff, N., & Shi, J. (2009). Type, source, and patterns of physical victimization: A comparison of male and female inmates. *The Prison Journal, 89*, 172–191.

Yahner, J., & Visher, C. (2008). *Illinois prisoners' reentry success three years after release*. Washington, DC: The Urban Institute.

Zamble, E., & Porporino, F.J. (1988). *Coping, behavior, and adaptation in prison inmates*. New York: Springer.

Zaw, K., Hamilton, D., & Darity Jr., W. (2016). Race, wealth and incarceration: Results from the National Longitudinal Survey of Youth. *Race and Social Problems, 8*, 103–115.

Zweig, J.M., Yahner, J., Visher, C.A., & Lattimore, P.K. (2015). Using general strain theory to explore the effects of prison victimization experiences on later offending and substance use. *The Prison Journal, 95*(1), 84–113.

CHAPTER 28

Ethical Considerations and Ramifications of Advance Care Planning and End-of-Life Decision Making for Older Adults

Pamela B. Teaster and E. Carlisle Shealy

> **Abstract**
> In the 1970s, the advance care planning movement gained momentum, reacting to improvements in medical technology allowing patients in life-limiting situations to survive longer than ever before. Ethical questions arose about end-of-life care and laws to address them. The United States continues to wrestle with treatment for dying patients related to treatment and quality of life. Against this landscape, the purpose of this chapter is to discuss how features of old age influence end-of-life and advance care planning. The chapter begins by characterizing old age and end of life, discussing ethical principles and the evolution of end-of-life decision making. Following, it considers mechanisms for end-of-life planning, including surrogate decision-making laws and guardianship for emergent health care situations. The chapter reviews ten years of research on advance care planning and introduces the diffusion of telemedicine. It concludes with questions yet to be resolved and how research, practice, and policy can help answer them.
>
> **Key Words:** older adult, end of life, advance directive, ethics, surrogate decision making

The authors gratefully acknowledge the assistance of Jacey Jarrell, Undergraduate Research Assistant of the VT Center for Gerontology, and Kathryn Ratcliffe, Graduate Research Assistant, VT Graduate Center for Gerontology.

In the 1970s, the advance care planning (ACP) movement gained momentum as a reaction to improvements in medical technology that allowed patients in life-limiting situations to survive longer than at any other point in history. Not surprisingly, a bevy of ethical questions arose about end-of-life care and laws and policies to address them. The United States continues to wrestle with the potential of life-lengthening treatment for patients at end of life, intervention that, in some instances, may produce questionable health outcomes related to burden of treatment and quality of life.

Issues concerning end-of-life decision making arose as capabilities arose to sustain them. A corpus of law and policy came into sharper focus as issues came to the fore (e.g., right to terminate treatment, termination of nutrition and hydration, right to withdraw treatment, physician-assisted suicide), often in the legal community. Important precedent-setting cases were determined at appellate courts and the Supreme Court. Decisions rested upon the case-by-case legal precedents established, among which were several major decisions, discussed throughout this chapter: *In re Quinlan* (1976), *Patricia E. Brophy vs. New England Sinai Hospital, Inc.* (1986), *Cruzan v. Director, Missouri Department of Health* (1990), *Helga Wanglie, Fourth Judicial District* (1991), *Washington v. Glucksburg* (1996), *Vacco v. Quill* (1997), *In re of Schiavo v. Schiavo* (2003), and *Oregon v. Ashcroft* (2004)). Associated laws were also enacted, including the Patient Self-Determination Act (1990), state surrogate consent laws, and death with dignity acts.

Against this landscape, the purpose of this chapter is to discuss how characteristics of old age influence end-of-life and ACP and decision making, particularly as they relate to law and policy (e.g., do-not-resuscitate and legal guardianship decisions). Objectives of the chapter are to provide a systematic review of law and policy regarding end-of-life decision making, highlight current salient research on the topic, and raise legal and policy-focused questions that have yet to be considered.

Our chapter begins with explaining the characteristics of old age and end-of-life issues for older adults. We then discuss ethical principles undergirding end-of-life planning, followed by the evolution of end-of-life decision making in the United States. We then explain surrogate decision-making laws as well as guardianship and its use for emergent situations in health care. After, we discuss the strengths and weaknesses of mechanisms for end-of-life planning (i.e., durable powers of attorney, living wills, portable medical orders [Physician Orders for Life-Sustaining Treatment]). Next, we provide a 10-year review of research on ACP and discuss the influence of actors and organizations. We also introduce the entrance of telemedicine and its diffusion due to COVID-19. We conclude our chapter with questions yet to be resolved and how research, practice, and policy can help answer them.

Characteristics of Old Age and End of Life for Older Adults

Older adults are the largest growing subset of the population within the United States. By 2030, one in five Americans is projected to be 65 years of age or older (Colby & Ortman, 2015). The trend of increasing age is expected to continue well into 2060, while the population of those 18 and younger is expected to decrease. The majority of present and future older adults are known as the "baby boomers" (Knickman & Snell, 2002), because between 1946 and 1964, 78 million of them were born, a significant spike from prior decades (King et al., 2013). Compared to previous generations, baby boomers are living longer but with more disease (King et al., 2013), creating issues around managing their medical and social needs along with future planning.

Advances in medicine and public health extended the average U.S. life expectancy despite a growing prevalence of chronic disease. In 2020, the average life expectancy was 77.8 years, nearly double that of 200 years ago (Arias, 2019), attributable to improvements in controlling infectious diseases, sanitation, public water treatment, and food safety (Ninde, 2017). Recent advances in antibiotics and surgical techniques, combined with improved nutrition, literacy, and housing conditions, have also pushed out life expectancy. However, living longer creates a domino effect, such that the longer someone lives, the more likely they are to develop a chronic disease. Those with chronic diseases often need adaptive care and support, which, in turn, creates a greater medical and economic burden on society.

Risks and Conditions

The increased risk of disease that may accompany older age can cause both mental and physical disabilities, including functional limitations (Toth et al., 2021). More than half of older adults turning 65 will develop a disability requiring some long-term service or support (e.g., personal care, mobility, and health) that can vary widely based on the condition or disability (Toth et al., 2021).

The three most deadly conditions older adults face are cardiovascular disease, cancer, and respiratory diseases (Centers for Disease Control and Prevention [CDC], 2020; Heron, 2019). Risk factors include hypertension, high cholesterol, obesity, and inactivity (CDC, 2021). It is not uncommon for older adults to have multiple chronic conditions requiring a continuum of medical care and attention (Davis et al., 2011). As a result, older adults are more likely to experience declines in physical functioning and social well-being and an increased risk of depression and other mental health problems.

Ongoing chronic conditions are often the underlying cause of acute and deadly medical events such as pneumonia, heart attack, and stroke (Fimognari et al., 2017; Heron, 2019). Subsequent hospitalizations can lead to the onset of new disabilities not previously recognized. The phenomenon called "hospitalization-associated disability" is particularly relevant to older patients, as it increases risk of long-term disability and death (Fimognari et al., 2017).

Cognitive Decline

Chronic and acute conditions are further complicated by subjective cognitive declines. Confusion and memory loss are typical symptoms of cognitive decline and early signs of more severe forms of dementia (CDC, 2020). Based on data from the Behavioral Risk Factor Surveillance System, adults over the age of 65 who reported cognitive declines were more likely to have three or more chronic conditions as compared to those without them (CDC, 2020). Alzheimer's disease, the most common form of dementia, is the fifth leading cause of death among older adults in the United States (Heron, 2019; Xu et al., 2020). On average, patients with Alzheimer's disease live 4–8 years after diagnosis and often require around-the-clock care in the late stages of the disease (Alzheimer's Association, n.d.). The prevalence of Alzheimer's disease–related death is expected to increase threefold by 2060 as compared to 2010 (Xu et al., 2020).

Although most adults wish to remain in their homes as they age, known as aging in place, this is not an option for all. Demands of the environment must match the abilities of the person (Fausset et al., 2011). When a mismatch occurs (e.g., the environmental demands exceed the older adult's abilities), aging in place becomes problematic. The severity and combination of diseases (e.g., having severe dementia and diabetes) may impact where older adults can and choose to live. Changes in the ability to manage activities of daily living (e.g., bathing, eating, cooking, finances, and medication management) along with managing a home can be unpredictable and impede aging in place (Fausset et al., 2011). If the demands of the environment exceed an adult's ability for any of these reasons, long-term care may become a necessary option.

Older Adults and End of Life

Places where older adults live are not necessarily where they die. An estimated 80% of older adults want to age in their own homes and 71% want to also die in their own homes (Fausset et al., 2011; Hamel et al., 2017). For some, dying at home is considered a cultural taboo, and so their preference is to die elsewhere. In 2017, 30.7% of older adults died at home, compared to 23.8% in 2003 (Cross & Warraich, 2019). While the number is rising, there is a significant gap between wishes and reality (Christensen, 2019), as 29.8% of older adults died in a hospital, 20.8% in a nursing facility, and 8.3% in hospice facilities according to 2017 estimates by Cross and Warraich (2019).

Often, declines in health require care or intervention that cannot be managed in the home setting. Health conditions can affect where and how death occurs. The care setting and subsequent place of death for someone with dementia or stroke may be far different than that of a cancer patient. For example, in 2014, 55.6% of dementia patients died in a nursing home or long-term care facility, and 21% died at home (Xu et al., 2020). In comparison, cancer patients predominantly died at home (37.8%) followed by a hospital setting (35.4%; Mitchell et al., 2005).

The longer lifespan and unique and personal circumstances surrounding one's death make end-of-life decision making more important than ever. Given the growing number of older adults, the increase in life expectancy, and medical interventions available to extend and prolong life, it is critical to understand and document individual choices and preferences around death and the principles supporting them.

Principles Undergirding End-of-Life Planning

Not surprisingly, complex issues related to end of life are highly ethical in nature. Applied to these difficult problems, modern bioethics often uses guiding principles, or principlism, notably articulated by Beauchamp and Childress (2012). Four principles (i.e., autonomy, beneficence, nonmaleficence, and justice) are typically used to guide decision making by health professions as well as other actors.

Autonomy

Autonomy, regarded as primary among the four principles, involves a patient's right to make decisions and life plans that are free from coercion (Pence, 2015). Highly valued, autonomy is emphasized in the United States and other democracies and makes it possible for individuals to guide their destiny. According to John Stuart Mill (1859, p.13):

> The only purpose for which power can rightfully be exercised over any member of a civilized community, against his will, is to prevent harm to others. His own good, either physical or moral, is not a sufficient warrant. Over himself, over his own body and mind, the individual is sovereign.

Autonomy is important to respect when an individual with a terminal illness accepts or refuses treatment.

Beneficence

Beneficence is associated with being and doing good as well as keeping others safe (Beauchamp & Childress, 2012). Pence (2015) suggested that beneficence is grounded in compassion. When determining a course of treatment for an older adult, the principles of autonomy and beneficence may compete. A classic example of the tension between the two is whether to continue to provide treatment that has little or no benefit to a dying older patient.

Nonmaleficence

The principle of nonmaleficence means to do no harm or that patients should not leave an encounter with a health care provider worse than before it. According to Pence (2015, p. 17), "This crucial principle of medical ethics prohibits corruption, incompetence, and dangerous, non-therapeutic treatments." Nonmaleficence protects patients from being harmed by an intervention or treatment and influences research studies. Pence (2015) observed that nonmaleficence bears an important relationship to autonomy because a patient has the right to be left alone. An example of the application of the principle of nonmaleficence is when a competent and dying patient decides to discontinue artificial nutrition and hydration.

Justice
The principle of justice is associated with David Hume (2006) and John Rawls (2009) and reflects fairness, equality, and equity. Justice encompasses a way of treating people without prejudice and of distributing goods and resources equitably. An example of the application of justice to end-of-life decision making, particularly during the COVID-19 pandemic, is the allocation of ventilators based on prognosis, not on ability to pay or a patient's age, gender, race, ethnicity, or location.

Evolution of End-of-Life Decision Making in the United States

Before the 1950s, end-of-life care was provided in the home setting, usually by family members who were guided by visiting health care professionals (Lee, 2002). As the modern hospital system came into being through such legislation as the Hospital Survey and Construction Act (1946), later referred to as the Hill-Burton Act, complex health care shifted to the hospital setting (Lee, 2002). At the same time, rapid technological advances in medicine occurred because of treatments needed for soldiers on World War II battlefields. Although the ability to prolong life increased more rapidly than at any other time in history, lacking was health care that included respect for patients' wishes rather than acquiescing to recommendations of the treating physician, labeled paternalism. Aware of the health care environment for depressed, heavily medicated, and bed-bound patients at end of life, in 1967, Cecily Saunders of the United Kingdom established the first hospice program, which started the modern end-of-life movement (Liegner, 1975). A decade later, in 1977, Florence Wald established the first home-based hospice program in the United States (Kaur, 2000). About the same time, Elizabeth Kubler-Ross published her ground-breaking work, *On Death and Dying*, describing stages of how dying patients approached their own demise and championing end-of-life care at home (Kübler-Ross, 1969).

Seminal and Precedent-Setting Legal Decisions on End of Life
Legal end-of-life decisions were forged on a case-by-case basis, winding their way through the court system. What follows is a description of select, seminal cases that served as the basis for present decision making concerning a patient's rights at end of life.

Cruzan v. Director, Missouri Department of Health (1975). In 1975, the case of Karen Ann Quinlan came before the nation and courts concerning the right to die. In April 1975, Ms. Quinlan, age 21, fell into a coma due to imbibing alcohol and taking tranquilizer pills. She stopped breathing for two 15-minute periods before arriving at a hospital and being put on a respirator. Over the course of months her condition deteriorated, and her physicians determined that she had suffered irreversible brain damage and was in a persistent vegetative state (PVS). By July of that year, Ms. Quinlan's parents asked medical staff to discontinue extraordinary treatment, which included turning off their daughter's respirator. Because medical staff refused, the Quinlans petitioned a New Jersey court asking that their daughter be allowed to die "with grace and dignity," even taking the petition to the New Jersey Supreme Court (McFadden, 1985). The court determined that Ms. Quinlan's respirator could be removed based on its ruling that the individual's rights take priority over the state's interests. After its removal, Ms. Quinlan lived another 10 years, dying in June 1985.

Patricia E. Brophy vs. New England Sinai Hospital, Inc. (1986). Another test of the legal limits of a patient's right to die (concerning removal of nutrition and hydration) involved Paul Brophy. In 1983, Mr. Brophy, a Massachusetts firefighter, suffered an aneurysm that destroyed large sections of his brain (Associated Press, 1986). When surgery failed to reverse his condition, his wife asked physicians at New England Sinai Hospital in Stoughton to remove his feeding tube. His physicians refused on ethical grounds. After an extended time in court, in 1985, the Massachusetts Supreme Court allowed Mrs. Brophy to discontinue his feeding tube by applying a substituted judgment standard. She based her decision on remarks made by her husband, who, upon returning from working scenes of fires, said that he did not want to be kept alive as a vegetable. After being kept alive for over 3 years, Mr. Brophy was transferred to Emerson Hospital in Concord, which discontinued his feeding tube. He died 8 days later.

Cruzan v. Director, Missouri Department of Health (1990). On the heels of the Brophy case was the landmark decision rendered by the U.S. Supreme Court, *Cruzan v. Director, Missouri Department of Health*, 497 U.S. 261 (1990). The court established that, absent a living will or clear and convincing evidence of what the incompetent person would have wanted, the state's interests in preserving life outweigh the individual's rights to refuse treatment and left to states the responsibility of determining right-to-die standards. In 1983, Nancy Cruzan, age 25, lost control of her car while driving at night, was thrown from the car, and landed face-down in a ditch filled with water. When paramedics arrived and attempted resuscitation, she had no vital signs. After 3 weeks in a coma, her physicians determined that she was in a PVS, and a feeding tube was inserted to provide nourishment. After 5 years, Ms. Cruzan's parents asked doctors to remove her feeding tube. The hospital refused to do so without a court order on the basis that removing the feeding tube would result in her death. Ms. Cruzan's parents filed for and obtained a court order at the trial court level to remove the feeding tube, but the state of Missouri and Ms. Cruzan's guardian ad litem appealed the decision, which reversed the lower court decision. The case was appealed to the U.S. Supreme Court, which found in favor of the Missouri Department of Health, ruling that the Constitution does not prevent the state of Missouri from requiring "clear and convincing evidence" before terminating life-supporting treatment, which upheld the ruling of the Missouri Supreme Court. The Cruzans then gathered clear and convincing evidence that their daughter would have wanted her life support terminated, and Ms. Cruzan's feeling tube was removed in December 1990. She died 12 days later (Glover, 1990).

Helga Wanglie, Fourth Judicial District, Minnesota (1991). Helga Wanglie was an 86-year-old woman from Minnesota who lived in a PVS for over a year after falling and breaking her hip in 1989. Upon experiencing a fall in her home, Ms. Wanglie was transferred to a nursing home. While there, she went into respiratory failure and was put on a respirator but experienced a cardiopulmonary arrest. Transferred to an acute care hospital, her diagnosis showed irreversible brain damage. The family regarded that withdrawing life support was unacceptable—that only God could take life—and that the doctors should not play God. Ms. Wanglie's case concerned a difference in treatment wishes of Ms. Wanglie's husband and children (who wanted her to remain on a respirator) and those of the treating team (who wanted to remove Ms. Wanglie from the respirator) because they determined that the treatment was inappropriate and futile (Angell, 1991). After months of back and forth with the family and the treating team, the hospital filed papers with the Fourth Judicial District in Hennepin County, Minnesota, for a judgment by the court concerning whether medical professionals were obliged to provide treatment they considered inappropriate and without benefit. The court ruled in favor of the family. Transferred to another facility, Ms. Wanglie died after suffering another cardiopulmonary arrest (Rie, 1991).

Washington v. Glucksburg (1997). Alleging a violation of the 14th Amendment's due process clause, the *Glucksburg* case involved a lawsuit brought by Harold Glucksberg, MD, and four other physicians, three terminally ill patients who have since died, and a nonprofit organization counseling people contemplating physician-assisted suicide. The plaintiffs sought to challenge Washington state's ban on physician-assisted suicide, which criminalized the promotion of suicide attempts by persons who tried to help another individual attempt suicide. Petitioners asserted that the state law denied competent terminally ill adults the liberty to choose death over life. In his majority opinion, U.S. Supreme Court Justice William H. Rehnquist held that the right to assisted suicide is not a fundamental liberty interest protected by the due process clause of the Constitution, maintaining that the practice has been and continues to be offensive to national traditions and practices. Moreover, employing a rationality test, the court held that Washington's ban was rationally related to the state's legitimate interest in protecting medical ethics, shielding disabled and terminally ill people from prejudice that might encourage them to end their lives (Schulman, 2019; *Washington v. Glucksberg*, 1997).

Vacco v. Quill (1997)**.** In another right-to-die case, *Vacco v. Quill*, 521 U.S. 793 (1997), the U.S. Supreme Court ruled in a 9–0 decision that a New York ban on physician-assisted suicide was constitutional. The court held that preventing doctors from assisting their patients, even those who were terminally ill and/or in great pain, was a legitimate state interest within the authority of each state to regulate. As with the *Glucksburg* decision, the *Vacco v. Quill* decision established that a constitutional guarantee of a right to die does not exist (Feinberg, 1998; *Vacco v. Quill*, 1997).

Oregon v. Ashcroft (2004). In this case, a doctor, a pharmacist, several terminally ill patients, and the state of Oregon challenged an interpretive rule issued by then attorney general John Ashcroft that physician-assisted suicide violated the Controlled Substances Act (CSA) of 1970, 21 U.S.C. §§ 801-904. This rule, dubbed the "Ashcroft Directive," criminalized conduct authorized by Oregon's Death With Dignity Act. The U.S. District Court held that the Ashcroft Directive was unlawful, was unenforceable, and violated the language and intent of the CSA, overstepping the bounds of the attorney general's statutory authority. Further, the court noted that doctors would be fearful of writing prescriptions sufficient to painlessly hasten death, pharmacists would fear filling the prescriptions, and patients could be consigned to constant suffering, thus dying a slow and agonizing death. Additionally, the court noted that patients attempting suicide without assistance from doctors and pharmacists may fail to do so or leave loved ones with the trauma of dealing with the aftermath (*Oregon v. Ashcroft*, 2004; Orr & Green, 2003).

In re of Schiavo v. Schiavo (2003). The euthanasia case of Terri Schiavo concerned a woman in her 30s in an irreversible PVS. In 1990, at age 26, Ms. Schiavo went into cardiac arrest at her home in St. Petersburg, Florida. Although she was successfully resuscitated, she suffered massive brain damage and was left comatose (Weijer, 2005). More than 2 months postarrest, showing no signs of improvement, her physicians determined that she was in a PVS. Despite heroic efforts by a multitude of therapists, she never returned to a state of awareness. In 1998, Michael Schiavo, her husband, petitioned Florida's Sixth Circuit Court to remove her feeding tube, arguing that his wife would not have wanted sustained artificial life support with no hope of recovery. Her parents, Robert and Mary Schindler, opposed the petition, disputing the husband's assertions and challenging their daughter's medical diagnosis, supporting continued artificial nutrition and hydration (Hook & Mueller, 2005). The ensuing 7-year legal battle (1998–2005) was highly visible and protracted, becoming both legal and political, going all the way to then president of the United States George W. Bush, before Schiavo's feeding tube was ultimately removed (Associated Press, 2005). In all, the *Schiavo* case involved a circus of 14 appeals and many legal motions, petitions, and hearings in the Florida courts; five suits in federal district court; political intervention by the Florida state legislature, then governor Jeb Bush, the U.S. Congress, and President George W. Bush; and four denials of certiorari (i.e., reviewing the lower court decision) from the U.S. Supreme Court (CDC, n.d.). After all the appeals finally wended their way through the federal court system, which upheld the original decision to remove the feeding tube, staff at the hospice facility at which Ms. Schiavo was a patient disconnected her feeding tube on March 18, 2005. She died 13 days later (Caplan, 2015).

Selected State and Federal Laws
Death With Dignity Laws
Death with dignity laws, physician-assisted dying, or aid-in-dying laws are premised on the belief that terminally ill persons have the legal right to make their end-of-life decisions and determine the extent of their pain and suffering. These state statutes permit mentally competent adults who have a terminal illness with a confirmed prognosis of 6 or fewer months to voluntarily request and receive prescription medication to hasten their death. Proponents argue that these laws give patients dignity, control, and peace of mind during their final days. Statutory protections require that patients are at the center of end-of-life care discussions. Existing physician-assisted dying laws mirror the widely acclaimed Oregon Death With Dignity Act. Two physicians must confirm a patient's residency, diagnosis, prognosis, mental competence, and voluntariness of the request. Two waiting periods are required—the first between the oral requests, the second between receiving and filling the prescription. U.S. jurisdictions with death with dignity statutes are California (End of Life Option Act; 2015/2016), Colorado (End of Life Options Act; 2016), District of Columbia (D.C. Death with Dignity Act; 2016/2017), Hawaii (Our Care, Our Choice Act; 2018/2019), Maine (Death With Dignity Act; 2019), New Jersey (Aid in Dying for the Terminally Ill Act; 2019), New Mexico (Elizabeth Whitefield End of Life Options Act; 2021), Oregon (Death With Dignity Act; 1994/1997), Vermont (Patient Choice and Control at the End of Life Act; 2013), and Washington (Death With Dignity Act; 2008; Death With Dignity Acts, n.d.).

The Patient Self-Determination Act
Concomitant national policies were also enacted, including the Patient Self-Determination Act (PSDA) in 1990. The PSDA requires that all hospitals, skilled nursing facilities, home health agencies, hospice programs, and health maintenance organizations receiving federal funds inform patients of their rights under state law to make health care decisions. The purpose of the act is to ensure that a patient's right to self-determination in health care decisions can be articulated and protected. Through advance directives—the living will and the durable power of attorney for health care—the right to accept or reject medical or surgical treatment is available to competent adults, so that in the event that adults become incompetent to make decisions, they may continue to control decisions affecting their health care (Kelley, 1995).

Surrogate Consent Laws
The purpose of surrogate consent laws is to guide decision making when an adult has not executed advance care directives. Without them, a patient must rely heavily on a state's default surrogate consent statutes. These statutes grant a person or particular class of people, usually in kinship priority, the authority to make health care decisions for a loved one when that loved one loses decisional capacity (Wynn, 2014) and when no guardian or agent has been appointed. Also, these laws fill in the gap as a way to secure consent to health care if there are no advance directives. Surrogate consent laws exist in nearly all states and enable physicians to consult a designated individual or group of individuals who can presumably convey the incapacitated or incompetent patient's health care wishes and provide informed consent or refusal for health care interventions (Wynn, 2014).

Some states have executed extremely narrow statutes; for example, California, Kansas, New Jersey, and Oklahoma limit their surrogate consent laws to consent to medical research, and Wisconsin's statute only applies to admission to certain facilities. According to Wynn (2014), statutes in most states include (a) a priority list of surrogates who may act, (b) limitations to the scope of decisions that they may make, (c) standards for making decisions, and (d) a dispute resolution process. Of particular interest are patients without family and friend decision makers who have been labeled as unbefriended or unrepresented persons (Chamberlain et al., 2020). In these instances in several states, physicians are added to the priority list of decision makers as well as those deemed "interested persons," which can include members of a hospital ethics committee. Although well intentioned and worthy of deeper examination, many statutes fail to account for cultural issues, the usefulness and equity of the priority list, and the appropriateness of decision makers for unrepresented persons (Bullock, 2011).

Guardians and Emergent Situations in Health Care

One of the most powerful of surrogate decision makers is a guardian, a person appointed by a court to make decisions for another person when they are unable to do so (Teaster et al., 2010). In some instances, there may be two surrogate decision makers—a health care agent and a guardian. When preferences of these two surrogates conflict, the deciding factor depends upon the state where the patient lives, as over half of states place the preference of the health care surrogate first, while 12 states regard that the decision of the guardian supersedes the health care proxy. One concern is the decisional standard to apply (e.g., best interest or substituted judgment). An appointed guardian may not know the person they represent and, barring finding any other information pertaining to the patient's wishes, can only apply a best interest standard. Guardians are often called upon by hospitals to serve in emergency situations when a decision maker outside the hospital needs to be found. The guardian may never have any information beyond that provided by the hospital. While serving an important legal function as court-appointed surrogate decision maker, the reality is that these emergency guardians typically act in accordance with the recommendations of the treatment team.

Mechanisms for End-of-Life Planning

Advance Directives

Because of the cases and decisions mentioned previously, laws were created in an attempt to specify and direct care when lives of patients were limited and when treatment appeared lengthy and onerous. The first advance directive document was the *living will*, enacted into law in many states with the intention of being a standard, comprehensible means by which seriously ill patients could communicate their wishes about end-of-life care (Sabatino & Karp, 2011).

An improvement on the living will, the *durable power of attorney for health care* (DPOAHC; i.e., designated health care proxy) emerged as a mechanism that allowed individuals to appoint a legal surrogate for health care decisions should they become unable to make and/or advocate for their own decisions. The living will and the DPOAHC became known as medical advance directives, with the consequence that approaches to health care decisions at end of life became highly legalistic. Not surprisingly, a legalistic approach developed due to the need of health care systems to avoid abuse, error, or litigation when carrying out a person's wishes, particularly if doing so meant limiting treatment options versus providing all possible care (Sabatino & Karp, 2011). Since the 1980s, limitations to the legalistic approach confused patients and their families because of the prescriptive language of the documents and the highly specific medical knowledge needed. In addition, early directives were not portable and were difficult to alter at a future time.

To counter the inadequacies of advance directives, another approach emerged—the communications approach (Sabatino, 2010). This strategy reflected a growing recognition that ACP could not and should not be reduced to "one size fits all" documents but instead should be an iterative process involving discussions held among a host of participants—especially the patient, as well as care providers, family members, clergy, and others important in the life of the patient.

DURABLE DO-NOT-RESUSCITATE ORDER

Health care professionals (e.g., emergency medical services and hospital staff) have a responsibility to help a patient whose heart has stopped or who has stopped breathing using an invasive and often painful technique called cardiopulmonary resuscitation (CPR). A durable do-not-resuscitate (DDNR) order is an order to prevent the administration of CPR should a patient's heart stop or if they cease breathing. Upon its execution, a patient's doctor will include the DDNR order, which is accepted in all states and hospitals in the United States, in the medical chart. The DDNR can be part of an advance directive or stand-alone (Bailey, 2021).

POLST/MOLST

The Physician Orders for Life-Sustaining Treatment (POLST) program was developed in Oregon in 1991 with the goal of improving end-of life care for patients with advanced, chronic, progressive illnesses whose death was imminent within a year or who wished to further define their preferences for treatment (Sabatino & Karp, 2011). POLST was intended to address problems created by advance directives—that most people fail to complete them, cannot understand the language and implications of the forms, neglect to revisit or to update directives, and rarely, if ever, review them with a surrogate who may fail to understand a loved one's stated preferences and thereby fail to execute their preferences (Hickman et al., 2008).

POLST emerged as a way to implement the communications approach, one that relied upon an exploration of the patient's values, goals of care, and preferences. POLST had "teeth" for emergency medical services (EMS) and for physicians because it relied on a physician's order to direct care at end of life. The paradigm included a form, content, and a process with three core tasks that quickly spread across the country—a discussion with a health care professional, incorporation of patient preferences into a physician order, and assurance that the form was portable with the patient. In the event of a medical emergency, the patient's wishes could be communicated with health care providers through the presence of a POLST form. Implementation of the POLST paradigm proliferated across the country because of the simplicity of its concept and its evidence-based effectiveness (Pedraza et al. 2017).

As of 2021, POLST exists in all states in the United States, although the manner in which POLST developed in each is unique. The nomenclature reflects the variation; for example, POLST is also called Medical Orders for Life Sustaining Treatment (MOLST) and Physician Orders for Scope of Treatment (POST; National POLST Paradigm 2020). The paradigms (i.e., programs) are intended to achieve broad goals, especially the use of the POLST conversation with appropriate patients and their families, which would result in POLST forms that become an order in the patient chart. Although POLST forms can be created in any venue (e.g., hospital, nursing home, assisted living facility, private practice location), which directs health care providers to carry out medical treatments according to the patient's wishes, the highest rates of completion are in hospice settings (Hickman et al., 2009).

Perspectives From Research Concerning End-of-Life Planning Documents
The following review of literature begins with defining ACP and a brief overview of one of the largest studies ever conducted on end-of-life care called the Study to Understand Prognoses and Preferences for Outcomes and Risks of Treatment (SUPPORT). Next, the prevalence of ACP and associated documentation including advance directives and assignment of a durable power of attorney (DPOA) are described. Study findings prior to the COVID-19 pandemic are presented first, with a focus on the United States. Reasons for poor uptake are explored along with how effective communication can positively impact ACP. The section concludes with a secondary review of studies on how COVID-19 changed awareness and demand for ACP in both the United States and the United Kingdom.

Defining Advance Care Planning
ACP refers to a process that supports adults of all ages in sharing their preferences and values in future medical care (Sudore et al., 2017). The goal of ACP is to ensure that those values and preferences are met in the event of serious illness (Sudore et al., 2017). While conversations are considered a part of the ACP process, experts agree that documentation of the conversation and/or legal documents are necessary to ensure that wishes are met. The definition of ACP was achieved through an interactive process whereby experts discussed and came to consensus on the meaning (Sudore et al., 2017).

The Call for Better End-of-Life Care
In 1995, the SUPPORT project was conducted in two phases with over 9,000 patients across five hospitals in the United States (Collins et al., 2006; Connors et al., 1995). In Phase 1, the study identified shortcomings in end-of-life care, including lack of known patient preferences, unmanaged pain, and poor communication between patients, families, and providers. In Phase 2, an intervention, which included prognostic information and enhanced communication, was implemented, the results of which unfortunately failed to show significant improvements to end-of-life care. The study nonetheless called attention to the need for better end-of-life care and sparked positive changes to both palliative and hospice care.

Prevalence of Advance Care Planning
The literature on ACP before the pandemic provides valuable insights into the prevalence of older adults who have initiated some aspect of the process as well as relevant factors and perceptions toward ACP. Reported prevalence of ACP before the pandemic ranged from 20% to 70% among older adults (Frechman et al., 2020; Waller et al., 2019). A study conducted by Bischoff et al. (2013) on Medicare beneficiaries assessed whether they had engaged in ACP and if so what type had taken place (e.g., conversations, advance directive, DPOA). Health proxies were interviewed following the death of the beneficiary. Over three quarters (76%) of respondents said the beneficiary had been involved in some type of ACP. Among those involved in ACP, 26% had conversations about preferences, made an advance directive, and assigned a DPOA. A study by Waller examined prevalence of ACP among 186 inpatient older adults and found that an even fewer number, 9%, had engaged in conversations, placement of an advance directive, and the assignment of a DPOA. The 27% without any type of ACP were largely unaware of the options (Waller et al., 2019). Similarly, Yadav et al. (2017) found that one in three adults completes an advance directive and that a slightly higher proportion of adults (38.2%) had an advance directive if they were seriously ill.

The Role of Communication in the Uptake of Advance Care Planning
An important way to improve uptake of ACP is to understand how patients feel about conversations concerning end-of-life care. Three primary themes—ambivalence, readiness, and openness—were identified by Zwakman et al. (2018), who described patients' experiences with ACP. Patients felt both positive and unpleasant feelings (ambivalence) from an invitation to complete an ACP. While the unpleasant feelings were distressing, they also saw the process as helpful. Likewise, Zwakman et al. (2018) reported some patients feeling shocked when invited to have a conversation about ACP. The last theme, openness, refers to the degree of comfort patients felt in sharing their wishes. When patients shared their deepest values, they felt future burden was reduced on their surrogate decision maker. Discomfort stemmed from patients feeling their family would not listen or would conflict with their provider.

Waller et al. (2019) identified other reasons for lack of patient engagement in ACP. Many patients thought their family and doctors would know what they wanted should they be unable to make decisions for themselves. Other patients reported that no benefit could be gained and ACP would burden others. Conversations about ACP most often take place informally. While informal communication can leave a gray area, it is far more beneficial than assuming the family already knows, as reflected in the findings by Waller et al. (2019).

A study by Fried et al. (2017) demonstrates how surrogate perspectives do not always match that of the patient. Fried questioned veterans and their surrogates about whether different types of ACP communication had occurred, and a substantial number of them did not agree. For some activities, such as communicating about quality versus quantity of life, 33% did not agree about participation. Among those who did agree, 50% failed to complete a living will or designate a health care proxy. Forty percent had not communicated about quality versus quantity of life, suggesting a significant need for reinforcing communication between the surrogate and patient and formally documenting the process.

Within the literature on ACP, effective communication is pivotal. While informal communication can create assumptions about what is understood, it may actually be more cross-culturally acceptable than formal processes (McDermott & Selman, 2018). Cultural factors (e.g., religion, trust in health care, race/ethnicity) impact acceptance of ACP and formal documentation processes. For example, non-White ethnicities are less accepting of formal approaches. Bridging informal communication with more formal communication through helping providers be more culturally aware may help more patients engage in more ACP. Knowledge of different communication strategies, careful language choices, and avoidance of medical jargon are approaches identified by McDermott and Selman (2018) as ways to create more cultural sensitivity toward ACP. Additional traits (e.g., empathy, readiness, and frankness) were also identified as necessary to enhance communication and uptake (Frechman et al., 2020).

COVID-19 and Its Impact on Advance Care Planning
During the COVID-19 pandemic, changes occurred around ACP practices and the type of language included in the plans. A recent study out of the United Kingdom by Hurlow et al. (2021) found a 333% increase in ACP for hospitalized patients in April 2020 as compared to April 2019. Within the United Kingdom, ACP initiatives are referred to as a Recommended Summary Plan for Emergency Care and Treatment (ReSPECT). ReSPECT is a process and treatment plan intended to incorporate decisions about resuscitation with other goals of care for patients with complex health conditions or nearing end of life (Huxley et al., 2021). Like POLST/MOLST in the United States, ReSPECT is intended to encourage conversations about ACP and travel with the patient in the event they cannot make their own medical

decisions (Huxley et al., 2021). The development of ReSPECT was informed by other systems like POLST (Hawkes et al., 2020). In the study by Hurlow et al. (2021), most plans were new, with less than 10% being revisions to existing plans. Increases were seen among participating adults both over and under 65, with a greater spike from the year prior among adults under 65. Among the same patient population, fewer wished to include a "do not attempt cardiopulmonary resuscitation" (DNACPR) in 2020 (63.5%) as compared to 2019 (97.4%). The increase in ACP among younger adults may be one explanation for a shift in exclusion of DNACPR. Hurlow et al. (2021) also found that the majority of older adults (84.5%) included a DNACPR even though it was lower than the year prior.

In another investigation in the United Kingdom, Straw et al. (2021) studied how many COVID-19-positive patients had documented ACP. Rather than assessing the change in new or amended plans, this study investigated whether admitted patients already had one in place. From early March to early May 2020, 84.3% of admitted COVID patients within a large teaching hospital had documented their "pre-emptive ceiling of care." "Ceiling of care" refers to the upper level of care preferred by the patient. An even higher number had documented CPR decisions (93%), with 74.5% having DNACPR. Noted in the studies from the United Kingdom was the availability of the ReSPECT process, which helped to standardize documentation of ACP.

Precise comparisons between the United Kingdom and the United States are challenging due to differences in the health care system and standardization of ACP; however, similarities can still be drawn. Like in the United Kingdom, the United States had an uptick in ACP. Auriemma et al. (2020) found a 4.9-fold increase in the use of a free online planning tool that guided families through ACP since the start of COVID-19. No new distribution efforts for the platform were made during the pandemic. Similarly, analysis of calls and requests for advance directives and medical orders from the West Virginia Center for End-of-Life Care revealed near-record numbers (Funk et al., 2020).

Among hospitalized patients in the United States who contracted COVID-19, many were admitted with documented CPR decisions (Alhatem et al., 2020); however, not all CPR documentation represents adequate ACP. A study of 520 inpatients found that, among those with a DNR, only 29% were placed before or within 24 hours of admission (Buzby, 2021). What makes the circumstances around COVID-19 and the placement of a DNR or non-DNR so unique is that only 10% of patients studied were able to do so after hospital admission due to the severity of their illness (Buzby, 2021). This meant surrogate decision makers had to make medical decisions for their loved one, often from a distance.

Actors and Organizations in the Right-to-Die Movement

In addition to the court cases, policy, and ACP documents described previously, there were at least two important actors in the right-to-die movement, who are profiled here. The first person was Jack Kevorkian, also known as "Dr. Death." The other and more recent figure was a former elementary school teacher, Brittany Maynard, who died early in her life.

Jack Kevorkian

A central figure who elevated the right-to-die-movement to the national stage, Jack Kevorkian was a colorful medical pathologist who willingly and willfully assisted approximately 130 terminally ill people to end their lives through procedures performed in homes, cars, and campgrounds (Schneider, 2011). As a condition of his assistance, Kevorkian required that his patients expressed a clear wish to die. In addition, they had to consult family physicians and mental health professionals and have at least a month to consider their decision, thus giving them the ability to change their minds. Kevorkian videotaped interviews with patients, their families, and their friends. He also videotaped the suicides, which he called "medicides."

Kevorkian's first assisted suicide patient was Janet Adkins, an Oregon schoolteacher who suffered from Alzheimer's disease. Immediately after her death in 1990, Kevorkian called the police, who arrested and held him briefly. From May 1994 to June 1997, Kevorkian stood trial four times in the deaths of six patients. Three trials ended in acquittals, with the fourth declared a mistrial. Kevorkian videotaped the lethal injection of Thomas Youk, a patient suffering from Lou Gehrig's disease, and sent the videotape to *60 Minutes*, which broadcast it shortly thereafter. The video showed Kevorkian performing the injection himself, not only prompting a national debate about medical ethics and media responsibility, but also serving as evidence for a first-degree murder charge brought by the Oakland County prosecutor's office in 1999. Kevorkian defended himself in the trial, which proved disastrous. After a trial of less than 2 days, a Michigan jury found Dr. Kevorkian guilty of second-degree murder. Though originally sentenced to 10–25 years in a maximum-security prison, he was released in 2007 upon promising not to conduct another assisted suicide (James, 1998).

Brittany Maynard
On New Year's Day 2014, Brittany Maynard, a 29-year-old woman, learned that she had terminal brain cancer. At first, treating physicians believed that she could live for several years; however, further tests revealed that she only had about 6 months to live. Ms. Maynard made the following post on a CNN website (Maynard, 2014): "After months of research, my family and I reached a heartbreaking conclusion: there is no treatment that would save my life, and the recommended treatments would have destroyed the time I had left." After deciding that she would end her life at the point her condition became unbearable, to receive the life-ending drugs legally, she uprooted her family from her home in Alamo, California, and moved to Oregon. An ardent traveler, during her last months of life, Ms. Maynard visited Alaska, Yellowstone National Park, and the Grand Canyon. She stated that being able to choose when to die allowed her to live. "I would not tell anyone else that he or she should choose death with dignity," she wrote on the CNN website (Maynard, 2014): "My question is: Who has the right to tell me that I don't deserve this choice?" Prior to her death, Ms. Maynard approached Compassion & Choices, an end-of-life rights advocacy group, which promoted her two videos that were viewed more than 13 million times by national and international viewers. Her death from barbiturates on November 3, 2014, was confirmed by her husband, who noted that, in accordance with Oregon law, her death certificate listed a brain tumor as the cause of death (Slotnik, 2014).

National Organizations Dedicated to End-of-Life Issues
The Hemlock Society. This society (1980–2003) began in 1980 after the success of the book *Jean's Way* (1978), which recounted how the author, Derek Humphry, assisted his wife in dying after her protracted battle with cancer (Humphry, 2003). Humphry founded the Hemlock Society in an effort to campaign for changes in law and to educate terminally ill people on assisted suicide. Beginning in Humphry's garage in California, the group eventually moved to Oregon but had several other homes before it disbanded. Humphrey published a number of texts, including *Let Me Die Before I Wake* and *Final Exit* (Derek Humphry Papers, 1989–2018, 2020; Hemlock Society, 2021; Humphry, 2005). At its height, the Hemlock Society had over 40,000 members nationally with 80 chapters worldwide. The Hemlock Society helped support the passage of the 1997 Oregon Death With Dignity Act (Hemlock Society, 2021).

National Hospice and Palliative Care Organization (https://www.nhpco.org/about-nhpco/). The National Hospice and Palliative Care Organization (NHPCO) is the leading membership organization representing hospice and palliative care providers (National Hospice and Palliative Care Organization, n.d.). Its stated goal is to "expand access to a proven person-centered model for healthcare—one that provides patients and their loved ones with comfort, peace, and dignity during life's most intimate and vulnerable experiences" (National Hospice and Palliative Care Organization, n.d.). Established in 1978, the NHPCO is headquartered in the Washington, DC metropolitan area in order to represent interests of individual and organizational members.

Compassion & Choices (https://www.compassionandchoices.org/about-us). Compassion & Choices is the nation's oldest, largest, and most active nonprofit that works to improve care, expand options, and empower people to chart their end-of-life journey (Compassion & Choices, 2021). Established in 1980, the organization has over 450,000 U.S. supporters. Its goals are (a) by 2028, that half the U.S. population will live in a location where medical aid in dying is an open and accessible medical practice; (b) to address disparities in end-of-life care and planning for communities of color and authorize legislation to advance equity in end-of-life care; (c) to transform how people with dementia die; and (d) to continue to grow a diverse, equitable, and inclusive movement in the areas of race, religion, party affiliation, sexual orientation, gender identity, and age.

World Federation of Right to Die Societies (https://wfrtds.org/mission/). The World Federation of Right to Die Societies (WFRTD) is an international federation of associations that promote access to voluntary euthanasia (Mission, Vision and Statutes- The World Federation of Right to Die Socieites, 2020). Founded in 1980, it is made up of 45 right-to-die organizations from 25 countries. The federation provides an international linkage for organizations working to secure or protect the rights of individuals to self-determination at the end of their lives. Its philosophy is that, regardless of nationality, profession, religious beliefs, and ethical and political views, all who appreciate the consequences of carrying out a wish to die and who take into account the reasonable interests of others should have access to a peaceful death at the time of their choosing. The WFRTD strives to have the following: the right to die with dignity, peacefully, and without suffering; the ability to make choices about death while taking into account the reasonable interests of others; and the right make well-considered end-of-life decisions in a safe and peaceful environment supported by the law (WFRTDS, 2020).

Telemedicine and Its COVID-19 Diffusion

The COVID-19 pandemic, which began in the United States in March 2020, created unprecedented challenges in delivering care to patients at the end of life. Restrictions to in-person care and visitation, lack of staffing, fear of contracting COVID-19, and the desire for many families to impede outsiders from entering the home contributed to a shift in how palliative and hospice care was offered (Acclivity Health Solution, 2020). While rarely used by palliative and hospice providers before the COVID-19 pandemic, telemedicine became a safe and accessible option to support and treat patients with serious or terminal illnesses. Telemedicine is defined as practicing medicine through the use of telecommunication infrastructure to deliver care to patients from a distance (American Academy of Family Physicians, n.d.). Delivery can be active, whereby information is exchanged in real time between the patient and provider, or passive, which does not require an immediate response (Steindal et al., 2020). Telemedicine is often considered a clinical service and provides patients with education, remote monitoring, and consultations with nurses and physicians (Gajarawala & Pelkowski, 2021).

Telemedicine was increasingly used in both hospitals and the home environment during the pandemic. Critically ill patients in intensive care units faced extreme social distancing and isolation to reduce the spread of the virus (Ritchey et al., 2020). During a time fraught with medical decisions and unknowns, the resulting loneliness made the experience that much more arduous. Palliative care teams used telemedicine to create communication channels with loved ones that had been diminished due to visitation restrictions. Essential palliative care services such as determining patient priorities, building connections with families, promoting comfort, and supporting patient dignity while dying were more effectively delivered via telemedicine.

In the home environment, telemedicine connected nonhospitalized patients with their provider without face-to-face visits. This enabled access to early interventions to reduce adverse events, unwanted trips to the emergency room, and close monitoring (Steindal et al., 2020). Patient monitoring systems remotely assessed blood pressure, blood sugar, heart rate, and oxygen levels (Vossel, 2020). For immunocompromised patients, staying out of the hospital and avoiding contact with others was more important than ever due to risks associated with COVID-19. Patients also had increased access to specialists, less travel time, and less waiting in doctors' offices. Hospice via telemedicine during the pandemic became an invaluable resource in delivering care while protecting the safety of many vulnerable older patients.

While telemedicine technology was available before the pandemic, hospice and palliative care providers were often skeptical that intimate care could be achieved remotely. Palliative care has often been considered a "high touch," not a "high tech" field of medicine (Steindal et al., 2020). The forceful push toward telemedicine proved to be advantageous for providers and patients. The pandemic sparked new conversations about serious illness and end-of-life choices. Patients had immense worry about being in an intensive care unit and potentially dying. To mitigate the worry, patients were more proactive about setting goals of care as compared to prepandemic times. In some instances, telemedicine actually allowed patients to open up more and "get to the heart of the problem" as compared to an in-person visit (Vossel, 2020). Providers were able to understand deeply held wishes of their patients and had the added benefit of minimizing their own risk of exposure.

Visual features also improved the telemedicine experience when having conversations about end-of-life care (Steindal et al., 2020). When conversations took place through video conferencing, providers could pick up on patients' cues of sadness, fear, happiness, or distress through their facial expressions and respond accordingly (Steindal et al., 2020). Providers could respond verbally and through body language to show they were listening, adding to the intimacy of the conversation (Lally et al., 2021). In return, patients felt comforted when seeing the face of the provider. As a result, providers could be more empathic and attuned to the patient's feelings and needs. In some instances, this meant allowing patients space and time to be deeply emotional, a critical component of palliative care telemedicine.

Challenges With Implementing Telemedicine

Patients who need or want to have conversations about end-of-life care are likely to be older in age and experiencing a significant illness. Ease of use when accessing the technology platform during a telemedicine visit is imperative for this patient population to feel comfortable and confident. Complicated technology can be an insurmountable barrier for those in the poorest health or with physical limitations. Facilitation of telemedicine visits needs to be simple, especially for older adults in poor health or those less familiar with technology (Steindal et al., 2020). While many patients will continue to see their provider in person because of perceived challenges, many palliative care patients wish to use telemedicine to complement in-person visits (Eastman et al., 2021). Solutions to mitigate some of the technology challenges associated with telemedicine include enlisting the help of family members and creating better access to tablets.

Lack of Reliable Internet Access. Initially, the purpose of telemedicine was to serve patients in remote and rural areas who were not geographically close to a provider. Ironically, those same people are disproportionately burdened with poor Internet access. Without adequate Internet service or a smartphone, video-based visits are not feasible. In addition to lack of Internet access, many are without Internet-capable devices. Among Medicare beneficiaries, 41% do not have an Internet-capable computer or a smartphone (Pearlstein, 2020). While nonvideo telemedicine may be an option, it is at the sacrifice of an intimate experience. Even then, persons with dementia or compromised hearing may have trouble making a phone call. The issue of Internet access and Internet-capable devices is even more pronounced among minority and lower income older adults (Pearlstein, 2020). Combined with the knowledge that older adults of color are already less likely to seek care in person, the challenge to create equitable access to telemedicine for the most vulnerable remains a monumental challenge.

Coverage and Reimbursement. The influx of telemedicine during the pandemic happened alongside changes to reimbursable services by the Centers for Medicare and Medicaid (CMS) and private insurers. Prior to the pandemic, options for telemedicine reimbursement were limited to patients in specific geographic locations, largely rural ones lacking adequate access to providers. However, only 21.5% of Medicare beneficiaries lived in rural areas, making telemedicine unobtainable for most. Other restrictions, like having a prior relationship with the provider, Health Insurance Portability and Accountability Act–compliant technology, and the need to see providers licensed in one's home state made telemedicine highly inaccessible (Showalter, 2020). Eliminating these restrictions and expanding coverage of services allowed more beneficiaries to receive care via telemedicine during the midst of the pandemic.

Since the pandemic, CMS made many services offered via telemedicine permanent. Combined with reimbursements that are no less than in-person visits, access to telemedicine for Medicare and Medicaid patients has grown over the course of the pandemic (Kaplan, 2021). Among private payers, one assessment indicated a 3,000% spike in telehealth claims, showing a strong need for remote access to telemedicine (Kaplan, 2021). While both CMS and private insurers saw more claims because of the pandemic, many cost reduction policies put in place by private insurers have not remained.

A new familiarity has developed around telemedicine and its use in end-of-life care. Whether this is a temporary shift from face-to-face interactions or a more permanent solution is yet to be determined. For many providers, especially those treating critically ill or dying patients, the convenience and frequent access to patients and families has made telemedicine a compelling option of care. Continued expansion of reimbursement for remote services and improvements to technology geared toward older adults will contribute to further adoption of palliative and hospice care via telemedicine.

Directions for the Future and Conclusion

Since the 1950s, end-of-life decisions and decision making have evolved rapidly. The information presented in this chapter reveals a general shift toward patient autonomy and enhanced ways of communication that accurately convey wishes and preferences at end of life. Essential is communication with health care providers, patients, and friends and family, conversations that can now be conducted (and reimbursed) both in person and virtually. While a variety of mechanisms exist to express wishes and values and guide others regarding treatment, we suggest that there is a continued need to erase taboos related to death and dying, normalize end-of-life conversations, create better ACP documents, widen the uptake of POLST/MOLST, improve surrogate consent laws, and finally, and most importantly, provide more equitable health care than in the past.

Erase Taboos Related to Death and Dying. Fear has long permeated conversations about death and dying. The unknown and elusive nature of death is largely to blame for this fear and has deepened taboo discussions within our culture. Today, death is out of sight, and many people are left grappling quietly with fears of their own death and that of loved ones, particularly true during the COVID-19 pandemic. The sadness, shock, and worry thought to be evoked through conversations of death often prevent the topic from ever being discussed. Moreover, although death happens every minute of every day, many go their entire adult life rarely, if ever, witnessing death. This is a sharp contrast from how people interacted with death centuries ago. The average life expectancy is now twice what it used to be, putting one's death in the distant future. For many, talking about death is unnecessary and uncomfortable. Combined with cultural unacceptability, conversations of death and dying are far too rare and too late.

To erase discomfort around death and dying, conversations should be embraced rather than avoided. If conversations are not held, families will be left unprepared for the inevitability of death. In some ways the reluctance to talk about death is the result of a feedback loop that needs to be shifted. Less avoidance would lead to less anxiety, more frequent conversations, more exposure to the topic, and less fear. As a society, creating an environment where death is less taboo will allow a greater emphasis on the quality of life of those living and dying.

Conversations and Communication. Talking about death through informal conversations is an important first step in creating an open, more comfortable dialogue about dying. Families play a critical role at the end of life because they are often the caregivers and surrogate decision makers relied upon by providers as a source of information. When intimate conversations are held with close family about preferences at the end of life, the family is more knowledgeable and prepared for the dying process. Benefits of these conversations are immense but not always recognized. The patient, family, or both may not be ready to talk about end-of-life decisions. Conversations about death that are rooted in stories or initially less personal can ease people into talking about their own death. Families who communicate about death are more likely to navigate the dying process with less stress, more peace, and a more positive experience of losing a loved one.

Improve Planning Documents. Despite many efforts, less than a third of adults prepare advance directives and other planning documents. This poor uptake creates problems when developing a treatment plan and establishing goals of care. The documents themselves can be problematic, as some are far too specific and lengthy while others reflect an outdated understanding of available treatment options. Some planning documents reflect conflicting goals, such that the treatment team is unable to interpret and execute the patient's wishes. Documents that are clear and succinct and updated at least every 5 years would be highly beneficial to the patient, the patient's family, and health care professionals. As with POLST/MOLST, discussed next, executing the document is only one part of the equation of ACP. The other component, just as important, is that the people who must execute the stated wishes are made aware of preferences *before* an acute situation presents itself.

Increase the Use of POLST/MOLST/POST. The intention and preparation of a POLST/MOLST document is not to supplant an advance directive but rather to ensure its implementation. A key component of POLST/MOLST is the conversation that a terminally ill person has with a specified health care provider who documents patient preference. Important about POLST is that it becomes a part of the patient's medical chart because it becomes a physician's order. The POLST can be portable should a patient transfer from one state to another, and POLST now has an electronic format—the e-MOLST. Movement to an electronic platform has the advantage of reaching and educating a broader audience, the necessity of which has been underscored by the COVID-19 pandemic.

Enact Stronger and More Person-Centered Consent Laws. Mentioned earlier, surrogate consent laws perform the important function of guiding decision making when a person has not executed advance directives. These laws provide important guidance for needed decisional authority, but they may be too narrowly fashioned, thus placing limits too great to be useful when complex health care decisions are needed and thwarting a patient-centered approach to health care. Additionally, the narrow authority as well as the priority list may, in fact, delegate the decision makers who are unable or unwilling to take into account the patient's gender, culture, and other preferences. The pervasive and problematic dilemma presented by patients who are unrepresented also deserves a far better approach than currently practiced.

Provide More Equitable Health Care. Finally, we make an important plea for health care that is more ethical and equitable. The COVID-19 pandemic, still raging across the planet, underscores well-known injustices related to access to health care, particularly for poor Blacks, Hispanics, and persons with disabilities. The pandemic has emphasized that place matters and that access to health care in most rural areas remains more problematic and limited than in most metropolitan areas.

Enter the necessity (and power) of the Internet, for which telemedicine has already been an important player and is now more so than ever. If politicians deliver on their promises, broadband in rural areas will increase access for those living there, and will help level the health care playing field at end of life. Health care professionals in urban areas can access those in rural areas and vice versa. Thus, we posit that it is imperative to expand and improve upon ways to maximize the use of telemedicine, particularly for special populations and particularly for those living in rural areas.

In conclusion, in this chapter we offer that, since the mid-1900s, the discussion about end-of-life decision making, invariably one rooted in ethics, has evolved considerably and swiftly. We have gone from decisions requiring the patient's expressed wishes to end a life for one whose life value is now questionable and whose pain is not well understood or controlled to a patient's right to choose when and how to die if disease, dementia, or both make life unbearable. End-of-life issues inevitably involve worth, dignity, self-determination, and quality of life. End-of-life circumstances also involve legalities, faith systems, money, advocacy, and politics. In some instances, end-of life issues also involve racism, ageism, and sexism. We stress that considerations at a person's end of life should be ethical, person centered, thoughtful, deliberate, and careful so that we embrace the unique preciousness of a life lived—one whose wishes should be honored as much and as well as humanly possible.

References

Acclivity Health Solution. (2020, June 9). *After COVID-19, will hospices still use telemedicine?* https://acclivityhealth.com/after-covid-19-will-hospices-still-use-telemedicine/

Alhatem, A., Spruijt, O., Heller, D. S., Chokshi, R. J., Schwartz, R. A., & Lambert, W. C. (2020). "Do-not-resuscitate (DNR)" status determines mortality in patients with COVID-19. *Clinics in Dermatology, 39*(3), 510-516. https://doi.org/10.1016/j.clindermatol.2020.11.013

Alzheimer's Association. (n.d.). *Stages of Alzheimer's*. https://alz.org/alzheimers-dementia/stages

American Academy of Family Physicians. (n.d.). *What's the difference between telemedicine and telehealth?* https://www.aafp.org/news/media-center/kits/telemedicine-and-telehealth.html

Angell, M. (1991). The case of Helga Wanglie—A new kind of right to die case. *New England Journal of Medicine, 325*(7), 511–512. https://doi.org/10.1056/NEJM199108153250712

Arias, E., Tejada-Vera, B., & Ahmad, F. (2019). Provisional Life Expectancy Estimates for January through June, 2020. *National Center for Health Statistics*. (010). https://www.cdc.gov/nchs/data/vsrr/VSRR10-508.pdf

Associated Press. (1986, October 24). Paul E. Brophy is dead at 49; tested rule on right to die. *New York Times*. https://www.nytimes.com/1986/10/24/obituaries/paul-e-brophy-is-dead-at-49-tested-rule-on-right-to-die.html

Associated Press. (2005, June 15). *Schiavo autopsy shows irreversible brain damage*. NBC News. https://www.nbcnews.com/id/wbna8225637

Auriemma, C. L., Halpern, S. D., Asch, J. M., Van Der Tuyn, M., & Asch, D. A. (2020). Completion of advance directives and documented care preferences during the Coronavirus disease 2019 (COVID-19) pandemic. *JAMA Network Open*, *3*(7), e2015762–e2015762. https://doi.org/10.1001/jamanetworkopen.2020.15762

Bailey, L. (2021, June). *Advance directives and do not resuscitate orders*. https://familydoctor.org/advance-directives-and-do-not-resuscitate-orders/

Beauchamp, T. L., & Childress, J. F. (2012). *Principles of biomedical ethics* (7th ed.). Oxford University Press.

Bischoff, K. E., Sudore, R., Miao, Y., Boscardin, W. J., & Smith, A. K. (2013). Advance care planning and the quality of end-of-life care in older adults. *Journal of the American Geriatrics Society*, *61*(2), 209–214. https://doi.org/10.1111/jgs.12105

Bullock, K. (2011). The influence of culture on end-of-life decision making. *Journal of Social Work in End-of-Life & Palliative Care*, *7*(1), 83–98.

Buzby, S. (2021, July 27). *Patient autonomy to place do-not-resuscitate order low in COVID-19 hospitalization*. American Society for Preventive Cardiology. https://www.healio.com/news/cardiology/20210727/patient-autonomy-to-place-donotresuscitate-order-low-in-covid19-hospitalization

Caplan, A. (2015, March 31). *Ten years after Terri Schiavo, death debates still divide us: Bioethicist*. NBC News. https://www.nbcnews.com/health/health-news/bioethicist-tk-n333536

Centers for Disease Control and Prevention (CDC). (n.d.). *The Terri Schiavo case*. https://www.cdc.gov/training/ACP/page52792.html.

Centers for Disease Control and Prevention (CDC). (2020). *Chronic diseases and cognitive decline—A public health issue*. National Center for Chronic Disease Prevention and Health Promotion. https://www.cdc.gov/aging/publications/chronic-diseases-brief.html

Centers for Disease Control and Prevention (CDC). (2021, January 13). *Heart disease resources*. https://www.cdc.gov/heartdisease/about.htm

Chamberlain, S. A., Duggleby, W., Teaster, P. B., Estabrooks, C. A. (2020). Characteristics and unmet care needs of unbefriended residents in long term care. *Aging and Mental Health*, *24*(4), 659–667. https://doi.org/10.1080/13607863.2019.1566812

Christensen, B. J. (2019, December 11). *More people in the US are dying at home than at the hospital*. CNN. https://www.cnn.com/2019/12/11/health/dying-at-home-hospital-study-wellness/index.html

Colby, S., & Ortman, J. (2015, March). Projection of the size and composition of the U.S. population: 2014–2060. *U.S. Department of Commerce* https://www.census.gov/content/dam/Census/library/publications/2015/demo/p25-1143.pdf

Collins, L., Parks, S., & Winter, L. (2006). The state of advance care planning: One decade after SUPPORT. *American Journal of Hospice & Palliative Care*, *23*, 378–384. https://doi.org/10.1177/1049909106292171

Compassion & Choices. (2021). *Compassion & Choices home*. https://www.compassionandchoices.org/

Connors, A. F., Jr., Dawson, N. V., Desbiens, N. A., Fulkerson, W. J., Jr., Goldman, L., Knaus, W. A., Lynn, J., Oye, R. K., Bergner, M., Damiano, A., Hakim, R., Murphy, D. J., Teno, J., Virnig, B., Wagner, D. P., Wu, A. W., Yasui, Y., Robinson, D. K., Kreling, B., . . . Ransohoff, D. (1995). A controlled trial to improve care for seriously ill hospitalized patients: The study to understand prognoses and preferences for outcomes and risks of treatments (SUPPORT). *JAMA*, *274*(20), 1591–1598. https://doi.org/10.1001/jama.1995.03530200027032

Cross, S. H., & Warraich, H. J. (2019). Changes in the place of death in the United States. *New England Journal of Medicine*, *381*(24), 2369–2370. https://doi.org/10.1056/NEJMc1911892

Cruzan v. Director, Missouri Department of Health, 497 U.S. 261 (1990).

Davis, J. W., Chung, R., & Juarez, D. T. (2011). Prevalence of comorbid conditions with aging among patients with diabetes and cardiovascular disease. *Hawaii Medical Journal*, *70*(10), 209–213.

Death with Dignity Acts. (n.d.). *Death with dignity*. https://deathwithdignity.org/learn/death-with-dignity-acts/

Derek Humphry papers, 1989–2018. (2020, June 22). Archives West. http://archiveswest.orbiscascade.org/ark:/80444/xv14471

Eastman, P., Dowd, A., White, J., Carter, J., & Ely, M. (2021). Telehealth: Rapid adoption in community palliative care due to COVID-19: Patient and professional evaluation. *BMJ Supportive & Palliative Care*. https://doi.org/10.1136/bmjspcare-2021-002987

Fausset, C. B., Kelly, A. J., Rogers, W. A., & Fisk, A. D. (2011). Challenges to aging in place: Understanding home maintenance difficulties. *Journal of Housing for the Elderly, 25*(2), 125–141. https://doi.org/10.1080/02763 893.2011.571105

Feinberg, B. (1998). The court upholds a state law prohibiting physician-assisted suicide. *Journal of Criminal Law and Criminology, 88*(3), 847–876. https://doi.org/10.2307/3491354

Fimognari, F. L., Pierantozzi, A., De Alfieri, W., Salani, B., Zuccaro, S. M., Arone, A., Palleschi, G., & Palleschi, L. (2017). The severity of acute illness and functional trajectories in hospitalized older medical patients. *Journals of Gerontology: Series A, 72*(1), 102–108. https://doi.org/10.1093/gerona/glw096

Frechman, E., Dietrich, M. S., Walden, R. L., & Maxwell, C. A. (2020). Exploring the uptake of advance care planning in older adults: An integrative review. *Journal of Pain and Symptom Management, 60*(6), 1208–1222.e59. https://doi.org/10.1016/j.jpainsymman.2020.06.043

Fried, T. R., Zenoni, M., Iannone, L., O'Leary, J., & Fenton, B. T. (2017). Engagement in advance care planning and surrogates' knowledge of patients' treatment goals. *Journal of the American Geriatrics Society, 65*(8), 1712–1718. https://doi.org/10.1111/jgs.14858

Funk, D. C., Moss, A. H., & Speis, A. (2020). How COVID-19 changed advance care planning: Insights from the West Virginia Center for end-of-life care. *Journal of Pain and Symptom Management, 60*(6), e5–e9. https://doi.org/10.1016/j.jpainsymman.2020.09.021

Gajarawala, S. N., & Pelkowski, J. N. (2021). Telehealth benefits and barriers. *Journal for Nurse Practitioners, 17*(2), 218–221. https://doi.org/10.1016/j.nurpra.2020.09.013

Glover, J. J. (1990). The case of Ms. Nancy Cruzan and the care of the elderly. *Journal of the American Geriatrics Society, 38*(5), 588–593. https://doi.org/10.1111/j.1532-5415.1990.tb02413.x

Hamel, L., Wu, B., & Brodie, M. (2017, April 27). Views and Experiences with End-of-Life Medical Care in the U.S. - Findings. KFF. https://www.kff.org/report-section/views-and-experiences-with-end-of-life-medical-care-in-the-us-findings/

Hawkes, C. A., Fritz, Z., Deas, G., Ahmedzai, S. H., Richardson, A., Pitcher, D., Spiller, J., Perkins, G. D., & ReSPECT Working Group Collaborators. (2020). Development of the Recommended Summary Plan for Emergency Care and Treatment (ReSPECT). *Resuscitation, 148*, 98–107.

Helga Wanglie, Fourth Judicial District (Distr. Ct., Probate Ct. Div.) PX-91-283, Minnesota, Hennepin County (1991).

Hemlock Society. (2021, March 22). https://en.wikipedia.org/wiki/Hemlock_Society

Heron, M. (2019). Deaths: Leading causes for 2017. *National Vital Statistics Reports, 68*(6), 1–77.

Hickman, S. E., Nelson, C. A., Moss, A. H., Hammes, B. J., Terwilliger, A., Jackson, A., & Tolle, S. W. (2009). Use of the Physician Orders for Life-Sustaining Treatment (POLST) Paradigm Program in the hospice setting. *Journal of Palliative Medicine, 12*(2), 133–141.

Hickman, S. E., Sabatino, C. P., Moss, A. H., & Nester, J. W. (2008). The POLST (Physician Orders for Life-Sustaining Treatment) paradigm to improve end of life care: Potential legal barriers to implementation. *Journal of Law, Medicine, & Ethics, 36*(1), 119–140.

Hook, C. C., & Mueller, P. S. (2005). The Terri Schiavo saga: The making of a tragedy and lessons learned. *Mayo Clinic Proceedings, 80*(11), 1449–1460. https://doi.org/10.4065/80.11.1449

Hospital Survey and Construction Act (Pub. L. 79–725, 60 Stat. 1040 (1946).

Hume, D. (2006). *An enquiry concerning the principles of morals* (Vol. 4). Oxford University Press.

Humphry, D. (2003). *Jean's Way*. Norris Lane Press.

Humphry, D. (2005, February 21). *Farewell to Hemlock: Killed by its name*. Assisted Suicide. https://www.assistedsuicide.org/farewell-to-hemlock.html

Hurlow, A., Wyld, L., & Breen, A. (2021). An evaluation of advance care planning during the COVID 19 pandemic: A retrospective review of patient involvement in decision making using routinely collected data from digital ReSPECT records. *Clinical Medicine, 21*(4), e395–e398. https://doi.org/10.7861/clinmed.2020-1036

Huxley, C. J., Eli, K., Hawkes, C. A., Perkins, G. D., George, R., Griffiths, F., & Slowther, A.-M. (2021). General practitioners' experiences of emergency care and treatment planning in England: A focus group study. *BMC Family Practice, 22*(1), 128.

In re Quinlan 70 N.J. 10, 355 A.2d 647 NJ (1976).

In re of Schiavo v. Schiavo, 851 So. 2d 182 (2003).

James, C. (1998, November 23). Critic's Notebook; "60 Minutes," Kevorkian and a death for the cameras. *New York Times*. https://www.nytimes.com/1998/11/23/us/critic-s-notebook-60-minutes-kevorkian-and-a-death-for-the-cameras.html

Kaplan, D. (2021, April 14). *Telehealth is poised for a post–COVID-19 future*. OneLive. https://www.onclive.com/view/telehealth-is-poised-for-a-post-covid-19-future

Kaur, J. S. (2000). Palliative care and hospice programs. *Mayo Clinic Proceedings, 75*(2), 181–184. https://doi.org/10.4065/75.2.181

Kelley, K. (1995). The patient self-determination act. A matter of life and death. *Physician Assistant (American Academy of Physician Assistants), 19*(3), 49, 53-6, 59-60.

King, D. E., Matheson, E., Chirina, S., Shankar, A., & Broman-Fulks, J. (2013). The status of baby boomers' health in the United States: The healthiest generation? *JAMA Internal Medicine, 173*(5), 385–386. https://doi.org/10.1001/jamainternmed.2013.2006

Knickman, J. R., & Snell, E. K. (2002). The 2030 problem: Caring for aging baby boomers. *Health Services Research, 37*(4), 849–884. https://doi.org/10.1034/j.1600-0560.2002.56.x

Kübler-Ross, E. (1969). *On death and dying*. Macmillan Company.

Lally, K., Kematick, B., & Gordon, D. (2021, February 3). *Optimizing telehealth palliative care beyond the COVID-19 pandemic*. American Society of Clinical Oncology. https://dailynews.ascopubs.org/do/10.1200/and.21.200458/full/

Lee, D. H. (2002). Approach to end of life care. *Ochsner Journal, 4*(2), 98–103.

Liegner, L. M. (1975). St Christopher's Hospice, 1974: Care of the dying patient. *JAMA, 234*(10), 1047–1048.

Maynard, B. (2014, November 2). *My right to death with dignity at 29*. CNN. https://www.cnn.com/2014/10/07/opinion/maynard-assisted-suicide-cancer-dignity/.

McDermott, E., & Selman, L. E. (2018). Cultural factors influencing advance care planning in progressive, incurable disease: A systematic review with narrative synthesis. *Journal of Pain and Symptom Management, 56*(4), 613–636. https://doi.org/10.1016/j.jpainsymman.2018.07.006

McFadden, R. D. (1985, June 12). Karen Ann Quinlan, 31, dies; focus of '76 right to die case. *New York Times*. https://www.nytimes.com/1985/06/12/nyregion/karen-ann-quinlan-31-dies-focus-of-76-right-to-die-case.html?.%3Fmc=aud_dev&ad-keywords=auddevgate&gclsrc=aw.ds

Mill, J. S. (1859). On Liberty. Batoche Books Limited: Kitchener, Ontario, Canada.

Mission, vision and statutes—The World Federation of Right to Die Societies. (2020, August 21). https://wfrtds.org/mission/

Mitchell, S. L., Teno, J. M., Miller, S. C., & Mor, V. (2005). A national study of the location of death for older persons with dementia. *Journal of the American Geriatrics Society, 53*(2), 299–305. https://doi.org/10.1111/j.1532-5415.2005.53118.x

National Hospice and Palliative Care Organization. (n.d.). NHPCO. https://www.nhpco.org/about-nhpco/

National POLST Paradigm. (2020). http://www.polst.org/

Ninde, C. (2017, April 3). *200 years of public health has doubled our life expectancy*. San Juan Basin Public Health. https://sjbpublichealth.org/200-years-public-health-doubled-life-expectancy/

Oregon v. Ashcroft, 368 F. 3d 1118 (*2004*). https://casetext.com/case/oregon-v-ashcroft

Orr, A., & Green, L. M. (2003). Oregon v. Ashcroft: Physician-assisted suicide with federally controlled substances. *AMA Journal of Ethics, 5*(1), 16-18. https://doi.org/10.1001/virtualmentor.2003.5.1.hlaw1-0301

Patricia E. Brophy vs. New England Sinai Hospital, Inc. 398 Mass. 417 (1986).

Pearlstein, J. (2020, September 9). *Access to telemedicine is hardest for those who need it most*. Wired. https://www.wired.com/story/access-telemedicine-is-hardest-those-who-need-it-most/

Pedraza, S. L., Culp, S., Knestrick, M., Falkenstine, E., & Moss, A. H. (2017). Association of Physician Orders for Life-Sustaining Treatment form use with end-of-life care quality metrics in patients with cancer. *Journal of Oncology Practice, 13*(10), e881–e888.

Pence, G. E. (2015). *Medical ethics: Accounts of ground-breaking cases* (7th ed.). McGraw-Hill Education.

Rawls, J. (2009). *A theory of justice*. Harvard University Press.

Rie, M. A. (1991). *The case of Helga Wanglie—Futile treatment*. Center for Practical Bioethics and Healthcare Educational Resources. https://practicalbioethics.org/case-studies-the-case-of-helga-wanglie.html

Ritchey, K. C., Foy, A., McArdel, E., & Gruenewald, D. A. (2020). Reinventing palliative care delivery in the era of COVID-19: How telemedicine can support end-of-life care. *American Journal of Hospice & Palliative Care, 37*(11), 992–997. https://doi.org/10.1177/1049909120948235

Sabatino, C. P. (2010). The evolution of health care advance planning law and policy. *Milbank Quarterly, 88*(2), 211–239.

Sabatino, C., & Karp, N. (2011). *Improving advanced illness of care: The evolution of state POLST programs*. AARP Public Policy Institute.

Schneider, K. (2011, June 3). Dr. Jack Kevorkian dies at 83; a doctor who helped end lives. *New York Times*. https://www.nytimes.com/2011/06/04/us/04kevorkian.html

Schulman, D. (2019, March 11). Schulman: Physician assisted suicide in America. *Yale Journal of Medicine and Law*. https://www.yalejournalmedlaw.com/examinations/blog-post-title-one-8gg22

Showalter, G. (2020, May 7). *Telehealth before and after COVID-19 telehealth in original Medicare fee for service*. Caravan Health. https://caravanhealth.com/CaravanHealth/media/Resources-Page/Telehealth_BeforeAfter_COVID19.pdf

Slotnik, D. E. (2014, November 3). Brittany Maynard, "death with dignity" ally, dies at 29. *New York Times*. https://www.nytimes.com/2014/11/04/us/brittany-maynard-death-with-dignity-ally-dies-at-29.html?.%3Fmc=aud_dev&ad-keywords=auddevgate&gclsrc=aw.ds

Steindal, S. A., Nes, A. A. G., Godskesen, T. E., Dihle, A., Lind, S., Winger, A., & Klarare, A. (2020). Patients' experiences of telehealth in palliative home care: Scoping review. *Journal of Medical Internet Research, 22*(5), e16218. https://doi.org/10.2196/16218

Straw, S., McGinlay, M., Drozd, M., Slater, T. A., Cowley, A., Kamalathasan, S., Maxwell, N., Bird, R. A., Koshy, A. O., Prica, M., Patel, P. A., Relton, S. D., Gierula, J., Cubbon, R. M., Kearney, M. T., & Witte, K. K. (2021). Advanced care planning during the COVID-19 pandemic: Ceiling of care decisions and their implications for observational data. *BMC Palliative Care, 20*(1), 10. https://doi.org/10.1186/s12904-021-00711-8

Sudore, R. L., Lum, H. D., You, J. J., Hanson, L. C., Meier, D. E., Pantilat, S. Z., Matlock, D. D., Rietjens, J. A. C., Korfage, I. J., Ritchie, C. S., Kutner, J. S., Teno, J. M., Thomas, J., McMahan, R. D., & Heyland, D. K. (2017). Defining advance care planning for adults: A consensus definition from a multidisciplinary Delphi panel. *Journal of Pain and Symptom Management, 53*(5), 821–832.e1. https://doi.org/10.1016/j.jpainsymman.2016.12.331

Teaster, P. B., Wood, E., Schmidt, W., Lawrence, S. A., & Mendiondo, M. (2010). *Public guardianship: In the best interest of incapacitated people?* Praeger Publishing Company.

Toth, M., Palmer, L., Bercaw, L., Voltmer, H., & Karon, S. L. (2021). Trends in the use of residential settings among older adults. *Journals of Gerontology: Series B. 77*(2), 424-428. https://doi.org/10.1093/geronb/gbab092

Vacco v. Quill. 521 U.S. 793 (1997). https://supreme.justia.com/cases/federal/us/521/793/

Vossel, H. (2020, August 19). *Rise of hospice telehealth can stoke patient satisfaction*. Hospice News. https://hospicenews.com/2020/08/19/rise-of-hospice-telehealth-can-stoke-patient-satisfaction/

Waller, A., Sanson-Fisher, R., Nair, B. R. Nair & Evans, T. (2019). Are older and seriously ill inpatients planning ahead for future medical care? *BMC Geriatrics, 19*(1), 212. https://doi.org/10.1186/s12877-019-1211-2

Washington v. Glucksberg. (1997). Oyez. https://www.oyez.org/cases/1996/96-110

Washington v. Glucksberg, 521 U.S. 702 (1996). National Hospice and Palliative Care Organization. (n.d.). NHPCO. https://www.nhpco.org/about-nhpco/

Weijer, C. (2005). A death in the family: Reflections on the Terri Schiavo case. *Canadian Medical Association Journal, 172*(9), 1197–1198. https://doi.org/10.1503/cmaj.050348

World Federation of Right to Die Societies (WFRTDS). (2020). *Mission, vision and statutes*. https://wfrtds.org/mission/

Wynn, S. (2014, October 1). *Decisions by surrogates: An overview of surrogate consent laws in the United States*. American Bar Association. https://www.americanbar.org/groups/law_aging/publications/bifocal/vol_36/issue_1_october2014/default_surrogate_consent_statutes/

Xu, W., Wu, C., & Fletcher, J. (2020). Assessment of changes in place of death of older adults who died from dementia in the United States, 2000–2014: A time-series cross-sectional analysis. *BMC Public Health, 20*(1), 765. https://doi.org/10.1186/s12889-020-08894-0

Yadav, K. N., Gabler, N. B., Cooney, E., Kent, S., Kim, J., Herbst, N., Mante, A., Halpern, S. D., & Courtright, K. R. (2017). Approximately one in three US adults completes any type of advance directive for end-of-life care. *Health Affairs, 36*(7), 1244–1251. https://doi.org/10.1377/hlthaff.2017.0175

Zwakman, M., Jabbarian, L., van Delden, J., van der Heide, A., Korfage, I., Pollock, K., Rietjens, J., Seymour, J., & Kars, M. (2018). Advance care planning: A systematic review about experiences of patients with a life-threatening or life-limiting illness. *Palliative Medicine, 32*(8), 1305–1321. https://doi.org/10.1177/0269216318784474

CHAPTER 29

Older Adults as Victims and Witnesses

Eve Brank

> **Abstract**
> The older adult population is one of the fastest growing in the United States due to advances in medicine and aging baby boomers. Developmentally, bodies and minds go through changes as they age that contribute to victimization risk and eyewitness accuracy. Although official crime statistics suggest that older adults are infrequently crime victims, they may fear being victimized at a greater rate than other age groups and they are at increased risk of being victimized by family members who are entrusted to care for them. Older adults who are victimized or who witness another crime can be called upon to serve as an eyewitness. Eyewitness research that has focused on older adults as eyewitnesses has found that they generally do not perform as well as younger adults due to both developmental and generational differences. Using older adults in research requires creativity and extra efforts, but it is a worthwhile pursuit, given their potential for victimization and other involvement in the legal system.
>
> **Key Words:** older adults, elder, victim, victimization, eyewitness, witness

The older adult population is one of the fastest growing in the United States due to advances in medicine and aging baby boomers. By 2034, there will be an estimated 77 million adults over the age of 65, more than twice the number in 2000 (U.S. Census Bureau, 2020). Older adults as a subpopulation are increasing numerically and proportionally, and these trends are expected to continue (Shrestha & Heisler, 2011). Given our better medical care and living conditions, average lifespan has generally increased across the past 100 years to approximately 78 years of age (Arias et al., 2021). More people are reaching ages that have customarily been considered "old" (Frolik & Kaplan, 2010). Not only are people living longer, but also there are more people because of the baby boomer generation. The first baby boomers turned 65 in 2011, with approximately 10,000 more celebrating their 65th birthday every year and continuing until the end of 2029 (Cohn & Taylor, 2010). Consequently, every aspect of life is expected to see an increase in the number of older adults (Rothman et al., 2000). As such, we should expect to see older adults becoming more involved within the legal system as both victims and witnesses (Brank & Wylie, 2014; Eglit, 2004; Rothman & Dunlop, 2006).

Who Are the Older Adults?

At what age is a person formally considered an "older adult"? This is more than a mere theoretical question and is a particular challenge when conducting and discussing research in this area. No clear boundaries exist for who is "old" (Brank, 2007). Unlike adolescence to adulthood when there are several age-defined milestones such as age of consent, transitioning to older adulthood is much more nebulous. An eligible 62-year-old can begin collecting reduced Social Security benefits, but to receive full benefits, they must wait until their full retirement age, which currently ranges from 65 to 67 years of age (with the ability to increase monthly payments by delaying collection until 70 years of age; Social Security Administration, 2021). At 65, an eligible adult qualifies for health care through Medicare (Medicare.gov, 2021). But other statutory definitions of the elderly define it as being anyone over 60 years of age (e.g., Adult Protective Services Definitions, 2022). The Age Discrimination in Employment Act (ADEA) applies to employees 40 years and older. Biologically, organs thicken and stiffen with age and start to become less efficient starting in the 20s. Indeed, even organizations that focus on older adults' needs are not especially obvious in their definitions by focusing instead on generic terms. For example, the American Geriatrics Society says it is "dedicated to improving the health, independence, and quality of life of *older people*" (emphasis added, American Geriatrics Society, n.d.). The National Academy of Elder Law Attorneys' mission is to "equip attorneys for the complexity of serving *older adults* and people with disabilities through education, advocacy, and community"" (emphasis added, National Academy of Elder Law Attorneys, n.d.). Not only does "old age" seem difficult to define today, but also it seems likely that it will continue to evolve as both life expectancies and retirement ages increase. For example, although 65 may have seemed the right age for Medicare benefits to begin, that may not continue to be true if most workers are willingly staying in the workforce until the age of 80 and living until 100.

In addition to the growth in the number of older adults, the current generation of adults over 65 years of age are also wealthier, more educated, and more involved outside their home than any generation prior (Eglit, 2004). Despite the increase in number and influence, our society clings to an underlying bias against the old (Butler, 1969). Most believe that older adults are in poor physical and cognitive health, and that leads to age-based stereotypes and bias against the old. Our modern, industrialized society tends to either fear (Brank, 2011) or fight against old age (Nelson, 2002). Indeed, research suggests that negative age stereotypes are more prevalent than gender and race stereotypes (Nosek et al., 2002), although the nature of the stereotype varies from the latter. Fiske and her colleagues have found that people often categorize based on two distinct dimensions—competence and warmth (Fiske et al., 1999). Older adults generally are categorized as low on competence and high on warmth (i.e., "doddering, but dear", Cuddy & Fiske, p. 3), which is similar to people with mental or physical disabilities (Cuddy & Fiske, 2002). The resulting prejudice is generally one of pity and sympathy—in other words, a paternalistic prejudice rather than an intentionally malicious prejudice.

Developmentally, our bodies and minds do go through changes as we age. Some of those changes are visible but nonpathological (e.g., wrinkling skin or graying hair), while other changes create cognitive and physical susceptibilities. For example, some cognitive disabilities (e.g., dementia and Alzheimer's disease) are more common among older adults as compared to younger adults, but most older adults have normal levels of cognitive functioning (Dunkin & Kasl-Godley, 2000). Importantly, even though fluid intelligence (ability to solve novel problems without prior training) generally declines with age, a person's crystalized intelligence (i.e., the knowledge a person has) either remains stable or improves with age (Stuart-Hamilton, 2003, but see Beier & Ackerman, 2003). In addition to the cognitive susceptibilities, old age can also create vulnerabilities in a person's physical body that increase the risks of injury, illness, and ultimately death (Miller, 1999). As such, there are additional risks when an older adult is victimized that may not be present or as prevalent for victims from other age subpopulations. As such, the next section addresses older adults as victims.

Older Adults as Victims

Official crime statistics suggest that older adults are infrequently crime victims, but they fear being victimized at a greater rate than other age groups (Weinrath & Gartrell, 1996). This victimization paradox may be due to the higher sense of physical vulnerability (Chu & Kraus, 2004) rather than an actual fear of crime (Kappes et al., 2013). Kappes and colleagues explain that the criminology research behind the paradox generally uses a question such as, "Would you feel safe being out alone in your neighborhood after dark?" which does not specifically mention crime. Therefore, an older adult answering this question may be thinking of their poor vision or a fear of falling and not a fear of crime. Indeed, in their experimental study, Kappes and colleagues did not find an age-related change in situational or dispositional fear of crime. When they are victimized, however, physical injuries can be more severe as compared to younger adults. Still, when an older adult is victimized, it is more likely to be financially motivated crimes rather than violent crimes and perpetrated by someone the older adult knows rather than a stranger. Indeed, estimates of older adult maltreatment by caregivers fall in a wide range from 5% to 30% prevalence rates (Dong & Simon, 2011). The imprecision results from the ill-defined parameters (Loue, 2001) and underreporting (Frolik & Kaplan, 2010). Additionally, there has been far less research and public attention to older adult maltreatment as compared to other areas of family violence (Kohn, 2003; Rathbone-McCuan, 2000). What research has been done is usually focused on detecting, defining, and reporting rather than preventing abuse (Kapp, 1995), which further suggests a lower valuing of older adult lives compared to children or younger adults (Goodwin & Landy, 2014).

Despite the devaluing of older adult life, many older adult maltreatment statutes are mirrored after the child maltreatment statutes (Brank et al., 2012). Indeed, some states have identical statutes with only the words "elderly person" substituted for "child" (e.g., Florida). Superficially, this could seem like legislative efficiency, but it is important to consider the unintended consequences given the unique patterns in abuse types—financial exploitation and fraud, sexual abuse, and self-neglect—among the elderly compared to children and youth.

Older Adult Abuse Is Different From Child Abuse

In general, children have very few financial resources, yet many older adults do, which means the statutes of older adult maltreatment that mirror those of child maltreatment effectively ignore abuse involving financial exploitation and fraud. Financial exploitation or fraud occurs when someone uses the financial resources of an elderly individual for that other person's benefit and does so with or without the elderly individual's consent (DeLiema, 2018). In practical terms, the exploitation or fraud occurs in a variety of forms including cashing checks without permission, forging financial or real property documents, and taking personal items without consent or through coercion.

Unfortunately, financial exploitation or fraud is one of the more common types of abuse perpetrated on older adults by both family and nonfamily (Acierno et al., 2010) even though it is thought to be underreported (Stamatel & Mastrocinque, 2011). Some estimates approximate that one of every 18 cognitively intact older adults living in the community experiences financial fraud each year (Burns et al., 2017). When a family member or other loved one is the perpetrator, it can be especially difficult to detect given how often people comingle their finances and fail to keep adequate records (Setterlund et al., 2007). Further, financial exploitation that occurs alone and financial exploitation that occurs in conjunction with other forms of elder abuse are inherently different types that warrant distinct interventions (Jackson & Hafemeister, 2012). When the abuse occurs with other forms of maltreatment as compared to alone, the victim is less healthy, and the perpetrator is more likely to be a person in the role of caregiver. As such, when financial exploitation is occurring with other abuses, the interventions need to be much more extensive, whereas when the financial exploitation occurs alone, the appropriate intervention is one that should focus on financial security and education about fraud (Jackson & Hafemeister, 2012).

A further complication with financial exploitation is that a person's priorities naturally change and develop as they age. Even classic developmental theory from Erik Erikson teaches that older adults tend to look back on their life to consider how meaningful of a life they have lived and what kinds of relationships they now want to foster (Erikson & Erikson 1998). Newer research confirms these priority shifts, which can mean that a person nearing the end of their life does not value financial resources the way someone in middle age may. Therefore, an older adult may competently decide they want to give their neighbor, a friend, or a new love interest a substantial monetary gift. Adult children of the older adult may find this suspect and completely out of character for their parent, but perhaps this is what we should expect of the older adult if their priorities are developing appropriately. It is especially important to remember that an older adult's bad decisions do not equal incompetence, just as a younger adult's bad decisions do not either. Eccentricity is allowed at any age of adulthood (Frolik & Kaplan, 2010), but its presence can make it very difficult to determine whether an older adult has simply developed new values and is eccentric or someone is taking advantage of the older adult.

Older adults have also reached the age of majority for consensual sexual activity, so there is no set upper age that is appropriate to forbid sexual activity the way the statutory rape and child sex abuse laws do so for children and adolescents. Despite the de-sexualization of older adults (Risen, 2010), many still experience and desire fulfilling sexual activity (DeLamater, 2012; Dominguez & Barbagallo, 2016). Somewhat related, although minors are restricted from entering a marriage, there is no similar restriction at the other end of the age spectrum (despite some familial concerns about late-in-life marriages). Because advanced age is not a legal proxy for competence, other determinations are required when a person may not have the requisite mental capacity to make decisions. For older adults, capacity is not a clearly defined concept (Eglit, 2004) and often cannot be answered with a simple yes-or-no answer. Rather, capacity should be thought of as a multifaceted continuum. Older adults may be competent for certain tasks but not others. Therefore, an older adult may not be competent to manage complex financial decisions but could be completely competent to decide whether to have sexual relations with another adult. Such a dichotomy underscores the importance of limited guardianships rather than the default of a full guardianship (Gavisk & Greene, 2007).

Another barrier to understanding and responding to elder maltreatment is the high prevalence of self-neglect among the older population (Connolly, 2008) and the virtual impossibility of distinguishing self-neglect from other neglect (Brank et al., 2012; Wylie & Brank, 2009). A competent and autonomous adult has the right to choose not to bathe, eat, socialize, and attend doctors' appointments, but when that person is in the care of another person, the caregiver must legally provide a requisite level of care. For self-neglect, there is no universal definition given the wide variability of what constitutes the necessities of life among cultures and socioeconomic classes (Pavlou & Lachs, 2008).

Although some believe that self-neglect of an older adult is an indication that the person lacks necessary capacity to care for themselves (Frolik & Kaplan, 2010), this belief negates the competent decision making of an older adult (Loue, 2001). Indeed, it is arguably ageist to believe that an older adult cannot competently yet eccentrically decide to be disheveled and antisocial (Butler, 1969; Loue, 2001). One study examining self-neglect among patients at a geriatric clinic found that only 50% of those patients characterized as self-neglecting had abnormal Mini Mental State Examination scores (Dyer et al., 2007). Competent adults are permitted to refuse medical treatment, even if such refusal will lead to death (Patient Self-Determination Act, *Cruzan v. Director, Missouri Department of Health,* 1990). Of course, both active and passive serious self-harm must not be taken lightly given the potential for terrible consequences (Wand, 2018), but it is important to distinguish between the protection and care versus paternalistic overreach.

In addition to the unique possibility for financial exploitation, consensual sexual activity, and self-neglect among the elderly as compared to children, there are also other complicating factors around reporting, responding to, and preventing older adult maltreatment. Most children leave their homes every weekday to attend school because of our compulsory education laws. Older adults do not have this type of potential built-in safety net when they are living in abusive situations without any outside involvement (Brank, 2007). Even if an abuse is reported, where will the older adult go? We do not have a foster care system or other similar place for older adults to be housed in the way we have for children. An adult protective service provider will likely get involved with a suspected maltreatment, but often the only placement alternative is in a nursing home—a place many older adults fear. Compounding all of this is the embarrassment that comes with the maltreatment when the abuser is an adult child of the older adult victim.

Informal Caregivers

Finally, an additional complication around older adult maltreatment is the real possibility that a person may not realize they are an older adult's caregiver. At first blush, such a scenario may seem difficult to imagine, but several cases exemplify this dilemma. For example, an adult son argued he was not his mother's caregiver and therefore could not be criminally responsible for the 82-year-old's death (*Peterson v. State,* 2000) resulting from a ruptured colon. The paramedics found the mother lying in human waste with extensive bedsores. The son and his brother lived with their mother, but the son argued his brother was the one who was responsible for caring for their mother given he worked long hours outside the home. The court disagreed with his defense that he had not assumed caregiving responsibilities and found him and his brother guilty of aggravated manslaughter. The court held that the son had a legal duty to oversee the care his brother was providing and ensure his brother was not abusing or neglecting their mother. In another case, a niece and her husband lived with her 74-year-old uncle who was described as chronically contentious, which they claimed made it difficult to ensure he was receiving appropriate care because he often angrily refused any care they tried to offer (*People v. Simester,* 1997). The uncle died with a variety of medical conditions including severe dehydration and a bedsore that had penetrated to within an inch of his hip bone. The court again was unsympathetic to the niece and her husband's defense and found the couple guilty of criminal neglect of an elderly person.

Perhaps these are simply instances of tough cases making bad laws, but the overarching theme with these two described cases and others like them is that the court believes people know when they are a caregiver to an older adult and know how to provide appropriate care. It is constructive to consider how different it is to become a caregiver for an infant versus an older adult. When a person becomes a caregiver either by birthing or adopting a child, there is an event that undeniably creates a parent–child relationship. In comparison, becoming a caregiver for an older adult is often a slow progression. It is not uncommon for a fully competent and physically healthy older adult to move in with an adult child for financial or convenience reasons. Indeed, sometimes the older adult is moving in to help take care of young grandchildren. Sometimes there is a clear event that precipitates a change in living situations, but research shows that this is not always the case and even when there is a clear health event, the new living arrangements are often intended to be only short term. Wylie and Brank (2009) experimentally examined older adult caregiving by asking study participants to imagine themselves in a variety of living situations with older adults who needed some form of care. As expected, the participants were not well attuned to the legal and medical requirements of caring for older adults. Wylie and Brank (2009) postulated that hindsight bias could be playing a role in some court decisions because once an elderly person has died, it is easy to conclude that something went wrong. Looking backward, it is difficult to miss all the warning signs that may not be as clear during a caregiving situation.

While caregivers are now handling far more medical responsibilities than ever before (O'Mara, 2005), many states also bar a family member from interfering with medical treatment decisions in competent adults (Glick, 2005). Because "a person who has the capacity to give informed consent to a proposed medical treatment also has the capacity to refuse consent to that treatment" (Cal. Prob. Code § 813), caregivers cannot force medical treatment on elders (Frolik & Barnes, 2007). Thus, caregivers face conflicting legal demands: On one hand they must make certain the elder's medical needs are being met, while on the other hand they cannot force medical compliance on a competent adult. If the caregiver is an official guardian for the older adult, then they may intervene and make decisions for the older adult, but guardianships do not automatically occur at a certain age (nor should they), and there can be a great deal of uncertainty when an official guardianship is not in place.

Juries and Older Adult Victimization

Despite the vast research attention to juries in the psycholegal literature (Wylie et al., 2018), there is only a small slice that has focused on jury decision making related to older adult abuse cases. In a series of studies, Jonathan Golding and his colleagues (2013) examined the way jurors view elder abuse cases in both criminal and civil court. Given the persistent stereotype of older adults as incompetent, Golding and colleagues examined the believability of an older adult victim and whether greater believability translated into more guilty verdicts (Golding et al., 2013). Although participants viewed the older adult victim of financial exploitation as equally believable whether she was described as cognitively impaired or healthy, they were more willing to convict the defendant when the older adult victim was described as healthy (Golding et al., 2013). Other related research found defendant guilt ratings and verdicts were positively related to more favorable attitudes toward the elderly victim (Dunlap et al., 2007). Extending an earlier and similar study (Wasarhaley & Golding, 2013), Wasarhaley and Golding (2017) examined the effect of jurors' ageism on a civil case against a nursing home facility for neglect of an elderly resident. Varying who (resident, resident's niece, or resident's floormate) provided the testimony, Wasarhaley and Golding found that participants' ageist attitudes led to negative perceptions of the resident victim, which further led to a lower likelihood of supporting the resident victim's case. Taken together, this body of research exposes how negative ageist attitudes can detrimentally impact a criminal or civil case of elder abuse.

If an older adult is a victim of abuse or witnesses some other crime, they may be called on to be a witness to the case. When that happens, their memory, competence, and credibility will be questioned. The following section addresses older adult memory in general and specifically as it relates to the eyewitness research that has compared older adults' eyewitness capabilities to those in children and younger adults.

Older Adults as Witnesses

If a young parent loses their car keys, we likely assume the reason is lack of sleep or distraction. If an older adult loses their car keys, we likely assume they have dementia. Research has demonstrated this attributional double standard. When a young person forgets, it is attributed to lack of effort or attention. In contrast, when an older adult forgets, it is attributed to memory decline or incompetence (Erber, 1989; Erber et al., 1992, 1993). Why is this? It is well documented that memory fades with time, but societally we also hold certain biased stereotypes about older adults. One prominent such stereotype is that older adults have poor memories. In truth, it is more complicated and nuanced than that. Although declines in memory ability are thought to be inevitable, they may be inflated by self-report. As a case in point, Parkin and Walter's (1992) older adult participants were significantly less confident than younger participants about their abilities even when they were correct in the memory task. Stereotype threat can negatively compound the impact on accuracy of older eyewitnesses (Thomas et al., 2020).

Older Adult Memory

To be an accurate eyewitness, there must first be an accurate memory. Memory is traditionally divided into the following three stages: encoding, storage, and retrieval. The encoding process involves converting sensory information into information that can be remembered. Encoding is impacted by how long or well the stimulus was experienced. A person's eyesight or hearing can impact how well they can acquire the information to encode, which means age-related hearing and eyesight loss can impact an older adult's encoding (Fozard & Gordon-Salant, 2001). The new encoded information then needs to be maintained, or stored, either for a short period of time or long term. We know that the longer the retention (i.e., storage) interval, the more memory fades (Deffenbacher et al., 2008). Finally, retrieving memories involves accessing the information that has been encoded and stored.

Each one of these stages plays a role in the accuracy and confidence of eyewitnesses, and given the impact of age on each stage, it is important to consider the role of old age for eyewitnesses. Indeed, older adult brains physically may not encode or retrieve the same way as younger adults as areas of the brain are activated differently. (Grady et al., 2005). And the length of storage between encoding and retrieval is negatively related with age such that the longer the retention interval, the worse the older adults do in retrieving memories compared to younger adults (Memon et al., 2004; Searcy et al., 2001).

Eyewitness Research

Eyewitness research is a ubiquitous psycholegal topic (Wylie et al., 2018) that has real-world implications given that mistaken eyewitness accounts are the leading cause of wrongful convictions according to the Innocence Project. Recently, researchers have been focusing more on older adults as eyewitnesses (Bartlett & Memon, 2007; Toglia et al., 2014). Eyewitness research generally focuses on three types of variables: system, estimator (Wells, 1978), and postdiction (Wells et al., 2006). System variables can be manipulated by the system, such as the structure of a lineup or the way in which investigators ask the witness questions. Estimator variables cannot be manipulated within the system, such as witness and perpetrator demographics or lighting at the time of the event. Postdiction variables are those related to explanations after the fact, such as the confidence a witness feels or how quickly the witness identifies a suspect.

SYSTEM VARIABLES FOR OLDER ADULT EYEWITNESSES

Given that system variables are those that are within the control of the legal system, much research attention is devoted to manipulating system variables to determine ideal eyewitness conditions. First, the way the witness is interviewed, that is, whether asking free recall or recognition questions, has been shown to have differing impacts depending on the age of the witness. Older as compared to younger eyewitnesses are less accurate on recall tasks (Coxon & Valentine, 1997) but tend not to perform significantly differently on recognition tasks (Bartlett & Memon, 2007). Similar to children, older adults are more likely to select someone in a lineup whether the perpetrator is present or not (Valentine et al., 2003). Older adults generally just do worse with lineups than younger adults, with fewer correct identifications and more choosing of foils (Wilcock & Bull, 2014). In particular, older adults are less accurate when the target is absent but perform similarly to younger adults when the target is present (Yarney & Kent, 1980).

Extensive research has demonstrated that investigators should instruct the eyewitness that the perpetrator may or may not be present in the lineup. When investigators do not say this, eyewitnesses are significantly more likely to choose someone whether the perpetrator is present or not (Steblay, 1997). Havard et al. (2017) found that adding a "mystery man" (i.e., a silhouetted image) to a lineup resulted in older adults more successfully rejecting a target-absent lineup and having no impact on a target-present lineup. The researchers speculated that this could be because it lowers the expectation that the perpetrator will be present in the lineup in a more concrete and memorable way than only the investigator saying so.

Another factor impacting lineup (i.e., photo array) performance is the way the photos are presented to the eyewitness. Traditionally, all the photos were presented at once, which results in a relative judgment and increased likelihood of selecting a false positive. Adjusting this method to present the photos sequentially—one at a time—results in far less false-positive identifications for younger adults (Steblay et al., 2001). Yet, Erickson and colleagues' (2016) meta-analysis demonstrated that using a sequential lineup for older adults does not have the same beneficial effect.

The Misinformation Effect for Older Adults. Unfortunately, eyewitnesses can receive misinformation from other witnesses or investigators after an event. Decades of research have demonstrated that when a person receives misleading information, it can distort the memory of the original event (Loftus et al., 1978). This phenomenon is referred to as the misinformation effect and is generally studied by exposing participants to an event, presenting them with some inaccurate information about the event that is intended to mislead about specific details, and testing their memory of the original event. Wylie and colleagues (2012) performed a meta-analysis comparing younger (average age of 22 years old) to older (average age of 71 years old) adults on misinformation and suggestibility effects across 23 studies (both published and unpublished). Across the 39 independent effect sizes, there was a small to medium effect demonstrating that older adults were more susceptible to misinformation. In fact, when the average age of the older adult sample was higher, the differences between older and younger adults were more pronounced. Wylie and colleagues postulated that these differences could be related to the developmental differences in memory functioning between young–older adults and old–older adults similar to differences in basic memory functioning between children and young adults that also contribute to age-related differences in misinformation effects.

Given the greater chance for the misinformation effect to impact older adults, researchers have sought to mitigate the impact of misleading information. Holliday and colleagues (2012) demonstrated a positive impact for using the Modified Cognitive Interview with older adults, which is an enhancement of the traditional Cognitive Interview that focuses on the eyewitness mentally recreating the environment at the time of the witnessed event. Holliday and colleagues' enhancement focuses on having the eyewitness report all remembered details regardless of their potential relevance, which can alleviate older adults' negative beliefs about their own memory. Another potentially positive intervention for older adults is the Self-Administered Interview, which is fully self-administered and therefore likely to avoid demand characteristics that could be present with the Cognitive Interview (Gawrylowicz et al., 2014). Wilcock and Bull (2014) suggest that future research on older adult eyewitnesses should focus on how to enhance their abilities given what we know about the developmental deficits.

ESTIMATOR VARIABLES FOR OLDER ADULT EYEWITNESSES

A variety of estimator variables have been examined in relation to comparing older adult eyewitnesses to younger. These also deserve attention here even though they are not within the control of the criminal justice system to address. First, the cross-race effect or own-race bias, which is a widely supported finding that people are better at identifying someone who is from their same race (Meissner & Brigham, 2001), is also present with older adults (Brigham & Barkowitz, 1978; Brigham & Williamson, 1979). Similarly, research has also demonstrated an own-age bias such that eyewitnesses are better at remembering people from their own group (Rhodes & Anastasi, 2012), but a recent meta-analysis determined that there does not seem to be an own-age bias for older adults (Erickson et al., 2016).

Eyewitnesses have no control over how long they will be exposed to the target when they are witnessing an actual crime. Therefore, researchers have examined the impact of exposure duration on identification. Unsurprisingly given what we know about the encoding process, eyewitnesses who experienced longer exposures to the target were more accurate in their identifications, and this was true for both older and younger adults (Memon et al., 2003). Similarly, an eyewitness cannot control how far away an event occurs, and older adults perform worse as eyewitnesses than younger adults the farther the distance (Nyman et al., 2019), with specific errors for estimating the perpetrator's gender (Nyman et al., 2021).

Another factor that occurs at the time of encoding is what has been called the weapons-focus effect (Loftus et al., 1987). Eyewitnesses are less likely to correctly identify a perpetrator if there was a weapon (or some other unusual object; see Pickel, 1998) because cognitive resources were attuned to the weapon (or other unusual object). Although the specific weapons-focus effect for older adults has not received much research attention, Garcia-Bahos et al. (2012) examined low- versus high-typicality scripts and found that when the participants viewed a high-typical script, there were no differences between the older and younger participants. However, when the participants viewed the low-typicality script, the older adult participants had significantly worse recall of the events as compared to the younger adults, which suggests that the impact of the weapons-focus effect could be even stronger with older adults.

Juries and Older Adult Eyewitnesses

Just as jury research on older adult victimization is scarce, so is jury research on the older adult eyewitness. It does seem clear that the older adult stereotypes described in a preceding section influence how people view older eyewitnesses. In general, an older eyewitness as compared to a younger one is seen as less accurate and competent; however, the older eyewitness is also seen as more honest (Kwong See et al., 2001; Mueller-Johnson et al., 2007; Ross et al., 1990). This assessment may not be unwarranted. Compared to young adult participants, older adult research participants provided fewer details and were more prone to suggestive questioning (Brimacombe et al., 1997).

Nunez and colleagues (1999) explored this phenomenon by also focusing on how the description of the older adult eyewitness affected perceptions of credibility. Not only did they manipulate the age of the described eyewitness, but also they varied the descriptions as either a generic older adult, a senior citizen, a grandfather, or an elder statesman. Participants rated all of the older adult eyewitnesses similarly in terms of believability, but their verdicts were impacted by the descriptions of the older eyewitness. The description of the older adult eyewitness as an elder statesman garnered the most guilty verdicts. Nunez and colleagues explained that this finding demonstrated that people are focused not only on numerical age but also on underlying stereotypes of old age, with the elder statesman phrasing being contradictory to the frail older adult stereotype, leading to greater believability in the former. More recent research suggests that some older adult bias may not be as influential as a written transcript as compared to testimony of the eyewitness because written transcripts do not include the visual cues of old age (Iida & Itsukushima, 2021). Taken together, there is much more work to be done to understand how older adults perform as eyewitnesses, how to improve that performance, and how jurors view and use their testimony.

Future Directions and Conclusions

Examining older adults is an important focus for a book such as this one. As an age group, they are increasing in size and societal influence. Unlike some other demographically distinguishable groups, everyone is likely to age into this one. With aging come developmental changes that can impact whether a person becomes a victim and how a person does afterward when providing evidence as a victim of or a witness to a crime. Despite more recent attention to the age group, they are still grossly underresearched in psychology and law (Wylie et al., 2018) and underdescribed in psychology and law textbooks (Brank, 2007). Indeed, it is well documented that social psychology research in general overrelies on samples of college students in artificial laboratory settings (Sears, 1986) and that developmental psychology mostly focuses on children rather than the full range of developmental age.

To remedy the lack of attention on older adults, this conclusion will focus on some suggestions for future researchers from my own work that is related to incorporating older adults into studies and factors to consider in doing so. First, scholars could consider developing an older adult participant pool at their university. Most psychology departments have student participant pools, which provide easy access to college student samples. Some departments have community participant pools, but those generally do not specifically target older adults. Advertising for a specific older adult participant pool can be very useful and done through a university's lifelong learning and alumni offices. To ensure socioeconomic diversity, participants could also be recruited from community centers, churches, assisted living facilities, and physicians' offices. Although panels from organizations like Qualtrics or online platform recruitment like that of Mechanical Turk have become popular, current older adults may be more inclined to participate in research that involves in-person data collection rather than online given generational experience with computers. If doing in-person data collection, it is also important to consider providing transportation for the older adults or meeting them in a community setting like a library or community center. Finally, unlike statutorily defined minimum age for research consent, there is no automatic age at which a person can no longer consent to participate in research. Moreover, it is important not to automatically exclude older adults because of paternalistic fear and ageist beliefs that they will not be able to adequately consent (Barron et al., 2004). As noted earlier in this chapter, an older adult may not be competent to make complex financial decisions but could be quite competent to decide whether to participate in a research study.

Assuming researchers can gain access to older adults and obtain their consent to participate, the next issue to consider is how to categorize older adult participants demographically. Often when older adults are included in research they are inappropriately categorized as one homogeneous group without considering the developmental changes that occur as one ages

(Dunlop et al., 2000). As such, researchers should consider using more nuanced categories such as young-old, middle-old, and old-old like some have already embraced (Memon et al., 2004). Further, the impacts of gender, race/ethnicity, sexuality, socioeconomic status, geography, and living situation are all important considerations when including older adults as participants because we know life experiences interact with age.

Ultimately, law–psychology researchers should seriously consider including older adults in their studies given that they are an increasing proportion of the population and more likely to be involved in the criminal justice system as both victims and witnesses. Additionally, older adult participants provide valuable insights because of their age both generationally and developmentally. Finally, because other demographic factors (e.g., gender, socioeconomic status, race) interact with age in a compounding way, age is an important consideration to fully understand the impact of intersectionality on law–psychology topics.

References

American Geriatrics Society (n.d.). *About Us.* https://www.americangeriatrics.org/about-us#:~:text=Founded%20in%201942%2C%20the%20American,of%20life%20of%20older%20people. Retrieved July 25, 2023.

Acierno, R., Hernandez, M. A., Amstadter, A. B., Resnick, H. S., Steve, K., Muzzy, W., & Kilpatrick, D. G. (2010). Prevalence and correlates of emotional, physical, sexual, and financial abuse and potential neglect in the United States: The National Elder Mistreatment Study. *American Journal of Public Health, 100*, 292–297.

Adult protective services definitions (2022) Ohio Rev. Code Ann. § 5101.60.

Arias, E., Tejada-Vera, B., & Ahmad, F. (2021, February). *Provisional life expectancy estimates for January through June 2020* (Report no. 010). Vital Statistics Rapid Release.

Barron, J. S., Duffey, P. L., Byrd, L. J., Campbell, R., & Ferrucci, L. (2004). Informed consent for research participation in frail older persons. *Aging Clinical Experimental Research, 16*, 79–85.

Bartlett, J. C., & Memon, A. (2007). Eyewitness memory in young and older adults. In R. Lindsay, R. Ross, D. Read, & M. Toglia (Eds.), *Handbook of eyewitness psychology: Memory for people* (Vol 2., pp. 309–338). Lawrence Erlbaum and Associates.

Beier, M. E., & Ackerman, P. L. (2003). Determinants of health knowledge: An investigation of age, gender, abilities, personality, and interests. *Journal of Personality and Social Psychology, 84*(2), 439–447.

Brank, E. (2007). Elder research: Filling an important gap in psychology and law. *Behavioral Sciences and the Law, 25*, 701–716.

Brank, E. M. (2011). Baby boomers at work: Growing older and working more. In R. L. Wiener & S. L. Wilborn (Eds.), *Disability and aging discrimination* (pp. 93–108). Springer.

Brank, E. M., & Wylie, L. E. (2014). Differing perspectives on older adult caregiving. *Journal of Applied Gerontology, 35*(7), 698–720.

Brank, E. M., Wylie, L. E., & Hamm, J. A. (2012). Potential for self-reporting of older adult maltreatment: An empirical examination. *Elder Law Journal, 19*, 351–384.

Brimacombe (née Luus), C. A. E., Quinton, N., Nance, N., & Garrioch, L. (1997). Is age irrelevant? Perceptions of young and old adult eyewitnesses. *Law and Human Behavior, 21*(6), 619–634.

Brigham, J. C., & Barkowitz, P. (1978). Do "they all look alike"? The effect of race, sex, experience, and attitudes on the ability to recognize faces. *Journal of Applied Social Psychology, 8*(4), 306–318.

Brigham, J. C., & Williamson, N. L. (1979). Cross-racial recognition and age: When you're over 60, do they still "all look alike"? *Personality and Social Psychology Bulletin, 5*(2), 218–222.

Burns, D., Hederson, C. R., Sheppard, C., Zhao, R., Pillemer, K., & Lachs, M. S. (2017). Prevalence of financial fraud and scams among older adults in the United States: A systematic review and meta-analysis. *American Journal of Public Health, 107*, e13–e21.

Butler, R. N. (1969). Ageism: Another form of bigotry. *Gerontologist, 9*, 243–246.

Chu, L. D., & Kraus, J. F. (2004). Predicting fatal assault among the elderly using the national incident-based reporting system crime data. *Homicide Studies, 8*, 71–95.

Cohn, D., & Taylor, P. (2010). *Baby boomers approach 65—glumly*. Pew Research Center. Retrieved from http://pewresearch.org/pubs/1834/baby-boomers-old-age-downbeat-pessimism

Connolly, M. T. (2008). Elder self-neglect and justice system: An essay from an interdisciplinary perspective. *Journal of the American Geriatrics Society, 56*, 244–252.

Coxon, P., & Valentine, T. (1997). The effects of the age of eyewitnesses on the accuracy and suggestibility of their testimony. *Applied Cognitive Psychology, 11*(5), 415–430.

Cruzan v. Director, Missouri Department of Health, 497 U.S. 261 (1990).

Cuddy, A. J., & Fiske, S. T. (2002). Doddering but dear: Process, content, and function in stereotyping of older persons. In T. D. Nelson (Ed.), *Ageism: Stereotyping and prejudice against older persons* (pp. 3–26). MIT Press.

Deffenbacher, K. A., Bornstein, B. H., McGorty, E. K., & Penrod, S. D. (2008). Forgetting the once-seen face: Estimating the strength of an eyewitness's memory representation. *Journal of Experimental Psychology: Applied, 14*(2), 139–150.

DeLamater, J. (2012). Sexual expression in later life: A review and synthesis. *Journal of Sex Research, 49*(2–3), 125–141.

DeLiema, M. (2018). Elder fraud and financial exploitation: Application of routine activity theory. *The Gerontologist, 58*, 706–718.

Dominguez, L. J., & Barbagallo, M. (2016). Ageing and sexuality. *European Geriatric Medicine, 7*(6), 512–518.

Dong, X. Q., & Simon, M. A. (2011). Enhancing national policy and programs to address elder abuse. *Journal of the American Medical Association, 305*, 2460–2461.

Dunkin, J. J., & Kasl-Godley, J. E. (2000). Psychological changes with normal aging. In B. J. Sadock & V. A. Sadock (Eds.), *Comprehensive textbook of psychiatry* (7th ed., pp. 2980–2988). Lippincott, Williams, and Wilkins.

Dunlap, E. E., Golding, J. M., Hodell, E. C., & Marsil, D. F. (2007). Perceptions of elder physical abuse in the courtroom: The influence of hearsay witness testimony. *Journal of Elder Abuse & Neglect, 19*(3– 4), 19–39.

Dunlop, B. E., Rothman, M. B., & Entzel, P. (2000). Epilogue: Policy implications for the 21st century. In M. B. Rothman, B. D. Dunlop, & P. Entzel (Eds.), *Elders, crime, and the criminal justice system: Myth, perceptions, and reality in the 21st century* (pp. 43–83). Springer.

Dyer, C. B., Goodwin, J. S., Pickens-Pace, S., Burnett, J., & Kelly, P. A. (2007). Self-neglect among the elderly: A model based on more than 500 patients seen by a geriatric medicine team. *American Journal of Public Health, 97*, 1671–1676.

Eglit, H. (2004). *Elders on trial: Age and ageism in the American legal system*. University of Florida Press.

Erber, J. T. (1989). Young and older adults' appraisal of memory failure in young and older adult target persons. *Journal of Gerontology, 44*, 170–175.

Erber, J. T., Etheart, M. E., & Szuchman, L. T. (1992). Age and forgetfulness: Perceivers' impressions of targets' capability. *Psychology and Aging, 7*(3), 479–483.

Erber, J. T., Szuchman, L. T., & Etheart, M. E. (1993). Age and forgetfulness: Young perceivers' impressions of young and older neighbors. *The International Journal of Aging & Human Development, 37*(2), 91–103.

Erickson, W. B., Lampinen, J. M., & Moore, K. N. (2016). Eyewitness identifications by older and younger adults: A meta-analysis and discussion. *Journal of Police and Criminal Psychology, 31*(2), 108–121.

Erikson, E. H., & Erikson, J. M. (1998). *The life cycle completed* (extended ed.). W. W. Norton & Company.

Fiske, S.T., Us, J., Cuddy, A.C., & Glick, P. (1999). (Dis)respecting versus (dis)liking: Status and interdependence predict ambivalent stereotypes of competence and warmth. *Journal of Social Issues, 55(3),* 473-489.

Fozard, J. L., & Gordon-Salant, S. (2001). Changes in vision and hearing with aging. In J. E. Birren & K. W. Schaie (Eds.), *Handbook of the psychology of aging* (pp. 241–266). Academic Press.

Frolik, L. A., & Barnes, A. M. (2007). *Elder law: Cases and materials*. Matthew Bender.

Frolik, L. A., & Kaplan, R. L. (2010). *Elder law in a nutshell* (5th ed.). West Publishing Co.

Garcia-Bajos, E., Migueles, M., & Aizpurua, A. (2012). Bias of script-driven processing on eyewitness memory in young and older adults. *Applied Cognitive Psychology, 26,* 737-745.

Gavisk, M., & Greene, E. (2007). Guardianship determinations by judges, attorneys, and guardians. *Behavioral Sciences and the Law, 25*, 339–353.

Gawrylowicz, J., Memon, A., Scoboria, A., Hope, L., & Gabbert, F. (2014). Enhancing older adults' eyewitness memory for present and future events with the Self-Administered Interview. *Psychology and Aging, 29*(4), 885–890.

Glick, J. B. (2005). Protecting and respecting our elders: Revising mandatory elder abuse reporting statutes to increase efficacy and preserve autonomy. *Virginia Journal of Social Policy and the Law, 12,* 714–743.

Golding, J. M., Hodell, E. C., Dunlap, E. E., Wasarhaley, N. E., & Keller, P. S. (2013). When a son steals money from his mother: Courtroom perceptions of elder financial exploitation. *Journal of Elder Abuse & Neglect, 25*, 126–148.

Goodwin, G. P., & Landy, J. F. (2014). Valuing different human lives. *Journal of Experimental Psychology: General, 143*(2), 778–803.

Grady, C. L., McIntosh, A. R., & Craik, F. I. M. (2005). Task-related activity in prefrontal cortex and its relation to recognition memory performance in young and old adults. *Neuropsychologia, 43*, 1466–1481.

Havard, C., Laybourn, P., & Klecha, B. (2017). The mystery man can increase the reliability of eyewitness identifications for older adult witnesses. *Journal of Police and Criminal Psychology, 32*(3), 214–224.

Holliday, R. E., Humphries, J. E., Milne, R., Memon, A., Houlder, L., Lyons, A., & Bull, R. (2012). Reducing misinformation effects in older adults with cognitive interview mnemonics. *Psychology and Aging, 27*(4), 1191–1203.

Iida, R., & Itsukushima, Y. (2021). Content vs age: Perceived credibility of older and young adult eyewitnesses with confidence inflation. *Psychology, Crime and Law, 27 (5),* 476–493.

Jackson, S. L., & Hafemeister, T. L. (2012). Pure financial exploitation vs. hybrid financial exploitation co-occurring with physical abuse and/or neglect of elderly persons. *Psychology of Violence, 2,* 285–296.

Kapp, M. B. (1995). Elder mistreatment: Legal interventions and policy uncertainties. *Behavioral Sciences and the Law, 13,* 365–380.

Kappes, C., Greve, W., & Hellmers, S. (2013). Fear of crime in old age: Precautious behaviour and its relation to situational fear. *European Journal of Ageing, 10*(2), 111–125.

Kohn, N. A. (2003). Second childhood: What child protection systems can teach elder protection systems. *Stanford Law and Policy Review, 14,* 175–202.

Kwong See, S. T., Hoffman, H. G., & Wood, T. L. (2001). Perceptions of an old female eyewitness: Is the older eyewitness believable? *Psychology and Aging, 16*(2), 346–350.

Loftus, E. F., Loftus, G. R., & Messo, J. (1987). Some facts about "weapon focus." *Law and Human Behavior, 11*(1), 55–62.

Loftus, E. F., Miller, D. G., & Burns, H. J. (1978). Semantic integration of verbal information into a visual memory. *Journal of Experimental Psychology: Human Learning and Memory, 4*(1), 19–31.

Loue, S. (2001). Elder abuse and neglect in medicine and law. *Journal of Legal Medicine, 22,* 159–209.

Medicare.gov. (2021). *Get started with Medicare.* https://www.medicare.gov/basics/get-started-with-medicare

Meissner, C. A., & Brigham, J. C. (2001). Thirty years of investigating the own-race bias in memory for faces: A meta-analytic review. *Psychology, Public Policy, and Law, 7*(1), 3–35.

Memon, A., Gabbert, F., & Hope, L. (2004). The ageing eyewitness. In J. R. Adler (Ed.), *Forensic psychology: Concepts, Debates and Practice* (pp. 96–112). Willan Publishing.

Memon, A., Hope, L., & Bull, R. (2003). Exposure duration: Effects on eyewitness accuracy and confidence. *British Journal of Psychology, 94,* 339–354.

Miller, R. A. (1999). Kleemeier award lecture: Are there genes for aging? *Journal of Gerontology, 54A,* 297–307.

Mueller-Johnson, K., Toglia, M. P., Sweeney, C. D., & Ceci, S. J. (2007). The perceived credibility of older adults as witnesses and its relation to ageism. *Behavioral Sciences and the Law, 25,* 355–375.

National Academy of Elder Law Attorneys (n.d.). *Who we are.* https://www.naela.org/Web/Web/Who-We-Are-Template.aspx?hkey=feb0efd3-bd62-4508-9ca4-20de373d4784 Retrieved July 25, 2023.

Nelson, T. D. (2002). *Ageism: Stereotyping and prejudice against older persons.* MIT Press.

Nosek, B. A., Banaji, M. R., & Greenwald, A. G. (2002). Harvesting implicit group attitudes and beliefs from a demonstration web site. *Group Dynamics: Theory, Research, and Practice, 6,* 101–115.

Nunez, N., McCoy, M. L., Clark, H. L., & Shaw, L. A. (1999). The testimony of elderly victim/witnesses and their impact on juror decisions: The importance of examining multiple stereotypes. *Law and Human Behavior, 23,* 413–423.

Nyman, T. J., Antfolk, J., Lampinen, J. M., Korkman, J., & Santtila, P. (2021). The effects of distance and age on the accuracy of estimating perpetrator gender, age, height, and weight by eyewitnesses. *Psychology, Crime and Law, 27*(3), 231–252.

Nyman, T. J., Lampinen, J. M., Antfolk, J., Korkman, J., & Santtila, P. (2019). The distance threshold of reliable eyewitness identification. *Law and Human Behavior, 43*(6), 527–541.

O'Mara, A. (2005). Who's taking care of the caregiver? *Journal of Clinical Oncology, 23*(28), 6820–6821.

Parkin, A. J., & Walter, B. M. (1992). Recollective experiences, normal aging, and frontal dysfunction. *Psychology and Aging, 7,* 290–298.

Pavlou, M. P., & Lachs, M. S. (2008). Self-neglect in older adults: A primer for clinicians. *Journal of General Internal Medicine, 23*(11), 1841–1846.

People v. Simester, 678 N.E. 2d 710 (1997).

Peterson v. State, 765 So. 2d 861 (2000).

Pickel, K. L. (1998). Unusualness and threat as possible causes of "weapon focus." *Memory, 6,* 277–295.

Rathbone-McCuan, E. (2000). Elder abuse within the context of intimate violence. *University of Missouri at Kansas City Law Review, 69,* 215–226.

Rhodes, M. G., & Anastasi, J. S. (2012). The own-age bias in face recognition: A meta-analytic and theoretical review. *Psychological Bulletin, 138*(1), 146–174.

Risen, C. B. (2010). Listening to sexual stories. In S. B. Levine, C. B. Risen, & S. E. Althof (Eds.), *Handbook of clinical sexuality for mental health professionals* (pp. 57–72). Taylor & Francis Group.

Ross, D. F., Dunning, D., Toglia, M. P., & Ceci, S. J. (1990). The child in the eyes of the jury: Assessing mock jurors' perceptions of the child witness. *Law and Human Behavior, 14*(1), 5–23.

Rothman, M. B., & Dunlap, B. D. (2006). Elders and the courts. *Journal of Aging and Social Policy, 18,* 31–46.

Rothman, M. B., Dunlap, B. D., & Entzel, P. (2000). Introduction. In M. B. Rothman, B. D. Dunlop, & P. Entzel (Eds.), *Elders, crime, and the criminal justice system: Myth, perceptions, and reality in the 21st century* (pp. xxix–xxxviii). Springer.

Searcy, J. H., Bartlett, J. C., Memon, A., & Swanson, K. (2001). Aging and lineup performance at long retention intervals: Effects of metamemory and context reinstatement. *Journal of Applied Psychology, 86*(2), 207–214.

Sears, D. O. (1986). College sophomores in the laboratory: Influences of a narrow data base on psychology's view of human nature. *Journal of Personality and Social Psychology, 51*, 515–530.

Setterlund, D., Tilse, C., Wilson, J., Mccawley, A., & Rosenman, L. (2007). Understanding financial elder abuse in families: The potential of routine activities theory. *Ageing and Society, 27*, 599–614.

Shrestha, L. B., & Heisler, E. J. (2011). *The changing demographic profile of the United States* (7-5700). Congressional Research Service.

Social Security Administration. (2021). *Retirement benefits*. https://www.ssa.gov/benefits/retirement/planner/agereduction.html

Stamatel, J. P., & Mastrocinque, J. M. (2011). Using National Incident-Based Reporting System (NIBRS) data to understand financial exploitation of the elderly: A research note. *Victims and Offenders, 6*, 117–136.

Steblay, N. M. (1997). Social influence in eyewitness recall: A meta-analytic review of lineup instruction effects. *Law and Human Behavior, 21*(3), 283–297.

Steblay, N., Dysart, J., Fulero, S., & Lindsay, R. C. L. (2001). Eyewitness accuracy rates in sequential and simultaneous lineup presentations: A meta-analytic comparison. *Law and Human Behavior, 25*(5), 459–473.

Stuart-Hamilton, I. A. (2003). Normal cognitive aging. In R. C. Tallis & H. M. Fillit (Eds.), *Brocklehurst's textbook of geriatric medicine and gerontology* (6th ed., pp. 125–142). Churchill Livingston.

Thomas, A. K., Smith, A. M., & Mazerolle, M. (2020). The unexpected relationship between retrieval demands and memory performance when older adults are faced with age-related stereotypes. *Journals of Gerontology: Psychological Sciences, 75*, 241–250.

Toglia, M. P., Ross, D. F., Pozzulo, J., & Pica, E. (Eds.). (2014). *The elderly eyewitness in court*. Psychology Press.

U.S. Census Bureau. (2020). *65 and older population grows rapidly as baby boomers age*. https://www.census.gov/newsroom/press-releases/2020/65-older-population-grows.html

Valentine, T., Pickering, A., & Darling, S. (2003). Characteristics of eyewitness identification that predict the outcome of real lineups. *Applied Cognitive Psychology, 17*, 969–993.

Wand, A. P. F., Peisah, C., Draper, B., & Brodaty, H. (2018). Understanding self-harm in older people: A systematic review of qualitative studies. *Aging and Mental Health, 22*, 289–298.

Wasarhaley, N. E., & Golding, J. M. (2013). Perceptions of institutional elder neglect in civil court. *Journal of Elder Abuse & Neglect, 25*(4), 305–322.

Wasarhaley, N.E., & Golding, J.M. (2017). Ageism in the courtroom: mock juror perceptions of elder neglect. *Psychology, Crime & Law*, 23(9), 874-898.

Weinrath, M., & Gartrell, J. (1996). Victimization and fear of crime. *Violence & Victims, 11*(3), 187–197.

Wells, G. L. (1978). Applied eyewitness-testimony research: System variables and estimator variables. *Journal of Personality and Social Psychology, 36*(12), 1546–1557.

Wells, G. L., Memon, A., & Penrod, S. D. (2006). Eyewitness evidence: Improving its probative value. *Psychological Science in the Public Interest: A Journal of the American Psychological Society, 7*(2), 45–75.

Wilcock, R., & Bull, R. (2014). Improving the performance of older witnesses on identification procedures. In M. P. Toglia, D. F. Ross, J. Pozzulo, & E. Pica (Eds.), *The elderly eyewitness in court* (pp. 118–134). Psychology Press.

Wylie, L. E., & Brank, E. M. (2009). Assuming elder care responsibility: Am I a caregiver? *Journal of Empirical Legal Studies, 6*, 899–924.

Wylie, L. E., Hazen, K. P., Hoetger, L. A., Haby, J. A., & Brank, E. M. (2018). Four decades of *Law and Human Behavior*: A content analysis. *Scientometrics, 115*(2), 655–693.

Wylie, L. E., Patihis, L., McCuller, L. L., Davis, D., Brank, E. M., Loftus, E., & Bornsetin, B. H. (2012). Misinformation effects in older versus younger adults: A meta-analysis. In M. P. Toglia, D. F. Ross, J. Pozzulo, & E. Pica (Eds.), *The elderly eyewitness in court* (pp. 38–66). Taylor and Francis.

Yarney, A. D., & Kent, J. (1980). Eyewitness identification by elderly and young adults. *Law and Human Behavior, 4*, 359–371.

CHAPTER 30

Aging in the Criminal Justice System: A Call for Age-Focused Research, Policy, and Practice

Lindsey E. Wylie and Sarah Hubner

> **Abstract**
>
> Adults aged 65 and older are the fastest growing subpopulation in the United States. Concurrent with general-population aging is a commensurate rise in the number of older adults involved in the criminal justice system, as both offenders and incarcerated individuals. Although older adults commit fewer and less serious crimes than younger adults, the proportion of older inmates continues to increase. This demographic shift precipitates rising costs, primarily associated with health care and end of life. To ensure older inmates' safety and meet legal requirements, facilities will have to make physical and social accommodations. These improvements, aimed at developing age-competent systems for adults, may also extend to reformation of policy and practices. However, research on older adults and aging within the criminal justice system is notably lacking. Thus, future studies should expand on the understanding of this aging experience, ultimately aiming to improve the aging crisis in U.S. correctional facilities.
>
> **Key Words:** aging offenders, aging inmates, compassionate release, normative aging, pathological aging

According to the U.S. Census, older adults are the fastest growing subpopulation in the United States. due to lower birth rates and increased longevity. The U.S. aging population increased rapidly for most of the 20th century, surpassing that of the total population and the population under 65, except during the 1990s, when the relatively smaller Depression-era cohort reached age 65 (Roberts et al., 2018). Rates are expected to continue to increase, especially as the baby boomer cohort reaches age 65 (Roberts et al., 2018). With the increase in older adults in the general population, there will also be a rise in older adults involved in the criminal justice system as persons committing crime and incarcerated individuals. In general, older adults (defined later) commit fewer of all types of crimes than any other age group. It begs the question, then, why study older offenders? First, as the general aging population increases, so too will the number of older adults arrested and incarcerated. Second, there are unique issues presenting with older adults as perpetrators of crime. Older adults may commit crimes for different reasons, may commit different types of crimes, and may have unique issues when it comes to arrest, sentencing, and incarceration. Third, older adults face unique issues when incarcerated, and as prisons continue to be overcrowded, finding solutions to address the needs of older adults and correctional facilities is imperative.

Despite these demographic trends, law–psychology scholarship with older adults in the criminal justice system has been somewhat limited—especially in comparison to other age groups (i.e., children, teenagers, young adults/college students). In a review of all published *Law and Human Behavior* articles from 1977 to 2016, Wylie, Hazen, and colleagues (2018) identified that fewer than 0.1% of articles included a sample of older adults, while 11.6% of articles included children under the age of 18. In a previous call aimed at increasing research with older adults, Brank (2007) noted that "as the discipline has demonstrated in other areas, [getting involved in elder issues] uniquely positions us to inform policy makers, physicians, attorneys, and the public" (p. 711).

The current chapter examines issues related to older adults involved in the criminal justice system as perpetrators of crime and inmates in correctional institutes. From the perspectives of psychology, law, gerontology, criminology, medicine, and social work, we will discuss the scholarship examining older adults through the various stages of the criminal justice process. First, we will explain how older adulthood is defined in various legal system structures and describe the aging process in terms of the physical and psychosocial changes that occur. Next, we will discuss older adults as the perpetrators of crime, including the rates at which they are arrested and the types of crimes for which they are most likely to be arrested. The next section describes older adults as defendants and the issues presented as they navigate court and sentencing practices. The last section includes discussion on older adults as inmates, how prison conditions affect older inmates, legal and psychological difficulties that emerge from housing older offenders, and potential solutions to address these issues. We conclude with implications for research, policy, and practice.

Review of Aging Issues
Defining Older Adulthood

"Age" as a concept is generally understood and can easily be measured as a continuous variable, but as a means to better understand how age is related to development, emotions, and behavior during varying life periods, age is conceptualized into stages (i.e., infancy, childhood, adolescence, middle age, and old age); however, there is no standardized age that separates one from each life stage (Kratcoski & Edelbacher, 2016). Although older individuals are often collectively termed "older adults," with the assumption they are a homogeneous age group, there is heterogeneity within the group. Within both psychological and legal scholarship, older adults may include "anyone over 65"; however, not only are there significant differences between a 65-year-old and a 90-year-old, for example, but also, even at the same age, individuals experience aging at varying rates. While one 70-year-old may be experiencing very little mental or physical impairment, another individual of the same age may be experiencing a series of comorbid mental and physical ailments.

What constitutes an "older adult" also has some considerable variability—both subjectively and within the legal system. Unlike childhood, which has a distinct end point of 18 years old (in most states), there is no consensus for when to define older adulthood. For instance, the Census includes those 65 and over as older adults. To become a member of the American Association of Retired Persons (AARP), one must be 50. To collect early Social Security benefits, one can be 62 years old, and to collect full benefits, one must be 65; however, even this is a moving target as the age for collecting benefits will gradually increase from 65 to 67 for those born in 1960 and later. State and federal statutes also vary with respect to what is considered old age. As we will further discuss in subsequent sections, some criminal sentencing statutes allow for downward departures from mandatory sentences based on an unspecified "old age," and when compassionate release statutes allow for release based on age, the specific age for eligibility varies by state.

Yet, there are even inconsistent definitions for old age within criminal justice settings and literature involving older adults as offenders. While some categorize older adults as aged 50 and above, others use 60 and above, and others 65 and above (Kratcoski & Edelbacher, 2016). Researchers within medicine, who study incarcerated older adults, have defined old age as 50 and older because individuals involved in the criminal justice system, and within correctional facilities specifically, are some of the unhealthiest individuals (Merkt et al., 2020). This is in part due to socioeconomic issues and unhealthy lifestyles prior to and during incarceration, but also because incarceration often exacerbates medical issues that already existed (Curran, 2000). For the purposes of this chapter, we generally consider older adults to be those aged 50 and older.

Normative and Pathological Aging Processes
While chronological and stage-graded age are useful for marking physical and psychosocial changes across the lifespan, aging is now increasingly defined by an individual's functional ability, disease status, and quality of life. Based on these domains of health and ability, populations can be categorized into aging patterns of successful, normal, or pathological (Rowe & Kahn, 1997). Successful aging is associated with minimal functional losses and disease, while pathological aging is conversely characterized by significant impairment or morbidity; normal aging is somewhere in between (Rowe & Kahn, 1997). While these patterns all include some normative, age-related changes, worse aging patterns are typified by pathological disease, dysfunction, and decline. Several factors, including sex, race, education, and lifestyle, contribute to cumulative (dis)advantage and help to predict aging patterns (Brinkley-Rubinstein, 2013; Dannefer, 2003; Merkt et al., 2020; Rodríguez-Rodero et al., 2011). Similarly, incarceration modifies aging patterns and is suggested to contribute to an accelerated functional aging process (Brinkley-Rubinstein, 2013; Merkt et al., 2020). Consequentially, some older prisoners may experience aspects of aging sooner and with greater burden than community-dwelling populations.

Aging is associated with a variety of normative physical and sensory changes, including reduced skin elasticity, graying hair, stooping posture, loss of muscle tone (sarcopenia), increased adiposity, and reduced auditory, visual, and olfactory acuity (Boss & Seegmiller, 1981). Deviating from the normative, older inmates specifically report poorer subjective health, high distress, and multiple chronic conditions, often at younger ages than the average population (Baidawi, 2016; Baidawi et al., 2016; Nijhawan, 2016). Reports suggest that, in incarcerated populations, these observable signs of aging may mark vulnerable targets and increase older adults' risk of victimization (Baidawi, 2016; Kerbs & Jolley, 2007). This risk is further exacerbated by physical, cognitive, and psychological comorbidities.

Considering physical age-related changes, older adults experience normative reductions in most body systems, although pathological processes can exacerbate these. For example, while cardiorespiratory fitness naturally declines with age (Hakola et al., 2011), diseases like hypertension and heart disease result in greater limits to function (Colón-Emeric et al., 2013; Petrie et al., 2018). Further, liver and kidney systems work less effectively with advancing age such that they metabolize and excrete drugs less efficiently (Bhutto & Morley, 2008; Boss & Seegmiller, 1981). This is especially relevant for inmates with substance abuse disorders (Gates et al., 2017). Older populations are also more vulnerable to infection due to depressed immune function (Oh et al., 2019). Infections in inmates may be related to a variety of factors including high institutionalized prevalence of communicable diseases (e.g., HIV/AIDS, hepatitis C, hepatitis B, tuberculosis), poor hygiene, and risky behavior (e.g., substance abuse, unprotected sex; Nijhawan, 2016). Other chronic conditions that affect inmate populations at high rates include diabetes, asthma, arthritis, and cancer. Uncontrolled pain, intensified by disease multimorbidity and high chronic stress, is also recognized as a major issue in prison populations, as it is associated with diminished quality of life (Lin & Mathew, 2005; Munday et al., 2019).

Cognitively, there are only minor declines associated with normative aging, mainly related to slight reductions in processing speed (Wilson et al., 2020). These small deficits are well compensated for by the aging brain and, in the absence of disease, generally do not impair older adults (Wilson et al., 2020). However, pathological impairments, including dementias, traumatic brain injuries, and developmental deficits, have been estimated at rates as high as 30%–44% within aging prisoner populations (Cipriani et al., 2017; Johanna du Toit et al., 2019; Maschi et al., 2012). Additionally, while no mental health disorders are associated with normative aging, among inmates 50 years and older, it is estimated that approximately 38.4% have at least one psychiatric disorder (Di Lorito et al., 2018), although a notable absence of empirical research limits exact estimates of the burden of cognitive and psychiatric disease in incarcerated populations. Moreover, the lack of adaptable infrastructure and health care for these especially vulnerable populations warrants additional focus, as discussed later in this chapter.

Psychological and Legal Frameworks

When asked to think of an elderly person, several attributes may come to mind. We may think of our grandmother who is wise but at times slightly forgetful, or we may think about the older person that lives next store who we would describe as a grumpy old man. Most often, people will not think of a person who is committing crime or incarcerated for life in prison. How, then, do our underlying attitudes about older adults guide our feelings and behavior toward older offenders moving through each stage of the criminal justice system?

Social psychological frameworks and theories may help to explain the unique perceptions we have toward older adults as offenders. Across studies examining old-age stereotypes, similar themes emerge. Older adults are often described with both positive and negative stereotypes (Barrett & Cantwell, 2007; Cuddy et al., 2005), with endorsements of negative stereotypes more prevalent (Chasteen, 2002; Hummert, 1993; Kite et al., 2002; Nelson, 2002). Similarly, perceivers prefer older adults exhibiting stereotype-consistent behaviors, as opposed to those that are stereotype inconsistent (Cuddy et al., 2005).

According to the stereotype content model (SCM; Fiske et al., 2002, 2007), targets are perceived according to two dimensions, warmth (e.g., are they trustworthy?) and competence (e.g., do they have the capacity or skill to compete?). Where a target group falls along these dimensions determines our attitudes and feelings toward the group. Studies indicate that older adults fall within the "warm but incompetent" dimensions and elicit feelings of pity and admiration (Cuddy et al., 2005). Because older adults are associated with these mixed warm–incompetent stereotypes, they are often targets of the most common form of ageist behavior, benevolent ageism, which results in "overhelping" (Bugental & Hehman, 2007; Cuddy et al., 2005). Variations in how older adults are perceived may also be contingent on contextual factors (Castelli et al., 2004; Schaller et al., 2003) that facilitate either desirable or undesirable stereotypes. According to the role congruity theory, biased responses develop from the interaction of stereotypic beliefs about the target and the context in which the target is evaluated (Eagly & Karau, 2002). When a group's stereotype is mismatched to valued social roles, prejudicial responses emerge.

Although issues of competency and capacity are relevant to all age groups (e.g., juveniles, people with mental illness), because there are noted declines in cognitive abilities, competency and capacity have additional relevance in the context of older offenders. At times these terms are used interchangeably; however, these terms have specific meaning within the legal system. While competency is a legal standard decided by a judicial body, capacity is an assessment by a medical professional of a person's ability to make certain decisions or perform certain tasks. One of the most significant differences between the two is that where competency is largely a binary legal decision of competent or incompetent, capacity is often thought of on a context-specific continuum (Arias, 2013; Moye & Marson, 2009). Although medical professionals recognize this graduated type of incapacity, legal outcomes often fail to recognize any intermediate determinations. As a result, judges must determine where along the capacity continuum a person should be considered incompetent and whether a person is incompetent in some or all areas of decision making (Arias, 2013).

Throughout the chapter, we note areas where various legal actors and entities make decisions about older adults as offenders and inmates. Negative aging stereotypes and attitudes may influence perceptions of capacity and competency, as well as contribute to assumptions about the character and behavior of older adults in the criminal justice system.

Current Scholarship in Aging Prisoners
Older Adults as Perpetrators of Crime

The study of criminal behavior has identified several variables that are reliable in predicting the level of crime and types of crime that are committed by certain groups of offenders. One of the strongest predictors is age, as research consistently finds a significant relationship between age and criminal behavior. As it is known, the age–crime curve demonstrates that criminal behavior peaks in the teenage years, then declines quickly, but then decreases more gradually as age increases (Farrington, 1986; Hirschi & Gottfredson, 1983; see Narvey & Piquero, this volume). According to Hirschi and Gottfredson (1983), this age–crime curve is universal. That is, the curve seems to apply, at least roughly, in all demographic and socioeconomic categories, as well as for all offenses. Nevertheless, recent studies indicate the precise age at which crime peaks depends on a variety of characteristics and conditions and varies across offenses (e.g., Fagan & Western, 2005). The study of criminal behavior, therefore, has often focused on juveniles and younger adults—the perpetrators of most violent and nonviolent crime; however, over the past few decades, even though the proportion of older adults committing crimes has not dramatically increased, statistics demonstrate growth in the number of older adults in state and federal prisons. As such, criminal behavior in older offenders warrants specific attention.

In the 1970s and 1980s, researchers predicted that we would have a "geriatric crime wave" (Flynn, 2000, p. 47) because of aging baby boomers and increases in the older adult population (Bachand & Chressanthis, 1988; Feinberg, 1984; Shichor, 1984). In the early 2000s, media reports and commentators even claimed a rise in serious crime committed by older adults based on gross national arrest figures (e.g., Marquart et al., 2000). Since then, the so-called geriatric crime wave has largely been dismissed, and once researchers applied methods of age standardization to arrest counts, they found little change in violent and nonviolent crime committed by older adults. Moreover, longitudinal analyses have indicated that the proportion of criminal involvement by older adults, as compared to other age groups, has been consistent over time (Feldmeyer & Steffensmeier, 2007; Steffensmeier, 1987). A more recent analysis of the Uniform Crime Report from 2000 to 2013 does suggest a small increase (from 1% to 2.2% for all index crimes) for those 60 and older (Kratcoski & Edelbacher, 2016).

With respect to the types of crimes that older adults engage in, statistics demonstrate that older adults are more likely to be arrested for minor offenses and alcohol violations (Feldmeyer

& Steffensmeier, 2007) than serious crimes. When examining overall rates, reports demonstrate that arrest rates were highest for property offenses (5%) and lowest for violent offenses (1%), but still relatively low compared to other age groups (Kratcoski & Edelbacher, 2016). Although arrest base rates remain low, some have documented increases in certain types of crimes. For instance, one report found that even though drug-related offenses were lowest for those aged 50 and older, the rate had increased from 2000 to 2018 (Butts, 2019). Another report found an increase for specific violent offenses (i.e., murder and manslaughter) and some property offenses (i.e., larceny-theft) for those 65 and older, and a slight increase in driving under the influence, liquor law violations, and vagrancy for those 60 and older (Kratcoski & Edelbacher, 2016).

The types of crimes older adults are likely to engage in are largely explained by the fact that for some crimes, older adults do not necessarily have the motivation, opportunity, or ability to commit the act. With age, there is a decline in physical strength and energy, as well as psychological drive. For older adults, therefore, it may be that even if they have the motivation to commit the crime, they may not have the opportunity or ability to do so. This likely explains why property offenses, such as shoplifting and minor theft (Kratcoski & Edelbacher, 2016), and drug- or alcohol-related offenses (Butts, 2019; Feldmeyer & Steffensmeier, 2007) are found to be the highest category of offenses committed by older adults. Lifestyle adaptations that accompany increased age likely contribute to older adults having fewer opportunities for crime, and older adults may actually be deterred by legal sanctions as they more fully appreciate that time is a diminishing, exhaustible, and increasingly valuable resource (Shover, 1996; Steffensmeier & Allan, 1995; Tittle & Paternoster, 2000). A related consideration is that aspirations and goals typically change with age, so older adults no longer strive for the same level of material fulfillment and recognition that they sought when they were younger. As such, the major sources of reinforcement for criminal behavior (e.g., money, sex, status, intense and lasting hostility toward others, and antisocial peer pressure) are absent or relatively weak in old age. Lastly, age differences may be built into enforcement policies and criminal statutes, such as diversion for elderly offenders, which may contribute to reported lower levels of elderly crime (Flynn, 2000; Rothman et al., 2000; Steffensmeier & Motivans, 2000; Terry & Entzel, 2000).

Within the literature on aging offenders, typologies have been identified to describe the various patterns observed with older offenders; these include the inveterate, the relapsing, and the first timer (Fattah & Sacco, 1989). The inveterate aging offender is the chronic offender who began engaging in criminal behavior in adolescence or early adulthood. Within the inveterate type, there are several subtypes identified, including the professional criminal (i.e., sophisticated crimes), the chronic drunk (i.e., homeless), the habitual petty criminal, the organized crime head, the inveterate psychopath (i.e., antisocial behavior—not necessarily from psychosis), and the chronic nonviolent sex offender. The next type is the relapsing older offender, which includes older adults who were thought to have been rehabilitated but who relapse into crime after a long period of successful adjustment and after staying crime free—possibly triggered by some life crisis or changes brought about by old age. There are two subtypes to the relapsing offender: the monomorphic, who engages in similar crime, and the polymorphic, who engages in different criminal activities later in life. The third type, the first timer, is characterized by having no prior delinquency or criminal history and is the most atypical. The first timer may become criminally involved because of psychiatric or behavioral changes caused by aging (loss of judgment or inhibitions, sudden mistrust), dementia, drug or alcohol abuse, personality changes from aging, or environmental changes (i.e., placement in assisted living or nursing home).

Older Adults as Defendants

Once older offenders reach the criminal justice stage of court and sentencing, there are unique issues that pertain to older adults but perhaps less so to younger and/or healthier counterparts. Although competency is at issue with all age groups, concerns with competency likely arise more so with older defendants—whether these concerns are warranted or become more of a concern because of aging stereotypes that older adults are less competent. Moreover, physical problems may also bring concern for competency and whether older defendants need accommodations within the courtroom. These concerns also become relevant once at the sentencing phase, as judicial bodies balance the needs of the older person and society.

THE ADJUDICATIVE PROCESS

There are several stages in the adjudicative process in which competency may be at issue to older adults (Frierson & Srinivasan, 2018; Wall, 2018), including standing trial, waiving their rights, pleading guilty, or being executed. As held in *United States v. Dusky* (1960) and later extended to other adjudicative constitutional rights in *Godinez v. Moran* (1993), to be mentally competent to stand trial a defendant must be able to assist their attorney in their defense and understand concepts related to the legal proceedings. Like all adults, older adults are presumed to be competent unless otherwise adjudicated incompetent through a formal court hearing. Although, as noted, older adults go through the process of aging at varying rates, issues of competency (either permanent or temporary) become more of a concern for older persons because of issues of neurocognitive concerns, possible alcohol or substance use disorders, physical health problems, and the stress of legal system interactions (Frierson & Srinivasan, 2018). In addition to mental competency to go through the adjudicative process, courts also may have to determine whether the older person has any medical conditions that will interfere with their physical competence to stand trial (*United States v. Doran*, 1971). Physical competency examines whether the defendant's medical condition or physical ailments will be exacerbated by subjecting them to trial. Assessing physical competency involves weighing the older person's health problems and any remedial measures, such as shortened trial days, medication, medical equipment, and medical personnel. Courts may also assess whether the physical problems are temporary or permanent when identifying a workable solution (Aprile, 2012).

In addition, courts must also consider whether courtrooms are accessible for older adults to ensure effective access to courts (Rothman & Dunlop, 2005). Although most of the discussion centers on accommodating older adults as victims and witnesses of elder abuse, as the population of aging offenders continues to increase, courtroom accommodations will become even more pertinent to the administration of justice with older defendants. For instance, an older defendant may need physical accommodations if they have difficulty with hearing, vision, or mobility (Aday & Kraybill, 2012; Rothman & Dunlop, 2005). Other solutions may involve the use of technology, which has become more commonplace in courtrooms following the COVID-19 pandemic (Pew Charitable Trusts, 2021). To illustrate, Stetson University's Eleazer Courtroom is the first courtroom specifically designed to be elder-friendly and includes hearing amplification devices, colored borders on the carpet to indicate courtroom pathways, a flat touchscreen panel outside of the courtroom that displays the courtroom and key players, nonglaring lighting, and a witness box located on the floor (Center for Elders and the Courts, 2020). Other accommodations may include specialized justice centers. For example, the 13th judicial circuit of Florida implemented the Elder Justice Center, which assists those 60 and older involved in either criminal or civil matters by offering accessible buildings, information and support, help with navigating the court system, and referrals to appropriate legal and social services (Elder Justice Center, 2021).

ISSUES IN SENTENCING: JUDICIAL

Although crimes may be similar, older defendants look physically, psychologically, and situationally different than younger defendants (Miller, 2011). What, if any, effect does this have on how the judicial system sentences older defendants? When sentencing older adults, there is limited research on whether there is a so-called "age bias." While it may be possible that there are no differences by age, it is also possible that older adults could be sentenced more leniently or more harshly than younger ones. Within the U.S. criminal justice system, there are two phases to sentencing. The first is the determination of guilt (i.e., guilty or not guilty), which may be determined by a judge or jury. The second is the sentencing phase, which is determined by a judge in all but six states. According to focal concerns theory (Hartley, 2014), in determining a sentence, judges generally think of three things: blameworthiness (i.e., culpability, crime severity, and criminal history), protecting the community, and practical constraints (i.e., ability to complete the sentence, health condition, special needs, costs to correctional system or family members). Because judges do not necessarily have all this information, they may rely on attributes about the defendant to assess whether they are likely to commit future offenses and are amenable to rehabilitation (Smith & Schriver, 2018). In considering research on attitudes toward older adults and stereotype theories such as the SCM (Fiske et al., 2002, 2007), it may be that judges are more lenient because they perceive an older person as being less blameworthy, find less of a need to protect the community (low risk of danger or recidivism), and perceive older adults as having higher practical needs that make incarceration less feasible (incarceration could be harsher, financial burden to corrections). On the other hand, if we consider research on stereotype consistency (Cuddy et al., 2005) and role congruity (Eagly & Karau, 2002), judges may give harsher sentences because older adults may be perceived as deviating from traditional aging stereotypes and deserving of punishment, "knowing better," or being less amenable to rehabilitation because of old age.

Of the limited research that has examined age bias in sentencing, these studies support that there is an age bias toward leniency. Most studies have examined how older offenders are sentenced using archival data from actual court cases with large samples. Early research, which typically treated age as a continuous variable and assumed linear effects, found small or insignificant effects on sentencing (Champion, 1987; Kramer & Steffensmeier, 1993; Peterson & Hagan, 1984). More recent research, however, has indicated a curvilinear effect on sentencing such that younger adults (under 21) and older adults (50–60+) were less likely to be incarcerated and received shorter sentences (Steffensmeier & Allan, 1995; Steffensmeier et al., 1998). Studies have also examined whether age interacts with other variables, such as gender and race, to affect sentencing decisions. Analyzing a large sample of cases from Pennsylvania, Steffensmeier and Motivans (2000) found that older adults received more lenient sentences than younger adults, but the leniency effect diminished for drug offenses. The interaction with age and gender revealed that the age effect was stronger for men than women, and that older women were the least likely to be incarcerated and received the shortest sentences. In examining sentencing based on age, gender, and race, older offenders still received more lenient sentences and there were significant interactions between all three demographic factors (Doerner & Demuth, 2010; Morrow et al., 2014).

Building on previous archival studies, Smith and Schriver (2018) administered a survey to examine the factors that a sample of 212 trial court judges considered in making sentencing decisions with older defendants, while considering their attitudes about aging and the judge's own age. Contrary to their hypotheses, the authors found that only 31% of judges acknowledged treating older defendants with greater leniency. Of those who indicated being lenient, the most frequent factors they considered were cognitive impairment and criminal history. When testing whether attitudes about aging or judge demographic variables predicted leniency, the models and variables were nonsignificant. Although leniency effects have been consistently found with archival research, the authors concluded that their findings differed from those findings because judges may not like to admit to treating groups differently and want to be perceived as being impartial. As such, additional prospective methodologies should be considered in gathering data on judicial sentencing decisions.

ISSUES IN SENTENCING: LEGISLATIVE AND SUPREME COURT INTERPRETATIONS

Even though a judge makes the final decision, sentencing options are largely controlled by the legislative branch, which provides a range of sentences for crimes within statute. Judges then use discretion to determine a sentence within those statutory guidelines. State and federal statutes, however, vary on the discretion they allow. While some jurisdictions impose mandatory minimum sentences and sentencing guidelines with little judicial discretion, especially for more serious offenses, other jurisdictions allow the judge more discretion to tailor the sentence to the crime and criminal. The U.S. Sentencing Commission (2018) established the Federal Sentencing Guidelines with the goal of establishing sentencing policies and practices for the federal courts. Although these guidelines only apply to individuals convicted in the federal system, many states have adopted the guidelines as part of their criminal code. Within the guidelines, each offense is assigned a base-level sentence, and then it can be adjusted up or down for mitigating or aggravating circumstances. Unlike other demographics, such as race, sex, national origin, creed, and socioeconomic status, that cannot be considered during sentencing, age and physical health are factors that can be considered (Chapter 6, Part H)—especially if home confinement might be as effective and less costly than incarceration. According to the guidelines, age should be considered only if the offender's characteristics are present to an unusual degree that distinguishes it from a typical case.

The Supreme Court of the United States has heard a series of cases that interpreted the Federal Sentencing Guidelines—specifically, whether age (which is not defined) is a per se (i.e., mandatory) reduction in sentence. In each case, the court held that a defendant's advancing age does not mean a mandatory downward departure (i.e., when a judge imposes a sentence that is lower than the minimum sentence suggested by the guidelines), but leniency may be granted if age contributed to frailness or poor physical condition (*United States v. Brooke*, 2002; *United States v. Bullion*, 2006; *United States v. Johnson*, 2012). In all three cases, although the court agreed the defendants were elderly and infirm, the justices' rationale for the decisions was that their age and health status would not deter them from committing future crimes—a fundamental rationale for sentence leniency.

To illustrate, the defendant in *United States v. Brooke* (2002) was arrested for selling cocaine at age 82, with several recent drug related convictions and probation violations. He was charged with conspiracy to sell cocaine, which has a maximum sentence of 60 months, and was given the maximum sentence because of his criminal history. During sentencing in the lower criminal court, the defendant presented his physical ailments (i.e., swollen knee, stiffness in hands, chest pains, respiratory problems, and arthritis) and argued that due to these health issues and his age, he should be granted a downward sentence. Although the judge recognized his discretion to adjust the sentence, the defendant was still sentenced to the maximum 60 months and appealed his case to the Supreme Court. The justices agreed with the lower court and held that the 60-month sentence should stand. The court did not disagree that the defendant was elderly and infirm; however, the justices focused on the third element of Section 5H1.1 in the sentencing guidelines: that an alternative "form of punishment such as home confinement . . . be equally efficient as . . . incarceration." The court concluded that home confinement would not be effective in restraining the defendant's criminal conduct because he already had a history of drug dealing in his home. The court also indicated that age alone would not grant a downward sentence and that health problems need to be "extraordinary," and in this case, the court did not think they were.

Little research has examined the sentencing guidelines and how age influences downward departures. In one known study, Burrow and Koons-Witt (2003) analyzed all cases from 1999 that included 25,333 defendants with data from the federal sentencing commission to investigate the extent to which factors related to age and physical condition influenced downward departures. In general, the authors found significant variations in the use of downward departures across circuits. With respect to older adult status (measured as 50+ for analysis), there was significant variation across circuits for whether older adult status was used as a criterion for a downward departure, and for three circuits, older adult status predicted whether a downward departure would be granted. The authors note that one of the "most salient findings is that the jurisdictions in which a defendant is tried and sentenced significantly influences" downward departures for old age (Burrow & Koons-Witt, 2003, p. 323). This means that the aim of the sentencing guidelines, to standardize sentences, was not achieved. The authors conclude that one reason for this may be the lack of a common definition for what age is considered "elderly" and suggest adopting a uniform definition (some have proposed the age of Social Security eligibility).

ISSUES IN SENTENCING: THE DEATH PENALTY AND EXECUTION

The United States has a growing death row population of older adults, and in many circumstances, these inmates are more likely to die from natural causes than to be executed because of the length of time they can spend on death row. The most recent area of case law involving the sentencing of older defendants is whether the death penalty is appropriate for older adults. Historically, the Supreme Court has placed a series of limitations for who can be sentenced to death, each time questioning whether the goals of punishment are being achieved by the death penalty. In *Ford v. Wainwright* (1986), the court held that it was unconstitutionally cruel and unusual punishment to execute defendants who are mentally incompetent, opining that such executions are neither a deterrent nor retributive. In the *Atkins v. Virginia* (2002) case, this rationale was extended to defendants with intellectual disabilities and low IQ (see Salekin & Wood, this volume), and in *Roper v. Simmons* (2005) the limits of the death penalty were extended to juveniles (see Zottoli et al., this volume).

In 2006, an inmate in *Allen v. Ornoski* (2006) filed for a petition in a California district court for writ of habeas seeking relief from his death sentence under the Eighth Amendment—arguing that he was elderly and "woefully infirm" from physical ailments. The lower district court did not stay his execution, stating: "Nothing about his advanced age or his physical infirmities (chronic heart disease, diabetes, legal blindness, and inability to ambulate), affected his culpability at the time he committed the capital offenses. There is no evidence now that he does not understand the gravity and meaning or his imminent execution" (*Allen v. Ornoski*, 2006, p. 12). After the lower court denial, Allen petitioned the Supreme Court, but the court did not hear the case. Most recently, the Supreme Court heard *Madison v. Alabama* (2019) and was asked to consider whether it was cruel and unusual punishment to execute an older inmate who over, the course of his confinement, developed a mental disability leaving him with no memory of the crime or understanding for the reasons behind the execution. The court held that the Eighth Amendment does not prohibit the state from executing someone if they do not remember the crime they committed, but it does prohibit the execution of someone who does not rationally understand the reasons for his execution—whether due to dementia or psychosis. Ultimately, the courts have asserted that physical ailments and age alone would not preclude execution, but once someone loses their rational understanding of why they are being executed, that crosses the threshold into cruel and unusual punishment.

Related, correctional systems have also dealt with issues on whether older adults are "too old" to be confined in death row because the conditions (i.e., confinement to room, isolation) are harsh for those who are ill or infirm, and inmates often spend a considerable number of years on death row awaiting execution. Regardless of one's opinion about whether the death penalty itself is cruel and unusual punishment, some argue that the length of time that inmates sit on death row is in and of itself cruel and unusual punishment (Rapaport, 2012). Under what has been termed a "*Lackey* claim" based on *Lackey v. Texas* (1995), inmates have sought relief from execution based on the notion that it is cruel and unusual punishment to be on death row for so long and that the conditions of death row are cruel and unusual punishment. Although *Lackey* claims have not been successful at staying executions, proponents of the claim suggest a modified "Lackey for the elderly" that may be more likely to succeed (Rapaport, 2012) given community sentiment and the "evolving standards of decency" test for limiting the death penalty (*Trop v. Dulles*, 1958).

Older Adults as Inmates

America's prisons are experiencing what some have called the "silver tsunami" (Jefferson-Bullock, 2018), in which an increase in the median age of inmates has brought new challenges for the correctional system. In an analysis of the state prison population from 1993 to 2013, the Bureau of Justice Statistics (BJS) reported that the number of state prisoners aged 55 and older increased 400%, from 3% of the total state prison population in 1993 to 10% in 2013 (Carson, 2020). During this time, most of the growth was attributed to those aged 40–54, while the fastest increase was for those aged 55 and older. Assuming trends remain constant, it is predicted that offenders over 50 will account for one third of inmates by 2030 (Rikard & Rosenberg, 2007; Williams et al., 2006). Two criminal justice system factors contributed to this growth: (a) a greater proportion of prisoners serving longer sentences for predominately violent offenses and (b) an increase in admissions for older adults from 1% to 4% of total admissions (Carson & Sabol, 2016). The increase is also likely due to social and medical factors, including generational population increases (i.e., baby boomers) and expanded life expectancy from advances in health care (Aday & Kraybill, 2013; Auerhahn, 2002).

The profile of the aging inmate, therefore, includes not only the three typologies discussed earlier (i.e., inveterate, relapsing, and first-time offender) but also the young offender with long or life sentences who ages while incarcerated (Fattah & Sacco, 1989). Even though statistics demonstrate that older adults are most likely to be arrested for minor offenses (Feldmeyer & Steffensmeier, 2007), the profile of the older inmate often includes more violent offenses (Lemieux et al., 2002)—not because older adults are more likely to commit more serious crimes, but because those who age in prison are more likely to be those offenders with longer prison sentences for violent offenses.

Older inmates have unique physical, psychological, and social needs compared to their younger counterparts. On average, older inmates have three chronic physical health conditions and require seven to 10 different medications (Mai & Subramanian, 2017). Because of this, it is considerably more expensive to house an inmate over the age of 60, with costs for older inmates estimated at $70,000 per year and $22,000 per year for younger inmates (Mai & Subramanian, 2017). Psychiatric illnesses are also twice that of younger inmates, and the psychological toll that the stress of prison can place on older adults can be more harmful to aging inmates than younger ones (Aday & Krabill, 2013; Caverley, 2006; Maschi et al., 2011).

With respect to social needs, older inmates may be more socially isolated than younger inmates from both outside and inside relationships. For instance, older inmates may not receive regular visits from family and friends because their social ties (i.e., family and friends) are also aging or they have fewer stable relationships because of divorce or estrangement from family (Flanagan, 1995; Leigey, 2010).

Studies have examined whether older inmates experience negative unintended consequences while incarcerated that affect overall well-being. A comprehensive literature review with 19 studies found that older adults experience stress over prison conditions, fear of victimization, physical health, access to health care, housing, fear of dying in prison, and death and loss (Maschi et al., 2011). In their mixed methods study of older adult prisoners, Kerbs and Jolley (2007) found a high prevalence of psychological, property, and physical and sexual victimization, mostly perpetrated on older prisoners by younger prisoners. Research demonstrates that the experience of being in prison can cause damaging psychological injuries, including psychological disorders and symptoms (i.e., depression, anxiety, posttraumatic stress disorder, dissociative symptoms, anger, and fear of safety) and substance abuse (Caverley, 2006). Perhaps the most noteworthy stressor was death anxiety among older adults in prison. For example, Aday and Krabill (2012) found that older adults in prison reported significant concerns about dying in prison settings, which was predicted by both inmate social support and several health-related variables. Fear of death was found to be higher for older prisoners than for similarly aged adults in community settings.

Research has examined the ways in which older inmates cope with the experience of incarceration and identified both internal and external coping resources that act as protective factors to ameliorate the adverse physical, mental, and behavioral consequences of stress and trauma among prisoners. Internal resources, such as self-control and emotional awareness, were significantly correlated with prisoners' overall positive functioning before and after prison release. External coping resources included religious activities, social and occupational functioning, and social support from family and friends in the community and peer support within the prison system (Day et al., 2008).

Health Care in Prison

With the number of chronic health conditions, it is important to provide adequate health care to older adults, which can be quite costly. Although prison is not an ideal place to get and receive health care, there are financial benefits both within prison and when prisoners are released into the community that make providing adequate health care cost effective in the long run. When prisoners return to the community, it is in society's best interest that they are as healthy as possible because good health has been linked to acquiring and retaining employment, reducing recidivism, and reducing costs of health care for society (Stal, 2013). However, prisons were designed to treat acute and not chronic health problems and often do not focus on preventative care. With the increase in medical issues that prisons will have to treat, prisons will need to consider improving their health services to reduce costs. For instance, one of the largest expenses is contracting medical care outside of prison; thus, creating in-house services that care for chronic illnesses (i.e., dialysis) could significantly reduce costs.

Providing health care to inmates is not only based on moral codes and medical oaths or financial incentives to provide treatment but also required by law. Under the Eighth Amendment to the U.S. Constitution, prisons must provide medical treatment. In *Estelle v. Gamble* (1976), the Supreme Court held that the Eighth Amendment was violated when corrections officials were "deliberately indifferent" to inmates' medical needs. In addition, under the Americans With Disabilities Act (ADA; 1990), prisons are required to accommodate people with disabilities. The ADA was passed in 1990 by Congress and was interpreted by the Supreme Court as applicable to prisoners in the Pennsylvania Department of Corrections in *Pennsylvania Department of Corrections v. Yeskey* (1998). In *Yeskey,* the defendant was sentenced to complete a first-time offender's motivational boot camp; however, because of his medical history of hypertension, the department of corrections refused to allow him to participate in the program. The court held that no public entity, including prisons, may discriminate against a qualified disabled individual due to their disability. For older or disabled inmates, accommodations may include grab bars in the showers, equipment for mobility, eliminating the need for stairs/installing elevators, or accommodating through lower bunk assignments.

Accommodations for aging prisoners constitute some of the highest expenditures for prison systems in the United States; as noted, the cost for housing an older inmate has been previously estimated at approximately $40,000 more than the average prisoner (Mai & Subramanian, 2017; Murolo, 2020). This inflated cost is largely attributed to concomitant increases in the number of aging prisoners and rising costs of care (Murolo, 2020). In-house accommodations for older prisoners may help to alleviate some of this financial strain while providing the added benefit of improving quality of life and minimizing victimization for vulnerable populations. Within the prison context, however, the correctional priorities to maintain safety, mitigate risk, and reduce vulnerability may be contradictory to the goals of ethical provision of health care for the sickest and most vulnerable groups (Hagos et al., 2022). Managing these groups requires special consideration of functional and cognitive ability, in addition to navigating logistical obstacles like prescription medication oversight and socio-emotional/spiritual support provision.

Among these vulnerable inmates are persons with dementia and cognitive impairment and those in end-stage disease or terminal decline processes, particularly those who would benefit from palliative and hospice care. Incarcerated populations are diagnosed with dementia at a higher rate than the general population and face a series of unique challenges given the juxtaposition of their disease process and environment (Brooke et al., 2020; Maschi et al., 2012). For example, prisoners with dementia may experience episodes of wandering but can be easily agitated or confused by restrictions and locked doors (Maschi et al., 2012). Recent recommendations from fieldwork have promoted maintaining general population integration in cognitively impaired groups for as long as possible, as segregation at early stages can hasten decline by way of reduced social and emotional opportunities, while unfamiliarity can be destabilizing as the disease progresses (Hagos et al., 2021; Maschi et al., 2012). Allowing inmates with dementia additional freedoms has unsurprisingly been shown to mitigate distress and improve prognoses; however, this is contradictory to institutional safety considerations aimed at reducing risk of injury and victimization (Hagos et al., 2022; Maschi et al., 2012). As such, memory care systems that are integrated directly into existing accommodations for offenders may be most feasible (Hagos et al., 2022). As symptoms progress, emphasis should be placed on maintaining safety and quality of life; in later stages, this may be best managed in specialized nursing units (Hagos et al., 2022; Maschi et al., 2012). Although specialized units are useful for oversight of the most advanced care within prison environments, they are costly and rare. This warrants future development of improved dementia management systems and protocols (e.g., correctional officer dementia education programs).

While dementia and specialized care units in prisons remain uncommon, an increasing number of facilities are implementing or ameliorating hospice and palliative care options for inmates (Hoffman & Dickinson, 2011; Prost & Williams, 2020). Some evidence has supported that state-operated facilities are more cost effective than geriatric release programs that rely on private contracting, emphasizing the utility of improved accommodations within prisons (Murolo, 2020; Virginia Department of Corrections, 2008). Ultimately, the need for end-of-life care in inmate populations comes in response to global improvements in health care and life expectancy, as a larger number of incarcerated individuals are requiring intensive and terminal care for longer periods of time (Stensland & Sanders, 2016). Other considerations for end of life in prison populations include (a) supporting spiritual and psychological wellness through chaplaincy and counseling, (b) facilitating end-of-life advanced care planning, and (c) managing funeral arrangements and body deposition with inmates and their family members (Cloyes et al., 2016; Gijsberts et al., 2011; Penrod et al., 2014).

Issues that arise in end-of-life care are often due to dissonance between health staff and correctional officers; for example, late-stage hospice patients require levels of care and attention exceeding the norm, which may be in discord with prison policy (Hagos et al., 2022; Stensland & Sanders, 2016). As discussed previously, it has often been recognized that safety policies (e.g., minimal physical contact with inmates) are direct barriers to ethical hospice care (Hagos et al., 2022; Stensland & Sanders, 2016). Similarly, the use of medications in hospice and general palliative care, namely for pain management, can be contrary to prison safety policy (Stensland & Sanders, 2016; Williams et al., 2014). Misuse and theft of prescription medications are high in inmate populations; however, failure to make these drugs available entirely is equally problematic as it markedly decreases inmates' quality of life (Hampton et al., 2015; Stensland & Sanders, 2016; Williams et al., 2014).

Of note, experiencing end of life in prison may be further complicated by suicide or prison homicide. Among inmate populations, older prisoners have the highest rates of suicide, consistent with suicide trends in community-dwelling populations (Barry et al., 2017; Carson, 2020). Older prisoners are at greater risk for suicidal ideation and eventual mortality based on higher rates of chronic disease, functional disability, pain, and affective disorders, primarily depression (Barry et al., 2017). On this same basis of heightened vulnerability, older prisoners are more likely to be victimized by younger inmates and are at greater risk of homicide in prison settings (Kerbs & Jolley, 2007, 2009; Reidy et al., 2017). This heightened vulnerability has been a leading argument in favor of age-segregated prisons, in addition to improving in-house accommodations for older offenders (Kerbs & Jolley, 2007, 2009).

Proposed Solutions for Aging Inmates and Overcrowding

As rates for the inmate population and long-term incarceration are rising, prison overcrowding has become problematic, and health care costs for treating older inmates continue to rise, correctional facilities and policymakers are tasked with employing potential solutions that address aging inmates. Generally, solutions to these issues fall within one of two types: (a) selective de-incarceration, where inmates are released to community-based alternatives, and (b) modifications to prisons and programming to fit the needs of older adults. De-incarceration includes laws and policies that reduce the number of inmates and length of sentences through sentencing and policy reforms, community reintegration programs, and compassionate release statutes. Proponents of de-incarceration argue that these measures would reduce costs (i.e., cost of health care), that older adults have low recidivism with advancing age, that accommodating older adults in prison is too costly, and that de-incarceration would reduce legal liabilities that come with having to accommodate and medically treat older and infirm inmates. Solutions aimed at making modifications to accommodate the changing demographics of prisons through building modifications and additional programs include having separate geriatric units within prisons and providing inmate health porters to assist aging and infirm inmates with day-to-day activities. Proponents of these measures support the underlying theories of punishment—retribution and deterrence—in maintaining that offenders should be held responsible for their actions and the public should be protected, which are the duties of the correctional system.

The first solution, reforming sentencing and parole policies, would encourage more flexibility in sentencing—for instance, reducing the use of life sentences without parole, restricting three-strikes policies to only include violent offenses, limiting the time for offenses that can be included in three-strikes policies, and reducing sentences for juvenile convictions. Punitive parole policies make it so inmates have no opportunity for parole, even if they can demonstrate rehabilitation. As supported by the age–crime curve, recidivism for older adults is lower than for younger adults. Parole reforms could include removing sentence options that do not allow for parole, allowing older adults to have more frequent access to the parole board as they age or become ill, and modifying the requirements for parole that may not apply to older adults (e.g., participation in vocational activities, having viable employment upon release). Other solutions are reintegration programs that assist older adults (and all prisoners) for release into the community to increase success upon release. For older adults, this may include applying for government services or providing subsidized housing for older inmates who do not qualify for other programs. Programs such as the Project for Older Prisoners (POPs), originating at George Washington University, can legally assist in getting older inmates who pose little threat to society released early. Law student volunteers at POPs conduct background investigations on older inmates, review prison records and medical history, and contact victims. If successfully released, the student volunteers serve as caseworkers and assist the older inmate in reentering the community (George Washington University, 1991).

Compassionate release statutes are one of the most discussed and researched proposed solutions (e.g., Berry, 2008; Green, 2014; Maschi et al., 2016)—though there still has not been much empirical attention. With a similar rationale to all de-incarceration solutions, compassionate release is based on the notion that older and infirm inmates pose little risk for committing more crime. The Sentencing Reform Act allows federal courts to release prisoners early for "extraordinary and compelling" reasons through court order and approval by the director of the federal Bureau of Prisons (BOP). In addition to the federal policy, most states have medical or compassionate release statutes (Chiu, 2010; Wylie, Knutson, & Greene, 2018) in which older and/or infirm inmates are eligible for release from prison into the community to live out their last days with family or friends. Jurisdictions vary considerably in terms of who grants release, criteria for release, and exceptions for release. In a content analysis of all state and federal statutes for compassionate release, Wylie, Knutson, and Greene (2018) found that the two most common eligibility requirements were based on chronic illness (67%) and having a terminal illness (60%), but fewer statutes mentioned age (31%) or mental health (26%), and approximately one third specified that an inmate could be released if the cost or burden of care was too high or the inmate would have adequate care outside of the facility (29%). When age was a criterion, 12 of 18 jurisdictions gave an eligibility age that ranged from 45 (e.g., Louisiana) to 70 (e.g., South Carolina). Some jurisdictions had ineligibility criteria specifying the types of offenses (i.e., sex offenses and murder), type of sentencing structure (e.g., mandatory minimums, sentences without parole), or the proportion of time served.

Although the public and wardens surveyed report supporting compassionate release (Wylie, Knudson, & Greene, 2018), the release of inmates under compassionate release is not widely utilized. Figures from 2006–2011 indicated that wardens and regional prison directors only moved 211 inmate requests forward to the BOP's office for approval. The BOP director considered those requests and approved 142 (68%). Although more were approved than not, the number of requests that actually moved for approval is low when considering the large proportion of older and/or infirm inmates in the population. In addition to the low frequency of requests forwarded to the BOP for approval, in 28 (13%) of cases, the inmates died while their requests were under consideration with the BOP's central office before a decision was made by the BOP director. In 2013, compassionate release was criticized by the Office of the Inspector General of the Department of Justice as "poorly run," not having clear standards, and not adequately tracking all requests (only the approved ones).

When compassionate release was first implemented, the BOP conducted a pilot program to examine its feasibility and effectiveness. The pilot program allowed for releasing eligible elderly inmates (e.g., over age 65, non–life-in-prison sentence for certain nonviolent crimes, no past escapes, and low risk of reoffending) from prison to home detention, which could include nursing homes or other residential long-term care facilities. Following the pilot program, the BOP concluded that it was more expensive to monitor older adults through private companies contracted to monitor inmates on home detention, as compared to keeping them in prison. Specifically, the report indicated that it did not achieve cost savings and actually imposed an additional $540,631 in costs. In further investigation, the BOP compared the daily marginal cost to house an inmate in a minimum- or low-security facility (estimated at $20.08 and $24.32 per day, respectively) with the regional average per diem paid to the private companies contracted to monitor inmates on home detention, which ranged from $34.86 to $47.76 per day. Although these findings were deflating to some, following this first report, the Government Accountability Office warned that the statistics presented may be misleading because the analysis did not account for factors such as construction of new prisons, certain modernization and repair projects, or depreciation of its existing facilities. Moreover, the report was limited in that home monitoring figures may not have been accurate because the cost of home monitoring was not separated from the costs of home detention for another reentry program.

Other than underutilization, there are some issues that have been identified with compassionate release. For one, there is often not a suitable place for released inmates to go. Because of their infirmity, they cannot live on their own. Many are estranged from their families and do not have alternative social support who will receive them upon release. Nursing homes are reluctant to take them, especially if they had violent or sex-related offenses. Moreover, there are financial difficulties. After release, the inmate would not have income or any ability to support themselves. As such, most will have to be supported by government programs, including Medicaid/Medicare and other monthly subsidies and services. Opponents argue, therefore, that compassionate release does not really reduce costs but rather shifts costs from one state or federal budget to another.

One of the central debates surrounding aging in prison is whether older inmates should be housed separately in "geriatric pods" from the general population because of health and safety concerns. Although most prisons do not currently have separate units for older adults, the trend has increased. In 2006, 16 states had separate housing, and some had special hospice care. Proponents of separate geriatric prison units assert that having an "age-friendly" environment is more suitable because older inmates have more medical issues and medical care would be centralized and cheaper, and older adults would be safer from attack if living separately. Moreover, separate units could address ADA concerns by having fewer stairwells, fewer upper bunk assignments, and fall-proof measures like nonwaxed floors and handrails. On the other hand, opponents assert that there are benefits to older adults remining in the general population, namely, that older inmates can benefit from the services that are centralized and available to inmates of all ages, and that all inmates could benefit from remaining in an intergenerational unit where older and younger inmates interact with each other. Research has examined the relationship between specialized geriatric care and services to see if geriatric units had more specialized services. In reviewing services for 918 prisons, only 4% provided specialized geriatric services. For those that did provide special services, the authors found that these services were most often mental health services, but not physical health–related services (Thivierge-Rikard & Thompson, 2007).

Although typically unsuccessful, some inmates have brought claims against prison administration for failure to protect the older inmates under the Eighth Amendment by way of separating them from the general population (*Brown v. Pattison*, 2004; *Edney v. Kerrigan*, 2004). To establish a failure to protect under the Eighth Amendment, an inmate plaintiff must satisfy a two-prong test: (a) prison conditions posed a substantial risk of serious harm and (b) prison officials were "deliberately indifferent" (had knowledge and disregarded the potential harm) to the plaintiff's health and safety. These are difficult prongs to meet because the plaintiff must show that prison officials had requisite knowledge that the older adult was at high risk for attacks. In fact, correctional officers have testified that they thought older adults would be *less* vulnerable to attack because of their status as an elderly inmate (*Edney v. Kerrigan*, 2004, p.17).

Another proposed solution that has been tried in some jurisdictions (e.g., Nebraska) is inmate health porters, which are inmates with specialized training (i.e., certified nursing assistant) who help older inmates with health care needs. The program was instituted to reduce costs for hiring outside help. Inmate porters undergo an intensive application process, including a security screening to identify recent misconduct and criminal history, a psychological interview, and an interview with a panel of security and medical personnel. If hired, the porters are compensated hourly at a rate that is much higher than other prison jobs. Although no research to date has evaluated the program, anecdotal communications indicate that porters feel the position allows them to gain redemption for prior mistakes and creates more meaning out of their time in prison. One inmate porter was quoted as saying, "I'm gonna die in here. I want to have a program like this available so when I need it, it is there" (Correctional News, 2013, para. 10).

Implications for Research, Policy, and Practice
Throughout this chapter we have described the unique issues faced by older adults in the criminal justice system, as well as a variety of considerations and potential challenges for developing age-competent systems. However, this is an expanding field of knowledge, and it should be noted that the implications for research, policy, and practice extend beyond what is herein defined. The topic of criminal offenders and aging in prison remains an understudied area in law–psychology, gerontology, medicine, and social work; to make meaningful improvements for aging offenders, additional cross-disciplinary work is vital. It is then necessary that recommendations from this research are purposefully applied to the police, courts, and corrections systems, to the benefit of not only the aging offender but also all incarcerated individuals.

The development of foundational knowledge on aging offenders from these disciplines may inform advancements to the criminal justice system, generating improvements in fairness, dignity, and quality of life for offenders and prisoners, as well as increasing systemic efficiency and reducing costs of care. The criminal justice system should be guided by geriatric models to prepare for the influx of older adults. The global aging crisis is projected to markedly change the demography of the United States and subsequently increase strain on existing programs. The criminal justice system is no exception, with these changes precipitating population aging in incarcerated individuals. Penal and judiciary systems are already overextended, reaching beyond their capacity to provide ample support for social services, health care, and infrastructure. The additional stress of accommodating older offenders and prisoners without age-competent systems could cause downstream institutional instability and decline at the operative and ethical level.

Understanding and application of the scholarship discussed in this chapter, namely the call for age-focused policy and practices, may help to address the aging crisis in the United States. Reform can serve to uphold the responsibility of correctional justice systems while helping to significantly reduce burden and costs, specifically those related to prisoners' changing functional and health care needs. Further, improved stability of the criminal justice system may be achieved via the primary solutions of sentencing and parole reform, given concurrent improvements to in-prison physical, social, and health care accommodations. Ultimately, it is vital that additional research is produced to inform reform measures, and that purposeful effort is subsequently aimed at improving the aging crisis in U.S. correctional facilities.

References

Aday, R., & Krabill, J. (2012). Aging offenders in the criminal justice system. *Marquette Elder's Advisor, 7*(2), 237.

Aday, R., & Krabill, J. (2013). *Special needs offenders in correctional institutions.* Sage Publications. http://dx.doi.org/10.4135/9781452275444.n7

Allen v. Ornoski, 435 F.3d 946 (2006).

Americans With Disabilities Act of 1990, 42 U.S.C. § 12101 et seq. (1990).

Aprile, J. (2012). Defending the elderly. *Criminal Justice, 27*(1), 55–56.

Arias, J. J. (2013). A time to step in: Legal mechanisms for protecting those with declining capacity. *American Journal of Law & Medicine, 39*, 134–159.

Atkins v. Virginia, 536 US 304 (2002).

Auerhahn, K. (2002). Selective incapacitation, three strikes, and the problem of aging prison populations: Using simulation modeling to see the future. *Criminology, 1*, 353–388.

Bachand, D., & Chressanthis, G. (1988). Property crime and the elderly offender: A theoretical and empirical analysis. In *Older offenders: Perspectives in criminology and criminal justice* (p. 76). Westport, CT: Praeger Publishers.

Baidawi, S. (2016). Older prisoners: Psychological distress and associations with mental health history, cognitive functioning, socio-demographic, and criminal justice factors. *International Psychogeriatrics, 28*(3), 385–395. https://doi.org/10.1017/S1041610215001878

Baidawi, S., Trotter, C., & Flynn, C. (2016). Prison experiences and psychological distress among older inmates. *Journal of Gerontological Social Work, 59*(3), 252–270. https://doi.org/10.1080/01634372.2016.1197353

Barrett, A. E., & Cantwell, L. E. (2007). Drawing on stereotypes: Using undergraduates' sketches of elders as a teaching tool. *Educational Gerontology, 33*(4), 327–348. https://doi.org/10.1080/03601270701198950

Barry, L. C., Wakefield, D. B., Trestman, R. L., & Conwell, Y. (2017). Disability in prison activities of daily living and likelihood of depression and suicidal ideation in older prisoners. *International Journal of Geriatric Psychiatry, 32*(10), 1141–1149. https://doi.org/10.1002/gps.4578

Berry, W. W., III. (2008). Extraordinary and compelling: A re-examination of the justifications for compassionate release. *Maryland Law Review, 68*, 850.

Bhutto, A., & Morley, J. E. (2008). The clinical significance of gastrointestinal changes with aging. *Current Opinion in Clinical Nutrition and Metabolic Care, 11*(5), 651–660. https://doi.org/10.1097/MCO.0b013e32830b5d37

Boss, G. R., & Seegmiller, J. E. (1981). Age-related physiological changes and their clinical significance. *Western Journal of Medicine, 135*(6), 434–440.

Brank, E. (2007). *Elder research: Filling an important gap in psychology and law.* Faculty Publications, Department of Psychology. University of Nebraska, Lincoln. https://digitalcommons.unl.edu/psychfacpub/389

Brinkley-Rubinstein, L. (2013). Incarceration as a catalyst for worsening health. *Health & Justice, 1*(1), 3. https://doi.org/10.1186/2194-7899-1-3

Brooke, J., Diaz-Gil, A., & Jackson, D. (2020). The impact of dementia in the prison setting: A systematic review. *Dementia (London, England), 19*(5), 1509–1531. https://doi.org/10.1177/1471301218801715

Brown v. Pattison, 2:01-CV-0411 (2004).

Bugental, D. B., & Hehman, J. A. (2007). Ageism: A review of research and policy implications. *Social Issues and Policy Review, 1*(1), 173–216. https://doi.org/10.1111/j.1751-2409.2007.00007.x

Burrow, J. D., & Koons-Witt, B. A. (2003). Elderly status, extraordinary physical impairments and intercircuit variation under the Federal Sentencing Guidelines. *Elder Law Journal, 11*(2), 56.

Butts, J. (2019). *Older adults responsible for total growth in drug arrests* (JohnJayREC DataBits 2019-02 422). John Jay College of Criminal Justice. https://academicworks.cuny.edu/jj_pubs/422

Carson, E. A. (2020). *Prisoners in 2019* (NCJ 255115). Bureau of Justice Statistics, U.S. Department of Justice. https://bjs.ojp.gov/library/publications/prisoners-2019

Carson, E. A., & Sabol, W. (2016). *Aging of the state prison population, 1993–2013* (NCJ 248766). U.S. Department of Justice. https://bjs.ojp.gov/content/pub/pdf/aspp9313.pdf

Castelli, L., Macrae, C. N., Zogmaister, C., & Arcuri, L. (2004). A tale of two primes: Contextual limits on stereotype activation. *Social Cognition, 22*(2), 233–247. https://doi.org/10.1521/soco.22.2.233.35462

Caverley, S. J. (2006). Older mentally ill inmates: A descriptive study. *Journal of Correctional Health Care, 12*(4), 262–268. https://doi.org/10.1177/1078345806295546

Center for Elders and the Courts. (2020, September 21). *Role and responses*. https://www.eldersandcourts.org/aging/aging-material-for-right-rail-menu-for-aging/the-role-of-the-courts

Champion, D. J. (1987). Elderly felons and sentencing severity: Interregional variations in leniency and sentencing trends. *Criminal Justice Review, 12*(2), 7–14. https://doi.org/10.1177/073401688701200203

Chasteen, A. L., Schwarz, N., & Park, D. C. (2002). The activation of aging stereotypes in younger and older adults. *journals of Gerontology, Series B, Psychological Sciences and Social Sciences, 57*(6), P540–P547. https://doi.org/10.1093/geronb/57.6.p540

Chiu, T. (2010). *It's about time: Aging prisoners, increasing costs, and geriatric release*. Vera Institute of Justice. https://www.vera.org/publications/its-about-time-aging-prisoners-increasing-costs-and-geriatric-release

Cipriani, G., Danti, S., Carlesi, C., & Di Fiorino, M. (2017). Old and dangerous: Prison and dementia. *Journal of Forensic and Legal Medicine, 51*, 40–44. https://doi.org/10.1016/j.jflm.2017.07.004

Cloyes, K. G., Rosenkranz, S. J., Berry, P. H., Supiano, K. P., Routt, M., Shannon-Dorcy, K., & Llanque, S. M. (2016). Essential elements of an effective prison hospice program. *American Journal of Hospice and Palliative Medicine, 33*(4), 390–402. https://doi.org/10.1177/1049909115574491

Colón-Emeric, C. S., Whitson, H. E., Pavon, J., & Hoenig, H. (2013). Functional decline in older adults. *American Family Physician, 88*(6), 388–394.

Correctional News. (2013). *Nebraska State Penitentiary implements new health programs*. https://correctionalnews.com/2013/06/19/nebraska-state-penitentiary-implements-new-health-programs/

Cuddy, A. J. C., Norton, M. I., & Fiske, S. T. (2005). This old stereotype: The pervasiveness and persistence of the elderly stereotype. *Journal of Social Issues, 61*(2), 267–285. https://doi.org/10.1111/j.1540-4560.2005.00405.x

Curran, N. (2000). Blue hairs in the bighouse: The rise in the elderly inmate population, its effect on the overcrowding dilemma and solutions to correct it. *New England Journal on Criminal and Civil Confinement, 26*(2), 225–264.

Dannefer, D. (2003). Cumulative advantage/disadvantage and the life course: Cross-fertilizing age and social science theory. *Journals of Gerontology: Series B, 58*(6), S327–S337. https://doi.org/10.1093/geronb/58.6.S327

Day, A., Davey, L., Wanganeen, R., Casey, S., Howells, K., & Nakata, M. (2008). Symptoms of trauma, perceptions of discrimination, and anger: A comparison between Australian indigenous and nonindigenous prisoners. *Journal of Interpersonal Violence, 23*(2), 245–258. https://doi.org/10.1177/0886260507309343

Di Lorito, C., Völlm, B., & Dening, T. (2018). Psychiatric disorders among older prisoners: A systematic review and comparison study against older people in the community. *Aging & Mental Health, 22*(1), 1–10. https://doi.org/10.1080/13607863.2017.1286453

Doerner, J. K., & Demuth, S. (2010). The independent and joint effects of race/ethnicity, gender, and age on sentencing outcomes in U.S. federal courts. *Justice Quarterly, 27*(1), 1–27. https://doi.org/10.1080/07418820902926197

Eagly, A. H., & Karau, S. J. (2002). Role congruity theory of prejudice toward female leaders. *Psychological Review, 109*(3), 573–598. https://doi.org/10.1037/0033-295X.109.3.573

Edney v. Kerrigan, 00-Civ-2240 (2004).

Elder Justice Center. (2021). Thirteenth Judicial Circuit Administrative Office of the Courts. https://www.fljud13.org/courtprograms/elderjusticecenter.aspx

Estelle v. Gamble, 429 U.S. 97 (1976).

Fagan, A. A., & Western, J. (2005). Escalation and deceleration of early offending behaviors from adolescence to early adulthood. *Australian and New Zealand Journal of Criminology, 38*, 59–76.

Farrington, D. P. (1986). Age and crime. *Crime and Justice, 7*, 189–250.

Fattah, E. A., & Sacco, V. (1989). *Crime and victimization of the elderly*. Springer-Verlag. https://link.springer.com/content/pdf/10.1007%2F978-1-4613-8888-3_6.pdf

Feinberg, G. (1984). *White haired offenders: An emergent social problem* [Paper presentation]. Annual meeting of the Gerontological Society of America, Boston, MA, United States.

Feldmeyer, B., & Steffensmeier, D. (2007). Elder crime: Patterns and current trends, 1980—2004. *Research on Aging, 29*(4), 297–322. https://doi.org/10.1177/0164027507300802

Fiske, S. T., Cuddy, A. J. C., & Glick, P. (2007). Universal dimensions of social cognition: Warmth and competence. *Trends in Cognitive Sciences, 11*(2), 77–88. https://doi.org/10.1016/j.tics.2006.11.005.

Fiske, S. T., Cuddy, A. J. C., Glick, P., & Xu, J. (2002). A model of (often mixed) stereotype content: Competence and warmth respectively follow from perceived status and competition. *Journal of Personality and Social Psychology, 82*(6), 878–902. https://doi.org/10.1037/0022-3514.82.6.878

Flanagan, T. J. (1995). Long-term incarceration: Issues of science, policy and correctional practice. In T. J. Flanagan (Ed.), *Long-term imprisonment: Policy, science, and correctional practice* (pp. 3–9). Sage.

Flynn, E. (2000). Elders as perpetrators. In M. Rothman, B. Dunlop, & P. Entzel (Eds.), *Elders, crime, and the criminal justice system* (pp. 43–86). Springer.

Ford v. Wainwright, 477 U.S. 399 (1986).

Frierson, R. L., & Srinivasan, S. (2018). Evaluation of elderly persons in the criminal justice system. In J. C. Holzer, R. Kohn, J. M. Ellison, & P. R. Recupero (Eds.), *Geriatric forensic psychiatry: Principles and practice* (pp. 163–169). Oxford University Press.

Gates, M. L., Staples-Horne, M., Walker, V., & Turney, A. (2017). Substance use disorders and related health problems in an aging offender population. *Journal of Health Care for the Poor and Underserved, 28*(2), 132–154. https://doi.org/10.1353/hpu.2017.0057

George Washington University. (1991). *Project for Older Prisoners (POPS*; NCJ 132249). Office of Justice Programs. https://www.ojp.gov/ncjrs/virtual-library/abstracts/project-older-prisoners-pops

Gijsberts, M.-J. H. E., Echteld, M. A., van der Steen, J. T., Muller, M. T., Otten, R. H. J., Ribbe, M. W., & Deliens, L. (2011). Spirituality at the end of life: Conceptualization of measurable aspects—a systematic review. *Journal of Palliative Medicine, 14*(7), 852–863. https://doi.org/10.1089/jpm.2010.0356

Godinez v. Moran, 509 U.S. 389 (1993).

Green, B. S. (2014). As the pendulum swings: The reformation of compassionate release to accommodate changing perceptions of corrections. *University of Toledo Law Review, 46*, 123.

Hagos, A. K., Butler, T. G., Howie, A., & Withall, A. L. (2022). Optimising the care and management of older offenders: A scoping review. *The Gerontologist, 62*, 508–519. gnab104. https://doi.org/10.1093/geront/gnab104

Hakola, L., Komulainen, P., Hassinen, M., Savonen, K., Litmanen, H., Lakka, T. A., & Rauramaa, R. (2011). Cardiorespiratory fitness in aging men and women: The DR's EXTRA study. *Scandinavian Journal of Medicine & Science in Sports, 21*(5), 679–687. https://doi.org/10.1111/j.1600-0838.2010.01127.x

Hampton, S., Blomgren, D., Roberts, J., Mackinnon, T., & Nicholls, G. (2015). Prescribing for people in custody. *Australian Prescriber, 38*(5), 160–163. https://doi.org/10.18773/austprescr.2015.057

Hartley, R. D. (2014). Focal concerns theory. In *The encyclopedia of theoretical criminology* (pp. 1–5). Wiley Onbline Library.

Hirschi, T., & Gottfredson, M. (1983). Age and the explanation of crime. *American Journal of Sociology, 89*(3), 552–584. https://doi.org/10.1086/227905

Hoffman, H. C., & Dickinson, G. E. (2011). Characteristics of prison hospice programs in the United States. *American Journal of Hospice and Palliative Medicine, 28*(4), 245–252. https://doi.org/10.1177/1049909110381884

Hummert, M. L. (1993). Age and typicality judgments of stereotypes of the elderly: Perceptions of elderly vs. young adults. *International Journal of Aging & Human Development, 37*(3), 217–226. https://doi.org/10.2190/L01P-V960-8P17-PL56

Jefferson-Bullock, J. (2018). Quelling the silver tsunami: Compassionate release of elderly offenders. *Ohio State Law Journal, 79*, 937.

Johanna du Toit, S. H., Withall, A., O'Loughlin, K., Ninaus, N., Lovarini, M., Snoyman, P., Butler, T., Forsyth, K., & Surr, C. A. (2019). Best care options for older prisoners with dementia: A scoping review. *International Psychogeriatrics, 31*(8), 1081–1097. https://doi.org/10.1017/S1041610219000681

Kerbs, J. J., & Jolley, J. M. (2007). Inmate-on-inmate victimization among older male prisoners. *Crime & Delinquency, 53*(2), 187–218. https://doi.org/10.1177/0011128706294119

Kerbs, J. J., & Jolley, J. M. (2009). A commentary on age segregation for older prisoners. *Criminal Justice Review, 34*(1), 119–139. https://doi.org/10.1177/0734016808324245

Kite, M. E., & Wagner, L. S. (2002). Attitudes toward older adults. In T. D. Nelson (Ed.), *Ageism: Stereotyping and prejudice against older persons* (pp. 129–161). MIT Press.

Kramer, J. H., & Steffensmeier, D. (1993). Race and imprisonment decisions. *Sociological Quarterly, 34*, 357–376.

Kratcoski, P. C., & Edelbacher, M. (2016). Trends in the criminality and victimization of the elderly. *Federal Probation, 80*(1), 58–63. https://www.uscourts.gov/federal-probation-journal/2016/06/trends-criminality-and-victimization-elderly

Lackey v. Texas, 514 U.S. 1045 (1995).

Leigey, M. E. (2010). For the longest time: The adjustment of inmates to a sentence of life without parole. *Prison Journal*, *90*(3), 247–268. https://doi.org/10.1177/0032885510373490

Lemieux, C. M., Dyeson, T. B., & Castiglione, B. (2002). Revisiting the literature on prisoners who are older: Are we wiser? *Prison Journal*, *82*(4), 440–458. https://doi.org/10.1177/0032885502238680

Lin, J. T., & Mathew, P. (2005). Cancer pain management in prisons: A survey of primary care practitioners and inmates. *Journal of Pain and Symptom Management*, *29*(5), 466–473. https://doi.org/10.1016/j.jpainsymman.2004.08.015

Madison v. Alabama, 586 U.S. __ (2019).

Mai, C., & Subramanian, R. (2017). *Price of prisons 2015: Examining state spending trends, 2010–2015*. Vera Institute of Justice.

Marquart, J. W., Merianos, D. E., & Doucet, G. (2000). The health-related concerns of older prisoners: Implications for policy. *Ageing & Society*, *20*(1), 79–96. https://doi.org/10.1017/S0144686X99007618

Maschi, T., Dennis, K. S., Gibson, S., MacMillan, T., Sternberg, S., & Hom, M. (2011). Trauma and stress among older adults in the criminal justice system: A review of the literature with implications for social work. *Journal of Gerontological Social Work*, *54*(4), 390–424. https://doi.org/10.1080/01634372.2011.552099

Maschi, T., Kwak, J., Ko, E., & Morrissey, M. B. (2012). Forget me not: Dementia in prison. *The Gerontologist*, *52*(4), 441–451. https://doi.org/10.1093/geront/gnr131

Maschi, T., Leibowitz, G., Rees, J., & Pappacena, L. (2016). Analysis of US compassionate and geriatric release laws: Applying a human rights framework to global prison health. *Journal of Human Rights and Social Work*, *1*(4), 165–174.

Merkt, H., Haesen, S., Meyer, L., Kressig, R. W., Elger, B. S., & Wangmo, T. (2020). Defining an age cut-off for older offenders: A systematic review of literature. *International Journal of Prisoner Health*, *16*(2), 95–116. https://doi.org/10.1108/IJPH-11-2019-0060

Miller, D. (2011). Sentencing elderly criminal offenders. *NAELA Journal*, *7*, 221–225.

Morrow, W. J., Vickovic, S. G., & Fradella, H. F. (2014). Examining the prevalence and correlates of a "senior citizen discount" in US federal courts. *Criminal Justice Studies*, *27*(4), 362–386. https://doi.org/10.1080/1478601x.2014.947029

Moye, J., & Marson, D. (2009). Assessment of decision-making capacity in older adults: An emerging area of practice and research. *FOCUS*, *7*(1), 88–97. https://doi.org/10.1176/foc.7.1.foc88

Munday, D., Leaman, J., O'Moore, É., & Plugge, E. (2019). The prevalence of non-communicable disease in older people in prison: A systematic review and meta-analysis. *Age and Ageing*, *48*(2), 204–212. https://doi.org/10.1093/ageing/afy186

Murolo, A. S. (2020). Geriatric inmates: Policy and practice. *Journal of Correctional Health Care: The Official Journal of the National Commission on Correctional Health Care*, *26*(1), 4–16. https://doi.org/10.1177/1078345819898465

Nelson, T. D. (Ed.). (2002). *Ageism: Stereotyping and prejudice against older persons*. MIT Press.

Nijhawan, A. E. (2016). Infectious diseases and the criminal justice system: A public health perspective. *American Journal of the Medical Sciences*, *352*(4), 399–407. https://doi.org/10.1016/j.amjms.2016.05.020

Oh, S.-J., Lee, J. K., & Shin, O. S. (2019). Aging and the immune system: The impact of immunosenescence on viral infection, immunity and vaccine immunogenicity. *Immune Network*, *19*(6), e37. https://doi.org/10.4110/in.2019.19.e37

Pennsylvania Department of Corrections v. Yeskey, 524 U.S. 206 (1998).

Penrod, J., Loeb, S. J., & Smith, C. A. (2014). Administrators' perspectives on changing practice in end-of-life care in a state prison system. *Public Health Nursing (Boston, Mass.)*, *31*(2), 99–108. https://doi.org/10.1111/phn.12069

Peterson, R., & Hagan, J. (1984). Changing conceptions of race and sentencing outcomes. *American Sociological Review*, *49*, 56–70.

Petrie, J. R., Guzik, T. J., & Touyz, R. M. (2018). Diabetes, hypertension, and cardiovascular disease: Clinical insights and vascular mechanisms. *Canadian Journal of Cardiology*, *34*(5), 575–584. https://doi.org/10.1016/j.cjca.2017.12.005

Pew Charitable Trusts. (2021). *How courts embraced technology, met the pandemic challenge, and revolutionized their operations*. https://www.pewtrusts.org/-/media/assets/2021/12/how-courts-embraced-technology.pdf

Prost, S. G., & Williams, B. (2020). Strategies to optimize the use of compassionate release from US prisons. *American Journal of Public Health*, *110*(S1), S25–S26. https://doi.org/10.2105/AJPH.2019.305434

Rapaport, E. (2012). A modest proposal: The aged of death row should be deemed too old to execute. *Brooklyn Law Review*, *77*(3), 1089–1132. https://brooklynworks.brooklaw.edu/blr/vol77/iss3/5

Reidy, T. J., Sorensen, J. R., & Bonner, H. S. (2017). Prison homicide: An extension of violent criminal careers? *Journal of Interpersonal Violence*, *35*(23–24), 5676–5690. https://doi.org/10.1177/0886260517721895

Rikard, R. V., & Rosenberg, E. (2007). Aging inmates: A convergence of trends in the American criminal justice system. *Journal of Correctional Health Care, 13*(3), 150–162. https://doi.org/10.1177/1078345807303001

Roberts, A. W., Ogunwole, S. U., Blakeslee, L., & Rabe, M. A. (2018). *The population 65 years and older in the United States: 2016* (ACS-38). U.S. Census Bureau.

Rodríguez-Rodero, S., Fernández-Morera, J. L., Menéndez-Torre, E., Calvanese, V., Fernández, A. F., & Fraga, M. F. (2011). Aging genetics and aging. *Aging and Disease, 2*(3), 186–195.

Roper v. Simmons, 543 U.S. 551 (2005).

Rothman, M. B., & Dunlop, B. (2005). Court Review: Volume 42, Issue 1—Judicial responses to an aging America. *Court Review: The Journal of the American Judges Association, 42*(1), 8–19. http://aja.ncsc.dni.us/htdocs/publications.htm

Rothman, M. B., Dunlop, B. D., & Entzel, P. (2000). *Elders, crime, and the criminal justice system: Myth, perceptions, and reality in the 21st century* (Springer Series on Lifestyles and Issues in Aging). Springer Publishing.

Rowe, J., & Kahn, R. (1997). Successful aging. *The Gerontologist, 37*(4), 433–440. https://doi.org/10.1093/geront/37.4.433

Schaller, M., Park, J. H., & Mueller, A. (2003). Fear of the dark: Interactive effects of beliefs about danger and ambient darkness on ethnic stereotypes. *Personality & Social Psychology Bulletin, 29*(5), 637–649. https://doi.org/10.1177/0146167203029005008

Shichor, D. (1984). The extent and nature of law breaking by the elderly: A review of arrest statistics. In E. Newman, D. Newman, & M. Gerwitz (Eds.), *Elderly criminals* (pp. 17–32). Oelgeschlager, Gunn, and Hain.

Shover, N. (1996). *Great pretenders: Pursuits and careers of persistent thieves* (Crime & Society Series). Westview Press.

Smith, M. S., & Schriver, J. L. (2018). Judges' sentencing decisions with older offenders. *Psychology, Crime & Law, 24*(2), 105–116. https://doi.org/10.1080/1068316X.2017.1390117

Stal, M. (2013). Treatment of older and elderly inmates within prisons. *Journal of Correctional Health Care: The Official Journal of the National Commission on Correctional Health Care, 19*(1), 69–73. https://doi.org/10.1177/1078345812458245

Steffensmeier, D. (1987). The invention of the new senior citizen criminal. *Research on Aging, 9*, 281–311.

Steffensmeier, D., & Motivans, M. (2000). Older men and older women in the arms of criminal law: Offending patterns and sentencing outcomes. *Journals of Gerontology, Series B, Psychological Sciences and Social Sciences, 55*(3), S141–S151. https://doi.org/10.1093/geronb/55.3.s141

Steffensmeier, D., Ulmer, J., & Kramer, J. (1998). The interaction of race, gender, and age in criminal sentencing: The punishment cost of being young, black and male. *Criminology, 36*, 763–797.

Stensland, M., & Sanders, S. (2016). Detained and dying: Ethical issues surrounding end-of-life care in prison. *Journal of Social Work in End-of-Life & Palliative Care, 12*(3), 259–276. https://doi.org/10.1080/15524256.2016.1200517

Terry, W. C., & Entzel, P. (2000). Police and elders. In M. Rothman, B. Dunlap, & P. Entzel (Eds.), *Elders, crime, and the criminal justice system* (pp. 3–18). Springer.

Thivierge-Rikard, R. V., & Thompson, M. S. (2007). The association between aging inmate housing management models and non-geriatric health services in state correctional institutions. *Journal of Aging & Social Policy, 19*(4), 39–56. https://doi.org/10.1300/J031v19n04_03

Tittle, C., & Paternoster, R. (2000). *Social deviance and crime*. Los Angeles: Roxbury

Trop v. Dulles, 356 U.S. 86 (1958).

United States v. Brooke, 308 F.3d 17 (2002).

United States v. Bullion, 466 F.3d 574 (2006).

United States v. Doran, 328 F.2d 535 (1971).

United States v. Dusky, 362 U.S. 402 (1960).

United States v. Johnson, 685 F.3d 660 (2012).

U.S. Sentencing Commission. (2018). *Federal sentencing guidelines: 2018 guidelines manual*. Retrieved from https://www.ussc.gov/guidelines/2018-guidelines-manual-annotated

Virginia Department of Corrections. (2008). *A balanced approach, 2008 Appropriations Act, Item 387-B Virginia Department of Corrections and Parole Board report on geriatric offenders*.

Wall, B. W. (2018). Working with the elderly defendant through the adjudicative process. In J. C. Holzer, R. Kohn, J. M. Ellison, & P. R. Recupero (Eds.), *Geriatric forensic psychiatry: Principles and practice* (pp. 213–218). Oxford University Press.

Williams, B. A., Ahalt, C., Stijacic-Cenzer, I., Smith, A. K., Goldenson, J., & Ritchie, C. S. (2014). Pain behind bars: The epidemiology of pain in older jail inmates in a county jail. *Journal of Palliative Medicine, 17*(12), 1336–1343. https://doi.org/10.1089/jpm.2014.0160

Williams, B. A., Lindquist, K., Sudore, R. L., Strupp, H. M., Willmott, D. J., & Walter, L. C. (2006). Being old and doing time: Functional impairment and adverse experiences of geriatric female prisoners. *Journal of the American Geriatrics Society, 54*(4), 702–707. https://doi.org/10.1111/j.1532-5415.2006.00662.x

Wilson, R. S., Wang, T., Yu, L., Bennett, D. A., & Boyle, P. A. (2020). Normative cognitive decline in old age. *Annals of Neurology, 87*(6), 816–829. https://doi.org/10.1002/ana.25711

Wylie, L. E., Hazen, K. P., Hoetger, L. A., Haby, J. A., & Brank, E. M. (2018). Four decades of the journal Law and Human Behavior: A content analysis. *Scientometrics, 115*(2), 655–693.

Wylie, L. E., Knutson, A. K., & Greene, E. (2018). Extraordinary and compelling: The use of compassionate release laws in the United States. *Psychology, Public Policy, and Law, 24*(2), 216–234. https://doi.org/10.1037/law0000161

CHAPTER 31

A Commentary on Adulthood/Aging, Developmental Psychology, and the Law

Nancy Rodriguez and Katherine Waggoner

> **Abstract**
> The current chapter is a commentary on the chapters on adulthood and aging in this volume. The authors of the chapters make excellent contributions on topics central to the intersection of adulthood and aging and the law. Based on this cumulative body of research, this chapter offers several themes that cut across the chapters. It begins by highlighting the role of social inequality in the life course and why it is increasingly relevant for advancing well-being and improving quality of life. The chapter discusses the alignment of legal policy, social norms around age, and developmental science, as well as how changing social norms are represented in legal policy. It moves on to a discussion on the relationship between criminal justice system outcomes in facilitating and/or inhibiting services for adults and the elderly. Finally, the chapter concludes with a discussion of the implications for research, policy, and practice.
>
> **Key Words:** social inequality, adulthood, aging, crime policy, legal policy, lifespan development

In this chapter, we seek to elevate the relationship between adulthood/aging, developmental psychology, and the law. Relative to adolescents, adults and aging populations not only are subject to different legal structures and expectations but also have unique needs.

While criminal justice policy, in large part due to advances in child and adolescent development research (National Research Council, 2013), has centered the need of developmentally appropriate and trauma-informed care for youthful individuals in the justice system, it has not addressed how to most effectively address the needs of adults and aging populations who come into contact with the justice system. To address this policy and practice gap, we need to ensure that policy reflects broader social contexts that characterize modern society, with both the knowledge produced by developmental science and a consciousness of current norms about aging represented in policy. We must also acknowledge and address how legal processes and outcomes impact the development of adults and the elderly.

We thank editors Allison Redlich and Jodi Quas for recognizing this void and ensuring that adulthood and aging are part of intellectual discussions around developmental science and the law. This section contains 10 excellent chapters written by experts across various disciplines, highlighting why and how adulthood and aging matter in the legal system. The authors address topics like adult deviancy (Narvey & Piquero, Chapter 21), the victimization of the elderly (Brank, Chapter 29), aging in the justice system (Wylie & Hubner, Chapter 30), and end-of-life care planning (Teaster & Shealy, Chapter 28). Subgroups like those with developmental disabilities (Salekin & Wood, Chapter 23), young adults (Gillespie et al., Chapter 22), and women's life circumstances like navigating reproductive rights (Whelan & Goodwin, Chapter 25) and motherhood (Shlafer et al., Chapter 24) also receive notable attention. Chapters also highlight the adverse effects of system contact such as policing (Burke et al., Chapter 26) and the crucial role of prisoner reentry (LeBel & Richie, Chapter 27). We draw from these chapters to highlight the role of social inequality in the developmental processes of adults and the elderly and in improving the well-being of justice-involved individuals. Since the COVID-19 pandemic, maintaining a healthy quality of life has become increasingly challenging for many. The pandemic not only had devastating health impacts on millions but also worsened existing racial and economic disparities (Bibbins-Domingo, 2020; García & Weiss, 2020). Thus, any consideration of policy with respect to adult development, aging, law, and justice needs to consider how changing contexts shape social inequality; in the current circumstances, this is most striking in terms of how inequity has been exacerbated by the pandemic.

Our chapter is organized as follows. We begin by discussing social inequality and why it matters in our conversation about adulthood/elderly and the law. We then move to a discussion on the relationship between changing social norms about aging and how such norms inform and shape policy and science. In particular, we note the need to consider how law reflects or fails to reflect changing norms and expectations of adults and the elderly. Our discussion shifts to the interactions with various stages of the criminal justice system, the consequences of system involvement, and the intersection with auxiliary systems such as health care and social service systems. We conclude the chapter by highlighting strategies for advancing research in these areas, as well as the policy implications for adulthood and aging in the legal system.

Social Inequality in the 21st Century

Society is stratified in ways that shape our experiences, opportunities, and behavior (Western & Pettit, 2010). Specifically, income inequality, poverty, and racial segregation have led to social stratification that dictates life for individuals across the life course (Lee & Wildeman, 2021; Turney & Wakefield, 2019). The stratified landscape of communities, along lines of race, employment, and opportunities, is a distinguishing and enduring characteristic of U.S. cities (R. J. Sampson et al., 2018). Despite the growing racial and ethnic diversity in the United States, cities remain highly segregated, leading to unequal opportunities and access to goods (Heimer, 2019). Racial disparities in educational outcomes, labor markets, health, and criminal justice contact have many drivers, but certainly, structural racism remains a fundamental cause of existing disparities. Structural racism is pervasive, and it impacts multiple systems that shape opportunities and outcomes across the life course (Z. D. Bailey et al., 2017).

Communities plagued by economic and racial inequality, created and perpetuated in large part by the lack of investments in certain communities, present an array of criminogenic risks that are particularly salient for adults and the elderly. Underserved communities are not only socially excluded but also characterized by a larger proportion of adult residents who may have poor family functioning, unstable employment and housing, histories of substance use, and mental health challenges. Parents and grandparents are looking not only to maintain their own well-being in these communities but also to promote the well-being of their children and other family members. Caretaking duties, especially for racial and ethnic minority groups for whom kinship care is part of cultural norms, may become difficult when faced with additional hardships of economic stain, limited access to the labor market and medical/behavioral health care. Accordingly, proper access to educational, health, and economic resources is fundamental to the long-term well-being of families and communities.

Not surprising, experiences of victimization and violence are concentrated in areas facing significant social inequality (National Research Council, 2014). Further, individuals experiencing social inequality are more likely to have contact with the legal system and receive more punitive outcomes in the system (Kurlychek & Johnson, 2019). The underinvestment in communities and unequal access to resources and goods have resulted in the disparate impact of system outcomes for adults, especially people of color. This includes contact at the front end of the justice system, via aggressive forms of police contact (Stewart et al., 2020), and in the pretrial stage of system processing, where people of color are less likely to avoid formal processing in the system. For instance, studies have found that minorities are far more likely to be stopped and arrested by police than Whites and to experience more aggressive forms of policing, including use of force (Geller, 2021). Amidst pretrial reform efforts, scholars have found that, despite a reduction in the number of people in jails, racial disparities have not decreased. Not only are people of color more likely to receive higher bail amounts, but also they are less likely to pay bail to receive pretrial release (Dobbie & Yang, 2021). Disparities in the pretrial stage are important because individuals who experience pretrial detention are more likely to receive punitive sanctions by the court. Importantly, racial disparities in the criminal justice system also exist at the back end, where people of color are disproportionately represented in correctional facilities. Indeed, contact with the criminal justice system can create, compound, and exacerbate inequalities for individuals, especially racial and ethnic groups who are over-represented in the legal system.

Criminal justice system disparities and resulting social inequality have implications for adults and the elderly. First, unlike many youthful justice-involved individuals, adults and the elderly will likely not be prioritized for treatment and programming that target substance use and mental health. This is important given the health disparities that exist in the community and among justice-involved populations. For adults and the elderly in the justice system, the aging process demands special care and attention. Further, the mental health and physical needs of this population are far greater than those of younger individuals (Wiley & Hubner, Chapter 30). In especially recent years, the health disparities that plague justice-involved individuals, coupled with COVID infections, led to health challenges and deaths among the confined. Studies have also found that older incarcerated persons have weaker social support systems and are less likely to have access to loved ones in prison (Wiley & Hubner, Chapter 30).

In addition to social inequity having important consequences for adults' and the elderly's experiences when they have contact with the justice system, contact with the justice system has important consequences for families and communities. Scholars have documented the adverse effects that system involvement has on children and families. The economic effects associated with justice system fees and fines lead to economic strain and leave limited resources for families. For adults who are incarcerated, even for short periods, their absence can result in significant disruption to childcare and caretaking duties. Family members of adults released from incarceration may have to help the formerly incarcerated adult reenter, including providing them with housing and basic amenities, alongside other forms of instrumental and emotional support. As a criminal record may cause challenges to obtaining employment opportunities for released individuals, families may need to step in and economically support aging adults during this reentry period.

A key consideration in relation to existing inequalities and those compounded by the legal system concerns how gender and racial background affect treatment, health care, and behavioral health services delivery and experiences. Importantly, social inequality shapes how women access the health care system (Heise et al., 2019). Access to reproductive education and contraception can shape educational and economic outcomes for women (Whelan & Goodwin, Chapter 25). Researchers have found that disadvantaged communities are characterized by poor access to reproductive education and affordable contraception (Whelan & Goodwin, Chapter 25). While policies have been implemented at various levels of government to ensure affordable access to health care and health equity, health care remains costly and is difficult to access.

At the federal level, the Affordable Care Act (ACA) was the most recent notable effort designed to provide Americans with health care. However, high out-of-pocket costs created medical financial hardships for many. Approximately 137.1 million adults reported any medical financial hardship in the past year (Yabroff, 2019). Such hardships, in addition to being difficult on their own, are also related to worse behavioral health, including higher levels of stress and poor coping. Further, medical financial hardship is linked to lower educational attainment and negative health outcomes (Carrillo et al., 2011). While the ACA is given credit for serving millions with no health care, disparities in access to health care persist. For example, unauthorized immigrants are prohibited from purchasing insurance via ACA, and when eligible, many immigrants are fearful of accessing public health resources due to the threats of surveillance and apprehension by immigration enforcement agencies (Perreira & Pedroza, 2019). This illustrates how policies and systems (i.e., health care and federal immigration system) can interact to shape outcomes that further marginalize certain communities. Although science may provide a path toward more equitable policy, gaps in research on development and system involvement have left many polices and norms unchallenged.

The Malalignment of Policy, Societal Norms, and Science

Norms regarding aging and conceptions of what it means to be young or old often shape policies aimed at protecting those vulnerable due to age. However, the conversation between societal norms and policy is often complicated by the contributions of science, which frequently contrast commonly held beliefs about aging and development. Societal norms regarding who is worthy of protection or punishment by the law are typically reflected in policies, which often reinforce these norms by setting standards for behavior and consequences of certain behaviors and by increasing the perceived validity of such standards. Yet, the validity and efficacy of many policies pertaining to criminal offending across the lifespan are questionable in the eyes of science. This malalignment is exhibited in myriad policies that are relevant to age, pertaining to both children and older adults, both of whom are often seen as highly vulnerable populations. Next, we highlight the many ways in which policy, norms, and science are contradictory as they pertain to young adults, women, and older adults. We conclude with a discussion on the extent to which criminal justice policies have been amended to reflect shifts in societal norms toward social equity.

Young Adults

As discussed by Gillespie et al. in their chapter on transition-age youth, policy in the United States regards the legal age of adulthood as 18 (Chapter 22; see also Hamilton, Chapter 17). If an individual commits a crime after their 18th birthday, they will be processed by the criminal justice system as an adult. Beyond this, depending on the state in which they live, some individuals under 18 may also be processed through the criminal justice system as an adult if they are convicted of committing certain crimes. Despite these common practices, neurological and developmental research indicate that psychosocial abilities are not fully developed until around age 26 (Steinberg et al., 2009). This means that, due to age-related underdeveloped brain networks, young adults, defined by Gillespie et al. as those 18–25, have a decreased capacity for self-regulation, risk perception, and emotional regulation relative to adults who are older than 25. Therefore, policies that regard those between the ages of 18 and 25 as fully developed adults are entirely misguided given developmental and neurological research.

The processing of young adults through the criminal justice system can be extremely harmful, such that these processes may damage future opportunities for young adults. Young people who are arrested and booked into jails may lose jobs and educational opportunities, and those who are convicted of a felony crime may risk a lifetime of stigma due to the mark of the "criminal" label (Denver et al., 2017). As noted in the previous section, the collateral consequences of system involvement are not equally felt across subpopulations (Burke et al., Chapter 26; Pinard, 2010). Youth of color are disproportionately incarcerated and left to deal with the lifelong impacts of criminal justice system involvement early in life. In all, the application of a criminal label to those under 25 may promote irreparable harm that shapes the opportunities and trajectories of young people throughout the life course.

Some policies and practices that guide the justice processes for young people who commit crimes have attempted to align with the conclusions of developmental and neurological research. Gillespie et al. (Chapter 22) focus on these practices, namely diversion programs and young adult courts. Despite common misconceptions associated with tough-on-crime movements that youth who commit crimes are irredeemable and in need of long-term incapacitation, Gillespie et al. highlight evidence that young adults are highly capable of change when offered rehabilitative treatments. Diversion programs, aimed at diverting young adults from further formal criminal justice system involvement and providing effective treatment components, may offer a valuable alternative to punitive consequences for young adults who engaged in crime. Evidence-based programs, like many diversion programs, exhibit an approach that is more in line with science.

Women

Social norms dictate that women, particularly those who are mothers, are a vulnerable population in need of extra protection through policies and practices (Hollander, 2001). However, for adult women who become involved in the criminal justice system, policies often create more harm than protection. In their chapter, Shlafer et al. (Chapter 24) explain that the majority of adult women who are incarcerated are also mothers. From the standpoint of developmental science, it is imperative that the children of incarcerated mothers maintain a bond with their parents, particularly if their incarcerated mother is the primary custodial parent. However, existing policies do very little to promote and support healthy parent–child relationships. Beyond this, the involvement of systems that are adjacent to the criminal justice system, such as family courts and child protective services, may introduce more challenges to mothers who have limited resources. For instance, mothers who are facing incarceration must also navigate many family court systems to ensure that loved ones, instead of the state, gain custody of their children. Beyond this, given such barriers, mothers who are unable to effectively navigate both family court and criminal court systems may be unable to maintain contact with their children or regain custody of them after incarceration (Shlafer et al., Chapter 24).

Relatedly, mothers of low socioeconomic status and mothers of color are most likely to have limited resources that may confound barriers to maintain custody and access to their children (Opsal & Foley, 2013). These processes, aimed at the protection of women and children, may exacerbate collateral consequences such as child trauma, financial strain, and health problems. A mother's health is deeply important to the health and development of her children. Therefore, when mothers in the criminal justice system are not receiving adequate health care, including physical and mental health, the development of their children is adversely impacted.

These processes often exacerbate generational inequity and further cycles of incarceration, poverty, and trauma experienced by mothers and their children (Lee & Wildeman, 2021). Although societal norms often place a great value on the protection of children, policies in place today often fall short of providing mothers, particularly low-income and/or criminal justice system–involved mothers, with the resources needed for healthy child development.

Older Adults

Although there are policies that clearly outline what ages constitute childhood, there are no clear parameters for "older adults." Brank (Chapter 29) underscores this fact, highlighting that policies range in their definitions of what age constitutes "old age" and that science provides very little clarity regarding what age could be generalized to all people as "old." Given this, we often rely on social norms and conceptions of old age to guide who is deserving of the informal social supports, such as the provision of meals, transportation, and conversation, commonly provided to older individuals. Notions of age and what constitutes old age are complicated by the fact that people today are living longer, working and remaining active in their communities at older ages, and remaining generally healthier. As a result, the needs of a population once considered highly vulnerable must be reconsidered with more nuance.

Given that older adults are perceived as highly vulnerable, their role in the legal system is usually conceptualized in terms of victims. Importantly, although processes of aging may naturally make physical bodies weaker and impair key mental faculties, victimization research suggests that older adults are violently victimized infrequently (Brank, Chapter 29). Despite the low statistical risk of violent victimization for this population, older adults often fear victimization. Exponentiating this is the reality that older adults are more likely to be financially victimized, particularly by loved ones, caretakers, or trusted individuals. The stress and fear of victimization is important to understanding the impact that the criminal justice system, as well as auxiliary systems such as Social Security and health care systems, may have on the lives of older individuals. Given the multifaceted needs of older adults for myriad services such as trusted caretakers and high-quality and affordable health care, there are an abundance of ways in which this population may be underserved by policies.

Research has established that the criminal justice system involvement of older adults is not limited to victimization. Instead, older adults make up an increasingly large proportion of the incarcerated population (Wylie & Hubner, Chapter 30). The presence of older adults within prisons and on community supervision mandates a reevaluation of how we understand incarceration, as this population presents unique health, employment, and reentry needs. In fact, the needs of incarcerated older adults may far exceed the general needs of nonincarcerated older individuals previously described. Beyond this, the incarcerated older adult population in particular may lack the necessary caretakers and advocates to ensure that such needs are met. Therefore, in thinking of how older adults interact with the system, we must ask who is caring for this population, how we are ensuring that physical and mental health needs are being met, and what additional considerations need to be made as older adults navigate the criminal justice system and reentry from incarceration. If norms and policies do not catch up to science, the needs of older adults who are involved in the criminal justice system will remain unmet (LeBel & Richie, Chapter 27; Wylie & Hubner, Chapter 30).

Changing Norms

In recent years many scholars, advocates, and policymakers have called attention to systemic inequities in policies. Addressing structural racism and social inequality within the criminal justice system will also require a greater alignment of policy and science. For instance, following the highly publicized and abhorrent murder of George Floyd, protests and activism in the summer of 2020 brought massive attention to the myriad inequities built into the criminal justice system and added fuel to long-standing calls for criminal justice reform. As a result of this normative shift, the United States has seen subsequent changes to criminal justice policies and practices (Grant & Smith, 2021; Legal-Miller, 2022). For instance, at the local level, many police departments reviewed and amended policies that guide the actions of officers (Bacon, 2022; Boxer et al., 2021). At the national level, President Joe Biden passed the Executive Order on Advancing Racial Equity and Support for Underserved Communities Through the Federal Government, which seeks to reduce social inequality in all sectors of government. Shifts in policy at every level of government represent a national shift toward prioritizing and reducing inequality. Looking forward, it is imperative that researchers are attuned to how these and ongoing policy shifts align with emerging and evolving evidence on crime and the life course.

System Involvement, Cumulative Disadvantage, and Collateral Consequences

For many individuals, criminal justice system involvement entails a process in which the decisions made early in the system shape subsequent outcomes. In other words, the experience of arrest shapes court proceedings, which ultimately shape outcomes of sentencing, incarceration, and eventually reentry. At any stage of involvement in the system, the happenings of earlier events will inform subsequent outcomes, and these outcomes often shape future behavior, including further participation in crime. This process is additive in nature, and the disadvantages encountered via system involvement may be confounded by challenges like systemic racism and individual-level characteristics, such as intellectual disabilities or older age (Kurlychek & Johnson, 2019). Therefore, although criminal justice system involvement can be bracketed off into stages, it is important to consider how experiences across the system impact each other sequentially and combine with other factors of disadvantage to shape outcomes for adults.

Understanding criminal justice involvement with the consideration of the impact of cumulative disadvantage is particularly important to fully realizing how policies impact system-involved adults and the elderly. A longer lifespan brings the accumulation of factors, including the stigma of prior criminality, financial debt, increased health needs, and the caretaking of others. The following section discusses the sequential stages of criminal justice system involvement with attention to how these stages may exacerbate existing inequities.

Law Enforcement

Contact with law enforcement is a common gateway to further criminal justice system contact. For many people, being arrested by the police is their introduction to the criminal justice system. This is important for a variety of reasons. First, empirical literature indicates that communities of color are heavily overpoliced (Burke et al., Chapter 26). Therefore, the likelihood of being stopped and arrested by the police in these communities is higher, resulting in a higher likelihood of subsequent criminal justice system involvement (Beckett et al., 2006). This is on full display in the literature that documents the school-to-prison pipeline. This research highlights that, largely due to increased police presence in schools with higher proportions of Black and Latino/a youth, children of color are more likely to be detained and arrested by police than White children.

As Burke et al. (Chapter 26) discuss, processes of racially discriminatory policing persist across the life course, with adults of color facing greater risks of arrest, fatal police encounters, and threats of force than White adults. Although there is some evidence that racial disparities in policing practices decrease in older adulthood, the harms of inequitable and overpolicing shape individuals across their lifespan. The harms of racially biased policing to both mental and physical health are paramount. Burke et al. call attention to the anxiety, depression, trauma, and hypertension that continued exposure to police violence and overpolicing produces for people of color. Beyond this, given the discretion that police have in making arrest decisions, racial bias at the officer level impacts who they arrest and for what. This discretion contributes to the disproportionate arrest rate of people of color, pushing more people of color into subsequent stages of the criminal justice system.

Court Processes
Often, following arrest, individuals are booked into jail, released on bond, and/or sent to await trial. These processes lead people into the complicated and costly U.S. criminal court system. A large body of research indicates that two major mechanisms of early court processes, cash bail and plea bargaining, are both racially and ethnically biased and discriminatory to those of low socioeconomic status. Cash bail presents a large barrier to individuals who lack the social and fiscal resources needed to satisfy the court or a bail bondsman (Martinez, Petersen, & Omori, 2020). As a result, poor individuals, who often include higher proportions of people of color, are more likely to be held in pretrial detention. When individuals await their trial in jail, they are more likely to accept pleas from prosecutors, which entail longer sentences, definitive convictions, and potentially greater long-term consequences (Johnson & Hernandez, 2021). Given that 95% of criminal convictions are the result of plea deals offered by prosecutors, plea bargaining is profoundly important to criminal justice system processes (Reaves, 2013). Research largely indicates that the acceptance of a plea results in more punitive sentencing outcomes than those associated with not accepting a plea (Wooldredge et al., 2015). Ultimately, court processes often take advantage of low-income minority defendants by limiting access to bail and to trials.

For many, involvement in the criminal court system often entails further involvement in other court systems, like family and child welfare courts. In these cases, factors of cumulative disadvantage are often exponentiated. As formerly discussed, the majority of incarcerated women are mothers, many of whom are also the primary custodial parent of their children (Glaze & Maruschak, 2008). As a result, parents who are facing incarceration or who are reentering must consider the court actions that are paramount to maintaining the custody and care of their children (Shafler et al., Chapter 24). Barriers in both the criminal justice court system and adjacent systems present massive challenges that those with limited resources, education, and physical ability may be unable to navigate effectively. The fallout of ineffective navigation of these systems impacts parents, their children, and those who may have to look after children when a primary caretaker is incarcerated. Outcomes of court processes, including criminal courts and adjacent systems, may exacerbate damage to bonds between parents or caregivers and their children. The presence of a parent or reliable caregiver is crucial for healthy child development. Parent–child separation can exacerbate trauma and harm for both parents and their children, potentially perpetuating inequality and trauma across generations.

Corrections and Reentry
Prison is often thought of as the last stage of the criminal justice system. Accordingly, it is within this stage that the cumulative disadvantage of prior system involvement culminates. Correctional and reentry experiences and outcomes are often shaped by prior trauma, mental health, physical health, and other individual factors. These individual-level factors and experiences interact with the structures built into the prison and reentry experience. As a result,

for many people, prison can exacerbate trauma and have extremely negative consequences for a wide range of health outcomes, physical and mental, the latter of which are often overlooked. LeBel and Richie (Chapter 27) explain that the prison experience can instill a sense of dependence, hopelessness, anger, and sadness in those who are incarcerated. Not only does the impact of incarceration on mental health matter for one's prison experience, but also trauma, poor mental health, and poor physical health can shape opportunities for a successful reentry after incarceration. This is particularly important for adults and the elderly who are incarcerated or reentering after lengthy periods of incarceration.

Adults and older adults reentering have health, financial, and social needs that vary distinctly from younger adults. Although older adults make up a smaller proportion of the incarcerated population compared to younger people, they represent a population that is quickly growing (Wylie & Hubner, Chapter 30). Understandably, incarcerated older adults have greater health needs than their younger counterparts. These include both physical and mental health needs. Importantly, the mental health needs of incarcerated adults and older adults are deeply tied to issues of physical health, with older prisoners at the highest risk of suicidality (Wylie & Hubner, Chapter 30). Additionally, the financial needs of older adults released from prison are likely significant, while opportunities for employment are severely limited. This is especially important among older adults reentering who may well lack caretakers and savings that could offset the burden of costs of health and housing expenses. Support systems such as Social Security and Medicare may help to offset these costs. However, research indicates that access to these systems may be made difficult due to formerly incarcerated individuals missing important documents and proper identification needed to receive benefits (Conly, 2005). In all, the incarceration and reentry experience is shaped and made complicated by cumulative disadvantage that may damage positive outcomes, particularly for adults and older adults.

Collateral Consequences of the Legal System

The consequences of criminal justice system involvement and policies are not isolated to the person who is involved; instead, criminal justice system involvement impacts entire families. While there are many collateral consequences associated with system involvement, we highlight the impact on families and the role of adults as caretakers of children and older adults. As discussed, most incarcerated individuals are also parents. This means that, due to incarceration, millions of children lose their primary caretaker for sometimes significant periods of time (Turney & Haskins, 2019). Research on these trends indicates that grandparents often gain custody, either formally or informally, of grandchildren when parents become incarcerated. Often, this caregiving comes without monetary benefit, like child support. Moreover, managing the needs of children can be challenging if the children act out, struggle academically or socially, and need additional intervention and assistance (Sampson & Hertlein, 2015; Turanovic et al., 2012). Beyond this, many grandparents may quit jobs to raise their grandchildren. However, there are some governmental programs aimed to help, such as congressional act HR 2628—Living Equitably: Grandparents Aiding Children and Youth Act, which was passed in 2003. This act was primarily aimed at providing housing assistance to custodial grandparents. Governmental assistance for grandparents may also come in the form of food stamps, the Special Supplemental Nutrition Program for Women, Infants, and Children, and Temporary Assistance for Needy Families (Bailey et al., 2019; Cox, 2009; Hayslip & Kaminski, 2005).

Even with some forms of support, the toll on grandparents who raise their grandchildren can be overwhelming as evidenced by the grandparents' high rate of mental health difficulties (e.g., depression). Grandparents often report feeling low levels of social support, which may compound mental health struggles (Poehlmann, 2003). These grandparents may be managing stressors and strain related to their own children while also raising their grandchildren (Hayslip & Kaminski, 2005). Mental health challenges may be confounded by physical health issues and fitness as 25% of custodial grandparents have disabilities and 38% are over the age of 60 (Bailey et al., 2019). Related, just as grandparents often care for their grandchildren when their children become incarcerated, they also lose a caretaker themselves. Many older adults rely on their children to provide care and advocacy as they age. However, when their children are incarcerated, they too lose this level of support.

Given that people of color are overrepresented in the criminal justice system, the collateral consequences of family disruption disproportionately impact people of color. In line with the discussion at the heart of this chapter, it is imperative that social inequality is recognized as a major contributor to the harms associated with criminal justice system involvement. In considering how collateral consequences impact older adults, issues associated with racial and ethnic discrimination in policy and practice in the criminal justice system are of the utmost importance.

Implications for Research, Policy, and Practice

The authors of the preceding chapters offer an array of suggestions for the next wave of research in this area. While most perspectives and criminal justice policies have focused on the development and deviance of children and youthful offenders, there is increasing awareness and attention to addressing the experiences of adults and aging adults as offenders, victims, and justice-impacted individuals. Here, we offer a few suggestions for expanding the evidence base in this space, ideally with the broader goal of turning that emerging evidence into action that will directly and significantly improve systemic responses, reduce inequities, and promote healthier functioning in legally involved adults of all ages. In line with this broader goal, we emphasize the importance of this work in fueling equitable and substantive changes to policy that will improve the treatment and outcomes of older adults with criminal justice system involvement.

Within the literature on development throughout the lifespan, there are clear data gaps that impact our understanding of the relationship between aging and the criminal justice system. Notably, due to the erasure of ethnicity in many official criminal justice records, we lack systematic data regarding system involvement and system harm for Latino/a individuals, who are often categorized as White (https://apps.urban.org/features/latino-criminal-justice-data/). Given that ethnicity is missing across various outcomes of the criminal justice system, the over- or underrepresentation of system involvement for ethnic groups, like Latino/a individuals, confounds our understanding of racial and ethnic disparities. Data regarding the needs and responses of adult and older adult populations are also missing. Because this population has received minimal attention in studies of developmental psychology and the law, we have very limited data on the needs and correctional outcomes for this group. As a result, we lack an evidence-based approach to understanding and implementing care for this population.

In light of increasing social inequality, there is a growing need to assess and explore how these factors shape criminogenic risks and needs in the lives of adults and the elderly. For example, as gaps in income inequality increase, do crime and victimization pathways among adults and the elderly change? Given this current gap in criminological literature, we are left wondering what perspectives might be best suited to explain the victimization and offending of older adults. Further, research that examines the varying definitions of what it means to be an "older adult" and the "elderly" and their implications for well-being would advance policy that can most effectively serve this population. An interdisciplinary approach may aid us in understanding victimization, offending, system involvement, and desistance of this older age group. Although age can shape behaviors and interactions with the legal system, other aspects such as gender, intellectual ability, and race/ethnicity intersect with each other and age to shape outcomes.

As such, we need better insight into the complexities of how justice system involvement shapes the lives of older adults. We lack a robust body of literature that considers how system interaction may impact older adults, especially how aging victims or perpetrators of crime cope with the collateral consequences of system involvement. As we reported, the collateral consequences associated with system contact are not uniformly felt. For those experiencing various forms of inequality (e.g., economic, health), the consequences for families and communities are significant. Better understanding these impacts can inform policies that untimely serve families and communities. Related, we know very little about how criminal justice system involvement is tied to involvement in auxiliary systems like Social Security, child services systems, and safety net programs for this older population. The intersection between the legal system and these auxiliary systems should be normative and part of effective policy responses when addressing adults and the elderly.

While there are numerous policy implications associated with adulthood, aging, and the law, making sure that the criminal justice system does not create or compound existing social inequalities should remain a national priority. There is substantial evidence that the criminal justice system can offer treatment for some, but it can also adversely impact health and economic well-being. Avenues to reduce system involvement for those that can be cared for outside of the legal system should be pursued. Sentencing schemes that appropriately address the needs and risks of adults and the elderly would lead to substantial reductions in the incarceration rate and, consequently, reduce disparities and adverse health outcomes for this subpopulation. Policies that reduce the incarceration of those vulnerable to health challenges should be pursued, and in instances where adults and the elderly are confined, mandatory participation in correctional programming that addresses their needs should be pursued.

We must reflect on the ways in which auxiliary systems confound adversity and consider how to reduce such disparities, particularly for highly vulnerable populations like older adults. Leveraging health care and social services in other systems to ensure that affordable and quality health care is accessible for this subpopulation can improve their quality of life and well-being. Further, improving the mental health and physical well-being of adults and the elderly should be cornerstones of criminal justice policies. We know that individuals in the legal system have disproportionately experienced trauma and that system involvement can create and compound existing trauma. Trauma-informed care should be integrated into criminal justice processes as well as the processes of auxiliary systems.

Lastly, as reported earlier, we know very little about evidence-based interventions that effectively serve this population. We encourage policymakers to advocate for older adults, many of whom are highly marginalized. Are correctional treatment programs and reentry programs addressing the age-based needs of individuals? What does reentry look like for a 35-year-old Black man with a history of mental health? A 55-year-old Black man with a history of victimization and substance abuse? A 40-year-old Native American woman who has been absent from her children for years? Reentry programs that work include cognitive-behavioral treatment and skill development; facilitating entry into the labor market and ensuring individuals have stable housing postrelease will yield effective outcomes. Ultimately, public health approaches that center continuity of care for aging populations should be standard practice in local, state, tribal, and federal criminal justice systems.

Conclusion

In conclusion, we stress the importance of approaching policy related to age, particularly that which pertains to adults and the elderly, with an understanding of the societal norms and science that inform such policy. Given that the United States is currently experiencing many normative shifts in response to greater recognition of social inequality in the criminal justice, health care, and economic systems, it is imperative that policy reflects these new social norms. Moving forward, policies must be responsive in the consideration of issues of social inequality and the evidence and science regarding processes of development and aging as they relate to crime and criminal justice system involvement. The consideration of age in this regard is perhaps more important than ever as the U.S. population ages and people live longer and healthier lives. Although policymakers and researchers must work diligently to fill the many gaps that we have identified in this chapter, we hope that this commentary offers greater insight on how we may begin to advance our understanding of and responses to issues of aging, criminal justice system involvement, and the many consequences endured by individuals and their families due to the incarceration of adults. Ultimately, as due attention is given to these issues, we hope that equitable and substantive changes to policy and practice will follow, improving quality of life over the lifespan for all people.

References

Bacon, M. (2022). Desistance from criminalization: Police culture and new directions in drugs policing. *Policing and Society, 32*(4), 522–539.

Bailey, S. J., Letiecq, B. L., Visconti, K., & Tucker, N. (2019). Rural native and European American custodial grandparents: Stressors, resources, and resilience. *Journal of Cross-Cultural Gerontology, 34*(2), 131–148.

Bailey, Z. D., Krieger, N., Agénor, M., Graves, J., Linos, N., & Bassett, M. T. (2017). Structural racism and health inequities in the USA: Evidence and interventions. *The Lancet, 389*(10077), 1453–1463.

Beckett, K., Nyrop, K., & Pfingst, L. (2006). Race, drugs, and policing: Understanding disparities in drug delivery arrests. *Criminology, 44*(1), 105–137.

Bibbins-Domingo, K. (2020). This time must be different: Disparities during the COVID-19 pandemic. *Annals of Internal Medicine, 173*(3), 233–234.

Boxer, P., Brunson, R. K., Gaylord-Harden, N., Kahn, K., Patton, D. U., Richardson, J., Rivera, L. M., Smith-Lee, J. R., Staller, M. S., Krahe, B., Dubow, E. F., Parrott, D., & Algrim, K. (2021). Addressing the inappropriate use of force by police in the United States and beyond: A behavioral and social science perspective. *Aggressive Behavior, 47*(5), 502–512.

Carrillo, E. J., Carrillo, V. A., Perez, H. R., Salas-Lopez, D., Natale-Pereira, A., & Byron, A. T. (2011). Defining and targeting health care access barriers. *Journal of Health Care for the Poor and Underserved, 22*(2), 562–575.

Conly, C. H. (2005). *Helping inmates obtain federal disability benefits: Serious medical and mental illness, incarceration, and federal disability entitlement programs: Prepared for National Institute of Justice*. Abt Associates.

Cox, C. (2009). Custodial grandparents: Policies affecting care. *Journal of Intergenerational Relationships, 7*(2–3), 177–190.

Denver, M., Pickett, J. T., & Bushway, S. D. (2017). The language of stigmatization and the mark of violence: Experimental evidence on the social construction and use of criminal record stigma. *Criminology, 55*(3), 664–690.

Dobbie, W. S., & Yang, C. (2021). The U.S. pretrial system. *Journal of Economic Perspectives, 35*(4), 49–70.

García, E., & Weiss, E. (2020). *COVID-19 and student performance, equity, and US education policy: Lessons from pre-pandemic research to inform relief, recovery, and rebuilding*. Economic Policy Institute.

Geller, A. (2021). Youth-police contact: Burdens and inequities in an adverse childhood experience. *American Journal of Public Health, 111*(7), 1300–1308.

Glaze, L. E., & Maruschak, L. M. (2008). *Parents in prison and their minor children* (NCJ 222984). Bureau of Justice Statistics.

Grant, P. R., & Smith, H. J. (2021). Activism in the time of COVID-19. *Group Processes & Intergroup Relations, 24*(2), 297–305.

Hayslip, B., & Kaminski, P. L. (2005). Grandparents raising their grandchildren: A review of the literature and suggestions for practice. *The Gerontologist, 45*(2), 262–269.

Heimer, K. (2019). Inequalities and crime. *Criminology, 57*(3), 377–394.

Heise, L., Greene, M. E., Opper, N., Stavropoulou, M., Harper, C., Nascimento, M., & Zewdie, D. (2019). Gender inequality and restrictive gender norms: Framing the challenges to health. *The Lancet, 393*(10189), 2440–2454.

Hollander, J. A. (2001). Vulnerability and dangerousness: The construction of gender through conversation about violence. *Gender & Society, 15*(1), 83–109.

Johnson, B. D., & Hernandez, R. (2021). Prosecutors and plea bargaining. In R.F.Wright, K.L Levine, & R.M. Gold (Eds.), *The Oxford handbook of prosecutors and prosecution* (p. 75).Oxford University Press.

Kurlychek, M. C., & Johnson, B. D. (2019). Cumulative disadvantage in the American criminal justice system. *Annual Review of Criminology, 2*, 291–319.

Lee, H., & Wildeman, C. (2021). Assessing mass incarceration's effects on families. *Science, 374*, 277–281.

Legal-Miller, A. (2022). Race, policing, and Black Lives Matter. In G. Peele, B. Cain, J. Herbert, & A.Wroe, (Eds.), *Developments in American politics* (p. 9). Palgrave Macmillan.

Martinez, B. P., Petersen, N., & Omori, M. (2020). Time, money, and punishment: Institutional racial-ethnic inequalities in pretrial detention and case outcomes. *Crime & Delinquency, 66*(6–7), 837–863.

National Research Council, Committee on Law and Justice, & Division of Behavioral and Social Sciences and Education (2013). *Reforming juvenile justice: A developmental approach* (Committee on Assessing Juvenile Justice Reform, R. J. Bonnie, R. L. Johnson, B. M. Chemers, & J. A. Schuck, Eds.). National Academies Press.

National Research Council. (2014). *The Growth of Incarceration in the United States: Exploring Causes and Consequences* (Committee on Causes and Consequences of High Rates of Incarceration, J. Travis, B. Western, & S. Redburn, Eds.).National Academies Press.

Opsal, T., & Foley, A. (2013). Making it on the outside: Understanding barriers to women's post-incarceration reintegration. *Sociology Compass, 7*(4), 265–277.

Perreira, K. M., & Pedroza, J. M. (2019). Policies of exclusion: Implications for the health of immigrants and their children. *Annual Review of Public Health, 40*, 147–166.

Pinard, M. (2010). Collateral consequences of criminal convictions: Confronting issues of race and dignity. *New York University Law Review, 85*, 457.

Poehlmann, J. (2003). An attachment perspective on grandparents raising their very young grandchildren: Implications for intervention and research. *Infant Mental Health Journal: Official Publication of the World Association for Infant Mental Health, 24*(2), 149–173.

Reaves, B. A. (2013). *Felony defendants in large urban counties, 2009—Statistical tables*. Washington, DC: US Department of Justice.

Sampson, D., & Hertlein, K. (2015). The experience of grandparents raising grandchildren. *Grandfamilies: The Contemporary Journal of Research, Practice and Policy, 2*(1), 4.

Sampson, R. J., Wilson, W. J., & Katz, H. (2018). Reassessing "toward a theory of race, crime, and urban inequality": Enduring and new challenges in 21st century America. *DuBois Review, 15*(1), 13–34.

Steinberg, L., Graham, S., O'Brien, L., Woolard, J., Cauffman, E., & Banich, M. (2009). Age differences in future orientation and delay discounting. *Child Development, 80*(1), 28–44.

Stevenson, M. T., & Mayson, S. G. (2017). Pretrial detention and bail. *Academy for Justice, A Report on Scholarship and Criminal Justice Reform (Erik Luna ed., 2017, Forthcoming), U of Penn Law School, Public Law Research Paper* (17–18).

Stewart, E. A., Warren, P. Y., Hughes, C., & Brunson, R. K. (2020). Race, ethnicity, and criminal justice contact: Reflections for future research. *Race and Justice, 10*(2), 119–149.

Turanovic, J. J., Rodriguez, N., & Pratt, T. C. (2012). The collateral consequences of incarceration revisited: A qualitative analysis of the effects on caregivers of children of incarcerated parents. *Criminology, 50*(4), 913–959.

Turney, K., & Haskins, A. R. (2019). Parental incarceration and children's well-being: Findings from the fragile families and child well-being study. In J. M. Eddy & J. Poehlmann-Tynan (Eds.), *Handbook on children with incarcerated parents* (pp. 53–64). Springer.

Turney, K., & Wakefield, S. (2019). Criminal justice contact and inequality. *RSF: The Russell Sage Foundation Journal of the Social Sciences, 5*(1), 1–23.

Western, B., & Pettit, B. (2010). Incarceration and social inequality. *Daedalus, 139*(3), 8–19.

Wooldredge, J., Frank, J., Goulette, N., & Travis, L. (2015). Is the impact of cumulative disadvantage on sentencing greater for black defendants? *Criminology & Public Policy, 14*(2), 187–223.

Yabroff, R. K., Zhao, J., Han, X., & Zheng, Z. (2019). Prevalence and correlates of medical financial hardship in the USA. *Journal of General Internal Medicine, 34*(8), 1494–1502.

INDEX

For the benefit of digital users, indexed terms that span two pages (e.g., 52–53) may, on occasion, appear on only one of those pages.

Tables and figures are indicated by *t* and *f* following the page number

A

AACWA. *See* Adoption Assistance and Child Welfare Act (AACWA)
AAIDD. *See* American Association on Intellectual and Developmental Disabilities (AAIDD)
AARP. *See* American Association of Retired Persons (AARP)
ABC. *See* attachment and biobehavioral catchup (ABC)
abortion
  deaths related to
    CDC on, 503
  impact on women's development and physical health, 501–3
  laws, policies, practices impacting, 495–98
    coercive/compulsory laws, policies, practices, 500–1
    federal laws, policies practices, 495–97
    "global gag rule," 497
    Hyde Amendment, 496
    Mexico City Policy, 497
    pivotal SCOTUS cases, 495–96
  medication
    federal laws, policies, practices on, 496–97
    mifepristone for, 486
    state laws, policies, practices on, 497–98
  stress after
    American Psychological Association on, 505
    World Health Organization on, 501–2
abuse
  baby, 11
  child (*see* child abuse)
  external validity of, 199
  false denials of, 199
  risky and antisocial behaviors in adolescence and, 217–18
  sexual (*see* sexual abuse)
  substance (*see* substance abuse)
ACA. *See* Affordable Care Act (ACA)
academic performance
  early adversity impact on, 172
ACE Study. *See* Adverse Childhood Experiences (ACE) Study
Achieving Best Evidence in Criminal Proceedings, 68
ACP. *See* advance care planning (ACP)
acquiescence
  defined, 264, 460
  described, 460
ADA. *See* Americans With Disabilities Act (ADA)
Adams, M., 324
addiction
  parenting effects of, 15–16
ADEA. *See* Age Discrimination in Employment Act (ADEA)
ADHD. *See* attention-deficit/hyperactivity disorder (ADHD)
adjudication
  deferred, 308
adjudicative process
  older adults and, 631
Administration for Children and Families, 11
adolescence. *See also under* adolescent(s)
  biological changes during, 211–12
  cognitive development in, 355–56
  described, 209
  desire for autonomy in, 237–38
  maltreatment during
    introduction, 4–6
  neurological changes during, 211
  risky and antisocial behaviors during (*see* risky and antisocial behaviors: in adolescence)
  socioemotional development in, 355–56
  unstructured socializing during risky and antisocial behaviors related to, 219
adolescence limited (AL) trajectory of risk and antisocial behaviors, 212
adolescent(s). *See also under* adolescence
  antisocial behavior in, 209, 321 (*see also under* risky and antisocial behaviors: in adolescence)
  awareness of police practices by, 262–63
  behaviors of
    SCOTUS on, 322
  biological changes of, 211–12
  CD in, 39
  in court, 160
  development of
    autonomy in, 237–38
    cognitive, 235–36, 239–40
    disclosures impacted by, 239–41
    features of, 234–38
    memory and suggestibility impacts of, 243–44
    socioemotional, 236–38, 240–41
  disclosures by, 238–41
    developmental effects on, 239–41

663

adolescent(s) (cont.)
  incarceration of, 321 (see also under adolescent incarceration)
  justice related to
    developmental research on, 385 (see also under youth justice system: developmental research on)
    in juvenile and criminal court, 279 (see also under criminal court: youth in)
    history of, 280–84
    introduction, 279–80
  memory of, 242–45
  Miranda comprehension by, 262–63
  Miranda waivers for, 272
  Miranda warnings for
    effectiveness of, 267–68
  rebellion among, 39–41
  risky and antisocial behavior in, 209, 321 (see also under risky and antisocial behaviors: in adolescence)
  roles of, 264
  sexual victimization of
    in adult correction facilities, 330
  suggestibility of, 242–45
  as suspects, 257 (see also under adolescent suspects: police interrogation of)
  TGNC
    incarceration impacts on, 332–33
  unaccompanied migrant, 149 (see also unaccompanied migrant youth)
  as victims and witnesses, 233
    factors impacting, 233
    introduction, 233–34
    investigative interviewing protocols, 245–49 (see also investigative interviewing protocols for adolescents: memory and suggestibility impacts of)
adolescent autonomy, 237–38
adolescent incarceration, 321
  impacts of, 323–33
    COVID-19 pandemic, 329
    on diverse populations, 331–33 (see also under diverse populations: adolescent incarceration impacts on)
    families, 324–25

future employment, 326–27
mental health, 327–28
peers, 325–26
physical health, 328–29
psychosocial development, 329–30
recidivism, 323–24
school, 326–27
victimization, 330–31
LWOP
  SCOTUS on, 334
rates of
  history vs. current patterns, 322–23
reform schools, 324
strategies to decrease, 333–36
  community-based treatment, 335
  DMC mandate, 336
  JDAI, 334–35
  justice reinvestment initiatives, 334
  laws/policy reforms, 333–34
  MST, 335
  risk assessment instruments, 335–36
  RNR model, 335
adolescent limited (AL) offenders, 407, 410t
adolescent offenders
  punishment vs. leniency for, 203–4
  Supreme Court's leniency toward, 203–4
"adolescent-onset" pathway
  "childhood-onset" pathway vs., 39
adolescent rebellion, 39–41
adolescent suspects
  interrogation law as applied to, 260
  police interrogation of, 257 (see also under juvenile interrogation)
  BJS on, 257
  constitutional laws governing, 259–61
  deception used by, 270–71
  developmental principles relevant to, 261–67
  implications for practice, policy, and research, 271–73
  interrogative suggestibility in, 263–64
  introduction, 257–59
  special care in, 260
  statements by
    constitutional laws governing, 259–61

youth of color
  legal procedures and experiences among, 265–67
adoption, 169
  child welfare
    contact in, 184
  as child welfare practice, 177–85
  as context for children's recovery after early adversity, 171–76 (see also under early adversity)
  critical/sensitive periods for, 173–74
  defined, 169
  developmental trajectories following, 172–76
  differential plasticity and, 174–75
  domestic infant
    contact in, 183
  foster care, 179–80
  by gay men
    policies/practices/laws related to, 181–82
  intercountry
    contact in, 184–85
    policies/practices/laws related to, 180–81
  introduction, 169–70
  by lesbians
    policies/practices/laws related to, 181–82
  loss and, 177
  open (see open adoption)
  policies/practices/laws related to, 177–85
    adoption by lesbians and gay men, 181–82
    changes in, 178–85
    developmental science contributions to, 185–87
    foster care adoption, 179–80
    intercountry adoption, 180–81
    open adoption, 182–85
    postadoption contexts for development, 175–76
  research related to
    in understanding human development, 170–77
Adoption and Safe Families Act (ASFA), 8, 12, 136–37, 179–80, 485
Adoption Assistance and Child Welfare Act (AACWA), 136, 179–80, 480
Adoptio naturam imitatur, 178–79
adoption diversity
  emergence of, 178–85

adoption identity
  development construction of, 176–77
adoption loss, 177
adoptive identity
  developmental construction of, 176–77
adult(s)
  antisocial behavior in
    predicting, 406–7
  with developmental disabilities
    in criminal justice system, 449 (see also under developmental disabilities: in criminal justice system)
  deviancy in, 403 (see also under deviancy: in adulthood)
  emerging
    in legal system, 425–27 (see also under transition-age youth (TAY): in legal system)
  older (see older adults)
  risky behavior in
    theoretical understanding of, 407–10, 410t (see also under adult risky behavior)
  young (see young adults)
adult abuse
  child abuse vs., 613–15
adult correction facilities
  "culture of violence" in, 330
  sexual victimization of adolescents in, 330
adult development
  law and, 399
adulthood
  deviancy in, 403 (see also under deviancy: in adulthood)
  emerging, 355
    cognitive and socioemotional development in, 355–56
    introduction, 400–1
    legally constructed status of, 348–54 (see also under age of majority)
  modern
    sociocultural conceptions of, 355
  older adults (see aging)
  transition to, 354–56
    in legal system, 423 (see also under legal system: transitioning to adulthood in; transition-age youth [TAY])
  sociocultural conceptions of, 355
  structural influences on, 354–55

adultification
  of youth of color, 266–67
adult-onset offending
  characteristics of, 409
adult risky behavior, 407–10, 410t
  Moffitt's developmental taxonomy and, 407–9, 410t
  theoretical understanding of, 407–10, 410t
advance care planning (ACP). See also under end-of-life planning
  communication role in uptake of, 598
  described, 587
  goal of, 597
  for older adults, 587
  research perspectives on, 597–99
    COVID-19 impact, 598–99
    prevalence-related, 597
advance directives
  in end-of-life planning, 595–96
Advancing New Standards for Reproductive Health (ANSIRH, 502
Adverse Childhood Experiences (ACE) Study, 132–33
adversity
  early (see early adversity)
AFCC. See Association of Family and Conciliation Courts (AFCC)
affect
  restricted/shallow
    antisocial behavior related to, 41–45
affective empathy
  described, 43
Affordable Care Act (ACA), 652
  contraceptive coverage guarantee under, 499
  Dependent Coverage Mandate of, 354
  "Preventive Care Guidelines" of, 499
age
  as concept, 626
  crime and
    relationship between, 405–7
  driving, 353
  as factor in antisocial behavior, 210
  as factor in liberate misrepresentation, 199
  as factor in offending behavior, 410t
  as factor in risky and antisocial behavior, 209–10

  as factor in suggestibility, 199
  in giving sexual consent, 353
  of juvenile jurisdiction, 392
  old age; older adults (see aging)
  in right to purchase, possess, and consume alcohol, 353–54
"age bias"
  in sentencing older adults, 632
age–crime curve, 405–6
age–crime trends, 403–4
Age Discrimination in Employment Act (ADEA), 611–12
age of legal majority, 347. See also age of majority
age of majority, 347
  categorical
    dismantling of, 356–58
    inadequacy of, 347–48
  exceptions to, 353–54
  introduction, 347–48
  legal effects of, 349–53
    contract rights, 351
    disentitlement to parental and/or state support, 349–50
    FLSA, 351–52
    freedom from parental authority, 350–51
    right to full labor market participation, 351–52
    right to medical and procreative choice, 352–53
    right to political civic participation, 352
  legally constructed status of, 348–54
  historical background, 348–49
  legal effects of, 349–53
  rethinking, 347
  transition to adulthood, 354–56 (see also under adulthood: transition to)
"age out"
  of propensity for antisocial behavior, 428
Aggression Replacement Training
  in decreasing adolescent incarceration, 334
aging. See also older adults
  cognitive-related changes in, 628
  in criminal justice system, 625 (see also under older adults: in criminal justice system)
  BJS on, 635
  cognitive-related changes, 628
  implications for research, policy, and practice, 641–42
  introduction, 625–26

INDEX | 665

aging (cont.)
　　normative and pathological
　　　processes–related, 627–28
　　social psychological
　　　frameworks and theories,
　　　628–29
　　introduction, 401–2
　　issues related to, 626–29
　　normative and pathological
　　　processes in, 627–28
　　normative physical and sensory
　　　changes in, 627
　　in place, 589
　　SCM of, 628
　　stereotypes of, 628
aging inmates
　　costs related to, 635–36
　　current scholarship related to,
　　　629–41 (see also under aging:
　　　in criminal justice system)
　　end-of-life care–related issues,
　　　638
　　health care–related issues, 636–38
　　issues related to, 635–41
　　overcrowding-related issues,
　　　638–41
　　prevalence of, 635
　　proposed solutions for, 638–41
Agnew, R., 365
Ahlin, E.M., 330, 331
AL. See under adolescence limited
　　(AL)
alcohol
　　prenatal exposure to, 13–14
　　right to purchase, possess, and
　　　consume
　　　age of, 353–54
Alger, H., 567
allegation(s)
　　false
　　　by child witnesses, 198–202
Allen, K., 7
Allen v. Ornoski, 634–35
Alper, M., 561–62
Alzheimer's disease
　　death related to
　　　prevalence of, 589
American Academy of Pediatrics, 11
American Association of Retired
　　Persons (AARP), 626
American Association on
　　Intellectual and
　　Developmental Disabilities
　　(AAIDD), 449–50
American Bar Association
　　on collateral consequences of
　　　felony convictions, 575

American Geriatrics Society, 611–12
American Immigration Council,
　　157–58
American Institutes for Research
　　of National Reentry Resource
　　Center, 575
American Law Institute, 140
American Professional Society
　　on the Abuse of Children
　　(ASPAC)
　　Handbook on Child Maltreatment
　　　of, 245
American Psychiatric Association
　　(APA)
　　on IDs and developmental
　　　disabilities, 450
American Psychological Association
　　on stress after abortion, 505
　　Zero Tolerance Task Force of,
　　　367–68
American Psychologist, 399–400
Americans With Disabilities Act
　　(ADA), 636–37
Anderson, S., 562
Annie E. Casey Foundation, 334–35
ANSIRH. See Advancing New
　　Standards for Reproductive
　　Health (ANSIRH
Antaki, C., 460
antisocial behavior, 37. See also
　　conduct disorder (CD)
　　ADHD and, 214–15
　　in adolescence, 209, 321 (see also
　　　under risky and antisocial
　　　behaviors: in adolescence)
　　adolescent-onset pattern of
　　　conceptualization of, 40
　　adolescent rebellion, 39–41
　　in adults
　　　predicting, 406–7
　　age and, 210
　　causal theories of, 39–47
　　CD and, 39
　　developmental pathways to, 37
　　　adolescent rebellion, 39–41
　　　causal theories, 39–47
　　　CU traits, 39, 41–43, 44–47
　　　effective components of
　　　　conscious, 41–45
　　　emotional and behavioral
　　　　regulation, 45–47
　　　empathy, 41–45
　　　future directions in, 48–51
　　　guilt, 41–45
　　　implications for policy, 50–51
　　　implications for practice,
　　　　48–50

　　　implications for research, 48
　　　introduction, 37–38
　　　early vs. late starting, 40–41
　　　limited remorse and, 41–45
　　　propensity for
　　　　"age out" of, 428
antisocial traits
　　prosocial traits vs., 215
APA. See American Psychiatric
　　Association (APA)
Apel, R., 563
Applebaum, L.K., 453, 458
Applebaum, P.S., 453, 458
Arnett, J.J., 355
AS. See Asperger syndrome (AS)
ASD. See autism spectrum disorder
　　[ASD])
ASFA. See Adoption and Safe
　　Families Act (ASFA)
Ashcroft Directive, 593
Askren, H.A., 503, 505
ASPAC. See American Professional
　　Society on the Abuse of
　　Children (ASPAC)
Asperger syndrome (AS)
　　in criminal justice system, 459
assault(s)
　　simple
　　　by TAY, 426–27
Association of Family and
　　Conciliation Courts
　　(AFCC), 110
asylum
　　described, 154–55
Atkins v. Virginia, 450, 459, 634
attachment. See also attachment
　　theory
　　assessment of
　　　Strange Situation procedure
　　　　in, 115–16
　　for children younger than 3 years,
　　　109
　　developmental timing and,
　　　112–13
　　disorganized, 131
　　early adversity impact on, 172
　　important aspects of, 112–15
　　intergenerational transmission
　　　of, 10
　　to multiple caregivers, 114–15
　　parent–child
　　　child development related to,
　　　　130–33
　　patterns of, 131
　　secure vs. insecure, 10, 113–14
　　in social–emotional
　　　development, 18–19

"Attachment, Brain Science, and Children of Divorce," 110
attachment and biobehavioral catchup (ABC)
for infant maltreatment, 20–21
attachment patterns, 131
attachment styles
of children
memory performance related to, 65
attachment theory, 109
attachment to multiple caregivers, 114–15
described, 111–15
developmental timing, 112–13
secure vs. insecure attachment, 113–14
translating into policies for overnight parenting time for infants and toddlers, 119–21
"Attachment Theory, Separation, and Divorce," 110
attention-deficit/hyperactivity disorder (ADHD)
antisocial behavior and, 214–15
attitude(s)
of children
criminal court impact on, 94–95
dependency court impact on, 99–100
attitudinal outcomes
for children in criminal court, 94–95
for children in dependency court, 99–100
attorney(s). *See also specific types*
defense (*see* defense attorneys)
prosecuting (*see* prosecutors)
for unaccompanied migrant youth
accessing of, 153
attorney–client relationships
youth of color–related disadvantages among, 289
"attorney-in-fact," 480–81
Auriemma, C.L., 599
Austin, J., 572
authority(ies)
juvenile's perceptions of and compliance with, 264–65
autism spectrum disorder (ASD). *See also under* developmental disabilities; intellectual disabilities (IDs)
in criminal justice system, 449
accommodations and reduced threshold for scrutiny, 467

balancing autonomy and vulnerability, 467–68
identification and screening efforts, 467
pathways into, 453–55
potential consequences of, 426–59 (*see also under* criminal justice system: cognitive defects in)
prevalence of, 451–53
social skills deficits impact, 459–66 (*see also under* criminal justice system: social skills deficits impact on)
defined, 451
described, 451
autobiographical memory, 58
of children
factors impacting, 158
described, 58
development of, 64
factors affecting, 59–60
autonomy
adolescent, 237–38
in end-of-life planning, 590
vulnerability and
balancing of, 467–68
Avery, B., 576

# B
baby(ies)
repeated abuse of, 11
Babylonian Code of Hammurabi
adoption and, 178
"Back the Blue" movement, 517–18
Baldwin, J., 517
Banks, M., 466
Barnert, E.S., 327, 329
Barnes, J.C., 216, 571–72
Bartholet, E., 139
basic research
youth justice system–related, 387
Basto-Pereira, M., 325
"battered-child syndrome," 135
Beauchamp, T.L., 590
Beaver, K.M., 216
Beckley, A.L., 410–11
behavior(s)
antisocial (*see* antisocial behavior)
deviant behavior (*see under* deviancy)
impulsive (*see* impulsive behavior)
offending (*see* offending behavior)
parenting (*see* parenting behaviors)

problems related to (*see* behavior problems)
risky (*see* risky and antisocial behaviors)
adult (*see* adult risky behavior)
behavioral regulation
development of, 45–47
Behavioral Risk Factor Surveillance System, 589
behavior problems
in social–emotional development, 19
BEIP. *See* Bucharest Early Intervention Project (BEIP)
beneficence
in end-of-life planning, 590
Berliner, L., 92
Bernstein, A., 506
Bernstein, N., 564
Bersani, B.E., 571–72
Best Practices in Forensic Mental Health Assessment series, 458
bias(es)
age
in sentencing older adults, 632
Biden administration
detention policy of, 161
Biden, J., Pres., 496, 654–55
Binswanger, I.A., 566
bio–ecological model. *See* social–ecological model
BIPOC. *See* Black, Indigenous, and other people of color (BIPOC)
Biringen, Z., 116
Bischoff, K.E., 597
Bixby Center for Global Reproductive Health
of UCSF, 502
BJS. *See* Bureau of Justice Statistics (BJS)
Black, Indigenous, and other people of color (BIPOC)
adolescent incarceration impacts on, 331–32
Black Lives Matter movement, 539, 541
Black youth. *See also* youth of color
punitive dispositions for, 293
Blair, L., 310
Blokland, A.A., 408–9
Bloom, K.C., 503, 505
"Blue Lives Matter" movement, 517–18
Boessen, A., 331–32
Bohnenkamp, J.H., 369

INDEX | 667

Bollich-Ziegler, K.L., 330
Bonell, C., 370
Bontrager Ryon, S., 323–24
BOP. *See* Bureau of Prisons (BOP)
Bor, J., 529–30
Bowlby, J., 111, 112–13
Brabeck, K.M., 149, 203, 204
Bradford, B., 533–34
brain
  cognitive control systems of, 235–36
  underdeveloped
    TAY in legal system related to, 427–29
brain development
  child development impact of, 131–33
  early adversity impact on, 171
  parenting quality impact on, 10
  stress effects on, 131–32
Brank, E.M., 611, 626, 654
Brewer, N., 452
Brockmann, B, 573
Brodzinsky, D.M., 169
Bronfenbrenner, U., 187, 365–66, 386, 518, 530–31, 545
Brophy, P., 591–92
Brown, D.A., 159
Browning, C.R., 223
Brown, J.D., 577
Brown, L.F., 85
Brown, M., 529–30
Brown, S.L., 327, 572
Brown v. Mississippi, 270
Bruck, M., 199
Bryant-Davis, T., 539
Bucharest Early Intervention Project (BEIP), 173
Buck v. Bell, 500
Bull, 618–19
Bureau of Justice Statistics (BJS)
  on adolescent incarceration victimization, 119–330
  on aging prison population, 635
  on maternal incarceration, 478–79
  on police interrogation of adolescent suspects, 257
Bureau of Prisons (BOP)
  on compassionate release statutes, 639–40
Burke, K.C., 517, 655–56
Burrow, J.D., 634
Burton, A.L., 576–77
Bush, G.W., Pres., 593
Bushway, S.D., 563
Byer, J., Judge, 374

C

CACs. *See* Child Advocacy Centers (CACs)
California Clearinghouse for Child Welfare, 20–21
callous–unemotional (CU) traits
  CD and, 39, 41–43, 44–47
  in early offenders, 203
Cambridge Study in Delinquent Development (CSDD), 408–9, 411–12, 413, 415
cannabis
  prenatal use impact of, 15
CAPE-1. *See* Clinical Assessment of Prosocial Emotions (CAPE-1)
capital punishment
  for persons with IDs
    SCOTUS on, 459
CAPTA. *See* Child Abuse Prevention and Treatment Act (CAPTA)
caregiver(s)
  multiple
    attachment to, 114–15
  for older adults, 615–16
caregiver–child relationship
  development shaped by, 10
caregiving
  maternal
    genetic effects of, 9–10
Carlson, J., 526
Carter, A.J., 454
categorical violence consequences (CVCs), 575–76
Cauffman, E., 331–32, 423, 532–33, 534
causal theories
  of antisocial behavior, 39–47
Cavanaugh, C., 391, 392, 393, 395, 534
CBCL. *See* Child Behavior Checklist (CBCL)
CBP. *See* Customs Border Protection (CBP)
CCTV
  children testifying via, 93–94
CD. *See* conduct disorder (CD)
CDC. *See* Centers for Disease Control and Prevention (CDC)
Ceci, S.J., 199, 461
"ceiling of care"
  defined, 599
Center for Policing Equity and Fair and Impartial Policing, 543
Centers for Disease Control and Prevention (CDC)
  on abortion-related deaths, 503
  Task Force on Community Preventive Services of, 294
  on unintended pregnancy, 494
Centers for Medicare and Medicaid (CMS)
  on telemedicine, 603
Chae, Y., 65
Chaplin, E., 454
Charles, V.E., 504–5
Chauvin, D., 517–18
"Checklist of Indicators," 467
child abuse
  adult abuse vs., 613–15
  brain development effects of, 131–33
  memory and suggestibility impact in children, 65–66
  memory performance related to, 65–66
  prevalence of, 7–8
Child Abuse Prevention and Treatment Act (CAPTA), 8, 11–12, 135–36
Child Advocacy Centers (CACs), 91, 101
Child Behavior Checklist (CBCL), 91
  Delinquency and Aggression subscales of, 416
childbirth
  impact on women's development and physical health, 503–4
child detention
  described, 151–52
  developmental impact of, 160–62
  history of, 152–53
child development, 129
  brain development effects on, 131–33
  child maltreatment and, 130–33
  CWS and
    interrelationship of, 133–38
    (*see also under* child welfare system (CWS): child development and)
  introduction, 129–30
  parent–child attachment impact on, 130–33
  risk factors impacting, 130–33
  state intervention related to risks associated with, 133
  stress effects on, 131–32
childhood. *See* children
"childhood-onset" pathway
  "adolescent-onset" pathway vs., 39

child maltreatment
  child development impact of, 130–33
  child welfare laws related to, 8
  costs associated with, 7–8
  developmental delays related to prevalence of, 11
  developmental impact of, 9
  forms of, 13–20
    prenatal maltreatment, 13–16 (see also under prenatal exposure to substances [PSE])
  in infancy
    consequences of (see also infant maltreatment)
    intervention following unique needs for, 10–11
  introduction, 2
child neglect
  brain development effects of, 131–33
child offenders
  CU traits in, 203
  punishment vs. leniency for, 203–4
child–parent psychotherapy (CPP)
  for infant maltreatment, 21
Child Protective Services (CPS), 10
  sexual abuse found by case example, 85–86
children
  autobiographical memory of factors impacting, 158
  beliefs of
    criminal court experience impact on, 94–95
    dependency court impact on, 99–100
  Black (see youth of color)
  CD in, 39
  in criminal court, 88–95 (see also criminal court(s), children in)
    developmental science of, 85 (see also under criminal court(s), children in)
  in dependency court, 95–101 (see also dependency court(s): children in)
    developmental science of, 85
  disclosure by, 66–67
  forensic interviewing of, 68–70
  in-court testimony by, 70–71
  legal involvement of
    causality-related questions, 87–88
    methodological considerations, 86–88

propensity score matching, 87–88
    random assignment, 87
    recruitment challenges, 87
  maltreatment of (see child maltreatment)
  memory in, 57 (see also under memory in children)
  suggestibility in, 57 (see also under suggestibility in children)
  as suspects
    police interrogation of, 257 (see also under adolescent suspects: police interrogation of)
  unaccompanied migrant (see unaccompanied migrant youth)
  welfare of
    early maltreatment–related parental rights vs., 196–98
  as witnesses
    false allegations vs. false denials, 198–202
  younger than 3 years
    attachment of, 109 (see also under attachment)
    parenting time for, 109 (see also under attachment)
children maltreatment
  introduction, 2
Childress, J.F., 590
child sexual abuse accommodation syndrome (CSAAS), 67, 200
child sexual exploitation and abuse (CSEA) victims, 239, 241, 247, 248
child testimony
  developmental perspective on, 158–60
  memory and, 158
  traumatic experiences impact on, 158
child welfare adoptions
  contact in, 184
child welfare laws/policies/practices
  adoption as, 177–85
  purpose of, 8
  types of, 8
child welfare system (CWS), 129
  child development and, 129
  early CWS, 135
  federal involvement, 135–37
  federal laws impact, 137–38
  focus-related concerns, 138–40
  future directions, 140–43
  legal standards, 138

poverty, 139
  racial disproportionality/racial disparities, 134–35
  risks associated with, 133
  scholarly debates, 138–40
  early, 135
  focus of
    concerns about, 138–40
    parenting interventions designed for, 8
  in Progressive Era, 135
  racial disproportionality/racial disparities associated with, 134–35
child witness(es)
  false allegations vs. false denials by, 198–202
CI. See Cognitive Interview (CI)
cigarettes
  prenatal exposure to, 14
civil citation programs
  for youth, 306–7
Clark, N.K., 460
Clark, S., 524
Clark, V.A., 570–71
Cleary, H.M.D., 257
Clinical Assessment of Prosocial Emotions (CAPE-1), 50
clinical research
  developmental research and integration of, 37–38
Clinton, B., Pres., 136
"cloak of competence"
  IDs and, 453
Close, D.W., 467
Cloud, M., 456
CMS. See Centers for Medicare and Medicaid (CMS)
cocaine
  prenatal exposure to, 14–15
Cochrane, D.M., 321
Cocker, A.G., 451–52
"Coffee with a Cop," 542
cognition
  cold
    described, 235
  deficits in
    in criminal justice system, 426–59 (see also specific types and under criminal justice system: cognitive defects in)
cognitive control system
  described, 356
cognitive decline
  confusion and, 589
  memory loss and, 589
  in older adults, 589

INDEX | 669

cognitive development
  of adolescents, 235–36, 239–40, 355–56
    disclosures impacted by, 239–40
    memory and suggestibility impacts of, 243–44
  maltreatment impact on, 19–20
  psychosocial development and "maturity gap" between, 427, 428f
cognitive empathy
  described, 43
cognitive functioning
  memory and suggestibility impact in children, 62–63
Cognitive Interview (CI), 245–46, 618–19
cognitive neuroscience
  impact on juvenile justice, 283–84
cognitive traits
  risky and antisocial behaviors in adolescence and, 214–15
Cohen, M.A., 415
Cohen, S.A., 506
cold cognition
  described, 235
Cole, T., 496
Colwell, L.H., 452
Comas-Díaz, L., 539
communication
  end-of-life planning–related, 604
  in uptake of ACP
    research perspectives on, 598
community-based treatment
  in decreasing adolescent incarceration, 335
community context
  risky and antisocial behaviors in adolescence related to, 222–24
compassionate release statues, 639
Compassion & Choices
  in right-to-die movement, 601
competence
  context-specific, 357–58
  defined, 286–87
competence to plead guilty
  social skills deficits impact on, 464–66
competence to stand trial (CST), 457–59
  social skills deficits impact on, 464–66
compliance
  defined, 264
Comprehensive Addiction and Recovery Act of 2016, 12

conduct disorder (CD)
  antisocial behavior and, 39
  childhood vs. adolescent types of, 39
  developmental pathways to, 37 (see also under antisocial behavior)
  emotional and behavioral regulation in, 45–47
  traits associated with, 39, 41–43, 44–47
Coney Barrett, A., Justice, 496
confabulation
  described, 460
conflict(s)
  family (see family conflict)
confusion
  cognitive decline and, 589
Connett, A.V., 565
Connolly, E.J., 216
conscience
  affective components of, 41–45
  described, 44
consent
  sexual
    age-related giving of, 353
contagion
  emotional
    defined, 43
Conte, J.R., 92
context-specific competence, 357–58
contraception
  impact on women's development and physical health, 503
  laws/policies/practices impacting access to, 498–501
    coercive/compulsory, 500–1
    federal laws/policies/practices, 498–99
    pivotal SCOTUS cases, 498–99
    state laws/policies/practices, 499–500
  Trump administration on, 499
contract rights, 351
Controlled Substances Act (CSA), 593
conversation(s)
  about past
    in language development, 64
  end-of-life planning–related, 604
Cook, D., 522
Cooper, A., 157
correction facilities
  adult (see adult correction facilities)

Couloute, L., 563, 568–69, 570
court(s)
  adolescents in, 160
  criminal (see criminal court)
  juvenile (see juvenile court)
  juvenile mental health, 310–11
  peer, 311–12
  processes of, 656
  specialty youth, 309
  teen, 311–12, 373–74
  truancy, 374
  young adult (see young adult courts [YACs])
Courtney, S.M.E., 571
court processing, 656
  informal
    rates of, 304–5
  traditional
    alternatives to, 303 (see also specific types and youth: alternatives to traditional court processing for)
courtroom(s)
  immigration
    unaccompanied migrant youth impact of, 162–63
courtroom testimony
  by children, 70–72, 92–94, 158–60
court-sponsored diversion
  for youth, 308–9
court teams
  infant–toddler
    for infant maltreatment, 22
COVID-19 pandemic
  ACP impact of
    research perspectives on, 598–99
  adolescent incarceration impact of, 329
  medication abortion impact of, 498
  telemedicine during, 601–3
Coyle, S., 366
CPP. See child–parent psychotherapy (CPP)
CPS. See Child Protective Services (CPS)
Crane, L., 463–64
Crane, M.G., 257
credulity
  defined, 460–61
crime
  age and
    relationship between, 405–7
  older adults as perpetrators of, 629–30

onset of
   defined, 410–11
criminal case
   progression of, 89
criminal court
   children in, 88–95
      attitudinal outcomes for, 94–95
      cross-examination of, 93
      developmental science of, 85
      future directions, 101–2
      introduction, 88–89
      legal questioning, 92–94 (see also legal questioning: of children in criminal court)
      process, 89–90
      socioemotional outcomes for, 90–92
   described, 279
   dispositions in, 292–94
   guilty pleas in, 290–92
   modern processes, 284–86
   plea process in
      parents' role in, 292
   sentencing in, 292–94
   trial stage in, 286–89
   youth in, 279 (see also under adolescent(s): in juvenile and criminal court)
      future directions, 295–96
      introduction, 279–80
criminal court process
   for children, 89–90
criminal justice system
   AS in, 459
   aging in, 625 (see also under aging, in criminal justice system)
   ASD in, 449 (see also under autism spectrum disorder [ASD])
   cognitive defects in
      capacity to waive Miranda rights, 455–56
      CST, 457–59
      culpability, 459
      potential consequences of, 426–59
   developmental disabilities in, 449 (see also under autism spectrum disorders (ASDs): in criminal justice system)
   IDs in, 449 (see also under intellectual disabilities (IDs): in criminal justice system)
   involvement of (see criminal justice system involvement)

older adults in (see also aging inmates)
   social skills deficits impact on, 459–66
      competence to plead guilty, 464–66
      CST, 464–66
      eyewitness identification, 461–63
      memory-related, 461–63
      waiver of Miranda rights and custodial interrogation, 463–64
criminal justice system
   involvement, 655–56
   court processes, 656
   law enforcement, 655–56
   prison-related, 656–58
criminal prosecution
   youth impact of, 294–95
Cross, D., 369
cross-examination
   goal of, 93
Cross, S.H., 590
Cross, W.E., Jr., 545
Cruzan, N., 592
Cruzan v. Director, Missouri Department of Health, 592
crystallized intelligence
   aging and, 612–13
CSA. See Controlled Substances Act (CSA)
CSAAS. See child sexual abuse accommodation syndrome (CSAAS)
CSDD. See Cambridge Study in Delinquent Development (CSDD)
CSEA victims. See child sexual exploitation and abuse (CSEA) victims
CST. See competence to stand trial (CST)
Cullen, F.T., 218, 404
culpability
   in criminal justice system, 459
cultural socialization
   by parents of color, 527–28
culture
   as factor in children's false memories, 60
"culture of violence"
   in adults correction facilities, 330
Cunningham, L., 351
custodial interrogation
   coercive nature of, 259
   described, 257

waiver of
   social skills deficits impact on, 463–64
custody
   determination of tests in, 259
Customs Border Protection (CBP), 151
CU traits. See callous–unemotional (CU) traits
CVCs. See categorical violence consequences (CVCs)
CWS. See child welfare system (CWS)

D

Daftary-Kapur, T., 279
Darling-Hammond, S., 370
David, H.P., 509
Davis, D., 264, 266
D.B. v. North Carolina, 260–61
DDNR order. See durable do-not-resuscitate (DDNR) order
death
   taboos related to erasing, 604
death penalty
   for older adults, 634–35
death with dignity laws, 594
deception
   police using
      with adolescent suspects, 270–71
decision making
   end-of-life (see end-of-life planning)
Deese Roediger McDermott (DRM) paradigm, 243
defendant(s)
   older adults as, 631–35
defense attorneys
   legal questioning of children in criminal court by, 92–93
deferred adjudication, 308
delegation of parental authority (DOPA), 480–81, 487
delinquency
   juvenile (see juvenile delinquency)
Delinquency and Aggression subscales
   of CBCL, 416
demographics
   memory and suggestibility impact on children in children, 59–60
Demuth, S., 565–66
denial(s)
   false (see false denial[s])

Denkowski, G.C., 451–52
Denkowski, K.M., 451–52
Dennison, C.R., 565–66
dependency court(s)
  children in, 95–101
    attitudinal outcomes for, 99–100
    developmental science of, 85
    future directions, 101–2
    introduction, 95–96
    process, 96–97
    socioemotional outcomes for, 97–99
  described, 95–96
Dependent Coverage Mandate of ACA, 354
de-sexualization
  of older adults, 614
detention
  child (*see under* child detention)
  developmental impact of, 160–62
  of unaccompanies migrant youth
    legal process for, 151–53
development
  adolescent
    features of (*see also* adolescent(s): development of)
    adoption research in understanding, 170–77 (*see also under* adoption)
  adult
    law and, 399
  of autobiographical memory, 64
  brain (*see* brain development)
  caregiver–child relationship in shaping, 10
  child (*see* child development)
  cognitive (*see* cognitive development)
  early (*see* early development)
  early adversity impact on, 171–72
  environment impact on, 8
  exosystem impacts on, 526–27
  language (*see* language development)
  macrosystem impacts on, 521*f*, 523–24
  maltreatment in infants impact on, 8–13, 9*f*
  mesosystem impacts on, 521*f*, 529–30
  microsystem impacts on, 532–35
  neurobiological (*see* neurobiological development)
  postadoption contexts for, 175–76
  psychosocial (*see* psychosocial development)
  socioemotional (*see* socioemotional development)
  of unaccompanied migrant youth immigration proceedings impact on, 160–63
  women's (*see* women's development)
developmental delays
  child maltreatment–related prevalence of, 11
developmental disabilities. *See also under* autism spectrum disorder (ASD); intellectual disabilities (IDs)
  AAIDD on, 449–50
  APA on, 450
  in criminal justice system, 449
    accommodations and reduced threshold for scrutiny, 467
    balancing autonomy and vulnerability, 467–68
    identification and screening efforts, 467
    introduction, 449
    pathways into, 453–55
    potential consequences of, 426–59 (*see also under* criminal justice system: cognitive defects in)
    prevalence of, 451–53
    social skills deficits impact, 459–66 (*see also under* criminal justice system: social skills deficits impact on)
  defined, 449–51
"developmental era"
  in youth justice reform, 386
developmental pathways
  to antisocial behavior, 37 (*see also* antisocial behavior: developmental pathways to)
developmental psychology
  impact on juvenile justice, 283–84
  questions related to, 170
  youth justice system–related, 385 (*see also under* youth justice system: developmental research on)
developmental psychopathology, 388
developmental research
  clinical research and integration of, 37–38
  policy-minded, 195
  youth justice system–related, 385 (*see also under* youth justice system: developmental research on)
developmental science
  adoption-related policies/practices/laws and, 185–87
  impact on juvenile justice, 283–84
developmental taxonomy
  Moffitt's, 404, 406, 407–9
developmental timing
  attachment related to, 112–13
deviancy
  in adulthood, 403
  age-related, 405–7
  introduction, 403–5
  policy and practice implications, 414–16
  research implications, 413–14
  age–crime trends, 403–4
DHS
  Office of Chief Counsel for, 154
Dianiska, R., 233
differential plasticity
  adoption and, 174–75
  described, 174
  examples of, 174–75
DiIulio, J., 282–83
DiPietro, S.M., 571–72
disability(ies)
  developmental (*see* developmental disabilities)
  "hospitalization-associated," 589
  intellectual (*see* intellectual disabilities [IDs])
disclosure(s)
  by adolescents, 238–41
  by children, 66–67
  substantiation dependence on, 199–200
disclosure and recantation
  memory and suggestibility impact in children, 66–67
disclosure processes
  memory in children–related, 68–72 (*see also under* memory in children: application in legal system)
disorganized attachment, 131
disposition(s)
  in juvenile and criminal court, 292–94
  punitive
    for Black youth, 293
  racial disparities related to, 293
disproportional minority contact (DMC) mandate

in decreasing adolescent
  incarceration, 336
diverse populations
  adolescent incarceration impacts
    on, 331–33
      gender and sexual minorities,
        332–33
      racial and ethnic disparities,
        331–32
diversion programs
  described, 425, 431f
  school-based, 372–74 (see
    also under school-based
    diversion programs)
  for TAY, 308–9, 430–41
    correctional-based, 432–33
    court-sponsored, 308–9
    described, 425, 431f
    diversion outcome research,
      433–34
    vs. formal system involvement,
      433
    introduction, 430–37, 431f
    limitations of, 434–37
    police-led, 306–7
    positive life outcomes related
      to, 434
    posttrial, 432
    prearrest, 432
    pretrial, 432
    quality of, 433–34
    racial disparities in diversion
      research, 434
    types of, 432–34, 435t (see also
      specific types)
    typology related to, 432–33
diversion research
  outcome-related, 433–34
  racial disparities in, 434
Division of Young Offender Parole
  and Reentry Services
  under Youthful Offender Act, 432
Dixon, T.L., 527
DMC mandate. See disproportional
  minority contact (DMC)
  mandate
Dmitrieva, J., 329
DNACPR. See "do not attempt
  cardiopulmonary
  resuscitation (DNACPR)
Dobbs v. Jackson Women's Health
  Organization, 493–94, 498
doctrine of emancipation, 350
domestic infant adoptions
  contact in, 183
dominance
  defined, 219

"do not attempt cardiopulmonary
  resuscitation (DNACPR),
  598–99
DOPA. See delegation of parental
  authority (DOPA)
Dowden, C., 572
Dowd, N.E., 143
DPOAHC. See durable power of
  attorney for health care
  (POACH)
driving age, 353
DRM paradigm. See Deese
  Roediger McDermott
  (DRM) paradigm
drug(s)
  prenatal exposure to, 14–15
Ducat, C., 303
Dudley, M., 161–62
due process
  absence of
    informal processing of juvenile
      offenders, 314–16
    criminalization of juvenile court
      and, 282–83
durable do-not-resuscitate (DDNR)
  order, 596
durable power of attorney for health
  care (DPOAHC), 595–96
Durose, M.R., 561–62
Dusky v. United States, 286–87, 288,
  457, 464–65
Dwyer, J.G., 139
dying
  taboos related to
    erasing, 603–5

E

early adversity
  child's recovery after
    adoption as context for,
      171–76
  developmental consequences of,
    171–72
  physical development effects
    of, 171
early development
  environment in, 9f, 9
  genetics in, 9f, 9
  maltreatment impact on, 9
  science of, 9f, 9–10
Early Head Start, 20–21
early maltreatment
  parental rights vs. children's
    welfare, 196–98
"early-starter" pathway
  "later-starter" pathway vs., 39
Eberhardt, J.L., 540–41

EBH–CRP intervention. See
  Emotional and Behavioral
  Health–Crisis Response and
  Prevention (EBH–CRP)
  intervention
economics
  education and
    reproductive rights and,
      506–7
education
  economics and
    reproductive rights and,
      506–7
EF. See executive functions/
  functioning [EF])
Eggleston, E.P., 410–11
Eisen, M.L., 61
Eisenstadt v. Baird, 498–99
Elder Justice Center, 631
elder law
  defined, 611–12
elderly
  defined, 611–12
Eleazer Courtroom
  of Stetson University, 631
Ellis, J., 458–59
Ellis, L., 214–15
emancipation
  doctrine of, 350
emergency medical services (EMS)
  POLST in, 596
emergency situations in health care
  in end-of-life planning, 595
emerging adulthood, 355
Emery, R.E., 117–18
emotion(s)
  prosocial
    described, 41
  regulation of (see emotional
    regulation)
Emotional and Behavioral Health–
  Crisis Response and
  Prevention (EBH–CRP)
  intervention, 363–64, 369
emotional contagion
  defined, 43
emotional reactivity
  defined, 43
emotional regulation
  development of, 45–47
  capacity in, 43
empathy
  affective
    described, 43
  cognitive
    described, 43
  components of, 43

empathy (cont.)
    defined, 43
    lack of
        antisocial behavior related to, 41–45
employment
    after prisoner reentry, 568–69
EMS. See emergency medical services (EMS)
end of life
    legal decisions on
        seminal and precedent-setting, 591–94
    for older adults
        characteristics of, 588, 589–90
end-of-life care
    for aging inmates, 638
    call for better
        research perspectives on, 597
end-of-life decision making. (see end-of-life planning)
end-of-life issues
    national organizations dedicated to, 600–1
end-of-life planning, 591–94
    documents related to, 597–99 (see also under end-of-life planning documents)
    evolution of, 591–94
    future directions in, 603–5
        conversations/communication, 604
        enact stronger/more person-centered consent laws, 605
        erasing taboos about death and dying, 604
        improve planning documents, 604
        increase use of POLST/MOLST/POST, 604–5
        provide more equitable health care, 605
    mechanisms for, 595–96
        advance directives, 595–96
        DDNR order, 596
        DPOAHCo, 595–96
        POLST/MOLST/POST, 596, 604–5
    for older adults (see also under older adults: end-of-life planning for)
    principles undergirding, 590–91
        autonomy, 590
        beneficence, 590
        justice, 591
        nonmaleficence, 590
    seminal and precedent-setting legal decisions on, 591–94

end-of-life planning documents, 597–99. See also specific documents
    improving, 604
    research perspectives on, 597–99
        ACP prevalence, 597
        call for better end-of-life care, 597
        communication role in uptake of ACP, 598
        COVID-19 pandemic impact on ACP, 598–99
        defining ACT, 597
England, B.G., 113–14, 119
Enriquez, R., 85, 200–1
environment(s)
    in early human development, 9f, 9
    epigenetics and, 9
    family (see family environment[s])
    impact on human development, 8
    school (see school environment)
EOIR. See Executive Office for Immigration Review (EOIR)
epigenetics
    environment and, 9
    in risky and antisocial behaviors in adolescence, 213–15
equifinality
    described, 38
Erickson, E.H., 614
Erickson, K., 456
Erickson, S.L., 464
Erickson, W.B., 618
Estelle v. Gamble, 636–37
ethical considerations
    in end-of-life planning for older adults, 587
ethnic disparities
    adolescent incarceration–related, 331–32
    in informal court processing for youth, 312–13
    in juvenile justice, 374–75
    in TAY arrests, 426
Evans, 244
event characteristics
    memory and suggestibility of impact on children, 60–61
Everington, C., 458–59
evocative rGE, 217
execution
    of older adults, 634–35
executive functions/functioning (EF)

described, 63
early adversity impact on, 172
intelligence and
    in children, 63
memory and suggestibility of
    impact on children, 62–63
memory recall and
    in children, 63
suggestibility and
    in children, 63
Executive Office for Immigration Review (EOIR), 162
Executive Order No. 13769, 522–23
Executive Order on Advancing Racial Equity and Support for Underserved Communities Through the Federal Government, 654–55
exosystem
    development and well-being impacts of, 526–27
    implications for policy and practice, 541–42
    policing as institution and in practice, 521f, 524–30, 541–42
experience(s)
    repeated
        children's memory impacted by, 60–61
    traumatic
        child testimony impacted by, 158
external validity
    of abuse, 199
eyewitness(es)
    older adults as (see older adult eyewitnesses)
eyewitness identification
    social skills deficits impact on, 461–63
eyewitness research, 617–19. (see also under older adults: as witnesses)
    described, 617–19
    older adults–related, 617–19 (see also under older adult eyewitnesses)

F

Fabricius, W.V., 109, 204–5
Fader, J., 578–79
Fair Labor Standards Act (FLSA), 351–52
false allegations
    false denials vs.
        by child witnesses, 198–202
false denial(s)
    of abuse, 199

by child witnesses, 198–202
false allegations vs.
   by child witnesses, 198–202
false memories
   cultural differences in, 60
Families First Prevention Services Act (FFPSA), 8, 12–13
family(ies)
   adolescent incarceration impact on, 324–25
   influence on risky and antisocial behaviors in adolescence, 215–18
family conflict
   risky and antisocial behaviors in adolescence and, 217–18
Family Court Review, 110, 116–17
family environment(s)
   trajectories of risky and antisocial behaviors in adolescence impact on, 216–18
Family First Prevention Services Act, 137
Family Law and the Indissolubility of Parenthood, 109
Family Preservation and Family Support Act, 136
family preservation programs
   "family support services" vs., 142
family relationships
   after prisoner reentry, 571–72
Family Sentencing Alternative Pilot Program, 482
"family support services"
   family preservation programs vs., 142
Farber, H.B., 269
Farrall, S., 568, 574
Farrington, D.P., 408–9, 411–12, 415
Farr, R.H., 176
FASD. *See* fetal alcohol spectrum disorders (FASD)
father(s)
   parenting by
      child development impact of, 114–15
father–child relationships
   overnight parenting time impact on, 118
Fazel, S., 451–52
federal child welfare permanency timelines
   incarcerated parents impacted by, 485
felony convictions
   collateral consequences of, 429*f*, 429–30, 575–77
Ferguson, G.M., 540

Fergusson, 223
fetal alcohol spectrum disorders (FASD)
   infants born with, 12
Feyerherm, W.H., 335–36
FFPSA. *See* Families First Prevention Services Act (FFPSA)
financial exploitation
   of older adults, 613–15
Fine, A.D., 363, 532–33
Fine, M., 545
Finlay, W.M.L., 460
Fiske, S.T., 612
Fissel, E.R., 368
Flinn, M.V., 113–14, 119
Flores settlement agreement, 152, 153, 156, 163
Flower, L., 424
Floyd, G., 376–77, 517–18, 524, 540, 541
FLSA. *See* Fair Labor Standards Act (FLSA)
Fondacaro, M., 393–94
Food and Drug Administration (FDA)
   on medication abortion, 496–97
foolish action
   defined, 461
Ford v. Wainwright, 634
forensic interviewing
   of children, 68–70
   protocols for, 68
Forslund, T., 110, 116–17, 122
Fortas, Justice, 282
foster care
   infants in
      PSE and, 13
   unique needs for, 11
foster care adoption, 179–80
"foster care drift," 136
Fountain, E.N., 289, 292, 303, 388
Fourth Amendment issues of consent to search and seizure
   SCOTUS on, 538
Frazier v. Cupp, 270, 464
Freckelton, 454
Frick, P.J., 37, 203–4
Fried, T.R., 598
Friendly Schools Project (FSP), 363–64
   in enhancing school safety, 369
FSIQ scores. *See* full-scale IQ (FSIQ) scores
FSP. *See* Friendly Schools Project (FSP)
full-scale IQ (FSIQ) scores, 458

future employment
   adolescent incarceration impact on, 326–27

G

Gaines, J., 573, 576
Gallup Student Poll
   on school safety, 364
Garcia-Bahos, 619
Garcia, S.R., 149
Gardner, M., 221–22
Garretson, H.J., 576
Gase, L.N., 311–12, 331
gay men
   adoption by
      policies/practices/laws related to, 181–82
gender
   as factor in memory and suggestibility in children, 59
gender minorities
   adolescent incarceration impacts on, 332–33
gene(s)
   described, 9
gene–environment correlation (rGE), 213–14
   evocative, 217
general strain theory (GST)
   in linkages between school safety and juvenile delinquency, 365
general theory of crime (GTC), 409–10, 410*t*
genetics
   in early human development, 9*f*, 9
   maternal caregiving impact on, 9–10
   in risky and antisocial behaviors in adolescence, 213–15
George, C., 119
George Washington University
   POP of, 639
Gianesini, J., 452
Gillespie, M.L., 423, 652–53
Gilman, A.B., 327
Giordano, P.C., 568
"global gag rule," 497
Glucksburg, H., 592–93
Glueck, S.S., 405–6
Godinez v. Moran, 465, 631
Goff, P.A., 523
Goldfarb, D.A., 100
Golding, J.M., 616
Goldstein, N.E.S., 542
Golombok, S., 175
Gonçalves, L.C., 327–28
Gonzalez, D., 149
Goodman-Brown, 248–49
Goodman, G.S., 85

Goodwin, M., 493
Goring, C., 210
Gorski, T.T., 566
Gottfredson, M.R., 210, 218, 407, 409, 629
Government Accountability Office report
    on consequences of felony convictions, 429–30
Graham, H., 568, 579
Graham, S., 531–32
Graham v. Florida, 293
grandparents
    assistance for, 657–58
Greene, E., 639
Greenspan, S., 455, 460–61
GRHs. *See* ground rules hearings (GRHs)
Griego, A.W., 462
Grisso, T., 262, 290–91, 385, 387
Griswold v. Connecticut, 498–99
Grotevant, H.D., 169
ground rules hearings (GRHs), 200–1
growth hormones
    release of
        in puberty, 211
GSS. *See* Gudjonsson Suggestibility Scale (GSS)
GST. *See* general strain theory (GST)
GTC. *See* general theory of crime (GTC)
guardian(s)
    in end-of-life planning, 595
Gudjonsson, G.H., 264, 458, 460
Gudjonsson Suggestibility Scale (GSS), 242–43, 263
guilt
    limited
        antisocial behavior related to, 41–45
guilty pleas
    competence for
        social skills deficits impact on, 464–66
    in juvenile and criminal court, 290–92
gullibility
    defined, 460–61
Gunasekaran, S., 454
Gunnison, E., 578–79
Guttmacher Institute, 506
    on reproductive rights, 494
    on state laws, policies, practices impacting abortion, 497–98
    on unintended pregnancy, 494
Guzzo, K.B., 508

H

Hague Convention on Protection of Children and Co-operation in Respect of Intercountry Adoption (1993), 180
Halsey, M., 568
Halushka, J.M., 569
Hamilton, V.E., 347, 353, 392
Handbook on Child Maltreatment of ASPAC, 245
Haney, C, 565, 566
Haney-Caron, E, 279
Hanrahan, K.J., 324
Harding, D.J., 563, 565, 566, 568, 571, 572
Havard, C., 618
Hawke, W., 184–85
Hawthorne Police Department, 542
Hayes Ability Screening Index, 467
Haynie, D.L., 216
Hazen, K.P., 626
health
    mental (*see* mental health)
    physical (*see* physical health)
health care
    aging inmates and, 636–38
    emergency situations in
        in end-of-life planning, 595
    in prison
        SCOTUS on, 636–37
health concerns
    after prisoner reentry, 572
health insurance
    parental coverage of
        age-related, 354
Health Insurance Portability and Accountability Act, 603
hearing(s)
    youth adjudicatory, 286–89
Heidbrink, L., 156
Helfgott, J.B., 578–79
Hellerstedt v. June Medical, 488
Helm, 291
Helverschou, S.B., 452
Hemlock Society
    in right-to-die movement, 600
Henderson, H., 233
Henggeler, S., 390
Henry, L., 463
Higgs, T., 454
Hill-Burton Act, 591
Hiller, M.L., 311
Hinton, E., 522
Hirschi, T., 210, 218, 407, 409, 629
Hobbs, S.D., 98, 101
Hoeben, E.M., 219

Hoge, R.D., 306
Holliday, R.E., 618–19
Holmes v. South Carolina, 202
Honeywell, D., 562
"hospitalization-associated disability," 589
houses of refuge, 281
    for adolescent incarceration, 324
housing
    after prisoner reentry, 570–71
Howland, M.A., 477
HPA axis. *See* hypothalamic-pituitary-adrenal (HPA) axis
HR 2628–Living Equitably: Grandparents Aiding Children and Youth Act, 657
Hubner, S., 625
"human frailty"
    in prisoner reentry, 572
Hume, D., 591
Hummer, D., 330
Humphry, D., 600
Hurlow, A., 598–99
Hutto, A.J., 462
Huynh, J., 158–59, 162
Hyde Amendment, 507
    abortion impact on, 496
hypothalamic-pituitary-adrenal (HPA) axis
    maltreatment impact on functioning of, 17–18
hypothalamic-pituitary-gonadal axis
    activation of
        in puberty, 211

I

IAC. *See* ineffective assistance of counsel (IAC)
ICDC. *See* Irwin County Detention Center (ICDC)
ICE. *See* Immigration and Customs Enforcement (ICE)
ICU traits. *See* Inventory of Callous–Unemotional (ICU) traits
IDEA. *See* Individual with Disabilities Act (IDEA)
identification
    eyewitness
        social skills deficits impact on, 461–63
IDs. *See* intellectual disabilities (IDs)
IMH–HV. *See* infant mental health–home visiting (IMH–HV)

immediate settings
  relations between police and, 521f, 527–30
immigrant youth
  prevalence of, 149–50
  unaccompanied, 149 (see also under unaccompanied migrant youth)
Immigration and Customs Enforcement (ICE), 151–52
immigration courtrooms
  unaccompanied migrant youth impact of, 162–63
Immigration Nationality Act (INA), 154, 157–58
Immigration Naturalization Service (INS), 152
immigration proceedings
  for unaccompanied migrant youth, 153–60, 153n.6 (see also under unaccompanied migrant youth: immigration proceedings for)
impulsive behavior
  among TAY, 426–27
INA. See Immigration Nationality Act (INA)
incarcerated parents
  impact of federal child welfare permanency timelines on, 485
  leaving prison
    legal considerations for, 487–88
  legal considerations for, 480–83
  legal intersections for, 479, 479f
  maintaining parent–child relationship for, 483–85
  parenting by, 477
  prison nursery programs, 483
  reasonable efforts at reunification for, 485–86
  release from prison
    reestablishment of parental rights following, 487–88
  terminating parental rights, 486–87
incarceration. See also under incarcerated parents; prison; prisoner(s)
  adolescent, 321 (see also adolescent incarceration)
  alternatives to
    for pregnant people and mothers, 481–83
  defined, 322
  maternal, 477 (see also under maternal incarceration)
  parental rights during, 477 (see also under incarcerated parents)
  parenting during, 477
  during pregnancy, 477
  state and federal population in, 561–62
  stigma associated with, 573–74
  of TAY
    prevalence of, 425–26
Inceglo, 235
in-court testimony
  by children, 70–71
Indian Child Welfare Act, 134–35
individual calendar hearing
  for unaccompanied migrant youth, 154
individual prevention objective, 393
Individual with Disabilities Act (IDEA), 12
ineffective assistance of counsel (IAC), 466
infancy. See under infant(s)
infancy defense, 351
infancy doctrine, 351
infant(s)
  abuse among
    prevalence of, 7–8
  FASD in, 12
  in foster care (see foster care, infants in)
  legal interventions related to, 2–4
  maltreatment of (see infant maltreatment)
  overnight parenting time for, 115–21
  POSC for, 12
infant maltreatment, 7. See also under child maltreatment
  developmental issues related to, 8–13, 9f
  interventions for, 20–22
    ABC, 20–21
    CPP, 21
    IMH HV, 21
    infant–toddler court teams, 22
    PFR, 21–22
    relationship-based, 20–22
  legal policies relevant to, 8–13
  substance use impact on, 16–20
infant mental health–home visiting (IMH–HV)
  for infant maltreatment, 21
infant–toddler court teams
  for infant maltreatment, 22
informal court processing. See under diversion programs
  for youth offenders, 303 (see also under youth: alternatives to traditional court processing for)
informal processing
  rates of, 304–5
inmate(s)
  aging (see aging inmates)
  older adults as
    issues related to, 635–41 (see also under aging inmates)
Innocence Project, 617
In re Elias V., 261
In re Gault, 282, 287
In re Winship, 282
INS. See Immigration Naturalization Service (INS)
insecure attachment
  secure attachment vs., 10, 113–14
insurance
  health (see health insurance)
intellectual disabilities (IDs). See also under autism spectrum disorder (ASD); developmental disabilities
  AAIDD on, 449–50
  APA on, 450
  "cloak of competence" associated with, 453
  in criminal justice system, 7
    accommodations and reduced threshold for scrutiny, 467
    balancing autonomy and vulnerability, 467–68
    capital punishment, 459
    identification and screening efforts, 467
    impact of, 461–63
    introduction, 449
    pathways into, 453–55
    potential consequences of, 426–59 (see also under criminal justice system: cognitive defects in)
    prevalence of, 451–53
    social skills deficits impact, 459–66 (see also under criminal justice system: social skills deficits impact on)
  defined, 449–51
  dispositional factors associated with, 465
  SCOTUS on, 450, 459
  suggestibility rates associated with, 63

intellectual disabilities (IDs) (*cont.*)
    victimization of persons with
        U.S. Department of Justice
        on, 453
Intellectual Disability: Definition,
    Diagnosis, Classification
    and Systems of Support,
    449–50
intelligence
    crystallized
        aging and, 612–13
    EFs and
        in children, 63
    memory and suggestibility
        impact in children, 62, 63
intelligence quotient (IQ)
    early adversity impact on, 172
"intelligent" waiver
    defined, 262
Intensive Supervision Service, 432
intercountry adoption
    contact in, 184–85
    open, 184–85
    policies/practices/laws related to,
        180–81
Interethnic Adoption Provisions Act
    (1996), 179–80
interrogation
    custodial (*see* custodial
        interrogation)
    juvenile, 257 (*see also under*
        adolescent suspects: police
        interrogation of)
interrogation law
    as applied to youth, 260
interrogative suggestibility
    defined, 460
    of juveniles, 263–64
interviewing protocols
    memory and suggestibility
        impacts of, 245–49 (*see*
        also specific types and
        investigative interviewing
        protocols for adolescents:
        memory and suggestibility
        impacts of)
intimate partner violence
    prenatal
        substance use impact of, 16
        SCOTUS on, 508
Inventory of Callous–Unemotional
    (ICU) traits, 49–50
investigative interviewing protocols
    for adolescents
    memory and suggestibility
        impacts of, 245–49
        ground rules, 246

individual differences, 248
    for LGBTQ youth, 248
    rapport building, 246–47
    reluctant victims, 248–49
IQ (intelligence quotient)
    early adversity impact on, 172
Ireland, C.A., 327
Irwin County Detention Center
    (ICDC), 500
Irwin, J., 565–67, 568–69, 572,
    573–74

J

Jack, 242
Jaffee, S.R., 216–17
Jarjoura, G.R., 223
JDAI. *See* Juvenile Detention
    Alternatives Initiative
    (JDAI)
JDCs. *See* juvenile drug courts
    (JDCs)
Jean's Way, 600
JJDPA. *See* Juvenile Justice and
    Delinquency Protection Act
    (JJDPA)
JJS. *See* juvenile justice system (JJS)
JLUSA. *See* JustLeadershipUSA
    (JLUSA)
JMHCs. *See* juvenile mental health
    courts (JMHCs)
John, A., 328–29
Johnson, R., 466
joint custody
    parents' rights and, 204–5
Jolley, J.M., 636
Jolliffe, D., 414, 415
Jones, J., 364
Jones, K.M., 506
JPOs. *See* juvenile probation officers
    (JPOs)
Juffer, J., 163
June Medical Services L.L.C. v.
    Russo, 495
jury(ies)
    on older adult abuse cases, 616
    older adult eyewitnesses and,
        619–20
Jury Selection and Service Act, 352
justice
    in end-of-life planning, 591
    juvenile (*see* juvenile justice)
    miscarriage of
        defined, 526–27
justice reinvestment initiatives
    in decreasing adolescent
        incarceration, 334
JustLeadershipUSA (JLUSA), 578

juvenile court
    criminalization of
        due process revolution and,
            282–83
    described, 279
    dispositions in, 292–94
    guilty pleas in, 290–92
    modern processes, 284–86
    plea process in
        parents' role in, 292
    rehabilitative alternatives
        through, 303 (*see also specific*
        types and youth: alternatives
        to traditional court
        processing for)
    SCOTUS impact on, 282
    sentencing in, 292–94
    trial stage in, 286–89
    youth in, 279 (*see also under*
        adolescent(s): in juvenile
        and criminal court)
    future directions, 295–96
    introduction, 279–80
juvenile delinquency
    school safety and, 364–67 (*see also*
        under school safety: juvenile
        delinquency and)
Juvenile Detention Alternatives
    Initiative (JDAI)
    in decreasing adolescent
        incarceration, 334–35
juvenile drug courts (JDCs), 310
juvenile interrogation, 257. *See also*
    under adolescent suspects:
    police interrogation of
    awareness of police practices
        during, 262–63
    constitutional laws governing,
        259–61
    developmental principles relevant
        to, 261–67
    implications for practice, policy,
        and research, 271–73
    interrogative suggestibility,
        263–64
    introduction, 257–59
    laws related to, 260
    legal procedures and experiences
        among youth of color,
        265–67
    Miranda comprehension during,
        262–63
    perceptions of and compliance
        with authority during,
        264–65
    policy and practice questions
        concerning, 267–71

Miranda warnings–related, 267–68
parents as adequate protectors of youth's rights during, 268–70
police using deception during, 270–71
rights associated with
parents as adequate protectors of, 268–70
special care in, 260
juvenile jurisdiction
age of
developmental research on, 392
juvenile justice
criminalization of, 282–83
developmental science era, 283–84
due process revolution, 282–83
early roots and Progressive Era, 280–82
future directions, 375–78
history of, 280–84, 424–25
SCOTUS in, 282
racial and ethnic disparities in, 374–75
schools and, 363 (*see also under* school[s])
Juvenile Justice and Delinquency Protection Act (JJDPA), 304, 336
juvenile justice system (JJS)
Reagan administration on, 424
school environment and, 363
juvenile mental health courts (JMHCs), 310–11
juvenile offenders
punishment vs. leniency for, 203–4
juvenile probation officers (JPOs), 363–64
as legal actors in schools, 371–72

K

Kaba, F., 328
Kassin, S.M., 267, 463
Katic, B., 370
Katz, N., 238–39, 459
Kazemian, L., 565–66
Kebbell, M.R., 458
Kelly, J.B., 120
Kemp, E.C., 37
Kempe, H., 135
Kennedy, Justice, 293
Kent v. United States, 282
Kerbs, J.J., 636

Kevorkian, J.
in right-to-die movement, 599–600
Khoury, M., 387
Kimonis, E.R., 49
Kim, S., 114
KiVa program
in enhancing school safety, 369
Klemfuss, J.Z., 57
Know Your Rights presentation, 152
Know Your Rights workshops, 153
Knutson, A.K., 639
Kochanska, G., 43–44, 114
Koons-Witt, B.A., 634
Kopf, D., 568–69
Kroll, K.M., 9–10
Kübler-Ross, E., 591
Kubrin, C.E., 364, 570
Kuhn, 218
Kunst, M., 566

L

labeling theory, 325
"*Lackey* claim," 635
Lackey v. Texas, 635
Laird, 218
Lamb, M.E., 120, 159, 160, 195
language development
early adversity impact on, 172
maltreatment impact on, 19–20
memory and suggestibility impact in children, 64
LARC methods. *See* long-acting reversible contraception (LARC) methods
latent trait theory, 409–10, 410t
"later-starter" pathway
"early-starter" pathway vs., 39
Lathrop, J., 424
Laub, J.H., 410–11, 568–69
Laumann-Billings, L., 117–18
law
adult development and, 399
childhood and, 2–4
law(s)
adolescence and, 4–6
adoption-related, 177–85 (*see also under* adoption: policies/practices/laws related to)
infant maltreatment and, 8–13
Law and Human Behavior, 399, 626
law enforcement, 655–56
Lawson, M., 65
Lay, B., 412
LCP. *See under* life course persistent (LCP)

Leach, 239–40
Leander, 238–39
Learning Disability Screening Questionnaire, 467
Learning Together Intervention (LTI)
in enhancing school safety, 370
LeBel, T.P., 561, 656–57
Lee, A., 424–25
Lee, J.M., 533
legal questioning
of children in criminal court, 92–94
alternate forms of testimony, 93–94
cross-examination, 93
prosecutors' and defense attorneys' questions, 92–93
via CCTV, 93–94
legal socialization
by parents of color, 528
legal status
purpose of, 348
legal system
collateral consequences of, 657–58
described, 423
emerging adults in, 425–27 (*see also* transition-age youth (TAY): in legal system)
memory in children in, 68–72 (*see also* memory in children: application in legal system)
within schools, 370–74 (*see also* school(s): legal system in)
TAY in, 423 (*see also* transition-age youth (TAY): in legal system)
leniency
punishment vs.
in adolescent offenders, 203–4
for child offenders, 203–4
for juvenile offenders, 203–4
Leo, R.A., 266, 464
lesbian(s)
adoption by
policies/practices/laws related to, 181–82
LGBTQ youth
rapport-building/interviewing strategies with, 248
liberate misrepresentation
age and, 199
Liem, M., 566
life course
prisoner reentry and, 561 (*see also under* prisoner reentry)

life course persistent (LCP) offenders, 407, 410t
life course persistent (LCP) trajectory of risky and antisocial behaviors, 212–13
life without the possibility of parole (LWOP), 203, 283, 284
　for adolescents
　　SCOTUS on, 322
　for youth
　　reductions in, 293
　　SCOTUS on, 293–94
Lilienfeld, S.O., 214–15
Lipscomb, A.E., 524
Li, S.M.Y., 321
Listwan, S.J., 565
Little, M., 325
Liu, 215
Lloyd, A., 303
Lofotus, E.F., 461
London, 244
long-acting reversible contraception (LARC) methods, 499, 503
Looney, A., 563
Lorek, A., 160–61
Loughran, T.A., 323–24
Love, M., 575
Lowery, B.S., 531–32
low self-control (LSC), 409–10, 410t
low self-control (LSC) theory, 409–10, 410t
LSC. *See* low self-control (LSC)
LTI. *See* Learning Together Intervention (LTI)
Luckasson, R., 458–59
Luecken, L.J., 117
Lunsky, Y., 432, 454–55
LWOP. *See* life without the possibility of parole (LWOP)
Lyon, E., 460
Lyon, T.D., 195, 244

M

MacArthur Competency Assessment Tool–Criminal Adjudication, 288
MacArthur Foundation, 386
Maclean, S.A., 161
macrosystem
　development and well-being impacts of, 521f, 523–24
　implications for policy and practice, 541
　policing at societal level, 521f, 522–24, 541
Madison v. Alabama, 634–35

Maimon, D., 223
Majd, K., 333
majority
　age of, 347 (*see also* age of majority)
　legal
　　age of, 347 (*see also* age of majority)
Malloy, L.C., 233, 240–41
Maloney, C., 335–36
maltreatment
　child (*see* child maltreatment)
　developmental impact of, 9
　HPA axis impact of, 17–18
　of infants (*see* infant maltreatment)
　language and cognitive developmental effects of, 19–20
　neurobiological development impact of, 17–18
　prenatal, 13–16
　prenatal maltreatment (*see also* prenatal exposure to substances [PSE])
　social–emotional developmental effects of, 18–19
　substance use defined as, 15–16
　telomere shortening related to, 18
Manasse, M.E., 209
Manchester Youth Justice service, 437
mandatory minimums
　for youth, 293
MAOA. *See* monoamine oxidase A (MAOA)
marriage
　after prisoner reentry, 571–72
Martin, G.E., 578
Maruna, S., 562, 567–68, 577, 578
Maryland Safe and Supportive Schools Survey, 366
Maryland v. Craig, 201
Mason, J., 467
Massachusetts Youth Screening Instrument, 389
MAT. *See* medication-assisted treatment (MAT)
maternal caregiving
　genetic effects of, 9–10
maternal incarceration, 477
　alternatives to, 481–83
　BJS on, 478–79
　prevalence of, 478
　prison nursery programs, 483
　in U.S., 478–79
Mathematica Policy Research, 442

Matthews, E., 576–77
"maturity gap"
　between cognitive and psychosocial development in young adults, 427, 428f
Maynard, B.
　in right-to-die movement, 600
McCann, W., 576
McCarthy, D., 324
McCuish, E., 330
McDermott, E., 598
McGee, T.R., 411
McGuire, 244
McNeill, F., 562, 568, 579
Meares, T.L., 528, 541
Mears, D.P., 314
Medicaid
　abortion coverage under, 496
Medicaid expansion
　under Patient Protection and Affordable Care Act, 142–43
Medical Orders for Life-Sustaining Treatment (MOLST), 596, 604–5
medication abortion
　COVID-19 pandemic impact on, 498
　federal laws, policies, practices on, 496–97
medication-assisted treatment (MAT)
　for opioid misuse during pregnancy, 14
Mehta, C.M., 399–400
Melinder, A., 65
memory(ies)
　of adolescents, 242–45
　　developmental effects on, 243–45
　autobiographical (*see* autobiographical memory)
　in children, 57 (*see also* memory in children)
　child testimony and, 158
　false
　　cultural differences in, 60
　inaccuracies related to among young children, 158
　of older adults, 617
　PTSD impact on, 236
　social skills deficits impact on, 461–63
　stages of, 617
memory care systems
　for aging inmates, 637
memory in children, 57
　application in legal system

courtroom testimony, 70–72
forensic interviewing, 68–70
future directions, 72–73
implications of, 72
development of, 58–59
disclosure processes related to, 68–73 (*see also* memory in children: application in legal system)
factors affecting, 59–66 (*see also specific factors*)
attachment styles, 65
child abuse, 65–66
cognitive functioning, 62–63
demographics, 59–60
disclosure and recantation, 66–67
event characteristics, 60–61
language development, 64
psychological factors, 65–66
PTSD, 62
repeated experiences, 60–61
stress, 61–62
inaccuracies of, 158
repeated experiences impact on, 60–61
memory loss
cognitive decline and, 589
memory performance
child abuse impact on, 65–66
memory recall
EF and
in children, 63
memory scripts, 60
mental health
adolescent incarceration impact on, 327–28
women's
reproductive rights impact on, 504–6
mesosystem
development and well-being impacts of, 521f, 529–30
implications for policy and practice, 542–43
relations between police and immediate settings, 521f, 527–30
metacognition
defined, 62
meta-theory
social–ecological model as, 365–66
Metcalf, S., 85
Metzger, C., 539–40
Mexico City Policy
abortion impact of, 497

Trump administration on, 497
microsystem
developmental and well-being impacts of, 532–35
direct interactions/personal factors, 521f, 530–39
officer-level risk factors, 521f, 530–32
situational-level risk factors, 521f, 532
impacts resulting from broader macrosystem context, 535–39
implications for policy and practice, 543–45
mifepristone
for abortion, 486
migrant youth
unaccompanied (*see* unaccompanied migrant youth)
Miller, J., 335–36
Miller, R.J., 575, 577
Miller v. Alabama, 283–84, 424, 442
Mill, J.S., 588–89
mind–mindedness
in attachment-based interventions, 10
Minnesota–Texas Adoption Research Project (MTARP), 183
Mioduszewski, M.D., 364
Miranda comprehension
by adolescents, 262–63
Miranda language, 267
Miranda rights
waiver of
capacity for, 455–56
social skills deficits impact on, 463–64
Miranda v. Arizona, 259, 267, 455–56
Miranda waivers
for adolescent suspects, 272
capacity for, 455–56
Miranda warnings, 268–70, 455–56
for youth
awareness of, 262–63
effectiveness of, 267–68
miscarriage of justice
defined, 526–27
misinformation acceptance, 461
misinformation effect, 461
for older adults, 618
misleading information
exposure to
IDs and, 461–62

misrepresentation
liberate
age and, 199
Mizrahi, J.:., 563
Mnookin, R.H., 138
Modified Cognitive Interview, 618–19
Moffitt, T.E., 40, 212–13, 216–17, 407–9
developmental taxonomy of, 404, 406, 407–9
MOLST. *See* Medical Orders for Life-Sustaining Treatment (MOLST)
Mondale, W., Sen., 135–36
monoamine oxidase A (MAOA)
childhood abuse related to
in antisocial behavior prediction, 215
Montes, A.N., 363
Montgomery v. Louisiana, 293–94, 424–25
Moore, A.A., 415
Morgan, A.B., 214–15
Morris, P.A., 365–66, 530–31
Mosotho, N.L., 452
Motivans, M., 632
Mountain View program, 432–33
MST. *See* multisystemic therapy (MST)
MTARP. *See* Minnesota–Texas Adoption Research Project (MTARP)
Mueller, D.J., 331–32
Multiethnic Placement Act (1994), 179–80
multiple caregivers
attachment to, 114–15
multisystemic therapy (MST)
in decreasing adolescent incarceration, 335
Mulvey, E.P., 321
Munn, M., 573–74
Murphy, G., 467

N

Nadel, M.R., 307
naiveté
defined, 461
Najdowski, C.J., 517
Narrative Elaboration procedure, 68
narrative practice
described, 247
Narvey, C.S., 403
NAS. *See* neonatal abstinence syndrome (NAS)
National Academy of Elder Law Attorneys, 611–12

National Academy of Sciences
  on adult development, 399–400
National Association of School
  Resource Officers, 376
National Center for Education
  Statistics
  on SROs, 370, 376
National Child Traumatic Stress
  Network, 20–21
National Educational Longitudinal
  Study, 368
National Epidemiologic Survey
  on Alcohol and Related
  Conditions (2001-2002),
  117–18
National Former Prisoner Survey,
  563
National Hospice and Palliative
  Care Organization
  (NHPCO)
  in right-to-die movement, 601
National Institute of Child
  Health and Development
  (NICHD), 159–60
National Institute of Child
  Health and Development
  (NICHD) Investigative
  Protocol, 68–69, 159–60, 246
National Institute of Child
  Health and Development
  (NICHD) Investigative
  Protocol, Revised, 69
National Inventory of Collateral
  Consequences of
  Conviction (NICCC), 429,
  575–76
National Longitudinal Study of
  Adolescent to Adult Health,
  565–66
National Reentry Resource Center
  of American Institutes for
  Research, 575
National Registry of Evidence-
  Based and Promising
  Practices
  Substance Abuse and
    Mental Health Services
    Administration of, 21
National Registry of Exonerations,
  526–27
National Research Council of the
  National Academies, 392
National Scientific Council on the
  Developing Child, 7
National Survey of Child and
  Adolescent Well-being
  (NSCAW), 11

Native American children
  in CWS
    racial disproportionality/racial
    disparities associated with,
    134–35
Naturalization Act of 1790, 522–23
neglect
  child
    brain development effects of,
    131–33
    physical, 139, 141
Neil, E., 184
Nelson, C.A., 173
NeMoyer, A., 288–89, 291–93
neonatal abstinence syndrome
  (NAS), 14
Nestor, P.G., 457
net widening
  defined, 313
  informal processing of youth
    offenders and, 313–14
neurobiological development
  maltreatment impact on, 17–18
neuroscience
  cognitive
    impact on juvenile justice, 283–84
neurotransmitters
  balance of
    in adolescence, 211
New Jersey v. J.L.G., 67
New Jersey v. Michaels, 461–62
New York City Police Department
  (NYPD)
  discriminatory policies of, 526–27
Ng, I.Y., 328
NHPCO. *See* National Hospice
  and Palliative Care
  Organization (NHPCO)
NICCC. *See* National Inventory of
  Collateral Consequences of
  Conviction (NICCC)
NICHD. *See* National Institute
  of Child Health and
  Development (NICHD)
Nielsen, L., 110
nondisclosure
  rates of, 200
nonmaleficence
  in end-of-life planning, 590
Notes of a Native Son, 517
"notice of referrals," 432
notice to appear (NTA), 154, 154n.7
NSCAW. *See* National Survey of
  Child and Adolescent Well-
  being (NSCAW)
NTA. *See* notice to appear (NTA)
Nunez, N., 619–20

Nurse–Family Partnership, 142
NYPD. *See* New York City Police
  Department (NYPD)

O

Obama, B., Pres., 328
Obergefell v. Hodges, 181–82
O'Brien, L., 221–22
O'Connell, M.J., 456, 464
OC YAC. *See* Orange County
  Young Adult Court (OC
  YAC)
offender(s). *See* juvenile offenders;
  specific types, e.g., child
  offenders
offending behavior
  age-specific risk factors for, 410t
Office of Chief Counsel
  for DHS, 154
Office of Juvenile Justice and
  Delinquency Prevention
  (OJJDP)
  on TAY charge types, 426–27
Office of Refugee Resettlement
  (ORR) "shelters," 150–54,
  150n.2, 156. *See also under*
  ORR "shelters"
O'Hear, M., 575
Ohio v. Clark, 202
OJIDP survey, 119
OJJDP. *See* Office of Juvenile
  Justice and Delinquency
  Prevention (OJJDP)
Okunda, 218
Olaguez, A.P., 57
old age
  characteristics of, 588, 589–90
older adult(s), 611. *See also* aging
  ACP for, 587 (*see also under*
    advance care planning
    [ACP])
  introduction, 587–88
  adjudicative process and, 631
  assistance for, 657–58
  capacity of
    described, 614
  caregivers for, 615–16
  cognitive decline in, 589
  in criminal justice system, 625
    (*see also* aging inmates)
  as defendants, 631–35
  death penalty for, 634–35
  defined, 611–12, 626–27
  described, 611
  de-sexualization of, 614
  end of life for
    characteristics of, 588, 589–90

end-of-life planning for, 587
   death with dignity laws related to, 594
   emergency situations in health care, 595
   ethical considerations/ramifications, 587
   future directions, 603–5 (*see also under* end-of-life planning: future directions in)
   guardians in, 595
   introduction, 587–88
   principles undergirding, 590–91 (*see also under* end-of-life planning: principles undergirding)
   PSDA, 594
   state and federal laws, 594–95
   surrogate consent laws, 594–95
financial exploitation of, 613–15
future directions, 620–21
memory of, 617
misinformation effect for, 618
as perpetrators of crime, 629–30
population of, 611, 625
risks/conditions of, 588–90
self-neglect among, 614–15
sentencing-related issues, 632–35
   age bias, 632
   death penalty and execution, 634–35
   judicial, 632–33
   legislative and SCOTUS court interpretations, 633–34
societal norms, policy, and practice malalignment in, 654
stereotypes of, 628
telemedicine for, 601–3
as victims, 613–16
   adult vs. child abuse, 613–15
   informal caregivers–related, 615–16
   introduction, 613
   juries on, 616
as witnesses, 617–20
   estimator variables, 619
   eyewitness research, 617–19 (*see also under* older adult eyewitnesses)
   juries and, 619–20
   memory and, 617
   misinformation effect, 618
   system variables for, 617–19
older adult eyewitnesses, 617–19
   estimator variables for, 619

juries and, 619–20
research on, 617–19
system variables for, 617–19
older adulthood. *See also* aging; older adults
   defined, 626–27
On Death and Dying, 591
onset of crime
   defined, 410–11
open adoption, 182–85
   benefits of, 183
   contact in, 182–85
      child welfare adoptions, 184
      domestic infant adoptions, 183
      intercountry adoptions, 184–85
   defined, 182–83
   described, 182–83
   policies/practices/laws related to, 182–85
   contact-related, 182–85
opioid use disorder (OUD), 14
Orange County Young Adult Court (OC YAC), 438–41, 440*f*, 441*f*, 442
Oregon Death With Dignity Act, 593, 594
Oregon vs. Ashcroft, 593
ORR. *See* Office of Refugee Resettlement (ORR)
ORR "shelters," 150–54, 150n.2, 156
   child/youth detention in developmental perspective on, 156
   unaccompanied migrant youth in developmental perspective on, 156
   self-representation in court, 156–58
Osgood, D.W., 219
OUD. *See* opioid use disorder (OUD)
overnight parenting time
   for infants and toddlers
      impact on father–child relationships, 118
      research on, 115–19
      translating attachment theory and research into policies for, 119–21
oxytocin system
   maternal care impact of, 9–10

P

PAE. *See* prenatal alcohol exposure (PAE)
Pager, D., 569

Palacios, J., 169
parens patriae, 281, 281n.2, 303–4, 350–51
parent(s). *See also under* parenting
   of color (*see under* parents of color)
   incarcerated, 477 (*see also* incarcerated parents)
   role in plea process, 292
parental reflective functioning
   in attachment-based interventions, 10
parental rights
   early maltreatment–related vs. children's welfare, 196–98
   during incarceration, 477 (*see also under* incarcerated parents)
   joint custody and, 204–5
parental support and benefits
   continued entitlement to age-related, 354
parent–child attachment
   child development related to, 130–33
parent–child relationships
   physical health related to, 111–12
parenting
   addiction impact on, 15–16
   by fathers
      child development impact of, 114–15
   in prison, 477 (*see also under* incarcerated parents)
   quality of
      brain development impact of, 10
parenting behaviors
   substance use impact on, 15–16
parenting interventions
   CWS–related, 8
parenting practices
   in risky and antisocial behaviors in adolescence, 218
parenting sensitivity
   in attachment-based interventions, 10
parenting time
   for children younger than 3 years, 109 (*see also* attachment)
   overnight (*see* overnight parenting time)
Parent-Report Strengths and Difficulties Questionnaire, 161
parents of color
   legal socialization by, 528
   racial/cultural socialization by, 527–28

Parke, R.D., 185–86
Parkin, A.J., 617
Parkinson, P., 109–10, 122
past
  conversations about
    in language development, 64
Pathways to Desistance Study, 321
Patient Protection and Affordable Care Act
  Medicaid expansion under, 142–43
Patient Self-Determination Act (PSDA), 587–88, 594
Patterson, E.J., 566
Patton, D, 568
PCL:YV. *See* Psychopathy Checklist: Youth Version (PCL:YV)
PDE. *See* prenatal drug exposure (PDE)
peer(s)
  adolescent incarceration impact on, 325–26
  delinquent and antisocial
    risky and antisocial behaviors in adolescence influenced by, 220–21
  risky and antisocial behaviors in adolescence influenced by, 219–24
    delinquent and antisocial, 220–21
    popularity impact, 219–20
    routine activities, 219
    unstructured socializing, 219
  in socioemotional development, 237
peer courts, 311–12
peer socializing
  unstructured
    risky and antisocial behaviors related to, 219
Pence, G.E., 590
Pendergast, A., 149
Pennsylvania Department of Corrections, 636–37
Pennsylvania Department of Corrections v. Yeskey, 636–37
PEPFAR. *See* President's Emergency Plan for AIDS Relief (PEPFAR)
perceived popularity
  defined, 219
"permanent incorrigibility," 203–4
persistent vegetative state (PVS), 591
personality traits
  risky and antisocial behaviors in adolesence related to, 214
Petersilia, J., 571, 573

Petrich, D.M., 324
Pettit, B., 563
PFR. *See* Promoting First Relationships (PFR)
physical development
  early adversity impact on, 171
physical health
  adolescent incarceration impact on, 328–29
  parent–child relationships impact on, 111–12
  women's
    reproductive rights impact on, 501–4
physical neglect, 139
  defined, 141
Physician Orders for Life-Sustaining Treatment (POLST), 596, 604–5
Physician Orders for Scope of Treatment (POST), 596, 604–5
PICS. *See* "Post Incarceration Syndrome (PICS)"
Pimentel, 244
Pine Grove, 432–33
Piquero, A.R., 403, 415
Pirius, R., 575
Pittsburgh Youth Study, 415
Plan B One-Step, 499
Planned Parenthood of Southeastern Pennsylvania v. Casey, 495, 508
Planned Parenthood v. Casey, 493–94
"plan of safe care" (POSC)
  for infants, 12
plasticity
  differential (*see* differential plasticity)
plea(s)
  guilty (*see* guilty pleas)
plea-bargaining process
  dispositional and situational factors in, 466
plead guilty
  competence to
    social skills deficits impact on, 464–66
plea process
  parents' role in, 292
Poehlmann, J., 484–85
police
  relations between immediate settings and, 521f, 527–30
police encounters
  perceived freedom during
    racial differences in, 537–39
  stereotype threat in, 535–37

police interrogation
  of adolescent suspects, 257
    (*see also under* adolescent suspects: police interrogation of)
police-led diversion
  for youth, 306–7
police practice(s)
  adolescents' awareness of, 262–63
police questioning
  types of, 257
policing
  direct interactions in, 521f, 530–39
  discriminatory, 518–20
  as institution, 521f, 524–30, 541–42
  personal factors in, 521f, 530–39
  racial disparities in, 517 (*see also* racialized policing)
  consequences of, 520–39, 521f (*see also under* social–ecological development framework: in racially disparate policing)
  evidence related to, 518–20
  implications for policy and practice, 540–45
  introduction, 545–18
  perceived freedom during police encounters, 537
  situational-level risk factors, 521f, 532
  social–ecological development framework application, 520–39, 521f (*see also under* social–ecological development framework: in racially disparate policing)
  racialized (*see* racialized policing)
  at societal level, 521f, 522–24, 541
  "warrior mindset" in, 524–26
policy(ies)
  defined, 479
  social norms, science and malalignment of, 652–55 (*see also under* societal norms, policy, and practice, malalignment of)
policy-minded developmental research, 195
policy reforms
  in decreasing adolescent incarceration, 333–34
POLST. *See* Physician Orders for Life-Sustaining Treatment (POLST)
polydrug use
  among prenatal substance users, 15

POP. *See* Project for Older Prisoners (POP)
popularity
  impact on risky and antisocial behaviors in adolescence, 219–20
  perceived
    defined, 219
  sociometric
    defined, 219
Porporino, F.J., 565
port of entry
  defined, 151, 151n.3
POSC. *See* "plan of safe care" (POSC)
positive psychological states (PPSs)
  recidivism related to, 567
Pösö, T., 180
POST. *See* Physician Orders for Scope of Treatment (POST)
postarrest diversion programs
  described, 432
"Post Incarceration Syndrome (PICS)," 566
Post-Traumatic Stress Disorder Reaction Index (PTSD-RI), 161
post-traumatic stress disorders (PTSD)
  memory function effects of, 236
  in children, 62
  of unaccompanied migrant youth, 150–51
posttrial diversion programs
  described, 432
poverty
  CWS and, 139
Powers, P.A., 460
PPSs. *See* positive psychological states (PPSs)
Pratt, T.C., 218
PREA. *See* Prison Rape Elimination Act (PREA)
prearrest
  for youth, 306–7
prearrest programs
  described, 432
prefrontal cortex
  restructuring of
    in adolescence, 211
pregnancy
  alternatives to incarceration during, 481–83
  impact on women's development and physical health, 503–4
  intimate partner violence before and during, 16

maternal substance use during, 15–16
  in prison, 477 (*see also under* incarcerated parents)
  introduction, 477–78
  prevalence of, 477–78
stress impact on, 9
unintended (*see* unintended pregnancy)
prenatal alcohol exposure (PAE), 13–14
prenatal drug exposure (PDE), 14–15
prenatal exposure to substances (PSE), 13–20. *See also under* child maltreatment: forms of
  alcohol, 13–14
  cannabis, 15
  cigarettes, 14
  cocaine, 14–15
  drugs, 14–15
  as maltreatment, 15–16
  opioids, 14
  PAE, 13–14
  PDE, 14–15
  polydrug use, 15
prenatal intimate partner violence
  substance use impact on, 16
prenatal maltreatment, 13–16. *See also under* prenatal exposure to substances (PSE)
  substance exposure, 13–16 (*see also* prenatal exposure to substances [PSE])
President's Emergency Plan for AIDS Relief (PEPFAR), 497
pretrial programs
  described, 432
"Preventive Care Guidelines" of ACA, 499
Pridemore, W.A., 566
prison(s). *See also under* incarceration; incarceration(s); prisoner(s)
  health care in, 636–38
    SCOTUS on, 636–37
  impacts of, 565–66
  life after
    harsh reality of, 572
  parenting in maternal incarceration (*see also under* incarcerated parents)
  parents leaving
    legal considerations for, 487–88
  pregnancy in, 477 (*see also under* maternal incarceration)

state and federal
  population in, 561–62
stigma of incarceration in, 573–74
prisoner(s). *See also under* aging inmates; prison(s)
  characteristics of, 563–64
  reentry of, 561 (*see also under* prisoner reentry)
prisoner reentry, 561, 646–47
prison(s); prisoner[s]. *See also under* incarceration(s)
  becoming "professional ex-" or "wounded healer," 577–78
  challenges related to, 568–72
    employment, 568–69
    family relationships, 571–72
    health concerns, 572
    housing, 570–71
    marriage, 571–72
  defined, 562
  felony convictions consequences upon, 575–77
  future research, 578–79
  harsh reality of, 572
  "human frailty" in, 572
  introduction, 561–63
  life course and, 561
  processes in, 562
  social bonds in, 571
  stigma of incarceration in prison impact on, 573–74
  as turning point, 566–68
prison nursery programs, 483
Prison Rape Elimination Act (PREA), 330
"professional ex-"
  becoming
    in prisoner reentry, 577–78
Progressive Era
  CWS rooted in, 135
  juvenile justice in U.S. during, 280–82
Project for Older Prisoners (POP), 639
Promoting First Relationships (PFR)
  for infant maltreatment, 21–22
Promoting Safe and Stable Families Act, 137, 142
propensity score matching, 87–88
prosecution
  criminal
    youth impact of, 294–95
prosecutors
  legal questioning of children in criminal court by, 92–93
prosocial emotions
  described, 41

prosocial traits
  antisocial traits vs., 215
Prowse, G., 528
PSDA. *See* Patient Self-
  Determination Act (PSDA)
PSE. *See* prenatal exposure to
  substances (PSE)
psychological factors
  memory and suggestibility
    impact in children, 65–66
psychology
  developmental (*see*
    developmental psychology)
psychopathology
  developmental, 388
Psychopathy Checklist: Youth
  Version (PCL:YV), 50
psychosocial development
  adolescent incarceration impact
    on, 329–30
  cognitive development and
    "maturity gap" between, 427, 428f
psychotherapy
  child–parent
    for infant maltreatment, 21
PTSD. *See* post-traumatic stress
  disorder (PTSD)
PTSD-RI. *See* Post-Traumatic Stress
  Disorder Reaction Index
  (PTSD-RI)
puberty. *See under* adolescence;
  adolescent(s)
punishment
  capital (*see* capital punishment)
  leniency vs.
    in adolescent offenders, 203–4
    for child offenders, 203–4
    for juvenile offenders, 203–4
PVS. *See* persistent vegetative state
  (PVS)

Q

Quas, J.A., 1, 85, 157, 399, 649–50
Queensland Longitudinal Dataset
  on adult-onset offenders, 413
questioning
  legal (*see* legal questioning)
  police
    types of, 257
    suggestive, 200
Quetelet, A., 405–6
Quinlan, K.A., 591

R

Rabior, E., 7
racial disparities
  adolescent incarceration–related, 331–32
  CWS–related
    child development impact of, 134–35
  dispositions-related, 293
  in diversion research, 434
  in informal court processing for youth, 312–13
  in juvenile justice, 374–75
  policing-related, 517 (*see also under* policing: racial disparities)
  in TAY arrests, 426
  in youth justice
    developmental research on, 391–92
racialized policing
  cumulative consequences of, 539–40
  implications for policy and practice, 540–45
  officer-level risk factors for, 521f, 530–32
  situational-level risk factors for, 521f, 532
racial–legal socialization, 528, 529
racial socialization
  by parents of color, 527–28
Rahr, S., 525
Raina, P., 432
"Raise the Age" efforts, 442–43
Rapley, M., 460
rapport building
  in interviewing adolescents, 246–47
Rawls, J., 591
reactivity
  emotional
    defined, 43
Reagan administration
  on JJS, 424
Reasoned and Equitable Community
  and Local Alternatives to
  the Incarceration of Minors
  (RECLAIM) initiative
  in decreasing adolescent
    incarceration, 334
Rebellon C.J., 209
recall
  memory
    EF and, 63
recall questions
  sensitivity of, 200
recidivism
  adolescent incarceration impact on, 323–24
  PPSs-related, 567
  substance abuse and, 572
  TAY–related, 425
RECLAIM initiative. *See* Reasoned
  and Equitable Community
  and Local Alternatives to
  the Incarceration of Minors
  (RECLAIM) initiative
Recommended Summary Plan
  for Emergency Care and
  Treatment (ReSPECT),
  598–99
Redlich, A.D., 1, 399, 649–50
reentry
  prisoner. (*see* prisoner reentry)
reform schools
  for adolescent incarceration, 324
refuge
  houses of (*see* houses of refuge)
rehabilitative alternatives
  through juvenile court system,
    303 (*see also specific types
    and* youth: alternatives to
    traditional court processing
    for)
Rehnquist, W.H., Justice, 592–93
relationship(s)
  age–crime, 405–7
  attorney–client
    disadvantages among youth of color, 289
  caregiver–child (*see* caregiver–child relationship)
  family (*see* family relationships)
  father–child (*see* father–child relationships)
  interpersonal
    reproductive rights impact on, 507–9
  parent–child (*see* parent–child relationships)
  promoting first (*see* Promoting First Relationships [PFR])
ReMerge, 482
remorse
  limited
    antisocial behavior related to, 41–45
removal proceedings
  for unaccompanied migrant youth
    commencement of, 154
REMS. *See* Risk Evaluation
  and Mitigation Strategy
  (REMS)
Repetti, R.L., 111–12, 113–14
reproductive rights
  Guttmacher Institute on, 494
  impact on women's development,
    493 (*see also* women's
    development: reproductive
    rights impact on)

contraception-related laws, policies, practices impacting, 498–501 (*see also under* contraception: laws, policies, practices impacting)
introduction, 493–94
laws, policies, practices impacting access to abortion, 495–98 (*see also under* abortion: laws, policies, practices impacting)
SCOTUS on, 493–94
social inequality impact of, 495–97
research
basic (*see* basic research)
clinical (*see* clinical research)
developmental (*see* developmental research)
diversion-related (*see* diversion research)
eyewitness (*see* eyewitness research)
translational (*see* translational research)
Research Network on Adolescent Development and Juvenile Justice, 386
resilience
evidence of cumulative consequences of, 539–40
ReSPECT. *See* Recommended Summary Plan for Emergency Care and Treatment (ReSPECT)
Restatement of the Law, Children and the Law, 140–42
restorative justice (RJ) programming, 363–64
in enhancing school safety, 369–70
"retraumatization" defined, 162–63
"Returning Home" studies, 563–64
Revised NICHD Protocol, 69, 199–200
Reyna, V.F., 291
rGE. *See* gene–environment correlation (rGE)
Riano, N.S., 423
Rice, D., 7
Rice, S.K., 525
Richardson, 242–43
Richie, M., 561, 656–57
right(s)
contract, 351

parental
joint custody and, 204–5
reproductive (*see* reproductive rights)
right-to-die movement
actors/organizations in, 599–601
Brittany Maynard, 600
Compassion & Choices, 601
Hemlock Society, 600
Jack Kevorkian, 599–600
NHPCO, 601
WFRTDS, 601
risk assessment instruments
in decreasing adolescent incarceration, 335–36
Risk Evaluation and Mitigation Strategy (REMS), 486
risks–needs–responsivity (RNR) model
in decreasing adolescent incarceration, 335
risky and antisocial behaviors
in adolescence, 209, 321
abuse and, 217–18
cognitive traits, 214–15
community context influence, 222–24
family environments and trajectories of, 216–18
genetic and epigenetic influences on interpersonal differences, 213–15
interpersonal variation in, 217–18
introduction, 209–10
parenting practices and interpersonal variation, 218
peak in, 210–12
peer influences on, 219–24 (*see also* peer(s): risky and antisocial behaviors in adolescence influenced by)
personality traits, 214
physiological influences on, 210–15
puberty manifestations, 210–12
routine activities and, 219
as status seeking, 221–22
supertraits, 214
trajectories of, 212–13
types of, 209
among TAY, 426–27
risky behaviors
in adolescence, 321
in adults
theoretical understanding of, 407–10, 410t (*see also under* adult risky behavior)

RJ programming. *See* restorative justice (RJ) programming
RNR model. *See* risks–needs–responsivity (RNR) model
Robbins, S.B., 452
Roberts, D., 138–40
Rodriguez, N., 649
Roesch, R., 157, 290, 458
Roe v. Wade, 493–94, 495
Rogers, R., 456
Roper v. Simmons, 424, 634
Roth, B.J., 156
Runyan, D.K., 98, 101
Rural Substance Abuse and Violence Project, 368
Rush, E.B., 61

S
Salekin, K.L., 449
SAMA. *See* Standardized Assessment of Miranda Abilities (SAMA)
Sampson, R.J., 568–69
Sarrett, J.C., 467–68
Sas, L.D., 102
Sauerland, 247
Saum, C.A., 311
Saunders, C., 591
SAVRY. *See* Structured Assessment of Violence Risk in Youth (SAVRY)
Scalia, A., Justice, 442
Schatz, S.J., 464
Scherman, R., 184–85
Scherr, K.C., 466
Scheweitzer, M., 334
Schiavo, T., 593
Schillaci-Ventura, J.M., 321
Schlussel, D., 575
Schnell, S.V., 94–95
Schnittker, J., 328–29, 566, 578
school(s), 370
adolescent incarceration impact on, 326–27
juvenile justice and, 363
future directions, 375–78
introduction, 363
racial and ethnic disparities in, 374–75
legal actors embedded in, 370–71
legal system in, 370–74
JPOs, 371–72
school-based diversion programs, 372–74
SROs, 370–74, 376
reform
for adolescent incarceration, 324

school-based diversion programs, 372–74
 teen court, 373–74
 truancy court, 374
school environment
 JJS and, 363
 juvenile justice and, 363
school resource officers (SROs), 363–64
 defined, 370
 as legal actors in schools, 370–74, 376
 National Center for Education Statistics on, 370, 376
school safety
 Gallup Student Poll on, 364
 interventions and prevention programs in enhancing, 367–70
  EBH–CRP intervention, 369
  interventions and prevention programs in (see also specific programs)
  KiVa program, 369
  LTI, 370
  RJ programming, 369–70
  zero-tolerance policies, 367–68
 juvenile delinquency and, 364–67
  GST, 365
  SDT, 364–65
  social–ecological model, 365–67
school-to-prison pipeline (STPP), 363–64
 zero-tolerance policies and, 368
Schriver, J.L., 632–33
Schwartz, I.M., 334–35
science
 policy, social norms and malalignment of, 652–55 (see also under societal norms, policy, and practice, malalignment of)
SCM. See stereotype content model (SCM)
Scott, E.S., 141, 295, 357
SCOTUS. See Supreme Court of the United States (SCOTUS)
script(s)
 memory, 60
SDS arrangements. See supported decision-making (SDS) arrangements
SDT. See social disorganization theory (SDT)
secure attachment
 insecure attachment vs., 10, 113–14

self-control
 defined, 409
 low (see low self-control [LSC])
 variables controlling, 409
self-incrimination
 protective measures in safeguarding suspects against, 259–61
self-neglect
 among older adults, 614–15
Selman, L.E., 598
sensitivity
 parenting
  in attachment-based interventions, 10
 of recall questions, 200
sentencing
 in juvenile and criminal court, 292–94
 of older adults
  issues related to, 632–35
  (see also older adults: sentencing-related issues)
 youth impact of, 294–95
Sentencing Reform Act, 639
Serious and Violent Offender Reentry Initiative, 565
Serpeloni, F., 215
sexual abuse
 CPS case example, 85–86
 substantiation of, 199–200
sexual consent
 age-related giving of, 353
sexual minorities
 adolescent incarceration impacts on, 332–33
sexual victimization
 of adolescents
  in adult facilities, 330
Shapland, J., 564
Shealy, E.C., 587
Sheidow, A.J., 223
"shelters"
 ORR (see ORR "shelters")
shift
 defined, 263
Shlafer, R.J., 477, 484
Shriver, E., 159–60
SIJ status. See special immigrant juvenile (SIJ) status
Sim, 160
simple assault(s)
 by TAY, 426–27
situational-level risk factors
 racialized policing–related, 521f, 532
Slobogin, C., 393–94
Slonecker, E.M., 57, 198–99

Smith, M.S., 632–33
smoking
 maternal
  prenatal exposure to, 14
SNAP. See Stop Now and Plan (SNAP)
social bonds
 in successful prisoner reentry, 571
social disorganization theory (SDT)
 in linkages between school safety and juvenile delinquency, 364–65
social–ecological development framework
 in racially disparate policing, 520–39, 521f
  exosystem, 521f, 524–30, 541–42
  introduction, 520–21, 521f
  macrosystem, 521f, 522–24, 541
  mesosystem, 521f, 527–30, 542–43
  microsystem, 521f, 530–39
social–ecological model
 Bronfenbrenner's, 545
 features of, 365–67
 in linkages between school safety and juvenile delinquency, 365–67
 as meta-theory, 365–66
social equality
 reproductive rights impact on, 507
 in 21st century, 650–52
socialization
 by parents of color
  cultural, 527–28
  legal, 528
  racial, 527–28
  racial–legal, 528, 529
social skills
 deficits in
  in criminal justice system, 459–66 (see also under criminal justice system: social skills deficits impact on)
societal level
 policing at, 521f, 522–24, 541
societal norms, policy, and science
 malalignment of, 652–55
  changing norms in repairing, 654–55
  in older adults, 654
  in women, 653–54
  in young adults, 652–53
socioeconomic development/well-being
 reproductive rights impact on, 506–9

economics and education, 506–7
interpersonal relationships, 507–9
social equality, 507
socioemotional development
of adolescents, 236–38, 240–41, 355–56
disclosures impacted by, 240–41
memory and suggestibility impacts of, 244
attachment in, 18–19
behavior problems related to, 19
described, 18
maltreatment impact on, 18–19
socioemotional outcomes
for children in criminal court, 90–92
for children in dependency court, 97–99
sociometric popularity
defined, 219
Solomon, J., 116, 119
Sonuga-Barke, E.J.S., 173
Sotomayor, Judge, 260
Spears, B., 500
special immigrant juvenile (SIJ) status, 154–55
specialized transition-age youth (TAY) diversions, 437–41. (see transition-age youth (TAY); young adult courts [YACs])
specialty youth courts, 309
Speck, J.S., 37
SPI. See Survey of Prison Inmates (SPI)
SROs. See school resource officers (SROs)
Stacks, A.M., 7
"staff security facility," 151–52
Standardized Assessment of Miranda Abilities (SAMA), 456, 464
Stanek, K.A., 363
Stanford Child Custody Study, 121
"star witness"
act as own, 158
State of Washington v. Woods, 86
status
defined, 348
legal, 348
status seeking
risky and antisocial behaviors in adolescence as, 221–22
statute(s)
defined, 479

Steffensmeier, D., 632
Steinberg, L., 211–12, 221–22, 237–38, 386, 427
Step-Wise Interview, 68
stereotype content model (SCM), 628
stereotype threat
in police encounters, 535–37
Stetson University
Eleazer Courtroom of, 631
Stevenson, M.C., 517
Stewart, E.A., 570
Stewart, R., 573, 575
Stinson, J.D., 452
Stolzenberg, S.N., 71
Stop Now and Plan (SNAP), 416
Stoughton, S.W., 525
STPP. See school-to-prison pipeline (STPP)
Strange Situation procedure
in assessing attachment in young children, 115–16
Strategies for Youth, 376
Straw, S., 599
stress
after abortion
American Psychological Association on, 505
child development and brain development impact of, 131–32
memory and suggestibility impact in children, 61–62
during pregnancy, 9
stressor(s)
of unaccompanied migrant youth, 150
Structured Assessment of Violence Risk in Youth (SAVRY), 51
Stuart, F., 575, 577
Study to Understand Prognoses and Preferences for Outcomes and Risks of Treatment (SUPPORT), 597
Sturges, J.E., 324
Stykes, J.B., 508
substance abuse
recidivism and, 572
Substance Abuse and Mental Health Services Administration
of National Registry of Evidence-Based and Promising Practices, 21
substance use
maltreatment in infancy related to, 16–20

parenting behaviors impact of, 15–16
prenatal exposure to, 13–15 (see also prenatal exposure to substances [PSE])
prenatal intimate partner violence impact of, 16–20
substantiation
dependence on disclosure, 199–200
Sufrin, C., 478
suggestibility
of adolescents, 242–45
age as factor in, 199
in children, 57 (see also suggestibility in children)
defined, 58–59, 263, 460
in forensic context, 460
interrogative
defined, 460
of juveniles, 263–64
suggestibility in children
EFs and, 63
factors affecting, 59–66 (see also specific factors)
attachment styles, 65
child abuse, 65–66
cognitive functioning, 62–63
demographics, 59–60
disclosure and recantation, 66–67
event characteristics, 60–61
language development, 64
psychological factors, 65–66
repeated experiences, 60–61
stress, 61–62
intellectual disabilities impact on, 63
suggestion(s)
suggestibility to, 59
suggestive questioning, 200
Sugie, N.F., 569
Suh, G.W., 116–17, 118, 120–21
superpredator(s)
defined, 424
described, 282–83
supertrait(s)
described, 214
risky and antisocial behaviors in adolescence and, 214
SUPPORT. See Study to Understand Prognoses and Preferences for Outcomes and Risks of Treatment (SUPPORT)
supported decision-making (SDS) arrangements
developmental disabilities–related, 467–68

Supreme Court of the United States (SCOTUS)
  on abortion
    pivotal cases, 495–96
  on adolescent behaviors, 322
  on capital punishment for persons with IDs, 459
  contraception-related cases, 498–99
  on Fourth Amendment issues of consent to search and seizure, 538
  on IDs, 450
  impact on juvenile court, 282
  on inmates' medical needs, 636–37
  on intimate partner violence, 508
  juvenile justice and
    history of, 282
  on LWOP for juvenile offenders, 334
  on LWOP for youth, 293–94
  "originalist" approach to interpreting constitutional rights, 201–2
  on reproductive rights, 493–94
  on sentencing-related issues for older adults, 633–34
surrogate consent laws, 594–95
Survey of Prison Inmates (SPI), 563–64

T

Taffe, R.L., 57
Tasker, F., 175
Task Force on Community Preventive Services
  of CDC, 294
TAY. *See* transition-age youth (TAY)
Taylor, 295
Team Kids Challenge, 377
Teaster, P.B., 587
Tedesco, F., 94–95
teen courts, 311–12, 373–74
telemedicine, 601–3
  challenges with implementing, 602–3
  CMS on, 603
  during COVID-19 pandemic, 601–3
  defined, 601
  for older adults, 601–3
telomere shortening
  maltreatment and, 18
temperament
  genetics impact on, 9
Ten Step Investigative Interview, 246

Terne, M., 462–63
testimony
  alternate forms of, 93–94
  courtroom
    by children, 70–72, 92–94, 158–60
testosterone levels
  in puberty, 211
TGNC adolescents. *See* transgender and gender nonconforming (TGNC) adolescents
The Case of Helga Wanglie, 592
The Case of Nancy Cruzan, 592
The Case of Terri Schiavo, 593
The Karen Ann Quinlan Case, 591
theory of mind (ToM)
  defined, 62
  described, 62
  memory and suggestibility impact in children, 62
The Paul Brophy Case, 591–92
"the talk," 528–29
Thompson, C., 412–13
threat(s)
  stereotype
    in police encounters, 535–37
Thronson, D., 163–64
Title IV-E funding, 485
Title IV-E program, 485
Tobin-Tyler, E., 573
toddler(s)
  abuse among
    prevalence of, 7–8
  overnight parenting time impact on, 115–19
Todres, J., 348
ToM. *See* theory of mind (ToM)
TRAC. *See* Transactional Record Access Clearinghouse (TRAC)
traditional court processing
  alternatives to, 303 (*see also specific types and* youth: alternatives to traditional court processing for)
Trafficking Victim Protection Reauthorization Act, 152
trait(s)
  antisocial vs. prosocial, 215
Transactional Record Access Clearinghouse (TRAC), 155
Transformative Justice program, 442
transgender and gender nonconforming (TGNC) adolescents
  incarceration impacts on, 332–33

transition-age youth (TAY)
  arrests among
    racial/socioeconomic disparities, 426
  of color
    arrests among, 426
  described, 423–24
  diversion programs for, 430–41 (*see also under* diversion programs: for TAY)
  incarcerated
    prevalence of, 425–26
  in legal system, 425–27
    described, 425–27
    felonies leading to failing trajectories, 429–30, 429f
    future directions, 442–43
    impulsivity among, 426–27
    introduction, 423–24
    overrepresentation of, 427–29
    policy implications, 442–43
    risk-taking behavior among, 426–27
    simple assaults, 426–27
    underdeveloped brain as factor in, 427–29
  recidivism rates among, 425
  simple assaults by, 426–27
  as understudied group, 427
translational research
  youth justice system–related, 387–91
    T1 research, 387–88
    T2 research, 388–90
    T3 research, 390–91
    T4 research, 390–91
TRAP laws, 488
trauma
  memory and suggestibility impact in children, 61–62
traumatic experiences
  child testimony impacted by, 158
Travis, J., 565–66, 575
"treatment without trial," 303–4, 314–16
  T1 research, 387–88
  T2 research, 388–90
    assessment tools, 389–90
    developmentally informed interview protocols, 389
    evidence-based interventions, 390
    introduction, 388–89
  T3 research, 390–91
  T4 research, 390–91
trial(s)
  competence to stand (*see* competence to stand trial [CST])
  youth adjudicatory, 286–89

trial stage
  in criminal court, 286–89
truancy court, 374
Trump administration
  on contraception, 499
  on Mexico City Policy, 497
  zero-tolerance policies of, 156, 161
Turnaway Study, 502–99, 503, 505, 506, 509–10
Turner, N., 563
T visas, 155
TVPRA, 152
20 Principles of Questioning, 200–1

U

UAC. *See* unaccompanied alien child (UAC)
Ucar, A., 467–68
UCSF. *See* University of California San Francisco (UCSF)
Uggen, C., 563, 573, 575
Umez, C., 573, 575, 576
unaccompanied alien child (UAC)
  defined, 149–50, 149n.1, 153
unaccompanied migrant youth, 149
  age of, 150
  defined, 149–50, 149n.1
  immigration proceedings for, 153–60, 153n.6
    adolescents in court, 160
    consequences of, 160–63
    courtroom experiences, 162–63
    developmental effects of, 160–63
    developmental perspective on child testimony, 158–60
    developmental perspective on ORR "shelters," 156
    impacts of, 163–64
    insights from developmental research on, 155–60
    self-representation in court, 156–58
  legal process for, 151–55
    accessing an attorney, 153
    commencement of removal proceedings, 154
    deportation hearings, 153–55
    detention-related, 151–53
    forms of relief, 154–55
    individual calendar hearing, 154
  in ORR "shelters," 150–54, 150n.2, 156 (*see also under* ORR "shelters")
  PTSD among, 150–51
  self-representation in court, 156–58
  stressors impacting, 150
"unaccompanied minor"
  defined, 149–50, 149n.1
UNCRC. *See* United Nations Convention on the Rights of the Child (UNCRC)
ungovernability action, 350
Uniform Crime Report, 629
unintended pregnancy
  CDC on, 494
  Guttmacher Institute on, 494
  prevalence of, 494
United Nations Convention on the Rights of the Child (UNCRC), 163–64
United Nations Global Study on Children Deprived of Liberty, 323
United States v. Brooke, 633–34
United States v. Dusky, 631
United States v. Texas, 493–94
University of California, Irvine study
  on YACs, 438–41, 440*f*, 441*f*
University of California San Francisco (UCSF)
  Bixby Center for Global Reproductive Health of, 502
Urban Institute's Returning Home study, 567
U.S. Border Patrol (USBP), 151
U.S. Citizenship and Immigration Service (USCIS), 154–55
U.S. Constitution's Sixth Amendment, 88–89, 91–92
U.S. Department of Justice
  on victimization of persons with IDs, 453
U.S. Immigration Legal System
  unaccompanied migrant youth in, 149 (*see also under* unaccompanied migrant youth: in U.S. Immigration Legal System)
U.S. Sentencing Commission, 633
U.S. Supreme Court. *See* Supreme Court of the United States (SCOTUS)
USBP. *See* U.S. Border Patrol (USBP)
USCIS. *See* U.S. Citizenship and Immigration Service (USCIS)

V

Vacco v. Quill, 593
Vagni, M., 62, 176
validity
  external
    of abuse, 199
van Koppen, M.V., 410–11, 412–13
Vázquez, C.P., 176
victim(s)
  adolescents as, 233 (*see also under* adolescent(s): as victims and witnesses)
  older adults as, 613–16 (*see also under* older adults: as victims)
victimization
  adolescent incarceration impact on, 330–31
  risk factors for, 331
Viljoen, J.L., 157, 288–89, 290, 321, 394
Villalobos, J.G., 264
violence
  culture of
    in adult correction facilities, 330
  intimate partner
    SCOTUS on, 508
visa(s)
  T, 155
Visher, C.A., 571
von Werthem, M., 161
vulnerability
  autonomy and
    balancing of, 467–68

W

Waggoner, K., 649
Wakefield, S., 563
Walker, H.M., 467
Walk, M., 138
Wall, B.W., 457–58
Waller, A., 598
Wallin, A.R., 99, 100
Walsh, A., 214–15
Walter, B.M., 617
Wang, E., 565
Wanglie, H., 592
Ward, H., 184
warn-and-release policies
  for youth, 306–7
Warraich, H.J., 590
"warrior mindset"
  in policing, 524–26
Warshak, R.A., 110
Wasarhaley, N.E., 616
Washington v. Glucksburg, 592–93

Way, S.M., 368
Weaver, B., 562
Weerman, F.M., 219–20
Weiss, B., 325
Weisz, V., 99, 100
well-being
  exosystem impacts on, 526–27
  macrosystem impacts on, 521f, 523–24
  mesosystem impacts on, 521f, 529–30
  microsystem impacts on, 532–35
  socioeconomic development and reproductive rights impact on, 506–9
Western, B., 326–27, 563, 569, 570, 572
WFRTDS. *See* World Federation of Right to Die Societies (WFRTDS)
Wheelock, D., 563
Whelan, A.M., 493
"Whiteness pandemic" in America, 543
Whittle, T.N., 576
Whole Woman's Health v. Hellerstedt, 495
Whole Woman's Health v. Jackson, 493–94, 495, 496
Wicklander-Zulawski training firm, 271
Wilberforce Act, 152
Wilcock, R., 463, 618–19
Wildeman, C., 563
Wilson, H.A., 306
Winningham, D.B., 456
witness(es)
  adolescents as, 233 (*see also under* adolescent(s): as victims and witnesses)
  child, 198–202
  older adults as, 617–20 (*see also under* older adults: as witnesses)
Woldgabreal, Y.A., 567
Wolfgang, M.E., 412–13
Wolf, T., Gov., 424–25
women
  societal norms, policy, and practice malalignment in, 653–54
women's development
  abortion impact on, 501–3
  childbirth impact on, 503–4
  contraception impact on, 503
  introduction, 493–94
  issues and synthesis of current scholarship and debate, 501–10

pregnancy impact on, 503–4
reproductive rights impact on, 493 (*see also under* reproductive rights: impact on women's development)
mental health and development, 504–6
physical health and development, 501–4
socioeconomic development/well-being, 506–9
Woodbury-Smith, M., 452
Woodhouse, B.B., 139
Wood, L.C., 161
Wood, M.E., 449
Woods, G.W., 455
Woods, J., 85–86
Woolard, J.L., 289, 292
Woolman, J., 477
Wooten, D., 500
World Federation of Right to Die Societies (WFRTDS)
  in right-to-die movement, 601
World Health Organization
  on abortion, 501–2
"wounded healer"
  becoming
    in prisoner reentry, 577–78
Wylie, L.E., 399, 616, 618, 625, 639
Wyman, J., 233, 389
Wynn, S., 595

Y

YACs. *See* young adult courts (YACs)
Yadav, K.N., 597
Yarborough v. Alvarado, 259
yield
  defined, 263
Yoder, J.R., 331
Youk, T., 599–600
Young Adult Court of Porirua, New Zealand, 437
young adult courts (YACs), 437–41
  collaborativeness of, 439–41, 441f
  components of, 437
  implementation of
    limitations of, 438–39, 440f, 441f
  mission, aims, purpose of, 437
  specialized TAY diversions in, 437–41
  University of California, Irvine study on, 438–41, 440f, 441f
  in U.S., 437, 438t
young adults
  "maturity gap" between cognitive and psychosocial development in, 427, 428f

societal norms, policy, and science malalignment in, 652–53
Young, R.L., 452
youth. *See also under* adolescence; adolescent(s); children)
  alternatives to traditional court processing for, 303
  civil citation programs, 306–7
  court-sponsored diversion, 308–9
  diversion programs, 306–7, 308–9, 372–74, 423 (*see also specific types and* diversion programs)
  future directions, 316–17
  implications, 316–17
  informal processing of juvenile offenders, 314–16
  introduction, 303–4
  JDCs, 310
  JMHCs, 310–11
  net widening potential, 313–14
  overview of, 305–11
  prearrest or police-led diversion, 306–7
  racial and ethnic disparities in, 312–13
  risks and pitfalls related to, 312–16
  specialty youth courts, 309
  teen courts, 311–12
  "treatment without trial," 314–16
  warn-and-release policies, 306–7
criminal prosecution of
  impact of, 294–95
incarceration of, 321 (*see also* adolescent incarceration)
interrogation law as applied to, 260
in juvenile and criminal court, 279 (*see also under* adolescent(s): in juvenile and criminal court)
LGBTQ
  rapport-building/interviewing strategies with, 248
LWOP for
  reductions in, 293
  mandatory minimums for, 293
prearrest for, 306–7
self-representation of
  in court, 156–58
sentencing of
  impact of, 294–95

as suspects
   police interrogation of, 257 (*see also under* adolescent suspects: police interrogation of)
   transition-age, 423 (*see also under* transition-age youth [TAY])
   unaccompanied migrant (*see* unaccompanied migrant youth)
   zero-tolerance policies impact on, 368
youth adjudicatory hearings and trials, 286–89
Youthful Offender Act
   Division of Young Offender Parole and Reentry Services under, 432
youth justice interventions
   measuring of "success" in, 393
youth justice reform
   "developmental era" in, 386
youth justice system
   developmental psychology impact on, 386 (*see also under* youth justice system: developmental research on)
   developmental research on, 385
      accessibility of, 395
      age of juvenile jurisdiction, 392
      basic research, 387
      credibility of, 395
      introduction, 385
      measuring "success" in interventions, 393
      racial disparities in, 391–92
      relevance of, 394
      sustaining developmental reform, 391–93
      toward different youth justice model, 393–94
      translational research, 387–91
      historical context of, 386–87
Youth Level of Services/Case Management Inventory, 389
youth of color. *See also under* Black youth
   adultification of, 266–67
   attorney–client relationships disadvantages among, 289
   in CWS
      racial disproportionality/racial disparities associated with, 134–35
   legal procedures and experiences among, 265–67
   policing of
      racial disparities in, 517 (*see also under* policing: racial disparities in)
   punitive dispositions for, 293
   TAY
      arrests among, 426
Youth Offender Act, 432
Yuille, Y.C., 462–63

Z

Zamble, E., 565
Zane, S., 503
Zapf, O., 458
Zara, G., 411–12, 413, 415
Zemishlany, Z., 459
zero-tolerance policies
   adverse outcomes for youth related to, 368
   in enhancing school safety, 367–68
   alternatives to, 368–70
   STPP and, 368
   of Trump administration, 156, 161
Zero Tolerance Task Force
   of APA, 367–68
Zottoli, T.M., 279, 389, 390, 393
Zwakman, M., 598
Zweig, J.M., 565